History of Computing

The *History of Computing* series publishes high-quality books which address the history of computing, with an emphasis on the 'externalist' view of this history, more accessible to a wider audience. The series examines content and history from four main quadrants: the history of relevant technologies, the history of the core science, the history of relevant business and economic developments, and the history of computing as it pertains to social history and societal developments.

Titles can span a variety of product types, including but not exclusively, themed volumes, biographies, 'profile' books (with brief biographies of a number of key people), expansions of workshop proceedings, general readers, scholarly expositions, titles used as ancillary textbooks, revivals and new editions of previous worthy titles.

These books will appeal, varyingly, to academics and students in computer science, history, mathematics, business and technology studies. Some titles will also directly appeal to professionals and practitioners of different backgrounds.

Author guidelines: springer.com > Authors > Author Guidelines

For other titles published in this series, go to www.springer.com/series/8442

Simon Lavington

Moving Targets

Elliott-Automation and the Dawn of the Computer Age in Britain, 1947 – 67

 Springer

Emeritus Professor Simon Lavington (retired)
School of Computer Science and Electronic Engineering
University of Essex
Wivenhoe Park
Colchester
CO4 3SQ
United Kingdom
lavis@essex.ac.uk

ISBN 978-1-4471-2636-2   ISBN 978-1-84882-933-6 (eBook)
DOI 10.1007/978-1-84882-933-6
Springer London Dordrecht Heidelberg New York

British Library Cataloguing in Publication Data
A catalogue record for this book is available from the British Library

Printed on acid-free paper

Springer is part of Springer Science+Business Media (www.springer.com)

Moving Targets – Elliott-Automation and the Dawn of the Computer Age in Britain, 1947–67

Introduction

In 1957 the Elliott-Automation company was formed from Elliott Brothers (London) Ltd., which itself had its origins in the Elliott Instrument Company founded in 1804. One way or another, Elliotts had been involved in the design of analogue computers since about 1916 and digital computers since about 1946. Elliott-Automation was thus an active participant in the birth of the *information age* in Britain. By 1961 the company, via its laboratories at Borehamwood a few miles north of London, was supplying 50% of the digital computers delivered to UK customers in that year. The company boss, Sir Leon Bagrit, was known as *Mr Automation* when he gave the BBC Reith Lectures in 1964. Yet by 1968 Elliott-Automation had effectively disappeared in a flurry of takeovers, leaving little apparent trace of the technical excellence that had once characterised the name *Elliott*.

Moving Targets charts the gradual take-up of information technology in Britain, as seen through the eyes of one innovative company and remembered by those who worked for that company. The electronic excellence, developed in the Borehamwood Laboratories of the Elliott company during the 1950s, forms the underlying theme of the story. This excellence grew out of government-sponsored work on secret defence projects. In this sense, the large numbers of Elliott computers that had permeated the market-place by 1961 represented the transfer of technology from military to civil applications, from swords to plough-shears.

The hopes and fears of ordinary citizens during the post-war period are now past history. It is as well to be reminded of these hopes and fears because they determined the priorities not only of those who designed the earliest digital computers but also of those who had to decide if, when and where such machines could be put to use. A quick review of the 1950s will serve to set the scene for much of this book.

Life in the 1950s

Two factors characterised the 1950s in Britain: economic austerity and the Cold War. The latter is the easier to comprehend. Churchill ominously remarked in 1946 that 'an Iron Curtain has descended on Europe' – an image first given meaning to most people in Britain by the Berlin Airlift, a tense confrontation with the Soviet Union which lasted from June 1948 to May 1949. The Cold War between the armed forces of *the west* and the communists of *the east* continued in varying degrees until the Soviet Union and its military manifestation, the Warsaw Pact, collapsed in 1991. The Berlin Wall which epitomised the separation of east and west Germany had effectively fallen in November 1989.

During the Cold War period, Britain had its own end-of-empire conflicts. From 1945 to the end of the 1960s and beyond, British troops were in action at various times in places such as India, Malaya, Cyprus, Kenya and Aden [1]. Britain also contributed forces to larger wars, particularly the Korean War (1950–1953) and the Vietnam War (1962–1975). Conscription, known as *National Service*, was introduced in 1947. This meant that most young men had some degree of military training right up until the end of the 1950s. In the immediate post-war years, science was assumed to be the servant of defence, operating through the mysteriously named Ministry of Supply, MOS. The surviving Visitors Books of Elliott's Borehamwood Laboratories show evidence of the frequent interchange between the company and the Ministry of Supply.

The resources available to the military were reflected in the country's annual defence budget. Since military applications provided the spur for many technologies, and in particular to Elliott's digital electronics, it is instructive to see how defence spending varied over the years covered by this book. This is shown in Table 1, taken from [2].

Table 1 The UK's annual defence budget, £m

	Budget (£m)	% change, adjusted for inflation
1945/46	4,410	...
1946/47	1,653	−62.8
1947/48	854	−50
1948/49	753	−16.3
1949/50	741	−3.5
1950/51	777	+2.5
1951/52	1,110	+31.3
1952/53	1,404	+18.6
1953/54	1,364	−5.7
1954/55	1,436	+3.3
1955/56	1,405	−6.1
1956/57	1,525	+2.6
1957/58	1,430	−9.7
1958/59	1,468	−0.7
1959/60	1,476	−0.7
1960/61	1,596	+6.3
1961/62	1,689	+2.2
1962/63	1,767	+1.6
1963/64	1,792	−1.0
1964/65	1,909	+2.0
1965/66	2,056	+3.0

Table 2	Approximate retail price index, UK
Year	Price index, 1974 = 100
1945	26.4
1955	40.9
1965	54.7
1975	124.2
1985	344.0
1995	542.1

The massive decreases in defence spending between 1946 and 1950 had consequences for companies such as Elliott Brothers (London) Ltd., whose activities in those years were still largely dependent upon contracts from the Admiralty. Likewise, the increased defence budgets between 1951 and 1953 helped to revive Elliott's fortunes. After 1960, the year-on-year changes in the UK's total defence budget were not dramatic so that any sudden impact upon Elliott's activities was due to the initiation or cancellation of individual major projects rather than on overall defence spending. One particular event that loomed large in the fortunes of the UK's aerospace industry was the cancellation of the TSR 2 fighter aircraft contract in 1965 – an event that certainly shook Elliott-Automation.

Translating contemporary expenditure into present-day equivalents is not an exact science. At various points in this book, prices are quoted and it is interesting to guess at the corresponding modern values. Table 2, which comes from [3], will help.

On a personal level, the emotional consequences of the Second World War persisted well into the 1950s. Ordinary people were used to making sacrifices. Economic austerity meant that war-time rationing of commodities such as food, clothes and petrol was only gradually phased out between 1948 and 1954, though coal rationing continued until 1958 [4]. People had to make the best of what was available: *make-do and mend* was a catch-phrase of the time. For those scientists and engineers whose contribution to the war effort had been an intellectual one, there was an unspoken assumption that post-war challenges could be met, difficult problems solved and that Britain was still at the forefront of scientific and industrial achievement. On a practical level, this spirit of confidence permeated most of the post-war digital computing projects and helps to explain group loyalties and the willingness to work hard for modest financial return. Resources were scarce, so great ingenuity was required.

The Arrival of the Modern Computer

To the general public, the stored-program digital computer first appeared in the late 1940s, heralded by newspaper headlines such as: 'A marvel of our time: the "memory machine" which can solve the most complex mathematical problems' [5]. Neither the computer nor its applications were understood by the journalists but both were somehow assumed to be important. The machines and their applications were taken to be products of the boffins who had come up with scientific wonders during the dark days of war.

Of course, not all pioneering digital computer projects had their origins in defence-related activities. Nevertheless, the great majority of projects were initially targeted at science and engineering calculations and the application of general-purpose computers to business and commerce was seldom considered at the outset. Certainly, it was not until the mid-1950s that Elliott's Borehamwood Laboratories investigated the possibilities for *electronic data processing* (*EDP*) and the needs of the business community. Marketing arrangements were established in 1956 with the National Cash Register Co. Ltd. (NCR).

In Table 3 we give a broad summary of the Elliott digital computers that emerged from Borehamwood. Of the 11 designs shown, six had their origins in classified defence contracts. Only one, the Elliott 405, was specifically aimed at the commercial data-processing market from the outset. The design of the Elliott 800 series and the 900 series were strongly influenced by the emerging requirements for industrial process control and factory-floor automation – areas in which Elliott-Automation excelled. If the numbers of each machine in Table 3 seem ridiculously small by modern standards, recall that by the end of 1949 there were probably only four prototype electronic stored-program computers that had come into hesitant operation anywhere in the world. Even by the start of 1955, there were still only about 17 operational digital computers in the whole of the UK and several of these were one-off research prototypes.

Besides stored-program digital computers, the Elliott company also designed analogue computers. Amongst the many analogue systems built by Elliotts was the huge TRIDAC machine, installed for missile research at the Royal Aircraft

Table 3 Elliott digital computers designed and delivered between 1947 and 1967. Accurate company records cease after 1967. Further details of costs, deliveries and applications are given in Appendix 8

Computer	Dates first working	No. built to 1967	Relative size	Initial application
152	1950	1	Medium	Defence
153	1954	1	Large	Defence
Nicholas	1952	1	Small	Defence
401, 402	1953, 1955	11	Small	General
403	1955	1	Large	Defence
311	1954	1	Medium/large	Defence
405	1956	33	Large	EDP
800 series and 503	1957–1962	219+32	Small, medium and large	Automation and general
ARCH101,1000, etc.	1962–1966	Many embedded	Small	Automation
502	1963	3	Large	Defence
900 series	1963–1970 and later	391+	Small	Defence and automation
4120, 4130	1965, 1966	160+	Medium	General

Table 4 Charting the gradual take-up of stored-program digital computers in Britain

Application area	Typical computing methods, before the move to stored-program digital computers	Approx. period during which the switch to digital computers took place
General science and engineering	Electromechanical numerical desktop calculators	1949–1954
Commercial data processing	Electromechanical numerical desktop calculators; electromechanical punched card accounting equipment	1953–1963
Special scientific simulations e.g. missile design; nuclear power stations	Electromechanical and electronic analogue computers; electromechanical differential analysers, etc. (see Chap. 4)	1958–1966
Automation and industrial process control	Electromechanical analogue instrumentation (see Chaps. 6 and 7)	1959–1966
Ship-borne naval weapons systems	Electromechanical and electronic analogue computers e.g. fire control tables (see Chap. 4)	1959–1969
Airborne flight control and weapons systems	Electromechanical and hydraulic analogue air data computers (see Chap. 12)	1965–1980

Establishment at Farnborough and costing £750,000 in 1954 – equivalent to about £15 million at the time of writing this book.

For some applications, notably airborne defence, the relative capabilities and cost-effectiveness of analogue versus digital computing was keenly debated for many years. In other areas such as commercial data processing, digital in the sense of numerical calculation had always been the natural choice. Generally speaking, the move to electronic stored-program digital computers occurred at different times in different application areas and depended upon a number of factors, of which technological considerations loomed large. Thus, the dawn of the *digital computer* age in Britain took place at various times between about 1949 and 1975, depending upon applications. Table 4 gives the flavour of the transitions for average users.

To describe all these interwoven computing threads and the resulting applications in a single book has been an interesting challenge. The challenge to the uninitiated reader is undoubtedly greater! In Fig. 1 we give a diagram of the book's chapters, arranged in three general themes. To the left of the diagram the growing importance of software and business applications is charted. The centre of the diagram highlights industrial process control, in which Elliott-Automation was a pioneer. To the right of the diagram, hardware considerations dominate the military arena. As an aside, the right-hand thread of Elliott's defence applications continues today, inherited via GEC and Marconi and now embedded in the multinational company BAE Systems. Amongst BAE Systems' many research and development sites is the former Elliott-Automation factory at Rochester.

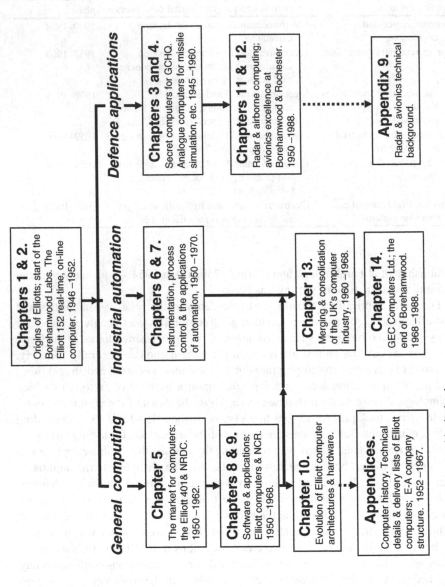

General computing

Chapter 5
The market for computers: the Elliott 401 & NRDC. 1950 –1962.

Chapters 8 & 9.
Software & applications: Elliott computers & NCR. 1950 –1968.

Chapter 10.
Evolution of Elliott computer architectures & hardware.

Appendices.
Computer history. Technical details & delivery lists of Elliott computers; E-A company structure. 1952 –1967.

Industrial automation

Chapters 1 & 2.
Origins of Elliotts; start of the Borehamwood Labs. The Elliott 152 real-time, on-line computer. 1946 –1952.

Chapters 6 & 7.
Instrumentation, process control & the applications of automation, 1950 –1970.

Chapter 13.
Merging & consolidation of the UK's computer industry. 1960 –1968.

Chapter 14.
GEC Computers Ltd.; the end of Borehamwood. 1968 –1988.

Defence applications

Chapters 3 and 4.
Secret computers for GCHQ. Analogue computers for missile simulation, etc. 1945 –1960.

Chapters 11 & 12.
Radar & airborne computing; avionics excellence at Borehamwood & Rochester. 1950 –1988.

Appendix 9.
Radar & avionics technical background.

Fig. 1 A guide to the subject matter covered in the book

Sources and Acknowledgements

Researching a book about Elliott-Automation, a company that effectively ceased to exist as a trading entity in 1968, has not been straightforward. In 1985, a survey of the historical records of British computer manufacturers [6] highlighted 'above all a widespread disregard for the value of archives. Of the twelve companies still in operation, only one (STC) has employed a qualified archivist and only four others make any effort at all to retain significant documents.' ICL and Ferranti Ltd. were fortunately amongst the four, and authoritative histories of these two important British computer manufacturers now exist (see [7, 8]).

Ferranti Ltd. and Elliott Brothers (London) Ltd. had together produced 75% of the British commercially available computers that had been delivered to customers by 1955 – indeed, the two companies became market rivals. Some of the computer endeavours of Ferranti and Elliott were in due course incorporated into ICL (respectively, in 1963 and 1968). ICL itself had had a long involvement in electromechanical punched card office equipment through its ancestor companies British Tabulating Machine Co. Ltd. (BTM) and International Computers and Tabulators (ICT).

More generally, the post-1967 successor companies to Elliott-Automation's activities have included at various times English Electric, GEC, ICL, Marconi, BAE Systems and Telent Ltd. Only the last two organisations have survived at the time of writing. M G D (Mike) Williams, who worked in Elliott-Automation's Head Office from 1956 to 1964 and then indirectly until the GEC takeover in 1968, has said: 'It is no surprise that company documents (both external and internal) for the period up to 1967 are hard to come by: reorganisations (frequently acrimonious) and repeated "new broom" exercises will have ensured that most if not all interesting papers held inside the company will have been disposed of' [9].

Whilst none of these successor companies appear to have made much official effort to preserve Elliott-specific historical material, enthusiastic employees have, from time to time, saved documents from oblivion. Thus, the Marconi Archive acquired some early Elliott papers in 2001, thanks to the efforts of H R (Ron) Bristow, a former Assistant General Manager [10]. These papers were passed with the rest of the Marconi Archives to the University of Oxford in 2005, upon the dissolution of the Marconi company.

Of more relevance to Elliott computers is the effort of S L H (Laurence) Clarke CBE, who retired in 1992 as Assistant Technical Director of GEC, to collect material for a history of Elliott's Borehamwood Laboratory. Clarke was obliged to abandon his project in 1997 for personal reasons but had by then accumulated written anecdotal evidence from a number of key employees who have since died [11]. Laurence Clarke gallantly passed his material to the present author in 2001.

Lacking official company archives, the computer historian is obliged to cultivate a network of former employees and hopefully, through them, access to original company documents and reports that have been kept for many years in attics and garages. The National Archives contains many relevant defence-related documents that were formerly classified (i.e. secret). Contemporary secondary source material, for example, Stock Exchange reports, National Research Development Corporation correspondence and trade journal articles, help to form a picture of the company's relative standing. Finally, personal histories and anecdotes, whilst often notoriously imprecise about dates and/or perceived rivals, do add colour to the picture and are sometimes invaluable in revealing the underlying causes of organisational changes.

Numerous former Elliott employees and related specialists have made original documents and notes available to the author. Besides Laurence Clarke and Ron Bristow, special mention should also be made of the following people who have been unsparing in their time spent in meeting with, and/or corresponding with, the author: Jonathan Aylen, Erik Baigar, John Barrett, Iann Barron, Tony Bartolome, Laurie Bental, John Blackburn, Gordon Brand, Allan Bromley, Heather Brown, John Brooks, John Bunt, Malcolm Burchall, Richard Burwood, Harry Carpenter, Mike Cochrane, Matthew Connell, Roger Cook, Doug Cornish, John Coulter, John Crawley, John Deane, Ninian Eadie, Dai Edwards, Marilyn Evans, Gerald Everitt, Ralph Erskine, Peter Excell, George Felton, Peter Fielding, Peter Freeman, Terry Froggatt, Andrew Gabriel, Steve Gilbey, Rob Gordon, Michael Healy, Peter Hearne, Ray Henville, Ed Hersom, Tony Hoare, Ron Howard, Roy Hynes, Michael Irish, Alex Kahan (grandson of Sir Leon Bagrit), Paul King, John Kinnear, Betty Laverick, Peter Lawrence, Jack Lonergan, Ian Merry, Colin Merton, Brian Millis, Gerry Mills, Rachel Monk, Frances Morley, Pierre-E. Mounier-Kuhn, Maurice Needham, Roger Newey, Peter Onion, Ian Ormerod, Richard Overill, Jack Pateman, David Pentecost, Paul Rayner, Lord William Rees-Mogg, Tony Ridlington, Dennis Rowland, Joseph Roth, Gavin Ross, Hugh Ross, Geoff Scammell, John Sinclair, Brian Spratt, Andrew St Johnston, Dina St Johnston (neé Vaughan), Harriett St Johnston, Alison Steer (neé Coales), Philip Tattersall, Colin Thurston, Nick Vince, Alan Wakefield, David Warman, Sally Whytehead (Charles Owen's daughter), Nigel Williams, Bruce Williamson, Ron Wilson, Linda Wolffe, Andrew Wylie and many others. Sadly, several of the aforementioned people have passed on since 2001 and others were in such frail health that they may not now be around to read these words of thanks. Nevertheless, the author is truly grateful to them all.

References

1. Amongst the end-of-empire conflicts were: India,1945–48; Palestine,1945–48; Malaya,1948–60; Suez Canal Zone,1951–54; Kenya,1952–60; Cyprus,1955–59; the Suez incident,1956; Borneo,1962–66; Aden,1955–67; Radfan (Federation of South Arabia),1955–67; Oman & Dhofar,1969–76. See for example: http://www.britains-smallwars.com/
2. Chalmers M (1985) Paying for defence – military spending and British decline. Pluto Press, London. ISBN: 074350023 5
3. Twigger R (1999) Inflation: the value of the pound 1750–1998. House of Commons Library. Research Paper 99/20, 23 Feb 1999, http://www.parliament.uk/commons/lib/research/rp99/rp99-020.pdf
4. The main sequence was as follows. 1948: bread rationing ended; 1949: clothes rationing ended; 1950: the points rationing scheme for many basic foods ended and petrol rationing ended; 1953: sweet rationing and sugar rationing ended; 1954: all food rationing officially ended; 1958: coal rationing ended

5. Anon (1949) The Manchester University computer. Photographs and article in the June 1949 edition of the Illustrated London News

6. Kelly S (ed) (1985) Report of a Survey of the Archives of the British Commercial Computer Manufacturers 1950–1970. Unpublished study by the Institution of Electrical Engineers, Nov 1985, 272 pages. This 6-month survey, funded by ICL, began in May 1985. It was one of the initiatives that led to the setting up of the National Archive for the History of Computing (NAHC) in Manchester in 1987 – (see page 9 of Serena Kelly's Report)

7. Campbell-Kelly M (1989) ICL: a business and technical history. Oxford University Press, Oxford. ISBN: 0-19-853918-5

8. Wilson JF (2001) Ferranti: a history. Building a family business, 1882–1975. Carnegie Publishing Ltd., Lancaster. ISBN: 1-85936-080-7
Volume 2: from family firm to multinational company, 1975–1987, published in 2007 by Crucible Books, Lancaster. ISBN: 978-1-905472-01-7

9. M G D (Mike) Williams, letter to Simon Lavington dated 14 July 2003

10. H R (Ron) Bristow joined Elliotts in Sept 1951 and, apart from a break between December 1952 and January 1955, stayed with the company until his retirement in 1992. His career with the company was predominantly within the Aviation sector, rising to the position of Assistant General Manager. He became interested in the company's history and was in a position to prevent the loss or destruction of many archival papers, including the 30-page typed document entitled 'Elliott Flight Automation History'. He eventually arranged for the documents to have a permanent home in the University of Oxford as part of the Marconi Archive. Since retiring in 1992, Ron Bristow has made a detailed study of Elliott's nineteenth-century instrument-making activities

11. S L H (Laurence) Clarke joined Elliott's Borehamwood Laboratory in 1951, having worked there the previous summer as a vacation student. Laurence's career was entirely within the computing sector, retiring as Assistant Technical Director of GEC in 1992. In 1994, with the active encouragement of John Coales, Laurence started work on a history of the Borehamwood Laboratories. He began by contacting former employees, with an emphasis on the period from 1946 to the early 1950s. By the end of 1995, Laurence had collected the written and verbal anecdotes of about 30 people, some of whom had joined the Laboratory when it was first set up by John Coales in October 1946. Due to other commitments, Laurence had abandoned his history project by 1997

Contents

1   The Navy Comes to Borehamwood   1
     1.1   A Place Called Borehamwood   1
     1.2   The Early Days of Naval Radar   4
         1.2.1   Setting up the UK's Research Establishments   4
         1.2.2   JF Coales and ASE   6
         1.2.3   Fire-Control Systems   8
         1.2.4   Action Information Organisation and CDS   10
     1.3   The Admiralty Decides   12
     1.4   Enter the Instrument Makers   14
     1.5   The Lewisham Factory of Elliott Brothers   20
     1.6   Leon Bagrit   25
     References   30

2   A Glint on the Horizon   33
     2.1   The Man for the Job   33
     2.2   Distant Targets   40
     2.3   The CDS Project   41
     2.4   The MRS5 Project   43
         2.4.1   Why Digital?   44
         2.4.2   Innovative Radar   48
         2.4.3   The Cancellation of MRS5   50
         2.4.4   The *Netting* Project and the Legacy of MRS5   52
     2.5   A Little Computer History   53
     2.6   The Elliott 152 Computer   58
     2.7   Enter the Entrepreneurs   64
     2.8   Borehamwood's Financial Struggles   68
     2.9   Pulling Out of the Mire   72
     References   75

3 The Secret Digit 79

   3.1 The Elliott 153: The DF Computer 80
      3.1.1 The Admiralty's Needs 80
      3.1.2 The Project at Borehamwood 81
      3.1.3 General Description of the 153's Architecture 84
      3.1.4 The Operation of the 153 at Irton Moor 87
   3.2 GCHQ and Oedipus 89
      3.2.1 The Problem of Super-Enciphered Intercepts 89
      3.2.2 The 311 Project at Borehamwood 91
      3.2.3 The Structure and Operation of Oedipus 94
   3.3 Australia and WREDAC 99
      3.3.1 The Needs of Woomera 99
      3.3.2 WRE Chooses Elliott 103
      3.3.3 The Performance of WREDAC 104
      3.3.4 The Architecture of WREDAC and WREDOC 107
   References 111

4 Analogue Expertise 113

   4.1 Introduction: Analogue Versus Digital 113
   4.2 Admiralty Fire Control Tables 114
      4.2.1 Developments up to 1945 114
      4.2.2 Flyplane Predictor Systems 118
   4.3 Early Analogue Computing Activity at Borehamwood 122
      4.3.1 The Differential Analyser 123
   4.4 TRIDAC: The World's Largest? 126
      4.4.1 Guided Weapons and Cold War Imperatives 126
      4.4.2 The TRIDAC Project and Borehamwood 127
      4.4.3 TRIDAC at RAE Farnborough 130
   4.5 AGWAC: An Australian Success 134
      4.5.1 The Joint Project Background 134
      4.5.2 The Birth of AGWAC 136
      4.5.3 AGWAC Grows Up 137
   4.6 Elliott Analogue Computers and Simulators for Nuclear Power 139
   4.7 Small Analogue Computers: GPAC 140
   References 144

5 NRDC and the Market 147

   5.1 NRDC Discovers Borehamwood 147
      5.1.1 Funding for the Small-Scale Prototype 151
      5.1.2 Hopes for an Advanced Computer 153
   5.2 The Elliott/NRDC 401: Of Men and Machines 157
      5.2.1 The Ideas Take Shape 157
      5.2.2 The First Public Appearance 160

          5.2.3   They Have Their Exits and Their Entrances 164

          5.2.4   The 401's Progress, via Cambridge, to Rothamsted 170

   5.3   Into the Marketplace: The Elliott 400 Series 174

          5.3.1   New Management 174

          5.3.2   The 402 Production Gets Going 176

          5.3.3   Early Scientific Applications 179

          5.3.4   The Flutter Problem 182

   5.4   NRDC as a Partner for the Future 184

          5.4.1   The Siemens Project 184

          5.4.2   Process Control 188

   References 189

6   Process Control and Automation: The Bagrit Vision 193

   6.1   What Is, or Was, Automation? 193

          6.1.1   The Historical Perspective 193

          6.1.2   The Reith Lectures Perspective 193

   6.2   The Origins: Industrial Instrumentation and Control 195

          6.2.1   Prehistory: B&P Swift 198

          6.2.2   Post-war Rationalisation of the Instrument Industry 200

          6.2.3   Elliott Acquires a New Image and a New Name 201

   6.3   Automation Comes of Age 205

          6.3.1   American Licences and the Grand Strategy 205

          6.3.2   Al Sperry, Panellit and the Elliott 803 Computer 206

          6.3.3   The Component Parts of a 1960s

                 Automation Application 211

   6.4   Computers Suitable for the Task in the 1950s 213

          6.4.1   The American Scene 213

          6.4.2   Early Days in Britain: The Growth of Elliott

                 and its Rival, Ferranti Ltd. 214

          6.4.3   The Computer Comes to Market in Britain: 1951–1955 217

   References 221

7   Automation: The Machines and the Applications 223

   7.1   The Need for Digital Control 223

          7.1.1   The ARCH Family of Industrial Control Systems 224

          7.1.2   ARCH Installations and the Market Competition 227

   7.2   Applications of Elliott Computers in Automation 230

          7.2.1   Steel and Other Metals Processing 231

          7.2.2   Electricity (or Power) Generation 235

          7.2.3   UK Government R&D Establishments 236

          7.2.4   Oil Refining and Related Activities 241

          7.2.5   Chemicals 242

          7.2.6   Ships and Shipping 244

            7.2.7   Paper Mills and Typesetting 244

          7.2.8   Road Traffic Control 246
          7.2.9   Other UK and Overseas Industrial
                   and Research Applications................................... 247
   7.3   Anecdotes from Elliott Programmers
         who Worked on Automation Projects 250
          7.3.1   From Ed Hersom.. 250
          7.3.2   From Peter Williams 253
          7.3.3   From Roger Cook 254
          7.3.4   From Richard Burwood 255
   References... 256

8 Software and Applications at Borehamwood 259

   8.1   General Introduction.. 259
   8.2   Early Days: 1947–1952.. 261
   8.3   Nicholas in the Theory Division: 1953–1958.............. 263
   8.4   The Computing Division Goes to Market: 1953–1957.................. 268
   8.5   The Golden Years of Elliott Computers: 1958–1965.................... 276
          8.5.1   Evolving Divisional Structure............................. 276
          8.5.2   Autocode.. 280
          8.5.3   Algol 283
          8.5.4   Systems Software and Operating Systems......... 287
   8.6   Defence Applications.. 294
          8.6.1   Ground-Based Air Defence.................................. 294
          8.6.2   Artillery Control for the Army............................ 297
   8.7   Computers in Education.. 299
   8.8   Last Days: A Plethora of (On-line) Applications 302
   References... 304

9 NCR, the 405 and Commercial Data Processing 309

   9.1   Early Commercial Applications of the Elliott 405 309
   9.2   How NCR Became Involved: 1956–1957.................... 312
   9.3   Processing the Army's Payroll: A Snapshot
         of EDP Capabilities... 316
   9.4   NCR's Activities in the Period 1956–1967................. 319
   9.5   Strategic Appraisal: An Alternative View.................... 324
   9.6   The Market Competition in 1965.................................. 326
   9.7   The End of the NCR Arrangements............................... 330
   9.8   Selling Computers: The Competition Increases 333
   References... 335

10 Evolution of Elliott Computer Architectures 337

   10.1 Early Years: High-Tech, High-Speed, High-Complexity.............. 337
   10.2 New Directions for Borehamwood's Digital Technology............. 338
   10.3 Into the Market Place: The Elliott 401, 402 and 405.................. 340

10.4   Address Modification, Indexing and General Register Sets 343
10.5   Pegasus: The First Implementation of a General Register Set..... 345
10.6   Word Lengths and Instruction Sets 347
10.7   Borehamwood and Transistors.. 350
10.8   Memory Management and Bulk Input/Output............................ 357
10.9   Magnetic Tape and Magnetic Film Storage 359
10.10   Other Peripheral Equipment 363
References... 367

11   EARS and Aerials: Elliott's Radar Achievements, 1950–1986 371

11.1   Introduction: John Coales' Legacy (1946–1950)....................... 372
        11.1.1   The Establishment of the Borehamwood
                 Laboratories 372
        11.1.2   Radar: The Core of the MRS5 Contract 374
11.2   The Borehamwood Research Laboratories in the Early 1950s.... 376
        11.2.1   Mopsy and the Cassegrain Aerial 376
        11.2.2   Reorganisation and the Start
                 of Elliott's Airborne Radar...................................... 377
11.3   Elliott-Automation and the Changing Role
        of Borehamwood (1954–1967)... 378
        11.3.1   The Microwave Division... 378
        11.3.2   The Communications and Radar Research Laboratory,
                 1957–1960... 379
11.4   Elliott Automation Radar Systems (EARS): 1960 Onwards 381
        11.4.1   Company Reorganisations 381
        11.4.2   Sensors and Signal Analysis... 382
        11.4.3   Proposed Airborne Early Warning (AEW)
                 Systems for the Navy 383
        11.4.4   EARS and the Aircraft Manufacturers: AEW Gathers
                 Momentum... 385
        11.4.5   Five Airborne Radar Projects
                 that Did Not Bear Fruit (1962–1968)............................ 387
11.5   Forward to the 1980s.. 388
        11.5.1   The End of an Era 388
        11.5.2   Airborne Interception (AI) and Foxhunter.................... 390
        11.5.3   Nimrod Airborne Early Warning System...................... 390
11.6   Conclusions... 394
References... 396

12   Airborne Computing System Developments
     at Elliott-Automation, 1958–1988 397

12.1   Digital Computing Takes to the Air... 401
12.2   The Verdan Computer... 402
12.3   The Elliott 920B and 920M Computers....................................... 405

12.4   Airborne Digital Computing Becomes a Separate Discipline   409
12.5   The 12 Series and the 920 ATC Digital Computers....................   413
12.6   Computers for Nimrod and Jaguar...   415
12.7   Tactical Aircraft Attack Systems and Head-Up Displays............   418
12.8   Expanding into America: The A7 Contract   420
12.9   Mirage, MIG and China..   423
12.10   Technological Marvels...   424
12.11   The Influence of the F16 and American Standardisation.............   425
12.12   The Tornado and Nimrod..   426
12.13   The Maritime Re-organisation..   429
12.14   The Microprocessor Arrives   430
12.15   Squeezing the Last Juice from the 920 ATC...............................   431
12.16   Epilogue   431
References..   433

13   Mergers, Takeovers and Dispersals...   435
13.1   The UK's Computer Landscape in the 1950s and 1960s............   435
13.2   The Zenith of Elliott-Automation
         as an Independent Company   436
         13.2.1   The Computing Sector of Elliott-Automation   436
         13.2.2   The Company's Overall Financial Position   440
13.3   Satisfying the UK's Business Data Processing Market   446
13.4   The Large Engineering Companies..   450
         13.4.1   The Electrical Giants...   450
         13.4.2   GEC and Arnold Weinstock..   451
         13.4.3   English Electric...   455
         13.4.4   Marconi, a Famous Name   456
13.5   The Coalescing of Computer Interests: EELM and ICT   457
13.6   The Merger Between Elliott-Automation and English Electric...   458
         13.6.1   The Letter to Shareholders..   458
         13.6.2   Government Encouragement for Rationalisation..........   461
13.7   The GEC Takeover and the Formation of ICL............................   463
References..   466

14   The End of the Line   469
14.1   All Change at Borehamwood...   469
14.2   Meanwhile, in the Wider World of Information Technology.......   473
         14.2.1   Formal and Professional Qualifications   474
         14.2.2   Computing and Journalism   474
         14.2.3   The BBC's Computer Literacy Project   475
         14.2.4   Minicomputers and Microprocessors............................   475
         14.2.5   Data Transmission and Wide-Area Networks...............   475
14.3   Sorting Out the Pieces...   476

14.4   GEC Computers at Borehamwood
       and Dunstable in the 1970s 484
14.5   The GEC Series 63: A Very Difficult Project 489
14.6   GEC Computers in the Mid-1980s:
       The End of Borehamwood's Independence 493
14.7   The Demise of Borehamwood 496
14.8   Post-script: John Coales and Leon Bagrit as Public Figures 499
References 503

Appendix 1: Technical Details of the Elliott 152 and 153 505

Appendix 2: Technical Details of the Elliott Nicholas Computer 515

Appendix 3: Technical Details of the Elliott 400 series Computers 531

**Appendix 4: Technical Details of the Elliott
800 Series & 503 Computers** 555

Appendix 5: Technical Details of the Elliott 502 Computer 569

Appendix 6: Technical Details of Elliott 900 Series Computers 579

Appendix 7: Technical Details of the Elliott 4100 Series Computers 597

Appendix 8: Elliott Digital Computer Deliveries and Costs 611

Appendix 9: Supplementary Avionics Details 637

**Appendix 10: Historical Notes on Early British
and Non-British Computers** 655

**Appendix 11: Elliott-Automation Group Structure
and Factories in 1965** 671

Bibliography 679

Index 689

Picture Credits 709

Chapter 1
The Navy Comes to Borehamwood

1.1   A Place Called Borehamwood

About a dozen miles north-west of the centre of London, just off the Great North Road, lies the village of Borehamwood. In the 1930s, this was in a rural part of Hertfordshire, in which were clustered several large film studios. Collectively known as the *Elstree Studios,* after the neighbouring village of Elstree, the Borehamwood area was, by 1939, home to the largest number of motion picture production facilities outside Hollywood.

The onset of the Second World War was to add a new dimension. When the Admiralty needed a relatively unpopulated site on which to build a dispersal factory or *shadow factory* for the production of fuses for naval gunnery, they chose a field to the north-east of Bullbaiter's Farm, about 2 miles outside the village of Borehamwood (see map in Fig. 1.1). After the war, when this factory's products were no longer required, the Admiralty arranged for the redundant building to house a rather special research laboratory specifically to allow an old-established company called Elliott Brothers (London) Ltd. to pursue classified naval contracts. From Elliott's Borehamwood Laboratory sprang some of the most interesting ideas in the history of early British computers.

This is the story of the Borehamwood computers, the people who designed and built them, and the applications to which they were put. It is in some senses the story of the birth of Information Technology in Britain, as seen through the eyes of Elliott Brothers (London) Ltd. and its successor company Elliott-Automation. Though Elliott-Automation was merged with other companies at the end of the 1960s, its spirit lives on today in the world-class avionics divisions of BAE Systems.

There are two remarkable things about Elliott's Borehamwood Laboratory. Firstly, there is its rapid growth from a cold start with a dozen scientists and engineers in October 1946 to a thriving establishment of over 400 by the autumn of 1950 – and this in a period of postwar austerity. Secondly, the projects undertaken by the Laboratory were mostly of a classified (i.e. secret) nature, requiring

S. Lavington, *Moving Targets*, History of Computing,
DOI 10.1007/978-1-84882-933-6_1, © Springer-Verlag London Limited 2011

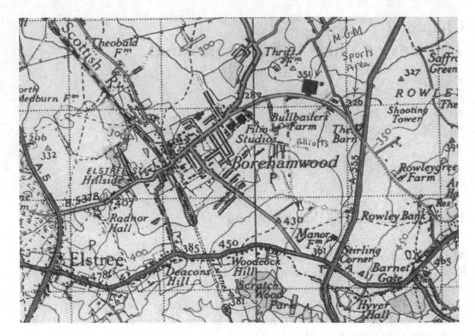

Fig. 1.1 A 1930s Ordnance Survey map of the village of Borehamwood in Hertfordshire, 12 miles north of the centre of London. To the right of the village, the locations *Elliotts, Sports Area* and *MGM* have each been marked by Ed Hersom, who joined the Borehamwood Research Laboratories of Elliott Brothers (London) Ltd. in 1947

the staff to work relatively independently from contact with other industrial and academic research establishments. It is only quite recently that some of the early Borehamwood defence reports have become officially available [1], allowing computer historians to appreciate just how exciting were the ideas generated by the Laboratory.

The need for commercial confidentiality has left another, more subtle, legacy. The reputation of individual scientists and engineers depends upon their ability to publish results openly. The work of the Borehamwood computer pioneers has remained largely unsung. With the effective takeover of the Borehamwood Laboratory's parent company Elliott Brothers (London) Ltd. by a succession of larger multinational companies in the late 1960s, archival records have been dispersed or lost. Although (to quote a wartime dictum) 'those who needed to know, did know', many former Elliott employees have gone to their graves without being able to explain their own contribution to innovative computer projects and related radar and aerospace developments. An aim of this book is to redress the balance.

Just how it was that advanced research came to rural Borehamwood in 1946, and why a company of scientific instrument makers called Elliott Brothers (London) Ltd. became involved, is a story that we will return to in a while. Firstly, it is necessary to explain why the Admiralty conceived the need for a new laboratory in

Fig. 1.2 The frontage of the former Admiralty Fuse Factory at Borehamwood, which became the Research Laboratories of Elliott Brothers in 1946. This neat photograph, from the early 1950s, belies the sparse, utilitarian, appearance of the rear buildings and open ground that extended for about 300 m behind the brick-built frontage

the first place. What sort of secret devices did the Navy require at the end of the war? Why could not the Admiralty's existing research establishments carry out the necessary development? The answer lies in the one word *Radar*.

Radar technology and the associated high-frequency (short wavelength) electronic know-how had dominated the Allies' scientific war effort and had contributed very significantly to victory. Realising the increased vulnerability of surface ships to attack by modern aircraft, the Navy attached great importance to the development of radar-directed anti-aircraft gunnery and, furthermore, to radar-directed command and control in multi-ship combat situations. Manual and electromechanical systems on warships were gradually to be replaced by electronic systems. In a remarkable leap of faith, the Admiralty decided in 1946 that the most advanced of their envisaged future systems (called *MRS5*) should be digital, rather than the customary analogue. We shall see in Chap. 2 how Borehamwood's first, and largest, Admiralty contract led to the design of the UK's first real-time online digital computer, the Elliott 152, for the control via radar of a warship's anti-aircraft guns. Later on we reveal how, by the early 1960s, Elliott digital computers accounted for about half the computers delivered annually in Britain and Elliott-Automation was the market leader in the online control of industrial processes.

Since many of the pioneering computer designers in the UK had learned their electronic trade at government wartime radar establishments, it is helpful to give a little background history. John Coales, the founding Director of the Borehamwood Laboratory, was a key figure in naval radar research. It will become clear later in this book that the development of early digital computer memory systems is intimately connected to 1940s radar work. Thus, a short review of UK radar developments, and an introduction to the sometimes confusing set of technical abbreviations, is a useful prelude to the Borehamwood story – and indeed to most of the other pioneering British computer projects of the late 1940s.

1.2 The Early Days of Naval Radar

It used to be assumed that radar was 'invented' by Robert Watson-Watt in England. The truth is not so simple. It is now clear that closely guarded research in Germany and America was proceeding along somewhat similar lines to British endeavours in the late 1930s – although at widely differing wavelengths. For example, in the Battle of the River Plate on 13 December 1939, the German pocket battleship *Graf Spee* was fitted with a radar rangefinder operating at a wavelength of 60 cm, whilst neither of the three British cruisers involved in the battle had radar. The previously unknown existence of the *Graf Spee's* radar was only revealed to British scientists when photographs of the wreck of the *Graf Spee* were examined shortly after the battle [2].

1.2.1 Setting up the UK's Research Establishments

It is believed that the concept of radio detection and ranging (radar) had been patented by LS Alder of HM Signal School, a naval establishment, in 1928. However, the then Director of Physical Research at the Admiralty could see no future in it, and did not authorise the expenditure to re-confirm the provisional patent [2]. Naval radar developments were approved in principle in October 1935, and serious work commenced in January 1938 [3].

Early practical experiments in radar or, as it was called until July 1943, RDF, were carried out in conditions of great secrecy at Orfordness, a remote site on the Suffolk coast (see also Appendix 9). In May 1936, the Air Ministry radar team at Orfordness led by RA (later Sir Robert) Watson-Watt moved to nearby Bawdsey Manor, where they were joined by the army's radar scientists. Meanwhile, naval radar research was carried out relatively independently at the Navy's Signal School (HMSS) at Eastney, Portsmouth.

Since several of the UK's future computer pioneers found themselves drafted to work on radar during the war, it is worth making a small detour to explain how the three services organised their radar research as hostilities began. The Air Ministry took the lead. On 1 September 1939, 2 days before war was declared on Germany, Watson-Watt's Air Ministry scientists moved to the safer location of

Dundee in Scotland, and from thence to Swanwich in Dorset, and finally in May 1942 to a permanent home in Malvern in Worcestershire. Meanwhile, the Army scientists at Bawdsey moved to Christchurch in Hampshire and then to Malvern. The Royal Navy retained its reputation as the Silent Service. Indeed, the Navy continued to conduct radar research relatively independently – first at its Eastney Signal School, and then from 1941 at dispersal sites in Surrey (at Haslemere and nearby Witley). In August 1941, the Navy's radar researchers at the Signal School had been formed into a separate command known as the Admiralty Signal Establishment (ASE). At Malvern, the RAF's Telecommunications Research Establishment (TRE) was the dominant partner, and by the end of the war, TRE had become the premiere allied site for innovations in radar and related electronic techniques.

For simplicity, we shall refer to all naval radar research as emanating from ASE, RAF radar research as emanating from TRE and army radar research as emanating from the Air Defence Experimental Establishment (ADEE). Of the people mentioned elsewhere in this book in connection with UK computer developments, the following had wartime connections with classified radar research and hence with state-of-the-art electronic pulse techniques:

At ADEE: WS Elliott
At ASE: J F Coales, A St. Johnston, E G Ludlow, T Gold, M Needham, C A Laws, A Cochrane and others
At TRE: H G Carpenter, T Kilburn, F C Williams, M V Wilkes, A M Uttley and others

Figure 1.3 is a conceptual diagram showing how wartime know-how at the various government establishments came to influence the design and/or construction of most of the pioneering pre-production British digital computers. In the case of the establishments at Bletchley Park and Dollis Hill, the know-how was mostly conceptual because, until the 1970s, the very existence of the UK's special-purpose code-cracking digital machines was not revealed outside the confines of the Government Communications Headquarters (GCHQ). In the case of ADEE, ASE and TRE, the flow of practical electronic expertise was more apparent.

We will return to Fig. 1.3 in later chapters, when the various projects are explained in a little more detail. In particular, we shall see how several of the computers shown in Fig. 1.3 had a particular relevance to Borehamwood. A general introduction to computer history is postponed to Sect. 2.3 and more details are given in Appendix 10.

As has been mentioned, John Coales became the first Director of the Borehamwood Laboratories after the war. Let us therefore continue the story of wartime naval radar, to convey a sense of the electronic priorities that motivated Coales in the late 1940s. The following information is largely taken from the book *Radar at Sea* [2]. This authoritative volume was compiled as a result of the activity of the Naval Radar Trust, set up in 1986 at a meeting attended by 150 wartime colleagues who had been associated with ASE. John Coales took a leading part in naval radar development [4] and in the formation of the Trust.

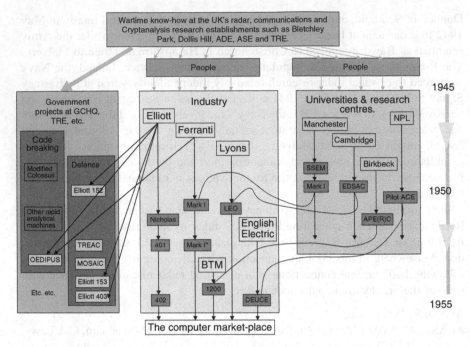

Fig. 1.3 The conceptual flow of British electronic expertise from government research establishments to academic and industrial organisations, immediately after the Second World War. The individuals who brought electronic know-how to computer development at Elliott's Borehamwood Laboratory after the war are identified by name in the text. Overall, the diagram shows that much behind-the-scenes activity was taking place whilst UK companies such as Elliott, Ferranti and English Electric were preparing computing systems for the open market. The left-hand box in the diagram includes six classified computer projects that came into operation in the period 1950–1955. In the right-hand box are shown five prototype research computers that came into operation in the period 1948–1952. The central box includes five types of production computer that came onto the market in the period 1951–1956

1.2.2   JF Coales and ASE

In the autumn of 1937, JF Coales, who had been working on Direction Finding (DF) equipment for the Navy since 1930, took responsibility at ASE for all naval radar research at wavelengths less than a metre. The Navy wished to work with shorter wavelengths than those used for the RAF's Chain Home (CH) stations (see Appendix 9) because: (a) this would allow smaller aerials to be used, hence more practical for ships at sea; (b) shorter wavelengths gave more precise information about a target; (c) shorter wavelengths were thought to be more difficult for an enemy vessel to trace.

As the threat of war increased in the late 1930s, the Navy's radar priorities emerged as:

1. Long-range air warning
2. Rangefinding for surface gunnery
3. Continuous short ranging on aircraft for anti-aircraft (AA) fire

By 1938, the Navy had decided to work on 7.5-m wavelength radar for long-range warning of aircraft (priority 1) and 50-cm wavelength for ship detection and gunnery control (priorities 2 and 3). By June 1939, Coales' team had a radar system working that transmitted 1.2 kW of power at 50-cm wavelength. This was world-beating, state-of-the-art radar. Yet in sea trials aboard ship, Coales' system was only able to detect ships at up to 5 miles distance and low-flying aircraft at up to 2.5 miles. Clearly, better performance was needed. Development proceeded at ASE at the highest priority.

Coales' *type 282* and *type 285* naval radar and their 50-cm derivatives became central to the vast majority of gunnery sets installed in British ships during the Second World War [3]. They were eventually superseded (in 1943 and 1945, respectively) by the *type 274* and *type 275* sets operating at 10 cm, which gave a narrower beam suitable for detecting small targets such as surfaced submarines and distant aircraft. Many of the naval applications of 10-cm radar were supervised by J F Coales. 10-cm wavelength radar was made possible by the invention in February 1940, by JT Randall and A H Boot of Birmingham University, of the multi-cavity magnetron valve – the result of an Admiralty contract. The magnetron was redesigned by E C S Megaw at the General Electric Company's (GEC's) Wembley Laboratories for operational use. The invention of the magnetron was of the utmost importance to the Allied war effort. By an inter-service agreement, the initial responsibility for 10-cm radar for all three services was placed with TRE, because of the RAF's urgent requirement for airborne radar sets. The *type 274* and *275* naval radar sets grew out of this TRE work.

At ASE, Coales would have been familiar with GEC at the start of the war because the company already had an Admiralty contract to develop naval communications equipment using a wavelength of 60 cm. Coales became an admirer of the way that GEC's Wembley Labs was organised and, as we shall see later, used Wembley as the pattern for the Borehamwood Laboratories.

Returning to the theme of naval radar, innovative electronic equipment became a major factor in the Battle of the Atlantic and other sea struggles. There were two side effects of these rapid electronic advances. Firstly, teams of scientists and engineers at establishments such as ASE and TRE grew skilled at state-of-the-art high-frequency pulse techniques, techniques that became very relevant to the postwar development of high-speed digital computers. Secondly, the teams were strongly motivated and well used to delivering innovative systems in short time-scales; this 'electronic confidence' would show through in the richness of digital designs which emerged in the UK postwar computer scene. As an indication of motivation, the following is J F Coales' description of ASE activity, as quoted in [2]:

'1941 opened in HM Signal School with everyone at fever pitch with excitement and enthusiasm, ... and this despite the fact that since the outbreak of war there had been no leave whatsoever and everyone had worked all the hours they could. Their Lordships [at the Admiralty] soon realised that this could not go on indefinitely, so we were ordered that everyone must have one day off a week and take a whole week's holiday in 1941'.

There are two applications of naval radar that were to have a direct influence on the Borehamwood story after the war: (a) gunnery control, more usually called *fire control*; (b) the collection and display of data on multiple targets, abbreviated as Action Information Organisation (AIO) or, originally, as the Comprehensive Display System (CDS).

1.2.3   Fire-Control Systems

At the outbreak of war, control of a ship's guns was normally carried out by a combination of optical, manual and electromechanical systems. Large ships had an installation called the Director (or Director Control Tower, DCT) mounted high up on the superstructure. The Director contained optical instruments for determining the range and bearing of a target. Originally, the Director was only intended for low-angle, or surface, gunnery. Later, radar antennae were added (e.g., for *type 274* radar), and later still radar nacelles were introduced to provide for High Angle gunnery (e.g. *type 275*) for use against aircraft. A gunnery control officer in the Director caused information to be fed to another part of the ship where the Fire-Control Tables, or Predictors, were housed. On larger ships, these 'tables' took the form of massive mechanical analogue calculators, weighing several tonnes, in which range and elevation of surface targets were set up on hand-wheels (see also Chap. 4). The Fire Control Table (FCT) then 'computed' the necessary settings for each gun, based upon own ship's course and speed, enemy ship's estimated course and speed, and predetermined wind and ballistics information. The resulting gun bearings and elevations were communicated to the gun crews. An adjunct to this was the fuse-setting equipment, for use with anti-aircraft shells which were designed to burst close to an enemy aircraft.

In the technical literature of the 1940s, the (electromechanical) analogue devices for fire control were sometimes called 'computers' – though of course this was well before the advent of what we would now understand as modern stored-program digital computers. The company Elliott Brothers (London) Ltd. had been making fire-control equipment, in one form or another, for the Navy since 1908. Elliott Brothers (London) Ltd. comes into the Borehamwood story in due course.

Towards the end of the war, advances in radar started to have two impacts on traditional methods of fire control. Firstly, as the performance of sea-going radar

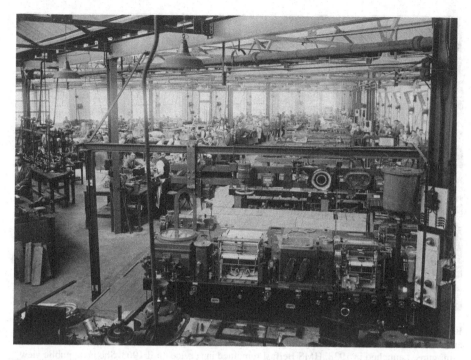

Fig. 1.4 Elliott's factory at Lewisham had been manufacturing fire-control (i.e. gunnery) equipment for the Royal Navy since just before the First World War. The photograph, taken in the 1920s, shows an Admiralty Fire Control Table (AFCT) being tested in the foreground. AFCTs were large electromechanical analogue computers

sets improved, it became possible to distribute accurate radar-derived range and bearing information, and to some extent height information, electronically throughout a ship. When fully developed, this rendered the traditional optical Director obsolescent. Secondly, it eventually became possible to mount a search-and-lock-on radar set onto each short-range anti-aircraft gun – giving each gun the capability (in theory, at any rate) to be controlled electronically. A late-1940s British development giving this capability to short-range weapons, for example Bofors guns, was the STAAG (Stabilised Tachymetric Anti Aircraft Gun) system. These and other analogue fire-control systems (FCS) are considered in more detail in Chap. 4, in the general context of analogue computers.

In 1944, the Admiralty produced a set of specifications for future gunnery radar, divided into short-, medium- and long-range systems (SRS, MRS, LRS). After the end of the war, the self-contained anti-aircraft gun radar systems were replaced by units known as MRS1. By about 1947, the Admiralty had contracted out to industry the development of three new MRS projects [5]. MRS3 (associated with radar *type 903*) was an anglicised version of the American Mk. 56 and Mk. 35 radar, with the contract being undertaken by Sperrys. MRS4 (with radar *type 904*)

Fig. 1.5 The Transmitting Station below-decks in the cruiser HMS Belfast. In the foreground is an Elliott Mark VI AFCT for computing elevation and training information for the cruiser's twelve 6-in. guns. Launched in 1938, HMS Belfast remained in service until 1963. She is on public view near Tower Bridge in London

went to Vickers at Crayford and Metro-Vick. MRS5 (radar *type 905* with a projected wavelength of 3 cm) went to Elliott Research Laboratories at Borehamwood. Good progress was made on MRS3, which is believed to have gone into service with the Royal Navy in the early 1950s. By the late 1940s, work on MRS4 had been abandoned, leaving MRS5 as an important research project involving J F Coales at ASE and, as we shall see, after 1946 at the Borehamwood Laboratories. The MRS5 (sometimes written *MRSV*) developments are described in the next chapter.

1.2.4 Action Information Organisation and CDS

Early radar sets had a simple cathode ray tube (CRT) display which gave a target's range, but not bearing. Targets were *blips* on a line traced electronically on the tube's screen. The Plan Position Indicator (PPI) was then introduced, whereby the CRT was made to display both range and bearings of targets as bright spots. Then came the Skiatron, which projected a PPI display optically onto a ground-glass screen. The Skiatron allowed operators to plot and annotate, by means of chinagraph

Fig. 1.6 HMS Vanguard, the last British battleship, was launched in 1944, commissioned in 1946 and decommissioned in 1960. Elliott AFCT Mark X equipment, together with two type 274 radar systems, was used for control of her 15-in. guns. In addition, HMS Vanguard had several other types of radar systems for controlling the anti-aircraft guns, etc

pencils, each target's movement as an action unfolded. The effective command of a ship under battle conditions began to rely more and more on the maintenance of an up-to-date plot. Towards the end of the war, efforts were in hand to provide electronic aids to automatic plotting. The Operations Room, rather than the bridge, was gradually becoming the tactical nerve centre of the ship. This was especially true for the direction of fighters during actions involving aircraft carriers. There was naturally a requirement to track multiple targets simultaneously and to deal with other incoming electronic information (e.g. Identification Friend or Foe, IFF).

By 1947, work had started at ASE on a new family of high-performance naval radar systems, to be connected to what was termed a Comprehensive Display System (CDS). By that time, J F Coales had left ASE to found the Borehamwood Laboratories. In principle, CDS was conceived as a data-extraction and display system for visualising target information received from (perhaps many) outlying radars (e.g., on picket ships). The outlying radars transmitted target information (range/bearing/elevation) into a central Command & Control system. To display this incoming information, a set of independent electronic markers was interleaved in the flyback of a normal radar system. These target markers were coded with numbers, letters or symbols. These markers could be selectively displayed at the grid-positions indicated by the range/bearing information. The target markers could be selected by a joystick activated cursor, and a target-marker's full supplementary information displaycd in a subsidiary 'window'. For a fuller description, see [6, 7].

The practical results of the CDS research, the integrated air defence control system type 984/CDS/DPT/CCA, first went to sea, in HMS Victorious, in 1957. In 1962, the US Navy held the first sea trials of its Naval Tactical Data System, the approximate equivalent of the British CDS [7].

As is described in Chap. 2, Borehamwood worked on Admiralty contracts for the CDS project as well as on contracts for the MRS5 project. More details of Borehamwood's work on CDS are postponed to Sect. 2.3.

1.3   The Admiralty Decides

John Coales was undoubtedly a principal player in ASE's plans to exploit the full potential of radar-controlled gunnery. Furthermore, he believed that it was essential for the MRS5 project to be undertaken by a multidisciplinary team of radar, control and gunnery scientists on a single site. The development of advanced naval fire-control equipment during the war had necessitated the cooperation of three Admiralty research establishments, at Teddington (Gunnery), Bath (Naval Ordnance) and Witley (Radar), with consequential frustrations and inefficiencies. Neither Coales nor Pat Brooking, the Admiral Superintendent, intended to repeat this bitter experience. Implicit in their vision for MRS5 was the necessity of combining two existing Admiralty research centres: ASE and the Admiralty Gunnery Establishment (AGE). At a time of rationalisation after the abnormally high wartime staffing levels, such an amalgamation of government-funded facilities might have seemed appropriate. Higher echelons in the Admiralty thought otherwise. They were not willing to countenance such a radical shake-up of tradition.

In what may have been a compromise plan, the Admiralty decided in the autumn of 1945 that the MRS5 project could best be undertaken by outsourcing the necessary R&D to industry. It may also have been felt that an industrial-strength laboratory would be better placed to assemble prototype systems and, after testing and acceptance, to go into production with a minimal discontinuity of control. Of course, all depended upon the Admiralty being able to 'sell' the MRS5 project to industry.

At the time, the Vickers-Armstrong company was the largest manufacturer of armaments in the UK, particularly for the Navy. It was Vickers who had developed the HACS system (see above). Naturally, the Admiralty first turned to Vickers for the MRS5 project. Vickers-Armstrong also made all the main Director towers for British ships but, being largely a mechanical engineering company, had contracted out all the electrical mechanisms to other firms. More particularly, at the end of the war Vickers-Armstrong had entered into an agreement with another company, Associated Electrical Industries (AEI), that AEI would undertake all the electrical and electronics parts of any future fire-control projects that were awarded to Vickers. When the Admiral Superintendent Pat Brooking realised this, he ruled Vickers out as a possible contractor for MRS5 because he firmly believed that both mechanical and electronic development of MRS5 should be undertaken at one site [8].

In 1946, there were several other large British engineering companies that had R&D facilities suitable for undertaking the MRS5 project. Amongst these were British Thomson-Houston (BTH), English Electric, Electric and Musical Industries Ltd. (EMI), Ferranti, GEC, Marconi, Metropolitan-Vickers, Mullard and Plessey – all names that we shall meet again later in this book when considering the embryonic computer industry. All these companies had recently been involved with the production of military electronic equipment of some form or other – though often as mass-producers rather than as originators of basic concepts. The range of manufacturing ability of some of these companies was magnificent – or at least so it must now seem to a twenty-first century audience all-too-familiar with the way in which heavy industry in the UK has declined. In the 1940s and 1950s, it was different. Consider English Electric, for example. Formed in 1918 by the amalgamation of four smaller engineering companies and with later additions in 1942 and 1946, English Electric designed and manufactured aero and marine engines and turbines, in addition to a host of smaller electrical consumer products. By the 1960s, the company had become especially famous in the public imagination for diesel-electric locomotives and for its P1 (Lightning) aircraft. The first truly supersonic British jet fighter, the English Electric Lightning, had its first test flight in 1954 and remained in service with the RAF until the late 1980s.

In the autumn of 1945, the Admiralty was, surprisingly, unable to find much enthusiasm amongst such companies for taking on the MRS5 project. Two reasons suggest themselves – one general and the other specific. In general, the war had had a profound effect upon all sectors of UK electrical and mechanical engineering. Companies had expanded their payroll dramatically, in response to government orders for urgently needed arms and munitions. The priority had been to meet ever-more demanding supply targets, in spite of disruptions by enemy action. By 1946, all this wartime activity had left British industry in need of a substantial re-focus on peace-time products. With peace came austerity and hardship. In 1946 and 1947, raw materials of all kinds were in short supply. Steel and petrol were strictly rationed. Infrastructures, particularly the national electricity and telephone utilities, were in dire need of repair and improvement. Getting involved in an ambitious, and secret, naval contract must have been low on the priorities of most company executives.

On a more specific topic, in 1945/46, the know-how surrounding radar technology was largely kept behind closed doors in government-run laboratories. Between 1939 and 1945, industry had been asked to manufacture to predetermined designs. Company-based and University-based blue-skies research had been scaled down; scientific effort had deliberately been concentrated in government establishments, such as ASE and TRE, which had close connections with the armed services. The development of radar, representing, as it did, the peak of electronic wizardry, was a prime example of this phenomenon. It is suspected that few UK company executives could comprehend, let alone be enthusiastic about, the technical requirements of the Admiralty's MRS5 project.

1.4   Enter the Instrument Makers

After unproductive discussions with Vickers-Armstrong and a number of other
large engineering companies, the Admiralty turned 'somewhat forlornly', according to John Coales, to Elliott Brothers (London) Ltd. Although a well-guarded
secret at the time, the Admiralty's 'forlorn' views of the Elliott company were
based on inside information about the firm's decline in performance during the war
[9], a subject to which we return in Chap. 2.

The early history of the Elliott company is ably described in [10–12], from
which the following brief notes are taken. The company was founded by William
Elliott, who was apprenticed to an instrument maker in 1795 and had set up in business on his own in London in about 1804. (The Elliott company letterhead in the
1960s actually said *Established 1800*, but this was on the basis of inaccurate
information.)

The onset of the *Industrial Revolution* in Britain led to a demand for precision
instruments. By the 1850s, the Elliott company products included drawing instruments, surveying instruments, telescopes and barometers. By the 1870s, telegraph
equipment and electrical instruments such as galvanometers were added. Naval instrumentation became an area of increasing activity and importance from the early years
of the twentieth century. From about 1911, Elliotts also included instrument panels for
aircraft in their repertoire. During its long existence, the company is said to have manufactured experimental apparatus for several notable scientists.

Elliott effectively ceased to be a family business in 1873 with the death of
Frederick Henry Elliott (a son of William) or, more strictly, with the death in due
course of his widow Susan.

Mrs Susan Elliott took Willoughby Smith as a business partner. Smith has been
described as 'a giant in the telegraphy business' but, being elderly at the time of
going into partnership with Mrs Elliott, he left the daily running of the Elliott
company to his son W O Smith. In turn, W O Smith had two sons L W and R O Smith,
who worked for the company. We shall meet LW and RO Smith in Sect. 2.7, when
they appear as Board members of Elliott Brothers (London) Ltd. in the autumn of
1945 (Fig. 1.10).

Returning to the 1890s, the instrument company Theilers and Elliotts combined
their activities in 1893 and traded as Elliott Brothers, with G K E Elphinstone as
managing partner and W O Smith as partner. The arrival of Elphinstone had
far-reaching consequences for Elliotts. Elphinstone came from an aristocratic
Scottish family and was well connected in government circles. He had a thorough
training in electrical engineering which was to bear fruit in many successful patent
applications. He was active in the development of gunnery-related equipment and
allied instrumentation for the Navy and was knighted at the conclusion of the First
World War. No doubt partly as a result of Elphinstone's enthusiasm, Elliotts moved
out of central London in 1900, when their new Century Works were opened in
Lewisham, about 8 miles south-east of the city centre – as described below in
Sect. 1.5. At that time, there were between 200 and 300 employees.

It is worth emphasising the importance of Elphinstone to the Elliott company. In the words of an Admiralty report written a couple of years after his death, 'Mr K G B Elphinstone brought to the firm his engineering ability and inventive genius and by his pressing enthusiasm and initiative he collected and animated an active group of working technicians and engineers..... His loss to the firm [in 1941] removed from the Directorate the only pronounced engineering qualifications available on the Board for undertaking Admiralty commitments and for endeavouring to match continued Naval requirements by a progressive policy and concern for the development of new products' [9]. The demise of Elphinstone certainly marked a decline in the company's fortunes.

The connection between Elliott Brothers (London) Ltd. and the British Navy is an emotive, but factually rather tenuous, part of the background to the Borehamwood story. The need for accurate gunnery at sea led to the development of several types of complex electromechanical predicting and plotting devices. Starting with the relatively simple hand-held *Dumaresq* analogue calculators, Elliotts worked with Royal Navy officers to develop and refine Fire-Control Tables which would today be recognised as complex analogue computers. These analogue computers required gears and motors designed with particular attention to precision and reliability – just the sort of challenge that inspired scientific instrument makers. It is not surprising that Elliott Brothers (London) Ltd. provided fire-control equipment to the Admiralty from 1908 until shortly after the end of the Second World War. Elliotts also supplied the first UK underwater ship's log and the first gyrocompass for the Royal Navy. During the war, the company had manufactured blind landing instruments, meteorological equipment, and gyro gun-sights (though production of this last item was very small in comparison with the output from another long-established company, Ferranti Ltd.). At the end of hostilities, a grateful country awarded medals to C A Gutsell, the Elliott company's chief designer, and to several other employees.

It might seem that the long-standing connection between Elliott Brothers and the Royal Navy would have led smoothly from the mechanical age to the electronic age, from analogue to digital, and that Elliotts would have been the Admiralty's first choice as contractor for the MRS5 project. However, the company's main factory, the Century Works at Lewisham in south London, had by 1945 become somewhat of a technological backwater. Although still skilled in manufacturing electromechanical equipment and precision electrical instrumentation, it had been bypassed by the huge wartime flow of government contracts for radar and allied electronic equipment. Compared with firms such as Ferranti Ltd., there was practically no electronic activity at Elliott's Lewisham factory. (This is exemplified in an analysis of patents for the Ferranti and Elliott Brothers, as given in Chap. 6.) The Elliott company had moved on from the days when their chief executive, G K E Elphinstone, was a well-known figure in Admiralty circles. Furthermore, a majority of Elliott shares had been acquired by Siemens Brothers of Woolwich, as described later. The influence of Siemens was, in the end, believed to have had a decidedly negative effect on Elliott's productivity and technical reputation – as illustrated in Chap. 2.

In 1946, when John Coales first came into contact with Elliott Brothers (London) Ltd., the company was run by a new, go-ahead, managing Director named Geoffrey Lee. How Lee became involved in Elliotts, and how Siemens Brothers' interests were bought out by the merchant bank Higginsons, is a fascinating story that sheds some light upon the evolution of the British instrument makers' industry and the path that was eventually to lead, as far as Elliott Brothers (London) Ltd. is concerned, to digital control and industrial automation.

In 1998, John Coales recalled the story, told to him many years before by Geoffrey Lee, of how Elliotts had been bought from Siemens Brothers in 1945 and how Lee had himself become the Managing Director of Elliotts with the help of Higginsons [8]. The tale is worth quoting in full but, before doing so, it is helpful to reveal some background facts about Dr. Wright, a leading player in the saga, so as to prepare the uninitiated for Coales' breathless prose. Dr. Wright was the most powerful figure within Siemens Brothers. To quote the Siemens company history [13]: 'Dr. Wright had died in office in 1951. For the last few years before his death, he had been chairman as well as managing director, but the double office had hardly increased his authority, for it was already paramount'. H R Bristow, himself a long-serving former employee of Elliotts, reminds us [12] that, in 1920, a working arrangement had been made between Elliotts and Siemens Brothers, Woolwich, 'to coordinate the two firms' experience in design and manufacture of electrical and mechanical instruments. Siemens took a share holding in Elliotts, which later became a majority holding'. Here, then, is the story of Elliotts, Siemens Brothers and Higginsons in 1945/46, as recalled by Coales [8]. Three paragraph-breaks have been added to Coales' text, to improve readability.

'Geoffrey Lee told me how J & E Stone of Deptford, who used to cast all the big phosphor bronze propellers for warships and liners, had been the empire of two families, the Pearsons and the Lees and that throughout the war he [Lee] and one of Pearsons had been joint managing directors. At some stage the Pearsons had started acquiring more shares whenever they could so that eventually they had a controlling interest. This resulted in Geoffrey Lee finding that the things he wanted to do were vetoed while the Pearson ideas were approved. Geoffrey Lee was not prepared to continue in such a situation so he resigned and found himself looking for a job.

'Now it so happened that at this time in 1945 Elliott Brothers was looking for a Managing Director, I believe because due to age the last of the Smiths had retired [probably L W Smith of the Smith family that became business partners to the original Elliott family in 1873, see Chap. 2 and [12]]. So Dr Wright, the head of the Siemens organisation in the UK, asked Geoffrey Lee to go and see him at Woolwich. They quickly reached an agreement but then Dr Wright asked Geoffrey Lee if there were any questions he wished to raise. [Lee did have a question, as described below, but Coales first gives some more background].

'Before the war three Jewish refugees had come to this country, one a Russian named Scholes [correct spelling?] who had made a fortune in Russia before the Revolution and then abandoned that and fled to Germany to make another. When Hitler came to power he had to abandon that one too and flee to this country where it is reputed he made another and became an expert on the instrument business which somehow introduced him to Higginsons, where he became a highly respected adviser. Lotti Ross on the other hand was a Hungarian and a very able mechanical engineer while Leon Bagrit was a highly intelligent Armenian [or Ukrainian? – see later] who among other things played the fiddle and was an art collector. Now in the 1930s W & T Avery had an almost complete monopoly of the manufacture and sale of weighing scales to the retailers in the UK. These scales were not mass-produced but had to be very accurately made and assembled and even so had to be tested and adjusted after installation by highly paid scale adjusters in order to satisfy the Weights and Measures Authority. Somehow Bagrit and Ross decided that by careful design and mass-production they could dispense with the scale-adjusters and still satisfy the Weights and Measures inspectors. They then apparently persuaded Higginsons of this, probably through the good offices of Scholes, then in his sixties, and Higginson, I believe [but see below in Sect. 1.6] bought a small engineering business, called B & P Swift, possibly making weighing machines, and installed Bagrit and Ross as Managing Director and Chief Engineer respectively. They were highly successful in achieving their aim and their mass-produced scales quickly undersold Avery's. During the war B & P Swift were able to get plenty of work making munitions of one sort or another and continued to expand. Then as the need for electronic instruments increased, no doubt also at Scholes's suggestion, they set up a small firm called Electromethods to develop and sell such instruments.

'Now at this time the British instrument industry was almost entirely made up of a large number of small family firms mainly based in London, the largest of them being the Cambridge Instrument Company based in Cambridge. Scholes had decided that this presented an opportunity for Higginsons to buy up a large number of them to form a larger company which would better compete with the much larger firms already operating in Europe and America, and he had already persuaded Higginsons to attempt to do this.

'Geoffrey Lee was already a part-time director of Electromethods and knowing Higginsons' intentions he did not wish to give it up. So when Dr Wright [at the above-mentioned Woolwich interview] gave him the opportunity to raise the matter he told him that he wished to continue this part-time directorship, which took up very little of his time. Apparently Dr Wright immediately took the attitude that if Geoffrey Lee came to work for him [at Elliotts] it must be absolutely full time with no part time jobs. To this Geoffrey Lee responded that in that case he would not take the position of MD of Elliotts. Geoffrey Lee was then completely taken aback when Dr Wright suggested that he [Lee] should buy Siemens out of Elliotts. Knowing what he did of Higginsons' plans, he apparently took a deep breath and asked Dr Wright if he could have 24 hours to consider the matter.

'The result we know. Geoffrey Lee went to Higginsons, who agreed to buy Elliotts from Siemens, installed Geoffrey Lee as Managing Director and Geoffrey Lee also remained on the Board of Electromethods'.

There is another, subtly different, version of this story, which we shall come to in Sect. 1.6 below but the final outcome of the story is not disputed.

Fig. 1.7 Leon Bagrit became the Managing Director of Elliott Brothers (London) Ltd. in 1947. He was responsible for breathing new life into an elderly firm, eventually becoming Chairman and Managing Director of the Elliott-Automation Group of companies until the takeover by GEC in 1968. This photo was taken in 1955

Fig. 1.8 Dr. Lawrence Ross, the long-time technical colleague of Leon Bagrit, became Technical Director of Elliott-Automation. Of Hungarian extraction, Ross was a very able mechanical engineer who had joined Bagrit's first company B & P Swift

Fig. 1.9 Edgar Herzfeld was the financial partner of the Bagrit/Ross/Herzfeld triumvirate that ruled the Elliott-related group of companies from 1947 to 1968. It was often said that 'Ross was the accelerator and Herzfeld was the brake'

Fig. 1.10 By 1945, the manufacturing facilities of Leon Bagrit's first company B & P Swift had expanded considerably due to war work. The photograph shows a section of B & P Swift's main machine shop. The original caption states 'The products of the best machine tool factories of Europe and America have been assembled to equip one of the most modern plants of its kind'. Bagrit was to contrast his up-to-date facilities with those of the old Elliott factory at Lewisham

Electromethods did not subsequently play much part in the fortunes of Elliott Brothers. Geoffrey Lee was the key player in the negotiations between Elliott Brothers and the Admiralty in 1946. Two other important names appear for the first time in the above story: Lotti Ross and Leon Bagrit. Dr. Lawrence Laslo (Lotti) Ross was born on 12 December 1900 with an original Hungarian surname variously recorded as Rossz or Roszwolgyi [14]. Leon Bagrit was born on 13 March 1902 and, because he soon became central to the whole Elliott and Borehamwood history, we shall introduce him properly in Sect. 1.6 below. In contrast, Lotti Ross was to remain an influential but shadowy figure, always there to give technical advice to his long-term friend and eventual boss, Leon Bagrit. Commander Henry Pasley-Tyler, who was eventually to become a Director of Elliott-Automation, described Ross as 'difficult to understand but a genius at heart' [15]. Few personal details of Dr. Ross have come to light, other than that he played the viola (see Chap. 6). Returning to the events of 1946, the focus was initially on Geoffrey Lee and John Coales and neither Bagrit or Ross had yet come into the Elliott/Borehamwood picture.

Discussions between the Admiralty and Elliott Brothers (London) Ltd. started in earnest early in 1946, with the objective of persuading the company to host a new research team whose prime objective, in the view of John Coales, was to work on the MRS5 contract. It was agreed that, with the help of the Admiralty, Elliotts would set up a new research laboratory of approximately 300 people in all. As well as leasing the redundant Borehamwood fuse factory to Elliotts at an annual rent of £4,615, the

Admiralty undertook to provide the capital required 'to equip the buildings and workshops' [8]. It was decided that Elliotts would transfer their Instrument research and development section, run by H D Hawkes, from Lewisham to Borehamwood. It was estimated that this section would represent 'about a tenth of the activity at Borehamwood, building up to about a third in the course of a few years' [8].

In a letter dated 28 May 1946, Geoffrey Lee, the Managing Director of Elliott Brothers, invited John Coales to take on the job of Research Director at Borehamwood at a salary of £1,600 a year. Coales recalls [8] that 'the more I talked to Geoffrey Lee the more I liked him and so I agreed to take on the job'.

Once agreement in principle had been reached with Elliotts, the Admiralty told Coales to proceed immediately with engaging staff for Borehamwood. Although still formally working at ASE, Witley, the Admiralty gave Coales permission to take as much time away from his ASE duties as required, in order to prepare Borehamwood for business by the autumn of 1946. Coales placed recruitment advertisements in newspapers and interviewed nearly 200 graduates and technicians during the summer of 1946 [8]. The difficulties of recruiting suitably qualified staff are discussed again in Sect. 2.1.

With hindsight, it seems that Elliott's guidelines for the financial management of Borehamwood were not sufficiently rigorously defined at the outset, and Coales' style of project management gave too much attention to technical features and too little attention to longer-term commercial benefits. We will see in Sect. 2.5 that, for various reasons, a clash of cultures and expectations gradually became apparent between the company's Lewisham headquarters and the Borehamwood Laboratory. However, all this was in the future when, on the 1 October 1946, the first batch of staff reported for duty at Borehamwood and Coales' bright new research team officially opened for business.

In the next chapter, we naturally concentrate on the technical activities of the new Borehamwood Research Laboratories. Before doing so, we should fill in two pieces of essential background to the Borehamwood story. Firstly, we describe Elliott's Lewisham headquarters in a little more detail because this gives a good impression of the company's long-established electromechanical manufacturing culture onto which the advanced electronic research culture of the Borehamwood Laboratories was due to be grafted. It will be evident that considerable managerial skills were to be required, if the old and new cultures were to work together in harmony. Secondly, in Sect. 1.6, we describe Leon Bagrit in more detail since he provided the long-term managerial skills within which the Borehamwood Research Laboratories were eventually to make such an impact on the British computing scene.

1.5   The Lewisham Factory of Elliott Brothers

Towards the end of the nineteenth century, it was clear that the Elliott company had outgrown its central London premises, which had successively occupied sites at High Holborn, the Strand, Charing Cross, and St Martin's Lane. A new and larger factory in the suburbs was required. The district chosen was Lewisham, about

5 miles (8 km) south-east of the city centre and just over 1 mile (2 km) south of the River Thames at Greenwich. Lewisham in the 1890s had an appropriate residential density of local labour and was well served by railway links to central London. The Lewisham site selected by Elliotts was a triangular area of water meadow bounded on two sides by railway lines and a housing estate and on the third by the Ravensbourne river. The southern apex of the triangle abutted Lewisham station. The site was approximately 7.5 acres (3 ha) in area [16], which certainly allowed for future expansion. Opposite on the eastern bank of the modest Ravensbourne lay an old Silk Mill with its mill pond.

Elliotts built their Century Works at Lewisham. Production started at Lewisham in 1900 – about 100 years after the effective foundation of the company by William Elliott in 1804. The photograph in Fig. 1.11 shows the site in the late 1940s, after the gradual expansion of factory buildings south-eastwards, towards Lewisham station which lies just outside the bottom right-hand corner of the photograph. By the start of the First World War, 400 or 500 people were employed at the site, many of them engaged in the production of naval fire-control equipment. Activity at the Century Works reached a peak during the Second World War. By 1943, the firm was said [9] to be employing 'about 1,800 workpeople of whom about half are directly employed on [Naval] Fire-Control Instruments and the other half on electrical and electromechanical apparatus to the present requirements of the

Fig. 1.11 The main factory of Elliott Brothers (London) Ltd. at Lewisham in the late 1940s. The dark-roofed trapezoidal building at the right-hand end of the factory was erected by the Admiralty in 1940 'for their special purposes' (i.e. fire-control equipment)

services and of Government Departments'. At its wartime peak, Lewisham is thought to have employed almost 4,000 people [17].

Being close to London docklands, Lewisham experienced considerable bomb damage during the war. To quote the description of Fig. 1.11 given in [17]: 'An industrial area close to a railway junction naturally suffered heavy bombing in the Second World War, but the Elliott factory itself escaped remarkably lightly. All around it bombsites can be seen, some of them occupied by prefabricated houses of various types. But oddly enough the most prominent derelict area, the dark square of rubble nearly in the centre of the picture, was not the result of bomb damage. That was the site of Lewisham Silk Mill, which had been demolished in 1937 or soon after'.

By 1939, the floor area of the factory was 155,000 ft^2. In 1940, an additional building with an area of 38,000 ft^2 was erected on the Lewisham site by the Admiralty 'for their special purposes' [16]. This bomb-resistant building was occupied by the company for the design and manufacture of naval fire-control (gunnery control) and associated equipment. The Admiralty building can be seen in the photograph in Fig. 1.11, towards the bottom right corner of the Lewisham site. In 1940 it had cost £50,000 [9].

The company also owned a sports ground of about 6 acres at New Eltham, approximately 4 miles to the south-east of Lewisham [16].

After the end of the war, Elliotts suffered a period of setbacks and regrouping, as hinted at earlier and described more fully in Chap. 2. Employment at the Century Works had dropped to 'less than 1,000' in 1947 [18, 19]. An impression of shaky morale at Lewisham in 1947/1948 may be gained by quoting from Harold Bowden [20], who had joined Elliott Brothers in the 1920s and worked his way up, staying with the firm until some time after the arrival of Bagrit and Ross in the late 1940s.

'When the war ended, the naval work which had sustained the firm dried up and the ageing directors could not undertake the revolution which would be necessary to succeed in the uncharted commercial world. New people took over and, after a few games of king-of-the-castle, Mr Bagrit and Mr Ross emerged as the new bosses. Mr Bagrit was the chief but we did not see much of him until a grand assembly at the Grosvenor Hotel when he lectured us on the supreme virtue of salesmanship. It was not very encouraging for technical men like myself but he certainly put his ideas into practice …

'Dr Ross was in evidence daily and started by assembling as many people as could be squeezed into the canteen to explain his empirical methods. He did not believe, he said, in planning things in great detail; if he had an idea he would try it and, if it didn't work - so what, he would scrap it. We must therefore not be surprised if a lot of confusing changes took place - it would all come out right in the end.

'Well, we had been warned but those who disliked change were shocked when he proceeded to do what he said. At this time there was no great difficulty in getting jobs and people left in droves … No-one was sacked, they found themselves some new niche and the shake-up did them a world of good. The foundry was shut down; this meant that the skilled joiners who made patterns were redundant but they were kept on the payroll. Mr Bagrit kindly found them work in panelling his house in Hampstead. [From the 1940s, the Bagrits lived at Vale Lodge and then at Upper Terrace House in Hampstead [21]].

Bagrit had a Bentley and a chauffeur who lived in Catford but had to be on call at all times of the day or night and took Mrs Bagrit shopping on Fridays. Dr Ross had no such perks, drove himself and lived in a modest house in Bickley'.

The Lewisham factory, and the Elliott company, survived. By the start of the 1950s, the research projects at Borehamwood and Leon Bagrit's entrepreneurial enthusiasm – of which more in later chapters – had breathed new life into the company. A new Electronics Division was set up at Lewisham in due course, to manufacture designs produced at Borehamwood. A certain amount of re-building activity was undertaken at the Century Works in the mid-1950s, according to the Elliott Annual Report of 1954. It was in this year that the Nuclear Reactor Controls Division was established at Lewisham and this Division was to be the Elliott activity that survived the longest on the site. Chap. 4 describes the Elliott Nuclear Reactor Computers and Simulators (i.e. analogue computers) and Chap. 7 gives examples of process control instrumentation for reactors.

Also in 1954, Century Works was undertaking work allied to the defence arena: the Mechanical Engineering Division included the manufacture of fire-control and gyroscopic equipment and hydraulic servos; the Aviation Division included auto-pilots, autostabilisers, and flight instruments.

Nevertheless, when Laurie Bental joined Elliott Brothers in 1955, he gained the impression [22] that 'the main part of the factory at Lewisham was still engaged on the manufacture and testing of electricity metres. I was fortunate to be allocated to very challenging work in the Automatic Weighing Division'. Laurie's first task was to design and build a digital adder for a crane sub-system, using type 3000 Post Office relays. He gives the impression that this digital unit was well outside the experience of his Lewisham boss. Soon after, Laurie happily transferred to the excitement of Borehamwood.

According to the collection of Elliott trade brochures now held at Lewisham Public Library, the products to emerge from the Lewisham factory in the 1950s and 1960s included the following:

- Torque motors – typical application: actuator for hydraulic valves, etc.
- Differential Pressure Transmitter – e.g. for flow measurement.
- Elliott load cell – a precision electromechanical force–measuring transducer based on resistance strain gauges. Amongst the applications were weighbridges and belt-weighers (for production-line belts containing (e.g.) lumps of coal); see Chap. 6.
- Bristol's 500-series recording thermometers.
- Bristol's air-operated free-vane controllers for process control.
- Electronic self-balancing potentiometric indicators, e.g., for industrial weighing applications. Also, the Elliottronic potentiometer recorder, a chart recorder for use with thermocouples etc. to produce a data-logging record of the control variables encountered in an industrial process; see Chap. 6.
- Mechanical automation – (sequence control systems) – e.g. for lathes and other machine tools.
- S S White industrial Abrasive Units.

- Beam switches, operating for tension or compression.
- Load cells used for testing jet engine thrust.

As an outward sign of the change in fortunes that Bagrit had brought to both Lewisham and Borehamwood, the marketing name of Elliott Brothers (London) Ltd. was effectively changed to Elliott-Automation Ltd. in the summer of 1957. Under Leon Bagrit's energetic expansion of the Elliott-Automation enterprise, the total people employed at the Century Works was to rise to about 2,000 by the mid-1960s, thereafter falling in response to mergers and takeovers. There is anecdotal evidence that, at some stage in the 1950s, Elliotts wished to expand the Century Works further but could not obtain the necessary planning permission from the local Lewisham Council. In any case, Elliott's manufacturing facilities had grown rapidly at other sites in the UK and overseas by the early 1960s. Appendix 11 documents the entire Elliott-Automation group structure and factories, as they existed at the zenith of Leon Bagrit's empire in 1965.

Elliott-Automation was absorbed into the GEC empire in 1968, as described in Chap. 13. By the time the Lewisham factory finally closed in 1989, there were only about 150 employees left on the site. By the early 1990s, the factory had been demolished and the site reused for residential housing.

In contrast to the demise of manufacturing at Lewisham, the fortunes of Elliott's Borehamwood Laboratories went from strength to strength. After the takeover of Elliott-Automation in 1968, research and development activity at Borehamwood continued under the GEC umbrella until at least the mid-1990s. As described in Chap. 14, computer design activity effectively dwindled from 1988 onwards, though various other avionics-related and radar activities continued at Borehamwood. A fundamental change of direction took place at Borehamwood in 1993, with the sale of the defence arm of GEC to BAE Systems. The rest of GEC was renamed Marconi plc. In May 2002, Marconic plc announced a loss of £5.7bn., at the time the biggest loss in British corporate history. Soon after (July 2002), the Borehamwood site was sold to a property-management consortium that included Legal & General and St. Modwen Properties plc. BAE Systems, however, continues today as a successful multinational company.

Besides Lewisham and Borehamwood, the Elliott company was to acquire several more manufacturing and development sites as the firm's fortunes strengthened during the 1950s and 1960s. Chief amongst the additional locations was a large factory at Rochester, whose acquisition is discussed in Chap. 2. Rochester was to become the heart of the company's aerospace activities and, in terms of innovation, the site where the spirit of Elliott technical excellence survived the longest within the GEC, and later the BAE Systems, organisations. A brief history of the Rochester site is given in Appendix 9.

All this was still to come when, in 1946, Geoffrey Lee and John Coales came to an agreement that established the new, forward-looking, Borehamwood Research Laboratories as part of the rather tired and war-weary company of Elliott Brothers (London) Ltd. Looming in the background was an entrepreneurial powerhouse named Leon Bagrit, to whose life history we now turn.

1.6 Leon Bagrit

There is little in the public domain about Leon Bagrit's early private life – so little, indeed, that one suspects Bagrit himself was not interested in anyone who looked backwards rather than forwards. Bagrit's entry in the *Oxford Dictionary of National Biography* [23] is perhaps the most informative account that has come to light. This entry was written by Bagrit's long-time business associate Edgar Herzfeld. Edgar Otto Herzfeld was born in London on 14 March 1909. He joined Elliott Brothers (London) Ltd. in about 1948, having previously been Secretary of B & P Swift [24]. Herzfeld quickly became the third member – and longest-surviving – of the ruling triumvirate of Bagrit, Ross and Herzfeld. Henry Pasley-Tyler has described Herzfeld as 'a most likeable man with an impish sense of humour, a real gentleman, enormously competent; his stability and financial management played an enormous part in the recovery of Elliott Brothers' [15].

The underlying chronology of Leon Bagrit, as extracted from Edgar Herzfeld's authoritative article [23], runs as follows.

1902   13 March: born in Kiev, Ukraine
1914   Arrived in London from Belgium
1926   Married Stella Feldman
1927   Becomes General Manager of Herbert & Sons, a weighing machine manufacturer
1935   Set up his own firm, B&P Swift, manufacturing weighing machines
1947   B&P Swift acquired by Elliott Brothers (London) Ltd.
1957   Establishment of Elliott-Automation Ltd., with Bagrit as deputy chairman and managing director
1962   Becomes a director of the Royal Opera House, Covent Garden, and is the founder and chairman of the Friends of Covent Garden
1962   Is knighted
1962   Becomes president of the British Friends of Haifa Technion, Israel
1963   Becomes a member of the Council for Scientific & Industrial Research
1963   Becomes Chairman and Managing Director of Elliott-Automation Ltd.
1964   Becomes a member of the Advisory Council on Technology
1964   Invited to give the BBC Reith Lectures
1965   Awarded the Albert Medal by the Royal Society of Arts for his work on the application of automation to industry
1966   Receives an honorary doctorate from the University of Surrey
1967   Elliott-Automation acquired by English Electric Co. Bagrit becomes a Deputy Chairman of English Electric
1968   English Electric acquired by the General Electric Company (GEC)
        Receives an honorary doctorate from the University of Reading
1973   Bagrit retires from being chairman of GEC-Elliott-Automation Ltd.
1979   22 April, dies in London

Leon Bagrit's 'wealth at death', according to [23], was £2,276,444 – not bad for someone from an impoverished background who did not speak a word of English before he was 12 years old! Bagrit's wife, Lady Stella Bagrit, died in March 2001, aged 95 [25]. They had two daughters and at least six grandchildren, of whom a grandson has provided more information about his grandfather's early life [26]. The following additional biographical comments on Leon Bagrit's early life are based largely on [23], supplemented by [21, 26–28].

Leon Bagrit was the second of three children of Manuel Bagrit, a jeweller, and his wife Rachel Yousopovich. The family left Kiev for Belgium, from which they soon moved on to England in 1914 'having lost all their possessions as a consequence of the German invasion' [27]. Upon arrival in Britain, the 12-year-old Leon spoke no English but the headmaster of St Olave's School, Southwark, took a personal interest in his education and in due course Leon gained a school prize for English Literature. Although [23] states that Leon read Law at Birkbeck College, University of London, such college records that have come to light simply show that he entered Birkbeck's one-year Matriculation course on 16 October 1923, being registered for English, Maths, Chemistry, French and History. At the time of his registration, Leon was aged 21. He was living at 458 New Cross Road, London SE14, and his occupation was given as *Commercial Traveller* – see Fig. 1.12.

Bagrit's Birkbeck registration form includes a section for giving *Schools attended with years of entering and leaving*. The single item in this section simply records 'St Olave's School, 1917 to 1920'. We may guess that Bagrit was very much a 'self-made man' whose natural abilities and energy propelled him upwards and onwards after leaving school. He had a talent for music and 'playing the violin in an orchestra helped him through the precarious early adult years … he had no formal training in engineering but possessed an exceptional understanding of engineering and related matters which was vitally important to his subsequent career.' [23].

Bagrit's 'precarious early adult years' are not revealed in any detail in [23]. Bagrit did, however, allow some of his pre-Lewisham career to creep into an official company document that appeared in the mid-1960s at about the time when Elliott-Automation was at its most profitable [28]. Here is an extract, which subtly re-tells the story recounted in Sect. 1.4 above by John Coales of how Bagrit's empire began.

'The history of the Elliott-Automation Group is really the story of the vision and drive of one man, Sir Leon Bagrit, and the confidence which his bankers, Higginson & Co. (now Philip Hill, Higginson Erlanger Ltd.) have had in him since the earliest days. In 1935 Leon Bagrit, who had previously worked for two weighing machine firms, Avery's and Herbert & Sons – set up his own company to manufacture weighing machines and food processing equipment. The company, B & P Swift, had an equity capital of only £100, of which two thirds was contributed by Leon Bagrit, but it expanded by raising preferential capital, discounting its hire purchase agreements, and by bank borrowing. In 1942 Rudolph de Trafford, a partner of Higginson & Co., joined the Board. By 1945 Swifts were established with two well-equipped factories on the North Circular Road.

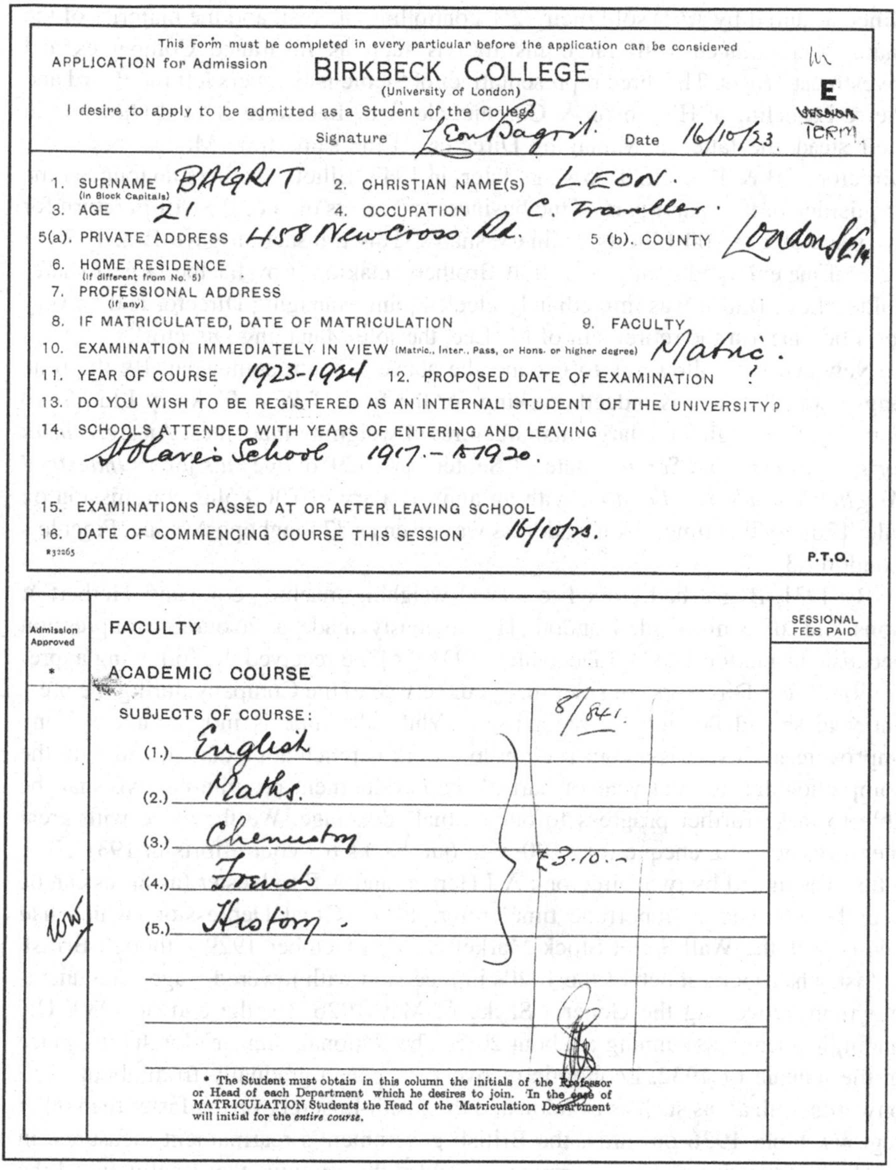

This Form must be completed in every particular before the application can be considered

APPLICATION for Admission   **BIRKBECK COLLEGE**
(University of London)

I desire to apply to be admitted as a Student of the College

Signature *Leon Bagrit.*   Date *16/10/23*

E
SESSION
TERM

1. SURNAME *BAGRIT*   (in Block Capitals)   2. CHRISTIAN NAME(S)   *LEON.*
3. AGE   *21*   4. OCCUPATION   *C. Traveller.*
5(a). PRIVATE ADDRESS   *458 New Cross Rd.*   5 (b). COUNTY   *London SE14*
6. HOME RESIDENCE   (If different from No. 5)
7. PROFESSIONAL ADDRESS   (If any)
8. IF MATRICULATED, DATE OF MATRICULATION   9. FACULTY
10. EXAMINATION IMMEDIATELY IN VIEW (Matric., Inter., Pass, or Hons. or higher degree)   *Matric.*
11. YEAR OF COURSE   *1923-1924*   12. PROPOSED DATE OF EXAMINATION   *?*
13. DO YOU WISH TO BE REGISTERED AS AN INTERNAL STUDENT OF THE UNIVERSITY?
14. SCHOOLS ATTENDED WITH YEARS OF ENTERING AND LEAVING
St Olave's School   1917. – 1920.

15. EXAMINATIONS PASSED AT OR AFTER LEAVING SCHOOL
16. DATE OF COMMENCING COURSE THIS SESSION   *16/10/23.*

#32265   P.T.O.

Admission Approved

FACULTY

* ACADEMIC COURSE

SUBJECTS OF COURSE :

(1.) *English*
(2.) *Maths.*
(3.) *Chemistry*
(4.) *French*
(5.) *History .*

SESSIONAL FEES PAID

8/84/.

£3.10.~

* The Student must obtain in this column the initials of the Professor or Head of each Department which he desires to join. In the case of MATRICULATION Students the Head of the Matriculation Department will initial for the *entire course.*

Fig. 1.12 Leon Bagrit arrived in Britain in 1914 as a 12-year-old refugee without a word of English. By the age of 21, he was working as a commercial traveller and had registered for a part-time Matriculation course at Birkbeck College, University of London

'In that year Elliott Brothers, the old-established firm of instrument makers, began running into difficulties. Elliotts had been kept going through the war largely by work on naval fire control equipment but their Admiralty contracts were cancelled at the end of the war. Accordingly in July 1945 Siemens Brothers and Co. Ltd.

(since acquired by AEI) sold their 72% controlling interest, and the majority of the shares were placed with large institutions such as Insurance Companies and Investment Trusts. The three representatives of Siemens Brothers left the Board and Pierre Lachelin, of Higginson & Co., and Geoffrey Lee were elected Directors in their stead, the latter as Managing Director. At the same time Mr Lee became a Director of B & P Swift. Two years later, in 1947, Elliott Brothers announced the acquisition of the major part of the business and assets of B & P Swift in return for the issue of £25,000 Elliotts ordinary shares. This transaction gave B & P Swift 22% of the enlarged equity of Elliott Brothers, making it by far the largest share-holder. Leon Bagrit was immediately elected joint Managing Director and he very soon became, on the retirement of Mr Lee, the sole Managing Director'.

New evidence allows us to expand the above account somewhat. By the time Bagrit was 27, he was indeed working for the firm of W & T Avery Ltd., Soho Foundry, Birmingham, a large manufacturer of weighing machines. An *Agreement for Employment and Service,* dated 1 September 1929, defines his job as *Industrial Weigher Salesman at London*, with an annual salary of £300 plus commission on sales [26]. By this time, Leon's address was given as 77 Stanhope Avenue, Finchley, London N3.

By 1931, Bagrit had moved to a rival weighing machine company, Herbert & Sons Ltd. of Smithfield, London. He obviously made a favourable impression because, in a letter dated 23 December 1931 [26], he received the following appre-ciation: 'Your Directors consider that your service to the Company during the pres-ent year should be suitably recognised. Whilst the time is inopportune for any improvement in salaries, your progressive work is much appreciated, and with the completion during next year of part of the development programme, we shall be able to make further progress to our mutual advantage. We therefore with great pleasure enclose a cheque for £100 with our thanks for your efforts in 1931'. The letter was signed by two Directors: A J Herbert and A E Sylvester (as far as can be deciphered). The 'inopportune time' refers to the Great Depression, which had begun with the Wall Street Stock Market crash in October 1929 – though British industry had spend much of the 1920s in recession with lowered wages and unem-ployment provoking the General Strike of May 1926. By the end of 1930, UK unemployment was running at about 20%. The National Hunger March took place in the autumn of 1932. Economic recovery happened gradually from about 1933 onwards, with areas such as London and the South-East recovering faster than other regions. From 1936 onwards, the British government's rearmament measures, in the face of the rise of Nazi Germany, provided the stimulus that finally ended the economic depression in Britain.

Whilst employed at Herbert & Sons, Bagrit's mind was turning to innovations in mechanical weighing machines or scales. A loose-leaf folder containing 36 pages of Leon's hand-written design notes has survived [26], of which one diagram is reproduced as Fig. 1.13. His machines all seem to be of the table-top variety (i.e. portable), for weighing groceries, etc. in retail outlets. Besides written comments, the pages contain formulae, calculations and some sketch drawings. The calcula-tions mainly concern dimensions of a beam and its bearings and the geometry of

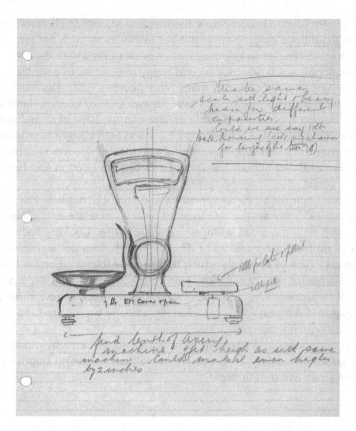

Fig. 1.13 Sketch of a weighing machine, taken from Leon Bagrit's design notebook covering the period 1932–1934. In 1935, Bagrit set up his own company, B & P Swift Ltd., to manufacture weighing machines and, in due course, food-processing equipment. During the Second World War, the company switched to government contracts, for example, gearboxes for aircraft controls and actuators for flaps and undercarriages

associated pointers. In one case, a comparison with an 'Avery' product seems to be made. The last page is dated 9 February 1934, and it seems likely that the notes were made in the period 1932–34.

In 1935, Bagrit left Herbert & Sons and set up his own company, B & P Swift, as recounted earlier. B & P Swift was located at 124–130 East Road, City Road, London N1, according to a patent filed in 1935 (see below). By 1945, the company's address for patent-application purposes was given as North Circular Road, London NW10 – probably synonymous with the Willesden district of London. A plausible explanation – see Appendix 9 and [29] – is that the B stood for Bagrit and the P for Dickie Pollard, a technical associate who became a close friend.

On the 24 October 1935, Bagrit filed his first patent (number 464832) for the improvement of knife-edges in scales. From that moment onwards, Leon Bagrit was on track to become the industrial entrepreneur behind much of the developments described in the rest of this book.

Bagrit's progression to become the Chairman and Managing Director of Elliott-Automation should not obscure his continued involvement with the arts. 'He had great breadth of vision and in business was more concerned with the broad sweep than with the detail, much of which he was happy to delegate to colleagues … this approach left him time to pursue his many other interests' [23]. His musical talent and his involvement with the Royal Opera House, Covent Garden, have already been alluded to. He was also 'a notable collector in the field of visual arts' [23]. Through charitable Trusts and scholarships, Leon and Stella Bagrit have bequeathed a number of grants that still support scientific and artistic endeavours at institutions such as the Royal Ballet School and Imperial College in London and Ben Gurion University in Israel.

As a person, Leon Bagrit could appear intimidating. His nephew Peter Fielding remembers him as: 'very austere. He found it difficult to relate or communicate in almost any way with me as an infant or even a teenager. Looking back, his eyes were kinder than his demeanour, and I think it was his stammer and stutter which inhibited an easy flow of humanity which he obviously felt based on his love of the arts' [21]. This stutter was seemingly not always apparent though Laurence Clarke, who joined Borehamwood in 1951 and rose to be a Technical Director, remembers that Leon Bagrit 'did repeat words occasionally when he was excited and somehow had to keep up with his thoughts' [30].

For most of this book, Bagrit, the private individual, remains hidden behind Bagrit, the leader of industry. In Chap. 14, we will catch up with Bagrit's persona in his mature years and in retirement.

References

1. It was in 2003 that Marconi/GEC finally left the Borehamwood Laboratories and the Strong Room at Borehamwood was 'cleared' by the relevant authorities. Copies of certain classified Reports were officially removed; the remainder were passed to the Science Museum in London, where they remain in storage
2. Derek H (1993) Radar at Sea – the Royal Navy in World War 2. MacMillan, London. See also Coales JF, Calpine HC, Watson DS (1946) Naval fire-control radar. J IEE 93(2): 349–379, part IIIA (Radiolocation)
3. (a) Kingsley FA (1995) The application of radar and other electronic systems in the Royal Navy in World War II. Macmillan, London; (b) The National Archive, file ADM 1/22753. 'Crown assistance to provide funds for Messrs Elliott Bros plant extension 1951'. Contains documents administered by the Admiralty's Director of Radio Equipment, to whom a request to extend Borehamwood was made. This request was, in the end, turned down. File ADM 1/22753 also, curiously, contains correspondence and historical notes concerning Information requested by Sir Robert Watson-Watt on 'radar in the Royal Navy', dated 1 Nov 1951
4. Coales JF, Calpine HC, Watson DS, Coales JF, Calpine HC, Watson DS (1946) Naval fire-control radar. J Inst Elect Eng 93(2):349–379, part IIIA
5. Morgan FC (1948) Hand-over notes. Admiralty Signal Research Establishment, Dec 1948. In File ADM 220/222: Fire control radar: outline of work in progress, Dec 1948, The National Archive
6. Benjamin R (1989) The post-war generation of tactical control systems. J Naval Sci 15(4):263–275

7. Benjamin R (1996) Five lives in one. Parapress, Tunbridge Wells. ISBN: 1-898594-25-2

8. Coales JF (1946) Elliott Research Laboratory – Borehamwood 1946. Seven typed pages and eight hand-written pages, covering the period mid-July 1945 to autumn 1946. Sent with an accompanying letter to S L H Clarke on 29 Apr 1998. A copy of the document exists in the Archive of the Institution of Electrical Engineers, London, catalogue number SC168/1/6/2/3. In the accompanying letter, John Coales says that he hopes to continue writing about Borehamwood 'because there is a lot during the next two years including the security problems and relationships with BTM etc. that now only I know about'. He explains in the letter that he has not been in good health. John Coales died on 6 June 1999, aged 92, having been unable to continue his account

9. The National Archive (1943) file ADM 178/309: Report on morale and output of Elliot Bros Ltd: suggestions for improvement, 1943. Produced by the Director of Naval Ordnance, Sept 1943, DNO. Note: this file was originally marked as 'Secret: closed until 2043'

10. Clifton, Gloria (March 1993) An introduction to the history of Elliott Brothers up to 1900. Bull Sci Instrum Soc 36:2–7

11. Bristow HR (March 1998) Elliott, Instrument makers of London: products, customers and development in the 19th Century. Bull Sci Instrum Soc 36:8–11

12. Bristow HR (2002) Development of the Elliott Company, 1804–1950. Paper presented at the Institution of Electrical Engineers summer conference on the history of electrical engineering, university of Greenwich, July 2002 (Available from the Institution of Engineering and Technology, Savoy Place, London WC2R 0BL)

13. Scott JD (1958) Siemens brothers, 1858–1958: an essay in the history of industry. Weidenfeld & Nicholson, London

14. Directors and Officers: Register of Secretaries and Directors of Elliott Automation Ltd., 1950–1958. This is a ledger with (mostly) hand-written entries in pre-printed columns, deposited in the Marconi Archives at the Bodleian Library, University of Oxford, where it appears under catalogue number E006

15. Commander Henry Pasley-Tyler CBE, un-dated audio-recording of an interview with Laurence Clarke. It may be inferred from letters to Laurence that this interview took place some time between 1 Feb 1995 and 24 May 1995, at which time he was 84 years old. Pasley-Tyler died in Dec 1995

16. Three-quarter page advertisement on page 11 of The Times newspaper for 11 May 1953, in compliance with the regulations of the Council of the Stock Exchange, London, 'for the purpose of giving information to the Public with regard to the Company'

17. John Coulter (2005) Around Lewisham and Deptford. Sutton, Gloucestershire, p 138. ISBN 0-7509-4136-7

18. Feature article in the Lewisham Journal & Borough News, 23 Nov 1951

19. Leon Bagrit in June 1963, quoted in the Elliott-Automation Annual Report for 1962

20. Harold Bowden, two-page typed transcription of his verbal account of life at the Lewisham factory, dated May 1997 when he was in his 90s

21. Dr LP (Peter) Fielding, e-mails to Simon Lavington in Apr–June 2009. (Dr Fielding is a nephew of Sir Leon and is a Trustee of the Sir Leon Bagrit Memorial Trust)

22. Laurie Bental (2001) The Elliott 803. 10-page typescript of a lecture given to the Computer Conservation Society in Manchester on 25 Sept 2001

23. Oxford Dictionary of National Biography (2004) vol.3. Oxford University Press, pp 244–245

24. CJ Whittall, two-page typed letter to C Dupen, dated 7 Mar 1966. Whittall was in charge of production at Elliott's Lewisham factory during World War Two. Dupen, in 1966 Secretary of the Elliotts Long Service Association, had started to write a history of the company. Whittall's letter summarized events at Lewisham during the period 1945–1948. A copy of Whittall's letter was sent to Simon Lavington by Ron Bristow on 16 Mar 2009, Bristow commenting that Dupen's History "didn't seem to get very far"

25. Marilyn Evans (2003) Departmental Administrator, Department of Bioengineering, Imperial College, London: letter to Simon Lavington dated 21 July 2003. The Bagrit Centre for

Biological and Medical Systems was founded at Imperial College in July 1991. See http://www.imperial.ac.uk/P3105.htm

26. Alex Kahan (2006) Documents loaned to Simon Lavington on 9 Oct 2006, with accompanying letter (Alex Kahan is a grandson of Sir Leon Bagrit and is a Trustee of the Sir Leon Bagrit Memorial Trust)

27. The Times Obituaries Supplement, 23 Nov 1979. Sir Leon Bagrit: Early faith in automation

28. Anon, Elliott-Automation Limited: History of the group. Type-written manuscript, undated but possibly written by E O Herzfeld in about 1966. This document was originally given the internal Elliott Archive catalogue number 4.18/2/8. It is now available at the Museum of the History of Science at Oxford, catalogue number to be assigned

29. Colin Thurston, Elliotts/B & P Swift/Swift & Swallow. A one-page typed manuscript of notes on Colin Thurston's time at Rochester from 1954 onwards, written for Simon Lavington on 3 Dec 2009

30. SLH Clarke (2009) e-mail to Simon Lavington dated 29 June 2009

Chapter 2
A Glint on the Horizon

2.1 The Man for the Job

John Coales was 40 years old when he arrived for his first day as Director of Elliott's Borehamwood Research Laboratory in October 1946. A brief chronology of John Coales' life to that point, largely taken from [1–3], is as follows:

1907   Born at Harborne, Birmingham, on 14 September, only child of John Coales and his wife Marion (née Flavell)

1926   Enters Sydney Sussex College, Cambridge, to read Mathematics. Transfers in his second year to Physics

1929   Graduates in Physics; joins the Admiralty Scientific Service and starts work at the Experimental Department, H M Signal School, Portsmouth

1931   Joins a small team working on Radio Direction Finding (RDF)

1936   Marries Mary Dorothea (Thea) Alison

1937   Leads a group of about a dozen people working on centimetric radar, for naval gunnery control. Team expanded to 40 people by 1940

1941   Admiralty Signal Establishment formed; Coales' section dispersed to Witley, near Haslemere, Surrey. Coales leads the naval gunnery radar development

1945   Awarded OBE for wartime services

1946   Leaves Admiralty to become Director of Elliott's Borehamwood Laboratory

Despite, or perhaps because of, the intense pressure and excitement of life at ASE during the war, John Coales was a youthful 40. He enjoyed tuning his elderly Sunbeam cars – he owned two of them. He was an enthusiastic member of a local Folk Dancing Group, an interest he had developed whilst an undergraduate [4]. He was fond of music and kept a viola in his office. A Cambridge graduate, he was sharp-witted, though his mild stutter and deep, booming voice sometimes made him seem abrupt in conversation. Colleagues spoke of his 'Forceful energy and disarming charm' and remarked that 'he was invariably smiling and in a good mood. His optimism irritated many people, but it made him drive through to completion

S. Lavington, *Moving Targets*, History of Computing,
DOI 10.1007/978-1-84882-933-6_2, © Springer-Verlag London Limited 2011

projects that others had despaired of' [1]. As Bob Ford remembers, 'Coales never considered that a thing could not be done' [5].

John and his wife Thea lived with their four children and John's mother, a trained concert pianist, in *Oakwood*, a large house in Radlett situated some 3 miles to the north of Borehamwood. There were two grand pianos in the large drawing room at Oakwood. At weekend house parties, his daughter Alison remembers [6] that there would sometimes be Morris Dancing in the drawing room.

John Coales' two Sunbeam cars, or bits of them, were a feature of the Borehamwood Laboratories that many former staff remember. The cars had names:

(a) 'Her Highness': registration number UW 23, a 1920s convertible
(b) The 'Ugly Duchess': registration number PO 4950, a 1920s saloon

In a way reminiscent of many family businesses of the era, laboratory technicians were called upon by Coales to minister to the needs of the Director's cars (see Fig. 2.1). Actually, *family business* gives the wrong impression: *family university* might be nearer the mark in the sense that Borehamwood was humming with intellectual endeavour and technical innovation. In the early days, Borehamwood

Fig. 2.1 John Coales, the founding Director of the Borehamwood Research Laboratories, was an enthusiastic character. Not only passionately committed to his work, his hobbies included country dancing and keeping his two elderly Sunbeam cars on the road. The facilities of the Laboratory were sometimes called upon to come to the aid of the Sunbeams, as shown here. Archer-Thomson, the stocky Laboratory Superintendent standing second-from-left, appears somewhat doubtful of the car's health!

was run in a relaxed style, more like that of a large university engineering department in the 1960s than an industrial laboratory in the 1940s.

On a personal level, John Coales took a lively interest in his staff. He had a reputation as someone who could see a person's potential. John Bunt, who arrived in September 1949, remembers [7] that: 'Some of the younger staff lived in a company-owned house at Radlett called *Lamorna*. It was conveniently close to John Coales' house, *Oakwood*, and John would bring staff from *Lamorna* in to work in the mornings in one of his two vintage Sunbeams. One of these was a saloon and one a coupé, but in other respects they were identical. One or other of these cars was usually to be found on blocks in the Research Lab. workshops being repaired or awaiting parts which had been stripped to keep the other car on the road...'.

Lamorna had an interesting history. Peter Atkinson remembers [8] it as 'a large house in Radlett which was bought to accommodate a number of German engineers who were to be brought from Germany to work at the Lab on a contract (probably MRS5) for the Navy. This was just after the war. In the event the Germans, when they finally arrived, chose to live in London and *Lamorna* was made available for a number of staff to live in. There were six flats, only one of them was self-contained ... we were all very young and it was a lively and interesting community'. Bill Pearse, a mechanical engineer, who was amongst the first group of six people to be recruited by John Coales, remembers [9] that the Germans included two engineers 'who had been recruited from Peenemunde with four others. The senior man, Weiler, held a position in the German hierarchy reporting directly to Goering and responsible for gyroscope design and supply across the Reich. Weiler (aged 65) was a very talented "natural" engineer'.

Returning to John Bunt's account of his early days, 'After I had been at Borehamwood a few months I was asked to dinner by John Coales at his home at Radlett. All new engineers were asked in due turn and it was a very pleasant evening in a lovely home and garden. I particularly remember the occasion because it was the day in June 1950 when the Korean War broke out. Another notable event was that it was my first introduction to Commander Henry Pasley-Tyler RN who was another guest at the dinner party, and had just joined the company. The Commander, who was always known to his senior colleagues as 'P-T', became the senior man at Borehamwood some while after John Coales' departure'. Commander Pasley-Tyler actually started work officially on 1 July [10]; his part in the Borehamwood story is picked up again later.

Coales' impressive wartime scientific reputation was well-known amongst his new staff, some of whom had come from government research establishments such as ASE and TRE. Most importantly for the success of the MRS5 project, Coales had built up a useful network of Admiralty and naval contacts.

In the immediate post-war years, recruitment of suitably qualified scientific and engineering staff was not easy because there were not enough experienced people available to drive the peacetime renewal of industry and academia. Coales recalls [11]: 'At that time it was extremely difficult for an unknown new laboratory to engage good staff because the Universities were all needing to replace staff lost to the armed services and government laboratories during the war... Although I did not approach any of my wartime colleagues in ASE, a number of the most able of them [for example, Cochrane and Laws] expressed a desire to join me at Borehamwood... Another and most unexpected advantage was that the end of the war had thrown out of work a very large number of technicians ... and many of these turned out to be naturally good engineers and some of them excellent research workers. So in the course of 2 years we built up a laboratory with a staff of two hundred, which acquired a high reputation for the quality of its work in instrumentation, radar, fire-control, automatic and remote power control and particularly in the development of digital and analogue computers and by the end of another two years [i.e. end of 1950] the number employed had risen to 400, of whom at least half were qualified engineers and scientists'.

Coales also developed a good working relationship with the Cambridge University Appointments Board (the 'careers unit' at his *alma mater*) and the Board was happy to send batches of final-year students for interview at Borehamwood. One of the early recruits was John Bunt, who was part of a group of 24 Cambridge final-year students who visited Borehamwood for interviews with Coales in 1949. Bunt's initial salary was £475 per annum which, he recalls, was £25 more than he had been offered anywhere else [12]. Laurence Clarke, another individual that we shall encounter later on in the story of Borehamwood computers, first appeared as a vacation student for a temporary summer job in 1950; he subsequently joined the Laboratory permanently in July 1951 after his graduation from Cambridge.

However, not all recruits were new to industry. A few 'old hands' moved to Borehamwood from Elliott's main factory at Lewisham. Besides H D Hawkes and his R&D staff, it was agreed that a senior designer named C A Gutsell and a few designer-draughtsmen would also transfer to Borehamwood from Lewisham [11]. One interesting arrival from Lewisham was C F (Chris) Phillips, an ex-Naval gunnery officer and mechanical engineer who had worked on the Admiralty fire-control tables manufactured at Lewisham. Phillips has been described [13] as 'the acme of practical engineering and jury rigging'. We will meet him later on as the first designer of the mechanical parts of Borehamwood computer disk storage. Another source of 'old hands' was the few staff who had remained on in the redundant premises of the Admiralty fuse factory. The factory had been operated by S. Smith and Sons Ltd., industrial aircraft instrument makers, but the building belonged to the Admiralty. Arthur Hemingway, who was amongst the first batch of a dozen new recruits to arrive in October 1946 (he recalls being offered the 'princely salary of £600 per annum') oversaw the transfer of infrastructure from Smiths to Elliotts [14]. Amongst the former Smith's employees to be re-engaged by Elliotts in October 1946 were some of the maintenance staff, the Librarian, the Medical Sister, and 'an elegant and soignée lady with glasses and pendant earrings, who was our telephonist. Once heard, she never forgot a voice, so that *Mr This* or *Admiral That* was always correctly addressed by name when he called us up' [11].

There was also the matter of machine tools and furnishings, originally the property of the Admiralty. Some of this equipment, notably lathes and jig borers, was of considerable value, and Elliott's Managing Director seems to have arranged for the more useful items to find their way to Elliott's Lewisham factory.

Summarising Coales' recruitment efforts, we may conclude that trying to poach experienced people from other, better-established, companies was not a fruitful strategy. Most of the Borehamwood staff in the early years were young people fresh from college or those recently released from wartime activity in government research establishments.

There was one large industrial concern that did have a profound influence on the shape of Borehamwood: the General Electric Company (GEC). Coales was a great admirer of the way in which GEC's Hirst Research Laboratory at Wembley was organised (see also Chap. 1, Sect. 1.2.2). Coales adopted this as his pattern. With the agreement of Sir Clifford Paterson, Director of GEC Research, Coales recruited GEC's Lab. Superintendent, H. Archer-Thomson, to oversee the organisation at Borehamwood. To the younger staff at Borehamwood, Archer-Thomson seemed somewhat like a formidable chief-of-police. He was in charge of site security, space-allocation, and the Strong Room. Into the Strong Room went all the secret documents, drawings and photographs pertaining to classified contracts. Coales insisted that the Laboratory notebooks of individual staff should be handed in at the end of every working day, and that all correspondence with the outside world should be handled by his office. Archer-Thomson's job was to enforce this regime. All staff of the rank 'of foreman and above' were required by the government to sign the Official Secrets Act.

Coales adopted two features of the GEC Laboratory organisation. Firstly, he placed staff into semi-autonomous Divisions, each Division being the repository of a particular skill-set. Secondly, he strove to relieve senior scientific staff of administrative duties so that they could devote all their energies to research. Coales had also observed similar arrangements at the Bell Telephone Laboratories in America, when he had visited them in 1944. He was convinced that the Divisional organisation and the devolution of administrative duties were two features that played a big part in creating the excellence that he had observed at the Hirst Labs. and at Bell Labs [11]. In the light of hindsight, we can see that the conditions that permitted these features to flourish were very dependent upon the industrial strength of the parent companies. Elliotts, the parent company of the Borehamwood Laboratory, was not in the same league as GEC or Bell. The wider consequences of Elliott's commercial weakness in the late 1940s have been alluded to in Chap. 1 and are picked up again in Chap. 5.

The number, nomenclature and scope of the Divisions at Borehamwood varied as the Laboratory evolved. The first set of Divisions to be established in 1946/1947 were, in probable chronological order: *Instruments, Circuits, Radio, Theory, Servos* and *Mechanical Engineering*. ('Radio' was a coded title for 'Radar'). Alec Cochrane, who headed the Radar/Radio Division, did not arrive on site until April 1947 [15]. The Computing Division was not formed until the end of 1948, when W S (Bill) Elliott joined Borehamwood.

The main Divisions that existed in 1949 are shown in Table 2.1. Commonly occurring synonyms are given in the left-hand column. The first name in each row in Table 2.1 is the one that we shall prefer to use throughout the rest of this book. In row two of the Table, 'Radio' was actually preferred to 'Radar' in the early Borehamwood days – probably because the British phrase *Radio Direction Finding*

Table 2.1 The principal divisions at Borehamwood in about 1949

Name and synonyms	Divisional head(s)
Circuits; Displays	C A (Coppy) Laws
Radar; Microwaves; Radio; Aerials	C A (Alec) Cochrane; Eric Whitehead
Computing; Computers	W S (Bill) Elliott; Andrew St Johnston
Electrical Engineering; Servos	H M (Harry) Gale; Arthur Hemingway
Theory; Mathematics	Norman D Hill
Instruments; Measurements; Standards	H D (Harry) Hawkes
Mechanical Engineering; Workshops	John Tindale; F Rock-Carling
Physics	Alan Brewer; Albert E De Barr

(RDF) was the original name for what the Americans called *Radar*. In the right-hand column of Table 2.1, we give the Division's senior person in 1949, followed where appropriate by the name of a subsequent Head where there had been a change by about 1953. In addition to the main scientific Divisions, Borehamwood had a Drawing Office, a Library and an Accounts section.

In the early history of the Borehamwood Laboratory, a Division was somewhat similar in scope and autonomy to a traditional University Department. That is, it represented a research discipline. It did not, however, have any say in wider company activities such as product marketing. By the mid-1950s, the concept of a Division at Elliotts had taken on an altogether more substantial and realistic pattern under the guidance of Elliott's renowned Managing Director, Leon Bagrit. Jack Pateman, who joined the Circuits Division at Borehamwood in 1948 and rose to lead Elliott's Flight Automation activities as described in Chap. 12 and Appendix 9, has described the Bagrit-style Division of the 1950s as being 'a semi-autonomous entity with its own engineering, sales production and commercial departments ... market oriented and responsible for a limited range of company products. Several of the new Divisions later became wholly owned Companies' [16]. We shall learn more of the substantial role played by Leon Bagrit as the Borehamwood story unfolds.

Returning to Table 2.1 and the late 1940s, W S (Bill) Elliott was the founding Head of the Computing Division. Bill Elliott, who had no family connection with Borehamwood's parent company Elliott Brothers (London) Ltd., was born in 1917 and entered Cambridge University to read physics in 1935. The following brief biographical details are taken from [17]. At Cambridge, Bill Elliott was Secretary/ Treasurer of the University Wireless Society, sharing an interest in amateur radio with Maurice Wilkes. We will meet Wilkes later in Sect. 2.5 below when we dip into computer history. Bill Elliott graduated in Physics from Cambridge in 1938 and commenced postgraduate research in the Cavendish Laboratory on transit time effects in thermionic valves. During the war, he was sent to work on radar at the Air Defence Research & Development Establishment. After the war, he remained registered as a Cambridge Ph.D. student for some time but eventually decided not to proceed with the valve work which had largely been superseded. He joined Powell-Duffryn's Research Labs. to work on carbon brushes and related electrical equipment. After 2 years with this company, he contacted Edward Shire at the Cavendish Laboratory and asked him for career suggestions. Shire passed the request to John

Coales. John and Bill had previously been in contact during the war regarding jamming and clutter in radar echoes. From the Borehamwood Visitors Books, we see that Bill Elliott came for exploratory talks with Coales several times in 1948 (on 8 and 21 August, 29 September, and 1 and 22 October), before finally joining Coales' team to set up the Computing Division in November or December 1948.

Coales recalled [18] that it seemed a little strange to some people that there should be both a Theory Division and a Computing Division at Borehamwood, implying that there was some overlap of responsibilities. He went on to say that he 'had to keep the peace between them'. We shall comment again on this aspect in Sect. 2.6 and in Chaps. 8 and 10. As far as *building* computer hardware, it was the Circuits Division that took the lead at first, somewhat to the puzzlement of Harry Carpenter and other new staff who had joined the new Computing Division early in 1949. As far as programming and software were concerned, it was the Theory Division that took the lead in the early days, as described in Chap. 8.

Recruitment of professional staff at Borehamwood gathered momentum in 1947, and by the end of that year, the Divisional structure was firmly established. There was, naturally, some transfer of people between Divisions, in an effort to match skills to needs. For example, John Bunt, after graduating in Physics from Cambridge, was originally recruited in September 1949 to work on the project known as the Comprehensive Display System (CDS) in the Circuits Division. He remembers that the research for CDS had largely been finished by then and so he found himself part of a large CDS construction team. After a few months, Bunt was transferred to the Electrical Engineering Division to work on a summing amplifier for the TRIDAC analogue computer (see Chap. 4). After a few more months, he was transferred to Harry Carpenter's team in the Computing Division, to work under Jim Barrow on the 152 computer (see Sect. 2.6). It was here that John Bunt learned the fundamentals of digital computers [12]. He went on to take a leading role in the design of Elliott computers in the late 1950s and the 1960s, eventually becoming Manager of the Mobile Computing Division. After the GEC takeover in 1968, John Bunt was appointed Technical Director of Marconi-Elliott Computer Systems Ltd.

Analysing the growth in the Borehamwood payroll is not always easy because surviving records seldom distinguish between categories of employee, and particularly between *professional* staff who were paid monthly and *support* staff who were paid weekly. For example, in addition to the initial batch of 12 professional staff who are known to have joined Borehamwood on day one (1 October 1946), we should add a modest number of support staff such as lathe operators, secretaries and cleaners who were inherited from Smith's fuse factory. By December 1946, W E (Ben) Bennett remembers arriving as 'employee number 40' and recalls that the Borehamwood group photograph of October 1948 depicted a total of 250 employees [19]. In December 1949, 261 people (most of whom would have presumably had professional qualifications) were recorded as having signed the Official Secrets Act [20]. The Borehamwood group photograph of 1 October 1951 shows 361 employees. By any measure, Coales' empire grew by leaps and bounds.

Coales had originally planned for a total payroll of about 300 people, 'of whom about half would be professional scientists and engineers'. Coales had originally hoped to appoint a Deputy Director as second-in-command to himself. He approached three extremely able people whom he had got to know through their war work but all had recently accepted senior posts – two at Universities and one at the new Atomic Research Establishment at Harwell. In the event, no Deputy was recruited.

Having to name some Borehamwood individuals, but not others, is a divisive but inevitable part of trying to write most retrospective histories. This book focuses on computer developments, with additional treatment of Elliott work in the areas of analogue computers, aerospace and radar. We must therefore pass over the other excellent, but unconnected, developments that were carried out at Borehamwood over the years.

The original organisation of Borehamwood into Technical Divisions was not inherently a bad thing, though in the case of Coales' rather autocratic style of management it proved somewhat unsatisfactory. Coales' divisional structure tended to favour a fragmented approach to equipment development, whereby the sub-units of a larger project were implemented by specialists without much reference to an overall systems architecture. For example, the interconnection of functional units tended to be considered too late in the design cycle. In short, there was a lack of project-centred (as opposed to technique-centred) management. We will return to this theme later, when describing the progress made by Borehamwood on the MRS5 and CDS projects.

2.2 Distant Targets

We saw in Chap. 1 that the 1946 agreement between the Admiralty, John Coales and the Managing Director of Elliotts, Geoffrey Lee, provided for the establishment of a Research Laboratory of about 300 staff. In 1946, Coales' prime objective was to work on two Admiralty contracts, MRS5 and CDS – of which the first was the darling of his eyes. The parent company, Elliotts, had also arranged to transfer their Instrument Research and Development section from Lewisham to Borehamwood, with the expectation that commercial activity in this section would build up to the point where it represented about a third of the work at Borehamwood.

In the light of hindsight, we can detect the seeds of an inconsistency of approach in these arrangements. Two types of research were being planned for Borehamwood:

1. Secret defence-related work, with clear Admiralty rules about allowable expenditure on capital equipment, overheads, etc.
2. Commercial development linked to specific products, guided by the market strategy and financial practices of the parent company

Although both areas would undoubtedly generate research challenges, they required completely different administrative management. We shall return to this theme in Sect. 2.7, when we pick up the activities of Geoffrey Lee and Leon Bagrit at Elliott's headquarters at Lewisham. On the technological side, there was also likely to be an initial divergence of activity between the two research areas. The Admiralty work involved high-frequency electronic pulse techniques and an emphasis, at least within the MRS5 project, on digital computation. The commercial work placed more emphasis on analogue signal-processing and electro-magnetic techniques. Over the next 20 years, the two areas would actually come closer, in the sense that analogue computation was replaced by digital processing as the latter became more reliable and cost-effective. This, however, was still in the unpredictable future in the post-war austerity of the late 1940s.

Putting commercial developments aside, Coales's principal concerns in 1946 were to make progress on the MRS5 and CDS Admiralty contracts. Of the two, MRS5 was the larger project, consuming about two thirds of the total Borehamwood effort during the period 1946–1950 and accounting for about two thirds of the income [18, 21]. We shall briefly describe CDS first because, having so to speak put that project to bed, we can then concentrate on MRS5 and the digital computers that sprang from the MRS5 work.

2.3 The CDS Project

The objectives of the Comprehensive Display System (CDS) were introduced in Chap. 1. From the list of Borehamwood internal research reports given in the Bibliography, it can be seen that 14 Progress Reports were produced for the CDS project between 31 July 1947 and 16 October 1951. The project leader was C A Laws, always known as 'Coppy Laws' because of his striking copper-coloured hair. Coppy was born in 1916. After working for companies making radios, he spent the war years at ASE, where his name appeared on eleven radar patents [22]. From ASE he went directly to Borehamwood, where he stayed until the 1968 merger between Elliotts and GEC described in Chap. 13.

At Borehamwood, the CDS project used *analogue* techniques whilst, unknown to Coales and Laws, Ralph Benjamin at ASE was working towards a *digital* version of the CDS concept. Many years later, Coales was to remember Borehamwood's CDS project with pride but also with some unease [18]. 'We weren't originally intended to have this contract; we were not told that Benjamin was doing some advanced, digital, CDS work at ASE, so we were working with what turned out to be obsolete (analogue) stuff'. In his rather self-centred book [23] Ralph Benjamin, a distinguished government scientist, described the Borehamwood CDS work retrospectively as follows.

'Initially a contract had been given to Elliott Brothers to produce the system. In a remarkably short time, their team, under two ex-ASE men, C A Laws and M V Needham, assembled two very sophisticated demonstration systems, one for the RN and one for 'loan' to the US Naval Research Laboratory. These early models did a great deal to demonstrate and 'sell' the operating concept, on both sides of the Atlantic. However, in line with the tradition of the firm, their approach was based heavily on electro-magnetic devices (relays, uniselectors, motors, magnetic clutches, potentiometers, monoscopes, etc.) and the system proved virtually un-maintainable. Meanwhile, work on the electronic (digital) solution continued at ASE'.

Technically, the Elliott CDS system at Borehamwood was ingenious. The CDS group was the first to devise the concept of an interlaced radar scan and operator-interaction via a joystick. The implementation used analogue electronics combined with electro-mechanical techniques. Historically, it was the first project to demonstrate real-time interaction between an operator and a screen. The CDS joystick controlled a symbol, known as a *hook*, interlaced with other data displayed on a CRT, to drag and drop screen information into memory [22]. The concept of interactive displays for general-purpose *digital* computers was not taken up by Elliotts, or by anyone else, for some years until digital memory technology had developed to the point where appropriate storage had become cost-effective. We shall return to the subject of computer history shortly.

As a demonstration prototype, CDS excited considerable attention, not least from the US Navy. A gathering of top US Navy brass and others was held at Borehamwood from 14 to 17 July 1950 (see Fig. 2.2), under the title *UK/US Conference on Data Transmission and Allied Subjects.* Two minor incidents are remembered about this visit [18]. Firstly, the MRS5 group was told not to power up their digital computer on the day of the visit because the Americans were not permitted to know about the MRS5 project and it was thought that the noise of the

Fig. 2.2 The photo shows some of the senior Borehamwood Laboratory staff and visiting Americans, assembled in July 1950 for the joint UK/US Conference on Data Transmission and Allied Subjects. The prime purpose of this mysteriously named, invitation-only, meeting was to discuss Borehamwood's Comprehensive Display System (CDS) – a classified project. John Coales is seated at the front of the photograph

computer's forced-air cooling system might attract awkward questions. Secondly, Coales thought that pre-lunch cocktails might be welcomed by his American guests. On the morning of the visit, he asked Andrew St. Johnston and Tom Ludlow, both young ex-RN officers, to 'fix the drinks'. In a manner reminiscent of the BBC comedy series *The Navy Lark*, the two young engineers went out and bought several bottles of spirits and mixed a wondrous brew. The effect on Anglo-American relationships is not recorded but, by design, Andrew and Tom ensured that there was plenty of the cocktail left over after the official guests had departed – 'dispensed to all and sundry in enamel jugs!' [24].

Returning to the CDS project, Maurice Needham was sent to America in 1951 to demonstrate the system to the Americans. Whilst there, John Coales instructed Needham to visit Bell Labs. He did so, and returned to Borehamwood carrying three transistors, the first such devices to be brought to Borehamwood. Needham has recalled [25] that Coales could not, regrettably, see clearly the future possibilities of CDS. At one point, Coales remarked to the CDS group, 'Hurry up and finish it so that you can get on with something more important'. This had a rather demoralising effect on the group and was uncharacteristic of Coales, whom Needham generally admired.

The CDS project was wound up at Borehamwood soon after Needham returned from America, the last CDS Progress Report to the Admiralty being dated 16 October 1951. All CDS reports were classified 'Secret'. Although apparently short-lived at Borehamwood, the legacy of the work on CDS is seen today in the Command and Control Centres on all modern warships.

2.4 The MRS5 Project

The specification of the Navy's Medium Range fire-control system MRS5 was, roughly speaking, as follows. Ship-borne radar was required to detect the range, bearing and elevation of an enemy aircraft when it was at least 8 miles away; the radar unit would then lock onto and track this target (*auto-tracking*) until it was either destroyed or had flown out of range. The radar unit was required to feed various parameters, relating to the target, continuously to a central on-board computer that would calculate in real time the target's trajectory. The computer would send appropriate aiming and fusing information periodically to the ship's main anti-aircraft guns, in order that the shells from each gun would explode at, or very close to, the target's predicted position. The central computer was to be *digital*, rather than analogue, and data was to be transmitted in digital form throughout the ship – see Fig. 2.3).

As Norman Hill explained [26], 'Bearing in mind that in practice the director would be on board ship subject to roll, pitch and yaw, the information coming from the radar system would need to be converted to a stable system of axes [derived from the *master reference gyro*], the future position of the target would then have to be predicted according to the time of flight of the shell fired from the naval guns

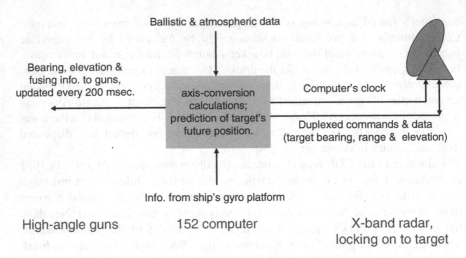

Ballistic & atmospheric data

Bearing, elevation &
fusing info. to guns,
updated every 200 msec.

axis-conversion
calculations;
prediction of target's
future position.

Computer's clock

Duplexed commands & data
(target bearing, range & elevation)

Info. from ship's gyro platform

High-angle guns   152 computer   X-band radar,
                                                                     locking on to target

Fig. 2.3 Simplified system diagram of the MRS5 *(medium range system)* fire-control project, showing the connections between the Elliott 152 real-time on-line digital computer, the target-tracking radar and the high-angle (i.e. anti-aircraft) guns. The radar was required to lock on to an approaching aircraft when it was still 8 miles away from the ship

and the information sent to the gun servos converted from the stable system of axes back to the ship's axes all in real time ie almost instantaneously. The mathematical problems were monumentally difficult. Ed Hersom in my team [i.e. the Theory Division] eventually produced a brilliant solution of this problem'. Ed Hersom specified the functionality of, and algorithms for, the MRS5's digital computer.

Alec Cochrane, who joined Borehamwood in April 1947 and became a leading light in the MRS5's radar developments, has said [15]: 'The operative principle as far as I could gather was to break with tradition and break new ground wherever possible.... However one defines the objective of the MRS 5 contract the emphasis was on innovation rather than further optimising the tried and trusted techniques ... The real attention was focussed on the enhanced computation possibility offered by the digital computer.'

2.4.1   Why Digital?

The choice of *digital* processing was a radical departure for the Navy in 1946. All gunnery predictors in service during the war, on land and at sea throughout the world, had used analogue computation. Furthermore, when Coales had visited America in August and September 1944 'to study US Naval Gunnery Radar, US Fire Control and the relation between them', the word *digital* did not appear anywhere in his report [27]. Besides US government departments and establishments, Coales and his colleagues visited MIT and the Radiation Lab., Bell Telephone Labs (at various

Fig. 2.4 Vice-Admiral Sir M M Denny, Controller of the Navy, came to inspect the MRS5 radar installation at Borehamwood early in 1951. John Coales is in the light grey suit, facing Denny. Leon Bagrit is on the far right of the photo

locations), the Ford Instrument Co., and Arma Corp. and were shown many new research projects. Of the Ford Instrument Company Inc., New York, Coales says: 'The [Ford] Mark I computer is, even now, almost certainly the finest high-angle computer in service at sea, and is doing excellent work in shooting down aircraft' (see also [28] for the background to Hannibal Ford's fire-control equipment). The Ford Mark I computer formed part of the US Navy's Mark 37 Fire-Control System, introduced in 1939. It was entirely analogue, and is described in Chap. 4.

It is true to say that, apart from MRS5, all other electronic research at Borehamwood in the period 1946–1949 was analogue. Nowadays, when the word 'computer' implicitly means a general-purpose digital machine, we tend to forget the debates that preceded the digital age. It is sobering, then, to recall the realities of yesteryear. For example, in the book *Electronic computers: principles and applications*, intended for the general reader and published in 1956, the technical content is approximately evenly balanced between analogue computers (42 pages) and digital computers (45 pages) – see [29].

It is interesting to speculate why, in 1946, the Admiralty chose to go digital. It seems quite likely that ENIAC was the spur. ENIAC, a special-purpose American electronic digital computer, had first come into operation in the autumn of 1945, as explained in Sect. 2.5 and Appendix 10. ENIAC's primary task was ballistics computations – not, it is true, real-time on-line ship-board gunnery computations but nevertheless precision computations that were loosely related to the MRS5 project's topic of fire control. Norman Hill, Head of the Theory Division at Borehamwood, recalled [26] that: 'Much interest was generated in ENIAC world-wide and

Mr Coales directed us to study the techniques embodied in it. Many visits were made to view ENIAC [by other British researchers], notably by Maurice Wilkes from Cambridge, Wilkinson from NPL, Professor Hartree from Manchester [later at Cambridge University from October 1946] and Uttley from TRE. These and other people decided to build digital computers at their various Establishments. Our problem [at Borehamwood] was how to seek information on these various plans and designs bearing in mind that we could not reveal our purpose since we were working on a secret contract. I remember going with John Coales in his vintage Humber [actually Sunbeam] registration number UW23, to the NPL for discussions with some of the above-mentioned people together with the great Turing who insisted on running to the canteen for lunch in pouring rain....'

In February 1945, the first non-American to be permitted to see the ENIAC project had been J R Womersley, the new Superintendent of the Mathematics Division at the National Physical Laboratory (NPL). At the end of 1945, when Alan Turing produced a document for the NPL containing what is probably the first complete design for a general-purpose digital computer, it was still uncertain how much memory would be required for practical problems, and whether the memory could be made to operate at sufficient speed and at an affordable price [30]. So although digital computers offered potentially more accuracy than analogue computers, going digital was a step into the unknown.

Besides accuracy, another reason why the Admiralty may have inclined towards digital techniques concerns data transmission. A major complication in ship-borne fire control prior to 1945 had been the means by which the components (director, predictor, guns) were linked. Data transmission was by stepper motors, later replaced by magslips [31] and then the metadyne, for moving pointers. Most of the control was, in the end, achieved by manually following a pointer. It goes without saying that electro-mechanical fire-control systems worked better against (slower-moving) surface targets than against (faster-moving) aircraft. Ships remained vulnerable to attack from the air. There was a need to speed up data-transmission – which may have suggested the need to explore *digital* transmission in projects such as MRS5.

A final, though admittedly tenuous, reason why the Admiralty might have inclined towards digital computing could have been the desire to outdo the Americans. The British analogue High Angle Control System (HACS) in use during the Second World War was a relatively poor performer compared with the American analogue Mark 37 FCS. More details of the differences between the two systems are discussed in Chap. 4. The Mark 37 FCS was introduced to the Royal Navy on a trial basis in one ship in late 1941. The Admiralty was impressed with the performance. More of the Mark 37 systems would have been ordered, but production in America was entirely consumed by equipping US Naval vessels. After the war, the battleship HMS Vanguard was equipped with Mark 37 FCS. In British naval circles, there must have been considerable pressure to develop a better, home-grown, fire-control system – especially since the critical balance-of-payments situation and the associated political problems made dollar purchases very difficult. The Admiralty chose to take a leap into the unknown and specify *digital* computing for the MRS5 project, perhaps in the hope of stealing a march on the Americans due to the expected increase in accuracy of digital systems?

Fig. 2.5 This cartoon, presented to John Coales for Christmas 1949, shows Coales in frantic *Morris dancing* mode whilst senior members of the Laboratory staff hold the secret MRS5 radar aerial – represented by a baby in a cot. The staff are thought to be (left-to-right): John Tindale, Arthur Hemmingway, C A Laws and H Archer-Thomson. The caption '*Ring out the old, ring in the not quite so old*' refers to the Admiralty's cancellation of the MRS5 project and its replacement by the 'Netting' project for radar evaluation

Certainly, the concepts that lay behind MRS5 were ambitious. Close interconnection was envisaged between three types of functional unit: the radar transmitter/receiver; the trajectory-predicting computer; the high-angle (i.e. *anti-aircraft*) guns. Of these three, the required pinpoint accuracy of the radar unit seemed to Coales to present the most challenging problems. Radar was also the topic about which he knew most, and it was advances in radar technology that had contributed most to the improvements in gunnery accuracy during the Second World War. In the event, it was indeed on the radar side of the MRS5 contract that the Borehamwood researchers were able to make the most obvious, world-class, advances. The significance of the MRS5 contract's digital computing innovations was more subtle and slower to blossom in the commercial world, but in the end, they, too, were substantial at the time of their introduction.

The interlaced threads of analogue and digital computing, of sequence-controlled and stored-program computers, and of special-purpose and general-purpose computers, are a fascinating part of the early history of the Information Age. We will describe some of these threads later in Sect. 2.5, as a prelude to Sect. 2.6 where we will describe the computer known as the Elliott 152 that lay at the heart of the MRS5 project. First, though, we continue with the MRS5 story as it unfolded during the period 1946–1949.

2.4.2 Innovative Radar

Returning to the MRS5 contract at Borehamwood, the first priority of Coales' scientists, and particularly of the radar teams led by Alec Cochrane and Eric Whitehead, was research into novel aerial (or *scanner* or *antenna*) systems for monopulse radar. New concepts in aerial design were necessary in order to obtain the very precise angular definition required for MRS5 automatic target-tracking.

The MRS5 radar operated in the X-band, that is, within a frequency band of about 8–12 GHz, equivalent to wavelengths between 4 and 2.5 cm. (A guide to microwave band terminology is given in Appendix 9). An innovative plate-type lens was developed at Borehamwood for the X-band microwave aerial, as shown in Fig. 2.6. In the egg-box construction of the lens, the spacings were determined by the wavelength and the front and rear contours determined the focal length. The lens was in four segments. The differences in target-reflections received by each segment were used to generate up/down, left/right, *misalignment signals*. Servo-mechanisms connected to hydraulic rams moved the whole aerial assembly so as to minimise the *misalignment signals* and thus lock the radar on to the moving target. The Borehamwood radar group was congratulated by the Admiralty in 1949, who were 'very impressed with the work that the firm [Elliotts] had done on plate lenses. A large amount of the work was quite original' [32].

Fig. 2.6 An innovative plate-type lens was developed for the MRS5's X-band radar. The lens was in four segments, here shown under test. The differences in target-reflections received by each segment were used to generate *misalignment signals*. Servo-mechanisms connected to hydraulic rams moved the whole aerial assembly so as to minimise the misalignment signals and thus lock the radar on to a moving target

Radar systems that tracked targets were not new in 1949: the innovative aspect of the MRS5 system was its high accuracy and ability to handle target glint. Glint is a term used to describe the small, dynamic, changes in the position of the returned echo. Glint is caused by the fact that practical aircraft reflect radar signals at a number of angles and from a number of surfaces. The Borehamwood team was to become expert at glint analysis.

The whole assembly of MRS5's radar system, complete with electronics and servo motors, was known as the Director, thus adopting the traditional warship terminology of the day. The MRS5's Director weighed approximately 14 t. Of this, the radar nacelle, containing the lens system, weighed about 2 t. The nacelle was mounted on heavy-duty elevating/training structures which formed a stabilised platform similar to those in use for naval guns (see Fig. 2.7). Coales' group invented, and patented in 1948, a binary encoding disk system for accurately representing the radar aerial's angular position as a bit-pattern. The encoder is described in more detail in Sect. 2.6 below.

The MRS5 Director was installed in the car park behind the main Borehamwood Laboratory in May 1950, with a clear view of the sky as required for practical tests on aircraft. A series of fly-past trials took place during the period October 1950 to

Fig. 2.7 The radar aerial and associated electronics for the MRS5 project was housed in a *Director* assembly weighing about 14 t. The photograph shows the Director as located on open ground to the rear of the Borehamwood Laboratory. Successful target-tracking tests involving Lancaster bombers and Mosquito fast reconnaissance fighters were carried out in the period October 1950 to November 1951

November 1951 – though the analysis of the target-tracking data was funded by a different Admiralty contract, as described below.

The MRS5 contract, number CP.12349/46, was placed with Elliotts by the Admiralty in October 1946. Activity on the MRS5 project spanned the years 1947–1950. The Admiralty's appraisal of the project half way through is reflected in the following quotation, taken from the ASRE's hand-over notes written by Commander F C Morgan in December 1948 to his successor, Commander T W Best [33]: 'Elliotts have a long term research and development contract for MRS5 and are tackling the problem as a whole quite fundamentally, without preconceived notions of how this or that should be done, and without tying their hands with past conservative practice. They have a highly competent, immensely keen team of scientists and engineers on the job, and are investigating new techniques and methods in a large number of fields. If we can be but patient I personally believe that something quite startlingly good will eventually be produced by this group. It is of more than passing interest that visitors from the USN and US Industry have been more impressed by the work going on at Elliotts than at anywhere else in this country'.

A listing of relevant Borehamwood Internal Technical Reports produced during this period is given in the Bibliography, from which it can be seen that the first MRS5 Progress Report was dated 1 October 1947 and the last Progress Report (number 11) was issued on 5 April 1950. Some time in late 1949, to the surprise of the entire team, the Admiralty gave notice that it intended to cancel the MRS5 project.

2.4.3   The Cancellation of MRS5

Why did the Admiralty suddenly consider withdrawing support from what was, at any rate from the radar standpoint, an excellent piece of development?

Cochrane's radar system of phase comparator simultaneous lober (based on the egg-box lens) was a world-beater, credited by C A Calpine (from Admiralty Operations Research) with being the most accurate angle measurer he had reviewed [15]. Cochrane was supported on the analytical side by Eric Whitehead, described as 'a brilliant theoretician' [34]. Whitehead recalled that: 'The times I spend at Borehamwood ... contained the most exciting professional experiences I have had at any time ...' [35]. The semi-official history of naval radar [3] says: 'Although the *type 905* [the MRS5 radar] never went into production, the study was of particular interest in that it incorporated electronic scanning for the first time in a British naval weapon radar'. Subsequent radar activities at Borehamwood are recounted in Chap. 11.

Although the cancellation of MRS5 came as a significant shock to the radar group, the team leader, Alec Cochrane, admitted in 1995 [15] that it had become clear to him at the time that 'MRS5 was doomed and the real problem at Borehamwood was survival'. By *survival* Cochrane was touching on the wider issues of the financial viability of Elliott Brothers (London) Ltd. and hence of the Borehamwood Laboratory. The Elliott company's finances are considered later, in Sects. 2.8 and 2.9. Cochrane continues: 'The only real alternative to naval contract work [for the radar team] was missiles and I nudged things in the direction of mil-limetre waves' [15]. It was whilst considering the problems of fitting a suitable aerial for a 9-mm wavelength guidance system inside a missile that Cochrane pat-ented the remarkable Cassegrain aerial ([15] and Appendix 9). This patent did, in the end, attract a considerable royalty payment to the company.

The Admiralty, of course, was well aware of the promising radar results that were emanating from Borehamwood in 1949/1950. In fact, they proposed to ask Borehamwood to continue this radar development, whilst ceasing to work on the larger digital fire-control activity. We will introduce Borehamwood's new radar contract, called the *Netting* project, in Section 2.4.4. First, though, it is interesting to speculate on exactly why the Admiralty wished to cancel MRS5. There appeared to be no single reason for cancellation, but amongst the factors for consideration would have been the following:

(a) Budgetary constraints being imposed by government in 1949 on all defence projects – see the defence-spending Table in the Introduction to this book. In [32] the Superintendent of the Admiralty's Gunnery Establishment (AGE), who effectively oversaw the MRS5 project, said that 'financial stringency has led to drastic modifications of all our development contracts'.
(b) The realisation by UK Defence chiefs that guided weapons, rather than guns, were going to be a more appropriate measure against attack by aircraft.
(c) The fact that Borehamwood appeared to be falling behind schedule with prog-ress on MRS5's digital computing and control system. At a progress meeting held on 16 June 1949, it was stated that 'the director and computer were the unknown dates, whereas the rest seemed reasonably well in hand' [32].
(d) A growing unease at AGE with MRS5 project-management procedures and the strained relationship that had developed between Coales at Borehamwood and the Elliott management at Lewisham led by Leon Bagrit (due in large measure to the financial weakness of the Elliott company at that time).
(e) The knowledge that a more modest, interim, analogue fire-control system based on the *Flyplane* principle (see below) could be brought into operation within 2 or 3 years.

We shall comment further on point (d) in Sect. 2.7, after we have described the MRS5's computer developments. With regard to point (b), some in the Admiralty had begun to consider guided weapons, at first called *Guided Anti-aircraft Projectiles (GAP)*, as early as 1943 [36]. Certainly, research in Britain for a beam-riding guided missile had begun at TRE during the latter stages of the war. The first flight tests of the *Long Shot* experimental missile were carried out on the Army's Salisbury Plain artillery range in 1948. Harry Carpenter, who joined the Borehamwood Computing Division in January 1949, was an electronics specialist at TRE who had been a member of the guided weapons team since mid-1945.

Regarding point (e) above, in 1947, the Admiralty had placed a development contract for an analogue fire-control predictor based on the *Flyplane* principle with the Instrument Department of Ferranti Ltd. at Moston, near Manchester [37]. The contract, worth £32,000 per annum in 1947, led to sea trials of fire-control systems incorporating Flyplane predictors from about 1950 onwards. In 1955, a separate Fire Control Department was established at Ferranti Ltd., by which time annual sales of Flyplane-related predictor systems had expanded to over £900,000 [37].

As recalled in a 1950 Admiralty report [38], the Flyplane system contained 'nothing sufficiently novel, i.e., novel in the sense that it had not previously been considered rather that previously used.... For at least 25 years there has been a recurrence of proposals for solutions of the anti-aircraft problem based on the use of the flyplane.... The starting point in all such solutions is that if we assume straight-line flight of the target during the time of flight of the shell, then that straight line and the point of observation (the gun position) define a plane known as the fly-plane; if now all our operations (computations and movements) can be carried out with no other reference than to this plane the problem, normally regarded as a 3-dimensional one, is reduced to a 2-dimensional one and so is simplified'.

The analogue Flyplane Predictor System (FPS), as installed in Royal Naval ships in the 1950s, is discussed in Chap. 4.

2.4.4   The Netting *Project and the Legacy of MRS5*

Coales has said [18] that, upon learning that the Admiralty had invoked the 3-month termination clause on the MRS5 contract, he went to see the Admiralty's Director of Physical Research, W R (Bill) Cook. Coales recalls that he spoke bluntly to him, as follows: 'Firstly, I cannot advise my Board to accept a purely radar contract, because this is not in line with the company's main business directions. Secondly, if the change in contract results in any redundancies then I will advise Elliotts to close Borehamwood down'. The Admiralty, Coales recalls, had never before been spoken to in such stark terms. Cook subsequently made strenuous efforts to find other government work for Borehamwood. It was thought by Coales to be largely thanks to Bill Cook that Coales' team obtained the TRIDAC contract for a massive analogue computer for three-dimensional simulations, as described in Chap. 4. The first TRIDAC Progress Report appeared on 14 July 1950 (see Bibliography). Additional government computer contracts of a more secret nature were also to come to Borehamwood, as described in Chap. 3.

Although the main MRS5 contract was, in fact, cancelled formally in 1950, the Admiralty did indeed award Borehamwood a subsidiary follow-on contract – referred to locally as the 'Netting' project (contract number CP.888/50). (It has not been revealed why the title *Netting* was used: Possibly, because of the image it conjured up of flying objects being captured in a net?) Anyway, the objective of the project was to use the MRS5's existing advanced radar unit and the soon-to-be-completed digital computer to carry out a comprehensive analysis of the radar system's performance, especially with respect to the glint phenomenon. It was arranged that two types of aircraft (the Mosquito fast reconnaissance fighter and the Lancaster heavy bomber) would over-fly Borehamwood, in a series of trials that spanned the period October 1950 to November 1951. Ben Bennett implies [19] that the fly-pasts actually started in June 1950, but he may have been referring to slow-moving initial tests that Norman Hill says [26] were performed first with a meteorological balloon and then with a helicopter, before the use of faster aircraft, 'all to the great interest of the locals'.

There was, naturally, liaison with the Fleet Air Arm and with Air Traffic Control and a naval officer was appointed by the Admiralty as Trials Officer. The broad conclusion of the Netting trials was that the radar system was capable of accurate measurement of target position around 10,000 yd (five nautical miles), with useful data being obtained at ranges as far out as about 20,000 yd (ten nautical miles). Ten miles was the limit of the high-performance optical cine-camera being used as a reference during the fly-past tests [39].

During the 'Netting' trials, the response-signals from the radar system were recorded in real time and then analysed off-line. The data from the 1950 trials was captured by analogue pen recorder because the digital system was not yet ready. Digital recording, on 35-mm film, took place from August 1951 onwards. This data-capture and subsequent analysis, performed largely under the direction of Ross Cameron [18], were to become the only useful task that the MRS5's digital computer, known as the Elliott 152, performed in earnest. However, the digital film-reader was the weakest part of the process and full-scale off-line digital analysis did not begin until about May 1952. Only a modest amount of actual digital computation had been completed by the project's deadline of 30 June 1952 [39]. There is anecdotal evidence that the central computer performed this small amount of analysis satisfactorily. However, a large quantity of (digital) recordings remained un-processed. These recordings were, 10 years later, still regarded by Eric Whitehead, by then Marconi's Chief Scientist, as the most comprehensive set of glint data in existence [40]. From the listing in the Bibliography, it can be seen that the 'Netting' project produced nine Progress Reports between 9 June 1950 and 5 August 1953.

So, what of the MRS5's computer? To understand how this, the first of the Borehamwood digital computers, stands in relation to other pioneering projects elsewhere, it is appropriate to remind ourselves of the state of play of high-speed digital computing developments worldwide in the 1940s. We will then return to the design of the MRS5 computer itself in Sect. 2.6.

2.5 A Little Computer History

There are probably three reasons why it is sometimes hard for succeeding generations to comprehend and trace the early development of the modern digital computer:

- *Complexity of cross-fertilisation*: Early pioneers may or may not have had knowledge of, or concerns for, what other contemporary groups were doing; interactions may or may not have taken place.

- *Storage technology*: The design of electronic circuits for the central computation and control functions of a digital computer was not too difficult, compared with the problem of devising suitable high-speed memory, or storage, technologies.
- *Limited end-user experience*: Whilst the basic concepts of the 'universal digital computer' soon became reasonably well-known, how to put those concepts to efficient use, and for what potential range of applications, was far less clearly understood.

To illustrate how such factors might have influenced events at Borehamwood, we need to remind ourselves of some of the pioneering landmarks of automatic digital computing.

In Appendix 10, we review a selection of 15 digital computing projects worldwide, most of which were conceived before 1947 and might therefore have been known to researchers at Borehamwood in late 1947. Firstly, there are five pre-1945 projects which, as shown in Appendix 10, are not really fully-fledged operational *stored-program* machines. These are:

(a) Charles Babbage's Analytical Engine, designed in the 1840s
(b) Konrad Zuse's Z3, which first worked in 1941
(c) Howard Aitken's Automatic Sequence-Controlled calculator (ASSC), also called the Harvard Mark I, which first worked in 1943
(d) The Colossus Mark I and Colossus Mark II cryptanalytical machines that worked at Bletchley Park in 1943 and 1944, respectively
(e) The ENIAC (Electronic Numerical Integrator and Computer), first working at the Moore School, Pennsylvania, in 1945

Although all were innovative at the time, none of the above projects possessed what we would now recognise as a practical internal read/write memory for the storage of program and data. Of these five machines, it is believed that the Borehamwood engineers would only have been familiar with the details of the last one, ENIAC. Furthermore, none of these five machines is within the scope of the chart of *post-war* British electronic digital know-how that has been presented in Fig. 1.3.

Appendix 10 describes a selection of ten later computer projects whose details would have potentially been more relevant to Borehamwood designers, if indeed sufficient details were readily available. These are:

(f) The small-scale experimental machine (SSEM), also called the Baby, which first ran a program on 21 June 1948 at Manchester University
(g) EDSAC, which first ran a program on 6 May 1949 at Cambridge University
(h) CSIRAC, first working at the Commonwealth Scientific and Industrial Research Centre (CSIR) at Sydney, Australia, in November 1949
(i) SEAC, the American Bureau of Standards' *Eastern Automatic Computer*, May 1950
(j) SWAC, the *Standards' Western Automatic Computer*, August 1950
(k) Pilot ACE, National Physical Laboratory, Teddington, Middlesex, May 1950

(l) Ferranti Mark I, delivered to Manchester University in February 1951

(m) UNIVAC I, delivered in March 1951

(n) Whirlwind, first working at the Massachusetts Institute of Technology (MIT) in March 1951

(o) IAS, first working at the Institute for Advanced Study (IAS), Princeton University, in the summer of 1951

What influence, if any, did the above 15 projects have on Borehamwood in 1947? It is clear from Norman Hill's remarks quoted earlier in Sect. 2.4.1 that, from the beginning, the general principles of stored-program computers were familiar to the Theory Division. Indeed, Norman Hill and John Coales visited NPL and met Alan Turing and others – probably in the first half of 1947, judging by Turing's movements [30]. Hill and Coales would, no doubt, have been made aware of Turing's plans for the ACE computer but the ACE project was not, at that stage, in a stable form that would have commended itself to those interested in robust digital hardware for a real-time on-line gunnery application.

Although the Computer Division was not established until the end of 1948, it is certain that its leader, Bill Elliott, already knew about computers from contact with his long-standing friend at Cambridge, Maurice Wilkes (later to become Professor Sir Maurice Wilkes FRS). Wilkes and Elliott had been fellow-undergraduates at Cambridge and shared an interest in amateur radio. Wilkes' Mathematical Laboratory at Cambridge remained an influence on the Borehamwood work, Wilkes himself becoming a Consultant to Elliott Brothers (London) Ltd. Norman Hill remembers [26] that: 'At around that time [1949 onwards?] Maurice Wilkes at Cambridge held a series of colloquia in the Mathematical Laboratory every two weeks at which experts on digital computing techniques were invited to give a talk followed by free discussion and tea and buns. As a forum for exchanging information these colloquia were invaluable and they greatly contributed to the growth of knowledge in this new and exciting field. We were able to keep up to date with progress on the different machines which were being designed and built. At about this time, 1947, Bill Elliott arrived at Borehamwood to lead the Computing Division. He had numerous friends at Cambridge, TRE and other places'. Actually, Bill Elliott did not join the staff at Borehamwood until after October 1948 – see above.

Apart from contacts via Cambridge, did individuals from other pioneering groups interact with Borehamwood? Looking at Fig. 1.3, one might reasonably assume that a general awareness of the SSEM, EDSAC and Pilot ACE projects would have found its way into the electronics industry by about 1950. Indeed, an inspection of the Borehamwood Visitors Books reveals the identity of several people who were (or were to become) knowledgeable about various aspects of digital computers. The purpose of their visits is not recorded, but it is interesting to quote names and dates, as shown in Table 2.2. The total period covered by Table 2.2 is October 1946 to December 1951. It is immediately apparent that very few computer-related names crop up over this 5-year period, indicating that the vast majority of visitors to Borehamwood had no known connection with digital computing.

Table 2.2 Computer-related visitors to Borehamwood between 1946 and 1951

Date	Person	Stated affiliation at that date
6 May 47	G G Scarrott	Cavendish Lab., Cambridge (later, at Ferranti Ltd)
6 June 47	A M Uttley	TRE
13 Oct. 47	J M Wilkinson	NPL
13 Oct. 47	H D Huskey	Ex-ENIAC, working at NPL (later, at SWAC).
2 Jan. 48	J M M Pinkerton	Cavendish Lab., Cambridge
10 April 48	M V Wilkes	Maths Lab., Cambridge
9 Nov. 49	L J Comrie	Scientific Computing Service, London
19 June 50	M V Wilkes	Maths Lab., Cambridge
2 Aug. 50	J M Bennett	Maths Lab., Cambridge (later, at Ferranti Ltd.)
23 Nov. 50	B V Bowden	Ferranti Ltd., Moston
23 Jan. 51	F C Williams	Manchester University
1 Feb. 51	J M M Pinkerton	J Lyons & Co.
19 Feb. 51	D Brunt	Royal Society
19 Feb. 51	B Lockspeiser	Dept. of Scientific & Industrial Research (DSIR)
25 Sept. 51	D R Hartree	Cavendish Lab., Cambridge
25 Sept. 51	M V Wilkes	Maths Lab., Cambridge
19 Nov. 51	C Strachey	National Research Development Corporation (NRDC)

In addition, NRDC staff (principally H J Crawley) came to Borehamwood on 10 Aug. 1950, 25 Sept. 1950, 19 Feb. 1951, 28 Sept. 1951, 16 Nov. 1951 and 19 Nov. 1951

Interestingly, in view of the mutual interest in CRT storage, members of the computer design group at Manchester University do not recall any visitors from Borehamwood coming to Manchester before the Ferranti Mark I Inaugural Conference in July 1951 [41]. However, as is explained in Appendix 1, Borehamwood researchers first met Professor F C Williams at an Institution of Electrical Engineers colloquium in London in November 1948.

Let us return to the 15 pioneering computers mentioned earlier, whose hardware performance is summarised in Appendix 10. In 1947, Borehamwood had a rather specialised interest in the entirely new field of real-time digital control, which required high computational speeds. On the key matter of performance, an obvious candidate for consideration by Borehamwood would have been the MIT Whirlwind computer, which was the only one having appropriately fast addition and multiplication rates. However, the first published report of this computer is probably Forrester's paper presented on 29 July 1948 at the Modern Calculating Machinery and Numerical Methods Symposium at the University of California, Los Angeles. Almost 3 years were to elapse before Whirlwind was fully operational.

In any case, information about Whirlwind and similar defence-related projects may have travelled slowly. Julian Bigelow, an IAS designer speaking in 1976, said: 'Several people have asked questions about what we were thinking at the time, when we got our ideas, and in particular how much we knew about – and possibly gained from – developments taking place at other places such as project Whirlwind at MIT and the ex-Moore School team in Philadelphia. The answer is that we had no communication contact except rumors, and as far as I know each of these groups proceeded along its own avenues, directed towards its own goals and developing its own criteria of what constituted excellence' [42].

The principal cause for delays in the Whirlwind project was problems with the MIT version of electrostatic (CRT) memory. When the first bank of memory tubes was attached to Whirlwind in July 1950, they proved unreliable and 'the behaviour of the storage depended on the programs used and their frequencies, and it varied when different areas of the storage surfaces were used. There was evidently much that we did not understand about the operation of the storage as an integrated part of the computer' (see Whirlwind Summary Report no. 24, third quarter 1950, page 6, as quoted in [43]. Borehamwood was to employ another, quite different, version of CRT storage, as described in Appendix 1.

More generally, storage issues had caused, or were causing, difficulties for several other computer design groups. In 1949, Nathaniel Rochester of IBM commented as follows in the premier US electronics journal of the time: 'The most difficult problem in the construction of large-scale digital computers continues to be the question of how to build a memory, and the few papers written do not reflect the greatness of the effort which is being exerted' [44].

Wartime radar experiments with equipment for permanent-echo calculation (e.g. at TRE) and Doppler radar (e.g. at ASE) had shown in principle that pulses could be stored as acoustic waves in a mercury delay line, but at that time, the techniques had not yet been applied to the long trains of pulses necessary to represent numerical information. Without a suitable read-write memory, general-purpose digital computers could not exist. The Cambridge EDSAC was, in May 1949, the first machine to exploit successfully the mercury delay line system in a fully functional stored-program computer. This system was not considered to be fast enough for MRS5. Other possibilities such as electrostatic CRT storage were still in the experimental stages in 1947.

In conclusion, the computer *hardware* developments at Borehamwood proceeded relatively independently from those of other contemporary design groups, principally because the MRS5 requirements for real-time operation placed severe demands upon arithmetic speeds obtainable with digital electronics. Furthermore, devising fast numerical algorithms for three-dimensional digital trajectory-prediction in MRS5 was a relatively new field of research. Finally, on a practical note, it was not certain that digital equipment based on thermionic valves (tubes) could be made reliable enough and compact enough to withstand the rigours of life at sea. One pulse lost from a radar system was recoverable; one pulse lost from a digital computing system could be catastrophic. It would not be until the mid-1950s that the inherently more reliable semiconductors began to replace valves. The basic properties of 'crystal triodes', or transistors, were demonstrated at the Bell Telephone Laboratories in America in 1947, but it was not until November 1953 that the first, modest, transistorised computer worked – at Manchester University [45].

2.6   The Elliott 152 Computer

The MRS5 project was given the internal number 152, in accordance with a Borehamwood classification system which, it is believed, gradually evolved over the years so as to reserve numbers in the range 100–199 for Admiralty-sponsored work, 300–399 for other classified Ministry of Supply work, and 400–499 for general-purpose computers sponsored by the National Research Development Corporation. We shall see later that this numbering system had largely become obsolescent by 1955.

Since the fire-control computer equipment lived on after the demise of the main MRS5 contract (see Sect. 2.4.4), it became usual at Borehamwood to refer to this first Elliott computer as 'the 152'. We shall henceforth adopt this convention.

The dominant requirements for the 152 computer were as follows. It should have sufficient speed to be able to send/receive data to/from the radar unit, compute the trajectory calculations from radar-derived data, and then send updated target information to the guns – repeating this sequence at sufficient speed to enable an aircraft flying at several hundred miles per hour to be tracked and destroyed. As is described in Appendix 1, this amounted to an ability to perform the necessary axis-conversions and to produce one update of {range, bearing and elevation} every 4 Milliseconds. In modern terms, the Elliott 152 computer was the brains at the centre of a real-time, on-line digital control system. In particular, each transmitted radar pulse was triggered by the 152 computer, the radar therefore being synchronised with the computer's internal clock. The central portion of the special 'egg-box' radar aerial, together with the Director's electronics and hydraulics, performed electronic scanning of the target as previously described. Radar-derived data, together with the aerial's angular position as read from an optical disc encoder, was transmitted as binary numbers back to the Elliott 152 computer.

The 10-in. diameter optical shaft-encoder disc on the MRS5 Director was a neat piece of advanced precision engineering [46]. Scribed with a pattern accurate to within one thousandth of an inch, the scale was projected onto a single photocell and photomultiplier, which was scanned by a CRT. The binary encoder not only gave a digital value of the current bearing but also the sine and cosine of this angle. The provision of trigonometric data produced a great saving of central computing time. (The alternative, namely sines and cosines stored in a fast look-up table within the 152, would have been very costly.) The 1948 shaft-encoder patent was filed in the names of J F Coales, N D Hill and S E Hersom (patent number 707212 dated 15 January 1948). This was also the first ever patent related to digital computing to emerge from the Elliott company. The encoder equipment is within the nacelle pictured in Fig. 2.7.

In the light of hindsight, the optical disc encoder patent could have been a huge money-earner for the company. However, as Norman Hill subsequently remarked [31], 'Although we and our patent agents tried to anticipate every possible application for this invention we failed to realise that the reading of the marks on the discs could be achieved by many small photocells in parallel instead of one single moving light spot. Subsequently these discs were widely used [by others] but our patent was of no use because in every case the reading was done in parallel instead of serially'.

Details of the Elliott 152 computer are given in Appendix 1. The architecture was complicated, being based on low-level functional parallelism imposed on a bit-serial ALU. There were separate data and instruction stores. Each of four programs was stored in a read-only memory so that the calculations for bearing, range and elevation could proceed relatively independently.

In the words of Norman Hill [31], 'It was decided to use a parallel system comprising essentially a series of units e.g. adder, multiplier, input, output, each operating in the same time scale with input and output gates which could be opened or shut simultaneously. Thus, at the expense of somewhat complicated programming, all the units could be set to operate at the same time and then reset to complete another series of simultaneous operations and so on. In this way we made a very fast, fixed-program real-time computer way ahead of its time'.

Here is a summary of the main characteristics of the Elliott 152, in modern terminology:

Word length	16-bit two's complement integers, with the binary point being *two* positions from the most-significant end (see below)
Instruction length	20 bits
CPU clock-rate	333 kHz
Multiplication-time	60 µs
Input/output data-rates	From radar director: 70,000 bits/s in; 10,500 bits/s out
Primary memory	CRT electrostatic RAM, using the Williams Tube *anticipation pulse* method. 16 tubes storing 256 digits each. In modern terms, this gave 512 bytes of RAM

Numbers were represented in the Elliott 152 as two's complement fractions, but with the implied point being *two* positions from the most-significant end. In the words of Ed Hersom, when describing a later Elliott computer called Nicholas [47]: 'I decided that the binary point should be two from the most-significant end, because I expected to be undertaking a lot of trigonometrical calculations such as axis conversion. The most-significant bit would be the sign, and the one next to it the overflow bit. (I never gave the idea of a separate register for overflow a single thought, again on economy grounds). The overflow bit also allowed a function like sin(x) to equal 1, or even slightly more due to rounding error, without causing severe mistakes'. This convention of imagining that an 'overflow' bit exists within each word has sometimes been used on other computers. The Apollo Guidance Computer, a 16-bit machine designed at MIT in the early 1960s, used a somewhat similar scheme [48].

The fastest storage technology available in 1947, anywhere in the world, was the CRT system being developed by Williams and Kilburn at Manchester University. Borehamwood chose to develop its own version of this CRT system for the Elliott 152. Williams had filed his first CRT storage patent, using the *anticipation-pulse* method, on 11 December 1946. The first Internal Report describing Borehamwood's CRT storage is dated 26 February 1948 (see Appendix 1). For a while, the storage

Fig. 2.8 The Elliott 152 computer in 1952, photographed during the off-line analysis of MRS5 radar data. The computer used 16-bit integers and 20-bit instructions, had a clock-rate of 333 kHz and a multiplication time of 60 μs. In modern terms the computer had 512 bytes of RAM, with instructions stored separately in ROM. The units in the foreground of the photograph are the set of six digital film cameras, each handling cassettes containing 400 ft reels of 35mm film on which was recorded radar tracking data. More photographs are given in [50]

group, first under M V Needham (Circuits Division) and then under R C Robbins (of the Circuits Division and then in the Computing Division), attempted to get the *anticipation-pulse* method of Williams-Kilburn storage to work at a pulse repetition rate of 1 MHz. Unsatisfactory results caused the clock-rate to be lowered to 333 kHz, some time in 1949. 333 kHz then became the standard clock-rate for all Borehamwood computers – and indeed for not a few Ferranti computers – for some years, as is described in Chap. 10. The 152's storage developments are discussed more fully in Appendix 1.

It would seem that initial development of digital techniques for use in the 152 computer began in the summer of 1947. In that year, D L Johnston of the Electrical Engineering Division started on the design of glass plate printed-circuit boards for the 152, intending to use the sub-miniature pentode valves (thermionic tubes) that were under development elsewhere. All through 1947 and 1948, therefore, the emphasis at Borehamwood was on developing the underlying technologies that would provide the necessary speed and reliability for the 152. It was probably not until the start of 1949 that work on what might be called the logical design of the arithmetic units of the 152 really got under way. By January 1949, when Harry Carpenter arrived, the overall systems architecture and the numerical algorithms for trajectory-prediction had not been decided upon. Carpenter was placed in charge of the central processor design. Incidentally, on the day that Harry first joined Borehamwood, Bill Elliott gave him a copy of Alan Turing's famous *On computable numbers* paper to read [49]. Harry, naturally, found it incomprehensible! He says [40] that he has often since wondered why Bill gave him (an engineer) this particular paper to read.

The people most closely associated with the implementation of the 152, under the general control of their respective Divisional Heads, included those named in Table 2.3. Since this list encompasses people from five Divisions, project co-ordination was sometimes problematic. The 152 project was supposed to have two types of regular (e.g. fortnightly) meetings: (1) A Steering Committee of Divisional Leaders and Archer-Thompson (the Laboratory's Security Officer), which mostly discussed non-technical matters; (2) a Systems Committee of engineers who were actually doing the design. Carpenter recalls that in his time at Borehamwood, the Systems Committee never met. He only found out about its nominal existence many years later, in retirement, when chatting about old times with Eric Whitehead [40].

In 1949, Carpenter, who was placed in charge of the central processor, decided on a modular architecture for the 152 (see Appendix 1).

In the rush to finish the Elliott 152 before the Admiralty money ran out, corners were cut. Carpenter was asked to take his engineers off the machine before he was satisfied about reliability. Matters came to a head when Coales ordered a partition to be erected which cut off the view of the machine from Carpenter's office across the open-plan factory bay at Borehamwood. One can imagine that tensions ran high!

The Elliott 152 computer carried out its first simple computations in mid-1950, according to a retrospective paper written in 1971 by Coales [46]. The first programs are described by S E Hersom, of the Theory Division, in an internal report dated 25 May 1950 (see Bibliography). The 152 can lay a claim to being the first

Table 2.3 Some of the people involved in the implementation of the 152

Name	Date joined EBRL	Area of design and implementation activity
Jim Barrow	Jan. 1948	Circuit & logical design
John Bunt	Sept. 1949	Circuit & logical design
Johnny Cane	Early 1948	Circuit & logical design
Harry Carpenter	Jan. 1949	Overall architecture; arithmetic unit design
D S Evans	1947	Optical disk encoder
Ed Hersom	Oct. 1947	Algorithms; functional specification; software
Andrew St Johnston	Autumn 1949	Circuit & logical design
Tom Ludlow	Jan. 1948?	Circuit and logical design
D L Johnston	Early 1947	Glass PCB design and construction
Norman Muchmore	1948	Power supplies
Maurice Needham	Oct. 1947	Initial CRT storage experiments
R C Robbins	Summer 1948	CRT storage
John Tyndale	1946 or early 1947	Cooling system

machine to attempt real-time digital process control, though a perusal of contemporary Borehamwood research reports suggests that it was only used for this purpose under test conditions, rather than in earnest. Taking a broader view, the field of process control is one in which Elliotts as a company, and John Coales as an academic researcher, were later to excel. The company's pioneering excursions into industrial automation are described in Chaps. 6 and 7; John Coales subsequently founded the Control and Systems Group at the University of Cambridge in 1953 after leaving Borehamwood.

The principal production work that the Elliott 152 performed was probably the analysis of MRS5 radar data, carried out in the spring and summer of 1952. This is described in Sect. 2.4.4 for the 'Netting' project. The radar specialists used the computer to analyse radar tracking data obtained from aircraft flight trials, with particular emphasis on the glint phenomenon. Data-capture was achieved in real time, but analysis was done later. The digital data, as described above, was first recorded optically on 400 – feet reels of 35-mm film, using six cameras simultaneously [50]. During subsequent analysis by the 152, the films were read back in a separate operation, using flying-spot scanners, tracking circuits, and high-speed servos to maintain alignment and to permit accurate start-stop. The optical films were developed at the Denham Film Studios, a few miles from Elliott's Borehamwood Laboratories. The subsequent use by Elliotts of 35-mm film stock for digital magnetic recording in the mid-1950s is mentioned in Chap. 10.

The 152 computer was, as John Bunt has remarked, 'a machine of remarkable power (when it worked), which employed every conceivable advance in technology known to man at the time. Printed circuits on glass plates, plated-through holes, deposited resistors, semiconductor diodes, plug-in units and so on. Some notable advances in techniques had been achieved in its construction, but unfortunately in a machine of its size, it was more often suffering from a breakdown than in robust health. I got to be quite good at locating faults in very quick time and Jim Barrow taught me how to repair faulty units by scratching out unwanted silver connections made by tracking across the glass and by using bits of wire to by-pass the plated-through holes. Between us we achieved quite remarkable running times for the machine before another breakdown occurred' [7]. To put the 'remarkable run times' in the context of 1950, John Bunt has also said [12] that: 'If the whole system could be made to work for a minute or two without breakdown – film readers and computer together – useful results were obtained'.

The problems of reliability had three main causes: (a) intermittent faults with the CRT storage system; (b) excessive heat generation; (c) rather optimistic physical design of the printed-circuit boards. The storage issues are described in Appendix 1. To cure overheating, Tyndale of the Mechanical Engineering Division designed what he called a *positive displacement wind engine*, *DPWE*, based on a large fan and wooden chamber or reservoir 'about 20 feet long and three feet high and wide', in the best Victorian engineering traditions. This solved the problem, but at the expense of excessive noise and oil pollution. The PDWE 'made a noise like the Gosport Ferry and had bearings that required greasing every morning' [7].

The printed-circuit problems, the responsibility of the Electrical Engineering Division, were not so easily rectified. There was electrolytic creep, or tracking, between adjacent printed silver conductors. The designer (D L Johnston) had, in the view of the Computing Division, tried to get more components per plate than was sensible, by doubling up on the edge-connectors. The mechanical design of the resulting edge-connectors left much to be desired, and many faults were found to be due to contact problems.

The lack of reliability notwithstanding, the 5-in. by 3-in. printed-circuit plates, shown in the photograph of Fig. 2.9, were a valiant attempt at packaging which was to influence Elliott's computer design philosophy long after the 152 had faded away. By the use of the (admittedly expensive) miniature pentodes that were becoming commercially available from Mullards in mid-1949, Borehamwood was able to pack a complete binary adder-stage on a single 5 × 4-in. plate. The multiplier consumed a total of 60 plates. The use of double-sided printing with plated-through holes, and deposited resistors etched to achieve the desired values, were two of the advanced features of Borehamwood's circuits that impressed visitors. More than one transatlantic visitor to the Laboratory urged Coales to take the technology to the market place and capitalise on the research [40].

Whilst all this hot technology was bubbling away to the north-west of London, there was another sort of activity coming to the boil at the main Elliott factory at Lewisham in the south-east of London.

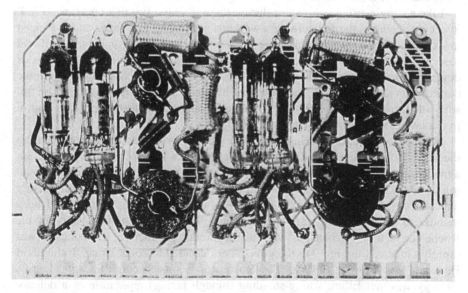

Fig. 2.9 The 152 computer used 5-in. by 3-in. glass printed-circuit plates, with double-sided printing, plated-through holes and deposited resistors. Four miniature pentode thermionic valves (tubes) are mounted on this plate

2.7 Enter the Entrepreneurs

We introduced Geoffrey Lee, the new go-ahead Managing Director of Elliott Brothers, in Chap. 1. Lee had by 1946 become a player in a wider circle of talented entrepreneurs whose ambition (it is deduced) was to run profitable companies that exploited the technical opportunities revealed by wartime R&D. By 1948, Lee was taking third place at Lewisham to Leon Bagrit and Lotti Ross, who were also introduced in Chap. 1. Of these three, Leon Bagrit provided the main entrepreneurial force. Behind all three of them lay the financial support of Higginsons.

Higginson and Company of Bishopsgate, London, a leading firm of merchant bankers, was founded in 1907. Higginsons was appointed managers from 1946 of the General and Commercial Investment Trust Ltd. – a fact which may have played a part in events at Lewisham. Subsequently, Higginsons merged with Philip Hill in 1951 to form Philip Hill Higginson & Co., then merged with Erlangers in 1959, then merged with M Samuels to form Hill Samuels in 1965, and finally became part of Lloyds Bank and the Lloyds TSB Group. It appears that Higginsons, knowing that the bank would have capital to place at the end of the war, sought advice on which industrial sectors were targets for profitable investment. They were told that the British instrument industry was ripe for development because it was character-ised by a large number of small privately owned firms. It is not necessary to describe the details of all Higginsons' interactions with the instrument industry in the 1940s. Instead, what follows is a summary of events as they affected Bagrit, Ross and the Elliott company, drawing largely on the information in [21].

Like all engineering companies during the war years, Bagrit's company B & P Swift obtained plenty of government work manufacturing munitions and continued to expand. After a while, seeing the need for electronic instruments, Bagrit and Ross set up a subsidiary called Electromethods to develop and sell this type of device. This was possibly the first tangible sign of Bagrit's passion for electronic control – an area that developed into what became known as Automation. The full story of Bagrit's seminal influence in the introduction of industrial process control in the late 1950s is given in Chaps. 6 and 7.

Needing more manufacturing space, B & P Swift had leased two factories during the war. As hostilities ended, one of these premises had to be relinquished. An agreement was reached with Geoffrey Lee that B & P Swift and Elliotts would jointly apply to the government for part of the huge Short Brothers aircraft factory at Rochester Airport, where the RAF's four-engined Stirling bomber had been manufactured during the war (see Appendix 9 for more on the history of the Rochester factory). When the war ended, aircraft production at Rochester was rapidly curtailed, and in 1946 the government decided to concentrate all the Short Brothers' activities at Belfast. The Rochester factory became vacant. Bagrit's strategy was that Elliott's long-standing (though fading) reputation as a defence equipment manufacturer would strengthen B & P Swift's chances of acquiring the Rochester property. The bid was successful, resulting in the acquisition of about five acres of potential floor space [51].

Meanwhile, by the end of the war, Elliotts at Lewisham was a company now showing definite signs of decline. The influential and technically gifted Chairman Sir Keith Elphinstone had died in 1941, leaving only one member of the Board, D C Harben, with any real technical knowledge of the company's products. This greatly disturbed the Admiralty, which was wrestling with the problems of updating and supplying fire-control equipment to its ships. Elliotts was the prime developer and provider of such equipment. In 1943, the Admiralty had written as follows. 'Having regard to the variety and complex character of its manufactured products it would be reasonable to expect the firm to maintain an exceptionally large design and drawing staff capable of feeding new developments. This section, however, is not large enough in relation to the whole works activities. In the period 1936–39 of pre-war re-armament programmes, the firm progressively enlarged its scope and volume of production to meet Admiralty requirements and achieved a considerable increase over the volume handled in the period 1932–35. Since the outbreak of war, however, the preceding rate of increase has not been maintained and in comparison with various other Admiralty firms the overall increase in this firm's contribution to the war effort is not outstanding' [52].

Criticism was not confined to technical matters. In 1943, the Managing Director, L W Smith, was described by Admiralty officers [52] as 'not endowed with a faculty for adjusting human relationships on a sympathetic and harmonious basis' and the working conditions and pay of the staff were said to be 'manifestly the reverse of generous'. In the same year, the Ministry of Labour carried out a survey report LC.13399/43 which contained 'severe criticism of the firm's management and indicates poor utilization of labour and facilities' [52]. It is also very probable that, under the financial dominance of Siemens Brothers of Woolwich who were majority shareholders, Elliott Brothers had been starved of capital during the war. Indeed, the financial control exercised by Siemens Brothers is described in [52] as 'a millstone round the necks' and a 'hostile parasitic incubus'. Strong words indeed.

As mentioned in Chap. 1, in the summer of 1945, Higginsons arranged to buy out Siemens Brothers' holdings in Elliott Brothers. £90,000 of Elliott Share Capital was purchased at £6 per share and distributed amongst Insurance Companies and Investment Trusts. G R Lee was appointed as Managing Director in July 1945. At the time, Lee was also on the Board of B & P Swift. Higginsons placed a nominated member on the Board of Elliotts, as shown in Table 2.4.

Table 2.4 The board of Elliott Brothers (London) Ltd. in the autumn of 1945

Board member	Comments
Sir Walter Jenkin	Chairman; resigned in November 1950; replaced by Rudolph de Trafford, a partner in Higginsons
G R Lee	Managing Director; installed by Higginsons as MD in July 1945
D C Harben	Works Director; resigned in May 1947
L W Smith	Brother of R O Smith; associated with the company for many years
P J A Lachlin	A partner in Higginsons
R O Smith	Secretary; brother of L W Smith (see above)

Shortly after his arrival at Lewisham, Lee appointed a young B & P Swift Works Manager, Woodruff, to understudy Harben and employed another young engineer, Klepp from Smiths Instruments, to take charge of development work at Lewisham. Klepp was to become the principal liaison person between the Elliott Directors at Lewisham and Coales at Borehamwood [21]. Klepp and Woodruff were nominally under Harben, but actually they reported directly to Lee. It seems very probable that Harben, and others of the *old guard* at Lewisham such as L W and R O Smith, found themselves gradually distanced from the policy-making processes and they soon faded from the scene.

During 1946, Lee approached various smaller instrument companies suggesting merger with Elliotts, but none would agree. Then in January 1947, Lee put a plan for merger with B & P Swift to the Elliott Board. The older-established Board members, particularly Harben, felt that B & P Swift's profits were too low and that the proposed price to be paid for their shares was too high, so they opposed the merger. Shortly after this Board meeting, the diligent Harben took extended sick leave due to stress and effectively left the company in May 1947. In this very month, the merger between B & P Swift and Elliott Brothers took place. Immediately, Bagrit was appointed Managing Director of Elliotts in place of Lee, and Dr Ross became Technical Director. From that moment onwards, things were never the same again at Lewisham.

At about this time, as Coales recalled [21], the British security services (MI5) visited him at Borehamwood and 'specifically warned him against admitting Directors of B & P Swift of alien origin who became Directors of Elliott Brothers to the secret work'. A perusal of the Visitor's book suggests that MI5's visit may have occurred on 10 April 1947. On his part, Bagrit announced at an Elliott Board meeting that he could not tolerate a situation in which he could not know what was going on at Borehamwood and that therefore he must have managerial access to classified projects. Discussion on the matter was postponed to the next Board meeting, by which time Bagrit reported that the matter 'had been settled'. The first recorded visit of Bagrit to Borehamwood was on 30 April 1947, according to the Visitors Book. Surviving correspondence shows that, certainly by 12 September 1950, Bagrit was enjoying the full confidence of the security services [53].

Bagrit set about re-positioning Elliotts. Bagrit employed business techniques that Coales, removed as he was from the cut-and-thrust of the marketplace, found extremely worrying. For a start, financial control of Borehamwood was placed firmly with Lewisham. Coales found that his orders for equipment and payments to suppliers were being deliberately delayed. In a letter to Geoffrey Lee (Elliott's former Managing Director and still on the Board) dated 21 January 1948, Coales wrote as follows:

'It has now come to my notice that the Company [i.e. Elliotts] has been blacklisted in at least one credit circle and it is rapidly becoming impossible to obtain the supplies necessary to carry out work either commercial or for the Admiralty.

'There is already a very great delay in the placing of orders on our behalf by Lewisham, and it now appears that the organisation has, to all intents and purposes, broken down.

There are, of course, two serious effects which arise from this situation. Firstly, that the sense of frustration of the staff here is increasing daily and it is impossible to prevent it becoming generally known that the Company is not paying its bills. The second effect is that not only is the goodwill of the Company as a whole being squandered but that, inevitably, the good name of the Laboratories is also being dragged down. So far, I have been able to maintain the high morale that was evident at the time of DNO's [Director of Naval Ordnance] visit but this is daily becoming difficult and unless immediate action is taken a crisis is likely to be reached within a few weeks.

'With regard to the second effect, it is clear that it is most important to maintain the good name of this Establishment [i.e. the Borehamwood Laboratories] since, if the Company does, in fact, founder, provided the goodwill of this Establishment is not impaired the Company can build up again around this Establishment.

'It is an intolerable situation that small firms should be put into serious financial difficulties because of the difficulties of this Company, particularly so when much of the work has been done under Admiralty contract for which the Company has, in fact, been paid by the Admiralty.

'Further, because the majority of our purchase orders are for materials to which the staff at Lewisham are unaccustomed, the fact that our orders have to go through Lewisham results only in very considerable delays and in a large number of queries which increases the work of our staff here. For this reason, a very great saving in manpower would be effected if the ordering was done direct from Borehamwood'.

After two more paragraphs of comment and suggestions, Coales' letter ends with this poignant paragraph:

'I very much regret having to issue what is to all intents and purposes an ultimatum but unless we can find some way of eliminating the delays, at any rate where the Admiralty work is concerned, I shall have to send copies of this letter to Mr Brundrett and Captain Lees and ask them what course of action they would suggest since under the present conditions I am unable to fulfil my obligations to the Admiralty. I realise that you are in a difficult position and I do not wish to embarrass you but there is no sense at all in my allowing the position to deteriorate to such a degree that there is little hope of retrieving it'.

We can now see that Lewisham was giving Borehamwood the cold shoulder, most probably because Bagrit considered that the activity at Borehamwood was not sufficiently directed towards either short-term or longer-term commercial profit. For his part, Coales clearly felt that Borehamwood was fulfilling its contractual research objectives and that Lewisham's problems were of its own making. Here, in truth, was an irreconcilable clash of cultures. On the one hand were Bagrit, Ross and Herzfeld, an entrepreneurial triumvirate who had ambitious plans to rescue the fortunes of the Elliott company. In the expression of the day, 'they meant business!' On the other hand was the scientist Coales who, as one loyal colleague was later to remark anonymously, 'was essential to the start-up of the Borehamwood Lab. but useless afterwards and not suited to the business world'.

In fairness to Coales, he did try strenuously to understand the economics of running an R&D department. The following section reveals the great personal struggle that consumed Coales in the period 1948–1951 as he fought to save the kind of research laboratory that he knew and loved. If the next section appears one-sided, it is because no official Elliott company documents have yet come to light that give Bagrit's responses to letters from Coales. Perhaps there weren't any. Bagrit had more than enough to think about at Lewisham, as he and Ross and Herzfeld struggled to turn round the fortunes of a seriously sick company.

2.8   Borehamwood's Financial Struggles

Coales has since stated that, at the end of 1947 and beginning of 1948, 'we thought Elliotts would go bankrupt. What we did not know was that Bagrit could go to Higginsons and borrow £500,000 on his note of hand! I made arrangements to borrow £5,000 from the bank on the security of my FSSU [Federated Superannuation System for Universities] Endowment Assurance policies, which were sitting in my safe at Borehamwood' [54]. Coales' plan was to go it alone. In January 1948, he produced a 16-page document entitled *Proposals for setting up the Research Laboratories of Elliott Brothers (London) Limited, Borehamwood as a separate company*. This report contained a detailed financial analysis of actual income and expenditure to date, plus estimates for 1948 and 1949. The proposal ends with the following note on the distribution of capital for the new Company:

'It is recommended that the Share Capital be limited to 15,000 ordinary shares of £1 each, of which 5,000 each be offered to the Business and Technical Directors. The remaining 5,000 shares should be offered to the employees of the Company. It shall be a condition that the ordinary shares must be held by the employees of the Company. The remaining £60,000 [required to float the Company] would, if possible, be obtained as a loan and it is proposed that the Government sponsored Industrial Finance and Investment Corporation for Industry be approached with a view to arranging this loan'.

Coales had obviously had enough of firms being bought and sold by City Suits! His document, however, was 'not yet distributed', according to a note on the title page signed by Coales and dated 29 February 1948.

A further draft report and financial analysis were produced at Coales' private request by Pennington & Son, solicitors, of Lincoln's Inn Fields, London, between March and October 1948 [21]. The invoice for £15-15s-0d, rendered to Coales by Messrs Pennington & Son on 29 October 1948, mentions 'long interviews with you with regard to the position of yourself and your staff and the Company's operations, and the proposed scheme for a new Company'.

In Table 2.5, extracted from information in [21], we summarise the actual research expenditure at Borehamwood from the start of operations to mid-October 1947 and Coales' predictions for 1948. It is seen that Admiralty contracts rise from about 50% of activity to 85% of activity, that a contract in the Physics Division to develop magnetometers for the Ministry of Supply (Air) rises from 0% to 8%, and that all other work is predicted to drop from 50% to about 7%. Under the 'Other work' heading comes the market-oriented developments being undertaken for Lewisham. John Coales' prediction of shrinking Lewisham work cannot have pleased Leon Bagrit.

Table 2.5 Analysis of percentage expenditure on labour and materials at Borehamwood, for the principal research projects in the years 1946–1948

Project, expenditure heading	1946 (%)	1947 (%)	1948 (%)
MRS5, labour	32	53	–
MRS5, materials	15	41	–
CDS, labour	19	10	–
CDS, materials	33	18	–
MRS + CDS, labour	–	–	85
MRS + CDS, materials	–	–	85
MOS (Air), labour	0	0	8
MOS (Air), materials	0	0	9
Other work, labour	49	37	7
Other work, materials	52	41	6

Coales described in [54] the usual basis in 1947 for calculating the annual profit allowed by the Admiralty on contracts. This was:

$$\{(7.5 \times \text{capital}) / (\text{annual turnover})\}.$$

Thus, if the capital is turned over once per annum, a profit at 7.5% of amount charged to the Admiralty would be allowed. If the capital is turned over twice per annum, then only 3.75% would be allowed, etc. When due allowance had been made for all items classed as 'capital', Coales was confident that the Admiralty would permit Borehamwood to make 7.5% profit on the MRS5 and CDS contracts. In addition to this, overheads were allowed to be charged at 108% on Admiralty contracts. These figures, of 108% overheads and 7.5% profit, are believed to have been considerably lower than the commercial and manufacturing targets to which Bagrit had been accustomed.

Later in 1948, Coales was to revise upwards his estimate in Table 2.5 of 'Other Work', which by then had included development of street lighting controls, colour printing controls, potentiometer recorders and plans to manufacture Flamitrol and Capacitrol devices under licence from the American company Wheelco. These estimates are shown in Table 2.6.

There is no evidence to suggest that Coales showed his private calculations to Bagrit. However, had he done so, the figures in Tables 2.5 and 2.6, encouraging though they appear, would hardly have impressed the industrialists unless more evidence had been forthcoming. One might conclude that Coales was now out of his depth. At the time, however, he was an honourable man, making great efforts to defend his staff and their research from what can only have seemed to many Borehamwood researchers to be the forces of darkness.

For Coales, this was indeed a most stressful period. In another letter to Geoffrey Lee dated 24 February 1948, but never sent [21], Coales opens with the following blunt statement: 'You are, I believe, going to the meeting at the Admiralty on Friday to discuss the future of the Research Laboratories at Borehamwood. Since I have

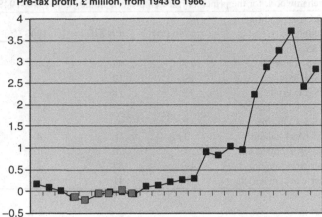

Fig. 2.10 Graph of the pre-tax profits of Elliott Brothers (London) Ltd. and Elliott-Automation Ltd., from 1943 to 1966. It is seen that Elliotts was trading at a loss from 1946 to 1951.The numerical data for this graph is given in Table 2.7

Table 2.6 Revised estimates on 'Other work' at Borehamwood, 1948–1949

	In 1948 (£)	In 1949 (£)
Estimated labour costs of other work	12,500	20,000
Estimated materials costs	12,500	20,000
Overheads (management, inspection, etc.)	5,000	8,000
Share of rent, rates, power, etc.	7,000	12,000
Notional profits on above	12,500	20,000
Therefore, total turn-over on other work	50,000	80,000

not been invited to attend the meeting, nor have you asked me to give you my views beforehand on a matter which vitally affects my own future and that of my staff, I am sending you our views uninvited'. Coales then goes on, for five typed pages, to state 12 points of issue, some of which are amplifications of the matters mentioned in his letter of 21 January (see above). Additional points raised include the following sentences:

(a) 'Failure to manufacture at Lewisham, equipment required by us after agreement has been reached that it should be done. The arbitrary stopping of work for Borehamwood without reference to me or anybody here and without even telling us that the work has been stopped'.

(b) 'There has been a complete refusal to spend the necessary Capital to provide even the bare necessities of furniture for staff engaged'.

(c) 'Before I joined, it was agreed that the Research Laboratories would be provided with a motor car, and later, it was specifically agreed with you and Mr Bagrit, that the black and white Vauxhall would be transferred to

Borehamwood as soon as a new Standard was delivered at Lewisham. This agreement was never implemented, apparently because Dr Ross damaged his own car and the Standard, as soon as it arrived, was handed over to him for his personal use'.

(d) 'Despite the fact that at Borehamwood we have had both people and facilities which could have helped the Company by the manufacture and sale of special instruments at a time when Lewisham's output was negligible, instead of being asked to help we were discouraged and even forbidden to do so'.

(e) 'The addition to the claims for payment by the Admiralty of what, in my opinion, are unreasonable sums for the work done at Lewisham and the failure to let me know what sums have, in fact, been claimed'.

(f) 'Although on my appointment as Research Director there was talk of my now being one of the "inner circle" whatever that may have meant, I have never been consulted about the Company's business, and I have, apparently, been kept as far as possible in the dark about the Company's financial position and the policy for the future. It is quite clear from this that either the Board of Directors has no confidence in my ability to help the Company through a difficult time and does not wish to enlist our help, or else it does not require a Research Director. This is born out by the fact that the Organisation Chart shows a Research Laboratory at Rochester of which I have not been officially informed and concerning which I have not been consulted. This is a very strange state of affairs'.

Coales concluded thus: 'To sum up, there is a clear indication of determination on the part of you and Mr Bagrit to maintain a tight control of all that goes on in the Research Laboratories by means of financial sanctions, even in the case of contracts for the success or failure of which we are entirely responsible. Research cannot flourish in such an atmosphere'. True though this last remark may have been, it would have taken a very well-established and wealthy parent company, such as GEC, to have supported the kind of research program that Coales had in mind. At that time, Elliotts could not afford the luxury.

Geoffrey Lee, the putative recipient of the above letter, quickly faded from the scene, and after 1948 Leon Bagrit became the main target of John Coales' frustrations. Although seldom mentioned specifically in surviving company documents, the name of Dr Lotti Ross should be implicitly coupled with that of Bagrit. This coupling is explained in a retrospective comment by Hugh McGregor Ross, who left Borehamwood to join Ferranti Ltd. in 1953: 'John Coales, who was and is one of my 'hero friends', is of the highest integrity and capability. ... Leon Bagrit was an entrepreneur of extreme skill and a true visionary ... Dr Ross was very acute in his appreciation of technical situations and tended to make up his own mind. Leon Bagrit relied exclusively and implicitly on Dr Ross in connection with all technical matters... Now it was obvious to me, even at my third level [down the management hierarchy], that John Coales and Dr Ross, who were as different as chalk from cheese, would have difficulty in agreeing on what was the right course of action, what were the right projects to work on, what was the best way of spending the limited funds. ... It was inevitable that any difference between them would turn into a difference between Coales and Bagrit. And equally certain that Coales would be the loser and have to leave' [55].

Coales battled on for four more years, finally leaving Borehamwood in April 1952, as described in Chap. 5. Both Coales and Bagrit and the research activity at Borehamwood all went on to achieve greatness in other directions – so we shall see that there *were* happy endings. However, let us finish this very stressful part of the Borehamwood story with two revealing anecdotes.

One lunchtime in about 1951, Leon Bagrit and Lotti Ross came into the canteen at Borehamwood with Coales. Ross (or was it Bagrit?) was seen to hand his hat and coat to Coales, as if to a cloakroom attendant at a Club. Many staff remember being shocked by this incident; indeed, Hugh McGregor Ross recalls it as his trigger for searching for a new job [56, 57].

A couple of years later, Laurence Clarke remembers that there was a row of parking slots outside Elliott's main Borehamwood building. 'The one nearest the front door was for important visitors. There was an enthusiastic security guard who, when a Rolls Royce pulled onto it, rushed up and told Dr Ross that he could not park there because it was reserved for the Managing Director. Ross merely said with a smile - "And who do you think I am – Robin Hood?"' [58].

2.9   Pulling Out of the Mire

John Coales resigned from Borehamwood in April 1952. Although he had not the satisfaction of seeing his cherished MRS5 project accepted for sea trials with the Navy, he did negotiate an arrangement with the National Research Development Corporation whereby the digital technology of the Elliott 152 computer was eventually transformed into a successful range of commercially available computers (the Elliott 400 series machines; see Chap. 5). After leaving Borehamwood, John Coales was invited in 1953 to form an Automatic Control Group in the Engineering Department at the University of Cambridge and was appointed an Assistant Director of Research. In 1957, he became a founding member of the International Federation of Automatic Control (IFAC), and by 1966 he had become the first Professor of Control Engineering at the University of Cambridge. He was elected a Fellow of the Royal Society in 1970, was the President of the Institution of Electrical engineers in 1971/1972 and was appointed CBE in 1974. One of his last professional activities was the initiation, in 1985, of a project to produce a history of naval radar during World War Two [3]. He died in Cambridge on 6 June 1999 aged 91. For further biographical details, see [1, 2].

Following Coales' departure from Borehamwood in 1952, there were a few months of uncertainty during which day-to-day administrative decisions at the Laboratory seem to have been the responsibility of W A P Wykeham, who had been appointed General Manager by Bagrit in the autumn of 1951 [59]. Coales has remarked [60] that Bill Wykeham was an old friend from ASE days and his appointment 'didn't cause any real trouble'. The summer and autumn of 1952 was a period during which research decisions at Borehamwood were the province of a group of senior divisional heads known to junior staff as the Fog Box – a reference to meetings held in a smoke-filled office under the effective chairmanship of Alex Cochrane and including Norman Hill and Bill Elliott. The 'fog' also gave a hint of uncertainly. Would Borehamwood be allowed to survive as a leading-edge electronics research centre, after Leon Bagrit had ordered what he called a necessary 'pruning' of staff numbers? Indeed, would Elliott Brothers (London) Ltd. survive as an independent company?

In fact, the period 1952/1953 did see staff resignations at Borehamwood but the net loss was nowhere near the rumour [10] that 'just after Coales left, 30% of staff was asked to find another job within 3 months'. Norman Hill remembers [26] that about 15% of staff were effectively sacked by the Fog Box, after 'many afternoons and evenings were spent in going through lists of staff selecting those who were to be asked to go, taking into account factors such as length of service, age, children, mortgages being repaid etc. while meanwhile the whole staff were in turmoil awaiting their individual fates.... We all felt that the astonishing technical achievements [of MRS5, CDS, etc.] had not been recognised, appreciated or understood by company management at Lewisham'. A consequence of all this was that some good people, such as Alex Cochrane, *chose* to leave (in 1954), but some of the new arrivals during this period were to prove equally talented. Bill Elliott managed to ensure that no member of the Computing Division was asked to leave the company during the Fog Box period [61].

Direction of the Borehamwood Laboratory was soon taken over by an ex-Naval man, Commander Henry Pasley-Tyler, known to all as 'P-T'. He had actually been appointed to the staff by Bagrit in July 1950, as someone who would liaise between the Admiralty and Elliotts at a time when tensions between Coales and Lewisham were threatening to disrupt the whole company. Regrettably, P-T became known as 'Leon's Spy' and Coales tended to freeze P-T out of Borehamwood staff meetings. However, by mid-1952 Pasley-Tyler seems to have gained the confidence of the research staff and henceforward became an effective and respected top-level negotiator in Borehamwood's research contracts, especially those involving the Ministry of Defence.

Meanwhile, Elliott Brothers (London) Ltd. was pulling back from the brink of insolvency. In Table 2.7, we give the pre-tax profits over the period 1943–1967, culled from the sources listed in [62]. It is seen that the company traded at a loss during the financial years 1946–1951. From 1952, although Coales' departure may have dented the morale of the research staff at Borehamwood, the company as a whole began to make real progress in the marketplace. From 1956, the company's main trading name was changed to Elliott-Automation Ltd.

Behind the scenes, the company's financial fragility remained for a couple of years after Coales' departure. An article in *The Statist* for 13 February 1954 stated that: 'The company still has, however, a substantial bank overdraft (amounting at present to approximately £290,000) and the directors consider it a matter of commercial prudence now to raise additional finance by the issue of further share capital.... The issued capital after the proposed rights issue has taken place will amount to £308,000 in Ordinary stock and £150,000 in Preference shares'. We pick up the financial threads again in Chap. 13.

Table 2.7 Pre-tax profit (£m), for Elliott Brothers (London) Ltd. and (from 1956) Elliott-Automation Ltd. over the period 1943–1966. This data is shown graphically in Fig. 2.10

Year	Pre-tax profit (£m)
1943	0.154
1944	0.079
1945	0.016
1946	−0.157
1947	−0.198
1948	−0.077
1949	−0.012
1950	−0.018
1951	−0.077
1952	0.102
1953	0.143
1954	0.223
1955	0.261
1956	0.293
1957	0.91
1958	0.82
1959	1.02
1960	0.96
1961	2.21
1962	2.86
1963	3.24
1964	3.70
1965	2.39
1966	2.81

Although the Elliott company's liquidity was modest in the early 1950s, Coales' legacy of research enthusiasm and innovative prototyping was flourishing at Borehamwood. Here are some technological highlights of the early 1950s, arranged chronologically:

1951 Mopsy shipborne anti-aircraft missile project initiated, leading in 1952 to a prototype radar with the renowned Elliott Cassegrain aerial (see Chap. 11)

1952 The Elliott Nicholas computer first worked (see Chap. 8)

1953 The Elliott 401 computer first worked (see Chap. 5). Also, an Aviation Division was established and research started on the design of a three-axis autostabiliser for the Lightning Mach 2 fighter. This was to lead to Elliott's involvement in world-class avionics, as recounted in Chap. 12

1954 The huge TRIDAC analogue computer was delivered to RAE Farnborough (see Chap. 4). The Elliott 153 computer and the 311 (Oedipus) were delivered to classified GCHQ locations (see Chap. 3)

1955   The Elliott 403 (WREDAC) was delivered to Woomera, Australia (see Chap. 3). The first of ten Elliott 402 computers was delivered (see Chap. 5). Elliotts get a contract to develop the inertial navigation system for the Blue Steel nuclear missile

1956   The first of 33 Elliott 405 computers was delivered (see Chap. 8)

The above list highlights computing achievements, in line with the main subject of this book. However, the sale of digital computers probably only accounted for less than 10% of the total sales income of the Elliott-Automation group of companies (see analysis in Chap. 13). Turning to other Borehamwood activities, Bob Ford, who joined Borehamwood in July 1951, describes the period 1955–1965 as 'the hey-day of the company when we were all inspired by Bagrit's vision of 'Automation' and thriving under his divisional structure was a great time' [5]. Bob worked in the Guided Weapons Division at Borehamwood when it was formed in 1952, went on to be Head of Airborne Radio & Radar Division and left the company in 1969 to join the Negretti & Zambra Group – eventually becoming Chairman.

We shall see in later chapters that the traditions of technological excellence, established by John Coales at Borehamwood, outlasted both Leon Bagrit and Elliott-Automation and thrived especially in the area of avionics under new company structures. In Chap. 3, we start by describing three secret digital computer projects that were completed in the period 1954–1956. Indeed, both Chaps. 3 and 4 are primarily concerned with defence-related applications, both analogue and digital. Readers with little interest in the military may understandably be tempted to skip to Chap. 5 where the civil applications – the ploughshares from swords – are introduced.

References

1. MacFarlane SA (2003) John Flavell Coales, CBE. Biogr Mem Fell Roy Soc Lond 49:119–131
2. Young P (1999, Oct) Professor John Flavell Coales, CBE, FRS, MA, Hon D Sc., C Eng, FIEE, FIEEE, FInstP, FICE. IEE Comput Control Eng J: 231–233
3. Howse D (1993) Radar at sea – the Royal Navy in World War 2. MacMillan, London. See also: Coales JF, Calpine HC, Watson DS (1946) Naval fire-control radar. J IEE 93, part IIIA (Radiolocation) (2):349–379
4. In 1928 John Coales was a co-founder of the group of English Country Dancers called the Cambridge Round. After the War, Coales hosted groups of ex-Cambridge dancers at Oakwood, his large house at Radlett, beginning in August in 1947 and subsequently at various times through to 1952. See http://www.srcf.ucam.org/round/history/coales for a history of the Cambridge University Morris Dancing group
5. RE (Bob) Ford (1995) Eight-page letter of Borehamwood anecdotes sent to Laurence Clarke and dated 18 Dec 1995
6. Alison Steer (née Coales) (2003) Conversations with Simon Lavington on 10 Dec 2003 and inspection of certain of John Coales' personal papers
7. John Bunt (1995) Un-titled and un-dated four-page typed notes of his time at Borehamwood. Almost certainly sent to Lawrence Clarke with an accompanying letter dated 16 Oct 1995
8. PD (Peter) Atkinson (1995) Letter to Lawrence Clarke dated 16 Oct 1995

9. WH (Bill) Pearse (1995) Letter to Laurence Clarke dated 9 Oct 1995
10. Commander Henry Pasley-Tyler CBE (1995) Un-dated audio-recording of an interview with Laurence Clarke. It may be inferred from letters to Laurence that this interview took place some time between 1 Feb 1995 and 24 May 1995, at which time he was 84 years old. Pasley-Tyler died in Dec 1995
11. JF Coales (1946) Elliott Research Laboratory – Borehamwood 1946. Seven types pages and eight hand-written pages, covering the period mid-July 1945 to autumn 1946. Sent with an accompanying letter to S L H Clarke on 29 Apr 1998. A copy of the document exists in the Archive of the Institution of Electrical Engineers, London, catalogue number SC168/1/6/2/3. In the accompanying letter, John Coales says that he hopes to continue writing about Borehamwood "because there is a lot during the next two years including the security problems and relationships with BTM etc. that now only I know about". He explains in the letter that he has not been in good health. John Coales died on 6 June 1999, aged 92, having been unable to continue his account
12. John Bunt (1994) Four-page typed manuscript of Borehamwood anecdotes, enclosed with a letter to Laurence Clarke dated 9 Nov 1994
13. Alan Essex (1995) Letter to Laurence Clarke dated 16 May 1995 enclosing 13 hand-written pages of Borehamwood anecdotes
14. Arthor Hemingway (1995) Letter dated 2 Nov 1995 to Laurence Clarke, enclosing five hand-written pages of Borehamwood anecdotes
15. CA (Alec) Cochrane (1994/1995) Letters to Laurence Clarke dated 14 Nov 1994 and 9 Oct 1995. The latter contains most of the historically important information
16. JE (Jack) Pateman (1994/1995) Letters dated 4 Nov 1994 and 7 Dec 1995, the latter with enclosed pages of Borehamwood anecdotes
17. No comprehensive biography of W S Elliott has come to light. In order of relevance to Borehamwood, the following references are of some use: (a) Ian Merry, July 2000, *A memorabilia of W S Elliott, physicist, Engineer and Professor Emeritus*. 2.5 page typed manuscript, dated July 2000 and copied to Simon Lavington. (b) "Professor W S Elliott and the Elliott-NRDC 401 computer". St Catherine's College Magazine, Cambridge. (Date and author unknown). (c) H McGregor Ross, obituary of W S Elliott, IEE News, Nov 2000, page 11. (d) Hannah Gay, *History of Imperial College, 1907–2007*. Published in 2007 by Imperial College Press
18. Audio tape of John Coales in conversation with Laurence Clarke, date unknown (but probably February 1995 or a little later). Duration: about 60 minutes, not all of which is relevant. This audio recording was made at a time when Laurence Clarke, with the approval of John Coales, was assembling material for a book about the history of the Borehamwood Laboratories. In the event, Laurence Clarke abandoned his project at the end of 1996 and passed his historical material to Simon Lavington on 10 July 2001
19. WE (Ben) Bennett (1994/1995) Letters to Laurence Clarke dated 5 Oct 1994 and 5 Jan 1995, the latter including two typed pages of historical notes
20. Foolscap hard-bound ledger entitled *Official Secrets Acts,* containing the names, dates and signatures of employees at Borehamwood. This book was recovered from the Strong Room at Borehamwood in 2003, at the time when the few remaining documents were being consigned to the rubbish skip
21. Copies of notes and papers resulting from discussions between JF Coales and Pennington & Son, solicitors, of Lincoln's Inn Fields, London, between Mar and Oct 1948. Sent by JF Coales to SLH Clarke on 10 Feb 1995. Copies of most of these papers are also held in the Archives of the Institution of Electrical Engineers, London, under catalogue number SC168/1/6/2/1
22. Unsigned obituary of C A Laws, IEE News, published by the Institution of Electrical Engineers, Dec 2002, p 7
23. Benjamin R (1996) Five lives in one. Parapress Ltd., Tunbridge Wells. ISBN: 1-898594-25-2
24. Laurence Clarke (2009) E-mail to Simon Lavington dated 14 Oct 2009
25. Maurice Needham (2007) Telephone conversation with Simon Lavington on 26 July 2007
26. ND (Norman) Hill (1995) A personal account of the early history of Elliott Brothers research laboratories. 6-page typed manuscript and accompanying letter to Laurence Clarke, dated 9 May 1995

27. The National Archive, file ADM 220/1668: Report on the visit to the United States in August and September 1944 of J F Coales and H C Calpine of the Admiralty Signal Establishment, with Mr H Clausen of the Naval Ordnance Department. Document dated Nov 1944

28. Clymer AB (1993) The mechanical analogue computers of Hannibal Ford and William Newell. IEEE Ann Hist Comput 15(2):19–34. See also: http://web.mit.edu/STS.035/www/PDFs/Newell.pdf

29. Ival TE (ed) (1956) Electronic computers: principles and applications. Iliffe & Sons Ltd. (Published for Wireless World), London

30. Hodges A (1983) Alan Turing: the enigma. Burnett Books, London. ISBN: 0-09-152130:0

31. Bell J (1947) Data transmission systems. J Inst Electrical Eng, Part IIA 94:222

32. The National Archive (1948–1950) Report ADM 294/15: MRS5 radar: minutes of quarterly meetings

33. Commander FC Morgan (1948) Hand-over notes. Admiralty Signal Research Establishment, Dec 1948. In File ADM 220/222: Fire control radar: outline of work in progress, Dec 1948, The National Archive

34. RB (Bob) Nichols (1995) Letter dated 19 Oct 1995 enclosing three typed pages of historical notes, sent to Laurence Clarke. Nichols joined Borehamwood towards the end of 1947, first in the Instruments Division and then moving to the radar group to work on MRS5

35. Eric Whitehead (1994) Letter to Laurence Clarke dated 22 Nov 1994

36. Kingsley FA (1995) The application of radar and other electronic systems in the Royal Navy in World War II. Macmillan, London

37. Wilson JF (2001) Ferranti: a history. Building a family business. Vol 1, pp 1882–1975. Carnegie, Lancaster, ISBN: 1-85936-080-7

38. Anon, *Appreciation of the general principles of Fly-Plane Fire Control Systems*, and *Comments on a proposal by Mr B M Brown, RNC, Greenwich, for a Naval fly-plane System.* Admiralty Gunnery Establishment, Teddington, Middlesex, Report number AGE/R1/25.00/Maths, 1950. Now in the National Archives as document ADM 263/149

39. Cochrane CA (1953) Netting Trials: final report. Borehamwood Research Report number 298, 5 June 1953

40. HG (Harry) Carpenter. Notes taken by Simon Lavington of nine lengthy telephone conversations with Harry Carpenter, during the period 16 May 2000 to 9 Dec 2002. Harry was unwilling to commit his historical anecdotes to paper but was more than happy to talk. Part way through these exchanges, in Nov 2001, Harry obtained clearance under the provisions of the Official Secrets Act to reveal certain details about his hardware design activities at Borehamwood (see also Chapter 3). More generally, Harry's reticence to write down anecdotes about Borehamwood was explained in a letter to Laurence Clarke, dated 10 Nov 1994: "I have never disguised the fact that I feel the organisational structure of the RLEB [Research Labs of Elliott Brothers] was badly flawed and ill-suited to the kind of development work we were trying to do (with, incidentally, an impossible time-scale).... 'if you can't say something nice, don't say anything at all'"

41. DBG Edwards, conversations with Simon Lavington, 2006–2008. (Dai Edwards joined Professor F C Williams' computer design team at Manchester University in Sept 1948, having graduated in Physics. Edwards remained at the forefront of computer design at Manchester University, becoming Professor of Computer Engineering in 1966 and retiring with the title Emeritus Professor in 1988).

42. Metropolis N, Howlett J, Rota G -C (eds) (1980) A history of computing in the twentieth century. Academic Press, New York, p 308

43. Redmond KC, Smith TM (1980) Project Whirlwind, the history of a pioneer computer. Digital Press, Bedford. ISBN: 0-932376-09-6

44. Rochester N (1950) Radio progress during 1949: electronic computers. Proceedings of IRE, Apr 1950, p 374

45. Lavington SH (1975) A History of Manchester computers. First edition published in 1975 by the National Computing Centre. Second edition published by the British Computer Society in 1998: ISBN 0-902505-01-8

46. Coales JF (1972, Jan) Computers and the professional engineer. Proc IEE119(1):1–16
47. Hersom SE (2002) Nicholas, the forgotten Elliott project. Resurrection, the Bulletin of the Computer Conservation Society, Issue number 27, spring 2002, pp 10–14
48. See: http://authors.library.caltech.edu/5456/1/hrst.mit.edu/hrs/apollo/public/
49. Turing AM (1937) On computable numbers, with an application to the Entscheidungsproblem. Proc Lond Math Soc 42(2):230–265. Corrigenda in Vol 43, pp 544–546
50. Clarke SLH (August 1975) The Elliott 400 series and before. Radio Electron Eng 45(8):415–421
51. (a) Anon, *150 years of instrument making.* Unsigned article in The Elliott Journal, vol. 1 number 1, March 1951, pp 3–10. (b) Elliott Brothers (London) Ltd.: large advertisement placed in The Times newspaper of Monday May 11 1953, "issued in compliance with the Regulations of the Council of the Stock Exchange, London, for the purpose of giving information to the public with regard to the Company". *In the matter of factory floor space, this advertisement gives the following figures: (i) Century Works, Lewisham, floor space of about 155,000 square feet. (ii) A factory at Rochester, Kent, is occupied under tenancy from the Ministry of Supply at an annual rental of £12,200. The premises consist of a modern single-storey building with a floor area of about 185,000 square feet. (iii) A research establishment at Borehamwood, Hertfordshire, is housed in a modern building with a floor space of approximately 80,000 square feet, under tenancy from the Admiralty at an annual rent of £8,750*
52. The National Archive, file ADM 178/309: *Report on morale and output of Elliot Bros Ltd: suggestions for improvement, 1943.* Produced by the Director of Naval Ordnance, September 1943, DNO. Note: this file was originally marked as 'Secret: closed until 2043'
53. Correspondence with the Ministry of Defence and associated government departments, in a confidential file labelled *From Commander H Pasley-Tyler's Lewisham files, 1950 – 1956,* formerly kept in the Strong Room at Borehamwood
54. Letter from J F Coales to S L H Clarke dated 10 Feb 1995, containing copies of papers written by JF Coales between Nov 1947 and 24 Feb 1948. The papers include the 16-page document entitled *Proposals for setting up the Research Laboratories of Elliott Brothers (London) Limited, Borehamwood as a separate company,* written in January 1948
55. Hugh McGregor Ross (1994) Letter to W S (Bill) Elliott, dated 1 Jan 1994
56. Hugh McGregor Ross (1994) After the Elliott 400 series. Resurrection, the Bulletin of the Computer Conservation Society, Issue number 9, spring 1994
57. Interpretations of this incident differ. In an e-mail to Simon Lavington dated 14 Oct 2009, Laurence Clarke remarked that he and Andrew St Johnston always found Lotti Ross "to be scrupulously polite". The incident itself is not denied
58. Laurence Clarke (2009) E-mail dated 29 June 2009, sent to Simon Lavington
59. Internal memo dated 5 Oct 1951, from Leon Bagrit to JF Coales and Mr Wykeham: *"Confidential. Arising out of the meeting held at Century Works on Friday the 28 September 1951, I confirm that as from Monday the 8 October 1951, Mr Coales will carry out the duties of Research Director of the Company and Mr Wykeham will assume the title and function of General Manager, Research Laboratories, Borehamwood"*
60. JF Coales (1994) Transcript of an interview by William Asprey of the Center for the History of Electrical Engineering, 21 Mar 1994. A copy of this is in the Archives of the Institution of Electrical Engineers, London, catalogue number SC168/1/6/2/4
61. Laurence Clarke (2009) E-mail to Simon Lavington dated 14 Oct 2009
62. The following sources have been used to obtain figures for the company's pre-tax profits: (a) A three-quarters page advertisement in The Times newspaper for Monday 11 May 1953, which gives a brief history of the company together with detailed financial detail for the years 1943–1952. (b) London Stock Exchange Yearbook for 1954 onwards (available at the Guildhall Library). Elliott's shares were first quoted on the London Stock Exchange in 1953, so the Yearbook gives financial information for Elliott Brothers (London) Ltd. from 1953 onwards. (c) Additional financial information may be gleaned from the surviving Elliott-Automation Annual Reports. Those for the years 1958 to 1966 have thus far come to light

Chapter 3
The Secret Digit

We describe three rather special Borehamwood digital computers in this chapter. Two of them were designed to perform tasks for the UK's intelligence services, via GCHQ (Government Communications Headquarters). The third went to a joint British–Australian long-range missile facility in Australia, to be used in analysing data from the Woomera test range. The time frame of all three computers, from conception to delivery, covers the period 1949–1956. Internally to the Borehamwood Research Laboratory of Elliott Brothers (London) Ltd., the projects were identified by sequence numbers in the company's list of orders. Table 3.1 summarises the connection between internal and external nomenclature.

Only one version of each of the machines in Table 3.1 was built. They were designed for specific tasks and indeed the 311 was not a general-purpose stored-program computer, being known within the cryptanalysis world as a Rapid Analytical Machine. Nevertheless, the 311 was the first GCHQ machine to really exploit the potential of high-speed digital storage [1]. Although the 153 and 403 computers were general-purpose, only the 403 was eventually used to run a variety of other (non-specific) programs during its life and only the 403 was to have any significant influence on the design of subsequent Elliott production computers.

The tasks for which the 153 and 311 computers were designed are still covered by the provisions of the Official Secrets Act. In this chapter, we concentrate on the innovative design of the machines at Borehamwood and the technology of their implementation, based on information released after 2001 by the relevant UK authorities. It is for others to speculate upon their wider strategic and military importance.

Table 3.1 Identification of the three Elliott computers

Elliott project ID	External name	Date delivered	Location	Organisation
153	DF computer	1954	Irton Moor, Scarborough	Admiralty and GCHQ
311	OEDIPUS	1954	GCHQ, Cheltenham	GCHQ
403	WREDAC and WREDOC	1955 and 1956	Salisbury, Australia	Long Range Weapons Establishment

S. Lavington, *Moving Targets*, History of Computing,
DOI 10.1007/978-1-84882-933-6_3, © Springer-Verlag London Limited 2011

3.1   The Elliott 153: The DF Computer

3.1.1   The Admiralty's Needs

The 153 computer was designed to calculate the most probable point of transmission of radio signals whose properties (principally direction-finding (D/F, or DF) bearings) had been deduced by Listening Stations located around the world. To quote from [2], 'The 153 computer has been built for faster handling of the DF data previously treated by the Admiralty Mathematical Method of plotting. It is a high-speed automatic electronic computer, and it uses an alternative method which is independent of gnomic charts'. The typical time taken by the Admiralty manual method of plotting bearings was between 15 and 30 min. The 153 computer reduced this time to about 10 s, plus 1 min for printing the Best Point Fix and a record of the input data used for this fix [3]. It was expected that 'up to 200 [plotting] tasks would be analysed per day and as many as 10 [Listening] Stations will contribute information on each of these' [3]. The computer was expected to 'digest the information as it becomes available', implying a requirement for reliable equipment and near real-time response.

The 153's logic circuits were based on wire-ended sub-miniature pentode thermionic valves (*tubes*), mounted on paxolin printed-circuit boards. The small primary memory (RAM) consisted initially of CRT electrostatic storage, later replaced by nickel delay lines. Secondary storage, of much larger capacity, was on magnetic disc. The 153's hardware architecture is discussed in Sect. 3.1.3, with Appendix 1 containing the finer points. First, though, we describe the birth of the project at Borehamwood.

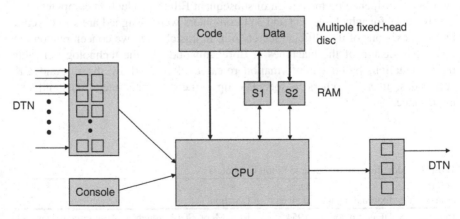

Fig. 3.1 An overall system diagram of the Elliott 153 Computer. This accepted direction-finding information coming in from remote stations via the *Defence Teleprinter Network (DTN)* on the left of the diagram and produced latitude/longitude output on the right of the diagram

3.1.2   The Project at Borehamwood

The government department ultimately requiring the results calculated by the 153 was GCHQ, as part of Signals Intelligence. In conjunction with the Admiralty, GCHQ placed the initial contract CP/12439/49 for the 153 computer with the Borehamwood Research Laboratories of Elliott Brothers (London) Ltd. in 1949. To quote [4], 'work made only slow progress. By January 1952 the original design had been improved, but delivery of a "development model" was not achieved until mid-1954, and it took a further eighteen months before the system was fully operational. No further models were built, but the original remained in satisfactory use until the late 1960s'.

The 'slow progress' was partly related to initial uncertainties about whether the computing for what was originally called the *D/F Calculator* should be analogue or digital. At a meeting with nine Admiralty scientists at Borehamwood on 2 March 1950, it was decided to go digital [3]. An examination of the Borehamwood Visitors Books show that regular twice-monthly meetings with the Admiralty liaison officer, L H F (Leslie) Nicholls, did not commence until July 1952. Up to that point, there had been some uncertainty about the digital technology to be used in the 153 computer. The initial plan was to employ the same circuit packages as the Elliott 152 computer but these were proving unreliable and were re-designed for the 153 project in 1952 by C E Owen, who then left Borehamwood in 1954. John Bunt remembers this as 'a difficult period for the company' [5]. He goes on to describe the 153 developments as follows:

'One effect of the financial problems that affected the Computer Division [at Borehamwood] was that they could not finance the development of the 401 and 153 at the planned rate and it was decided to delay the 153 programme by about a year, much to the disappointment of the Admiralty Research Laboratory (ARL). At that time, Charles Owen who designed the 153 left the company as did Bill Elliott, leaving the management of the Computer Division in the hands of Andrew St Johnston. Charles Owen deserves much credit for the logical design and wiring schedules of the 153, which were excellent'.

Andrew St Johnston had joined Elliott's Borehamwood Laboratories in 1949, becoming Manager of the Computing Division in 1953 and staying in a senior role within Elliott-Automation until leaving the company in 1968. More details of his outstanding contribution to Elliott computing projects are given in Chap. 5. Charles Owen, who joined the Circuits Division at Borehamwood in the latter half of 1951 and left in 1954, was a first-class electronic circuit engineer who also designed the Elliott Nicholas computer (see Appendix 2). To continue with John Bunt's account of the 153 project:

'The team working on the 153 was basically J E (Johnnie) Cane working on the disc, G G (Geoff) Ballard working on the CRT stores and me [John Bunt] working on the logic system. This would have been the set-up in late 1952 or 1953. The disc was the responsibility of Chris Phillips, a mechanical engineer, but I don't remember who designed the [disc] electronics. Cane was his assistant. The CRT stores were designed by R C

Robbins. Ballard was his assistant. So there was a period of delay before the construction began, during which time Cane, Ballard and I familiarised ourselves with the design and checked every detail. This turned out to be very worthwhile, since the commissioning went very well. The three of us took the machine to Scarborough [in 1954]. We were shortly followed by Dina Vaughan [later Dina St Johnston] who was writing the program specified by ARL [and using background notes provided by Bruce Bambrough and A J Wakefield [3, 6]]. When the machine was working, Cane and Ballard returned to Borehamwood, leaving me to maintain the whole thing. I had to learn about the disc and the CRT stores in quick time.

'All went well for a time, until it became necessary to replace the tube in one of the CRT stores. The stores worked on the focus-defocus principal, but instead of using the focus electrode which would have required a large signal, the focussing was achieved with a much smaller signal using the grid of the CR tube. Whoever made this design decision was unaware that the tube manufacturers were working to avoid the variation of the focussing when the brightness was varied by applying a signal to the grid. So it soon became apparent that there would be a day when a replacement would no longer be available, and since the life of the tubes was relatively short, the system was not viable.

'Accompanied by officers of ARL we searched the Admiralty stores at Warrington in vain and failed to find any old tubes with the defocusing characteristics. So it was decided to replace the whole store section with nickel delay lines, which were [by 1954] well established and proved on other machines – 401, 402, etc.

'I have the idea that in the early days of [the 153's] design it was intended that each [CRT] store would have a capacity of 32 words and that it was necessary to reduce this to 16 words. So when the change to nickel lines was decided, a compromise was sought by reconfiguring the stores to be 10 single words and 6 four-words which could be housed in the same space and use the same 4-bit addressing. This would not affect the design of the logic system. The capacity of each store was now $(10 \times 1) + (6 \times 4) = 34$ words. If we could have started from scratch with nickel delay lines, we would almost certainly have gone for 32 single words and five address bits, but at this stage that would have meant reconstructing the logical section of the machine as well as the stores and this was not acceptable.

'When the new store section was complete, I installed it at Scarborough. This was a fairly simple job and was completed without any difficulty.... ARL now took over the remaining software work, which was undertaken by Mrs Beryl Kitz. The ARL officer with overall responsibility for the installation was L H F (Leslie) Nicholls. His senior officer who paid a number of visits to Scarborough was Dr S Vajda, sometimes accompanied by the ARL Superintendent.... Fortunately faults were comparatively few and the machine turned out to be far more reliable after the change of stores'.

Delivery of the Elliott 153 computer to Scarborough took place in August 1954. It was a water-cooled giant occupying 15 cabinets of electronics and about 30 ft (9 m) in length – see Fig. 3.2. It cost the Admiralty about £125,000 [7]. The 153 was operated by a team of four people: two girls handling the punched paper tape and the teleprinters and two operators on the computer and the visual plotter (performing a rough manual check on the DF fix). Results of a computed fix were sent via teleprinter to GCHQ, etc. Monthly analysis figures would typically show about 230 DF fixes being processed every 24 h [8]. Although the computer was general-purpose in design, the 153's software was normally read-only since the machine was dedicated to a single, strategically important, task. Occasionally, an

Fig. 3.2 The Elliott 153 computer, installed at the joint Admiralty/GCHQ establishment at Irton Moor near Scarborough in 1954. The Elliott 153 used 16-bit integers and a 64-bit instruction format. Programs and other data were stored on a 45-kB disc. The CPU contained two 68-byte RAM caches

Admiralty programmer called Beryl Kitz came and made a minor adjustment to the 153's program [8].

The 153 was located at the Irton Moor naval shore establishment, about 5 miles south-west of Scarborough in Yorkshire. It is believed that Irton Moor was, in the 1950s, the largest remaining wartime W/T (wireless telegraphy) station in the UK, with well in excess of hundred staff. It is still active, in greatly expanded form. Irton Moor, Scarborough, had been established as a naval W/T station long before the outbreak of the Second World War. During the war, it acted as a D/F and Y station and was well served by connections to the Defence Teleprinter Network (DTN). The construction of the DTN had begun before the outbreak of war. It was independent of, but alongside, the normal GPO public telephone network. The DTN is thought to have grown to be larger than the normal GPO network by the end of the war, at which point it involved more than 10,000 Creed teleprinters. These were mainly the Creed Model 7 machines. The Creed company manufactured more than 150,000 Model 7 teleprinters between 1931 and the late 1960s.

Shore-based DF stations could obtain bearings at ranges of up to 3,000 miles. During the Second World War, these stations were best known for their part in detecting the position of German U-boats. For the background to this and to related naval wartime intelligence, see [9]. During the Cold War, the emphasis moved to embrace not only submarines but also Soviet bloc land-based military installations, including (it is believed) pinpointing the radio transmissions coming from individual tanks. The DF Listening Stations included a number of overseas locations. Irton Moor is still believed to be very much an active part of what used to be called the Composite Signals Organisation (CSO) – see for example [10]. Irton Moor is now explicitly referred to as *GCHQ Scarborough*.

Back in the 1960s, Ray Henville worked for the Admiralty as one of the maintenance engineers on the 153 computer at Irton Moor. Ray had trained as an electrical apprentice at Portland dockyard, had served as a *Radio Electrical Artificer* during National Service in the Royal Navy, and had subsequently returned to work on radio and radar at Portland. He was recruited in 1959 to join the Elliott 153 maintenance team. He remembers [8] that 'In the late 1950s there wasn't a pool of IT personnel with digital experience to recruit from, but anyone with a radar background would at least have knowledge of pulse techniques and I believe that was the basis for selection of personnel to work on the 153'.

During his time at Irton Moor from 1959 to 1964, Ray Henville remembers [8] that data input was 'by means of mechanical Creed tape readers. These were extremely noisy in operation, sounding something like a machine gun as the tapes were read in. Since a Ferranti high-speed optical tape reader was used to read in the *program* tapes, a program was [later] written to use this for data input also. We tried to input the data at 50 characters per second but at this speed the mechanical clutches on the reader went out of adjustment very quickly. I think we eventually settled for 30 characters per second'.

As for maintenance, Henville remembers that the 153 initially operated day shifts (9.00 a.m.–5.00 p.m.) but then switched to operating throughout the 24 hours with a short regular maintenance period (15–30 min) per day. During this maintenance period, the engineers carried out two activities. Firstly, they systematically changed logic cards, delay lines and other valves, such that every removable subunit was changed and tested within 1 month. (Besides the miniature pentodes employed in the logic circuits, the 'other valves' included 6CH6 tetrode power valves and 12AT7/12AU7/12AX7 double triodes). Secondly, with a test program running, the engineers would 'margin' each section of the computer by gradually reducing the HT voltages with a rheostat until the machine failed; this could reveal incipient faults which might otherwise occur whilst the machine was being used live. The total number of valves (thermionic tubes) in the Elliott 153 was about 2,000. The overall reliability record became very good, typically 97%, probably helped by keeping the computer permanently powered up. At Irton Moor, the engineers used to receive down-time statistics on each of seven government (defence?) computers then in operation. The 153 regularly came top of the list in reliability [8].

3.1.3   General Description of the 153's Architecture

The design of the 153 followed that of its predecessor, the Elliott 152 computer used in the MRS5 project. Although basically serial – except for the parallel reading of instructions from disc – speed was gained by functional parallelism: the 153's 64-bit instruction allowed for the specification of several concurrent ALU and RAM tasks. The RAM caches were known as S1 and S2. Each of S1 and S2 contained 34 words. Because the machine was serial, it could be arranged that a new operand may be written into a RAM address at the 'same' time as the original contents were being read out. Numbers were represented as 16-bit two's complement fractions, but with the implied point being two positions from the most significant end. This follows the scheme used for the earlier computers designed at Borehamwood, namely the 152 and Nicholas (see Chap. 2). This convention, of imagining that an 'overflow' or 'guard' bit exists within each word, has since been used on other computers, for example on the Apollo Guidance Computer, a 16-bit machine designed at MIT in the early 1960s [11].

The 153's digit-period was 3 µs – in common with many of the early Elliott computers. The basic cycle-time of the machine, which was the time for fetching or for executing each instruction, was 24 bit-times, that is, 72 µs. A cycle consisted of 16 digit-periods plus an 8-digit gap. The gap allowed for the fast multiplier to yield its result and/or for tracks to be switched on the disc.

The main memory was a large, two-sided, magnetic disc. Side A had 48 tracks for program storage, plus a clock track and an address track. The 48 program tracks were organised as 12 groups of four. Two tracks were used for an input routine (Initial Orders) and for test programs. A group of four tracks could be read simultaneously, thus allowing one quad-word instruction to be read per machine cycle. Side B of the disc had 40 tracks. These were employed for storing incoming DF records associated with up to 255 DF tasks, Listening Station constants for up to 20 DF stations, and a directory. Fast electronic track-selection was used for side A; slower relay-tree selection was used for side B. Side A was normally read-only; side B was read/write. The total disc storage in modern 8-bit bytes, as seen by a programmer, is: (48 tracks × 256 × 2) + (40 tracks × 256 × 2) = 45 kB.

The 153's central processor (CPU) technology was based on the use of type CV466 sub-miniature pentode thermionic valves (tubes) and CV425 germanium semiconductor diodes. Use was made of a family of standard plug-in circuits or 'packages' – see Fig. 3.3. The CPU consumed about 9.2 kW of power, provided by a bank of trickle-charged batteries. More hardware details and the instruction set are given in Appendix 1.

Input to the 153 computer came from any 10 from a maximum of 20 teleprinter tapes – (the desired 10 being connected manually via a jackfield). Each input was more precisely described as a 'teleprinter reperforator and tape reader pair', and each pair formed a direct connection with a remote DF Listening Station (e.g. in the eastern Mediterranean). The paper tape acted as an input buffer store, smoothing out asynchronies between the real-time, unpredictable, arrival of messages and the 153's internal operation. The 5-track paper tape readers operated at ten characters per second. Output was to three teleprinters.

The 153 was a general-purpose stored-program electronic digital computer whose design and operation had been tailored to a specific application. With a cycle-time of 72 µs for fetch and for execute, the 153's equivalent rate of obeying instructions was 7 kilo-instructions per second (KIPS). However, each of the 153's instructions could do the work of several conventional orders. When summarised in modern terminology, the 153's instruction set appears to offer the programmer approximately 15 identifiable operations, as follows:

Fig. 3.3 The unreliable glass printed-circuit plates of the Elliott 152 computer were re-designed as less ambitious but more robust paxolin boards for the Elliott 153 computer. Underneath the aluminium sleeve, towards the right of the photo, are four miniature pentode valves

- Add, subtract, reverse-subtract, multiply, AND, logical shift left, logical shift right.
- Unconditional absolute jump; Jump if acc < 0; Jump if acc = 0.
- Read (a word) from disc; write (a word) to disc.
- Read handkeys from control desk.
- Input a character from a selected paper reader; output a character to a selected teleprinter.

However, this simple picture gives no real idea of the speed or power of the 153. Firstly, all operations (including multiply) are completed within one machine cycle of $(24 \times 3) = 72$ μs. (An exception is some control transfers: if the destination-address for a jump instruction lies less than about ten instructions from the present one, an extra delay of one disc revolution (10 ms) is incurred.) Secondly, each instruction allows the programmer to select operands from several sources concurrently, including from the two RAM caches S1 and S2. Thirdly, every instruction carries with it a 16-bit constant (literal) which may be used either for computation or for address-generation purposes. Fourthly, the 153 is designed to allow the functional sub-units within the CPU to operate concurrently, thus offering a degree of low-level parallelism. It is as if each 64-bit instruction has the power of a microprogram macro. For example, the 153 can perform the following functions in one machine cycle (72 μs):

(a) Read a character from tape reader 6 and store this in address 12 of S1
(b) Transfer the previous contents of the above address to location 5 of S2

(c) Multiply the previous contents of location 5 in S2 by $\pi/4$, a constant contained within the present instruction, holding the result in the multiplier register

(d) Add the previous contents of the multiplier register to the previous contents of location 5 in S2 and hold the result in the accumulator

If we were to express the above sequence in symbolic instructions suitable for a modern computer with a general-register instruction format, the following program fragment would perform the same action as the single instruction executed by the 153 computer:

$R3$:= $\pi/4$;
$R4$:= $R2*R3$;
ACC := $R2 + R4$;
$R2$:= $R1$;
$R1$:= *char read from PTR6*;

It seems reasonable to multiply the 153's rate by about four, when seeking to compare its performance with conventional production computers of the same historical period. Assuming a non-overlapped fetch-execute cycle, that is, 2×72 μs, this yields a figure of $4 \times 7 = 28$ KIPS (kilo-instructions per second) for the 153. On this basis, Table 3.2 gives a comparison between the Elliott 153 and six other computers of the 1950s when performing fixed-point arithmetic.

3.1.4 The Operation of the 153 at Irton Moor

The disc of the 153 computer held 24 words of fixed data (e.g. geographical position) for each of up to 20 DF receiving (listening) stations located around the world. When sending reports to the 153 computer at Irton Moor, each remote DF Listening Station necessarily had to include information that identified the station (as three 5-bit characters) and the date/time of the report. Based on [2], a typical

Table 3.2 Comparing the performance of the Elliott 153 with that of other contemporary computers

Computer	Year delivered	KIPS	Typical on-line storage (kB)
Ferranti Mark I Star	1953	0.8	82
IBM 650	1954	0.2	40
Elliott 153	1954	28	45
IBM 704	1955	42	162
English Electric DEUCE	1955	31[a]	34
Ferranti Pegasus	1956	3	25
Ferranti Mercury	1957	17	165

[a] Assumes that DEUCE was able to sustain its maximum rate by using optimum programming. The average DEUCE rate was typically rather lower

operational sequence for the 153 computer at Irton Moor, Scarborough, is believed to have been as follows:

Step 1. Read incoming DF reports from up to ten Listening Stations and assemble all reports relating to the same radio transmission (which might have come from an individual submarine, a tank, a building, etc.). Store this set of DF data on disc and give the set a *task serial number*. Indicate to the operator that a new set of task-data is available. Note that the disc may already contain sets of data from previous tasks. DF data for up to 255 tasks may be held at any one time. (By convention, 'task 0' is defined to signify 'no task'.)

Step 2. The operator selects an appropriate set of DF data, by setting the task serial number up on a row of switches on the 153's control desk. In this context, the operator sees a 'task' as the calculation of a Best Point fix, etc., from one radio transmission. If for GCHQ operational reasons the DF data from one or more Listening Stations is currently suspect, the operator can set a switch which causes the data from one or more stations to be ignored during the task calculation. The data from rejected stations remains on disc, so that it may be included in subsequent calculations if required. The Best Point Fix calculations proceed under automatic program control, as soon as the program has read the switch-settings provided by the operator.

Step 3. The computer performs the indicated task on the relevant set of DF data and produces the following output:

(a) The latitude and longitude of points defining both a 'Best Point' fix and a 'Probability Rectangle'

(b) A printed record of the relevant DF reports

(c) The statistical deviation of each station's bearing from the Best Point found by the machine

This output is sent to a tape reperforator for possible onwards transmission to GCHQ, etc., and also to a page teleprinter for a local record. Finally, a third page teleprinter produces information of use to the control desk operator, including an indication, by serial number, of the total number of DF reports so far received in respect of each radio transmission from an individual source (submarine, tank, etc.)

Step 4. Every time a new DF report arrives, the sequence repeats from step 1. At step 2, the operator can choose to re-calculate a result for one incident or calculate a result for a new incident.

As indicated in [4], the Elliott 153 computer remained in satisfactory use at Irton Moor until the late 1960s. Andrew St Johnston left Borehamwood in April 1968. Some months before he left, he is believed to have been contacted by Irton Moor and asked whether Elliott-Automation wished to acquire the 153 computer (minus its power supply of submarine accumulators!) as a potential historical exhibit. Andrew authorised the acquisition and the machine was placed in storage at Borehamwood [12]. Sometime after Andrew had left Elliotts, Laurence Clarke was ordered to scrap the 153. The company was in the throes of mergers and takeovers and was not in a position to accept the remains of this historic piece of early digital technology.

3.2 GCHQ and Oedipus

3.2.1 The Problem of Super-Enciphered Intercepts

The intense code-breaking activity at Bletchley Park during the Second World War, which reached an electronic high point with the introduction of the Colossus cryptanalytical machines, reduced but did not cease after the end of hostilities. Several different *Rapid Analytic Machines* were designed and built in the period 1945–1955 [1]. The first general-purpose digital computer to be installed at GCHQ was a Ferranti Mark I Star, which became fully operational at Cheltenham in mid-1954. Perhaps the most interesting Rapid Analytical Machine to be used by GCHQ in the mid-1950s was Oedipus. Borehamwood played a significant part in its design. Although special-purpose rather than general-purpose, Oedipus contained arithmetic capabilities and large amounts of digital storage and could search through data very much faster than contemporary production computers.

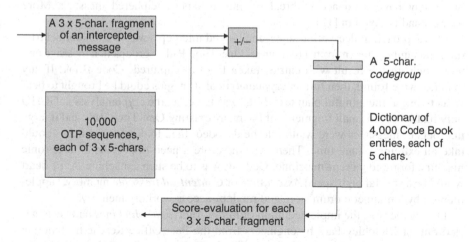

Fig. 3.4 The Elliott project number 311 became GCHQ's OEDIPUS cryptanalytical computer. This overall diagram shows the basic computational sequence, in which it is believed that fragments of intercepted messages were combined with trial random numbers taken from captured One-Time Pads and then compared with a dictionary of known code words. The code words were contained in a semiconductor associative (i.e. content-addressable) memory, thus permitting very rapid comparison. OEDIPUS processed 10,000 trial matches in 1.6 s, about 10,000 times faster than a contemporary 40 KIPS general-purpose computer

The code-breaking tasks for which Oedipus was designed are still classified. However, we may use the general problem of super-enciphered intercepts to illustrate Oedipus' structure and possible use. The encoding of super-enciphered messages took place in two stages. First, a standard *Code Book* was used by the sender to convert each letter, word or common phrase into a unique numerical equivalent (called a *codegroup*). Then a number chosen at random was added (or sometimes subtracted) to/from each codegroup in the message, using non-carrying arithmetic. The sender took random numbers from a pre-printed list of additives, the list having first been generated by hand, or electromechanically or electronically. For example:

> If the codegroup 'Enemy convoy in sight' is   67095
> and the random additive is   33432
> then the enciphered group will read   90427

It was, of course, important that the printed list of random additives was not re-used by the sender. Lists of random numbers often took the form of so-called *One-Time Pads (OTP)*. A typical pad might have 60 five-digit numbers per page. If the numbers on the OTP were truly random and the additives only used once, then the message was undecipherable to anyone not possessing a copy of the sender's Code Book and OTP.

In practice, mistakes were made in the construction, distribution and use of OTPs. In addition, fragments of a particular Code Book might be recovered by capture or stealth, or cryptanalytically – though Code Books were changed periodically (say every 2 years). In summary, there were practical reasons why a cryptanalyst might have a chance of breaking into a super-enciphered message. More background is given in [13].

One approach to decrypting super-enciphered intercepts was to add/subtract trial random numbers taken from a (captured) One-Time Pad to groups in a message and then compare the result with entries taken from a (captured) Code Book. If any matches were found, then further cryptanalytical strategies could be brought to bear so as to reveal meaningful plaintext. If, as was the case, the cryptanalysts at GCHQ only had access to small fragments of the many existing One-Time Pads and if large numbers of messages were waiting to be decoded, then looking for matches could take an extremely long time. There was therefore a need to provide an electronic machine for rapid pattern-matching. Oedipus was to be such a machine. At its heart would be a special high-speed *Associative* or *Content-addressable* memory, supplemented by a magnetic drum store and random-access working memory.

During the war, the implementation of *Rapid Analytical Machines* had been carried out for Bletchley Park by engineers from the Post Office Research Station at Dollis Hill, north London [14]. In particular, the Colossus team had been led by the Post Office engineer T H (Tommy) Flowers. After the war, GCHQ began to recruit its own engineers. S D (Toby) H, an ex-Naval signals officer who had worked directly for Tommy Flowers at Dollis Hill for at least 2 years on electronic telephone exchange research, moved to GCHQ in January 1951 and became involved in the Oedipus project. The initial intention was that the design and construction of

Oedipus would be entirely outsourced. According to the former GCHQ historian, the late Peter Freeman CMG, it is believed that Toby H was instrumental in advising that the Borehamwood Laboratory of Elliott Brothers (London) Ltd. should be given the contract for 'the production of designs, the development of sub-assemblies, and the integration of the whole' of the Oedipus project and that Oedipus's magnetic drum should be purchased from Ferranti Ltd. [15]. The first of many recorded visits of GCHQ personnel to Borehamwood occurred on 22 September 1950, according to the surviving Borehamwood Visitors Books. It is of passing interest to note that Tommy Flowers and his Dollis Hill colleague S W Broadhurst attended a Borehamwood meeting on 26 June 1951.

3.2.2   The 311 Project at Borehamwood

The formal Oedipus contract reached Borehamwood in the spring of 1951. At the time of initial discussions with GCHQ, the number 310 had been allocated by Borehamwood to the project. However, such was the secrecy that when the formal contract arrived in 1951 the Borehamwood administrators were unaware of the link with the earlier discussions and gave the project a new number: 311. Because of security considerations, nobody at Borehamwood, then or since, was aware of the internal GCHQ name Oedipus.

The principal engineer at Borehamwood responsible for the 311 project was H G (Harry) Carpenter. Harry had joined the Telecommunications Research Establishment (TRE) in September 1941 to work on 10-cm Airborne Interception radar, after completing an accelerated Mechanical Sciences Tripos degree at Cambridge. He stayed on at TRE after the war to work on beam-riding guided weapons – principally the Long Shot project. From TRE he joined the Computing Division at Borehamwood in January 1949. He quickly became the principal digital hardware logic designer for the Elliott 152 computer. Indeed, Harry was still very much involved in the 152 project when, on 15 March 1951, he was given full security clearance to begin work on the 311 project.

This was an extremely stressful period of Harry's life [16]. It is worth digressing to explain the sources of the stress because these have a bearing on the progress of the Oedipus project at Borehamwood. The initial cause of stress in 1950, according to Harry, seems to have been the Elliott 152 computer's glass printed-circuit plates which had been designed by D L Johnston of the Mechanical Engineering Division. Visitors to Borehamwood were impressed with the glass plates, one American observing that 'a mint of money' could be made by exploiting the plate technology. John Coales, who was the Laboratory Director and Harry Carpenter's ultimate boss, decided to invest significantly in special tools so that many glass plates could be produced, on the assumption that they would be used in several digital projects. However, the plates were not well engineered, especially in respect of the mechanical edge-connectors that were the source of much unreliability. Coales did not agree with Harry that the glass plates were to blame for the 152 computer's unreliability and ordered Norman

Hill, head of the Theory Division, to run some statistical experiments to prove that the computer's faults had little to do with the glass plates. This resulted in an inevitable clash of priorities between Hill as a potential user of the 152 computer, and Carpenter as an engineer trying to improve the hardware. Matters came to a head when John Coales ordered a partition wall to be erected that cut Harry's office off from the 152 computer. In Harry's view [16], the incident illustrated the flaw in Coales' insistence that Borehamwood be run as a *Technique-oriented* Laboratory rather than as a *Project-oriented* organisation. At TRE, Harry had been used to working under extreme pressure, but within a good project management framework. In contrast, at Borehamwood 'it felt as if you had your feet in treacle' [16].

Harry Carpenter's engineering responsibilities for the 152 computer overlapped with the start of his work on the 311 project. The first version of the 152 computer was completed in September 1950. Aircraft fly-past tests for the MRS5 radar took place in the period October 1950–November 1951, as described in Chap. 2. The principal production work that the 152 performed was probably the analysis of MRS5 radar data, carried out in the spring and summer of 1952. Harry started work on the 311 project in the spring of 1951.

For the 311 work, Harry took over a room formerly used as a staff social area. There were lots of moans from colleagues when Harry locked the door and the Laboratory Superintendent, Archer-Thompson, would not let anyone near the place. Harry remembers that he 'sat there on my own, grappling with the design problems and sometimes getting very depressed'. When Harry needed to make dye-line copies of engineering drawings, he was instructed to lock himself into the Duplicator room. He was given a special safe in the Borehamwood Strong Room for the 311's paperwork. At some point in the 311 project, probably during 1952, Harry went into hospital for a hernia operation after helping to jump-start the sports car of a visiting GCHQ liaison person. Harry had an adverse reaction to the anaesthetic, became depressed, and was prescribed a drug that, he remembers, 'distorted my mental picture'.

When Harry had been working on the 311 for about 8 months, a high-level GCHQ deputation came to Borehamwood to see John Coales and to review progress. Judging from the Visitors Book, the date was 21 Nov 1951 and the GCHQ group consisted of A D V (Tony) R, S D (Toby) H and 'G W M'. After a while, Harry remembers [16] that he was summonsed to come to the meeting. Coales asked Harry to confirm that he was 'deploying maximum effort' on the 311 project. Harry replied that, although he was working hard on the 311, he also had some responsibilities for the 152 computer. At that, Coales banged the table and became very angry, saying that he would sack Harry tomorrow if Harry could not do both jobs. The meeting then ended and, once outside the Director's Office, the three GCHQ people 'formed a sympathetic circle' round Harry and said that GCHQ would give Harry a job tomorrow if he wished to move!

At around this time it became clear to GCHQ that the Oedipus project, in the words of Tony R, 'was too much for Borehamwood, so it was decided that GCHQ would do the project in-house with Elliotts and Ferranti as major sub-contractors' [1]. A D V (Tony) R had been recruited by GCHQ in September 1951 to be GCHQ's project leader for Oedipus. Prior to joining GCHQ he had been working for 2 years at Dollis Hill, on an electronic telephone exchange project under Tommy Flowers.

The date of the first entry in Harry Carpenter's 311 Lab. Notebook, fortuitously preserved in the Library at GCHQ Cheltenham, is 3 April 1951. Judging from the visits of GCHQ personnel to Borehamwood, Harry's main Oedipus design activity spanned the period April 1951 to July 1952. Testing and associated Borehamwood involvement extending until the summer of 1953.

Although Harry Carpenter was closest to Oedipus, other Borehamwood engineers helped with certain subsections of the implementation without knowing anything about the overall project. A G W Edmunds and Andrew St Johnston from the Computing Division assisted with some of the CRT memory circuits and F Rock-Carling from the Mechanical Engineering Division assisted with the physical design of the Dictionary's framework – (described later). Meanwhile, the 20 or so engineers in the comparatively small Computing Division had also been involved with the 153 and 401 projects (see earlier this chapter and Chap. 5).

Ferranti Ltd. was given the contract for the Oedipus drum store. The contract number was 6/WT/16872/C.B19(a), dated sometime in mid-1951 and handled by Ferranti's Moston factory near Manchester. The 10-in. drum was delivered to Cheltenham (the new GCHQ premises) by the end of March 1953, or soon thereafter. The Ferranti drum, and Oedipus, started to become operational in May 1954. The whole system was deemed to have become fully operational by mid-1955. Oedipus worked satisfactorily until dismantled in February 1962 – though it had actually been 'retired' from active service late in 1959 [1].

The hardware architecture of Oedipus is described in detail in [1] and in outline in the next section. Initially, Elliott Brothers (London) Ltd. was the prime contractor. Subsequently, the engineering design-effort for Oedipus was finally re-apportioned as follows:

Fig. 3.5 H G (Harry) Carpenter joined Borehamwood in 1949, having worked at TRE on guided missiles. He contributed to the design of the Elliott 152 and 401 computers, before becoming the team leader for Elliott's contribution to OEDIPUS

Items	Responsibility
Basic circuits (trigger, delay, clock, etc.)	Elliott
Shift registers	GCHQ
CRT stores and associated circuits	Elliott
Matrix adder	GCHQ
Dictionary	Elliott
Score adder	GCHQ
Input/output equipment (paper tape and cards)	GCHQ
Drum store	Ferranti
Counters, etc. for drum	Ferranti
Plug board and associated circuits	Elliott
Control and monitoring	GCHQ
Power supply, racking, cabling	GCHQ
Testing and commissioning	GCHQ

By the autumn of 1952, Harry Carpenter's responsibilities for the 152 computer had ceased. Since his Oedipus tasks were beginning to diminish, his involvement in the 401 computer at Borehamwood began to increase. The Elliott 401 first ran a program in March 1953 – see Chap. 5. The National Research Development Corporation (NRDC), sponsors of the 401, arranged for the 401 to be moved to Cambridge on 14 June 1953, at a time of management upheaval at Borehamwood. Harry Carpenter resigned from Borehamwood and joined NRDC to work at Cambridge on further development of the 401 computer, staying there until the machine was installed at the government's Rothamsted Research Station in March 1954. After more consultancy work for NRDC and others, Harry worked for Tube Investments from 1955 to 1958, for IBM at Hursley from 1958 to 1962, and then as an independent Consultant until his retirement in 1986 aged 66. He died in December 2010.

3.2.3 The Structure and Operation of Oedipus

We take the generic example of super-enciphered intercepts as introduced previously in Sect. 3.2.1 to illustrate the structure and possible operation of Oedipus. Refer also to Fig. 3.6, which shows the main components of the machine.

During a setting-up phase, Oedipus' **drum** would be loaded with approximately 10,000 fifteen-character strings, each string representing 3 five-character random numbers taken from captured One-Time Pads. Next, the dictionary would be loaded with approximately 4,000 five-character groups, taken from a captured Code Book. Along with each group in the dictionary was stored an importance-score. Once set up, it is believed that Oedipus' use for cryptanalysis then proceeded as follows.

Step 1: Read into the **Text Store** (implemented as a shift register) the next 15 characters of an intercepted message. Treat these 15 characters as 3 five-character groups.

Step 2: Read the next 3 five-character random numbers from the **Drum** and add (or subtract) these, modulo 10, to the 3 five-character groups of the current

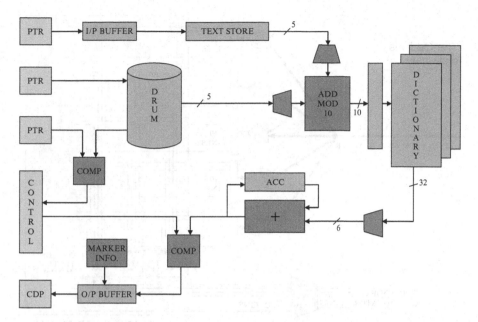

Fig. 3.6 A conceptual system diagram of OEDIPUS. Input/output equipment is on the left of the diagram. The Ferranti drum is towards the centre and the Elliott content-addressable dictionary is at the right of the diagram

fragment of intercepted message. The effect is to reveal 3 plausible five-character groups that might have come from a Code Book.

Step 3: Compare each of the 3 plausible five-character groups with all the 4,000 five-character groups stored in the **Dictionary**. For all groups which match, add up the corresponding importance-scores so as to produce an overall indication of ranking (Fig. 3.7).

Step 4: Compare the accumulated ranking with a predetermined threshold. If a threshold is exceeded, output the result to punched cards, together with marker-information.

Step 5: Repeat steps 2–4 for all 10,000 sets of five-character random numbers stored on the drum.

Step 6: Go back to step 1, unless there is no more text to be read.

The overall effect was to produce an indication of the likelihood that the intercepted message had been encoded using a particular One-Time Pad and a particular Code Book. This information could then be used off-line to refine the decryption process and, if all went well, to produce meaningful plain text.

More details of the Oedipus hardware will be found in [1]. In the context of early 1950s technology, the outstanding feature was the amount of on-line storage (equivalent to 200 kB) and the rapid rate of searching (equivalent to 100 kilo-instructions/second (KIPS), based on Oedipus's rate of 10 μs per character). Comparison may be made with the figures given in Table 3.2, where the nearest rival is seen to be the IBM 704, delivered in 1955. Oedipus processed 10,000 trial

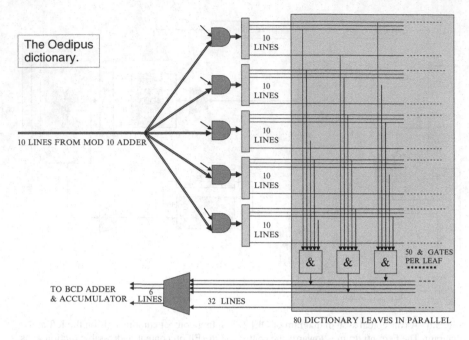

The Oedipus dictionary.

10 LINES FROM MOD 10 ADDER

10 LINES

10 LINES

10 LINES

10 LINES

10 LINES

&

&

&

50 & GATES PER LEAF

TO BCD ADDER & ACCUMULATOR

6 LINES

32 LINES

80 DICTIONARY LEAVES IN PARALLEL

Fig. 3.7 4,000 five-input *AND* gates were used in the OEDIPUS dictionary. All 4,000 *AND* gates were activated in parallel, causing a simultaneous comparison to be made between a new five-character interrogand and 4,000 stored five-character groups once every 50 μs

matches in 1.6 s, about 10,000 times faster than a contemporary 40 KIPS general-purpose computer of the mid-1950s.

Oedipus's drum, very similar to the one used in the production Ferranti Mark I Star computers, contained 256 tracks, each holding 3,000 digits plus a 200-bit *dead space* to allow time for switching between tracks. The tracks were organised into 50 switchable bands of five tracks each. Additionally, there was one timing track for providing 100 kHz clock pulses, a special 5-track band of fixed information intended for certain special applications, and about 30 spare tracks 'in case of damage'. A phase-lock loop controlled the drum speed by comparing the clock track with a 100 kHz reference source (crystal). The total capacity of the main group of 250 tracks was 150,000 five-bit characters. Characters were initially loaded onto the drum from a 200-characters/s Ferranti optical paper tape reader, prior to the main computational cycle. Drum loading proceeded at an average speed of 160 characters/s. and a complete load could take about 20 min. Two paper tape readers, reading identical tapes displaced by one character position, were employed to ensure that no data errors occurred during loading. At run-time (step 2 above), the maximum transfer-rate from the drum determined the timing of the whole computer. In summary, Oedipus processed information *on-the-fly*.

The Oedipus dictionary was the most unusual, and crucial, section of the computer. It was *content-addressable*, or *associative*, in the sense that the presentation of an interrogand caused all entries in the dictionary to be searched at once, in parallel. The Oedipus dictionary differed from modern semiconductor associative memory (CAM) in three respects: (a) the Oedipus capacity (i.e. number of stored entries) was

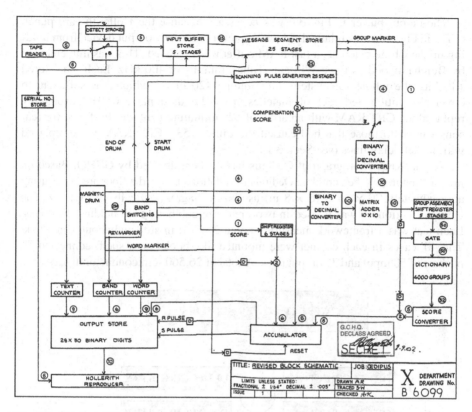

Fig. 3.8 Original GCHQ drawing B6099, entitled 'revised block schematic of OEDIPUS'. The orientation of this diagram is the same as that of the schematic shown in Fig. 3.6

relatively large compared with that available using modern CAM chips; (b) the Oedipus entries were fixed (i.e. read-only) rather than being dynamically changeable by program; (c) if a match with one of the Oedipus-stored items occurred, then that item caused an *importance* value, or score, in the range 0 –> 31 to be output; modern CAM chips usually just signal the presence or absence of a match.

The Oedipus dictionary was implemented by semiconductor diode *AND* gates and, as explained in [1], the read-only contents were pre-wired at the time of manufacture. There were 50 *AND* gates per physical *leaf* (or segment) and 80 leaves in a complete dictionary. All 4,000 *AND* gates were activated in parallel, causing a simultaneous comparison to be made between a new five-character interrogand and 4,000 stored five-character groups once every 50 µs.

There was provision for changing the dictionary manually, according to the demands of particular applications. Several *sets*, each of up to 80 dictionary leaves, were constructed. The unused sets for any operational run were kept in special storage cabinets in the computer room at GCHQ. One could change from one set to another by plugging in the new set by hand – taking perhaps half a day to change sets, including testing. It is conjectured that each set consisted of a selection of entries taken from a particular captured Code Book.

The output buffer in Fig. 3.6 was necessary because the Hollerith card punch (CDP in Fig. 3.6) was relatively slow. To prevent this slow output device from holding up the whole machine, a fast RAM buffer was provided. This was implemented by Borehamwood as three Williams Tubes, running at 400 kHz. Each tube stored 140 bits, the whole sub-system thus holding 420 bits – which was sufficient to cover the anticipated rate of matches from the dictionary. GCHQ eventually replaced the CRT RAM with an array of 420 miniature pentode flip-flops, for reasons similar to those that had caused the Elliott 153's CRT RAM to be replaced with nickel delay lines (see Sect. 3.1.2),

No surviving photograph of Oedipus has yet been located by GCHQ. Based on information in [1], the complete Oedipus installation occupied a floor area measuring approximately 20 × 25 ft (6 × 8 m) as shown diagrammatically in Fig. 3.9. The Oedipus dictionary was housed in two operating cabinets, each holding 40 leaves. Each leaf was a framework measuring about 2 × 3 ft in area and about 1 in. thick. The 40 leaves in each cabinet were mounted like books on a shelf, connected by busbars of 50 input and 32 output lines. A total of 26,560 semiconductor diodes were

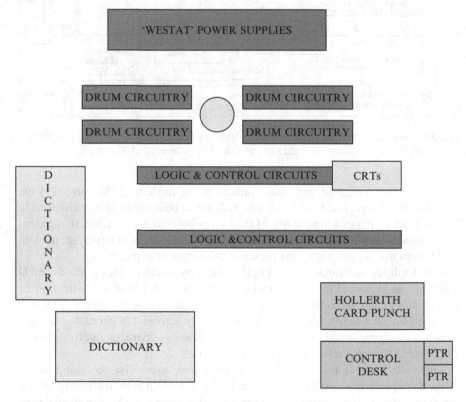

Fig. 3.9 No photographs of OEDIPUS seem to have survived. However, based on a sketch by Tony Ridlington, one of the original GCHQ designers, the machine occupied a floor area of approximately 20 by 25 ft (6 by 8 m). The diagram shows the disposition of the equipment when viewed from above

employed. The cumulative back-resistance of the many diodes, which aggregated to a non-infinite value, was a physical limitation to the dictionary's overall capacity. Germanium diodes were used in the first leaves to be constructed. Thereafter, the recently introduced silicon diodes were used. Both types operated successfully.

One should really consider the whole of GCHQ's cryptanalytical procedures before attempting to assess the overall strategic usefulness of Oedipus. This is outside the scope of the present account. It is known that the program parameters for the machine could be changed by plugboards or switches. It has been suggested [17] that Oedipus might have been used to deal with a huge backlog of unbroken One-Time Pad (OTP)-enciphered messages that had been accumulating since about 1943. The UK and American Intelligence Services set up the Venona programme, which is thought to have spanned the period 1943–1980, to deal with these super-enciphered intercepts [18]. It is believed that the use of Oedipus at GCHQ was at its most intense during the period 1955–1959. It might therefore be significant that one of the turning points in the Venona programme seemed to have occurred in 1957. To quote Venona Monograph Number 4 [19]: 'The Naval GRU systems resisted the best efforts of Arlington Hall, NSA and the UK SIGINT service until 1957, when a UK analytic attack provided the first results in detecting reused key'. Any relevance of Oedipus to all of this is, of course, pure speculation but it is interesting to think that the efforts of Harry Carpenter and others at Borehamwood might have contributed to something significant.

3.3 Australia and WREDAC

3.3.1 The Needs of Woomera

The origins of the Woomera missile-testing range in South Australia and its support base at Salisbury near Adelaide – see Fig. 3.10 – lie in the Anglo-Australian Long Range Weapons Organisation (LRWO) Joint Project. Initiated at a time of intense post-war interest in the development of guided weapons, the Joint Project came into formal being on 1 April 1947 and lasted until 1980 [20]. The first rocket-firing at the Woomera range was in February 1949. Woomera and Salisbury, together forming what was at various times called the Weapons Research Establishment (WRE) or the Long Range Weapons Establishment (LRWE), went on to employ thousands of people over several decades. Throughout its life there was interchange of personnel, know-how and equipment between WRE and the UK's relevant Ministry of Supply establishments such as the Royal Aircraft Establishment (RAE) at Farnborough, the Telecommunications Research Establishment (TRE) at Malvern, and the UK's modest test ranges at Aberporth on the Welsh coast and Orfordness on the Suffolk coast. More comments on the strategic significance of WRE will be found in Chap. 4, when the Elliott analogue computer AGWAC is discussed.

By the mid-1950s, the Elliott-built AGWAC was meeting WRE's need for the analogue simulation of missile behaviour. An equally important requirement was for

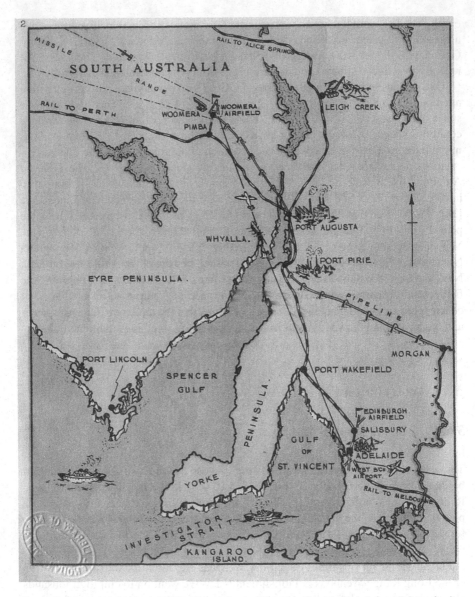

Fig. 3.10 The joint Anglo-Australian Long Range Weapons Organisation is best known for its Woomera rocket range in the South Australian desert, shown at the top left of the map. Salisbury, just to the north of Adelaide, is where WREDAC, the Weapons Research Establishment's Digital Automatic Computer, was located. WREDAC was the name given to the Elliott 403 computer

a digital computer to capture and analyse the large quantity of data produced each time a missile was launched at the Woomera range. For this, a greatly enhanced version of the Elliott 402 computer, at first known as the Elliott 403 or *Cobber* but later known as WREDAC (Weapons Research Establishment's Digital Automatic Computer), was designed and constructed at Borehamwood to a specification produced by WRE. Before describing WREDAC, it is helpful to give some idea of the data-gathering and data-analysis problems for which this computer was required. Most of the following information is based on the official history of WRE [20].

At least one third of the many hundreds of WRE staff were engaged on instrumentation. We use *instrumentation* as an umbrella term for all the Woomera equipment necessary for tracking a missile and for capturing telemetry data produced by the missile in flight. A variety of optical and electronic devices was needed for tracking because the individual instruments differed in their capabilities – for example accuracy, useful working range, pureness of data, ease of deployment and use in the Australian desert.

The optical tracking instruments at the Woomera range included several kinetheodolites – that is, theodolites incorporating recording ciné cameras. On each frame of each film was recorded the image of the missile (which might be offset from the cross hairs), the azimuth and elevation scale-values of the cross hairs at the frame's centre and the frame-number. After a missile-firing, each frame of each film had to be inspected off-line to produce a numerical record of {azimuth, elevation, offset, frame-number}. These records were at first processed manually. Later on in WRE's history they were digitised onto (for example) punched paper tape, for input to a computer. In passing, recall that the task of optically tracking a moving target was also tackled at Borehamwood, on a much smaller scale, during the fly-past testing of the MRS5 radar (see Chap. 2).

The electronic tracking instruments at Woomera included: (a) anti-aircraft radar which could lock onto a target and feed back the polar co-ordinates; (b) reflection Doppler radio equipment, recording an analogue beat-signal on to magnetic tape; this tape then had the 'noise' removed electronically off-line and the cleaned data recorded onto magnetic tape for input to a computer; (c) missile-tracking systems that received a signal from a transmitter in the missile and worked out the trajectory by triangulation.

Finally, there was telemetry equipment. Each missile usually contained many on-board transducers, measuring parameters such as acceleration, pressure, temperature, etc. All transducer outputs were fed to a multi-channel transmitter carried by the missile. A ground station recorded all the signals, which were converted off-line into a form suitable for input to a computer.

All of the above instrumentation depended, of course, upon the existence of a common timescale. Timing signals were distributed via field cables at Woomera to each monitoring instrument. The output from all the Woomera range instruments was then sent to WRE's support base at Salisbury, near Adelaide, for analysis.

In 1949, early in the history of the range, a group of about a dozen young women were the 'human computers' at Salisbury who performed the numerical analysis after each test-firing. A Mathematical Services Section was set up at Salisbury and another 20 *computing girls* joined in 1950. At that time, before the arrival of automatic electronic digital computing equipment, much of the data-preparation work was manual. For example, the optical data from Woomera's kinetheodolite films was inspected manually and transcribed to paper. Manual trajectory-calculations were then carried out using mechanical desk calculators such as the Friden or Marchant varieties. For optical trials data, inspecting and transcribing 10,000 points from kinetheodolite film was said to take about 50 h, plus another 50 h to calculate the results, plus 20 h to present and display the final trajectory information. Another perspective on the data-mountain facing Salisbury is given in [20]: 'In the two years 1955 and 1956 they [the Salisbury staff] had the prospect of reading 400,000 points of trajectory, velocity and attitude data, or about 800 points a day. In addition they would be calibrating six million telemetry points. Even at 100 % efficiency, this was around 200,000 man-hours of work. It would take up to 200 more [human] Computers to tackle such a load manually, from a specialised labour market already drained dry. And finally WRE would be processing as much as 600 kilometres of film a year!'

More generally, when all forms of instrumentation were considered, it was said that numerical calculations only accounted for about a third of the total data-processing effort required: reducing the source data to a form suitable for numerical analysis was the larger component of the whole exercise [20]. As the programme of missile tests gathered momentum at Woomera, there was clearly a need to speed up the analysis operations at Salisbury. In 1950, it was evident that the rate of acqui-sition of new data was outstripping the rate at which such data could be processed. Attention therefore focused upon the design of suitable electronic equipment to deal with the potential mountain of data.

As for reducing data to machine-readable form, the first improvement came when WRE acquired some American Boscar (Ballistic film analyser and recorder) machines for the semi-automatic reading of the optical film and transferring the trajectory data to paper tape. The second step, proposed by John Ovenstone of WRE (see below), was for WRE to design some input data-conversion equipment that would take the analogue source data from telemetry, Doppler, radar and missile-tracking systems, as recorded on analogue magnetic tape, and convert this to digital data on digital magnetic tapes to be read by a standard computer. A telem-etry data-converter was accordingly designed and built by WRE, using about 300 thermionic valves. It produced machine-readable digital magnetic tapes suitable for input to a digital computer. However, at that point in history when there were few working digital computers anywhere in the world, and only one such in Australia (the CSIR, Commonwealth Scientific Research Centre) Mark I at Sydney [21], the provision of an actual data-analysing computer for Salisbury represented a signifi-cant technical and organisational challenge.

In passing, we note that Salisbury may have been unique in having to support what was probably the world's largest test-range with the potential of producing vast amounts of trials data for analysis. However, Salisbury was not the only estab-lishment considering digital processing of trajectory instrumentation. For example the MOSAIC computer, built between 1947 and 1953 by a British Post Office team headed by Dr Allan Coombs of Colossus fame, was installed at TRE, the UK's radar establishment at Malvern, for processing radar tracking data. In this case, the tracking data was produced directly onto 3-in. wide punched paper tape by two data recorders mounted on trucks. MOSAIC was the largest of the pre-1954 British computers, containing 6,000 thermionic valves, 2,000 germanium diodes and having internal storage for 1,024 forty-bit words in mercury delay lines [22]. MOSAIC's data-analysis tasks were certainly not as demanding as those faced by Salisbury and, in any case, the MOSAIC computer was very much a one-off project.

3.3.2   WRE Chooses Elliott

In 1950, LRWE planned to design its own digital computer, to be called LEDAC (Long Range Weapons Electronic Digital Automatic Computer). The initial idea was to copy Trevor Pearcey's CSIR Mark I computer [21], for which the project's cost was estimated as £40,000. However, the plan for LEDAC was later rejected, in favour of a proposal to buy a Ferranti Mark I to be financed by the UK government, at a quoted price of £95,000. In turn, this proposal came to nothing – for reasons that are unclear (but see below). The next, and crucial, step was for John Ovenstone to present his 21-page Report entitled *Notes on Data-processing at LRWE* to the Data Processing Committee at Salisbury in October 1953 [20].

John Alan Ovenstone [23] was born in Sydney in 1925, did doctoral research in physics at the University of Cambridge from 1949 to 1952 and worked for WRE from 1953 to 1958. From 1964 to 1971, he was the first Professor of Computing Science at the University of Adelaide. He died in July 1984. Whilst undoubtedly a leading light amongst early Australian proponents of digital computing, he also attracted a certain amount of controversy during his professional career. One former colleague, admittedly an analogue rather than digital expert, has described Ovenstone as a person well ahead of his time who tended to advocate goals that proved to be beyond the reach of an organisation's practical resources.

To continue with WRE's search for a digital computer, we may quote the official history [20] as follows:

'Ovenstone's *Notes* offered a broad specification for the prospective [digital] computer and for the various converters that would take recordings from the telemetry, doppler, radar and missile tracking systems and transform them into the digitised form readable by the machine. In addition, Ovenstone described the output converters which were necessary for the computer to print its results or draw its graphs. Altogether the notes comprised a bold and perceptive plan which was almost wholly realised over the next few years....

'By early 1954 LRWE had given up any thought of building its own computer.... Ovenstone's specification in his *Notes* for an ideal computer were not [sic] extremely oner- ous. The capacity to handle input in large quantities was more important than sheer calculat- ing power. The total storage which he saw as necessary, both internal memory and that on a magnetic drum store, was in modern terminology less than 64 kilobytes. Even so, it was by no means simply a matter of placing the order and taking delivery of a device in a crate. In the mid-1950s computer manufacture was entirely a bespoke trade, and it was impossible to buy one 'off the peg'. When the suppliers spoke of having a computer 'in commercial pro- duction' they meant they were making a few, or at most a few dozen, machines; and each one was probably being tailored to the customer's requirements during manufacture.

'[Ovenstone's] specifications were circulated among interested British firms, and George Barlow and Ovenstone went to England in May 1954 to spend some six weeks looking at the various machines on offer. Two contenders were the English Electric DEUCE and the Ferranti MARK I, but Barlow and Ovenstone decided both had insurmountable problems. The prototype DEUCE was barely complete and an unknown quantity; nor could a copy be built and delivered by June 1955. The Ferranti machine's neat appearance concealed the fact that it was not built out of the replaceable plug-in units that were thought essential for easy servicing. Ferranti made a valiant last ditch effort to overcome the servicing objection, but it could do nothing about the technical disadvantage that its machine stored data electrostatically, which raised questions about radio interference when there were large transmitters nearby, as at Salisbury. Eventually the contract for the supply of a 'High Speed Digital Computer No. 403 (and Ancillary Equipment)' went to the London-based firm of Elliott Bros, for a machine at a total quoted cost of £106,625. Elliott's analog computers had a good reputation, and also their 403 used nickel delay lines for the volatile memory, storing 136 pulses in each line, and so were less susceptible to electrical interference. But Elliotts secured the contract for WREDAC (originally called 'Cobber', for no obvious reason) mostlybecause of their low quoted price....'

The official WRE history goes on to say that 'there were those who had misgivings' about the Elliott contract, urging WRE to go for an American computer and specifically for an IBM 701. Given the normal bureaucratic delays, if the IBM route had been followed then the eventual machine delivered to WRE might well have turned out to be an IBM 704. However, dollar currency shortages and the political realities of a 'buy British' policy for the joint Anglo-Australian project meant that an American solution was unlikely in 1954.

Laurence Clarke believes that the basic logic design of WREDAC was carried out in the space of about a week after the initial visit of Ovenstone and Barlow at Whitsun 1954. Laurence was in North Wales on holiday visiting family and was called back by Andrew St Johnston because of the importance of the project [24]. On 29 September 1954, the first manufacturing progress meeting for WREDAC was held at Elliott's Borehamwood Laboratories, 'amid a flurry of telexes querying and replying to minor details'. A crucial matter was the interface between the Woomera instrumentation's data-converters, then being built by WRE at Salisbury, and WREDAC. A completion date of July 1955 was set for the manufacture of WREDAC. For much of the autumn of 1954 and spring of 1955 Jack Bowie, Ovenstone's technical assistant, stayed at Borehamwood as the WRE representative. Laurence Clarke recalls [24] that: 'Bowie was always threatening us with a "crutching knife" if the project ran late. This is a horrendous tool used by the sheep shearers!'

The machine eventually arrived in Adelaide by sea in September 1955, accompanied by three Elliott personnel including the engineers Bob Cudmore and John Cane. John remained for about 3 months and Bob for 9 months to supervise WREDAC's installation and commissioning [24]. At this stage, the special Elliott Output Converter, to be called WREDOC (see below), was still being built at Borehamwood.

3.3.3   The Performance of WREDAC

A delay of 6 months elapsed before the main WREDAC computer was judged ready, by about March 1956, to run the acceptance tests at Salisbury. Not least of the initial problems was overheating. Ambient temperatures at Salisbury were in the mid-thirties centigrade and Salisbury's 'uncertain' air conditioning plant was often unable to cope with the computer's 25 kW power consumption. Laurence Clarke was sent out from Borehamwood to Australia for 9 weeks early in 1956 to investigate why WREDAC's acceptance tests were being delayed. Clarke recalls

[25, 26] that he found the air conditioning not working and, in some trepidation (he was 25 years old), Clarke informed the Salisbury Director that he [Clarke] was switching WREDAC off until Salisbury had fixed their air-conditioning plant.

Overheating was certainly not the only cause of unreliablility. Peter Goddard, who took over from John Ovenstone in 1958, recalls that the Elliot 402 circuits, upon which WREDAC was based, used 32 bit words and allowed a 2-digit recovery time before the next serial word was processed. 'Unfortunately John Ovenstone realised we needed 34 bit words in the one-off 403 for the calculating precision we needed. So WREDAC had no recovery pause. When pulses had been through four or five cathode following circuits we had problems' [27].

Furthermore, it was found that in some of WREDAC's circuits, the 12AT7 double-triode thermionic valves were being driven too close to their performance limits. This resulted in an unexpectedly rapid deterioration in valve characteristics over time, leading to a need for frequent valve replacement in certain heavily loaded sections of the computer. The same problem was later identified with similar heavily loaded 12AT7 circuits in the Elliott 405 computers. Joseph Roth was given the task of investigating the 405's performance at Borehamwood in 1957. He recalls [28] that 'The [405] computer could not be relied on to operate for more than six to eight hours before a valve failed, so halting operations. So I developed a testing routine in which a section of the computer was tested each day at the start of work on a specially designed test rig. The loading of any switch [ie logic circuit] was categorised under three headings – high, medium and low – depending on the result of the emission test on each triode. New valves were placed where the load was high and as they aged they were moved to the next lower stress level. In this way all the valves in the computer were tested each week and as a result valve failure during operation was very significantly reduced'. The engineers at WRE had arrived at similar conclusions about the need for 'preventive maintenance' for WREDAC.

Meanwhile, in 1955 and 1956, a team back at Borehamwood headed by Barry Cole and Paul Rayner was designing and building an Output Converter which had been specified by John Ovenstone. Called WREDOC, this consisted of seven cabinets of electronics plus magnetic tape units, fast printer and graphical output units (see the full specification below). WREDOC, which was delivered to Salisbury in the autumn of 1956, handled the huge amounts of output data produced by the main WREDAC computer. When completed, the total equipment for processing Woomera trials data digitally consisted of about 36 tall racks of electronics [20]. A little over half of these racks held the WRE-designed converters for telemetry, Doppler and radar data, all of which fed their digitised data (via magnetic tape) into WREDAC. In turn, WREDAC fed the analysis results (via magnetic tape) to WREDOC for off-line printing and graphical display.

At Salisbury, the reliability of the Elliott equipment was not living up to expectations. Nevertheless, at the end of the December 1956 quarter Ovenstone reported optimistically [20]: 'For the first time since the [Woomera] Range commenced operation there was no backlog of trial calculation over the Christmas period and, despite the shortage of skilled programming and maintenance staff, a reasonable service to the establishment was maintained'. Ovenstone predicted that WREDAC would soon be working for 8 h of a 10-h day. In the event, this proved wildly over-optimistic. As the official history goes on to recall:

'In the time-honoured way, supplier and customer tended to blame each other for WREDAC's teething troubles. WRE criticised the poor standard of workmanship, while Elliotts accused the Salisbury engineers of fiddling with precision equipment without knowing what they were doing. In a generous move Elliott eventually replaced the entire disk unit at no charge, but this cut no ice at WRE, where the firm's performance in rectifying the faults was later judged to have been 'something less than spectacular'. A more balanced judgment should stress that everyone at the time was down near the bottom of the learning curve when it came to computers. Elliotts' Computer Division was desperately overloaded with orders [for 402s and 405s]'.

In 1959, WREDAC was still only providing about 30 h a week of useful computing time. In that year it was reported that 'despite its limited hours WREDAC was processing very much more data than had been handled before its introduction …. In November 1960, Trials Superintendent J. Clegg was able to report at last that the reliability of WREDAC had risen above the 80 per cent mark. By then, though, the statistic was of little moment. WREDAC was thoroughly obsolete and WRE had ordered its successor [an IBM 7090]' [20].

In retrospect, it may be said that the unreliability of WREDAC was not the only factor that determined the overall rate at which missile test-data could be processed and analysed digitally. There was also the efficient operation of the various pieces of (locally designed) electronics required to convert the instrumentation source-data onto punched paper tape or magnetic tape, ready for input to WREDAC. Finally, there were the demands of other users for WREDAC computing time. Being a general-purpose stored-program computer, WREDAC began to be applied to other tasks that competed with the original workload of test-data analysis.

The successor to WREDAC, an IBM 7090, was delivered to WRE at the end of 1960 and formally handed over on 13 February 1961. WREDAC continued to run in parallel with the IBM 7090 until the end of 1962. The 7090 remained in operation until 1976, then effectively being superseded by a new IBM 370/168 installed in September 1975.

Unfortunately, the official history does not give enough data on WREDAC's later performance to judge whether the computer was indeed, as some have since curiously claimed, 'a complete disaster'. The only set of comparative trials data-analysis figures, given below, certainly shows that WREDAC's first 2 years at Salisbury were disappointing:

Machine and years	Trajectory points calculated per day	Cost of each calculated point, in Australian dollars
Pre-WREDAC (1955–1956)	800	4.00
(WREDAC) 1956–1957	1,000	0.50
(IBM 7090) 1963–1964	3,000	0.10

However, by the end of 1960, as previously mentioned, WREDAC's reliability had risen above the 80% mark so, in the end, the computer was certainly capable of making a useful contribution to Salisbury's operations. In retrospect, Laurence

Clarke remembers [24] that 'people were working their socks off to perform very stretching tasks – possibly the impossible'. Many people at LRWE were aware of the immense potential of digital computers. If this potential was not realised *immediately,* they were naturally going to experience some disappointment.

We conclude the WREDAC story with an account of the machine's internal architecture and how this fitted into Borehamwood's evolving plans for the design of other computers in the Elliott 400 range.

3.3.4   The Architecture of WREDAC and WREDOC

At Borehamwood, the 403 computer, known as WREDAC, was an enhanced version of the Elliott 402 machine with significant architectural changes. In turn, the 402 had been developed from the Elliott/NRDC 401 computer, as discussed in Chap. 5. One 401 and approximately ten 402 computers were built between about 1955 and 1960. At Salisbury, South Australia, WREDAC was used in conjunction with an Elliott-designed off-line unit called WREDOC, which was required for the production of bulk output as mentioned in Sect. 3.3.3.

Below we give a summary of the main differences between the production 402 and the one-off 403 installation (WREDAC combined with WREDOC), each of which used the same family of Elliott logic packages based on 12AT7 double-triode thermionic valves:

	402	403
Number of cabinets	6 (+3[a] if floating-point hardware)	9 for main computer + 7 for WREDOC
Word size	32 bits visible to programmer	34 bits visible to programmer
Instruction length	32 bits – (one per word)	17 bits – (two per word)
Instruction format	*(1 + 1)* – *address* format	*1-address* format
Clock frequency	333 kHz (= 3 μs digit-period)	333 kHz (= 3 μs digit-period)
Basic add-time	2 × (34 × 3) μs	2 × (34 × 3) μs
Multiply, divide	32 word-times	32 word-times
Fast storage	15 × one-word	512 words, as (127 × 4) + 4 × 1
Disc storage	2,944 words, at 4,600 rpm	16,384 words at 2,300 rpm
Magnetic tape storage	None	2 Pye 1/4-in. decks (100 digits/in., at 100 in./s, giving 2,000 chars/s).

[a]Contemporary photos show nine cabinets for the 402F complete with floating-point hardware. Laurence Clarke remembers [29] that the floating-point unit itself consisted of only one extra cabinet but this depends upon whether only fully populated logic cabinets are being counted – see for example the photograph of an Elliott 401 in Fig. 5.6

Other differences between the 402 and the 403, as recalled by Laurence Clarke [26, 30], were as follows (see also Appendix 3). The 403 included look-ahead at branch instructions and a form of instruction-pipelining, autonomous data transfers and hardware binary/decimal and decimal/binary conversion. The 403's fixed-head magnetic store was physically drum-like rather than disc-like (see Appendix 3 for

Fig. 3.11 The Elliott 403 computer, WREDAC, at Borehamwood in 1955 just before shipment to the Long Range Weapons Establishment, Salisbury, South Australia. Nine of the computer's cabinets held the main electronics, the other cabinets housing power supplies, cooling equipment, etc. Paper tape input/output equipment is shown on the table in the left foreground

more details). The quarter-inch-wide magnetic tape units were manufactured by the radio and television company Pye Ltd. of Cambridge, to a design of Donald Willis of Cambridge University. Willis was part of Maurice Wilkes' team, afterwards leaving to join the Decca company. It was said at Salisbury that 'the two tape drives on WREDAC ran with vacuum pockets to cushion the braking, but often that feature proved inadequate, snapping the tape when their servo mechanisms responded inadequately. They were slow by any subsequent standards' [31]. A detailed discussion of Borehamwood's own subsequent development of magnetic tape storage is given in Chap. 10.

It is the bulk handling of output that really distinguishes the 403 from the 402. Before WREDOC, the main forms of input/output for all Elliott (and indeed all Ferranti) computers had been via five-track punched paper tape – a technology derived from pre-war teleprinter equipment. Andrew St Johnston recalls [32] that 'Two novel aspects [of the 403] come to my mind. Firstly it needed a line printer whereas Elliotts had been paper tape and teleprinter users. We used the Bull printer [see below] which worked well. Barry Cole did the development. The second point on the 403 was a requirement for a plotter. There were of course no plotters on the market in those days so I picked on the standard Muirhead fax machine [Mufax]

Fig. 3.12 WREDAC generated large volumes of numerical and graphical data, which necessitated the design of a special output converter, WREDOC, connected to the main WREDAC computer. The photo shows the rear of WREDOC's seven racks of electronics, during commissioning at Borehamwood before shipment to Australia. Barry Cole is to the left and Paul Rayner is to the right in the picture

Fig. 3.13 The front of WREDOC at Borehamwood, just before shipment to Australia in 1956. On the left of the photo are four *Mufax* facsimile machines, specially converted to draw two-dimensional graphs. Next to these is the Bull lineprinter. At the right-hand side is one of the Pye half-inch magnetic tape decks

and put a coded disc on the shaft with the one turn spiral so that we could, by timing, put dots anywhere across the page. This worked sufficiently for the job'.

Paul Rayner, who designed WREDOC with Barry Cole, has expanded on St Johnston's account and corrected certain details. Rayner describes [33] the photograph of WREDOC shown in Fig. 3.13 as follows: 'I believe the cabinet underneath the Bull Printer was its power supply and drive electronics. The "device" on the side of the printer nearest the main cabinets was the coded disk: we made it for the printer, not the plotters which took serial information anyway in their facsimile role. We had to digitise the rotation of the printer print wheels to one part in 1024 and to do this we designed a glass disk of about 12 in diameter with a photographically produced Grey code pattern on it. The coded tracks had to be staggered to line up with the ten lamps and photocells you can see clearly in one of my photos [see Fig. 3.12]. For each line of print, the print wheels were spun and had to be stopped with the appropriate character lined up for the print operation itself. The bank of print wheels hinged forward to impact on the paper with a tremendous clonk that I can still hear today. This was repeated every few (one or two) seconds. Quite a beast! The printers were synchronous devices and once started it was necessary to present a line of data at the right instant required by the printer every few seconds. The data had to be read from the magnetic tape, formatted and buffered to synchronise with the printers. Not an easy task with the technology of the day. [WREDOC] needed almost as much hardware as the 403 [WREDAC] itself'.

The idea of having separate autonomous units for input and output on the Elliott 405 computer came from the WREDOC experience. The architecture of the Elliott 405, which represented the company's first excursion into the commercial data-processing arena, is described in Chap. 9 and Appendix 3. The first production 405 was installed in July 1956 in Elliott's Computing Service Bureau at Borehamwood.

We may end the rather complex story of the 403 (WREDAC and WREDOC) on a positive note, by quoting from an internal National Research Development Corporation memo [34] that described H J Crawley's visit to Borehamwood on 15 February 1955, at a time when the 402 and the 403 were both in the process of being manufactured:

'The first production 402 (the one for France) is nearing completion.... The design of the plug-in units has changed very little from the design of the plug-in units employed in the 401, but the cabinet and chassis designs have been very considerably improved and the arrangements for mounting plug-in units in the cabinets for arranging the interconnecting wiring and for supplying cooling air appear to be very good indeed.... Adherence to this modular principle has enabled Elliott Brothers to design rapidly and easily the 403 machine which is the special machine to be delivered to the Long-Range Weapons Establishment.

'The 403 machine will comprise sixteen cabinets of standard form, the contents of the cabinets being made up of all standard pieces including power supplies employed in 402, together with long nickel delay lines, the design of which has also been based on the modular principle. The magnetic store of 403, however, does not employ a three microsecond drum as in the 402, but employs a much larger disc store based upon the design of the large disc store (with replaceable disc) employed in a recently-delivered Admiralty Machine [the Elliott 153, see Sect. 3.1]. Assembly of the 403 has not yet commenced. Construction of the large disc store was well advanced, however, and here again construction appears to be of an impressively high standard.... The general impression which I received from this visit was one of bustle and activity and very considerable satisfaction with the way work is going'.

Notwithstanding the digital enthusiasm apparent both at Borehamwood and at the National Research Development Corporation, in the early 1950s it was still *analogue* computing that remained the natural choice for many strategic applications of computers. In the next chapter, we make a necessary digression to cover the important analogue computers that were designed at Borehamwood.

References

1. Lavington S (April/June 2006) In the footsteps of Colossus; a description of Oedipus. IEEE Ann Hist Comput 28(2):44–55. Invaluable help with the preparation of this paper was given to the author by Tony R (especially in a letter to Simon Lavington dated 16 July 2002) and by Peter Freeman (especially in a letter to Simon Lavington dated 2 Dec 2002)
2. Bunt JP. The 153 computer. Volume 1. Borehamwood Internal report 371(A), dated 1 Jan 1956. The diagrams are bound separately as Volume 2, report 371(B), also dated 1 Jan 1956. Volume 3, report 371(C) of the same date, contains test programs. Some amendments to report 371 were dated 30 Sept 1957. A related report by John Bunt is entitled: 153 computer maintenance handbook. Borehamwood Internal report 386, dated 1 Oct 1955
3. Bambrough B (1951) Design proposals for D/F calculator. Borehamwood Internal report 246, dated 29 July 1951
4. Anon (2001) Unsigned one-page typed note, attached to a letter dated 2 Oct 2001 from Gill Bennett, Chief Historian, Foreign and Commonwealth Office, to Simon Lavington. It is assumed that the source of the attached note was GCHQ
5. John Bunt (2002) The history of the 153. Two-page typed manuscript, sent to Simon Lavington with an accompanying letter dated 13 May 2002
6. Wakefield AJ (1954) Mathematics of the D/F calculator programme. Borehamwood Internal report 348, dated 5 Feb 1954
7. Mitchell EF (1954) Internal NRDC Memo dated Sept 1954. National Archive for the History of Computing, Manchester. NRDC records Box 86/15/4
8. Ray Henville (2009) E-mail to Simon Lavington 25 Feb 2008 and three-page typed manuscript plus sketch diagram, dated 24 Nov 2009
9. Beesley P (2000) Very special intelligence – the story of the Admiralty's Operational Intelligence Centre, 1939–1945. Greenhill Books, London
10. Wood DFJ (2001) The hidden geography of transnational surveillance – social and technological networks around signals intelligence sites. Ph.D.thesis, University of Newcastle upon Tyne. See http://www.staff.ncl.ac.uk/d.f.j.wood/thesis.htm and, in particular, the section on CSO (Composite Signals Organization) Irton Moor
11. Bell CG, Newell A (1971) Computer structures: readings and examples. McGraw-Hill, New York
12. Andrew St Johnston (2001) Interview with Simon Lavington at Hedgegrove Farm (Andrew's home) on 29 Oct 2001
13. Stephen B (Oct 2001) Codebreaking with IBM machines in World War II. Cryptologia 25(4):241–255, See also http://www.jproc.ca/crypto/otfp_otlp.html
14. (a) Flowers TH (July 1983) The design of Colossus. Ann Hist Comput 5(3):239–252. (b) Coombs AWM (July 1983) The making of Colossus. Ann Hist Comput 5(3):253–259. (c) Chandler WW (July 1983) The installation and maintenance of Colossus. Ann Hist Comput 5(3):260–262
15. Peter Freeman (2004) Letter to Simon Lavington, dated 20 Sept 2004

16. HG (Harry) Carpenter (2000–2002) Notes taken by Simon Lavington of nine lengthy telephone conversations with Harry Carpenter, during the period 16 May 2000–9 Dec 2002. Harry was unwilling to commit his historical anecdotes to paper but was more than happy to talk. Part way through these exchanges, in November 2001, Harry obtained clearance under the provisions of the Official Secrets Act to reveal certain details about his hardware design activities at Borehamwood

17. Ralph Erskine, Philip Marks, Frode Weieud (2006) E-mail exchanges with Simon Lavington, September/Oct 2006

18. General information on the Venona programme is (or was in 2006) given at: http://www.nsa.gov/publications/publi00039.cfm)

19. Venona Monograph Number 4, page 7, is (or was in 2006) publicly available at: http://history.acusd.edu/gen/text/coldwar/venona4.html

20. Morton P (1989) Fire across the desert: Woomera and the Anglo-Australian joint project 1946–1980. Australian Government Publishing Service, Canberra

21. McCann D, Thorne P (2000) The last of the first: CSIRAC: Australia's first computer. Department of Computer Science and Software Engineering, University of Melbourne, Parkville, Victoria, Australia. ISBN: 0-7340-2024-4. See also: http://www.csse.unimelb.edu.au/dept/about/csirac/

22. Coombs AWM. An electronic digital computer. Parts 1–4, Post Office EEJ, vol. 48, July and Oct 1955 and Jan 1956, pp 114, 137 and 212, and vol. 49, Apr and July 1956, pp 18, 126. A summary of MOSAIC will be found in chapter 10 of: Lavington SH (1980) Early British computers. Manchester University Press, Manchester. ISBN: 0-7190-0803-4. Co-published by Digital Press, 1980. ISBN: 0-93237-08-8. http://ed-thelen.org/comp-hist/EarlyBritish.html

23. *Bright Sparks:* a register of people involved in the development of science, technology, engineering and medicine in Australia, including references to their archival materials and bibliographic resources. See: http://www.asap.unimelb.edu.au/bsparcs/biogs/P003832b.htm

24. SLH Clarke (2008) E-mails to Simon Lavington, Mar 2008

25. SLH Clarke (2007) Conversation with Simon Lavington, 7 June 2007

26. SLH Clarke (1993) Recollections of the Elliott 400 series. Computer Resurrection, the Bulletin of the Computer Conservation Society, Issue number 6, summer 1993, pp 15–21

27. Peter Goddard (2008) E-mail to Simon Lavington, dated 10 Mar 2008

28. J Roth (2008) E-mail to Simon Lavington on 24 Feb 2008

29. SLH Clarke (2009) E-mail to Simon Lavington, dated 14 Oct 2009

30. SLH Clarke (2001) Conversation with Simon Lavington on 10 July 2001

31. Don Fenna (July 2004 and May 2006) communication with David Pentecost. Don Fenna worked at WRE from 1956 to 1969 and later became Emeritus Professor of Applied Science in Medicine at the University of Alberta, Canada. See the Computer Conservation Society's *Our Computer Heritage* website: http://www.ourcomputerheritage.org/wp/ for more WREDAC comments compiled by David Pentecost

32. St Johnston A (1995) History of the Research Laboratories of Elliott Brothers (London) Ltd.: Andrew St. Johnston's Contribution. Typed manuscript sent to Laurence Clarke on 31 May 1995 (eight pages)

33. Paul Rayner (2008) E-mail correspondence with Simon Lavington, Aug/Sept 2008

34. Crawley HJ (1955) Progress on the 402 at Elliott Brothers. Two-page typed NRDC internal memo dated 15 Feb 1955, addressed to Mr Hennessey and Lord Halsbury. Describes a visit made by Crawley to Borehamwood on 8 Feb (available at the National Archive for the History of Computers, NAHC file reference NRDC/86/13/8)

Chapter 4
Analogue Expertise

4.1 Introduction: Analogue Versus Digital

Computing devices based on analogue methods have a long history. Physical quantities such as fluid pressure, linear position or speed of rotation had been used as the analogy of numerical quantities long before electromechanical digital computing came into use. Some of the largest and most powerful electronic analogue computers, for example, the TRIDAC described in Sect. 4.4, were designed and built in the 1950s, at a time when electronic digital computers were still in their infancy. In the mid-1950s, the applications of analogue versus digital computing were topics for informed debate (see, e.g. [1]). In some specialist areas such as airborne computing and flight control, digital computers did not become dominant until the 1980s. As far as Marconi–Elliott Avionics Systems is concerned, Ron Howard CBE, a former Managing Director and Chairman of GEC Avionics Ltd., has said [2] that the breakthrough into fully redundant flight controls based on microprocessors did not come until 1979 with the design of a *slats and flaps* control system for the A310 Airbus wings. More comments on the suitability of analogue and digital techniques for airborne computing will be found in Chap. 12.

John Coales, the founding Director of Elliott's Borehamwood Laboratories and certainly an early advocate of digital techniques, made an interesting retrospective observation in December 1955 [3]: 'When I first became involved in the design of [the TRIDAC analogue] computer in 1948, I thought that analogue computers were on their way out and digital computers would replace them. I now think quite differently, partly because of the experience of TRIDAC, but partly because of other considerations met in solving non-linear problems, where one great value of the analogue computer is that a very much better appreciation is obtained of how the process being investigated really behaves. With an analogue computer one can see what is going on in different parts of the system while it is actually happening, whereas with the digital computer, although one can make provision for doing this by printing out different results from within the process, one cannot easily see what is happening while the process is being worked out.'

Coales' remarks raise the topic of what is now called *visualisation*: techniques for presenting the end-user with a graphical representation of the results of a computation.

S. Lavington, *Moving Targets*, History of Computing,
DOI 10.1007/978-1-84882-933-6_4, © Springer-Verlag London Limited 2011

Graphical output units for digital computers, initially consisting of point-plotting systems giving two-dimensional line-drawings, were introduced in the late 1950s. Simple ones employed chart recorders, for example for the Elliott 403 (WREDAC) in 1956, see Chap. 3. Later graphical output systems displayed images on a cathode-ray tube, possibly with the facility to obtain a photographic record of the screen during computation – for example on the Ferranti Mercury computer in 1959. However, user interfaces were still primitive at that time. David Edwards, speaking of the Mercury graphical output unit, has said [4]: 'The disappointing aspects of it for me at the time [1959] was the problem of getting any software designers inter-ested in providing suitable support for the users, so we only got desperate users who had to provide all their own software.'

Elliott Brothers (London) Ltd. was reasonably well-placed to continue manufac-turing electromechanical analogue computing devices after the Second World War. Having been left behind in the acquisition of electronic experience, one might even say that analogue instrumentation was the *only* viable product line at Elliott's main factory at Lewisham in 1945. It was at Lewisham in the 1930s that Elliott's electro-mechanical analogue computing had reached a high point of technical excellence for gunnery control, usually called *fire control*, equipment for the Royal Navy. Although somewhat outside the timeframe of the rest of this chapter, it is worth touching on Elliott's analogue fire-control computers because they formed a back-ground to the work at Borehamwood between 1946 and 1950 on *digital* fire control – as described in Chap. 2 – and also to the *Flyplane* analogue ship-borne equipment that, in the event, the MRS5 digital project failed to replace in the 1950s.

4.2   Admiralty Fire Control Tables

4.2.1   Developments up to 1945

The connection between Elliott Brothers and the British Navy went back well before the First World War, to a time when precision instruments were being intro-duced not only for navigation but also as aids to ballistics prediction and fleet station-keeping. Some of the instruments were of modest size, not much larger than handheld, such as the Battenberg Course Indicator and the Dumaresq Instrument, both of which solved problems involving the relative bearing and velocities of two ships. An Elliott company booklet [5] produced in 1937 describes the company's Battenberg and Dumaresq equipment and also proudly featured the Gyrostat, 'used for the stabilisation of optical parts and for eliminating the effect of the ship's roll on them'. The squirrel-cage rotor of the Gyrostat's three-phase 20,000 rpm induction motor was a good example of Elliott precision engineering, being turned in one piece, including the spindles, from an ingot of nickel steel of $5^{3}/_{8}$ in. diameter. 'Bearing in mind the fact that the air gap is only 0.013-inch, it must run with absolutely no vibration ... The gyro runs on specially designed ball bearings of our own manufacture ...' [5]. However, pride of place in the same 1937 Elliott booklet was given to descriptions of the company's naval fire-control analogue computers.

Instruments designed to aid precision gunnery became more complex in operation from 1908 when Lieutenant F C Dreyer invented a mechanical device the size of a very large table that combined 'time and range' with 'time and bearing'. In 1911, Elliott Brothers had produced the first Dreyer Fire Control Table for the Navy and installed it in the battleship HMS Prince of Wales [6]. The Dreyer Table was operated by a crew of eight ratings, each being responsible for turning a handle that, via pointer-following, controlled the value of a particular variable. Over the next 25 years, this arrangement led to a succession of ever more sophisticated electro-mechanical analogue computers (which the Navy called *Tables* or *Clocks* or *Boxes*) for fire control, allowing secondary parameters such as wind speed to be included in the ballistics equations that were solved. For convenience, we shall often use the general term Admiralty Fire Control Table (AFCT) to represent all types of gunnery analogue computers. Strictly speaking, however, the Admiralty Fire Control Clock was a simplified AFCT and the Admiralty Fire Control Box was a further simplification of the AFCT.

To set the scene for all these developments, a small reminder of naval terminology is helpful. For more details, see [7]. The general arrangement for surface gunnery control aboard warships involved three physically separated units:

N.1656

Fig. 4.1 Part of the mechanisms for calculating gun *bearing* or *training* (i.e. the horizontal movement necessary for aiming a gun), in an Elliott AFCT analogue computer of the 1920s. The large heart-shaped cam in the centre of the photo was cut according to the inverse-tangent function. More details will be found in Ref. [15]

- The *Director* (strictly, the *Director Control Tower (DCT)*) which was situated high up on the superstructure; this contained equipment for estimating the target's range, bearing, course and speed and transmitting this continuously changing information to:
- The *Fire Control Table(s)*, situated below deck in the *Transmitting Station, TS*; this included one or more analogue computers for calculating gun elevation, gun-bearing and projectile (e.g. fuse-setting) parameters and transmitting this continuously changing information to:
- The ship's gun turrets, where each gun crew adjusted the required parameters and fired rounds as ordered by the *Director*.

The equipment in the *Director* for estimating range and bearing was at first optical. After about 1944, radar gradually became the preferred technique. From the late 1940s, a fourth physical location was added to the traditional elements of Director, Transmitting Station and Guns: this was the *Operations Room*, where the tactical *Plot* was maintained from radar and other electronic information received both from the ship's own equipment and from neighbouring friendly vessels and aircraft.

Of course, the ship's roll, pitch and yaw, together with subtler factors such as wear on the rifling of a gun's barrel, added complications to the above simple description. When one considers that, at a range of 15 miles, a projectile's time-of-flight could take the better part of a minute during which the target's position might have changed by almost a mile, the need for precision computing is apparent.

The fully developed Admiralty Fire Control Table (AFCT) was thus an analogue computer for solving differential equations. It required, amongst other things, integrators, possibly torque amplifiers or servomechanisms, and means for inputting updated values to the many parameters of the ballistics equations. Some of the parameters varied slowly, for example barometric pressure and wind strength, and could be set up via simple hand wheels. Other parameters, for example target range, could be varying continuously and were either adjusted manually (pointer-following) or semi-automatically (using selsyns, magslips, etc. for electrical transmission of data from point to point through the ship). It was only during the 1950s that *auto-following* via radar began to be seriously used operationally – and even then optical and manual target-following equipment remained alongside the radar installations, as is shown below.

Good technical accounts of naval fire-control equipment will be found in [6–8]. In the period 1910–1960, during which they were developed and refined, these mechanical and electromechanical analogue computers came in many sizes with differing degrees of sophistication, the British versions being described variously as Admiralty Fire Control Tables/Clocks/Boxes as mentioned previously. They all had to be real time and robust. Elliotts' Lewisham factory was the prime supplier to the Admiralty of all of these devices up to 1950. Maurice Needham remembers [9] that: 'Everything had to be designed, quite rightly, to cope not only with shock from gunfire – quite unbelievable on a capital ship firing a broadside – but also with the not always delicate touch of the matelots! The Fire Control Table on a capital ship was manned by members of the Royal Marines band and had a standby electrical supply in the form of a generator attached to a bicycle frame which would be peddled by a bandsman in emergency! I remember seeing the Elliott label on the Fire Control Table in HMS Howe, during working up gunnery trials of the new *type 274* 10cm radar, blissfully ignorant of the fact that I would join the firm after the war.'

Judging by serial number, approximately 300 Elliott Admiralty Fire Control Tables and Clocks saw service in the Second World War [8]. They were fitted to all battleships and cruisers and to large numbers of destroyers. Figure 1.4 shows an early Fire Control Table being assembled and tested at Elliott's Lewisham factory. Figures 1.5 and 4.2 show Elliott equipment installed in the Main Armament Transmitting Station below decks in the cruiser HMS Belfast. The Admiralty Fire Control Table Mark VI in Fig. 4.2 measures approximately 84 in. (213 cm) long by 38 in. (97 cm) wide. Distributed around it during an action was a crew of one officer and 12 ratings, four of whom were responsible for telephone/WT communications. HMS Belfast, one of the largest of the Royal Navy's cruisers during the Second World War , was ready for service in August 1939 and was finally retired from active service in 1963 [10]. The ship has been restored and is moored as a permanent historical exhibit near Tower Bridge in London (see: http://hmsbelfast.iwm.org.uk/).

Fig. 4.2 A close-up of HMS Belfast's AFCT analogue computer, showing the handles for setting values of enemy ship's speed, range and bearing data, etc., as received from observers high up in the ship's superstructure. Ballistics parameters such as wind speed, direction and barometric pressure were also set manually on the AFCT. The AFCT computer received other data on own ship's speed, etc., and then worked out gun elevation and training and fed this information to the turrets

In summary, the commitment of Elliott's Lewisham factory to the supply and maintenance of Admiralty Fire Control Tables and Clocks was long standing and persisted for a few years after the end of the Second World War.

Surface gunnery, and the associated electro-mechanical analogue computers, changed little through the 1950s – if only for the reason that the *Low-Angle*, large-calibre surface guns had themselves become obsolescent relics of an outmoded form of warfare at sea. From 1945, attention turned to *High-Angle* guns, anti-aircraft measures and guided missiles. Research into guided weapons had intensified during the Second World War, with the Germans well in the lead with their HS293 airborne anti-ship missile and, of course, the V1 and V2 [11]. It was, however, not until 1961 that the *Sea Cat* guided missile came into service in British ships, followed by others such as the *Sea Dart* and *Sea Wolf.* Meanwhile, anti-aircraft fire-control equipment for *High-Angle* guns continued to be developed during the 1940s and 1950s.

It has to be said that the standard British fire-control equipment for wartime naval anti-aircraft guns, the High Angle Control System (HACS), was a relatively modest performer compared with the American Mark 37 FCS. The Mark 37 FCS was introduced into the US navy in 1939 and had both high-angle and low-angle functionality. Unlike the HACS, the Mark 37 was a fully predictive or *tachymetric* system in which the Mark 37's analogue computer calculated where the target aircraft would be in three-dimensional terms, not the two-dimensional terms of the HACS [12].

A good description of the Mark 37's analogue computer, which was produced by the Ford Instrument Company Inc. of New York, may be found in [13]. It is worth summarising this description here, because it gives a sense of the high point of *analogue* computing capability just before Borehamwood's *digital* computing activities commenced. The electro-mechanical 'Mark I' analogue computer at the heart of the Mark 37 FCS included the following computational sub-units in addition to a large number of data transmitter/receiver units:

Nine component solvers
One vector solver
Six disc integrators
Four component integrators
Nine multipliers
Six computing multipliers

The whole Ford computer measured approximately 62 in. long by 38 in. wide by 45 in. high ($157 \times 97 \times 114$ cm^3). It weighed about 3,125 lb (1,417 kg). In 1939, it cost about \$75,000 – perhaps equivalent 70 years later to about £1 million in 2009 terms.

4.2.2 Flyplane Predictor Systems

Back in Britain at the end of the war, Admiralty-sponsored research projects such as MRS3, MRS4 and MRS5 sought to promote a new generation of high-angle gunnery control equipment. None of these MRS (medium-range systems) seems to have had much practical effect on the post-war anti-aircraft performance of Royal Naval ships on active service. Instead, a somewhat pedestrian fire-control system based on the *Flyplane* principle was introduced in about 1950 to bridge the gap until fully operational guided missiles were installed. The Flyplane Predictor System, FPS, illustrates the transition from manual optical target-following to radar-based auto-tracking and from electromechanical to electronic analogue computing. To quote [14], from which much of the following details are taken, 'the FPS Mark 5 was a fully-stabilised tachometric AA and surface (SU) fire control system'. The main difference between this and earlier systems was that 'purely mechanical computing mechanisms have been eliminated and all calculations are done by electromechanical servos'.

The component parts of the complete FPS5 consisted, for various de facto operational and availability reasons, of an amalgamation of tried-and-tested old technologies together with newer electronic equipment. To quote Alan Bromley's general observations in [8], 'This entire complex of apparatus, which evolved throughout World War II, gives very much the impression of a cludge on top of a cludge. No doubt the development took the direction it did as a response to finding rapid solutions to the problems raised by battle experience and a need to use, as far as possible, the considerable amount of complex equipment already in service and the existing experience of trained personnel.'

Referring to Fig. 4.3, the main units of the FPS5 when controlling 4.5-in. guns were as follows:

(a) Director Mark 6M, which included *type 275* radar in two nacelles
(b) Gyro Rate Unit (GRU) stabiliser Mark 3
(c) Elevation, Training and Range control electronics for the *type 275* radar
(d) The Flyplane tracker/predictor analogue units
(e) Admiralty Fire Control Box (AFCB) Mark 10 (a simplified AFCT)

Unit (a) was positioned high up on the ship's superstructure, as can be seen in Fig. 4.4. The remaining units were below decks in the Transmitting Station. A good example of a complete FPS5 installation dating from 1955 can be seen today aboard the Second World War destroyer HMS Cavalier, preserved in Chatham Historic Dockyard. Referring to HMS Cavalier's system and to Fig. 4.3, the Gyro Rate Unit (manufactured by Ferranti Ltd.) is the size of an office filing cabinet. The *type 275's* Elevation, Training and Range control electronics measures about 6 ft high by 6 ft wide (1.8×1.8 m^2); it is not clear who manufactured this equipment. Physically, the complete Flyplane Tracker/Predictor Mark 5 system, manufactured by Ferranti Ltd., is contained in six sections of racking, each section being about 6 ft high and 19 in (0.5 m) wide. The AFCB Mark 10 has three main parts: (1) the calculating unit; (2) an Applications Unit; (3) the Gun Data Unit, used to transmit gun aiming (i.e. elevation and training) information to the actual guns. HMS Cavalier's AFCB Mark 10 unit was manufactured in 1955 by Laurence Scott & Electromotors Ltd., Norwich, and measures about 6 ft high by 6 ft wide.

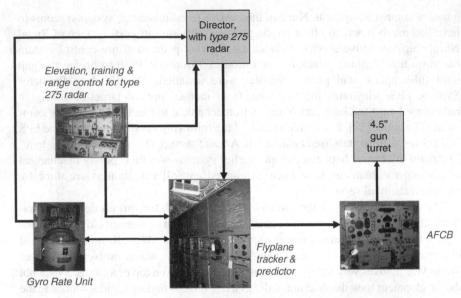

The principal flow of information in the Flyplane FPS5 Fire Control system.

Fig. 4.3 A simplified schematic of the FPS Mark 5 fire-control system of the mid-1950s, as installed in the destroyer HMS Cavalier. Radar and/or optical range and bearing data is fed from the Director to the *Flyplane* tracker and predictor units and from thence to the AFCB, which in turn controlled the ship's 4.5-in. guns. The AFCB (Admiralty Fire Control Box) was a reduced-function version of the electro-mechanical AFCT (Admiralty Fire Control Table)

It is believed that the Mark 10 AFCB was the last of the electro-mechanical AFCBs. The Mark 11, also manufactured by the Instrument Department of Laurence Scott & Electromotors Ltd., was electronic and was physically much smaller. The Instrument Department's naval weapons activity continues today, within a successor company called MSI Defence Systems.

Apart from the gun crews, the total personnel required to operate Flyplane systems when at action stations was typically four officers and 17 ratings – indicating that manual intervention was still very much part of practical gunnery control. Taking a historical perspective, all this makes Borehamwood's 1947 vision of automatic real-time on-line control by digital computer – see Fig. 2.3 – look very ambitious.

The performance of the FPS5 was expressed as 'a plus-or-minus 20 yards miss-distance, at target ranges of less than 6,000 yards'. The maximum range of the *type 275* radar was said to be 36,000 yards [14]. Other FPS versions existed; see for example [15].

One of the first ships to conduct sea trials of an early Flyplane system was HMAS Tobruk, shown in Fig. 4.4. She was a Battle class destroyer laid down in August 1946, built at Sydney, launched in December 1947 and commissioned in May 1950 [16]. In August 1951, HMAS Tobruk joined the UN naval force for operations in Korean waters. However, the ship combined the Flyplane system with

Fig. 4.4 HMAS Tobruk was one of the first ships to be fitted with the *Flyplane* electronic analogue fire-control units. HMAS Tobruk was a Battle Class destroyer built in Sydney, launched in December 1947 and commissioned in May 1950. The twin nacelles of the *type 275* radar can be seen on the Director, above the bridge. In 1951, HMAS Tobruk joined United Nations naval forces for Korean War operations

AFCC Mark 8 fire-control equipment, which could not make use of auto-following by radar. In 1950, the early Flyplane analogue computer seems to have been a special add-on unit and, as such, is hardly mentioned amongst other gunnery-related issues in HMAS Tobruk's Flyplane evaluation report [16].

Returning to the theme of analogue computing, the Ferranti Flyplane *Tracker* and *Predictor* consisted of electro-mechanical servos and electronic amplifiers. In the mode known as *aloft control*, radar was firstly roughly aimed manually via two ratings with precision binoculars in the Director. In the mode *blind control*, radar sought out a target and attempted to lock on to this. The FPS Tracker contained 13 computing servos for processing the lateral, vertical and range information. The FPS Predictor contained 14 computing servos. The servos were mostly operating on AC voltages. In general terms, the servo-systems used transformers for addition/subtraction, inductive potentiometers (I-pots) for multiplication and division, and magslip resolvers and composers for resolving an input voltage V into components $V_1 \sin \theta$ and $V_2 \cos \theta$. Axis changing was also done via magslips. The computing servos were used for integration and differentiation and to solve simultaneous equations.

We may conclude this section with a quote from [8]: 'It is also interesting to realise that the mechanical analogue technology was expensive.... The fire control systems, including mechanical computers, for the battleship King George V cost

£213,000 in 1939, equivalent to perhaps £20 million in 2009 ... It is likely that this experience led the Admiralty to accept computation as a complex and expensive art. Perhaps their readiness to support the expensive and complex development of digital computers at Borehamwood in the post-war years is, in part, directly attributable to their wartime experience of mechanical analogue computing systems.'

As it happened, probably the largest and most expensive defence-related UK computer project in the 10 years after the end of the Second World War was analogue, not digital, as described in Sect. 4.3. The mechanical production skills of Elliott's Lewisham factory, honed on the Fire Control Tables, had an input to this huge analogue project which was called TRIDAC. However, the development of TRIDAC spanned the period 1950–1954, by which time *electronic* analogue amplifiers had replaced much of the functionality formerly implemented via precision mechanical engineering. More generally, it was electronic expertise that was at a premium after the war and in this respect Lewisham had lagged behind its industrial competitors. If the Elliott company had not agreed to host the Borehamwood Laboratories in 1946 and hence become involved in Admiralty contracts with an electronic focus, it is most unlikely that Elliotts would have been active in the design of TRIDAC or indeed any pioneering post-war computers, either analogue or digital.

In Elliott's transition from electro-mechanical to electronic analogue computers, the two Admiralty digital contracts (*MRS5* and *Netting*) described in Chap. 2 and the consequential rapid expansion of skilled staff at Borehamwood, provided the essential impetus. Fortunately, a contemporary technical summary of Borehamwood's entire analogue and digital computing ambitions survives and, in the next section, we draw upon this to introduce Elliott's emergence as a major UK producer of electronic analogue computers in the 1950s.

4.3   Early Analogue Computing Activity at Borehamwood

John Coales resigned as Director of the Borehamwood Laboratories in March 1952 and left in April of that year, as described in Chap. 2. In the resulting interregnum before the formal instalment of Commander Henry Pasley-Tyler as Director, C A Cochrane of the Radio Division (actually, radar and microwave techniques) assumed responsibility for co-ordinating Borehamwood's research activities. In a ten-page internal document entitled *Organisation for Research and Development* dated 14 May 1952, Cochrane devotes almost half the text to a description of analogue and digital computing activity. This activity is, somewhat confusingly, distributed across five of the eight Borehamwood divisions as follows.

The scope of the Computing Division under W S Elliott is defined as 'the study of computing methods and circuit techniques for digital computing and responsible for design and construction of complete machines'. The scope of the Electrical Engineering Division under H M Gale is defined as 'electromechanical servo mechanisms and analogue computing; printed circuits and magnetic amplifiers'.

However, in addition the Circuits Division includes responsibility for 'circuit techniques for analogue computing'. Finally, the Theory Division 'advises on the best type of machines for the solution of particular mathematical problems', and the Physics Division includes 'study of the properties of materials, in particular those used in computers'. It is clear that, by mid-1952, the development of computing techniques was a significant activity in Borehamwood.

Cochrane goes on to describe various computing machines which were either 'in use' or 'under development' in May 1952. In the former category, the only analogue computer in use at that time was a Differential Analyser that had been designed and built by K L Selig and others – most probably in the Theory Division [17]. This is described in Sect. 4.3.1. Of the analogue computers under development in May 1952, two are mentioned by Cochrane. The first, TRIDAC, is considered in Sect. 4.4. The second was a small special-purpose analogue computer of which little is now known. Cochrane describes it as 'a high-speed electronic analogue machine designed to handle an input data rate of 1000 [points] per second. It incorporates two multipliers, one squarer, three adders and five integrators. An overall accuracy of about 3% is required and the size will be 5ft by 3ft by 3ft 6 inches (approximately 152cms × 91cms × 107cms). Input is on variable density or variable area tracks on film and the output is printed on a paper roll.'

4.3.1 The Differential Analyser

The design of the Elliott differential analyzer was started in 1947 and the machine was in operation by 1950 or earlier. Only one version was built, as an internal computing facility for the Theory Division within Borehamwood. However, as noted in [18], the fact that this analyser was chosen as an exhibit in the Dome of Discovery during the Festival of Britain in 1951 'is an indication that it is representative of modern engineering methods'. Continuing from [18]: 'It is intended to deal with the more usual day-to-day engineering problems that normally remain unsolved because of the time and labour involved in step by step methods. The accuracy aimed at is not high, as not only is high accuracy rarely required for this type of work but the available data are usually only approximate'. When compared with the early classic differential analysers, for example that of Vannevar Bush [19], the Elliott machine was of lower accuracy and handled problems of rather limited magnitude. However, it was more robust and able to be configured more rapidly on account of its flexible interconnections.

The Elliott differential analyser was built from mechanically independent units, connected by servo-systems which communicated via Magslips (Fig. 4.6). The overall electrical connections necessary to solve a particular problem were configured as desired via a central patch panel. In its system design, one can detect both the influence of robust electro-mechanical data transmission as seen in the Admiralty Fire Control Tables and the modular approach to computer construction as seen in the MRS5's 152 digital computer. It is probable [17] that the differential analyser's ball-and-disc

Fig. 4.5 Elliotts had several exhibits in the Dome of Discovery at the 1951 Festival of Britain. The photo shows the Elliott Differential Analyser at the exhibition. On the right are three plane input/output tables and one rotary output table. The integrators, adders, etc. are in the racks to the left

Fig. 4.6 A ball-and-disc integrator unit of the Elliott Differential Analyser. The complete machine had six such units, six adders and various input/output units, all interconnected by *magslip* servos

integrators were based on the Argo-pattern variable-speed drives used by Elliott's Lewisham factory in the Admiralty Fire Control Tables – perhaps even constructed from parts left over from what may have been the final production batch of Elliott-built AFCTs for the KING GEORGE V class battleships [20].

The computing facilities of the Elliott differential analyzer are summarised in Table 4.1. The plane (i.e. flat) and rotary (i.e. cylindrical) input tables used special

Table 4.1 Characteristics of the Elliott differential analyser

Unit	Number available	Characteristics
Integrator	6	Integrator constant $K = 20$
Adder	6	Sum $S = A/n + B$, where $n = 1, 2, 5$ or 10
Plane input table	3	Useful area = 27×17 in.^{2} (69×43 cm^2)
		Max. gradient of curve = $70°$
		Max. speed: 10 in./min along the curve
		Lead screw pitch: 0.1 in.
Rotary input table	1	Useful area = 31.4×17 in.^{2} (80×43 cm^2)
		Max. gradient and speed as above
Plane output table	1	Useful area = 27×17 in.^{2} (69×43 cm^2)
		Number of pens: 2
		Lead screw pitch: 0.1 in. (both co-ordinates, each curve)
Independent variable	1	Speed range = 0–300 rpm (both directions)

photo-electric curve followers designed by K L Selig [18]. An example of the machine's use is given in [21]. This is a problem specified by the Services Electronics Research Laboratory and involving the investigation of a cylindrical diode when the anode is acting as a waveguide at 10,000 MHz. The differential equation for this problem specified the trajectory of an electron. It was required to find the value of the dc potential which just prevents all electrons from reaching the anode. The solution required four integrators, one plane input table, the rotary input table (for the sine function), an adder and an output table. Further details of the Elliott differential analyser are given in [18, 21–23].

To conclude on a lighter note, Roy Hynes was one of the Borehamwood engineers who took turns at demonstrating the Elliott Differential Analyser to the public in the Dome of Discovery at the Festival of Britain in 1951. He recalls [24] that 'people were fascinated by the patterns being drawn out on the plotting tables. After my spiel, I asked a woman if she had understood. "No", she said, "but my daughter would, she's got Matric." I had also explained to a group of schoolboys that the machine did difficult mathematics and one asked "Does it do decimals?" When I answered "Well, more difficult than decimals", they were devastated to think that such things could be!' Other Elliott exhibits elsewhere at the Festival included an aerial magnetometer and an automatic acid controller for a glass absorber plant [25].

More generally, analogue computers such as the Elliott Differential Analyser often involved precision mechanical engineering. Bill Pearse, who joined the Mechanical Engineering Division at Borehamwood in October 1946 and became the first head of the Aviation Division in 1952, has described the design of sine–cosine generators with swash-plate drive for a missile simulator (most probably the TRIDAC project, see below). Pearse was helped considerably in his design of the sine–cosine generator by Weiler, a senior Peenemunde engineer who had been brought from Germany after the war to work at Elliotts (see also Chap. 2). Bill Pearse remembers [26] that the design was of such precision 'that we could not find a manufacturer in the UK to undertake the manufacture of the several units needed.

Ultimately I went to Berlin [with Weiler] and placed the work with a factory that had just been fully fitted out with high precision machinery from Switzerland. Just one of the many penalties, in my experience, which resulted from us winning the war.'

Substantially all differential analysers in the period 1930–1955 were analogue devices. Digital differential analysers (DDA) then emerged for a brief period until general-purpose digital computers completely took over – and improved upon – their functionality. An example of a DDA is contained within the Verdan airborne digital computer, discussed in Chap. 12.

4.4   TRIDAC: The World's Largest?

4.4.1   Guided Weapons and Cold War Imperatives

The development of a British nuclear bomb had begun in 1947 – independently from the Americans, since by the McMahon Act passed by Congress in 1946 the USA was prohibited from sharing any more atomic secrets with its allies. The first test of a British nuclear weapon was in October 1952, at the Monte-Bello Islands off the north-west coast of Western Australia. Meanwhile, the Cold War was generating several other kinds of hot spots, of which the Korean War (1950–1953) was the most intense. The Korean War coincided with a significant reassessment of the UK's military spending. In August 1950, the British government announced a large increase in the defence budget [27], which increased again the next year; see also the table given in the Introduction. In 1951/1952, UK defence spending was 7.5% of GDP and rose to 8.7% in 1952/1953 – a higher proportion than in any other western country except America.

One of the UK's post-war priorities was the development of a long-range ballistic missile, or *Independent Deterrent*, a complete weapon system that ideally did not rely upon American technology. A major result in the early 1950s was the development of the fixed-site *Blue Streak* missile, intended to deliver UK nuclear warheads with an air-frame to be built by de Havillands and with Rolls-Royce engines [28]. The design of the Blue Streak missile required massive amounts of simulation and testing that were beyond the capabilities of individual aerospace companies, who had to call upon the research facilities at the Royal Aircraft Establishment (RAE) at Farnborough, Hampshire.

Blue Streak was one driver for the development of a very large RAE analogue computer, which became known as TRIDAC. Another, perhaps more important, driver for TRIDAC was the need to defend the UK against incoming hostile ballistic missiles – implying the development of interceptor missile technologies that again demanded large amounts of simulation and testing. Indeed, in the original 1949 RAE report [29] that made the technical case for TRIDAC, the development of interceptor-type guided missiles was assumed to be the priority.

G W H Gardner, the then Director General of Technical Development (AIR), Ministry of Supply, and soon to be the Director of the Royal Aircraft Establishment, gave the prestigious James Clayton lecture [11] at the Institution of Mechanical Engineers on 19 November 1954. His lecture was entitled *Guided Missiles*. He described the early history of guided weapons and the technical challenges of the immediate post-war years. To quote from Gardner: 'It is hard to imagine a more difficult engineering problem than that of developing a guided missile of the kind discussed in this lecture to a satisfactory degree of reliability before it is outmoded by counter-measures or by advances in the art.... The missile is a complex of advanced aerodynamic, structural, propulsion, hydraulic, electronic and instrument techniques... The problem of achieving reliability which may be the greatest of those mentioned, requires the attention of our best engineers at all levels in order to ensure that sound engineering principles and practice are followed and that the potential value of these important weapons becomes a reality.' Outlining the major development facilities necessary for guided weapons (as compared with conventional aircraft), he pointed out that a suitable wind tunnel would, at that time, cost about £10 million. Faced with this scale of investment, comprehensive flight simulation facilities had become increasingly important. The Royal Aircraft Establishment had therefore conceived the need for the huge TRIDAC three-dimensional analogue computer, to be described in Sect. 4.4.2.

A large-scale simulator was not the only R&D requirement. Gardner pointed out that, as far as missile engines were concerned, a modern propulsion-test plant would also cost about £10 million. This is where the National Gas Turbine Establishment's facilities at Pyestock, near Farnborough, came into the picture for testing propulsion units such as ram jets. The role of an Elliott 405 computer in the online control and data analysis of the Pyestock engine-testing facilities is discussed in Chap. 7. Finally, Gardner drew attention to the need for a very large, preferably uninhabited, testing area and associated instrumentation for the live firing of long-range missiles. This is where Woomera in South Australia came into the picture, as discussed further in Sect. 4.5.

The need for missile simulation was not, of course, confined to the UK. In America, a group at the Massachusetts Institute of Technology (MIT) had set up the Dynamic Analysis and Control Laboratory in 1946, to begin work on a large analogue computer called the Flight Simulator [30, 31]. This became operational by 1948 and remained in use for the next 10 years. In about the same time-period as the Flight Simulator, two more large analogue computer projects called Cyclone and Typhoon were initiated in America [31]. None of these three machines was believed to have been as big as TRIDAC.

4.4.2 The TRIDAC Project and Borehamwood

Work on TRIDAC, which was at first called the *Three-dimensional Simulator*, began at Borehamwood in 1950, in collaboration with the Royal Aircraft Establishment (RAE). The first joint technical meeting between representatives from Elliotts and RAE was attended on Borehamwood's behalf by John F Coales (as Research Director), John Gale and Arthur Hemingway (from the Electrical Engineering Division) and S E (Ed) Hersom (from the Theory Division). Ed Hersom, who had some experience both of analogue and digital computing procedures, remembers [32] that: 'The proponent of the [analogue] electronics was W.R. Thomas (then at RAE). I suspect it [the TRIDAC project] was someone's idea of providing Elliott's with another contract to replace the now defunct MRS5. Thomas's original report [29] had an estimate of £20,002! I tried to maintain that a digital solution would be better but I was shot down in flames! JFC was curiously silent. I suspect he agreed with me but he badly needed the contract. I believe, moreover, that I was technically correct because I hear that the project ran to millions!'

Borehamwood's first Progress Report for the *Three-dimensional Simulator* project appeared in July 1950, to be followed by 25 more classified internal reports, the last one dated 1 June 1956. The pace of work increased in 1952, with the name TRIDAC coming into use in the spring of that year – (see the list of Borehamwood Research Reports given in the Bibliography). Towards the end of 1952, a new divisional structure was introduced at Borehamwood (see also Chap. 2), with Commander Henry Pasley-Tyler in overall charge. A Guided Weapons Division was formed, with W R Thomas as Divisional Manager, taking responsibility for the final technical specification of TRIDAC.

Before 1952, the early TRIDAC implementation at Borehamwood had largely taken place within the Electrical Engineering Division, headed by H M Gale, and especially within the *Light Servo* sub-group which was headed by Arthur Hemingway. When the contract for TRIDAC was formalised, Roy Hynes, who worked in the Electrical Engineering Division at Borehamwood from January 1948 to September 1954 before moving to Australia to join the Long Range Weapons Establishment, recalls that 'Hemingway became responsible for its overall design' [24]. Over 50 years later, it is difficult to derive a complete list of people who contributed to the TRIDAC project at Borehamwood. Until the spring of 1952, only Coales' name appeared as the author of the various TRIDAC internal research reports. After Coales left Borehamwood, the following names (in alphabetical order) appeared as authors:

C H (Hugh) Devonald (of the Theory Division)
H M Gale
R C Gold
R E (Ron) Hare
A V (Arthur) Hemingway
R W (Roy) Hynes
A J Ide
D J W Marsh
JCN (Jack) Nutter
A J (Albert) Wakefield (of the Theory Division)
G A White
P (Peter) Wilde

Roy Hynes remembers that Peter Atkinson, Cliff Lock and Carl Selig also played a part in the TRIDAC design process. Bill Pearse implies that he and Staff Ellis (an Australian) were involved with the design of a rate gyroscope assembly [26].

The Computing Division was also reorganised in 1953, with Andrew St. Johnston becoming the Divisional Manager (W S Elliott had left Borehamwood by May 1953, see Chap. 5). Andrew himself had taken no part in the design of TRIDAC but recalls [33] that Commander Pasley-Tyler 'used me as a hatchet man to get the other computing projects that had languished under the old regime to work properly.... I was also given TRIDAC to sort out and complete. TRIDAC was a massive analogue computer for the RAE Farnborough. It was intended both to simulate a missile's flight and also to test guidance heads in real time. To this end it had a large number of analogue amplifiers, but also several fast response hydraulically actuated platforms on which missile guidance components could be mounted. (These platforms were not, in the event, implemented, see below.)

'The TRIDAC team [at Borehamwood] had two good electronic engineers in the shape of Jack Nutter and his winger Ron Hare, but the project needed more hands, more brains and more project management. I hauled in a number of my digital team including Albert Wakefield who was the only mathematician apart from Ed Hersom who could do the analogue mathematics. I took him off the 153 and put Dina Vaughan who was in Norman Hill's department on to the 153 – [see also Chap. 3]. Norman Muchmore helped in the power supplies, Berwick Stallworthy produced an analogue recorder which was required but hadn't even been started. John Halsey did his normal invaluable managing and rushing around role.

'Tony Jefferies was my right hand man. His first action was to close all the existing TRIDAC Research Orders (ROs) at Borehamwood, to which people booked their time. All over the [Borehamwood] plant there were cries of 'You've closed my RO' to which the question was 'what part of TRIDAC are you working on?' The answer was, only too often, 'what's TRIDAC?' There were rather a lot of 'home jobs' going on at that time'.

Like many pioneers trying to recall events that had taken place almost 50 years earlier, Andrew St. Johnston's memories do not give the full story. Roy Hynes [24] commented after St. Johnston's death that, by 1953, 'the development of TRIDAC was virtually complete and I don't think that it should be thought that anything needed to be "sorted out" then.... Although Wakefield's contribution was very much appreciated I don't think the comment that "he was the only one who could do the analogue mathematics" is warranted. ...However, in 1953 there must have been at least two things that needed to be completed: (1) The installation of the equipment at RAE, and (2) the establishment of methods and procedures for setting up actual Guided Weapons problems on TRIDAC. The first of these tasks was taking up the full-time efforts of Jack Nutter and Ron Hare. This must have presented a number of problems if only because of the computer's large size. For the second task, Albert Wakefield and I made a first attempt as reported in our paper on test problems [34]. To actually set up these problems, would again require Jack Nutter's services. I had left Borehamwood before this was done. Perhaps it was these things that Andrew referred to that needed to be "sorted out"'.

4.4.3   TRIDAC at RAE Farnborough

According to the definitive account [3], the construction of the Three-Dimensional Analogue Computer TRIDAC and its installation at the Royal Aircraft Establishment was completed in 1954. However, it appears not to have become fully operational until about 1956. The primary use of the computer was the real-time simulation of two independent three-axis vehicles, typically a guided missile attacking an incoming target. This was a topic of more than academic interest at this stage in the Cold War.

TRIDAC occupied a large building at RAE (see Figs. 4.7 and 4.8) and cost £750,000 in 1954. To quote from the introduction to the definitive paper [3], 'TRIDAC ... has been built to assist in solving guided-weapons problems, has electronic, mechanical and hydraulic components, and operates on a 1:1 timescale so that real components can be included in the computation. TRIDAC is intended to assist system understanding and development by constructing system models with which mathematical computations can be carried out. Each computing section, the parameters of which can be easily changed, represents a particular part of the real system. The mathematical operations of summation, integration, multiplication and resolution are carried out using either drift-corrected dc amplifiers or electrically controlled servo motors, with hydraulic or electric power. Connections to the

Fig. 4.7 Arthur Hemingway, shown on the right, was the first engineer to arrive at the Borehamwood Laboratories in October 1946. He headed the *Light Servo Group* within the Electrical Engineering Division and became the leader within Elliotts of the TRIDAC project. The photo shows him discussing a model of the buildings in which TRIDAC was installed in 1954

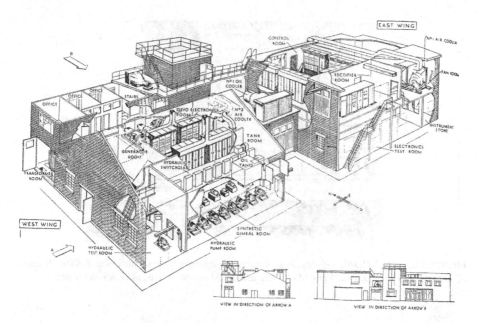

Fig. 4.8 The initial specification for TRIDAC came from the Royal Aircraft Establishment (RAE), Farnborough. The photo shows how TRIDAC's electronic and hydraulic equipment was distributed throughout a group of buildings at RAE

servo motors and interconnections between the various cabinets, which contain some 2,000 electronic units, are arranged to facilitate the simulation of the flight of a guided missile.'

The real-time, three-dimensional flight problems, which involved six degrees of freedom and included aerodynamic cross-coupling effects, kinematic couplings and control and guidance cross-couplings, were of such complexity that contemporary conventional analogue or digital computers were totally inadequate for the task. An exceptionally large analogue computer was the only answer. The Americans were developing three such machines, as mentioned earlier. TRIDAC was the British response to the challenge.

The critical issue faced by the TRIDAC team at RAE and Borehamwood was the design of a directly coupled (dc) electronic amplifier with good long-term stability. In TRIDAC, each high-gain (factor of 60,000) dc amplifier was coupled to an ac amplifier which provided the drift correction, the ac amplifier being provided either with a relay chopper or with a magnetic modulator. The resulting ac/dc combination achieved accuracies to within 0.1%. The features that made the TRIDAC amplifier so special were its very high input impedance, its extraordinarily high gain, its very low output impedance, and its freedom from drift resulting from input chopper stabilisation. The electronics was mounted in standard plug-in units measuring $12 \times 8 \times 3$ in.^{3} (approximately $30 \times 20 \times 8$ cm^3), of which TRIDAC contained a total of about 2,000. A set of up to 224 such plug-in units was assembled into

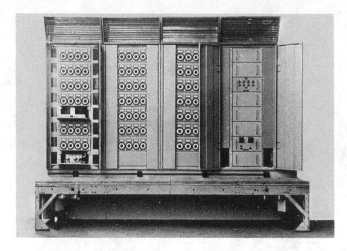

Fig. 4.9 Critical to TRIDAC's success as an analogue computer was the stability of its 2,000 high-gain dc amplifiers. Sets of up to 224 amplifiers were assembled into steel rafts, as shown in the photo

Fig. 4.10 This is the rear view side of the raft shown in Fig. 4.9. Eleven such rafts housed the analogue amplifiers in TRIDAC

a steel structure called a *raft*, there being 11 such rafts in the complete computer (see Figs. 4.9 and 4.10). On the front panel of each raft were coefficient potentiometers, patchboards and monitoring equipment.

TRIDAC's electronics, totalling about 8,000 thermionic valves (tubes) was complemented by nine hydraulic servomechanisms, having oil delivered at two pressures: 250 lb/in.^{2} and 2,000 lb/in.^{2}. The high-pressure oil system, which took up a large amount of space in the computer building, allowed the servomechanisms to respond rapidly enough for TRIDAC to simulate missile responses up to a frequency of 100 Hz. The entire computer consumed a peak power of 600 kW, of which 200 kW was dissipated in the electronic units and 400 kW in the hydraulics. Output from TRIDAC was via multi-channel recorders and plotting tables.

It was originally intended that TRIDAC's hydraulic servos should be used to drive an actual gimbal system on which Guided Weapons components could be mounted for test purposes [24]. However, consideration of weight and power requirements to meet the expected angular accelerations eventually ruled this out and a four-axis synthetic gimbal system was developed using four of the servos in which the four axes are physically separate. This was for the computation of axis resolution and multiplication only; there was no platform on which guided weapons (GW) components could be mounted. It is believed that, after TRIDAC was made operational, RAE developed a Single Axis Flight Table which was installed on the roof [24].

TRIDAC has been described as 'probably the world's most ambitious analogue computer project' [35] and as 'the largest analogue computer in the world' [36]. Certainly, TRIDAC's total of 8,000 thermionic valves is about twice the number in Typhoon, which was said to be the largest analogue computing facility in America in 1952 [31]. Because of 'engineering problems and the sheer size of the machine' TRIDAC did not become operational until early in 1956 [35]. Was it a success? Simulations on TRIDAC contributed generally to the UK's missile technology and saved a great deal of money by reducing the need for live test firings. TRIDAC, and its derivative AGWAC (see below) 'saved many thousands of pounds and their introduction marked a turning point in the testing of expensive rocketry [for example the UK's *Blue Streak* ballistic missile] and, ultimately, in the testing of many other things as well' [35]. Although Blue Streak was eventually cancelled as a weapons-delivery system in April 1960, it was used briefly for civil satellite launching for the European Launcher Development Organisation (ELDO). Blue Streak was the first stage of ELDO's Europa launcher, which had its maiden flight at the Woomera site in June 1964. Of the many shorter-range guided missiles to be developed with the aid of TRIDAC, amongst the more successful were the ground-to-air *Heathen* (which led to *Bloodhound* and *Thunderbird*) and several ship-to-air missiles such as *Sea Cat* and *Seaslug*.

In about 1965 RAE is believed to have replaced much of TRIDAC's simulation capabilities with two large analogue/hybrid computer systems manufactured by Redifon-Astrodata Ltd. [31] However, these did not meet RAE's operational requirements and so in 1967 RAE sold both of the analogue/hybrid systems and bought two AD4 analogue computers manufactured by the American company Applied Dynamics Inc. The AD4 system remained in use until 1982 [31]. By that time digital computing had gained undisputed prominence across the whole of the aerospace field. The younger generation of Mathematical Services staff at RAE even described the original TRIDAC as "a bit of a joke" [37] – but nobody had been laughing in 1950.

Fig. 4.11 TRIDAC's control room. The entire complex was understandably described as 'the biggest computer in the world'. It cost £750,000 in 1954

4.5 AGWAC: An Australian Success

4.5.1 The Joint Project Background

There is a long history of scientific co-operation between Australia and Britain, fuelled particularly by initiatives such as the Anglo–Australian Long Range Weapons Organisation (LRWO) Joint Project, which came into formal being on 1 April 1947 and lasted until 1980 [38]. The Joint Project was the main recommendation of the Ministry of Supply's 1946 Evetts Mission to Australia, led by Lt. Gen. J F Evetts. The Mission team had included an Admiralty scientist named H C Calpine, a fact that may have had some subsequent significance for Elliotts: John Coales and Calpine had been close colleagues at ASE since 1937 and had been joint authors of the 1946 post-war paper describing naval fire-control radar [39]. Calpine had also visited Coales at Borehamwood in 1947.

The physical embodiment of the Joint Project was the Woomera rocket-testing site in the South Australian desert and the Long Range Weapons Establishment. The latter, known from 1955 as the Weapons Research Establishment (WRE), was located in Salisbury, near Adelaide in South Australia. Salisbury lies about 20 km north of Adelaide – (see Fig. 3.10). Woomera itself is about 430 km NNW of Adelaide. Woomera is still the largest land-based test range in the world, equivalent in area to England [38].

Fig. 4.12 AGWAC, the Australian Guided Weapons Analogue Computer, started off as a smaller version of TRIDAC. Nevertheless, it still weighed 32 t! It was installed at Salisbury, South Australia, at the end of 1954 and was enhanced over the next few years. AGWAC had a long and successful life, finally being dismantled at the end of the 1960s

Throughout the life of the Joint Project there was interchange of personnel, know-how and equipment between LRWE and the UK's relevant MoS establishments such as RAE, TRE, RRDE, the Aberporth range in Wales and the Orfordness range in Suffolk. On the Australian side, the Joint Project touched the lives of many eminent scientists and engineers, not least of whom was the computer pioneer Trevor Pearcey (1919–1998) whose CSIR Mark I digital computer first ran a program in Australia in November 1949 [40] as mentioned in Chap. 3. Of more relevance to Borehamwood's analogue activities was John P (Jack) Lonergan who, amongst other things, went on to hold the post of Superintending Research Scientist at the Australian Department of Defence.

As far as Lewisham was concerned, a modest technical relationship between Elliotts and Australia had been formed in 1948. In that year the specification was issued for a small jet-propelled, unmanned target aircraft, the *Jindivik*, to be designed (with RAE input) and built in Australia. A revised version of the Elliott Type A autopilot was developed at Lewisham for *Jindivik* [41]. The first successful flight of the unmanned *Jindivik* was at the LRWO's Woomera range in August 1952. The Aeronautical Research Labs (ARL) located at Fishermans Bend in Melbourne was also involved in the Jindivik project. Jindiviks have certainly proved their worth and are still believed to be in service.

Staff at RAE, Borehamwood, Woomera and Salisbury were in contact with each other during the development phase of TRIDAC [35]. Many Australian scientists had spent time at RAE and it was natural for the Australians to be interested in acquiring powerful computing facilities for themselves, for missile simulation and flight-data analysis. This included the later requirement for a digital computer, the Elliott 403 computer (WREDAC), as described in Chap. 3.

4.5.2   The Birth of AGWAC

On the analogue side, a smaller simulator based on TRIDAC technology and called AGWAC (Australian Guided Weapons Analogue Computer) was felt to be desirable. In the autumn of 1952, J P (Jack) Lonergan and E G (Ted) Hayman, two Australians attached to the simulators group at RAE, drew up a preliminary specification for AGWAC [35]. Elliott's TRIDAC contract was eventually extended to provide for the bulk of the AGWAC hardware. Jack Lonergan remembers the events surrounding AGWAC's birth as follows [42].

> 'I was working at the RAE from late 1951 till early 1954. I had been sent there from the then Long Range Weapons Establishment, Salisbury, South Australia (later the Weapons Research Establishment, WRE) to study guided weapon technology and in particular their simulation. Whilst at RAE I had a lot of interaction with Eggy Burt and Jack Gait (who were masterminding the conceptual design of TRIDAC) and with Elliott Brothers' people, especially W R Thomas, the Manager of the Borehamwood Guided Weapons Division and Ken Simmonds who was the Elliott Chief Engineer covering Lewisham and the satellite factory at the Chatham Works near Rochester Airport.

> 'When the UK decided that LRWE Salisbury should have a weapons simulator they first asked Elliotts to design and construct it. Elliotts at Borehamwood decided that they were too overloaded to take the job on in the foreseeable future. However, Ken Simmonds at Lewisham offered to plug the gap on two conditions: (i) that I be formally appointed as Design Authority who would be responsible for all the conceptual design of the simulator, and (ii) his task would be to engineer hardware to my design, with no responsibility for its working later as a simulator. I found myself working for a time at Lewisham and later at Elliott's Rochester site.

> 'A considerable amount of dust then went up into the air with the UK MOD and its Australian counterpart engulfed underneath. Surprisingly it took only a relatively short time for the air to clear, and AGWAC came into being under Simmonds' proposal. AGWAC went on to be a great success in LRWE/WRE'.

Lonergan remembers that 'Construction and its supervision went ahead very smoothly, largely facilitated by Elliott goodwill and the empathy that developed between Simmonds and his works manager, Phil Keeble on the one hand and myself on the other.' Elliotts had committed themselves to finishing the construction of all AGWAC hardware by March 1954 and they were as good as their word. Their final administrative act was to hold a farewell dinner at Oddenino's Hotel in Regent St., London, chaired by Dr. Ross, the Elliott's Technical Director, with Jack Lonergan as the guest of honour.

Units for AGWAC began to be assembled in Australia towards the end of 1954. To quote [43]: 'The over 12,500 components of AGWAC weighed more than 32 tons, and arrived in Australia by sea and air in the first half of 1954. On arrival, the computer was first installed [at Salisbury] in Building 77, Labs Area, and was incorporated into the Flight Research Division. Its introduction prompted the renaming of the Flight Research Division to the Systems Assessment Division which "began developing and validating mathematical models of weapons systems as part of the Australian contribution to the Joint Project". AGWAC's ability to simulate missile firing was both cost and time efficient. AGWAC allowed laboratory studies of the simulated missile, reducing the use of missile firing at Woomera. This saved both time and money although actual firings were still needed to validate laboratory findings. The development of this computer technology helped process the large amounts of data compiled during tests and trials (*Blue Jay, Bloodhound, Thunderbird, Rapier*) and thus was a vital tool for DSTO [Defence Science and Technology Organisation]'.

According to [35], by April 1955 'AGWAC had been in operation for about three months'. It was immediately successful, 'unlike the Elliott WREDAC digital computer, which was got working only with difficulty and not for some time after installation'. Besides having fewer operational amplifiers than TRIDAC, totalling somewhat over 1,000 thermionic valves (tubes) instead of TRIDAC's total of 8,000, WRE designed their own choppers based on a modification of simple tungsten vibrators used in commercially available car radios. This gave a cost-saving of about 30 times, compared with the more expensive RAE-designed choppers used in TRIDAC. More significantly in respect of cost and physical size, AGWAC did not have hydraulic servos. However, WRE found that their own electrically powered servos could respond to perhaps 10 Hz, which proved adequate for most simulations.

On 10 October 1954, *The Kent Messenger* carried a story about both TRIDAC and AGWAC with the headline: 'Kent-made robot brain for rocket experiments'. The article included comment about Elliott's Rochester factory, where some of the electronics was being assembled. This was causing Elliotts to take on relatively unskilled labour in a factory that had, up to that point, been noted more for its skilled mechanical workshops. The training opportunities thus created were clearly of benefit to the locality. Turning to more specific comment, in the opinion of the Australian rocket scientist Alex Biggs 'The Elliott-built mechanical servomechanism computing elements which were used in both AGWAC and TRIDAC were, at their best, superb examples of the metal machinist's art' [35].

4.5.3 AGWAC Grows Up

In Australia, AGWAC was extended over the next few years, firstly with a WREDAC to AGWAC converter to enable digital trials data to be converted into analogue voltages. By 1958, 'AGWAC's original 95 drift-corrected amplifiers, of which 21 could be used for integration, had in addition, 20 single product high speed electronic multipliers, five general purpose servo multipliers with 106 associated amplifiers, five electro-mechanical sin-cosine resolvers with 96 amplifiers and additional power supplies, automatic sequencing equipment and the WAC Mk. 2 Digital to Analogue Converter' [35].

More details of the life of this analogue computer are given in [43]: 'Major expansions were carried out on AGWAC: one being completed by 1958 and the other commencing around the end of 1961 for the Bloodhound Mk. 2 work. As W.R. Dickson noted in April 1979, 'In its final form [after this last update], the computer had more than 450 computing amplifiers, 52 electronic multipliers, and extensive servo-multipliers and servo-resolver equipment. It also had sophisticated control equipment and very comprehensive input and output peripheral equipment, including IDAC Mk. 2, a 24-channel digital to analogue converter.'

AGWAC also eventually contained more than one Co-ordinate Converter [43]. As Bob Arstall noted in 1992:

'It is a co-ordinate converter which, in analogue form, did the trigonometric sums which are needed to translate from missile axis to earth axis and suchlike simultaneously in three dimensions, a comparatively trivial task in this era of digital computing, but quite a problem then. There were a number of these converters in AGWAC, mounted on a large rack. The drive motors were controlled by servoamplifiers which have unfortunately now long since gone to salvage. This portion of the huge complex was quite significant and illustrated well the peak of analogue ingenuity which was reached at that time'.

AGWAC was dismantled towards the end of the 1960s.

Returning for a moment to the digital computing scene, WREDAC (aka the Elliott 403) was delivered to WRE, Salisbury, in the autumn of 1955 and started handling data from the Woomera range about a year later (see Chap. 3). It was replaced by a magnetic tape-based IBM 7090/1401 combination in 1961 or 1962. At this point, however, digital computers were still not fast enough for the WRE scientists. Alex Biggs remembers [35] that 'Although we were not so sure about it at the time, we were about to enter the age of digital simulation. The IBM 7090 computer acquired in 1961 was 70 times faster than WREDAC. However, it was still much slower than AGWAC which simulated missiles in real time. We could live with computations performed at up to ten times real time, but not much slower. Initial estimates of computing speed and problem size placed us tantalizingly close to this goal.'

Given the classified nature of AGWAC's applications, the successful development and use of analogue techniques in Australia has, perhaps inevitably, faded into an unremarked corner of conventional computer history. This is a pity because, in the long run, AGWAC appears to have made a bigger contribution to the field than did TRIDAC. There must therefore have been justifiable satisfaction at WRE from 3rd to 8th June 1957, when a conference on Data Processing and Automatic Computing Machines was held at WRE. Both AGWAC and WREDAC and their associated equipment were demonstrated to about 300 visitors. Amongst the visitors were people from universities and government establishments in England.

British digital computer pioneers attending the associated May 1957 Australian Computer Conference included M V Wilkes and A S Douglas (Cambridge), T Kilburn and J C West (Manchester) and J H Wilkinson (NPL) – all travelling courtesy of the Ministry of Supply.

4.6   Elliott Analogue Computers and Simulators for Nuclear Power

In about 1953, Maurice Needham moved from Borehamwood, where he had been working on the CDS project (see Chap. 2), to be Head of Elliott's Nuclear Instrumentation Division at Lewisham. The formation of this Division was the suggestion of Dr. Lotti Ross. Their initial contract was to provide instrumentation for the UK's first nuclear submarine, HMS Dreadnought. The work took place before digital technology had been applied to this type of measurement and control application. Maurice Needham's team used analogue techniques and, at first, magnetic amplifiers. Magnetic amplifiers or *transductors*, a development of the dc-controlled ac inductance, were not new: they had been in use for motor control and lighting control for many years. By the end of the 1940s, Elliott Brothers had accumulated considerable expertise in magnetic amplifier design [44]. Compared with the newer electronic amplifiers based on thermionic valves (tubes), magnetic amplifiers of the 1950s were generally bulkier and had a very limited frequency response. However, they were high-gain devices that allowed electrical isolation between input and output. Of greater significance for nuclear submarine applications, magnetic amplifiers were much more reliable and robust than electronic ones.

Maurice Needham's Division at Lewisham eventually became Elliott's Nucleonics Division and went on to design and supply equipment for nuclear power stations. For this, there was a requirement to devise analogue computers specifically tailored to deal with reactor kinetics.

A contemporary article and a brochure [45, 46] describe what Elliott called their Nuclear Reactor Computers and Simulators, both devices being analogue computers intended for reactor control purposes. The Elliott ND111 analogue computer, completed in about 1957 and shown in Fig. 4.13, comprised seven cabinets of electronics. One of the cabinets simulated the six basic reactor kinetics equations, with adjustable preset controls for inputting the coefficients of the particular fissile material being studied. Step changes in reactivity, as well as changes in factors such as poisoning, etc., could be inserted. The remaining six cabinets simulated the surrounding power-station equipment such as heat exchangers, turbines and alternators.

The ND111 analogue computer was built upon the experience of TRIDAC and AGWAC. The DC amplifier unit, a re-design of earlier Elliott ones, used *Synchroverter* choppers manufactured under licence from the Bristol Company of Waterbury, Connecticut, with whom Elliotts had developed an agreement in 1954. Multiplication in the ND111 was performed by plug-in servo-multipliers, each capable of multiplying up to five quantities.

As stated in the company brochure [46], 'The Nuclear Division of Elliott Brothers (London) Limited, in studying the design of instrumentation for both research and power station reactors, has developed analogue computing techniques for simulation of the many mathematical relationships involved. This is probably the fastest method available for determining the overall design requirements of a system, and for assessing the effects of individual features of a design on the performance of the complete system.'

Fig. 4.13 The Elliott ND111 analogue computer, completed in about 1957, was used to simulate the operation of nuclear power stations. Several ND111 computers were delivered to customers

Maurice Needham recalls [47] that several of the ND111 analogue computers were delivered to external customers. 'The first was for GEC Simon-Carves Ltd who were in the nuclear reactor business at that time. Others went to Imperial College and to Birmingham University. The designs were originated by A Ross Cameron, who joined me in the Nuclear Division. Later Jack Nutter joined my team and obviously brought great analogue computing experience with him.' Ross Cameron authored an article jointly with a member of the Simon-Carves Atomic Energy Group that mentions Elliott's nuclear reactor computers and simulators [48].

4.7   Small Analogue Computers: GPAC

From about 1954, Elliott Brothers produced a range of relatively small general-purpose analogue computers called GPAC. The amplifier design was a cheaper version of the one used for TRIDAC. For GPAC, a simplified chopper function was employed based on an oscillating post-office relay. There were two main versions of GPAC: 20- or 40-amplifier varieties. The need for, and subsequent use of, GPAC mainly arose from Borehamwood's early excursions into the field of stability and control of military aircraft. It is not known how many GPACs were delivered to external customers but GPACs were certainly well-used for aerospace calculations within the Elliott company for about 10 years (Fig. 4.14).

Peter Chinn, who joined the Guided Weapons Division at Borehamwood in 1956, remembers [49] that 'my first computer was a G-PAC analogue computer. It was a set of half a dozen or thereabouts bays – probably 19-inch racks, and I guess the minimum kit was one bay. Above desk height there were rows of chopper-corrected high gain DC amps – four rows of 5, I think … Across the front were plug-in panels

Fig. 4.14 The Elliott GPAC analogue computer, in its basic form, was a 20-amplifier general-purpose machine of modest cost that first appeared in about 1954

with slots to plug in input resistors and feedback resistors and capacitors, plus lots of facility for cross links…. It was really quite a good machine, if a mite twitchy, and needed a team of two or three guys full time to "mend" amplifiers. The G-PAC(s) represented the total computing capacity for the systems study and trials analysis teams for *Caravan*, which was the homing head which flew from Aberporth in the Short Brothers GPV trial missile.'

GPACs lasted about 10 years at Borehamwood. Early in the 1960s, Elliott's Guided Weapons Division moved to Frimley, about 25 miles south-west of London. Ron Howard [50] remembers that by the mid-1960s 'the American PACE computer had become the world leader for aviation systems development and one was acquired at Rochester for all subsequent Elliott-Automation work'.

This is a good place to say a little more about Elliott's use of GPAC for aircraft calculations, because this provides an analogue perspective that usefully augments the account of digital airborne computers given in Chap. 12. What follows is based on Ron Howard's memoirs, as recounted in [50, 51]. Further comments on flight automation will be found in Appendix 9.

After working on 3-axis electro-hydraulic systems in the UK RTV1 (Research Test Vehicle 1) beam-riding missile at Woomera (Australia) and Aberporth (Wales),

Fig. 4.15 GPAC analogue computers formed the basis for the simulation facilities available in the Guided Weapons Division at Borehamwood, as shown in this 1958 photo. Enhanced GPAC systems performed useful work until at least the mid-1960s

Ron Howard joined the Aviation Division at Borehamwood in October 1954. Shortly after he arrived, he was asked by Jack Pateman to configure the first GPAC analogue computer for stability and control studies for a Mach 2 Interceptor, which was to become the English Electric P1, or Lightning, fighter aircraft. The task was to set up an analogue simulation based on partial differential equations covering the short-period auto-stabilisation of the pitch, roll and yaw axes for the aircraft. Since the 20-amplifier GPAC had limited facilities based on the operations of addition and integration only, the equations had to be simplified and answers derived for groups of a few equations at a time. The computing procedure was to insert an artificial gust of wind as a disturbance and then record on a pen recorder or an oscilloscope the effect on the output variables being studied. Adjustments could then be made to the auto-control loop gains to get the desired performance and stability of the aircraft. Besides Ron Howard, other Borehamwood staff involved in this activity included Eric Priestley and Tony Richards.

   Although relatively simple compared to the TRIDAC or AGWAC missile calculations, the Lightning calculations became the first significant analogue programming activity to have been undertaken in-house at Borehamwood. Ron Howard remembers that Andrew St. Johnston often came to the Aviation Division's laboratory with visitors, to demonstrate the company's application of GPAC to real-world problems. Andrew St. Johnston recalls [33] that 'The TRIDAC work did allow us to start a business selling small analogue computers [GPAC] mostly to Government Departments.'

Ron Howard believes that the prototype GPAC computer was pensioned off in about 1957, to be replaced by a 40-amplifier GPAC equipped with precision potentiometers with geared rotary scales. This computer was coupled to an actual aircraft in a hangar at English Electric's Warton factory so as to close autostabiliser control loops – the first time such total system simulation activity had been attempted at Warton. The 40-amplifier GPAC was also used for autopilot simulation work. It was transported to a Rolls-Royce engine test bed at Derby to operate the Lightning automatic throttle on an actual Avon engine at simulated approach speeds where the relationship between thrust and airspeed was variable due to non-linear engine rpm and fuel burn characteristics. This GPAC then went on to become the core of the simulator design and testing for the Vickers VC10 airliner, the testing process continuing until automatic landing was certificated in early 1967. The success of the Elliott analogue computer for the Lightning and VC-10 projects led to the establishment of a full 3-axis rig for the TSR 2 fighter project, including control surface loading, a big step in ground simulation. This activity was entrusted to Elliott, as the flight control system suppliers for TSR 2, and took place at Rochester. The TSR 2 simulations used a later twin cabinet version of GPAC with integrated overhead potentiometer setting panels. The TSR 2 contract was cancelled in 1965 – marking the effective end of GPAC's life within the Elliott-Automation organisation.

Fig. 4.16 Units of an analogue automatic flight control system, inserted in a Flight Laboratory ground test development rig in about 1957–1958. The units in the photo with black handles come from either a Lightning or a Buccaneer fighter. Within a unit, the small black rectangular boxes with labels are magnetic amplifiers. The two separate black boxes with connectors, opposite the engineer's knees, are gyro units

References

1. Scott WE, Haley ACD (Oct 1954) Some comparisons between analogue and digital computers. J Br IRE 14:476–486
2. RW (Ron) Howard (2006) E-mail to Simon Lavington dated 14 Nov 2006
3. Spearman FRJ, Gair JJ, Hemingway AV, Hynes RW (1956) TRIDAC, a large analogue computing machine. Proc IEE 103B:375–395
4. DBG (Dai) Edwards (2007) E-mail to Simon Lavington dated 2 Nov 2007
5. Anon (1937) A century of progress, 1800–1937. Publicity booklet produced by Elliott Brothers (London) Ltd.
6. Padfield P (1973) Guns at sea. Hugh Elvelyn Ltd., London
7. Brooks J (2001) The Admiralty Fire Control Tables. Warship, 2002–2003, pp 69–93. See also: Fire control for British dreadnoughts: choices of technology and supply. Brooks J (2001) Ph.D. thesis, Department of war studies, King's College, London
8. Bromley A (1984) British mechanical gunnery computers of World War II, University of Sydney, Basser Department of Computer Science, Technical Report number 223. Jan 1984. ISBN: 0 909789 63 X
9. Mourice Needham (2007) E-mail dated 18 Nov 2007 to Simon Lavington
10. Wingate J (1971) HMS Belfast. Profile Publications, Windsor, Berkshire. ISBN 085 3850835
11. Gardner GWH (1955) Guided missiles. Proc Inst Mech Eng 169:30–40
12. DiGiulian T. The British High Angle Control System (HACS). http://www.navweaps.com/index_tech/tech-066.htm
13. (a) Clymer AB (1933) The mechanical analogue computers of Hannibal Ford and William Newell. IEEE Ann Hist Comput 15(2):19–34. http://web.mit.edu/STS.035/www/PDFs/Newell.pdf (b). See also the web-based Analog Computer Museum and History Center. http://dcoward.best.vwh.net/analog/ford.htm
14. The National Archive, file ADM 234/680: Flyplane Predictor System Mk 5: user handbook 1953–1958. BR 1644(1), first issued May 1953
15. The National Archive, file ADM 234/148: Fire control drill for flyplane system Mark 3, 1955–1961. This practical manual, originally BR779, was first issued in Nov 1955
16. Australian National Archives, file MP981/1: HMAS TOBRUK – Flyplane control system Mark 2 – Summary of progress report. Contents date range: 1949–1950.
17. ND (Norman) Hill (1995) A personal account of the early history of Elliott Brothers research laboratories. 6-page typed manuscript and accompanying letter to Laurence Clarke, dated 9 May 1995
18. Ashdown GL, Selig KL (Sept 1951) A general purpose differential analyser: part I, description of machine. Elliott J 1(2):44–48
19. Bush V, Hazen HL (1927) Integraph solution of differential equations. J Franklin Inst 204:575
20. John Brooks (2002) E-mail to Simon Lavington, dated 21 Mar 2002
21. Hersom SE, Selig KL (July 1952) A general purpose differential analyzer: part II, application of machine. Elliott J 1(3):76–80
22. Selig KL (1951) The Elliott differential analyzer. Borehamwood Internal Research report 226, 24 Feb 1951
23. Selig KL (Mar 1951) A photo-electric curve follower. Elliott J 1(1):25
24. RW (Roy) Hynes (2008) Series of e-mails to Simon Lavington in Mar 2008
25. Anon (Sept 1951) Elliott exhibits at the Festival of Britain. Elliott J 1(2):67
26. WH (Bill) Pearse (1995) Letter to Laurence Clarke, dated 9 Oct 1995
27. Chalmers M (1985) Paying for defence – military spending and British decline. Pluto Press, London
28. Dommett R. The Blue Streak Weapon. http://brohp.org.uk/downloads/prospero2_article.pdf
29. Thomas WR (1949) A design for a three-dimensional simulator for guided missiles. Technical note GW 52, Oct 1949. RAE reference GW/S.100A/WRT/55. Thanks are due to Geoffrey

Rowlands, of the Farnborough Air Sciences Trust, for identifying and obtaining a copy of this report in Aug 2009

30. Hall AC (1950) A generalized analogue computer for flight simulation. Trans Am IEE 69:308–320

31. Small JS (2001) The Analogue Alternative – the electronic analogue computer in Britain and the USA, 1930–1975. Routledge. ISBN: 0-415-27119-3. See also: Stout TM, Williams TJ (1995) Pioneering work in the field of computer process control. IEEE Ann Hist Comput 17(1):6–18

32. SE Hersom (2001) E-mail to Simon Lavington, dated 17 Nov 2001

33. Andrew St Johnston (1995) History of the Research Laboratories of Elliott Brothers (London) Ltd.: Andrew St. Johnston's Contribution. Typed manuscript sent to Laurence Clarke on 31 May 1995 (eight pages)

34. Hynes RW, Wakefield AJ (1953) Test problems for Tridac on beam-riding and homing missiles. Borehamwood internal research report number 315, dated 27 May 1953 and classified as 'Secret'

35. Polomka BJ, Bigg A. Guided weapons: the development of mathematical models and computer simulations in Australia. National Library of Australia archive: http://purl.nla.gov.au/nla/pandora/guided) See also http://members.iinet.net.au/~alexandergbiggs/histpt2.html and http://members.iinet.net.au/~alexandergbiggs/histpt3.html

36. Arthur V Hemingway (1995) Elliott Brothers research labs – notes. Eight-page handwritten anecdotes, sent to Laurence Clarke on 2 Nov 1995

37. John Barrett (2002) E-mail to S H Lavington, dated 23 Oct 2002. John had worked at RAE Farnborough

38. Morton P (1989) Fire Across the Desert: Woomera and the Anglo-Australian Joint Project 1946–1980. Australian Government Publishing Service, Canberra, 1989. (For AGWAC, see especially pages. 200, 379 and 380). See also: http://www.woomera.com.au/history.htm

39. Coales JF, Calpine HC, Watson DS (1946) Naval fire-control radar. J IEE 93, part IIIA (Radiolocation)(2):349–379

40. McCann D, Thorne P (2000) The last of the first: CSIRAC, Australia's first computer. Department of Computer Science and Software Engineering, University of Melbourne, 176 pages. ISBN: 0 7340 2024 4

41. Anon (1992) Elliott Flight Automation Limited: a brief history. This 30-page typed document gives varying degrees of coverage for period 1948 to 1985, with some staff listings to 1992. H R (Ron) Bristow, who has a long-standing interest in the history of the Elliott company (see below), provided the following further information on the provenance in an e-mail to Simon Lavington in March 2007. "It is an updated version of the document 'Elliott Flight Automation History' by David Broadbent which, in 1970, had the Elliott Archive catalogue number 1004/10/1. Broadbent was a senior engineer and manager in Elliott Brothers (London) Ltd., and in particular in Elliott Flight Automation, for many years in the 1950s and 1960s. After his death, Broadbent's notes were added to by C.R Reese, an engineer and manager in Elliott Flight Automation from about 1955 to 1993, using press releases and company announcements". The document is now part of the Marconi Archives at the Bodleian Library, Oxford, for which the cataloguing process was still in progress in 2007

42. JP (Jack) Lonergan (2008) E-mail to Simon Lavington dated 29/1/08. As at March 2008, Jack Lonergan was preparing an illustrated article on AGWAC for the Defence Science and Technology Organsiation's website. The ten-page draft manuscript was sent to Simon Lavington on 3 Mar 2008

43. Information from the Australian Archives of the DSTO (Defence Science and Technology Organisation) in the State Library of Victoria, as quoted by Andy Moffatt in an e-mail dated 21 May 2007 to Ron Howard. This e-mail also contains the following eight relevant references: (a) Arstall B (1992) Internal minute, Co-ordinate Converter – Ex AGWAC, Serial No. 1, Electronic Warfare Division, 15 July 1992, typewritten (including three Polaroid photographs of converter). (b) Department of Defence, 'General Matters Associated with the DRCS Historical Collection Committee', Edinburgh, A5728/7/1, Part 1, Folio 26. (c) Department of

Defence, DRC Salisbury, 'Items not considered worth preserving for the DRCS Historical Collection', A5728/7/5, Folio 3, 27 April 1979. (d) Department of Supply, Progress Reports: 1952/53, January–June 1957, January-June 1958, D3703/1, Box 2, National Archives (but stored at Edinburgh). (e) Dunne LJ, Parkhill S (June 1963) Department of Supply, The Extended and Modernised Analogue Computing Facilities at W.R.E., Adelaide, p 4. (f) Lonergan JP (Feb 1958) Department of Supply, Weapons Research Establishment, Design Principles for a General Purpose Axis Transformation Unit for AGWAC, Salisbury, 35 pp. (g) Lawrence TFC, Hayman EG, Benyon PR (Sept 1961) Use of a mathematical model in the evaluation of guided missile performance. J I. E. Aust. (h) Beltrame GE, Biggs AG, Benyon PR, Possingham ML (April 1972) Systems simulation: the development of computer models to evaluate weapon system performance. Electrical Eng Trans, I.E. Aust

44. Gale HM (Mar 1951) Magnetic amplifiers and their application to industrial purposes. Elliott J 1(1):11–15
45. Cameron R, Austin DA (1957) An electronic reactor simulator. Nucl Power 2:146–51
46. Anon (1958) Elliott nuclear reactor computers and simulators. Brochure ND1, Elliott Nuclear Division, Lewisham. (Undated but probably about 1958)
47. Maurice Needham (2007) E-mail dated 30 Nov 2007 to Simon Lavington
48. Cameron R, Austin DA (Apr 1957) An electronic reactor simulator. Nucl Power 2:146–151
49. Peter Chin (2002) Letter to Terry Froggatt, dated 4 Jan 2002
50. RW (Ron) Howard (2005) Elliott analogue computers in aviation. Manuscript of four typed pages, written on 16 May 2005. Copy e-mailed to Simon Lavington on 8 Dec 2005 by H R (Ron) Bristow
51. RW Howard (2007) E-mail of 18 May 2007 to Ron Bristow, forwarded to Simon Lavington in May 2007

Chapter 5
NRDC and the Market

5.1 NRDC Discovers Borehamwood

The National Research Development Corporation (NRDC) was set up in July 1949 to encourage the commercial exploitation of the flood of British ideas that had emerged during and after the Second World War. Fortunately, the early NRDC documents have been catalogued and preserved in the (British) National Archive for the History of Computing (NAHC), currently housed at the University of Manchester. As explained in the preface to the NAHC's holdings of NRDC papers, 'during the 1950s, computer development was the single most important aspect of the NRDC's activities'. The broad-brush story of government policy on the exploitation of computer technology and the role of the NRDC has been presented by John Hendry in his 1989 book [1] and summarised by John Crawley, formerly of NRDC [2]. However, neither of these sources provides detailed assessments of computer hardware and software, nor of the deeper interactions between NRDC and Elliott Brothers (London) Ltd.

The 'deeper interactions' are indeed still surrounded with a certain amount of mystery as far as official accounts are concerned and, to this day, personal loyalties of the few surviving players tend to produce selective memories. In this chapter, we try to disentangle the complicated technical web which linked Elliott Brothers (London) Ltd. and the NRDC in the 1950s. The background theme is the emergence at Borehamwood of a relatively small and young computer systems design team that went on to make a relatively large impact in the emerging market place.

The first formal contact between the National Research Development Corporation (NRDC) and Borehamwood occurred on 10 August 1950 when, at the invitation of John Coales, H J Crawley and D Hennessey visited the Laboratories [3]. John Crawley was the Computer Projects Manager for NRDC and, though junior to Hennessey, was to become the more important player in NRDC's attempts to stimulate a British computer industry. Dennis Hennessey was NRDC's overall Patents Manager, covering all areas of science and engineering.

Hennessey's report of the 10 August visit [4] gives a revealing glimpse of a Laboratory emerging from the confines of classified Admiralty research contracts.

S. Lavington, *Moving Targets*, History of Computing,
DOI 10.1007/978-1-84882-933-6_5, © Springer-Verlag London Limited 2011

After briefly describing the Elliott 152 fixed-program computer which, at that time, 'has obeyed the test programme satisfactorily', Hennessey says:

'The approach of the firm [Elliott Brothers (London) Ltd.] to the design of computing equipment is based on an appreciation that such equipment contains a number of basic circuit arrangements very well suited to construction as replaceable sub-assemblies, and two lines of progress have been pursued in parallel. The first involves the engineering of these sub-units in forms which it is expected will make them suitable for use in a range of computers of various orders of complexity. The second is co-ordinated with the first, and is a general study of requirements and the various organizations of machines to meet these requirements. That is to say, the firm is attempting to design a range of integral sub-assemblies from which it hopes to be able to build up various properly engineered computing machines.'

Crawley and Hennessey were clearly intrigued by what they saw at Borehamwood, no doubt contrasting the forward-looking plans of Elliott Brothers (London) Ltd. with the sluggishness exhibited by most other British electronics manufacturers at that time. Hennessey took the view that 'the Company [Elliott Brothers] is making good progress towards its declared object, and has learnt a good deal about the unit construction techniques which it is employing. We formed the impression that the level of the work done by the firm is technically high, and that attention is being paid to design considerations such as those of reliability, ease of access and service ability which are of primary importance for commercial production'.

Borehamwood's strategy in August 1950 for the commercial exploitation of computing equipment was reported by Hennessey to cover three avenues:

1. Use of fixed-program computers for process control applications;
2. Design of universal, stored-program computers;
3. Manufacture of small electromechanical accounting equipment.

The first avenue was clearly an extension of the 152's real-time, on-line, experience; this would contribute, within a few years, to the ARCH project and industrial automation (see Sect. 4.4.2 and Chap. 7). The second avenue was the one that was of immediate interest to NRDC; this is described in greater detail below. The third avenue probably arose from an idea of Leon Bagrit. By August 1950, Bagrit had an associate company which (said Hennessey) 'is shortly coming on the market with an electro-mechanical, non-digital [sic] desk calculator, which will be marketed under the name "Logabacs". This is a machine in which 96 mechanical registers are provided. The associate company is organised to sell and service these machines, for which Elliott Brothers are satisfied there will be a good demand'. Logabacs, or more correctly Logabax, was predicted by Hennessey to herald Borehamwood's entry into the commercial applications of universal digital computers. It is not clear why Hennesesy came to this conclusion. Logabax was the name of a French company that made electromechanical calculators, one model of which did indeed have 96 registers. A first British Logabax collaborative venture had been attempted with the Powers-Samas company in the mid-1930s [5]. By the 1950s, the Logabax company was desperately seeking commercial partners [6]. Later, in the 1970s, Logabax manufactured printers and desktop microcomputers. The Logabax company was wound up in 1981, having played no part in the Elliott story.

In conclusion, Hennessey and Crawley 'felt that the firm's activities, grasp of the problems involved, and clear-headed ideas about plans for the future would justify the Corporation's giving serious attention to some kind of collaboration ...' [4].

During the meeting of 10 August 1950, Coales had readily acknowledged the need for a licencing agreement between Elliotts and NRDC to cover Elliotts' use in the 152 computer of NRDC storage patents (particularly, F C Williams' patent for the *anticipation-pulse* form of CRT electrostatic storage). Once such an agreement was in place, both parties assumed that some form of fruitful collaboration was both possible and desirable. The process of turning this assumption into reality actually proved to be a long drawn-out affair.

From the start, NRDC appears to have had two strands of collaboration in mind. The third Earl of Halsbury (1908–2000), NRDC's Managing Director, made his first visit to Borehamwood on 25 September 1950 during which he and Crawley talked to Coales, Bagrit, and W S Elliott. In an Internal NRDC memo of the visit [7], Crawley wrote cautiously that:

'Various suggestions were made concerning arrangements whereby the Corporation might finance work at Elliott Bros. No commitments were made, but the proposition appeared to be generally acceptable that Elliott Bros. should take a small study contract to enable them to consider the circuit developments involved in the Manchester machine, and to report on the possibilities of applying their miniaturisation and circuit techniques to the development of a machine based upon the Manchester machine. It also appeared possible that Elliott Bros. would look favourably, perhaps more favourably, upon the possibility of a contract to enable them to develop, or study the development of, a machine based upon their own circuit developments.'

The *Manchester machine* referred to above is the Manchester University Mark I computer which had been in operation in various forms since the spring of 1949 and the fully engineered production version that, in the autumn of 1950, was nearing completion in Ferranti's factory at Moston near Manchester [8]. In the light of discussions between Elliott Bros. and NRDC over the next few months, we can now see that Crawley was predicting two separate contracts between Borehamwood and NRDC. For convenience, we may call these the *Small-scale Prototype* and the *Advanced Computer*.

For the *Small-scale Prototype*, NRDC had in mind a marketable computer of modest cost which would utilise the Borehamwood packaged-circuit techniques of small, replaceable, sub-assemblies based on those developed for the 152 computer (see Fig. 5.1). Initially, it was assumed that the *Small-scale Prototype* would combine the Borehamwood packaged-circuit techniques with the proven Manchester University memory technology and systems architecture.

For the *Advanced Computer,* NRDC probably had no fixed plan other than to trust the enthusiasm and electronic skills of Borehamwood. For its part, the Computer Division at Borehamwood saw the possibility of an *Advanced Computer* contract as their chance to bring to fruition the multiple-functional

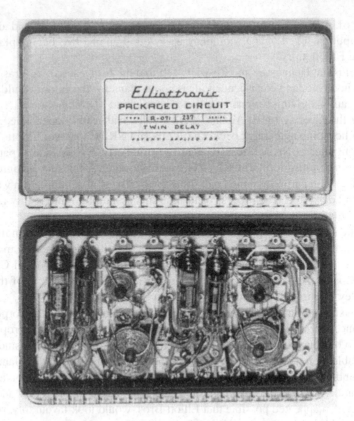

Fig. 5.1 By about 1950, Elliotts was considering whether to exploit commercially the printed-circuit technology developed for the 152 computer. Elliottronic was the name of a subsidiary company used for this exercise. One of the factors that led the National Research Development Corporation (NRDC) to approach Elliotts was the belief that Borehamwood might be well placed to develop medium-priced computers based on packaged-circuit units

unit, high-performance, systems architecture that had begun to emerge before the Admiralty effectively pulled the plug on the 152 project (see Chap. 2 and Appendix 1). This high-performance system was also to be proposed by Borehamwood for the DF computer project then under discussion with the Admiralty and GCHQ (see Chap. 3).

Underlying these two NRDC notional contracts were various unspoken, and sometimes contradictory, aspirations. For its part, NRDC trusted the opinion of Professor F C Williams at Manchester University and saw the CRT storage technology as probably the most promising memory system then in existence. (Certainly, the interest of IBM in the CRT patents [8] supported this view). However, the Manchester computer then being re-engineered by Ferranti Ltd. was a top-of-the-range design and what was now needed, in NRDC's view, was a small- or medium-scale alternative. For its part, Borehamwood had been unable to get CRT memory technology to work at the speeds originally desired for the 152 computer (see Chap. 2) and some of the Borehamwood engineers were not happy with the current state of development of CRT storage. We shall see that Borehamwood was soon to develop its own, more robust, memory system based on nickel delay lines. Furthermore, Borehamwood's early experience with fast multiplier design and concurrent ALU activity supported their view that Borehamwood was possibly better placed than Manchester to pursue high-performance designs – provided, of course, that an external source of R&D funding was forthcoming. For Borehamwood, still reeling from the sudden decrease in Admiralty support for the MRS5 contract, and aware of the perilous financial position of Elliott's Lewisham factory, the acquisition of R&D funds was crucial.

5.1.1   Funding for the Small-Scale Prototype

The first step was a study contract. At an NRDC Board Meeting held on 27 September 1950 authority was given 'for the placing of a contract for this purpose up to a total sum of £1,500'. By mid-November 1950, the contract had been extended by £1,000, and in the words of an NRDC memo [9]: 'the bull's eye [of the contract's extension] would be the actual design of a saleable computer'. The first version of the formal contract was not sent to EBRL until 22 March 1951. Coales replied on 10 April 1951, asking for two minor modifications to the contract and then commenting thus: 'As regards the development of a machine, we shall, according to our present plans, have capacity available to proceed with the work at the end of this year, i.e. immediately after the completion of the study. We cannot, however, undertake to keep this development capacity available without having any undertaking that it will be required to do work for the Corporation. This is a difficult problem and we should like to discuss it with you in the hope of finding a solution which would adequately safeguard the interests of both parties'.

Coales clearly wanted some guarantee of NRDC support for a production machine, in order to keep his team of engineers together. This request for a guarantee caused much internal debate within NRDC during the latter half of April. At length Crawley wrote to Coales on 2 May 1951, saying, in effect: 'sorry; NRDC can't give any guarantees, but let's deal with this when the occasion arises'. Coales finally replied on 26 June 1951 saying: 'We confirm that we are glad to accept the [study] contract ... We are also agreeable to the starting date being recorded as the 10th June 1951; we expect to begin work on the contract immediately'.

To further complicate the story, the study contract resulted in Borehamwood Internal Report number 267, dated 30 January 1952, which describes not a *small-scale* but a *high-performance* computer that, furthermore and much to NRDC's disquiet, did not propose to use CRT memory. In his letter to NRDC of 12 February 1952 enclosing report 267, Coales admits that 'we have included in the report a good deal of forward thinking, almost certainly beyond the terms of reference of the existing development contract'. The high-performance theme is discussed in Sect. 5.1.2.

Fig. 5.2 In order to reduce costs, the logic circuits of the Elliott 152 and 153 computers were redesigned by Laurence Clarke so that the expensive sub-miniature pentode valves (seen in Fig. 5.1) could be replaced by the cheaper double-triode valves. The photo shows prototype packages for the Elliott/NRDC 401 computer

As far as a small-scale computer was concerned, the study contract did eventually lead to a positive funding decision. At the 32nd NRDC Board meeting held on 23 April 1952, the Board 'gave authority for the expenditure under the Corporation's contract with Elliott Bros. Ltd. to be extended to £25,000 to cover the cost of construction of a prototype machine embodying various techniques proposed by Elliott Bros. Ltd., subject to the Company's position as the Corporation's licencees being appropriately established, including their liability to pay royalties to the Corporation under such licence'. At the 35th NRDC Board meeting held on 23 July 1952, the Elliott contract ceiling was raised from £25,000 to £30,000, at Borehamwood's request.

The legal niceties of the various contracts with Elliott Brothers took several months to resolve. In a letter from Borehamwood to Crawley dated 23 February 1953, it is suggested that Saturday 12 July 1952 be taken as the termination date for the first (study) contract and Monday 14 July 1952 be taken as the commencement for the new 'development and construction' contract. NRDC agreed this in a letter to Borehamwood dated 3 March 1952. 12 July was chosen because this was the date when the total expenditure on the first contract reached the round figure of £4,500. In practice, there was no boundary between work done at Borehamwood under the 'study' contract and the 'construction' contract. By 26 June 1951, expenditure on work for NRDC had been given the internal Borehamwood accounting number 401. The computer that eventually resulted from this expenditure was naturally called the NRDC/Elliott 401.

The final contractual specification of the small-scale machine (the 401) was agreed on 12 December 1952. The formal date of signing is recorded on the contract as 17 February 1953. In the light of Bill Elliott's subsequent career moves,

Fig. 5.3 By mid-1952, the production of logic circuits for the 401 computer was under way at the modest electronics workshop that served the Computing Division at Borehamwood in the early 1950s

it is interesting that clause 2 of the 11-page Contract has a specific provision: 'Elliotts shall arrange that so long as Mr William Sydney Elliott is in the employment of Elliotts he shall during the continuance of this Agreement be employed upon the project and shall devote so much of his working time thereto as shall be necessary for the proper furtherance of the project'.

Before describing the small-scale computer that was actually built by Borehamwood with NRDC support, we should pause to consider the fate of the high-performance aspirations of both parties.

5.1.2 Hopes for an Advanced Computer

Whereas the small-scale computer was to be serial, Lord Halsbury had other ambitions for the *Advanced Computer*. In his report to the NRDC Board on 20 December 1950 [10] he says:'An alternative type of machine is the "parallel" one.... In the United Kingdom, there is at present only one team working on the design of a parallel machine, namely that under Dr A M Uttley at the Ministry of Supply's Telecommunication Research Establishment [this computer was known as TREAC]. In the United States, however, there is a markedly greater concentration on the design of parallel machines, and a greater rate of progress. The parallel machine has a substantial advantage in speed over the serial one, at the expense of some increase in complexity.

'It is recommended that the Corporation should support a second design of parallel machine in the United Kingdom, and it is further recommended that Elliott Brothers Ltd. be invited to undertake this work. It is considered that the firm is the most suitable of all firms and organizations working in the field to attack the design of a parallel machine, and the most likely to produce a satisfactory design with despatch.'

From the 1970s onwards, *parallelism* became a Systems Architecture term describing multiprocessor computers exhibiting Single Instruction Multiple Data (SIMD) parallelism, Multiple Instruction Multiple Data (MIMD) parallelism, etc. In the 1950s, however, the adjective 'parallel' simply described uniprocessors that treated all digits in a word in parallel rather than in series. Although it was true (as Lord Halsbury implied) that about half the contemporary American arithmetic units were of parallel design in 1950, the main technical challenge at that time was to match the (slower) memory-access speeds to the (faster) arithmetic unit speeds. Experts on both sides of the Atlantic differed as to how to achieve this in a cost-effective manner. In the light of hindsight, we can see that the Borehamwood philosophy of what was called *multiple transfers,* meaning that a single instruction could cause multiple functional units within the central processor to operate concurrently, was unusual for 1950. Novelty aside, the philosophy did nothing to address the basic data-bandwidth limitations of the memory system. A more detailed technical description of the Borehamwood approach to high-performance design, as exemplified by the Elliott 152 and 153 computers and others, is given in Chap. 10 and Appendix 1.

Lord Halsbury ended his Report of 20 December by seeking the authority of the Board for the expenditure 'of a sum not exceeding £100,000' on the *Advanced Computer* project. This was a substantial sum – equivalent to approximately £4 million at 2009 prices.

It is perhaps worth remembering that, in contemplating the sponsorship of an expensive high-performance computer, NRDC was entering the unknown. The NRDC Board, in the words of Halsbury in a letter to Coales dated 20 February 1952, 'consists largely of businessmen and even the scientists on it know very little about computers'. Halsbury was therefore keen to take advice from the Brunt Committee on High Speed Calculating Machines. This was an Advisory Committee of the Department of Scientific and Industrial Research, set up in 1949 and chaired by Professor Sir David Brunt, an eminent meteorologist. The Brunt Committee's members included Prof. F C Williams (Manchester University) and Dr M V Wilkes (Cambridge University) – both gentlemen afterwards to become Fellows of the Royal Society and to be knighted. Throughout the period from the spring of 1951 to spring of 1952 NRDC sought the detailed comments of the Brunt Committee, and others, on whether to sponsor Borehamwood to design a high-performance computer. NRDC supplemented the Brunt advice with direct approaches to four established groups: F C Williams' team at Manchester, M V Wilkes' team at Cambridge, S H Hollingdale's group at RAE Farnborough and J M Wilkinson's group at NPL. Finally, and (as we shall see) of direct relevance to subsequent events, NRDC sought comments from a private individual: Christopher Strachey.

Christopher Strachey (1916–1975) was to make many notable contributions to Computer Science [11]. He graduated from Cambridge in Natural Sciences in 1939, following this with war work at Standard Telephones and Cables Ltd. (STC) on microwave valves. At STC, he used a differential analyser for the solution of equations. In 1951, whilst a mathematics teacher at Harrow School, Strachey was given the opportunity to write programs for both the NPL Pilot ACE and the Ferranti Mark I computer at Manchester University. His obvious programming skill brought him to the attention of Lord Halsbury, who interviewed him in November 1951 and employed him as a technical consultant at NRDC from June 1952 to 1959. (It is said [12] that Alan Turing recommended Strachey to Lord Halsbury, having observed Strachey's programming ability first-hand at Manchester.) On 22 November 1951, Crawley sent Strachey a copy of Borehamwood's report number 247B, dated 3 August 1951, being their first formal proposal for 'a general purpose mathematical electronic digital computer'. Report number 267 (dated 30 January 1952) followed in February 1952, by which time NRDC was relying increasingly on Strachey's advice.

Predictably, the experts differed in their detailed technical advice to NRDC on the evolving Borehamwood plans. Perhaps the spirit of their initial comments is best summed up by those of F C Williams, who wrote as follows to Crawley on 19 February 1951: 'I feel it would be an excellent idea to encourage Elliott Bros. to produce a machine but that the requirements put on them should be that it must use highly developed circuit elements of the kind they are working on now and that it must be a fast machine; leaving to them a certain amount of latitude as to the degree of parallelism incorporated. Furthermore I think it would be sound policy not to press them too severely on the matter of delivery date, firstly because the major service they can perform is in the development of techniques of construction which activity would be prejudiced if "blitzkreig" methods of production were adopted, and secondly because until the Ferranti machine has operated for a considerable period we are really in no stronger position to assess any proposed new design than we were when the Ferranti design was crystallised'.

On receipt of this type of advice, NRDC felt it inappropriate to rush into any definite contractual specifications for an advanced computer. Interestingly, however, by May 1951 NRDC had begun to discuss the *destination* of any eventual high-performance machine that Elliotts might build. Amongst suggestions were the Royal Aircraft Establishment at Farnborough and what was euphemistically referred to as a 'Ministry of Supply location' (which could have meant such places as the Atomic Weapons Research Establishment or GCHQ). However, no firm decision on an *Advanced Computer* contract was made during 1951.

To Coales, whose own position at Borehamwood was becoming increasingly difficult for the reasons described in Chap. 2, the lack of substantial funding from NRDC was weighing heavily on his mind. On 22 February 1952, Coales wrote a long letter to the NRDC (starting, uncharacteristically, 'Dear Sir' instead of to Halsbury personally) in which he sets out the cost of building one machine and doing preliminary research for a second, more advanced, machine. The 'preliminary research' was quite substantial, involving work on transistors, magnetic logical elements and static magnetic (i.e. core) stores. Depending upon exactly how the wording in the letter is interpreted, Coales was asking NRDC to guarantee funding in the region of £100,000. This letter seems to have been Coales' swansong – a forthright attempt to get some commitment from NRDC before Coales himself resigned. John Coales formally left Borehamwood in April 1952.

The news of Coales' departure from Borehamwood quickly reached NRDC. In a letter dated 27 March 1952 to Coales, addressed to Coales' home in Radlett, Halsbury says:

'I was very sorry indeed to hear that you had severed your connection with Elliott Brothers. I am naturally a little anxious about the position there as we looked to you for the leadership and direction of the enterprise, though of course [W S] Elliott was known to be in charge of the theoretical side of it. I would welcome a private conversation with you on this matter as soon as possible ....'

On 28 March 1952 Bagrit wrote to Halsbury, to reassure him that Coales' departure was not serious to the computing endeavours. Bagrit wrote: '... the fact that Mr. Coales is no longer with us will not, in any way, affect the proper and active development of the computer which you propose entrusting to us. The administration of the Laboratory, and its activity, has for some time past been in the hands of Mr. Wykeham, who is of course a technical man, and the scientific development of computers has, in any case, been in the hands of [W S] Elliott. Mr. Coales has, of course, had an important part to play in overall research policy and in that sphere we shall miss him'.

Nevertheless, NRDC's faith in Borehamwood was severely rattled. To further complicate matters, W S Elliott was on sick leave for all of April and most of May 1952. Finally, Halsbury was by this time getting signals that must have considerably reduced his former enthusiasm for a large Borehamwood machine. In a letter dated 9 May 1952 from Patrick Blackett (then Professor of Physics at Manchester University) to Halsbury, Blackett says: 'For instance Brooker, in casual conversation, said that for every problem that needs the whole of the Williams machine [meaning the Ferranti Mark I], there are 100 which need only one tenth of it'. R A (Tony) Brooker was at that time in charge of the Computing Service and software development at Manchester University. In a reply letter to Blackett dated 12 May, Halsbury said 'You are quite right in saying that Williams is dead against the big Elliott project ....I am quite sure that Brooker is probably right in his comments. This fully bears out what Strachey has told me'.

Interestingly, Halsbury's personal confidence in Bill Elliott remained undiminished. Writing to 'My dear Elliott' at his home address on 23 April 1952, Halsbury says:

'There are a number of factors on which Williams, Wilkes and the NPL do not agree, neither with you nor with one another, but I think there is a sufficient margin of opinion on every point which could be argued more than one way to justify us going ahead with your design.

'The feature upon which Williams feels most strongly is the multiple transfer system [explained in Appendix 1]. As you know, we have never been in love with this ourselves, though not for the reasons on which Williams bases his criticisms. Wilkes and the NPL, however, do not altogether share Williams' views on the subject of the multiple transfer system and in these circumstances we are not prepared to oppose it strongly as yet.

'Everybody is in agreement that the first stage should be to make a prototype embodying all the various different principles which you propose to employ, and get some idea of the practical difficulties. The construction of a full-scale machine will come later. The final decision on the multiple transfer idea can be made when the prototype has been operated [sic] and you will then have a great deal more experience to go on. Wilkes was most emphatic that we should not allow the decision to go head with the development contract to turn on the issue of who did, or who did not, like some features of the original design, and I think this point has been fully taken. At any rate, I hope so.

'At my Board meeting today I got a decision to go ahead with your design up to what might be called demonstration prototype stage. I am leaving for the moment the question of what this is going to cost and propose to go ahead on the basis of the present contract up to £25,000, subject to clarification on one or two drafting points in the contract and licence agreement between ourselves and Elliott Brothers, and one ought to be able to sort these out fairly readily.

'From this you will see that I have brought the matter to as happy an issue as could be hoped for at present, and feel that you have been supported as far as was possible, having regard to the speed at which we are trying to work.

'I hope, therefore, that this will dismiss a load of worry from your mind and that you will now sit down, or lie down, or stand up, or walk about, or whatever it is that will help you to concentrate upon your convalescence and full restoration to health and vigour, which happy consummation is, I think, the best contribution you can make at this stage to the development of digital computers.'

From this point onwards, all thought of an *Advanced Computer* contract for Elliott Brothers was set aside and NRDC concentrated instead on arranging for Borehamwood to build what had originally been seen as the *Small-scale Prototype*. This computer, as was mentioned in Sect. 5.1.1, became known as the Elliott/NRDC 401.

5.2 The Elliott/NRDC 401: Of Men and Machines

5.2.1 The Ideas Take Shape

Whilst all the contractual debate between the company and NRDC was grinding on, the electronic engineers at Borehamwood had not been idle. There were two significant technical developments that emerged during the period late-1950 to mid-1952.

Firstly, the printed-circuit packages of the 152 computer had to be redesigned by:

(a) Using widely available miniature double-triode valves rather than the more expensive special sub-miniature pentodes
(b) Replacing glass substrates with conventional paxolin ('plastic') boards and point-to-point wiring
(c) Using a more reliable system of edge-connectors

For technical details, refer to [13], the photograph in Fig. 5.2, and the list of relevant Borehamwood research reports in the Bibliography – especially numbers 217 dated 5 December 1950, 301 dated 2 September 1952, and 303 dated 27 October 1952.

Secondly, an alternative to the Williams/Kilburn CRT electrostatic memory had been developed at Borehamwood. Hearing that nickel variable delay lines had been employed for pulse storage in the USA in 1950 for NAVAR and similar radar-based air navigational systems [14], Ron Millership of the Physics Division at Borehamwood realised that nickel delay lines might also be used for a computer's primary storage system [15, 16]. The nickel delay-line technology turned out to be more robust and more reliable than CRT storage, but more expensive per bit. However, nickel delay lines were cheaper per bit and more robust than mercury delay lines (Fig. 5.4).

The first public manifestation of the new memory technology was a device called SNARC – short nickel line accumulating register calculator – demonstrated at the Physical Society's Exhibition in London early in 1952. The Physical Society's annual exhibition was, at the time, the only national annual showcase for new developments in electronics and instrumentation. Exhibitors came from industry, the research establishments and academia. The SNARC demonstrator was a chance to combine a one-word experimental nickel delay-line register with the double-triode versions of the former Elliott 152 miniature pentode circuits. Some years later, it was realised that dual triodes had problems with gradual cathode decay, whilst miniature pentodes did not suffer the same problems [17].

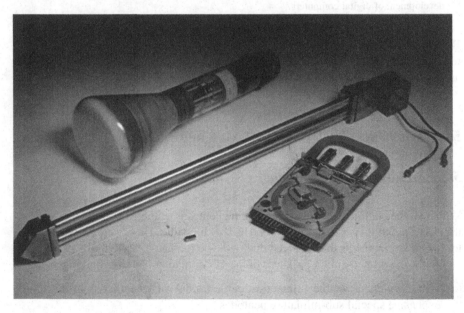

Fig. 5.4 The main problem faced by all early digital computer projects concerned memory technology. The photo shows three systems employed in different machines over the period 1948–1955. At the top is a cathode ray tube (CRT) used for electrostatic storage. In the centre is a twin steel tube filled with mercury, giving a form of delay-line storage. To the right is another form of delay-line storage using the magneto-strictive properties of nickel wire. Devices similar to these three could each store approximately 1,000 bits. Nickel delay lines, invented at Borehamwood, were more robust and more reliable than CRT storage, but more expensive per bit. Furthermore, nickel delay lines were cheaper per bit and more robust than mercury delay lines

Independently of SNARC and the NRDC work on the 401 project, nickel delay lines were also used successfully at Borehamwood for the in-house computer called NICHOLAS (see Chap. 10 and Appendix 2). Finally, SNARC was used in-house as an accurate digital timer to calibrate a novel microwave Torque Vane Wattmeter designed by Betty Laverick of the Radar research group at Borehamwood. Laurence Clarke was responsible for the implementation of SNARC, using a three-package version of the single-word nickel delay line. Laurence remembers [18] that 'the very clever development of the single package version that allowed a few more registers in the 402, was done by Garnet Edmunds [A G W Edmunds], known possibly only behind his back as *Nimble*'.

Once the new packaged circuits and the new nickel memory technology had proved satisfactory in a test set, the design of the 401 computer proceeded rapidly and had been substantially completed by September 1952 – though the main disc store was not fully operational until a few months later. Fortunately, Andrew St Johnston's contemporary laboratory notebook has survived to give an idea of how things progressed. Judging by the dated entries, this red foolscap-sized hard-backed notebook was used more or less on a daily basis from 25 February 1952 throughout 1952 and then intermittently until about November 1953. Entries are in pencil and are mostly of a technical nature, with many circuit diagrams appearing. From time to time, there are notes of meetings or of visits to outside organisations. This so-called *Red Book* was inherited by Laurence Clarke, upon the death of Andrew in 2005.

From the 24 June 1952 entry in the *Red Book* we see that responsibilities for implementing the 401 had been assigned as follows:

Planning	Andrew St Johnston and Harry Carpenter
Logical design; programs	Andrew St Johnston; Hugh Devonald
Circuit boards and short nickel delay lines	Laurence Clarke
Disc and associated circuitry	Berwick Stallworthy
Power supplies, test gear, etc.	Norman Muchmore

It is interesting that Bill Elliott's name does not appear on this list.

By the summer of 1952, Christopher Strachey was being employed as NRDC's principal consultant to watch over the 401 developments. In an Internal memo from Strachey to Halsbury, dated 25 August 1952 and entitled: *401 Mark I Computer – Elliott Brothers*, Strachey reports: 'I have had a talk with Elliott Brothers about the logical design of this machine. As it is only intended to be a simple machine, and is, moreover, subject to a number of technical restrictions on design, I have made very few suggestions to them. I think they have accepted most of these, and there are virtually no points on which we disagree'. Within a week of writing this, Strachey departed for Toronto, where he worked for NRDC writing programs for a Ferranti Mark I computer in connection with the Saint Lawrence Seaway project. This computer, the second production Ferranti Mark I, was installed at the University of Toronto where it was called *Ferut*. Strachey did not return to the UK until March 1953.

The Elliott 401 first became operational at Borehamwood, in the sense of running its first program, in March 1953. Elliott Brothers, being in the scientific instrument business, generally had a stand at the annual Physical Society Exhibition. A last-minute decision was taken to include a demonstration of the new 401 and so the machine was transported to Imperial College, London, for the Physical Society Exhibition held from 3 to 8 April 1953. This must have been the first time ever that a general-purpose stored-program computer was put on public display at a trade show. The 401 performed well at the exhibition – more reliably, it was later realised, than during the following weeks back at Borehamwood. Chris Strachey took the lead in writing the demonstration programs for the exhibition. It is recalled that at one stage he worked through the night. In the morning he was discovered, not with the remains of coffee and sandwiches, but happily surrounded by a carpet of cigarette ends and one dead matchstick – he was known for his chain-smoking habits.

The public success of the Elliott 401 did not go unnoticed by the Elliott top management. As soon as the exhibition ended, the young Computing Division engineers were summoned to the company's Head Offices at St. Annes Gate, London, for celebratory drinks. Laurence Clarke well remembers being button-holed by Dr Lotti (Lawrence) Ross, who impressed upon him the future importance of computers for 'Ze Cat Crackers'. Tired, befuddled with alcohol and confused by Ross's heavy Hungarian accent, it took Clarke some time to work out that Catalytic Crackers in the oil industry were being predicted by Ross to be an application ripe for automated process control. In retrospect, perhaps April 1953 was the first occasion on which Ross communicated his enthusiasm to the Borehamwood engineers for what came to be called Automation. We pick up the Automation theme again in Sect. 5.4.2 and in Chaps. 6 and 7.

Interestingly, the Elliott 401's debut took others by surprise. M H (Harry) Johnson, from the Operational Research Group of the Ministry of Civil Aviation, had already gained practical programming experience on the Cambridge EDSAC, the NPL Pilot ACE and the Ferranti Mark I. He recalls [19] that the 401 at the Physical Society Exhibition 'amazed everyone involved in computer activity, particularly as most of us had been completely unaware of any Elliott Brothers interest in computers'. This is a reflection of the tight security that surrounded most of Borehamwood's projects.

5.2.2   The First Public Appearance

It is instructive to quote from the Elliott-NRDC 401 brochure printed for the April 1953 Exhibition, since the brochure's emphasis on physical details gives us an insight into the way in which, at that time, informed members of the public regarded computers as rather special scientific instruments. After stating that 'one of the principal aims has been to produce a machine of moderate cost, good reliability, and extreme ease of servicing', the brochure launches enthusiastically into the following description:

'The main store, which is of the rotating magnetic disc type, comprises 8 tracks closely spaced near the outer rim of a 9-inch diameter disc, each track carrying 128 words of 32 binary digits each. The disc rotates at a speed of approximately 4,600 rpm which corresponds to a rotation period of 13.1 milliseconds and a digit rate of 333,000 per second. In addition to these 8 tracks the disc carries three special tracks for address information and the production of timing signals. Each of the 8 main store tracks is provided with a common writing and reading head, and the track selection is performed electronically. It is possible to extend the capacity of the main store from 8 tracks, 1,024 words, to 23 tracks, 2,968 words by the provision of relay switches, pre-selecting under program control, any one of 16 tracks, the pre-selected track being then available as one of the 8 electronically selected tracks.

'The arithmetic registers are composed of single-word length magneto-strictive delay-line storage loops. Six such registers are provided in this machine. Two are used for the accumulator, which can operate single-length or double-length, the other four being used as multiplier, multiplicand, instruction and general-purpose registers. The arithmetic and control sections of the machine are built up from a set of standard circuits which had been developed to operate at a digit frequency of 333,000 per second.

'The input system includes a mechanism which employs a ratchet-type driving motor and five photocell tubes for parallel sensing of the holes in the teleprinter-type punched tape on which information to be fed into the computer is recorded.

'The results of calculations issuing from the computer are converted into an easily comprehensible form by an electric typewriter which is operated by a set of solenoids energised under the control of the computer.'

After describing the instruction set in detail (for which see Appendix 3), the brochure then specifies the performance of the 401, of which the following is a summary:

Addition time: 200 µs
Multiplication time: between 7 and 10 ms, depending upon sign
Input from paper tape: 40 characters per second
Output to electric typewriter: ten characters per second

In a 1975 retrospective paper [20], Laurence Clarke implies that the multiplier in the first version of the 401 'had only been useable with positive numbers' and that after the April 1953 exhibition this was corrected.

The exhibition brochure contains several photographs of the 401 and its components, including the images shown in Figs. 5.2 and 5.5. The main computer, including power supplies and cooling fans, occupied seven cabinets. Two mobile trolleys then carried, respectively, the input/output equipment and maintenance facilities (oscilloscopes and engineer's switches). The total dimensions of the computer, excluding the two trolleys, were: 13 ft long, 2 ft deep and 7 ft 6 in. high (equivalent to approximately 3.96 m by 0.61 m by 2.29 m). The weight was 22 cwt (equivalent to 1,109 kg). The machine required a three-phase electricity supply and consumed 5 KVA of power. The 401 contained approximately 500 thermionic valves (tubes).

It is bemusing to recall that, in 1953, a 'small' computer weighed over a tonne, had only 4 Kbytes of memory and a clock-rate of 0.33 MHz. Fifty years later, a commodity PC available in any High Street store would have offered at least 512 Mbytes of RAM

Fig. 5.5 The Elliott/NRDC 401 computer, as exhibited at the Physical Society Exhibition in London in April 1953. The left-hand unit standing in front of the computer is an engineers' test-trolley. The unit to the right is an electric typewriter for printed output. Input was via five-track punched paper tape (not shown in the photo) and results could also be punched on paper tape

plus many Gbytes of disc memory and would have a clock-rate of at least 2 GHz. In round figures, the performance of a 'small' computer in 2003 had improved by at least 1,000 times whilst the physical weight has fallen by about 1,000 times and the cost has dropped by about 100 times. Such is the present-day rate of progress of semiconductor technology that these 2003 figures themselves are now looking quaint.

The Elliott 401's exhibition brochure concludes with this assessment:

'Although the machine is essentially an experiment in construction rather than an embodiment of an ideal logical design it is believed that the simple design chosen can be of very considerable practical utility in many branches of scientific computation. For example, it will determine all the roots of a set of 20 simultaneous linear equations in about three minutes or all the roots of a set of 30 equations in about 20 minutes. Using desk machines [i.e. electro-mechanical desk-top calculators] the determination of a dominant root of a set of 20 equations requires about 10 days work and a set of 30 equations is liable to be too formidable a problem to be tackled on desk machines.

'The nature of the construction is such that the logical design may be modified readily, and machines of considerably different logical organisation can easily be assembled using the same components as the present machine. For instance, additional functions may be provided or extra arithmetic units such as a fast multiplier might easily be installed. The storage capacity can also be increased to provide a limited quantity of immediate access storage or intermediate storage and the machine can be arranged to operate in conjunction with a variety of input and output mechanisms for any special data handling requirements.

Fig. 5.6 The 401 with covers removed. On the top shelf of the right-hand bay is the magnetic disc memory, which originally held 1 K of 32-bit words – (extended later)

'For any further particulars or general enquiries about the computer 401 please apply to: The National Research Development Corporation, 1 Tilney Street, London W1.'

For NRDC, the significance of the 401's successful demonstration was that it introduced a second player to the UK marketplace. Ferranti Ltd. was already producing limited numbers of large-scale computers for sale, at a price of about £90 K each. Now the hope was that Elliott Brothers, or some derivative of Elliott Brothers, could produce small- or medium-scale machines in commercially realistic quantities at a price in the region of £20 K each.

The significance for Elliott Brothers of the 401's success was threefold. Firstly, the Borehamwood Laboratories had emerged from the cloak of defence-contract confidentiality into the bright lights of the marketplace. Secondly, it was a matter of pride that the 401 (or more strictly the production version, the 402) was the first commercially available computer to have been designed without dependence upon an academic or government research establishment as the source of ideas. Thirdly, the 401 strengthened the company's hope that further NRDC funding might now become available.

NRDC, however, was having doubts. By the spring of 1953 Crawley, for one, knew that W S (Bill) Elliott had given notice of his intention to resign from Borehamwood and that he wished to take several members of the computer design team with him. In order to understand subsequent events, we need to make a short digression into the realms of 'who did what, and to whom'.

5.2.3   They Have Their Exits and Their Entrances

After the exhibition of 3–8 April 1953, the Elliott 401 computer was moved back to Borehamwood. At this point, the team's morale started to wobble. Whilst everyone knew that further refinements were necessary to the 401's electronics, they also knew that Bill Elliott, their Computing Division Manager, intended to take the 401's expertise elsewhere. It is known that he had made informal approaches to at least one American company and then, in turn, to English Electric, Mullard and finally to Ferranti [21]. In fact, Bill Elliott left Borehamwood for a spell at Cambridge in May 1953 and then joined Ferranti Ltd. with effect from 1 November 1953. By that time, the 401 had been physically removed from Borehamwood by NRDC and at least one Ferranti employee (Ken Johnston) was being given access to the machine's engineering details (see Sect. 5.2.4 below). On 3 June 1954, Crawley sent Bill Elliott (by then based at Ferranti Ltd., 18 Manchester Street, London W1) copy no. 4 of the Final Borehamwood Report (no. 339) on the 401, plus one complete set of drawings of the machine.

It is difficult to describe the effect of all this on individuals within the 401 team at Borehamwood. Even 50 years later, the surviving members of the team have strong, and in some cases, conflicting opinions about the turn of events. Any retrospective

Fig. 5.7 The Computing Division (plus one) at Borehamwood in 1952/1953. *Front Row L–R:* Charles Owen (of the Circuits Division), RC Robbins, W S (Bill) Elliott, Harry Carpenter, Mr Moffatt (administration), Mrs Cox (secretary). *Middle Row*: Laurence Clarke, Andrew St Johnston, Johnnie Cane, Jock Gerrard, Berwick Stallworthy, Norman Muchmore, John Halsey. *Back Row*: Tom Ludlow, Garnet Edmunds, Mr Anderson, Bob Cudmore, Jim Barrow, Peter Atkinson, Len Thomas, Stu Ellis, Bert Calver and John Bunt

Fig. 5.8 Charles Owen (1918–1984) joined the Circuits Division at Borehamwood in 1951 and left in 1954 to join Ferranti Ltd. He was the 'father' of a succession of carefully designed logic circuits that were used (with appropriate modifications) in the Elliott 153 and 400 series computers and the Ferranti Pegasus and Perseus computers. He joined IBM in 1956 and in 1969 was awarded an IBM Fellowship

analysis of motivations, necessary to understand subsequent computer developments, has to proceed cautiously.

The first question for the historian to resolve is: Who were the principal players? A little detective work is required to reveal the names of those closest to the spirit of the 401, since the formal Borehamwood Divisional structure was in transition from one based on techniques to one based on projects. Help comes in the form of an unsigned news item, headed *New Electronic Digital Computer Techniques*, appearing in the May 1953 edition of the magazine *Electronic Engineering*. The foreword states that 'Electronic Engineering obtained the following information about '401' from Mr. W S Elliott, Head of Computing Division of Elliott Brothers (London) Ltd., Mr. H G Carpenter, Leader of the design Group which developed '401' and Mr. A St. Johnston, the '401' Project Leader, and Mr. H J Crawley of NRDC during the showing of the machine at the Physical Society Exhibition'. After describing the computer, the article ends with the following paragraph:

'A team of several engineers collaborated in the design of 401, under the leadership of W S Elliott, H G Carpenter and A St. Johnston. The collaborators were S L H Clarke, B V Stallworthy and N W W Muchmore. Three of the basic circuits for logical operations had been previously developed by C E Owen and the magnetic disc store was developed by P D Atkinson. The magnetic disc and its bearings and heads were designed by C F Phillips. R C Robbins was a consultant on storage development. Two other engineers J R Halsey and J P Bunt, also assisted. C H Devonald collaborated in the preparation of the initial orders and programmes for the machine. In this connection Mr C Strachey of the National Research Development Corporation gave valuable help.'

Reading between the lines of the above quotation, there were evidently some issues of *amour-propre* between the three personalities who were all introduced as 'leaders'. Hindsight permits the following disambiguation. In mid-1952, at the time of finalising the 401's specification, Harry Carpenter was the most experienced electronic engineer of the three. However, he was heavily committed to the secret GCHQ project (see Chap. 3) and had little time to spare for the 401 before the end of 1952. Bill Elliott was a Divisional manager, already thinking of his next career move and unlikely to have had much day-to-day involvement with the 401's electronic implementation. Indeed, when Bill was involved with modifications to the 401 at Cambridge in the summer of 1953 (see below), ex-colleagues at Borehamwood have said that they then realised how little Bill knew of the 401's operation at the hardware level. Andrew St Johnston, the youngest of the three and the one most closely associated with the 401's detailed design, quickly became the de facto team leader. Andrew was the sole author of the first 401 internal Borehamwood publication to appear, namely report T11 dated 2 September 1952. He was the senior author of the end-of-project report, no. 339 dated 29 March 1954. Although both Harry Carpenter and Bill Elliott had resigned several months before publication, Harry Carpenter (but not Bill Elliott) was cited as a co-author of report 339. The full list of authors is: A St Johnston, S L H Clarke, N W M Muchmore, C H Devonald, B V Stallworthy, H G Carpenter and J P Bunt. The ordering in this list may well reflect Andrew St Johnston's feelings about the relative electronic engineering effort contributed to the project. Fifty years later, S L H Clarke remembers just five people as being central to the 401's hardware implementation: A St Johnston, S L H Clarke, N W M Muchmore, B V Stallworthy and J R Halsey [21].

In the electronic context, it is not surprising that the disc contribution of the experienced mechanical engineer Chris Phillips was omitted from authorship of the 401's end-of-project report. Chris Phillips was formally based at Lewisham, where he had been a principal designer of the electromechanical fire-control tables used by the Navy during the war. Chris commuted daily from Portsmouth to Borehamwood and was remembered as a first-class engineer. Also understandably, the original contribution of R W Millership (Physics Division) to nickel magnetostrictive delay-line techniques was felt to be too far removed from the logical design of the 401 itself.

In truth, any commercially viable computer design team in the early 1950s required contributions from many types of individual. This was still the pioneering age, when ideas were being tried out for the first time and there were no such things as international standards. Fifty years later, commodity chip-sets, standard interfaces and operating systems and standard applications-packages now ensure that there is much less scope for individual innovation in the marketplace. Any home enthusiast can 'build' a personal computer by assembling off-the-shelf hardware and software modules. It is therefore worth digressing briefly from the NRDC/Elliott 401 story to remind ourselves of computer design activity at the very beginning of the information age.

In addition to the support services present in any large engineering company, for example workshop, secretarial, drawing office, purchasing and accounts services, a computer design team of the 1950s would ideally include four kinds of professionals:

Fig. 5.9 Christopher Strachey (1916–1975) started his computing career writing programs in his spare time for the Pilot ACE at NPL and the Ferranti Mark I at Manchester. He worked for NRDC from 1952 to 1959. After a short period as an independent consultant, he entered academia – first at Cambridge and then at Oxford as the first Director of the Programming Research Group. At Oxford, his interest in the theoretical aspects of programming led to the development of Denotational Semantics

(a) Team leader(s)
(b) Conceptual thinker(s)
(c) Hardware and software engineers – (typically 25% of the total team by number)
(d) Hardware and software technicians – (typically 65% of the total team)

Actually, the software side as such would be very thinly represented on the early design teams since computers were sold with the barest minimum of software. With the notable exception of Chris Strachey and, earlier, Ed Hersom, 'pure' programmers and mathematicians seldom took much part in detailed computer design.

A good team leader was aware of current computer R&D worldwide, had many useful contacts in industry and academia, and was good at producing high-level plans for new projects and then finding appropriate sources of funding. Bill Elliott was such a person.

A good conceptual thinker was able to abstract away from particular technologies and particular end-user applications and apply mathematically sound insights to generic problems, understanding both the hardware and software sides of candidate solutions. Such people were as rare in 1950 as they are today. A 1950s computer project was unlikely to go down in history as truly innovative unless the team included a good conceptual thinker. Christopher Strachey (of NRDC) was one such person. Laurence Clarke has stated [22] that Strachey 'was a real inspiration to us'.

Amongst the computer-related people employed at Borehamwood in the period 1950–1953, no individual seems to have made their mark on history as a good conceptual thinker, though perhaps Charles Owen and Ed Hersom might each be considered serious candidates. (IBM was certainly to champion Owen in 1969, when he was awarded a prestigious IBM Fellowship.)

Of good hardware engineers and technicians, Borehamwood had plenty. They were competent at practical implementation and the day-to-day management of production resources, though few of them in 1950 knew much about what we would now call computer systems architecture. In fact, Maurice Wilkes (of Cambridge University), when asked in April 1952 by NRDC to comment upon Borehamwood's plans for a high-performance computer as embodied in Report 267, said that: 'the machine bears evidence of being designed by a group who have not built a machine before ...'

Based on the above skills-categories, we may trace the movement of individuals through the Borehamwood-derived computer projects that spanned the period 1951–1955. There are four such projects: first, the paper study for an *Advanced Computer* as discussed in Sect. 5.1.2 above; secondly, the 401 computer itself; thirdly, the Elliott 402/403/405 computers, these being the commercially available successor machines produced at Borehamwood (see later); finally, the Ferranti Pegasus computer which was produced by Bill Elliott and others after he had left Borehamwood (see Chap. 10). Table 5.1 shows the movements of the principal players, highlighting those whose names appear (or might be expected to appear) as authors of technical publications. The four main columns in Table 5.1 represent the four computer projects. The three main rows represent the categorisation of individuals as either conceptual thinkers (theory), project leaders or hardware/software engineers. Of course, one person (e.g. Andrew St Johnston in the 402 project) may have had more than one role but the entry in the Table 5.1 gives the main responsibilities.

Here is an alphabetical identification of individuals whose initials appear in Table 5.1, with their original Borehamwood division, where applicable, in parenthesis. Those with no divisional annotation were recruited from elsewhere by Ferranti for the Pegasus project [23].

P D Atkinson (Computing), J P Bunt (Computing), T G H Braunholtz, H G Carpenter (Computing), S L H Clarke (Computing), C H Devonald (Theory), W S Elliott (Computing), G Emery, J W Fairclough, G E Felton (Theory), J R Halsey (Computing), S E Hersom (Theory), D Hogg, I W Merry, B G Maudsley, N W W Muchmore (Computing), C E Owen (Circuits), C F Phillips (Mechanical), R C Robbins (Computing), B M Rose (Theory), A St Johnston (Computing), B V Stallworthy (Computing) and C Strachey (NRDC).

Table 5.1 Movement of people between computer projects, 1951–1955

Principal skill	Paper design (1951–1952)	401 (1952–1953)	402/3/5 (1953–1956)	Ferranti Pegasus (1954–1956)
Theory	?	?	?	CS
Project leadership	WSE	WSE	ASJ	WSE
Hardware/ software engineering	SEH, CHD, CEO, BMR	ASJ, CEO, SLHC, CHD, HGC, CFP, JPB, NWMM, BVS, PDA, RCR, JRH	SLHC, CFP, (JPB), NWMM, BVS, PDA, RCR, JRH	CEO, GEF, IM, CHD, BGM, TGHB, JWF, GE, DH

Looking at Table 5.1, one might predict that the fourth project (the Ferranti Pegasus) would be more likely to make a significant impact on the worldwide development of computer design concepts and systems architectures than the third (the Elliott 402). This indeed proved to be the case, as is discussed more fully in Chap. 10. Events need not have turned out this way, but they did, and Bill Elliott's departure from Borehamwood was the trigger which caused the insights of people such as Chris Strachey, Charles Owen and George Felton to coincide briefly, but effectively, during the development of Pegasus.

Perhaps the last word on the departure of Bill Elliott and its effect upon NRDC's attitude to Borehamwood should come from Lord Halsbury. In an internal NRDC memo reporting on a lunchtime meeting with Bagrit and Ross on 9 April 1954, Halsbury recorded that he 'had not at present sufficient confidence in the strength of their organisation' for NRDC to give the company [i.e. Elliotts] the financial backing that it would have liked. In reply, Bagrit and Ross 'reserved their views on whether they were in fact as weakened by the exit of a number of their staff' as Halsbury seemed to think. 'Mr Bagrit in particular insisted that it was an overdue house-cleaning'. Although Halsbury repeated that he regarded Elliott Brothers as weak, he had, he said, 'every hope that they would make a satisfactory recovery in due course'. Ending on a positive note, Halsbury had heard that the company had become interested in the application of a computer to the running of an oil refinery and he told Bagrit and Ross that he attached 'the highest importance to making a beginning on work of this kind in the field of automatic control techniques'. The topic of automation re-emerges in Sect. 5.4.2 and in Chap. 6.

Table 5.1 demonstrates that, though Bill Elliott may have temporarily deprived the Computing Division at Borehamwood of managerial experience, he did not persuade his immediate colleagues to move. What he *did* do was to persuade three key members of *other* Borehamwood Divisions and, most importantly, Christopher Strachey of NRDC, to participate in his new computer project at Ferranti Ltd. Charles Owen (Circuits Division), Hugh Devonald and George Felton (both of the Theory Division) had all moved from Borehamwood to Ferranti by the end of 1954. (Harry Carpenter had by that time become a Consultant for Tube Investments Ltd.) There was an implication that the old Borehamwood Divisional structure was not conducive to new projects. Although Bagrit soon rectified this by successful re-organisations, Bagrit's changes did not come soon enough to avert NRDC's temporary loss of faith in Borehamwood.

Retrospectively, there is a hint that Halsbury's own lack of faith in Borehamwood may have had more to do with personalities than with technical competence. Laurence Clarke remembers the 'disastrous misunderstanding on NRDC's part brought about by WSE misrepresentation' [18]. Furthermore, John Crawley has said [2] 'the situation as presented to NRDC appeared much more serious than it eventually turned out to be'. After explaining that Halsbury was 'convinced that Elliott's computer R&D effort was just going to disintegrate', Crawley asks: 'Why did we form this view so strongly? I don't really understand now.... What subsequently emerged was that we were quite wrong in our forecast of what was going to happen at Elliott Bros; they went on from strength to strength and did very well'.

5.2.4   The 401's Progress, via Cambridge, to Rothamsted

From the spring of 1953 to the end of that year, the story of the 401 had some similarities with a mediaeval fairytale which might go as follows:

Once upon a time there was a young girl of great promise called Fourowun, the pride of her home village of Borehamwood. One of the villagers, a tearaway fellow called Bill, had fallen out with his mates, left the village, and wanted to take Fourowun with him. He planned to set up home with Fourowun in a rival village called Ferranti in the forest of Manchester. The elders of Ferranti were not so sure: the villages of Borehamwood and Ferranti had become rivals and in any case the Ferranti elders found Bill a bit too boisterous. Rich Uncle Halsbury, from his palace in the big city, saw all these events and puzzled about them. Uncle Halsbury had friends in both villages. He had great affection for young Fourowun. He had watched her grow from a baby, had lavished gifts upon her, and now almost regarded her as his own daughter. Uncle Halsbury also admired the spirit of tearaway Bill and eventually came to the conclusion that Bill was the right man to give Fourowun a happy life. If the couple could not live in Borehamwood, then a home for them must be found elsewhere. Bill wanted to move at once to Ferranti but Uncle Halsbury knew that things were not so simple. Fourowun should finish her education first, so Uncle Halsbury arranged for her to go to Cambridge University, where he asked his wise friend Christopher to be her tutor. Eventually, Bill made new friends in Ferranti and found himself another girlfriend, Pegasus, who was even more beautiful than Fourowun. Bill, Pegasus and Bill's new friends set up home in the big city, well away from the forest of Manchester. But Bill only stayed with Pegasus a short while before moving on once again, to a village called IBM in the forest of Hursley.

Like all good fairytales, there were moments of deception, misunderstanding, anger and reconciliation. The heroine, Fourowun, actually went to a nunnery called Rothamsted where she served faithfully for many years. Her life inspired both villages to great efforts in the marketplace and, in that sense, the tale had a happy ending. However, Uncle Halsbury reflected that producing happy endings in both villages had caused him more stress than he could possibly have imagined (paraphrasing [24]).

Anyone doubting the appropriateness of words such as 'deception' and 'anger' in the fairytale should read the verbatim transcription [25] of a tense meeting held on 5 November 1953 between NRDC and the following Borehamwood representatives: Dr L L Ross (General Manager of Elliott Bros.), Commander H Pasley-Tyler (Borehamwood Laboratory Director), Mr. D H Marlow (Commercial Manager, Computing Division) and Mr. A St. Johnston (Chief Engineer, Computing Division).

Returning to non-contentious facts, NRDC arranged for the Elliott 401 to be moved to Cambridge on 14 June 1953 where, over the next few weeks, an assessment of necessary improvements was drawn up. Then NRDC's Sub-Committee on Electronic Computers, at its meeting held on 21 July 1953, approved 'a programme of work for improving the 401 prototype machine which had been conceived as the result of studies made of the machine at Cambridge, and was estimated to cost

£12,000 over a period of four months'. The improvements included the construction of a new disc assembly, new means for inserting constants into programs (the 'number generator'), provision of a circuit-board tester ('plate tester') and provision of a full set of spare circuit boards. From Borehamwood's viewpoint, the lack of easy day-to-day access to the 401 at Cambridge, and the presence at Cambridge of Ferranti-oriented people with whom they would rather not work, created unnecessary difficulties.

The one relevant engineer at Cambridge who had the trust of all players was Harry Carpenter. Harry had suffered a minor nervous breakdown during the 311 (Oedipus) project for GCHQ, had resigned from Borehamwood and had gone to Cambridge as a Consultant to NRDC. NRDC, for its part, also sent its own technical experts Christopher Strachey and Donald Gillies to Cambridge. Their brief was to advise on modifications to the logical design of the 401 and to develop applications programs. Patent application 23735/53 covers improvements to the 401 devised by Strachey and Gillies whilst the 401 was at Cambridge.

Maurice Wilkes' group at the Cambridge Mathematical Lab., having their own research agenda, had little day-to-day connection with the Elliott 401 though Wilkes wrote a program for it early in 1954.

Harry Carpenter stayed with the 401 at Cambridge until its move, in March 1954, to the government's Rothamsted Agricultural Experimental Station in Hertfordshire. By this time, the specified modifications to the 401 had been carried out to NRDC's satisfaction. Just before leaving Cambridge at the end of March 1954, the 401 ran for 26 h non-stop without a breakdown – 'a remarkable feat then for a machine with thermionic valve logic', as the magazine *Electronics Weekly* said in its commemorative issue of 10 August 1965.

5.2.4.1 Why Did NRDC Install the 401 at Rothamsted?

As early as May 1951, Lord Halsbury had been considering possible destinations for any computer that might arise from NRDC's sponsorship of Borehamwood's design efforts. Professor Douglas Hartree of Cambridge University, a respected adviser on all aspects of early computing endeavours, wrote to Halsbury on 19 May 1951 saying: 'It seems desirable that there should be one of these machines in Scotland, both to spread the interest in these machines and their possibilities and to provide a local service, and to disperse the available equipment in case of war'. Halsbury replied: '... I believe that the Brunt Committee are much better qualified than we are to say where the proposed Elliott machine should go ...'. Candidate destinations must have included the defence-related establishments – GCHQ (Eastcote and later Cheltenham), AWRE (Aldermaston), TRE (Malvern), RAE (Farnborough), AERE (Harwell), etc. – with RAE an apparent front runner in 1951.

By 1954, when the 401 project was pronounced complete, the defence-related establishments were making their own provision for computing facilities. This left the civil establishments. The National Physical Laboratory had designed and built its own computer (the Pilot ACE). The interested universities (Cambridge,

Manchester, Birkbeck College and Imperial College) had also designed and built their own machines.

NRDC could in principle have installed the machine at their London offices at Tilney Street where it could have served as a bureau machine for demonstration to prospective computer users. However, NRDC lacked the technical staff necessary to operate and maintain the computer and so searched for a suitable national establishment willing to take on what was, in 1954, still a piece of leading-edge technology of unknown reliability.

It is most probable that the arrival of the 401 at Rothamsted was largely due to the enthusiasm and influence of Frank Yates [26], the then Director of Rothamsted. Frank had been active in what would now be called Operational Research during the war. He was elected a Fellow of the Royal Society in 1948. He had contacts in high scientific places. Michael Healy, who worked in the statistics section at Rothamsted at the time and who 'went to Cambridge to learn about programming in the early days', remembers events thus [27]. 'The acquisition of the 401 by Rothamsted seems to have been almost entirely Frank Yates' doing. He was on excellent terms with the Agricultural Research Council at the time, and had incorporated a suitable room in the "temporary" building that was put up at the time, but the idea was pretty far-sighted, although it followed naturally from our work on punched card equipment. He contrasted in this respect with Peter Medawar, head of the National Institute for Medical Research at Mill Hill, who wanted nothing to do with the nasty things.... I did a lot of programming for the machine, which arrived with almost no software – I may have spent my most productive years programming a one-off machine in machine code'. An example of a 401 program, the square root routine, is given in Appendix 3; see also [28]. Gavin Ross, a long-time statistician at Rothamsted, has added [29]: 'I understand that the original idea was to buy the [401] machine outright, but the Agricultural Research Council did not have the money. So Michael [Healy] suggested that they should just lease it from NRDC'.

Returning to events of 1954, Maurice Wilkes of the Cambridge Mathematical Laboratory says, in a letter to Lord Halsbury dated 29 March: 'The 401 has now left us and I would like to say how much we appreciated having it here. It is quite stimulating to be brought into close contact with a new machine and I hope that opportunities for similar arrangements will occur in the future. The performance of the machine during the last few weeks removed any remaining doubts there were about the quality of the technique....

'It did not take me long to pick up the elements of programming for the 401 but I must say I found the necessity for optimum programming rather tiresome. I believe that in the new models you are proposing to provide more registers to which rapid access can be obtained and I shall look forward to hearing what you decide to do in this respect.'

At Rothamsted, the Elliott 401 gave valuable service to the statisticians and continued as a focal point for other real-world applications, as described in Sect. 5.3.2. The 401's hardware was enhanced in several respects (see Appendix 3) during its useful life at Rothamsted, eventually being retired in July 1965. The machine lay in pieces in a Science Museum store in London for some years. Restoration by volunteers from the Computer Conservation Society began in a small way [30] in 1993, then languished for a few years and has recently re-commenced.

Whilst events were taking their course at Cambridge in 1953, NRDC was taking steps to secure its Intellectual Property. At a Board meeting dated 25 March 1953, NRDC 'decided that in order to make provision for the recovery of the Corporation's development expenditure on the Elliott machine, out of which few patents had emerged, the Company [Elliott Brothers] should be required to agree that they would not manufacture computers on their own account embodying the Corporation's industrial property rights such as designs without the express consent of the Corporation and appropriate payment for using those designs'.

Only three of Borehamwood's many patents were considered relevant to NRDC's 401 computing interests in 1953. These were:

Number	Date	Inventor(s) and subject
26800/52	24/10/52	Millership and Owen: number generator and nickel delay line
29845/52	25/11/52	Owen: improved delay network
29846/52	25/11/52	Owen: the circuits for three standard modules used in the 401

Borehamwood was confident that it could incorporate these ideas into market-able computers. By June 1953, in discussion with NRDC, Bagrit boldly stated that Elliott Brothers 'would have no difficulty in producing' a batch of between 6 and 24 machines, the cost of each machine being, he estimated, of the order of £12,000. At an NRDC Board meeting held on 24 March 1953, enquiries from IBM, Remington Rand and Bendix Corporation had been reported. Over a year later, an NRDC Board meeting held on 22 September 1954 heard that: 'It is reported that Elliott Bros. have sold four '402' computers – one for the Operational Research Group for War Office use, one for the Australian Long Range Weapons Department, one to a French Computing Corporation and the fourth to Mars Chocolate Bar firm. The Corporation will receive royalties on these machines plus a development recovery charge of £2,000 from Elliott Bros. in respect of each one sold'. Details of the 402, the fully engineered version of the 401, are given in Sect. 4.3.1 and in Appendix 3. The sale of a 402 to Mars was not actually consummated, though the detailed requirements analysis for Mars was to awaken in Borehamwood a realisation of the differences between scientific applications and commercial data-processing applications. The theme of commercial data processing is taken up again in Chap. 9. The Australian sale referred to above by NRDC was in fact the Elliott 403 computer, also known as WREDAC (see Chap. 3), and not a 402 machine.

Whilst NRDC did not fully recover its costs for the 401 project, few would carp at the final account. In a retrospective paper, written in July 1965 to mark the final decommissioning of the 401 at Rothamsted, Crawley summarised the financial returns to NRDC thus:

'The expenditure by the Corporation on the development contract and certain other minor expenses associated with [the 401] during its early life amounted to approximately £62,000. Arrangements with Elliott Bros. provided for a limited development recovery to be paid on some of the range of 400 series machines (the 402 and 405). This produced a development recovery return of just over £21,000. The rental arrangement with Rothamsted provided for an annual rental of £2,000 and a share in any moneys earned by the machine when hired by outside users. Little outside work has been done, which has been charged for, and the Corporation's receipts for the machine during its [11-year] sojourn at Rothamsted has been approximately £22,000.'

So, for an outlay of £62,000, there was a return of £43,000 plus the satisfaction of having firmly established the production, by two UK companies (Elliott and Ferranti), of successful small- and medium-range computers. Furthermore, the Elliott 401 at Rothamsted had acted as a catalyst for many emerging practical uses of digital computers, as discussed later.

5.3   Into the Marketplace: The Elliott 400 Series

5.3.1   New Management

At Borehamwood, the computer design team under Andrew St Johnston produced a re-engineered version of the 401 called the 402. In due course, the team went on to produce the Elliott 403 (see Chap. 3) and the Elliott 405 (see Chaps. 8 and 9) and other ranges of computers. Technical details of all the 400 series machines are given in Appendix 3.

Before launching into the story of the Elliott 402, this is a good place to say more about Andrew St Johnston who was, by the summer of 1953, the Manager of the Computing Division. In the words of John Bunt [31], 'after the departure of John Coales and Bill Elliott, Andrew was the natural leader of the team and he succeeded in giving the team confidence in their future at Borehamwood'. The following biographical data comes from [32, 33].

Andrew St Johnston was born on 28 August 1922. In 1943, he graduated in Electrical Engineering (Communications) at the City & Guilds College, then part of Imperial College. He immediately joined the Royal Navy, serving as a radar officer and being posted to the Far East. He returned to join the Admiralty Signal Establishment (ASE), ending his service with the rank of lieutenant commander. Interestingly, he first met Commander Henry Pasley-Tyler at ASE [17]. After a short spell at a small company called Midgley Harmer, Andrew joined the Computing Division at Borehamwood in 1949 to work under Harry Carpenter on the Elliott 152 computer. From 1953 to 1968 Andrew led the computer engineering activities at Borehamwood, overseeing the design, production (and in the case of the 400 series much of the initial marketing) of the Elliott 400 series, 800 series, 502, 503, 900 series and 4100 series computers. He left the company in March 1968, after the merger with English Electric. Laurence Clarke has said [34] that 'I always felt he was disappointed not to get the top job in English Electric Computers'. Upon leaving Elliott-Automation, Andrew joined his second wife's software company Vaughan Systems Ltd. [35], latterly becoming Managing Director. Andrew retired at the age of 77 in 1999 and died on 3 April 2005.

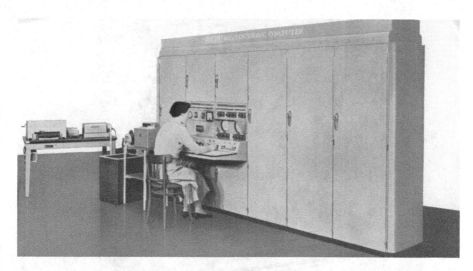

Fig. 5.10 The Elliott 402, the improved production version of the 401, was first delivered in 1955. The paper tape input/output equipment is on the left of the photo. The actual computer shown is a 402E; the larger 402F had floating-point hardware. As far as can be ascertained, a total of ten 402 machines were built. The great majority of applications were in science and engineering

Andrew inspired great loyalty amongst his team members, particularly when outside pressures made great demands upon their time. Laurence Clarke summed up Andrew's career at Borehamwood thus [34]: 'His immense contribution to the development of the computer industry in Britain has never been sufficiently recognised. It started in secrecy, was hidden by the political machinations of NRDC and Ferranti, and finally kept from ultimate fruition by the lack of financial stamina in Elliott-Automation'.

On *financial stamina,* this is an appropriate point to recall the physical and organisational difficulties within which Andrew St Johnston's group was working. David Ince, an engineering graduate who was a fighter pilot in the Second World War, joined the Aviation Research Laboratory at Borehamwood in the late summer of 1954. Here are David Ince's impressions [36] of Borehamwood in 1954: 'A dark and scruffy works building, fronted by a brick office block ... the whole set-up had a part worn look about it, suggesting an acute shortage of funds for capital expenditure and non-essential maintenance. In one respect these impressions were correct. ... for the triumvirate which ruled over Elliott Brothers, brilliant as they were unconventional, were in permanent danger of overtrading. The Chairman, Leon Bagrit, later to be knighted and to become known as *Mr Automation,* was master behind the scenes, rarely seen. In earlier times, when the cash position was even tighter, legend had it that he would strip the company of its component stocks – selling these off one day and buying them back the next – in order to pay the wages... The building at Borehamwood ... was a hive of activity behind its seedy image. Divided into separate cells by internal partitions, or sometimes just chalk marks on the floor, it reflected the operational and organization policy of a dynamic,

Fig. 5.11 Andrew St Johnston, who became Manager of Elliott's Computing Division in 1953, joined Borehamwood in 1949 and left in 1968. In the photo, Andrew is discussing the Elliott 803's re-styled console with Prince Philip, during Prince Philip's visit to Borehamwood on 17 May 1963. In the *left* foreground of the photo is Commander Henry Pasley-Tyler, who had become the effective Director of the Borehamwood Laboratories after the resignation of John Coales in 1952. Sir Leon Bagrit (who was knighted in 1962) is on the *right* of the photo

free thinking, top management. [Elliotts were] one of the first companies to grasp the true potential of electronics ... there was rapid growth through a proliferation of highly motivated product oriented divisions'.

5.3.2 The 402 Production Gets Going

Returning to the plans for a commercial successor to the Elliott 401, a copy of the first 402 descriptive brochure was sent to NRDC on 23 April 1954. Apart from constructional improvements noted below, the main functional improvements were:

- Improved multiplier design, multiplication taking 3 ms regardless of sign
- Provision of hardware division, taking 3 ms

- Fifteen words of immediate-access storage (as nickel delay lines)
- Capacity of magnetic store (called a *drum* rather than a *disc*) increased from 1,024 words (as 8 tracks of 128 words) to 2,944 words (as 23 tracks of 128 words, selected electronically in groups of eight tracks)
- A motor-alternator set, installed a short distance away from the computer, was provided for better AC mains-transient isolation

By the start of 1955, it was clear that peace had broken out between NRDC and Borehamwood. In an internal NRDC memo recording his visit to the Laboratories on 15 February 1955, Crawley is full of enthusiasm:

'The first production 402 (the one for France) is nearing completion, and at least constructionally this machine is very impressive. The machine uses the new Elliott three microsecond drum store instead of a three microsecond disc store, and here again the construction of the drum appears to be first-class. The design of the plug-in units has changed very little from the design of the plug-in units employed in the 401, but the cabinet and chassis designs have been very considerably improved and the arrangements for mounting plug-in units in the cabinets for arranging the interconnecting wiring and for supplying cooling air appear to be very good indeed. There is no evidence, however, that there has been any significant circuit development work carried out on the design of the plug-in units for the magnetic store.

'The power supply arrangement in the 402 appears to be particularly good. The power supply equipment is considerably distributed through the machine and consists of a number of standard small power supply units. Standard stabiliser units have also been developed on plug-in chassis, the whole resulting in extreme flexibility. It is noteworthy that this idea of breaking down power supplies on a modular principle has not been followed in the design of the FPC 1 [Pegasus, see [23]]. Adherence to this modular principle has enabled Elliott Brothers to design rapidly and easily the 403 machine which is the special machine to be delivered to the Long-Range Weapons Establishment [Australia].

'The 403 machine will comprise sixteen cabinets of standard form, the contents of the cabinets being made up of all standard pieces including power supplies employed in 402, together with long nickel delay lines, the design of which has also been based on the modular principle. The magnetic store of 403, however, does not employ a three microsecond drum as in the 402, but employs a much larger disc store based upon the design of the large disc store (with replaceable disc) employed in a recently-delivered Admiralty Machine [the Elliott 153 computer]. Assembly of the 403 has not yet commenced. Construction of the large disc store was well advanced, however, and here again construction appears to be of an impressively high standard.

'The Computing Division at Borehamwood will shortly be installed in new premises [in Warwick Road] adjacent to the existing buildings, where they will have considerably more space than at present, and be substantially self-contained. The move to the new premises has already started but will not be completed probably for quite a few weeks. The new premises will give ample space for assembly of machines.

'The general impression which I received from this visit was one of bustle and activity and very considerable satisfaction with the way work is going.

'The staff appears to have been expanded considerably and no doubt was expressed to me about the ability of the company to meet dates which it had promised on machines. It is expected that the first 402 machine will be ready for shipment in less than two months. French technicians are at present working with the team who are commissioning the machine.

'A humorous side-note is that internally the 402 machine has been christened "Eccles", who is apparently a moronic radio character [in the soon-to-become famous BBC Goon Show]. An alternative interpretation suggested by Mr. Marlow [Commercial Manager, Computing Division] is "Elliott Computers Cost Less". Needless to say, the team putting the final touches to the first 402 are known as the Ecclesiastical Commissioners.'

Laurence Clarke remembers [18] that the name *Eccles* first appeared in connection with a prototype 402 that was used to verify the new features of the production 402.

The *French 402,* referred to above, was delivered to the Institut Blaise Pascal in 1955, on the initiative of the Director, Louis Couffignal. It cost £27,000. Pierre Mounier recalls [37] that: 'The 402 was located in Chatillon, a suburb of Paris whose access was not as easy as the computing facilities of Bull or IBM in the capital. And the early users I have interviewed seemed to dislike the 402 also for technical reasons. Consequently, the 402 often stood idle – a rare fate for the expensive computers of that time. The 402 was replaced or backed up somehow with an IBM 650. The whole Couffignal period at the Institut fell into oblivion, or institutional amnesia, when Couffignal was replaced with René de Possel in 1957, who gave the Institut a considerable impetus. An Elliott 803 was bought in 1962, indicating that the Institut Blaise Pascal still appreciated Elliott's innovative spirit. The 803 was mostly used for teaching programming and numerical analysis, and for crystallographic structures calculations'. The Institut also purchased an Elliott 4130 computer when this became available in 1967/1968 (see Chap. 8 and Appendix 7).

Andrew St Johnston has another anecdote [32] about the French 402. Professor Cuffignal 'wanted Elliotts to make his [own] design of computer, but could see the point of buying an existing design. However he wanted all the labels [of the 402] in French. Some of these concerned waveforms in the machine that could be monitored on the control console CRT. Charles Owen's circuits used not only a clock, but a reset waveform that cut off lengthy tails of pulses. This feature was one of the strengths of his design. Cuffignal thought about these waveforms and identified Reset as *Le Coupure*, the cutting down: fairly reasonable. To my amusement, Clock became *Le Timing*! (in a suitable French accent)'.

A general account of the activity at Borehamwood in this period is provided by Laurence Clarke [13]. Although the surviving records are not precise, it is probable that a total of ten Elliott 402 computers were built [38–40]. At least one of these ten machines was used in-house at Borehamwood to run a Computing Service from 1958 (or before?). It is also evident that seven Elliott 402 computers were delivered to the following external customers on the dates shown:

1955	Institut Blaise Pascal, Paris, France
1956	Imperial Chemical Industries Ltd., Billingham Division, Co Durham
1957	Bomber Command, RAF High Wycombe, Buckinghamshire
1957 (?)	Rank, Taylor and Hobson Ltd., Leicester
1958	Rotol Propellers Ltd., Gloucester
1958	British Railways, probably to the Research Department at Derby
1958	Ernst Leitz GmbH, Wetzlar, Germany

Although dates are not precisely known, the remaining two Elliott 402 computers were most probably delivered to the following customers:

1955   Army Operational Research Group, West Byfleet, Surrey
?   British Railways at Wolverton, Bedfordshire

At one time, one of the external 402s probably came back to Borehamwood so as to provide *two* Computing Service machines on the premises. It is known that in 1961 a second-hand 402 went to Rothamsted, the gift of Elliott Brothers [41]. In March 1965, this 402 computer was passed on by Rothamsted to Watford Technical College (subsequently called West Herts College). By 1969, Watford Technical College had acquired another second-hand machine, namely the 402 formerly used by ICI at Billingham [42]. In 1965, Rotol, by then known as Dowty Rotol, had acquired the 402 formerly used by British Rail at Derby. Rotol coupled their two machines together electrically, when processing jobs requiring large amounts of storage [42]. There may have been other instances of second-hand machines being donated or sold on to new sites but details are unclear. It is said [42] that five Elliott 402 computers were still in operation in 1969.

Eight of the ten original computers were the standard 402E variety. The Ernst Leitz computer and one of the British Railways machines were 402F models with floating-point hardware. Curiously, there is confusion about exactly how many of the delivered Elliott 402s had the hardware floating-point unit which was designed by Laurence Clarke. Clarke himself remembers that there was only one such variant: this was the Leitz machine, formally distinguished as a 402F and delivered to Germany as recounted in Chap. 8. However, John Bunt, alas now no longer with us, wrote [31] in 2001 as follows:

'One of the company reorganisations created the Scientific Computing Division [in about 1958] of which I was the Technical Manager.... So, I had to support the 402 (E & F) at a time when sales were really finished. I had had no previous experience of the 402, but the 402E was a straightforward production job. However we had a second order for a 402F. I think it was from British Rail at Derby. So at a time when almost all my energies were involved with the Elliott 802, I had to commission the 402F and support the machine at Leitz. I spent a very pleasant few days with Leitz at Wetzlar in West Germany, but the second 402F for BR I had to commission myself, in evenings and weekends, because there were no further sales to support a team to look after it.'

It is apparent that the great majority of applications in the mid-1950s were in science and engineering. To appreciate how it was that the organisations, named above, decided to take a step into the unknown and purchase their first-ever digital computer, we need to go back a few years and consider the type of scientific problems that initially seemed suitable for solution by the 400 series machines.

5.3.3   Early Scientific Applications

The presence of a working 401, first at Cambridge and then at Rothamsted, was the signal for several organisations to apply to NRDC for use of time on the machine.

Exploring new applications was encouraged as part of NRDC's role in promoting the use of digital computers in the UK. On behalf of NRDC Strachey, Gillies and Carpenter all, at various times, helped first-time users map their problems onto the 401's computational facilities. In certain cases, as with Dr Gillies and the aircraft industry, NRDC personnel did much of the detailed programming.

Early users of the 401 were not charged for machine time. Writing to a potential customer in September 1954, Crawley said: 'NRDC permitted the use of the machine free of charge when it is a case of people wishing to introduce themselves to the use of the 401 and like machines, or wishing to develop the technique of applying the machine to their problems'.

In consultation with Dr Frank Yates, Head of Statistics at Rothamsted, NRDC worked out a charge for production work and routine computing, once the 401 had settled down at Rothamsted. In September 1954, Crawley had suggested to Yates that the charge be £40 per hour. Yates' reply, in a letter to Crawley dated 16 September 1954, said that £40 seemed high; he suggested £20 per hour, adding: 'At present the machine is by no means fully extended – I reckon that it could easily be run on a two-shift basis of, say, 16 hours a day …'. By January 1955, the standard charge for the 401 was settled at £25 per hour.

As a comparison, the Theory Division at Borehamwood permitted outside users to hire time on the Elliott Nicholas computer (see Chap. 8), for which the charge in 1954 was 'one penny per second' [43]. One old penny was 1/240th of a pound, equating to a charge of £15 per hour. Nicholas was a less-powerful computing resource than the Elliott 401.

The first set of problems for which NRDC's help was sought covered an interesting spectrum of applied science and engineering. Summarising the surviving correspondence, the tasks included the following areas and organisations, approximately ordered by the date at which an enquiry was first received by NRDC:

- Statistics, linear programming, time series analysis, etc., for the Army's Operational Research Group (May 1953).
- Structure and stability calculations for the Bristol Aeroplane Co. Ltd. (August 1953).
- Structure and stability calculations for the De Havilland Aircraft Company (October 1953).
- Solution of simultaneous non-linear differential equations for the British Electricity Authority which, by May 1955, had become the Central Electricity Authority (February 1954).
- Structure and stability calculations for the Hawker Aircraft Company (May 1954).
- Statistical analysis and statistical data processing and queuing theory, for the Road Research Laboratory (June 1954).
- Solution of some unspecified problems for the Directorate of Colonial Surveys (August 1954).
- Solution of sets of simultaneous equations for a research project on acetylene production at Imperial College, London (November 1954).
- Cyclotron design problem for CERN (European Council for Nuclear Research), Geneva. (Work substantially completed by August 1955, at which time the total bill for the 401's time had amounted to just under £194).

- Statistical analysis for the Research & Development Department of the Distillers Company (August 1955).
- Statistical analysis of experimental results for the National Institute of Industrial Psychology (October 1955).

NRDC's correspondence with the above organisations reveals some interesting insights into the practical difficulties faced by early users. Here is a selection.

In a letter dated 24 June 1954, Dr R D Smeed of the Road Research Laboratory, Harmondsworth, states that they had already used relay computers, punched-card equipment, and NPL's Pilot ACE computer – but there was limited availability on the Pilot ACE and in any case Dr Smeed's source data was on five-track paper tape and, with Pilot ACE, the necessary prior tape-to-punched-card conversion took nearly as long as the rest of the analysis. Dr Smeed's statistical problems included frequency distributions and moments, multiple linear regressions with up to 15 variables, queuing problems and 'data processing of various kinds'.

On 15 June 1955, Dr Yates (Rothamsted) wrote to H H Brazier, the Chief Computer [sic] of the Directorate of Colonial Surveys at Surbiton, reporting that the total [401] machine time for two production runs on Brazier's problem was 50 min. Yates added: 'Our girl took a full working day to punch the data tapes. I think a fair charge for this [data preparation] service would be £2 as she is a very skilled operator'.

P G Smith, of the Distillers Company's R&D Department at Epsom, explained in a letter dated 17 August 1955 that they had already had some computational work done for them at Borehamwood (Elliott 402), at NPL (Pilot ACE), and on LEO at Lyons' premises at Cadby Hall, London, but that 'none of these have immediately available any statistical analysis routines'. Hence, Smith approached NRDC for time on the 401 at Rothamsted where staff had developed considerable know-how on computational statistics. The Distillers Company clearly made satisfactory use of the facilities for, according to an internal NRDC memo dated 3 January 1956, the company was by that date considering computers 'not only for scientific calculation but also from the accountancy angle'.

The Electricity Authority's task was to calculate the theoretical impedances of the new power lines (i.e. transmission lines) being designed for the 270 KV National Grid system. The solution of simultaneous non-linear differential equations was required, where the non-linear function was in tabular form. J P Holland of the Electricity Authority, Bankside House, London, writing to NRDC on 11 February 1954, explained that he had prepared 'a complete sub-routine for interpolation and also a Runge-Kutta routine in outline'. By October 1954, Harry Carpenter estimated that the time required on the 401 for each transmission line calculation would be:

Program input	4–5 min
Data input	10 s
Calculating time	30 s
Output time	4 min

On 30 March 1955, Carpenter wrote to Holland describing the production runs carried out on the 401 on 25 March: 'Measured computing time = 90 secs. per set of parameter values; total of 64 sets of parameter values; therefore, total time

(at £25 per hour) is 1 hr 36 minutes'. Carpenter added that 'no charge was made for checking the program, or for repeat runs of doubtful values'.

5.3.4   The Flutter Problem

In the light of hindsight, applications of the Elliott 401 in the aircraft industry were to have the most beneficial impact on the engineering sector of British industry. As aircraft became larger and travelled faster, so the problems of structural vibration or 'flutter' began to have a relatively more serious effect on flight-control and on metal fatigue. The design of airframes, which had always involved a deal of computational analysis, became an area demanding huge computational resources.

Matters came to a head, as far as public awareness of the problems was concerned, with the apparently inexplicable crash of two De Havilland Comet airliners in January and April 1954. The Comet, which had its first test flight in 1949, was a standard-bearer for British aviation expertise. In May 1952, after exhaustive testing, a Comet took off from London to Johannesburg for the world's first all-jet flight with fare-paying passengers. The Comet flew faster and higher and offered a smoother ride than other contemporary airliners. 30,000 passengers were carried during the first year of service and over 50 Comets were ordered. Comets were designed and built at de Havilland's Hatfield factory, about 6 miles north of Borehamwood.

Fig. 5.12 The application of computers to aircraft design was a hot topic in the early 1950s, particularly after the crash of two De Havilland Comet airliners in 1954 due largely to metal fatigue. Elliotts and NRDC collaborated with aircraft manufacturers in developing programs for so-called *flutter calculations* to analyse stress in airframes

Then in 1954 disaster struck. After careful analysis of the two 1954 Comet crashes, the accident investigators came to the conclusion that metal fatigue was the most likely cause of both accidents. Further experiments revealed that stress-concentrations round the square corners of the Comet's windows were much greater than had originally been expected. The Comet was accordingly re-designed. Modified Comets then performed well for many years, both in the civilian and military sphere. We shall meet the Comet in a military context in Chap. 12. The Comet 4 design was developed to meet a requirement for a maritime patrol aircraft for the Royal Air Force, becoming the Hawker Siddeley Nimrod. Nimrods entered service in 1969 and the latest variant was still in service with the RAF in 2007.

Peter Hunt of the de Havilland Aircraft Company was an early (1953/1954) outside user of the Elliott Nicholas computer at Borehamwood, where he carried out flutter calculations for the original Comet airliner, using a 10×10 matrix of floating-point numbers [44].

In a letter to De Havillands dated 12 March 1954, Crawley says: 'We have been thinking further on the subject of your problem and have had consultation with Mr. (Peter) Hunt of your Company, and it would appear that a method of analysing this problem, suggested by one of our staff, Mr. D B Gillies, offers the possibility of a more comprehensive and faster solution than the solution that you have so far contemplated. This method has not been worked out in detail or tried on the [401] machine, but we suggest that it would be well worthwhile for us to collaborate to finish the study of this method and try it out on the computer.

'Should you be agreeable to this we are quite prepared to devote machine time to the testing of the program, without charge. We suggest that a solution of this type would represent a step forward in the technique of flutter analysis and would be well worth writing up and publishing in a suitable technical journal. This would achieve the dual object of making the information available to the aircraft industry in this country and stimulating interest in the use of digital computers for this type of design problem.'

R M Clarkson, the assistant Chief Engineer at De Havilland, wrote back immediately stating that the company was 'very anxious to co-operate'. By the following summer, the job had been substantially completed. Writing to NRDC on 17 June 1955, Clarkson says:

'From the amount of program which has been written so far we can conclude that the 401 solves this problem in a suitable manner and fairly quickly. The program has been checked for problems appropriate to two, three and four degrees of freedom, but for five and six degrees of freedom it still requires modification in the form of double length working being incorporated at certain stages in the calculation or by new matrices being used.

'In this connection a different method appropriate only to the case of two degrees of freedom (and which we have coded up) produces the critical speeds and frequencies in 10 seconds. It is also interesting to note that since the stick-free stability equations for an Aircraft are a particular case of the flutter equations the above program can be used for this stability work as well ....

'In conclusion we would like to thank you very much indeed for giving us this opportunity of using the 401 in an attempt to solve the flutter determinant by digital methods, and in particular would like to thank your engineers and programmers who have given us so much help in getting this program working at Rothamsted.'

De Havilland's experience was not lost on other aircraft designers or other computer manufacturers. By May 1954, the Hawker Aircraft Company had run their version of the flutter problem with four degrees of freedom on the Pilot ACE computer and on a Ferranti Mark I Star. (The 'four degrees of freedom' involves four simultaneous second-order linear differential equations of the second degree in velocity, from which the eight modes of vibration, equivalent to the eigenvalues of the corresponding matrices, are required.) In May 1954, Hawker was thinking of buying its own 402 computer from Elliott Brothers and wished for a demonstration of a flutter program on an Elliott 402. However, a 402 was not yet working at Borehamwood. It was felt by the Borehamwood sales staff that the demonstration of a related problem on the 401 at Rothamsted would convince Hawkers to place their order, so they asked for NRDC's assistance. A meeting took place between Borehamwood, Hawkers and NRDC on 15 May 1954. In proposing to help with such a demonstration (but only as a matter of low priority), Gillies also observed in his note of the meeting that: 'Mr Hunt [of De Havillands] and I were planning a method which would be several times faster than the ACE or MUC methods, and would give all the desired answers, but this program would certainly not be available within 3 months'. [By 'MUC', Gillies was referring to the Manchester University Computer, which, in the context of the meeting, was his informal way of describing the Ferranti Mark I installed at Manchester University].

Peter Hunt joined Ferranti Ltd. on 1 July 1955. The landmark Gillies/Hunt paper describing their solution to the flutter problem was published in 1956 [45].

5.4   NRDC as a Partner for the Future

The deliveries of Elliott 402 and 403 computers covered the period 1955–1963. Although no 404 machine was produced, a paper specification for an Elliott 404 appeared in May 1956 [46]. As indicated in Appendix 3, the 404 was to have been a cross between the 403 and the successful Elliott 405 business data-processing system.

The final member of the 400 series was the commercial data-processing machine called the Elliott 405. Deliveries of the 405 spanned the period 1956–1962. The development of the 405 and the marketing arrangements with NCR are described more fully in Chap. 9. Delivery lists, and estimated costs, for all Elliott computers are given in Appendix 8.

Although NRDC personnel took no part in the specification or design of the 405, NRDC did take what turned out to be an indirect, and traumatic, part in promoting this computer.

5.4.1   The Siemens Project

In January 1956, NRDC decided to involve itself in an exemplar project that would demonstrate the usefulness of digital computers in support of industrial management and decision making. This can be seen as a natural follow-on from the type of applied engineering applications described in the previous section. The particular demonstration chosen by NRDC was the use of an Elliott 405 computer for 'stores inventory control and production control and planning, associated with the manufacture of automatic telephone exchanges'. The location selected for the work was the Siemens Edison Swan factory at Woolwich in south London. At that time, the Woolwich factory was said to be using about 100,000 items of raw materials and parts. Any inefficiencies in stock control had serious implications for the amount of money tied up in stock and in work-in-progress. As Hendry says [1], 'the cost of stock and work-in-progress was running at between £2 million and £3 million, and the production cycle was much longer than was desirable'.

The plan for the project was that NRDC provided 'two full-time and one part-time programmers and Siemens provided three, initially untrained, programmers and a number of assistant staff, plus over six persons engaged on organisation and methods'. NRDC would provide initial funding to purchase the Elliott 405 and all necessary ancillary equipment. Siemens would, upon satisfactory completion of the development, purchase the whole hardware/software system, take over all maintenance, reimburse NRDC's costs plus 5% of capital expenditure and pay NRDC an additional fee set at 5% of NRDC's total expenditure. The final cost to Siemens was estimated (by January 1958) to turn out at about £128,500, of which the cost of the 405 and all necessary ancillary equipment amounted to £84,000.

The delivery of the 405 to the Woolwich factory was promised for September 1957. NRDC then allowed 2 years for completion of the software development, after which time Siemens, if satisfied with the resulting system, was required to take over the hardware and software and pay NRDC the amounts described above.

At the time of initiating what became known as the 'Siemens project', NRDC was breaking new ground. The first Elliott 405 had not yet come off the production line at Borehamwood; Siemens had no experience of digital computers nor, crucially, had they any experience of conventional electromechanical punched-card procedures; neither NRDC programmers nor Borehamwood programmers had any real experience of clerical data processing. Probably the only UK concern that had, by January 1956, accumulated any experience of digital computers in an office data-processing environment was the catering company J Lyons & Co. Ltd., who had previous familiarity with electromechanical punched-card procedures. The company's new LEO (Lyons Electronic Office) computer, whose central processor was a re-engineered version of the Cambridge University EDSAC, had run test programs as early as February 1951 but the first full-scale trial of the company's payroll program did not take place until 1 January 1953. The LEO computer and all its considerable input/output equipment was finally declared complete at a party held on 23 December 1953. Such was the success of LEO within the catering company that Lyons founded a new enterprise, Leo Computers Ltd., in November 1954 to build and sell a new machine called LEO II. The first LEO II was delivered in 1957. LEO computers are discussed further in Appendix 10.

What distinguished LEO, and later the Elliott 405, from other contemporary UK computers was their mechanisms and procedures for dealing with the transfer of large amounts of data in character form. Commercially realistic quantities of alphanumeric data required bulk storage, preferably via magnetic tape equipment, and bulk input/output, normally via punched-card equipment and rapid 'line-at-a-time' printers (line printers). In America, the first UNIVAC computer had successfully faced these challenges. UNIVAC I, the *tour de force* of the Presper Eckert/John Mauchley partnership, was installed in mid-1951.

As is described in Chap. 9, the 405 was considered to be the largest UK-designed commercially available business data-processing computer in 1956. It was also Borehamwood's first foray into the business data-processing area – an area that NRDC wished to promote.

To continue the Siemens story, it was on the 25 January 1956 that NRDC first decided to commit money for the purchase of an Elliott 405 for the Siemens project. Although initially promised for September 1957, a 405 computer was not delivered to Siemens' Woolwich factory until April 1958. Meanwhile, the NRDC programmers had arranged to do some initial development on a 405 at Borehamwood. Time on the Elliott 405 was normally charged at £50 per hour but a special rate was agreed for NRDC staff working towards the Siemens project. Colin Merton and B G (Brian) Millis were the programmers chiefly associated with the project, though several other NRDC employees such as Tony Keeping contributed from time to time [47]. Christopher Strachey was involved only at the commencement of the activity. Siemens employed three programmers. John Halder was the senior; the second was Barry Wilkinson, straight from A levels (the school leaving examination); the third was an older employee of Siemens, Bill Rees [47]. At a later stage, Prof. R W Revans of Manchester College of Science & Technology acted as a consultant to the project, spending 2 days per week at Woolwich.

The summer and autumn of 1958 was a time of stress for all concerned with the project, as the engineers worked to improve the reliability of the Woolwich installation and the programmers worked to tame the complexity of the end-user application. Strachey had specified an extremely rigorous set of Acceptance Tests for the 405, designed to exercise all the bulk data-processing facilities required for what was to be a substantial workload. By the end of 1958, software development was on track but hardware unreliability continued to cause problems.

At a meeting of NRDC's electronic computing sub-committee held on 16 December 1958, it was reported that 'the Elliott 405 installation at Woolwich had so far not passed its Acceptance Tests and was also performing unsatisfactorily on dummy acceptance trials conducted by Elliott Brothers. Dr Ross of Elliott Brothers had been told that, if the machine had not passed the agreed Acceptance Tests by the end of January 1959, the Corporation would consider the machine to be unacceptable'. Borehamwood was just able to save the day. At a meeting of the electronic computing sub-committee held on 17 February 1959, NRDC was informed that the 405 'had now successfully passed a stringent Acceptance trial specified by the Corporation, and had been accepted, subject to minor reservations'.

During 1959, the original intention of handling 'stores inventory control and production control and planning, associated with the manufacture of automatic telephone exchanges' did not proceed as planned, largely due to events that were beyond the control of either Borehamwood or NRDC. It seemed that there were shortcomings on the part of Siemens staff in inadequately specifying the total list of stock items. The Siemens Edison Swan Company's Woolwich enterprise was re-organised by the parent company, AEI, and the production of telephone equipment eventually ceased at Woolwich. In January 1961 the company, by then called AEI (Woolwich) Ltd., gave formal notice of dissatisfaction with the Siemens project.

Summarising his retrospective comments [47], Brian Millis highlights his three main reasons for the failure of NRDC's *Siemens Project*:

1. It was too ambitious for the time. The 405 computer was a new design, with practically no software. 'The Siemens project programmers developed our own basic packages, even re-writing the 405's Assembler so as to incorporate essential checking facilities. This all consumed time and effort'.
2. At the outset, Siemens' Woolwich factory only had a manual clerical system: 'no punched cards –the knowledge of what was really going on was in Jack's head'. When the team started planning the data structures for the 405, the Siemens Head of Organisation and Methods, A J Jones, 'told us that, while many of the parts were not coded in a systematic way, they had recently introduced a new coding system'. However, the new system was not rigorously adhered to and anomalies continued to occur. 'The lack of any punched card predecessor also gave rise to a huge data preparation load – all the parts had to be typed up and verified (on paper tape). I remember amongst others the multiplicity of different types of screws, head type (countersunk or whatever), standard (BSF or Whitworth), thread length and size...'.
3. The AEI takeover of Siemens and the associated management review was the last straw. 'AEI had its own computer design – the AEI 1010 – and to the AEI management the obvious thing was to scrap the 405-based project and replace it by a project based on their own new machine. I do not think this actually came to anything'.

By March 1961, the 405 was deemed to be surplus to the company's requirements and the future of the computer at Woolwich was under discussion by NRDC, still the machine's legal owners. Over the next few months, eight organisations were considered as potential destinations for the machine. The 'Siemens 405' was finally installed in the Engineering Department at Cambridge University at the request of Professor John Coales, in February 1962. Thus ended a project that had, once again, strained relations between Elliott Brothers and NRDC.

In retrospect, this was a difficult time for NRDC on more than one front: relations with Ferranti Ltd. had also soured over the cost of NRDC's involvement in the Ferranti Pegasus project. Whilst many thought that the government should be directing considerably more money towards UK computer manufacturers in order to compete with American companies, the plain fact was that NRDC was not set up to be a lavish patron. NRDC was obliged to recover its costs by licencing agreements and by levies on any products that resulted from initial NRDC sponsorship.

We end this chapter by considering the final major partnership between NRDC and the Elliott company which, from 1957 onwards, was known as Elliott-Automation.

5.4.2 Process Control

Whilst all the manufacturing and marketing activity for the 400 series computers was proceeding apace, the Borehamwood engineers were busy developing their new 800 series machines – this time completely independently of any NRDC support. The 800 series covered the small-to-medium end of the market. Deliveries started in 1958 and several hundred 803s were sold over the next few years, as described in Chap. 10 and Appendix 4. By the end of 1961, Elliott Brothers or, as it had by then become known, Elliott-Automation Ltd., could justly claim to be providing about half of all computers manufactured in the UK. (The precise market share is analysed in Chap. 13.)

In parallel with the success of the 800 series, Borehamwood had been refining its long-held belief in the need for better industrial control systems and process automation as recounted in Chaps. 6 and 7. The way ahead seemed to lie in the development of a hierarchy of control equipment, comprising customised selections of modules ranging from simple analogue computing elements to complete general-purpose digital computers. Accordingly, in September 1959 Elliott-Automation approached NRDC for help in developing what was to become known as ARCH: the Articulated Control Hierarchy. In November 1959 NRDC agreed to make available up to £150,000 for one half of the cost of developing the ARCH concept.

The technical details of ARCH and the incorporation of 800 series and 900 series computers into ARCH systems are covered in more detail in Chap. 7. The purpose of mentioning the project here is to round off the account of how NRDC interacted with Elliott Brothers and Elliott-Automation during the 1950s and 1960s.

ARCH was launched at a Press Conference held at the Savoy Hotel, London, on 7 May 1962. The first public demonstration of specific ARCH equipment was at the Instruments, Electronics & Automation Exhibition at Olympia, London, from 28 May to 2 June 1962.

The Minutes of NRDC's Project Committee meeting of 26 June 1962, under the heading 'Elliott's Automation (ARCH) project', record the events as follows: 'The Committee were also impressed with the technical and commercial potential of the [ARCH] project, which was of a much greater order than the previous one [the Siemens project]. In this case there was no question of action to counter inadequacy of the exploitation effort but rather of a need to recognise that the Corporation had an enthusiastic collaborator in Elliott-Automation Ltd. One thing which was noted by the Committee was the declaration by the collaborator that their association with NRDC had in their view an important prestige value to them. The financial aspect of the agreement should be watched with care'.

The ARCH project was essentially the last major partnership between Borehamwood and NRDC. It ended on a happy note. Lord Halsbury had retired from NRDC in the spring of 1959. His successor as Managing Director of the National Research Development Corporation, John Duckworth, had less of a personal interest in computers. In the mid-1960s, by which time the role of NRDC had been taken over by the Ministry of Technology, government again began to play a part in stimulating – or rather, rationalising – the UK computer industry. Indeed, the Ministry's Industrial Reorganisation Corporation (IRC) was to play a role in events at the end of the 1960s that saw the demise of Borehamwood as an independent player. We will return to these momentous events in Chap. 13. First, we go back a few years to give a more thorough introduction to Leon Bagrit's concept of automation and how the ARCH project came to play a part in Elliott-Automation's early pre-eminence in the field of industrial process control. This is in the next chapter.

The NRDC source documents forming the background to Chap. 5 are stored in the National Archive for the History of Computing (NAHC) at the University of Manchester. See: www.chstm.manchester.ac.uk/research/nahc/. The NAHC collection comprises 49 boxes of archival material, formerly classified as 86/1, 86/2, etc., but re-numbered in 1985 as NAHC/NRD/C1, NAHC/NRD/C2, etc. Of particular relevance to Elliott Bros (London) Ltd. are the following boxes:

C11 and C12:	Elliott 405
C13:	correspondence with Elliott Bros (London) Ltd., 1950–1965.
C14:	specifications of Elliott contracts, 1949–1953
C15:	correspondence, agreements, finance, etc.
C25:	Christopher Strachey, correspondence 1956
C35:	Elliott ARCH project, 1959–1962
C39:	401 at Rothamsted; 405 at Siemens

References

1. Hendry J (1990) Innovating for failure: government policy and the early British computer industry. MIT Press, London. ISBN 0-262-08187-3
2. (a) Crawley HJ (1957) The National Research Development Corporation Computer Project. NRDC Computer Sub-Committee, paper 132, Feb 1957. (b) John Crawley (1993) NRDC's role in the early British computer industry. Resurrection, the Bulletin of the Computer Conservation Society, Issue number 8, winter 1993, pp 25–32
3. Research Laboratories, Elliott Brothers (London) Ltd., Visitors Book
4. D Hennessey, three-page confidential NRDC Internal Memorandum MDR 14/Annexe B, dated 12 Aug 1950 (on page 1) and 14th August (on page 3). Addressed to: Managing Director. NAHC file 86/13/1
5. (a) Campbell-Kelly M (1989) ICL – a business and technical history. Oxford University Press, Oxford. (b) Mounier-Kuhn P-E (1994) Product policies in two French computer firms: SEA and Bull (1948–1964). In: Bud-Frierman L (ed) Information Acumen – the understanding and use of knowledge in modern business. Routledge, London
6. Mounier-Kuhn Pierre-E (2008) E-mails to Simon Lavington, Nov 2008

7. Crawley HJ (1950) Note on visit to Elliott Bros on Monday 25th September. NRDC Internal Memo dated 27 Sept 1950

8. Lavington SH (1975) A history of Manchester computers. First edition published by the National Computing Centre, 1975. Second edition published by the British Computer Society, 1998. ISBN: 0-902505-01-8

9. Johnson WEP (1950) NRDC Internal Memo dated 24 Nov 1950. NAHC file 86/13/1

10. Managing Director's Report *Electronic computers, Elliott Brothers Ltd.*, to the 18th NRDC Board meeting, 20 Dec 1950. NAHC file 86/13/1

11. Campbell-Kelly M (1985) Christopher Strachey, 1916–1975 – A biographical note. IEEE Ann Hist Comput 7(1):19–42

12. Hodges A (1983) Alan Turing: the enigma. Burnett Books, London, p 447. ISBN: 0-09-152130-0

13. Clarke SLH (1993) Recollections of the Elliott 400 series. Computer Resurrection, the Bulletin of the Computer Conservation Society, Issue number 6, summer 1993, pp 15–21. See also a similar paper by Laurence Clarke entitled *Early computer production at Elliotts*, Computer Resurrection, Number 41, Autumn 2007

14. Bradburd EM (1951) Magnetostrictive delay line. Electrical Commun 28(1):46–53

15. Millership R, Robbins RC, De Barr AE (Oct 1951) Magnetostriction storage systems for high-speed digital computers. Br J Appl Phys 2(10):304

16. De Barr AE (May 1953) Digital storage using ferromagnetic materials. The Elliott J 1(4):116–120, See also Borehamwood Internal Research Reports numbers 309 dated 30 Dec 1952 and 325 dated 22 Feb 1953

17. Andrew St Johnston (2001) Interview with Simon Lavington at Hedgegrove Farm (Andrew's home) on 29 Oct 2001

18. Laurence Clarke (2009) E-mail to Simon Lavington dated 14 Oct 2009

19. MH (Harry) Johnson (2002) My work with computers: from the Ferranti Mark I to the ICT 1900 (1952–1966). 84-page typed manuscript, circulated privately, June 2002

20. SLH Clarke (Aug 1975) The Elliott 400 series and before. Radio Electron Eng 45(8): 415–421

21. SLH Clarke (2007) Conversations with Simon Lavington on 7th June 2007

22. SLH Clarke (1993) Recollections of the Elliott 400 series. Computer Resurrection, the Bulletin of the Computer Conservation Society, Issue number 6, summer 1993, pp 15–21

23. Lavington SH (2000) The Pegasus story: a history of a vintage British computer. Science Museum, London. ISBN: 1-900747-40-5. (Second edition to appear in 2011)

24. The Rt. Hon. the Earl of Halsbury (1959, Jan) Ten years of computer development. Comput J 1(4)

25. See file NAHC/NRD/C13/4: *Verbatim note of meeting with Elliott Bros, 5th November 1953*. Present at this meeting were (for NRDC): Mr D Hennessey, Mr J F Lockwood and Mr H J Crawley, and (for Elliotts): Dr L L Ross, Commander H Pasley-Tyler, Mr A St Johnston and Mr D H Marlow. At this tense meeting, accusations and insinuations flowed back and forth. Although the name of W S Elliott was not recorded, Dr Ross was moved to make the following observation half-way through the meeting: "Ever since the machine [the 401] went to Cambridge and ever since a certain person left the Bros. [i.e. Elliott Brothers (London) Ltd.] we have heard rumours to the effect that we have lost interest in the machine. This is incorrect. Our team is an excellent one and is very much larger than it has been at any time since the inception of the machine"

26. Healy M (1995) Frank Yates, 1902–1994 – the work of a statistician. Int Stat Rev 63:271–288

27. Michael Healy (2009) E-mail to Simon Lavington, 11 June 2009

28. Yates F, Lipton S (April 1957) An automatic programming routine for the Elliott 401. J ACM 4(2):151–156

29. Gavin Ross (2009) E-mails to Simon Lavington, June 2009

30. See the editorial comment entitled *40 years of the Elliott 401* on page 6 of the Summer 1993 edition of Resurrection, the Bulletin of the Computer Conservation Society

31. John Bunt (2001) Eight-page typed letter sent to Simon Lavington, dated 11 Dec 2001

32. Andrew St. Johnston (1995) History of the research laboratories of Elliott brothers (London) Ltd. – Andrew St. Johnston's Contribution. Nine-page typed manuscript dated 31 May 1995 and sent to Laurence Clarke
33. Obituary of Andrew St Johnston in *The Times* newspaper on 2 May 2005
34. Laurence Clarke (2004) Oration at the funeral of Andrew St Johnston, 15 Apr 2005
35. Lavington SH (May 2009) An appreciation of Dina St Johnston, 1930–2007, founder of the UK's first software house. Comput J 52(3):378–387
36. Ince, David (1992) Combat and competition. Newton, Swindon. ISBN 1-872308-23-6
37. Mounier-Kuhn P-E (2008) (CNRS & Centre de recherches en Histoire de l'Innovation Université Paris-Sorbonne): e-mails to Simon Lavington, Nov 2008
38. Anon, *Elliott Automation: Computers and Orders, 1947–1966.* Brochure published in early 1967 by the Directorate of Information Services, Elliott-Automation Ltd., 21 Portland Place, London W1
39. Anon, *Computer and data processing installations.* Elliott Computing Division. Issued 31st August 1963 by Elliott Brothers (London) Ltd., Borehamwood
40. See: *Computer Survey,* vol. 1 number 1, June 1962. Published by United Trade Press Ltd., London
41. See the Rothamsted Annual Reports for the following years: 1961 (p 164), 1962 (p 173), 1963 (p 168), 1964 (p 205) and 1965 (p 206)
42. Woodland L (1969) The 402 story. Computer Weekly, 8 May 1969, p 10. This was Part 5 in a series of Computer Weekly articles on early British computers
43. Hersom Ed (2007) Nicholas, the forgotten Elliott Project. Resurrection, the Bulletin of the Computer Conservation Society, vol 27, spring 2002, pp 10–14. Also quoted by G E Felton, in his presentation at the BCS@50 Conference, London, 12–14 July 2007
44. Felton GE (2006) Getting the job done. Resurrection, the Bulletin of the Computer Conservation Society, Issue number 38, summer 2006, pp 13–17. See: http://www.cs.man.ac.uk/CCS/res/res38.htm#e
45. Hunt PM (1956) The electronic digital computer in aircraft structural analysis, parts 1–3. Aircraft Engineering, Mar 1956 (pp 70–76), April 1956 (pp 111–118), May 1956 (pp 155–165)
46. Mills RG (1956) A general description of the Elliott 404 Electronic Digital Computer. Report S64 published by the Computing Machine Division, Elliott Brothers (London) Ltd., Borehamwood, in May 1956 (42 typed pages)
47. Brian Millis (2007) E-mails to Simon Lavington, Aug 2007

Chapter 6
Process Control and Automation: The Bagrit Vision

6.1 What Is, or Was, Automation?

6.1.1 The Historical Perspective

Automation, broadly defined as the computer-assisted control of industrial processes, covers a wide spectrum of applications. Here we need to narrow the spectrum somewhat, so as to focus on the word *automation* as it might have been understood by people such as Leon Bagrit during the period 1948–1968. Of course, Bagrit's view evolved over this period, just as the capabilities of digital computers evolved over the same period. This chapter charts the evolution.

For some computer historians, the 1950s indeed offers a good starting-point for understanding automation, since the 1950s may be considered to cover the first decade of what has been called the *Digital Information Age* – though both analogue and digital techniques actually existed side by side during the 1950s as far as process control was concerned. Other computer historians would go much further back in time, pointing out that the Jacquard loom, invented in 1802 [1], can be said to have embodied automation. Jacquard's loom used punched cards to specify the weaving of complicated patterns and pictures. Finally, for yet other commentators the word *automation* carries no particular links with industrial mechanisms. Instead, automation is primarily associated with data-processing software. Hence, an article in the *Insurance Journal* [2] selects 1972 as the start of automation since it was in this year that the Association for Cooperative Operations Research and Development (ACORD), based in New York, introduced the ACORD Standard Forms for the insurance business.

6.1.2 The Reith Lectures Perspective

By the early 1960s, Leon Bagrit himself had a clear view that automation was particularly relevant to the manufacturing industry but was not to be confused with mere mechanization. In his 1964 BBC Reith Lectures [3], he stated that

S. Lavington, *Moving Targets*, History of Computing,
DOI 10.1007/978-1-84882-933-6_6, © Springer-Verlag London Limited 2011

automation would liberate humans, whereas mechanisation, as exemplified by Charlie Chaplin in the film *Modern Times,* enslaved them. To quote from Bagrit's book of the Reith Lectures:

'Automation has been, and still is, a greatly misused word, but its proper meaning, and therefore its implications, is gradually becoming better understood. Perhaps I could attempt an explanation, if not a definition, by saying that it is a concept through which a machine-system is caused to operate with maximum efficiency by means of adequate measurement, observation and control of its behaviour. It involves a detailed and continuous knowledge of the functioning of the system, so that the best corrective actions can be applied immediately they become necessary.

'Automation in this true sense is brought to full fruition only through a thorough exploitation of its three major elements, communication, computation and control – the three 'C's'....

'I myself prefer the word cybernation, because it deals with the theory of communications and control, which is what genuine automation really is....

'I have always thought it was most unfortunate that the word "automation" was invented in the motor car industry, in fact by a works manager at Ford's in Detroit ... [probably in 1953; see for example [4]]. The word is only ten years old, but in these ten years it has unfortunately developed the connotation, not of cybernation, but of automaticity and there is the greatest difficulty in getting rid of this unfortunate meaning'.

Were it not for the fact that the Reith Lectures addressed a general audience of non-specialists, Bagrit could have gone on to mention some of automation's enabling technologies. Bagrit's assessment of the necessity for these enabling technologies is illustrated by remarks to shareholders in various Company documents. For example, in the Elliott-Automation Report for the year 1959, the Chairman said that 'Automation depends to a very large degree upon knowledge of advanced techniques in a surprisingly varied number of fields, and this inevitably requires intimate contact with the latest scientific ideas and technologies'. This thought was amplified in the Report for the following year, when the Chairman's Statement included this paragraph:

'I would like to recall that after the end of the War, the then newly appointed management of Elliott Brothers (London) Ltd. set out as a matter of policy to enter the new developing field of *Control Engineering,* subsequently called *Automation.* To that end, and in pursuance of an overall plan, it steadily assembled in the one Company, and subsequently in your Group, the widely different techniques and equipment necessary for the automation of plants in a vast variety of industries. Consequently, we engaged in such diverse fields as Process Control Instrumentation, Automatic Control Valves, Digital and Analogue Computing, Data Reduction, Telecommunications and others, all of which are essential ingredients of automation. As shareholders know, to handle this immense variety of equipment and techniques, the Group is organised into many separate divisions, the number of which has again grown appreciably during the year and now exceeds sixty.'

For his Reith Lectures, in contrast, Bagrit focussed on extolling automation as the enabler for industrial efficiency and wealth creation, from which would grow prosperity for all. To quote for the dust jacket of Bagrit's book [3]: '*The Age of Automation* presents a fascinating brave new world with man saved from the drudgery of routine work, rich enough to help the underdeveloped areas, with leisure to cultivate cultural and sporting interests and with the prospect of comfortable retirement from an industrial to a rural area at 55'. These words betray some of the social preoccupations of Britain in the 1950s, when war-time austerity was still a vivid memory, the Cold War a reality. As computers emerged from the laboratory into the workplace, there were considerable misgivings about the consequences for employment: 'Will computers take our jobs?' A hidden agenda for Bagrit's book was therefore a need to demonstrate that the man they called *Mr Automation* was actually an influence for the good.

6.2 The Origins: Industrial Instrumentation and Control

Setting aside the above utopian sentiments, we need to delve deeper into the technology of industrial automation and return to the late 1940s and early 1950s before the word *Automation* had been coined. The origins of the concept lie in the techniques evolved for instrumentation and control of industrial processes. Bagrit and his close technical adviser Dr. Lawrence (Lotti) Ross had seen the possibilities for automated process control several years before Bagit's Reith Lectures. For example, in a visit to Borehamwood in August 1950, Hennessey of the National Research Development Corporation (NRDC) had noted Bagrit's intention to exploit the 'use of fixed-program computers for process control applications' (see Chap. 5).

The in-house publication *The Elliott Journal*, a Borehamwood-inspired organ whose first issue appeared in March 1951, contains several indications that the process control theme was being actively developed by the company under the general heading of *instrumentation*. For example, a 1951 advertisement for a Lewisham-produced instrument called the *Elliottronic potentiometer recorder* (see Fig. 6.1) suggested that the production of a data-logging record of variables encountered in an industrial process could also be used 'to provide various combinations of two- and three-term control' [5]. This idea was put into practice for blast furnace temperature control at the Ebbw Vale steelworks of Richard Thomas & Baldwin Ltd. in about 1952/3 [6]. In another issue of the journal, a paper touching on the connection between instrumentation and automatic control [7] suggested that a box labelled 'controller' in a system diagram could be regarded as a 'computer': this computer received inputs such as temperature and pressure from the industrial process and passed outputs that activated pumps and valves associated with the process. By 1954, the last year of publication, the journal was advertising Elliott's services to industry through the company's

36   THE ELLIOTT JOURNAL

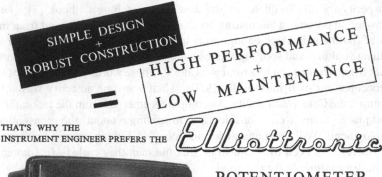

THAT'S WHY THE
INSTRUMENT ENGINEER PREFERS THE *Elliottronic*

POTENTIOMETER
RECORDER

The Elliottronic Potentiometer Recorder is a
masterpiece of sound electrical engineering.
Fewer moving parts than in any comparable
instrument and plug-in unit construction
permit unusual ruggedness, guarantee that
its high performance will be maintained
under the most arduous conditions and without
specially skilled attention. For use with thermocouples and resistance
thermometers and, with associated Elliott equipment, for the measurement of conductivity, pH,
flow, pressure and other variables. The Elliottrol Controller may be incorporated in the instrument
case or fitted externally to provide various combinations of two and three-term control.

Speed, 3¼ secs. for full travel of 10″ chart span.   Single colour continuous recording
type (illustrated) or multi-colour instrument recording at 5 sec. intervals available.

ELLIOTT BROTHERS (LONDON) LTD., CENTURY WORKS, LEWISHAM, LONDON, S.E.13 ● TIDeway 3232

Fig. 6.1 This advertisement for an Elliottronic potentiometer recorder appeared in March 1951,
in the first volume of *The Elliott Journal*. The description says: 'For use with thermocouples and
resistance thermometers and, with associated Elliott equipment, for the measurement of conductivity, flow, pressure and other variables. The Elliottronic Controller may be fitted to provide
various combinations of two and three-term control'

several Divisions [8]. Amongst the Elliott Divisions at that time were *Process
Control* (which was stated to include instrumentation) and *Computing* (both analogue and digital).

It was several years before digital (as opposed to analogue) computers had
evolved to become an essential ingredient of industrial automation. In general

Fig. 6.2 In 1957, Meaford B power station in the West Midlands was equipped with Elliott-Automation's *Electroflo* instruments and controls. Automatic controllers attached to each instrument constantly adjusted the plant's parameters so as to give maximum efficiency for the load conditions at any one time

terms, digital computers were initially introduced to extend the facilities of data loggers. A conventional data logger of the 1950s monitored inputs from transducers, compared readings with upper and lower limits, printed a record at predetermined intervals and sounded an alarm if values went outside predetermined limits. Users then began to ask for more flexible monitoring (e.g. different points at different rates according to different transient conditions, or alarms based on rates of change) and on-the-fly calculations to determine process efficiencies. The gradual arrival of more compact, rugged and reliable computers facilitated such advances in data logging. This new breed of computer was eventually to become the link between the 1950s world of data recorders with manual control panels and the 1960s era of completely automated control.

Possibly Bagrit and probably Ross had seen this evolution coming. In April 1953, as recounted in Chap. 5, Dr Ross had enthused to Borehamwood staff about the opportunities for computer-controlled catalyst-cracking processes in the petrochemical industry. It seems most likely that, in the petrochemical example, Bagrit and Ross had been influenced by their interactions with American control and instrumentation companies such as Fisher Controls (see below). The influence of one particular American industrialist, Al Sperry, is described in Sect. 6.3.2. Although by the mid-1950s several companies were certainly interested in expanding the scope of automatic digital control, real progress had to await the introduction of production computers that were sufficiently rugged and reliable to operate in harsh industrial environments. Dr Ross' 1953 vision of computers being used in catalyst-cracking processes was frankly not understood at the time by the designers of the Elliott 401 at Borehamwood. But then these electronic engineers had not served their time in a mechanical engineering company grappling with the challenges of accurate measurement, as had Bagrit and Ross.

6.2.1   Prehistory: B&P Swift

The start of Leon Bagrit's 30-year journey from the small engineering firm of B&P Swift to the world-class company Elliott-Automation Ltd. has already been summarised in Chap. 1. It is tempting to imagine that, throughout this journey, Bagrit was driven by his 1960s Reith Lecture vision of automation. In reality, the vision was unlikely to have been so focused at the outset. Rather, Bagrit gradually realized the possibilities of making money by applying precision engineering to instrumentation and control, especially in industrial applications where the key to success lay in the ability to perform accurate measurements of physical quantities. Without accurate measurements, efficient control is not possible.

From 1935 onwards, Bagrit's company B&P Swift had specialised in weighing equipment, particularly in scales for the food preparation and retail industry. During the Second World War, B&P Swift, like many engineering firms, turned to war work and manufactured aircraft equipment under contract for the Ministry of Aircraft Production. B&P Swift's contracts, to quote [9], included 'flap and under carriage actuators, which called for good gear and screw-cutting facilities, for which the company, though small, developed a high reputation. After the war, the aircraft industry continued with the design of larger and faster aircraft, and it began to appear that pilots would have difficulty in controlling them because of the larger forces required. The Ministry of Supply therefore initiated the development of electromechanical power assistors, and placed a contract with Swift. This contract represented the first aircraft design work undertaken by the company and installations were completed in a large flying boat built by Short Brothers, the *Shetland*, and in *Tudor* commercial airliners built by A V Roe'. B&P Swift's extensive machine tool facilities are shown in Fig. 1.10.

Exposure to the challenges of controlling mechanisms within aircraft must have opened up possibilities, both in the mind of Bagrit and of his close friend and technical adviser Dr Lotti (Lawrence) Ross, for the wider application of measurement and control devices. The Short Brothers' contract may also have given Bagrit advance knowledge of the departure of Short Brothers from Airport Works at Rochester in 1946 and the consequential opportunities for acquiring space in this huge factory. For completeness, in Appendix 9 we tell the story of the Airport

SCIENTIFIC FLUID

CONTROL BY . . .

Fisher Valves, Level and Pressure Controllers as used extensively by the world's petroleum, chemical and gas making plants, as well as by other industries in which fluid handling is involved . . ARE NOW MADE IN ENGLAND

DIAPHRAGM MOTOR VALVES

generally for pneumatic operation, where the operating pressure is transmitted from a controlling instrument or pilot. All valves are designed to give throttling action as required for applications associated with the automatic or manual control of flow, pressure or temperature. Inner valves of various types and characteristics are available.

Types 57T Direct action or 555T Reverse action valves. Standard in high tensile iron or cast steel with stainless steel or bronze trim, single or double port, screwed or flanged for pressures up to 1500 PSI at 750°F; sizes ½" to 12".

Available with skirt guided characterised V-port, top and bottom guided V-port, throttle plug or ratio percentage flow plug inner valves.

LEVEL-TROL AUTOMATIC LEVEL CONTROLLERS

Fisher Level-Trols, which operate on the displacement principle, are designed for external or internal mounting on all types of vessels, giving a pneumatic output proportional to the variation of level. Float cage type Level-Trols are available for installations where obstructions or turbulence occur within the vessel.

Type 2405-249. For external mounting. Fabricated steel or high tensile iron float cage. Pressure-tight weather-proof pneumatic pilot case. Adjustable proportional band and level position. Flanged and screwed equalising float cage connections available with 9 standard cage lengths from 14" to 120".

FISHER GOVERNOR COMPANY LIMITED
CENTURY WORKS, LEWISHAM, LONDON, S.E.13   *Telephone:* TIDeway 3232

Fig. 6.3 Elliott acquired a manufacturing licence for the American-designed Fisher valves in 1948 and was producing them in quantity at the Rochester factory from about 1950. As this 1951 advertisement states, diaphragm motor valves were used for automatic control of flow, pressure or temperature

Works at Rochester in Kent and the chronology of Elliott's gradual acquisition of a historic manufacturing site. For now, though, let us continue with the immediate post-war evolution of Bagrit's ideas for industrial process control.

Fig. 6.4 The Aden refinery of the British Petroleum Company. Many pipes, controlled by more than a hundred valves, took oil from the oil fields to storage tanks. The Fisher valves were operated from a central control room. As the 1960 Elliott-Automation Annual Report stated, 'If it flows through pipes anywhere in the world, the chances are that it is controlled by Fisher'

6.2.2 Post-war Rationalisation of the Instrument Industry

The connection between *instrumentation* and *industrial control* has already been alluded to. At the end of the Second World War, the UK's instrument industry consisted of many small firms and there was scope for rationalization. Higginsons, the merchant bank, came to play a prominent role in this process.

There are implied connections, on a personal level, between Leon Bagrit and Higginsons bank that would benefit from further research. It is unfortunate that it has not thus far proved possible to locate original source documents that reveal what Bagrit himself thought of Higginsons, or vice versa. What is clear is that Higginsons took a particular interest in the coming-together of B&P Swift and Elliotts, as described in Chap. 1. For an outsider's view of these events, we may quote Harry Johnson who, after war service, joined the Operational Research Group of the Ministry of Civil Aviation and then, from 1954, worked for Ferranti's Computer Department in Manchester. In his memoirs [10], Johnson says: 'Shortly after the war ended Elliott Brothers had come under the control of a merchant bank [Higginsons] as part of a government inspired move towards rationalising the British instrument industry. In 1947 the bank engineered a take-over of Swifts by Elliotts and made Bagrit managing director. This gave him an excellent base from which to pursue his interest in computerised automation and he strengthened it in 1948 [or 1950?] by the purchase [licence, actually] of Fisher Controls'. We will return to the topic of Fisher Controls later, in Sect. 6.3.

John Coales provides a closer insight into the relationship between Bagrit and Higginsons. Writing to Laurence Clarke in 1995 with a description of the events in 1947/48 when, as he says, 'we thought that Elliotts would go bankrupt'. As recalled in Chap. 2, Coales remembers that: 'What we did not know then was that Bagrit could go to Higginsons and borrow £500,000 on his note of hand!' [11]. Higginsons was indeed an important player in the Elliott company history, propelling Leon Bagrit to supreme power within the company. On the way, heads were to roll. Besides the demise of the old guard at Lewisham H A Stevenson, the Managing Director of the small instrument company Ether Ltd., effectively taken over by Elliott Brothers in 1945/46, was another casualty. In summary, we may conclude that, after the rationalising of several instrument-manufacturing companies in post-war Britain, Elliott Brothers (London) Ltd. came out on top.

6.2.3 Elliott Acquires a New Image and a New Name

Bagrit's Grand Strategy at Elliotts did not at first include the word *automation,* which seems to have appeared for the first time in company literature in 1955. In the Annual Report for 1954 of Elliott Brothers (London) Ltd. (written in 1955), the word appears in capitals within the *Chairman's Report.* The precise quotation is as follows:

'Process Control. Your company is prominently engaged in this branch of instrumentation for industry, which, as its name implies, provides the automatic control of processes by means of instruments. This branch of instrumentation is now developing into a more advanced form of these controls, namely, AUTOMATION, covering a wide range of manufacturing and other activities applied in oil refineries, chemical plants and steel works and they are gradually spreading to other industries'.

A year or so before the above report was written, *The Statist* carried an article [12] on the company that made no reference to the word 'automation', preferring 'process control'. Under the heading Elliott Brothers (London), *The Statist* said: 'One of the principle activities of this London firm of instrument makers and electrical and mechanical engineers, whose shares were introduced to the Stock Exchange last year, is the manufacture of process control apparatus. It is the directors' policy to strengthen this section of the business and to this end the assets and goodwill of Bristol's Instrument Company of Weymouth have recently been acquired and a licence agreement entered into with that company's former parent concern, the Bristol Company of Waterbury, Connecticut, USA.

'Announcing this in a circular to shareholders, the directors state that Bristol's business will make a direct contribution to the company's earnings, and that they are confident that the acquisition and the arrangement with the Bristol Company of America should together enable the company in due course to effect considerable economies in development and production costs as well as to expand successfully its activities in the process control field.'

The name of Elliott Brothers (London) Ltd. was effectively changed to Elliott-Automation Ltd. in the summer of 1957. Before that, Bagrit had experimented with

Fig. 6.5 In January 1962,
Elliott-Automation (E-A)
acquired Spencer (Melksham)
Ltd., suppliers of bulk
materials-handling equipment.
The acquisition comple-
mented E-A's existing
expertise in bulk-weighing
instrumentation. The photo
shows Spencer (Melksham)'s
£500,000 sugar handling
installation in Barbados

the awkwardly sounding name Elliottomation Ltd., a minor entity that occurs in the
list of Directorships held by Leon Bagrit in July 1958 as recorded in the ledger
Register of Secretaries and Directors of Elliott-Automation Ltd. [13]. The final trigger for the adoption of Elliott-Automation may have been Hall Telephone
Accessories Ltd. of Willesden, north London, a company manufacturing coin-
operated apparatus for the GPO (the UK's national telephone authority) that
changed its name in 1955 to Associated Automation. Bagrit's close colleague
Lawrence Ross was a Director of Associated Automation. In 1957, Associated
Automation was taken over by Elliott Brothers.

By the time that Elliott-Automation was launched, Leon Bagrit was 55 years
old. His capacity for hard work was undiminished and he was a rising star in the
firmament of entrepreneurial British industrialists. A rare glimpse of the man
behind the suit is afforded by his nephew, Peter Fielding. In 1958, Leon Bagrit had
a transient ischemic attack (TIA) and was told by his doctor to take 6 months off
work. Peter remembers [14] that, not one to do things by half measures, Bagrit
'rented a most wonderful villa in Cap Ferrat in 1958. I remember the year because
I hitchhiked down to the South of France and went to stay with Stella and Leon for

Fig. 6.6 The photo shows Elliott control panels at Calder Hall in Cumbria, the world's first industrial nuclear power station which was connected to the National Grid in August 1956. In 1960, the first Elliott 803 computer to be used for on-line control applications in the UK was installed at Calder Hall. The computer, initially badged as a Panellit 609, was connected to 410 different monitoring and control points in the reactor. Some of the alarm functions were based on rates of change, illustrating an early benefit of digital control

Fig. 6.7 A control panel supplied by Elliott Process Automation for a fertilizer plant exported to the Soviet Union in about 1965

a week or 10 days in what was for me the total lap of luxury. I can remember the warm sun, the patio, and being served breakfast which included my first experience of fresh figs. During that time Leon and I would occasionally walk around the grounds, and as he came to the gardeners he would walk over to them. A few words were exchanged and he gave them something. As we walked on he said, "It is very interesting. These people do not ask for a big salary, but really love it when I give them some extra money. I would be quite willing to give them a higher wage, but they seem to prefer it this way." Not that much humanity in this interchange, more of a pragmatic cynicism. However, he at least recognized that they were poor.... The week-end I was there, there were some very interesting house guests that included Sir Simon Marks [later Lord Marks] of Marks and Spencer and Erich Leinsdorf, the Austrian-born American conductor'. More insights into Leon Bagrit's personality are given in Chap. 14.

By 1961, Elliott-Automation, as personified by Leon Bagrit himself, had found a niche on the nation's topical agenda. With a foreword that praised Leon Bagrit as the man who has, 'perhaps more than any other, made Britain aware of the vital place of automation in industrial progress', a long article [15] by Goronwy Rees in the *Sunday Times* in 1961 went on to say:

'Automation is a word which has been in general use in the English language only during the last six or seven years, but even in so short a time it has acquired such a variety of meanings that it may be thought already to have outlived its usefulness. It is applied indifferently to devices which link machine tools in automatic production lines; to techniques of automatic control over manufacturing processes; to the processing of information by electronic computers.

'Automation means all this and much more; so much more, indeed, that by now it might be held to be simply a general term covering all the latest applications of scientific discovery and invention to industrial processes.

'In recent years, however, automation has begun to produce effects which may properly be called revolutionary, among them the effect of showing that in some respect machines may behave in ways which closely resemble human beings ....

'No one has tried harder or more persistently to explain the kind of problems created by automation, or the immense social and industrial changes it is likely to bring about, than Mr Leon Bagrit, who is deputy chairman and managing director of Elliott-Automation Ltd., a firm which is today very much the child and product of his own very original ideas. It is therefore not surprising that, just as Mr Bagrit is a remarkable man, so Elliott-Automation is a remarkable firm; indeed it is in some respects unique, because it is the only firm in the world which covers the entire field of the automation industry, from electronic computers for industry to automatic homing heads for guided missiles'.

This *Sunday Times* eulogy is somewhat over the top – although there is good reason to believe that Elliotts had responded quicker to the possibilities of automation than any other UK company. Joseph Roth, who worked for Elliott Brothers from 1951 to 1969 and who became intimately involved with industrial control applications has said [16]: 'It is I believe correct to say that at the time, Elliotts were considered to know more about industrial automation than any other company in the UK. I was often introduced as "the man who knows more about the application of computers to process monitoring and control than any other person in the UK". I was never that sure myself and found it somewhat embarrassing but it helped to promote the company'.

There were at least three substantive reasons why even the sceptical observer could not deny that Elliott-Automation was a force to be reckoned with by 1961. Firstly, there was the company's strong research base at Borehamwood. Secondly, one of the outputs from Borehamwood, the Elliott 800 series of fully transistorised computers, had achieved UK market dominance in the area of small machines eminently suitable for industrial automation applications. Thirdly, there were the company's capable manufacturing bases at Lewisham and Rochester where, amongst many other things, leading-edge American control technology was being made under licence. We will consider the Elliott 800 series computers and their competitors below and in Chap. 10. Firstly, we should say more about the relationships that had grown up between Elliotts and relevant American companies.

6.3 Automation Comes of Age

6.3.1 American Licences and the Grand Strategy

According to a retrospective company history [17] written by a senior manager in the early 1960s, 'Sir Leon's first tasks, on obtaining full control of Elliott Brothers [in 1947], were to set about reorganising the management structure and modernising the plant. … Two major decisions were then made which have profoundly affected the course of the business in the last 15 years. The first decision was to branch out from instrumentation into an entirely new activity, preferably one that would enable Elliotts to benefit from one of the major technical advances of World War II. An obvious choice was atomic energy but this was rejected since it was considered too large a field for a small firm to tackle successfully. The choice eventually fell on control engineering, or what is now known as automation.

'The difficulty was that at this time British knowledge and experience of control engineering techniques was several years behind that of the Americans. How to catch up? Sir Leon Bagrit has said that "the gigantic cost of research and development appalled us". The decision was therefore made that know-how in the new field should be built up piecemeal, not by Elliotts undertaking the basic research and development themselves, but by the leap-frog policy of obtaining UK manufacturing and selling licences from the leading companies in the world, usually American, specialising in particular aspects of automation. The first of these agreements was signed in 1948 with the Fisher Governor Company of Iowa and covered the sole manufacturing rights outside the USA of Fisher fluid control equipment, valves and regulators [see Fig. 6.3]. This was followed by agreement in 1953 with the Bendix Aviation Corporation of Detroit, covering automatic pilots, flight instruments and process control equipment; and in 1954 with the Bristol Company of Waterbury,

Connecticut, covering Bristol instruments and process control equipment. As part of the agreement with Bendix, new shares equivalent to 34 per cent of Elliott's equity were issued to the American company (the holding was eventually sold by Bendix in 1960) and as part of the agreement with Bristol, the UK manufacturing subsidiary was acquired by Elliott Brothers. Apart from this, the agreements with American and Continental Companies (the number of such agreements now exceeds 30) have all followed the same pattern with Elliotts being granted the sole manufacturing and selling rights in the UK, and often in other parts of the world, in return for royalty payments.

'It is now clear that in forging these links with American companies it was Sir Leon Bagrit's intention right from the beginning to build up Elliotts into one of the world's leading specialists in the whole field of automation but for obvious reasons this "grand strategy" was not revealed to the Americans at the time the original agreements were signed'.

Naturally, not all of the American developments found favour with Elliotts. To quote John Bunt [18]: 'During my first visit to the USA in 1957 I visited Bendix in Detroit to see their G15 computer designed for use in the field of machine tool control. It was an attractive system. However Elliotts did not go into the machine tool control market and so we did not pursue this'. In contrast to this, the story of Bagrit's links with Al Sperry and the Panellit company of Chicago is altogether more interesting and is worth recounting in full.

6.3.2   Al Sperry, Panellit and the Elliott 803 Computer

Albert Francis Sperry (see Fig. 6.8) was born on 8 May 1900 in Odessa, Russia [19]. He must have come to the USA as a child because he graduated from Rensselaer Polytechnic Institute, 150 miles north of New York City, in 1923 with BSEE. He worked from 1922 to 1937 for the Republic Flow Meter company, applying for his first patent within a few months of joining the company. He rose to become Director of Research and, later, Vice-President in charge of Engineering and Research. In 1937, Sperry started Hubbard Engineering Company, consulting in the field of instrumentation with special relevance to power plants and industrial automatic control.

From 1942 to 1945, Sperry was carrying out projects for the war effort, particularly for the Signal Corps, Air Corps and US Navy. More crucially, he was the Consulting Engineer for EI DuPont de Nemours Inc. for the design of the complex monitoring system for the atomic plant at Hanford, Washington – part of the top-secret Manhattan atomic bomb project. The Hanford instrumentation was required to monitor over 2,000 pressure readings in the atomic pile, as part of the Safety Shut-down System.

In 1945 Sperry founded his own company called Panellit. The name 'Panellit' is said to be derived from the phrase *Panel instruments*. Panellit grew in strength during the 1950s. A highlight was their involvement with the design of the Tidewater Refinery at Delaware City, the first major multi-process petro-chemical plant to be built as a single unit [19]. An Elliott 803 was delivered to the Tidewater Refinery in 1960 – see Chap. 7. During the same year, three Elliott 803 systems were delivered to EI DuPont de Nemours Inc., also undoubtedly due to the connection with Panellit.

Panellit was merged into Information Systems Inc. in 1960 and in 1961 with Scientific Data Systems. Al Sperry died in 1962 after having been, so his ISA (Instrument Society of America) obituary says, 'in semi-retirement for two years' [19].

Fig. 6.8 America led the way in the use of digital computers for industrial process control. The first Ramo Wooldridge RW300 computer went online at the Texas Oil Company's catalytic polymerisation process at Port Arthur, Texas in April 1959. The photo shows the American engineer Al Sperry (1900–1962), a leading light in the process-control world. Sperry's company Panellit Inc. encouraged Elliott-Automation to upgrade the Elliott 802 computer so that it became more suitable for industrial automation

Fig. 6.9 The Elliott 802 computer, first delivered in 1958, used a mix of transistors and thermionic valves (tubes). The 802 heralded a new breed of compact, robust and reliable computers suitable for industrial process control

Fig. 6.10 The first Elliott 803 to be delivered went in November 1959 to E.I. Du Pont de Nemours Inc., Beaumont, Texas, for the on-line control of a nylon process. Of the 21 Elliott 803 computers to have been delivered during 1960, 10 were exported to America. Many of these were rebadged as Panellit 609 computers

Sperry was highly regarded in the fields of instrumentation and control, being the inventor of over 50 patents concerned with electrical instruments, automatic control, data reduction, and scanning and annunciator systems. In 1952, the Industrial Instruments and Regulators division of the American Society of Mechanical Engineers honoured Sperry 'for the elements which added to the mathematical structure of process control, for his aids to operation of complex systems, and for his professional leadership and inspiration to others'. The Instrument Society of America (ISA), founded in April 1945, nominated Al Sperry as its first President. ISA grew from 900 members in 1946 to a total of about 40,000 members from more than 110 countries in 2007. Being international in scope, ISA changed its legal name in 2000 to *ISA – the Instrumentation, Systems, and Automation Society.* The Society has an Albert F Sperry Award, created in 1956. Sperry gave evidence to the US Congress Joint Economic Committee hearings on automation in the same year.

Sperry's Panellit company attracted the attention of the media. In an article dated 30 December 1957 on the US Space Program, *Time* magazine said: 'In Skokie, Illinois, two bright young scientists named Leonard and Albert Sperry started out during World War II with an idea for electronic information-gathering systems for civilian and military customers. Today, the Sperrys' Panellit Inc. builds monitoring devices for the Army's Jupiter ballistic missile, is at work on a portable atomic reactor, and produces a series of central control systems for atomic submarines, oil refineries and electric utility plants. Estimated 1957 sales: $9,000,000, up 25% from 1956'.

By the early 1950s, Sperry's reputation had crossed the Atlantic. On page 9 of Al Sperry's semi-autobiographical notes [19], held in the ISA Archives, Sperry writes: 'This broad spectrum of activity in industrial automatic control attracted the attention of a group of men in England who were beginning to build a similar automation complex. They approached Mr. Sperry and agreements were reached for cross-licensing and exchange of information between [the] two companies. They invited Mr. Sperry to become a director of Associated Automation, which is now part of Elliott-Automation Limited. Later, the English company formed a Panellit Division in an effort to duplicate the unique services offered by Mr. Sperry's activities in industry in the United States and to make it available to the European Industrial Community'. It can be deduced from the Elliott-Automation Annual Reports that the Division known as Panellit Ltd. was formed sometime before mid-1958. The 'group of men in England', to whom Sperry refers, included Leon Bagrit, Dr Lotti Ross, Andrew St. Johnston and John Bunt. The first two were, respectively, the Managing Director and Group Technical Manager of Elliott-Automation; the last two were, with SLH Clarke, the leading lights of Elliott-Automation's Computer Division at Borehamwood.

Staff from Elliott-Automation were indeed frequent visitors to Al Sperry and Panellit Inc. at Skokie, Chicago. Here's how John Bunt, writing in December 2001, recalled the relationship between Panellit and Elliott-Automation:

'Associated Automation and later Elliott-Automation had a licence agreement with a US company called Panellit, later called ISI [Information Systems Inc.]. This was run by Al Sperry in Skokie, a suburb of Chicago, in Illinois. Sperry was developing his own computer [see [20]] to use in process control systems which they called the 609.

'There was a very close personal relationship between Bagrit, Ross and Sperry. Sperry was a very capable pianist. Bagrit and Ross respectively played the violin and viola and the three of them spent their leisure times together making music.

'I was invited to the Sperrys for dinner one evening. He had two concert grands in his lounge and the hall was dominated by a very large Jackson Pollock, which his wife had just bought. Another dinner guest was a well known concert pianist. Sperry's wife was a member of one of the leading families of Chicago the Sears Roebucks, the Marshall Fields and the Adlers. They were the leading supporters of many cultural activities in Chicago. Al's brother Leonard Sperry lived in Los Angeles and was a financier or entrepreneur. He lived in a house next door to Esther Williams, the swimming film star, in Beverley Hills.

'Bagrit and Ross persuaded Al Sperry to abandon his own computer development and buy his computers from Elliotts. So I delivered an 802 to them in Chicago and spent some time showing Sperry how to operate it. [This was one of the first Elliott 802s to be built and it was delivered to Panellit in September 1958; see Appendix 8]. Sperry said that he could not sell the 802 because it had some valves (or tubes as he called them) in it. The valves provided the trigger pulses to the ferrite core logic and the ferrite core store drivers. So we developed the 803 using British made power transistors which had by that time become available.

'Sperry bought quite a large number of these machines (803A) and having acquired quite a lot of operating experience gave us ideas for improvements in the computer.

'ISI moved from Chicago to Los Angeles and I went over there to tell them what we had decided about these improvements, which were to lead to the 803B. Sperry was quite impressed that we had acted to such a degree on his company's suggestions and was in favour of further purchases of our computers.

'However, ISI negotiated a merger with another company in the same line of business, called Genesys and Sperry lost control. I think the orders for the 803B dried up.

'Sperry was a very hospitable host and looked after me well when I was in Chicago in January. He wanted to lend me his Cadillac for the weekend, but since the roads were thick with ice, I wisely declined the offer. He was "Al" to all his staff and always lunched with me and other engineers in his canteen. At that time this practice was unknown in the UK.

'A consequence of using the ferrite core logic and ferrite core store was that it was necessary to be sure that temperature compensating circuits worked properly. So the production department [at Borehamwood] had to install temperature controlled rooms to test all the 803s in both hot and cold temperatures, as required for the process control environment'.

Andrew St Johnston, the Manager of Elliott's Computer Division, also remembers the influence that Al Sperry had on the development of the Elliott 802 and 803 computers. Writing in 1995 [21], St Johnston has this to say about the period 1955–1960:

'A new factor that entered the scene at this point was due to the fact that Elliotts had many licence agreements with American companies particularly in the Process Control field. One such was a small company called Panellit (from Panel Instruments) the boss of which was Al Sperry. Al, Bagrit and Ross played trios. Bagrit had earned his living at one point as an orchestral violinist, Dr. Ross played the cello and Sperry was on piano.

'Al Sperry was an enterprising gentleman and was looking for a computer to run in Process Control applications. The 802 with its reliability clearly would fill the role but he insisted that his market wanted no valves; a bigger core store; and a cubicle layout that would go behind a panel and not take up half the floor. Fortune was on our side again. Mullard produced drive transistors that could cope with John's [John Bunt's] cores, they also provided a large 4K word core store which could be driven by the same drive transistors. Bagrit had seen the [Elliott] 405 at an exhibition on a stand which was next door to the Olivetti stand with its very elegant equipment. We were therefore instructed to get the 803 cabinets designed by an industrial designer. Peter Bell did the honours.

'The result was the 803 which was highly successful. Five were sold in the USA [but see the list in Appendix 8]; others went to many places including Moscow and

Cuba. The 405 [magnetic] film was used to make it an NCR-Elliott business system, and they were also used in defence and process control'.

Joseph Roth, who we met earlier, was able to confirm the favourable impression made by the Elliott 803 in America. He recalls that 'Andrew St Johnston told me that Sperry, recognising that he was not getting anywhere in trying to build his own computer, went round the world looking for someone who could provide a suitable computer for process control and when he came upon Elliott's he found what he was looking for' [16].

As is indicated in Appendix 8, an apparent total of 18 (or 21 if another company brochure [22] is to be believed) Elliott 803 computers were delivered to the USA between 1960 and 1963. Of these eighteen, the five (?) computers that were sold via Panellit would have been known in America not as Elliott 803s but as Panellit 609s. This was most probably the case with the 803 computers installed at EI DuPont de Nemours Inc. and at the Tidewater Refinery, Delaware. At the time (1960–1963), a sale of *any* British computer to the Americans was cause for celebration. As sometimes happens in periods of unusual success, the facts may subsequently have been enthusiastically embellished. Joseph Roth recalls [16] that: 'I was always under the impression (for that is what I was told) that the number [of 803 computers sold to America] was 32 and this is the figure I used when lecturing, writing and in discussion and no one ever thought to correct me (of course the bigger figure sounds better!!)'.

We round off this account of the Elliott 803s successful debut by standing back and considering the hardware and software systems that surrounded the actual computer, when applied to a practical industrial control project. This also allows some relevant terminology to be introduced.

6.3.3   The Component Parts of a 1960s Automation Application

To fix ideas, it is helpful to take a case study of the period, namely: process control at the Spencer Steelworks of Richard Thomas & Baldwin's company at Llanwern, 3 miles east of Newport in Wales. This was a substantial project that became a landmark in the automation of the UK's steel industry as well as an early test of Elliott-Automation's ability (or struggle) to manage the software development necessary for novel and complex systems. Leon Bagrit's initial involvement was a personal one. Joseph Roth, who managed Elliott Process Automation at that time, has said [16]: 'The story I was told, by those that should know, was that Harold Wilson (Prime Minister at the time) introduced Harry Spencer to Leon Bagrit. Harry Spencer wanted his new steel works to be "the least obsolescent in the world" (so acknowledging that by the time it was operational technology would have moved on) on the one hand and Leon Bagrit, said the Prime Minister, was the man who knew all about automation'. The connection between Leon Bagrit and Harold Wilson is discussed again in Chap. 14.

Elliott-Automation Systems Ltd. had been engaged early in 1960 by Richard Thomas & Baldwins (RTB) 'to advise on and to introduce, throughout RTB, automation both of processes and of administrative procedures' [23]. In March of that year, RTB had also asked the British Iron and Steel Research Association's Operation Research Department 'to survey the potential for computers in a modern integrated steel works and to make proposals for Spencer Works in particular'.

In October 1960, as a result of these two studies, Elliott-Automation Systems Ltd. defined a four-level hierarchy of computer systems for the Spencer Works [23]:

Level 1: Planning, accounting, stores control and general off-line data processing
Level 2: Production scheduling, on the basis of customers' orders
Level 3: Production and quality control; data-gathering and progress-monitoring
Level 4: Process control and the automation of machinery

All four levels of computers in this hierarchy were envisaged as being interconnected. In this respect, there are echoes of ARCH, the Articulated Control Hierarchy concept, for whose development NRDC gave support in November 1959 (see Chap. 5). We will describe particular details of the Spencer steelworks implementation later. Before doing this, we need to consider how the computer technology available in the 1950s and early 1960s measured up to the implied requirements of the four-level hierarchy.

Levels (1) and (2) required general information-processing capability, little different from other contemporary computer applications. Levels three and four, however, necessitated interconnection with machinery and instrumentation on the factory floor. Sensors of real-world quantities, such as temperature and pressure, converted these physical measurements into digital form for input to the computer(s) at levels three and four. Likewise, the results of digital calculations often had to be converted into voltage signals, capable of actuating real-world factory-floor devices such as flow-valves, heating elements, conveyor-belt motors etc. The computers at levels three and four were often *online* – that is, intimately attached to the production machinery that they controlled. Finally, the computers usually had to respond within a certain critical time, *real time,* to incoming signals. By way of further explanation, associated with each piece of machinery there was usually a *crisis time*, this being the maximum allowable time between that machine signalling a need for attention and a computer responding with an appropriate action. If a particular computer could not reason and act fast enough to replace a skilled human operator of a machine, then that computer was not adequate for the real-time, on-line control of the machine. In some critical applications, for example fighter aircraft, the controlling computer had to be able to react *faster* than a human operator.

In summary, reliability, robustness and speed of operation, combined with appropriate communication and control hardware (sensors/actuators) and software, were the essential attributes of computers at levels three and four in the automation hierarchy. These were demanding attributes – especially in respect of the software.

Few of the production computers available in the 1950s, on either side of the Atlantic, were up to the challenge.

6.4 Computers Suitable for the Task in the 1950s

6.4.1 The American Scene

American computer manufacturers were the first to enter the market in practical automation systems. Although the concept of a digital computer controlling a manufacturing plant may have first surfaced in an article in *Scientific American* in 1948 according to [24], 'actual applications had to wait until relatively small, reliable, and also relatively inexpensive machines were available, along with vendor companies with the will and the initiative to pursue this field vigorously'. Amongst the leading American vendor companies was Ramo-Wooldridge (RW), later known as Thompson-Ramo-Wooldridge (TRW) and then Bunker Ramo. According to [25], quoting [26], 'Ramo Wooldridge announced the first computer specifically designed for industrial process control – the RW300 – in September 1957'. In January 1958, the Texas Oil Company announced the purchase of a RW 300 to control its catalytic polymerisation process at Port Arthur, Texas which went on-line in April [or March?] 1959' – (see also [27]).

Of course, special-purpose military applications on both sides of the Atlantic, such as the MRS5 and Whirlwind projects described in Chap. 2 and Appendix 10, did produce interesting results in the field of real-time, on-line computer control that pre-dated the RW 300 installations. The comprehensive US Office of Naval Research (ONR) survey of 99 computers, carried out in 12 countries in February 1953 [28], lists 6 computers that mention *real-time control problems* as their entry for the 'best suited for' category in the survey's tabular data. These six computers, all American and all the result of government support (mostly for defence purposes), are summarised in Table 6.1.

About a year after the above survey was undertaken the DIGITAC computer, developed by the Hughes Aircraft Corporation, was used by the US Air Force for the experimental control of an airborne automatic pilot system. DIGITAC has been given credit by some commentators for being the first computer system to be applied to process control [27].

Notice that according to this ONR survey Britain and Europe had, by early 1953, no significant candidate computer with real-time capability, either in the military or civil domain. Focussing on the UK, we should for completeness take a closer look at the immediate post-war years to list the commercially available British computers and identify any candidates for industrial process control. This historical exercise also provides an opportunity to introduce some British manufacturers, especially Ferranti Ltd., whose computer products were to become market competitors to those of Elliott-Automation.

Table 6.1 Six early American computers that had some form of real-time capability

Computer	Best suited for	Available
DYSEAC (the second SEAC)	General-purpose, simulation, some classes of real-time control	July 1953 'at the earliest'
ERA1103	General large-scale computation; real-time control and simulation	Sept. 1953
Hughes Airborne Control Computer	Calculation of real-time control problems	Feb. 1952
JAINCOMP-B1 (Jacobs Instrument Co.)	Real-time computation with fixed program and little input	Spring 1951
JAINCOMP-C	Real-time or general-purpose computing	Summer 1953
Whirlwind I	Real-time control problems, also general-purpose computation	Dec. 1950[a]

[a]Whirlwind was working reliably enough to do useful work by March 1951; see Appendix 10

6.4.2 Early Days in Britain: The Growth of Elliott and its Rival, Ferranti Ltd.

From its foundation in 1949, the National Research Development Corporation (NRDC) made great efforts to encourage the development of electronic computers in the UK [29, 30]. In particular, in 1949 the NRDC approached the following ten companies with the aim of promoting interest in the manufacture of digital computers:

1. British Tabulating Machine Co. Ltd. (BTM)
2. British Thomson-Houston (BTH)
3. English Electric Co Ltd. (which included Marconi)
4. Elliott Brothers (London) Ltd.
5. Electrical and Musical Industries Ltd. (EMI)
6. Ferranti Ltd.
7. General Electric Co. Ltd. (GEC)
8. Metropolitan-Vickers Ltd. (MetVic)
9. Plessey Company
10. Powers-Samas Accounting Machines Ltd. (Powers)

On 14 December 1949, these companies were invited by NRDC to the first and, as it transpired, only meeting of an Advisory Panel on Electronic Computers. The outcome of the meeting was, from NRDC's viewpoint, disappointing. Quoting HJ Crawley's report for the Corporation [29]:

'The outcome of the Advisory Panel was that both the electronic manufacturers [particularly numbers 2, 5, 6 and 7 in the above list] and the punched-card machine manufacturers [numbers 1 and 10 in the above list] respectively represented that they were individually in positions to tackle the problems of an electronic computer development project as well as, for example, the International Business Machines Corporation in the United States. It was pointed out to the punched-card machine manufacturers that, in the opinion of the Corporation, they had inadequate electronic staff and resources. It was apparent also that the manufacturers were not willing that the Corporation should take the initiative in launching a development project but agreed that the Corporation could usefully coordinate activities'.

Recalling the events some years later, Lord Halsbury, the Managing Director of NRDC from 1949 to 1959, described it as 'trying to drive mules uphill'. By 1953, only Elliott Brothers, Ferranti and, to some extent, English Electric had shown any signs of responding to the challenge. As is illustrated in Chap. 5, NRDC initially concentrated its efforts on the two most promising candidate companies: Elliotts and Ferranti. Meanwhile, English Electric developed a comparatively modest but ultimately fruitful relationship with the National Physical Laboratory in respect of the Pilot ACE and DEUCE computers, as discussed below.

The subsequent growth in the fortunes of Elliott-Automation, compared with its market rival Ferranti, is a remarkable story. To set the scene, it is necessary to go back a few years and recall the origins of Ferranti. The origins of Elliott have already been described in Chap. 1.

The Ferranti company was founded in 1882 by Sebastian Ziani de Ferranti, an inventive *Manufacturing Engineer* who had been born in Liverpool in 1864 [31]. Ferranti set out to promote the 'all electric' age and had soon achieved substantial success in the fields of electrical generation and supply, transformers and electricity meters. Like Elliott Brothers (London) Ltd., work on electrical measuring instrumentation was one of the themes of Ferranti's Research and Development (R&D) activity. However, Ferranti Ltd. had many other concurrent activities and was much more of a general electrical manufacturer because it included heavy-current equipment in its portfolio.

By the end of the 1930s, Ferranti was larger than Elliott Brothers (London) Ltd. although, as far as process control was concerned, the future prospects of the two companies might reasonably have been judged to be similar. However, the Second World War was to have markedly different consequences for the two firms. Whereas Ferranti was able to build on its radio and radar activity to become a leading UK electronics player, Elliott lost out in the vital field of electronics.

An analysis of the subject matter of patent applications emanating from the two companies adds weight to this view. The UK Patent Office used to publish regular listings of inventions, entitled *Index to Names of Applicants in Connection with Published Complete Specifications*. The volumes of listings appeared periodically, each consisting of either a group of 20,000 patents or, from 1965, a group of 25,000 patents. The time-period covered by each volume naturally varied somewhat. This was especially true of the war years, where shortage of paper held up publication and the backlog was spread over several post-war publications.

In the extracts from the *Index* given in Table 6.2, we have concentrated on patents issued by Elliott Brothers (London) Ltd. and by Ferranti Ltd. during two sample periods: immediately pre-war and immediately post-war. The information in the *Index* is based on the date of an invention's initial Application. (A complete patent specification, with its serial number and final description, was usually published between 2 and 6 years after the initial Application.) In Table 6.2, we place the subject matter of each invention in one of four categories of electrical

Table 6.2 Analysis of Elliott and Ferranti patent applications

Approximate years covered	Range of patent Application numbers considered	Elliott patents by subject and number	Ferranti patents by subjects and numbers
1937	440,001–460,000	I=3	24: I=5; R=8; M=6; X=5
1938	460,001–480,000	I=7	30: I=8; R=16; M=1; X=5
1944–1946	580,001–600,000	I=5	28: I=6; R=16; M=3; X=3
1944–1946	600,001–620,000	I=1	19: I=2; R=13; M=0; X=4
1944–1946	620,001–640,000	I=4	16: I=3; R=9; M=0; X=4

I = Electrical instrumentation, measuring and indicating apparatus
R = Electronics (mainly radio and radar) and related light-current electrical apparatus
M = Electrical machines (generators, motors, transformers); heavy-current and high-voltage devices
X = Other (e.g. domestic appliances; non-electrical devices)

Table 6.3 Profits, in £million, of Ferranti Ltd. and Elliott Brothers (London) Ltd.

Year	Ferranti: gross profit, £m	Elliott: pre-tax profit, £m
1943	+0.481	+0.154
1944	+0.648	+0.079
1945	+0.748	+0.016
1946	+0.002	−0.157
1947	+0.349	−0.198
1948	+0.374	−0.077
1949	+0.321	−0.012
1950	+0.551	−0.018
1951	+1.228	−0.077
1952	+1.320	+0.102

engineering, denoted in the Table as I, R, M and X (as defined in the Table). The purpose is to distinguish those patents that were likely to contribute enabling technologies to the manufacture of process control equipment.

Table 6.2 shows that, both before and after the war, Elliotts retained its R&D in the single area of light current instrument manufacture. The R&D of Ferranti, in contrast, continued strongly in the electronics area whilst reducing in the heavy machines area.

How did the above technical innovations translate into commercial success, as measured by profitability? After the end of hostilities, Elliotts' fortunes declined and in fact the company traded at a loss for 6 years, as described in Chap. 2. In contrast, as Table 6.3 shows, Ferranti's profits quickly recovered from the effects of the cancellation of war-time defence contracts, then went through a plateau, finally rising again in 1950. It was not until 1952 that Elliott's profits began to look healthy.

Paradoxically, 1952 marked the nadir of morale at the Borehamwood Research Laboratories: the inspirational John Coales had resigned and high-tech Admiralty contracts were evaporating (see Chap. 2). Unable to rely mainly on defence contracts, the cold wind of short-term commercial wealth-creation had begun to blow through the bountiful research pastures of the Borehamwood Laboratories.

Table 6.4 State of Ferranti Ltd. and Elliott Brothers (London) Ltd. in 1954

	Ferranti Ltd.	Elliott Brothers (London) Ltd.
Issued capital	£3,000,000	£612,000
Gross profit (before tax)	£1,446,649	£222,878
Number of employees	10,560	3,500

Minds were focused. The rich reservoir of electronic excellence that had been built up by John Coales was henceforth directed to irrigate Elliotts' product developments, enabling the company, within a few years, to catch up with Ferranti in the production and delivery of electronic computers. Of more relevance to Leon Bagrit's ambition and Lawrence Ross's technical intuition, Borehamwood's electronic skills began to bring their vision of truly automatic control to life. But this took several years.

Meanwhile, continuing the comparison of the two companies in the early 1950s, payroll is another indicator of relative commercial activity. The number of employees at Elliott's Lewisham works peaked at about 4,000 during the war but had dropped to 'less than 1,000' in 1947 [32], Coales putting the figure at 800 [33]. The total for Elliott's Lewisham, Borehamwood and Rochester sites is not known accurately but is estimated to have been about 1,500 in 1950 and 3,500 in 1954. The figure is known to have reached 7,200 by 1958 and to have risen steadily for the next few years [34]. The number of Ferranti employees expanded from 5,800 in 1939 to over 11,000 in 1945, dropping sharply after the end of hostilities but then recovering to 7,000 by 1950 [31].

In summary, the overall state of both companies in 1954 is shown in Table 6.4. It can be seen that, at this time, Ferranti Ltd. was about three times as large a company as Elliott Brothers (London) Ltd.

1954 is a reasonable year to choose as the datum for the establishment of Ferranti's and Elliott's mainframe computer credibility in the marketplace. To demonstrate this, we have to widen the discussion to include other UK companies that were, somewhat reluctantly and in due course, to become interested in digital computers.

6.4.3   The Computer Comes to Market in Britain: 1951–1955

The first two production Ferranti Mark I machines, judged at the time to be relatively large and expensive computers, were sent respectively to Manchester University and Toronto University in 1951 and 1952. Manchester University's Ferranti machine, delivered in February 1951 and officially inaugurated in July of that year, is believed to have been the world's first production computer to be installed in a customer's premises [35]. The first Ferranti Mark I* (*pronounced 'Mark One Star'*) went, in conditions of great secrecy, to GCHQ Cheltenham in 1953 [36]. As far as the open market was concerned, these first three Ferranti computers were associated with research establishments at a time when most people regarded a computer as a specialist mathematical tool. The story of the Elliott 401, first publicly demonstrated in 1953 and subsequently installed at the Agricultural Research station, Rothamsted, in 1954, is given in Chap. 5. The production version, the 402, judged at the time to be relatively inexpensive and easy to install and maintain, was first delivered to a customer in 1955. The approximate prices by 1956 of a Ferranti Mark I* and an Elliott 402 were, respectively, £90K and £25K.

Ferranti and Elliott computers dominated the embryonic UK market at the start of 1955. Two other companies, British Tabulating Machines (BTM) and English Electric, were not far behind.

BTM based their Hollerith Electronic Computer, HEC, on the pioneering work of AD Booth at Birkbeck College, London [37]. The HEC1 was first demonstrated in 1953. Seven HEC2(M) computers, the 'marketable' version of the prototype, were built and delivered to customers, the first one in 1955. The HEC2(M) was retrospectively renamed the BTM 1200.

The English Electric Co. of Stafford had been in formal contact since 1949 with the group designing the Pilot ACE computer at the National Physical Laboratory. The Pilot ACE first ran a program in May 1950. English Electric produced a successful production version called DEUCE, of which the first of 33 DEUCE computers was delivered to a customer in 1955 [38]. Interestingly, 12 of the 33 DEUCE machines were retained for in-house work (including bureau activity) within the various divisions of the substantial English Electric engineering empire. The full DEUCE delivery list is given in Appendix 10. Chap. 13 provides more background information on the English Electric company.

Whilst all of this was going on, J Lyons & Co., the London-based catering company famous for its restaurants (known as Tea Shops) had taken the basic design of the Cambridge University EDSAC computer and enlarged the architecture to accommodate the bulk input and output of commercial data. The resulting LEO computer, the Lyons Electronic Office, first ran a program in the spring of 1951 [39]. Useful computing followed a year later and by the spring of 1953 full-scale payroll work was being undertaken. By the time the project had been completed in the autumn of 1953, the machine had become known as LEO I. In November 1954, Lyons founded a new company, Leo Computers Ltd., to build and sell a new computer, LEO II, the first one of which was installed at J Lyons & Co. in May 1957. The first LEO II to go to a third-party customer was delivered in September 1958 to WD & H O Wills Ltd., the tobacco company. The story of LEO II continues in Chap. 13, in connection with the link to English Electric Computers Ltd.

More background on all the above early British computers will be found in Appendix 10 and in [40]. Delivery lists will be found at [41] though, in the case of Elliott computers, there is some ambiguity about the exact number of machines built and their destinations – as discussed, for example, in Chap. 5 and Appendix 8.

Table 6.5 shows all British-designed computer deliveries during the first 5 years of commercial activity. It is seen that Ferranti were, during this initial period of

Table 6.5 The first 5 years of UK computer production: deliveries to external customers, 1951–1955

Year	Computer	Customer	Application
1951	Ferranti Mark I	Manchester University	Scientific and engineering
1952	Ferranti Mark I	Toronto University	Mathematical research
1953	Ferranti Mark I*	Ministry of Supply (GCHQ, Cheltenham)	Classified work
1954	Elliott 401	Agricultural Research Council, Rothamsted	Agricultural statistics
1954	Ferranti Mark I*	Royal Dutch Shell Labs., Amsterdam	Oil refining studies
1954	Ferranti Mark I*	Atomic Weapons Research. Est., Aldermaston	Research work
1954	Ferranti Mark I*	A V Roe & Co. Ltd., Manchester	Aircraft design calculations
1955	Elliott 402	Institut Blaise Pascal, France	Mathematical research
1955	Elliott 402	Army Operational Research Group, West Byfleet	Operational research
1955	BTM1200 (HEC2M)	GEC Research Labs, Wembley	(Application unknown)
1955	BTM1200 (HEC2M)	ESSO Oil Refinery, Fawley	Scheduling and planning
1955	Ferranti Mark I*	National. Inst. for Applications of Maths., Rome	Research work
1955	Ferranti Mark I*	Ministry of Supply, Fort Halstead	Defence-related research
1955	English Electric DEUCE	National Physical Labs., Teddington	Mathematical applications
1955	English Electric DEUCE	RAE, Farnborough	Aircraft research
1955	Elliott 403	Weapons Research Est., Woomera, Australia	Guided missile trials

mainly scientific applications, the market leaders. At approximately £90,000 each, the Ferranti Mark I* was by far the most expensive computer in Table 6.5, followed by the English Electric DEUCE at a little less than £50,000, then the Elliott 402 at about £25,000. Cheapest was the BTM 1200 at about £18,000 – all expressed as 1955 prices. For an everyday comparison of prices, an average British four-door family saloon car typically cost a little less than £600 in 1955.

The next year, 1956, saw continued production of the Elliott 402, the Ferranti Mark I*, the BTM 1200 and the English Electric DEUCE. (Background to the DEUCE, and a complete delivery list, is given in Appendix 10). 1956 also saw the first deliveries of a burst of new production computers in the UK, including the first

Ferranti Pegasus (delivered to Ferranti's London Computing Service in March 1956), the first Elliott 405 (delivered to Elliott's Borehamwood Computing Service in July 1956), the first BTM 1201 (originally called the HEC4), and the first production transistorised computer, the Metropolitan-Vickers MV950. October 1956 also saw the first arrival on UK shores of an American-designed computer, the IBM 650. This machine was first delivered to US customers in 1954. By 1962, about 1,800 IBM 650s had been sold worldwide, outselling all other contemporary computers by an order of magnitude.

Returning to Table 6.5, the conclusion is that by the end of 1955 there were still less than a dozen production computers in use in the whole of the UK. These were all British-designed. None of the computers mentioned in Table 6.5, nor indeed most of those British machines that followed in the next 4 or 5 years, was really suitable for factory-floor applications in on-line process control. This was because they lacked sufficient robustness, reliability and cost-effectiveness for the job. There was also little interest at the time in developing the necessary repertoire of special input/output devices necessary to interface a digital computer to the largely analogue world of industrial processes. (There was one exception: the Elliott 405 installed in September 1957 at the National Gas Turbine Establishment, Farnborough, for on-line monitoring of jet engine testing – as described in Chap. 7 – but this was a special case with defence requirements.)

That Borehamwood was principally responsible for changing the above picture is due to a combination of two factors: Leon Bagrit's drive for Elliott to be *First in Automation* (the title of a company booklet [42]), coupled with the legacy of electronic excellence at Borehamwood. Out of Brehamwood came the Elliott 800 series of computers and the concept of the ARCH Articulated Control Hierarchy, originally conceived as a modular system of standard analogue and digital sub-units sharing a common communication protocol. The 800 series was eminently suitable for industrial automation tasks.

As for Ferranti Ltd., the Ferranti Argus was to become the company's main offering for industrial process control applications [25]. Originally developed in 1958 for real-time use in the Bloodhound missile's launch control post, the Argus range of computers was gradually improved and expanded over the years to fulfil a variety of civil and military tasks. Ferranti's Wythenshawe factory maintained control of the Argus developments after 1963, when the mainstream Ferranti computing activities had been absorbed by ICT (later ICL). The first use of an Argus computer for industrial automation was in 1962, for control of an ammonia/soda plant for ICI at Fleetwood, Lancashire.

English Electric was also not far behind. Their KDN 2 computer, first delivered in 1962, found favour in many process control areas, particularly in steel manufacturing as is shown in Chap. 7.

Generally speaking, it was not until 1960 that process control by digital computer had reached the factory floor in British industry – somewhat later, it is true, than the advent of similar applications in America. In the next chapter, we consider how the Elliott 800 series machines and, in due course, their partners, the Elliott 900 series and ARCH systems, were applied to practical process control.

References

1. Campbell-Kelly M, Aspray W (1996) Computer: a history of the information machine. Basic Books, New York. ISBN 0-465-02990-6
2. Mingo S (2000) A brief history of automation: the past, present and future of the industry. Insur J 15 May 2000, www.insurancejournal.com/
3. Bagrit L (1965) The age of automation. The BBC Reith lectures 1964. Weidenfeld & Nicholson, London
4. Ashburn A (1962) Detroit automation. Ann Am Acad Political Soc Sci (Automation) 340(March):21–28
5. See the company's advertisement in Elliott J, vol. 1, no. 1, March1951
6. Olah G, Andrews R (1953) Automatic control of hot blast temperature. Elliott J 1(4) May 1953
7. Klepp EC (1952) Recent developments in instruments. Elliott J 1(3):86–89
8. See the company's advertisement in Elliott J, vol. 2, no. 1, Aug 1954
9. Anon, Elliott Flight Automation Limited: a brief history. This 30-page typed document gives varying degrees of coverage for the period 1948–1985, with some staff listings to 1992. It is an updated version of a document entitled 'Elliott Flight Automation History' by David Broadbent which, after his death, was added to by C.R. Reese. The document is now part of the Marconi Archives at the Bodleian Library, Oxford. See also Appendix 9
10. MH (Harry) Johnson (2002) My work with computers: from the Ferranti Mark I to the ICT 1900 (1952–1966). June 2002. 84 typed pages. Circulated privately
11. JF Coales (1995) Letter to SLH Clarke, dated10 Feb 1995. This assertion was also stated by Coales in an audio interview with William Aspray on 21 Mar 1994 (Transcript available as interview number 192, Centre for the History of Electrical Engineering, Rutgers University, New Jersey, a copy of which is deposited as document SC168/1/6/2/4 in the IEE Archives, London)
12. (Anon). Elliott Brothers (London). Article in The Statist for 13 Feb 1954
13. Directors and Officers: Register of Secretaries and Directors of Elliott Automation Ltd., 1950–1958. This is a ledger with (mostly) hand-written entries in pre-printed columns deposited in the Marconi Archives at the Bodleian Library, University of Oxford, where it appeared under provisional catalogue number E006
14. Dr LP (Peter) Fielding, e-mails to Simon Lavington in Apr to June 2009. (Dr Fielding is a nephew of Sir Leon and is a Trustee of the Sir Leon Bagrit Memorial Trust)
15. Rees G (1961) Men of achievement – 2: *Sunday Times* magazine section, page 28, 23 Apr 1961. The photo of Leon Bagrit had the superimposed legend 'Prophet of Automation'
16. Joseph Roth (2008) E-mail communication with Simon Lavington on 24 Feb 2008
17. (Anon) Elliott-Automation Ltd.: History of the Group (Two sheets, typed, unsigned and undated but placed in the informal Elliott Archives by RW Bristow. From dates given in the text of this History, it must have been written between 1962 and 1965. It can be inferred that the author was at that time a long-serving senior manager – such as Edgar Herzfeld)
18. John Bunt (2001) Letter and eight pages of accompanying typed notes, sent to Simon Lavington by John Bunt on 11 Dec 2001
19. Al Sperry: Biographical notes. Documents held in the library of ISA, the Instrument, Systems and Automation Society (formerly the Instrument Society of America), PO Box 12277, 67 Alexander Drive Research Triangle Park, NC27709, USA
20. See Control Engineering, vol 6, no 8, p 52
21. Andrew St Johnston (1995) History of the Research Laboratories of Elliott Brothers (London) Ltd. – Andrew St. Johnston's Contribution. Nine-page typed manuscript, dated 31 May 1995 and sent to SLH Clarke
22. Anon, ARCH in action: on-line computing and data handling systems. Publication number R31 (48 pages) produced by Elliott Process Automation Limited. Undated but a date of mid-1966 may be deduced
23. Massey RG (1963) Computers in a new steelworks. Comput J 5(4):271–275

24. Stout TM, Williams TJ (1995) Pioneering work in the field of computer process control. IEEE Ann Hist Comput 17(1):6–18
25. Aylen J (2007) Bloodhound on my trail: Ferranti's adaptation of military hardware to process control computer. Paper presented at a symposium on Technological Innovation and the Cold War, held at the Center for the History of Business, Technology and Society, Wilmington, Delaware, 9 Mar 2007
26. Anon (1965) Bunker-Ramo dropping process control computers. Control Eng 12(6):22
27. Anon (1992) The computer control pioneers: a history of the innovators and their work. A 123-page book produced in 1992 by the Instrument Society of America and compiled by the ISA Ad Hoc Committee on the computer control pioneers. ISBN1-55617-370-9
28. Anon (1953) A survey of automatic digital computers, 1953. Office of Naval Research, Washington, DC, Survey co-ordinated by NM Blackman. The data for this comprehensively technical 109-page document was gathered in Feb 1953 in twelve countries. It gives details of "99 automatic digital computers intended for more or less general-purpose computation"
29. Crawley HJ (1957) The National Research Development Corporation Computer Project. NRDC paper no. 132, Feb 1957
30. Hendry J (1989) Innovating for failure: government policy and the early British computer industry. MIT Press, London. ISBN 0-262-08187-3
31. Wilson JF (2001) Ferranti: a history. Building a family business, 1882–1975. Carnegie Publishing Ltd., Lancaster, 2001. ISBN:1-85936-080-7. Volume 2: From family firm to multinational company, 1975–1987, published in 2007 by Crucible Books, Lancaster. ISBN:978-1-905472-01-7
32. Leon Bagrit in June1963, quoted in the Elliott-Automation Annual Report for 1962
33. John Coales, An attempt at an explanation of the happenings of the last year. Ten pages of un-dated hand-written notes and an accompanying chart of dates and names covering the period 1944 to 1947 and probably drawn up with the help of Penningtons, solicitors, between March and October 1948. Part of this set of papers is deposited as document SC168/1/6/2/1in the IEE Archives, London)
34. Elliott-Automation Ltd., Report and accounts for 1962. A year-by-year employment graph is given on page 2
35. Lavington SH, A history of Manchester computers. First edition published in 1975 by the National Computing Centre. Second edition published in 1998 by the British Computer Society, ISBN:0-902505-01-8
36. Lavington SH (2006) In the footsteps of Colossus: a description of Oedipus. IEEE Ann Hist Comput 28(2):44–55
37. (a) Campbell-Kelly M (1989) ICL: a business and technical history. Oxford University Press, Oxford. ISBN:0-19-853918-5. See also: (b) Hanley D, Compiled notes and personal memories of HEC2(M) and DEUCE IIA computers. 26-page typed Memorandum sent to Simon Lavington on 3 Nov 1999 (refer to David Hanley: dehanley@acm.org). Other HEC information may be found at: http://www.vk2bv.org/sb/hec4.htm#H3
38. A tentative delivery list for DEUCE computers, reproduced in Appendix 10, will be found at: www.ourcomputerheritage.org/wp/. This is based on DEUCE information obtained from several sources, principally: http://users.tpg.com.au/eedeuce/ and http://www.old-computers.com/museum/computer.asp?st=1&c=1089 and http://www.members.optusnet.com.au/deucepix/pjwalker.htm
39. Bird PJ (1994) LEO: the first business computer. Hasler Publishing Ltd., Wokingham. ISBN 0-9521651-0-4
40. Lavington SH (1980) Early British computers. Manchester University Press, Manchester. ISBN: 0-7190-0803-4. Co-published by Digital Press, 1980. ISBN: 0-93237-08-8. See also: http://ed-thelen.org/comp-hist/EarlyBritish.html
41. The Computer Conservation Society's Our Computer Heritage website is a collection of technical information on computers manufactured by six British companies. At the time of writing, the Pilot Study for this collection embraces the following companies: Elliott Bros (London) Ltd., Ferranti Ltd., English Electric Ltd., EMI, LEO Computers Ltd. and BTM/ICT/ICL, http://www.ourcomputerheritage.org/wp/
42. First in automation.20-page company brochure published by Elliott-Automation in about 1967

Chapter 7
Automation: The Machines and the Applications

7.1 The Need for Digital Control

As implied in Chap. 6, the general-purpose digital computer made a hesitant entry into the field of process engineering in Britain. In a retrospective note [1], John Bunt implies that Dr. Lawrence Ross was probably the first person within Elliotts to encourage the development of small digital computers as vital components of future industrial automation projects. Bunt recalls that: 'of all the [Elliott] directors, it was Dr. Ross that we most frequently saw [at Borehamwood]. In addition to his appointment with Elliott Brothers (London) Ltd., Dr Ross held a position with another company, Associated Automation, based at Willesden. It was the takeover or merger between these two companies which created the company called *Elliott-Automation*'.

John Bunt continues: 'In recounting the company's activities in the computer field, it should not be forgotten that the company's main objective lay in the field of Industrial Automation and computer developments were not always obviously central to that objective except in so far as they contributed to developing the necessary technology and making enough money to support the development work. I was invited once to lunch at Portland Place with Dr. Ross, who explained that and who said that the development of small digital computers was a vital part of the company's development plan as they were a necessary component in future industrial automation projects. They were the link between the Data Loggers, Display and Control Panels then in existence and the fully automated systems of the future'.

As was indicated in Chap. 6, the advent of compact, rugged and reliable computers transformed manual control via data logging into the more automated forms of control. The next step towards true online digital control also required computers that included good *Interrupt-handling* facilities, flexible interfaces to large quantities and types of measuring and actuating devices and good communications hardware. It goes without saying that the software to integrate all these hardware resources was both vital and complex. Writing appropriate software was a task to which Elliotts, in common with other manufacturers of digital control systems, initially allocated insufficient resources.

S. Lavington, *Moving Targets*, History of Computing,
DOI 10.1007/978-1-84882-933-6_7, © Springer-Verlag London Limited 2011

7.1.1 The ARCH Family of Industrial Control Systems

The year 1959 marks the start of R&D at Borehamwood aimed at meeting the specific hardware requirements for practical digital control of industrial processes. As discussed in Chap. 5, Elliott-Automation approached NRDC in 1959 for help in developing what was to be known as ARCH: the Articulated Control Hierarchy, originally conceived as a modular system of standard analogue and digital subunits sharing a common bus. The idea was that tailor-made ARCH online installations could be configured to suit the particular process(es) being controlled. Subsequent enhancements could readily be accommodated, due to the modular nature of the ARCH system. Although it is natural to focus on the digital computing and storage components of ARCH systems, one should not neglect the wide use of analogue computing elements in many ARCH systems. The derivation of production indicators such as plant efficiency, as functions of continuous variables, was often more conveniently calculated in analogue form, using combinations of standard analogue modules such as the adder/subtracter, the multiplier/divider and the integrator.

The design of ARCH family members in the range ARCH 100 – ARCH 1000 came out of the Process Control divisions of Elliott-Automation. Family members ARCH 2000–9000 were systems built round standard computers designed in the Computing divisions of the company – as implied by the categorization in Table 7.1. In 1964, the ARCH 101 (later 102) and ARCH 9000 were the first members of the family to be described as *Direct Digital Controllers, DDC.* As far as Borehamwood was concerned, the spur for DDC development came in April 1963 when a group

Table 7.1 Guide to Elliott-Automation ARCH process-control systems

ARCH variant	Word-length	Add time (μs)	Max. core size, words (K)	Related to	First delivered
101	12	?	?	–	1965 (one known)
102	13	23	8	902	1966
1,000	18	280	8	–	1962
2,000	24	14	32	?	?
2,020/2,030	24	6 or 12	8 or 16	4100	1965
5,000	39	7	128	503	? (none known)
6,000	20	2.3	16	?	? (none known)
8,000	39	576	8	803	1960
9,000	18	21 (or 23)	8	920[a]	1965
Panellit 609[b]	39	576	8	803	1960

[a] ARCH 9000 may have incorporated a 903 CPU; ARCH 9050 may have incorporated a 905 CPU

[b] The Panellit 609 was an 803 packaged for process-control applications and marketed via a licencing arrangement with the Panellit Corporation of Skokie, Chicago. More information on the Panellit Corporation and its UK offshoot Panellit Ltd. will be found in Sect 6.3.2. Of 17 Elliott 803 computers that were delivered to the USA, those that were sold via Panellit would have been known in America not as Elliott 803s but as Panellit 609s. The exact number of machines to which this re-naming applied is not known

of process industry representatives met in Princeton under the auspices of the Instrument Society of America to formulate guidelines for the kind of computer that would be needed for DDC. As reported in [2], *inexpensive* and *reliable* were the most important attributes demanded by the users.

Elliott-Automation launched ARCH at a Press Conference held at the Savoy Hotel, London, on 7 May 1962. The first public demonstration of ARCH equipment was at the Instruments, Electronics & Automation Exhibition at Olympia, London, from 28 May to 2 June 1962. Bill Willison was the chief engineer of the Process Control Division (later called the Process Computing Division) which developed the ARCH system. To quote from an advertisement for ARCH that appeared in the magazine *New Scientist* for 5 September 1963, 'ARCH is:

- A vital new concept in process computing which permits step-by-step introduction of computer control in any plant at low cost;
- A range of compatible and proven transistorized analogue and digital modules which work on their own or teamed in a system – ultimately as a network of systems interlinked to give integrated control over interdependent process areas.
- If there is a way of measuring a process variable then there is a way into ARCH. Any kind of input – pneumatic, shaft position, ac or dc voltage or current – every conceivable form of transducer, every possible type of signal, could be the start of an ARCH control network'

Besides the technical features, the ARCH scheme also offered financial benefits to end-users. In a paper written in 1964 [3], Leon Bagrit highlighted the economic risks associated with the 'monster' computers of the 1950s and contrasted these with the simplicity of ARCH:

'Enough has been said to show that while the concept of automation is revolutionary, its implementation must be progressive and this is dictated by consideration of capital investment as much as by technical developments. Each step provides knowledge and experience to signpost the next. For this reason I believe that, although the massive general purpose computing machine, itself a crude precursor of the machine of tomorrow, is still of importance in certain fields, it already fails to satisfy our automation needs. Such machines involve very large capital outlay which our industry cannot afford. Even in those few cases where such investment could be contemplated, there would be a need for lengthy investigations and detailed prior planning before any go-ahead could be given. The time-lag would be such that in the meantime problem emphasis would shift and new knowledge would re-orientate the methods and goals. In these circumstances there would be a grave danger either of never getting the system into operation or, by precipitate action, of creating a 'white elephant'.

'We have a practical solution to this difficulty based on the principle of the hierarchical automation system outlined in my reference to the steel industry. In following up the ideas embodied in this concept, we have turned away from the monster, expensive, all-embracing computer installation, towards a system of very much smaller and inexpensive special purpose units, which we call 'ARCH', constructed like building blocks, from both digital and analogue modules. These allow an engineer familiar with his own process and not an outside computing expert, to build up progressively anything from a simple process controller to a system for the automation of a works complex. With this versatile range of modular units progressive automation has become a reality. Today a start can be made with modest capital outlay in the knowledge that extension is easily achieved on the firm basis of later experience. Moreover, should a wrong choice have been made at any stage, the resulting modifications are easy and no catastrophic financial loss would be incurred'.

The ARCH family evolved over the same time-period (1959–1965) as the Elliott 800 series, 900 series and 4100 series computers were being developed. It is therefore not surprising that ARCH installations made use of various standard Elliott digital computers in the 800, 900 and 4,100 range. They also incorporated a range of general digital building-blocks of the Elliott Minilog family in addition to analogue computing elements and special signal-processing and interfacing equipment. The Minilog components were developed at Borehamwood and were available from about 1962 [4]. Each Minilog component was an encapsulated transistorised logic circuit, usually based on NAND gates, the whole device looking rather like an early (and slightly larger) version of the TTL integrated circuits that were widely used in digital design from the 1970s onwards. More details of Minilog elements will be found in Chap. 10.

The ARCH nomenclature is a trifle confusing. For example, in [5] and Sect. 7.3.1, Ed Hersom recalls: 'Coming back to ARCH there seems to have been a bit of "retro-naming" since I left Elliotts in 1967'. Hersom's last project was to commission the Lee Valley Water Works monitoring system, involving an Elliott 102 which was a cut-down version of the Elliott 902. The Lea Valley computer was subsequently referred to as an ARCH 102 in a company brochure. To add to the confusion, there was a time shortly after the 1968 GEC takeover when 'M' for Marconi was added, to produce the 'MARCH' appellation.

Table 7.1 shows the principle ARCH variants and their relation (if any) to the mainline Elliott computer products.

The ARCH 101 and 102 Direct Digital Controllers (Fig. 7.2) in their standard form were each capable of handling up to 30 control loops – expandable to nearly 100 (see [2]). They provided proportional or proportional-plus-integral non-interacting control actions. The analogue inputs to the ARCH 101 were converted to 12-bit words (in the ARCH 101) and all calculations were performed internally to double-length (24-bit) accuracy. Outputs were to 10-bit accuracy, available either as DC voltages or as pulse-trains suitable for devices containing stepper motors such as the Digitair pneumatic transducer which converted an input of 0–1,024 pulses into an air output change of 3–15 lb/in.^{2}

The ARCH 9000, based on a 900-series Elliott computer, also used 12-bit analogue-to-digital converters for the control system's input variables [2]. For direct digital control, the ARCH 9000 could be programmed to perform two- or three-term control functions, ratio control, cascade control and other complex functions. In addition to looking after a hundred or more loops, the central processor had ample time left over for other activities such as data logging and data reduction. Interrupts were organised into four levels of priority. Output signals could be in any of four forms: analogue voltages, pulse-trains, a pulse rate for velocity actuation of control valves, or a combination of any of the preceding three types. In addition, the usual logging typewriters, alarm printers, alarm displays and trend recorders were available as output equipment.

Finally, there was at least one special, tailor-made ARCH system configured for a particular contract. An example is the ARCH 105 system installed in 1968 for the process control of a pilot plant for Unilever.

7.1.2   ARCH Installations and the Market Competition

The first Elliott 803 computers to be used for on-line control applications (but without the *ARCH* appellation) were delivered from November 1959 onwards (803 model A up to the end of 1960 and then 803B thereafter). It is believed that the first actual on-line 803 in the UK went to the UKAEA system at Calder Hall. This was a month or so ahead of what was retrospectively called an ARCH 8000 that went, in July 1960, to Samuel Fox & Co. Ltd. (later known as British Steel Corporation, Special Steels Division) in Sheffield for an on-line billet cutting application (see also Sect. 7.2.1). The project manager for this Samuel Fox application was Tony Ide [6].

ARCH variants were still being delivered after 1970, though records are sparse after 1966. The number and types of Elliott-Automation computers delivered in each calendar year during the period 1960–1966 for *on-line* control applications are supposedly given in [7] together with details of customer and application though, as pointed out in Appendix 8, there are some inconsistencies. Table 7.2 summarises the approximate numbers of on-line machines delivered per year.

The figures per year in Table 7.2 can be aggregated to yield a total of 54 Elliott computers installed for on-line applications by 1965. To this should be added the Elliott 405 computer installed in 1957 at the National Gas Turbine Establishment (NGTE; Pyestock, Farnborough). This was the only 405 to have been used in an on-line application; it was replaced at Pyestock by an SDS 9300 in 1966 [8]. The Elliott company's own total of 54 (or 55) on-line applications may then be contrasted with the figure of 39 given in [9] (as reproduced in Table 7.3) which appears to have been derived from two contemporary surveys. The discrepancy may be due to different interpretations of the terminology *process control* or *on-line*, and/or missing data in the contemporary surveys. Another survey compiled in 1965 from an apparently wider number of contemporary sources [10] gives higher overall numbers, as shown in Table 7.4. It also illustrates the very rapid growth in industrial process control worldwide in the 1960s.

Raw numbers aside, what is indisputable is that Elliott-Automation was the clear leader amongst UK computer companies in 1965 but fell far short of the American

Fig. 7.1 Starting in 1959 with support from the National Research Development Corporation (NRDC), Elliott-Automation developed a modular system of analogue and digital sub-units sharing a common bus. This was launched in 1962 as ARCH: the Articulated Control Hierarchy. Some members of the ARCH family were built round standard Elliott digital computers. Other ARCH variants were tailor-made and incorporated special signal-processing and interfacing units. The ARCH system in the photo was being prepared for the Steel Company of Wales

Table 7.2 Delivery of Elliott-Automation computers for *on-line* process control

Computer	1960	1961	1962	1963	1964	1965	1966
803 or ARCH 8000 (or Panellit 609)	11	1	4	4	4	–	2
502	–	–	–	–	1	–	1
ARCH 1000	–	–	1	4	6	9	5
4120 or ARCH 2020	–	–	–	–	–	–	6
4130 or ARCH 2030	–	–	–	–	–	–	4
900 or ARCH 9000	–	–	–	–	–	9	7
ARCH 102	–	–	–	–	–	–	2
Total of all types	11	1	5	8	11	18	27

leaders in process-control applications. By 1968, it is estimated [9] that Bunker-Ramo's market share had dropped to just 3%. The joint world leaders in 1968, each with an 11% market share, were estimated to be General Electric (326 installations) and English Electric (which by that date included Elliott-Automation) with 307 installations. The English Electric KDN2 computer, in particular, had achieved good sales for control applications in the metals industry, as discussed below.

Fig. 7.2 The ARCH 101 Direct Digital Controller (DDC) was introduced in 1964. The unit accepts 30 or more analogue signals, implements a variety of control functions digitally, and provides resulting analogue output signals to the processes being controlled. Other forms of output are possible, for example digital pulses can be converted to pneumatic pressure-changes. In summary, a DDC could in principle take the place of a human operator in supervising the control of a simple industrial process

Table 7.3 Perceived market share in process-control computers: estimated total installed by March 1965, as reproduced from Table 3 in [9]

Manufacturer	Number sold	Market share (%)
Bunker-Ramo (TRW, CAE)	107	19
IBM	84	15
General Electric	81	14
Westinghouse (PRODAC)	57	10
Honeywell	40	7
Elliott	39	7
Control Data (CDC)	24	4
Bailey Meter	14	2
English Electric (KDF, KDN)	14	2
Ferranti (Argus)	13	2
Foxboro	13	2
Leeds and Northrup (LN)	12	2
Others	79	
Total installations worldwide	565	

Table 7.4 Perceived total of online process-control installations worldwide in November 1965, as estimated in [10]

	1958	1959	1960	1961	1962	1963	1964	1965
World total of on-line systems	2	5	20	70	185	380	605	810
Of which, number in metal industries	0	1	5	14	25	46	66	139

Fig. 7.3 Commissioning ARCH systems at Borehamwood in 1966. In that year Elliott-Automation was given a Queen's Award to Industry, in recognition of 'outstanding achievements in the technical development of process-control computers'

7.2   Applications of Elliott Computers in Automation

By 1966, according to [11], 'ARCH systems have been provided to meet the wide range of varying needs – data logging, alarm scanning, DDC multivariable control, sequencing, process optimization and combinations of these roles. The size and configuration of a system for a given application depends upon the particular objectives and needs. No two system requirements are identical. However, experience to date with over 125 ARCH systems in operation indicates that the potentially infinite range of system requirements can be met. The majority of these systems are working in the Oil and Chemical fields on distillation columns, platinum reformers, ammonia production, ethylene production and natural gas fractionation'.

To quote from the Introduction in another Elliott-Automation brochure [7]: 'To the end of 1966 Elliott-Automation had sold 728 computers: of these 578 were of its own design and manufacture and the remaining 150 were NCR 315 computers manufactured for the National Cash Register Company.... Of the total 578 Elliott-designed computers on order or already delivered, approaching one third (177) were for direct on-line control applications. Of these, 82 had been delivered and 95 were included in the order book. Out of 177 on-line applications, 63 were for operational military weapons systems, leaving 144 other on-line computer control systems ordered from the Company. This figure is believed to exceed substantially the achievement in this field of any other computer manufacturing company outside the United States of America and to be the fifth highest of any company in the world'.

The customers for these on-line applications are summarised in Appendix 8, which also contains comments about discrepancies between the different sources used to compile the data. The difficulty of obtaining a definitive list of all on-line applications in the 10-year period 1960–1970, accurate as to dates of computer delivery, dates of full system operation and technical details of the application, may readily be appreciated. The area-by-area picture given in the following sections necessarily contains gaps, which can only be filled if and when more source documents come to light.

The applications of Elliott computers to automation cover a wide spectrum, from military weapons systems to paper mills, and from road traffic control to ships' boilers. For illustrative purposes we focus on the eight areas that seemed, in the 1960s, to be the most important:

Steel and other metals processing
Electricity (power) generation
UK government research establishments
Oil refining and related activities
Chemicals
Ships and shipping
Paper mills and typesetting
Road traffic control

According to [10], in 1965 'metals, chemicals and power generation, together account for about 75% of the world's installations of on-line computers for industrial control'.

Incidentally, the background histories of many of these areas also serve to highlight ways in which the UK's industrial profile in the 1960s was very different from that of today. Since modern readers may be unfamiliar with the identity or significance of some of the company names given in Appendix 8 due to evolutionary changes that have occurred since the 1960s, background notes are provided for five of the eight sample application areas. In some cases these background notes mirror the decline in British manufacturing industry; in other cases they mirror the gradual move from public to private enterprise as key sectors of British infrastructure were in due course *de-Nationalised* by right-of-centre governments.

7.2.1 Steel and Other Metals Processing

In 1965, Joseph Roth, the Projects Manager at the Metal Industries Division of Elliott Process Automation Ltd., identified 18 functional uses of computers, of which 'basic oxygen converters' was the most common [10]. The applications included the following:

Use	Total number worldwide in 1965	As percentages
Basic oxygen converters	34	19
Hot strip mill	25	14
Reversing hot mill	18	10
Production control	14	8
Cold mill	12	7
Blast furnace	12	7
Coating	12	7
All other metals applications	52	≈28
Total	179	100

Of the 179 metals installations worldwide, 23 (13%) were in UK and 104 (58%) in USA. The first such application seems to have been in 1959, when a GE 312 computer was used for on-line logging and data reduction in the sinter strand at the Youngstown Sheet and Tube Company's Indiana Harbor Works, USA.

Fig. 7.4 An Elliott 803 computer was delivered in July 1960 to the steelworks of Samuel Fox & Company Limited, Stocksbridge, Sheffield, for billet cut-up (shearing) optimization

By 1965, the three principal UK computer manufacturers who had penetrated the metals sector are believed have been [10]:

Elliott-Automation   Nine ARCH/800 series installations
English Electric   Seven KDN2 installations
Ferranti   Four Argus installations

A general survey of early automation in the iron and steel industry is given in [12].

7.2.1.1 UK Industrial Background

In 1951, the UK's Steel industry was nationalised, only to be denationalised in 1953. About 90% of the UK's steel industry was again nationalised in 1967 when 14 large companies were grouped together as the British Steel Corporation. In 1988 came another denationalisation, when the assets of the Corporation were transferred to a company known as British Steel. In 1999, this company merged with Koninklijke Hoogovens to form Corus. Then Corus itself was taken over in 2007 by the Indian organization Tata Steel. The Steel Company of Wales, the Richard Thomas and Baldwins Group and Samuel Fox & Company Ltd. were all absorbed into the British Steel Corporation in 1967. The following steel companies and applications are amongst those mentioned for Elliott computers in Appendix 8.

Samuel Fox & Company Limited, Stocksbridge, Sheffield. Application: billet cut-up optimization. An Elliott 803 (aka ARCH 8000) computer was delivered in July 1960. A contemporary Elliott-Automation Press Release [13] claimed that: 'The installation is the first application of an electronic digital computer to an actual steel process anywhere in the world and the first such application to any industrial process in the United Kingdom'. Anecdotes from an Elliott employee involved in this Samuel Fox project are given in Sect. 7.3.1. Sometime later, an Elliott ARCH 1000 was installed at Samuel Fox for 'soaking pits logging' [10].

Richard Thomas & Baldwins Limited (RTB), Spencer Works, Llanwern, Newport, Monmouthshire. This substantial strip-mill project [12, 14] is believed to have been the first successful use, worldwide, of computers for complete mill control. It involved two 803 (ARCH 8000) computers: one for ingot/slab control and on-line information handling, the other for production control for steel plant, slabbing mill and hot strip mill. The 803 for ingot/slab control was installed at the end of August 1962, according to [14]. A third Elliott 803 (actually, the first to be installed at Llanwern in November or December 1961) was used for program development, operational research, training and back-up. Some background descriptions of software development carried out by Vaughan Programming Services, on behalf of Elliott-Automation, are given in [14, 15].

The hot mill automation at RTB, the most complex part of the process, was preformed by an American GE 412 computer with an 8 K RAM (core) and a 56 K word drum backing store. The main reason for choosing the GE412, manufactured by the General Electric Company of Phoenix, Arizonia, was instruction-speed. The GE412's fixed-point add time was 40 ms [16], whereas that of the 803B was

576 ms. In addition, the GE412 had an Automatic Priority Interrupt, Variable Elapsed Time Counters and Program Variable Time Control – all designed specifically for real-time control. The GE412 was available from July 1962 whereas the Elliott 503, the faster version of the 803, was not available until 1963. The 503's add time was 7.2 ms – though an Elliott 503, with its 39-bit word and floating-point hardware, would have been overkill for the Llanwern project. A year later, the Elliott 502, with an add time of 2 ms and fast program switching according to eight levels of priority interrupts, was Elliott's specific answer to the most challenging applications in real-time radar control (see Appendix 5) – but an Elliott 502 would certainly not have been cost-effective for the RTB application.

Commissioning of the complete steelworks project at Llanwern took place in stages, starting in 1963. The automatic crop shear started in July 1963 and gauge control in October 1963. Slab tracking, logging and all of the mill set-ups and temperature controls were fully operational by October 1964 [12].

The new Spencer Works had actually been formally opened before the computer systems were fully operational. Joseph Roth, whose first job at Borehamwood in 1957 had been as Deputy Chief Engineer in the Business Computing Division, remembers the RTB project as follows [6]: 'I was the project manager for the hardware aspect of the computer systems installed at Spencer Works and still have quite a few memories of the trials and tribulations of that exercise including for instance the formal opening of the works by the Queen [in October 1962]. Of course, the computer system was one of the prime exhibits and when the Queen and Prince Philip came into the computer room which housed the two 803's and the computer system was explained to her, she said to Harry Spencer "Is the equipment actually working? I get so tired of being asked to open plants when they are not actually in working order!"'

Whilst those who worked on the RTB implementation may have had a less-than-rosy view of the technical quality of this early Elliott-Automation installation, the opening of the Spencer Works did provide useful publicity to the company. In an article entitled *The Wages of Automation* in *Time* Magazine for Friday 2 November 1962, we read that: 'Elliott-Automation in barely 16 years has established itself as one of the world's most sophisticated manufacturers of automatic controls, and the largest outside the US. Elliott's 38 divisions and 25 factories turn out hundreds of complex products ranging from industrial computers to automatic homing heads for missiles. Since 1959 the company's sales have increased 122% to $756 million, and its annual profits have soared almost 83% to $6.6 million'.

More anecdotes from an Elliott employee involved in the RTB project are given in Sect. 7.3.1.

Steel Company of Wales Ltd. (SCoW), Tinplate Group, at Trostre near Llanelly and at Velindre about 15 miles north of Ebbw Vale. One Elliott ARCH 1000 computer was installed in 1963 at Velindre and two ARCH 1000 computers were installed in 1965 at Trostre, for quality recording of continuous electrolytic tinplate production. These three systems logged the locations of imperfections in the tinplate so that customers such as the Metal Box Company could avoid using imperfect areas of tinplate which, if used for food tins, would result in *bleeding* of the contents.

An ARCH 1000 Five-Stand Cold Mill Logger was also installed at Velindre in 1966. Software development for some of the tinplate applications was carried out by Vaughan Programming Services [15].

Imperial Smelting Corporation, Avonmouth. In 1967, an Elliott ARCH 2020 with 16 K words of 2 ms cycle-time core store was installed to control an ISF Zinc smelting operation. This involved the ARCH 2020 in handling over 500 measurements, more that 800 contact closure signals and over 120 direct digital control (DDC) loops, thus making it 'the largest [DDC] of this type known in the world' [17]. Elliott-Automation supplied the whole of the automation system, including data logging and materials-handling equipment, bringing the value of the work done at Avonmouth to almost £1 million (1967 prices). To quote [17]: 'It is the largest automation system ever devised for a non-ferrous metal plant and one of the largest automation systems ever installed anywhere'. The same brochure also looks forward to future improvements: 'In the sinter plant … sinter quality varies but it could be accurately determined by x-ray fluorescent analysis techniques. The computer could take the result of this analysis, perform the numerous complex calculations involved and send out corrections to the settings of the constant-weight feeders in the proportioning plant…. The solution of these problems will be aided considerably by an optimisation technique which has recently been pioneered by an Elliott-Automation team working on an experimental plant at the Ministry of Technology's Warren Spring Laboratory. This new advance in automation technology is now established under the name CUDOS – Continuously Updated Dynamic Optimisation System'. (See below for more on the Warren Spring installations and Figs. 7.10 and 7.11 for Elliott-Automation's X-ray fluorescent spectrometer.)

Royal Netherlands Blast Furnace & Steelworks Co. This is most probably the entry in Appendix 8 called 'Royal Dutch Steelworks', for which an Elliott ARCH 1000 computer was installed in 1963 for 'investigation of blast furnace operations'. By 1965, the applications were 'logging and control' [10]. The steelworks, located at Ijmuiden in Holland, was known by various names such as Konijilkee Hoogovens. Software development was carried out by Vaughan Programming Services [15].

7.2.2 Electricity (or Power) Generation

7.2.2.1 Background

The Central Electricity Generating Board (CEGB) was created from the Central Electricity Authority (formerly the British Electricity Authority) in 1957. Although electricity privatisation began in 1990, the CEGB continued to exist until 2001. The assets of the CEGB were broken up into three new companies: Powergen, National Power and the National Grid Company. In the 1960s, most power stations were coal-fired. The National Coal Board (NCB) was created in 1947 as part of the Labour government's nationalisation of key industries. Coal mining employed over 700,000 people in Britain in 1950. Many coalfields were closed in the 1980s. In 1987, the NCB was privatised to become the British Coal Corporation.

Early examples of the use of Elliott 803 computers in power station control occur at two American utilities: Boston Edison Co. and Gulf States Utilities, both installations dating from 1960. In the UK, an ARCH 1000 was installed at CEGB Croydon 'B' power station in 1964 and an ARCH 102 at CEGB Fawley, Hampshire, in 1968. Elliott-Automation control equipment of one sort or another (usually including data logging) was installed at many other power stations, including CEGB Barony, South Ayrshire, CEGB Berkeley Nuclear Laboratories, CEGB Northfleet, Kent, CEGB Trawsfynnyd, Gwynedd and CEGB Tilbury, Essex. In the Elliott-Automation Annual Report for 1962, Leon Bagrit wrote: 'We consider our work in the new Spencer Works of Richard Thomas and Baldwins, and in a project as important and advanced as the Tilbury Power Station, as milestones of progress in industrial automation'.

Under *Electricity Generation*, we should really include the atomic power station at Calder Hall. Instead, because of its links with the UK government's Atomic Energy Authority, this landmark project is included in the next section.

7.2.3 UK Government R&D Establishments

7.2.3.1 Background

The National Gas Turbine Establishment

The Royal Aircraft Establishment (RAE) at Farnborough came into being in 1918, having its origins in HM Balloon Factory, founded in 1908 – the year that Samuel Cody made the first aeroplane flight in Britain at Farnborough. In 1936 Frank Whittle formed his company Power Jets Ltd to develop gas turbine (ie jet engine) technology. In 1944 Frank Whittle's company Power Jets merged with the gas turbine division of RAE and set up headquarters at Pyestock, adjacent to Farnborough. In 1946 the Pyestock site was reconstituted to form the *National Gas Turbine Establishment (NGTE)*. In 1988, RAE was renamed the Royal Aerospace Establishment. In 1991, it was merged into the Defence Research Agency (DRA), the Ministry of Defence's new research organization. In 1995, the DRA and other MOD organizations merged to form the Defence Evaluation and Research Agency (DERA). In 2001, DERA was part-privatised by the MOD, resulting in two separate organizations: the state-owned Defence Science and Technology Laboratory (DSTL), and the privatised QinetiQ, a Public-Private Partnership. It is believed that a supermarket distribution centre now occupies the former NGTE site at Pyestock.

An Elliott 405 was installed at NGTE for the on-line monitoring of aero engines in the autumn of 1957, remaining operational until 1966. Much of the NGTE work was classified. It is believed that the four engine-testing cells, any one of which could be switched on-line to the Elliott 405, gave a research facility unrivalled throughout Europe. An ARCH 102 was delivered to the NGTE site in 1969.

From [8, 18] it may be deduced that the NGTE facility at Pyestock had four test cells, each of which could contain a jet engine whose performance was being

Fig. 7.5 The National Gas Turbine Establishment, at Pyestock near Farnborough, had facilities for evaluating jet engines. The photo shows the test area of four cells, each of which could contain a jet engine whose performance was being studied. The horizontal cylinder to left of centre in the photo is Test Cell number 1. An identical-looking Test Cell 2 is further away within the same complex, with a control room between them. Note the cloud of engine exhaust (mixed with cooling water) billowing up from Cell 2

studied – see Figs. 7.5 and 7.6. During an engine evaluation, a test rig was successively stabilised at a number of predetermined monitoring points, each one defined as a set of values of {altitude, flight-speed and air temperature}. Changes in altitude were simulated by changing the ambient air pressure round the engine under test. Speeds of up to Mach 3 and altitudes up to 70,000 ft could be simulated. A complete test sequence might last about 2 h, during which there might be say 10–20 pre-defined monitoring points. The rig might take a few minutes to stabilise at each new position. Each time a stable point was reached, a button was pressed by the test controller and a set of between 300 and 600 parameters was recorded digitally. These parameters represented such things as fuel-flow, temperature and pressure at various points on the engine. The parameters were then transmitted as bit-patterns to the Elliott 405 computer, situated in another building about half a mile away.

DSIR Laboratories

The UK's Department of Scientific and Industrial Research (DSIR) was formed in 1917 with the aim of enhancing scientific and industrial R&D through government funding. DSIR was disbanded in 1965. Amongst DSIR laboratories were

Fig. 7.6 An Elliott 405 computer was installed at Pyestock in 1957 for on-line analysis of jet engine test data, remaining operational until 1966. During a test, sets of between 300 and 600 parameters were recorded digitally. The windows to the right of the photo look out on to Test Cell 1. A duty fire officer stands to the left of the photo. The engine's parameters were digitised and transmitted as bit-patterns to the 405 situated safely in another building about half a mile away

Warren Spring, opened in 1959 in Stevenage, Hertfordshire and the *National Physical Laboratory* at Teddington, Middlesex (originally founded in 1900).

DSIR's Warren Spring Laboratories had a close relationship with Elliott-Automation – indeed, Laurence Clarke's father was, for several years from 1959 until his retirement, the Director of the Warren Spring Labs. In 1962, an ARCH 1000 was installed at Warren Spring and linked to a Water Gas Shift plant (an example of a *transfer line* reactor) for the further development of the ARCH architecture. Warren Spring then went on to use the ARCH 1000 to develop practical methods of adaptive control, making it available to other research groups at universities, etc. In 1965, an ARCH 9000, and in 1968 another ARCH 1000, were installed for what was described as 'Experiments in on-line control and optimisation of continuous process plants including direct digital control'. (See also the Imperial Smelting Corporation, above.)

Atomic Energy

In 1946, the Atomic Energy Research Establishment was set up at Harwell in Berkshire. From this, the *United Kingdom Atomic Energy Authority (UKAEA)* was formed in 1954. Apart from Harwell, the UKAEA's Laboratories included one at

Fig. 7.7 The Elliott-Automation Data Logger for the Euratom Dragon nuclear reactor at Winfrith Heath, Dorset, in 1962. The Data Logger was required to monitor one thousand measurement points at the rate of five per second. As well as raising the alarm if any off-normal condition arose, the equipment provided a printed log of all readings

Culham and one at Winfrith Heath (where the Dragon reactor was located). From 1965, UKAEA branched out into various commercial and non-nuclear activities that had grown from nuclear technology. The European Atomic Energy Community EURATOM, established in 1957, partnered UKAEA in some research projects.

From the late 1950s, Elliott-Automation was involved in nuclear instrumentation. To quote [19], written in 1958, 'Elliott Brothers were also responsible for the instrumentation of the experimental reactor *Neptune* at the UK Atomic Energy Establishment, Harwell, and have been entrusted with the design and development of the reactor instrumentation and instrumentation for the steam-raising plant for the first British sea-going nuclear submarine HMS Dreadnought'. Actually, in the end HMS Dreadnought used an American nuclear reactor. HMS Valiant, the second UK nuclear submarine, was the first to have an all-British reactor system.

7.2.3.2 Calder Hall

Sellafield in Cumbria, the site of an old Second World War munitions factory, was re-named Windscale in 1947 and chosen by the UK government as the place at which weapons-grade nuclear material was to be produced. In due course, with the creation of the United Kingdom Atomic Energy Authority (UKAEA) in 1954, ownership of Windscale Works passed to the UKAEA and R&D activity at the site was broadened. The first of four Magnox nuclear reactors went operational at Calder Hall, adjacent to Windscale. Calder Hall was the world's first commercial nuclear power station. Construction started in 1953 and the station was first connected to the National Grid in August 1956. Calder Hall had four Magnox reactors, each capable of generating 50 MW of power [20].

A reactor at Windscale (but not at Calder Hall) was the focus of great concern when, on 10 October 1957, the graphite core caught fire, releasing substantial amounts of radioactive contamination into the surrounding area. Nevertheless the Windscale disaster indirectly provided an opportunity for Elliott-Automation to introduce on-line digital techniques to the Calder Hall nuclear power station. The events, as remembered by Joseph Roth [6], were as follows.

'Associated Automation at Willesden – where the Panellit Division of Elliott-Automation was first based – had obtained an order in 1958 from the UKAEA to provide an analogue monitoring and control system for the No 4 Reactor at Calder Hall. This order followed the Windscale disaster, about which the subsequent Committee of Inquiry concluded that a major problem was due to the lack of proper monitoring equipment, it being necessary to monitor the double differential of the rate of change of temperature in the reactor core which the Windscale (analogue) instrumentation had been unable to do. Unfortunately the analogue approach being adopted by Associated Automation for Calder Hall also proved not to be up to the task and UKAEA wanted the company to return the progress payments which had been made, up to the contracted project cost.

'At that time [1959] the first 803 had just been developed and I was seconded to Willesden to first persuade UKAEA to give Elliotts a second chance with a digital solution and then to produce the computer based digital solution. This I did and UKAEA gave us a year to complete the system but with no further payments. The Calder Hall system was my first project of an industrial control computer system and at the time we were of the opinion that this was one of the first – if not the first – on-line system in the world. It operated on a 24/7 basis.'

The Calder Hall project involved an Elliott computer being connected to 410 different monitoring and control points in the reactor. Some of the alarm functions were based on rates of change, illustrating an early benefit of digital control. Besides being amongst the first few applications of the new Elliott 803 computer (or indeed *any* digital computer) to industrial on-line control, the system involved prototype Elliott 803 hardware marketed as the Panellit 609. The Panellit Division of Elliott-Automation did not itself have the necessary in-house resources for software development and so placed a contract with Vaughan Programming Services (VPS) for the task. VPS, which had been set up by Dina St. Johnston, wife of Andrew St. Johnston, in February 1959, was the UK's first Software House [15].

In a letter dated 11 December 1959 to Panellit, VPS quotes £200 for 'writing and testing the necessary computer programmes', the programs to be ready 'by about the 20th February 1960 to meet a UKAEA deadline of 31st March'. In a subsequent letter dated 8 March 1960 to Panellit, Dina St. Johnston of VPS wrote: 'As became apparent during the limited running obtained with the previous programme, the complexity of the system is such that all effects of any manual intervention must be anticipated for the programme to be proved to be correct'. Dina then quotes a total of £210 for the further work which had become necessary to rewrite the program to the new specification. Panellit later paid a retaining fee of £400 per annum for Dina's continued services. To place such remunerations in context, in 1962 a four-bedroom terrace house in Manchester could be bought for £1,200 and a four-door family saloon car typically cost about £700. (Specifically, the motoring extremes in 1962 were represented by an Austin Mini at £496 and a Rolls-Royce Silver Cloud II at £6,272).

During the complex Calder Hall project VPS designed their Master Control Executive (MACE), a robust timesharing mini-operating system with predictable and precise response times. More details of MACE will be found in Chap. 8 and in [15].

The EURATOM Dragon Nuclear Reactor

Around 1962, a large Elliott-Automation Data Logger was installed at UKAEA Winfrith Heath, Dorset, for the EURATOM *Dragon* nuclear reactor, where it monitored approximately one thousand measurement points at the rate of five per second [21]. In 1962, it was stated that 'every nuclear reactor in Britain contains Elliott equipment' [21]. In 1966, an ARCH 9000 was installed at the Ceramics Division, UKAEA Harwell, for the on-line control of four X-ray diffractometers.

7.2.4   Oil Refining and Related Activities

Probably the first computer control of a catalytic polymerization process was the installation of a Ramo-Wooldridge RW-300 computer at Texaco's Port Arthur refinery in the USA [22]. The RW-300 had an 8 K word drum as its main memory. Inputs to the computer included 26 flow-rates, 72 temperatures, two pressures and three propylene analyses. A paper feasibility study for the Port Arthur project was completed in 1957 and the system went live in March 1959. The benefits were reported to be as follows: the conversion of propylene to polymer had increased to about 92% from a historic average of about 83%; catalyst savings of about $75,000 per year had occurred. The computer hardware costs were estimated to be $300,000 (Fig. 7.8).

Elliott-Automation was involved with several oil companies. Exact installation-dates and applications have not been determined with any reliability in some cases but the following are indicative.

- Tidewater Refinery, Delaware, USA. In 1960, an Elliott 803 was installed for the control of a petrochemical process (Naphthalene).
- Tidewater Oil Company, San Francisco. An Elliott 803 computer was installed.
- United Fuel Gas Company, West Virginia.

Fig. 7.8 An Elliott-Automation *Viscometer,* as installed at the Esso Fawley oil refinery near Southampton. The instrument gave continuous automatic analysis of viscosity, leading to greatly improved control of product quality

- Austrian Mineral Oil Company.
- Esso.
- British Petroleum Co. Ltd., London. In 1965, an Elliott ARCH 101 was installed for direct digital control in conjunction with an analogue computer.
- BP Chemicals (UK) Ltd., Hull. In 1965, an ARCH 9000 was installed for direct digital control and plant optimisation.
- Mobil Oil Co. Ltd., Research and Technical Service Laboratory, Coryton, Essex. In 1967, an ARCH 9000 was installed for control of an internal combustion engine test centre, plus data logging.

7.2.5   Chemicals

7.2.5.1   Background on the Relevant Companies

Imperial Chemical Industries (ICI) was formed in 1926 from the merger of four British chemical companies. In 1984, ICI was the first UK company to achieve £1 billion in annual pre-tax profits. From 1993 onwards, ICI started to re-position itself (or 'slim down'), starting with the demerger of the ICI Pharmaceuticals Division to form Zeneca (later AstraZeneca). From about 2000 onwards, ICI has been chiefly known for its specialty chemical products and paints.

Eleuthère Irénée du Pont founded EI DuPont & Company in 1802 in America as an explosives company that later turned to chemicals, materials and energy. Today, DuPont operates in more than 70 countries.

Dista Products Ltd. grew out of the Distillers Company Ltd. (DCL), an enterprise formed in 1877 from an amalgamation of six Scotch whisky distilleries. DCL had a site at Speke in Liverpool, on which the government built a factory to manufacture vital antibiotic penicillin towards the end of the Second World War. After the war, DCL established a new division, Distillers (Biochemicals) Ltd., specialising in deep fermentation techniques; it produced a series of antibiotics and used the prefix *Dista* on many of its products. In 1963, the Speke site was bought by Eli Lilly and Company, of USA, for manufacturing and distributing antibiotics to the European market. At this time (1963), DCL's Speke facility was formally re-named Dista Products Ltd.

It has not proved possible to determine the exact installation-dates and other details of the many applications of automation in the chemical industry. Amongst early examples were three Elliott 803 computers installed in America in 1960 in three separate nylon or Mylar processing plants run by the EI DuPont & Company Limited. In 1966, an ARCH 1000 was installed at ICI Ltd., Plastics Division, Wilton, Middlesborough, Teesside, for data logging and synthetic process control. Other Elliott-Automation installations existed at ICI Limited, Billingham; Shell Chemicals Limited; Distillers Company Limited; the Spencer-Weatherly fertiliser plant near Dublin; the Ministry of Chemical Industries, USSR; the Ministry of Chemical Industries, Poland; Chemoprojekts, Bratislava, Czechoslovakia; Badlsche Anilin-und-Soda Fabrik, Germany; Dista Products, Liverpool.

More information has come to light on the last of the above applications. In 1967, an ARCH 102 was installed at Dista Products Ltd., Speke, Liverpool, for the control of batch fermentation of antibiotics such as penicillin [23, 24]. The system, involving 114 control loops under the direct digital control (DDC) of an ARCH 102 computer, cost about £100,000 (1967 prices) to implement. The result was greater accuracy of controlling parameters such as temperature, giving a higher yield. The actual computer at Dista was ARCH 102 serial number 7, ordered in February 1966 and installed in April 1967. According to [25], the long console shown in the background of Fig. 7.9 included both manual and automatic control modes. Dista insisted, against the advice of Elliott-Automation, in the ability to revert to manual mode because they were uncertain about the reliability of what was, in 1967, a novel computer installation upon which Dista's entire antibiotics production would depend. Manual mode was, in fact, used on several occasions during the first few months of installation because of faults in the mercury-whetted electro-mechanical rotary switches that Elliotts had installed to sample the many transducers at high speed. Elliotts replaced these switches with solid-state multiplexers and 'reliability was established overnight'. Cost figures of the Dista operation are given in Appendix 8.

Fig. 7.9 In 1967 an ARCH 102 was installed at Dista Products Ltd., Speke, Liverpool, for the control of batch fermentation of antibiotics such as penicillin. The system, involving 114 control loops, cost about £100,000 (1967 prices) to implement. The Elliott 902 processor at the heart of the ARCH 102 system represented about 20% of the cost of the whole Speke project

7.2.6 Ships and Shipping

Elliott-Automation instrumentation and control equipment found its way into many large ships, particularly for engine room and boiler control. Apart from photographs, few technical details have come to light. The companies involved included Shell Tankers UK Ltd.; Trident Tankers Ltd.; Port Line Shipping Company; Maritime Fruit Carriers Company Ltd.; and Welsh Ore Carriers Ltd. Elliott-Automation was proud to have equipped the 103,000 t BP tanker *British Admiral*, said to be 'the largest ship ever built in Britain' when it was launched on 17 March 1965 by the Queen at Vickers' yard in Barrow-in-Furness.

7.2.7 Paper Mills and Typesetting

7.2.7.1 Background

The Thomson organization became involved in newspaper publication in Canada in 1934. In 1954, the company's founder, Roy Thomson, moved to Scotland to begin a new phase of his career in the UK, by which time he owned the largest number of newspapers of any group in Canada. In 1959, Thomson acquired the Kemsley

Group, publishers of many UK national and regional newspapers – including the *Reading Post* which was to become the object of an Elliott typesetting project. By 1995, Thomson Regional Newspapers had become the largest publisher of regional and local newspapers in Britain, but in that year Thomson made a strategic decision to withdraw from the UK newspaper market. Amongst the newspapers released in 1995 were *The Times* and *The Sunday Times*, titles that Thomson had acquired in 1967; these were sold to News International Ltd. By 2006, The Thomson Organization had become a multi-national company of some 32,000 employees, active in the fields of law, tax, accounting, financial services, scientific research and healthcare. The company's headquarters are now in America. The revenues in 2006 amounted to $6.6 billion [26].

The origins of Reed International date from 1894 when Albert E Reed established his newsprint manufacture at Tovil Mill, near Maidstone in Kent. In 1920, the building of a new mill at nearby Aylesford was started. By 1958, Aylesford Paper Mills had become the largest in the UK. The name of the company was changed to Reed International Limited in 1970, when (amongst other assets) it acquired the International Publishing Corporation (IPC). By 2002, the company was known as Reed Elsevier PLC. In 2006, Reed Elsevier's revenues were £5,398 million and the organization employed 36,000 people.

Two Elliott-Automation paper mill installations are known: the Albert E Reed & Co. Ltd. paper mill at Aylesford, Kent, and Oxford University Press's mill at Wolvercote, a few miles north of Oxford. The Wolvercote mill, one of the oldest in the country, was the first in the world to incorporate on-line, direct computer control of the paper-making process [27]. An Elliott ARCH 1000 system was installed in 1965. As a result of automation, closer control of the process parameters enabled the Wolvercote paper-making machinery to run faster without loss of quality. Furthermore, switching the plant to new settings required for the production of different grades of paper was easier and quicker, since the computer stored the standard running conditions for each grade. To quote [27]: 'The immediate effect of on-line computer control on Wolvercote's economy is expected to be a 5% increase in output. This is basically comprised of a 50% time-saving for grade changes, and a 15% reduction of waste due to off-specification paper. Taken together, these increases in efficiency are expected to yield a saving of at least £50,000 in the first full year of operation, and the whole cost of the project is expected to be recovered in less than two years. Wolvercote should now be in a stronger competitive position and should benefit from an enhanced customer relationship as a result of the exceptionally consistent grade quality. Wolvercote is an example of what can be achieved by forward-looking management in a business of medium size'. Wolvercote imported all its raw materials. About 25% of its output went to Oxford University Press who, in turn, exported about 60% of its book output. For a comment on the influence of Wolvercote on the Elliott system at Reed's Aylesford Mills, see Sect. 7.3.1.

In 1966 and 1967, a total of four Elliott ARCH 9000 systems were installed at Thomson Regional Newspapers, for computer typesetting at the *Reading Post* and other publications. Each system enabled a number of control desks to share one computer. The first typesetting system, developed from 1964 onwards in collaboration with The Thomson Organization, was described in the Elliott-Automation Annual Report for 1964 as 'the most advanced in the world'. It was thought sufficiently novel for Elliott-Automation to plan wider commercial exploitation. Accordingly, a revenue-sharing agreement with The Thomson Organization was drawn up in the spring of 1965 – though this appears to have been overtaken by events and never to have been formally signed [28].

7.2.8 Road Traffic Control

The first Elliott-Automation entry into the road traffic control arena was a system developed for Munich City Council. An Elliott ARCH 9000 was installed at Munich in 1965, followed by an Elliott 4120 in 1967. According to the Elliott-Automation Annual Report for 1966, the Munich system was formally inaugurated in the spring of 1967 and 'this has now led to even more substantial contracts from both Madrid and Barcelona'. No further evidence of the Spanish projects has yet come to light.

Within the UK, an Elliott ARCH 1000 was installed in 1966 by the Ministry of Transport, for toll registration and traffic control for the new River Severn road bridge. This was followed by Ministry of Transport orders for seven systems [29–31] in the period 1968–1972, which together formed the National Motorways Communication System. Surviving records are not entirely clear, partly because these seven systems span the period of re-organization following the takeover of Elliott-Automation by GEC in the autumn of 1968 and partly because the seven systems themselves were subject to reconfiguration throughout their active life. At Borehamwood, the production of Elliott 900-series machines used for road traffic control was continued under the label Marconi-Elliott Computer Systems Limited (MECS), which was then re-named GEC Computers Ltd. in 1971. Another source of confusion is the fact that some of the seven traffic control sites were eventually shut down, their functionality being incorporated into other sites within the same region of the country. Finally, most sites were subject to hardware and software upgrades (e.g. increased primary memory).

Piecing all the available evidence together, the probable locations and processors at the seven sites (CP1–CP7) of the National Motorways Communication System are shown in Table 7.5, ordered according to their date of installation. The two earlier sites (CP2 and CP7) were closed down and their functionality incorporated into one of the larger sites based on dual 905 processors, when these larger sites became operational. There was then a period of re-adjustment of controlled areas. All the 905 systems were then gradually phased out or replaced over the period from 1980 to August 1994 [30, 31].

Some of the software development for the seven road traffic systems shown in Table 7.5 was undertaken by Dina St. Johnston's company Vaughan Programming Services, later known as Vaughan Systems Ltd. [15], under contract from GEC's Traffic Division. Richard Burwood joined Vaughan Systems in 1978 and eventually became responsible for most of the software upgrades [30, 31].

Table 7.5 UK traffic control systems based on Elliott 900 series computers, installed subsequent to the takeover of Elliott-Automation by GEC

Date installed	Processor	Initial highway designation, location and subsequent history
1968	ARCH 9000 with a single 903	CP7: Heston, near Heathrow. Initially controlling the section of the M4 from Hammersmith to Heathrow airport. Eventually replaced by a new London West system
1969/1970	ARCH 9000 with a single 903	CP2: Tinsley (M1, J34), near Sheffield. Later replaced by a subsection of CP1
1971/1972	ARCH 9000 with dual 905	CP1: Westhoughton near Preston (M6). Controlled the areas including Manchester, Preston, Hull, Wakefield, etc.
1971/1972	ARCH 9000 with dual 905	CP4: Almondsbury, Bristol. Controlled the M5 and M4 areas including Cwmbran, Exeter, Cheltenham, etc.
1971/1972	ARCH 9000 with dual 905	CP5: Scratchwood, Hertfordshire (M1). Controlled the areas including Bedford, Guildford, Maidstone, north London, etc.
1971/1972	ARCH 9000 with dual 905	CP6: Hook, Hampshire (M3). Intended to control the areas including Winchester and Maidstone but functionality soon transferred to other sites
1972/1973	ARCH 9000 with dual 905	CP3: Perry Bar, Birmingham. (M5, M6). Controlled the areas including Birmingham, Cheltenham, County Durham, Shropshire, etc.

7.2.9   Other UK and Overseas Industrial and Research Applications

Below is a list derived mainly from [11] of other known UK applications, not necessarily all strictly *on-line* process control but certainly process control, for which no further details have yet come to light:

Grimethorpe Colliery (instrumentation and automatic control for five boilers)
Hawker Aircraft Company Limited
Vickers Armstrong Limited
Birmingham College of Advanced Technology
University of London
J. Lyons & Company Limited
J & E Hall Limited
Babcock & Wilcox Limited
Gas Council
Humphreys and Glasgow Ltd.
Medical Automation at University College Hospital

Here is another list, again mainly derived from [11], of additional known overseas online applications for which no further details have yet come to light:

Czechoslovakian Research Institute
BASF, Ludwigshafen am Rhein
Mashpriborintorg, USSR
Societa Montecantini S.p.A., Italy

Slovnaft, Bratislava, Czechoslovakia
SNAM Progetti S.p.A., Italy
Gulf State Utilities, LA., USA
Farbenfabriken Bayer A.G., Germany
Buromaschinen Export GmbH, Germany
D.D.R. Technoimport Rumania
Boliden Gruv A.B., Sweden
Goldsworth Mining Pty. Ltd., Australia

Joseph Roth also mentions [6] an ARCH installation at a steelworks near to Cologne.

In the period 1960–1966, approximately 165 Elliott computers were applied to on-line process-control applications (see delivery lists in Appendix 8). The computers were as follows:

The Elliott 800 series (16% of the 165 total)
The 900 series (54%, many to defence applications)
The ARCH variants (21%)
The 4100 series (9%)

Of course, sales continued after 1966 but no detailed Elliott-Automation, or successor-company, records have come to light for the years 1967 onwards. The post-1967 sales of 900-derived computers for avionics and defence applications probably number several thousand (see Chap. 12). Many of these later applications were embedded in military hardware and many would be classified as on-line control (Fig. 7.10).

Fig. 7.10 In 1964 Elliotts developed an online multi-fixed-channel X-ray fluorescent spectrometer, for automatic ore analysis in mining operations

Table 7.6 List of process-control applications running on Elliott computers for which the software development was outsourced to Vaughan Programming Systems

Approx date	Application	Customer	Computer
1960	Calder Hall Data logger	Panellit (Elliott-Automation)	Arch 609 (aka Elliott 803)
1962	Ingot & Slab Controller, RTB, Spencer Steel Wks	Elliott-Automation	Elliott 803
1963	Hoogovan Furnace Controller (steel mill)	Panellit (Elliott-Automation)	Arch 1000
1964	Early Warning Display System at RAF Fylingdales	Elliott-Automation	Elliott 803
1965	Severn Bridge Toll Collection (Poss. 1963, not 1965)	Elliott-Automation	Arch 1000
	Montecatini Data Logging System	Elliott-Automation	Arch 1000
1966	Steel Co. of Wales, Tinning Line Systems	Elliott Process Automation	Arch 102
	Data logger for Metronex (Poland)	Elliott Process Automation	Arch 102
	Spectrometer Analysis, Mt. Goldsworthy (Australia)	Elliott-Automation	Arch 1000
	Spectrometer Analysis, Bolidens (Sweden)	Elliott-Automation	Arch 9000
1967	Engine Test for Mobil Oil	Elliott Process Automation	Arch 9000
	Air Traffic Control Simulator	Elliott-Automation	Elliott 503
	Complex Process Monitoring for Ludus (Rumania)	Elliott Process Automation	Arch 1000.
1968	M4 Motorway Control	Elliott Traffic	Arch 9000
	Process Control of Pilot Plant	Unilever	Arch 105
1969	RTB Tinning Line System (steel mill)	Elliott-Automation	Arch 9000
1970	N.E. Gas Board logger	GEC/Elliott	Arch 9000/105
1971	Hillside Monitoring, Almondsbury	Dept. of the Environment (DOE)	Elliott 903
	Motorway Assistance (Lane Driver)	DOE	Elliott 903
1975	Motorway Control (Sheffield)	DOE	Elliott 903
1979	Post Design Services (Fylingdales)	Ministry of Defence	Elliott 803
1980	Enhanced Motorway Signalling	Dept. of Transport/TRRL	Elliott 905

An idea of the overall range of civil industrial process-control applications may also be judged by noting the software tasks outsourced to Vaughan Programming Services (VPS), as presented in Table 7.6. This is an extract from the full list of all VPS projects from 1959 to 1988, which has survived and is given in full in [15]. Table 7.6 also hints at the continuing need of Elliott-Automation and latterly GEC to supplement its own in-house software-writing resources (Fig. 7.11).

There is a final niche of the automation sector that could be mentioned, namely, numerically controlled machine tools such as lathes and jig-borers. Elliott-Automation initially decided not to be active in this area. No information has come to light to indicate whether or not GEC became involved in this sector after 1968.

Fig. 7.11 The X-ray fluorescent spectrometer being installed for on-stream analysis of mineral ore in South Africa. An added benefit was that the mining company could process much lower grades of ore economically. Similar applications opened up in the chemical and allied industries, where many Elliott computers were installed

7.3   Anecdotes from Elliott Programmers who Worked on Automation Projects

These sample anecdotes have been chosen to illustrate the spirit of adventure experienced by those whose task it was to write programs for the early applications of computers to industrial control. The reminiscences, though rich in human detail, are sometimes meagre on technical facts. As is to be expected with anecdotal evidence recorded about 50 years after the event, the following stories give a general impression of the times rather than an accurate account of equipment and procedures. The anecdotes are grouped by author, rather than chronologically.

7.3.1   From Ed Hersom

The following five snippets come from e-mails sent to the author in 2001 by H E (Ed) Hersom (born 1921, died 2002). Ed graduated from Oxford with a Maths degree, interrupted by war service at Bush Radio where he worked on military communications. He joined the Theory section at Borehamwood in 1947, leaving Elliotts in 1967 to join the Numerical Optimisation Centre at Hatfield Polytechnic. He retired in 1981. At Borehamwood, Ed was initially involved in the specification and applications of the Elliott 152 and Nicholas computers (see Chap. 10 and Appendices 1 and 2), after which he devoted increasing amounts of time to software development for novel end-user applications.

Here are Ed's anecdotes concerning process-control software in the late 1950s and early 1960s. As he said in an introductory e-mail: 'I was more concerned with the industrial area and we were certain that computing would play a very large part in factory control. But what an uphill task to make others see this!'

7.3.1.1   Billet Cut-Up Optimisation at Samuel Fox & Co. Ltd., Stocksbridge, Sheffield

After Coppy Laws' CDS Admiralty contract ended (see Chap. 2), Ed formed a group to discuss with industrialists how they might improve their productivity. 'In particular, a joint team of Coppy's people and OR [Operational Research] folk at Sam Fox (Sheffield) was formed to look at their particular problems. I was a member of that team (as a consultant to Coppy Laws). We concentrated on Sam Fox's cut-up line after the last mill. Sam Fox rolled to customers' orders so their products varied rapidly. This last mill therefore produced bars of various cross-sections and so of various lengths (the ingots from which the steel came from were nearly constant [in cross-section].) When they rolled a bar of 2 inches × 4 inches its length would be about 140 feet. If uncut this would go through the ladies' lavatory at the end! They had therefore installed a flying shear which cut the bar into two or three lengths and these were shunted back to a gang shear which cut them to the customers' requirements. These had tolerances but they were often of the form: *bars to be 10′ to 12′ but must be a multiple of 3′*. If the flying shear did not cut the appropriate length there would be a lot of wasted bits at the gang shear and these were of good steel – not like the ends of the original bar. My main contribution to this project was to devise a scheme to predict the final length of the bar before it had completely emerged from the mill so that the flying shear could be set correctly and the required settings could be displayed at the gang shear.

'It took literally years for this project to mature. The original intention was to have a relay computer [electro-magnetic] but before that was designed the earlier models of the 803 were available and an 802A (I think) was installed initially. Albert Wakefield, one of my original Nicholas programmers, then with the computer boys, actually did the programming.

'To finish this narrative, Sam Fox had installed the equipment but did not insist the men used it. They encouraged them, of course, and after a while three of the four crews (they worked shifts) used it but one held out against. Their pay depended on the amount of good steel produced and sometime later the crew that did not use the new equipment found their pay consistently less than that of the others. Then they did! [This is an interesting instance of the suspicion in which computers were initially held in some quarters, because it was feared that 'computers will take away our jobs'].

7.3.1.2 Nuclear Instrumentation

'Maurice Needham and Geoff. Ballard (man & boy) started up the nuclear business at Elliotts. It became a good business and was housed at Lewisham. As Maurice said, if you land a nuclear contract, say to instrument a nuclear submarine, a small part of the instrumentation is nuclear the rest is a vast amount of conventional instrumentation – pressure/temperature gauges, flow-meters etc. A bit of nuclear know-how was very useful! Eventually, Geoff took over the running of that division and Maurice took over the work Coppy Laws had started in Lewisham'.

7.3.1.3 Richard, Thomas & Baldwins Limited, Spencer Works, Llanwern

'As I said [in an earlier e-mail] Maurice Needham took over the work Coppy Laws had started in Lewisham. This was known as E-A Automation Systems Ltd. (a consultancy operation bringing computers into industrial control) and I went with Maurice. The headquarters were at Greenwich and I had an office there (as well as Borehamwood). ... Coppy Laws had been in charge of a group which was, *inter alia*, responsible for the cut-up line system at Sam Fox. Around 1959, Maurice Needham took over his work and ran a newly-formed company, E-A Automation Systems. (I never liked the tautology but now we have 'PIN Numbers'!). I joined him and had an office at their new premises at the old site of Submarine Cables just south of the southern end of the Blackwall Tunnel but I still kept one at Borehamwood (southwest corner of the first floor, old building).

'Now some back-ground history. Pre-war a chap called Harry Spencer ran a steel stock-yard. That is, he would buy steel, in particular, rolls of plate for bodies of cars, from the steel mills and sell them on to the car manufacturers. One day he landed the order from one car manufacturer, probably Morris or Austen, for all their requirements for rolled steel plate. R.T.B. who actually supplied the steel regarded this as a dangerous situation so invited H Spencer on to their board. Cuckoo-like, he rose to be in charge when the steel industry was nationalised and a new mill was to be built at Llanwern.

'This is when we came in. Leon Bagrit sold to Harry Spencer the idea that this should be an 'Automated Mill' and that Elliotts were the chaps to do it! [See also anecdote in Sect. 6.1.3]. So began two of my most stressful years!

'We were not confined to recommending our own equipment so as part of a hierarchy of computing systems we planned for controlling this mill we got G.E. (US) to 'automate' the slab-to-coils section and we proposed 803's for the (heat)-soaking pits and for the one above in this tree of controls. (There is an IEE paper by Roger Massey and me showing this scheme.)'

7.3.1.4 Lea Valley Water Company: Telemetry Scheme
and Water Distribution Control

'Coming back to ARCH, there seems to have been a bit of 'retro-naming' since I left Elliotts (1967). Having given in my notice I had 6 months 'free' so I took on the job of commissioning the Lee Valley Water Works monitoring system. The computer involved was an Elliott 102, a cut-down version of the 902, but I see from your notes that that became the ARCH102. The hardware was more-or-less in place when I came but no programming had been done (not untypical in those days!). I don't remember the precise code I used but I do remember the following:

'It was a paged machine with four levels of interrupt of which I used only two or three. I recall that I was surprised to discover from my study of the system that the device that needed the highest level of interrupt was the IBM output printer despite the fact that we had to monitor the alarms of all the pumping stations and reservoir levels in the area!

'The pages were only 128 words. The system I devised was a lowest level doing not much more than wait for an interrupt. When one came, the machine would go off and service that interrupt. The various programs would 'talk' to each other by a battery of buffers, there were no stacks then. This meant there were many short programs or modules which I termed 'Produles' but that never caught on.

'All programs were input by punched paper tape and these little produles had to be fitted into the pages. I well remember laying out these tapes on a bench column-wise so that the total length of each column did not exceed 128 words. I was surprised how easy and efficiently, space-wise, I was able to do this'.

7.3.1.5 Paper Mills

In a document entitled *Ed Hersom's Memories*, sent to Laurence Clarke on 1 December 1994, Ed Hersom writes as follows: 'Many years after I had left "The Bros" [in 1967] I was down in Kent visiting Reed International. Someone at Reeds, then holding quite a responsible position, remarked that "it took a little company to show us how [to automate a paper mill]". He was referring to the small paper making firm Wolvercote at Oxford, which had been "automated" by Elliotts. One wonders how many such remarks have, or could have been, made'.

7.3.2 From Peter Williams

Peter Williams contributed the following anecdotes on 21 August 2007, concerning the installation and programming of Elliott computers at the Spencer Steelworks of Richard Thomas & Baldwins company at Llanwern, near Newport in Wales, from 1962 onwards.

'I joined Elliott Brothers in 1962 from GKN, where I had worked in various steel production departments for 5 years direct from National Service which I opted to do post Uni. I suspect it was my steel industry experience that they [Elliotts] were interested in. I was sent on a programming course and then located to Newport offices as part of a small project team defining the system. At this stage I was called a systems analyst and was never required to programme.

'The overall manager was a young man whose name I forget. His immediate subordinate was a middle aged bloke called Ed. Lund, an ex Indian Army major.

He was not a graduate, but was formidably bright. This was reflected in meetings when he found the solution to problems while the rest were still trying to articulate them. He would then become bored and go to sleep.

'Another very bright man at my level was Tudor Morgan, whose first action each morning on arriving at the office was to spend 10 minutes doing the Times crossword. The highlight of his week was Thursday when the Listener was published and he could tackle the Listener crossword. This normally took some 20 minutes. I'm afraid I couldn't understand the clues, let alone solve them.

'Our task was, in talking to the various operatives at Spencer Works, to define the programmes to be written for the Scheduler 803, which took in the steel orders and sorted them in the most efficient sequence for the Blast furnaces, Steel Plant and then Rolling Mill. This took a great deal of computer processing and the finalised schedule (which I believe was done weekly) was passed automatically to the Controller 803 which issued the correct instructions to the various plants at the appropriate time. Specially designed data entry terminals were located throughout the processing plants for operatives to update the controller on what had been produced. At the end of each shift, the Controller would then update the Scheduler's order book.

'It was very exciting work and with the best of people. Unfortunately the 803s ran out of steam when it reached the point of controlling the actual steel rolling process. I am somewhat hazy about this but believe that OEM process control computers [GE 412] were linked to the rollers at different stages and controlled the width and thickness of the rolling process on direct instructions from the Controller.

'Programming was done by an organization called St. Johnson Associates [actually, Vaughan Programming Services], a computer programming and consultancy organization run by a formidable lady, Dina St. Johnson, the wife of Andrew St. Johnson who was, I believe, MD of Elliotts at Borehamwood. There were two programmers I remember distinctly who were superb: Rene Arnold and Phil Tattersall.

'Needless to say the lack of system power led to acrimonious discussions between the companies, which at my level one could only guess at. In any case I was transferred to a project in Israel in late '63.

'I am not sure if this is of any use to you. I can only say that I thoroughly enjoyed my time with Elliotts and particularly working on the Spencer Works project despite its demise. It seemed to me that it was pioneering and way ahead of anything that IBM would attempt at the time'.

7.3.3   From Roger Cook

R L (Roger) Cook joined Borehamwood in 1954 and stayed with Elliotts until the merger with English Electric in 1967. He transferred to ICL in 1968. Roger became the leading systems software expert at Borehamwood.

'Eventually the transistor arrived although the 802 still had valve power supplies. This was rapidly replaced by the 803, probably the first all transistorised machine. For the first time there was talk of manufacturing in bulk and about 200 machines were eventually delivered. The reliability [of the Elliott 803] to us programmers, used to continuous interruption while nickel delay lines were adjusted and while valves were removed daily for preventive maintenance, was obvious. One early model was installed in the USA to control a power supply [i.e. generating station]. After 18 months we had a call saying there was a fault and they had lost the key to open the cabinet. Although probably apocryphal, it has the ring of truth.

'I gathered the reputation of being able to test and discover, always by chance, the situation to cause a hiccup. During a visit to discuss steel cut-up at Samuel Fox I asked what happened when a red hot steel billet, which was nearly twice the height of a man, fell over. I was assured this never happened; a little later I pointed to one lying on the ground.... Eva Ney developed an efficient program to cut the rolled steel to meet the order book but I do not remember whether it was actually implemented. Eva had caused some problems in the rolling mill, which was not designed to accommodate women with thin heels.

'It was, I think, 803s that were used at the *Reading Evening Post* for computer assisted typesetting. This was the very first system I had personally sold. I remember standing outside the board room awaiting a decision. Later, Lord Thomson, at that time proprietor of *The Times*, assured me that a strike by newspapermen would be the end of the paper. It was for this reason that he was first using computers at a new newspaper in the provinces. Later still there was a year long strike at *The Times*. At that time, other companies were planning for full automatic composing. Our plan was for staff to type in as they did on their existing hot metal machines, to provide basic line layout according to font, whilst requesting assistance if hyphenation was needed. The output drove a new film printer that would provide off-set litho plates. I was present when the first day's edition was made up and appreciated the excitement of seeing the first print of the new paper'.

7.3.4 From Richard Burwood

After working for the Admiralty at ASWE for 2 years, Richard Burwood joined Elliott Process Automation at Borehamwood in 1969. He moved to STC from 1972 to 1978 and then worked for Dina St. Johnston's company Vaughan Systems from 1978 to 1995. During his years at Vaughan Systems, Richard took on more and more responsibility for the software of the Elliott/GEC ARCH 9000 computers used in the National Motorways Communication System. Writing in 2009 [30], he remembers a particular motorway incident as follows.

'I designed and implemented the Tidal Flow changes for the Aston Expressway [Birmingham] – (GEC had shied away from that part of the purchase spec.). Some years later, there was a heavy thunderstorm in the Birmingham area, and three police forces tried to set a speed limit on all their signals, because of the poor visibility. The computer set most of the signals on one area, but did not complete the report, and would not accept further signaling instructions although the telephones seemed to be functioning correctly.

'My [CP3 technical] contact happened to be in Perry Barr control office that day (I have no idea why he was there). They re-programmed the standby half-system and switched to that half, which started up as normal, but did not complete the initial report of signal settings found. My contact 'phoned me to ask for help. Luckily, I had a *snoop* command available to print out memory locations, and by examining various data locations, I was able to spot that there was excess activity on one of the outstation lines. I asked them to unplug the modem receive card for that line, and the system reverted to normal working.

'They discovered later that lightning had struck a box beside the motorway and it was transmitting replies continuously afterwards. Dina's interrupt level code had assumed that replies would cease within the specified period, so I had to alter the code to give up waiting for cessation after filling a buffer with replies. That change enabled the computer to detect the problem and report a fault pointing the engineers towards the problem'.

***

It has been evident throughout Chaps. 6 and 7 that the application of computers to industrial process control was of paramount importance to Leon Bagrit in the 1960s. It has to be admitted that, 50 years later, process control is now seen as a niche market. In Chap. 8 we therefore return to a more general history of the Computing Division at Borehamwood to recall other applications of Elliott computers in the 1950s and 1960s and the part played by programmers such as Ed Hersom and Roger Cook.

References

1. JP Bunt (2001) Nine-page typed letter, sent to Simon Lavington on 11 Dec 2001
2. Direct Digital Control. 10-page Company brochure, published by Elliott Process Automation Ltd., describing Type 1 and Type 2 direct digital controllers and how these may be part of the ARCH equipment and architecture. Undated but probably 1964. (For the Instrument Society of America's background to the DDC meeting, see [22] below)
3. Leon Bagrit (1964) Automation – an extension of man. 12-page typed paper including the comment 'prepared for the Imperial Defence College,' dated May 1964
4. Anon (1962) An introduction to system design using Minilog switching elements. A 16-page illustrated technical brochure published by Panellit Ltd., a company within the Elliott-Automation Group. Undated, but it can be inferred by the reference on page 10 of the brochure that the date is not earlier than 1962
5. Hersom SE (ed) (2001) information contained in a series of e-mails sent to Simon Lavington in 2001
6. Joseph Roth (2008) E-mail communication with Simon Lavington on 24 Feb 2008
7. Elliott-Automation: Computer Orders and Deliveries, 1947–1966. 23-page brochure, published by Elliott-Automation early in 1967. The main data in this brochure is believed to be more or less correct up to the end of 1966 – but see Chapter 5 for comments on the 402 computer discrepancies. A loose insert gives the revised totals of all deliveries up to 31 Mar 1967 but does not give customer-details of the post-December 1966 computers

8. Airey L (1959) A digital instrumentation system for use in the testing of jet engines. Paper read on 11 Feb 1959 at a meeting of the Society of Instrument Technology, Manson House, Portland Place, London. Later published in the Society's Transactions

9. Aylen J (2007) Bloodhound on my trail: Ferranti's adaptation of military hardware to process control computer. Paper presented at the conference on Technological Innovation and the Cold War, held at the Center for the History of Business, Technology and Society, Delaware, Mar 2007. Jonathan Aylen's sources for Table 7.3 in this chapter are: (a) Freeman C (1965) 'Research and development in electronic capital goods. Natl Inst Econ Rev Nov 34:40–91. (b) Control Engineering (1965a) Process computer scorecard updated. Control Eng 12(3) Mar, pp 57–62

10. Roth JF (1965) On-line computer systems in the metals industry: a survey. Metal Industries Division, Elliott process Automation Ltd. Report number 576/JFR/CR, Nov/Dec 1965. (38 typed pages). Joseph Roth's references for Table 7.4 above were stated to be: (a) Process Computer Scoreboard. Control Eng. Issues for Sept 1963, Mar 1965, Aug 1965. (b) Numerous issues of the following journals and magazines for the period 1963–1965: Control Engineering, Control, Iron and Steel, Iron and Steel Engineer, Electronics Weekly. (c) Kirkland RW (1965) Process computers – their place in the steel industry. Iron and Steel Engineer, Feb 1965. (d) Anon (1965) A review of on-line digital computer applications in the British steel industry. British Iron & Steel Research Association report. (e) Anon (1965) Automation in iron and steel works. Proceedings of the international congress of ferrous metallurgists

11. ARCH computer Control Systems Data Logging. Ten-page brochure produced in 1966 by Elliott Process Automation Ltd., to mark the granting of a Queen's Award to Industry for 1966

12. Aylen J (2004) Megabytes for metals: development of computer applications in the iron and steel industry. Iron Steelmaking 31(6):465–478

13. Press Release from John Geddes, Public Relations, Elliott-Automation Ltd., 34 Portland Place, London W1. Undated but probably before 30 Nov 1961. See also: www.smecc.org/panellit_computers.htm

14. Massey RG (Jan 1963) Computers in a new steelworks. Comput J 5(4):271–275

15. Lavington S (2009) An appreciation of Dina St Johnston, 1930–2007, founder of the UK's first Software House. Comput J 52(3):378–387

16. Weik MH (1964) A Fourth Survey of Domestic Electronic Digital Computing Systems. Report BRL 1227, Jan 1964, Ballistics Research Laboratories Aberdeen proving Ground, Maryland, USA. Available from http://ed-thelen.org/comp-hist/BRL64.html#TOC

17. Automation at No. 4, Avonmouth. 8-page Company brochure, published by Elliott-Automation, describing the zinc and lead smelting plant of the Imperial Smelting Corporation (part of Rio Tinto Zinc Corporation). Undated but probably 1967

18. Clothier PM (1965) Electronic instrumentation for the engine test facility. NGTE Note number NT 556, May 1965. Published by the Ministry of Aviation, National Gas Turbine Establishment, Pyestock, Hants (27 typed pages)

19. First in Automation. 45-page Company brochure, first published by Elliott-Automation in June 1958. Subsequent (undated) versions seem to have been produced with the same title. Possibly the last of these, with only 20 pages and undated, was produced in about 1967

20. see: http://en.wikipedia.org/wiki/Sellafield#Calder_Hall_nuclear_power_station

21. Elliott-Automation Annual Report for 1962

22. The Computer Control Pioneers: a history of the innovators and their work. A 123-page book produced in 1992 by the Instrument Society of America and compiled by the ISA Ad Hoc Committee on the computer control pioneers. ISBN 1-55617-370-9

23. Automation in Action: Batch Fermentation. An 8-page undated booklet published by Elliott-Automation Ltd. Since Elliott-Automation is described in the booklet as 'an English Electric Company', the likely date of publication is late 1967 or early 1968

24. The End of an Era. Article dated 21 Feb 1986 in issue 251 of Speke Today, a Dista company newsletter

25. Letter from John Thorley, ex-Dista employee, to Jonathan Aylen (Manchester Business School), 26 Mar 2007. John Thorley designed the layout of the Auto/Manual console

26. See: http://www.thomson.com/about/history/
27. The Wolvercote Story: Automation in Action. 10-page Company brochure, published by Elliott Process Automation Ltd., describing the automation of a paper mill. Undated but probably 1965
28. File of correspondence entitled Thomson Computer Typesetting, containing papers dated between early-1965 and early-1969. File passed to Simon Lavington on 2 June 2003 at Borehamwood, rather than being destroyed when GEC/Marconi finally vacated the Borehamwood premises
29. Computer Survey, vol 9, no 6, Nov/Dec 1970
30. (a) RW Burwood (2009) Elliott Computers for Motorway Signalling. Three-page typewritten note, dated 18 Feb 2009. This note later formed the basis for an article by Richard Burwood submitted to Resurrection, the Bulletin of the Computer Conservation Society (see [31]).
(b) RW Burwood (2009) letter dated 22 July 2009 to Simon Lavington, giving more details of the National Motorways Communication System
31. Burwood R (2010) Elliott computers for motorway signalling. Resurrection, the Bulletin of the Computer Conservation Society, Issue number 49, winter 2009/2010

Chapter 8
Software and Applications at Borehamwood

8.1 General Introduction

Software is an ephemeral artifact. Programmers are, of course, tangible but the results of their labours survive more in the consequences than in the detail. This chapter and the next can only give a mere glimpse, through the eyes of the participants, of what it was like to program and market the Elliott digital computers that emerged from Borehamwood in the period 1947–1967. The machines themselves are summarised in Table 8.1, which is similar to the table given in the Introduction to this book but with the 900 series computers split into two rows. This split indicates that the development of the 900 series machines continued at Rochester for aerospace applications, long after Elliott-Automation itself had been taken over by GEC in 1968. The post-Borehamwood story of the 900 series computers is given in Chap. 12 and Appendix 6.

The architectures of the Elliott computers in Table 8.1 are compared in Chap. 10 and hardware details will be found in the appropriate Appendices. Some of the Elliott computers, for example the 152, 153, 311 and 403 machines, were one-off, defence-related projects whose classified nature ensured that their influence on the contemporary computing scene was minimal. Other computers, particularly the Elliott 405, had a significant influence on early British commercial electronic data processing (EDP) that merits a separate chapter (following the present one) where the link between Borehamwood and the British arm of the National Cash Register Co. Ltd. (NCR) is also described.

To begin at the beginning, the total number of people employed at the Borehamwood Research Laboratories of Elliott Brothers (London) Ltd. in 1947 numbered well under a 100. Of these, the first tentative programming steps were taken by the small *Theory Group* of just three people which, as remembered by Hersom [1], 'was headed by N.D. Hill with myself and a *computer*, i.e. a girl who operated a Marchant electro-mechanical calculator...'. By 1952 the total number of

S. Lavington, *Moving Targets*, History of Computing,
DOI 10.1007/978-1-84882-933-6_8, © Springer-Verlag London Limited 2011

Table 8.1 Elliott digital computers designed at Borehamwood

Computer	Dates first working	Number built	Relative size	Initial application
152	1950	1	Medium	Defence
153	1954	1	Large	Defence
Nicholas	1952	1	Small	Defence
401, 402	1953, 1955	11	Small	General
403	1955	1	Large	Defence
311	1954	1	Medium/large	Defence
405	1956	33	Large	EDP
800 series and 503	1957–1962	219+32	Small, medium and large	Automation and general
ARCH 102, 1000, etc.	1962–1966	Many (see Chap. 7)	Small	Automation
502	1963	3	Large	Defence
903, 905, ARCH 9000	1963–1965	144+	Small	General and automation
920, 902, 12/12	1962–1976, and later	Many hundreds	Small	Defence
4120, 4130	1965, 1966	160+	Medium	General

Not included in the table: the NCR315, manufactured at Borehamwood from 1961 but designed by NCR in America and marketed by NCR

employees at Borehamwood had risen above 400, organised into seven divisions whose relative size may be ordered as follows:

Electrical Engineering
Circuits
Mechanical Engineering
Radio (which was really Radar)
Computing
Physics
Theory

Two of these, *Circuits* and *Computing*, were developing digital hardware in 1952, whilst such programming activity as existed was still confined to the Theory division. G E (George) Felton, who joined Borehamwood in 1951, remembers that, by 1952, 'a small digital computer (Nicholas) was being built [in the Theory division]. There were other computers that did hush-hush jobs that none of us were supposed to know anything about' [2].

In Sect. 8.2 we give an impression of the 'hush hush' computing atmosphere in the Theory Division before the Nicholas computer existed. This is followed by an account of the Nicholas days, when programming at Borehamwood really got under way. The Computing Division comes to the fore in Sect. 8.4, by which time Elliott computers had begun to be sold on the open market. We concentrate on the general and scientific areas and early attempts to address business applications; the full story of commercial data processing and the NCR connection is continued in the next chapter. By 1958, Elliott computers were selling well and software activity at Borehamwood had matured. The high-level language and operating system developments are covered in Sect. 8.5, which continues the story up to the point of the English Electric merger in 1967 and subsequent GEC takeover in 1968.

General and scientific applications of Elliott computers are covered in this chapter. Industrial process control has been dealt with in the *Automation* Chaps. 6 and 7 and business data processing will be covered in Chap. 9. The more specialised field of airborne and aerospace applications is covered in Chap. 12.

8.2 Early Days: 1947–1952

In the early days of the Elliott 152 project, the Theory Division at Borehamwood was responsible for specifying most of the algorithms – and hence programs – to be used for naval gunnery or *fire control*. The Computing Division did not come into effective existence until the arrival of W S (Bill) Elliott in the autumn of 1948. Ed Hersom of the Theory Division took the lead with the 152 programming activity for the MRS5 contract, notably by writing time-critical axis-conversion routines. The on-line, real-time nature of the 152's tasks is explained in Chap. 2. The Elliott 152 computer first worked in reduced (and somewhat unreliable) form in September

Fig. 8.1 The photo shows (*left to right*) George Felton, Ed Hersom and Bobby Hersom (née Lewis), all of whom worked in the Theory Division at Borehamwood. Amongst other programming projects, Ed Hersom specified the axis-transformation algorithms for the Elliott 152 computer. Pre-1952 programming at Borehamwood was idiosyncratic, due to the secrecy of the tasks and the uniqueness of the early Elliott computer architectures. In due course, George Felton's provision of a subroutine library for the Elliott Nicholas computer in 1953 was influenced by the design of the systems software of the Cambridge EDSAC

1950 and then, in enhanced form, in March 1951. The 152 computer had effectively ceased activity by the end of June 1952. There is very little reference to this work in the open literature. However, microfiche copies of most of the classified Internal Reports, covering the period 1946–1952, have survived. These are listed in the Bibliography.

The Theory Division was responsible for other calculations during this period, in support of the R&D activities of the various Borehamwood Divisions. Between 1947 and 1952, the Theory Division relied on 'human computers' – women undertaking manual calculations on one electro-mechanical desktop machine (a Marchant) and one purely mechanical one (a Brunsviga) [1]. The Division also made use of the Elliott Differential Analyser for analogue calculations from 1950 onwards. This Differential Analyser is described in Sect. 4.3.1, in the context of other Elliott analogue computers.

A significant change of emphasis occurred in 1953, with the availability of the in-house designed Nicholas stored-program digital computer, described in [1, 4–7] and in Appendix 2. It is interesting to note that the idea for this computer, its funding and its overall specification came from the Theory Division. Nicholas' conception and birth are recalled by Ed Hersom [1, 6] as follows.

'At the end of 1951 or early 1952 Bruce Bambrough visited RAE, Farnborough, to discuss a computing project. This was part of RAE's study of a "guided bomb" i.e. a guided weapon but with only gravity for propulsion. What was required was the "airspace" in which this bomb could be dropped and still hit the target. This is easily translated as: for a variety of heights and a given forward velocity, what was the perimeter on the ground of the area which could be hit? This entailed the integration of many trajectories and hence a large computing project for manual computing. Next day Bruce came into my office and, after a brief explanation of the RAE project, said, "for the money they talked about we could build a machine to do the job". That was how the Nicholas project started.'

The circuit design and logical design for Nicholas was largely carried out by one man, Charles Owen of the Circuits Division, with the nickel magneto-strictive memory technology originally coming from the Physics Division. Further hardware details of Nicholas are given in Appendix 2. It might seem odd that the Computing Division was not more closely involved in the Nicholas project. At this time (1952) the Computing Division was in fact busy developing its own ideas for computing machines which were first to bear fruit in 1953 as the Elliott 401 – see Sect. 8.4 and Chap. 5. It is also possible that the Computing Division's *amour propre* played a part.

8.3   Nicholas in the Theory Division: 1953–1958

The Theory Division was entirely responsible for the system software and applications programming for the Nicholas computer, which first worked in December 1952. Nicholas had a primary memory consisting of 1,024 words (equivalent to 4 KB). There was no backing store. The word length was 32 bits, with the Elliott 152's arrangement of the binary point being *two* places from the most-significant end – as explained in Chap. 2. A single-address instruction format was employed. Input/output was via five-track paper tape and teleprinter (Fig. 8.2).

At first, the process of booting up Nicholas and then programming it in five-track teleprinter code was extremely tedious. Ed Hersom explained this as follows [1, 6]:

'Nicholas was equipped with two 5-hole paper tape readers – called Main and Auxiliary. When an input command *I* [upper-case I] was executed the five bits corresponding to the five holes on the tape in the Main reader were fed into the five least significant bits of the accumulator, and the tape advanced one row. To input a longer string there had to be a series of *I*s, each followed by several *D*s (doubles, ie left shifts). The Auxiliary reader had its contacts (which were mechanical "peckers") directly connected to the control section of the machine. This reader was only used at boot time, when control was switched to it. It then issued a string of *I*s and *D*s and store commands until a complete program was read in and stored in memory. The code on the tape in the Main reader was the so-called Initial Orders (*IO*s). When the Auxiliary reader was finished, control was passed to these *IO*s, and they generated a program enabling Nicholas to read in a binary coded tape via the Main reader.

Fig. 8.2 The Elliott Nicholas, which first worked in December 1952, was built in the Theory Division for trajectory calculations for a guided bomb project. Nicholas went on to give an in-house computing service until 1958. In 1955 the BBC used Nicholas to predict the results of the General Election

Initially both readers were electrical/mechanical devices whose peckers rapidly destroyed a tape. The Main reader was quickly replaced by a home-made photo-electric device, which was crude but surprisingly reliable.

'The *IO*s were written by Brighid Rose (now Mrs Simpkin). She claims to be the first programmer employed by Elliotts – [though the term *programmer* was not then in use]. Brighid went on to code the guided bomb project [Nicholas's first task], which had to be done using the old teleprinter code (CCITT Alphabet No 2), not ASCII. George Felton joined us when Nicholas was operational, but still incomplete, and he managed to shorten these *IO*s. We realised that, if they could be made even shorter, the inadequate Auxiliary reader could be replaced by a standard stepper switch – a 50-way Uniselector common on telephone exchanges at that time. One morning George announced, "If the *I* instruction could be replaced by a combination of *D* and *I*, I could reduce the auxiliary tape to the required length" (the required length was determined by the number of commands which could be wired in around the stepper switch).

'When we turned to Charles Owen's logic diagram (see Figure A2.2), we found that he had specified a connection to one of the plates [circuit packages] just to prevent this occurring! I made the necessary disconnection, while George punched out a new auxiliary tape. The mod worked, so the tape reader was replaced by a Uniselector and life became less fraught!

'This change was the only one ever found necessary to Charles' original drawing, which speaks volumes for the quality of his work.

'Ruth Felton had joined us before George, but had been employed on other work. Now she joined the Nicholas team, and devised what we called the Translation Input (*TI*) – what would now be called an Assembler. The TI's enabled an alliterative tape to be punched: C = Clear the acc., A = Add from address, S = Subtract from address and so on. These were represented by 3 bits of the 6-bit field for instructions. Some "doubles" were available e.g. CA = Clear & Add to the acc. In theory there were 64 combinations but only 47 were possible [6]. A visiting IBM executive who was touring computer installations worldwide told us ours was the first site he had seen where such a program was actually in use. George Felton subsequently developed the Nicholas subroutine library. He has said it was much influenced by the library developed at Cambridge University for EDSAC.'

Two sample programs that use the Nicholas *Translation Input* assembler, namely the *Print* and *Multiply* subroutines, are given in Appendix 2.

Back in 1953, G E (George) Felton and his wife Ruth were substantially responsible for the new Nicholas programming scheme, or *system software* as it would later be called. To quote [7], 'The heart of the [Nicholas] programming system was an elaborate symbolic input routine known as *Translation Input* that was heavily influenced by the EDSAC input routine and was a considerable extension of it. The Nicholas input routine was probably the most polished British programming system of mid-1953.'

George Felton remembers [2] that: "In 1952 Ruth wrote the first *Initial Orders* or assembler for Nicholas, made up of about 400 commands". [Actually, the date must have been 1953 and Ruth was writing the newer input scheme known as *Translation Input* – see [3]]. Anyway, George continues: 'These [400 commands] helped users to write programs and had preset parameters, which allowed blocks of code to be moved. David Wheeler's EDSAC Initial Orders were influential .... Nicholas was relatively easy to program, and we developed things for it including floating-point routines. It was very important to do things by floating-point; otherwise you had to scale everything to avoid overflow, which was a very unfortunate thing to happen. The result was that we built a library of routines such as floating-point, and later an interpreter for floating-point. The following year we also had a matrix interpretive scheme so that we could do operations on modest-size matrices, but the store was only 1024 words.'

Another comment on the influence of EDSAC and Cambridge comes from Ed Hersom [8], when describing the work of Brighid Rose who, as has been mentioned, was the main programmer for the Guided Bomb contract which was Nicholas' first task. Brighid joined Borehamwood at the end of 1951 and left in mid-1953. The Guided Bomb was thought to have been code-named *Red Cheeks* [9]. Hersom remembers that 'Brighid's trajectory calculations required an integration routine and, for simplicity, we chose Runge-Kutta. We frequently attended the EDSAC seminars in Cambridge (just up the road!) and heard, in particular, Stanley Gill [co-author of the seminal programming book by Wilkes, Wheeler & Gill [10]] give his talk on his extension to the R-K routine. I remember vividly discussing with Brighid whether we ought to do the same but concluded that for Nicholas (and this project) it gave no significant benefit and took more code (very important!).'

At this point, the Theory Division started to recruit people specifically as programmers. Two newcomers arrived who were subsequently to make a big contribution to the development of software at Borehamwood: A N Vaughan in 1953 and R L (Roger) Cook in 1954. Vaughan's first name Aldrina was universally abbreviated to Dina, except by her father! Both Dina and Roger have recalled the excitement of coming to work at Borehamwood and it is interesting to recount the circumstances of their arrivals.

Dina was 23 years old when she joined Elliotts [11]. She had been working for 6 years with the British Non-Ferrous Metals Research Association in London whilst studying for an external mathematics degree and had found that, upon graduating, she was not offered any promotion or salary increase. In 1953 she answered an advertisement for a position at Borehamwood. Ed Hersom recalls [8] that: 'I was the first to interview Dina Vaughan (after the routine vetting by personnel). Nicholas was in full swing but I had no establishment for another programmer. I remember going to Eric Whitehead who was looking after the general research interests at that time and saying to him "Look, you must find a place for this girl". The necessary arrangements were made. Dina was quickly recognized as a high-flyer and was sent to attend the Cambridge University Summer School on Programming in 1954. Dina soon transferred to the Computing Division where, amongst other responsibilities, she was entrusted with writing the in-house payroll program for Elliotts in 1956. She married Andrew St Johnston in 1958 – she was Andrew's second wife – and left Elliotts at the end of that year to found her own company, Vaughan Programming Services, the UK's first software house [11]. Dina remained a hands-on Director of Vaughan until 1996.

Roger Cook remembers [12] that: 'In 1954 [having graduated in mathematics] I was employed by the Sun Life to become an actuary but found it incredibly dull and wrote to Elliotts and to English Electric for employment as a programmer. I was interviewed by George Felton and Ed Hersom, offered a job and started work before I received the invitation for interview by EE. I remember the first day when, after a short introduction, I was invited to write my first program for Nicholas and to make it operational before I went home that night. Subsequently, there was a set of ten mathematical problems to program before being given a "real" job. Being of a somewhat impetuous and impatient nature I completed these over the next few days in a somewhat slapdash fashion, eager to get on with real work.' Roger Cook became, in due course, Manager of Elliott's Scientific Computing Division and later Assistant General Manager of the Computing group, in both cases reporting to Andrew St Johnston as the General Manager. Roger stayed with Elliotts until the merger with English Electric in 1967; he transferred to ICL in 1968.

Returning to Nicholas, the computer performed both in-house tasks in support of Borehamwood projects and some outside applications (acting as a bureau service) in the period up to 1958 – much of the in-house work being of a classified nature such as the computing of trajectories for guided weapons. For outside work, Nicholas could be hired at one old penny a second, which worked out at £15 an hour [1]. George Felton recalls the following example of outside work [2]: 'I remember Peter Hunt visiting Elliott Brothers from de Havillands [aircraft company] in 1953. In July of that year I wrote a Programming Manual, which included an outline of the subroutine library. I also showed Peter Hunt how to program Nicholas. He programmed and executed the flutter calculations for the Comet 1, the world's first jet airliner. He used the floating-point matrix scheme, limited to 10-by-10 size matrices. Later I flew to Australia in a Comet 1, before they discovered the metal-fatigue problem that led to the crashes.' Two De Havilland Comet airliners crashed in January and April 1954, focusing mathematical minds throughout the aircraft industry on the effects of vibration on airframes. In Chap. 5 we described how the National Research Development Corporation (NRDC) encouraged the use of the Elliott 402 and other computers in investigating the flutter problem as a matter of some urgency.

A full list of Theory Division staff is hard to compile because the Elliott company employee records, if indeed they still exist, have not yet come to light. Individuals naturally came and went – some transferring to/from other Divisions within Borehamwood. Amongst the programmers active in the Theory Division at various times during the period from 1953 to 1958 are believed to have been: Bruce Bambrough, Albert David Beeching, Roger Cook, Hugh Devonald, George Felton, Ed Hersom, Ruth Holt (later Ruth Felton), Bobby Lewis (later Bobby Hersom), Susan Morris, Henry Orde, Sheila Quinn, Brighid Rose, Dina Vaughan, Albert Wakefield, Bill Williams and Sue Williams.

George Felton, Laurence Clarke, Bobby Lewis and Ruth Holt all started work at Borehamwood in the late summer of 1951 – though Laurence had been a *vacation student* there in 1950. They were all members of The Round, the English folk dancing club in Cambridge, and thus well known to John Coales [13]. Laurence remembers that Ruth, Bobby and he used to sit together in university lectures – all doing the Maths tripos [14]. Susan Morris was also at Cambridge University.

Norman Hill, who had been the Head of the Theory Division from its earliest days and, as a Divisional leader, heavily involved in the administrative changes at Borehamwood in the period 1952–1953, moved out of Theory to become briefly part of the Computing Division in about 1955 as described later. George Felton and Hugh Devonald moved to Ferranti in 1954 where they worked on Pegasus (see also Chaps. 5 and 10). Roger Cook soon transferred to the Computing Division, where he started work on matrix inversion routines for the Elliott 402. Dina wrote programs for the Elliott 153 computer (see Chap. 3) for a GCHQ/Admiralty Direction Finding application at Irton Moore, Scarborough until about 1955 and then transferred to the Computing Division at Borehamwood. She left Borehamwood to found the UK's first software house, as described in [11]. Henry Orde also transferred to the Computing Division to work on commercial data-processing applications in about 1955. Then in the mid-1960s, he moved to NCR (London) and from thence in due course to NCR in America. Ed Hersom worked on many programming applications at Borehamwood, latterly on process control, and left Elliotts in 1967 to join the Numerical Optimisation Centre at Hatfield Polytechnic in 1967.

8.4   The Computing Division Goes to Market: 1953–1957

As far as software is concerned, the Computing Division under W S (Bill) Elliott appeared to make a rather slow start. This is because Bill Elliott had other priorities. In the period 1948–1953, the Computing Division was heavily involved in developing, modifying and maintaining the hardware for the 152 computer as part of the MRS5 project. The MRS5 contract was Borehamwood's number one priority as far as the Director, John Coales, was concerned. Nevertheless out of the 152 activity came Bill Elliott's abiding interest in packaged logic circuits. A family of these circuit modules was initially developed by of D L Johnston of the Electrical Engineering Division who used glass printed-circuit plates with plated-through holes and deposited resistors [15]. The glass plates, though technically advanced, proved very unreliable. After his arrival in the Circuits Division in 1951, C E Owen made a fresh start, using the same sub-miniature pentode thermionic valves but mounting them on less-ambitious paxolin plates [16]. Extensions of Owen's ideas were to be developed and refined over the next 4 years to appear in various guises as the underlying logic technology of several Elliott and Ferranti production computers – latterly using circuits based on triodes to replace the expensive sub-miniature pentodes used in the 152. Bill Elliott and the Computing Division quickly became champions of *package technology*.

In contrast to the agendas of other Borehamwood divisions, Bill Elliott's group became interested in developing reliable digital computers for the open market. The first tangible evidence of this, as far as non-defence circles were concerned, was a device called SNARC – short nickel line accumulating register calculator – demonstrated at the Physical Society's Exhibition in London early in 1952. This was followed by the demonstration of the new Elliott/NRDC 401 computer at the Physical Society Exhibition held from 3 to 8 April 1953, as discussed in Chap. 5. It is significant that the NRDC contract included the prior construction of an *Interference Test Set* – to prove to NRDC that the circuit packages proposed for the 401 were robust in the presence of electro-magnetic noise from nearby equipment such as electric motors. The Computing Division soon became immersed in the task of establishing a manufacturing capability at Borehamwood for the 402 computer, the fully engineered production version of the 401.

Going back a few months to 1953, the Initial Orders for the Elliott 401 were devised by Hugh Devonald of the Theory Division with early assistance from Harry Carpenter of the Computing Division. The demonstration programs for the 401 at the Physical Society Exhibition in April 1953 were written by Christopher Strachey of NRDC. After that date, the programming effort associated with the 402 computer was carried out by members of the Computing Division. Albert Wakefield, initially a member of the Theory Division but transferring in due course to the Computing Division, wrote the definitive Initial Orders for the Elliott 402, which he reduced to 13 instructions. His program was known as *Albert* [14]. About ten Elliott 402 computers were built. From the delivery list given in Appendix 8, it may be seen that the applications come under the heading of 'scientific and engineering'. The main deliveries span the period 1955–1958.

Roger Cook [12] remembers writing applications programs for Elliott 402 computers: 'The first 402 was to be delivered to Paris [in April 1955, to the Institut Blaise Pascal] and Henry Orde, who had a French wife, caused the system to be painted *402 calculateur electronique* – unfortunately he got the gender wrong. [Actually, Pierre-E. Mounier-Kuhn has since said that Henry Orde did not necessarily get the gender wrong: "Calculatrice électronique" fitted perfectly, just as "Calculateur" would have [17]]. The customer had required an acceptance test comprising inversion of a matrix. Inversion times were advertised in the enormous 402 coloured brochure but, in fact no program had been written. I was instructed to write the program. The 402 was a fixed point machine and I was concerned at the possible inaccuracy that might result. I think I applied scaling factors to each row. In the event the matrix provided was well behaved and produced excellent results. The 402 was controlled by a drum with rotation time 1.4 msec during which time 128 32-bit words could be serially read. The problem is to extract two numbers, multiply them and add during this time. Subsequently, I remember several visits to Paris and the entertainment that followed but not what I did at the computer site....

'A little later, the CEGB asked to use the matrix program to correlate electricity demand against specified stimuli, especially the time at which TV programs ended. I wrote a little program using the matrix routines, ran the program, sent the results and an invoice and forgot about it. A year later a letter arrived with new data requesting a another run; I had never thought of keeping the program nor was there, at that time, a requirement or facility for registering operational programs for future use....

'I remember spending much of a long hot summer helping the IPC (Iraq Petroleum Company – this was before the days of modern Middle East politics) implement a simulation of their oil field. Most oil fields are localised but, in Iraq, the field extends over hundreds of square miles while the oil is located in 14 different levels of rock. We had data for the whole area, for each rock level for the last 30 years. The 402 had a total storage of perhaps 16K numbers, less program space. The solution was to hold the data on a sequence of rolls of paper tape and for each calculation read the whole set at 1000 cps (see below). I think this took about half an hour per run. After many weekends of processing the paper tape we demonstrated that we could reproduce the known annual data and started the simulation runs for future years. The results were kept from my prying eyes but I learnt a lot about oil, rock porosity, pumping et al.'

The fast paper-tape reader referred to above, an impressive piece of engineering, was introduced by Elliotts in 1957. Paul King was recruited in October of that year, straight from Cambridge University to work for Gerry Mills as a *programmer-investigator* – in effect, a technical salesman. A few years later Paul became Sales Manager of the Scientific Computing Division at Borehamwood. He recalls [18] that: 'One of my first tasks was a hardware-oriented bit of programming. We had recently developed a high speed paper tape reader, capable of operating at 1000 characters per second, and were offering it as the main input device for the 402. However the 402's main memory was a magnetic drum which rotated 75 times per second so a normal program stored on the drum with a loop back to "read another character" would not have been capable of reading the tape faster than 75 characters per second. The 402 had a very limited amount of high speed memory, 16 words I recall, on nickel delay lines and I wrote a very compact program which was stored on these delay lines. This read the data from the tape and stored it on the high speed memory. The result was a silent high speed operation interspersed by a single click every time a batch of data was dumped from the high speed memory onto the drum. The data had to be presented in a special format so I wrote a complementary program which output data in that format from the drum to the paper tape punch.'

At around this time the capabilities of the Elliott 402 computer were further enhanced by the provision of a hardware floating-point unit, in response to the needs of a particular customer. By 1957 it was not uncommon to see built-in floating-point facilities on high-performance, high-cost, scientific computers such as the IBM 704 and the Ferranti Mercury. However, the Elliott 402 represented the smaller, cheaper, end of the market to which floating-point hardware had not generally penetrated. The first 402 with floating-point hardware, designated the '402F', was delivered in February 1958 to Ernst Leitz GmbH (of *Leica* cameras) in Germany for ray-tracing and optical lens systems design. Paul King remembers that 'An unusual feature of this machine was that it was capable of calculating with infinity, needed for representing parallel beams of light' [18]. Roger Cook recalls that: 'The word length remained at 32 bits, resulting with poor precision compared to today's Personal Computers. Moreover, there was no agreed standard on representation…. The computer replaced a prewar relay machine [at Leitz] programmed by punched 35 mm film. The film used showed pictures of Greta Garbo in her prime but somewhat maltreated by the punched holes.' The 'prewar relay machine' at Leitz was in fact a Zuse Z5, ordered in 1950 and delivered to Leitz in 1953 [19]. It was a floating-point relay machine with an add-time of 0.1 s. The Z5's punched 35 mm film had originally come from Zuse's friend H. Schreyer [17]. Incidentally, the 402F is believed to be the first digital computer to have been exported from the UK to Germany [20].

The Elliott 402F that went to Ernst Leitz was one of two production 402s to be equipped with a hardware floating-point unit – which (according to contemporary photographs, see Fig. 8.3) took up three extra cabinets of electronics. Meanwhile at Borehamwood, the hardware designers were directing their efforts towards the new Elliott 800 series computers, advertised as 'small, medium-speed digital computers, flexible in operation and economical to run'. Although the first production machine, the 802 launched in November 1958, did not have floating-point hardware, the 803 (first delivered in 1960) did. The 803 had a 9-bit binary exponent and a 30-bit mantissa. Further hardware details are given in Appendix 4.

Returning to applications, Elliotts were asked by the BBC on at least three occasions to help predict the results of a General Election – in 1955, 1959 and 1964. Nicholas was used at Borehamwood on the first occasion, then a 402 was moved to a BBC studio for the second election and an 803 installed at the BBC for the third event.

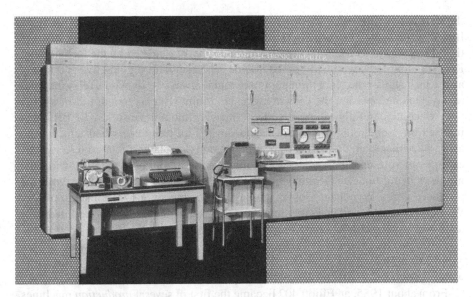

Fig. 8.3 The Elliott 402F, first delivered in 1958 to the Ernst Leitz company in Germany for ray-tracing and optical lens systems design, had floating-point hardware. At Leitz the 402F replaced an electro-mechanical relay machine, the Z5, designed by Konrad Zuse

Ed Hersom remembers [6] that: 'Prior to the 1955 General Election we had been in touch with Reuters who had pre-calculated a forecasting method that relied on the median swing (Conservative/Labour) of the initial returns. We wrote a simple program and, come the day, we had:

- one person who viewed a TV and wrote the returns onto a piece of paper;
- another took these papers to a tape-punch operator;
- a third took these (short) pieces of tape and inserted them into Nicholas's tape reader.

The printed result was conveyed to yet another person who was glued to the 'phone connected to Reuters and gave them the latest result verbally. We had no practice run beforehand.

'All went well until a mistake occurred. An erroneous return had been entered into the machine. I stopped Nicholas, and Susan Morris, who had written the program, and I went into a huddle to work out how we could correct the accumulated results in Nicholas and still be able to carry on. This we did to our immense relief. The girl on the 'phone to Reuters heard them say we had been twenty minutes behind hand but were now catching up! Apart from that manual glitch the machine worked perfectly for the 3–4 hours whilst the majority of the returns came in.'

Roger Cook remembers the next election predictions in 1959 [12]: 'There was the Elliott 402 which the BBC wanted to be installed in the studio.... A young man David Butler was introduced who would define the program required, which two of us wrote. We were installed in a large studio with the programme scheduled for a 9.00 pm start. Fortunately the 402 worked without a failure and the prediction, after the first two results, was so unexpected that David Butler and Richard Dimbleby [the BBC presenters] refused to broadcast the results. Later in the night we realised that the prediction was, in fact, very accurate! I was fascinated by the technique of Richard Dimbleby, who had one 30 minute rehearsal before going live and acting as the mainstay of the team throughout the night, always ready with a relevant word to say. On one occasion the camera switched to him with his mouth full of a large bun which he carefully removed and continued without a pause…. The BBC had insisted on "something that moves" and the [Elliott] engineers had attached an array of perhaps hundred flick-over number units displaying total votes, swings, changes in vote and the camera spent many minutes filling in time showing the numbers being updated. I remember we went off the air about 4.00 am with the producer, Grace Wyndham-Goldie, saying back on the air at 6.00 am sharp please. We then continued until well after lunch time. Throughout this time the commentator team was expected to be ready to speak at 2 seconds notice.

'The third election [in 1964] was less exciting as the novelty had worn off but again I think we installed an Elliott 803 in the studio. All this was, I think, done without cost to the BBC in the belief that publicity would result.'

From about 1955, an Elliott 402 became the first of several *production* machines to be used at Borehamwood to run a Computing Service, or Bureau, for outside users (though the Nicholas in-house machine had had limited external users before 1955). There was, at first, very little use made of the 402 facility for in-house tasks. Roger Cook remembers [12] that: 'Payroll was the first application [in 1956] and we all had to leave the computer hall at pay day to avoid seeing the print out of the payroll. The first technical application was a simple program we wrote to print out systematically the back-plane wiring showing the colour and number of wires expected on each pin. This simple program reduced the pre-commissioning checking significantly as well as reducing the number of errors to be found during live testing.' The Borehamwood Computing Service was enhanced in July 1956 with the instal- lation of the first Elliott 405 computer with four magnetic film decks and a 16K word disc [21].

Returning to the mid-1950s, the one-off Elliott 403 computer, designed for the Long Range Weapons Research Establishment in Australia, was delivered towards the end of 1955 as described in Chap. 3. The 403 was also essentially a scientific computing machine, though there was a requirement to handle large amounts of numeric data and to print and display the results graphically. The 403's bulk output unit, a significant piece of equipment occupying as many racks of electronics as a 402 computer, took data from magnetic tape that had been prepared by the main computer and then printed and displayed the results off-line. This experience of designing hardware for large data-transfers was to contribute to the design of the Elliott 405.

Examples of machine-code programs for the Elliott 401, 402, 403 and 405 com- puters can be found at [22] and Appendix 3.

As a general rule, applications programming in the early 1950s was not something to which hardware manufacturers devoted much effort. Speaking of the Elliott 405 installed at Littlewoods Mail Order company in 1958, Gerald Everitt says [23]: 'Elliotts provided a small library of utility programs and subroutines, but only the two programs for translating input of programs were regularly used [at Littlewoods]. These were known affectionately as Albert and Roger after the authors – [probably Albert Wakefield and Roger Cook]. Programmers at Littlewoods were on their own. They had half a sheet of machine code instructions and ready access to the engineers. Who could ask for anything more?' Programmers of the day knew that they were pioneers and acted accordingly. At the end of each computer task (at Littlewoods) Gerald Everitt caused the cryptic message *OMT* to be printed out on the console typewriter. Onlookers assumed this stood for something technical. Actually, it stood for 'One More Time' and was the punchline of an old army joke that Everett used to tell. At the conclusion of rehearsing a squad for the Sunday Church Parade, the sergeant-major announced: 'All right, lads, we'll sing 'Oly 'Oly 'Oly one more time and then we'll all f**k off for a cuppa.' More on the Littlewoods 405 will be found in Chap. 9.

Dina Vaughan, by then Dina St Johnston and celebrating 10 years as an independent programmer, gives a more reflective view of the age. Writing in 1969 [11], Dina observed that:

'Computers [in the early 1950s] were first applied to mathematical work and the user did his own programming entirely. Later a small library of common mathematical functions was organised or supplied by the manufacturer. The users were scientifically minded people, usually with considerable mathematical training. When computers started to be applied to business data processing and other non-mathematical fields, the users were seldom scientifically inclined and hence expected much more support from the computer manufacturers. Alternatively, the bigger user companies built up teams of their own covering business data processing and scientific applications.'

The Elliott 402 was mainly used for science and engineering tasks, as described in Chap. 5. These included statistics and time-series analyses, a Cyclotron design task for CERN (European Council for Nuclear Research) and, most importantly, work for several aircraft manufacturers on structural vibration in high-performance aircraft (the so-called flutter problem). In addition, attempts were made as early as 1954 to interest the business community in the Elliott 402 – see for example [24]. Three years later and looking back on [24], Andrew St Johnston was able to remark on the two most important lessons learned from his attempts to apply the 402 computer to commercial data processing [21]. Firstly, Elliotts realised that businesses come in a variety of shapes and sizes, implying an ability to configure a computing system from a variety of hardware options. Secondly, Elliotts realised the importance of giving end-users large amounts of bulk storage, exemplified by magnetic tape or film devices. These lessons underlie Borehamwood's transition from the 402 to the 405 computer.

Elliott's entry into the commercial data-processing market really had to await the arrival of the 405 system, the first one being delivered in July in 1956. In June of that year, a marketing collaboration was agreed between Elliotts and the UK arm of the National Cash Register company (NCR), whereby NCR took over responsibility for marketing the 405 'for all business applications' (see Chap. 9). This also led in due course to the provision by NCR of some software support for the 405. There was naturally a period of overlap, during which the Computing Division at Borehamwood began to explore the new field of commercial applications whilst continuing to exploit the more familiar areas of scientific and engineering applications and the emerging field of industrial process control (automation). Furthermore, NCR took some time to fully embrace the stored-program digital computer culture since NCR had a long historical involvement with retail and financial applications based on electro-mechanical accounting machines and small cash-register systems.

Norman Hill, who had been the Head of the Theory Division, moved into the Computing Division to become the Commercial Manager in about 1955, staying in this role until late 1956. Early in 1957, Hill joined the EMI company as Computer Sales Manager [25], though exactly why he chose to leave Borehamwood is not clear. At EMI, he was responsible for the sales of 'nearly all the EMIDEC 1100s and 2400s' [26]. By 1960 Hill had become EMI's 'Chief Computer Executive with responsibilities for computer policies and planning' [27]. Hill's place as Commercial Manager in the Borehamwood Computing Division was taken by R L (Ronnie) Michaelson, an actuary by training, who was recruited from BTM. At BTM, Michaelson had proved a perceptive convert to the world of digital data processing [28]. His book *Rambles through Binland and Electronia* was enjoyed by many. In turn, Ronnie Michaelson moved up the Elliott-Automation hierarchy to become Assistant Controller (Admin.) in about 1959. His position as Commercial Manager was taken over by Eddie Nash, of whom more later.

Back in 1955 Norman Hill had helped to establish a technical sales team that sought out applications for the Elliott 402 and 405 computers. This represented perhaps the first systematic excursion by the company into the area of end-user software. R G (Gerry) Mills, who graduated in mathematics from Cambridge, then spent time at STC working on electronic telephone exchanges and then joined Borehamwood in the spring of 1955. He describes the start of this new phase of activity at Borehamwood as follows [29].

'Norman Hill was Commercial Manager in 1955 when he recruited a team of six people, to work on various scientific and commercial applications of computers for practical sales. There was Pat Shackleton, myself, John Cox, Joe Burton, Des Preston and Doug Honeyman as a "sales force". I was half mathematician, half electronic engineer; Pat was a mathematical thinker; Joe Burton was a chartered accountant; Doug a qualified Cost and Works accountant; John was a qualified Local Authority accountant and I forget Des's specialty, possibly insurance or accounting. None of us, including Norman, knew anything about selling! We all got on well together, even though the accountants were a bit out of their depth to start with. Quite soon Pat Shackleton got me interested in the commercial applications of computers, showed me his sorting program, and explained how vital it was.'

In this last comment one may detect an enthusiasm for commercial data processing that was, some years later, to bring Gerry Mills into disagreement with the Elliott management's handling of the Computing Division. Gerry has since explained his position, identifying various ways in which he believed the company ought to have acted differently in the early 1960s – (see the next chapter on commercial data processing). We pick up this theme again in Chap. 13, when discussing the context in which the main computing interests of Elliott-Automation were to be swallowed up in a flurry of mergers and takeovers towards the end of the 1960s.

Whereas the advantages of a digital computer for calculations, modelling and analysis were reasonably obvious to scientists and engineers, the application of computers to business data processing was far from obvious to the commercial world in 1955. Even as late as 1960 when he arrived at Borehamwood, David Pentecost recalls [30] 'sitting within earshot of some Elliott sales staff, hearing them discussing prospects amongst themselves, racking their brains to try to think of the types of commercial organisation to whom they might sell the Elliott 803, and how a computer could be used, (apart from the obvious payroll application, which by itself would not justify the cost of a computer except perhaps by the very largest of companies)'.

By 1957, however, Borehamwood was undeniably a buzzing part of the dawning commercial data-processing scene. The *Financial Times* newspaper described Elliotts as 'One of the three manufacturers of large digital computers for office use in this country – the others are Ferranti and Leo Computers .... The 405 accounts for nearly 90% of Elliott's current computer output (by value), and has been responsible for most of the recent expansion. In the last 12 months the computing division's workshop floor space has increased by 20,000 square feet, a rise of over 50 per cent, while manpower has similarly risen to over the 400 mark. Annual turnover last year reached £1m., and is expected to double by 1958' [31].

Borehamwood's involvement in *marketing* the 405 computer tailed off after early 1957, the torch having been passed to NCR as described in the next chapter. Thereafter, the Computing Division mostly pursued their exploitation of the scientific market, expanding into industrial process control and portable military applications by the end of the decade. The first of Borehamwood's S-series Reports on applications of the new Elliott 802 computer appeared on 4 September 1959. D A Smart was the author of many of the feasibility studies for the 802/803 systems. Although sales of Elliott computers to commercial data-processing customers was nominally the province of NCR, the dividing line between 'business' and 'scientific' applications was a fuzzy one and Borehamwood certainly exploited a range of general applications such as *point-of-sale*, *typesetting* and *operational research* which spilled over into the business world. An example of the latter is remembered [18] by Paul King, as follows:

'To sell a computer it was sometimes necessary to demonstrate that it could really deal with the customer's problem. One was the British Aluminium Company. They had a hydro electric power station at Fort William near the base of Ben Nevis. I wrote a simulation programme on the Elliott 803 which modelled two reservoirs up in the mountains, with dams over which water would flow to waste and connected by a pipe whose flow capacity depended on the water level. The lower reservoir was connected by another pipe to the generators far below. The electricity output depended on the head of water available. The first task was to explore different operating rules to see which would produce the most electricity and hence the most aluminium: it might not pay to run at maximum flow rate if this would cause the reservoirs to run dry later. Input data was the daily record of rainfall over the last 10 years and output, for a given set of operating rules, was the amount of electricity generated. The next task was to simulate possible physical changes to the system such as higher dams, second underground pipe etc. to see whether the increased output of electricity would justify the expense of the changes. Altogether this was a classical piece of Operational Research.' An Elliott 802 computer was delivered to the British Aluminium Co. Ltd. in 1961, for 'Simulation studies, operating research & stock control' (see Appendix 8 for deliveries).

8.5   The Golden Years of Elliott Computers: 1958–1965

8.5.1   Evolving Divisional Structure

The first Elliott 802 computer was delivered to a customer in 1958 and the first 803 computer in November 1959. The success of the 800 series computers and the early dominance of Elliotts in the UK's industrial process control market (see Chap. 7) heralded a golden age for Elliott computers. The growth in Elliott's UK sales, compared with that of other computer manufacturers, is given in Table 8.2, taken from contemporary issues of the magazine *Computer Survey* (Fig. 8.4).

During this time the company organisation was expanding and evolving, in line with Leon Bagrit's strategy of creating divisions to exploit market opportunities. The name *Elliott-Automation* had first been registered as a public company on 20 August 1957. An analysis of the Annual Reports of the Elliott-Automation group of companies reveals that by the spring of 1960 approximately 1,700 employees were engaged in R&D at Borehamwood – of whom perhaps 500 were directly involved in designing and producing the hardware and systems software for electronic computers. At the time, the total number of Elliott-Automation employees (all sites) was approximately 14,000. The main locations were still at Lewisham, Rochester and Borehamwood, with practically all of the digital computer hardware and software design taking place at Borehamwood.

In 1960 the organisation of computing activity at Borehamwood was mostly integrated into a single Computing Division of Elliott Brothers (London) Ltd.,

Table 8.2   Annual deliveries of computers to UK customers, 1958–1963

	Total computers delivered in the UK per year (excluding defence)	Percentage of these which were manufactured by Elliotts at Borehamwood
1958	50	20
1959	44	30
1960	68	32
1961	84	50
1962	120	38
1963	200	38

Fig. 8.4 The Borehamwood site of Elliott-Automation had expanded considerably in 1958/1959 with the construction of a large building containing offices, manufacturing and research space. This 1970s photo shows the 'new building' in the background, with a GEC sign prominently displayed. The two-storey brick building in the left foreground is the original Admiralty Fuse factory which, in 1946, became the Research Laboratories of Elliott Brothers (London) Ltd.

trading as Elliott-Automation Computers Ltd., although by 1960 the industrial process control activities had caused two new sections to be distinguished: the Process Automation Group and the Automatic Data Processing Group. Shortly after this, a new subsidiary company, E-A Automation Systems Ltd., had been added to the Elliott-Automation empire as discussed in Chap. 6.

Definitive company staff lists appear not to have survived. However, Peter Lawrence [32] remembers that 'the senior Computing Division staff in 1960 were as follows:

Manager:	Andrew St Johnston
Sales:	H.E.C. (Eddy) Nash
Engineering (Hardware):	John Bunt
Software:	Roger Cook
Research:	Lawrence Clarke

Other groups within the Division covered areas such as: manufacturing, test/ commissioning, maintenance, contracts, training, publications.' Peter continues:

'From 1st January 1962 Elliott-Automation Computers was divisionalised as follows, with Andrew St Johnston being the General Manager:

- Elliott Computing Division (400 series, 503, 800 series and, later, 903 and 905 software and sales)
  Manager: Eddy Nash, followed by J.W. (Peter) Reffen
  Sales: R.G. (Gerry) Mills, followed by P.F. (Paul) King

Development: – not sure of structure but senior staff included Geoff Rowley,
                Laurie Bental, Roger Cook, Tony Hoare.

* Mobile Computing Division (502, 900 series, except for sales and software for
  ES market)
  Manager: John Bunt
  Sales: W.T.M. (Warren) Gaskell, followed by C.C.H. (Cedric) Dennis
  Chief Engineer: Jim Barrow followed by L.C. (Len) Handley and then Doug
        Libby.

* Panellit Division (ARCH systems) – *(but see below for alternative name)*.
  Manager: Lawrence Clarke
  Technical: – unsure but G.B. (Barry) Cole was one senior.

* Computing Research Laboratory:
  Manager Peter Kellett, followed by Mike Downer.

* National Computing Division (a small engineering group manufacturing the
  NCR 315 under license)

Peter Lawrence's memory may be slightly in error regarding the 'Panellit'
Division which, though certainly growing out of links between Elliotts and the
American company Panellit (see Chap. 6), was by 1962 called the Industrial
Process Automation Division (IPAD). Laurence Clarke believes that, by that date,
he (Laurence) was Assistant General Manager primarily responsible for IPAD and
for the Computing Research Laboratory, and that Trevor Roberts was the IPAD
Divisional Manager [14].

At some later date [about 1964] Mobile Computing Division was moved to a
different subsidiary, Elliott Space and Weapon Automation Ltd. under D (Paddy)
Hunter, and Panellit Division was split off as Elliott Process Automation Ltd.
The Elliott Space and Weapons company was located at both Borehamwood and
at Frimley in Surrey. Frimley is about 30 miles south-west of the centre of
London.

The reorganisations of 1 January 1962 caused dismay in some quarters. Gerry
Mills recalls [29] that 'the decision of Bagrit and Herzfeld to break up the Computing
Division in 1962 led to the resignations of Nash and myself at a time when Elliott
computers were number 1 in the UK and doing well worldwide'. Describing the reorganisation as 'bureaucratic nonsense', Mills continues: 'it was an amazing period,
and the number of really good people who left Elliott's [at this time] saying the same
thing shows what a fantastic opportunity to lead the UK computer industry was
missed'. Mills is of the opinion that Bagrit should have severed the agreement with
NCR, floated the entire Computing Division as a separate company and raised
the capital required independently of the rest of Elliott-Automation. 'Given the right
Chairman, the City would have thrown money at the new company.' Mills' analysis
is considered again in the next chapter, after the role of NCR has been described.
It is not clear whether Mills' *new company* could have survived the competitive era
of mergers and takeovers that beset the British computing scene in the period
1963–1968, events that are described more fully in Chap. 13.

Fig. 8.5 In the mid-1960s Sir Leon Bagrit was at the height of his influence in government circles. He was able to arrange for an Elliott 803 computer to be installed in the Palace of Westminster, for a Computer Appreciation course for Members of Parliament

The structure of the Elliott-Automation group continued to evolve, reaching what seems in the light of hindsight to be the high point of complexity in May 1965 [33]. At this time the group contained 15 main *Operating Companies*, divided into approximately 64 *Divisions* plus a number of *Laboratories, Technical Centres*, etc. – as detailed in Appendix 11. At Borehamwood the operating company known as Elliott-Automation Computers Ltd. contained the following seven subsections, all reporting to Andrew St Johnston as the General Manager:

- Scientific Computing Division
- National Computing Division (linked with NCR)
- Educational Computing Division
- Data Processing Division
- Computing Services Division
- Computer Maintenance Division
- Computing Research Laboratory

Other companies within the Elliott-Automation Group contained further Divisions relevant to digital computers, particularly:

- Elliott Flight Automation Ltd. (which included the Airborne Computing Division)
- Elliott Space and Weapon Automation Ltd. (including the Mobile Computing Division)
- Elliott Brothers (London) Ltd. (including the Microelectronics Group)

Finally, operating companies that clearly exploited the use of computers (analogue or digital) included: Elliott Process Automation Ltd., Elliott-Automation Nucleonics Ltd., Elliott Traffic Automation Ltd., Elliott Mechanical Automation Ltd. and Associated Automation Ltd. Again, no official Elliott company records have come to light for this period so it has not proved possible to discover a definitive list of senior managers for the various computing-related Divisions.

By 1965, the development of hardware and software for Elliott-Automation digital computers had become dispersed. Whilst Borehamwood continued to be, as it were, the spiritual home, airborne computing was being driven more and more from Rochester (see below). From about 1964 Military (mobile) computing had an outpost at Frimley in Surrey. Process control and automation activities were carried out at various premises within the Greater London area, including Lewisham, Willesden, Park Royal and Greenwich.

Back at Borehamwood, Roger Cook has recalled the atmosphere as follows [12]. 'My overall memories are of a frantic but enjoyable time with ideas for new equipment and new application areas arriving more rapidly than could be contemplated. Considerable frustration when the gestation period exceeded the mean time for arrival of the next idea. The Elliott concept of setting up independent units for each market area was basically sound but the overall management and financial funding never permitted the individual divisions to stay in existence for long enough to bring products to market. We [at Borehamwood] tried our hand at typesetting, CAD, flight simulation, on-line medical analysis, education, rail and road signalling, real-time control, point-of-sale, and many others all of which today are recognised computer market areas. I was not part of the airborne computer side [which gradually migrated to Rochester] but always felt that their side of the fence was more coherent and logically developing.' By 1962 Rochester had become the headquarters for Elliott Flight Automation. Airborne computing is briefly mentioned below under *defence* but is covered more fully in Chap. 12.

8.5.2 Autocode

Until the end of the 1950s all programming for Elliott computers was carried out in machine code or assembler. In this respect, Elliotts lagged behind many other computer manufacturers. As Roger Cook has observed, 'during this time there was no operating system as such. A set of library routines and programs were provided but all customers' programming was in machine code written with the minimum of mnemonic naming, translated and loaded via a simple program. Curiously, although the programs were not proven and tested by anyone other than the author, I cannot remember any level of customer queries or support requirements for the provided programs – perhaps they were not much used' [12] (Figs. 8.5 and 8.6).

Then in about 1960 Elliott Autocode was introduced [34]. As Roger Cook has said [12]: 'We wrote a simple program that enabled users to write in algebraic format and released it as Elliott Autocode. This was just before the first issues of BASIC appeared [the BASIC language actually appeared in 1964, see [35]]. Our Autocode was a great success with the customers; I wonder, in retrospect, why we had not thought of it sooner. We bypassed FORTRAN, because, in 1960, the ALGOL specification was released and Tony Hoare was given the task of writing our first proper compiler. Sensibly, he wrote it in Algol, using recursion, and a fully working version was released to the customers in less than a year. There is some debate whether we were the first to release a "proper" Algol compiler; personally, I think we were. It worked in the limited memory of the Elliott 802 and 803 using punched paper tape as an intermediate store for the first phase output of the compiler. This then had to be read in backwards to enable the compiler efficiently to fix up the variables with actual addresses.' The Elliott Algol story is recounted later, after we have given a taste of Elliott Autocode. Jill Pymm, who was responsible for the 803 Autocode, subsequently became a member of Tony Hoare's Algol implementation team.

The syntax of Elliott Autocode was similar to other contemporary autocodes, but with differing local conventions for distinguishing between types (principally just *integer* or *real*). Other presentational differences were due to the limitations, or richness, of the particular character set chosen for each computer manufacturer's designated data-preparation and input device. This is illustrated by the following four fragments of autocode programs, each produced by paper-tape input equipment, for calculating the Root Mean Square of 100 real (i.e. floating-point) variables. The fragments are presented in chronological sequence, ordered by the date in which the respective manufacturers introduced their language and accompanied by a reference to the literature. A historical progression of readability may be observed, foreshadowing an underlying progression towards high-level languages such as Algol. Indeed, the last example (Atlas Autocode) is an Algol-like block-structured language with certain improvements.

(a) *Ferranti Mark I autocode, introduced in Manchester in 1954* [36]:

```
n1 = 1
v101 = 0
2v102 = vn1 × vn1
   v101 = v101 + v102
   n1 = n1 + 1
   j2, 100 ≥ n1
   v101 = v101/100.0
  *v101 = F1(v101)
```

Note that the symbol * caused printing to ten decimal places on a new line; F1 signified the intrinsic function *square root*.

(b) *Ferranti Pegasus autocode, introduced in 1957* [37]:

$$n1 = 1$$
$$v101 = 0$$
2) $$v102 = vn1 \times vn1$$
$$v101 = v101 + v102$$
$$n1 = n1 + 1$$
$$\rightarrow 2, \; 100 \geq n1$$
$$v101 = v101/100$$
$$v101 = SQRT\,v101$$
$$PRINT\,v101$$

(c) *Elliott autocode, introduced in 1960* [34]:

```
A = 0
CYCLE J = 1:1:100
B = C(J)*C(J)
A = A + B
REPEAT J
B = B/100
B = SQRT B
PRINT B, 5:2
```

Fig. 8.6 In efforts to open up markets, Elliott 803 computers were demonstrated in many places. The photo shows part of an 803 being installed in Sheffield, where the company organised a symposium on *Computers in Industry* at the Sheffield Industries Exhibition Centre in November 1963. This attracted several hundred visitors over 4 days, and dozens more to an evening lecture course on *Algol Programming*

(d) *Ferranti Atlas Autocode, introduced in 1964* [38]:

integer j; real a; array mydata(1:100)
comment calculate the RMS of the real variables mydata(1) -> mydata(100)
a = 0
cycle j = 1, 1, 100
a = a + mydata(j)*mydata(j)
repeat
print(sqrt(a/100), 5, 2)

8.5.3 Algol

Whilst Elliott Autocode was being promoted, a small group of programmers at Borehamwood was taking a bolder step. As Paul King remembers [20]: 'Probably the most important piece of programming work at that time was the development of an Algol Compiler, which was primarily the work of Tony Hoare. My involvement was only indirect. We showed our 803 computer in Moscow in 1960 and we needed an interpreter on the exhibition stand. We found this young Englishman (well, only about 2 years younger than me) who had taken a first class honours [actually, second class [39]] in Greats at Oxford and was now doing a post graduate course in numerical analysis in Moscow. He quickly learnt about our computers and soon did far more than interpret for us. I was so impressed that I persuaded him to take a job with us back at Borehamwood, which proved to be a really smart recruitment move. A year or so later Tony, Roger Cook, Jeff Hillmore and I attended a seminar in Brighton where Dijkstra presented his Algol 60 programming language and we decided almost on the spot, to implement it.'

Edsger Dijkstra (1930–2002) was the first to implement an Algol compiler: 'In August 1960 our implementation was working, more than a year before the one of our nearest competitor, the group of Peter Naur in Copenhagen' [40]. Dijkstra's work took place at the Mathematical Centre (Mathematisch Centrum), Amsterdam, under the direction of Adriaan van Wijngaarden and their computer was the Dutch-designed Electrologica EL-X1 [41]. The meeting with Tony Hoare at the 'Seminar in Brighton' was remembered by Dijkstra years later as follows [42]: 'The first time we met was in 1961 and neither of us remembers it. It was a lecture series on Algol 60 at Brighton. I can be forgiven that I don't remember Tony for I was one of the few speakers and he was only a participant in the audience. His amnesia is harder to forgive, but he has explained it to me by the presence of Peter Naur, the other bearded speaker with a continental accent, claiming that in his memory Peter and I merged into one person....'

The Algol language, originally known as *International Algorithmic Language, IAL*, was proposed by a committee composed of European and American representatives from academia and industry, meeting in Zurich in 1958. This was refined in January 1960 at a further meeting in Paris which produced the Algol 60 Report. Elliotts was not represented at either meeting, the only British attendee at Paris being Mike Woodger from NPL. Peter Naur and Adriaan van Wijngaarden were present.

More should be said about C A R (Tony) Hoare, since he is almost certainly the most distinguished Computer Scientist ever to have worked at Borehamwood. Summarising the biographical notes that appear in [43, 44], Tony Hoare graduated from Oxford University with a degree in Philosophy (together with Latin and Greek). During his National Service (1956–1958), he studied Russian in the Royal Navy. Then he took a qualification in statistics at Oxford, which included a course in programming. In 1959, as a graduate student at Moscow State University, he studied the machine translation of natural languages. To assist in efficient look-up of words in a dictionary, he developed the well-known sorting algorithm *Quicksort* [45].

Tony Hoare joined the Computing Division at Borehamwood in August 1960, as mentioned earlier. He led a team (that included Jeff Hillmore and Jill Pym, who subsequently became Tony's wife) 'in the design and delivery of the first commercial compiler for the programming language Algol 60' [46]. Promoted to the rank of Chief Engineer, he then led a larger team on a 'disastrous project to implement an operating system' (this was for the Elliott 503 computer – see later). After 'managing a recovery from the failure', he moved as Chief Scientist to the Computing Research Division at Borehamwood, where he worked on the hardware and software architecture for future machines – to be known as Alpha, Beta and Gamma – see Chap. 14. These projects were put on hold when Elliott-Automation merged with English Electric in 1967 and was then taken over by GEC in 1968. In that year Tony left the company and was appointed Professor of Computing Science at the Queen's University, Belfast. In 1977 he moved back to Oxford to lead the Programming Research Group (PRG), after the untimely death of another distinguished Computer Scientist, the PRG's founder Christopher Strachey in 1975. (Chris Strachey had himself been associated with Elliotts during his period with the NRDC between 1952 and 1959: see Chap. 5.) At the PRG, Tony Hoare's teams 'pursued an ideal that takes provable correctness as the driving force for the accurate specification, design and development of computing systems, both critical and non-critical. Well-known results of the research include the Z specification language and the CSP concurrent programming model.' Tony received the prestigious ACM Turing Award in 1980. In 1982 he was made a Fellow of the Royal Society and in 2000 he was knighted for services to education and Computer Science. On reaching retirement age at Oxford, Emeritus Professor Tony Hoare became a Senior Research Fellow with Microsoft Research in Cambridge.

Tony Hoare provided a fascinating insight into his 8 years at Borehamwood, in his ACM *Turing Award* address [47]. The following extracts, from the first section of his address, describes his 'Algol years'.

'My first task [upon arrival at Borehamwood] was to implement for the new Elliott 803 computer, a library subroutine for a new fast method of internal sorting just invented by D L Shell [see [48]]. .... My boss and tutor, Pat Shackleton, was very pleased with my completed program. I then said timidly that I thought I had invented a sorting method that would usually run faster than *Shellsort*, without taking much extra store. He bet me sixpence that I had not. Although my method was very difficult to explain, he finally agreed that I had won my bet. I wrote several other tightly coded library subroutines but after six months I was given a much more important task – that of designing a new advanced high level programming language for the company's next computer, the Elliott 503, which was to have the same instruction code as the existing 803 but run sixty times faster.... By great good fortune there came into my hands a copy of the Report on the International Algorithmic Language ALGOL 60. Of course, this language was obviously too complicated for our customers. How could they ever understand all those begins and ends when even our salesmen couldn't?

'Around Easter 1961, a course on ALGOL 60 was offered in Brighton, England [at Brighton College of Technology], with Peter Naur, Edsger W. Dijkstra, and Peter Landin as tutors. I attended this course with my colleague in the language project, Jill Pym, our divisional Technical Manager, Roger Cook, and our Sales Manager, Paul King. It was there that I first learned about recursive procedures and saw how to program the sorting method [Quicksort] which I had earlier found such difficulty in explaining.

'After the ALGOL course in Brighton, Roger Cook was driving me and my colleagues back to London when he suddenly asked, "Instead of designing a new language, why don't we just implement ALGOL 60?" We all instantly agreed – in retrospect, a very lucky decision for me. But we knew we did not have the skill or experience at that time to implement the whole language, so I was commissioned to design a modest subset. In that design I adopted certain basic principles which I believe to be as valid today as they were then....

'... As the design and implementation progressed, I gradually discovered methods of relaxing the restrictions without compromising any of the principles. So in the end we were able to implement nearly the full power of the whole language, including even recursion, although several features were removed and others were restricted.

'In the middle of 1963, primarily as a result of the work of Jill Pym and Jeff Hillmore, the first version of our compiler was delivered. [Interestingly, the very first simple 802 Algol program was run on 15th February 1962 – see [46a]]. After a few months we began to wonder whether anyone was using the language or taking any notice of our occasional reissue, incorporating improved operating methods. Only when a customer had a complaint did he contact us and many of them had no complaints. Our customers have now moved on to more modern computers and more fashionable languages but many have told me of their fond memories of the Elliott ALGOL System and the fondness is not due just to nostalgia, but to the efficiency, reliability, and convenience of that early simple ALGOL System.'

Several other computer manufacturers were also working on Algol implementations. Was Elliott's compiler indeed the first to be released commercially, as Tony Hoare indicated? In the UK the compiler of Brian Randell and Lawford Russell at English Electric's establishment at Whetstone, south of Leicester, was certainly early in the field and became highly regarded. Randell has said [49] that the Elliott Algol compiler 'was, I believe, ready before the KDF9 implementation of the Whetstone Algol system and, as far as I can now recall, any of the preceding systems that were based on the Whetstone system's design'.

Affection for Algol is well-illustrated by a quotation from Peter Chinn, who joined Elliott's Guided Weapons Division at Borehamwood in 1956 to work on systems study and trials analysis for homing heads used in guided missiles. To begin with, Peter used Elliott's GPAC analogue computer (see Sect. 4.7), supplemented by a Rheinmetal desk calculator 'for doing sums'. His first digital computer was an Elliott 802, followed by the 803 in the early 1960s. Chinn says: 'Up till that time, I had only ever programmed in machine code. Elliott Autocode was around, but somehow I leapfrogged it. I particularly remember my first brush with high level languages. Les Broad & I shared an office, we needed to solve a quintic equation and had been failing to do so for a couple of days. The next morning I walked into the office at 9·30 & said "Les, I've booked half an hour on the 803 at 3·00 o'clock – we've got 5½ hours to learn Algol & write a program to solve quintics". And we did! I'm not sure that we deserved to, but it all worked like a charm. I've had a soft spot for Algol ever since' [50].

Tony Hoare's publications and his growing contacts with academia and the international programming community meant that Borehamwood became better known for its software efforts than hitherto. For example, in August 1962 Tony was invited to serve on the new Working Group 2.1 of the International Federation for Information Processing (IFIP), charged with responsibility for maintenance and development of Algol. Other contacts opened up. In April 1960 ECMA (the European Computer Manufacturers Association) was established with headquarters in Geneva [51]. The organisation, which still exists as an international standards body for information technology and consumer electronics, changed its name to *ECMA International* in 1991. In 1960, 20 manufacturers formed the initial membership of ECMA, Elliotts being one of eight UK companies represented. Eddie Nash, by that time a Manager of Elliott's Computing Division, was the official Elliott representative. Roger Cook became a member of ECMA Technical Committee 2 (programming languages) and also a member of ECMA TC 5 (Algol). Significantly, NCR was not itself a full ECMA member but was permitted associate status. To quote [46]: 'The National Cash Register Co Ltd is not as such a member of ECMA but by virtue of their association with Elliott Brothers, employees of NCR may represent Elliott on ECMA committees.' H L S Orde was designated *the alternate NCR member*.

Looking back to ECMA in 1961, Roger Cook recalls [12] that: 'At that time there were over 20 independent companies in Europe, nearly half of them UK companies. We met and discussed problems for two days at a time. IBM and other US companies with strong European development, were allowed to be members. Later on in the 60s, I became chairman of the Algol committee. I thought we had reached agreement on a possible standard for Algol input/output, there being no mention of this in the Algol standard. Little, if any, briefing was given to me or, I suspect to the other European members. The IBM delegate had however been very precisely briefed; when I put the proposal that we publish our agreements he became a skilled proponent of why not; we did, in the end, publish our document although no-one took much notice of it.' Between 1965 and 1970 Tony Hoare served on ECMA, as chairman of one of ECMA's Technical Committees.

The Algol language was never to achieve the popularity amongst scientific users that Fortran enjoys, nor was it to have much impact on the commercial data-processing world. Nevertheless, the Elliott Algol implementation certainly put Borehamwood on the international software map in the 1960s. This was because, as Tony Hoare remarked in 1973, 'the more I ponder the principles of language design, and the techniques which put them into practice, the more is my amazement and admiration of Algol 60. Here is a language so far ahead of its time, that it was not only an improvement on its predecessors, but also on nearly all its successors' [52].

8.5.4 Systems Software and Operating Systems

In the 1950s most Elliott computers, in common with the machines of other manufacturers, normally executed one user program at a time. Towards the end of the 1950s experiments with multiprogramming began to appear. Roger Cook remembers [12]: 'The Elliott 802 had an interrupt line enabling one program to be orderly shut down and another started. During a computer exhibition [probably at Olympia, London, in November 1958], we amused ourselves by demonstrating a user participating system while a background job continued. I wrote a naive article on multiprogramming on the 802 which was published by the British Computer Society [53]. Some year or so later I received a letter from the USSR with a copy of my article translated into Russian'.

The first serious attempt to write a small operating system for an Elliott computer may have been Dina St Johnston's *Master Control Executive* (MACE), written for an Elliott 803 in 1960.

As was mentioned earlier, Dina had left Borehamwood at the end of 1958 to found Vaughan Programming Services (VPS) in February 1959. VPS's first real challenge came in 1960, with a contract to write software for the UKAEA's Calder Hall atomic station at Windscale (Sellafield). An Elliott computer was to provide a logging and alarm-scanning system for the prototype Magnox gas-cooled reactor, in what became the world's first industrial scale nuclear power station. As described in Chap. 7, the project involved connecting the computer to 410 different monitoring and control points, some of the alarm functions being based on rates of change. The Calder Hall contract was an early example of industrial on-line control.

As part of the programming effort for the complex Calder Hall project, Dina St Johnston designed and wrote Vaughan's Master Control Executive (MACE), a robust time-sharing mini operating system 'with predictable and precise response times', which went on to perform satisfactorily well into the 1980s. MACE had seven principal sections: initial settings, main computational cycle, process modules, common subroutines, device routines, interrupt routines, a common database and interface storage area. The database, which included the parameters of the particular application (alarm limits, scaling factors, telemetry data, etc.), was seen as a particularly useful feature, making MACE systems adaptable, expandable and easily

Fig. 8.7 The Elliott 503, first delivered in 1963, was software-compatible with the 803 but was about 70 times faster. Approximately 32 Elliott 503 computers were built – (see the delivery lists in Appendix 8). The machine in the photo was installed at The Hague (Netherlands), where it was used for land reclamation calculations

testable. Over the next 10 years, VPS proved the point by using MACE in over 20 different applications running on 8 different types of computers (see [11] for details).

Vaughan Programming Services also wrote various pieces of system software for Elliott computers, under contract from Borehamwood. Examples listed in [11] include:

- Sort Generator and System Software (Elliott 503)
- CRT Format Generator (Elliott 903)
- Fortran Compiler for Mobile Computer for Schools (Elliott 903)
- Test and Diagnostic Programs for Elliott 4100
- Implementation of Common Language Assembler, several models

It seems that, on occasions, Elliotts found it more efficient to outsource certain systems' software tasks. Paul King remembers [54] that Borehamwood was 'certainly short of resources ourselves so no doubt that was the reason, rather than cost-effectiveness. This would apply to the Elliott 503 work. Programs for the 903 were the responsibility of the Mobile Computer Division …likewise, programs for the NCR 4100 would have been the responsibility of the NCR division, I think'.

Fig. 8.8 'Not since the famous descent on our shores of Mr Kruschev and Mr Bulgarin in April 1956 has a Russian political visit to this country roused so much interest as that this week of Alexei Nikolaevitch Kosykin, Prime Minister of the Soviet Union', wrote the London Evening News. On 8 February 1967, Kosygin visited Borehamwood, his only excursion outside London. Andrew St Johnston is in the left foreground with arm raised, guiding Mr Kosygin. Sir Leon Bagrit is second from the right

This was not entirely true – for example software was developed for 4100 graphical applications at Borehamwood.

Gerald Everitt, who worked for Vaughan Programming Services during the relevant time, takes the view that Borehamwood's practice of outsourcing 'helped Elliotts spread the load and import some expertise indirectly from other manufacturers. It was particularly useful when a self-contained product could be identified. It was not unusual. We [VPS] wrote a cut down version of a Fortran Compiler that would fit into a 903 whilst Computer Analysts and Programmers (CAP) were doing the same for Algol. We later used the Algol from CAP on a project at London Airport. It seemed far more elegant and flexible than our Fortran but was prohibitively slow' [55].

By 1963, Elliotts had developed the 503 computer, the first three production machines being installed that year as bureau/service computers at Borehamwood (two) and NCR in London (one). All Elliott 803 programs worked unchanged on the 503, which was about 70 times faster. For example, the fixed-point *ADD* times for the 803 and 503 were respectively 576 and 7.2 µs. Both machines could have up to 8K words (approximately 40KB) of primary RAM but, in the case of the 503, this was backed by up to 128K words of slower RAM, access to which was normally via autonomous block transfers at 15,800 words/s, though single words could be accessed in 71.9 µs. Further hardware details may be found in Appendix 4. A full operating system was planned for the 503 – a project that was to run into severe difficulties. The problems have been famously described by Tony Hoare in his *Turing Award* paper [47]. Here are extracts from Tony's account of events that took place at Borehamwood between 1963 and 1966.

'After the unexpected success of our ALGOL Compiler, our thoughts turned to a more ambitious project: To provide a range of operating system software for larger configurations of the 503 computer, with card readers, line printers, magnetic tapes, and even a core backing store which was twice as cheap and twice as large as main store, but fifteen times slower. This was to be known as the Elliott 503 Mark II software system. It comprised:

1. An assembler for a symbolic assembly language in which all the rest of the software was to be written.
2. A scheme for automatic administration of code and data overlays, either from magnetic tape or from core backing store. This was to be used by the rest of the software.
3. A scheme for automatic buffering of all input and output on any available peripheral device – again, to be used by all the other software.
4. A filing system on magnetic tape with facilities for editing and job control.
5. A completely new implementation of Algol 60, which removed all the nonstandard restrictions which we had imposed on our first implementation.
6. A compiler for Fortran as it was then.

'I wrote documents which described the relevant concepts and facilities and we sent them to existing and prospective customers. Work started with a team of fifteen programmers and the deadline for delivery was set some eighteen months ahead in March 1965. After initiating the design of the Mark II software, I was suddenly promoted to the dizzying rank of Assistant Chief Engineer, responsible for advanced development and design of the company's products, both hardware and software.

'Although I was still managerially responsible for the 503 Mark II software, I gave it less attention than the company's new products and almost failed to notice when the deadline for its delivery passed without event. The programmers revised their implementation schedules and a new delivery date was set some three months ahead in June 1965. Needless to say, that day also passed without event. By this time, our customers were getting angry and my managers instructed me to take personal charge of the project. I asked the senior programmers once again to draw up revised schedules, which again showed that the software could be delivered within another three months. I desperately wanted to believe it but I just could not. I disregarded the schedules and began to dig more deeply into the project.

'It turned out that we had failed to make any overall plans for the allocation of our most limited resource – main storage. Each programmer expected this to be done automatically, either by the symbolic assembler or by the automatic overlay scheme. Even worse, we had failed to simply count the space used by our own software which was already filling the main store of the computer, leaving no space for our customers to run their programs. Hardware address length limitations prohibited adding more main storage.

'Clearly, the original specifications of the software could not be met and had to be drastically curtailed. Experienced programmers and even managers were called back from other projects. We decided to concentrate first on delivery of the new compiler for ALGOL 60, which careful calculation showed would take another four months. I impressed upon all the programmers involved that this was no longer just a prediction; it was a promise; if they found they were not meeting their promise, it was their personal responsibility to find ways and means of making good.

The programmers responded magnificently to the challenge. They worked nights and days to ensure completion of all those items of software which were needed by the Algol compiler. To our delight, they met the scheduled delivery date; it was the first major item of working software produced by the company over a period of two years.

'Our delight was short-lived; the compiler could not be delivered. Its speed of compilation was only two characters per second which compared unfavorably with the existing version of the compiler operating at about a thousand characters per second. We soon identified the cause of the problem: It was thrashing between the main store and the extension core backing store which was fifteen times slower. It was easy to make some simple improvements, and within a week we had doubled the speed of compilation – to four characters per second. In the next two weeks of investigation and reprogramming, the speed was doubled again – to eight characters per second. We could see ways in which within a month this could be still further improved, but the amount of reprogramming required was increasing and its effectiveness was decreasing; there was an awful long way to go. The alternative of increasing the size of the main store so frequently adopted in later failures of this kind was prohibited by hardware addressing limitations.

There was no escape: The entire Elliott 503 Mark II software project had to be abandoned, and with it, over thirty man-years of programming effort, equivalent to nearly one man's active working life and I was responsible, both as designer and as manager, for wasting it.

A meeting of all our 503 customers was called and Roger Cook, who was then manager of the computing division, explained to them that not a single word of the long-promised software would ever be delivered to them....

'At that time I was reading the early documents describing the concepts and features of the newly announced [IBM] OS 360, and of a new time-sharing project called Multics [at Massachusetts Institute of Technology]. These were far more comprehensive, elaborate, and sophisticated than anything I had imagined, even in the first version of the 503 Mark II software. Clearly IBM and MIT must be possessed of some secret of successful software design and implementation whose nature I could not even begin to guess at. It was only later that they realized they could not either.

'So I still could not see how I had brought such a great misfortune upon my company....

'Of course, the company did everything they could to help me. They took away my responsibility for hardware design and reduced the size of my programming teams. Each of my managers explained carefully his own theory of what had gone wrong and all the theories were different. At last, there breezed into my office the most senior manager of all, a general manager of our parent company, Andrew St. Johnston. I was surprised that he had even heard of me. "You know what went wrong?" he shouted – he always shouted – "You let your programmers do things which you yourself do not understand." I stared in astonishment. He was obviously out of touch with present day realities. How could one person ever understand the whole of a modern software product like the Elliott 503 Mark II software system?

'I realized later that he was absolutely right; he had diagnosed the true cause of the problem and he had planted the seed of its later solution.

I still had a team of some forty programmers and we needed to retain the good will of customers for our new machine and even regain the confidence of the customers for our old one. But what should we actually plan to do when we knew only one thing – that all our previous plans had failed? I therefore called an all-day meeting of our senior programmers on October 22, 1965, to thrash out the question between us.... Our main failure was overambition.....

'How did we recover from the catastrophe? First, we classified our 503 customers into groups, according to the nature and size of the hardware configurations which they had bought – for example, those with magnetic tapes were all in one group. We assigned to each group of customers a small team of programmers and told the team leader to visit the customers to find out what they wanted; to select the easiest request to fulfill, and to make plans (but no promises) to implement it. In no case would we consider a request for a feature that would take more than three months to implement and deliver. The project leader would then have to convince me that the customers' request was reasonable, that the design of the new feature was appropriate, and that the plans and schedules for implementation were realistic. Above all, I did not allow anything to be done which I did not myself understand. It worked!

'The software requested began to be delivered on the promised dates. With an increase in our confidence and that of our customers, we were able to undertake fulfilling slightly more ambitious requests. Within a year we had recovered from the disaster. Within two years, we even had some moderately satisfied customers.'

Tony Hoare's frank and perceptive analysis of a major project's failure was, and is, unusual for the software industry. Two or three years before Elliott's 503 troubles, Ferranti avoided what might have been a similar tale of woe with the Supervisor (Operating System) for the joint Manchester University/Ferranti Atlas computer. Work on the Atlas software commenced in about 1959, at which time the magnitude of the task of writing the Atlas Supervisor was not fully appreciated. Unlike the Elliott 503, however, Atlas had a large-paged virtual address space with hardware memory management. The Atlas Supervisor, consisting of about 35,000 machine instructions, was implemented by a team led by David Howarth that at no time numbered more than six programmers [56]. Without David Howarth, whose capacity for hard work was legendary, the Atlas story might have been different.

To continue our review of Borehamwood software, it is interesting to quote from a 1965 company brochure that sought to reassure customers about the scale of Elliott's commitment to programming systems [57]. A section entitled *The Elliott Investment in Programming Languages* contains the following explanations:

'Today there are over 300 Elliott computer installations. The value of exports alone in 1964 was £3,000,000. 175 fully qualified programmers are available in Elliott-Automation to solve data processing problems. The investment in programming languages can be gauged by the fact that 50 man years has been spent on developing ALGOL compilers ... Economic necessity requires that the programs written by general purpose system programmers should be of use to as many users as possible. Currently, for example, there are probably 5,000 programmers using the 200 Elliott 803 computers in the field and our systems programming costs can be attributed to 200 sales.

'The following summary of the software which has been developed for the Elliott 503 is typical of the facilities offered by the Company for use in the scientific field:

ALGOL, SAP (Symbolic Assembly Program), FORTRAN, AUTOCODE
The STAR operating system
A central package of programs (PCP and SPAN) which controls all peripheral
    devices.'

Language H (see Chap. 9) was also mentioned in the Report as being available for the Elliott 803 and 503 computers. In the case of the Elliott 4100 series, 'the above [503] programming systems are either completed or in an advanced stage of development'. In addition, 'the Elliott 502 programming system will contain the CORAL subset of JOVIAL. The Elliott 920 programming system will contain ALGOL, CORAL and the CORAL subset known as CORALette.' By way of explaining the relationship between some of these languages, the Report gives the following comparison of main memory requirements for various languages when running on an Elliott 920 computer:

JOVIAL, an offshoot of Algol	32K words
CORAL, (Computer On-line Radar Applications Language)	16K words
CORALette, Elliott's subset of CORAL	8K words

Finally, looking ahead to period 1966–1968, Borehamwood does not seem to have fully utilised the Elliott 4100 series' architectural features in the development of forward-looking, multi-user, operating systems. Specifically, the Elliott 4130 computer found favour with several UK universities, as described below. At the end of the 1960s the on-line use of terminals was beginning to catch on. Nevertheless, at first neither Elliott nor its successor ICL offered a 4100 series operating system that met the needs of universities trying for the first time to teach computer programming to large classes of students. The Elliott 4130's hardware assistance for multiprogramming environments, described in Appendix 7, appears not to have been used by the manufacturer's system software before a group at the University of Kent used it to implement the Kent On-line System, KOS, in 1971 [58]. KOS allowed both on-line terminals and batch jobs to run concurrently. Appendix 7 cites the names of several other universities that adopted KOS for use with their 4130 computers.

8.6 Defence Applications

This chapter's account of Elliott computer software and applications has thus far omitted mention of military and aerospace applications. The exciting, and ultimately longer-lasting, story of airborne computing and avionics is recounted in full in Chap. 12. An Elliott-Automation Airborne Computing Division was originally established in 1959/1960 at Borehamwood. By 1962 Rochester had become the headquarters for Elliott Flight Automation and between that date and 1969 the focus of airborne computer developments gradually moved away from Borehamwood to Rochester.

After 1968, of course, the airborne computing activity was pursued under the GEC umbrella though, interestingly, the name *Elliott* was used on products until about 1988. At Rochester, Elliott Flight Automation Ltd. became Marconi-Elliott Avionics Systems Ltd. in 1969, then Marconi Avionics Ltd. in about 1978, then GEC Avionics Ltd. in 1984, then GEC-Marconi Avionics Ltd. in 1993, and then BAE Systems in 1999. Digital hardware and software is still very much part of Rochester's interests at the time of writing (2010).

8.6.1   Ground-Based Air Defence

Back in the 1950s Borehamwood, and later also Frimley in Surrey, were the locations for Elliott-Automation computer projects in ground-based air defence and in army gunnery. Army applications are covered later, in Sect. 8.6.2. Before describing these, we firstly focus on the RAF.

Simple experiments in fighter interception control for the RAF were first conducted by Borehamwood in July 1957, using telephone landlines connecting facilities at the Central Fighter Establishment at West Raynham, Norfolk, to an Elliott 402 at Borehamwood [59]. The demonstration involved an English Electric Lightning supersonic fighter. The project gained momentum with the arrival of Laurie Payne and Keith Oughton, who left the Decca company and joined Borehamwood when Decca cancelled its own computer project for the RAF's *Linesman* air defence system. (*Linesman* was the name of a major and long-standing UK air defence system whose development spanned many years [60].) At Borehamwood, Payne, Oughton and others developed the Elliott-Automation

Fig. 8.9 In autumn 1967, an Elliott 4130 was due to be installed at the Institut Blaise Pascal's new Institut de Programmation (IP) building at Orsay, south of Paris (in the event, the computer went to a new faculty building at Quai Saint-Bernard, Paris). This Asterix-type cartoon was drawn by Bernard Robinet, then a student at the IP. The caption, when translated, reads: *'Say, Algorithmix, you will let me use it, won't you?'* – *'Yes, Technologix, but don't dismount the peripherals!'* The reference to 'dismounting' relates to magnetic tape reels and exchangeable disc packs. Notice that Asterix's flask contains the magic potion *Algol*

Fire Brigade system [61]. This provided computer-aided control of fighter interception and surface-to-air missile deployment. The first versions were implemented with Elliott 803 computers, each 803 being able to control three aircraft. At the time, the RAF was calling for a total capability of about 100 aircraft [62] in the defence of the UK during the Cold War.

From about 1963, a new version of *Fire Brigade* went into service [61]. This was based on the Elliott 920 computer, also called the MCS 920 where MCS signified Elliott-Automation's Mobile Computing Systems Division based at Frimley. Each 920 could handle 12 aircraft. A basic 12-target *Fire Brigade* system

Fig. 8.10 Operators at RAF Patrington near Hull (now RAF Holmpton) at a radar control desk as part of the Fire Brigade air defence system in the mid-1960s. Elliott computers, firstly the 803 and then the 920, provided Fire Brigade's computer-aided control of fighter interception and surface-to-air missile deployment

incorporating the MCS920 was said to cost £120,000 in 1964 [63]. The *Fire Brigade* systems, which remained in service until about 1972, initially commended themselves to NATO air defence organisations on account of being modular, using standard off-the-shelf computers, and being relatively cheap and easy to install.

Air defence is naturally intimately connected with radar developments. An account of Elliott's radar activities after the departure of John Coales is given in Chap. 11. In about 1960 the computing and radar divisions of Elliott-Automation became involved with the Royal Radar Establishment (RRE), Malvern, and other firms such as the Automatic Telephone and Electric Company of Liverpool (later part of the Plessey Group) in a classified real-time, on-line data-processing application. This was most probably part of the *Linesman* proposals mentioned above. Borehamwood designed the high-speed Elliott 502 computer to meet the stringent challenges of real-time response implied by the *Linesman* air defence proposals. The Elliott 502 was so named because it was at first conceived as a successor to the Elliott 402; neither its architecture nor its software had much connection with the later Elliott 503. It is believed that the first Elliott 502, delivered in 1963, was the core of the *Linesman* SIMULATOR X project at RRE Malvern. More details of the 502 computer will be found in Appendix 5. General comments on Elliott's air defence applications from 1962 to 1969, including SIMULATOR X and SIMULATOR M, are given in [64].

8.6.2 *Artillery Control for the Army*

This sector of military computer applications saw the birth of the successful Elliott 900 series machines, which were later to be taken to even greater heights, so to speak, by the Airborne Computing Division in the late 1960s and 1970s. The origins of the 900 series go back to about 1960 or 1961. John Bunt, who was intimately connected with the development, recalls the birth [65].

'The origin of the 900 series lay in a development contract for a tank-borne gun fire control computer, placed with our company at Frimley, by the West German Government. The development work was carried out by my team at Borehamwood and was the reason for setting up the Mobile Computing Division.

'Jim Barrow, who I had worked with years before on the 152 project, joined us as Chief Engineer and he was largely responsible for the circuit design and for the packaging. I think that the computer was the 901 (although 902 is possible). It had a fixed store for the programme, wired on ferrite cores and a small core store for the working space. It used parallel arithmetic. Although the development was completed the army's tank did not go into production, so the 901 (or 902) was a one-off. The importance of this contract was that some of the technology was applied to a general purpose computer, the 920A which was also built into a cast iron casing and forced air cooled.

'The Royal Artillery were interested in Gun Fire Control [initially using the American-designed FADAC] and bought a system to evaluate in 1959. I remember standing at Larkhill, the Royal Artillery's establishment on Salisbury Plain, with the guns nine miles behind me and the target one mile in front. The NCOs were suitably protected in a dugout, but I and the officers stood on an elevated mound for good visibility, while shells whistled overhead. The shoot was successful apart from one round which landed in the vicarage garden and did nothing to improve the standing of the Royal Artillery with the Church of England.

'Part of the [Elliott] development work was to prove that the 18 bit computer could produce a sufficiently accurate calculation. The trajectory was calculated using double-length arithmetic and 18 bits was shown to be quite adequate. The R.A. decided against the cast iron casing and decided to opt for a lighter weight casing which became the 920 B. The development work and proving trials were monitored by RARDE [the Royal Army Research and Development Establishment at Fort Halstead] at Sevenoaks in Kent. The first production order was for 76 computers and received widespread press publicity [see below]. The development work on the 900 series was financed entirely by the [Elliott] company.

'Development work, under Jim Barrow continued in order to produce a miniature version of the 920 using integrated circuits and once again a ferrite core store. All the joints were welded for reliability. This was called the 920M and was adopted for the Jaguar Aircraft and by ELDO for the rockets which they launched from French Guiana. The ELDO trials were generally successful, but one rocket did veer off course. It turned out that the computer had switched off before the satellite had

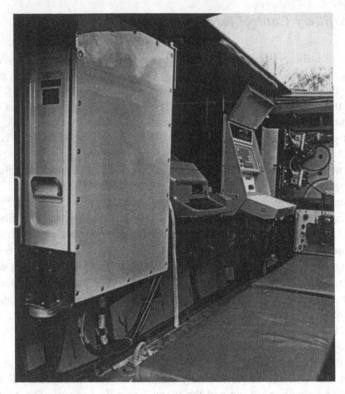

Fig. 8.11 The inside of a battery command post vehicle, with an Elliott 920B computer in the left foreground. The FACE (Field Artillery Computer Equipment) control console is towards the far end of the bench seat. Elliott Space and Weapon Automation Ltd. received the first order for 76 FACE systems in 1967

been put into orbit. This was the result of a lightning strike. The computer was cleared of blame as the specification to which we were working had required it to shut down in such an eventuality.'

The production equipment for gun control for the British army was called FACE: Field Artillery Computer Equipment [66], based on the Elliott 920B computer. FACE equipment was carried either in FV432 tracked battery command-post vehicles (see Figs. 8.11 and 8.12) or in Land Rovers. A compatible survey computing centre using an Elliott 920B was mounted in six-wheeled Saracen FV610 vehicles. Both systems communicated with the 920B-based AMETS portable meteorological station. Together, the three components could be used to control a variety of self-propelled guns, ranging from 175 mm heavy artillery to 105 mm howitzers. Elliott Space and Weapon Automation Ltd. received the first order for 76 FACE systems in about 1967. At the time this was believed to be, numerically, the largest single order for computers ever placed outside the USA [66].

Fig. 8.12 Looking down into the FACE command vehicle, as the soldier on the right enters numerical data into the computer. The console can control up to ten remote guns

8.7 Computers in Education

Until the late 1950s, the provision of generally available computing facilities in British universities was sparse. For those institutions that did equip themselves, the emphasis was on science and engineering applications – the main academic areas keen to adopt digital computing. The University of Cambridge used its in-house designed EDSAC I computer from 1949 and then EDSAC II from 1957. Manchester University had the Ferranti Mark I from 1951 and then the Ferranti Mercury from 1957. London University installed a Mercury computer in 1958. These were all, in their time, large and powerful machines and London and Manchester were to continue to equip themselves with the latest large computers, starting with the Ferranti Atlas in 1962 and 1964 respectively. Cambridge was not far behind with Titan, an Atlas variant giving service there from 1963. Edinburgh University installed an ICL 4/75 computer in September 1968, thereby establishing the Edinburgh Regional Computing Centre. This took its place alongside the London and Manchester Regional Computing Centres to become the UK's three regional providers of powerful computing resources for higher education from the end of the 1960s onwards.

The remaining UK universities were not so well equipped. The Elliott 803 was the first Borehamwood-designed computer to recommend itself to the smaller universities because of its relatively low cost at the time. Starting with a delivery to Brunel College of Technology, west London, in 1961, a total of 33 Elliott 803 computers had been installed in 24 UK and 9 overseas universities and colleges by 1966 (see delivery lists in Appendix 8). An Elliott 503 was installed at Bristol University in 1964 and another at Battersea College of Technology in the following year. But by 1965, the new Elliott 4100 series was being demonstrated to customers and this was clearly going to be of greater interest to higher education institutes.

In the autumn of 1965, the Flowers Report [67], which assessed the future computer requirements of UK universities, made its findings known. The Flowers Committee suggested upgrading one Elliott 803 site (Hull) and one Elliott 503 site (Bristol), and recommended the installation of new Elliott computers (mostly the 4100 series) at the following universities: Aberystwyth, Bangor, Brunel, Cardiff, Durham, Hull, Leicester, Warwick, York. No complete records of Elliott 4100 series computer sales have come to light but the following additional universities are believed to have taken delivery of 4100 computers in the period up to 1970, latterly under the ICL banner [68]: Aberdeen, Dundee, Edinburgh, Exeter, Heriot-Watt, Keele, Kent, Kings College London, Reading, Stirling, Sussex. Most of these machines were the 4130 variety and they gave an institution-wide computing service. A few, in contrast, were for dedicated Departmental use – as was the case with the Elliott 4120 installed in 1966 in Professor Donald Michie's Department of Machine Intelligence and Perception at Edinburgh University. This department had begun life as the Experimental Programming Unit in January 1965 and had changed its name in October 1966 [69].

A full account of the Flowers Report recommendations cannot be given here. Suffice it to say that Flowers showed that UK computer manufacturers were no longer able to satisfy the top-end requirements for very powerful machines and that, at the lower end of the spectrum, Elliott machines were considered appropriate for many institutions.

In the arena of further (as opposed to higher) education, polytechnics and colleges that installed Elliott 4100 systems are believed to have included Dundee Technical College, Northern Polytechnic, Huddersfield College of Technology, Napier College (Edinburgh), Robert Gordon's Institute (Aberdeen) and Kingston College of Technology [68, 70, 71].

Turning to schools, early use was sometimes obtained either via limited access to the facilities of larger organizations located nearby or by 'gifts' of second-hand computers. An example of the former is provided by Hatfield School in Hertfordshire, which was set up in the late 1950s as a state school with a deliberate bias towards science and technology. This bias was motivated by the nearby presence of the De Havilland aircraft factory which had also been a factor in the establishment of Hatfield New Town and Hatfield College of Technology (later Hatfield Polytechnic and now the Hatfield campus of the University of Hertfordshire). As a former pupil of the school remembers [72], the school shared the same campus as the Technical College and was housed in a connected building. A limited amount of sharing of facilities occurred between the school and the college, an innovative example arising when the college installed its first computer, an Elliott 803, in 1963. School pupils had limited access, about 2 h per week, and wrote programs using Elliott Autocode and Algol.

An example of the gift scenario is provided by Forest Grammar School, Winersh, Berkshire, which in 1965 or 1966 obtained an Elliott 405 that had first been delivered in September 1959 to Crosse and Blackwell, the food suppliers. Steve Gilbey, a pupil at the time, says [73] that he 'clearly remembers weekend trips to Crosse and Blackwell's offices in London (Soho Square) to dismantle it and I also recall the various printouts we acquired with [the 405] listing cases of baked beans and so on. I vaguely remember that we cannibalised another 405 for spare parts ....' The cannibalised machine was the Elliott 405 first delivered to Siemens at Woolwich in April 1958, then passed to Cambridge University in February 1962 and finally donated to Forest Grammar School in August 1966.

Forest Grammar School's computer was featured in a BBC *Tomorrows World* programme first broadcast on 5 February 1969 [74]. The 7-min film sequence shows boys operating and helping to maintain the Elliott 405, doing everything from switching on the motor-alternator set, to using a CRO to monitor logic signals, changing a delay-line package, and playing the game of noughts-and-crosses interactively. Junior boys are shown in a classroom, acting out register-to-register binary arithmetic and we hear from a senior boy who had written a special programming language called *Minigol.* The computer, which the school called *Nellie,* was said to have a mean time between faults of 12 h. Watching this film clip, which is available on the BBC's website, gives a fascinating – some may say scary – insight into the inspirational and pioneering work of dedicated teachers in the years before personal computers arrived.

Few schools could afford to install new computers in the 1960s, even if they had staff keen enough to organise the facilities. It was not until 1978 that the BBC initiated its *Computer Literacy* project, followed by the specification of the BBC Micro in 1980. The first IBM Personal Computer (PC) was launched in America in August 1981. Computers were not commonly present in most UK schools until the mid-1980s.

As far as Borehamwood was concerned, the announcement of the Elliott 903 in mid-1965 at a basic price of about £12,750 opened up wide educational possibilities. Rob Gordon, who joined Elliott's Educational Computing Division in September 1965, recalls [70] that: 'Elliott-Automation must be applauded for having the foresight at such an early stage to see the need to get computers into schools and smaller technical colleges. Today all schools have their IT facilities but 45 years ago computers were alien to teachers ... As it turned out, the venture was somewhat premature to reap real rewards in terms of volume sales from a market that was some years from maturity. However, there was one notable user at the Royal Liberty School in Romford. Bill Broderick, a teacher of mathematics, was the enthusiast who reflected Elliott's wish to expose young people to computers at a very early age. The school had a 903 installed [in mid-1966 – see Fig. 8.13]. I am unable to set out the other successes at school level but I do recall a 903 being taken to Eton College and Martin Clinton [Elliott's Sales Manager] giving a presentation there [late in 1966], which I believe came to nothing.'

The Royal Liberty School's Wikipedia entry in 2009 stated enthusiastically that 'Royal Liberty was the first school in Europe to install an electronic computer' – probably not quite true but certainly very close to the mark. The first computer to

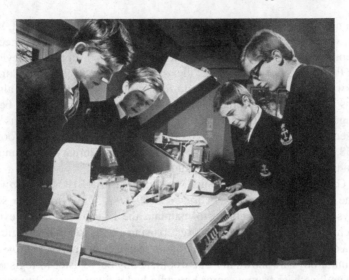

Fig. 8.13 The Royal Liberty School in Romford, Essex, installed an Elliott 903 computer in 1966. The photo shows the 903's paper tape input/output equipment. The Royal Liberty School is believed to have been the first British school to have bought a new computer, though Forest Grammar School, Winersh, Berkshire, had been given a second-hand Elliott 405 about a year earlier

be installed at Eton College, in 1969, was indeed an Elliott 903. Professor J. Kolbuszewski, head of the Department of Transport & Environmental Planning at the University of Birmingham, arranged for an Elliott 903 to be supplied 'at the advantageous price of £9,000' [75]. Professor Kolbuszewski's department at Birmingham had developed a software applications package for the 903 [76]; his son was at Eton College.

Deliveries of the 903 commenced in mid-1966, so the Royal Liberty School must have been amongst the first customers. From late 1966, Elliott-Automation equipped a large Bedford van with a generator and an Elliott 903 as a mobile classroom. It was big enough to cope with quite a large group of people so could be used to support on-site courses and demonstrations. Roger Cook remembers [12] that 'the plan was for these [903s] to be sold to primary/junior schools. We spent nearly a fortnight touring Europe with two 903s in a van demonstrating to education establishments.' Before the 903 was available, sales staff needing a mobile demonstration had made use of an Elliott 920 (the military version of the 903) in a Land Rover.

8.8   Last Days: A Plethora of (On-line) Applications

In 1966, by which time the Borehamwood software group 'had recovered from the 503 disaster', the Elliott 800 series, 900 series and 4100 series computers had been launched and were selling well. All these machines were smaller than the 503 and, in consequence, addressed different markets. For many customers, typical applications still involved the running of single programs at a time, using input/output equipment of limited throughput. There was therefore little call for Borehamwood to design complex operating systems for the 800, 900 and 4100 machines – though in certain areas such as academia the need did arise, as mentioned earlier. On the other hand, Elliott's continuing sale of 800 and 900 series computers, and their ARCH derivatives for industrial process control, did create a requirement for a different kind of systems software. In many on-line control applications, there was a need to respond in real time to many tens, and sometimes hundreds, of input/output signals. In the early days of industrial automation, each new application called for dedicated, bespoke, software – not all of which was written at Borehamwood. Besides the Elliott-Automation sites at Lewisham, Willesden, Park Royal and Greenwich, outsourcing to software houses such as Vaughan Programming Services was introduced. This is discussed in Chap. 7.

Returning to more general topics, software staff at Borehamwood continued to be involved in applications programming, selling existing computers and helping to specify future products and instruction sets. Roger Cook has told of intense activity, ranging from demonstrations to schools to the development of the Elliott graphical output unit (see Chap. 10) to the specification of new computer systems. In particular, Roger Cook recalls the birth of the Elliott 4100 series as follows.

'I remember taking a week off [in about 1963/4] to specify the 4100. The result was implemented in both the 4120 and 4130 machines. A proposal for a high speed 4150 was presented at a later date to all scientific and university establishments via a travelling road show for which we had, for once, taken professional guidance in preparation and presentation techniques. We carried our own spotlights, chairs and stands to each location. The 4100 was to be offered to NCR as well as to be marketed directly by Elliotts. It included a couple of instructions to ease packing and unpacking of characters to words and instructions to help the implementation of stacks [see Appendix 7].

'NCR and Elliotts were very different companies. I remember discussing with them pre- delivery testing; they suggested a period of 2 years intensive proving – we, I think, were talking in terms of one month. They specified an assembler to be delivered on 1st May: I had a sense of elation as I handed it over on 30th April. A number of 4130s were sold shortly before the take over of Elliotts by English Electric. I become the sales manager for ex-Elliott equipment and we concluded a bulk deal for 4130s shortly after. The ex-Elliott sales value in the first 3 months exceeded the total English Electric sales.

'The day of the announcement of the English Electric takeover [June 1967 – see Chap. 13] I was with Andrew St Johnston in Brighton selling the idea of computers in public libraries. We had, I think, just arrived when there was an urgent call for Andrew to return immediately. We were all told the news the following morning.'

In the next chapter we recount the full story of the link between Borehamwood and NCR and the efforts of Elliott-Automation to address the data-processing requirements of business and commerce.

References

1. Hersom SE (2002), Nicholas, the forgotten Elliott Project. Resurrection the Bulletin of the Computer Conservation Society, Issue number 27, spring 2002, pp:10–14
2. Felton GE (2006) Getting the job done. Resurrection Summer(38), http://www.cs.man.ac.uk/CCS/res/res38.htm#e
3. Felton GE (1953) Programming Nicholas. Borehamwood Internal Research Report M12, 6 July 1953
4. Hill ND (1953) Nicholas. In: Proceedings of the NPL symposium on automatic digital computers, pp 44–45, HMSO, 1954
5. Hersom SE (1965) Operating experience with Nicholas. Proc IEE 103(Part B 1–3):276–277
6. SE Hersom (2000) Nicholas: reminiscences. Typewritten document sent to Simon Lavington, Jan 2000
7. Campbell-Kelly M (1982) The development of computer programming in Britain (1945–1955). Ann Hist Comput 4(2):121–139
8. SE Hersom (2002) E-mail exchanges with Simon Lavington over the period 24 Aug 1999 to 17 Apr 2002. Ed Hersom died later that year
9. Rose BM (1953) Trajectory calculations for Red Cheeks. Borehamwood Internal Research Report number 328, 27 Aug 1953
10. Wilkes MV, Wheeler DJ, Gill S. The preparation of programs for an electronic digital computer. Addison-Wesley, 1951 (1st ed.); 1957 (2nd ed.). See also: Campbell-Kelly M, Programming the EDSAC: early programming activity at the University of Cambridge. IEEE Ann Hist Comput 20(4), Oct 1998, pp 46–67
11. Lavington SH (2009) An appreciation of Dina St Johnston, 1930–2007, founder of the UK's First Software House. Comput J 52(3):378–387
12. Roger Cook, Letter to SLH Clarke dated 4 Feb 1995, augmented by various e-mails to Simon Lavington in Aug and Sept 2007
13. In 1928 John Coales was a co-founder of the group of English Country Dancers called the Cambridge Round. After the War, Coales hosted groups of ex-Cambridge dancers at Oakwood, his large house at Radlett, beginning in August in 1947 and subsequently at various times through to 1952, http://www.srcf.ucam.org/round/history/coales for a history of the Cambridge University Morris Dancing group
14. Laurence Clarke (2009), E-mail to Simon Lavington dated 14 Oct 2009
15. The following Borehamwood Internal Research Reports are relevant to the Elliott 152's glass printed-circuits: (a) Johnston DL (1949) Glass printed circuit units (report 142B, 16 Oct 1949); (b) Johnston DL and Chitty JA (1950) Pilot production of printed circuit units (report 173, 26 Apr 1950); (c) Johnston DL (1950) Estimated cost of production for printed circuit units (report 196B, 1 May 1950)
16. Owen CE (1952) Three standard circuits for serial digital computers. Borehamwood internal report no. 301, 2 Sept 1952
17. Pierre-E Mounier-Kuhn (CNRS & Centre de recherches en Histoire de l'Innovation Université Paris-Sorbonne): E-mails to Simon Lavington, Nov 2008
18. Pau King, E-mail to Simon Lavington, 27 Aug 2007
19. The Zuse Z5 computer is described at: http://user.cs.tu-berlin.de/~zuse/Konrad_Zuse/en/rechner_z5.html
20. First in automation. Brochure published by Elliott Automation Ltd., first edition (43 pages) dated June 1958
21. St Johnston A, Clarke SLH (1957) The development of a business computer system. Presented at the Convention on electronics in automation, Cambridge, 27 June 1957. Published in the J Br IRE 17(July):351–364
22. DJ Pentecost has collected some example Elliott 400 series programs for the Computer Conservation Society's Our computer heritage project, http://www.ourcomputerheritage.org/wp/upload/CCS-E2X4.pdf

23. Everitt G (2006) Making money while the world slept Computer Resurrection, the Bulletin of the Computer Conservation Society, Issue number 37, spring 2006, http://www.cs.man.ac.uk/CCS/res/res37.htm
24. St Johnston A, Clarke SLH (1954) Applications of a high-speed electronic computer to a business-accounting problem. J Br IRE 14:293–302
25. Hendry J (1990) Innovating for failure: government policy and the early British computer industry. MIT Press, Cambridge. ISBN: 0-262-08187-3
26. Claydon R (1996) Early computer developments at EMI. Resurrection, the Bulletin of the Computer Conservation Society, Issue number 16, Christmas 1996
27. EMIDEC Computer News, issue 1. Undated but one can deduce from the contents that it was published at the very end of 1960 or in Jan 1961, http://www.iansmith.myzen.co.uk/emidec/emipicbr.pdf
28. Bird, Raymond (Dickie) (1999) BTM's first steps into computing. Resurrection, the Bulletin of the Computer Conservation Society, Issue number 22, spring 1999 http://www.cs.man.ac.uk/CCS/res/res22.htm#c
29. Gerry Mills (2009) E-mails to Simon Lavington, Sept 2008 to Jan 2009
30. David Pentecost (2008) E-mail to Simon Lavington, Sept 2008
31. Article in the Financial Times, 3 May 1957, as Part 12 of a series on the Modern British Factory
32. Peter Lawrence (2001) E-mail to Simon Lavington dated 3 Dec 2001
33. List of Elliott-Automation companies, taken from the booklet *Reports and Accounts for the year ended 31st December 1964* as presented at the Annual General Meeting held on 24 June 1965
34. (a) Anon (1960) 803 autocode specification, July 1960 (this document appears in a typed list of Borehamwood technical documents in the possession of Laurie Bental. No further details have yet come to light); (b) Anon (1962) A specification of the mark 3 autocode for the 803 electronic digital computer, July 1962
35. The original BASIC language was designed in 1963 by Kemeny JG and Kurtz TE at Dartmouth College, New Hampshire, USA. It was released in 1964. BASIC is an acronym for Beginner's All-purpose Symbolic Instruction Code, http://en.wikipedia.org/wiki/BASIC_programming_language
36. Brooker RA (1955) An attempt to simplify coding for the Manchester electronic computer. Br J Appl Phys 6:307–311
37. Clarke B, Felton GE (1959) The Pegasus autocode. Comput J 1(4):192–195
38. Brooker RA, Rohl JS, Clark SR (1965) The main features of the Atlas autocode. Comput J 8:303–310
39. CAR Hoare (2008) E-mail to Simon Lavington dated 20 May 2008
40. Dijkstra EW (1980) A programmer's early memories. In: Metropolis N, Howlett J, Gian-Carlo R (eds) A history of computing in the twentieth century: a collection of essays. Academic, New York, pp 563–573, See also: Document EWD 1166, From my Life, at: www.cs.utexas.edu/users/EWD/
41. For an overview of the Dutch Electrologica EL-X1 computer, http://en.wikipedia.org/wiki/Electrologica_X1
42. Dijkstra E, Letter catalogued as document EWD 1287 in the University of Texas' Dijkstra Archive, www.cs.utexas.edu/users/EWD/
43. A good biographical summary for Tony Hoare will be found at www.research.microsoft.com/users/thoare/
44. Hoare CAR (2009) My early days at Elliotts. Resurrection, the Bulletin of the Computer Conservation Society, Issue number 48, Autumn 2009, pp:21–29
45. (a) Hoare CAR (1961) Algorithm 64, Quicksort. Commun ACM 4(7):321–322; (b) Hoare CAR (1962) Quicksort. Comp J 5(1):10–15
46. (a) Hoare CAR (1962) Report on the Elliott ALGOL translator. Comput J 5(2):127–129; (b) Hoare CAR (1963) The Elliott ALGOL input/output system. Comput J 5(4):345–348; (c) Hoare CAR (1964) The Elliott ALGOL programming system. In: Wegner P (ed) Introduction to systems programming. Academic Press, New York, pp 156–166

47. Hoare CAR (1981) The emperor's old clothes. Commun ACM 24(2):75 – 83. This is Hoare's *Turing Award* paper

48. Shell DL (1959) A high-speed sorting procedure. Commun ACM 2(7):30–32

49. Randell B (2010) Presentation at the joint seminar of the BCS Advanced Programming Group and the Computer Conservation Society to celebrate the 50th anniversary of Algol. Science Museum, London, 14 Jan 2010

50. Peter Chinn (2002) Letter to Terry Froggatt dated 4 Jan 2002

51. (a) ECMA: European Computer Manufacturers Association: Memento 1964 (a 38-page official historical and organisational document), http://www.ecma-international.org/publications/files/ECMA-MEMENTOS/Ecma%20memento%201964%20public.pdf; (b) For a modern summary, http://en.wikipedia.org/wiki/Ecma_International

52. Hoare CAR (1973) Hints on programming language design. Stanford Artificial Intelligence Laboratory, Memo AIM-224: STAN-CS-73-403, Dec 1973. Written whilst Tony Hoare was on leave of absence from Queen's University, Belfast, http://www.eecs.umich.edu/~bchandra/courses/papers/Hoare_Hints.pdf

53. Cook RL (1960) Time-sharing on the National-Elliott 802. Comput J 2(4):185–188

54. Pau King (2009) E-mail to Simon Lavington dated, 18 Jan 2009

55. Gerald Everitt (2007) E-mail to Simon Lavington dated 23 Aug 2007

56. Kilburn T, Howarth DJ, Payne RB, Sumner FH (1961) The Manchester University Atlas operating system: Part 1, Internal organization. Comput J 4(3):222–225 (Part 2: User description, Comput J 4(3) 1961, pp 226–229)

57. Anon, Mini Firebrigade and programming languages. 12-page typed report published by Elliott Airspace Control Division. Undated, but the contents strongly suggest 1965

58. Brown PJ (July 1971) The Kent on-line system. Software Pract Experience 1(3):269–277

59. Anon, A practical demonstration of a method of recovering and marshalling aircraft, assisted by the electronic computer. Small, three-page leaflet giving the programme of events and a photograph of an Elliott 402 computer. Leaflet dated July 1957

60. See: http://en.wikipedia.org/wiki/Linesman/Mediator

61. (a) Anon (1961) Fire-brigade: air defence control. 22-page pre-sales brochure, published September 1961 by Elliott Brothers (London) Ltd., Borehamwood. Document number SCP2; (b) Anon (1963) *Fire-Brigade: Elliott Air Defence System,* a 15-page brochure published in May 1963 by the Aircraft Direction Division, Borehamwood

62. SLH Clarke (2007) Meeting with Simon Lavington, 7 June 2007

63. (a) Flight International, 2 Jan 1964, p 3; (b) Flight International, 3 June 1965, p 891

64. Mike Cochrane. Summary of Elliott projects developed between 1962 and 1969. Three-page typed manuscript, with two-page typed accompanying letter to Simon Lavington dated 9 Feb 2002. Mike Cochrane worked on air defence applications for Elliott's Airspace Control Division (originally Aircraft Direction Division) from mid-1962 to late-1969

65. John Bunt (2001) Eight-page typed letter sent to Simon Lavington, dated 11 Dec 2001

66. Anon, FACE: Field artillery computer equipment. Seven-page illustrated brochure produced by Elliott Space and Weapon Automation Ltd., Chobham Road, Frimley, Surrey. Undated, but most probably some time between 1963 and 1967

67. Report of the Flowers Committee on the Computer requirements of Universities and Research Councils. Published Jan 1966, London, HMSO, Cmnd 2883, http://www.chilton-computing. org.uk/acl/literature/manuals/flowers/foreword.htm (The Flowers Working Group was set up in March 1965. The date of the Report was 14 June 1965)

68. RG Wilson (2009) E-mail to Simon Lavington dated 7 Jan 2009. Ron Wilson joined Elliott-Automation as a graduate trainee in the autumn of 1962. In Sept 1964 he joined Elliotts' Scientific Computing Division (SCD) as a sales engineer, based at Elliotts' Manchester area offices in Bramhall, Cheshire. In Jan 1966 he moved to Glasgow. He transferred, with E-A and EE sales staff, to ICL in May 1968

69. Howe J (2007) Artificial intelligence at Edinburgh University: a perspective. Revised June 2007, http://www.aiai.ed.ac.uk/events/edcomphistory2007/AIhistory.htm

70. Gordon R, Rob Gordon's recollections. Four-page manuscript dated 4 Feb 2009. Rob joined the Educational Computing Division (sales section) at Borehamwood at the end of Sept 1965, transferring to be a lecturer at Borehamwood in late 1966. In 1968 he joined EECL's much larger education and training department and was based at Radley House in Ealing. Later that year EECL and ICT merged to form ICL. Rob continued to work for the company in various roles over the following 30 years (including a return to front line sales from 1977 to 1983) until his retirement on 31 Dec 1998
71. Anon (1967) Elliott automation: computers and orders, 1947–1966. Brochure published in early 1967 by the Directorate of Information Services, Elliott-Automation Ltd., 21 Portland Place, London W1
72. Professor Peter S Excell (2000) A pioneer initiative in school computing. Five-page typewritten manuscript sent to Simon Lavington with a covering letter dated 13 Jan 2000
73. Steve Gilbey (2005) E-mail to Simon Lavington dated 13 Sept 2005
74. Seven-minute film clip, first broadcast on 5 Feb 1969, in the BBC's *Tomorrow's World* series, http://www.bbc.co.uk/archive/tomorrowsworld/8008.shtml
75. See the Minutes of Provost and Fellows, Eton College, Dec 1969. There are also three letters relating to this purchase: COLL/P10/33/57
76. Beilby MH (1970) Manual of Workshop system. 40-page booklet published in 1970 by Marconi-Elliott Computer Systems Ltd., Borehamwood. Issue 1, ESD, 5/70. Workshop was a formula-evaluation program, developed by Beilby MH in the Department of Transportation and Environmental Planning, University of Birmingham, Birmingham

Chapter 9
NCR, the 405 and Commercial Data Processing

9.1 Early Commercial Applications of the Elliott 405

The first investigation into the possibility of applying an Elliott 402 computer to commercial data processing was published in 1954 (see [1]). There then appear to have been at least two events that persuaded Borehamwood that the 402 was not, after all, a suitable architecture for business applications and that new, specially designed, hardware would be required [2]. The first event was Andrew St Johnston's unsuccessful attempt to sell an Elliott 402 to the Mars confectionary company. During this exercise, it was realised that the transfer of large amounts of data was a critical issue and that the 402 was not up to this task. The second event was the approach to Borehamwood in May 1954 by the Long Range Weapons Establishment (LRWE), who urgently needed a computer that was also required to deal with very large volumes of data. LRWE awarded Borehamwood a contract for a one-off Elliott 403 computer, also known as WREDAC (see Chap. 3), which was delivered to Salisbury, Australia, in the autumn of 1955 to support the Woomera rocket range. WREDAC, and its bulk data output unit WREDOC, became the spur for the design of a new Elliott 405 computer.

The 405 contained autonomous units able to perform a range of Input/Output operations on bulk data, including character conversion, currency conversion (pounds, shillings and pence) and on-the-fly searching. A fuller description of the architecture of the Elliott 405 is given in Appendix 3. The first Elliott 405 was installed at Borehamwood in July 1956, where it became a computing service and software development resource. The 405 actually struggled to cope with extremely large volumes of commercial bulk data, as is illustrated by the comparison with the IBM 705 given in Appendix 3.

In 1955, when Norman Hill recruited a team of six people to work towards selling Elliott computers to scientific and commercial organisations, the starting-point was usually feasibility studies for prospective customers. The challenge was to demonstrate potential advantages to managers who had probably had no previous contact with, or knowledge of, digital computers. In Table 9.1, we give the titles of the feasibility studies for the Elliott 405 computer, as published in the form of Borehamwood S-series Internal Reports between the autumn of 1955 and the spring

S. Lavington, *Moving Targets*, History of Computing,
DOI 10.1007/978-1-84882-933-6_9, © Springer-Verlag London Limited 2011

Table 9.1 Borehamwood feasibility studies of data-processing applications, autumn 1955 to spring 1957

Title of Borehamwood S-Series Report	Date	405 Delivery?
Legal and General Assurance Society	9/8/55	Oct. 58
Parts Division, Ford Motor Co., data processing	31/10/55	–
Agricultural census, Inst. Nat. Statistique/Economiques	–/10/55	–
Brit. Insulated Callender's Cables, centralised accounting	11/11/55	Feb. 58
National Gas Turbine Establishment, test data	16/11/55	Sept. 57
Unilever Group of Companies, centralised accounting	9/12/55	Nov. 57
Colgate-Palmolive Ltd., data processing	28/12/55	–
(a spare parts supply organisation, data processing)	5/1/56	–
Littlewood Mail Order, pilot data-processing scheme II	13/2/56	Feb. 58
Mercantile Credit Co., data processing	12/3/56	–
Yarrow & Co. Ltd., engineering and accounting departments	15/3/56	–
Post Office, London area, centralised accounting	12/4/56	Dec. 58 & 59
Group Life and Pension schemes, administration	5/5/56	–
Midland Counties Diary Ltd., data processing	22/5/56	–
Stewart & Lloyds Ltd., payroll accounting	23/5/56	–
A stockbroker's office	15/6/56	–
Courtaulds Ltd., centralised accounting	15/6/56	May 59
Radio Rentals Ltd., maintenance of subscribers' accounts	20/6/56	–
British Extracting Co. Ltd., sales office procedures	6/6/56	–
H.M. Customs and Excise, overseas trade statistics	25/6/56	–
North Thames Gas Board, coke order processing	12/7/56	–
Austin Motor. Company Ltd., data processing	17/7/56	–
United Africa Co. Ltd., mercantile trading activities	25/7/56	–
North Western Gas Board, customer accounting	(Undated)	Oct. 58
A stockbroker's office	24/8/56	–
Messrs. A.C. Nielson Co. Ltd., Oxford, statistical work	30/8/56	–
Richardsons Westgarth Group of Cos, production control	17/9/56	–
South African National Life Assurance Co.	17/9/56	–
North Western Electricity Board, energy accounts	2/10/56	–
British European Airways, electronic inventory system	25/1/57	–
Messrs. Newton Chambers Ltd.	8/1/57	May 58
Messrs. J Sainsbury Ltd., branch stock control and ordering	24/1/57	–
Hertfordshire County Council, payroll and budgetary control	27/2/57	–
Govt. of New Zealand, salaries and treasury accounting	3/3/57	–

of 1957. In the final column of Table 9.1 is a note indicating the resulting sale of an Elliott 405 computer, if any, to the organisation featured in the corresponding earlier feasibility study.

An analysis of authorship of the Borehamwood S-series Reports in Table 9.1 indicates that the following programmers were, in the order of their involvement, the principal staff concerned with these Elliott 405 marketing activities: H L S (Henry) Orde, A J (Albert) Wakefield, Patrick Shackleton, A N (Dina) Vaughan, A D (Doug) Honeyman, D M (Des) Preston, R G (Gerry) Mills, J W Cox and A J Burton.

As a back-up to feasibility studies, a company considering purchasing, or actually buying, an Elliott 402 or 405 computer would normally send two or three of its own staff to a programming course. Such courses were held at Borehamwood or, in due course, held at one of the NCR centres in London. The staff then returned to their end-user companies to write applications-specific software. It is not certain when these programming courses started. Laurence Clarke seems to recall that the first one may have been held in 1955 [3]. No details of this first course have come to light.

An early example of an *Electronic Computing Course* which covered more than just programming was the one held at Borehamwood from 20 February to 9 March 1956. This was attended by 21 customers, representing organisations such as Lever Brothers (Port Sunlight), Norwich Corporation, British Petroleum, National Gas Turbine Establishment, Mars Ltd., Boots Pure Drugs Ltd., General Motors Ltd. and the United Africa Company. Besides basic programming (total of six lectures and 12 exercise sessions), the topics included introductions to the Elliott 402 and 405 systems architectures and a number of applications such as stock control, centralised banking, payroll and process control. The lecturers were: A St Johnston, J R Halsey, H Mitchell, R G Mills and N D Hill on the hardware and systems side; N D Hill, E T Mountford, S E Hersom, H L S Orde, A N Vaughan and R L Cook on programming; M Browner, P Shackleton, A D Honeyman, J W Cox, D Preston, A J Burton and A J Wakefield on business-oriented applications; A St Johnston and C A Laws on process control; E O Herzfeld on 'a businessman's approach to the use of computers' and M V Wilkes (later to become Professor Sir Maurice Wilkes FRS) from Cambridge University on 'the organization of a computing centre'. Maurice Wilkes was a consultant to Borehamwood at that time.

Judging by an undated contemporary team photograph, the Computer Training Group at Borehamwood numbered 15 staff in about 1958. This team was no doubt responsible for both in-house and external courses. The Head of the group was F S Ellis.

The first Elliott 405 to go to an external customer was installed in the City Treasurers' Department at Norwich City and County Offices in late 1956/early 1957. It is believed to have been the first computer to have been purchased by local government [4]. Dina Vaughan wrote the initial applications software.

In 1956, in a joint project led by the National Research Development Corporation (NRDC), Borehamwood became involved in demonstrating the use of an Elliott 405 computer for stores inventory control and production control and planning, associated with the manufacture of automatic telephone exchanges. The location selected for what was intended as a UK-wide exemplar was the Siemens Edison Swan factory at Woolwich in south London. At that time, the Woolwich factory was using about 100,000 items of raw materials and parts. For various reasons described in Chap. 5, the *Siemens Project* did not turn out to be the shining exemplar that NRDC had anticipated.

Borehamwood was much prouder of the Elliott 405 installed in February 1958 for inventory control at Littlewoods Mail Order organisation in Liverpool, a project excellently described in [5]. There was an added bonus of the Littlewoods activity: some of the staff who were at Littlewoods during the build-up of the project went on to work with Elliott computers elsewhere. H E C (Eddie) Nash came from Littlewoods to Borehamwood in 1959 to take on a managerial role in the Computing Division. The Littlewoods programmers Gerald Everitt and Philip Tattersall joined Dina St Johnston's software house Vaughan Programming Services respectively in 1961 and 1962 (see [6]). Applications running on Elliott computers accounted for 92% of Vaughan Programming Service's contracts during the period 1959–1964.

Turning to Gerald Everitt's description of the Elliott 405 project at Littlewoods [5], he summarises the application as essentially one of inventory control. It was to show an excellent return on investment – certainly greater than other early commercial applications of computers such as payroll. Littlewood's mail order business alone had a turnover of £75 million in 1958 and stock levels were generally about 6–8 weeks. After the development of the computerised control system, stock levels were reduced by about 2 weeks [7]. The cost of saving a week's stock (at 5%) would have been about £70,000. Now the purchase price of the Littlewoods 405 computer was about £110,000, creating an annual amortised cost of between £10,000 and £20,000. The Computer Department at Littlewoods had a staff of about 60. It is unlikely that staffing costs of the Computer Department exceeded £50,000 at 1958 prices. Comparing savings on stock with capital and staff costs, the financial benefit of the Elliott 405 to Littlewoods is obvious.

Part of Littlewood's investment had been to recruit programmers, some of whom had to 'learn on the job' in order to write low-level software for the 405 computer. The 405 gave the programmer up to five separate, programmable local machines – one for input, one for output, one for disc memory, one for magnetic film, one for central processing. Philip Tattersall recalls [7] programming the *output compiler* (an autonomous unit), 'starting from logic diagrams and learning how to use a CRO [Cathode Ray Oscilloscope]'. He goes on to say 'Forecasting techniques were also developed to extend the Littlewoods inventory control systems. These techniques required the writing of a program for the inversion of matrices in order to enable multiple regression to be performed. This was not 405 country since the 405 was, par excellence, a data processing machine and not a computing machine. The 405 was painfully slow [at matrix inversion] but it coped and we produced some interesting results.'

The Littlewoods project had broken new ground. The fertile fields of general commercial applications were soon to be cultivated further, by NCR on Elliotts' behalf.

9.2   How NCR Became Involved: 1956–1957

The National Cash Register Company of Dayton, Ohio, was effectively established in 1884 to manufacture and sell the first mechanical cash registers – forerunners of what would now be called *point-of-sale* equipment for retail outlets. The company was incorporated in the USA in 1925/26. Known universally as *NCR*, the company developed a worldwide business designing and selling electro-mechanical accounting machines, cash registers and adding machines. NCR was, however, relatively slow to become involved with stored-program digital computers. In the early 1950s, 'NCR's view was mixed and its strategy undefined' [8].

In [10] it is recalled that: 'NCR's business in the 1950s was based primarily upon data collection rather than data processing. The big question was how to best develop from scratch, not having a punched-card base, a data processing capability that would complement the data-capturing abilities of NCR's accounting machines, cash registers and adding machines.... One of the errors committed by NCR in the 1950s and early 1960s was the assumption that the computer business would simply be another layer on the cash register, accounting machine and adding machine cake. The theory was that to NCR's three [existing] departments – cash registers, accounting machines and adding machines – a fourth would be added in the computer business department'.

At its Dayton, Ohio, headquarters, NCR attempted to acquire a computer-manufacturing capability in 1952 by buying a small Californian producer of scientific computers, Computer Research Corporation. This was not a great success. Thus, it was not until 1959 that the first NCR business computer series, the NCR 304, was shipped in America, with the General Electric Company being contracted to provide the production engineering and manufacturing. After its release for sale, 'the 304 was downplayed by NCR both internally and externally ...NCR became so pessimistic about its chances that the company contracted with GE to make only 24 systems' [8]. It was not until the early 1960s that NCR at Dayton had created its own computer design and production base to produce the NCR 315 as a successor to the 304.

Meanwhile, the British branch of NCR was moving rather more rapidly into the electronic data-processing arena. The seed of a collaboration with Elliott Brothers (London) Ltd. was sown at the National Conference of the Office Management Association, held at Brighton on 19–22 May 1955. The Conference is believed to have included papers from Elliotts, Leo, NCR, Ferranti, Burroughs, IBM and English Electric, which were later published in a book entitled *The Scope for Electronic Computers in the Office*. The Elliott paper in particular (which drew on [1]) came to the attention of Bill Woods of NCR. Laurence Clarke, one of the authors, recalls the moment [9]: 'Our paper was presented at a conference at which the Managing Director of NCR (UK) was present. The MD was impressed with the payroll application given in our paper. The MD said that NCR (UK) was ready to exploit commercial applications of computers in Europe, but that at that time a US-designed NCR computer was not yet ready. The MD later approached Bagrit & Ross, to see whether a deal with Elliotts could be done.' Laurence was sent to the USA at the end of 1955 to investigate the matter further.

In June 1956 Elliotts made an announcement in the press of arrangements with NCR 'under which that company would market in this country our digital electronic computers, particularly the Elliott 405, for all business applications' (see also [10]). This was followed by an undated illustrated brochure issued jointly by both

Fig. 9.1 A marketing agreement between Elliotts and the British arm of NCR, National Cash Register Co Ltd., was announced in mid-1956 and formally signed in 1957. This celebratory luncheon in 1957 shows Leon Bagrit (*centre*) talking to (*left-to-right*) J E Warring (Director, NCR Overseas Sales, Dayton, Ohio), J S Scott (NCR Dayton) and D A F Donald (Managing Director, NCR Great Britain) who were visiting Borehamwood

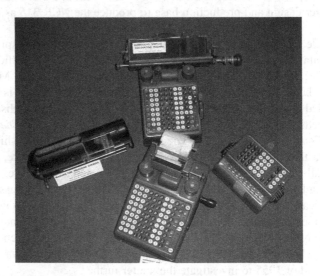

Fig. 9.2 In 1958, the Royal Army Pay Corps (RAPC) decided to move from electro-mechanical calculators, such as those shown in the photo, to electronic digital computers. The task of processing the pay of about 200,000 soldiers had previously been carried out using 850 hand calculators such as the Burroughs Class 9 Simplex accounting machine shown at the top of the photo. The Elliott 405 computer was the British front-runner in an attempt to win the huge RAPC contract. The 405 was not, in the end, able to match the performance of the IBM 705 computer

companies, stating that: 'As recently announced in the editorial columns of national newspapers and all leading business journals, an arrangement has recently been concluded by which the marketing and installation of Elliott computors [sic] for business data processing applications will now be undertaken by the Electronics Section of The National Cash Register Company Limited, 206–216 Marylebone Road, London NW1.' A footnote added that 'Elliott Bros (London) Limited remain responsible for the business data processing equipment which they have already sold, and will themselves continue to market analogue and digital computers for scientific applications and specially designed automation equipment for plant process control and similar purposes.'

A special NCR *Overseas Electronics Meeting* was held in London from 27 to 29 May 1957. An enthusiastic article on the front page of issue 7b of the company's magazine *Overseas News,* published by NCR's headquarters in Dayton, describes the meeting as 'intended to give overseas delegates from most [NCR] Overseas Sections and many countries a more complete picture of the "405" National-Elliott Business Computer Systems and their applications, and the organisations required to handle the equipment'. The highlight of the conference was a trip to see the Elliott R&D, manufacturing and testing facilities at Borehamwood. An accompanying brochure stated that 'During 1957 the [NCR] Company announced the signing of a long-term agreement between Elliott Bros (London) Ltd. and NCR London. NCR London now has the sales agency for the Elliott computer [the 405], which will be marketed as The National-Elliott Data Processing System. Selling rights have also been awarded covering France and Germany, and certain other countries will be added from time to time.' Indeed, NCR went on to market Elliott 405 computers everywhere *except* in the USA.

The arrangement between the two companies was judged at the time to be mutually beneficial. Laurence Clarke remembers that 'in 1956 the resources of Elliotts' Computing Division at Borehamwood were at breaking point and the deal with NCR gave us breathing space. Elliotts could not have sustained the marketing and software activity taken on by NCR' [11]. For NCR, the deal allowed them to exploit what was, in 1956, the leading British commercial data-processing system – as judged by the technical evaluation undertaken for the Royal Army Pay Corps by Post Office engineers (see below in Sect. 9.3). Notwithstanding the clear win-win nature of the deal, it does seem remarkable that a large American-based company had teamed up with a relatively small British player. The sizes of the two organisations, and some other companies relevant to the development of digital electronics at that time, may be judged from the amounts of issued capital as presented in Table 9.2.

NCR seemed to have taken to the marketing of the Elliott 405 with reasonable enthusiasm. A complete list of deliveries is given in Appendix 8. In November 1956 the second 405 to be built went to NCR's head office in Marylebone Road, London, for demonstration purposes and for running the *National-Elliott Computing Service.* A further machine was installed at Marylebone Road in January 1959, at which time it was described as 'the largest and most comprehensive 405 system in the world. This seems to make one area of London the most 'computer concentrated'

Table 9.2 Issued capital (London Stock Exchange) for six companies

	1955	1960	1965
BTM/ICT	£2,800,000	£10,400,000	£18,268,750
Elliott/Elliott-Automation	£612,000	£6,574,487	£17,832,153
English Electric	£13,252,037	£32,774,850	£40,131,304
Ferranti	£3,000,000	£4,500,000	£4,500,000
GEC	£19,314,680	£23,600,000	£61,260,000
NCR	£11,747,801	£12,577,249	£14,841,929

The NCR capital, originally quoted in US dollars, has been converted to sterling using the ratios 2.80, 2.81 and 2.796, respectively, for the years 1955, 1960 and 1965

district in Europe' [12]. NCR installed a 405 system for 'demonstration and computing service' in Frankfurt, Germany, in November 1958 and another in Sydney, Australia, a year later. The Sydney machine, parts of which are now preserved in the Powerhouse Museum in Sydney, gave the first demonstrations of electronic data processing in Australia [13].

Such tangible displays of EDP were to open up important markets for NCR. For example, in December 1959, NCR sold a 405 system to Sumitomo Bank in Osaka, Japan. 'This was the beginning of our long relationship with that bank as their computer supplier in addition to the many other products we sold them. In time, Sumitomo became NCR's largest customer anywhere in the world' [8].

Standing back from NCR, who were clearly just getting up to speed in 1957, it is helpful to review the UK's other suppliers of business data-processing hardware at a time when the Elliott 405 was gaining acceptance. An opportunity to judge the EDP capabilities on offer is afforded by the records of a major procurement exercise that tested all UK competitors to the limit. The case study involves the requirements of the Royal Army Pay Corps.

9.3 Processing the Army's Payroll: A Snapshot of EDP Capabilities

By 1956 the pay and accounting system used by the British army was in need of modernisation. Since the Second World War, staff from the Royal Army Pay Corps (RAPC) had been operating a manual payroll system based on the use of Burroughs Class 9 Simplex accounting machines (see Fig. 9.2). Approximately 850 of the Burroughs units were in use, the majority of which were first installed during 1942/43. By 1956 these electro-mechanical desktop calculators were wearing out and the time for electronic digital computing had come.

The army required a payroll system with a minimum capacity of 180,000 soldiers' accounts, expandable to 240,000 accounts, based on single-shift working (nominally 8 h in every 24 h). This would leave the option of further expansion to two- or three-shift working in the event of emergency military mobilisation.

Even by 1958, the RAPC computerisation was still the most ambitious of the UK government's projected clerical computer projects (see [14]). At the time, commercial electronic data processing was in its infancy. Setting up and running a computer centre to provide a reliable payroll system for an army of several hundred thousand soldiers was a major challenge which broke new ground. There was very little contemporary UK experience to guide the authorities. It is instructive to follow the RAPC's computer procurement process, not only because the project was an ambitious one but also because the technical assessment has been recorded in some detail [15, 16]. The evaluation process gives a snapshot of contemporary commercial data-processing platforms in 1956, comparing computers of UK origin with those of America.

Based on the specification produced by the RAPC's Electronic Computer Investigation Committee, an Invitation to Tender for a computer payroll system for the army was sent to 14 electronic and office equipment suppliers, ten of whom were British companies and four American. The returns were due by 1 April 1956. Table 9.3 presents a summary of the results, with minor comments added in the light of hindsight.

From the responses listed in Table 9.3, seven companies had clearly failed to submit anything tangible. This left seven companies whose products merited some analysis. In its report, the RAPC Working Party commented that it was 'disappointed that manufacturers such as English Electric Co. Ltd. and Ferranti Ltd. who have operational machines and are pioneers in the development of scientific computers in this country, were unable to submit firm proposals for an automatic data processing system'. In the event, the proposals from the British Tabulating Machine Co. Ltd. and from EMI fared little better. Upon close examination, the Working

Table 9.3 Companies responding to the Royal Army Pay Corps' *Invitation to Tender*, April 1956

Company	Relevant EDP project in 1956	First delivery of this as a product?
The Plessey Co. Ltd.	(None)	–
Remington Rand Ltd.	UNIVAC II	1958
British Tabulating Machine Co. Ltd.	BTM 1400 (scrapped in 1959)	1961 (ICT 1300)
Burroughs Adding Machines Ltd.	(None)	–
Decca Radar Ltd.	(None)	–
English Electric Co. Ltd.	(None)	–
Ferranti Ltd.	Pegasus; Perseus	1959 (Perseus)
EMI Sales and Service Ltd.	EMIDEC 1100	1960
NCR/Elliott Bros. (London) Ltd.	National/Elliott 405	1956
IBM United Kingdom Ltd.	IBM 705	1956
LEO Computers Ltd.	LEO II	1957
Powers Samas Accounting Machines Ltd.	(None)	–
Standard Telephones and Cables Ltd.	(None)	–
Underwood Business Machines Ltd.	(None)	–

Party concluded that both the BTM 1400 and the EMIDEC project were 'in the development stage and there is insufficient evidence to establish feasibility'. The Working Party was of the opinion that 'there is a gap of something like three to five years between a machine in production, such as the National/Elliott 405, and machines under development, such as the BTM1400 and EMIDEC, and although we have no evidence that leads us to doubt the ability of either British Tabulating Machine Co. Ltd. or EMI Electronics Ltd. to produce a workable system at some future date, we feel that considerable risk would attach to the acceptance of proposals of this nature'.

In passing, it may be observed that EMI did come to market with the successful EMIDEC 1100 system. The first delivery was to Boots the Chemists at Nottingham in April 1960, the installation becoming operational in September of the same year. Gerry Mills recalls [17] that during the RAPC discussions Elliotts 'were quite worried about the EMIDEC competition'. More on the EMIDEC 1100's emerging transistor technology will be found in Chap. 10.

The RAPC Working Party still had three potential contenders from Table 9.3. The proposal from LEO Computers Ltd. was given serious consideration, as was natural for an organisation that had pioneered business computing applications in 1951 [18]. However, the proposal was eliminated because the computer concerned (LEO II) had inadequate drum storage for the total task. The proposal was, in effect, considered to be not much more than a conventional punched-card system because it involved several computer runs to process standing record files and the consequential inputting of large numbers of cards. The total LEO payroll processing cycle was judged to involve 'the continuation of clerical processes which ought to be eliminated in an automatic system'. The number of separate computing runs could result in 'anything up to 4000 cards being out of collation at any one time and may easily lead to a state of chaos'. Furthermore, the LEO proposal made no provision for the handling of audit queries and various other essential accounting activities.

The upshot of the tendering process was that only two systems, the Elliott 405 and the IBM 705, went through to the detailed evaluation stage. A fuller account of this evaluation is given in Appendix 3, since it includes an analysis of how the two computers compared at the instruction level when carrying out various common data-processing tasks. This, in turn, sheds light on the relative suitability of various architectural features of the Elliott 405. It can be seen from Appendix 3 that *three* Elliott 405 computers were required to yield the same performance as a single IBM 705 computer for the RAPC's huge payroll task.

The IBM bid was accepted by the RAPC in 1958. An IBM 705 system was eventually delivered to the RAPC's main establishment at Worthy Down, about 5 miles north of Winchester, at the end of 1960.

Looking back to 1957, it is instructive to review the UK's installed base of business data-processing computers. By the end of 1957, about six Elliott 405s and one LEO II had been installed in the UK. These two types of machine addressed the *large business data-processing* market sector, the top end of which was exemplified by the RAPC application. In the *small business data-processing* sector, 13 BTM

1201 computers had been installed by the end of 1957. In contrast to this rather modest number of large and small UK installations, the RAPC evaluation committee had noted that by the end of 1957 in America 'the IBM 705 is a standard machine which is coming off the production line at the rate of 7–9 machines a month. Many IBM 705s are in operational use in the USA and their reliability is regarded as proven'. The message to Elliotts and to all other UK computer manufacturers in 1957 was clear: IBM was the world leader in the provision of large commercial data-processing systems and its penetration of the lower end of the market could be expected quite soon.

9.4 NCR's Activities in the Period 1956–1967

Sales of the NCR/Elliott 405 covered the period 1956–1961. NCR also marketed the Elliott 803 to commercial data-processing customers from 1960 onwards, the Elliott 503 from 1963 onwards, the Elliott 4120 from 1965 onwards and the 4130 from 1966. The full delivery lists are given in Appendix 8, though no distinction is made in the lists between the various market sectors or indeed whether a particular sale was due to NCR or Elliott sales staff. All that can be said is that the Elliott 802, 502 and 900 series computers were *not* primarily directed at the commercial EDP sector and therefore NCR would have played little or no part in their promotion.

Overlapping with the Elliott-designed computers, the Dayton-designed NCR 315 was marketed by NCR from 1960 onwards. The sole UK manufacturing of the 315 was for a time carried out at Borehamwood by arrangement. By 31 March 1967, the number of Borehamwood-built NCR 315 computers to have been delivered was 123, with a further 27 on order [19]. 'After sales of the 315 got under way, NCR did not push the Elliott 803 machines' according to Michael Irish [20]. They were rather more enthusiastic about selling the 4100 computers – with good reason, as may be deduced from the comparative performance given in Sect. 9.6. Roger Cook is of the opinion that 'The 4100 series was designed with NCR in mind – the 4120 for NCR and the 4130 for more 'scientific' applications' [21].

To support all the above EDP platforms, NCR's software teams developed a business-oriented language and applications programs. Amongst the people associated with these NCR teams were Arthur Bevan, Sandy Cormack, Michael Irish and Nick Vince. Prominent amongst NCR's output at this time was *Language H*. This was a business-processing language 'designed to permit COBOL style operations in a simpler language, and suitable for running on a smaller machine' [22]. The first Language H compiler for the NCR/Elliott 405M 'was completed in August 1961 and checked out to be effective by December 1961. January 1962 saw the start of a project to develop a Language H compiler that ran on a 405M but produced object code for an NCR-Elliott 803B' [23]. In time, Language H compilers were produced for the Elliott 803 and the 4120/4130 and for the NCR 315. Language H is believed not to have been implemented on later NCR computers such as the Century.

Fig. 9.3 The first external delivery of an Elliott 405 was to Norwich City Council in February 1957. The photo shows part of the system arriving at the Norwich City Treasurer's Department. In the previous year, the first two 405 computers to have been built were installed, respectively, at Borehamwood and at NCR's Marylebone Road headquarters in London, where they offered a computing service to external customers

Incidentally, Michael Irish, who joined NCR straight from college in January 1961 and remained for 10 years, believes that the 'H' in *Language H* stood for John C Harwell. This has been confirmed by others [24]. It is known that John Harwell was Manager of Computing Services at Honeywell Controls Ltd. in London in 1962 and 1963. He later moved to NCR and then, in about 1967, he founded a software house in London called *Harwell Data Processing* [24].

Another Elliott/NCR product was the NEAT Assembly language for the NCR 315 and for the Elliott 4100 series computers, the first NEAT manual for the 4100 series being dated June 1966. The NEAT assembler for the 4100 series was developed at Borehamwood by a team led by Roger Cook.

On the hardware side, NCR at Dayton developed several special input/output devices in addition to designing complete computer systems such as the NCR 315. NCR produced the successful CRAM (Card Random Access Memory) using magnetically coated cards, as an alternative to magnetic tape storage. Nick Vince, who was with NCR from late 1963 to late 1975, remembers [23] that: 'CRAM was an amazingly powerful storage medium for data storage and information retrieval applications in which it would easily out-perform the big disk drives of the day but I found all too often that the techies of the day would not believe just how good CRAM was'. More details of CRAM will be found in Sect. 9.6. In the

Fig. 9.4 Commissioning the Elliott 405 at Norwich City Council in 1957

mid-1950s, NCR was also an early player in the field of Magnetic Ink Character Recognition (MICR) – a technology that was adopted by most banks by the mid-1960s. Nick Vince recalls that: 'NCR (UK) never really cracked the Banking sector with the 315 computer but I can well remember Lloyds Bank using NCR's very large and powerful MICR cheque reader/sorters with their IBM mainframes. I can also remember we could run NCR's 2000 cpm Punched Card Reader flat out on a 315 which sounded like an aero engine when we did. The 315 when processing punched paper tapes read the data at the full 1000 cps maximum of the paper tape reader due to the principles of "single-shot data preparation" of NCR's Accounting Machines.'

The *single-shot data preparation,* mentioned above, refers to the way in which NCR's existing range of electro-mechanical manual accounting machines were gradually integrated into the world of electronic stored-program computers. Basically, an NCR accounting machine was fitted with a paper tape punch. Each time the accounting machine operator completed a transaction-entry, a record was automatically punched onto paper tape. At regular intervals, perhaps weekly, the reel of paper tape was taken to a computing centre for off-line processing. This was a procedure that appealed to small businesses who could not justify purchasing their own digital computer. Such businesses could continue to use the cheaper accounting machines with which they were familiar, whilst hiring time at a computer bureau to produce periodic statistics for management purposes.

Fig. 9.5 The 405 system allowed a number of configuration options, as explained in Appendix 3. The photo shows a larger 405 installation, probably the first one as installed at Borehamwood. The legend across the top of the left-hand cabinets says: 'National-Elliott Data Processing System'. When NCR took over responsibility for marketing, the 405 computer sometimes confusingly appeared in alphabetic listings of manufacturers under 'National' and sometimes under 'Elliott'

A specific example of the integration of small and large (or 'old and new') technologies is provided by the wholesale jewellery firm of Walter Graham (Jewellery) Ltd., London [25]. In 1963 this company bought an NCR Sterling Compu-Tronic accounting machine to prepare invoices, which were required at the rate of between 100 and 150 invoices per day. (Such invoices were formerly prepared by five typists, who were replaced by one Compu-Tronic operator.) The NCR Compu-Tronic accounting machine simultaneously punched records on paper tape. Reels (spools) of paper tape produced by the Compu-Tronic were taken each week to an NCR 405 computer bureau in London for processing digitally. The checks and statistics required by Walter Graham Ltd. took between 20 and 30 min of 405 computing time each week. Then every month an additional 5.25 h of computing time was required to produce monthly analyses of products, customer records and stock records, which were printed off-line from magnetic tape. Then every 6 months, an additional 20 min of computing time was required for 6-monthly turnover reports.

As a further example of combining old and new retail practices, the NCR 315 operator's console could be fitted with an accounting-machine keyboard having the usual invoice-preparation features. Sales data could then be entered into the 315 computer manually – an office procedure which was clearly to become widespread some years later, when on-line VDUs were introduced.

NCR was active in providing computing bureaux and data-processing centres in large cities, in due course extending the bureau concept to cover both training and self-service facilities. For training purposes, NCR established its own special centres, for example, in Baker Street, London, independently from the original training facilities which had been organised by Elliotts at Borehamwood since the mid-1950s. The NCR company magazine *NCR Post* for October 1962 reports on customer training for an Elliott 803, which had been delivered to Northamptonshire County Council's Treasurer's Department. The 803 at Northamptonshire was used for two initial tasks: (a) monthly analysis of income and expenditure under about 10,000 headings; (b) costings for 17,000 meals served each day in 70 schools throughout the County. The *Post* article enthuses that: 'Programs for both tasks were written by a member of the Treasurers' Department trained in the NCR Education Centre at 88 Baker Street.'

The introduction of novel self-service bureau facilities occurred in 1966, being described in an *NCR Post* article as follows.

'On 1st June 1966 a new service, NCR Elliott Computer Workshops Ltd., was announced by NCR and Elliott-Automation Ltd., under which time can be hired on an electronic computer with magnetic tape files and high-speed printer, for as little as fifty shillings [£2.50 in decimal currency]. The inclusive charge for using one of the Workshop's [Elliott] 4100 computing systems is £20 per hour at peak periods and £10 per hour at off-peak periods. This means that a minimum 'time-segment' of 15 minutes, during an off-peak period, can be purchased for fifty shillings. ... Unlike conventional computing centres, which do everything for their customers, the Workshops provide a 'launderette' service with customers writing the computer programs and operating the equipment themselves.... The new company has established a schedule of short courses to train people to program and operate the computers. Lasting two or three days, these will be held periodically at the Workshops.... A jointly owned company, NCR Elliott Computer Workshops, will operate the service as a development of the unique Workshop facilities that Elliotts have made available to many users over the last three years. The four established Workshops, which use NCR Elliott 803 computers, are being augmented by a countrywide chain of all-purpose Workshops which will be equipped with the much more powerful NCR Elliott 4100 system. The first of these is already in operation at Greenford and a further three will be opened during the next nine months at Manchester, Birmingham and Borehamwood.'

The *NCR Post*, in a subsequent edition, was able to announce that: 'The NCR Elliott Computer Workshop at Broad Street, Birmingham, was opened on 20th September [1966] by Sir Eric Clayson, Chairman, Birmingham Post & Mail Ltd.' In January 1968, after the arrangement between Elliotts and NCR had been terminated (see below), S J Conway, the Chairman and Managing Director of NCR's British Selling Organisation, was able to look back and observe [26] that: 'The new wing at the Greenford Training Centre is now in full use, providing an extra 15 classrooms as well as other facilities, and raising the total number of classrooms to 27.' Conway also reported that 'The continued success of our Data Processing Centres has created further expansion in this field. Towards the end of 1967, the splendid work which has been done in London and Dundee was augmented by the opening of a third centre in re-built premises attached to our Birmingham office.'

All the above user-oriented and applications-oriented activities of NCR need to be set in an economic and historical context. How effective was NCR really being in promoting Elliott products (rather than NCR's products)? What was the view of contemporary Borehamwood staff? This is perhaps a good point at which to step back and re-examine the relationship between Elliott-Automation and NCR and to revive the doubt expressed by some programmers at Borehamwood that the 1956 marketing arrangement with NCR was not likely to bear fruit.

9.5   Strategic Appraisal: An Alternative View

Once sales of the Elliott 405 had taken off in 1957 and the potential for business applications had become a reality, many at Borehamwood were keen to see the new market exploited with vigour. Indeed, some Borehamwood staff gradually became impatient and had begun to question the wisdom of handing the control of the commercial EDP sector over to NCR. A major proponent of this viewpoint was R G (Gerry) Mills, who has been introduced in the previous chapter.

Briefly, Gerry Mills joined Borehamwood in 1955. He became disenchanted with what he describes [17] as 'the restrictions caused by the NCR link-up' and left in 1958 to join ICT, where he worked at Hyde Park Corner for ICT's Special Projects Department. Mills returned to Borehamwood in 1961 as Sales Manager, at the invitation of Eddie Nash who had meanwhile become Commercial Manager of Elliott's Computing Division. There is little doubt that Eddie Nash was a powerful influence on programmers such as Mills. An ex-RAF bomber pilot, Nash had come to Borehamwood from Littlewoods in 1959. He has been described by Laurence Clarke [27] as a dynamic personality who 'started a culture change at Elliotts, introducing a commercial/sales approach in which all engineers represented the company and were there to sell – (not backroom boys)... One of Eddie's flamboyant gestures was to take a full- page ad in *The Times* announcing that Elliotts had sold more computers in the UK than IBM – probably true by quantity if not by value'. Nash had a vision for the wider dissemination of Elliott computers. Mills shared this vision, a vision that was soon to be blurred.

Mills left Borehamwood for the second time in 1962, along with Eddie Nash, both men disagreeing with the way in which the organisation of Elliott's Computing Division had been broken into four parts in 1962 by Leon Bagrit. In the opinion of both Mills and Nash, the whole of Elliott's Computing Division should have been floated off as a separate company and the agreement with NCR cancelled. The new company should then have made no distinction between 'scientific' and 'commercial' markets and should have recognised, in Gerry Mill's view, 'the interchangeability of hardware and software'. Mills goes on to say that 'the point that was not understood by senior [Elliott] management was that once the concept of multi- tasking had been sorted out, one processor design with accompanying software could handle all applications. Subsequent development could then concentrate on faster and cheaper hardware, without the need to write new software and, in particular, new operating systems.'

In Chap. 8 we saw that Mills' phrase 'sorting out multi-tasking' was not so easily achieved in practice. Nevertheless, Mill's implied vision of a compatible *range* of computing systems was certainly seen as a desirable target by most computer mainframe manufacturers in the early 1960s.

The Mills analysis does not appear to allow for Elliott-Automation's specialist computing areas such as avionics and industrial process control. Mills has, however, remarked [17] that 'there was a clear role for separate ruggedised products for mobile/defence markets, and a separate sales division would have been appropriate, with product design and construction part of the main Computing Division'. It is very doubtful that Peter Hearne and Jack Pateman in Elliott's Airborne Computing Division would have agreed with Mills' concept of centralised product design and construction (see Chap. 12).

Of course, Mills' vision of a separate new company would not have been possible without new funding. Could the necessary capital be raised in 1962 in the City of London? Evidently, Mills thought that the chances were good. He has said [17] that 'given the right Chairman the City would have thrown money at it. The management of Elliott's was not highly regarded in the City, though there was a lot of interest in what they were doing. My first job in 1962 after I left Elliott's was to design and install the first stockbroker system (using an 803); in 1963 my company [see below] designed and implemented the first Unit Trust system, and we were nearly the first to design and implement a share registration system. I obtained a very good idea of how the City worked in those two years'.

It is unlikely that funding or encouragement for a new, separate, computer-manufacturing company would have come from within the Elliott-Automation Group itself, which is of course why Mills suggested that new capital should have been sought elsewhere. In this connection, it is worth recalling the reason why people such as Andrew St Johnston had welcomed the idea of a link with NCR in the first place. In 1956 the Computing Division at Borehamwood was hard-pressed and under-resourced. This, in turn, reflected the precarious financial position of the parent company, Elliott Brothers (London) Ltd., in the 1950s. The struggle to get Elliott Brothers out of the red and into profitability between 1946 and 1951 has already been mentioned. Pre-tax profits remained distinctly modest until about 1960, when they climbed to a peak in 1964 and then started to fall.

In Table 9.4 we give some key parameters for the Elliott-Automation group, for the years covered by the agreement with NCR. The data is taken from the company's Annual Reports and from the Stock Exchange Yearbooks. During the period under review, Elliott-Automation grew rapidly, judging by the number of employees and the group's total factory floor area as shown in the Table. Subtracting pre-tax profit from top-line profit in Table 9.4 gives some indication of the cash necessarily set aside by the company to cover interest and depreciation each year. This is seen to rise alarmingly after 1964 – a sign of fragility. The conclusion is that Leon Bagrit, whose empire seemed to depend more and more on digital electronic expertise as the years went by, would not have tolerated Gerry Mills'

Table 9.4 Some characteristics of Elliott-Automation Ltd. during the main years of the agreement with NCR

	1957	1958	1959	1960	1961	1962	1963	1964	1965	1966
TLP = Top-line profits (£m)	1.14	1.10	1.36	2.27	2.95	3.92	4.76	5.60	5.59	6.47
PT = Pre-tax profits (£m)	0.91	0.82	1.02	0.96	2.21	2.86	3.24	3.70	2.39	2.81
(TLP – PT), giving provision to cover interest and depreciation	0.23	0.28	0.34	1.31	0.74	1.06	1.52	1.90	3.20	3.66
Number of employees (K)	NA	7.3	7.8	10.6	12.9	15.9	17.3	22.4	23.5	23.1
Av. factory floor area (million sq. ft)	NA	NA	1.3	1.7	1.8	2.2	2.6	NA	NA	NA

recommendation of a mass defection of computing staff to a new and separate company in 1962.

As for the career of Gerry Mills after leaving Borehamwood, he started his own company, Mills Associates Ltd. (MAL). He recalls [17] that 'I opened my first of eventually eleven computer bureaux 18 months later. Initially I used 803's, which (once we bought line printers) were very effective at business computing, this demonstrating that Eddie and I were right and Elliott's management were wrong.... Once ICL and IBM had announced their 1900 and 360 series, I no longer regarded the NCR/Elliott offerings as credible, and Mills Associates Ltd (MAL) decided to abandon Elliotts (we had four Elliott 803s) and switch to ICL. We also switched to an industry-standard language (COBOL). This made it much easier to recruit and retain staff, and we could use slightly lower quality staff. The muddly NCR/Elliott situation was bad for Elliotts in almost every way. For the first few years of MAL our entire bureau revenue derived from processing by-product paper tape from NCR adding and accounting machines.' By 1979 [28], MAL was making an annual profit of £120,000.

Turning back to what actually happened after Gerry Mills and Eddie Nash left Elliott-Automation, we need to consider how the NCR/Elliott computing platforms compared with the offerings of their rivals in the field of small- and medium-sized commercial data-processing systems. A snapshot of the competition in the mid-1960s is provided in the next section.

9.6   The Market Competition in 1965

Very significant changes had occurred in the business data-processing market since the start of the agreement between NCR and Elliott. The picture presented by the Royal Army Pay Corps market survey of 1956/57 – see Sect. 9.3 – had become completely out of date by 1965. The main changes over the 9-year period, as discussed in more detail in Chap. 13, may be summarised thus:

(a) IBM had grown rapidly as a computer supplier in Europe. IBM computers accounted for about 18% of all UK installations in 1962 and about 29% by 1967.

(b) The sales of traditional punched-card office machinery (mainly electro-mechanical) showed a rapid collapse in 1961/62, indicating a willingness of more and more commercial organisations to move into the digital computing era. One contributory factor was the popularity of the modestly priced IBM 1401 computer, which had first appeared in Britain in 1960. During 1961–2, IBM installed nearly a hundred IBM 1401s, accounting for about a third of new computer sales in Britain during that period. The new 1401 computer installations usually replaced older electro-mechanical office equipment.

(c) Upwards-compatible *ranges* of computers had emerged. These systems allowed users to migrate reasonably smoothly from smaller to larger systems, should the need arise, without changing their supplier. IBM announced its System/360 range in April 1962, at about the same time as ICT announced its 1900 range. The first ICT 1900 system was installed in 1964.

In 1965 the NCR/Elliott products, which by that time mainly covered the lower EDP price-range, were facing stiff competition. A two-page NCR/Elliott internal information memo dated 26 January 1965 [29] gives a summary of the perceived market rivals to the Elliott 4120. The principal technical parameters, which should also ideally be cross-checked against contemporary source-documents for accuracy, are presented 'as found' in Table 9.5.

Fig. 9.6 Most of the surviving images of Elliott 4100 series installations focus on the ancilliary equipment such as tape decks, disc stores and lineprinters because by the late 1960s bulk input/output and storage facilities tended to dominate the requirements of many users. Here is a 4130 Central Processing Unit which, when its doors were shut, was the least-photogenic cabinet in the entire computer room

Fig. 9.7 An operator is shown standing at the middle of three 4100 series Exchangeable Disc Storage (EDS) units. In his right hand is a pack of discs, which are ready to be mounted on the middle EDS unit. In the background may be seen four 4100 series magnetic tape units. The photo was taken at Borehamwood in about 1967 (see also Fig. 13.2, which gives an overall view of the same computer room)

The original NCR/Elliott internal memo [29] is prefaced by this caveat: 'The following comparison of NCR and the main competition in the lower price range computers shows the configurations, prices and basic timings. Basic arithmetic timings should, of course, not be taken as direct comparisons of speed of performance of a commercial job. For example, the 315 commands are very powerful and perform many functions by hardware that have to be done by program on other computers. On the other hand, however, very fast internal speeds (eg on the 4120) mean that even allowing for the extra instructions the peripherals can be kept closer to their rated maximum speeds'.

Of the five computers featured in Table 9.5, the IBM 360/20 is the only one lacking the option of punched paper tape input/output (abbreviated PT in Table 9.5), instead relying solely on punched-card input/output. All the other manufacturers offer both paper tape and punched-card input/output. The 360/20 is also exceptional in not offering magnetic tape equipment, choosing instead to offer only disc packs, each having between 7.3 million and 58 million characters of on-line storage. ICT and Honeywell also offer disc packs of broadly similar capacity but running at only about half the transfer rate of the IBM 360/20's 158 Kilo-characters/second (abbreviated KC in Table 9.5) discs. Later, Elliott offered exchangeable

Table 9.5 Comparison of some competitors to NCR and Elliott in the smaller computers available in 1965 for commercial data processing

	Elliott 4120	NCR 315–900	ICT 1902	IBM 360/20	Honeywell 200
Primary memory size (RAM) in characters	32K–128K	10K–80K	16K–64K	4K–16K	2K–32K
Cycle time (µs)	6	6	6	3.6	2
BCD or binary	Binary	BCD	Binary	Binary or BCD	BCD
Word length (bits)	24	12	24	8	6
ADD time (µs) (6 + 6 decimal digits)	12–18	48	18	125	44
MULT. time (µs) (6 × 6 decimal digits)	87–93	582	1,412	680	408
Index registers	1	64	8 (also as accs)	8 (also as accs)	16
Software	NEAT, Lang. H Algol SAP	BEST Lang. H Cobol Fortran Algol NEAT	PLAN Rapidwrite Fortran (Algol coming)	Fortran IV New Fortran Cobol	Easycoder Bridge Cobol Automath
Sample system (*see notes in text*)	32K RAM 4 × 12KC PT in/out 600 lpm	10K RAM 4 × 12KC PT in/out 600 lpm	16K RAM 4 × 20KC Card in/out 300 lpm	4K RAM 2 discs Card in/out 300 lpm	8K RAM 4 × 20KC PT in/out 650 lpm
Approx. price (£)	60,000	78,000	88,000	68,000	77,000

disc packs, for the system 4100 computers' Exchangeable Disc Storage (EDS) units (see Fig. 9.7). For comparison, the magnetic tape options offered by the other four manufacturers in Table 9.5 have the following respective minimum and maximum transfer rates:

Elliott 4120	12–33 KC
NCR 315–900	12–120 KC
ICT 1902	20–60 KC
Honeywell 200	20–83 KC

The option of various forms of magnetic card input was, in January 1965, available only for the NCR 315 and the ICT 1902 systems: NCR offering its CRAM system and ICT its Magnetic Card File. The range of lineprinter options is similar across all five manufacturers, typically yielding printing speeds from 300 lines per minute (abbreviated lpm in Table 9.5) to 1,000 lpm.

The NCR CRAM (Card Random Access Memory) deserves more explanation, especially in view of its high transfer rate of 100 KC. Here is a brief technical description, taken from a contemporary NCR brochure [30].

'CRAM reads and records data on mylar magnetic cards approximately 14 inches long and 3 inches wide (36 cms by 8 cms). Each card has seven data recording tracks that can be individually addressed for reading or recording data. A single track has a storage capacity of 3,100 alphanumeric characters. Thus, each magnetic card has a total storage capacity of 21,700 alphanumeric characters. Each CRAM file is designed to handle a deck of 256 magnetic cards with a storage capacity of over 5.5 million alphanumeric characters of information. *[For comparison, another NCR brochure noted that "This represents more information than could be punched into 69,000 punched cards"].*

'Like reels of magnetic tape, the decks of magnetic cards have been designed in such a way that they can be easily mounted and removed from the CRAM unit. For ease of mounting and convenience in storing, the decks are housed off-line in a cartridge. Any number of these cartridges of cards can be stored off-line; any one of which can be interchanged on the CRAM unit in approximately one minute when required for processing. When mounted on the CRAM unit, the deck of magnetic cards is suspended from two gating rods. The cards are individually selected by eight electronically controlled two-position rods. Each of the 256 magnetic cards has a unique binary notching configuration that permits it to be released from the deck when selected. ... Once a card has been called for by the computer, and the rods in the CRAM unit have been properly set, the magnetic card is dropped from its hanging position on the rods. The cards are separated by 256 jets of air that permit the selected card to fall freely. After the card has been released, it will be pulled by means of a vacuum onto a rotating drum and quickly accelerated to a speed of 400 inches a second. ... Thus, CRAM provides a tremendous transfer rate of 100,000 characters per second. ... Up to 16 of these unique magnetic card handlers can be operated on-line in an NCR 315 Computer System.'

Returning to Table 9.5 (taken from [29]), the sample systems presented in the penultimate row of Table 9.5 show that, on the face of it, the Elliott 4020 seems to offer good value for money. However, a proper evaluation for a given customer should certainly have included appropriate benchmarking results and many other factors such as available applications packages and quality of after-sales hardware and software support. Perhaps, at this distance in time, the safest general conclusion is that the NCR/Elliott sales force was able to offer products that compared favourably with the rest of the market in January 1965. Confirmation that the Elliott 4100 system offered good value came in 1968, when ICL took over sales of this computer – as indicated below.

9.7   The End of the NCR Arrangements

Elliott-Automation merged with English Electric in August 1967, the merged companies then being taken over by GEC in September 1968 a couple of months after the formation of ICL in July 1968. By that time, ICL had effectively brought together the commercial data-processing capabilities of all the major UK manufacturers, including BTM, ICT, Ferranti, EMI, English Electric, Leo, Marconi and Elliott-Automation (see Chap. 13). ICL was only interested in the commercial data-processing side of Elliott computers, confining its acquisition to the Elliott 4120 and 4130 computers. Since NCR was obviously not interested in the scientific, military or process control aspects of Elliott-Automation computers, the clear message was that, after the turbulent events of 1967, NCR had no option but to stand on its own. By this time, it is believed that the NCR 315 was being manufactured at NCR's Dundee factory – which was also looking forward to producing the new NCR Century computer. There was thus no longer a need for NCR (UK) to rely upon the manufacturing facilities at Borehamwood. NCR's main digital computer design and manufacturing facilities at Dayton, Ohio, were also well established by the mid-1960s. Indeed, Laurence Clarke was of the view that 'NCR never really wanted Borehamwood to have a manufacturing clause for the 315 and so got out of the agreement as soon as they could' [31].

All agreements between NCR and Elliott-Automation effectively came to an end in October 1967 [26]. In a move designed to reassure NCR staff in the face of persistent rumours S J Conway, the Chairman and Managing Director of NCR's British Selling Organisation, issued a long statement to employees in January 1968 [26]. Here are some extracts:

'The reason why NCR is always "on the move" is that we are working in a highly competitive industry where new developments occur with almost frightening rapidity... This is particularly true of the electronic data processing field. Although we have been trading in Britain for the best part of a century, our computer business is little more than ten years old....

Fig. 9.8 The American-designed NCR 315 computer was manufactured under licence at Borehamwood, as shown in the photo, from about 1962. Elliott-Automation merged with English Electric in August 1967 and all agreements between NCR and Elliott-Automation effectively came to an end in October 1967

'At this point it seems appropriate to discuss the change in our association with Elliott-Automation. As you know, this association has lasted ten years. It began because we believed, when business computers came on to the scene, that it would be in our interest to draw on the expertise and manufacturing resources of an established British company that had already gone a long way in the development of scientific computing techniques.

'That decision is not regretted now. With the help of Elliott-Automation, NCR were first in the field of commercial EDP; and today we can look back on an impressive list of highly successful installations.

'But over the years a new situation has developed. The first significant change in the association was in 1960, when Elliott-Automation began to make certain parts of the NCR-designed 315 computer. This development continued through the introduction of the 4100 data processing system. More recently, we started to "go it alone" by setting up a [NCR] 500 Series production line in Dundee. This, of course, was done with Elliotts' agreement.

'During 1967 it had become apparent that we were getting ready for a big step forward in our "NCR first" policy. Discussions had already begun when Elliott-Automation was taken over by a competitor. Our first thought was to safeguard the interests of firms which had bought Elliott-built computers from NCR – an important factor in maintaining our reputation for service. Now, however, the last links have been formally broken. NCR stands on its own in computers; and I believe that it is a time of great opportunity.'

NCR was certainly able to survive without the Elliott-Automation link but there was much to be done. Of immediate concern was the imminent onset of decimal currency in the UK which, for a company specialising in what we would now call *point-of-sale* equipment, meant that 'hundreds of thousands of [our NCR] machines will have to be replaced by the end of 1972, if not sooner' [26].

NCR continued as a supplier of computers and associated information-processing equipment, including Automated Teller Machines (ATM) for banks. In the 1980s, for example, the company introduced its Tower 16/32 series of UNIX-based machines and then went on to supply various other computers that were compatible with the IBM PC. NCR was acquired by AT&T in 1991 but was spun off by AT&T in 1996 and now retains its original NCR name. The company is still trading at the time of writing, the manufacture of ATMs being its principal activity. In 2010 there were over 21,000 employees worldwide.

With the light of hindsight, it appears that the culture and business traditions of Elliott-Automation and NCR had not really mixed. The duo had failed to sustain the expectation of the late 1950s that Borehamwood's technological excellence and NCR's reputation in the business world would together propel Elliott computers into a dominant market position within the UK. With a background of leading-edge defence electronics on the one hand and electro-mechanical cash registers on the other hand, it is not surprising that the clash of cultures had not resolved itself by the time the agreement between the companies came to an end in 1967.

We end this chapter by returning the focus to the general hopes and fears of Elliott computer sales staff, comparing the responses of both Borehamwood's and

NCR's efforts to meet the challenges of increased market competition in the last few years of an independent Elliott-Automation.

9.8 Selling Computers: The Competition Increases

We start with an account of a Borehamwood-based sales engineer's experiences in the mid-1960s. M A (Alan) Wakefield joined Borehamwood as a graduate management trainee in September 1961 and became a fully fledged sales engineer in November 1963. His market specialities were scientific, industrial and engineering applications and higher educational establishments in the Midlands region. Alan remembers the period 1963–66 as follows [32].

'When I joined Elliotts and started in sales, I think it is fair to say that Elliott was in a pretty good market-leading position with its products, technology etc. Such competition as occurred in selling situations was either from Ferranti, with the latter day Pegasus – getting a bit *passé* by then? – and sometimes the Sirius. Occasionally, the IBM 1620 (a small scientific machine) showed up, and the odd appearance of a Stantec Zebra. English Electric didn't seem to have any small scientific machines, though their KDF 9, for example, would compete with Elliott's larger 503 computers. There was also ICT: well they were really Ferranti at that time, weren't they! The top end of the scientific market was Ferranti Atlas territory against which we, in the stand-alone research, technical and educational area, weren't really competing.

'But by 1965/66 the picture was changing quite significantly. ICT had introduced their 1900 Series computers, including the 'scientific' variants 1905/1907, and started to offer more direct competition to Elliotts across the range. Following on from its world wide launch of the System/360 in 1964, IBM had introduced a rather different computer in 1965, the IBM 1130, which was aimed directly at the low-cost end of the engineering and education sector – ie straight into Elliott's back yard! The IBM 1130 [33] was a 16-bit machine with between 8K and 32K words of core storage. It was offered with a wide range of optional peripheral equipment, including a popular removable-cartridge hard disk drive (the *Ramkit)* which had a formatted capacity of 512K words. Other American companies began to make an impact, such as DEC (Digital Equipment Corporation) with their early PDP range of systems. These included the popular low-cost PDP8 which was much favoured in laboratory data logging, data capture and on-line instrumentation applications in University departments. Life was definitely getting harder for Elliott's sales engineers!

'Generally speaking, as I have indicated, our own Borehamwood-oriented sales situations were frequently non-competitive, or only mildly so, prior to 1965. Our main challenge was often in helping our prospective buyers and customers seek out, compete for, and gain budgetary allocation and approval from the funding bodies themselves, that is to say the Public Sector grant approvers and the R & D budget authorisers in the larger industrial corporations, whose available cash was often variable and limited.

By 1965/66 Elliott's commercial partner, NCR, was also experiencing more severe competition from the major data-processing suppliers, especially the Americans who were by then more firmly established in the UK. We can get a general idea of the relative performance of the Borehamwood-based sales engineers compared with their NCR-based equivalents by reproducing some statistics that appeared in an internal Borehamwood publication [34]. Table 9.6 shows the cumulative yearly Elliott 4100 order/delivery statistics as at October 1966, where the figures in brackets refer to the situation in the previous month (i.e. September 1966). For comparison, the last row in the Table gives the final 1966 yearly totals according to another company document [19]. As is usual with the few surviving Elliott-Automation company records, it is today impossible to resolve the minor anomalies in Table 9.6.

The Elliott 4130 became available in 1966, a year after the 4120 appeared: hence the lack of actual 4130 deliveries recorded in Table 9.6. The 4130 was more oriented towards the scientific and educational market (see Appendix 7), which might account for NCR's relative lack of interest in the 4130 as revealed in the Table. It might also be inferred from Table 9.6 that the NCR sales force was rather slow off the mark in promoting the 4120, even though the 4120 was reckoned to be more suited to their market area.

Alan Wakefield has reflected on the background to selling Elliott hardware as follows [32].

'What I gathered after the first two years was that Elliott-Automation was an organisation, especially in the computer field, which struggled somewhat with the transition from being a technology led, major project and contract focused, largely public sector funded operation into a more market driven, competitor-aware, commercially astute enterprise which needed to operate on a more global basis. And despite its early technical and sales successes, Elliott-Automation had focused its computer products on rather too narrow a set of market segments, namely scientific and technical, rather than seriously addressing the larger opportunity for commercial data processing. Elliott's scientific market was largely constrained by the availability of public funding which was often quite variable and limited, whereas the larger private sector commercial and public administration bodies were developing more rapidly, and with more available financing, in the broad field of data processing.'

The above comments might also impinge upon the relative performance of the Elliott and NCR marketing efforts. Was it true, as some believed, that Elliotts regarded

Table 9.6 Cumulative month-by-month sales figures for the Elliott 4100 series computers for 1966, as at October of that year, from [34]

Division responsible for the sales	4120 delivered	4120 on order	4130 on order	Totals, both computers
Scientific Computing Div	18 (16)	13 (14)	13 (13)	44 (43)
Other Divisions	11 (11)	2 (2)	1 (1)	14 (14)
Overseas	2 (2)	1 (1)	0	3 (3)
NCR	11 (11)	23 (22)	4 (4)	38 (37)
Total	42 (40)	39 (39)	18 (18)	99 (97)
1966 Annual total, from [19]	*40*	*40*	*20*	*100*

Figures in brackets are for September 1966

NCR sales staff as 'cash register people who did not really understand computers and advanced technology', whereas NCR regarded Elliott sales staff as 'boffins and tekkies who had little experience of selling in the real commercial world'? Borehamwood-oriented sales engineers such as Alan Wakefield, who had joined Elliott-Automation long after the formal arrangement with NCR had been initiated, simply assumed that Elliotts covered the scientific, technical and research applications, and, of course, process control and defence, and NCR covered commercial data processing, accounting, finance, business organisation and similar segments. Alan Wakefield remembers that 'There was occasional overlap of selling and customer requirements, but usually these were resolved at senior sales management level in the two companies. Personally, I had very little liaison or overlap with our opposite numbers in NCR during my four years on the patch in the Midlands area. Was Elliott dissatisfied with NCR Sales performance? If we look, for example, at the overall computer orders and deliveries for the Elliott 803 and 4100 systems, then one could infer that NCR was less successful than they should have been, given the relative market potential and sizes of the two market segments. But conversely, in the commercial data processing segment NCR was facing stiff competition from the established names (IBM, ICT, Burroughs, English Electric, etc.), whereas the competition in the scientific market segments was rather less fearsome, and often minimal or nonexistent'.

Competition was indeed to get fiercer for the whole of the UK's computer-manufacturing sector. In Chap. 13 we discuss the orgy of mergers and takeovers that left Borehamwood and Rochester somewhat in the role of specialist suppliers to niche markets such as aerospace and communications whilst ICL became more or less the UK's single supplier of computers for general scientific and business applications. The phrase *niche markets,* though true in the sense of general computing, certainly does not imply any lack of innovation or indeed profit. In the next three chapters we broaden the technical history to review Elliott-Automation's contribution to the evolution of computer systems architectures (Chap. 10) in the 1950s and 1960s, and to catch up on the company's parallel endeavours in the related areas of radar (Chap. 11), airborne computing and aerospace applications (Chap. 12) – where the Elliott marque was to gain world-class recognition.

References

1. St Johnston A, Clarke SLH (1954) Applications of a high-speed electronic computer to a business-accounting problem. J Br IRE July:293–302
2. Andrew St Johnston (2001) Conversation with Simon Lavington at Hedgegrove Farm on 29 Oct 2001
3. SLH Clarke (2009) E-mail to Simon Lavington dated 14 Oct 2009
4. Barnard AJ (1958) The first year with a business computer. Comp J 1(1 April):29–36, This describes the Elliott 405's tasks at Norwich
5. Everitt G (2006) Making money while the world slept. Computer Resurrection, the Bulletin of the Computer Conservation Society, Issue number 37, spring 2006
6. Lavington SH (2009) An appreciation of Dina St Johnston, 1930–2007, founder of the UK's first Software House. Comput J 52(3):378–387
7. Philip Tattersall (2007) E-mails and telephone conversations with Simon Lavington, Aug/Sept 2007

8. Anderson WS, Truax C (1991) Corporate crisis – NCR and the computer revolution. Landfall Press, Inc., Dayton. ISBN 0-913428-74-4

9. Laurence Clarke (2001) Conversation with Simon Lavington at Southwold on 10 July 2001

10. Stock Exchange Yearbook for 1956: Annual Report for Elliott Brothers (London) Ltd. (Available at the Guildhall Library, London)

11. Clarke SLH (2007) Presentation at the BCS@50 conference, London, 13 July 2007. See also Clarke SLH (2007) Early computer production at Elliotts. Computer Resurrection, Issue number 41, autumn 2007 http://www.cs.man.ac.uk/CCS/res/res41.htm

12. Anon (1959) News item on page 85 of the Computer Bulletin for Apr/May 1959

13. Connell M, Curator, Computing and mathematics, The Powerhouse Museum, PO Box K346, Haymarket, NSW 1238, Australia

14. (a) The National Archives, document PRO T 222/1304 (1958) General summary of major ADP systems in hand or being planned, Feb 1958 (b) Document PRO T 222/1331: Progress summary of ADP projects as at December 1960. See also Agar J (2003) The government machine: a revolutionary history of the computer. The MIT Press, Cambridge

15. Royal Army Pay Corps (1957) Report of the Electronic Computer Investigation Committee. The War Office (F9), Dec 1957

16. Royal Army Pay Corps (1957) Electronic Computer Investigating Committee: Report of Working Party. Application of automatic data-processing to soldiers' pay accounting. The War Office, Aug 1957

17. Gerry Mills (2009) E-mails to Simon Lavington, Sept 2008 to Jan 2009

18. Lavington SH (1980) Early British computers. Manchester University Press, Manchester. ISBN: 0-7190-0803-4. Co-published by Digital Press, Bedford. ISBN: 0-93237-08-8. http://ed-thelen.org/comp-hist/EarlyBritish.html

19. Elliott automation: computers and orders, 1947–1966. Brochure published in early 1967 by the Directorate of Information Services, Elliott-Automation Ltd., 21 Portland Place, London W1

20. Michael Irish (2007) E-mails and 'phone conversations with Simon Lavington, Aug 2007

21. Roger Cook (2007) E-mails to Simon Lavington in July and Aug 2007

22. Cormack AS (Oct 1962) Early operating experience with Language H. Comput J 5(3):158–161

23. Nick Vince (2007) E-mails to Simon Lavington in Aug 2007

24. David Pentecost, Harry Lawrence (2008) E-mails to Simon Lavington in Oct 2008

25. Capturing invoice data for computer processing (1963) Data Process Mag Mar–Apr:4–11

26. Statement by Conway SJ, the Chairman and Managing Director of NCR's British Selling Organisation, to employees (Jan 1968). Three pages, possibly issued in conjunction with the company's magazine NCR Post

27. SLH Clarke (2007) In conversation with Simon Lavington, 7 June 2007

28. Ryan J (1979) It can be done. Scope Books, Newbury, Berkshire. ISBN: 0 906619009. This book, describing 23 small UK start-up companies, gives a snap-shot of the business strategy and activities of Mills Associates Ltd. in 1979

29. Anon (1965) Machine comparisons. NCR/Elliott Information memo number 5, 26 Jan 1965 (Two pages, type-written, internal company document)

30. NCR CRAM. Illustrated brochure, undated but believed to be 1960. Reproduced at: http://archive.computerhistory.org/resources/text/NCR/NCR.CRAM.1960.102646240.pdf. For more background on the use of CRAM with the NCR 315 computer, see also: http://archive.computerhistory.org/resources/text/NCR/NCR.315.1960.102646242.pdf

31. SLH Clarke (2007) E-mail to Simon Lavington dated 29 June 2007

32. Wakefield A (2009) On the road to selling computers: recollections of a Graduate Management Trainee at Elliott Automation Ltd, Borehamwood, from Sept 1961. Document written in Jan 2009. Also, accompanying e-mail exchanges with Simon Lavington, Jan 2009

33. www.ibm1130.org/

34. News Bulletin of the Scientific Computing Division, number 10, Oct 1966 (Nine-page typed newsletter, published by Elliott-Automation Computers Ltd. and circulated to staff at Borehamwood)

Chapter 10
Evolution of Elliott Computer Architectures

10.1 Early Years: High-Tech, High-Speed, High-Complexity

Computer design at Borehamwood was initially driven by the demands of real-time on-line control of ship-borne radar. From January 1949 Harry Carpenter and Ed Hersom became jointly responsible for defining the systems architecture of the Elliott 152 computer, as discussed in Chap. 2. They had some difficulty in meeting the speed of operation required by the MRS5 project. By 1949 the building blocks available at Borehamwood included a relatively fast random-access CRT storage system based on the *anticipation-pulse* method, a family of innovative printed-circuit logic modules based on miniature pentode thermionic valves (tubes), and a design for a fast serial multiplier. The real-time requirements stretched these building blocks to the full – exemplified by John Coales' disappointment that Borehamwood's CRT memory could only operate at one third of his desired frequency of a million cycles/ second (1 MHz). These practicalities obliged Carpenter and Hersom to devise complicated means of achieving speed by introducing functional parallelism into a basically serial computer. The resulting architecture was deliberately tailored to the particular real-time tasks of tracking airborne targets and controlling a ship's high-angle guns – tasks that placed a premium on rapid axis-conversion algorithms. The 152's program resided in a fast, read-only, instruction store.

The architecture of the Elliott 153, the *DF computer*, followed closely that of the 152 in respect of functional parallelism at the register level. The 153 is fully described in Chap. 3 and in Appendix 1, where it is explained that the ALU, the separate fast multiplier and two RAM caches could all be given sub-tasks to perform within a single program instruction. In this respect, the 153's exceptionally long instruction word of 64 bits had the bit-significant flavour of a modern micro-program instruction.

Perhaps of more lasting significance to the company, the 153 project saw the in-house development during the period 1952–1954 of a relatively large fixed-head disc store of capacity (in modern terminology) of 45 KB. Although this capacity was overshadowed by the IBM 704's capacity of 162 KB in 1955, the Elliott 153's disc technology paved the way for Borehamwood to equip the 403 computer with

S. Lavington, *Moving Targets*, History of Computing,
DOI 10.1007/978-1-84882-933-6_10, © Springer-Verlag London Limited 2011

a 64 KB disc in 1955 and the 405 computer with options for either a 64- or a 128-Kb disc in 1956. We pick up the theme of bulk storage again in Sect. 10.8 below.

In the light of hindsight, we can see that the internal CPU architecture of the Elliott 152 and Elliott 153 was unlikely to be cost-effective for general-purpose medium-priced production computers. On the practical side, the 1949 Borehamwood version of CRT storage was subsequently proved to be relatively unreliable compared with the CRT systems developed by Williams and Kilburn at Manchester University. The Elliott 152's family of glass printed circuits was also found to be too unreliable for sustained useful computation. Although the Elliott 153 was built with improved paxolin-mounted printed circuits of good reliability, both the 152 and the 153 computers used expensive miniature pentode thermionic valves. For classified defence projects, cost had been of secondary consideration in pursuit of state-of-the-art solutions to specific military objectives. Clearly, a fresh approach was required if Borehamwood and Elliott Brothers (London) Ltd. wished to make a competitive entry into the general-purpose digital computer market.

10.2   New Directions for Borehamwood's Digital Technology

On the building block front, two independent improvements were introduced at Borehamwood as discussed in Chap. 5. Firstly, nickel magnetostrictive delay-line storage was successfully developed. These memory devices were extensively used by both Elliott and by Ferranti throughout the 1950s, only being replaced in due course by the American invention of the ferrite core store.

The second improvement to building blocks was introduced by Charles Owen, a first-class circuit designer who joined the Circuits Division at Borehamwood in 1951. Owen developed a new and reliable family of digital logic packages using miniature pentodes. The intended target for this improved family of circuits was the Elliott 153 computer. Owen's circuit family was adapted by Laurence Clarke for the Elliott 401 computer to use the cheaper double-triode valves. Later on still, further slight adaptations of the Owen/Clarke circuits were to find their way into the Ferranti Pegasus and Ferranti Perseus computers. The clock-rate for all these circuits was 333 kHz, a frequency originally determined in 1949 by the limits of reliable operation of Borehamwood's anticipation-pulse CRT storage system. This clock-rate persisted in the Elliott 400 series computers and the Ferranti Pegasus and Perseus computers to the end of the 1950s.

Nickel delay-line storage and Owen's improved miniature pentode circuits were first put to practical use in the Nicholas computer at Borehamwood, which first ran a program in December 1952. Nicholas was in no way a production machine – the epithet *home made* having more than a grain of truth [1]. Nevertheless, it had an apparently straightforward architecture with a one-address instruction format and, thanks to the influence of the EDSAC team at Cambridge University and the innovative software developed by the Theory Division at Borehamwood, was easier to program than many contemporary early computers. Appendix 2 describes the complicated interaction between Nicholas' hardware and software.

Chronologically, the next Elliott computer to have a simple one-address (as opposed to *one-plus-one*) instruction format was the 403, also known as WREDAC. The design for the 403 was commenced by the Computing Division in some urgency in the spring of 1954, delivery to Australia taking place in September 1955 (see Chap. 3). The 403 owed nothing to Nicholas. There are several reasons why the overall architecture and systems software of Nicholas did not appear to have much immediate influence on the Elliott 401/402/403/405 design activities of the Computing Division at Borehamwood. The reasons are complex, interspersed with personalities, but the following factors have a bearing on the story:

(a) Nicholas was a one-off computer, rapidly designed by Charles Owen of the Circuits Division, for the Theory Division's internal use on classified problems. It used the expensive miniature pentodes, whereas the 401's circuits used the cheaper equivalent triodes (particularly the 12AT7 thermionic valves).
(b) The authors of the Nicholas systems software, George and Ruth Felton, had both left Borehamwood by 1954, as had Charles Owen.
(c) During the period of Nicholas's conception, birth and infancy (1952–1954) the Computing Division was preoccupied with other design commitments, namely the 311 (Oedipus) project for GCHQ (from the spring of 1951 until the summer of 1953); the 153 computer for the Admiralty and GCHQ (effectively mid-1952 to end 1954); helping to complete the TRIDAC analogue computer for RAE (effectively during 1953 and 1954). Andrew St Johnston had had a plan to turn the 153 machine into a general-purpose stored-program computer [2], but this plan was superseded by the 401 developments sponsored by the National Research Development Corporation (NRDC).
(d) NRDC contracts relating to the design of the Elliott 401 computer commenced in the autumn of 1950 (see below). Leon Bagrit and Lawrence Ross had 'decided that the 401, rather than Nicholas, was the way forward for computer development because the 401 was to have a larger store than [the 1K words (4Kbytes) of] Nicholas' [2].
(e) There were unsettling Computing Division staff changes during the relevant period: the empire-building Bill Elliott left Borehamwood in the spring of 1953 and Andrew St. Johnston thereupon became the Divisional Manager. Andrew 'opted for the magnetic drum type of memory because it clearly could be expanded more readily than the nickel delay lines [of Nicholas' main memory]' [3].
(f) Finally, as Laurence Clarke has remarked, 'Andrew's design method was very personal' [4].

Coming at the end of 1952, Nicholas marks the effective conclusion of the first phase of computer development at Borehamwood. It was a phase of defence-oriented, security-shrouded, largely task-specific, digital design activity. There was a brief period of organisational uncertainty at Borehamwood, which no doubt helped to convince Bill Elliott to resign in 1953 as head of the Computing Division, his place being taken by Andrew St Johnston.

It is believed that Bill Elliott wished to take the majority of the Computing Division with him in 1953 but his grand ambitions only appealed in the end to three key colleagues: Charles Owen, Hugh Devonald and George Felton, all of whom eventually moved with Bill Elliott to Ferranti Ltd. to form the core of Ferranti's London Computer Centre. This Centre was established in 1954 at 21 Portland Place, an elegant four-storey house that had been built in 1777 by the Adams Brothers just north of Oxford Street [5]. It was here that the Ferranti Pegasus computer was developed, running its first program in October 1955 and at first using nickel delay-line storage only – the drum backing store was still in the final stages of development and was not in use by programmers until mid-March 1956 [5]. At about the same time, the Mercury higher-performance computer was being developed by Ferranti in Manchester, based on the design of a Manchester University prototype called Meg [6]. There were at that time significant differences of approach between Ferranti's London and Manchester computer design activities, due not only to architectural and technological perspectives but also to personalities. In the light of hindsight, the architecture of Pegasus was to have a greater historical impact than the architecture Mercury. Since Pegasus in some senses grew out of Borehamwood, we will refer to this important machine later in Sect. 10.5, after catching up with Borehamwood's own computer design initiatives.

10.3   Into the Market Place: The Elliott 401, 402 and 405

In the period 1950–1952 the task of the Computing Division, encouraged by NRDC, was to build upon its experience of digital design, memory technologies and packaged circuit modules so as to produce a marketable computer. But was there, indeed, any realistic market for digital computers? Expert opinion at the time was divided. As mentioned in Chap. 5, Professor Douglas Hartree of Cambridge University, a respected mathematical physicist and an enthusiastic advocate of digital computing in the immediate post-war years, appeared cautious. And yet, in 1951 Ferranti Ltd. took the unusual step of appointing Vivian Bowden as the company's first – and the UK's first – computer salesman. Professor Douglas Hartree was still doubtful. In September 1951 he remarked to Bowden: 'We have a computer here at Cambridge; there is one at Manchester and one at the NPL. I suppose there ought to be one in Scotland, but that's about all' [7].

The Ferranti Mark I, delivered to Manchester University in February 1951, was the world's first production computer – marginally ahead of UNIVAC I in America. However, the Ferranti Mark I was very expensive. The engineering challenge that Borehamwood, with NRDC's help, set itself was to produce a computer that was 'of moderate cost, good reliability, and extreme ease of servicing' [8]. Only thus, in NRDC's view, was the market to be opened up to industry at large.

Apart from one important item mentioned in Sect. 10.4, the Elliott 401 and its improved successor the 402 are not now regarded as particularly innovative, historically speaking, as far as systems architecture is concerned. The 401 and 402 both had *one-plus-one* address formats, preferred because their main stores were

Fig. 10.1 Various Elliott logic circuits during the period 1954–1964. The larger units to the rear of the photo are from an Elliott 503 system controller (*left*) and an Elliott 402 arithmetic unit (*right*). In the foreground (*left-to-right*) are three transistor daughter-board modules from early 803 computers, a Minilog element, and two tunnel diode experimental modules – the small black item at the right being two tunnel diodes configured as a *Goto Pair*. The small circular object at the centre of the photo is a coin: a *threepenny bit*

sequential discs. Each instruction contained both an operand address and the address of the next instruction, thus permitting *optimum programming* as pioneered by the NPL Pilot ACE computer which had first run a program in May 1950. The Pilot ACE's instruction format was very complicated and obliged the programmer to have a detailed knowledge of the computer's internal timing [9]. In contrast, the Elliott 401's instruction format was straightforward – see Appendix 3 – whilst retaining a hint of the Elliott 153's microprogram-like generality.

In terms of the contemporary marketplace, the most attractive features of the Elliott 401/402 computers undoubtedly concerned their physical construction. By using well-engineered, easily replaceable circuit packages, the reliability and maintainability were potentially very high (once the ageing effects of double-triode thermionic valves had been understood). By the use of nickel delay lines for central registers and a straightforward disc memory of modest capacity, the overall cost was kept relatively low. The production 402 computer, of which approximately ten were sold between about 1955 and 1960 as described in Chap. 5, cost approximately £25,000 each in 1955 [10]. For comparison, the Ferranti Mark I and Mark I Star, of which nine machines were built between 1951 and 1957, cost in the region of £95,000 each at 1955 prices. Of course, the Ferranti Mark I was a much more powerful computer.

In terms of moderate-cost scientific computers of the mid-1950s, the Elliott 402's British rival was undoubtedly the Ferranti Pegasus computer which, in hardware terms but not architecturally, owed much to the Elliott 401 [5]. Forty Pegasus computers were sold by Ferranti between 1956 and 1962, at an approximate cost (normalised to 1955 prices) of about £35,000, rising to somewhat over £45,000 by the end of its selling life [5].

The dates of first delivery of the Ferranti Mark I, the Elliott 402 and the Ferranti Pegasus computers spanned the period 1951–1956 – five fruitful years of early

Table 10.1 Approximate characteristics of four British computers available in the mid-1950s

	Ferranti Mark I and Mark I Star	Elliott 402	English Electric DEUCE	Ferranti Pegasus
Delivery period	1951–1957	1955–1960	1955–1960	1956–1962
Approx. price, normalised to1955	£95,000	£25,000	£45,000	£35,000
Number sold	9	10	33	40
Fxpt ADD (ms)	1.2	0.204	0.3	0.3
Fxpt Multiply (ms)	2.16	3.2	2.08	2.0
Immediate-access store (words)	416	15	384	55
Drum capacity, words (KB)	16K words (80 KB)	3K words (12 KB)	8K words (32 KB)	4K words (20 KB)

British computer design when many new hardware and software ideas were being tested in the market place. Adding the English Electric DEUCE computer [11] to the story, we may compare the cost and performance of these four machines that ushered in the computer as an essential tool for scientific and engineering enterprises in the UK. Table 10.1 sets out the main physical characteristics of the four products and illustrates the advances not only in architecture and in technology, but also in market confidence, made in the period 1951–1955.

Table 10.1 should be interpreted with caution, since the figures are approximate and, in any case, a proper comparison of the four computers depends upon many other factors not represented in the table. For example:

(a) The times for fixed-point addition are the minimum. Optimum programming techniques are necessary on the Elliott 402 and the English Electric DEUCE in order to achieve best performance. At worst, an Elliott 402 *ADD* could take one complete drum revolution time, i.e., 13 ms.

(b) The DEUCE's *immediate-access* mercury delay-line store consisted of several sections of different capacities and therefore of different access times, whereas the other three computers gave *random-access* across the whole of the primary memory. (By *random-access* in this context of bit-serial memories we mean that the time to access any one word is independent of the physical location of that word. If our definition was to be more rigorous and demand that access-time to any *bit* was to be independent of the physical location of that bit, then only the Ferranti Mark I and Mark I Star met this criterion.)

(c) There were subtly different versions of all of the computers in Table 10.1, representing various degrees of hardware upgrade.

(d) The three manufacturers represented in Table 10.1 provided various degrees of software support over the life of their computers. By the end of the 1950s, Ferranti was arguably providing the most support and Elliott the least.

Table 10.1 indicates that, after 1956, the Elliott 402 had a hard job competing with Pegasus on price/performance grounds. If we include the provision of software support, then the Elliott 402 slipped further behind as time went on. By 1957

Ferranti had provided Pegasus with an Autocode, which was a primitive high-level language similar to the autocode developed at Manchester University for the Ferranti Mark I computer in 1954 (see Chap. 8). Borehamwood did not develop an autocode (for the Elliott 800 series computers) until about 1960. By 1962 the Pegasus library of documented subroutines contained about 200 useful programs, in addition to a Matrix Interpretive Scheme and the Autocode [5]. It has been said that Pegasus 'opened up a new era in the provision of high-quality programming systems by manufacturers of computers in Britain … it marks a turning-point from a situation of laissez-faire to one of strong involvement' [12].

The Ferranti Pegasus computer is mentioned again in Sect. 10.5 below. First, however, we should step back in time a few years and introduce an important architectural theme within which Elliott computers played an interesting historical part.

10.4 Address Modification, Indexing and General Register Sets

The concept of address-modification by means of index registers was invented at Manchester University in 1949 (patent number 16588/49, 22 June 1949, in the names of F C Williams, M A H Newman, T Kilburn and G C Tootill). Ten years later, this invention was still being described as 'probably the most important single advance in the recent history of computing' [13]. In the Manchester Mark I and Ferranti Mark I implementations, it was convenient to hold the index registers (called B-lines at Manchester) in a separate store with its own arithmetic unit – a concept that, in later Manchester/Ferranti computers such as Atlas (see [14, 6]), enabled B-arithmetic operations in the B-accumulator to be overlapped in time with computation in the main (A) accumulator. This speeded up computations involving the address-generation of structured data such as arrays and matrices.

In 1953 the Elliott 401 was one of the earliest non-Manchester computers to employ an index register for address-modification. (The IBM 704, delivered in 1955, was the first IBM computer to use them [15].) It is very probable that Christopher Strachey suggested to Andrew St Johnston that the 401 should incorporate an address-modification register [2]. In turn, Andrew remembers that 'After the Exhibition [in London in April 1953] Strachey had a discussion with me on improvements to the 401 and at that point I suggested to him the concept of multiple accumulators. Probably he had had the same idea himself' [3]. Laurence Clarke remembers [4] that 'Strachey definitely suggested B-lines to me and worked out how we'd do it on 401'.

The 401 actually introduced two working registers known as X and Y, in addition to the double-length accumulator A and the multiplier register M. As is shown in Appendix 3, an incoming instruction could be modified by adding the contents of either the X or Y register to the instruction before it was obeyed. The X or Y register could also be either the source or the destination for an arithmetic operation, as specified by bits in the 401's generalised instruction (see Appendix 3).

Unlike Manchester, however, Borehamwood used a single ALU for both address-calculations and for main computation.

The Elliot 402 computer, first operational in 1955, further generalised X and Y into a set of 15 *Immediate-Access* registers which were mapped into the first 16 locations of the 402's address space (location 0 always contained zero). This was most probably the first step towards what later became known as a *general register-set* architecture. In its pure form, *general register-set* architectures provide a small number (usually 8 or 16) of fast registers that can be used both for address-modification and for main computation. We will return to the subject of general register-sets shortly. The Elliott 402's instruction had three *B-digits*, allowing *Immediate-Access* registers 1–7 to be used for address-modification purposes (the contents of B0 was always taken to be zero).

Taking an overall view of all Elliott computer designs in the period 1947–1967, the number of explicit address-modification, or index, registers available for each of the major Elliott machine types is shown in Table 10.2. More details will be found in Appendices 1–7.

Referring to Table 10.2, it is seen that Borehamwood adopted a new policy in the late 1950s and early 1960s for the Elliott 800 series and the software-compatible Elliott 503 computer. Apart from the main accumulator and an accumulator-extension register, these machines had no other working registers visible to programmers (though of course there was by implication a *Program Counter* register). As is explained in Appendix 4, two 19-bit instructions are packed into each 39-bit word for the Elliott 803 and 503. The pair of instructions is separated by a 'B-line' bit.

Table 10.2 The number of explicit address-modification, or index, registers in various Elliott computer designs

Elliott computer	Number of explicit index regs	Names of these registers and comments on their use
153	–	–
Nicholas	–	–
401	2	X, Y
402	8*	B0–B7, being the first 8 of 16 fast *Immediate-Access Store* locations
403	4*	Any set of four B-lines, B0–B3, chosen from 12 fast registers
405	4*	B0–B3
803/503	0	All memory locations available, via the previous instruction
502	1	B. The accumulator and PC could also be used for address-modification
900(18-bit)	1	B
900(12-bit)	0	All memory locations available, via the previous instruction
4100	1	R. (This register also used as the *reserve accumulator*)

An asterisk indicates that the contents of B0 was always taken to be zero, indicating 'no modification' in this case

When this bit is set, the second instruction is modified by adding to it the contents of the memory location specified by the address portion of the first instruction of the pair. Thus any storage location could, in effect, act as an index register. In computer design terms, this brings to mind the compiler-writer's dictum that there are only three satisfactory choices for the number of programmer-visible working registers in a machine: zero, one or infinity. (The zero case is exemplified by stack-based, zero-address, instruction sets such as that of the English Electric KDF9 computer which was first delivered to a customer in 1964 [16].)

There are a number of small address-modification details glossed over by Table 10.2, for which the interested reader is referred to the appendices. For example, in Appendix 3, it may be seen that the Elliott 403's *Use Logic* instruction allowed various B-line options to be configured, including arranging that the contents of *two* B-lines be added together before being used as modifiers. The concept of double B-modification was a feature of the Ferranti Atlas computer, first operational in 1962 [14]. Another matter of detail relates to the well-known but hazardous 'side-effect' of classical address-modification whereby *all* of an instruction, including the function (op code) bits, could be altered dynamically by program. Elliott computers from the 800 series onwards did not allow the function bits to be altered during address-modification.

Returning to the theme of general register sets, none of the Elliott computers covered by Table 10.2 can be said to exhibit a general register-set architecture in its pure form. For this, we have to turn to the Ferranti Pegasus. As is explained more fully in Chap. 5, the Elliott 401 and the Ferranti Pegasus computers shared a common technical heritage. If politics and personalities had been different, the Pegasus design would very probably have emerged earlier from the Borehamwood stable instead of from Ferranti's new London Computer Laboratory somewhat later. In view of the Elliott connection and the historical importance of Pegasus in the wider world, it is worth making a digression to give an overall description of the Pegasus architecture.

10.5 Pegasus: The First Implementation of a General Register Set

The Ferranti Pegasus, first delivered in 1956, is considered to be the first computer with a clear *general register-set* architecture. Specifically, in their seminal book *Computer Structures: Readings and Examples* [15], Bell and Newell state that 'Pegasus has the nicest ISP [instruction-set processor] structure discussed in this section – perhaps in this book … It is probably the first machine to use an array of general registers as accumulators, multiplier-quotient registers, index registers, etc.' The first American-designed computer to adopt this general register organisation was the UNIVAC 1107, delivered in 1962. By the 1980s the concept had become the de facto starting point for the design of most processors world-wide. An exception is the small number of computers using a zero-address, or stack-oriented, architecture such as the English Electric KDF9 referred to earlier (Fig. 10.2).

Fig. 10.2 The Ferranti Pegasus computer was an outgrowth of the Elliott 401 project. First delivered in March 1956, Pegasus was more expensive than the Elliott 402, was slightly faster, had more memory and better systems software, and more were sold (40 delivered compared with ten of the Elliott 402)

The Pegasus computer grew out of Borehamwood's experience with the Elliott 401 [5], especially in Pegasus' use of a family of packaged logic circuits and a primary memory based on nickel delay lines. Charles Owen, ex-Borehamwood, took the lead in refining and improving Laurence Clarke's double-triode packaged circuits – which were, in their turn, adapted from an earlier Charles Owen family based on sub-miniature pentodes. George Felton, also ex-Borehamwood, took the lead in designing and implementing Pegasus systems software. Christopher Strachey, working as a consultant for the National Research Development Corporation (NRDC), took the lead as Pegasus logical designer and instruction-set originator. A brief introduction to Christopher Strachey has already been given in Chap. 5 and more information may be found in [17]. Strachey had also been in Canada from the end of August 1952 to March 1953, working for NRDC writing programs for a Ferranti Mark I computer (given the local name *Ferrut*, signifying the University of Toronto) in connection with the Saint Lawrence Seaway project. Whilst in Canada, he was able to visit several computer installations in the United States and study their instruction sets. Upon Strachey's return to England in March 1953, he wrote the first demonstration programs for the Elliott 401 and advised Harry Carpenter on modifications to the 401 during his 8-month stay in Cambridge in 1953/1954. Strachey's accumulated experience, no doubt, led him to formulate a novel arrangement of registers for Pegasus, as now explained.

A Pegasus 19-bit instruction has the following format for the main computational orders:

N	X	F	M
Address or constant	Accumulator	Op code	Modifier
7 bits	3 bits	6 bits	3 bits

Into the first eight locations of the N-field are mapped the eight X-accumulators which also act as the eight Modifier (M) registers – though location zero always contains the value zero. The Pegasus programmer is thus provided with seven general-purpose registers, available for all computational and address-generation activity.

The main arithmetic and logical operations in the Pegasus instruction set are symmetrical. For example, there are three forms of an ADD instruction:

$$x' = x + n;$$
$$x' = x + c;$$
$$n' = n + x.$$

where x is the contents of one of the seven general registers, n is the contents of a location in the immediate-access store (into whose address space the seven general registers are mapped), and c is a constant (i.e., literal).

It was not until the advent of the Elliott 803 and 503 computers at the start of the 1960s that Borehamwood adopted and expanded the above Pegasus arrangement for flexible arithmetic and logical operations – see Appendix 4.

For Pegasus, the input and output devices are also mapped into the immediate-access address space. Single-word or block, read or write, transfers from/to the drum backing store are performed by a group of four dedicated instructions.

The Elliott 402, designed a year or so before Pegasus, had a 32-bit instruction. This included 10 bits of next-instruction-address and 10 bits for specifying the address of the operand. The remaining 12 bits gave a somewhat reduced repertoire of operations compared with Pegasus, especially in respect of testing and control-transfer instructions. The addressing options between the two machines were similar, except for the following points. The 402 mapped *all* operand-locations, both immediate-access and backing-store locations, into the same 10-bit address space, all but 15 locations of which were held on the drum backing store. However, input/output was not memory-mapped. Pegasus mapped only the immediate-access (RAM) locations into the 7-bit address space; backing-store transfers to/from this 7-bit space had to be performed by separate instructions. Pegasus included input/output locations in the 7-bit space, so that normal computational instructions could be used for input/output. The 402 had specific input/output instructions.

10.6 Word Lengths and Instruction Sets

The early Elliott computers favoured word-lengths of 16-bits (the 153, Nicholas) or 32-bits (the 400 series). In response to calls for greater fixed-point accuracy and competition from other manufacturers, 39-bit words were used for the 800 series and the 503 computers. The Elliott 502, designed for special high-performance on-line projects, reverted to 20-bit words. Then the Elliott 4100 series of medium-performance general-purpose computers settled for 24-bit words. In between these extremes, the defence-oriented 900 series of compact mobile computers had 18-bit words and also later, in reduced form, 12-bit words. Fixed-point data was normally represented in all Elliott computers in two's complement fractional form.

The arithmetic of early Elliott machines such as the 153, Nicholas and the 400 series was bit-serial, employing thermionic valve (tube) technologies. A change came in the early 1960s, by which time semiconductor logic was firmly established, initially using germanium junction transistors. (The story of Borehamwood's entry into the transistor era is recounted in the next section.) The 803, though still basically using bit-serial arithmetic, employed some internal parallelism for data transfers. The 800 series were the first Elliott machines to have magnetic core memory. The 502, 503, 900 series and 4100 series were all bit-parallel throughout. The original 900 series and 4100 series designs employed magnetic core memories, but by the early 1970s all Elliott 900 series developments were turning to silicon semiconductor memory.

Instruction formats was an area where all Borehamwood designs showed some similarity. Setting aside the Elliott 153 with its special functional parallelism, all other Elliott computers basically conformed to the one-address instruction format – with the 401 and 402 also carrying the address of the next instruction (the so-called *1 + 1* instruction format). The Nicholas, 403, 405, 803 and 503, all packed two instructions per word; the 4100 had both one and two instructions per word; the remaining Elliott computers had just one instruction per word.

The repertoire of common arithmetic instructions employed by computers designed at Borehamwood differed little from those found in the products of the other main British and American computer manufacturers of the period 1955–1965. All Elliott computers incorporated an ADD and a MULTIPLY instruction, with the Elliott 403 having additional MULTIPLY-AND-ADD and MULTIPLY-AND-SUBTRACT versions. Borehamwood's views on subtraction evolved somewhat over the years, as can be seen from Table 10.3, particularly regarding the inclusion

Table 10.3 The inclusion of some sample fixed-point arithmetic operations in Elliott computers

	Subtract	Reverse-subtract	Negate	Divide	Hardware square root
153	Y	Y			
Nicholas	Y		Y		
401	Y			Y	
402	Y		Y	Y	
403	Y			Y	
405	Y	Y		Y	
803/503	Y	Y	Y	Y	Y – see text
502	Y	Y		Y	Y
900 (18-bit)		Y		Y	
900 (12-bit)		Y		Y	
4100	Y	Y		Y	

of the REVERSE-SUBTRACT (or *negate-and-add*) instruction. Table 10.3 also charts the inclusion of hardware DIVIDE and hardware SQUARE ROOT facilities, the latter being provided for the Elliott 502 and for the 800-series computers in cases where an 800-series machine was being used for industrial process control applications.

All Elliott computers *except* the 401 had a logical AND instruction, referred to in the earlier machines as COLLATE. The 401 had the more general EXCLUSIVE-OR operation, referred to in the Elliott literature as NEQ (logical non-equivalence). The Elliott 4100 series included AND NOT, as well as the AND operation. All Elliott computers incorporated SHIFT LEFT and SHIFT RIGHT instructions, though it was not until the 4100 series that programmers had the specific means for choosing between logical, arithmetic or circular shifts.

From the Elliott 153 onwards, Borehamwood computers had the ability to read into the accumulator a word set up on handkeys on the operator's console, such handkeys being referred to in the early literature as the *number generator*.

The Elliott 403 was the first Borehamwood design to incorporate a *normalise* instruction. Hardware support for floating-point operations was provided on the Elliott 402F, 803B and 503 and 4130 computers. Floating-point was performed by extracodes on the 4120 computer. The germ of the general concept of extracodes can actually be discerned in the Nicholas instruction set. The Nicholas programmer could issue a single instruction which had the effect of inhibiting the incrementing of the Program Counter whilst hardware went through an automatic sequence of behind-the-scenes low-level tasks, for example the manipulation of the double-length accumulator during multiplication (see Appendix 2). However, the Elliott 4100 series was the first Borehamwood design to have explicit extracodes.

The Elliott 405 was an early Borehamwood design that gave explicit assistance with subroutine entry/exit. As Elliott entered the on-line control arena, more attention was given to fast program swapping. For example, the 503's *Switch* instruction took 19.5 µs to load registers and transfer control. A similar operation in the 502 computer, the *Program Break* instruction, took rather less than 10 µs to perform an automatic context switch. A feature of the Elliott 502 was that it allowed the apparently simultaneous running of several programs on a time-division basis, according to pre-assigned priorities. Up to eight levels of priority were catered for. The Elliott 502's processor was also unusual in being *asynchronous* – that is to say, there was no fixed-frequency clock. This is explained further in Appendix 5.

Many Elliott computers offered a type of instruction known generically as *read-modify-write*, whereby the contents of a memory location could be altered, or perhaps tested, in one indivisible hardware action. Examples are: *increment memory*, and *swap accumulator and memory*. As may be seen in Appendices 3–7, this form of instruction first made its appearance in the 403 and 405 computers, then in the 502, then was seen at its richest in the 803 and 503 computers, and then appeared rather less abundantly in the 4100 series machines. The 900 series computers also had a small number of this type of instruction. One reason for the richness of *read-modify-write* instructions in the 800-series computers may have been the need to provide easy manipulation of a main memory location when it was being used as a modifier or index register. (Recall that the 800-series machines had no explicit modifier registers.)

The 900 series, designed to meet the need for compact, mobile computers operating in hazardous environments, had reduced instruction sets compared with other contemporary Elliott machines. The 12-bit members of the 900 family, in particular, had minimalist instruction sets that were not particularly easy to use. These 12-bit members were often embedded in special-purpose avionics equipment – see Chap. 12 and Appendix 6.

In contrast, the 4100 series had, for its generation, a reasonably sophisticated instruction set that gave considerable help to high-level compiler writers. The concept of a stack (push/pop), as used for example in block-structured languages, was given explicit hardware support. There was hardware assistance for packing and unpacking characters. There was a *Conditions* register. The four forms of operand-addressing (literal, direct, modified, indirect) were made conveniently available for all instructions. There was a flexible set of instructions for register-to-register moves. There were plans for datum/limit registers to aid memory management, though it is not clear to what extent the available 4100 series operating systems made use of these (see comments in Appendix 7). As has been mentioned, the 4100 series had extracode instructions. Finally, the Elliott 4100 series had a Standard Interface for all input/output devices, the physical manifestation of which was a standard plug and socket arrangement for all peripherals. More details will be found in Appendix 7.

We now need to pause in the architectural discussion and consider how semiconductor technology, and in particular the arrival of the junction transistor, affected the implementation of digital circuits at Borehamwood and other UK computer design centres.

10.7   Borehamwood and Transistors

Andrew St Johnston recalls [3] that 'We were lucky with transistors. The first usable transistors came out in the mid-1950s [actually, early 1950s]; these were point contact transistors and had the advantage that you could make a bistable with one transistor. Many eminent folk started to work on this component. We were too busy trying to make 405s and also commissioning the 153 computer and therefore could put no effort into this development.'

Amongst the 'eminent folk' was R L (Dick) Grimsdale at Manchester University, whose early point contact transistor computer was first working in November 1953 [6]. The reliability was not good. Significantly, when Metropolitan-Vickers based their MV950 on the Manchester design, they converted many of the circuits to junction transistors. The MV950 was completed in 1956 for internal use within the company and six machines were produced [6]. Meanwhile, a point-contact transistor computer known as CADET burst into life in 1955 at the UK's Atomic Energy Research Establishment at Harwell [18]. In America, the TRADIC (TRAnsistor DIgital Computer) was produced for the US Air Force in 1954 [19].

Also in America, the *surface barrier* transistor was proving successful, being used in the MIT Lincoln Laboratory's TX-0 computer (first working in 1956) and the Philco Corporation's TRANSAC S-1000 computer (first working in about 1957) – see [20].

John Bunt remembers [21] some interaction with Philco, as follows. 'Philco, the US company, designed one of the first fully transistorized computers and offered Elliotts a licence to manufacture to their design. It was ahead of anything we had at that time. Andrew St J. and I attended a meeting with Sir Leon Bagrit in London with representatives of Philco, who asked what we would offer them for a licence. When pressed, they quoted their terms which were a down payment of some magnitude and royalties on sales. Sir Leon told Philco that he had negotiated many licence deals but he had never offered a down payment. He said that if the project was successful, royalties should be satisfactory to Philco. A down payment suggested a lack of confidence by Philco in their product. He suggested that Philco's terms might be more satisfactory to a gramophone records manufacturer (meaning EMI).' We shall return to pick up the EMI story a little later (Fig. 10.3).

Andrew St Johnston continues [3]: 'The point contact transistor proved unreliable when used in computer quantities. The junction appeared just at the right time when John Bunt was free from the 153, and Jim Barrow was also freed from the research work he was doing. The folk working on point contact devices went on for several years before giving up. This gave us a head start. My wife Dina had joined Elliotts in 1953 and worked with John on the 153 for a long time at Scarborough (before our marriage). John dined with us on the way back from Scarborough

Fig. 10.3 A printed-circuit board from an Elliott 803B computer in about 1963. Mullard OC84 germanium transistors are used for logic, with OC23 power transistors shown on the right-hand side. This particular printed-circuit board contains three sections of logic, namely part of the Instruction Register control, the Interrupt control logic, part of the CPU timing control

Fig. 10.4 Borehamwood introduced Minilog elements for logic design in 1962, a year or two before TTL integrated-circuit chips came onto the market in America. Each Minilog element was an encapsulated transistorised logic circuit based on NAND gates, measuring 5.1 cm x 2.2 cm x 1.6 cm. The photo shows an engineer extracting a printed-circuit board upon which are mounted 18 Minilog elements, part of a telecommunications project

[probably towards the end of 1954] which in those days took a long time even at John's speed. I proposed to him over the table that he start a small team on developing junction transistor circuitry. Jim Barrow was already at work on the more conventional technique using two junction transistors as a bistable.

'John's circuitry was really rather remarkable because it used core logic, and the OC72 transistors were really only re-shapers. [The pre-1959 OC series of transistors were AF (audio frequency) devices whose modest switching properties limited their use in high-speed computing circuits]. John's bistable technique was [similar to that used in] the 152/153 of a looped back single bit delay. His logic cores needed valves to drive them as did the core store at the time. He built an 801 (the other numbers had been used elsewhere). Laurie Bental was part of the team. This core circuitry showed more reliability than the bistable technique, so this design technique went forward as a scientific computer to become the 802. This worked and some were sold. One of the long established programmers Roger Cook advised John on the order code. Iann Barron was involved as a Vac student but played no part in the real design'.

The OC series of low-power germanium junction transistors was produced in the UK by the Mullard company from mid-1954 onwards, the OC72 becoming commercially available in late 1955 [22]. The OC72 had a common-base 3dB cutoff frequency of only 350 KHz – relatively poor for high-speed computing circuits. By 1959 the superior-speed OC42 had become available and then, about three years

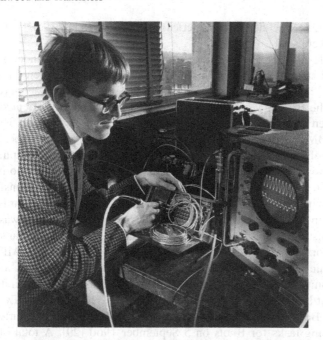

Fig. 10.5 In about 1963, Borehamwood started research into the design of high-speed logic circuits based on tunnel diodes. The photo shows Iann Barron with an experimental system working at 50 MHz. The target, a computer working at 250 MHz, was not achieved before the research project was scaled down

later, the OC84. The final design of the production Elliott 803B was based largely on the OC84, with the OC42 and various other transistors also appearing in places. The Mullard OC28 or OC23 power transistors were used where large current-driving capability was required.

John Bunt's main logic circuits for the Elliott 800 series computers used Mullard type OC84 junction transistors and ferrite magnetic cores. The system for the 803A employed two cores per logic gate in a master/slave configuration (but see below for later 803B developments). The master/slave configuration is believed to be somewhat similar to the technique adopted by EMI in their EMIDEC computer. It is interesting to wonder whether there was any informal contact between Borehamwood and EMI at Hayes, about 14 miles away across the outer-London suburbs. There was unlikely to have been formal contact since the EMIDEC 1100 was poised to become a competitor to the Elliott 405 in the business data processing market. Remember, however, that Norman Hill had left Borehamwood's Computing Division to join EMI early in 1957 (see Chap. 8).

Laurie Bental, who joined John Bunt's team at Borehamwood in late 1955 or early 1956, remembers [23] that 'during 1957 the laboratory prototype 801 computer was developed and used to test the new core technology'. The production version, the Elliott 802 computer, was on display at the Automation Exhibition at Olympia, London, in November 1958 and an 802 was delivered to a customer (the Natural Gas Pipeline Co. of America) towards the end of 1958 [24]. A total of seven 802s were sold.

Meanwhile over at EMI's Laboratories at Hayes, a team under R T (Ron) Clayden had started to build a simple thermionic valve computer, CP401, at the end of 1954 [25]. Before this was completed, in 1956 Clayden's team received an order from the British Motor Corporation for a larger, payroll-oriented, machine that was given the name CP407 or, colloquially, the *BMC computer*. The technology of the BMC computer [26] was mostly thermionic valves (tubes). A small section controlling the punched-card input and lineprinter output equipment is said to have employed OC 72 transistors and magnetic cores – though no mention of these is given in [26]. This section was designed by Godfrey Hounsfield (later Nobel prizewinner Sir Godfrey Hounsfield CBE, FRS, who afterwards achieved fame as the inventor of CT scanners). The BMC computer (CP 407) was delivered to BMC's Austin Longbridge factory in 1958. Starting in 1958, the transistor ideas were taken forward by Godfrey Hounsfield for the circuitry of the EMIDEC 1100 machine, which Hounsfield later enthusiastically described [27] as 'the first all-transistor computer to be constructed in Britain'. This claim had initially been made in print by Norman Hill in August 1960 [28]. The first EMIDEC 1100 was delivered to Boots, Nottingham, on 20 April 1960 [28] and had started running data processing tasks for Boots on 5 September 1960 [29]. A total of about 22 EMIDEC 1100s were sold.

Back at Borehamwood, the Elliott 802 had not been entirely transistorised because no high-power semiconductor devices were obtainable for the core logic reset pulses and the core memory driver pulses at the time of designing the circuits. Mullard's OC16 high-power transistor, capable of handling 24 W, became available in about 1956. Using these, the Elliott 803A, a fully transistorised version of the 802, was first working in 1959. The first Elliott 803 was delivered to E I DuPont de Nemours Inc., Beaumont, Texas, in November 1959 for the control of a nylon processing plant and a further 23 Elliott 803s were sold to external customers during 1960 [30] – though the exact delivery-months have not yet come to light. It might be inferred from [31] that the first Elliott 803 had actually been delivered before October 1959. A total of over 200 Elliott 803s were eventually sold (see Appendix 8). Some first-hand memories of the 803 hardware are given in [32]. As is discussed in Appendix 4, there were actually two versions of the 803: the 803A up to about the end of 1960 and the 803B thereafter. Minor differences in the type and use of transistors between the A and B versions and the layout of printed-circuit boards are noted in Appendix 4.

Perhaps one reason why both Norman Hill and Godfrey Hounsfield claimed precedence for the EMIDEC 1100 as the UK's first fully transistorised computer was that the EMI machine was a substantial, high-profile, business data processing system typically costing £250,000. In contrast, the Elliott 803, priced at about £25,000, was targeted at the less visible market of scientific applications and industrial process control. Though smaller, the 803 was probably first into the field by a few months.

Meanwhile, Ferranti had also been busy investigating transistors. In common with several other groups, Ferranti had been looking at so-called *ballot box* logical circuits which employed ferrite cores to sum the net contribution of current pulses in several windings. The investigations of Ken Johnson and others led to the *Neuron* logical circuit, for which a test-bed called *Newt* was produced in 1957 [33]. When the fully developed circuits were described at an IEE meeting in February 1959, the *Neuron* arrangement invoked much comment from the audience. Laurie Bental, of Borehamwood, is recorded [34] as saying that the circuit 'was more complicated than it need be. He was familiar with an element with similar properties which made use of the square loop property of a ferrite material and used only about a quarter of the number of components.' The *Neuron* was used in the Ferranti Sirius computer, announced on 19 May 1959 and first delivered in June 1960 to Ferranti's Newman Street bureau in London [35]. Sirius was a serial fixed-point decimal computer having a 500 kHz clock rate and a main store (extensible) of 1K words arranged in 50-word loops of torsional delay lines. Approximately 22 Sirius computers were sold, each costing £20,000 [33].

To continue the story of Borehamwood's entry into the transistor era, it is worth mentioning the Elliott Minilog circuit building blocks. Each Minilog component was an encapsulated solid-state transistorised logic element based on NAND gates, measuring $5.1 \times 2.2 \times 1.6$ cm^3. The initial series of nine Minilog elements included various NAND gates for composing such building blocks as binary counter stages, differentiators, oscillators and delay elements. To quote the introductory technical brochure of 1962 [36], 'Minilog is used exclusively in Panellit Data Loggers and Alarm Scanning Equipment, for the 609 Industrial and Computing System and to drive the peripheral equipment of the Elliott 803 Computer. Other applications include conveyor systems, automatic lift control, automatic test equipment and Optimat, an on line optimising controller.' Minilog elements were first introduced by Borehamwood as replacements for relays in industrial switching and sequencing devices. Thereafter, they found a wide use in bespoke process control and automation systems. The price of each Minilog element in 1967 lay between about £1.20 to £4.50, depending upon functionality [37].

In common with many computer manufacturers of the time, Elliotts naturally kept themselves informed about advances in semiconductor device technologies. This kind of forward-looking endeavour was often carried out on the advice of Elliott's consultants. One consultant, Professor W J (Ted) Poppelbaum of the University of Illinois, suggested the establishment of a small research group to investigate high-speed logic and storage elements based upon tunnel diodes. The group was led by Iann Barron, who had spent the summers of 1955, 1956 and 1957 working at Borehamwood as a vacation student and had joined Elliotts full time in 1961 after National Service [38]. Having played a large part in commissioning the Elliott 502 computer (see Appendix 5), Iann took responsibility for the tunnel diode experiments at Borehamwood using the technique of *Goto pairs*. The Elliott-Automation Annual Report of 1963 proudly states that 'Research in the Borehamwood Laboratories into the use of tunnel diodes in fast logic circuits has put Britain ahead of the world in this branch of computer technology.' The eventual aim was "to build a computer (not just a store) operating at 250 MHz. In practice, the original circuits worked at 10/15 MHz, and the systems in the photograph [in Fig. 10.5] worked at 50 MHz. A much smaller package was required to achieve 250 MHz; this was designed but only a few prototypes were delivered before I left" [38].

Iann Barron left Borehamwood 'rather suddenly' in 1965 to found his own company, Computer Technology Ltd., producing the *Modular One* minicomputer which first came onto the market in 1969. Iann had not always seen eye to eye with his seniors at Borehamwood over matters of computer design. Iann went on to found Inmos Ltd. in 1978, the developers of high-performance parallel computer systems based on *transputers* which first hit the market in 1985. He has remarked retrospectively [38] that 'my education in computers was completed by Elliotts: I had worked as a programmer [on Nicholas], a logic designer [on the 802], a computer architect [on the 502] and a circuit designer [tunnel diodes]'.

To return to 1964, in that year Elliotts considered setting up their own semiconductor manufacturing facility. Laurence Clarke and Edgar Herzfeld were sent to America to investigate possible licencing agreements. Laurence had meetings with Fairchild between 25 February and 8 March 1964, and with Motorola early in May 1964. He remembers the occasion as follows [39].

'When Elliotts were thinking of entering the microelectronics business (eventually setting up in Glenrothes under Ian Mackintosh in 1966) I was deputed to visit the bosses of Motorola and Fairchild to look into the possibilities of a licence deal. As you know it was Elliott policy, wherever possible, to build on the basic work of the world leaders. I went to San Francisco to visit Bob Noyce of Fairchild in Palo Alto and then Motorola in Phoenix (Lester Hogan). By this time I was well into the Californian mode of dress and always dressed informally. I reported each evening to Edgar Herzfeld down town. What other business he was about I don't know. However the arrangement was for him to come to Palo Alto on a Friday morning to talk "Turkey". He was always a very proper person so I put on a suit for the day and was really shaken to find that he turned up in an open-necked flowery shirt! Like Dr Lawrence Ross, Herzfeld had a very nice sense of humour and teased me about it very gently. Incidentally his wife, who was accompanying him, was a very charming person and was, I believe, a fairly distinguished chemist in her own right. With hindsight I can say predictably, the Motorola option did not get selected because they demanded a large up-front payment and guaranteed turnover – Elliotts just did not have the stamina for that sort of thing. Whether that was the only stumbling block I just don't remember. We recruited Mackintosh from Westinghouse and I guess he was responsible for the details of the final [Fairchild] deal.'

Elliotts opened their Microelectronics facility in Glenrothes, Fife, in the latter half of 1966, starting with Fairchild know-how. For some, Glenrothes seemed a step too far, bearing in mind the wobble in the financial status of Elliott-Automation at that time (see Chap. 13). Shortly after the English Electric merger and the GEC take-over, the Glenrothes facility was closed down.

We now step back in time to the early 1950s and resume the systems architecture story by considering how Borehamwood developed the technology of magnetically coated drums and discs as a means of storing large quantities of data. Allied to this is the problem of integrating fast-access (but small-capacity) memory devices with slower-access (but larger-capacity) devices.

10.8   Memory Management and Bulk Input/Output

Probably the first attempt to combine primary and secondary memory into a single hierarchy occurred at Manchester University in 1949 [6]. The Manchester Mark I computer had a CRT primary RAM backed by a fixed-head drum, with software-controlled swapping of 64-word pages between primary and secondary memory. A dozen years later, Manchester University was to pioneer virtual addressing and hardware assistance for memory management.

At Borehamwood, as with many other computer design teams of the early 1950s, the engineering aim was to obtain a cost-effective balance between speed and capacity, using memory technologies that were essentially sequential in nature. In Borehamwood's case, the technologies were nickel delay lines and magnetic surface recording on discs or drums. The Elliott 403 (WREDAC, see Chap. 3 and Appendix 3) had a particularly complex hierarchy which is now briefly described. Firstly, the 403 had a fast, four-word, instruction buffer. Instructions were fetched in groups of four and, if no control transfers occurred, the 403 was pipelined so that

Fig. 10.6 Close-up of the read/write head structure for an Elliott disc memory for a 400-series computer. The disc is mounted vertically, and the heads are recording on each side of the magnetically coated surface

decoding of a following instruction took place whilst the current instruction was being executed. Then the 403 had three levels of addressable storage for operands: an *Immediate-Access* section nominally containing $(12+512)$ words, a disc backing store of 16K words (approximately 64 KB) and finally up to four magnetic tape units. The topic of magnetic tape storage is considered in Sect. 10.9.

The problem of bulk input/output, so crucial to the requirements of commercial data processing applications, had exercised Borehamwood since 1953 (see for example [40]). The movement of large amounts of numerical data had been a major concern in the design of the Elliott 403 (WREDAC) in 1954/1955, especially in respect of the printing and graphical display of flight data for the Woomera weapons trials range in Australia. The Elliott 403 received trials data both in paper tape form and from magnetic tape. The results of analysing programs were written to magnetic tape. Then a special off-line output unit called WREDOC accepted the data from magnetic tape, carried out the necessary buffering and formatting, and (a) printed results on a fast lineprinter and (b) displayed information graphically on four graph-drawing devices. WREDOC required a significant amount of hardware to fulfil its bulk data-handling tasks and was, in effect, almost a separate computer (see Chap. 3).

The hardware lessons of WREDOC, and the many case studies carried out for businesses of varying size and complexity (see Chap. 9), convinced the Borehamwood team that their new commercial data processing computer, the Elliott 405, should include two features that were, it is believed, reasonably novel in the mid-1950s:

(a) The 405 should be flexible in configuration, each particular installation being built up by choosing from a repertoire of interconnecting units.
(b) One of these units, to be called the *Input/output Compiler*, should allow for the fast autonomous transfer of large volumes of characters, including any necessary formatting and binary-to-decimal and decimal-to-binary conversion.

Further technical details of the Elliott 405 are given in Appendix 3.

A word should be said about Elliott's definition of *drum* and *disc* in connection with secondary storage equipment. During the 1950s at Borehamwood, the terms *drum* and *disc* both referred to devices employing fixed-head recording on a magnetically coated rotating surface. The main difference between an Elliott drum and disc was the obvious one of physical shape of the rotating device and the location of the fixed-position read/write heads in relation to the device's axis of rotation.

Generally speaking, in the early days of computers, a fixed-head drum was usually assumed to have a smaller capacity than a fixed-head disc. From the 1960s onwards, the term *disc* came to be used generically by computer manufacturers for devices that had moving heads, implying that there were more information tracks than heads – and hence an even larger overall memory capacity. The access-time on a moving-head disc has two basic components: the seek-time, during which head(s) is/are positioned in line with the chosen track, followed by latency, during which the disc spins round until the start of a desired block of data is reached. A refinement is the exchangeable disc store, for which a group of one or more removable discs (called a disc-pack or cartridge) could be mounted in turn on a single mechanism. This is analogous to the way in which several separate reels of magnetic tape can be mounted, one at a time, on a given tape deck.

Compared with conventional magnetic tape systems, moving-head disc systems gave much more rapid access to a particular block or record of information. In business data processing parlance, discs were often said to give *direct-access,* sometimes also called *random-access,* to blocks or records within a file, when compared with systems that held files on magnetic tape. The IBM 305 RAMAC computer, first introduced in 1956, held files on an IBM 350 moving-head disc device. RAMAC stood for 'Random Access Method of Accounting and Control', implying the great advantage over competitors of the relatively rapid access to bulk data held on the IBM 350 moving-head disc.

In comparison with IBM and many other manufacturers, Borehamwood was very slow to appreciate the advantages of moving-head discs. It was not until the mid- or late-1960s that Elliott introduced a moving-head disc system for the Elliott 4100 series computers. By October 1967, for example, a disc handler was available that employed ten disc surfaces, each having hundred tracks and giving a total on-line capacity of one million 24-bit words. A maximum of eight handlers could be attached to one standard interface channel of an Elliott 4100 series computer.

R G (Ron) Wilson, who joined Elliott-Automation as a graduate trainee in 1962 and became a sales engineer in Elliotts' Scientific Computing Division (SCD) in September 1964, recalls the backing storage situation at that time as follows [41]: 'There was no disc offering on the 803 and 503, and my recollection of the 4100 Series is that the disc option was at first offered only in a rather diffident and off-hand manner. With the 903 the lack of storage peripherals was a longstanding embarrassment. I think the 903 was initially offered with cassette magnetic tapes as its only external storage.'

10.9   Magnetic Tape and Magnetic Film Storage

Early British computer manufacturers were relatively slow to adopt magnetic tape storage, compared with American companies. In America the UNIVAC I, delivered in June 1951, had a magnetic tape system (called Uniservos) of novel design, using phosphor-bronze metal tape with nickel-cobalt coating. By 1953 IBM had successfully introduced magnetic tapes of a more reliable and cost-effective type for the IBM 700 series computers, using a plastic (Mylar) backing coated with iron oxide. In Britain, the Lyons LEO computer was the first machine for which magnetic tape for bulk data input and output was proposed. In 1950 Standard Telephones and Cables Ltd. was contracted to design and supply the magnetic tape equipment for LEO, for delivery early in 1951. However, by mid-1953 no satisfactory magnetic tape system had become operational and so punched cards were chosen for bulk data input/output for LEO [7].

The National Research Development Corporation (NRDC) became aware that Britain was seriously lagging behind in the development of magnetic tape systems. Accordingly, from June 1953 onwards, the NRDC placed contracts with several firms including Pye Ltd. of Cambridge, Epsylon Research & Development Co. Ltd. of Twickenham and EMI of Hayes, Middlesex [42]. None of these contracts had produced entirely satisfactory results and by the end of the 1950s most British computer suppliers still felt obliged to use tape decks manufactured in America by companies such as Ampex. It was not until the early 1960s that the UK caught up – and by that time, or shortly thereafter, it was prudent for computer suppliers every-where to demonstrate that their magnetic tape systems were 'IBM-compatible'.

In 1954/1955 Borehamwood's initial excursion into the field was to provide the Elliott 403 (WREDAC) with magnetic tape decks originally designed for EDSAC by Donald Willis of Cambridge University Mathematics Laboratory and manufac-

Fig. 10.7 A magnetic film deck from an Elliott 405 computer. The reel of magnetically coated 35-mm film is mounted on two spools beneath the removable cover at the bottom of the photo-graph. The wires from the white amplifier boxes at the top of the photograph lead down to the read/write heads. The Elliott system used sprocket-driven film, which gave a relatively slow transfer rate. However, the system was relatively robust and reliable when compared with other contempo-rary magnetic tape systems of the1950s

tured by the radio and television company Pye Ltd. The decks employed quarter-inch (6.35 mm) plastic tape – similar in width to that used at the time for reel-to-reel audio recording – but operating at a much faster linear speed of about 100 in./s, recording at approximately 100 frames/in. and each reel containing about 1,500 ft (approximately 450 m) of tape. The mechanical design of the tape deck presented some difficulties: vacuum pockets were used to cushion the stop/start braking, 'but often that feature proved inadequate, snapping the tape when their servo mechanisms responded inadequately' [43]. In addition, the tape's 'toffee paper substrate seemed too flimsy for robust commercial use' [44].

The Pye quarter-inch magnetic tape system was chosen for the Elliott 403 because of its availability. However, Andrew St Johnston and Laurence Clarke had already been thinking of alternatives. In May 1954 they had proposed a magnetic *film* system for the Elliott 402 computer [40] though it was not until a year or two later that their ideas were to become a reality, as is now related.

The pressure was on by 1955, when Borehamwood was certain that a satisfactory magnetic tape technology was essential for the new Elliott 405 computer. Inspiration came from the data-recording days of the MRS5 and 152 project, when 35 mm optical film had been used by Borehamwood to capture the huge amounts of radar trials information at high data-rates. Laurence Clarke remembers [44] that 'at the peak time of our trials we were creating several times the film output of the studios getting their film processed at the nearby Denham Labs. This meant that we had the connections and familiarity with the film substrate.' The reference to the Denham Labs deserves a brief digression to describe what, collectively, were known as the Elstree Film Studios.

The village of Elstree, about a mile to the south-west of Borehamwood, was larger than the village of Borehamwood before the First World War. Consequently, the name *Elstree Studios* came to be used informally for all of the six large film studios that grew up in this region of Hertfordshire during the 20-year period from 1914 [45]. The district became home to the greatest number of motion picture production facilities outside Hollywood, although five of the six 'Elstree' studios were actually located in the parish of Borehamwood. The largest such studio occupied a 200-acre site almost opposite the Elliott Research Laboratories on Elstree Way, Borehamwood. Originally begun as Amalgamated Studios Ltd. in 1935, this site was purchased by Metro-Goldwyn-Mayer (MGM) in 1944. Metro-Goldwyn-Mayer Inc., founded in America 1924, was the biggest of the Hollywood giants. MGM continued production at their Borehamwood site until 1970 when they moved to the EMI Studios on Shenley Road, Borehamwood – a facility that is still very much in business as a high-quality Film and Television Studio.

Elliotts at Borehamwood were familiar with the 35-mm film stock used by all the Elstree Studios both for optical images and, when suitably coated with magnetic material, for sound recording. The robust mechanical characteristics of the 35-mm film equipment suggested that the medium could be adapted by Elliotts for the reliable recording of digital information. Thus Borehamwood developed their 35-mm (approximately 1-in. wide) Magnetic *Film* Store as a practical rival to the half-inch wide Magnetic *Tape* Stores of IBM and other American computer manufacturers.

Laurence Clarke remembers [28] that when he gave one of the Cambridge Mathematical Laboratory colloquia on the Elliott 405, 'I was rather stumped by someone asking the question "Why film?". Before I could think of a snappy answer, Fairthorne of RAE adjusted his hearing aid and said "because it demonstrates the non-trivial advantage of existence!"'

The first Elliott magnetic film systems for the 405 were in use by late 1956. The mid-1950s was still an era of experimentation before there was any attempt at international standardisation. Thus there were at least seven varieties of American magnetic tape systems in operation in 1957, using tape widths that varied between a half-inch to three inches, giving transfer rates ranging from 6K to 40K characters/s, and employing reels of length 1,500 feet to 2,700 ft with each reel able to hold between 1.4 and 24.8 million characters [10]. Meanwhile, Ferranti Ltd. was using half-inch magnetic tapes for their Pegasus and Mercury computers, with mechanisms manufactured by the American company Electrodata. Later, similar mechanisms manufactured by the British company Decca were available (Donald Willis had moved to Decca from Cambridge). Interchangeability between manufacturers, and between different systems offered by the same manufacturer, presented challenges to all computer users in the period 1955–1965 (see for example [46]).

The emerging standard was that of IBM, whose half-inch magnetic tape system gave a transfer rate of 15K characters/s, with each reel holding up to 5 million characters. In contrast, Elliott's 35-mm Magnetic Film system had a very pedestrian performance of 0.3K characters/s in normal use, or 1.8K characters/s when used in a special off-line unit for direct printing of data to lineprinter. Each Elliott 1,000-ft reel held approximately 1.2 million characters.

The low transfer-rate performance of the Elliott system was largely a consequence of its sprocket drive, which allowed the tape to run out of contact with the heads. This, in turn, meant that environmental control, particularly dust filtration, was less of an issue than in rival systems. The Elliott system also allowed bi-directional reading/writing. For this, the film was imagined as consisting of two halves. Each half had four tracks – three for information and one for clock. In addition, there was a block marker track shared by both. Only one half of the film is used at any one time, one half being read from or written to when the tape is moving in one direction, and the other half when it is moving in the other direction. In response to the challenge of the Royal Army Pay Corps procurement exercise in 1957, where the Elliott 405 came head-to-head with the IBM 705, Borehamwood offered to increase the transfer rate of the 405's magnetic Film Store to 12K characters/s by doubling the film speed and changing to unidirectional reading/writing [47]. This offer was not, in the event, taken up because IBM won the Royal Army Pay Corps (RAPC) contract (see Chap. 9 and Appendix 3).

One interesting comment on IBM magnetic tape systems did emerge from the RAPC study. On reliability, it was stated [47] that in 1957 an IBM 705 in use by the Domestic Corporation of New York experienced the following average error rates:

Tape errors	0.65/8 h shift
Memory errors	0.06/8 h shift
Other errors	0.18/8 h shift

This indicates that in the mid-1950s magnetic tape units were likely to be amongst the most unreliable components in a typical IBM computing installation. No comparative figures for Elliott 405 magnetic film units have come to light, but anecdotal evidence from a meeting of the 405 Users' Association [44] indicated that reliability was good, relative to the other systems then in use.

Borehamwood's Magnetic Film system lasted for the life of the Elliott 405 computers and was also used for the 803, until being replaced (rather tardily, many would say) by a more conventional half-inch magnetic tape system in the early 1960s. The Elliott 503, the high-performance version of the 803, had a maximum of eight half-inch, 7-track, magnetic tape decks. The instantaneous transfer rate was 42,000 characters/s. Variable length records were employed. With a normal packing density of 556 characters/in. and tape-reels of up to 2,400 ft in length and records of 128 words, one reel could typically store about 1,730,000 words in total. For this record-length, the effective maximum transfer rate is about 35 records/s.

The Elliott 903 offered 9K characters/s magnetic tape mechanisms, having seven tracks and recording at 200 bits/in. These were compatible with the ECMA (European Computer Manufacturers' Association) standards. By 1965 the magnetic tape system on offer for the Elliott 4120 had minimum and maximum transfer rates of 12K and 33K characters/s respectively – which was typical of the medium-priced systems of other manufacturers at that time [48] but well below the high-cost, high-performance systems then available elsewhere. For example, the Ampex TM2 decks used by the Ferranti Atlas computer used 1-in. wide, pre-addressed, tapes that transferred blocks of 512 words at an effective rate of 64K characters/s [49]. Bi-directional reading/writing was catered for.

10.10   Other Peripheral Equipment

Perhaps because of an early emphasis on engineering applications that were computationally intense, Elliott began to lag behind its competitors in the commercial data-processing sector since Borehamwood did not provide a wide enough range of input/output equipment. This was certainly the opinion of R G (Ron) Wilson, a sales engineer in Elliotts' Scientific Computing Division (SCD) who has been introduced earlier. Wilson recalls [41] that 'It was easy to see that Elliott-Automation Computers Ltd. had a strong technical and academic bias, and that most of the brilliant minds there were concentrated on sophisticated and efficient processor design. As a result the more mundane aspects such as peripherals took a back seat.... their relative neglect of peripherals meant that for a long time we (or rather NCR) did not compete too well in the commercial marketplace.' Wilson goes on to quote Elliott's bias towards paper tape input, compared with which

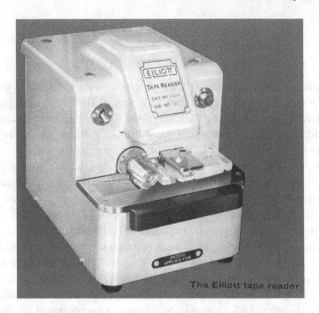

Fig. 10.8 In 1958, Borehamwood produced Elliott's fast paper tape reader, capable of transferring information at 1,000 characters/s. The early Elliott 400 series computers had used a 40 characters/s paper tape reader, later replaced by various Ferranti paper tape readers operating at speeds between 100 and 300 characters/s

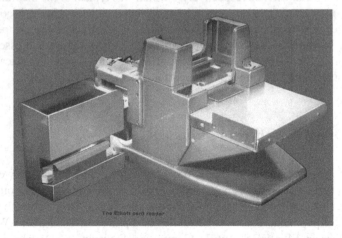

Fig. 10.9 Elliott's fast (400 cards/min), 80-column card reader in 1958. The first, primitive, provision of card-reading facilities for the 401 computer simply read 32 columns from 80, at a rate of about 15 cards/min

punched card readers were 'regarded with distain'. He also remembers that 'line-printers were for the favoured few'.

Wilson's remarks are not entirely fair. Borehamwood did actually design a fast (1,000 characters/s) paper tape reader and a fast (400 cards/min) card reader in

1958 or early 1959. Both devices were successes. For example, the Elliott card reader was also used by EMI for their EMIDEC 1100 computer.

Like many computer companies, Borehamwood also bought in equipment designed by other manufacturers. For example, the Elliott 900 series lineprinter was a Potter chain printer, model HSP 3502/A; this was rated at 315 lines/min, each line having 132 printing positions. The Elliott 900 series magnetic tape unit incorporated an Ampex TM7 tape drive; this was rated at 9K characters/s. Nevertheless, Elliott's repertoire of advertised peripherals in the mid-1960s was slender compared with that of ICT.

ICT was rapidly moving into pole position as the major British supplier of computers. At the start of the 1960s, ICT's range of peripherals was not much better than Elliotts – though ICT did include Magnetic Ink Character Recognition devices and the company offered several choices of magnetic tape systems. However, by 1964 and the launch of the ICT 1900 range of computers, things had changed dramatically. The first machine, an ICT 1905, was delivered to a customer early in 1965. A comparison of the Elliott 4120 and the ICT 1902 is given in Chap. 9. The ICT 1900 Standard Interface allowed compatibility between all processors and all peripherals. By 1966 ICT's peripheral repertoire included [50]: three types of card reader; four types of card punch; lineprinters of widths 96,120 or 160 characters per line operating at 300 or 600 or 1,350 lines per minute; magnetic tape systems at 20.8K, 41.7K, 60K or 96K characters/s; three sizes of magnetic drum providing capacities of 128K, 512K or 2 million characters; three versions of fixed disc stores giving capacities of 100, 200 or 400 million characters; exchangeable disc stores utilising cartridges, the 6 discs in a cartridge giving capacities of either 4 or 8 million characters. In addition, ICT offered paper tape input/output equipment, graph

Fig. 10.10 A model 928 graphical display unit for use with an Elliott 900 series computer in the mid-1960s. In the photo, the user is pointing a *Light Pen* at the screen to identify an item of interest, to achieve much the same effect as a modern mouse and cursor

Table 10.4 Characteristics of the common input/output devices typically installed on Elliott computers in the 1960s, in addition to standard 100 characters/s. paper tape punches and 10 characters/s. teleprinters

Computer/date	Paper tape reader (characters/s)	Card reader (cards/min)	Lineprinter (lines/min)	Digital plotter (steps/s)
803A, early1960	140	–	–	–
803B, April 1964	500	340	300	300
503,December 1963	1,000	340	1,000	300
4100, October 1967	1,000	400	1,250	300

Data obtained from Elliott FACTS booklets

plotters, CRT displays and magnetic ink character recognition devices. By comparison, Elliott's view of peripheral equipment was rather limited.

In Table 10.4 are the specifications of the standard peripherals normally offered for the Elliott 803, 503 and 4100 series computers at various times, as noted in the company's FACTS booklets. By 'normally' we mean that, although additional equipment may have existed as options at the stated time, its availability was not specifically noted in the booklet. The FACTS booklets were pocket-sized manuals containing technical specifications of the instruction set, register layout, speeds, memory capacities, physical properties, input/output equipment and principal software available for a particular Elliott computer. The booklets were issued from about 1960 onwards and were updated as necessary. The transfer-rate figures in Table 10.4 are the highest (fastest) given for a particular input/output medium in a particular FACTS booklet. Of course, lower-performance devices, for example the ubiquitous 100 characters/s paper tape punch and the 10 characters/s teleprinter, were always available.

There are two areas where Borehamwood peripherals did make a market impact in the mid-1960s. The first was the Card Random Access Memory, or CRAM, an American NCR invention that was manufactured (assembled?) for a while at Borehamwood. More details of the CRAM system will be found in Chap. 9. CRAM devices were offered on the NCR 315 computer (manufactured at Borehamwood) but not on Elliott computers.

The second peripheral, this time designed and built at Borehamwood and very much used with Elliott computers, was a graphical output unit. Much of the early work on computer graphical displays was linked to military radar surveillance and aircraft interception – especially in the United States. Apart from the display facilities on the Digital Equipment Corporation's PDP1 computer in 1961, probably the first true, commercially available, graphics terminal was the IBM 2250, introduced with the IBM 1130 computer in 1965 [51]. The Elliott graphical output unit was developed during 1965 and made available from 1966 for 4100 series computers. Laurie Bental, whose group carried out the development, said that their work was 'based on research done at MIT' [52]. Roger Cook has added the following comments [53]. 'I cannot remember the year when we built and demonstrated a graphics display [probably 1965]. This had dedicated electronics for the trigonometric conversions and would cope with the rotation of a wire frame. We experimented with solid bodies and removal of hidden lines but found that the demand exceeded the speed capabilities. If someone had more vision, money and could have allowed work to continue for another year or so then who knows what might have resulted. Meanwhile, we were charging on with the next idea.'

The Elliott graphical unit was said to have been the first such British equipment to become commercially available [54]. Certainly, ICL regarded it favourably upon taking over Elliott's 4100 series in 1968 – see Chap. 13.

Typical of Elliott graphics units were the model 4280 and model 928 [55], which had 1024×1024 pixels on screens varying from 10 to 17 in. The units came with hardware for vector, character and arc generation, a light pen and a keyboard. Software such as the DISMAN display manipulation package was provided, together with Algol and Fortran library routines. The units were found especially useful for engineering design applications.

This concludes the picture of Borehamwood computer architectures. Broadening the perspective, the following two chapters deal with Elliott-Automation's radar and airborne computing activities from the early 1950s to the end of the 1980s. The applications are largely defence-oriented. The story of Elliott's mainstream computer fortunes at Borehamwood during the period of rationalisation and reorganisation in the late 1960s is then picked up in Chap. 13.

References

1. Hersom SE (2002) *Nicholas, the forgotten Elliott project*. Resurrection, the Bulletin of the Computer Conservation Society, Issue number 27, spring 2002, pp. 10–14
2. Andrew St Johnston, comments to S H Lavington at a meeting at Hedgegrove Farm (Andrew's house) on 29 Oct 2001
3. Andrew St Johnston, History of the Research laboratories of Elliott Brother (London) Ltd.: Andrew St Johnston's Contribution. This is an 8-page typed manuscript dated 31 May 1995, written for Laurence Clarke (who had at that time started to collect relevant historical material). See also [2] above
4. SLH Clarke (2009), E-mail to Simon Lavington dated 14 Oct 2009
5. Lavington SH, The Pegasus Story – a history of a vintage British computer. Published by the Science Museum, London, in 2000. ISBN:1-900747-40-5. Second edition, published by the British Computer Society, is in press
6. Lavington SH, A History of Manchester Computers. First edition published by the National Computing Centre in 1975. Second edition published by the British Computer Society in 1998. ISBN:0-902505-01-8
7. Lavington SH (1980) Early British Computers. Manchester University Press. ISBN:0-7190-0803-4. Co-published byDigital Press, 1980. ISBN:0-93237-08-8. Available on the web at: http://ed-thelen.org/comp-hist/EarlyBritish.html. The specific letter from Hartree to Swann is quoted in: Swann BB (1975) An informal history of the Ferranti Computer Department. Circulated privately. Copy available at the National Archive for the History of Computing (NAHC) at the University of Manchester. See www.chstm.manchester.ac.uk/research/nahc/
8. St Johnston A, Clarke SLH, Muchmore NWW, Devonald CH, Stallworthy BV, Carpenter HG, Bunt JP (1954) 401 Mark I computer. Elliott Brothers (London) Ltd., Borehamwood internal report 339, 29 Mar 1954
9. Wilkinson JH (1975) The pilot ACE at the National Physical Laboratory. Radio Electron Eng 45:336–340

10. Comparative data on machines available in the United Kingdom for clerical users. Comput Bull Oct 1957, pp 88–115
11. Haley ACD (1956) DEUCE: a high-speed, general-purpose computer. Proc IEE103B (Supplement 1–3):165–173. The English Electric DEUCE is also amply described in the following website, which includes electronic versions of original technical manuals: http://users.tpg.com.au/eedeuce/intro.htm. A list of DEUCE deliveries will be found in Appendix10
12. Campbell-Kelly M (Apr 1982) The development of computer programming in Britain (1945–1955). Ann Hist Comput 4(2):121–139
13. Burnett-Hall DG, Samet PA (1959) A programming handbook for the DEUCE computer. Royal Aircraft Establishment, Farnborough. Technical Note MS 38, UDC number 518.5: 531,791. Apr 1959. This is a 200-page manual, available electronically at: http://users.tpg. com.au/eedeuce/raeprog.htm#list#list
14. Kilburn T, Edwards DBG, Lanigan MJ, Sumner FH (Apr 1962) One level storage system. IRE Trans Electron Comput EC-11(2):223–235
15. Bell CG, Newell A (1971) Computer structures: readings and examples. McGraw-Hill, New York
16. Allmark RH, Lucking JR (1962) Design of an arithmetic unit using a nesting store. Proceedings of the IFIP Congress, Munich, 1962, pp 694–698 (Reprinted in Bell and Newell – see [15] above)
17. Campbell-Kelly M (1985) Christopher Strachey, 1916–1975: a biographical note. IEEE Ann Hist Comput 7(1):19–42, Jan–Mar1985
18. Cooke-Yarborough EH, Barnes RCM, Stephen JH, Howells GAA (1956) A transistor digital computer. Proc IEE 103B (Suppl 1–3):364–370
19. Felker JH (1954) Performance of TRADIC transistor digital computer. Proceedings of the AFIPS Eastern Joint Computer Conference: Design and application of small digital computers, Dec 1954, pp 46–49
20. Maddox JL, O'Toole JB, Wong SY (1956) The Transac S-1000 computer. Proceedings of the AFIPS Eastern Joint Computer Conference: New developments in computers. Dec 1956, pp 13–16
21. John Bunt, letter dated 11 Dec 2001and eight pages of accompanying typed notes, sent to Simon Lavington
22. Andrew Wylie, in an e-mail to Simon Lavington dated 1 Mar 2009, said: 'The OC72 is first mentioned in *Wireless World* in the issue for December 1955, in a construction article, so at that time it was more than just a laboratory type. It then appears several times in 1956. This certainly suggests that it was commercially available in late 1955. Note that Mullard's OC70 and OC71 junction transistors were available from mid-1954 onwards'. For more on the history of transistors, see Andrew's interesting website: http://ourworld.compuserve.com/homepages/ Andrew_Wylie/semics.htm from which the following additional facts are taken. The OC series was very widely used in Europe for a period of almost twenty years and many millions were made…. Mullard produced the first true high-power transistor in Europe, the OC16, in about 1956, which was capable of handling about 24 watts. The early OC series were AF (audio frequency) devices whose switching properties limited their use in high-speed computing circuits. Mullard's first RF (radio frequency) junction transistor, for example the OC170 used in the Atlas computer, was available from1959
23. Laurie Bental, The Elliott 803. Talk given to the North West branch of the Computer Conservation Society, Manchester, 25 Sept 2001
24. Anon, Elliott Automation: Computers and Orders, 1947–1966. Brochure published in early1967 by the Directorate of Information Services, Elliott-Automation Ltd., 21 Portland Place, London W1
25. Ron Clayden (1996) Early computer developments at EMI. Resurrection, the Bulletin of the Computer Conservation Society, Issue number 16, Christmas 1996
26. Froggatt RJ (Dec 1957) Logical design of a computer for business use. J Br Inst Radio Eng 17:681–696

27. Godfrey N Hounsfield (1980) Autobiographical note from: From Les Prix Nobel. The Nobel Prizes 1979. Wilhelm Odelberg (ed) [Nobel Foundation], Stockholm. See http://nobelprize. org/nobel_prizes/medicine/laureates/1979/hounsfield-autobio.html

28. The Times Supplement on Computers in Commerce, a 12-page illustrated addition to The Times newspaper of Tuesday 4 Oct 1960. This contains two items of relevance to the EMIDEC 1100 computer: (a) An advertisement placed by EMI Electronics states that the Boots EMIDEC machine was delivered on 20 Apr 1960 and that two further computers had been delivered so far that summer: to Glaxo on 18 May and to ICI on 15 June. (b) Hill ND, The modern transistor – a far cry from cat's whisker. 'The first commercially available transistor computer was the EMIDEC 1100'. Article in the above-mentioned Supplement

29. EMIDEC Computer News, issue 1. Undated but we can deduce from the contents that it was published at the very end of 1960 or very beginning of 1961. See http://www.iansmith.myzen. co.uk/emidec/emipicbr.pdf

30. Anon (1963) Computer & data processing installations. Brochure published by the Computing Division, Elliott Brothers (London) Ltd., on 31 Aug 1963

31. De Kerf JLF, A survey of European digital computers. A collection of three articles published in Computers and Automation, Feb, Mar and Apr 1960 (Berkeley Enterprises, MA, USA). This paper contains the following sentences: 'The new computer, National-Elliott 803, is being used by Information Systems Inc. of Skokie (Illinois) as the control unit of their 609 process control system (cf Control Eng 6(8): pp 52). About forty Elliott computers have been delivered and about twenty are on order (Oct 1959)'

32. (a) Adrian Johnstone (1991) The young person's guide to The Elliott 8O3B. Resurrection, the Bulletin of the Computer Conservation Society, Issue number 3, spring 1991. (b) Graham Phillips (2007) Memories of the Elliott 803B. Resurrection, the Bulletin of the Computer Conservation Society, Issue number 40, summer 2007

33. Wilson JF, Ferranti: a history. Building a family business, 1882–1975. Carnegie Publishing Ltd., Lancaster, 2001. ISBN:1-85936-080-7. Volume 2: from family firm to multinational company, 1975–1987, published in 2007 by Crucible Books, Lancaster. ISBN:978-1-905472-01-7

34. Scarrott GG, Johnson KC, Haley G, Naylo R (1959) The design principles of the neuron and resonant-circuit logical elements. Proc IEE, part B 106:468–469

35. Swan BB (1975) An informal history of the Ferranti Computer Department. 98-typed pages, circulated privately. A copy is now held in the National Archive for the History of Computing, catalogue reference NAHC/FER/C30

36. Anon, An introduction to system design using Minilog switching elements. A16-page illustrated technical brochure published by Panellit Ltd., a company within the Elliott-Automation Group. Undated, but it can be inferred by the reference on page 10 of the brochure that the date is not earlier than 1962

37. Anon, Minilog elements and accessories Price List, Sept 1967. Four-page typed internal leaflet produced by Elliott-Automation Microelectronics Ltd.

38. Iann Barron, seminar given to the Computer Conservation Society in London on 4 May 2006, followed by several e-mail exchanges with Simon Lavington between May and Oct 2006

39. SLH Clarke (June 2009) E-mails to Simon Lavington

40. St Johnston A, Clarke SLH (July 1954) Applications of a high-speed electronic computer to a business-accounting problem. J Br Inst Radio Eng 14:293–302

41. RG Wilson, From Elliott to ICL. 11-page typed manuscript dated 1 Feb 2009. Ron Wilson joined Elliott-Automation as a graduate trainee in the autumn of 1962. In Sept 1964 he joined Elliotts' Scientific Computing Division (SCD) as a sales engineer, based at Elliotts' Manchester area offices in Bramhall, Cheshire. In Jan 1966 he moved to Glasgow. He transferred, with E-A and EE sales staff, to ICL in May1968

42. John Hendry (1990) Innovating for Failure: government policy and the early British computer industry. MIT Press, London. ISBN 0-262-08187-3

43. Don Fenna, communications with David Pentecost, July 2004, and May 2006. Fenna worked at WRE from 1956 to1969 and later became Emeritus Professor of Applied Science in Medicine at the University of Alberta, Canada. See the Computer Conservation Society's Our

Computer Heritage website: http://www.ourcomputerheritage.org/wp/ for more comments on the Elliott 403 compiled by David Pentecost

44. SLH Clarke (2008) E-mail to Simon Lavington on 21 Aug 2008. See also: Clarke SLH (1993) Recollections of the Elliott 400 series. Comput Resurrection the Bulletin of the Computer Conservation Society, Issue number 6, summer 1993, pp:15–21

45. For more information on 'The Hertfordshire Hollywood', see the following websites:http://www.elstree.co.uk/index.php?page=history. http://www.localauthoritypublishing.co.uk/councils/elstree/hollywood.html. http://en.wikipedia.org/wiki/Elstree_Studios

46. Anon (July 1959) Interchangeability and compatibility of magnetic tapes. Ferranti Ltd., publication CS234

47. (a) Royal Army Pay Corps: Report of the Electronic Computer Investigation Committee. The War Office (F9), Dec 1957. (b) Royal Army Pay Corps: Electronic Computer Investigating Committee: Report of Working Party. Application of automatic data-processing to soldiers' pay accounting. The War Office, Aug 1957

48. Anon, Machine Comparisons. NCR/Elliott Information memo number 5, 26 Jan 1965 (Two pages, type-written, internal company document)

49. See section F5/X2on the Ferranti Atlas, at the Computer Conservation Society's Our Computer Heritage website: www.ourcomputerheritage.org/wp/

50. The content of an ICT brochure describing the ICT 1900 product range, dated Nov 1966, is given at: http://www.ourcomputerheritage.org/wp/upload/CCS-T5X2.pdf

51. For a readable history of computer graphical units, see http://www.columbia.edu/acis/history/2250.html. For information on the IBM 2250, see http://www.ibm1130.net/functional/DisplayUnit.html

52. Laurie Bental, (2002) Letter to Simon Lavington dated 30 Jan 2002

53. Roger Cook (1995) Letter to SLH Clarke dated 4 Feb 1995, augmented by various e-mails to Simon Lavington in Aug and Sept 2007

54. Anon, Elliott-Automation; 1966 Reports and Accounts. Illustrated brochure dated 30 May 1967 and presented to the Annual General Meeting of the company on 23 June

55. Anon, 928 Graphical Display System.17-page technical brochure published by Marconi-Elliott Computer Systems, 1970. Brochure number 928/ST L/1.

Chapter 11
EARS and Aerials: Elliott's Radar Achievements, 1950–1986

By John Kinnear and Elizabeth Laverick

Preamble by Simon Lavington

The primary source for this chapter is a 6,000-word draft history of Elliott's radar work in the period 1950–1970, written for the author by Dr Elizabeth Laverick, OBE and John Kinnear in May/June 2005. Subsequent minor comments and explanations have been incorporated where appropriate.

Betty Laverick and John Kinnear were, second only to Peter Mariner, the leading lights of Elliott-Automation's radar developments at Borehamwood throughout the period under review. Regrettably Peter Mariner, the Chief Executive of the main radar division within Elliott-Automation from the mid-1950s, died in 1995 and was therefore unable to comment on the text of this chapter. John Kinnear died suddenly in January 2007. Betty Laverick died on 12 January 2010.

John Kinnear joined Borehamwood in 1951, after war service with the Royal Signals and a Physics degree from Oxford. He remained with the company until his retirement in 1990. He became the Divisional Manager of Elliott-Automation's Airborne Radar Division in 1962. By 1975 he was the General Manager, Market Development, of Marconi Elliott Avionics Systems Ltd. (later renamed GEC Avionics Ltd.). Dr Elizabeth Laverick joined Borehamwood in 1952, after obtaining a Ph.D. in Physics from Durham University and working for GEC (Stanmore) for three years. In 1960 she became the Manager of the Research Labs in Elliott-Automation Radar Systems Ltd. She became the Technical Director of Marconi Elliott Avionic Systems Ltd. in 1970 and left the company in the following year to become the Deputy Secretary of the Institution of Electrical Engineers. From 1985 until her retirement in 1988 she was a part-time Consultant for the IEE on a DTI contract on Advanced Manufacturing in Electronics.

In the words of Laverick and Kinnear, when writing this chapter: 'This account draws on the best recollections of the authors and some of their erstwhile colleagues, long after many of the events described, and in the absence of much documentary evidence. They recognise that there are omissions due to uncertainties of recollection, and that there may be other aspects and opinions of the events of which they may be unaware.'

S. Lavington, *Moving Targets*, History of Computing,
DOI 10.1007/978-1-84882-933-6_11, © Springer-Verlag London Limited 2011

11.1 Introduction: John Coales' Legacy (1946–1950)

11.1.1 The Establishment of the Borehamwood Laboratories

At the end of the Second World War, Elliott Brothers (London) Ltd., like many other companies that had devoted the major part of their resources to the manufacture of war materials, found itself with an empty order book and no customer base. Amongst several other defence-related projects, the company had been the major designer and supplier of mechanical fire-control tables (electro-mechanical analogue computers – see Chap. 4) to the Navy. In 1946, wishing to extend the field of naval gunnery fire-control into the new electronic era, the Admiralty backed the creation of an Elliott research laboratory at Borehamwood, Hertfordshire, by funding research into a medium range radar-controlled gunfire directing system designated MRS5 (see Chaps. 1 and 2, and Sect. 11.1.2 below). John F Coales, an eminent scientist who had been heavily involved in the Navy's wartime Radar developments, was appointed to head the laboratory. He enlisted a number of experienced Admiralty scientists and engineers to form the core of the future laboratory. Progressively over the next few years he recruited many more engineers, expert in their specialist fields, and a number of university graduates, all interviewed and *handpicked* by himself. It is worth pointing out that Elliotts had substantially no radar or electronics experience before the arrival of John Coales. In contrast, all the UK's pre-war radio and electronics firms such as Plessey, Ferranti, Cossor, Decca, EMI, Standard Telephones & Cables, Mullard, Marconi and E.K. Cole had gained valuable experience from wartime contracts connected with radar.

By 1950, Elliott's Borehamwood Research Laboratory was basically youthful: the scientific staff looked like the students of the day and were motivated by John

Fig. 11.1 John Kinnear joined Borehamwood in 1951, remaining in the radar divisions of Elliott-Automation and its successor companies until his retirement in 1990. He rose to be General Manager Market Development, Marconi Elliott Avionics Systems Ltd. (later renamed Marconi Avionics Ltd. and subsequently GEC Avionics Ltd.). John Kinnear died in 2007

Fig. 11.2 Dr Elizabeth Laverick joined Borehamwood in 1952 and left in 1971, by which time she had become Technical Director, Marconi Elliott Avionic Systems Ltd. From 1971 until her retirement in 1988 Betty Laverick was associated in various roles with the Institution of Electrical Engineers, being appointed OBE for her services to women in engineering. She died in 2010

Coales in a very professorial way. Indeed, the workshop technicians referred to the Lab staff as *the students*. More generally, the Borehamwood salaried staff, whatever their speciality, were all officially known as *Engineers* – a sociologically interesting indication that the Lab's task was to implement novel solutions to practical problems.

The Admiralty's MRS5 radar fire-control project and the CDS project (see Chap. 2) provided the critical mass for the laboratory, occupying the major part of its effort, alongside a number of lesser projects directed towards the Company's Lewisham businesses and outside customers, all intended to exploit the newly emerging areas of electronic technology. The laboratory, as set up, comprised nine groups. Titles varied slightly over the years but, in practical terms, the groups comprised the following: Radio (which really meant radio-location or *Radar*), Circuits, Computing, Theory, Heavy Servomechanisms, Light Servomechanisms, Measurements and Instruments. These were backed up by service departments including accounts, publications, library, drawing office, machine shops, electrical, carpentry, and a small physics/chemistry facility providing, inter alia, glass-blowing, electro-deposition and vacuum physics.

The first five of these groups were predominately engaged in the Admiralty projects while the others worked on such diverse tasks as magnetometry for mineral prospecting, meteorology (e.g. an automated dew-point hydrometer), precision positioning for such applications as colour printing and cigarette manufacture, and industrial weighing. Some of these activities fed into the production facilities at the main Lewisham factory of Elliott Brothers (London) Ltd.

In the subsequent reorganisation of the Borehamwood Laboratory in 1952/1953, the Radio and Computing Groups were amongst those that continued as entities and grew into major Elliott-Automation businesses. Some of the other groups were dispersed and their members reassigned to set up new spheres of activity in areas such as Avionics, Guided Weapons, Nuclear, and Industrial Processes and Automation. The story of Elliott-Automation's successful entry into the Avionics market is described in Chap. 12.

Over the years, the Borehamwood Physics/Chemistry facility built on its vacuum physics skills, making specialist vacuum tubes in conjunction with the Services Electronics Research Laboratory (SERL/CVD) at nearby Baldock in Hertfordshire, as well as devising and producing tubes of its own design. In due course, following Elliott Brothers' Licence agreements, first with Leybold, then with Litton Industries, it produced high-voltage vacuum tubes and devices and later became a separate division: Elliott Electronic Tubes Limited. It was eventually incorporated into Elliott-Automation Radar Systems as its Neutron Division. It became a sizeable business with activities that included the design and manufacture of Microwave Klystrons and Magnetrons, Ionisation Chambers and Radiation Detectors, Helium Neon low-power lasers, Carbon Dioxide high-power lasers and cutting devices, laser distance-measuring equipment and laser rangefinders, X-ray tubes, high-power rotating anode X-ray tubes and X-ray generators, X-ray topography, X-ray Diffraction and X-ray Activation Analysis equipments, Neutron tubes, Neutron Radiography and the Hiletron Neutron Therapy machines.

We will now return to the late 1940s and describe how the facilities assembled at Borehamwood were put to work on an advanced radar project for the Admiralty.

11.1.2   Radar: The Core of the MRS5 Contract

The first research contract (CP.12349/46) placed on the Borehamwood Research Laboratory of Elliott Brothers (RLEB), in October 1946, was for the Royal Navy's envisaged Fire-Control system MRS5. One of the teams set up for this purpose was the Radio Group, which was concerned with the design of the Radar Director. The *Director*, a naval term, referred to a unit mounted high up on a ship's superstructure for directing gunfire. In the MRS5 manifestation, the Director was a moveable structure weighing about 14 t, containing the radar transmitting/receiving aerial and associated electronics for precise positional control – see Fig. 2.7. The Radio Group at Borehamwood was headed by Alex Cochrane backed up by Eric Whitehead, a brilliant theoretical physicist/mathematician and comprised some ten staff.

The concept of the MRS5 system required the radar detection and ranging on a target aircraft out to at least 8 miles from the ship, with the three-dimensional position information fed into a digital computer which would track the target in real time. The computer would calculate and feed to the ship's guns the appropriate aiming and fusing information so that their shells would explode at or very near the target's position. The accuracy of the radar was seen as the most demanding and challenging requirement of the MRS5 system.

Fig. 11.3 Peter Mariner joined Borehamwood in 1951 and, from the mid-1950s to the mid-1980s, headed the radar activities of Elliott-Automation which were mostly based at Borehamwood. The radar division became successively known as Elliott-Automation Radar Systems (EARS), Marconi Elliott Avionic Systems Limited (MEASL), Marconi Avionics Systems Limited (abbreviated to MAV) and subsequently, in 1984, GEC Avionics. Peter Mariner died in 1995

A crucial factor in the ability of a radar to accurately determine the spatial coordinates of a target was a phenomenon termed glint. This was the variation of the apparent position of an aircraft due to the varying combination of echoes from different parts of its structure as its aspect with respect to the radar changed. The novel technique of *monopulse static-split* was seen by Borehamwood as offering the most accurate basic technique for radar tracking, superseding the sequential lobbing method which was in earlier use during the war. It was therefore essential to determine if the monopulse technique would offer the necessary accuracy.

One of the most important tasks carried out in the Radio Group was an analytical comparison by Eric Whitehead of the performance against glint of the two alternative implementations of monopulse reception: phase-comparison and amplitude-comparison systems. Phase comparison seemed better for this purpose. To implement such a system, techniques were developed for the design and fabrication of novel *egg-box* lenses and a four-lens phase-comparison monopulse radar head was incorporated into the prototype Radar Director. This entailed the design of a range of microwave components, together with equipments for the measurement of their characteristics and performance.

The main MRS5 project was terminated by the Admiralty in 1950, but the Director was used to carry out a series of fly-past trials to evaluate its capability against radar glint (see Chap. 2). This glint data proved to be a useful reference for other high-precision radar target-tracking work at Borehamwood for several years to come. Nevertheless, the termination of MRS5 came as a disappointment to the radar team. Fortunately, a much smaller and unrelated Admiralty contract came along to provide the challenge for some innovative research into radar aerials. The results of this research were to have far-reaching consequences.

11.2   The Borehamwood Research Laboratories in the Early 1950s

11.2.1   Mopsy and the Cassegrain Aerial

After the termination of the MRS5 contract, a further Admiralty contract was obtained by Borehamwood in 1951 for the design of a miniature (6-in. [15 cm] diameter) homing head as part of the Mopsy ship-borne anti-aircraft missile project, the work to be carried out in the Radio Group. Mopsy was a 1950 joint US/UK initiative, an outcome of the Admiralty's 1948 Popsy project for a semi-active surface-to-air homing missile, together with the propulsion unit developed by the Americans for the US Meteor missile. For further details, see [1].

To achieve the necessary tracking accuracy for Mopsy with such a small aerial, operation in the comparatively short 8-mm band was necessary and the Services Electronics Research Laboratory (SERL/CVD) at nearby Baldock was responsible for developing a Magnetron for the 8-mm band. (Appendix A9.4 gives a brief introduction to microwave and radar terminology, including a table of frequencies, wavelengths and bands.)

As well as requiring the development of a range of waveguide components and test instruments in the new 8-mm waveband, the Mopsy project required a miniature aerial of very high performance in the Monopulse mode. It was in the consideration of forms for this aerial that Cochrane and Whitehead had come up with the concept of the Elliott Twist-reflector aerial on the Cassegrain principle (Patent No.700868: Feeding Aerials). Peter Mariner joined the group in 1951 and was given responsibility for aerial work. Shortly afterwards he was joined by John Kinnear, who was given the task of *reduction-into-practice* of the twist-reflecting Cassegrain aerial concept.

While awaiting materials for an experimental aerial, a number of alternative forms of aerial were made as yardsticks and their performance assessed. These included a dielectric lens, a stepped dielectric lens, spun aluminium parabolas and centrifugally cast parabolas. When the awaited materials arrived, test pieces were made for the parabolic reflector and the twist-refracting element. These were individually tested and found to perform well. The elements were then assembled into an experimental aerial and tested. Results were encouraging and equalled the performance of the best of the earlier forms of aerial. A prototype aerial was then designed and made which confirmed the good results and established the feasibility of the concept.

In the course of this work it was realised that there were several variants of the Elliott aerial concept that also offered attractive properties. The first, the use of a small hyperbolic-profile sub-reflector in front of a large twist-reflecting parabolic main reflector, offered a compact design, and was to find many future applications.

The second variant arose from the realisation that the plane twist-reflecting plate could be tilted so as to change the angle of the emerging beam (Patent No. 716939: Scanning rotated polarisation aerials). The plate deviation required was only half the angle by which the beam was deviated. This, together with the low inertia of a very light plate, offered the prospect for very rapid beam scanning. A brilliant mechanical linkage invented by the group's mechanical designer, Doug Stewart, took care of the resolution of the complicated angles involved.

The third variant was that the twist-reflecting element could be designed to be effective at two widely separated frequencies, enabling a radar to be designed to operate simultaneously in two wavebands. This also was to find important future applications. Indeed, the Cassegrain developments earned considerable revenue for Elliott-Automation, once an American patent infringement had been successfully challenged. The fascinating story of Elliott's defence of the Cassegrain patent is given in Appendix A9.5: the result of a prolonged legal battle came in 1972 with a cheque for $1,150,000.

11.2.2 Reorganisation and the Start of Elliott's Airborne Radar

By 1952, Borehamwood activity on Admiralty contracts had been severely reduced and the Elliott Laboratory faced a financial crisis. Leon Bagrit, who had risen to become the driving force behind Elliott Brothers (London) Ltd., saw the need for a more business-oriented way of going about things: research was to be a means to an end and not an end in itself. A divisional structure was set up which envisaged each Division as a self contained business (see also Chap. 2).

John Coales resigned as Director of the Research Lab. and left Borehamwood in April 1952. In the subsequent reorganisation, Alex Cochrane was promoted to be in charge of what was now termed The Borehamwood Establishment of Elliott Brothers, but was shortly to leave the company. The Radio Group, under Peter Mariner, became part of the Elliott Brothers' Research Division led by Eric Whitehead. The Radio Group itself was split into two complementary sections: one under the leadership of John Kinnear; the other under Dr Elizabeth Laverick who had just joined from the GEC Research Laboratory at Stanmore, initially to extend the group's radar capability into the 4-mm band.

The higher frequencies associated with the 4-mm band required new methods. Initially harmonic generation from 8 mm had to be employed for 4 mm, as thermionic tubes (valves) were not yet available at the higher frequencies. The small size of the waveguides meant that conventional methods of measurement could not be used and new techniques had to be devised. Eric Whitehead conceived and Dr Laverick designed a novel form of waveguide reflectometer, the Rotary Standing Wave Indicator, which was particularly suitable for measurements in the 4- and 8-mm bands (UK Patent No.742948 Standing Wave Meter).

There were two valuable areas of technological expertise in the Radio Group, now led by Peter Mariner, that were the basis on which future business would be grown. The first was the expertise in the design of microwave aerials, especially the Elliott twist-reflecting Cassegrain aerial. The second was the expertise in the design of microwave waveguide components, devices and instruments.

Around this time (late 1952), a bench-top radar employing the prototype Elliott Cassegrain aerial (see Sect. 11.2.2) was constructed (Patent No.782734 – Aerial Construction). This was demonstrated to several of the American defence companies who had been brought to visit the Borehamwood Research Laboratory in the course of Leon Bagrit's wooing of potential licensors. The Cassegrain aerial was also demonstrated to visitors from the Government's Signals & Radar Research Establishment (RSRE) and to Robert Clayton the Head of the Government sponsored GEC Stanmore Research Laboratory. The RSRE took a keen interest in the device and provided funding for further work. The GEC Laboratory went on to build an X-band (3 cm) aerial of the scanning version but found that the beam offset was not exactly twice the angle of the scanning (twist-reflector) plate. This was considered sufficiently serious by RSRE that Dr Laverick's team was funded to investigate. Her team determined that the position of the gimbal axis of the plate in relation to its surface was critical. When this was correctly located, the 2:1 criterion was satisfied and accurate positioning was achieved. The Laboratory was then contracted to make a scanner for RSRE's ongoing Airborne Radar research programme. Thus began the Elliott Company's involvement in the Airborne Radar field.

Meanwhile, work was going on in the design of an 8-mm radar system to be mounted on an armoured vehicle. This included the design of an Elliott Cassegrain scanning aerial with the parabolic reflector formed from thin wires embedded in a hemispherical shell of low-density foamed plastic with an amplitude comparison monopulse feed and waveguide comparator. The system's Transmit/Receive (T/R) system also broke new ground in using ferrite circulators and ferrite switches.

11.3   Elliott-Automation and the Changing Role of Borehamwood (1954–1967)

11.3.1   The Microwave Division

A further reorganisation at Borehamwood in 1954 created the Microwave Division, managed by Peter Mariner, with Elizabeth Laverick and John Kinnear as the departmental heads. In various guises, in the course of successive Elliott-Automation company reorganisations and until the merger into GEC in 1968 this team, under Mariner's drive and entrepreneurship, was to form the core of the Company's notable expansion in radar applications and allied fields.

As well as continuing the development of the Cassegrain and other novel forms of aerial, the Microwave Division designed and made a range of top-grade microwave instruments and test equipment in several frequency bands. These included absolute waveguide measuring instruments (the Torque Vane Wattmeter, operated by the radiation pressure on a small vane), the Rotary Attenuator (Patent No. 691939 – Rotary Attenuator) and the Rotary Standing Wave Meter (RSWI) (Patent No.742948 – Standing Wave Meter) – all inventions of Eric Whitehead. The Division also developed automatic measuring equipment, notably Aerial Near-field Phase and Amplitude Plotters in X and S-band (APAP) and a Q-band automatic swept-frequency waveguide-impedance measuring instrument (ASFIM).

11.3.2   The Communications and Radar Research Laboratory, 1957–1960

Another Elliott-Automation company reorganisation in 1957 saw the microwave instruments business split off and ultimately discontinued. Mariner became Head of the Communications and Radar Research Laboratory (CRRL) at Borehamwood, with his former departments merged into this Laboratory.

Fig. 11.4 Peter Mariner (*left*) explaining the ZB298 Battlefield Surveillance radar to Sir Herman Bondi, FRS, Chief Scientific Adviser to the Ministry of Defence, during the latter's visit to Borehamwood in 1976

By now the pattern for future successful growth was established. The Research Laboratory at Borehamwood was to advance the technological expertise and experience base, augmenting and complementing projects funded by the Government Research Establishments with Elliott company-funded research. With the expertise it so gained, the Laboratory would propose and design prototype equipments to meet government and commercial requirements and these activities would be spun off into Product Divisions, formed as necessary, for further development, manufacture and marketing. A small group of engineers from the Laboratory who had been involved in the prototype would be transferred or loaned to set up the new Division and the Laboratory would continue to provide expert help and advice.

The reconstituted Communications and Radar Research Laboratory's first venture into airborne radar was for John Kinnear to provide a short statement on radar, to be included in a proposal that the Elliott-Automation Aviation Division was making in 1958 against a NATO requirement for a fighter bomber aircraft, NBR2. The project did not proceed and in fact it is believed that no NATO-initiated attempt at a common aircraft ever bore fruit. However, the aviation and radar activities within Elliott-Automation continued to be coordinated as the years went by. John Kinnear was specifically tasked by Peter Mariner to ensure that the Radar's role and design was envisaged in the context of the overall aircraft avionic and weapon systems.

At this time the CRRL was familiarising itself with the military aircraft scene. Although an earlier Minister of Defence, Duncan Sandys, had declared in the 1957 Defence White Paper that there was no future for manned aircraft, a major evaluation of the air defence scenario had been compiled by R.V. Jones (then a principal scientific adviser to the government). One conclusion was that it was realistic for aircraft to penetrate below radar cover by flying fast at low altitudes. This led to an RAF requirement for an aircraft for this role and the project for the ill-fated TSR 2 was commenced. In parallel with this, the Royal Navy's Blackburn Buccaneer project was in progress – specifically designed to withstand the rigours of very low-level flights.

Meanwhile at the same time a group at RSRE led by Reg Willmer was considering what was necessary to counter similar tactics on an enemy's part. It concluded that what was required was a fighter aircraft which would fly at a high enough altitude to allow line of sight to a sufficiently long range to give time for threat assessment and target engagement. For target engagement, this aircraft must be fitted with radar having a long-range look-down detection and tracking capability and it must be armed with medium range look-down/shoot-down guided missiles. This, the RSRE group judged, required a high-power coherent Doppler radar. A research programme was initiated at RSRE into this type of radar and the Elliott Cassegrain aerial was considered appropriate for such a radar. Thus Elliott-Automation's Communications and Radar Research Laboratory (CRRL) was brought into the programme to design a prototype aerial and scanner, in the course of which they became familiar with RSRE's thinking on the subject. The requirement for long-range look-down radar was to re-emerge later, as described below in Sect. 11.4.4.

11.4   Elliott-Automation Radar Systems (EARS): 1960 Onwards

11.4.1   Company Reorganisations

In 1957 the Board of Directors, hitherto comprising solely Leon Bagrit (Managing Director) and Dr L.L. Ross (Technical Director), was expanded. Edgar Herzfeld joined as Financial Director – Herzfeld had in fact been part of Bagrit's inner team since the late 1940s. George Fairbanks became Commercial Director with Cdr. H. Pasley-Tyler and Maurice Gartside as Directors, these comprising the Management Committee based at the Company's headquarters at Portland Place. Pasley-Tyler had supervisory responsibility for Military business throughout the Company and Gartside for the Industrial. When the new building at Borehamwood opened in 1958, Pasley-Tyler took up day-to-day residence there while retaining his Director's office at Portland Place.

In 1960 Elliott-Automation again reorganised into groups of management companies, one of which was Elliott-Automation Radar Systems (EARS) at Borehamwood with Peter Mariner as General Manager. (From the Elliott-Automation Annual Reports, the first mention of Elliott-Automation Radar Systems as a separate company was actually in 1964.)

Other Management Companies formed at this time included Elliott Flight Automation Ltd. (EFA) under Jack Pateman, to be based at Rochester, Kent; Elliott Space & Weapon Automation Ltd. (ESWAL) under Cdr Malim to be located at Frimley, Surrey; and Elliott-Automation Space and Advanced Military Systems (EASAMS), a systems-management company, at Camberley Surrey under Howard Surtees.

Within EARS, Dr Laverick became Head of the Radar Research Laboratory (RRL) at Borehamwood and a new Division, Airborne Radio & Radar (AR&R), was formed under Bob Ford to support and improve the Royal Navy's AN/APS 20 Airborne Early Warning (AEW) radar in its Fairey Gannett aircraft (a task transferred from the now disbanded Elliott Radar Division at Rochester); to spearhead the Company's drive to break into the wider Airborne Radar market; to exploit and build on the Company's Licence agreements with the Bendix Corporation for aircraft radio equipments, the quantity manufacture of Radio and Radio/Navigation equipments and Sonarbuoys for the RAF and the design of a range of aircraft audio and Public Address (PA) systems for commercial and military aircraft. (A sonarbuoy, or *sonobuoy* or *sonabuoy* is a device which, when dropped from an aircraft into the sea, uses active or passive devices to detect (audio) signals emanating from a submarine. The sonarbuoy then transmits locational information back to the aircraft.)

In 1962 the Airborne Radio & Radar Division was split: The Airborne Communications Division (ACD) was formed to continue and advance the radio and sonarbuoy business. Later, following the merger with GEC in 1968, this Division was subsumed into the Marconi Aeronautical Division to form the Airadio Division later to become part of avionics. The Airborne Radar Division (ARD) was created to continue the drive into airborne radar systems, with a nucleus from AR&R augmented by a strong contingent from the Radar Research Laboratory who joined together with the airborne radar projects that they had been working on. The Radio Service and Repair Division was created in 1962 to continue the support of the APS20 radar and the company's other radio and radar products. Particularly, they were to incorporate into the APS20 radar an IFF/SIF (Identification Friend or Foe/ Selective Identification Facility), a parametric rf. amplifier and a video integrator.

11.4.2   Sensors and Signal Analysis

In the early 1970s a prototype Battlefield surveillance radar was designed within the Radar Research Laboratory (RRL) with RSRE support, carrying on from an RSRE *evaluation of concept* programme, and a cell from the laboratory was split off as the nucleus of the Mobile Radar Division. Development was completed and a large quantity was manufactured for the British Army. A considerable number was sold to 13 countries overseas and this was believed to be the only project where the royalties paid to the Government exceeded the funding it had provided for the development. The Radar Research Laboratory and the Division produced a number of new products for armies, among them: a seismic intruder detection equipment (Tobias); a smaller Private Venture battlefield radar, Vampire; an infrared detection device Iris; a smaller battlefield radar (Shrimp); and PASS (Precision Angulation and Support System) for the British Army comprising a novel form of medium level tripod and a precision Common Mounting System for battlefield sighting, ranging and target-marking devices, of which over 1,000 were sold.

The Division's technologies and experience led to the design of Intruder Detection Systems for high security sites using both seismic and infrared methods. Whereas the military devices were man-operated and transportable, for civil purposes they needed to be fixed installations of varying extent and complexity and not usually manned. Sophisticated signal processing was therefore developed and incorporated to preclude false alarms such as might be caused by wind and rain, traffic, animals, birds or insects. The basic system went under the name CIRCE (The Greek goddess who turned intruders into stone), and a more elaborate system AIDA which could be used to advantage where a location was manned or guarded.

In 1972 the Research Laboratory designed, and the Lightweight Structures department of Advanced Projects Division made, five very accurate 1-m diameter aerials for the Radio and Space Research station for use in a European Synchronous Satellite research programme. The aerials were required to be operable continuously without degradation of performance in poor weather conditions and in particular ice and snow must not accumulate on them. The aerials were of fibreglass sandwich construction with heating elements under the front skin. Following the success of these aerials a 10½ ft aerial was ordered, designed and delivered in 1973, for uninterrupted operation for 10 years to track and receive centrimetric and millimetric signals from the Sirios II Satellite.

The Radar Research Laboratory at Borehamwood went on to design the Q-band aerial for the Army's Rapier Blind-fire anti-aircraft missile system under sub-contract to Elliott Space and Defence Systems.

The Laboratory's signal processing expertise led to contracts from AUWE (the Admiralty Underwater Weapons Establishment) for the design and manufacture of Naval sonar signal analysis equipments and the Special Projects Division was created under Alan Tonkin for this market.

Over the 10 years from the late 1950s to the late 1960s, the Borehamwood Laboratory and the Airborne Radar Division, both in due course becoming part of the GEC empire, carried out a number of projects for the Blind Landing Experimental Unit (BLEU) at the Royal Aircraft Establishment at Bedford. These included an experimental microwave beacon system aimed at providing an all-weather landing capability for the UK's V-Bombers, the supply of a precision-tracking radar facility, using the US Navy's SPN10 deck landing radar together with an analysis computer and recorder in a vehicle, and the development and manufacture of an ILS (Instrument Landing System) ground monitor.

This was followed by the design and manufacture of a prototype system ALMS (Aircraft Landing Monitoring System) for the automatic recording of aircraft landing performance. This comprised three types of sensor: photo-electric (Skyscreens) for measuring an aircraft's height, lateral position, speed and rate of descent at several distances prior to its crossing the runway threshold; seismic to determine moment and position of touchdown and bounce; and photo-optical (infrared) for determining its roll-out path along the runway. Following success-ful trials at BLEU in 1969, a contract was placed for a system to be installed on runway 28L at London's Heathrow Airport to form a part of the Aircraft Landing Quality Assessment Scheme. Over 50% of flight accidents occur in the landing phase and the programme aimed at gathering comprehensive data by which this rate might be reduced. The ALMS data on each landing was to be coordinated with Aircraft Identification (airline, flight number, aircraft type) from the *Telemove* System and Meteorological data (visibility, wind speed and direction, etc.) from the MOTNE (Meteorological Operational Telegraphic Network), to be analysed daily by computer. The system was installed and became operational in 1972.

Of course Blind Landing, or *Auto-land*, also requires complex and highly reliable flight-control equipment and instrumentation in the aircraft, certified by regulatory bodies and subject to extensive trials and evaluation. The Aviation Division of Elliotts and its successors did pioneering work in this field, as is described in Chap. 12.

11.4.3 Proposed Airborne Early Warning (AEW) Systems for the Navy

One of Elliott-Automation's tasks as the Support contractor for the Royal Navy's AN/APS20 radar was to propose and implement improvements to the system. The Radar Research Laboratory had been developing a *Bandwidth Compressor* for the

Fig. 11.5 The Blackburn Buccaneer high-speed, low-level, fighter saw service with the Royal Navy between 1962 and 1968, thereafter serving with the Royal Air Force. In the 1960s, Elliott's radar team made two proposals for upgrading the radar unit in the Buccaneer and was awarded a contract in 1967. The contract was cancelled the same year. However, the successful Elliott Foxhunter radar was flight-tested on a Buccaneer in about 1980

RAF's reconnaissance aircraft to compress the data from its reconnaissance sensors so that it could be transmitted in real time by data link back to base during its mission (a predecessor of MPEG?). By adapting the technology, the Airborne Radar Division conceived and proposed a Moving Target processor (MTI) to give the APS20 radar a look-down capability. With this adopted and put into service, the Division started to give consideration to a new generation of Airborne Early Warning (AEW) radars.

At this time the Royal Navy had a specialist low flying attack aircraft, the Buccaneer 2, supersonic at low level and with a high wing loading which made it a very stable weapon delivery platform. Its role was for attacking ships at sea and to support landings on hostile territory. Elliott's radar team prepared an unsolicited proposal for an upgrade of the radar unit of the Buccaneer, which they referred to as the Buccaneer 3. This embodied the dual frequency version of the Elliott Cassegrain aerial to provide long detection range over the sea combined with high-definition mapping to show up details of the coastline on landfall. It also provided ground mapping and high accuracy position and range measurement of radar-prominent targets over land or sea. The proposal aroused considerable interest but was not taken up.

11.4.4   EARS and the Aircraft Manufacturers: AEW Gathers Momentum

One of the frequent government defence reviews decreed that the Navy was not to replace its aircraft carriers and that the Royal Air Force was to provide air protection to the fleet and its task forces and to detect and report shipping to a long range. By 1963 the Royal Air Force had come up with its concept for future air defence. This envisaged a fighter aircraft capable of prolonged loitering at altitude with an Airborne Interception (AI) radar capable of detecting an intruder at any altitude at long range and, importantly, to be able to track aircraft flying very low against the background of radar returns from surface features. An aircraft with variable wing sweep (variable geometry) would give the possibility of prolonged loiter on patrol with the wings extended, combined with a high-speed dash for interception with wings swept. This would be complemented by a high-flying AEW aircraft giving coverage from ground to high altitude and within very long range to direct fighters into position to make successful interceptions. Also, in support of the land battle, the RAF required the capability of tracking the movements of land vehicles, friendly and hostile.

An Air Staff Target was drawn up and in 1964 Elliott-Automation Radar Systems (EARS) was given a 4-month contract to study and make proposals for the Airborne

Fig. 11.6 The Hawker Siddeley Nimrod was primarily a maritime patrol aircraft, based on an extensively modified de Havilland Comet jet airliner. Nimrods saw service with the RAF from 1969 to 2010 in various forms, including the Maritime Reconnaissance (MR) variant and the Airborne Early Warning (AEW) variant. The Nimrod AEW3 project incorporated a new Elliott radar system, for which flight trials commenced in 1981. The project ran into severe problems and was cancelled by the government in December 1986. Instead, the RAF in due course obtained the American AWACS system

Early Warning (AEW) System in conjunction with several airframe companies. With the whole-hearted backing of Henry Pasley-Tyler, who had overall authority for the Company's Military business, Peter Mariner set up a team comprising everyone in his Group who could contribute. Mariner was able to call on the participation of other units under Pasley-Tyler's command. The team was led by John Kinnear supported by Eric Daboo, the Chief Scientist in EASAMS, with Frank Adams responsible for the radar aspects. As well as the Airborne Radar Division, the Airborne Communications Division and the Research Laboratory participated and substantial contributions were made by Airspace Control Division, the designers of the Fire Brigade Fighter Direction System, on tracking of targets, fighter control, and situation and data displays. The Airborne Computing Division contributed on the computer and software implications and Elliott Flight Automation on navigation. At the end of the 4 months the report, in 8 volumes and some 3,000 pages in all, was delivered to MOD(PE), and a presentation given.

Discussions continued between the RAF, the MOD(PE) and EARS in respect of AEW. The study had considered several alternative locations for the aerial on the aircraft, and had concluded that to meet all aspects of the requirement the best solution would employ large circular or near circular aerials mounted at the front and rear of the airframe. The dual frequency version of the Elliott Cassegrain aerial would provide co-aligned beams for both radar and IFF (Identification, friend or foe).

The proposals from the aircraft companies had entailed both the design and manufacture of new aircraft and, to avoid the consequential considerable expense and risk, MOD(PE) and EARS were asked to look at the possible use of existing aircraft. The RAF had a number of Andover aircraft, the military version of the Avro 748, which could be made available. After detailed consideration this option was ruled out because space and weight limits were marginal with consequent risk and the possibility that reflections from the propellers could jeopardise the operation of the radar system. A jet aircraft was indicated and the BAC 111 was considered but, eventually, the conversion of some Maritime Reconnaissance Nimrod airframes, which would be surplus after their mid-life update, was seen as the best option, with their ability to fly fast to the patrol zone and slowly when there.

A contract for the Project Definition phase was placed with EARS for a flying test bed to be carried in a Comet 4 aircraft shortly becoming free from trials at Boscombe Down. The aircraft would be modified to carry a typical large aerial at the front, with an experimental radar, albeit operating at much reduced power since a transmitter valve for the full power proposed was not immediately available. This would allow confirmation that the anticipated detection and clutter rejection performance could be expected to be achieved and could identify any unforeseen problems. The airframe was modified with the characteristic nose and radome and the trials radar produced. Then suddenly in 1970, the Government, in the midst of a financial and industrial crisis, sought spending cuts and the programme was abandoned. Had this programme run its course it would probably have identified many of the problems which dogged and delayed a fresh AEW development programme (involving the Nimrod aircraft) that was initiated by the Government a couple of years later; this is described in Sect. 11.5.3 below. With the loss of the first AEW programme the Advanced Special Projects Division, led by Frank Adams, was created to replace the Airborne Radar Division and to carry on work on advanced radar systems.

As an interim solution to its AEW commitment, the RAF decided to fit the improved AN/APS20 radars, at that time becoming free from the Navy's Gannet aircraft, into Shackleton Airframes and in 1972 the Borehamwood product support team was contracted to provide the backing for this. One of the Company's tasks as the Support contractor for the Royal Navy's AN/APS20 Radar had been to propose and implement improvements to the system. The Research Laboratory had been developing a *Bandwidth Compressor* for the RAF's reconnaissance aircraft to compress the data from its reconnaissance sensors so that it could be transmitted in real time by data link back to base during its mission. Using similar technology, the Airborne Radar Division had conceived and proposed a Moving Target processor (MTI) to give the APS20 radar a look-down capability. The Special Projects Division was contracted to produce units for incorporation into the Shackleton AEW system. With this adopted, manufactured and put into service the Division started to give consideration to a new generation of AEW radars (see Sect. 11.5.3).

11.4.5 Five Airborne Radar Projects that Did Not Bear Fruit (1962–1968)

In 1962 the Airborne Radar Division was requested to prepare proposals for radars for Ground Attack and Interceptor versions of the prospective P1154 V/STOL (Vertical/Short Take-off & Landing) aircraft – a projected big brother to the P1127/ Harrier. The Proposals were submitted in 1963, but, before any follow up had been arranged, the aircraft was cancelled by the government in the same wave of 1965 cutbacks that saw the demise of the TSR 2 project. The Elliott proposals had been well received by the RRE Airborne Radar Group, who involved the Elliott radar team in their programme to build and fly, in a Canberra test vehicle, an experimental low-power FMICW (Frequency-Modulated Interrupted Continuous Wave) AI radar as a test vehicle for the gathering of clutter performance data and the signal processing necessary to separate signals from clutter. This programme, which was ongoing into the 1970s, included the design and construction of a scanning aerial, receiver and signal processor, as well as the full-time inclusion of two members of the Elliott team at Malvern to participate in the assembly of the radar and in the flight trials.

In 1964, EARS was asked to make proposals for the radar for an envisaged Anglo-French Variable Geometry aircraft (AFVG), in competition with Ferranti and French companies CSF and Electronique Marcel Dassault. A comprehensive assessment and proposal embodying the Elliott Cassegrain Aerial was submitted to the Ministry of Defence Procurement Agency (MOD(PE)) who exchanged the British and French documents with the French defence agency. The French reports were not disclosed to the British firms involved. The project did not go ahead. However, the French went ahead with their own Mirage aircraft with a radar embodying a Twist-reflecting Cassegrain Aerial! The idea of a Variable Geometry Aircraft was to emerge again, however, as described in Sect. 11.5.

In the mid-1960s a mid-life update was under consideration for the Buccaneer, to be called the Buccaneer 2* (2 Star). EARS was invited by MOD(PE) to update its earlier radar proposal. The new proposal was presented to MOD(PE) and early in 1967 there came a contract for development and manufacture. A few weeks later a formal cancellation followed – yet another result of external factors that were outside the control of the companies involved in defence contracts.

In mid-1966 discussions were held with the Department of Naval Air Warfare (DNAW). The Navy felt that its Through-Deck Cruisers and task forces could be required to operate in parts of the world where the RAF could not give air cover and would be highly vulnerable with no indigenous Airborne Early Warning (AEW) capability. A study was carried out and a proposal made for a helicopter-borne medium range AEW system. This was well received by DNAW but funding was not forthcoming. Had this project gone ahead, the Falklands story might have been very different in 1982.

In 1968 MOD(PE) wished to place competitive studies for a new radar as part of the envisaged update of the Nimrod Maritime Patrol Aircraft. Two consortia were formed to participate: one, the incumbent EMI with Racal; the other comprising Elliott, Ferranti and Decca (self-styled EFD). This bid was unsuccessful.

11.5   Forward to the 1980s

11.5.1   The End of an Era

In 1967 Elliott-Automation merged with English Electric and the next year English Electric was taken over by GEC. Henry Pasley-Tyler was retired. Elliott-Automation Radar Systems (EARS), now without Pasley-Tyler's enthusiastic and whole-hearted backing, was put into the newly formed GEC Marconi Electronics company together with Elliott Flight Automation (EFA) and the Marconi Aeronautical and Electro Optical Divisions at Basildon to form Marconi Elliott Avionic Systems Limited (MEASL). Bob Telford, the Managing Director of GEC Marconi Electronics, became Chairman of MEASL and Dr. Bernard O'Kane Managing Director, both from the Marconi Company. Jack Pateman was Assistant Managing Director of MEASL and Chief Executive of the Rochester organisation and Peter Mariner an Executive Director of MEASL, Managing Director of EARS and Chief Executive of the Basildon Site.

Eric Whitehead became Chief Scientist of the Radiation Systems Group (RSG), and Dr Laverick Technical Director with John Welsh, her erstwhile deputy, Head of the Research Techniques Laboratory. Frank Adams, as Manager of the Advanced

Projects Division, was to continue the co-operation with RRE in the experimental FMICW radar programme.

In 1972 Dr O'Kane became Chairman and Jack Pateman became Managing Director of MEASL. Peter Mariner and Bill Alexander became Assistant Managing Directors; Alexander with responsibility for the Divisions at Rochester and Mariner for the Divisions at Borehamwood and Basildon. Frank Adams was given technical coordinating responsibility, reporting Eric Whitehead. The Special Projects Division was created under Peter Harris to continue the work on AEW and AI Radars

In 1973, after the formal winding up of Elliott Brothers, the Company name was changed to Marconi Avionics Systems Limited (Marconi Avionics or MAV) and subsequently, in 1984, to GEC Avionics.

Highlights of the post-1970 work of Elliott-Automation Radar Systems (EARS), as re-constituted under the GEC umbrella of MEASL, are discussed in the next section in respect of two major radar projects for the RAF: Airborne Interception (AI) and a re-visited Airborne Early Warning (AEW) system for Nimrod. With these two projects in progress, the Elliott-derived radar systems group had grown in strength from a few hundred employees in the mid-1950s to some 4,500 employees by the mid-1980s. The Airborne Interception radar, known as Foxhunter, came to a successful conclusion but the new AEW project was plagued by setbacks outside the control of EARS. Nimrod AEW was axed by the government in 1986, in favour of the American's Boeing AWACS.

There is one further project that should be described at this point because it marks what turned out to be the passing of an era at Borehamwood.

In 1970 Elliott-Automation Radar Systems (EARS) and Ferranti Ltd. were funded to study and bid for the Ground Attack and Reconnaissance radar for another variable geometry aircraft (VGA) in an Anglo-German-Italian Aircraft collaboration. On the completion of the studies Elliott and Ferranti were asked to get together to work out how they might share the avionics system which was understood to be the British responsibility within the collaboration. John Kinnear from Elliotts and Alan Wesley from Ferranti were nominated by their respective Companies to come to an arrangement as to how the radar, the largest and most valuable single item in the avionics, might be shared. They reached an agreed division and a joint radar project management team was set up. However, despite several meetings at higher levels the companies could not reach an agreement on the sharing of the overall system. Admittedly, the background to the discussions was complicated. On the one hand, EFA (Rochester) had experience of several inertial navigation systems, for example in the Blue Steel stand-off missile project, and was competing/collaborating on other systems on the VGA. Ferranti Edinburgh, for their part, had produced the successful Airborne Interception radar AI type 23 in the period 1956–65 and had designed the terrain following radar for the TSR 2 and the attack radar in the Royal Navy's Buccaneer aircraft. In the end, neither Jack Pateman on EFA's part nor Don McCallum (Director and General Manager of Ferranti Edinburgh) and Mal Powley on the Ferranti side were willing to give up the Inertial Navigation System which was seen as a future money-spinner for their respective organisations. Rough justice was then imposed by the government: the Inertial Navigator was allotted to Ferranti and selection of the radar was transferred to Germany who opted for licensed production of American radars.

In 1971 Dr Laverick, frustrated at the outcome of the VGA radar competition, left the Company to become Deputy Secretary of the IEE (The Institution of Electrical Engineers). Shortly after, with John Kinnear now in a marketing and business development role, came the end of the era that had continued since the days of the Elliott Brothers Research Laboratory at Borehamwood. The future of radar in the GEC/Marconi empire was henceforth in the hands of a new young generation of engineers.

11.5.2   Airborne Interception (AI) and Foxhunter

A collaborative programme for an Anglo-German-Italian ground-attack aircraft had resulted in the Panavia Tornado, which made its maiden flight in August 1974 and was in service with the RAF from 1979. In about 1979, the RAF produced its Requirement for an interceptor aircraft based on the Tornado and termed the Air Defence Variant (Tornado ADV). EARS were invited to submit proposals for the AI radar and were requested to involve Ferranti. The design was generally similar to their earlier proposals employing the Elliott Cassegrain Aerial, updated in the light of advances in technology especially in computing and signal processing.

The proposal was submitted and accepted and contracts placed for the radar, with Ferranti contributing the high-power transmitter. The Russian Foxbat aircraft having been recently in the news, Peter Mariner chose the name Foxhunter for the Radar, designated by the RAF AI24. This project demanded a major expansion at Borehamwood and the Airborne Radar Systems Division was created to undertake the project. As the teams grew, development progressed and production approached, new premises were sought. Eventually, after several frustrated attempts to secure premises local to Borehamwood, in 1980 a new factory was acquired at the fast-growing new town at Milton Keynes where housing for new and transferred staff was plentiful and relatively inexpensive.

The radar was flight tested on a British Aerospace Buccaneer and first flew in a Tornado F2 in June 1981 – see [2]. The development was completed and the system entered RAF service in about 1985. In all, several hundred Foxhunter radars were manufactured for the RAF and the Italian and Saudi Arabian air forces.

11.5.3   Nimrod Airborne Early Warning System

The imperative for an RAF AEW aircraft as a key element in Britain's air defence had not gone away. In 1972 the Airborne radar team in EARS commenced a further evaluation of the options. Visits were made to General Electric and Quonsett US Naval air base in the USA to assist an appraisal of the stretch potential of the

Fig. 11.7 Inside a Nimrod AEW aircraft. The photo shows six operator consoles, whose function is believed to have been as follows: four for radar, one for communications and one for Electronic Warfare Support Measures

Hawkeye's ANAPS 110 radar, possibly in a British airframe. The earlier Elliott proposals were reviewed and revised and a Pulse-Doppler form instead of the previous FMICW (Frequency-Modulated Interrupted Continuous Wave) technique was judged to be more acceptable – both forms having their pros and cons. Alternative airframes were considered, with the British-designed Nimrod ultimately considered as the best option.

At the same time the American company Boeing was also active in pressing their AWACS airborne early warning system. AWACS more than satisfied the RAF's requirements for their role in the air defence of the UK and the NATO flanks but it had no maritime surveillance or overland vehicle detection capability, since it had been designed deliberately to reject returns from slow-moving objects so as to avoid overloading the track computing. Since AWACS was very expensive, Boeing sought the participation of the NATO countries – but without success.

Senior members of EARS also made a succession of visits to Defence Ministries and Industry in France, Germany, Italy, Sweden and Japan in search of collaborators or purchasers.

New proposals were submitted by EARS and in March 1977 a go-ahead was given by the UK Ministry of Defence for AEW Nimrod (see [3] for further information). EARS was reorganised by the formation of the Airborne Radar Systems Division (ARSD) to handle the AI radar business, Airborne Warning Systems Division (AWSD) for the AEW project and the Airborne Software Division (ASD), EARS' software house, to concentrate software expertise and to provide a career structure for programmers.

In the early stages of the AEW project, the AWSD engineers with the critical expertise found themselves giving up an excessive proportion of their time to interviewing new recruits for their teams and, subsequently, initiating them into their tasks. The Airborne Warning Systems Division, created for the project, was grown from a few score of engineers in the early stages of the project to a total of over 2,000. This meant, however, that the programme was thereafter always under pressure. To house the enlarged team, new factories were acquired at Radlett and Hemel Hempstead and laboratories and workshops fitted out and equipped.

With the simultaneous growth of the AI Radar programme in the Airborne Radar Systems Division, the radar systems group had been grown from a few hundred in 1970 to over 3,000. One consequence, however, was that Peter Mariner who had driven the activity in a hands-on manner as de facto Head of Marketing, Head of Engineering and Head of Production, became involved with the location and acquisition of additional premises, initiating new buildings and their fitting out, and then became largely office bound with administration and the volume of paperwork that beset him. The conduct of day-to-day matters devolved onto his subordinates.

Design and development went on and in August 1980 a full working AEW system, albeit not radiating, in a rig at Radlett was demonstrated to the Chief of the Air Staff and senior representatives from organisations associated with the project. The first modified Nimrod airframe flew for testing in July 1980, and the first aircraft for radar trials was completed in 1981.

In the time-honoured way, the overall responsibility for the AEW Nimrod programme within the UK's Ministry of Defence had been placed on the Director of Military Aircraft Projects. He had a Nimrod Director and an Assistant Nimrod Director who was given the responsibility for Nimrod AEW3. This arrangement appeared to ignore the fact that the electronic system, which was by far the major and more innovative and challenging part of the programme, was under the direction of the Director of Air Weapon Systems and his Assistant Director Electronics Radar (Airborne) – DLRA/1.

Consequently the whole AEW programme was treated as an aircraft project and the Ministry decided that the radar trials were to be based at the British Aerospace airfield at Woodford, where the Nimrod airframes were being modified. This was a major contributor to the ultimate failure of the project. For one thing, the workforce at Woodford was rigidly unionised and inflexible. By the time all preparatory procedures had been carried out each morning, test flights could not commence until the middle of the day and the aircraft had to be back by mid-afternoon for the necessary checks to be made before closing time. For EARS personnel who had been used to working all hours to get things done, this was acutely frustrating. Also, any items of this extremely complex equipment that developed a fault or required rechecking or even minor modification had to be extracted and sent back to Radlett for repair and retest, often causing several days' delay.

The flight trials showed a considerably larger than expected concentration of *false plots*, which overloaded the tracking system. Progress was so slow that the worried management of EARS, backed by up their Ministry opposite numbers, eventually pressed for the trials aircraft to be based at the British Aerospace airfield at Hatfield, only a few miles from Radlett – albeit too late. One of the benefits, once this move had taken place, was a greater flexibility and urgency. Among the trials that it was now possible to arrange was a night flight, carried out over Scotland and the North Sea, when it was found that the numerous false alarms virtually died out by the small hours of the morning and started to spread out again from around Aberdeen towards dawn. It seemed, therefore, that these false alarms originated from road vehicles. When the original design was conceived in the 1960s, the M1, Britain's first motorway, had only just opened and there were no 30- or 40-t Juggernaut lorries on the roads. It had not perhaps been appreciated that there were now so many large slab-sided vehicles on the roads. These vehicles could return huge radar echoes, causing more numerous and much bigger echoes than had been originally envisaged. These echoes *flashed* as the vehicle's aspect changed with twists and turns and dips in the road. In fact it was not the radar and its tracking system which was the fundamental source of the false-alarm problem but the changed scenario in which AEW operated. The implications of this change had not been appreciated, since it presented a different and more severe problem to the pulse-Doppler radar than to the originally conceived FMICW form.

A unit had been designed, interposed between the radar and the tracking computer, to separate the low-speed returns. This proved very critical to set up, possibly because of the unappreciated strength of the false echoes. On many flights high expectations were dashed but eventually it came good and a very successful sortie was achieved in September 1983 (or 1984?). However, it was too late in the day: the RAF had become very impatient and the AEW project was chopped at the end of 1986. NATO agreed to accept AWACS, by now augmented to give it a sea surveillance capability, as a consequence of the French concluding a valuable deal for licensed production of the engines (which would also then be used in versions of the Airbus), and the RAF got the AWACS that it had sought all along. More comment on the cancellation of the AEW project is given in Appendix A9.5.

Despite its termination, the project resulted in the design, construction and commissioning of a system larger and more complex than had ever been put into a British aircraft previously. This must be recognised as a major achievement. Many factors contributed to its end. No adequate flight trials to gather data for the radar design had been possible before the first high-power transmitter and transmitter tube had been designed and were available for the flight model of the radar. The design of the transmitter and its associated valves, providing and consuming a power two to three orders of magnitude greater than had previously flown in a British aircraft, was a considerable achievement which, however, needed further development time. In the absence of data from high-power flight trials, the design of the target tracking system had to be worked out against a postulated scenario. The scenario that was revealed by the flight trials turned out to be more severe.

It had been envisaged from the start that the small number of AEW radars required would not constitute a production run, but they would be equivalent to the conventional B-models. Nevertheless, it now seems unreasonable that the first airworthy development model of a system of great complexity and high power, which had not flown before, could have been expected to operate without the need for a significant period of development recursions and optimisation. The arrangements for the flight trials were unhelpful from the viewpoint of the timely radar development. And finally: the ultimate customer, the RAF, had always wanted AWACS.

11.6   Conclusions

Taking a retrospective view of the radar-related defence contracts described in this chapter, there are several lessons to be learned – some of them technical, some political. The influences that the Borehamwood Laboratory in particular, and Elliott-Automation in general, had come to recognise in planning their strategy for radar in the 1960s and 1970s included the following:

Inter-service rivalry. The Company realised that it had to recognise and respond to the parochial and differing attitudes of the Services. As one example, the Royal Air Force required a low-level attack aircraft, a role for which the Royal Navy's Buccaneer was designed. However, the Buccaneer was derided by the RAF. When the Navy was giving up what was assumed, before the Falklands War, to be its last aircraft carriers, the Buccaneer aircraft were transferred to the RAF. The RAF pilots who flew them then became devotees.

International collaboration. Throughout the 1960s, the UK government was seeking to join the European Economic Community (EEC). To establish its credentials, the UK sought to make major projects collaborative with one or more of the existing EEC members. This often entailed Britain divulging her technology to countries and companies less advanced in the art, who in due course were to become the UK's competitors.

Financial difficulties. Because of repeated financial crises in the UK's economy, otherwise desirable programmes were liable to be abandoned by the government at any stage. Cutting costs through international collaborative programmes had an (apparent) appeal, though it has been a matter of dispute whether any significant saving has ever been realised in the event.

American Goodies. RAF Requirements Officers saw exciting new aircraft being designed in the USA and could go across and fly them. The aircraft existed and, understandably, the officers wanted them for the RAF. It has to be said, however, that there was a counterbalance to this transatlantic envy: Mod(PE) and the UK's Research Establishments realised that if US aircraft and systems were widely adopted then the UK would lose its technological and manufacturing base. Once this base was lost, it would be gone forever and the country would be dependent on other nations and have no negotiating strength.

If the above catalogue of concerns seems to focus on the airborne applications of radar, this is because military aircraft provided by far the most important market for advanced radar technology from the mid-1950s onwards. It is not surprising that, especially within the Marconi Avionics organisation, the various radar divisions became more and more closely linked with the aircraft divisions. There were, however, differences in technical cultures. For example, the radar business consisted of a relatively small number of high-value equipments while the avionics business usually comprised much larger numbers of lower-value equipments. Such culture differences were, perhaps, not fully understood by EFA. For various reasons, therefore, there was a gradual reversal of fortunes that may well have had its effect on the morale of senior staff within Elliott-Automation Radar Systems (EARS).

In the very early days at Borehamwood under J.F. Coales, radar was the driver of *research* (though not, it has to be said, of production and marketing). However, in relation to other UK radar manufacturers such as Ferranti and Decca, it was not until the end of the 1970s and the ADV Tornado contract and Foxhunter (described in Sect. 11.5.3) that the Elliott name was associated with large-scale radar *production*. In contrast, the Aviation Division was not formed at Borehamwood until about 1953 or 1954, but by 1970 the resulting Avionics endeavours had reached world-class strength. The story of Elliott-Automation's aircraft and aerospace computational activities is given in Chap. 12. As for the Borehamwood radar legacy, Dr Elizabeth Laverick and John Kinnear have summarised the impact in the following paragraphs.

A measure of the achievement of the radar team is demonstrated by some figures. Numbering some ten staff of all denominations at Borehamwood in 1952, it had grown from 200 by the end of the 1950s, to 1,150 at the end of the 1960s, to 3,200 by the end of the 1970s and to over 3,250 by 1984. The order book figure of £250,000 in 1969–1970 had grown to £170 million by 1980. Floor space of some 155,000 ft^2 in 1969 reached 545,000 ft^2 by 1980 and 700,000 ft^2 in 1984. In addition to several premises at Borehamwood, the radar activities had extended to sites at Radlett, Hemel Hempstead, Welwyn Garden City, Peterborough and Milton Keynes.

The growth from the small radar team in 1952 to the 4,500 strong organisations in the mid-1980s derived from Peter Mariner's ambition, purposefulness and drive. From the start he had a personal involvement at *every* level with his staff, his customers and his associates at the Ministry of Defence and its research establishments, until the dispersal of his Divisions and the administrative demands of his enlarged organisation made him virtually office bound. Peter Mariner led by example: he rarely left work before 10.30 p.m. and often worked at home until the small hours. His application brushed off on his staff. As a result he had the whole-hearted support throughout of talented, dedicated and hard-working people of all skills and disciplines, widely appreciated for their competence, all of whom made their personal contribution to the radar team's achievements. Peter Mariner retired in 1984, at which point he was an Assistant Managing Director, GEC Avionics.

References

1. http://www.skomer.u-net.com/projects/popsy.htm
2. Anon (1981) Tornado radar. Aviation Week Space Technology (A McGraw-Hill Magazine) 6 June 1981:63
3. Williamson B, BAe Nimrod AEW. http://www.spyflight.co.uk/Nim%20aew.htm – which consists of about a dozen pages of text plus several photographs

Chapter 12
Airborne Computing System Developments at Elliott-Automation, 1958–1988

A personal account By Peter Hearne, 2006

Preamble by Simon Lavington

Peter Hearne, F R Eng., was born in 1927. His posts have included that of Director and General Manager of Elliott Flight Automation (subsequently GEC Avionics) from 1965 to 1986, Assistant Managing Director of the GEC Marconi Group 1986/90, and Chairman of GEC Marconi Avionics from 1992 to 1993. His personal account of the application of digital computers to aircraft was written in 2007. Whilst Peter Hearne drew largely from his own considerable experience, he also had available certain background material from ex-colleagues, as given in [1, 2]. Peter's draft text was shown to three other former Elliott colleagues, R W (Ron) Howard, Paul Rayner and Terry Froggatt, who provided some additional information as detailed respectively in [3–5].

The story of the various aircraft divisions within Elliott-Automation started in earnest with the establishment of an Aviation Division at Borehamwood in 1953. The pace changed in 1968, following the merger of Elliott-Automation with English Electric and then English Electric's takeover by GEC. However, after 1968 the name 'Elliott' continued to be intimately associated with aviation, *Elliott Brother (London) Ltd.* remaining as a registered trading name of GEC Avionics until 1988. In 1999 GEC sold all its defence-related divisions, including Avionics, to BAE Systems (which itself grew from British Aerospace). By that time, it had become the fourth largest aircraft electronics company in the world with some 16,000 employees.

Peter Hearne is an avowed digital man. Peter's former colleague Ron Howard CBE, a former Managing Director and Chairman of GEC Avionics Ltd., was the company's authority on Flight Control Systems (FCS). The development of FCS has its roots in analogue computing. Although the story of Elliott-Automation's analogue computing activities is generally covered in Chap. 4, more should now be said about the interwoven history of both analogue and digital avionics before moving on to Peter Hearne's purely digital chapter. This also provides an opportunity to define a few terms and mention the historic connection between early American digital airborne computing and Elliott's entry into the same arena. Helpful notes from Peter Hearne and Ron Howard have underpinned these scene-setting introductory remarks.

S. Lavington, *Moving Targets*, History of Computing,
DOI 10.1007/978-1-84882-933-6_12, © Springer-Verlag London Limited 2011

Computers in aircraft are now used for two classes of activity:

- *Flight Control*: augmentation of aircraft's natural aerodynamic stability and handling, automatic control of flight vector and manoeuvring, engine control and associated instruments, which allow the aircraft to fly safely throughout its speed range at all altitudes and weather conditions.
- *Mission Systems*: navigation, target detection, weapon aiming and delivery equipments and complementary situational displays which allow the aircraft to find or detect its target and complete its operational task in all weather conditions.

In the 1950s analogue techniques were used for both Flight Control and Mission Systems purposes, with flight control the predominating concern. The Air Data Computer of the 1950s was an entirely analogue device, a vital part of the instrumentation system of all high-performance aircraft – see Fig. 12.1. Indeed, electromechanical analogue signal-processing equipment in aircraft persisted well into the 1960s and 1970s, there being by that time an overlap between airborne analogue and digital techniques. More background information on the analogue side of Elliott's *flight control* projects in the 1950s and 1960s is given in Appendix 9, as are the definitions of key phrases such as *Fly-by-Wire*.

The emergence of self-contained inertial navigation systems in the mid-1950s put a premium on very low drift, very high accuracy analogue circuitry – particularly in the area of open loop functions. Whereas closed loop control functions have a

Fig. 12.1 Computers in aircraft are used for two general classes of tasks: *Flight Control* and *Mission Systems*. The photo shows an early Elliott analogue computer for flight control, known as an *Air Data Computer*. This type of equipment was typical of the late 1950s

degree of self-correction in the feedback process, no such correction is possible in the integration of acceleration, speed and distance in an inertial navigator unless there is a separate and different navigation sensor present, which often defeats the purpose of maximum independence and minimum size and weight of the installed navigation system. Hence the very high precision, low electronic drift – and sometimes very high speed (e.g. ICBM) or very long flight times – demanded a different and in this case a *digital* approach to navigation system calculation and control.

Although the initial application was directly related to the calculation and control functions of inertial platforms, it was quickly realised that the various types of digital outputs would allow a significant simplification of communication between sub-system elements and other aircraft systems as well as being of considerable help in other types of self-contained navigation system such as Doppler. Moreover, digital computation allowed many complex calculations and control functions to be performed with a much greater ease than equivalent highly refined and complex analogue components such as ball resolvers.

The first *miniature* digital computer made its appearance in the inertial navigation system of the USS Nautilus, which was launched in 1954 and completed the first sub-polar crossing in 1958. A production version of the Nautilus' navigation computer, VERDAN (Versatile Digital Analyzer), was incorporated in the North American A3J Vigilante Mach 2 twin engine carrier-borne strike aircraft, later re-designated the A5. The A3J system was based on the combination of the Verdan computer with the Autonetics inertial navigation platform.

In addition to carrying out all of the navigation functions, the A3J system acted as a central data source for attitude, heading and velocity data which it fed to the aircraft's radar, TV optical sight and Head-Up Display. All of the hardware and the totality of the system was produced by North American Aviation's electronic systems group which was known by the trade name of Autonetics. This was the first instance of the use of a digital computer in a production military aircraft. The Hughes Aircraft integrated radar/interception computer system in the later Convair F102s and in the F106s which came later in the early 1960s.

The A3J's system, known as REINS (Radar Enhanced Inertial Navigation), first flew in the Vigilante in 1960 but its operational use was curtailed by the intractable problems of weapon release at Mach 2 and 40,000 ft from the A3J's very unorthodox weapon release system. This basic design defect resulted in the Vigilante's operational service being confined to the vital, but far more hazardous, medium-level target reconnaissance and Electronic Countermeasures role in Vietnam from 1965 on, where its effectiveness and losses were proportionately high.

As set out below, Elliott's first venture into airborne digital computing came with the TSR 2 strike aircraft for which they had had the foresight to license the Verdan computer. Whilst the American Vigilante system was closely focused around the inertial navigation/digital computer pair, the British TSR 2 introduced a much wider system functional concept and can be seen as one of the forerunners of the widespread use of digital computers in aircraft. The TSR 2 prototype first flew in September 1964 – see Fig. 12.2.

Fig. 12.2 The TSR 2 (*Tactical Strike and Reconnaissance*) was an ambitious aircraft, specified by the government at the end of the 1950s. The photo shows a prototype TSR 2, which first flew in 1964. The project was cancelled in 1965, to the dismay of the UK's aerospace industry.TSR 2's specification included the first UK defence requirement for a real-time airborne digital system

Of course, the Borehamwood Research Laboratory of Elliott Brothers (London) Ltd. had begun to think of real-time digital control during the late 1940s. The prototype Elliott 152 computer, built under an Admiralty contract for radar-directed naval anti-aircraft fire control systems, was working under test conditions in the summer of 1950 (see Chap. 2). The 152 computer was orders of magnitude too large and uncertain to be used in aircraft systems. Although Elliott's Borehamwood establishment had originally been set up in October 1946 to pursue radar-related Admiralty contracts, the main Elliott factory in Lewisham had for very many years been involved in a variety of electro-mechanical and electrical instrumentation and control projects, including aircraft instrumentation, as discussed in Appendix 9. Therefore when, in 1952, there was a need for Borehamwood to diversify its research activities it was natural to consider flight control applications as one of several possible areas for expansion. More generally, industrial process control, or automation, emerged as the main driver for Elliott's future, as discussed in Chaps. 6 and 7.

As for flight control, Ron Howard remembers the manner in which Borehamwood was encouraged along this path [3]: 'The Smiths company was the traditional supplier of autopilots for transport and bomber aircraft and the RAE [Farnborough] with the UK government wanted an alternative supplier to tackle the new supersonic combat aircraft field. Elliott Brothers (London) Ltd., with its long history of making aircraft instruments, and another company, Louis Newmark Ltd., were asked to go into competition for the honour, by bidding for the two systems required for a 3-axis autostabiliser and the MK13 autopilot. During 1954 Elliott was chosen for both contracts and Newmark was directed into the helicopter controls business. This took place at the time I joined the company in October 1954.'

An Aviation Division was formally established at Borehamwood in late 1953 or early 1954. Initial projects involved the development of analogue autopilots for unmanned experimental aircraft and an analogue 3-axis autostabilisation system for a Mach 2 fighter under the official requirement F23/49, which was to become the English Electric Lightning. By 1960 this activity had expanded to cover the autopilots for both the Lightning and Buccaneer transonic strike aircraft as well as complementary development of analogue air data systems for these aircraft.

Most importantly work had begun, also under Ron Howard's leadership, of a dual channel fail-operative autopilot/automatic landing system for the Vickers VC10 long-range jet airliner. In 1960 Elliott's expertise in advanced flight control systems in the UK was recognised by the award of the triplex automatic terrain following autopilot and autostabliser contract for the Mach 2-plus TSR 2 strike aircraft. These two systems, along with the earlier Lightning system, can be considered as the foundation stones of much of what was to follow in Flight Control system developments at Elliott's. All this had a powerful influence on thinking throughout the industry and operators.

Now that the scene has been set for digital techniques, let Peter Hearne take over.

12.1 Digital Computing Takes to the Air

The first UK defence requirement for a real-time airborne *digital* system emerged in 1958/1959, as part of the specification for the TSR 2 project. This required a computing system which integrated the output of the inertial platform (provided by Ferranti Ltd.) and other sensors including forward and sideways looking radars, and generated advanced navigation and steering information to the crew as well as bomb aiming and delivery displays. Because the TSR 2, and its subsequent cancellation, had such a profound influence on most British aerospace companies, including Elliott-Automation, it is worth spending a little time explaining the background.

In 1956 the Ministry of Supply (MoS) began talks with English Electric about the need to design a replacement for the *Canberra* bomber. (Operational Canberras were first delivered to the RAF in 1951; photo-reconnaissance versions were still in service in 2006). In 1956 the Canberra replacement aircraft was required to have a range of 2,000 nautical miles, a speed of Mach 1.5 at altitude, able to carry reconnaissance equipment and a variety of weapons (including, for example, six 1,000-lb bombs), to attack at very low level, and to have a short field take-off capability: clearly a very ambitious project! By 1959 the project had been designated TSR 2, the Canberra being regarded as the TSR 1. The initials originally stood for Tactical Support and Reconnaissance, though it later became Tactical Strike and Reconnaissance once the possibility of a nuclear role was considered. On the 27th of September 1964, the first test flight of XR219, the TSR 2 prototype, took place [6].

As far as Elliotts was concerned, the TSR 2 digital computer project involved a detailed knowledge of aircraft systems. As a result, an Airborne Computing Division was formed in the Flight Automation group at Borehamwood. The activity was headed by Paul Rayner, initially as Chief Engineer but later as Divisional Manager, who was poached from Elliott's mainstream scientific /commercial computing business headed up by Andrew St. Johnston, plus a software specialist John Bussell also from the same stable. On my second day in the company, 12 May 1959, I was told by Jack Pateman that as one of the company's few aircraft design specialists I was going to be responsible for growing the Airborne Computing business – a severe shock to my own system.

12.2 The Verdan Computer

Our competitor for the TSR 2 contract was the Dexan computer, produced by GEC Stanmore Research Laboratories under contract and guidance from RAE (Farnborough). Although by 1959 the Computing Division at Borehamwood was well underway with the development of the 800 series general-purpose digital computers using transistors – the first production 802 was completed in November 1958, see Chap. 10 – Elliotts had nothing at all suitable in time or size and packaging for the TSR 2 project. Jack Pateman had several months earlier had the good fortune and inspiration to start negotiations for a licence from the Autonetics Division of the North American Aviation Corporation for their Verdan computer, which was already in production for aircraft, cruise and ballistic missiles and submarine projects in the USA (see above).

The Verdan computer was primitive by today's standards but offered 2,000 words of disc storage, which could be allocated between General-Purpose (GP) and Digital Differential Analyser (DDA) functions. We found the DDA very useful for the real-time control tasks and we had many arguments as to which functions should be GP and which should be in the DDA. I seem to remember that we finally adopted a policy of using the GP to initialise the DDA.

However, the Verdan computer was small enough to go into an aircraft – see Figs. 12.3 and 12.4 – highly reliable for its day, well engineered to military aircraft specification standards and had substantial existing test and programming/software infrastructure which did not exist for the Dexan competitor. The Verdan is believed to have been the first digital computer to be installed in a European aircraft, the prototype TSR 2 [1]. Paul Rayner was chosen to lead the Verdan developments for Elliott's part of the TSR 2 project. Paul was undoubtedly the single most capable individual in terms of engineering knowledge and leadership, team management and foresight from the start of the airborne digital saga until his promotion to MD of GEC Computers in the mid-1980s. There is no doubt that without his outstanding contributions our successes would have been much less marked. Paul remembers the Verdan activities as follows [4].

'As well as for submarines and the A3J Vigilante aircraft, the Verdan computer/ inertial platform pair, along with a star tracker, was the guidance system for the B 52 air launched Hound Dog (Elvis!) nuclear cruise missile. Hound Dog went into

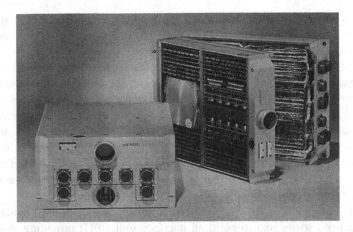

Fig. 12.3 Lacking a suitable airborne computer of their own at the time, in 1958 Elliott-Automation's Airborne Computing Division obtained a licence from the Autonetics Division of the North American Aviation Corporation to use the Verdan digital computer. This had been developed for a US missile project

Fig. 12.4 The Verdan is believed to have been the first digital computer to be installed in a European aircraft, namely the prototype TSR 2

service in 1959 and I believe about 600 of these missiles were built. The North American Aviation Corporation were prime contractors for the missile and their Autonetics Division developed both Verdan and the IN (inertial navigation) system providing the primary navigation data for the missile and to which Verdan was tightly coupled.

'Being a missile, there was no man-machine interface involved (at least, not on board the missile). Also the missile avionics were completely solid state, mostly digital and Verdan was designed specifically to integrate with them. Although the internal design of Verdan was modular and maintainable there were no equipment racks in the conventional sense: equipment was fixed down in any convenient place in the missile.

'The TSR 2 on the other hand was a multi-role aircraft, had a pilot and a navigator, was basically an analog aircraft fitted for the most part with conventionally designed aircraft equipment, including the IN system, and had its avionics mounted in standard ATR (*Air Transport Racking*) racks for ease of front line servicing.

'So – Autonetics were paid to repackage Verdan into an ATR box and re-qualify to UK aircraft standards. One Verdan quickly became two as we explored its programming limitations. The aircraft power supplies were not sufficiently stable for digital equipment, so a motor-alternator, American sourced and approved by their military (more about that later) was fitted.

'Aircraft equipment with which we had to interface mostly used synchros for communication, so we had to build an interface unit (IFU) providing synchro to digital and digital to synchro converters. Nothing like this existed, so we had to design and build these from scratch. It was state of the art electronics all the way through. We started designing this and other boxes using germanium transistors (Verdan used germanium throughout). Halfway through the design, much more reliable silicon transistors became available and I remember the rather traumatic design review where we decided to switch. This meant turning the electronic circuitry "upside down" [pnp versus npn transistors].

'The space we were given for the Navigator's Control and Display Unit (NCDU) was tall and irregularly shaped, spanning the upper and lower halves of the cockpit. This was in the days before CAD and was a mechanical design nightmare. It used Nixie (*note spelling*) gas discharge tubes for the numerical display and we had to design our own ruggedised keyboard from scratch. Another first – a digital data transmission system was developed to connect the NCDU to the computer.

'Another box we had to design was the Reconnaissance Buffer Store (RBS) to interface the Verdan system to the reconnaissance recorders. The timescale for this was a year or two after the other units and by this time prototypes of the first integrated circuits were becoming available from Texas Instruments. Without telling MOD we decided to use them in the RBS.

'The stability of the aircraft power generators and the RFI specifications were largely governed by the requirements of the aircraft communication systems. Voltage fluctuations and spikes from unsuppressed switches could be tolerated but continuous frequencies in the RF bands were a definite no-no. This was exactly the opposite of the requirements for digital equipment. We got over most of the problems by installing the motor-generator to supply the digital equipment, but meeting the stringent RFI specifications continued to be a problem, particularly from the Digital Data Transmission to the cockpit.

'Having selected the motor-generator supplier, recommended by the Americans and agreed by MOD, I went over to check out the company at their premises located half way between Los Angeles and San Diego. I was dismayed to find that they were a small back-street company with no quality systems whatsoever. This highlights a major difference of approach at that time between American and UK procurement procedures. While every component and all material we used in our designed equipment had to be MOD approved and purchased against tightly controlled specifications (most of which didn't exist and had to be written by us), the Americans qualified their equipment at black box, or even system level and left it to manufacturers' normal commercial practice to look after the innards of their boxes. This meant that American timescales were much shorter and costs were less. We had the added problem of persuading component suppliers to accept rigorous specifications and control procedures for what was only a very small part of their total output.'

The wisdom of putting the TSR 2 computer project in the hands of Paul Rayner and the aircraft systems specialists, rather than Andrew St. Johnston's in-house Borehamwood computer designers, was shown by the innovative system design which evolved using two interlinked Verdan computers, one being primarily for Navigation but with a reversionary bombing mode and the other being primarily Bombing but with a reversionary Navigation capability. This concept was based upon the *fail-operative* automatic landing system, which Ron Howard had conceived and was developing for the civil side of Vickers for the VC10 airliner. (It was in fact the direct ancestor of the subsequent Concorde system – see later).

The TSR 2 system was the first of its kind in Europe and indeed more advanced than any existing US system [7]. I had very mixed feelings when some 5 years later Autonetics rather shamefacedly revealed that they had copied the Elliott systems concept for the very similar system they had supplied later to the F111 aircraft. Intellectual Property Rights (IPR) had not yet got the attention that exists today but I felt that we had been screwed. Had it been the other way round, I am sure that the US firm would have sued us.

The TSR 2 project came to a sad end (in May 1965) because the RAF had over-egged the requirement and escalated the cost enormously. Actually, a less demanding aircraft specification had been evolved over an earlier period of time. This was the English Electric P17A, which did not have all the bells and whistles of the TSR 2 but would have been affordable – and incidentally infinitely more effective operationally, than the Tornado which ultimately emerged after the TSR 2 cancellation (see also Sect. 12.12).

12.3   The Elliott 920B and 920M Computers

Whilst the TSR 2 project was underway, we realised that Verdan would have a rather short life as a *central computer* and we began to look at the 920 derivative of the Elliott 901 computer which had started to emerge in the main stream computing side at Borehamwood. By the early 1960s, the 901 had evolved into the 920A, having an 8K store with about 10 μs access time but still in an outer package form which allowed soldiers to stand on it whilst getting into a tank. We actually flew a 920A in the test-bed Comet which had a TSR 2 system used for airborne trials and it worked well. We now started urging the Borehamwood Computing Division, led by Andrew St Johnston, to develop a suitable airborne version of the 920A computer.

At this moment in time, 1964, the factors dominant in the aircraft systems designer's mind were as follows:

- Meeting military aircraft environmental design specifications.
- Computer speed and memory storage capacity. This was dominated by storage (memory) technology, which in turn was affected by environmental requirements – particularly temperature and vibration.
- Maintainability and reliability.
- Size and weight and, increasingly, cost.

With our then lack of foresight in the Airborne Computing Division, we did not even consider that software support was of prime importance. Software was less than 5% of the engineering effort on the TSR 2 project. Instead, we continued to bias technical and system solutions towards minimising hardware complexity and costs, even though additional software problems might sometimes result.

The machine we wanted was designated the 920M. It had to have microcircuit technology and multilayer printed-circuit boards (PCBs) to be competitive with the rapidly developing US machines. We wanted a 1 μs, 8K-core store, excellent reli-

Fig. 12.5 Elliott-Automation's aviation activities saw many name-changes after the GEC takeover of 1968, the principal ones being Marconi–Elliott Avionics Systems Ltd. (1969); Marconi Avionics Ltd. (1978); GEC Avionics Ltd. (1984); GEC-Marconi Avionics Ltd. (1993) and finally BAE Systems (1999 onwards). The photo shows the Board of Marconi–Elliott Avionic Systems Ltd. (MEASL) in about 1969 or shortly thereafter, *(left to right)*: Ron Howard, Director; Peter Hearne, Director; Jack Pateman, Managing Director; Bernard O'Kane, Chairman; Peter Mariner, Assistant Managing Director; Bill Alexander, Assistant Managing Director; Wally Paterson, General Manager; David Rickard, Finance Director

ability and maintainability at squadron level and a standardised aircraft equipment form factor, namely ATR, which was fully compliant with military aircraft equipment specifications. The relevant ATR form factor was about 20–25% of the volume of the existing 920A and since we needed to operate at around 55°C with cooling air it posed a considerable challenge to Borehamwood.

Common sense suggested that we should go for a laboratory demonstrator, which included the system design, circuitry and functional aspects of the computer but not the fully engineered form factor.

This machine, developed in the mainstream Computer Research Laboratory at Borehamwood by Laurence Clarke, Geoff Monk and Peter Lawrence, turned out to be a roaring success. What was meant to be a demonstrator configuration in terms of power consumption and operating temperature prior to squashing it into a ¾ ATR short box, became a best seller in a wide range of applications and some 600 or 700 were sold. It was called the Elliott 920B.

Terry Froggatt worked as a 900 series programmer from 1966 to 1976, starting in the Airborne Computing Division at Borehamwood and ending with the Maritime Aircraft Systems Division in Rochester. Terry has added the following retrospective comment about the 920B [5]. 'The earlier Verdan had been hard to program because the instructions had to be scattered round the disk to get the timing right, as with all sequential stores such as drums or long mercury delay lines. The later Minim and the 12-series computers (both 12-bit 900 Series derivatives – see Appendix 6) were hard to program because, with their short word lengths, only a small part of the memory was directly addressed; this also made it difficult to accumulate any reusable software. In contrast, a 920B with its 18-bit word length and 8192-word memory was relatively easy to program, the whole memory being directly and uniformly addressable.' More technical details on the whole of the 900 series machines will be found in Appendix 6.

The Elliott 920B was a big advance for Airborne Computing. We successfully used it as the main computer in the Nimrod Mark 1 ASW (anti-submarine warfare) to integrate all of the navigation, radar, sonar and EW (Electronic Warfare) system outputs and to drive a very comprehensive large target situation display. The first Nimrod Mark I MR (Maritime Reconnaisance) flew in June 1968, entering service with the RAF in October 1969. Note that the 920B did *not* process the raw sensor information itself: that was done by the individual sensor suites and separate sensor operators themselves. Nevertheless, the 920B did allow an accurate situation picture to be built up from the combination of some five complementary information sources, which greatly improved the ASW localisation and attack capability of the Nimrod aircraft.

The 920B also found itself as a key element in our expanding Automatic test equipment business and was widely used in RAF applications. It also appeared in Air Defence systems, Army battery fire control and Met data and many other functions. It also assumed a civil form known as the Elliott 903, repackaged in more of a cabinet form rather than the cross between a small- and medium-sized grey suitcase, which was its military persona.

However, despite its functional success it did *not* fulfil the prime requirement of being small enough and light enough to fit it into a military fighter/attack type

Fig. 12.6 The Elliott 920M computer, which used a form of multi-layer printed-circuit boards and flat-pack integrated circuits, was developed in the Computer Research Laboratory at Borehamwood and first delivered in about 1967

Fig. 12.7 The fold-out construction of the Elliott 920M computer. After about 1966, Elliott-Automation's Airborne Computing division started designing its own machines for aerospace applications, the first of which was the 920 ATC computer

aircraft. For that we need the 920M, which we had previously specified for the anticipated growth of the TSR 2 system. The Elliott 920M, which eventually emerged, was good enough and unique enough in the UK to give us an edge in the market. The computer is shown in Figs. 12.6 and 12.7. Unfortunately at that early stage, the Elliott company lacked access to multi-layer PCB technology which the aircraft side regarded as essential. Instead, the Airborne Computing Division was forced to rely upon a Borehamwood Computer Laboratory development of etching mini-windows to allow metal tag cross-connections between layers of metallic coated Mylar type sheets. This process was used in small blocks to produce the three-chip slab elements which made up the computer, as well as in larger sheets to form the much more elaborate multi-layer motherboard. We promoted the fact that the three-chip slabs, which were wire-wrapped into the motherboard pins, allowed us to have a throw-away maintenance philosophy as well as giving great rigidity and heat conduction to counteract vibration and temperature effects. This went down well with the customers, although the rapid fall in the price of chips soon began to undermine part of the justification. However in its production form, initially with an 8K, 2-μs store, the 920M was widely used in its intended role in the Jaguar navigation attack system and eventually grew to a 64K machine and was adopted for a number of naval inertial navigation applications.

The TSR 2 project was cancelled in May 1965 but Elliotts decided that, rather than retrench and cut back, they would continue to support the technology initiatives which they had initiated to support future TSR 2 developments. These initiatives included the 920 series and also, fatally as it turned out, microelectronics. Though I cannot prove it, many of us thought that the costs of the microelectronic effort under Ian Macintosh [at Glenrothes] was the straw that broke the camel's back and hastened the merger with English Electric in September 1967 (see Chap. 13).

12.4 Airborne Digital Computing Becomes a Separate Discipline

We are now in the period 1966/1967 and it is worth taking a break in the narrative to examine some of the undercurrents which were affecting the growth of airborne digital computers. There were three major influences.

Perhaps the most fundamental was the realisation in the Airborne Systems Group that a large central digital computer, what we now call a *Mission Computer*, was not of general application for all types of aircraft systems. It was so expensive and so complex that it could only be justified when there were a great many tasks to be performed in a number of closely associated aircraft systems. However, the reliability implications of using a centralised computer for so many different functions were disturbing. Even if multiple computers were considered, the difficulties of providing a *fail-operative* multiplex interface unit for all of the individual systems' inputs and outputs looked even more complex and expensive.

One evening in 1964 John Shepherd (a very bright young systems engineer who had joined us some 4 years previously after graduating from Cranfield) and I were having a drink after work in the engineering laboratory extension opposite the main Borehamwood factory, otherwise known as a pub called the Elstree Way. Many an intractable design problem was solved in that bar and this was one such occasion.

'You know John', I said, 'What we really need is a small digital computer which is no bigger, no heavier and no more expensive than any single analogue computer which it replaces. If we don't do that we're going to be stuck with analogue electronics for a long time to come.'

As a result of this conversation, development started in the Airborne Systems Laboratory, quite independently of the mainstream Elliott Computing Systems activities and laboratories, of what was initially called the *MINIM*, then the *DEC* and in its production form the *12 Series* computer. Initially, core store prices drove the cost too high but the microchip revolution started to eat away at the costs and a successful design emerged. The ultimate sales of this machine, and its close derivatives, which were somewhere in the 30,000s and which was adopted by Marconi Space and Defence Systems (MSDS) for their tank and torpedo systems as well as aircraft EW, will be described in more detail later.

At one swoop we had made progress on two very pressing tasks. Firstly we were able to go ahead with the development of cost-efficient *federated* systems which solved the problems of reliability, computing cycle times, the emerging software problems and all of the other difficulties which were beginning to emerge from the concepts of large Central Computing systems in aircraft. In later years it was an infinite pleasure when the Elliott concept of federated computers defeated IBM Germany on their proposal for such a single central computing system for the Tornado.

The second task involved the introduction of the basic advantages of digital computing into the traditionally analogue world of Automatic Flight Controls.

As described briefly above, by 1962 Elliotts had become the prime UK company in advanced thinking in Flight Control and their views and opinions were respected

Fig. 12.8 The supersonic Concorde incorporated an Elliott analogue automatic flight control system. The aircraft's specification dates from the early 1960s. Concorde had its first test flight in 1969, entered service in 1976 and was withdrawn from commercial flights in 2003

by international bodies such as the American FAA and the International Air Transport Association. Elliott's leading position in the field was now confirmed by their selection as the UK lead contractor for the Concorde automatic flight control system. This brought together the supersonic experience of the Lightning and TSR 2 teams and the extensive work on fail operative system thinking and technology developed on the VC 10.

The late 1950s was a time of significant change in the automatic flight control field. Although the advent of higher speed jet aircraft with their attendant stability problems and more demanding handling had set a new pace in the electronic control system components, up to this time the automatic systems had tended to be an add-on to the basic flying control system. With the emergence of requirements for fail-operative control functions in critical flight regimes where no disturbance was allowable in the event of system malfunction, the design and layout of the main flying control system and its actuators and even the layout and functional partitioning of the aerodynamic control surfaces themselves became an important feature and increasingly a major joint responsibility of the airframe designer and the flight control system supplier. Elliott made a major contribution to this evolution by the design and development of actuation systems which integrated the electronic control input with the hydraulics of the main flying control power actuator. In turn this led to considerable shared responsibility with the airframe designs of the Vickers VC10, where the main control surfaces were split into several separate units, and in the TSR 2 with its critical yaw instability above Mach 2 and transonic 200 ft automatically controlled terrain following.

By the time that the Tornado programme was underway, the Borehamwood team had evolved a quadruplex channel electro-hydraulic actuator which became the principal actuator used through the automatic flight control system on all Tornado aircraft. And of course the provision of fail operative control systems had a direct bearing on the configuration of the basic electrical power and hydraulic systems of the aircraft – which was yet another field in which the Flight Controls Group had to develop a strong background of engineering understanding and competence.

Even with the earlier background of VC10 and TSR 2, the Concorde project posed a considerable challenge. Unlike the VC10 where the critical fail operative functions were principally centred around the 1-min duration segment of the approach and landing, the Concorde was designed to fly in an artificially stabilised fly-by-wire mode throughout its 3-h flight. Manual reversion was possible but it is a matter of record that this was very rarely, if ever, used in any passenger carrying flight – such was the in-service integrity and reliability of the system and hardware design.

Moreover even the basic physics of controlling the aircraft were demanding, the supersonic cruise aerodynamics of the aircraft requiring minute angular movement of the main controls at significant bandwidths at the end of a fuselage some 200 ft long.

Faced with these problems, there is no doubt that the fundamentally correct decision was to forego the opportunity to introduce hitherto untried digital flight control technology into the Concorde and to rely upon the proven background of analogue electronic flight control, stretching back over the last 20 years.

Ron Howard [3], an expert in analogue techniques who had joined Borehamwood in 1954, remembers that: 'The apparent slowness in the adoption of digital computing in automatic flight controls was due to very real problems not presented by the relatively straight forward centralised computing required of navigation and display systems. All flight control systems are feedback closed loop in nature. So stability and control, particularly at high gain low signal levels is critical and hence data discrimination, accuracy and rates must be very high and comparable with the previous results achieved by continuous analogue predecessors. The prime motivation to move to digital technology was to develop high integrity failure-survival active control systems which were as safe as airframe and could substitute for it and so free aircraft performance from the bonds of classic aerodynamic design. The existing digital computer designs were too inflexible and too large and heavy to meet these demands.'

The resulting analogue automatic flight control system for the Concorde was undoubtedly complicated and challenging but as mentioned above it did its job outstandingly well in service, pilots in particular being envious of its superior ability to pull off a really smooth landing consistently. Talking to Ron in later years he admitted that he would have liked to have the benefits in system design which a digital system would have brought but that the engineering risk was undoubtedly too high, a judgment with which I fully agree.

With the appearance of the 12 series computer (see below) in actual airborne hardware form, the digital team began to press the Flight Controls Group to consider the plunge into the digital sea. The original 12/12 had been designed as a gas turbine engine controller to replace the hydraulic *Meccano* which had evolved over the years from the original ad hoc engine control systems of the early jet age. The 12/12 was originally called DEC (acronym for Digital Engine Controller) until the Digital Equipment Company objected. The digital enthusiasts thought that if it could control a sometimes idiosyncratic turbo jet, which it did very successfully on an engine test bed, why not an aircraft?

The reason was of course that, as set out above, the digital controller was just one component – albeit a crucial one – of a number of equally complex and critical units, e.g. pilot's controllers, actuators and gyros, which together made up the totality of an automatic flight control system.

As these facts sank into the digital group, they also came to realise that the design authority and leadership for any flight control system design must reside with the appropriate specialist group of flight control system specialists and that the digital group's role was that of a high grade component supplier and not a system designer. In its way this was somewhat like a re-run of the original contretemps between the Aviators and Borehamwood computers in 1966 (see below). With this realisation, and the willingness of the digital computer designer to work with the various specialised control groups to produce processor designs optimised for their particular purposes, digital technology started to become widely accepted in Marconi–Elliott Avionics some 5–7 years before it entered into our competitors' product ranges. Looking forward, this was a critical element in the company's growth in the 1970s and 1980s, particularly in the Head-Up Display field where we rapidly became a world leader.

As Ron Howard has pointed out, it took some little time before digital techniques spread throughout flight control system design and even in 2007 some of the important elements still related to the conversion of digital signals to high integrity analogue outputs to drive the control system actuators. Digital processing was first adopted for the lower bandwidth outer loop functions of the Tornado autopilot whilst the more safety critical high bandwidth inner loop autostabilisation/fly-by-wire block remained strictly analogue. The wisdom of such a step by step decision was clearly demonstrated when the demands of a full digital autostabiliser on a 'foreign' prototype jet fighter exceeded the available cycle time of the processors, causing the aircraft to go unstable and crash.

Looking further ahead, the rapid development of microprocessors in the 1980s gave the Flight Control system design groups themselves the tools which they needed to achieve their particular requirements for integrity, speed and software control of a complete inner and outer loop control system without the need to recourse to specialist computer suppliers. This is touched on again in Sect. 12.13. This development, greatly aided by the arrival of low cost semiconductor stores, was the beginning of the new age where computers became a universal engineering technique rather than an individual end in themselves.

12.5 The 12 Series and the 920 ATC Digital Computers

Returning to the late 1960s, the 12 series computer was designed to have a 12-bit instruction word and also, as far as possible, the same instruction set throughout all the different variants of the machine. However, different length data words (9, 12, 16, 18, or 24 bits) were provided to suit the particular applications. With the price and performance of today's microelectronics, such a degree of hardware tailoring seems absurd, but in the late 1960s and early 1970s the cost and sometimes speed implications were such that it was well worth the extra trouble.

Whilst the various divisions of Marconi–Elliott Avionics were allowed to design and implement their own hardware and system versions of the 12 series machine for use in their various flight control, air data, display and similar applications, the design was closely guarded at the Rochester factory. Other parts of Marconi had to buy the complete 12 series computer element from us and this was a substantial profit earner over many years.

The Third Major event of this time was the fairly rapid onset of the divorce of the Flight side from the activities of the mainstream Borehamwood computing business. Although Andrew St Johnston had collaborated willingly enough when Airborne Computing Division was originally established in1959/1960 and had transferred the key individuals Rayner and Bussell, who got it going, the increasing independence of thought and action by the aviators had begun to disturb the mainstream of computing system developments.

Fig. 12.9 The Elliott 920 ATC (Advanced Technology Computer), the first version of which went into production in about 1977. This was the first 'Elliott' airborne computer to be designed at Rochester, rather than at Borehamwood. After the mid-1970s, most airborne computers looked similar when placed in standardised aircraft equipment containers known as ATR (Air Transport Racking), as shown in the photo

Basically, Elliott Computers Ltd. (ECL) at Borehamwood thought that they would continue to design all the various types of computers, both civil and military, to their own specifications and the aviators would gratefully buy them and somehow squeeze them into their aeroplanes.

The first ripple in this idyllic concept had come when the aviators rather off-handedly told ECL that the 920A computer was useless for our future purposes and that we intended to seek to licence Verdan successors – which we indeed tried to do. Common sense and company policy, however, led to the 920B and 920M, as described above, but these were only just keeping up with US competitors and we needed to get ahead. Friction was already growing between John Bunt, in charge of Mobile Computing Division, and ourselves when we started insisting on defining the main characteristics of the 920M machine which he was developing as a common user machine.

Relations got tenser still when we started up on the MINIM/12 series development, which represented a completely new series of computers which owed nothing to the mainstream Elliott activities.

I happened to be present at the meeting at which the divorce went from degree nisi to absolute. In our quest for a 920M successor we had been agitating for the development of an airborne version of the more powerful 920C machine, which existed but only in the present limited 920M-technology implementation and also in a non-aviation form factor and construction.

Conscious now of the growing software problem, we were anxious to stick with compatible 920 instruction code and support tools. However, by this time we *had* to have a multi-layer board construction and, what is more, we had found an external source for such boards from which we could purchase them.

In early 1966, Commander Pasley Tyler, the head of all military groups and computing companies at Elliotts, held a meeting at which Andrew St Johnston and John Bunt represented ECL, Lawrence Clarke represented Process Control interests, and Jack Pateman and myself represented the Aviators. The key question was this: 'Where would the Board of Elliott-Automation put its by now very scarce development funds for the next generation of military computers?'

John Bunt and Laurence Clarke argued strongly for continuing with something very like the existing 920C, which we felt would be obsolete for our purposes before it got into production. Jack and myself stated clearly that we wanted a sub-microsecond 32K machine on multi-layer boards and a 1 ATR form factor.

The argument raged, with the usual points, as to why could we (the Aviators) not accept what was so obviously right for the computer group? Finally, Pasley Tyler asked both groups to quote their forward sales estimates. It became apparent that the forward estimates of UK sales of the *airborne* configuration were much higher (by a factor of about 10) than those for the early type 920C *standard* computer. In the event, the 700 plus airborne versions that were sold found their way into the advanced Marconi–Elliott Avionics AQS 901 sonic processing system of the Nimrod Mark 2 and Australian Air Force's P3C (see later), as well as into the Nimrod's tactical navigation system. They were also included in a repackaged form factor as the mode control and track generation computer (but *not* the digital signal processing (DSP) of raw radar signals) for the Tornado F3s' Foxhunter radar as well as other smaller projects.

That was the parting of the ways. Avionics went on to design and manufacture the new airborne central computer which I christened the 920 ATC (Advanced Technology Computer). The 920 ATC was the first 920-derivative to have floating-point hardware. The 920 ATC performed its flight trials in 1976/1977 and went into production in mid-1977. The 920 ATC and the 12/12 series provided the basis of all of our future airborne computer developments. In addition, we were to become the first company to design and produce the new standard USAF 1760 series computer – a development in the 1990s that is described in Sect. 12.10.

As for Elliott Computers, the portion that subsequently became GEC Computers (see Chap. 14) never did produce any further new military machine designs in the 1970s or 1980s – although they might have done so if the Nimrod AEW project had been handled differently.

12.6 Computers for Nimrod and Jaguar

Let us take a step back and consider where Airborne Computing had got to by the start of 1966. Firstly, in the field of 'larger' airborne computing systems, we were now hard at work on the Nimrod Mark 1 Central Tactical System. The Nimrod maritime patrol aircraft, which first entered service in 1969 as the MR1 version, was based on the civilian Comet airliner. Following various upgrades, Nimrods were still in service with the RAF in 2006.

For the Nimrod Mark I Central Tactical System in the late 1960s, the 920B computer correlated the inputs from the sensor operators of the various sensor suites on the aircraft (Radar, Sonics, EW, MAD (Magnetic Anomaly Detector)) and enabled a much more accurate position of past and predicted target-track, sonar buoy positions and attack profiles to be built up and displayed on a very large circular Plan Position Indicator (PPI) CRT. This greatly improved the operational capability of the aircraft but it must be stressed that the processor was *not* processing sensor information.

The Mark 1 Nimrod was a big advance but it still retained much of the analogue interfaces that had given us complications on the TSR 2. Where possible on the TSR 2 aircraft, we had used shaft encoders (optical and otherwise) for shaft position measurement. However, in many cases for the conversion of existing synchro signals we had to go to a dedicated digital servo with a common shaft encoder/synchro receiver or transmitter unit. Although this worked, it was an obvious source of future unreliability and the final interface unit, which contained a number of these servo units, was big and rather heavy.

Fortunately by the time of the Nimrod Mk1, we had arrived at the point where multi-channel A/D conversion and synchro-to-digital conversion had begun to become available in solid-state form. They were, however, still space consuming and the interface unit remained a major component in the system. In the Nimrod we had the additional advantage that the majority of the displays appeared on the comprehensive set of CRTs provided at the central Navigator's station; these plus the large keyboard produced a logical and useable Control and Display Unit (CDU).

On the TSR 2, in one of the first digital systems of its type to be fitted into an aircraft, we had to develop a complete Nixe tube display, along with drives to the moving map servos and inputs to various radar and other systems CRT display units. All this was necessary to make the considerable additional information content, which the computing system was now generating, available to the crew. Cockpit display panel space in any fighter/strike aircraft is *always* at an absolute premium. The problem of control and display for increasingly capable *information-rich* digital systems continued to pose difficulties until the widespread adoption of CRT/LCD systems from the 1980s onwards.

The second major development was our bid activity to UK MoD (Ministry of Defence), ultimately successful, for the Navigation Attack Weapon Aiming System (NAVWAS) in the Jaguar single-seater strike aircraft, using the emerging 920M computer. Originally specified in 1965 as a dual-role advanced/operational trainer and tactical support aircraft, the Jaguar was later transformed into a powerful fighter-bomber. Deliveries began in 1973. Several Jaguar upgrades have taken place since. As an aside, a Jaguar was used by Marconi Avionics Ltd to demonstrate *Active Controls Technology* and Fly-By-Wire in October 1981. For test purposes, this Jaguar 'Was made thoroughly unstable with a quarter of a ton of lead in the tail and a pair of large leading edge wing strakes' [3]. Jaguars were still in service with the RAF in 2007. A glossary of terms used in Fly-By-Wire systems is given in Appendix A9.2.

The Jaguar NAVWAS design, strongly derived from the TSR 2 background, provided all of the outer loop navigation and steering functions of the Inertial Navigation platform as well as a comprehensive range of different types of weapon

Fig. 12.10 The Anglo-French Jaguar ground-attack fighter first flew in 1968 and went into service with the RAF in 1974. The Elliott 920M computer was used in the Jaguar's navigation and attack system

delivery attack profiles for a large number of different weapons, including nuclear. It also integrated all of the various sensors such as Air Data and radio navigation into the central core inertial platform and computer, to give a wider range of reversionary capabilities. The result was a one-man crew aircraft which had a superior payload (in terms of bomb load/range) to the seven-man crew, four-engined, Halifax of the Second World War, and having much more accurate navigation and bombing and capability and flying at three times the speed.

To achieve all of this with a 920 core store of 8,192 eighteen-bit words was a challenge, to say the least. We managed to do it by developing a very competent engineer-led integration/software team, using a great deal of hardware in the loop system testing for verification and development. Paul Rayner remembers [4] that 'Having learnt the hard way on TSR 2, I persuaded my system engineer in charge of the project, Roger Strange, to make his number one priority the definition and control of system interfaces and these in effect became part of the contract.' Even though we had now a production 2-μs cycle time store, the speed and capacity requirements did not allow even the consideration of HOL (high-order languages, also known as high-level languages) compilers, which were just beginning to emerge [8]. For example, in a 550-knot low-altitude lay down weapon drop the Jaguar aircraft is travelling at 1,000 ft/s. To get the accuracy needed for weapon delivery we were forced to a predictive system based on a 150 cps iteration rate somewhat similar a pseudo DDA. Likewise, we had to consider special programs for various unusual roles since there was no room for the loading of the total range of multi-role software in the store.

Again, we had a very elaborate interface unit, rather larger than the computer in fact. This used a new form of cold wall construction in which the cooling air is blown through a hollow wall of the box to which the heat from the components is conducted via a metal ladder grid overlaid on the multilayer PCBs, which were now entering our inventory. This method of construction became almost universal throughout the company during the 1970s and 1980s, because of the considerable increases in reliability arising from cooler components with no cooling air contamination and the ability to tailor the heat profile throughout the box.

For the Jaguar's Control and Display units, we drove a projected film Moving Map display of Elliott design and manufacture and an electronic Head-Up Display (manufactured by Smiths) along with a series of digital counters and interfaces with existing synchro analogue instruments. But overall, since we were in at the beginning of the aircraft design, it eventually turned out to be a considerable improvement on mid-1960 strike aircraft cockpits and helped to point the way to today's cockpits.

Two hundred Jaguar aircraft were produced for the RAF with a further 80 or more going to India and some 36 for Oman and even some for Nigeria and Ecuador. The Omani aircraft and, I believe, some Indian aircraft received the upgraded 920M computer with 32K of 1-μs store which was christened 920M GT. Something like 450 systems were produced, well ahead of any similar UK or European contemporary system of this type. However, we suffered from the very rapid change in electronic technology (mainly in the inertial platform) which was taking place at that time, and when in 1986 the RAF chose to upgrade their Jaguars only 13 years after they entered service in 1973 the inertial platform and much of the early electronic system was replaced by later generation units from Ferranti – which had the advantage for the RAF of some commonality with Tornado. However, the export aircraft retained the existing fit for some years after that; hence the 32K store upgrade to the 920M.

The performance of the Jaguar in both Gulf wars and elsewhere proved the soundness of the basic system design concepts. Indeed, it is only now as I write this in 2005 that we are seeing a projected 'withdrawal to storage' forecast for 2008, 35 years after the Jaguar first entered service.

But though the Jaguar contract in 1966 looked like, and indeed was, a saviour of some parts of Elliott-Automation's Aviation Division after the TSR 2 cancellation, it was in fact a much smaller contract opportunity in the USA which first led to the remarkable growth of Elliott-related avionic system activities in the USA and ultimately provided one of the main building blocks of BAE Systems America, now in 2006 the largest unit in the BAES Company.

12.7   Tactical Aircraft Attack Systems and Head-Up Displays

The system in question was called ILAAS (Integrated Low Attack Avionic System). It was to be procured from Sperry as the system integrator and Sperry were looking for a very advanced digital Head-Up Display (HUD) system, well ahead of the existing state of the art.

The misguided UK procurement of US-built aircraft to replace TSR 2 and other cancelled UK projects opened up a slight chink in the previously highly protected US defence equipment market. UK firms were now allowed to bid but, as someone said, 'A UK company needs a knockout win just to achieve a draw.'

However Ken Warren, a highly energetic and personable ex De Havilland graduate apprentice then running the Airborne Displays Division (ADD), thought otherwise. It was undoubtedly almost entirely due to his tireless efforts that we turned the key in the door which gave us our first, and as it turned out continuing, access to the magical kingdom of US military procurement. Whilst Head-Up Displays and associated systems led the way, the general opening up of the US market also became 'a widespread company effort' involving several other Divisions [3].

Ken had been with me in the engineering side of the Comet operations in BOAC and had later joined Smith's Industries. Becoming disillusioned with the unaggressive nature of Smiths, he had joined Elliott-Automation's Aviation Division in 1961 as the deputy manager of the military autopilot group, responsible for the Lightning and Buccaneer systems. Later he moved to run the Head Up Displays division, which was the renamed Rank Cintel unit that Elliott-Automation acquired in 1963 and which became part of my group of major *mission systems* divisions .These dealt with the 'nasty' operational functions of the aircraft: dropping bombs, firing missiles, finding and destroying or shooting down the target, etc. (Ron Howard, heading the Flight Controls group, was the other side of the coin, since he dealt with flight control systems, automatic pilots, air speed and altitude measuring systems, engine instrumentation, etc., which enabled the aircraft to fly safely in any place, anytime, in any weather.)

It is worth perhaps jumping ahead here to say that it is a measure of Ken Warren's ability that he was elected to the House of Commons as a Conservative MP for Hastings and Rye in 1970. He ended his parliamentary career as Chairman of the House of Commons Select Committee for Trade and Industry, becoming Sir Kenneth Warren on retirement. The Nice Guys sometimes win!

That, of course, was yet to come but Ken felt strongly that we ought to try to crack the US market. Ron Howard and I both agreed but it was only with some reluctance that Bill Alexander and Jack Pateman agreed that, as early as November 1964, Ken should spend a larger proportion of his time in Sperry, Long Island (a sort of American Hounslow!).

Space does not permit the telling of the whole ILAAS saga but there is one memorable quote which became a company catchphrase. In the middle of an argument, Sperry's Chief buyer, who had developed quite a taste for Glenfiddich, turned to Ken and said 'Come on Warren, I want facts not Fiddich!'

By January 1966, some seven or eight key members of the ADD (Airborne Displays Division) team began to join with Ken in haunting the halls of the Sperry plant, which was located in the old Lake Success building where the UN had held its first meetings. As the year went on, we got closer to an advanced Head-up Display (HUD) design which just might work. It involved a very high speed digital waveform generator (a world first), a ROM fixed-memory main core store and a number of other features that broke the mould – such as a 6.5-in. exit optic-and-ceramic body CRT. One of Jack Pateman's visits came when we were getting near to estimating a production price for 500 HUD units. Jack was so horrified at the development unknowns that he walked out of Sperry and went home, leaving us with very red faces trying to explain why he was no longer in the USA. It truly was a high-risk business attempting to estimate for something which nobody had yet designed, let alone built, before so we were, to say the least, not entirely confident. However, we had a lucky break when Sperry suddenly said that they only wanted us to bid a firm price for just 5 prototype units. This was easy by comparison (though we still lost money on them) and by twisting Pateman's arm over the transatlantic 'phone we were able to get Board permission to quote and to accept the order in July 1966.

The next day, Ken and other team members all packed up to go home to start work in the UK or to attend some other US meetings with potential subcontractors, leaving me to go into Sperry alone. After initialling the outline award paper work, I went back to the motel. At about 3 p.m. in the afternoon, I went to the pool (it was about 90°F in the shade) and dived in. As I came up on the opposite side, a guy leaned over with an iced daiquiri. 'I know you like these, Peter' he said. 'I want to congratulate you on your ILAASS award. National Semiconductors will be delighted to give you an improved quote for your production batches'. Bush telegraph and pony express could not have been quicker!

Some 2 weeks later Ken Warren, who was 99% responsible for this success, went over to the US with Pasley Tyler, the Elliott Board Director to whom we all reported, for an arranged and more formal signing ceremony with press releases etc. and, of course, more Fiddich!

So we got into our first full-scale US development programme. It turned out to be the first step towards a fully engineered version of the 12 series computer and, as such, a tremendous boost for the future. Equally importantly, the new US requirements introduced us to some much more demanding formal engineering disciplines of reliability and maintainability engineering and guarantees: the 'ilities' as they came to be called in time. Our involvement in these formal US disciplines had an immensely advantageous effect on all of our product range and helped to set the Elliott-related aviation companies on the road to continuing success in the USA.

12.8   Expanding into America: The A7 Contract

Let me break again for a moment to say that, while all this was going on, Ron Howard had been attacking the Lockheed Company in Atlanta who were in the early stages of designing the new giant C5A military transport. Ron had some exceptionally competent people in the analogue control technologies and was able to win no less than three major contracts for the complex electro-mechanical (analogue) Elliott central Air Data Computer system, together with a hybrid performance monitoring computer and an undercarriage control system. Excellent results for a first time out, which made up for the fact that the production run of the aircraft (somewhat bigger than a 747) was limited to 58 aircraft [3].

But even more important to the whole future of our US programmes was the fact that Ron was introduced to Lloyd Flatt, a graduate aerospace engineer turned business consultant, who turned out to be the best thing since sliced bread as far as Elliotts was concerned. Lloyd had been a NASA employee at the start of the great space programmes and had become involved in sub-contracts administration, a very critical occupation since NASA did not have either the in-house or out-of-house resources to execute these vast programmes themselves. Lloyd accurately foresaw that many of the sub-contractors who were drawn into the Saturn/Apollo programmes were quite new to the game and needed educating and strengthening in order to be able to meet the stringent performance success requirements of US contracts in the space and aviation sectors. Lockheed considered that potential overseas contractors needed similar assistance and advised Ron to find a local representative, which resolved itself into Ron being introduced to Lloyd C. Flatt by the UK consulate in Atlanta [3]. Lloyd rapidly became a most valuable member of our marketing organisation and remained so until he retired in the mid-1990s. Sadly, Lloyd died in January 2008. His advice and counsel on the relative importance and differences between our existing UK design and engineering practices and the much tougher needs of the US market was a key element which helped us to join the ranks of successful US contractors, rising to a place in the top ten US Defense System Electronic contractors by 1992.

The idea of a digital waveform generator which formed the heart of the ILAAS system had originally been proposed by Dick Barltrop and strongly endorsed and promoted by Ken Warren. Barltrop was the former Chief Ordnance Artificer on the battleship HMS Vanguard. After making major contributions to high integrity flight control systems when Chief Engineer of the civil aircraft autopilots group, Barltrop was promoted to be Technical Manager of Elliott's Airborne Displays division, now headed up by Ken Warren. Up to that time, all displays had used simple-minded analogue waveform generators with a fixed range of formats which were both limited in content and difficult to modify.

Dickie Barltrop suggested that we use one of the proposed high speed 12 Series computer family which was being developed by, amongst others, Jim Machin and David Hussey two of our more creative engineers (but which, incidentally did not at that stage exist). With this approach we could generate displays by calculating the co-ordinates of the start and finish of a line and its length and then apply the bright-up pulse signal between them accordingly. Circles used a sine/cosine function. This gave us order of magnitude improvements in flexibility and also performance and display content. There was just one snag though: high-performance jets can roll at around 400–700°/s. Could we operate fast enough to present an accurate picture whilst the aircraft was manoeuvring energetically?

In fact, we could. However, the UK Government scientists at Farnborough refused to believe that the system would ever work. For a period of some 5 years (1966/1971), we built and delivered some thousand HUDs to the US Navy and USAF which were used extensively and very successfully in combat in Vietnam. During this period, Farnborough and MoD PE staff absolutely refused to visit the

Rochester plant to witness any demonstrations of the system since, so they said, 'they knew it would not work, so why waste everybody's time?' Galileo, thou shoulds't have been living at this hour!

Some historical highlights of the Rochester factory are given in Appendix 9. Rochester was, by the turn of the century, destined to keep the Elliott spirit alive after first Lewisham and then Borehamwood slipped out of the picture. As far as digital computing was concerned, a turning point came during the HUD developments when, according to Jack Pateman [1]: 'The production version of the display equipment was originally developed at Rochester under Brian Wolf, with the digital computer section being developed at Borehamwood under Paul Rayner, where most of the digital expertise in Elliott-Automation existed. However it soon became apparent that this arrangement was causing severe programme slippage and it was decided to take the risk of moving the digital computer development to Rochester.' Actually, not all members of the team were able to move. Terry Froggatt [5] remembers that 'half our team were attached ladies, who stayed at Borehamwood, and became the Nimrod AEW team. With hindsight it is interesting to see how the relatively small team of programmers who moved with ACD from Borehamwood to Rochester, nominally to program the 920M for Jaguar, and later the 920 ATC for Nimrod, also seeded the work of other divisions, such as the ILAAS HUD (Mandy Pearson neé Clarke) and the Minim/12-series (me).' The ACD programmers were also involved in a proposal for CHLL: the Compacted High-Level Language machine.

Getting back to the drawing board, the Waveform generator electronic unit for ILAAS was sensibly allocated to Airborne Computing division led by Paul Rayner. The unit which emerged used a 2K *rope core* memory (ROM with wires threading or bypassing ferrite cores) with a store cycle time of around 1 µs. It had a central cold wall, on each side of which were mounted a series of separate modules: store, processor, appliqué (i.e. specific aircraft type interface), power supply and test. This concept of separate function modules, a US navy ship-borne maintenance brain-wave, was inefficient and unnecessary and though it did not detract from the functioning it was more costly and expensive than it needed to be. It never found its way into any serious production equipment.

The ILAAS contract award for some six prototype systems came in the summer of 1966 but very rapidly things began to change. Sperry had hoped to become the system integrator for all of the new US Navy aircraft. However, the airframe manufacturer Ling Temco Vought (LTV), whose A7 Corsair II was designated to be the first aircraft update, had quite different ideas. They insisted on being their own systems integrator and suddenly the big prize of a production order for 1,290 aircraft sets was up for grabs from the LTV purchasing group, instead of coming to us as a follow on directly from Sperry. Moreover, the big prize was up for grabs to all of the competitors whom we had previously beaten.

The saga of the A7 contract award would fill a book on its own. The myriad stories include: how we had to adjust from the Long Island fraternity to the Texans, who turned out to be a pretty nice bunch; how, frustrated by our competitor's dirty tricks, I arranged for an RAF transport aircraft fitted with one of our HUDs to arrive at LTV's airfield for their test pilots to fly and how, whilst it was airborne, another aircraft had a minor prang on the runway – thus giving us a very useful 4 h in the air with the LTV pilots, who became thoroughly indoctrinated with our HUD. On the downside, there is the story of how we shot ourselves in both feet by our reluctance to accept what we all regarded as a lunatic compressed timetable, how our competitors Kaiser were awarded the contract and then declared that they *too* could not meet the timetable, and how a dash to Dallas by Jack Pateman and Lloyd Flatt at LTV's request finally brought the prize home.

The A7 contract awarded to Elliotts in summer 1967 was truly the start of the major Elliott presence in the USA, leading, amongst other things, to HUD production work beginning in about 1969 in our Atlanta facility. (A support facility had been set up in Georgia in mid-1966 [3], in connection with the supply of Elliott modular Air Data Computers for the Lockheed C5A Galaxy transport.) But the technology and capability of the digital HUD system which had been created was even more important.

The first of these later developments came when John Shepherd, later to become our resident systems guru genius and subsequently Director of Research of all of the Marconi company, rolled into my office and said: 'How would you like a complete weapon aiming system for the price of a HUD *all* on its own?' John had recognised the fact that all of the information which we used in the weapon aiming calculations was already being supplied to the HUD to draw the symbology format for the attack phase. A somewhat tweaked interface design, faster logic and expanded store in the waveform generator gave us a very effective and self-contained, greatly improved, gun, bomb and missile sight and aiming system which could be installed in many different existing aircraft. Most importantly, because the unit had its own highly capable A to D interface, it could use the existing sensors, gyros, etc. in any aircraft without requiring major internal systems modifications in the aircraft.

First to use this system was the US Marine Corps' A4 M Skyhawk attack jet, followed by a number of export orders for overseas A4 operators. By the time we had exhausted the A4 market, some 700 A4 jets in some five different airforces had been upgraded.

12.9   Mirage, MIG and China

The upgrade market was especially fertile. Aeroplanes in the 1970s did not go faster or fly higher than the types designed and built some 10 or 15 years earlier. Instead, the new aircraft had much better combat capability because they had much better avionic systems. So there were a lot of earlier aircraft flying around in different air forces such as Mirages, Northrop F5s, Saab Drakens and, very attractively, MIG21's which were ripe for improvement. We targeted the Mirage, MIG 21 and F5 as the principal candidates. We also hoped to collect the F4 Phantom at some point. The pay-off came first on the Mirage, which in turn led us to the even more astonishing 7,000 systems contracts for all of the F16 fighters produced up to 2001.

At the same time, our foresight in targeting the MIG 21 as a potential market gave us first a major contract in Egypt. Then in 1978 the Chinese came looking in the West for defence equipment. After presentations in England and a game of hide and seek with the French competitors at the Paris Air Show, our offer of a modification of the Egyptian system was readily accepted and led to orders for around 600 systems and trips to China in 1979 by Jack Pateman, as the Managing Director, for detailed negotiations and formal acceptance of the contract. Incidentally, this contract included the supply of head-up displays, an air data system, new VHF radios, and new ranging-radar equipment. It was one of the first contracts to capitalise on the integration of a Borehamwood airborne radar with the Rochester core avionics, thus maximising the technical strength of the enlarged company. Later we collected smaller contracts on F5s and Drakens but the F4 remained tantalisingly out of reach despite a very successful trial with the USAF.

12.10   Technological Marvels

Getting back to technology, we were finding that the accuracy and flexibility and functional capability of the combination of electronic displays and high-speed digital computers was enabling us to develop products which had previously been restricted to Marvel Comics. Thus, our ability to generate and display continuously the theoretical bullet trajectory through space before any bullets were actually fired brought a threefold improvement in air to air gunnery scores. Likewise, our ability to do the same for accurate air to air missile launch within the launch-success envelope was yet another feature which was unique to Marconi Avionics and helped win us in 1972 what became contracts of over $1 billion in value over the life of the F16 aircraft.

On the hardware side, the F16 posed us a challenge as it encouraged the development of the first of the range of a new standard embedded processor designated MIL-STD 1760. Taking a deep breath, we went for it and became the first ever company to supply such a system in production to the USAF. They in turn used to chide their stateside contractors that the Brits were beating them and that they should pull their socks up.

Another major advance was the introduction of the MIL STD 1553 ring main digital highway which greatly simplified interfaces and aircraft wiring and retrofit opportunities. This was something we would have loved to have had on TSR 2. By now the design of the system was being driven by a powerful combination of Airborne Computing Division, Airborne Display Division and Flight Automation Research Laboratory. The latter had done a great deal of experimental work on digital highway structures which produced the serendipitous outcome of them designing the first chip set version of the highway. Manufactured at GEC Wembley, this was sold extensively to electronic manufacturers throughout the USA for several years before the competition caught up.

The last versions of the F16 electronic unit have advanced from the original 16K 16-bit word using the new USA Jovial language to a 64K word machine, considerably faster with Ada implementation. Along the way, we had introduced the integrated night attack capability which is the last chapter in this part of the business.

Very importantly, too, the integration of the hardware of some of the other product groups of the Marconi company which had been brought into Rochester's orbit produced some major advances in night vision systems in military aircraft. Used in combination with the Head-Up Display developments, it gave attack aircraft the ability to carry out attacks by night almost as effectively as they could by day, a capability which was enthusiastically developed by both our US and UK customers.

More specifically related to the digital area was the evolution of the cruise missile navigation technique, of digital terrain profile matching, to a manned aircraft system implementation. Known as Terrain Referenced Navigation (TRN), the central core system provided an extensive associated data store not only of terrain features and profile but of operationally critical areas such as missile sites and engagement zones. Such systems greatly reduce, or eliminate, the need for detectable RF and radar transmissions from the aircraft and complement the stealth technologies used in many modern-day aircraft designs. The prototype demonstrator system, installed in a Grumman A6 Intruder, used to draw gasps of astonishment from US 'brass' observing in the navigators seat, as it traversed the Blue Ridge mountains and valleys at low altitude in complete darkness and radar silence.

12.11   The Influence of the F16 and American Standardisation

The introduction of aircraft digital highways was not without its complications. At one point, the Controller of MoD Research Establishments, Sir Colin Fielding, attempted to decree that the British standard should be based entirely on the system developed for ships by the Admiralty Surface Weapons Establishment. Fortunately, by this time the Air branch of MoD PE were sufficiently switched on to realise that it was essential to adopt the American standards if we were to achieve future interoperability between US and UK equipment and aircraft. However, they were temporarily outgunned within the MoD. Accordingly, a joint meeting between MoD and industry was arranged at which the MoD tried to get their ship data highway blessed as the standard. The Air branch put me up to make some brutally rude remarks in order to derail the naval case. I attacked by saying that we were hard at work building 1,000 US systems and that: 'anyone who turned their back on that market simply did not understand the rapidly developing world needs for standardisation and the imperatives of flight critical system design' (direct quote). After a lot of huffing and puffing, the Air Branch was allowed to adopt the 1553 standard. Whatever happened to the ship standard I do not know.

At about this time, there were some important tectonic plate movements in the way in which new airborne computers were developed. Airborne Display Division had, with the very large ongoing A7 HUD contract, become a powerhouse of know-how on digital displays and their systems applications. Their engineering group was rapidly developing the capabilities needed to carry on the development of the small RISC

12 series family for their own applications. Robin Sleight, who was a long time member of the division, with a similar background of aeronautical engineering and flying to my own, had recently completed a 4-year stint as the company representative at the LTV plant, ensuring that the HUD production deliveries in production and in operational testing went smoothly. After a short spell in Inertial Navigation Division as a programme manager on a new Naval gyro compass system, Robin was promoted to head the engineering department of Airborne Display Division at about the time (1975 onwards) that we started to develop the first production version of the F16 system. (The first version of the F16 fighter aircraft entered service with the USAF in 1979; F16s were still in service in 2006). Robin's American exposure and his understanding of the customer base, engineering possibilities and operational applications made him one of the most effective of the senior managers at Rochester, not only in the mid-1970s but through all of the advanced HUD system developments, described later, and one of the leading contenders for the future CEO. By the end of his career, he had become Business Development Director for the entire GEC Avionics company, thus steering the whole company product range development objectives and marketing in the direction which needed to go.

As described above, the F16 unit led the US companies in its adoption of the new USAF standards for digital equipment, sometimes tripping up on deficiencies in the USAF-promulgated definitions of standard and protocols. However, the combination of Airborne Displays Division (ADD), Airborne Computing Division (ACD) and Flight Automation Research Lab. (FARL) was such that these problems were overcome in a timely manner and the new F16 unit emerged with a 16K 16-bit semiconductor store in what was basically a 12/16 RISC computer implementation. It is of interest to note that the last versions of the F16 electronic unit have advanced from the original 16K 16-bit machine which used the new USA Jovial language to a 64K word machine, considerably faster, with Ada implementation.

Whilst the F16 system was in development, Airborne Computing Division had metamorphosed into Maritime Aircraft Systems Division in 1973 – as is discussed later. The change had come about because, as the F16 programme was showing, airborne computing was rapidly becoming an enabling technology for a large number of different end user applications rather than a discrete business area.

12.12   The Tornado and Nimrod

Meanwhile, starting in 1969, Airborne Computing Division had been going through the process of evolving and developing the prototype 920 ATC computer. This was originally intended for the next generation military aircraft which in fact became the Tornado. The original GR1 version of the Tornado was first delivered in 1980 as a low-level attack aircraft. Upgraded Tornados, including the tactical reconnaissance version, were still in service in 2006. The 920 ATC computer was tailored for the Tornado task with 32K of 1-μs store, expandable to 64K. (The maximum size a program could be was 131,072 words; any memory beyond this could only be

Fig. 12.11 The specification for the Tornado multi-role combat fighter dates from 1970. The Tornado first flew in 1974 and the first batch was delivered to the RAF in 1979. Production of the aircraft ceased in 1998. It was hoped that the Tornado would use the Elliott 920 ATC but, in the end, international collaboration determined that the computer contract went to Litton Industries, Germany

used for data.) Even with this upgrade and an existing-software support system in the RAF Jaguar/Nimrod fleets with a degree of portable software modules, 'International Collaboration' work-sharing issues determined that the contract went to Litton Germany with a new computer, the Spirit 3, with none of these features. In fact, the Spirit 3 was a computer which had no past, a continuing difficult service life and eventually no future.

But all was not lost. Airborne Computing Division under Paul Rayner was recognised by the MoD to be the most innovative UK company in the field of airborne digital computers and we were awarded the contract for the very advanced sonobuoy processing system to be fitted to the midlife update of the Nimrod maritime reconnaissance ASW (anti-submarine warfare) aircraft version. This system eventually used two 128k 'mainframe' 920 ATCs, each backed by a 256k bulk store unit.

Planning by the MOD for a comprehensive avionics upgrade for the Nimrod Mark I MR ASW had begun in 1975. The new equipment suite included a Thorn EMI Searchwater radar in place of the aging ASV-21D unit, a new GEC Central Tactical System and the AQS-901 acoustics system compatible with the latest 'Barra', Cambs and Dicass sonobuoys. Thirty-five MR.1 were upgraded to the new Maritime Reconnaissance 2 standard, with the first aircraft being redelivered to the RAF on 23 August 1979 [9].

Paul Rayner remembers [4] that:

'There were two parts to our involvement in Nimrod maritime ASW system, each based on a 920 ATC. The first part involved taking Navigation data from the IN (Inertial navigation unit) and other sensors, combining it with information about targets from the Radars, Magnetic Anomaly detector (MAD), Autolycus ("a snap-

Fig. 12.12 The first Nimrod Mark I MR (Maritime Reconnaisance) aircraft flew in June 1968, entering service with the RAF in October 1969. It employed an Elliott 920B computer. The aeroplane in the photo is a Nimrod MR2. The sonobuoy processing system fitted to the Nimrod ASW (anti-submarine warfare) aircraft version used two Elliott 920 ATC computers

per-up of unconsidered trifles") and the Sonobuoy Processor (see below), and displaying this for the Tactical Navigator on a large circular CRT display manufactured by our IN division.

'The second part of the Nimrod ASW system, known as AQS901, was the processing and display of the information received from Sonobuoys. We had two major subcontractors for this part of the programme, Computing Devices of Canada who developed the Fast Fourier Transform (FFT) Analyser and Rank Pullen who developed and provided us with four chart recorders. This was a world beating system, also sold to the Australians for their Orions. In competitive ASW exercises, Nimrod frequently embarrassed the Americans by comprehensively outperforming them with Nimrod's superior search system. Together with our major subcontractors I had about 1000 people involved in this development programme. We later developed a cut-down version of AQS901 for the Westland Sea King helicopter retrofit programme and, later still, developed an enhanced system for the Agusta-Westland EH101 helicopter (now known as the Merlin).'

The Nimrod AQS901 displayed the processed sonobuoy signal outputs to two operators seated behind two large keyboards with five very high definition CRTs and two multi-function pen recorders. A further component, also supplied by Marconi Avionics, was the very high capacity digital recording system which enabled, amongst other modes, target signature capture and playback either in the air, after landing or when airborne on the next mission. The system operational capabilities are still shrouded in 'need to know' but on several occasions it embarrassed USN submarine commanders. It was undoubtedly well ahead of the equivalent

US Navy P3C system, supplied by IBM, for much of the 1980s and will not be fully replaced until the Nimrod 4 has been in service for several years.

12.13   The Maritime Re-organisation

The scale of the Nimrod acoustic signal processing system, known as the AQS 901, was such that Airborne Computing Division had to concentrate on the Maritime aircraft market. This led on to other smaller systems, known as the AQS 902 series, for helicopters and other lighter aircraft which were supplied to a number of different navies, including the Swedish. Remember that the Swedes suddenly started detecting Russian submarines in their coastal waters and harbours (Guess how!) Starting in 1983, the AQS 902 system was developed into the AQS 903, which went into production in 1985. In 1983, Maritime Aircraft Systems Division (MASD) was the first division of GEC/Marconi Avionics to be awarded the Queen's Award for Technological Innovation for its successful acoustic processor developments over the past 10 years.

As a result of its transformation into Maritime Aircraft Systems Division some time between August 1972 and May 1973 [5], the re-titled group started taking less interest in the attack aircraft systems field. The Central Tactical System (CTS) for the Nimrod update was transferred to Inertial Navigation Division (IND), which in retrospect was a wrong decision because of the historic reluctance of that division to adapt to new concepts and technology. However, this did not prevent IND from making a success of the new CTS in the Nimrod, using a 920 ATC with 64K plus bulk store to update the previous 8K 920B computer. At the end of that exercise the responsibility for new maritime CTS systems was transferred back to MASD, who produced some very effective systems for Sea King updates and other types of aircraft and helicopters.

At the same time, Airborne Display Division (ADD), who had been the original exploiter of the 12 series computer, began to assume responsibility for the ongoing work on its development. This resulted in special versions for Marconi Defence Systems which were used in such diverse rugged environments as Tanks, Torpedoes, and special podded systems for external carriage on aircraft wings. Several thousand discrete computer packages were produced for these applications.

Although ADD was, as we see now, the ancestor group for the 12 series, it had also been adopted in one form or another first by Flight Controls Group as a starting point for design of the Tornado outer loop autopilot. This led on to its experimental use in a Boeing military transport as a system component in a full triplex Fly-By-Wire system which also introduced a limited amount of fibre optic data transmission. The success of the Flight Controls Group's very innovative flight control system design on the Boeing Y14 transport and a related demonstrator Fly-By-Wire system on an experimental BAE Jaguar were the harbingers of the Group's entry into their own specialised developments of advanced digital based systems with, among other essentials, their very specific requirements for both hardware and software reliability levels.

Fly-By-Wire flight control systems literally determine the total flight safety of the aircraft, at least as much as the structure of the wings and tail or the operation of the engines and fuel supply. Over the years, Flight Controls Group had gained a worldwide reputation for the performance and reliability of its systems in such aircraft as the Concorde and Tornado and now they extended it into the acquisition of the Fly-By-Wire system contracts for the Boeing 777 airliner and the Typhoon 'Euro' fighter.

Based on the rapidly developing use of microprocessors which replaced the 'old' discrete computer concept, Flight Controls Group pioneered world-leading advances in high integrity software development and proving and such new concepts as consideration of the use of dissimilar microprocessors in multi-channel systems and solar radiation events and effects on 'in-flight' system operation.

Of the Boeing 777 Primary Flight Controls Computers contract, Ron Howard remembers this as 'the largest contract from the 1990s' [3]. The road from the dauntingly complex analogue system of the 1960s Concorde to the Boeing 777 system of the 1990s was, for the Flight Controls Group, a long and arduous one whose innovations and pioneering concepts demonstrated once again that the *zeitgeist* of Elliotts still flourished.

12.14   The Microprocessor Arrives

But by now it had become apparent that, with the advent of the microprocessor, the day of the specialised embedded computer was over. These newer systems were based upon carefully selected microprocessor designs, used in a very high integrity *fail operative* system configuration and not on the use of the older discrete computer configurations.

Likewise on the new AQS 903 system for the Merlin ASW helicopter, the powerful dual 920ATC core gave way to an even more powerful network of pipeline processors which distributed the computing load throughout the system, rather than concentrate it in the centre.

In other systems too, the need for a specialised mission computer was eroded by the fact that new generations of microprocessors with EPROM stores could not only each provide the distributed computing functions but one of them could readily be expanded to provide the mission computing functions which had previously been the domain of the main mission computer.

Thus, advances in semiconductor storage technology, by replacing the need for core storage, eventually banished the discrete computer in both its main and distributed roles.

Perhaps the last and most widespread use of a discrete 12 series computer module, albeit in microprocessor form, was in the multi-platform Standard Central Air Data

Computer (SCADC), some 7,000 of which were supplied to the USAF by Instrument Systems Division of the Flight Controls Group, a fitting tribute to their design.

12.15 Squeezing the Last Juice from the 920 ATC

In its last stages the 920 ATC found itself repackaged into a segmental shaped volume and used in the nose radar of the Tornado Foxhunter radar, where it carried out the main system management and switching and outer loop target tracking and interception calculations. But the sign of the times was that the really difficult problem of target extraction from the radar signals was done by a dedicated Digital Signal Processor which bore little resemblance to the General Purpose computers of the past.

The 920 ATC was also scheduled to play an important part in the Nimrod AEW system. However, as the problems of multiple false target returns and other complexities became known from flight trials (see Chap. 11), it became apparent that it was inadequate for the system functions which had to be met. A proposal that GEC should spend their own money in providing an alternative ruggedised COTS (commercial off-the-shelf) version of one of the more powerful GEC 4100 series was, in my view, foolishly rejected by Pateman and Weinstock. Had this been done, the project might well have been saved before the RAF marshalled their arguments for cancellation of the Nimrod AEW system (in December 1986). To add detail to the Nimrod AEW saga, refer to Chap. 11 for the radar side of the project and to Appendix 9 for comments about the capabilities of an existing GEC 4080M computer which was used to process radar data.

Taking into account the approximately 250 computers supplied to the Nimrod Mk 2 ASW and RAAF P3C and the 300 or so for the Tornado ADV radar together with other applications, something over 700 ATC computers were supplied in various forms. This is not a bad record but not as good as if the 920 ATC computer had also served in its original form in all of the 700 or so Tornados that were delivered.

12.16 Epilogue

In the end the airborne digital computer, whether it was a small embedded microprocessor or large-scale data cruncher, became just another component which the system designer acquired from specialist ranges produced by dedicated computer manufacturers such as CDC (Control Data Corporation).

This followed the traditional history of specialist products worldwide. In the early days when no supply sources or markets exist, the system companies' desire is to design and manufacture them in-house. But as demand grows, it becomes economically worthwhile for specialist groups to develop who concentrate upon that particular component. At this point, the system designer has to decide whether he will use his often overstretched technology resources to be in this new component market or whether he will concentrate on the systems field where he has a more unique position and experience.

Most system suppliers chose the latter route, recognising that the specialist component groups will inevitably develop a greater expertise in their speciality, due to their exposure to a much wider market. Perhaps the best example of this is the increasing use of Commercial Off The Shelf (COTS) hardware and other derivatives from the commercial IT sector whose investment in some technologies and software developments is many times greater than the more limited defence market numbers. So the evolution of the industry has seen the passing of the age of the more personal contributions of individual engineers and, with it, much of the day-to-day excitement when your colleague on the next bench produced some yet unknown new concept or solved a hitherto intractable problem.

Borehamwood, where this all started, was principally about people and for that one must praise the wisdom and influence of John Coales. Coales, who was a pre-war and wartime senior member of the Royal Navy Scientific Service, later became Professor John Coales FRS FREng of Cambridge University. Universally respected by all the staff that he had recruited at Borehamwood, it was he who encouraged the atmosphere of scientific enquiry which infused the factory and laboratory in the late 1940s/early 1950s which produced a generation of engineers who were always prepared to look towards innovation rather than tradition.

Leon Bagrit, who took over the Elliott company, managed to keep the best of this spirit whilst curtailing the obvious commercial risks by dividing the company up into Divisions – relatively self-contained groups of engineers, production and commercial staff who were responsible for a particular business sector. An example is Airborne Radio. Almost always led by engineers, who were also responsible for the financial results, these Divisions generated intense team loyalties which helped carry on the original spirit of endeavour.

Divisional rivalries helped to raise the standard across the Elliott company and the mixture of the ethos of *Band of Brothers* and *Creative Tensions* contrasted very favourably with that of companies structured along more traditional lines.

A further factor which often surprised me was the strong historical thread which ran through our activities and was a source of pride to many employees. A visitor to the Science Museum in London will see an Elliott 'integrated flight instrument display system' dating back to the First World War and the more knowledgeable can trace the successful developments of bomb delivery systems to Elliott's work with H E Wimperis, between the wars on improved bomb sighting instruments, and inertial navigation to a pre–First World War Elliott licence for the Anschultz floated mercury gyro.

Time passes and whilst it would have been nice to encapsulate the spirit of creativity which inspired those at Borehamwood, and later Rochester, events have dictated otherwise.

But today, as some 40 years ago, one can continue to take pride in recognising that at any time in the 24 hours, high in the stratosphere over all of the continents and oceans of the world, from the Poles to the Equator, *Elliott* equipment continues to play a major part in the commerce and defence of the world's nations.

References

1. JE (Jack) Pateman (2004) A 10,300-word draft history of the Aviation Division, assembled for the author by J E Pateman, CBE, in March 2004 – a short while before his death in August of that year. Jack Pateman drew on material provided by his ex-Elliott colleagues David Broadbent and Ray Reece who, in turn, were contributors to [2] below

2. Anon (2007) Elliott Flight Automation Limited: a brief history. This 30-page typed document gives varying degrees of coverage for the period 1948 to 1985, with some staff listings to 1992. Ron Bristow, who has a long-standing interest in Elliott company history, provided the following further information on the provenance in an e-mail to Simon Lavington in March 2007. *"It is an updated version of the document 'Elliott Flight Automation History' by David Broadbent which, in 1970, had the Elliott Archive catalogue number 1004/10/1. Broadbent was a senior engineer and manager in Elliott Brothers (London) Ltd., and in particular in Elliott Flight Automation, for many years in the 1950s and 1960s. After his death, Broadbent's notes were added to by C.R Reese, an engineer and manager in Elliott Flight Automation from about 1955 to 1993, using press releases and company announcements"*. The document is now part of the Marconi Archives at the Bodleian Library, Oxford, for which the cataloguing process was still in progress in 2007

3. RW (Ron) Howard (2006) E-mail to Simon Lavington, dated 14 Nov 2006

4. Paul Rayner (2007) E-mail to Simon Lavington, dated 17 Sept 2007

5. Terry Froggatt (2007) Comments sent to Simon Lavington by e-mail, dated 1 Jan 2007

6. See the History of the British Aircraft Corporation, as recorded at: http://www.thunder-and-lightnings.co.uk/tsr2/history.html

7. Forbat J (2006) From TSR 2 to Tornado. Published by Tempus Publishing Ltd. A very good account of the intricacies of the overall TSR 2 weapons system

8. The Ada language, developed for the Department of Defense in America between 1977–1983, was initially known as "the DoD HOL"). An Elliott 803 compiler for the Algol high-level language was developed in 1962, marking Borehamwood's first foray into high-level languages – see Chap. 8

9. See: http://www.aeroflight.co.uk/types/uk/bae_systems/nimrod/nimrod.htm

Chapter 13
Mergers, Takeovers and Dispersals

13.1 The UK's Computer Landscape in the 1950s and 1960s

The 10-year period 1959–1969 saw significant changes – one might almost say upheavals – in the fortunes of British computer manufacturers. In this chapter we show how Elliott-Automation Ltd. was eventually to be pulled apart, the mainframe computing interests being absorbed into ICL which, by the end of the decade, emerged as the primary embodiment of the British computer industry. The story of ICL's birth has been carefully charted in Martin Campbell-Kelly's well-researched book on ICL history [1], which had the benefit of unrestricted access to BTM and ICT company records in the 1980s. We shall draw on [1] from time to time in this chapter, adding such material as is needed to do justice both to the wider Elliott-Automation company's history and to the role of Borehamwood as a source of computing activity.

Between the years 1948 and 1970, approximately 80 distinct stored-program digital computers were designed in the UK, resulting in well over 2,000 installed machines of British provenance. The number and nature of computer installations in Britain changed over the years, as charted more fully in Appendix 10. In 1955 there was probably a total of less than 30 computers in operation (including research prototypes), the majority in science and engineering applications and all of the machines designed in the UK. By 1970 the majority of installations in Britain were in business and commercial applications and increasing numbers of these computers were imported from America. As described in Appendix 10, about 29% of UK installations were IBM machines by 1967, and IBM's percentage was set to expand. The most striking change in emphasis came during the period 1960–1963, when there was a very rapid growth in the perceived needs of the commercial data processing market – an area that IBM was well placed to exploit. The events of the early 1960s set the tone for the British computer company amalgamations discussed later in this chapter.

S. Lavington, *Moving Targets*, History of Computing,
DOI 10.1007/978-1-84882-933-6_13, © Springer-Verlag London Limited 2011

As has already been shown in Chaps. 6 and 7, 1960–1964 also saw the rapid expansion of process control applications – an area in which Leon Bagrit made sure Elliott-Automation played a leading role. In the light of hindsight, it seems as if Bagrit's enthusiasm for, and success in, the process control market may have caused him to miss opportunities in other computer markets. Nevertheless, the broader Elliott-Automation empire was at the height of its power by 1964.

In this chapter, our account of the mergers and takeovers that convulsed the British computer industry proceeds as follows. Firstly, we establish the position of Elliott-Automation in the early 1960s and comment on the financial factors influencing Leon Bagrit as he planned his company's activities towards the end of the decade. We then take a general look at the business and commercial computing arena and show how Elliott-Automation was in fact losing ground to competitor companies. The competitive battles were to lead to the formation of ICL. All this took place within the context of British electrical and electronics manufacturing industry. We provide brief histories of the largest industrial players, showing how GEC came out top and in due course swallowed Elliott-Automation. Finally, we detail the events of the fateful years 1967 and 1968 that led to the demise of Bagrit's Elliott-Automation group of companies and divisions as an identifiable trading entity.

13.2   The Zenith of Elliott-Automation as an Independent Company

13.2.1   The Computing Sector of Elliott-Automation

In his 1961 Annual Report, Leon Bagrit stated with some pride that 'Over 60% in number of the computers manufactured in the United Kingdom in 1961 were made at Elliott-Automation's Borehamwood factory'. In the 1962 Annual Report, he said: 'Deliveries of Elliott 803 computers for office and scientific purposes are now approaching the one hundred and fifty mark, far in excess of the numbers of any other British computer'. In the 1963 Annual Report, Bagrit was of the opinion that: 'Electronic computing is a key element in all forms of automation and it is therefore particularly important that we retain our leading position in that technique'. Interestingly, and typically, Bagrit did not choose to comment on the use of computers in the business and commercial arena.

Continuing with extracts from the Annual Reports, it was also in 1963 that Elliott-Automation decided to 'engage in a major way in the design and manufacture of microelectronic integrated circuits', starting with a licencing agreement with a world leader at that time, the Fairchild Camera and Instrument Corporation of America. Entry into the semiconductor manufacturing sector was subsequently regarded by some at Borehamwood as a step too far. Finally, the 1963 Annual Report produced the following figures (see Table 13.1) for the number of computers delivered to UK customers (excluding deliveries for defence purposes) in the

Fig. 13.1 Sir Leon Bagrit in the early 1960s, at about the time when he received his knighthood and Elliott-Automation was approaching its zenith. The equipment shown in the background is believed to be part of a large Elliott ARCH system for industrial process control

Fig. 13.2 The large front-of-office computer room at Borehamwood served both as a computer bureau and as a showroom for the company's products. This photo, taken in about 1967, shows an Elliott 4130 system in foreground and a 4120 system in the background

Table 13.1 Annual deliveries of computers to UK customers, 1958–1963

	Total computers delivered in the UK per year (excluding defence)	Percentage of these which were manufactured by Elliotts at Borehamwood
1958	50	20
1959	44	30
1960	68	32
1961	84	50
1962	120	38
1963	200	38

year shown. The data is based on material obtained from the journal *Computer Survey* and is copied for convenience from the table given earlier in Chap. 8.

Elliott's moderately declining market share by numbers (static at 38%), as hinted at in Table 13.1, should perhaps have caused some soul-searching in the company. Actually, the market share by *value* in 1963 was even lower – more like 23%, as is shown below in Sect. 13.2.2. Certainly, 1961/2 was for some people at Borehamwood a turning point, with the realisation that Elliott's penetration into the commercial data processing market had faltered. In the view of Gerry Mills, who in 1961 was a Sales Manager in the Elliott Computing Division under Eddie Nash as Commercial Manager, the link between Elliott and NCR was no longer effective because 'NCR's first concern was protecting their accounting machine business and they were not really very interested in computers' [2].

Notwithstanding the gainsayers, by 1964 the Elliott-Automation Group's profits were at an all-time high (see Sect. 13.2.2) and Bagrit remained optimistic overall. In the 1964 Annual Report, he said: 'Although digital computing is but an element in Automation it is an important one and we are pleased that our business in this field has once again made substantial progress. Our sales of 803 computers are well past the 200 mark. We have now moved into quantity production, both of the high-speed Elliott 503 scientific computer and of the small 920, originally developed for defence purposes, but which is finding wide and varied applications. We continue to produce NCR 315s in substantial numbers. Quite recently we launched our first all-silicon general purpose computer, the Elliott 4100, which will be marketed by us in collaboration with NCR. Apart from the special case of the NCR 315, which was designed in the United States but is made by us in this country, and which as a result of our manufacturing arrangements, adds substantially to computer exports from the United Kingdom, it is important to record that all our computers which have been so successful were conceived and designed in this country by our own scientists and technologists.' Whilst all this may be true, Bagrit remained silent about Elliott's performance in the most rapidly expanding market sector, business and commercial data processing.

Returning to the general picture, let us expand upon Bagrit's view that 'digital computing is but an element in Automation'. As is shown in detail in Appendix 11, the headquarters company of Elliott-Automation Limited, whose prestigious head office was at 29 Portland Place, London, had 16 subsidiary groups of companies. Amongst these, the following 12 groups were relevant to various aspects of computing and control in 1964/5:

Elliott Brothers (London) Ltd., with six subsidiary companies, 11 Divisions (including the Integrated Circuits Division), the Microelectronics Research Laboratory and 11 Service Centres

Elliott-Automation Computers Ltd., with six Divisions and one Research Laboratory

Elliott Flight Automation Ltd., with 11 Divisions and two Laboratories

Elliott Space and Weapon Automation Ltd., with eight Divisions and one Laboratory

Elliott-Automation Radar Systems Ltd., with four Divisions and one Laboratory

Elliott Process Automation Ltd., with 14 Divisions/subsidiaries and one Laboratory

Elliott-Automation Nucleonics Ltd., with four Divisions and subsidiaries

Elliott Medical Automation Ltd., with three Divisions/subsidiaries

Elliott Mechanical Automation Ltd., with four subsidiary companies and three Divisions

Associated Automation Ltd., with three subsidiary companies, six Divisions and one Laboratory

E-A Control Valves Ltd., with three subsidiary companies

Satchwell Controls Ltd., with nine subsidiary companies

Within the hierarchy of Elliott-Automation companies, much of the digital computer design and marketing activity in 1964/65 still resided in the following seven component parts of Elliott-Automation Computers Ltd. at Borehamwood:

Scientific Computing Division
National Computing Division (manufacturing the NCR 315 under licence)
Educational Computing Division
Data Processing Division
Computing Services Division
Computer Maintenance Division
Computing Research Laboratory

Coming on strongly in 1964 was the Airborne Computing Division, originally established at Borehamwood in 1959/60. As shown in Chaps. 8 and 12, airborne computing was gradually to move from Borehamwood to Rochester over the years 1962–1969, where computers were applied with outstanding success to avionics applications in the 1970s and beyond. The Mobile Computing Division, also originally at Borehamwood in 1960, gradually moved to Frimley under the banner of Elliott Space and Weapon Automation Ltd., where computer applications in ground-based air defence and in fire-control for the army were pursued with vigour.

In the background to all of this in 1964 was the newly formed Microelectronics Group of Elliott Brothers (London) Ltd. Finally, there were NCR's London-based efforts at applying Elliott computers to the business and commercial sector. Keeping track of the growing influence of computers within the Elliott-Automation hierarchy is not easy, especially as the names and number of Divisions tended to change almost annually in response to Leon Bagrit's strategy of exploiting market opportunities.

We now need to consider how the income derived from Borehamwood computers related to the performance of the overall Elliott-Automation enterprise – which was, after all, manufacturing and marketing a wide range of other electronic, electrical and mechanical products.

13.2.2 The Company's Overall Financial Position

An analysis of the Elliott-Automation Annual Reports reveals that the company as a whole was at its largest in 1964 and 1965, thereafter shrinking slightly. The comments in the city pages of *The Times* reflect the Stock Market's reaction to the rise and fall in the company's fortunes. On 20 November 1963, *The Times* talked about 'the unassailable growth status of this remarkably successful group ...'. A year later, on 14 November 1964, the company's interim dividend statement was 'one of the most keenly awaited of the week. Further marked growth in profits is hoped for, along with a bigger dividend...'. But on 25 May 1965, *The Times* reported that 'Elliott-Automation has all the things a company could best do without under corporation tax. Investment allowances have always been high as Elliott is in a growth field. The preference dividend takes close on a quarter of what is required to pay the present ordinary dividend. There is an overseas tax charge, admittedly small but likely to increase. And, of course, a hefty capital appetite. Taking this with the cutbacks in defence expenditure already announced, 1965 is not likely to be Elliott's easiest year. Yet the chairman, Sir Leon Bagrit, is looking for satisfactory results, though not specifically a satisfactory "advance in sales and profits".' By 12 November 1966, the Elliott-Automation interim report was, said *The Times,* 'awaited with a mixture of hope and apprehension over the extent to which the group's fortunes have recovered...'.

As for quantifiable indicators, the company's zenith may be charted with reference to data contained in the Annual Reports. If both UK and overseas units are included, the number of employees and the factory floor area for the entire Elliott-Automation empire peaked approximately as follows:

	1964	1965	1966
Number of employees	22,400	23,500	23,100
Factory floor area	4.2 million square feet	4.4 million square feet	?
Profit before taxation	£4,129	£2,391	£2,806

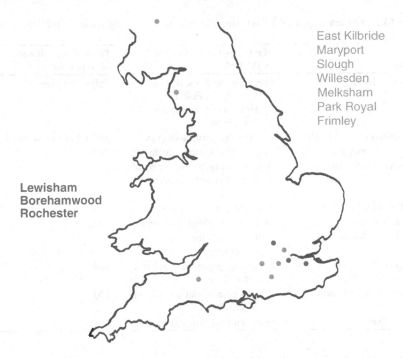

East Kilbride
Maryport
Slough
Willesden
Melksham
Park Royal
Frimley

Lewisham
Borehamwood
Rochester

Fig. 13.3 By 1964, ten of Elliott-Automation's factory sites in the UK each had a floor area of over 100,000 ft². Chronologically, the oldest-established site was at Lewisham, dating from 1900. Borehamwood was acquired (rented from the Admiralty) in 1946. The company began operations at Rochester in about 1947. Rochester grew to become the largest of the company's sites

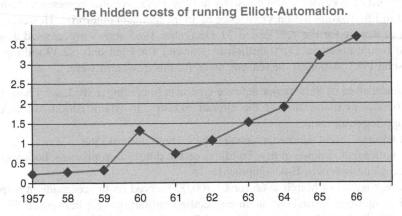

Fig. 13.4 Graph of Elliott-Automation's *top-line profits* minus *pre-tax profits*, in £ million, for the years 1957–1966. The graph gives an indication of the annual cost to the company of interest on loans and depreciation of assets

Table 13.2 The ten largest of Elliott-Automation's manufacturing plants in the UK in May 1965

Location	Main activities on the site in 1964/65	Floor area, in thousands of square feet
Rochester, Kent	Precision mechanical workshops; Fisher fluid valves; aerospace equipment	560 + 295 planned
Borehamwood, Hertfordshire	Computers; radar; aerospace	346 + 115 to come in 1965
Lewisham, south-east London	Instruments; sensors; nucleonics	222
Willesden, north London	Automatic equipment for retail and telecomms; process control	206
East Kilbride, Scotland	Manufacturing (various)	200
Slough, Berkshire	Satchmo switching equipment	190
Melksham, Wiltshire	Bulk materials handling equipment	170
Maryport, Cumbria	Electroflo; process control and automation	144
Park Royal, west London	Process control and automation; Electroflo	120
Frimley, Surrey	Space and weapon automation	107

The complete list of Elliott-Automation companies and Divisions is given in Appendix 11. A total of 25 of the subsidiary companies in the Elliott-Automation organisation were located overseas. Elliott-Automation had some 50 factories, service centres and branch offices in the UK and a further 40 factories and places of business in Europe, Australia and South Africa [3]. Of the UK establishments, ordered by size, the ten sites shown in Table 13.2 and Fig. 13.3 had more that 100,000 square feet of floor area [3].

The list of companies and divisions in May 1965 probably represents the high point of Elliott-Automation's existence as an independent enterprise. However, the Annual Report for the year ended 31 December 1965 shows a decreased annual profit before taxation: £3.70 million to year-end 1964 but only £2.39 million for year-end 1965. Amongst the reasons given for this downturn were:

• Cancellation of three major defence contracts (including TSR 2, see Chap. 12)
• Consequent dislocation of the aircraft industry, to whom Elliott-Automation supplied equipment
• A national credit squeeze, characterised by high interest rates
• A national slowdown in new buildings and in domestic appliances, both sectors being consumers of E-A equipment
• A writ issued in March 1966 for £3,700,000 served on the company in respect of some work carried out on an unspecified military project between 1958 and 1964. (In the following year's Annual Report it is stated that the legal hearing for this claim was expected to take place in early 1968 and a successful outcome for the company was predicted. The nature of the 'military project' has not yet been discovered; it was possibly related to radar.)

The cancellation of TSR 2 had a devastating effect upon the R&D activities of many UK companies associated with avionics. According to Henry Pasley-Tyler, who was at that time a Board-level Director of Elliott-Automation and in overall charge of the company's military projects, the cancellation also had a fundamental effect upon Leon Bagrit himself [4]. Pasley-Tyler noticed that Bagrit gradually became less interested in detailed administration of the company – whilst remaining (in Pasley-Tyler's words) 'an extraordinarily interesting man, competent and artistic'. A year or so later, according to Pasley-Tyler, Bagrit seemed to have begun to look around for someone to succeed himself as boss of Elliott-Automation.

Pre-tax profits of the company were to bounce back to £2.81 million in 1966, the final year for which detailed figures have come to light. The Annual Report for 1966 was presented at the AGM held on 23 June 1967. The city pages of *The Times* for 31 May commented that: 'If stock market optimism were a horse with a rational appetite, Elliott-Automation's annual report and accounts would look like an empty manger...'. News of the proposed merger with English Electric appeared in the Press on 23 June 1967, as described later. It is not surprising that very few financial records of Elliott-Automation after June 1967 seem to have survived the turbulent period of mergers and takeovers.

Even by 1966 the signs of impending problems for the company were evident. Table 13.3 shows *top-line profits* less *pre-tax profits*, the difference representing such factors as interest payable on Elliott-Automation's bank borrowings and depreciation of company assets.

It was a worrying sign that the business overheads, charted in Fig. 13.4, were increasing. The consequences of this trend and related commercial factors are dealt with in due course. First we need to complete the picture of Elliott-Automation at the height of its power in the mid-1960s by considering the position of the company's computer-related revenues, relative both to the company's own trading position and that of its market competitors.

Notwithstanding the growing influence of computers in the 1960s, specific digital computer *design and production* activity at Borehamwood remained a financially modest part of the whole of Elliott-Automation's manufacturing resources. This may be illustrated with reference to sales income from the digital computers themselves – though of course the sale of a computer might be related to the sale of other equipment as well. In particular, many 800 and 900 series computers, and their ARCH derivatives, were used for process control applications where the cost of the central processor was often dwarfed by the cost of the surrounding Elliott-Automation instrumentation and interfacing equipment. For example, in 1967, the company installed an automation system at the Imperial Smelting Corporation, Avonmouth, of total value nearly £1 million, of which the central digital processing equipment probably only represented 5% of the cost.

Table 13.3 *Top-line profits*, TL, minus *Pre-tax profits*, PT, for Elliott-Automation Ltd.

	1957	1958	1959	1960	1961	1962	1963	1964	1965	1966
(TL – PT)	0.23	0.28	0.34	1.31	0.74	1.06	1.52	1.90	3.20	3.66

By combining the computer costs and deliveries figures in Appendix 8 with overall company sales figures given in the Elliott-Automation Annual Reports, we can derive an idea of the value of digital computer sales as a proportion of other sales. This is presented in Table 13.4. The underlying data is necessarily very approximate as explained in Appendix 8, due to the sparseness of surviving company records. A single source [5] from about 1965 does boast that 'today there are over 300 Elliott computer installations. The value of exports alone in 1964 was £3,000,000'. This may make our estimates given in Table 13.4 rather too small.

Notwithstanding the lack of absolute accuracy, the last two columns of Table 13.4 do illustrate three general points. Firstly, the annual income derived from digital computers was, it appears, always likely to have been less than ten percent of total Elliott-Automation group sales income. Secondly, computer income suffered a dip in 1960/63 relative to other Elliott-Automation sales, although in absolute terms the computer income continued to increase. Thirdly, income noticeably increased, both relatively and absolutely, after 1964 as the Elliott 900 and 4100 series computers began to penetrate the small-to-medium end of the market. If the sale of computer-related communications and industrial control equipment were to be added in to the penultimate column in Table 13.4, in line with the imperial Smelting Corporation experience quoted above, it would become clearer that computing was actually a well-performing sector of the Elliott-Automation enterprise by 1967 – even if Elliott's performance relative to other computer manufacturers was faltering.

Another source of sales information comes from the contemporary report of a Parliamentary Select Committee on Science and Technology [6], which compiled statistics for the period leading up to the formation of ICL in 1968. The Committee's data was derived from users' returns and, in the words of the Report, 'is not necessarily comprehensive'. The Committee also used weighted averages when attempting

Table 13.4 Estimate of approximate income from the sale of Elliott digital computers, in £ million, as a percentage of the total sales income of the Elliott-Automation group of companies

	402	405	800 series	503 series	900 series	4100 series	All computers, less defence	All computers, incl. defence	Total E-A sales	Comps as % of E-A
1954							0	0.125	?	
1955	0.054						0.054	0.161	?	
1956	0.027	0.170					0.197	0.197	?	
1957	0.054	0.340					0.394	0.394	?	
1958	0.108	0.765	0.030				0.903	0.903	10.4	8.7
1959		0.935	0.120				1.082	1.082	13	8.3
1960		0.255	0.720				0.975	0.975	20	4.9
1961		0.255	0.780				1.035	1.035	27	3.8
1962	0.027	0.085	1.590				1.675	1.675	36	4.6
1963	0.054		1.260	0.390			1.650	1.650	39	4.2
1964			1.020	1.300			2.320	2.620	55	4.8
1965			0.720	1.690	0.300	0.360	3.070	3.370	59	5.7
1966			0.300	0.780	0.725	2.040	3.845	4.145	64	6.5

to estimate the notional price of each computer – a near-impossible task. Notwithstanding these limitations on accuracy, some useful indicators of the value of annual sales attributable to various computer manufacturers, was estimated in [6]. These are displayed in Table 13.5.

The figures for Elliott computer sales in Table 13.5 appear to include the NCR 315 and the figures in this row should therefore be reduced somewhat if comparisons are to be made with Table 13.4. The American-designed NCR 315 computer was manufactured under licence at Borehamwood from about 1962 to 1967 and was sold from about 1963 onwards. As at 31 December 1966, Borehamwood had delivered 115 of these NCR computers and a further 35 machines were on order [7]. The precise number of sales in each year is not known. The approximate price of a typical NCR 315 was about £78,000 – see Chap. 9.

Taking all factors into account and making the necessary adjustments, the value of sales of Elliott computers shown in Tables 13.4 and 13.5 are not too dissimilar.

The Moonman Report [6] also estimates the percentage share of the UK's computer market enjoyed by each computer manufacturer. This information is summarised in Table 13.6.

It can be seen that Elliott-Automation's market share held steady, apart from a dip in 1966. The fortunes of Elliott's traditional competitor, Ferranti, also held reasonably steady but at a much lower level. The reason for the lower level is as follows. Looking back in time, Ferranti had struggled to recoup after the high development costs of the large Ferranti Atlas and Orion computer projects. The Atlas sales to the scientific sector were disappointing (see Appendix 10). Orion was

Table 13.5 Notional value, in £K, of manufacturers' share of the total UK computer market (After Moonman [6])

	1964 (£)	1965 (£)	1966 (£)	1967 (£)	1968 (£)
ICL (incl. ICT & English Electric)	22,389	20,488	28,875	38,563	49,297
Elliott (incl. NCR 315, etc.)	4,108	6,160	5,134	11,302	12,835
Ferranti	116	414	476	390	767
GEC/AEI	485	1,246	395	350	304
IBM	21,461	22,574	36,264	50,526	28,130

Table 13.6 Manufacturers' percentage share of the total UK computer market by value (After Moonman [6])

	1964 (%)	1965 (%)	1966 (%)	1967 (%)	1968 (%)
ICL (incl. ICT & English Electric)	41.4	32.0	34.4	32.4	41.0
Elliott (incl. NCR 315, etc.)	7.6	9.6	6.1	9.5	10.7
Ferranti	0.2	0.6	0.6	0.3	0.6
GEC/AEI	0.9	1.9	0.5	0.3	0.3
IBM	40.0	35.1	43.2	42.5	23.4
Other (non-UK) manufacturers	9.9	20.8	15.2	15.0	24.0

Table 13.7 Share of installed base of British computers, as in January 1963, and before the takeover by ICT of Ferranti's main-frame computer interests

	Value (£m)	Percentage share (%)
Ferranti	6.620	24.5
ICT (including EMI)	6.614	24.5
Elliott (including NCR)	6.238	23.1
English Electric	3.565	13.2
Leo	1.740	6.4
AEI	1.140	4.2
STC	0.540	2.0
Others	0.570	2.1
	27.027	100.0

aimed at the large business data processing market and achieved somewhat more success. Thirteen Orion 1 computers had been delivered between early 1963 and January 1965 [8]; this was followed by an Orion 2 design. Ferranti's Computer Department had made a record loss of £1,804,241 in 1963 [9]. Ferranti's mainframe computer interests were taken over by ICT in 1963, so the figures in Table 13.6 represent the remaining Ferranti military and process-control computer interests.

A better idea of the value of British computers installed in Britain in January 1963, shortly *before* the ICT takeover of Ferranti, was obtained by the organisation Computer Consultants, as quoted by Bernard Swann on page 77 of [8]. This is shown in Table 13.7.

As has been mentioned, Ferranti's general-purpose computer activities were taken over by ICT in 1963. From the wider perspective of *all* computer applications, it should be noted that the acquisition by ICT of Ferranti's mainframe computer interests in 1963 only applied to six of the Ferranti computers listed in Appendix 10, together with associated manufacturing plant such as Ferranti's factory at West Gorton. This still left the Ferranti company with the military computers such as Argus and some substantial computer-related R&D sites at Bracknell, Wythenshawe, etc. Thus, Ferranti continued as a competitor to Elliotts in the military sector and, in due course, in the process control market when the Argus series was applied with increasing success to industrial automation.

It is now necessary to see how the sale of Elliott computers compared with those of other rival UK and American manufacturers, especially in the commercial and business sectors where the growing influence of IBM was sharpening minds.

13.3 Satisfying the UK's Business Data Processing Market

Prior to 1960, very few British-designed computers were considered suitable for large business applications, although BTM had started to address the smaller end of the market. Prior to 1960, there were indeed only three credible British-designed contenders for large business applications, as shown in Table 13.8.

Table 13.8 British-designed computers available before 1960 and considered suitable for large business data processing applications (See Appendix 8 for detailed costings for the Elliott 405)

	First delivered	Approximate price (£)	Number delivered
Elliott 405	1956	85K	33
LEO II	1957	95K	11
Ferranti Perseus	1959	100K	2

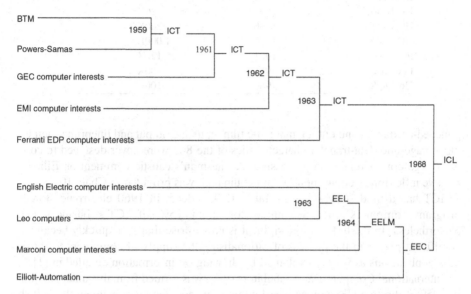

Fig. 13.5 The chart shows the approximate evolution of ICL, from 1959 to 1968, based on information derived *ICL: a business and technical history* – see [1]. The two British electromechanical punched-card equipment manufacturers, BTM and Powers-Samas, came together in 1959 to form ICT. By 1961 ICT was firmly committed to electronic data processing and, over the next 7 years, gradually acquired the mainframe computer interests of all the other major British stored-program computer manufacturers. In 1981, ICL went into partnership with Fujitsu. By 2001 Fujitsu had gained control and had dispensed with the name ICL

All three computers in Table 13.8 were based on thermionic valve technology. None of these could match the power of the IBM 705, as is demonstrated in Chap. 9 when discussing the evaluation of tenders for the Royal Army Pay Corp's payroll task. At this juncture, more British manufacturers began to respond to the challenges, since it had become obvious that markets were rapidly opening up. By 1962, Table 13.9 shows that five new British and six new American computers were considered suitable for large business data processing applications. All the computers in Table 13.9 were based on transistor technology.

Smaller transistorised computers such as the Elliott 803 and the Ferranti Sirius are not included in Table 13.9 because they were not considered to offer the bulk data-movement facilities required for large commercial applications. Whilst it is true that the Elliott 803 did eventually offer business-oriented peripheral equipment such as

Table 13.9 British and American computers available between 1960 and 1962 and considered suitable for large business data processing applications (Data based on [1])

	First UK delivery	Approximate price (£)
EMI 1100	1960	180K
EMI 2400	1961?	500K
English Electric KDP10	1961	400K
Honeywell 800	1962	400K
IBM 305	1960	70K
IBM 1401	1960	120K
IBM 1410	1960	200K
IBM 7090	1960	1,000K
ICT 1301	1961	120K
Leo LEO II	1962	200K
Univac SS-80	1960	100K

punched-card input and output, magnetic film input and output and lineprinter output, the storage and data-transfer characteristics of the 803 were never designed to cope with large commercial data processing. A salesman's caustic comment on Elliott's relative inflexibility about input/output equipment was provided in Chap. 10.

ICT has a modest presence in Table 13.9. Indeed, in 1960 electronic stored-program computers only accounted for about 15% of ICT's business [1]. Nevertheless, in the light of hindsight, it is no surprise that ICT quickly became a significant player in the process of rationalising the supply of computers for business applications as is now explained by drawing on information detailed in [1].

International Computers and Tabulators (ICT) was formed from the amalgamation in 1959 of the two UK punched-card equipment manufacturers, namely the British Tabulating Machine Co. (BTM) and Powers-Samas. BTM had been founded in 1904, and re-incorporated in 1907, to exploit Herman Hollerith's invention in America of punched-card tabulating machines. Powers-Samas had grown from the Accounting and Tabulating Machine Company, established in 1915 as the British agency for the American Powers Accounting Machines. From this grew the Powers-Samas company in 1929. Thus ICT, through its two ancestor companies, had many years of experience in the provision of office machinery based on electromechanical punched-card equipment. Critically, ICT understood the day-to-day data processing needs of the business community.

Up to the late 1950s, punched-card machinery formed the overwhelming data processing resource for business and commerce. Indeed, sales of this type of equipment in the UK were increasing right up until 1961. The punched-card machinery market collapsed between the autumn of 1961 and spring 1962 'with devastating suddenness' [1]. One of the reasons for the sudden collapse was the popularity of a new IBM product, the 1401, that had first appeared in Britain in 1960. During 1961–1962, IBM installed close on 100 of its 1401 electronic computers, which accounted for about a third of the computer sales in Britain during that period. The new 1401 computer installations usually replacing older electromechanical equipment, encouraging others to make the move to stored-program machines.

Because ICT concentrated on the ever-expanding area of business and commercial applications, the company's fortunes quickly became the concern of city financiers and government advisers. As time went on, the hopes for the survival of an independent UK IT industry were focused more and more on ICT. Looking ahead, the progress of ICT's gradual acquisitions of rival companies in this area is roughly illustrated by Fig. 13.5, taken from [1].

Bernard Swann, Ferranti's long-serving computer Sales Manager, writing in 1975 [8] was of the opinion that 'The competition situation among the British machines continued far too long, putting the Government in a difficult position as it tried to decide which horse to back. They were in the end compelled to bring the engineering companies together with the unified punched card companies [combined in 1959 as ICT]. The long delay had, however, made unity more difficult to achieve so that the new ICL [formed in 1968] was only viable with a good deal of Government support which it has continued to need ever since'.

Several of the amalgamations inherent in Fig. 13.5 were indeed encouraged by government. Why was this? Some of the companies whose names appear in the figure, particularly GEC and English Electric, were industrial giants who had many more manufacturing interests other than computers. If the product at the heart of Fig. 13.5 had been light bulbs or refrigerators, rather than computers, surely the government at the time might have been content with diversity and *natural selection* rather than intervening to encourage a single-company monopoly?

There were probably four related factors that predicated government intervention in the UK computer industry by the mid-1960s. Firstly, digital computers had, by that time, clearly become essential to the wealth-creating capabilities of the nation – not to mention the nation's defence. Secondly, the hardware and software incompatibility of different makes of (British) computer was causing unnecessary and costly overheads. Thirdly, the advances in underlying computer technologies, particularly memory systems and semiconductors, were producing a rapid evolution of computing practices and expectations; there was a practical need to help end-users make transitions. Fourthly, American computer manufacturers enjoyed a voluminous home market that allowed them to develop cost-effective products; these products were gaining ground in Europe and elsewhere, to the disadvantage of UK computer manufacturers.

Taking the above four factors into consideration, the government of the day certainly felt obliged to intervene. The situation was a world away from today's laptop suppliers, most of whom make use of common underlying technologies (for example, Intel chips, Microsoft software and the Internet). In 1964/65, Prime Minister Harold Wilson's Labour government set up a Ministry of Technology and an Industrial Reorganisation Corporation, to make a stab at maximising public benefit from, amongst others, the UK's computer manufacturers.

Many companies became involved in the turmoil of amalgamations in the 1960s. Several, like GEC, English Electric, Elliott-Automation and Ferranti had wider interests than computers. Since these four were soon to become intertwined, we now give a brief historical overview of these engineering companies. There is another reason for looking at these former paragons of British manufacturing industry: their names have now vanished and the modern reader might be excused for misunderstanding their former importance.

13.4   The Large Engineering Companies

13.4.1   The Electrical Giants

Relative to the UK's broad industrial capability in the year 1960, at least three of the companies swept up in the computer amalgamations of the 1960s would have been classed as very large electrical engineering concerns. Table 13.10 shows these and other companies of interest, arranged in order of their capitalisation [10]. Of course, the amount of authorised or issued capital does not necessarily relate directly to the size or success of an enterprise, but it does give a general idea of the ambitions of an organisation.

The 1960s was still the era of intense manufacturing in Britain, when the above companies each employed several tens of thousands of people. The larger engineering concerns made practically everything they needed 'in house'. For example visitors to Ferranti's computer factory at West Gorton, Manchester, in 1962 would see steel girders going in at one loading bay and complete computers coming out of another loading bay. Furthermore, the larger companies were active across the whole spectrum of electrical engineering. Electronics, and in particular digital electronics, was but one part (sometimes a modest part) of their total product range. This was especially true of AEI and GEC, neither of which chose to pursue its general-purpose computer interests much after 1961 when compared with the efforts of the main players in the market at that time.

EMI in Table 13.10 is a rather special case, insofar as it was not a traditional electrical engineering company but a business firmly rooted in entertainment. Electric and Musical Industries Ltd (EMI) was formed in 1931 from a merger of two gramophone (phonograph) companies. From its beginning, EMI was involved in the manufacture of audio recording and playback equipment, in sound recording facilities at its famous Abbey Road studios in London and in the provision of records to play on its gramophones [11]. During and after the Second World War, the EMI Laboratories in Hayes, west London, developed electronic equipment for both defence projects and, at the end of hostilities, for television. EMI was encouraged to use its electronic expertise for computer design in the late 1950s, but this activity was never going to become the company's major concern. On the engineering front,

Table 13.10   Seven large UK engineering companies, ranked according to their capitalisation in 1960

Company	Authorised capital (£m)	Issued capital (£m)
AEI (including BTH and Met. Vic.)	48.7	47.1
English Electric (including Marconi)	35.0	32.7
GEC	23.6	23.6
EMI	17.5	12.5
ICT	12.0	10.4
Elliott-Automation	10.0	6.5
Ferranti	4.5	4.5

EMI was noted for its provision of high-quality colour television cameras and, in the 1970s, for CAT scanners and medical imaging. Towards the end of the 1970s, EMI's manufacturing activities were run down, and it became much more of a media organisation. At the time of writing (2010), it is still well known as one of the world's Big Four recording companies.

The larger electrical engineering companies in Table 13.10 were all well established, having their origins in the nineteenth century. AEI, Associated Electrical Industries Ltd., was first registered as British Westinghouse in 1899. It changed its name to Metropolitan-Vickers Electric in 1919 and then to AEI in 1928. As is amplified in Sect. 13.4.2 below, GEC, the General Electric Co., was first registered in 1900. Mergers and partnerships were certainly not uncommon amongst similar companies. English Electric was itself the result of a conjunction, in 1918, of four older companies (see also Sect. 13.4.3). By the end of the 1950s, English Electric attempted a further rationalisation, observing that its business was in heavy electrical products, whereas 82% of GEC's turnover was in light electrical goods. So in September 1960, EE tried to merge with GEC. However, the merger was turned down by the GEC Board [12]. In 1963, Arnold Weinstock became Managing Director of GEC and began a process of acquisitions that would see his company emerge as the top dog of electrical engineering in the UK. The saga of GEC's eventual triumph extended over some 60 years [12].

Since GEC was to swallow up most of Elliott-Automation, it is worth devoting a little space on the company's history.

13.4.2   GEC and Arnold Weinstock

GEC had its origins in an electrical goods wholesaler established in London during the 1880s by two German immigrants, Gustav Binswanger (later Gustav Byng) and Hugo Hirst (later Lord Hirst) [12]. In 1889, the General Electric Company Ltd. (GEC) was formed as a private limited company to trade in *Everything Electrical*, a phrase by which GEC became well known. Rapid success in electrical components, particularly the Osram range of tungsten filament lamps, ensured that GEC was well placed to take advantage of the manufacturing opportunities of the First World War, supplying products such as radios, signalling lamps and searchlights.

GEC took over the heavy engineering firm of Fraser and Chalmers in 1918, thus widening its product portfolio. In the 1920s GEC was a major contractor in the creation of the UK's National Grid for countrywide distribution of electricity. GEC opened its own Research Laboratories, later called the Hirst Laboratories, at Wembley in north London in 1923. It was here that the cavity magnetron was developed, based on the pioneering research of Randell and Boot at the University of Birmingham at the outbreak of the Second World War. As mentioned in Chap. 1, the organisation of GEC's Hirst Laboratories was taken by John Coales in 1946 as the pattern for Elliott's new Borehamwood Research Laboratories.

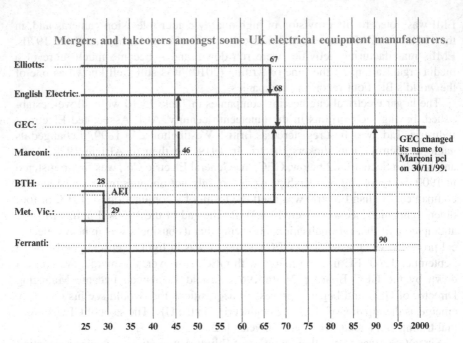

Fig. 13.6 The mergers and takeovers amongst the major British electrical engineering companies in the period 1920–1990. GEC, which had acquired Elliott-Automation's military and process-control computer interests in 1968, had emerged as the winner by 1990. In 1999 GEC changed its name to Marconi. This diagram shows the corporate view. Some company names, for example Metropolitan-Vickers and Marconi, continued to be used after the date of formal takeover or merger

Fig. 13.7 Arnold Weinstock (1924–2002) served as Managing Director of GEC from 1963 to 1996. From 1970 Weinstock guided GEC to ever-increasing profitability at a time when manufacturing industries were generally declining in Britain. In 1999 most of GEC, except for the defence-related sections known collectively as Marconi Electronic Systems, was re-named Marconi plc. At the same time, British Aerospace purchased Marconi Electronic Systems, to form BAE Systems. Marconi plc subsequently got into severe financial difficulties and most of the company was acquired by Ericsson in 2006. Marconi's remaining UK operations were renamed Telent Ltd

Hugo Hirst died in 1943. Perhaps as a result, the post-war years saw GEC's profits begin to fall for the first time. Nevertheless, a period of dramatic recovery and expansion was heralded in 1961 when GEC took over a company called Radio and Allied Industries and, with it, an outstanding manager called Arnold Weinstock (later Lord Weinstock).

Arnold Weinstock was born in Stoke Newington, north London, in 1924, the son of a Polish master tailor who had come to England in 1904. The story of Weinstock's amazing life is ably told in a *Guardian* obituary [13], of which the following is a summary. Orphaned at the age of eleven, evacuated from London at the outbreak of war, Weinstock graduated from the London School of Economics (LSE) in 1944. At LSE, he came under the influence of Friedrich von Hayek, said to be one of the intellectual influences behind the Thatcherite economics of the 1980s. After war service spent as a statistician in the production and priority branch of the Admiralty at Bath and a spell working for a property company in London, Weinstock met and married Netta Sobell, the daughter of Michael Sobell, an entrepreneur who had made his fortune manufacturing radios.

In 1954, Weinstock joined Sobell's Radio and Allied Industries. So impressed was the City with Weinstock's management skills that, when the larger GEC was floundering in 1961, Radio and Allied Industries was encouraged to make a reverse takeover of GEC. This echoed the process, albeit on a more modest scale, whereby Leon Bagrit arrived with the smaller B&P Swift Ltd. to become Managing Director of the larger Elliott Brothers (London) Ltd. in 1947 (see Chap. 1). Weinstock became managing Director of GEC in 1963.

For more than three decades at GEC, Weinstock was to lead one of the UK's most successful industrial conglomerates at a time when manufacturing was steadily declining in Britain. It is said [13] that Weinstock was a forbidding figure, before whom his senior managers would quake. He is described [12] as 'abrasive, ruthless, aggressive'. There are anecdotes of managers being reduced to tears in budget meetings [14]. In particular, Weinstock insisted that each separate company within the GEC Group of companies had to be profitable annually. This tended to mean that no company could support a strategic investment that significantly impacted its profit. As is discussed in Chap. 14, in the 1980s GEC Computers appears to have found that Weinstock would initially approve a strategic growth and then constrain the necessary R&D by month-by-month tactical accounting.

Weinstock kept a tight control on costs, was willing to close uneconomic factories and was able to take on the trade unions. 'When the economy was going through one of its most severe recessions, under John Major's stewardship in 1990–1992, GEC demonstrated a rare consistency, breaching the £1bn profit mark despite the problems of a high exchange rate as a result of the exchange rate mechanism. This was only possible because of the strict cost regime at GEC, which set it apart from the crowd' [13]. By 1984 GEC was ranked third amongst UK companies, coming behind British Petroleum and Shell Transport and Trading. At that time, GEC's market capitalisation was £4.915 billion. Weinstock retired as Managing Director of GEC in 1996. During his life, he received many honours, being knighted in 1970 and made a Life Peer in 1980. He died in 2002.

Back in the 1960s, Weinstock returned GEC to profit. GEC acquired Associated Electrical Industries (AEI) in 1967, at which time the AEI Group included Metropolitan-Vickers, BTH, Edison Swan, Siemens Bros., Hotpoint and W.T. Henley. There then followed a succession of takeovers and mergers in which GEC gained control of many other companies, amongst which the following have some relevance to the history of computers (see also Fig. 13.6):

1968   GEC acquires English Electric (including Marconi) and Elliott-Automation
1988   The creation of GEC-Plessey Telecommunications (GPT)
1989   GEC acquires Plessey's avionics and naval systems businesses
1990   GEC acquires Ferranti (the sections not acquired by ICT in 1963)

Backtracking in time, GEC had developed a modest interest in computers in 1956. In that year, GEC had entered into an agreement with BTM and had jointly set up a company called Computer Developments Ltd. (CDL). As described in [1] CDL began operations in November 1956, with a staff of six people focussed on semiconductor digital circuits. The first step for CDL was to design a simple experimental computer operating at the very slow rate of 20 kHz. It contained about 1,000 transistors, 1,500 diodes, and had a magnetic drum for storage. From this grew the 1301 project, intended to be developed and manufactured at GEC's Coventry telecommunications factory. ICT provided the drum, card reader, punch and printer. By the end of September 1959, the prototype 1301 computer ran its first program. Attention then focused on the newly formed ICT (see Fig. 13.5) and CDL was subsequently wound up.

GEC retained a relatively modest interest in the application of computers to industrial process control. In about 1962 or 1963, when Laurence Clarke was Elliott-Automation's Assistant General Manager responsible (amongst other things) for E-A's Industrial Process Automation Division, he remembers [15] 'detailed discussions with GEC about taking on their computer business in the process field. They had agreements with TRW [Thompson-Ramo-Wooldrige, see Chap. 6] in the States. We had got right to the point of the distribution of GEC staff within Elliotts. At the very last minute – again I was away on leave in the lake District expecting to return to a signed and sealed situation, having had some documents notarised – Joe Wiltshire, the future MD of GEC Elliott-Automation, persuaded Arnold Weinstock of the foolishness of giving up computer interests. The deal was then off!'

Summarising GEC's long march to dominance in the field of general electrical engineering, Fig. 13.6 shows the chronology of takeovers.

We now give a more detailed account of the English Electric company, as an example of the UK's electrical engineering capabilities in war and peace. This helps to fix early computers in a general manufacturing context, thereby complementing the more usual descriptions based on applications and market areas. The English Electric story is also a useful yardstick by which to compare the progress of smaller companies such as Elliott-Automation. Finally, of course, the English Electric culture had a direct bearing on the fortunes of Elliott's Borehamwood Laboratory. As we shall see later in Sect. 13.6, at the end of August 1967 the merger of

Elliott-Automation and English Electric was announced and then, on 6 September 1968, the takeover of English Electric by GEC was agreed.

13.4.3 English Electric

Summarising the company's history, four firms joined together in 1918 to form English Electric Co. Ltd. [16]:

Siemens Dynamo Works	(Main business: electrical energy)
Dick Kerr & Co.	(Main business: electric traction)
Williams & Robinson	(Main business: marine steam engines)
Phoenix Dynamo Manufacturing Co.	(Main business: small electrical machines)

The English Electric (EE) company's principal pre-war factories were at Stafford, Preston, Rugby and Bradford. In 1938, in what became the run-up to the Second World War, the work on defence-related contracts included the following:

Emergency switchgear for towns; electrical equipment for Shadow Aircraft factories
Aircraft frames for Hampden bombers (designed by Handley Page)
Diesel generating sets; electric motors for submarines

Many such war-related product lines continued during the war [17]. In addition, the following items were amongst the products manufactured during hostilities:

Bombsights; repeater compasses for aircraft
Covenanter tanks, Centaur tanks, Comet tanks
Metadyne remote power equipment for gun mountings
Vampire single-seat jets

An order for 120 Vampires was placed in May 1944; the first one was delivered on 20 April 1945.

On 23 December 1942, English Electric (EE) had acquired D Napier & Son Ltd., an automobile, marine and aero engineering firm. The growth rate of the EE group during the war is apparent from the following employment statistics [17]: payroll at 1 January 1939: 1,200 employees; payroll at the end of the war: nearly 30,000 employees.

In 1946, the Marconi group of companies joined EE (see also Sect. 13.4.4 below). Up to that point, the EE Group's activities had not really included electronics. Perhaps as a result, Marconi's electronics expertise of the late 1940s appeared not to impinge much on the main EE interests. For the next 20 years, there remained somewhat of a cultural gap between EE and Marconi.

In 1955, two locomotive manufacturing companies joined EE: (a) the Vulcan Foundry Ltd.; (b) Robert Stephenson & Hawthorns Ltd. By the late 1950s and early 1960s, EE was particularly well known in the public mind for its Canberra jet bomber, Lightning supersonic fighter aircraft and the Deltic diesel-electric locomotive. The English Electric Canberra first flew in May 1949, entered service with the RAF in May 1951 and was finally retired from RAF photo-reconnaissance duties in June 2006. It has been described as one of the most successful British military aeroplanes of all time. One thousand three hundred and fifty-two Canberras were built.

Of more relevance to Elliott Brothers (London) Ltd. was the English Electric Lightning, of which the prototype, known as P1, first flew in August 1954. Lightnings were in service with the RAF from 1959 to 1988. This high-performance fighter required a new generation of (analogue) avionics, for which Borehamwood carried out much of the R&D, as touched on in Chap. 4.

The story of English Electric computers, which formed but one part of the company's total manufacturing activities, is continued in Sect. 13.5, after we have filled in a few details about the Marconi company.

13.4.4 Marconi, a Famous Name

The radio pioneer Guglielmo Marconi (1874–1937) founded his *Wireless Telegraph & Signal Company* in 1897. In 1898 he opened the world's first wireless factory in Chelmsford. In 1900 the company's name was altered to Marconi Wireless Telegraph Co. At the same time, the Marconi International Marine Communication Co. Ltd. was formed because ship-borne radio had become an important and specialised part of the business. As for the main Marconi company, electronics, communications and, in due course, radar were the principal activities. The main laboratories and factories remained in the Chelmsford region, both within the town and also at nearby places such as Great Baddow and Writtle. In the 1960s it was at Chelmsford that the company developed an independent interest in computers for military applications, for example radar, as recounted in a little more detail in Sect. 13.5.

Back in 1946, as noted above, Marconi became part of the English Electric group. Hence, Marconi eventually became part of GEC when GEC took over English Electric in 1968. Such was the reputation attached to the name *Marconi* that, far from vanishing after 1968, it surfaced in several guises, and at various times, within the GEC group. Below we give examples of a somewhat complicated assortment of names, the majority of which were associated with companies within GEC's defence divisions. The dates signify when each entity came into being.

1969	Marconi-Elliott Avionics Systems Ltd.
1969	Marconi Elliott Computer Systems Ltd.
1978	Marconi Avionics Ltd.
(Date?)	Marconi Defence Systems Ltd.
(Date?)	Marconi Underwater Systems Ltd.
(Date?)	GEC-Marconi Radar and Defence Systems Ltd.
(Date?)	Marconi Space & Defence Systems
1987	GEC-Marconi Ltd.
1993	GEC-Marconi Avionics Ltd.
1998	Marconi Electronic Systems.

In 1999 most of GEC, except for the defence-related sections known collectively as Marconi Electronic Systems, was re-named Marconi plc (later to become the Marconi Corporation). At about the same time, British Aerospace purchased Marconi Electronic Systems to form BAE Systems. At this point, the name GEC, for many years associated with a large and powerful organisation, vanished from public gaze. Of the old Elliott/Marconi sites of the 1970s, Borehamwood was gradually disposed of – as described in Chap. 14. The Rochester site and the sites in and around Chelmsford became part of BAE Systems and Rochester remains so at the time of writing.

After 1999 Marconi plc embarked upon a major re-alignment, making substantial acquisitions of companies relevant to telecommunications and Internet equipment. However, the company got into severe financial difficulties and in May 2002 announced a loss of £5.7 billion, at the time the biggest loss in British corporate history. The Marconi Corporation naturally became a likely target for a takeover, most of the Corporation finally being acquired by Ericsson in January 2006. Marconi's remaining UK operations were renamed Telent Ltd., a relatively small company with its headquarters in Coventry. Thus in 2006 the name Marconi effectively vanished, amidst public wonder that so mighty an industrial giant had, so to speak, evaporated.

The events of the 1970s, 1980s and 1990s were, of course, still a long way ahead when English Electric, Marconi and Elliott-Automation found themselves part of Arnold Weinstock's GEC empire in 1968, their general-purpose computer interests having been passed to ICL. We now describe in more detail the run-up to the formation of ICL, emphasising those elements of the story that have the closest connection with the fortunes of Elliott-Automation.

13.5 The Coalescing of Computer Interests: EELM and ICT

As Fig. 13.5 implies and [1] amplifies, the computer interests of English Electric, Leo and Marconi rapidly came together for mutual comfort in the turbulent period 1963–1964. Their comfort zone was not to last long. In 1964 the English Electric Leo Marconi company (EELM) soon began planning a new range of computers. In the light of the announcement in April 1964 by IBM of the System/360 range, EELM and all other large computer manufacturers came under pressure to devise their own systems that were either distinct from, or compatible with, the instruction set of the new IBM range. Whatever strategy EELM adopted, it could not afford to ignore IBM's dominance of worldwide markets.

In America, RCA chose to be compatible with IBM, quickly announcing its Spectra 70 range. In Britain, ICT chose not to follow RCA but to continue with an in-house design study (the FP6000) and to announce the ICT 1900 range in September 1964. EELM chose compatibility. The EELM System 4, based on the RCA Spectra 70, was announced in September 1965. It is perhaps a mark of Leon Bagrit's relative lack of interest in the business use of computers that the IBM announcement of 1964 did not appear to trigger any sudden increase in enthusiasm

for commercial applications in the Elliott-Automation camp – nor indeed at NCR
in London.

By 1967, at the time of the merger between English Electric and Elliott-
Automation, EELM had begun deliveries of System 4 computers. At that time, the
members of the System 4 range were as follows [1]:

System 4/10   (Subsequently cancelled)
System 4/30   First delivered June 1967; typical price: £172K
System 4/50   First delivered May 1967; typical price: £271K
System 4/70   First delivered mid-1968; typical price: £600K

The development, production and installation of System 4 computers was not with-
out its difficulties, and the company's resources were stretched. The System 4 activity
was not really helped by the merging of the English Electric Group and Elliott-
Automation in July 1968 and EELM's name-change to English Electric Computers.
In parallel with this larger corporate merger, talks had been going on between English
Electric Computers and ICT. On 10 August 1968, the business of English Electric
Computers Limited was merged with ICT to form International Computers Limited
(ICL), as described in Sect. 13.7. First, though, we need to backtrack slightly and deal
with English Electric and Elliott-Automation's corporate dance.

13.6   The Merger Between Elliott-Automation
and English Electric

In Chaps. 7 and 8 we left Elliott-Automation at an apparent high point in its fortunes, especially regarding the application of its computers to defence and industrial
control. However, the signs of impending financial trouble were already beginning
to appear, for those analysts able to see behind the glossy photographs in the company's upbeat 1966 Annual Report. On 9 June 1967, rumours of a merger were first
aired in the Press. Here's how the bad news was officially broken to shareholders.

13.6.1   The Letter to Shareholders

In a letter to Elliott-Automation shareholders dated 17 July 1967, Sir Leon Bagrit
explained that the E-A Directors had given considerable thought to the company's
prospects, both in terms of development and of profitability, and of whether or not
it would be in the Company's best interests to accept an offer by English Electric
to acquire the whole of the issued capital of Elliott-Automation [18]. Bagrit
continued thus:

'During the last decade Elliott-Automation has become a leading manufacturer of
a uniquely wide range of automation equipment and has, as a result of building up
and maintaining a highly skilled technical organisation, gained a world-wide

reputation for the quality and variety of its work. The ability of your Company successfully to develop and market advanced technological products is evidenced by an unbroken record of increased sales but the build-up of assets required to implement this increasing turnover has resulted in exceptionally heavy working capital requirements.

'Elliott-Automation has a high level of existing borrowings and the Group's ability to raise additional capital has been materially reduced by the cancellation of Government contracts which led to the fall in our profits in 1965. Very substantial expenditure on research and development and on the exploitation of new advanced technological products is essential if your Company is to remain in the forefront of the automation field and compete effectively in world markets. In addition there will be a further considerable demand for working capital to meet the expanding turnover. With continuing success these factors would necessarily put an excessive burden on the finances of a Group of the size of Elliott-Automation.

'The arrangements made in connection with the proposed merger of your Company with English Electric include the provision by the Industrial Reorganisation Corporation of £15 million for the development of the combined activities in the fields of advanced technology in which we both operate [see also below]. The provision of this finance will ensure that your Company will have sufficient funds available to satisfy its requirements both for development finance and working capital.

'English Electric is already heavily involved in electronics, computers and automation systems and in 1966 its turnover in these fields exceeded £80 million. The merger of these interests with Elliott-Automation will create an advanced technological complex (with an annual turnover of approximately £150 million, representing even now over 40% of the combined turnover of English Electric and Elliott-Automation) which will be the largest unit in Europe operating in these fields of advanced technology. Due to the complementary nature of the products at present produced by English Electric and Elliott-Automation, it will also create a group capable of supplying a uniquely wide range of fully integrated systems and automation products. The importance of such a unit to the national economy is recognized in the Governmental support which this merger has attracted'.

Bagrit went on to explain the financial details. 'The terms of the merger will result in the Ordinary Shareholders of Elliott-Automation receiving, on the basis of English Electric annual dividends of 11% (less tax), an increase of 25.7% in annual income and value each Ordinary Share of Elliott-Automation at 13s. 4d. [equivalent to £0.67], based on the middle-market quotation for the ordinary Shares of English Electric on 11th July 1967. This compares with a middle-market quotation for the Ordinary Shares of Elliott-Automation of 11s. 3d. on 8 June 1967, the day prior to the publication of Press reports regarding a possible merger of your Company. Based on the profits after taxation of Elliott-Automation in the year to 31 December 1966, the terms value the Ordinary Shares at a price/earnings ratio of 29.2.

'Your Directors have considered these factors and, while the level of current trading indicates that the profits before taxation of Elliott-Automation for the year to 31st December 1967 should, in the absence of unforeseen circumstances, show a significant increase over those earned in the previous year, they consider that the

greater prospects before the merged Company, compared with those of Elliott-Automation as an independent organisation, make the merger desirable from the point of view of the long-term interests of the shareholders of Elliott-Automation....
Your Directors, therefore, recommend both Preference and Ordinary shareholders to accept the Offers and intend to accept in respect of their own shareholdings'.

Bagrits concluded thus: 'If the Offer for the Ordinary Shares of Elliott-Automation becomes unconditional, I will join the Board of English Electric as a deputy Chairman with special interest in the development of automation, electronics and computer activities. I will continue to be Chairman and Managing Director of Elliott-Automation, to the Board of which representatives of English Electric will be elected.'

The last day for acceptance of the Offer was set at 14 August 1967. The merger went ahead shortly after this date.

Accompanying Bagrit's letter of 17 July was a 5-year financial analysis of the two companies, prepared by the merchant bankers Lazard Brothers & Co. Ltd. This included data on the following annual parameters:

TVR = turnover for the year ended 31 December
PBT = profit before taxation and interest
PAS = profit applicable to Shareholders
DIV = dividends paid out to Shareholders from PAS
RET = profits retained by the company from PAS
ISC = issued share capital

In Table 13.11 we compare these six parameters, as measured in £ million, for English Electric (EE) and Elliott-Automation (EA) over the 5 years preceding their merger.

It can be seen from Table 13.11 that Elliott-Automation's retained profits (RET) fell in 1965 and became negative in 1966 (meaning that the company felt it necessary to subsidise the dividend paid to shareholders in 1966). Between the same

Table 13.11 Comparison of six financial parameters, in £ millions, for English Electric and Elliott-Automation, 1962–1966

	1962 (£)	1963 (£)	1964 (£)	1965 (£)	1966 (£)
TVR:EE	199.7	209.0	227.3	244.8	270.3
EA	36.0	39.0	55.0	59.0	64.0
PBT: EE	9.9	11.8	14.6	17.9	20.3
EA	3.3	3.8	4.9	3.6	4.3
PAS: EE	3.1	4.3	6.4	9.4	9.6
EA	1.5	1.9	2.2	1.6	1.6
DIV: EE	1.6	1.9	2.8	2.9	4.5
EA	0.7	0.9	1.0	1.0	1.8
RET:EE	1.5	2.3	3.6	6.5	5.1
EA	0.8	0.9	1.2	0.5	−0.2
ISC: EE	33.7	33.7	40.1	47.9	58.6
EA	10.4	11.2	17.8	18.6	18.6

years, 1965 and 1966, issued capital (ISC) remained static although turnover (TVR) had increased. It was not surprising that a merger seemed a good option to the Directors of Elliott-Automation in the summer of 1967.

There was also something more sinister looming in the background. Ron Howard, who joined Borehamwood in 1953 and went on to become a Divisional Manager within GEC Avionics at Rochester, remembers a presentation to senior Elliott-Automation staff at 29 Portland Place on 4 September 1967. In their presentation, Leon Bagrit (E-A) and Lord Nelson (EE) remarked that the merger of their companies had 'staved off a dreaded takeover of both companies by GEC!' [19]. This anecdote is echoed in [12].

13.6.2 *Government Encouragement for Rationalisation*

The Labour government of Harold Wilson, first elected with a slim overall majority in October 1964 but re-elected with a substantial majority in March 1966, set itself the goal of rationalising the UK's manufacturing industries. Wilson promptly established a Ministry of Technology in November 1964 and, about a year later, the Industrial Reorganisation Corporation (IRC). The IRC's purpose was to 'promote industrial efficiency and profitability and assist the economy' [1]. This was the period of the so-called *white heat of technology*, during which the UK's computer industry was the government's prime target for remedial action to save it from being engulfed by the American giants – particularly IBM. Deciding on the practical nature of 'remedial action' proved to be less than straightforward for the government.

The relative fortunes of some of the main players in the government's plans were changing. Some idea of these movements may be gained from examining the amount of issued capital, year-on-year, in the run-up to the creation of a single UK mainframe manufacturer. The summary given in Table 13.12 for five companies hints at, amongst other things: the comparatively rapid growth of GEC after Arnold Weinstock gained control; the steady rise in the growth of English Electric, ICT and Elliott-Automation; and the relatively static state of Ferranti's capitalisation.

GEC, however, was at that time not seriously interested in the computer market. Of the other companies in Table 13.12, more details are available in [1, 9] and in

Table 13.12 Issued capital, in £ millions, of five of the several companies involved in the rationalisation of the UK's computing industry

Company	1955	1960	1965
BTM/ICT	2.800	10.400	18.269
Elliott-Automation	0.612	6.574	17.832
English Electric	13.252	32.775	40.131
Ferranti	3.000	4.500	4.500
GEC	19.315	23.600	61.260

Table 13.13 The profit and staffing figures for Elliott-Automation, Ferranti and ICT over the period 1960–1967

	E-A profits (£)	E-A employees	Ferranti profits (£)	Ferranti employees	ICT profits (£)	ICT employees
1960	1,777	10,600	4,015	13,649	2,452	19,616
1961	2,206	12,900	3,401	15,917	2,518	21,823
1962	2,862	15,900	2,171	18,809	2,115	24,285
1963	3,238	17,300	1,671	20,849	1,437	21,129
1964	4,129	22,400	1,824	18,865	2,593	20,359
1965	2,391	23,500	2,751	19,272	−509	22,883
1966	2,806	23,100	2,848	19,097	2,331	23,708
1967	?	?	3,258	19,565	3,029	24,765

the Elliott-Automation Annual Reports. From these three sources, the data in Table 13.13 can be derived.

The entries under 'profit' in Table 13.13 are broadly compatible between companies though, for completeness, the definitions used in [1, 9] and in the relevant E-A Annual Reports are now quoted as follows: for ICT: *pre-tax profits*; for Ferranti: *gross profit after deduction of depreciation, directors' fees, auditors' fees and interest charges*; for Elliott-Automation: *profit before taxation but after depreciation and interest charges have been subtracted.*

Drawing further on [1], we an see that by 1965 ICT was the UK's largest seller of computers and in that year ICT was suffering a financial crisis due to at least two internal factors: the continuing decline of the electromechanical punched-card machine business and the strains of introducing ICT's new 1900 range of computers. In 1965 the Ministry of Technology was in favour of English Electric taking control of ICT, but this idea was rejected by both companies. By the following year, the position had changed: ICT's success with its 1900 series computers and English Electric's difficulties with its System 4 computers meant that ICT was emerging as the stronger of these two computer manufacturers. In 1966 the IRC then began to favour a merger between ICT and Elliott-Automation because (a) the incompatibility between the 1900 series and the System 4 computers tended to eliminate English Electric as a partner for ICT and (b) there were signs that Elliott-Automation was running into financial difficulties and could benefit from an association with a larger partner.

Elliott-Automation, however, at first favoured a liaison with a large electrical engineering company. Early in 1967, Elliott-Automation began exploratory negotiations with GEC. When these came to nought, attention was turned to English Electric – with the results described above in Sect. 13.6.1. The government's Industrial Reorganisation Corporation facilitated this merger to the tune of £15 million, via the following mechanism. In 1967 English Electric created £15 million of *Subordinated Unsecured Loan Stock*, issued to the government's Industrial Reorganisation Corporation (IRC). Under the terms of the Agreement between IRC and English Electric, the £15 million Stock was free of interest up to 31st August 1969, with interest thereafter at 8% per annum. The Stock was finally to be repaid not later than 31st August 1975. It was a condition of the loan that the £15 million be applied 'only towards assisting the development of the electronic activities of English Electric and Elliott-Automation'.

13.7   The GEC Takeover and the Formation of ICL

At the same time as the merger between English Electric and Elliott-Automation was going ahead, a joint ICT-English Electric Technical Working Group met in great secrecy [1] in the Hotel Cavendish, London, from 3 to 5 July 1967 to consider merging the mainframe computer interests of the two companies. The Working Group's motivation was both technical and financial: each company needed to plan its next range of computers for the 1970s, for which considerable investment was going to be necessary; both companies were in danger of losing market share to competition from large American companies such as IBM. On the financial side, it had become clear that government aid would be necessary to support future R&D. On the technical side, it was far from clear whether a new range could be designed that would allow existing customers to migrate from current 1900 and System 4 machines. The Working Group's conclusions were cautiously optimistic: 'We are agreed that there is no *prima facie* reason why it should not be possible to plan a range of systems meeting the basic requirements of competitiveness and of acceptable compatibility with the current ranges of both companies' [1].

The secret computer talks between ICT and English Electric Computers did not at first impinge upon life at Borehamwood or the general management of English Electric Computers. However, at the end of August 1967 ICT received an informal takeover bid from the Plessey Company and, 2 weeks later, another bid from EMI. This caused much alarm at ICT. The Ministry of Technology thereupon urged ICT and English Electric to merge their data processing endeavours in the national interest and offered a government grant to help the process along. The pressure for action increased towards the end of 1967, as the UK's economic climate worsened, the pound was devalued, cuts were made in public expenditure and English Electric's problems with the System 4 deepened. On 21 March 1968, the Minister of Technology presented to the House of Commons plans for a new company, International Computers (Holdings) Ltd., whose shareholders were to be as follows ([1] quoting the ICL Annual Report for 1968):

ICT	53.5%
English Electric	18.0%
Plessey	18.0%
Ministry of Technology	10.5%

Interestingly, the ICT Press Release of 10 August 1968, entitled *ICL Profile* [20], chose to give a different analysis of the ICL shareholders:

English Electric	18%
Plessey	18%
Ministry of Technology	10.5%
Vickers	12.6%
Ferranti	5.7%
22,000 other small shareholders	35.2%

Plessey obtained its 18% shareholding in exchange for a cash injection of £18 million; English Electric obtained its 18% shareholding in exchange for its main-frame computer assets and manufacturing facilities, valued at £17 million. The result was that all System 4 activity was transferred to the new company ICL, leaving behind the process control and military computer activities.

ICL was formally registered as a company on 9 July 1968, to become the UK's principle manufacturer of general-purpose computers covering data processing applications in science, engineering, business and commerce. Shortly afterwards, the mainframe computer business of English Electric Computers Limited was formally merged with that of International Computers Limited (ICL). This brought the System 4 and the Elliott 4100 series computers into the ICL stables. Several tens of ex-Elliott computer engineers were transferred to ICL (see also Chap. 14).

The remaining process control and military computer activities of English Electric and Elliott-Automation were to be carried on by a company called Marconi-Elliott Computer Systems Ltd. (MECS). This included the remaining engineers at Borehamwood (but not Rochester) working on the 900 series comput-ers, a small team developing process control computers (KDF7, KDN2) at the English Electric factory at Kidsgrove, Staffordshire and the Marconi team develop-ing the Myriad computer at Chelmsford. Little attempt was made to integrate Borehamwood computer activity with that at Kidsgrove or Chelmsford.

Meanwhile, the main English Electric company had been approached by GEC. The frenzied activity between the emissaries of English Electric and GEC during late August and early September 1968 is chronicled by two leading business jour-nalists who conducted interviews with the leading players at the time [12]. On 6 September 1968, the takeover of English Electric by GEC was agreed. Perhaps 'agreed' is not the most appropriate word. Two senior English Electric executives, William (later Sir William) Barlow and Robin Inskip the second Viscount Caldecote, disagreed so strongly with this move that they resigned from English Electric after many years service.

Although GEC had a modest interest in computers in its Telephone Exchange business at Coventry, no attempt was made to merge this with the ex-Elliott team at Borehamwood. The many-sided fortunes (eventually misfortunes) of Borehamwood in the 1970s and beyond are touched on in Chap. 14. On the positive side, the Elliott 900 series computers, and their successors, continued to be developed at Rochester for aerospace applications as described in Chap. 12, where they made a name for themselves and helped GEC/Marconi/BAE Systems become world leaders in avion-ics. Other Elliott-Automation activities such as traffic control, radar and instrumen-tation, were added to, or in some cases absorbed into, the expanding GEC empire.

It would be true to say that the acquisition of English Electric by GEC, and the consequential arrival of Arnold Weinstock's management culture, caused a distinct downturn of morale amongst the Elliott staff. Andrew St Johnston, who had been Elliott's Computer Division Manager since 1953, left Borehamwood in 1968 to join Vaughan Programming Services (later Vaughan Systems), latterly as Managing

Director. Vaughan Systems had been set up in 1959 – arguably Britain's first software house – by Dina Vaughan who had become the second Mrs St Johnston in the summer of 1958 [21]. John Bunt, who had become Technical Director of Marconi-Elliott Computer Systems Ltd., took early retirement in 1972 as recalled in Chap. 14. Meanwhile, ICL showed little interest in maintaining non-ICT computers. Largely because of this, three ex-Elliott-Automation engineers left to start an independent company Systems Reliability Ltd. (SRL) in 1968, specialising in the maintenance of Elliott 800, 900 and 4100 series computers. They were soon joined by other ex-Elliott-Automation engineers, as described in Chap. 14.

Ninian Eadie, who started with Leo Computers and went on to become a Board member of ICL before retiring from ICL in 1997, has added the following retrospective comment [22]. 'I had a lot of experience of mergers and acquisitions during my time with ICL, but of all those I encountered the Elliott merger was certainly handled the worst.... When English Electric bought Elliott in 1967 David Caminer, who was then Sales Director of English Electric LEO Marconi Computers, seems to have decided from the outset that Elliott had nothing to offer. No attempt was made to sell the hardware, and he showed little respect for the staff. I think everything had melted away within the year. I am happy to say that I had no hand in this.'

Within the GEC empire Marconi Elliott Computer Systems continued its activity, being re-named GEC Computers Ltd. in 1971. The company developed the GEC 2050 computer (intended to replace the Elliott 905) in 1970 and the GEC 4080 (intended to replace the Elliott 4130) in 1973. The story of the post-1970 GEC computers ended in 1993 with the GEC4310, the last of the 4000 series machines, as mentioned in Chap. 14.

As for ICL, the company was initially saddled with three incompatible ranges of computers: the ex-ICT1900 series, the ex-English Electric System 4 and the ex-Elliott 4100 series. ICL judged the 4100 series to be of modest potential, mainly of interest to scientific users and universities. Enhancements were curtailed and manufacture of the 4100 series was discontinued in 1970. As for the 1900 and System 4 ranges, in the context of the company mergers it was politically imperative to keep both systems going. At the time of ICL's birth in 1968, several hundred 1900 series machines had been installed, compared with only a handful of System 4 machines [1]. Furthermore, it became apparent that there were significant production problems with the System 4. Nevertheless, ICL continued to market both existing ranges whilst beginning to plan ahead for a new range.

IBM's announcement of its own new range, the System/370, in June 1970, and an economic crisis that adversely affected computer sales in 1971–72, added complications to ICL's marketing strategy. Nevertheless, when ICL announced its new range, the 2900 series, in October 1974 customer confidence in ICL was high.

The subsequent history of ICL is recounted in [1] and elsewhere. Briefly, by the end of 1976 ICL's fortunes were looking very promising but by 1980 competitive pressure from IBM and the Japanese plug-compatible mainframe manufacturers had caused ICL to look very carefully at its costs. Profits were falling. Early in 1981 ICL had exploratory talks with several American computer companies, including Univac, but these got nowhere. ICL at that time lacked the fully fledged in-house semiconductor technology that would have given it access to low-price chips. Therefore, in October 1981 ICL reached an agreement with Fujitsu, whereby the Japanese company provided ICL with semiconductor chips and design tools to complement ICL's in-house CAD facilities. By 1983 ICL's profits were again healthy.

ICL's fortunes over the next 15 years were mixed. A link-up with STC in the mid-1980s turned out not to have been such a good thing. ICL proved to be the stronger partner and the STC culture faded. In 1989, ICL acquired Regnecentralen of Denmark, known for its front-end communications handling equipment. In 1991 ICL acquired Nokia Data, thus bringing in a PC manufacturing capability and a range of desktop software products. Meanwhile, ICL had become increasingly reliant upon Fujitsu [23]. Eventually, Fujitsu acquired ICL and in June 2001 Fujitsu decided to dispense with the name ICL. At that time, ICL employed 19,200 people in Europe, the Middle East and Africa, over 10,000 of whom were in the UK. A press announcement describing the company's name-change stated that a modest operating profit had been recorded lately but, year-on-year, the company was still trading at a loss. The loss for the last year was put at £22.6 million, compared with a loss of £48.2 million in the previous year. In 2002 the residue of the ICL company was rebranded as Fujitsu's European Services arm. By 2006 the Fujitsu Group had become 'a leading provider of customer-focused IT and communications solutions for the global marketplace'. As their website said in 2009 [24]: 'Pacesetting device technologies, highly reliable computing and communications products, and a worldwide corps of systems and services experts uniquely position Fujitsu to deliver comprehensive solutions that open up infinite possibilities for its customers' success.' So there! The headquarters is in Tokyo.

Although we have by now indicated the eventual demise not only of Elliott-Automation but also of GEC and ICL as distinct trading entities, it would be wrong to let the story of Borehamwood simply evaporate in the fog of financial machinations. In the next chapter we tell the story of the somewhat varied fortunes of ex-Elliott personnel and GEC Computers at Borehamwood in the 1970s and 1980s, leading to the final closure at the turn of the century of the whole Borehamwood site as a high-tech location.

References

1. Campbell-Kelly M (1989) ICL: a business and technical history. Oxford University Press, Oxford. ISBN: 0-19-853918-5
2. Gerry Mills (2009) E-mails to Simon Lavington, Sept 2008 to Jan 2009
3. Elliott-Automation factories (1964) 32-page company booklet of photographs and statistics, produced in 1964
4. Commander Henry Pasley-Tyler CBE, un-dated audio-recording of an interview with Laurence Clarke. It may be inferred from letters to Laurence that this interview took place some time between 1 Feb 1995 and 24 May 1995, at which time he was 84 years old. Pasley-Tyler died in Dec 1995
5. Anon (1965) Mini Firebrigade and programming languages. 12-page typed report published by Elliott Airspace Control Division. Undated, but the contents strongly suggest 1965

6. Moonman E (ed) (1971) British computers and industrial innovation: the implications of the Parliamentary Select Committee. Allen and Unwin. Eric Moonman MP was Chairman of the Parliamentary Labour Party's Committee on Science and Technology. His book was subtitled: 'The considered and expanded majority report of Subcommittee D of the Parliamentary Select Committee on Science and Technology'

7. Anon (1967) Elliott automation: computers and orders, 1947–1966. Brochure published in early 1967 by the Directorate of Information Services, Elliott-Automation Ltd., 21 Portland Place, London W1

8. Swan B (1975) A history of the Ferranti computer department. 98-page typed manuscript, produced in 1975 and circulated privately. Catalogue item NAHC/FER/C30 in the National Archive for the History of Computing. www.chstm.manchester.ac.uk/research/nahc/

9. Wilson JF (2001) Ferranti: a history. Building a family business, 1882–1975. Carnegie Publishing Ltd., Lancaster. ISBN: 1-85936-080-7. Volume 2: from family firm to multinational company, 1975–1987, published in 2007 by Crucible Books, Lancaster. ISBN: 978-1-905472-01-7

10. Stock Exchange Year Book, published annually by the London Stock Exchange

11. For a brief history of EMI, see: http://en.wikipedia.org/wiki/EMI

12. Jones R, Marriott O (1970) Anatomy of a merger: a history of GEC, AEI and English Electric. Jonathan Cape, London. ISBN: 0-224-61872-5. For a more recent overview of GEC, see: http://en.wikipedia.org/wiki/The_General_Electric_Company

13. Lord Weinstock's obituary appeared in the Guardian newspaper on Wednesday 24 July 2002. http://www.guardian.co.uk/news/2002/jul/24/guardianobituaries.alexbrummer

14. Thurston C (2010) Telephone conversation with Simon Lavington on 11 Jan 2010 when discussing GEC Computers Ltd. in the 1970s and 1980s

15. SLH Clarke (2009) E-mail to Simon Lavington dated 14 Oct 2009

16. English Electric House (1961) A 47 page pamphlet published by the English Electric Co. Ltd. ISBN: 016972

17. War diary of the English Electric Co. Ltd., March 1938 to August 1945. Published by the English Electric Co. Ltd, UK. ISBN: 027504

18. Leon Bagrit (1967) Two-page letter dated 17 July 1967 'to the members of Elliott-Automation Limited' and included in a document sent to shareholders and entitled: Offers by Lazard Brothers & Co. Ltd. on behalf of The English Electric Company Ltd. to acquire all the Preference and Ordinary shares of Elliott-Automation Ltd

19. RW (Ron) Howard (2006) E-mail to Simon Lavington, 14 Nov 2006

20. Papers of Birkett DA, the ICT Company Information Officer, filed as document COM/1993/1433 at the National Museum of Science and Industry, South Kensington, London

21. Lavington S (2009) An appreciation of Dina St Johnston, 1930–2007, founder of the UK's first Software House. Comput J 52(3):378–387

22. Nirian Eadie (2007) E-mail to Simon Lavington dated 10 July 2007

23. The Wikipedia entry for ICL gives a good overview of the company's history, especially the latter period until its demise. http://en.wikipedia.org/wiki/International_Computers_Limited#Fujitsu

24. For an overview of the current operations of the Fujitsu Group, see: http://www.fujitsu.com/global/

Chapter 14
The End of the Line

14.1 All Change at Borehamwood

In the words of the hardware engineer Laurie Bental, who worked there from 1957 to 1994, 'The demise of computing activities at Borehamwood was a long and painful process, spanning the years 1968 to 1988' [1]. Although 1968 marked the end of Elliott-Automation Computers Ltd., the 'long and painful process' had actually begun 2 or 3 years earlier in the opinion of some market-oriented staff.

Notwithstanding the undoubted success of Elliott computers in areas such as industrial process control and military applications, Elliott's and NCR's disappointing level of sales to the commercial data processing sector was becoming all too apparent. Paul King, the Sales Manager, recalls [2] that: 'By 1965 it was becoming clear to me that Elliott-Automation did not have the financial strength to invest in computing on the scale which was necessary to compete with the larger players especially IBM, DEC, Hewlett Packard. So in 1966 I left to become Management Services Manager of the Steel Company of Wales, thus drawing to a close the most exciting and enjoyable phase of my career'.

A number of experienced senior staff had also decided to leave Elliott-Automation. For example, Tony Hoare, who had joined in 1960, left Borehamwood in 1965; Henry Orde, who had joined in about 1953, left in about 1967 or earlier; Ed Hersom, who joined in 1947, left in 1967; Andrew St Johnston, who joined in 1949, left in March 1968; Roger Cook, who joined in 1954, left in 1968.

There was another factor at work that might have tended to dilute senior managerial skills. In the mid-1960s Leon Bagrit had, in the opinion of Andrew St Johnston, 'extended himself too much', creating what Andrew believed were too many small Divisions within the Elliott-Automation group. This caused several accelerated promotions to managerial positions, a process that was said by Lawrence Ross to 'free up innovation and enterprise'. Andrew St Johnston, however, felt a little apprehensive at the influx of some relatively inexperienced managers. Andrew's second wife, Dina (neé Vaughan), has said [3] that the mid-1960s marked the point where Andrew first became critical of Leon Bagrit's managerial style.

In what proved to be a turbulent period for Elliott-Automation, middle-management was usually unaware of the pressures placed upon Leon Bagrit. John Bunt, writing

S. Lavington, *Moving Targets*, History of Computing,
DOI 10.1007/978-1-84882-933-6_14, © Springer-Verlag London Limited 2011

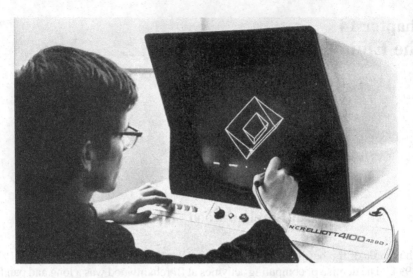

Fig. 14.1 In 1968 the commercial data-processing ('mainframe') computer interests of Elliott-Automation were taken over by ICL, who saw little value in promoting anything but the 4100 series computers and its peripherals – such as the 4280 Graphical Display Unit shown in the photo. GEC took over Borehamwood and all the 900 series small machine applications in areas such as defence and industrial process control

retrospectively in 2002 [4], remembers the events of 1967 thus: 'The first knowledge I had that Elliott-Automation was to be merged with another company came about when I was told, as Manager of Mobile Computing Division, to show Michael Clarke of the Plessey Company over my Division [in 1967]. He was Deputy Managing Director of the Plessey Company and younger brother of John Clarke, the Managing Director. The next thing that we knew was that the company was to be acquired by the English Electric Co. It was later said that English Electric was the choice of the E-A Board, because they felt that E-A would be better off with the management style of English Electric rather than that of the Plessey Company'. Indeed, Lord Nelson, Chairman of English Electric, got on well on a personal level with Leon Bagrit [5].

Notwithstanding these omens, the merger of Elliott-Automation and English Electric in August 1967 had at first brought little perceptible change to Borehamwood. English Electric was presented with 'a glorious opportunity for rationalisation … yet the greater part of Elliotts was left to run as before under the executive direction of its chairman, Sir Leon Bagrit, and only two small parts moved to English Electric product groupings' [6]. In particular, English Electric, as the dominant partner, appears not to have managed the absorption of Elliott-Automation's computer activities in a very creative manner. It will be remembered from Chap. 13 that English Electric Leo Marconi (EELM) had started delivery of their System 4 range in the early summer of 1967 and that the development, production and installation of System 4 computers was not without its difficulties.

Wilf Scott of English Electric was destined to become Manager of the merged EELM and Elliott-Automation Computing groups, but he died almost immediately after the merger, in the summer of 1967. Many believed that Andrew St Johnston should then have got the job, but instead an English Electric man with a power engineering background was given the post. At a level above this, Robert Telford, the Managing Director of Marconi, was given the task of sorting out strategy. Laurence Clarke of Elliott-Automation became, in Laurence's words, 'Bob Telford's bag man' [3]. Andrew St Johnston, as has been noted earlier, left Borehamwood in March 1968 to join Vaughan Programming Services. In about 1969/70 Laurence Clarke became Technical Director of GEC-Elliott-Automation, which took in the GEC, AEI, English Electric and Elliott interests in the field. In 1974 he became Technical Director of GEC Marconi, with responsibilities in Computing and Automation.

Notwithstanding the pressures that the System 4 developments undoubtedly exerted upon English Electric, Ninian Eadie has recalled the merger with Elliott-Automation with some misgivings (see Chap. 13). Ninian Eadie had joined Leo Computers as a graduate and remained with the company when it became a part of ICL. Doug Comish, a colleague of Ninian Eadie, agrees with Ninian but goes on to say [7]: 'There were important differences [between EELM and Elliotts] that limited the synergy possible from the merger and as a result only limited effort was expended on it. First of all, Elliott's main strengths were in process control and automation and these did not fit easily into the English Electric strategy. And secondly, on the EDP side, Elliott's had worked very closely with NCR with whom I think they had a Marketing agreement [see Chap. 9]. There was probably a shortage of effort to devote sufficient time to do a thorough evaluation of possibilities. For sure there were some very talented technical staff of all types at Elliotts and some smart salesmen too. But most of these people drifted away and English Electric Computers did not take maximum advantage of their talents'.

The 'drifting away' is vividly recalled by John Sinclair [8]. John Sinclair started with Elliott-Automation in August 1967, having been interviewed by Eric Tommey, who was the service manager at the Perry Barr office in Birmingham. John says: 'My first period (of 16 weeks) was at the maintenance engineers' training school at Borehamwood to learn about the 803. The chap in charge of the school was Stuart Ellis. In June 1968 I started working for English Electric, the take-over becoming effective at this time as far as I was concerned'. However, John Sinclair was still operating under his Elliott-Automation Computer Division Conditions of Service when, in the autumn of 1968, he found himself transferred to ICL. This caused anomalies. For example, Sinclair's line manager at ICL was only allocated a Morris 1000 Traveller car, whilst Sinclair was allowed the superior Vauxhall Viva. This illustrates the administrative confusion that followed the events of 1967/68, when first EE and then ICL and then GEC came on the scene.

Sinclair says that ICL was not interested in maintaining non-ICT computers when he, along with what Roger Cook remembers as being 'about 100 Borehamwood computer people', was transferred to ICL. Largely because of this lack of interest, three ex-Elliott-Automation engineers (Eric Tommey, Derrick Haden and Harold Allsop) founded Systems Reliability Ltd. (SRL) at Luton in 1968. They were soon joined by between 20 and 40 ex-Elliott-Automation engineers, including Sinclair and, in due course, Stuart Ellis. SRL became the first *third party maintenance company* in the UK, principally to maintain the old Elliott machines. SRL not only maintained Elliott computers: in due course SRL began to offer its own hardware enhancements for these machines. An example was the replacement of the core store on Elliott 4120 and 4130 computers by a semiconductor store that offered a speed improvement of about six times whilst being physically smaller. SRL also attempted to offer maintenance on non-Elliott ICL computers but fell foul of ICL's management on this issue. In 1984, by which time the old Elliott computers were being superseded, SRL became a plc and started developing new products of its own in the area of computer-based telephone management systems. In 1991 Sinclair was made redundant. In 1993 SRL collapsed. At its height, SRL was an organisation of approximately 300 employees, still based at Luton.

David Warman, who joined Borehamwood in 1967 and became a 4100 Series commissioning engineer, transferred to ICL Putney in 1968. As he remembers [9], 'It was very clear, at least to those of us in the little corner they gave us for 4100 commissioning in Putney, that the machines were not long for this world by the end of 1968. It felt that we were pretty much forgotten already. We were surrounded by dusty relics of other inductees – such as the slowly decaying RCA Spectra system at one end of our section. Leaving there was pretty easy by then, though I wish I had known about SRL at the time.' David Warman left ICL in January 1969.

Back in July 1968, when ICL was formally registered as the company to take on the mainstream computing interests of ICT and the English Electric/Leo/Marconi/Elliott-Automation amalgam (see Chap. 13), ICT was clearly in the driving seat. The formation of ICL was announced with a six-page Press Release by the ICT Company Information Officer, Dennis Birkett, dated 10th August 1968. This document [10], entitled *ICL Profile*, naturally devotes a great deal of space to the 1900 range and the System 4 range of computers. In the entire six-page document, there are only two small sections where anything connected with Elliott/Borehamwood is mentioned – and actually the name Elliott is not explicitly used at all. The only Borehamwood product to be mentioned is described thus: 'The ICL 4100 Series was also announced in 1965. There are two models in the range: the 4120 and the 4130. They have been most successful in universities, research establishments and for industrial automation schemes. The graphical display system associated with 4100 central processors is a recognised leader in computer design technology'. Towards the end of the Press Release, there is a list headed *Production Centres*, which in its entirety is as follows:

ICL 1900	Letchworth, Croydon, West Gorton, Castlereagh
ICL System 4	Kidsgrove, Winsford, Cowdenbeath
ICL 4100	Cowdenbeath, Borehamwood
Magnetic Recording	Data Recording Instrument Company, Staines

It is not difficult to imagine the downturn of morale in some sections of Borehamwood in August 1968.

Not long after the GEC takeover, Sir Leon Bagrit was retired by GEC in 1973 after serving on the board of English Electric and as chairman of GEC-Elliott-Automation Ltd.

Dr. L.L. Ross and Commander Henry Pasley-Tyler 'retired' even quicker than Bagrit, having fulfilled no executive positions within the GEC empire. Of the Elliott-Automation *Old Guard*, only Edgar Herzfeld – younger than Bagrit by 7 years – survived to play an active role. Herzfeld became Director of Contracts and an Associate Director of GEC, retiring in the early 1980s. He was replaced as GEC Director of Contracts by Norman Scott, who had been the Contracts Director of GEC-Elliott-Automation under Joe Wiltshire.

The year 1973 marks the effective end of Sir Leon Bagrit's career as a business-man, but we cannot let him slip out of the wider Elliott story without describing more about his public life as a man of some eminence. This is best postponed until Sect. 14.8. We shall pick up the threads of GEC Computers, both at Borehamwood and at Rochester, in Sect. 14.3. First, however, it is helpful to review some of the changes that were taking place in the wider world of Information Technology whilst Elliott-Automation was in the process of being dispersed, dissolved and re-grouped.

14.2   Meanwhile, in the Wider World of Information Technology

The 15-year period 1965–1980 saw the transition from mainframe to minicomputer and then the start of the microcomputer era. Of course, it was not only the physical size that was changing. The computer as a concept, with all its potential advantages and limita-tions, was becoming better understood by a broader range of companies and organisa-tions, leading to an increase in the sales of computers of all types, but especially in the rapidly expanding area of commercial business data processing.

Advances in technology, particularly in semiconductor devices and magnetic surface recording, led to better reliability and to price/performance improvements in processor speed and memory capacity. The quality and scope of systems software and applications programs became more relevant to an organisation's smooth run-ning than the raw speed or capacity of the underlying hardware – though, of course, the capabilities of hardware and software were still inextricably linked as far as the end-user was concerned. Fortunately, the 'national pool' of programmers, able to write software of reasonable quality, increased rapidly between 1965 and 1980.

Looking back, all of the above might seem obvious. And yet, it is as well to remind ourselves that computing in the 1970s was still, by today's standards, primi-tive. The Internet had not arrived. Access via keyboard, mouse and icon was unknown. Computers were still the domain of the expert – and these 'experts' were having to learn fast.

Below we give a few illustrative examples of how the Information Age was still at a primitive state of development but growing rapidly. These examples are taken largely from the historical review given in [11]. The UK, not surprisingly, lagged behind the USA in the uptake of Information Technology and so the dates which follow, being specific to the UK, were in general a couple of years later than equiva-lent events on the other side of the Atlantic.

Fig. 14.2 This photo of the computer room at Chelsea College of Advanced Technology in the early 1970s indicates that, by then, equipment from a variety of manufacturers was beginning to coexist side-by-side – though not necessarily directly connected. In the background against the wall are the darker cabinets of a Digital Equipment Corporation's PDP 11 system. The operator in the foreground stands at some Elliott 4130 equipment whilst behind her are units of an Elliott 900 system. Two Calcomp (?) graph plotters (one a drum type, the other a flat bed) are to be seen to the right foreground

14.2.1 Formal and Professional Qualifications

In 1957 the British Computer Society (BCS) was founded with about 600 members. A BCS report was drawn up which recommended a scheme of professional qualifications and examinations in computing. This recommendation was formally ratified in March 1968, at which time the BCS membership was 18,000 – said at the time to be 'well short of the total IT working population'. In October 1965, Manchester University accepted its first intake (of 26 students) to the UK's first university undergraduate course in Computer Science. The BCS devised its own syllabus and examination system at around the same time. In 1983 the BCS started to accredit University and College courses in Computer Science.

14.2.2 Computing and Journalism

In 1966 the newspaper Computer Weekly was launched. By the end of the year, sales were running at 15,000 per week. Ten years later, sales had risen to 80,000. The first issue of the magazine Computing appeared in January 1973. In America,

Byte magazine and Creative Computing were launched in 1975 for the home computing market. The UK equivalents, Personal Computer World and Practical Computing, came out in 1978.

14.2.3 The BBC's Computer Literacy Project

This project was started in 1978, at a time when popular computing 'was in the hands of enthusiasts', but with some public awareness that interesting things were happening. In December 1980 the specification of the BBC microcomputer was put out to tender. In February 1981 Acorn was chosen as the supplier. 1982 was declared 'Information Technology Year' in the UK. By the spring of 1984, 250,000 BBC Micros had been sold, finding their way into schools and homes throughout the country.

14.2.4 Minicomputers and Microprocessors

The American company Digital Equipment Corporation (DEC) produced its PDP8 minicomputer in 1965. Whilst comparatively modest in computing power – it had an 8-bit word – the PDP8 was readily transportable: it was the size of a chest of drawers and could fit onto a table-top. The PDP8 was the first minicomputer to achieve substantial sales worldwide, thereby becoming the standard by which all other early minicomputers were judged. The British-designed Modular One, an innovative 16-bit minicomputer, was first delivered in 1968. In 1971 the American company Intel produced the 4004 microprocessor chip, a 4-bit building block from which commodity microcomputers could be constructed by others. The first IBM Personal Computer (PC) was launched in America in August 1981. By November 1989, IBM's Personal Computer revenues had overtaken the company's mainframe revenues.

14.2.5 Data Transmission and Wide-Area Networks

In 1959 it was reported [12] that 'for some time now the Post Office has been receiving enquiries about line transmission facilities available for use with automatic data processing machinery'. A booklet was issued by the Post Office, the government monopoly that was the precursor of British Telecom (BT), with the title Facilities for DataTransmission. By the early 1960s a small number of telephone line data-links had been set up on an ad hoc basis between individual computer sites that wished to exchange digital data. Then in 1965/66 Donald Davies at the National Physical Laboratories (NPL) conceived the idea of packet switching, building a prototype system at NPL about 5 years later [13]. The UK government and the Post Office were unwilling to get involved at a national level and so the prototype system, which might have led to the development of a wide area network within the UK, remained local to NPL. Meanwhile, by mid-1969 in America the first four nodes of *Arpanet* had been established using packet switching. By 1971 *Arpanet* had become a robust and flexible system for interconnecting computers over long distances at 56 kb/s, with about 20 nodes active. In 1971 the European Informatics Network (EIN) was proposed. However, it was not until about 1976/77 that it became operational. Email facilities were introduced into the UK from about 1981 but did not reach ordinary computer users for several years. The Internet and World Wide Web were still to come.

In the light of hindsight, events such as those described above heralded the *democratisation* of computers. It became possible for greater numbers of people, at ever humbler positions in the work-place hierarchy, to take the initiative in acquiring – and benefiting from – computing resources. Computing power began to be distributed in smaller physical units, each unit requiring less and less in the way of infrastructure such as air conditioning, on-site maintenance engineers, etc. After the formation of ICL as the major UK computer manufacturer in 1968, the remaining smaller computer manufacturers such as Ferranti and GEC (which included relevant parts of Elliott-Automation, English Electric and Marconi) were for all practical purposes excluded from the business data processing area. However, there remained plenty of opportunities for expanding into other markets where *democratisation* was having its effect. Laboratory and educational systems, industrial process control, traffic control and telecommunications are examples of areas where the demand for smaller systems grew dramatically during the 1970s. These areas, and the ever-present needs of the military, should have provided Borehamwood with enough revenue to flourish. Would GEC's re-structured computing enterprise at Borehamwood rise to the challenge?

14.3   Sorting Out the Pieces

At its zenith in the mid-1960s, the Elliott-Automation group employed about 23,400 people and comprised some 50 factories, Service Centres and Branch Offices in the UK, and a further 40 factories and places of business in Europe, Australia and South Africa (For the full list of facilities, refer to Appendix 11). In 1967, just after the merger with English Electric, much of the Elliott-Automation empire remained intact.

In October 1967 the agreement between Elliott-Automation and NCR ended. In the summer of 1968 ICL was created, taking over the business data processing (EDP) activities of the merged English Electric and Elliott-Automation companies. The removal by ICL of the EDP interests left behind the following computer-related components:

- In the Elliott-Automation sphere: most of the computing activities at Borehamwood, including the manufacturing capability for 800-series and 900-series computers

Fig. 14.3 An aerial view of Elliott-Automation's former Borehamwood site from the north, after ownership had passed to GEC. The original two-storey brick-fronted offices of Elliott's Laboratory are to be seen at the *right-centre* in the photo. This view dates from 2002, by which time the area outlined in light grey had passed to a property-management company who were advertising the site as comprising '265,000 sq. ft. of office space available for hire'. Other adjacent ex-Elliott buildings to the *top* of the photo on Warwick Road were not included in this advertisement

Fig. 14.4 John Bunt, who joined Borehamwood in 1949, became Technical Director of Marconi-Elliott Computer Systems Ltd in 1969. The company's name was changed to GEC Computers Ltd in 1971 and within a couple of years John Bunt had resigned. The Computer Research Laboratory at Borehamwood had begun the design of a new range of small computers, which eventually became the GEC 2050, GEC 4080 and related machines. Sales of the GEC 2000 series and 4000 series computers spanned the period from about 1971 to the end of the 1990s

and the Computer Research Laboratory; the Mobile Computer Division at Frimley; the airborne computing activities at Rochester; various process-control and automation activities distributed between Borehamwood, Lewisham, etc.; the microelectronics facility at Glenrothes

- In the English Electric sphere: a small group at Kidsgrove working on industrial process control computers (particularly KDN7)
- In the Marconi sphere: the Computer Division and the Automation Division at Chelmsford and associated microelectronics facilities

The Marconi sites in the neighbourhood of Chelmsford and the principal Elliott-Automation sites at Rochester, Borehamwood and related properties and Lewisham were independently pursuing many projects that contained significant elements of digital electronics – especially in the fields of avionics, radar and industrial process control. Defence contracts were recovering after the setback of the TSR 2 cancellation of May 1965. At some point in 1968 the Computer Research Laboratory at Borehamwood was, for managerial purposes, attached to E-A Space & Weapons (at Frimley). The Research Laboratory supported the real-time computer interests of Space & Weapons, Flight Automation and Process Automation. In 1969 Marconi-Elliott Avionics Systems Ltd. was established at Rochester and flourished in a manner that was, in due course, to impact upon the fortunes of the computing activity at Borehamwood, as discussed in Sect. 14.6 below.

When GEC took over in the autumn of 1968, most of the former Elliott-Automation factories became part of a new holding company called GEC-Elliott-Automation, which was a wholly-owned subsidiary of English Electric of which, in turn, the ultimate holding company was GEC.

Of course, the formal winding-up of the Elliott-Automation company could not take place overnight. For instance, there were Debentures with fixed maturity dates which meant that a legal entity had to be maintained until they expired. Another example of a legal difficulty is the matter of Elliott's Cassegrain radar aerial patent-infringement activity, which had been pursued through the US Department of Justice since the mid-1960s (see Appendix 9). The process was long and tedious because of the US defence implications. By 1972, a substantial case against American companies had been drawn up and because Edgar Herzfeld needed to close Elliott-Automation's books to complete the takeover by GEC, a date was set for a court hearing in America. At the last moment, the Justice Department agreed a settlement and Judgment was given in Elliott-Automation's favour on 28th July 1972, for the sum of $1,150,000. As far as can be determined, the summer of 1972 marks the formal demise of Elliott-Automation as an active entity – though *Elliott Brother (London) Ltd.* continued as a registered trading name of GEC until 1988.

No copies of any Elliott-Automation Annual Reports or Accounts seem to have survived for the financial years 1967 or 1968. The profits of the new GEC-Elliott-Automation group are not directly comparable with any entity prior to 1969 because some unrelated GEC business activities had been transferred into GEC-EA

Table 14.1 Financial summary for GEC-Elliott-Automation Ltd.

	1969/70	1970/71
Sales (£m)	87.395	128.776
Trading profit (£m)	6.523	8.107
Profit after tax (£m)	2.714	3.733

and some EA businesses had been transferred out of GEC. However, for what its worth, a summary of the GEC-EA group accounts for the financial years 1969/70 and 1970/71 are shown in Table 14.1 (extracted from [14]).

The task of integrating all of the computer-related activities smoothly into the existing GEC framework after 1968 was almost impossible. Given the aggressive, profit-motivated, goals of GEC's boss Arnold Weinstock, GEC's approach to integration favoured the axe rather than the warm embrace. In 1967 the Management Consultants MacKinsey had been called in by English Electric to recommend a strategy for integrating Elliott-Automation and Marconi with the parent English Electric Group. John Bunt recalls [4] that 'All the Elliott-Automation Managers were interviewed by MacKinseys. I don't think they ever completed their study, because they were dismissed [in 1968] by Sir Arnold Weinstock, the Managing Director of GEC, who circulated a note to the newly enlarged company saying that he did not require any management consultants to tell him how to organise his business.' Arnold Weinstock's impressive, but abrasive, track record has been described in Chap. 13.

In 1969 a company called Marconi-Elliott Computer Systems Limited (MECS) was established at Borehamwood to pursue non-EDP applications in areas such as small military computers and industrial process-control. At this point, the 'current range' of computers was described in the MECS Newsletters as comprising: MYRIAD series, M2100 series (a small-scale 16-bit multiprocessor for real-time control [15]) and 900 series. About 50% of the applications for these computers was given as 'military'. The other 50% was made up roughly equally of the following applications areas: Industrial, Laboratory, Marine, Education, Traffic control, Communications, Medical. In 1971 the name of the company was changed to GEC Computers Limited. The first distinctive product, the MECS 2050, was launched in 1970. This 8-bit computer, re-named the GEC 2050 after 1971, was in production until the end of the 1970s. The 2050 was used, amongst other things, as a Remote Job Entry workstation, supporting a card reader, line printer, console, and a communications link to a remote mainfame system [16].

In May 1969 John Bunt was appointed Technical Director of Marconi-Elliott Computer Systems Ltd. His retrospective view of computer-related events at Borehamwood over the next 3 years highlights the difficulties of integrating the cultures and skills of the various constituent parts. Quoting extensively from [4]:

'The final shape of the computer business [at Borehamwood] was based almost entirely on ex-Elliott-Automation personnel. The [English Electric] development work at Kidsgrove under Ken Chisholm was wound up, and although we wanted to move him to Borehamwood, he preferred to remain at Kidsgrove. The [Marconi] Chelmsford group was more of a problem. Myriad 2 was in small scale production, but it required only limited technical support from the engineers and Marconi's production was not divisionalised like the E-A production, so that it was only the engineering personnel in the Computer Division at Chelmsford and the Automation Division who were affected by the merger. We had no suitable position for the Manager of the Computer Division (Eric Atkins?) and he left the company. A few technical staff from Chelmsford moved to Borehamwood, including Arthur Young, a senior software and systems design man from the Automation Division.

'At Borehamwood, the Computer Research Lab., which had been a part of E-A Computers, was not transferred to ICL, and it joined the new company which was [soon] called GEC Computers Ltd. Other parts of E-A to join new the company were the Display Division under Eric Kirk and the Manager of the Magnetic Tape Division, Ray Matthews, both transferred from the old Elliott Space and Weapons Company.

'GEC Computers had as its Managing Director, Desmond (Paddy) Hunter, who had been one of the Managing Directors of Elliott Space and Weapons. He had been a radar and weapons systems engineer and involved with computers in that field. When I was in charge of Mobile Computing, he was instrumental in obtaining the FACE (Field Artillery) contract with the Elliott 920B computer. However, my responsibility for contracts with the Army and for future development work arising from the FACE contract passed to the Military Data Systems Division at Frimley.

'The Computer Research Lab. was run by G.W. (Geoff) Monk who had succeeded Laurence Clarke in that position some years before. He had a small team of very talented engineers, among them Neil Gammage, Mike Bradshaw and Mike Melliar-Smith. They had been working on a high speed system of logic circuits using tunnel diodes. This was under the guidance of one of our consultants Prof. W.J. (Ted) Poppelbaum, of the University of Illinois.

'The Managing Director of Marconi was Robert Telford, later Sir Robert Telford. He welcomed us at Borehamwood as new colleagues and did his best for us during the difficult times which followed the takeover. He arranged a visit to Chelmsford of some of the senior managers from ICL and a few of us from Borehamwood were invited to partake, a gesture which made us feel a part of the same family.

'The Research Director of Marconi was Dr. Eastwood. He was nearing retirement and although very interested to see what we were doing at Borehamwood, I think he played little part in shaping our future.

'The Borehamwood establishment, like all the ex-E-A factories, formed part of the new GEC subsidiary GEC-Elliott-Automation, which was headed by Joe Wiltshire. He had his office at Borehamwood. He replaced Sir Leon Bagrit who was retired by GEC after being on the board of English Electric for a short time. Other E-A Directors were Dr. L.L. Ross, who retired, Edgar Herzfeld, who took on a senior contracts role in GEC and Commander Henry Pasley-Tyler who was for many years in charge of the Borehamwood establishment. He also retired.

'Joe Wiltshire came to us at Borehamwood with a reputation for harsh treatment of personnel during his time in dealing with the integration of Associated Electrical Industries following the takeover of that company by GEC [in 1967 – see Chap. 13]. He soon made savings in the overheads in E-A, but for a time, at least, he had little impact on the technical staff.

'The Technical Director of GEC was Robert (later Sir Robert) Clayton. He took a great interest in our work, but was not a 'computer man' and unlike the E-A Directors he did not regard computers as an essential part of the GEC stock-in-trade. The same applied to Microelectronics and Large Scale Integrated Circuits. GEC did research work on new semi-conducting materials, but the factories of both E-A at Glenrothes in Fifeshire and of Marconi at Witham [near Chelmsford] in Essex, were closed. The E-A team was headed by Dr. Ian MacIntosh who had recently returned from the U.S.A., to head the E-A team at Glenrothes.

'Old GEC had an interest in computers through the work it was doing for the Post Office on computers for telephone exchanges. This was being done by a small team at Coventry, who visited us at Borehamwood to see our work and learn of our future plans. Bob Clayton was keen to arrange the exchange of visits, but it was clear that there was no question of merging their work with ours, although our computer development plans could have met the P.O. requirements quite easily. There may have been contractual reasons why this activity had to remain independent, but if so, I never heard them. Following visits by our top technical men to Coventry, the report was made that we were uncooperative and not prepared to listen. Knowing the members of our [Borehamwood] staff who this report referred to, I considered this a political report aimed at preserving the independence of the Coventry team.

'The senior people in GEC Computers now felt that the formation of the new company presented an opportunity which might not occur again, to produce a new range of computers to cover as far as possible all the applications known to us in the enlarged GEC Group. None of the existing ranges were ideal and not designed with Large Scale Integration in mind. So we decided not to base our designs on the existing ranges – the KDF7, the 900 Series, [the 4100 series] and the Myriad. So, Geoff Monk and his team set about designing the new range. They called the computers, ALPHA, BETA and GAMMA. They were to be upwards software compatible [Actually, this is more accurately expressed as 'upwards memory architecture and high level language compatible', since the instruction sets were not planned to be exactly compatible [17]]. ALPHA was to have 8-bit hardware, BETA was to have 16-bit hardware and GAMMA 32-bit hardware. GAMMA was never more than a concept, aimed at protecting us in the marketplace for the most powerful applications, such as air traffic control, but ALPHA and BETA development was started'.

Alpha, Beta and Gamma were conceived in the Computer Research Laboratory (CRL) at Borehamwood in about 1969. Alpha became the GEC 2050, an 8-bit computer. Beta became the GEC 4080; it had the hardware (i.e. microcode) Nucleus, for which a Queen's Award for Innovation was given to the company in 1979 [18]. The GEC 2050, launched in 1970 as the MECS2050, was intended to take over from the Elliott 905 and the 4080 from the Elliott 4130. Later, the 2050 was replaced by the 4060. The GEC 4080, the first of the 4000 series computers, was officially launched in 1973. About 20 more varieties were announced over the next 10 years or so [16], though some of the variants differed little from others. Andrew Gabriel recalls [19] that 'the lower model numbers were slower cheaper systems (the 4070 being the first slower system, but it was artificially slowed and was no cheaper to manufacture). The 406x systems replaced it and were much cheaper to manufacture. The higher model numbers (4082, etc.) were the larger (more store) more expensive systems'. At the start of this progression of computers, Roger Newey remembers [17] that 'the three original architectural designers from CRL were J W J (Bill) Williams, N D (Neil) Gammage and Mike Melliar-Smith. In essence, Bill did specifications, Neil hardware concepts, Mike computer science and real-time architecture. Neil & I did the final 2050 design (he the microcode, me logic); there was an earlier design that did not work out'.

Continuing the Alpha, Beta and Gamma story in 1969, John Bunt remembers [4] that:

'It was necessary to sell our plans to the GEC management, to a number of the GEC subsidiaries, to the Ministry of Technology and to other Government personnel. A sophisticated sales presentation, lasting about an hour, was worked up with audiovisual displays and presentations by Paddy Hunter, me, Geoff Monk and a number of others. We hired an actor to coach us in the presentation, which proved to be very effective. I think it is fair to say that the driving force behind this was Geoff Monk, who had the enthusiastic support of Paddy, me and the marketing team.

'In about 1970, because of matters concerned with our budget, Paddy was sacked by Joe Wiltshire. This came of something of a blow to us in GEC Computers. Paddy was a popular Managing Director, a good manager, very hard working and a very enthusiastic driving force behind the new company. GEC looked for a new Managing Director and eventually Alan Fraser was appointed'.

John Bunt continues:

'In the interim period, Laurence Clarke was drafted in to fill the gap on a temporary basis. This was an unsatisfactory arrangement for us, as I expect it was for him. In the short space of time, he could not hope to understand the workings of our various departments, and all he could hope to do was to be a channel of communications between Joe Wiltshire and the managers of GEC Computers. Fortunately this arrangement only lasted for a few months in 1971 [or was it 1970? See below for another comment on this unsatisfactory period].

'I think it was late in 1971 that Alan Fraser arrived. His earlier career had been as a General Manager in the Elliott Flight Automation company at Rochester, before moving to Borehamwood as Joint Managing Director with Andrew St. Johnston mainly looking after production matters. After the creation of ICL he moved to Kidsgrove to look after the production of the English Electric KDF9, in which role he was very successful. But the KDF 9 was wound down and his position at Kidsgrove came to an end. While Alan was an old colleague to many of us at Borehamwood, he had no experience of computer technology or of any of the applications we were concerned about.

'So, in 1971 and 1972, the 900 series computers provided GEC Computers with a steady income and the development of ALPHA and BETA was proceeding very satisfactorily. However it was clear that GEC did not believe that an in-house computer capability was essential or an integrated circuit capability either. We were subjected to political pressure from other parts of GEC, many of whom wanted to develop their own computers or buy them in from outside suppliers.

'Geoff Monk left the company in 1970 [to join Vaughan Systems [20]] and eventually, late in 1972, I came to the conclusion that the strain of working in the environment existing at Borehamwood was excessive and that I should leave the company before I was forced to do so for health reasons. It is sad to reflect on the fate which a number of my colleagues suffered, probably at least in part, for the same reason. Alan Fraser died in office [in August 1986, aged 68, at which point he was Chairman of GEC Computers but with very little input to the day-to-day running of the business] and several others were also affected.

'My job was advertised and pending any permanent appointment, Peter Reffen, who had been my assistant looking after production matters, was appointed on a temporary basis.

'Robert Clayton and Dr. Eastwood invited me to a farewell lunch at Wembley, which was a friendly gesture. Alan Fraser and my colleagues at Borehamwood made me a small presentation and we parted on good terms.'

The computer scene as painted by John Bunt depicted three emerging loci of power within Weinstock's empire in 1971:

- Marconi-Elliott Computer Systems Ltd., which became GEC Computers Ltd., based at Borehamwood
- GEC Communications, Coventry
- Marconi-Elliott Avionics Systems Ltd., Rochester

In Bunt's admittedly Borehamwood-centric view, the computer R&D effort of all three players should have been concentrated at Borehamwood. This would, he believed, have produced a strong team which could have been backed by the microelectronics facilities of either E-A at Glenrothes or Marconi at Witham (near Chelmsford). In the event, both Glenrothes and Witham were shut down. In Bunt's view, neither Sir Arnold Weinstock nor his Technical Director, Sir Robert Clayton, were sufficiently computer-minded to realise just how essential computers and microelectronics were for GEC's future. As for arranging close collaboration between Borehamwood, Coventry and Rochester, this would, in Bunt's view, have meant removing GEC Computers from the control of Joe Wiltshire – something that Weinstock was not prepared to do. GEC Computers at Borehamwood ploughed its own furrow for some years, as described in Sects. 14.4 and 14.5 below.

Of the three 1971 sites identified by Bunt, Rochester was in the end to become the most successful. In 1978 Marconi-Elliott Avionics Systems at Rochester was renamed Marconi Avionics, changing to GEC Avionics in 1984, to GEC-Marconi Avionics Ltd. in 1983 and then to BAE Systems in 1999. If any site deserved to inherit the spirit of technical innovation begun at Borehamwood in 1946 by John Coales, it is BAE Systems at Rochester. More on the Rochester story and airborne computers will be found in Chap. 12 and Appendix 9. As for Borehamwood, GEC Computers existed there and, for a time, at Dunstable (see below), relatively independently until about 1988, when GEC Computers was absorbed by GEC Communications (or Telecommunications) at Coventry as described in Sect. 14.6. In 1999, after a major company reorganisation, GEC Telecommunications became part of Marconi plc and the initials 'GEC' were dropped. Marconi plc got into severe financial difficulties in 2002 and had disappeared by 2006, as mentioned in Chap. 13.

Of course, many other GEC activities were located at Borehamwood in the period 1970–2003 – some of them direct progressions of Leon Bagrit's empire. Initially Borehamwood was the headquarters offices of the GEC-Elliott-Automation Group, which in 1970 had a turnover of about £80 million [21] and consisted of five product companies and four systems companies whose factories were mostly located elsewhere. In the product group were: Elliott-Automation Control Valves, Elliott Process Instruments, English Electric-AEI Industrial Controls, Elliott Mechanical Automation and AEI Scientific Apparatus. The four systems companies were: AEI-Elliott Process Automation (which included power automation activities), English Electric-AEI Projects (which included marine automation), GEC-Elliott Traffic Automation and GEC-Elliott Mechanical Handling. Making business sense of this collection of nine companies was not easy. The man chosen by Weinstock to do the job, Joe Wiltshire, had embarked on 'a year of careful pruning' [21] though others saw him more as a hatchet man. For many, 1969/70 was not a happy time. Joe Wiltshire did indeed take some decisive, rapid actions to unite the interests of various competing companies in the process control sector. However, he eventually fell from grace in about 1974.

Other, later, GEC companies that were to occupy space on the Borehamwood site had no connection with the Bagrit era. An example is GEC Plessey Telecommunications, a company commonly known as GPT, which was set up by GEC and Plessey in 1988. The name GPT lasted until 1997, when it was changed to SGCS (Siemens GEC Communication Systems). We give more details of GPT in Sect. 14.6.

Returning to 1969, Marconi-Elliott Computer Systems Ltd. was kept separate from the GEC-Elliott-Automation group, as were other GEC activities such as radar and avionics. The separation was not just organisational. Laurie Bental remembers [22] that 'In contrast [to the former Elliott practice], GEC System companies bought their computers largely from outside the Company, mainly from DEC [the American manufacturers of the PDP range of machines].'

Marconi-Elliott Computer Systems became GEC Computers Ltd. in 1971, and we now recount the fortunes of GEC Computers at Borehamwood.

14.4   GEC Computers at Borehamwood
and Dunstable in the 1970s

Detailed company records have not come to light for the post-Elliott period – and indeed may possibly not now exist. Andrew Gabriel, who worked for GEC Computers from 1983–1990 at Dunstable and then from 1991–1995 at Borehamwood, had become interested in the history of the company. He remembers [19] that some time in the early 1990s 'I was offered all the marketing materials, archived in the print room at Dunstable, providing I took them there and then, but it was in many filing cabinets, and I simply had nowhere to store them and no means to take them away that afternoon. This was in a "slash and burn" phase of the management, who were determined to chuck everything out.... The main archive which was in the print room at Dunstable was never recovered.'

The 1970s and 1980s were periods of highs and lows. For the highs, sales of the GEC 4000 series computers swelled in the mid- and late 1970s when they were used for X25 packet-switched systems and for Prestel systems [16]. The X25 protocol for wide area networks enabled publicly accessible data communications in the 1970s and 1980s, activity that was later largely taken over by the Internet protocols now familiar to users of the World Wide Web. Prestel, the brand name of the UK Post Office's *Viewdata* technology, was launched as a public service in 1979 [23]. Again, Prestel has largely been superseded by the World Wide Web and search engines such as Google.

Mainly as a result of X25 and Prestel sales, GEC Computers opened a development and manufacturing presence on the Woodside Estate in Dunstable, Bedfordshire in the late 1970s [16] whilst retaining Borehamwood as the headquarters. However, by 1989, the sales of GEC 4000 systems were declining and a decision was made to cease manufacture completely. Geoff Scammell, who joined GEC Computers as a graduate programmer in 1976 and who (at the time of writing) is the Customer Services Manager for Telent Technology Services Ltd., has been responsible for managing the support of the GEC 4000 systems for over 2 decades. Geoff remembers the post-manufacturing era as follows [24]. 'What was left of the manufacturing team effectively became the core of the hardware repair workshop which stayed in Borehamwood for a short while and then moved to Wellingborough in Northamptonshire. The repair shop stayed there until December 2008 and the very last remaining member of that repair shop retired at the end of March 2010 – with the GEC4000 hardware support rigs now being based at Telent's headquarters building in Warwick.'

When the decision was made to stop manufacture of the GEC4000, a parallel decision was made to port its OS4000 operating system onto the Motorola MVME187 RISC single-board computer. The new system, known as the GPT 4300, was launched in the early 1990s. However, less than 50 GPT4300s were ever sold, though 18 are still in operation today as command-and-control centre computers for a number of UK county fire brigades, and in military applications [24].

Returning to the Dunstable story, at its zenith the Dunstable presence had covered three factories, which included activities such as computer manufacture and systems assembly, field service, and the *Dunstable Development Centre* (DDC) which 'was mostly two giant open plan offices holding almost two hundred developers at the peak' [19]. The three Dunstable factories were closed down gradually during the period 1989–1992.

Andrew Gabriel recalls [19] that 'Customer Support remained rattling around in the otherwise empty [Dunstable] building for a while, together with the print/copy room and archives. After Customer Support moved out, just a few racks of wide area networking equipment remained (it was the hub linking many GEC sites' wide area network (GECnet) together, and there was still building lease remaining).

Table 14.2 Financial summary for GEC Computers Ltd. in the mid-1970s

	1973–74	1974–75	1975–76
Turnover (£m)	3.31	4.38	5.15
Exports (£m)	0.048	0.099	0.020
Profits before tax (£m)	−0.233 (loss)	−0.340 (loss)	0.215

After the place was broken into one weekend and a small rave held, followed by the sprinkler system freezing and then flooding the building, GEC (or GPT by now) moved out.'

Let us move back in time to the early 1970s and to Borehamwood. Amongst scant company information to have come to light is the following financial snapshot of GEC Computers in the mid-1970s, at which time the Elliott 900 range of computers was still being produced alongside the GEC 2000 and 4000 series machines. Table 14.2 is based on data compiled by the National Computing Centre [25], the figures relating to financial years ending on the 31st March.

It is clear from Table 14.2 that GEC Computers was not performing in a manner likely to please Arnold Weinstock. At Borehamwood part of the trouble was deemed to be loss of market penetration, due to the success in the UK of the American minicomputer manufacturers, particularly Digital Equipment Corporation (DEC) with its PDP8 computer and, from 1973, the 16-bit PDP/11 range. At the time, there were a few UK minicomputer start-up companies such as Computer Technology Ltd. with its Modular One product (from 1968) and Digico with its Micro 16 (from 1968). Such companies were not thought to be in a position to offer a robust challenge to the growing numbers of American minicomputer imports. Of course, ICL was having great success with its 1900 range computers but these did not really extend 'downwards' to intersect with the needs of typical minicomputer users – nor was ICL really interested in entering this market. ICL was more concerned with commercial data processing and large applications areas, for which it was poised to announce its New Range, the 2900 series.

It occurred to some that GEC Computers, based at Borehamwood, and Ferranti Computers, based at Wythenshawe (near Manchester) and Bracknell (west of London), might pool their efforts and win back ground lost to US companies such as DEC, Hewlett-Packard, Data General and Prime. Both Borehamwood and Wythenshawe had good track records in the areas of computers for military applications and for industrial process control. The Elliott 900 series continued to sell well, as did the Ferranti Argus series. Both series had been successively upgraded since the mid-1960s.

The formal suggestion for some form of UK challenge to the US minicomputer companies seems to have come from a letter from Martin Lam of the Department of Trade and Industry (DTI) to Bob Telford, Managing Director of GEC/Marconi Electronics, dated 6th May 1976. Laurence Clarke was asked to respond to this on behalf of Borehamwood. In an internal memo on 25th May 1976, Clarke was not sanguine that the UK government would be willing to put up sufficient finance (say up to £100 million) for an effective local competitor to DEC, who at that time had a turnover in the range £600–800 million, even if a UK competitor was felt to be desirable.

However, after a few months confidential discussions were initiated between GEC Computers (Borehamwood) and Ferranti Computers (Wythenshawe). The objective was to achieve a strong presence in the civil mini- and midi-computer markets and to act as a vigorous UK competitor to encroaching American computer manufacturers such as DEC, Hewlett-Packard, Data General and Prime. The principal products of the collaboration were to be OEM sales of minicomputers, starting from a 'close association with existing experience in 8-bit and 16-bit microprocessors within GEC and Ferranti'. Laurence Clarke later recalled [26] that 'we had in mind the upward compatibility of "beta" including the Ferranti machines'. At the time, Clarke also remarked that the discussions would have been 'easier three or four years ago' and that they needed to hurry to a conclusion 'before it is too late' [27].

The National Economic Development Office became involved in the discussions in the autumn of 1976. By 31st March 1977 John Pickin of Ferranti was able to report to Martin Lam that the two companies had had '12 meetings over the last three months'. By 10th June 1977, the two companies had come to the following conclusions about a joint enterprise:

(a) *Partners*. It was believed that a US partner for any collaboration would not be forthcoming. It was recommended holding fire on a possible EEC partner until the proposed new GEC/Ferranti company had been established. Other possible UK partners such as Plessey were considered but, again, it was decided to delay any decision on the matter of other partners. It was decided that ICL, with its commercial data processing bias, would not offer much collaborative advantage as a partner for the marketing of OEM minicomputers.

(b) *Strategy*. It was envisaged that the new company would develop a new range of upwardly compatible computers – clearly a very costly notion at a time when GEC was already committed to the 4080 and Ferranti to the Argus 700. It was hoped that the new company 'would take the market shares of CTL, Digico and Micro Computer Systems [all current small UK computer manufacturers] by agreement, acquisition, or otherwise'. It was predicted that the new company's total personnel (including engineering, sales, servicing, manufacturing and administrative staff) would grow from 1,600 in 1977/78 to 6,200 by 1981/82.

(c) *Equity*. It was proposed that GEC Computers and Ferranti Computers should have equal equity in the new company. It was further envisaged that £21 million should be provided by the National Enterprise Board as loan stock, repayable in instalments beginning 8 years from the founding of the new company.

It appears that the proposal for a merged company died a natural death. The most plausible reason for this death was that government was hardly likely to put large sums of money into a new computer manufacturing venture, since it was already under pressure to help ICL. The American company DEC was meanwhile extending its product range, closing the few gaps into which GEC/Ferranti might have been able to insert new products.

Whilst the above discussions were taking place, GEC Computers and Ferranti Ltd. continued to sell reasonable numbers of their existing product lines. The eventual fragmentation and demise of Ferranti Ltd. in the 1980s and 1990s is covered in [28]. Briefly, the most significant event occurred in 1987 when Ferranti purchased the American defence company International Signal and Control. Consequential financial and legal difficulties eventually forced Ferranti into bankruptcy in 1993. Various computer-related parts of Ferranti were acquired by GEC-Marconi and thence, in due course, by BAE Systems.

Returning to GEC, company documents detailing the year-on-year deliveries of Borehamwood computers have not come to light, but some idea of the number of Elliott 900 series computers to have been sold by the spring of 1977 may be gauged from a telex sent by I P (Iorweth) Evans to Laurence Clarke on 13th April 1977. Evans writes: 'Regrettably our records no longer list the customers for each machine and there may be some confusion between different types of 920M, and between 920B and 903. Whenever I am asked the question ['how many have been delivered?'] I always say that we have built in excess of 1,200 900 series machines. We are continuing to produce 920Ms and the rate could vary between 3 and 5 per month (say 40 per year). MSDS [Marconi Space and Defence Systems] have been producing 920Bs (it is rumoured at least 50 last year) and a recent Press Release suggests they could be making now approximately 12 per month. (These figures you would need to check with MSDS). Please remember also MEASL [Marconi-Elliott Avionics Systems Ltd.] who are producing the 920ATC'.

Evans then goes on to give the following delivery statistics for the 900 Series computers originating from Borehamwood:

920A	20
902	18
920B	530
903	110
920C	23
905	94
920M	480
Total	1,275

Laurence has added a pencilled note suggesting 14 more 903 machines had been built by the spring of 1977. To these figures should be added the 900 Series computers built elsewhere, particularly at Marconi Space and Defence Systems (Stanmore) and at Marconi-Elliott Avionics Systems (Rochester), the detailed sales of which were, interestingly, apparently not known by Evans or Clarke. The innovative developments of the 900 Series computers in the late 1970s and 1980s for avionics purposes, at Rochester and Stanmore, are discussed further in Chap. 12 and in Appendix 6.

The above remarks about Rochester do not necessarily imply that Borehamwood itself had ceased to be innovative. As has been said, in October 1979 GEC Computers Ltd. received a Queens Award for Technological Achievement for the *Nucleus 'hardwired central executive'* of the 4000 series. The Nucleus performed activities such as memory management and asynchronous message passing [18].

Continuing with estimates of 900 Series sales and gathering the evidence of avionics applications presented in Chap. 12, it seems that the following might represent the total sales of airborne computers whose design was related to the 900 Series:

920	600 or 700
920ATC	550
12 Series	7,000 or more

The 12 Series, or 12/12 airborne computers started off by being generally compatible with the 12-bit version of the Elliott 900 Series. The 12 Series was originally called *Minim*. According to Chap. 12, the sale of *derivatives* of the 12 Series went on to number approximately 30,000 machines.

Returning to mainstream 900 series applications, the software house Vaughan Programming Services, later Vaughan Systems Ltd., was writing new programs for Elliott 900 series computers from time to time until the end of the 1970s – (see Chap. 8). The last Vaughan contract involving an Elliott 905 computer was in 1980, for an enhanced motorway signalling system for the Department of Transport.

14.5   The GEC Series 63: A Very Difficult Project

By 1978 all talk of a link with Ferranti had been abandoned but sales of the GEC 4000 series were buoyant. By this time Laurence Clarke had moved upwards and outwards. Since 1974, at the time of Joe Wiltshire's demise, he had been based at Chelmsford rather than at Borehamwood. Alan Fraser was still Managing Director of GEC Computers Ltd (GECCL) at Borehamwood. Colin Thurston was Director in charge of the Commercial side of the company and George Hinchliffe the Director in charge of the Military aspects.

After lengthy debate, it was decided that GECCL should embark on the design of a new computer, in due course named *Project R* (the R standing for *Roadrunner*), that was 'powerful, state of the art, capable of being produced in a number of variants, have as its basic operating system an industry standard (there was not one at that time but it was decided that UNIX was the best bet) and most importantly that it should be able to run 4000 series software so that the investment made by our customer base was protected' [29]. It was agreed with Bob Telford, the Marconi Managing Director to whom Alan Fraser reported at that time, that GECCL did not have enough skilled personnel available to handle *Project R* and so contact was made with a computer design company based in the Los Angeles area.

Discussions were advancing very satisfactorily when higher GEC politics intervened. What follows is a condensed paraphrase of Colin Thurston's more detailed account [29].

At about this time GEC bought AB Dick, a reprographics company based in Chicago whose main product line was small printing machines used in the *Mom & Pop* printing shops which were common throughout the US. More surprisingly, it was then announced that Geoff Cross, who had been Managing Director of ICL

Fig. 14.5 At the end of the 1970s, GEC Computers began the design of a new machine, initially called *Project R,* in collaboration with the American company A B Dick. The collaboration was beset with difficulties, both technical and financial. Re-named the GEC Series 63, the computer was formally announced in 1983 and sales began in 1984. Within a couple of years the Series 63 development had been cancelled. By the end of the 1980s Borehamwood had ceased to be associated with innovative computer design

Fig. 14.6 Laurence Clarke, seen here in 2010, was born in 1929 and joined Borehamwood upon graduation in 1951. He spent all his working life with the computer design side of Elliott-Automation and related companies, retiring in 1992 as Assistant Technical Director of GEC. He lives in Suffolk, where he remains active in community affairs

from 1972 to 1977, was to become MD of AB Dick. Cross had collected some ex-ICL people round him including Ed Mack, described in [30] as 'an abrasive character brought in from Univac'. Cross's team also included John Coleur, described in America as a computer designer of some renown, who had started work on a new computer design for AB Dick. The suggestion was made that GECL should form a joint project with AB Dick, pooling their efforts to produce a new computer to be marketed on both sides of the Atlantic. Indeed, it was made clear that higher GEC budgetary approval for a new GECCL computer would be conditional upon it being a joint venture between GECCL and AB Dick.

Alan Fraser and colleagues at GECCL were not keen on the idea of a joint project, which seemed open-ended compared with the tight specification for *Project R* that was already making good progress. Furthermore, prior experience with US regulatory problems had inclined GECCL away from the American market. Nevertheless, exploratory joint technical meetings were held. John Coleur was able to convince GECCL that the needs of both companies could be met by a modification of his new design, and it was agreed to go ahead subject to budgetary approval from Arnold Weinstock. Alan Fraser appointed Roger Newey from GECCL as joint Project Manager with Dick Ruth from AB Dick. Detailed plans were formulated to set up a joint design centre in Phoenix (Scottsdale), Arizona. This involved a number of GECCL staff and their families temporarily re-locating to Phoenix.

Then in about 1981, as the design effort ramped up, two things happened. Firstly, contrary to his earlier indications, Weinstock now began insisting that *Project R* be financed from GECCL's existing resources without affecting GECCL's year-on-year bottom-line profits. Secondly, the differing end-user requirements of AB Dick and GECCL became more obvious, causing 'considerable argument' at joint meetings [29]. Alan Fraser was under extreme pressure every month, as GECCL faced the almost impossible task of trying to keep the project going and properly funded whilst maintaining bottom-line profits.

The project began to run late from both the hardware and software viewpoints and consequently costs increased. Geoff Cross is said to have fallen out with Arnold Weinstock [26]. In March 1983 Alan Fraser became Chairman of GEC Computers and Colin Thurston took over as Managing Director. Colin was an Elliott protégé. Having joined Elliott Brothers (London) at Rochester as a 16-year-old apprentice in 1954, he eventually went to university as the first Elliott-funded student. Upon graduating in 1961, he moved to Borehamwood where he became involved with computers for the first time.

There was now enormous pressure on GECCL to finish the project and bring the new computer to market. *Project R* was formally re-named the GEC Series 63 and was publicly announced in May 1983, 'well before it was ready' as Colin Thurston has remarked retrospectively [29].

According to a brochure dated 1986, there were to be six models in the Series 63 range, as shown in Table 14.3. For all models, the normal GEC Series 4100 peripherals could be attached, an SCSI adapter gave data transfers up to 1.5 MB/s, Ethernet was available, and the UX63 (UNIX-compatible) Operating System was

Table 14.3 Specification of various models of the GEC Series 63 computer

	63/15	63/20	63/30	63/40	63/50	63/60
Processor speed (MIPs)	1.5	2	3	3	3	3
Maximum memory (MB)	4	8	16	16	32	32
Comments				Integrated X.25		Integrated X.25

installed. Actually, only two models (the 63/30 and the 63/40) seem to have been produced [19].

Approximately 22 Series 63 systems were sold. Early in 1984 the first ten went to academic sites, under the UK's Alvey collaborative research programme (see later). The sites were the Universities of: Cambridge, Edinburgh (Dept. of Artificial Intelligence), Edinburgh Regional Computing Centre, Essex, Imperial College (two systems), Oxford, Rutherford Appleton Laboratory, Sussex and UMIST. Six of these sites also had DEC VAX computers and academics were not slow to pronounce the VAX a more desirable machine. The eventual role for many of the Series 63 systems at Alvey-sponsored sites was as fileservers for SUN workstations.

Producing the Series 63 had involved tremendous efforts by staff at Borehamwood and Dunstable. There were serious financial repercussions that are described more fully in Sect. 14.6. According to a GECCL company review leaflet (undated, but probably 1983): 'In 1982 we spent more than 20% of our total turnover on research and development – about twice as much as a computer company of our size would normally expect to spend ... much of this was upgrading the GEC 4000 Series and the development of the Series 63... Orders for defence products were seriously affected by the review of defence expenditure carried out by the Conservative government and we are now only beginning to recover ... We have recently completed delivery of GEC 4080M computer systems to Marconi Avionics for the Airborne Early Warning (AEW) processing system. The order for the first production run of GEC 4080M systems for Project Wavell (military Command and Control system) has recently been received. ...' Development was also proceeding on the GEC 4150, 4160, and enhancements to the GEC4180 and the 4190 computers. The sad tale of the 4080M computer in the Nimrod AEW project is recounted in Appendix 9.

Before describing the 'serious financial repercussions' of the Series 63 project, a word should be said about the Alvey collaborative research programme [31], in which many of the Series 63 computers were put to use. Prior to the Alvey Programme, Information Technology research at UK universities was primarily funded through a mechanism whereby individual academics made unsolicited grant applications to the UK's Science and Engineering Research Council (SERC). Each application was assessed on its merits and either accepted or rejected. SERC was not proactive; there was no strategic plan to identify key areas and very little collaboration with industrial R&D. The situation began to change in the late 1970s, when SERC experimented with *Specially Promoted Programmes* under which academics were invited to bid for funds to support particular areas of computing research. One such programme was overseen by SERC's *Distributed Computing Systems* (DCS) panel which was active from 1977 to 1984 [32]. For a time, Roger Newey chaired the DCS panel.

Then, stemming from his involvement with the Ministry of Technology, Laurence Clarke was instrumental in organising a SERC Workshop in January 1982. The Workshop proposed a 5-year directed, centrally funded programme of joint university/industry/government research into certain key areas of computer science and applications. The government responded by inviting John Alvey, Director of Technology at British Telecom (BT) to chair a study group to refine the proposal. The result was the establishment in mid-1983 of the Alvey Directorate. Brian Oakley, who was at the time Secretary of SERC, became Director of the Alvey Programme with Laurence Clarke as his deputy. Laurence had been Chairman of SERC's Information Engineering Committee. Funding of £350 million (at 1982 prices) over 5 years was made available by the government. This spawned a portfolio of 210 collaborative research projects, each lasting on average 3 years, and involving a total of about 2,500 people at its peak. For his work for the Alvey Programme, Laurence Clarke was appointed CBE.

During the Alvey Programme, Laurence Clarke had been based at Wembley. He retired in 1992, but had been working only two days a week for some two years before that, largely involved in ESPRIT activity. (ESPRIT was a collaborative research programme funded by the European Commission). He had first come to Borehamwood in 1950 as a Cambridge vacation student and had been associated with digital computers all his working life. He recalled [26] that, upon graduating and joining Elliotts full-time in July 1952, 'I had the advantage of already knowing the arcane language of computers which put me in an advantageous position to work closely with Harry Carpenter and Andrew St Johnston, a relationship which lasted until Andrew left the company [in 1968]'. At the time of writing (2010), Laurence fortunately survives in good health, active in the community and one of the very few sentient survivors of the formative years of Borehamwood. His collection of source documents and his anecdotal contributions to this book have been invaluable.

14.6   GEC Computers in the Mid-1980s: The End of Borehamwood's Independence

Going back a few years and turning to the wider picture, in 1982 the main GEC Group included over two hundred operating companies, employing 190,000 people and recorded an annual turnover of almost £5 billion. At this time GEC Computers was occupying two main sites: Borehamwood (for Engineering, Programming, Sales and Administration) and Dunstable (mainly for production and a smallish 'forward thinking' team – see earlier description). There were also sales offices in Bristol and the Netherlands. The main GEC conglomerate was structured into a number of management companies that controlled the majority of the business. These included Avionics (at Rochester), Defence Systems (at Stanmore) and Telecommunications (at Coventry). GEC Computers at Borehamwood, where about 1,000 people were employed, was one of several smaller units that did not conveniently fit into any of the major groupings – though for a time it formed part of GEC Information Systems Ltd., in association with some of GEC's telecommunications enterprises. Generally speaking, GEC Computers reported directly to Arnold Weinstock.

GEC Computers Ltd. (GECCL), though a comparatively small part of the GEC group, fiercely defended its independence from the larger units and was in principle not unhappy to be reporting directly to Weinstock. However, Weinstock had become displeased with what he saw as the poor financial performance of GEC Computers. 'Not understanding the technology himself, he put GECCL into what he considered to be a safe pair of hands, those of J E (Jack) Pateman, the Managing Director of Marconi-Elliott Avionics Systems at Rochester' [33].

Precise data on GECCL's financial performance has not come to light. The sales figures in Table 14.4, extracted from various issues of *Datalink*, the in-house newsletter, merely indicate a reasonably steady level of computer sales.

Of the 1982/83 sales figures, 48% of the total were to military applications; 45% of the total were to other GEC companies; 10% of the total were for export.

Nevertheless, as remembered by Paul Rayner [33], 'By 1984 GEC Computers had lost millions of pounds'. In that year, Jack Pateman asked Paul Rayner to take over the Borehamwood company as Acting Managing Director and sort it out. This he did, returning GEC Computers to profitability in 1988 and overseeing the transfer of GEC Computers to GEC Plessey Telecommunications (GPT). Thus, 1988 was the year in which Borehamwood finally lost its independence as a site of innovative computer development.

In parenthesis, the formation of GPT was driven by the need to bring all the System X telephone exchange manufacturing into one company. System X had been developed jointly by the Post Office (later British Telecom), GEC, Plessey and STC and had first entered public service in 1980. In 1982 STC left the consortium, leaving GEC and Plessey as the main suppliers of System X. GEC Computers itself had not, however, been involved with System X. In the lead up to the formation of

Table 14.4 Annual sales of GEC computers

Year	Orders received (£)	Actual sales (£)
1978/79	25.3	11.3
1979/80	17.4	16.6
1980/81	26.4	26.6
1981/82	19.9	24.1
1982/83	20.5	23.4
1983/84	31.5	24.4
1984/85	23.6	23.7
1985/86	25.2	26.8
1986/87	21.9	24.9

GPT, it was unclear whether GEC Computers should remain a separate entity within GEC or be transferred with the other GEC communications companies into GPT [19]. In the event, it was transferred under the GPT umbrella and was renamed GPT Computers Limited.

Let us return to 1984. Before describing the actions that Paul Rayner took at Borehamwood, it is appropriate to establish his credentials. Paul joined Borehamwood as a hardware engineer in 1955, having graduated in Electrical Engineering from Imperial College. His first project was the complex output converter, known as WREDOC, for the Elliott 403 computer (see Chap. 3). Involvement in a number of other projects followed, including transistor logic for the Elliott 802 (see Chap. 10), hardware for on-line process applications of the 803, in particular the real-time billet cutting system for the Samuel Fox steelworks (1960, see Chap. 7) and the Verdan airborne computer for TSR 2 high-performance aircraft (see Chap. 12). Largely because of his involvement in TSR 2, in the early 1960s Paul was appointed Chief Engineer of the Airborne Computing Division. He then served as the Divisional Manager from 1965 to 1980. During this time, he acquired much experience of 900 Series computers in connection with avionics projects. In 1969 Paul moved to Rochester, where his boss within Marconi-Elliott Avionics Systems was Peter Hearne, the General Manager who ran a group of Divisions of which Airborne Computing was one. After his secondment to GEC Computers from 1984 to 1988, Paul returned to Rochester as Special Assistant to the Managing Director, GEC Avionics Ltd., in which role he was concerned with strategic development and R&D policy. Paul retired in 1990.

Of his tenure at GEC Computers from 1984 to 1989, Paul Rayner remembers events as follows [33].

'There were three main problems [at Borehamwood] identified when I took over. Firstly, money was being poured into the development of a new small computer [the Series 63] to compete in a market that was already becoming very competitive. Secondly, our commercial products were frequently being sold at a loss because, although our sales teams were motivated by commission on the value of sales they brought in, there was no relationship between commission and profitability to the Company. For instance they concentrated on selling the most attractive products which generally had the lowest margin, they were able to offer discounts to clinch a sale, and they were able to offer variations on the standard product which were never properly costed. Thirdly, commercial software was given away free to make our products appear more attractive.

'I stopped all work on the new small computer [the series 63] immediately and restructured the commission scheme to link it more closely to profitability. There were howls from the salesmen but it had the desired effect. The software problem was more difficult and we attempted to limit further new software to externally funded projects. The Company had over 1000 employees when I took it over and, in order to cut costs, we reduced this to about 600 – not a process that I enjoyed. Turnover went down a little, but profitability improved remarkably. We concentrated on our core activities of military products, process control, sales to the universities and the rapidly growing field of digital communications.'

Fig. 14.7   Andrew St Johnston, seen here in retirement, was born in 1922, served as a radar officer in the war, joined Borehamwood in 1949 and became Manager of the Computing Division in 1953. He led the computer developments at Borehamwood until 1968, when he left to join his wife's software company Vaughan Programming Systems. He served as Managing Director at Vaughan until his retirement in 1999. Andrew died in 2005

14.7   The Demise of Borehamwood

Borehamwood was a large site, its several buildings housing employees of several GEC companies and sub-groups that had little formal connection with GEC Computers Ltd. Many of these sub-groups were engaged in classified defence projects. Radar-related activities accounted for much of the activity at Borehamwood, both before and after the arrival of GEC – see Chap. 11. Tony Bartolome, who was located at Borehamwood between 1976 and 2000, has described the atmosphere as follows [34] (Fig. 14.7).

'When I started at Borehamwood in 1976 I was a young software engineer with no real concept of the Elliott-Automation history. I joined a group of about 50 software engineers which, in the scheme of things, was a small percentage of the total number of employees on the site. I cannot go into the detail of the work I was involved with at the time as it may still be restricted, but I was involved in the software developments associated with the ill fated AEW Nimrod and the [successful] Tornado Foxhunter radar [see Chap. 11]. The cancellation of the AEW Nimrod at Christmas 1986 dealt a huge blow to GEC and impacted the work force at Borehamwood. I do not know how many people this actually affected, but there were quite a few redundancies because of it.'

'There wasn't really any interfacing with the other companies in the building. Our group, which was an outpost of Rochester, kept very much to ourselves and in actual fact, up to the end of the AEW, didn't get involved with Rochester at all at the engineering level. Some of those that I worked with may well have been ex-Elliott-Automation employees but it was transparent to those of us who weren't. I didn't detect any friction between employees at the site until I reached the Management level, where the different business divisions within GEC as a whole, fought for their survival, sometimes at the expense of their sister companies. This was the way Arnold Weinstock ran GEC and positively encouraged this type of 'lean and mean' attitude.

'The relationship that there was with Rochester, mostly at the management level, was generally good and after the demise of the AEW, Rochester threw the Borehamwood site some lifelines by either contracting work out to us, or seconding some of our staff to the Rochester site to work there. This helped keep the number of redundancies to a minimum. During this period between 1986 and the mid 1990's my Division always had a good working relationship with Rochester and the engineering staff interfaced with each other extremely well.

'In the late 1980's and early 1990's manufacturing dropped off dramatically, but the software industry developed at a pace and in particular in support of other GEC sites such as Rochester, Basildon, Chelmsford, Milton Keynes and Stanmore.'

Changes were afoot in other sites. In 1993 the GEC Hirst Research Laboratories at Wembley finally closed and the remaining Hirst staff transferred to Borehamwood. 'The Hirst people only occupied a small fraction of the available accommodation. In general, at this time one or more different companies occupied each available floor' [34], amongst which were divisions as disparate as GEC General Signals Ltd. and Marconi Defence Systems Ltd. The remains of GEC Computers still existed in 1995 when Andrew Gabriel left the company, though at that point he remembers [19] that there were just 55 staff remaining, out of a total he estimates to have been between 1,200 and 1,600 in GEC Computers a dozen years previously.

Tony Bartolome continues: 'The biggest change that took place while I was at Borehamwood was the sell-off of the defence arm of GEC to BAE [in 1999]. At this point, it was always on the cards that the BAE elements in the building would rationalise and be dispersed to other sites around the UK. I left Borehamwood in 2000 whilst working for EASAMS [Elliott-Automation Space and Advanced Military Systems]. This company was sold off as part of the planned Marconi reorganisation. Marconi hit the buffers and shortly afterwards folded.'

As implied in Sect. 14.4, the support of GEC4000 series computers is actually continuing at the time of writing, based at Telent Technology Services Ltd.'s headquarters building in Warwick. Geoff Scammell, Telent's Technology Services Manager, recalls [24] that 'there are still a few GEC4000s in service today, most notably controlling the mills and furnaces at Corus's steelworks in Llanwern, and controlling several of London Underground's lines (linking the signalling systems, trackside monitors, timetabling systems and platform-based passenger information systems). Indeed, London Underground has stated that without the incredible reliability of the GEC4000s, London would today be grinding to a halt on a daily basis. My understanding is that on at least one line, there are no plans to replace the GEC4000 control computers until 2022, which would be around 40 years after they were installed.'

Going back to Borehamwood, January 2002 saw the start of the clearing-out process as Marconi/GEC finally prepared to leave their remaining space at Borehamwood. The irrevocable point was reached towards the end of 2002 when a decision was made to clear out the contents of the Strong Room.

The Borehamwood Strong Room was entered down steps from the ground floor of the original Admiralty war-time *shadow factory*. It was built to withstand bomb damage, being a cross between an air raid shelter and a bank vault. It had a huge metal, safe-like door. The Strong Room contained sensitive records dating back to 1946, including the collection of Elliott Research Laboratory Visitors Books for which the first entry was recorded as 4th October 1946. The 'men from the Ministry' visited the Strong Room at Borehamwood towards the end of 2002 and removed certain documents still classified as 'secret', after which some of the remaining declassified research reports during the period 1947–1955 were passed to the National Museum of Science and Industry in London and some boxes of photographic negatives found their way – more by luck than judgement – to the Marconi Archives at Chelmsford and from thence, in due course, to the University of Oxford. Most of the residual documents were destroyed in 2003 though, with the cooperation of the Marconi Security Officer, the author of this book managed to save some key items – including the complete set of Visitors Books. By this time, much of the Borehamwood site had passed to a property-management consortium that included the Legal and General Insurance Company and St. Modwen Properties plc. A large part of the site was promoted as comprising '265,000 sq. ft. of office space available for hire' – see Fig. 14.3.

Thus ended the scientific and technical associations of a former field, lying to the north-east of Bullbaiter's Farm and about 2 miles outside the original village of Borehamwood. From 1946 to 2001 Elliott Brothers (London) Ltd. and its successor companies had occupied premises on the old Bullbaiter's Farm field. Starting in October 1946 with an ex-Admiralty shadow factory of about 70,000 sq. ft. and about 50 employees, the Borehamwood Laboratories peaked at about 350,000 sq. ft. of floor space housing perhaps 6,000 employees – though this estimate may be a little too high [24]. The Laboratories had seen innovative engineering of the highest order which had made significant contributions to areas such as defence, aerospace and industrial automation. Fuelled by these innovations, the Elliott-Automation company had played a significant part in the birth of the Information Age in the UK, most especially in the formative years 1955–65 when the digital computer came into the marketplace as a useable and affordable tool. Although the Borehamwood Laboratories have now, like many similar organisations, been consigned to the dustbin of outmoded empires, the name Borehamwood surely deserves to be remembered as part of the rich historical tapestry of British electronic innovation.

We should not end the Borehamwood story without remembering the contributions of hundreds of unsung Elliott heroes: the scientists and engineers, men and women, whose names remained invisible to the outside world – especially if they worked on classified projects. Without their ideas and dedication, Elliott Brothers (London) Ltd. would surely not have survived as an independent company after the end of the Second World War. A few Borehamwood digital pioneers, such as Tony Hoare and Iann Barron, became well known in the computing arena after leaving Elliotts. Others, such as Andrew St Johnston who had been an active player in a remarkable progression that saw digital computers start as a gleam in the Admiralty's eye and end as a tool in the hands of every schoolchild, have remained relatively unfêted.

Perhaps two individuals stand out as having had a major impact on Borehamwood's 40-year reputation for technical excellence: John Coales as the originator and Leon Bagrit as the sustainer. Both men became, for a short time, widely known outside their respective academic and industrial circles. In the final section we examine and contrast their public personae.

14.8 Post-script: John Coales and Leon Bagrit as Public Figures

The decade after resigning from Borahamwood in 1952 was, for John Coales, not easy. However, by 1966 he had become the first Professor of Control Engineering at the University of Cambridge and President (from 1963 to 1966) of the International Federation of Automatic Control (IFAC). He was, indeed, by then a leading light in the creation of the new profession of control engineering and this was recognised when the UK's Science Research Council (the precursor of SERC) established Cambridge as one of three national *Centres of Excellence* in the subject. Interestingly, John Coales and Leon Bagrit crossed pens, so to speak, in the letters section of *The Times* newspaper at the end of 1963. On 20th December, in a letter headed 'Research into Automation: how it can best be furthered', Coales wrote as chairman of the newly formed UK Automation Council lamenting the fact that there was no National Institute of Automation carrying out government-funded research into the subject. Instead, he suggested that universities be provided with about £250,000 annually to carry out the same task. On 23rd December, *The Times* published Bagrit's response, his main thrust being that theoretical research was all very well but what was needed today was fiscal incentives for industry to adopt

Fig. 14.8 John Coales, seen here in 1971, was born in 1907, joined the Admiralty Scientific Service in 1929 and by 1937 was leading the Admiralty's radar research team. In 1946 he left to found the Borehamwood Research Laboratories of Elliott Brothers (London) Ltd. He resigned in 1952 and started the Automatic Control research group at the University of Cambridge. In 1966 he became Professor of Control Engineering at Cambridge. He died in 1999

Fig. 14.9 Sir Leon Bagrit, seen here in 1976, was born in Kiev, Ukraine in 1902, arrived in England in 1914, and set up his own manufacturing company, B & P Swift, in 1935. In 1947 he became Managing Director of Elliott Brothers (London) Ltd. He became Chairman and Managing Director of Elliott-Automation until its takeover in 1968, when he became Chairman of GEC-Elliott-Automation Ltd. He retired in 1973 and died in 1979

existing automation techniques. In a sense, this interchange contained echoes of the fundamentally differing views of Coales and Bagrit in the period 1949–1952 over the future of Borehamwood.

At Cambridge, one speciality of Coales' group was hybrid computation for which he had acquired a large analogue computer, a PACE 231R Mark V, connected to an Elliott 4130. At its peak, the Cambridge control group comprised about 50 post-graduate students and research workers, over which Coales exercised 'a largely benign, occasionally irascible, paternalistic supervision' [35]. He was elected a Fellow of the Royal Society in 1970, was the President of the Institution of Electrical engineers in 1971/72 and was appointed CBE in 1974 – the year in which he retired. He remained a keen fell walker, mountaineer and Morris dancer, being described as 'a large man, in body and spirit, with great physical energy and sustained enthusiasms … he was a remarkable gentleman, in the true sense of that word' [35]. Coales died in 1999 at the age of 91, sustaining his enthusiasms till the last.

For Leon Bagrit, the period 1962–1967 saw Bagrit expand his contacts and influence in the national arena. He had been knighted in 1962 for his services to industry. In 1962 he also became a director of the Royal Opera House, Covent Garden, and the founder/chairman of the Friends of Covent Garden. On 17th May

1963 the Duke of Edinburgh visited Elliott-Automation at Borehamwood and on 24th October 1963 Bagrit was invited by the Queen and the Duke of Edinburgh to a luncheon party at Buckingham Palace. The high noon of Bagrit's popular exposure started soon after, in 1964, when he was invited by the BBC to give the prestigious Reith Lectures.

However, it was probably a chance meeting in 1963 with William Rees-Mogg (later Lord Rees-Mogg) that was to open more doors for Bagrit. William Rees-Mogg was, *par excellence*, a networker. Coming from a Somerset family of landowners, a Balliol man and President of the Oxford Union, Rees-Mogg had joined the *Financial Times* in 1952, rising to be chief leader-writer. He moved to the *Sunday Times* in 1960 as city editor and then political and economic editor and from there to *The Times*, of which he was the editor from 1967 to 1981. During this time, Rees-Mogg recalled [5] that he had developed a particular interest in the UK's electronics industry. Indeed, one of his many directorships was of GEC (from 1981 to 1997).

Leon Bagrit and William Rees-Mogg and their wives met in 1963 whilst on a voyage to America on the luxury liner *SS France*. Rees-Mogg has recalled that he became impressed with Bagrit's 'wonderful, imaginative mind', and they soon became firm friends [5]. William Rees-Mogg's wife Gillian and Leon shared the same birthday and a joint celebration was to become an annual event. After Leon Bagrit's death in 1979, Rees-Mogg became Chairman of the *Sir Leon Bagrit Memorial Trust*, a charity which still (in 2010) supports good causes such as scholarships at the Department of Bioengineering at Imperial College and at various ballet schools.

Rees-Mogg remembers that he introduced Bagrit to Harold Wilson, shortly before Wilson became Prime Minister in 1964 (Wilson may actually have been aware of Bagrit before this time, as is implied by the RTB Llanwern steelworks project described in Chap. 6). In any case, friendship with Harold Wilson opened up many opportunities for Bagrit to explain his ideas of industrial automation to a labour government that had created a Ministry of Technology to support the modernisation of industry. Perusal of the *Court Circular* section of *The Times* indicates that Bagrit became a familiar figure at official dinners – for example being a guest when Prime Minister Harold Wilson gave a dinner party for Hubert Humphrey, the Vice-President of the United States, on 3rd April 1967. Leon Bagrit's name – and photograph – regularly appeared to readers of *The Times*, a publication known in that period as 'the top peoples' newspaper'. Excluding conventional social items, the number of articles in *The Times* that mentioned Leon Bagrit by name rose annually from 6 in 1962 to 17 in 1963, peaked at 18 in 1964 and only fell back to single figures in 1968. Most of these articles were naturally in the business and technical areas, though Leon Bagrit's interest in the Arts also surfaced from time to time. His support of Covent Garden merited regular mentions and on 20th July 1964, in a piece about Tate Gallery acquisitions, *The Times* noted that 'Three sculptures from Michael Arton's recent one-man exhibition at the Grosvenor Gallery have been lent to the Gallery by Sir Leon Bagrit.'

Throughout the 1960s and the early 1970s, Sir Leon and Lady Stella Bagrit lived at an elegant London property known as Upper Terrace House, adjoining Hampstead

Heath. Dating from about 1700, the house was described by *The Times* in 1967 as having 'four main reception rooms including a dining room in the Adam style, a library with a barrel-vaulted ceiling, and a Georgian staircase hall. There are four bedroom suites, including one with a Georgian Gothic interior removed from Lee Priory, near Canterbury. There are staff quarters and a separate flat. The garden runs to about three-quarters of an acre.' For a time, Sir Leon also owned 'an extraordinary country house, to which I never went, near Windsor Park, and he reconverted it back to its original 16th Century (I think) glory' [36]. Lord Rees-Mogg also recalls [5] that 'I went to a party that the Bagrit's gave in their house at Windsor Great Park. I cannot remember the reason for the party, though it had a charitable purpose of some kind. I do remember that it was attended by Her Majesty the Queen, and I remember walking with her by the side of the lake. The house, as I remember it, was a very fine 18th century house'.

An ironic final touch to Leon Bagrit's public persona as an establishment figure came on 28th May 1968 when, in an article headed 'protest planned', *The Times* reported that 'Sir Leon Bagrit, the industrialist, will be the target for an anti-Vietnam protest by students when he receives an honorary doctorate of science at Reading University on Saturday. The students plan to picket the great hall of the university. Sir Leon is chairman and managing director of Elliott-Automation which, the protest organisers claim, has at least five contracts from the United States defence department for the supply of military equipment, but a spokesman for Elliott-Automation said: "It is totally untrue that any Elliott equipment is being used in Vietnam".'

Sir Leon Bagrit retired from being chairman of GEC-Elliott-Automation Ltd. in 1973. His contract with GEC was not due to expire until 1976, though he also had a life contract with Elliott (Brothers) London at nominal pay after 1976 [37]. By 1973, however, Lord Rees-Mogg remembers that Sir Leon 'was disillusioned, out of favour with GEC and not in the best of health' [5]. By about 1976, Sir Leon and Lady Stella Bagrit had sold Upper Terrace House and their Windsor house and had moved to a flat just off Grosvenor Square. Sir Leon 'took his collection of miniature bronzes with him, and had on the walls some of their smaller but wonderful works from the Impressionists and others [36]. Their two children, Valerie and Patricia, were both married and had gone to live in America. Sir Leon Bagrit became too unwell to travel [36], gradually slid from public gaze and died on 22nd April 1979. Below are some extracts from his obituary, published in *The Times* on 23rd November, which shed light on his human side. More biographical details of his early life are provided in Chap. 1.

'Sir Leon Bagrit, sometimes called the *father of automation in Britain*, and an industrial visionary of undoubted significance, died on April 22 at the age of 77. He was chairman of Elliott-Automation, Ltd. from 1963 to 1973, a firm very much the child and product of his own original ideas ...He was a figure of European importance in the development and expansion of that series of self-actuating engineering techniques now known generally as automation. The significance and importance of Bagrit's contribution to industry was his realisation, just after the Second World

War, that there must come a great and increasing use of mechanical processes which would constitute something like a new industrial revolution.

'By the time he had reached middle life Bagrit had developed a striking and most versatile personality, which manifested itself not only in the fields of invention and business management but in those of music and the visual arts....

'Bagrit believed in a very large measure of decentralization in each of the companies comprising the [Elliott-Automation] group.... Commercial success, of course, he achieved in full measure; but behind his operations as a business man there lay much deep thinking about the needs of British industry in the second half of the twentieth century and the steps necessary to achieve success in a new age – an age which, he firmly believed, would see a second industrial revolution having economic and political consequences of immense significance to the country's future. He felt that the opportunity was wide open, and must not be neglected. Of a type not often encountered in the business world, Bagrit added to his technical and scientific genius a broad general culture. He was widely read, and had keen interest in music and the visual arts, especially sculpture.'

The above obituary writer used a curious phrase: *deep thinking*. Were any of Sir Leon's thoughts, we may wonder, deep enough to be judged significant by today's standards? Here's one to ponder. It comes from Sir Leon's second BBC Reith Lecture in 1964 [38]: 'Perhaps the most far-reaching use of the new generation of computers will be in the retention and communication of information of all sorts within a national, possibly a world-wide information system. This will enable decisions to be taken by people at all levels on a much more informed basis'.

References

1. Laurie Bental (2002) Letter to Simon Lavington, 20 Mar 2002
2. Paul King (2007) E-mail to Simon Lavington, 27 Aug 2007
3. Dina St Johnston, Laurence Clarke (2007) In conversation with Simon Lavington on 7 June 2007
4. John Bunt (2002) The end of the road. Typed four-page document written for Simon Lavington, March 2002. A post-script, entitled An Opportunity Missed: being wise after the event, was added in Apr 2002, a few weeks before John Bunt's death
5. Lord William Rees-Mogg (2009) Conversation with Simon Lavington on 9 Dec 2009 and subsequent e-mails
6. Jones R, Marriott O (1970) Anatomy of a merger: a history of GEC, AEI and English Electric. Jonathan Cape, London. ISBN: 0-224-61872-5
7. Doug Cornish (2007) E-mail to Simon Lavington, 20 July 2007
8. John Sinclair (2007) E-mails and telephone conversations with Simon Lavington in Apr and May 2007
9. David Warman (2010) E-mail to Simon Lavington dated 3 Feb 2010
10. Papers of Birkett DA, the ICT Company Information Officer, filed as document COM/1993/1433 at the National Museum of Science and Industry, South Kensington, London
11. These examples of the progression of Information Technology are taken from the BCS@50 conference, held in London in July 2007, when invited pioneers of computing reviewed their

various fields. The Conference celebrated the 50th anniversary of the British Computer Society

12. Anon (1959) Automation in the post office. Comput Bull Feb/Mar:78–79
13. Roberts LG (1978) The evolution of packet switching. Proc IEEE 66(11):1307–1313. http://www.packet.cc/files/ev-packet-sw.html
14. GEC-Elliott Automation Ltd (1971) Report and Accounts for year ended 31 Mar 1971
15. Anon (1970) M2140 computer system. 56-page technical brochure published in 1970 by Marconi-Elliott Computer Systems Ltd., Borehamwood
16. Technical information on GEC 2000-series and 4000-series computers may be found on Andrew Gabriel's web-site: http://www.cucumber.demon.co.uk/geccl/ and in his contributions to Wikipedia: http://en.wikipedia.org/wiki/GEC_Computers
17. Roger Newey (2009–2010) E-mails to Simon Lavington dated 7 Nov 2009 and 7 Feb 2010
18. Anon (1977) Central Processor Unit Nucleus. (User hardware handbook: computer, reference number DD1196). Published by GEC Computers Ltd., Borehamwood, 77 p. http://www.computinghistory.org.uk/userdata/files/nucleus.pdf
19. Andrew Gabriel (2010) E-mails to Simon Lavington, Feb 2010
20. Lavington S (2009) An appreciation of Dina St Johnston, 1930–2007, founder of the UK's first Software House. Comput J 52(3):378–387
21. Anon (Feb 1970) Divide and rule: the GEC-Elliott Automation Group. Dataweek 10(9)
22. Laurie Bental (2002) Letter dated 20 Mar 2002 to Simon Lavington
23. Broadhead WR (July 1981) Prestel: the first year of public service. Post Office Electr Eng J (Institution of Post Office Engineers) 74 (Part 2):129–133
24. Geoff Scammell (2010) E-mails to Simon Lavington, Mar 2010
25. Data compiled by the National Computing Centre in Nov 1976
26. SLH Clarke (2009) E-mail to Simon Lavington dated 14 Oct 2009
27. Laurence Clark (2007) Personal contemporary notes and files loaned to Simon Lavington in June 2007, dealing with the proposed collaboration between GEC Computers and Ferranti
28. Wilson JF (2001) Ferranti: a history. Building a family business, 1882–1975. Carnegie Publishing Ltd., Lancaster. Volume 2: from family firm to multinational company, 1975–1987, published in 2007 by Crucible Books, Lancaster. ISBN: 978-1-905472-01-7
29. Thurston C (2009) GEC Computers Ltd and the series 63. Three-page typed manuscript produced for Simon Lavington on 15 Dec 2009
30. Campbell-Kelly M (1989) ICL: a business and technical history. Oxford University Press, Oxford. ISBN: 0-19-853918-5
31. Oakley B, Owen K (1990) Alvey: Britain's strategic computing initiative. MIT Press, Cambridge
32. Newey R, The Distributed Computing Systems Programme, 1977–84. This Overview was the opening talk at the DCS Conference at Sussex University in September 1984. The Proceedings of this conference were published in 1984 by Peter Peregrinus Ltd., on behalf of The Institution of Electrical Engineers, as Distributed Computing Systems Programme, edited by DA Duce. ISBN 0-86341-023-5. http://www.chilton-computing.org.uk/acd/dcs/overview.htm
33. Paul Rayner (2007) Memoirs sent as a series of e-mails to Simon Lavington, Aug/Sept 2007
34. Tony Bartolome (2007) Memoirs sent as a series of e-mails to Simon Lavington, Aug 2007
35. MacFarlane Sir A (2003) John Flavell Coales, CBE. Biogr Memoirs Fellows R Soc Lond 49:119–131
36. LP Fielding (Leon Bagrit's nephew) (2010) E-mail to Simon Lavington dated 13 Jan 2010
37. The Times newspaper, 15 Oct 1968
38. Bagrit Sir L (1965) The age of automation – the Reith lectures 1964. Weidenfeld & Nicholson, London

Appendix 1
Technical Details of the Elliott 152 and 153

Introduction

The Elliott 152 computer was part of the Admiralty's MRS5 (medium range system 5) naval gunnery project, described in Chap. 2. The Elliott 153 computer, also known as the D/F (direction-finding) computer, was built for GCHQ and the Admiralty as described in Chap. 3. The information in this appendix is intended to supplement the overall descriptions of the machines as given in Chaps. 2 and 3.

A1.1   The Elliott 152

Work on the MRS5 contract at Borehamwood began in October 1946 and was essentially finished in 1950. Novel target-tracking radar was at the heart of the project, the radar being synchronized to the computer's clock. In his enthusiasm for perfecting the radar technology, John Coales seems to have spent little time on what we would now call an overall systems design. When Harry Carpenter joined the staff of the Computing Division at Borehamwood on 1 January 1949, he recalls that nobody had yet defined the way in which the control program, running on the 152 computer, would interface with guns and radar. Furthermore, nobody yet appeared to be working on the computational algorithms necessary for three-dimensional trajectory prediction. As for the guns that the MRS5 system was intended to control, not even the basic ballistics parameters seemed to be known with any accuracy at Borehamwood [1, 2].

A1.1.1   Communication and Data-Rate

The physical separation, between radar in the Borehamwood car park and digital computer in the laboratory, necessitated an interconnecting cable of about 150 m in length. It is true to say that the electronic problems of interfacing radar and computer had not been considered at the time of positioning the aerial. There were

S. Lavington, *Moving Targets*, History of Computing,
DOI 10.1007/978-1-84882-933-6, © Springer-Verlag London Limited 2011

two coaxial cables, each about 0.25 in. in diameter, connecting computer and radar: one carried a signal derived from the computer's clock, the other duplexed commands and data. On receipt of a command, the radar unit responded by sending back an integer. Parameters received from the radar unit were used by the 152's software to calculate an updated position of the target aircraft. The computer sent 1,000 pulses per second to the radar (one pulse every millisecond). It was assumed that perhaps one pulse in three would not yield a meaningful return, so there was a need to average over four radar returns when computing trajectories. Therefore, the 152 was required to perform the necessary axis-conversions and to produce one update of {range, bearing and elevation} every 4 ms. Each of the {range, bearing and elevation} parameters was represented to 14-bit accuracy, as were the sine and cosine of the bearing. Fourteen bits gave a precision of better than 1 minute of arc. In addition to any control and/or addressing commands, the data-rates coming into and out of the 152 computer were thus:

$14 \times 5 \times 1,000 = 70,000$ bits/s inwards;
$14 \times 3 \times 250 = 10,500$ bits/s outwards.

A1.1.2 Memory System

It was clear that input/output activity would have to be overlapped with computational activity and that the rate of obeying instructions would have to be extremely rapid. Potentially the fastest-access storage technology available in 1947, anywhere in the world, was the CRT electrostatic system being developed by Williams and Kilburn at Manchester University. To begin with, the system was based on William's original *anticipation-pulse* method, as patented on 11 December 1946. By the autumn of 1947 this had been refined by Kilburn into two alternative schemes: the *dot-dash* and the *focus-defocus* methods. The digit period chosen by Manchester in June 1948 for the University's small-scale experimental machine (the SSEM) was 8.5 μs. This was considered too slow for the 152 computer which, in 1947, was aiming for a 1-μs digit period (i.e. 1 MHz clock-rate).

M V Needham joined Borehamwood in September or October 1947. Maurice remembers [3] that, somewhat later, John Coales came into the Lab one day and said that he had learned that F C Williams was working on electrostatic CRT storage and had discovered that one could obtain a pulse that anticipated the present position of the spot on the screen. Coales said that 'this sounded just the sort of thing that the MRS5 project could make use of for its memory system', so Borehamwood 'had got to get on with it'. Maurice set up an experiment to investigate what this anticipatory effect might be. He produced a demonstration of the physical effect and indeed found an anticipation pulse. At this point, their experimental device 'was not yet computer-oriented'. Coales then informed Maurice that F C Williams was due to give a talk at the Institution of Electrical Engineers (IEE) on 2 November 1948. Maurice was instructed to be present at the talk and 'to ask an intelligent question!'

Maurice did indeed ask more than a question. He briefly described Borehamwood's experience of the anticipation-pulse method, showed a film of their stored patterns, and suggested that the anticipation-pulse method seemed to allow greater speeds of operation than other electrostatic methods. Maurice remembers that F C Williams was scornful of this claim at the time. However, when the results of the meeting were written up and appeared in print [4], Williams and Kilburn stated that 'we now agree with Mr Needham'.

The anticipation-pulse method of CRT storage was used for the Elliott 152 computer and, initially, in the Elliott 153 computer.

A1.1.3   CPU Design

In 1949 Harry Carpenter, who was placed in charge of the central processor, decided on a modular architecture for the 152. The computer was to have multiple functional units, each addressable and each connected to a bus [1]. Multiple simultaneous transfers of data could occur between stores and the various parts of the arithmetic unit. In this respect, the 152's architecture was markedly different from that of contemporary projects elsewhere. The 152's working memory was parallel-access Williams Tubes, with 16 tubes storing 256 digits each [5]. In modern terms, this gave the computer 512 bytes of RAM (random-access memory).

The general layout of highways and functional units for the 152 computer (see Fig. A1.1) was similar to that of the 153 computer, illustrated later in this appendix.

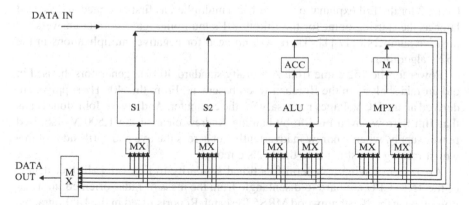

Fig. A1.1 The few original research reports for the Elliott 152 computer to have survived are not easy to interpret. This conceptual diagram shows, in modern terminology, how the 152's architecture was based on low-level functional parallelism. Concurrent transfers between sub-units were permitted within a single instruction. In the diagram, S1 and S2 are RAM caches. MX indicates multiplexer units. MPY is a fast multiplier unit and ALU provides other functions such as ADD, SHIFT, etc.

Having devised the fastest practicable memory-access time, the next challenge was to design a fast multiplier. With 16-bit words and a digit period of 3 μs, it was found possible, with a series/parallel 'wiffle-tree' design, to perform a complete multiplication every 60 μs. The basic control cycle of the machine was then based upon a 'beat' of 60 μs, corresponding to 16 digit periods plus a 4-digit gap. A serial addition could be performed within this 60-μs period.

Harry Carpenter knew that the above memory and arithmetic unit characteristics, if used in the conventional single-instruction, single-data mode of computer operation, would still not have given sufficient performance for real-time digital fire control. Therefore, provision was made for a number of instruction streams to be executed in parallel. Each of four programs was stored in a read-only memory so that the calculations for bearing, range and elevation could proceed simultaneously. Other sequences co-ordinated the overall trajectory-prediction activity and controlled input and output to/from the 152. Each of the fixed programs was held on a glass slide or card (both systems were tried), with binary ones and zeros being represented by clear or opaque spots (or by punched holes or no holes in the card). The slides (or cards) were read by a CRT flying-spot scanner. No further details have come to light.

The 152's instruction length was 20 bits. Each slide (or card) held 16 instructions. The instruction format would seem complex to modern eyes, since it gave the programmer the sort of low-level control normally associated with microprogramming. Having a series of fixed programs held in read-only memory (ROM) meant that the 152 was not, strictly speaking, a *universal* stored-program computer. The emphasis was on speed of access to predetermined standard program sequences, for which some form of fast ROM was the main requirement.

Numbers were represented in the Elliott 152 as two's complement fractions, but with the implied point being *two* positions from the most significant end – (see Chap. 2 for the full explanation). The 152's multiplier, as first designed and as used later as the starting point for the Elliott 401's multiplier, gave correct answers for positive numbers only [1]. There was no need for negative multiplications in the 152's algorithms.

Power for the 152 came from Admiralty standard 400 Hz generators, housed in old air raid shelters in the Borehamwood basement. From this 400 Hz supply were derived all the DC voltages necessary for the computer. Andrew St. Johnston recalls that Jim Barrow saved his life by hauling Andrew clear of the 1,500 V stabilised power supply, when Andrew inadvertently got across the live and earth sides of this whilst making adjustments to the 152's circuits!

Apart from having a general functional similarity to Fig. A1.1, further details of the 152's CPU are hard to disentangle from the mass of radar-oriented information given in the Borehamwood MRS5 Research Reports listed in the Bibliography. Similarly, it is not easy to extract a definitive instruction set, nor to transcribe the numerical algorithms for axis-conversion, etc., into comprehensible program listings. Some general insights are provided by the retrospective papers [5, 6]. However, producing hardware and software descriptions of the 152 that are understandable to modern readers is a task that remains to be done by other computer historians.

A1.2   The Elliott 153, the D/F Computer

A1.2.1   The 64-bit Instruction for the Elliott 153

In some respects, each of the relatively long instructions for the Elliott 153 appears more like a modern *microinstruction,* in that it specifies the interconnection of highways and registers at the hardware level [7–10]. The 153 follows the design

The four 16-bit words making up each instruction for the Elliott 153 are partitioned as shown diagrammatically below. The following abbreviations are used:

s	Spare, i.e. unallocated, bit(s)
S1	RAM store number 1
S2	RAM store number 2
S3	A 16-bit constant contained in the fourth word of an instruction
Input/Output	The Elliott 153 has ten paper tape readers for input and three teleprinters for output. These devices can be individually selected and activated by digits 10–15 of instruction-word 1
J	A *Jump if* indicator, used in conjunction with the three Control bits in the third word of an instruction
Md	Multiplicand register
Mr	Multiplier register
Acc	The main accumulator
Acc F	The function (op code) for the main ALU. These two bits specify one of the following basic operations: Add, Subtract, Reverse-subtract, logical AND
Task	These two bits control the interrogation of certain *Task selector* and *Station rejector* switches in the operator's console – see later
Control	These three bits have two distinct uses. When *J* = 1, they define the possible conditions for transfer of control. The possibilities are: *jump if acc negative* or *jump if acc zero* or *jump unconditionally.* If *J* = 0, the three Control bits are used for disc transfers, the possibilities being the three commands to *Set Relay Tree, Read from disc* and *Write to disc.* The detailed action is described later

2	4	3	6	1
s	S1 addr	S1 in	Input/output select	J

2	4	3	3	3	1
s	S2 addr	S2 in	Md in	Mr in	s

3	3	2	3	2	3
s	Acc in 1	Acc F	Acc in 2	Task	Control

16
S3, a constant (i.e. literal)

The format for the four 16-bit words that make up a 64-bit instruction for the Elliott 153 computer.

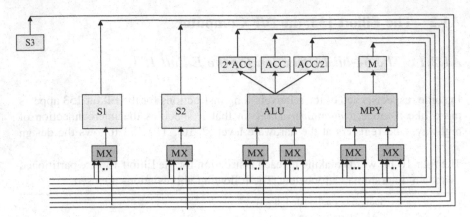

Fig. A1.2 The internal architecture of the Elliott 153 was similar to that of the 152, since it allowed several arithmetic and logical operations to be carried out within a single machine instruction. In the diagram, S1 and S2 are RAM caches and S3 holds a 16-bit constant (i.e. *literal*), brought in via the present instruction. The input/output and bulk storage facilities of the Elliott 153, as described in Chap. 3, were completely different from those of the 152

of its predecessor, the Elliott 152 computer, in arranging for more than one functional unit to be active simultaneously. This low-level parallelism results from the arrangements of multiplexed serial highways, as shown in Fig. A1.2.

The detailed allocation of particular groups of bits in the four words shown above is now given, based on information contained in [7]. For convenience, the bits are numbered 1–16 starting at the left-hand (most significant) end.

Word 1

Bits 7–9: Source of the Data for RAM Cache S1

000	Regenerate (see note (a))
100	Input from the multiplier register, M
010	Input from S2
110	Input from the selected Tape Reader
001	Input from S3, the constant specified in the present instruction
101	Input from the accumulator, A
011	Input = 2A (i.e. acc shifted one place left)
111	Input = A/2 (i.e. acc shifted down one right)

Bits 10–12: Tape Readers and Teleprinters

000	No action
100	Read from Tape Reader 6
010	Read from Tape Reader 7
110	Read from Tape Reader 8
001	Read from Tape Reader 9
101	Read from Tape Reader 10, and step on all Readers
011	Teleprinter 1
111	Teleprinter 3

(continued)

Word 1   (continued)

Bits 13–15: Tape Readers and Teleprinters (continued)

000	No action
100	Interrogate Tape Readers
010	Teleprinter 2
110	Read from Tape Reader 1
001	Read from Tape Reader 2
101	Read from Tape Reader 3
011	Read from Tape Reader 4
111	Read from Tape Reader 5

Word 2

Bits 7–9: Source (Routing) for RAM Cache S2

000	Regenerate (see note (a))
100	Input from multiplier register, M
010	Input from Tape Readers
110	Input from S1
001	Input from S3
101	Input from the accumulator, A
011	Input = 2A (i.e. acc shifted one place left)
111	Input = A/2 (i.e. acc shifted down one place right)

Bits 10–12: Source (Routing) for the Multiplicand

000	Input is unity
100	Input from multiplier register, M
010	Input from S2
110	Input from S1
001	Input from S3
101	Input from the accumulator, A
011	Input = 2A (i.e. acc shifted one place left)
111	Input = A/2 (i.e. acc shifted down one place right)

Bits 13–15: Source (Routing) for Input to the Multiplier

000	Retain the previous number in the M register
100	Input from multiplier register, M
010	Input from S2
110	Input from S1
001	Input from S3, the constant specified in the present instruction
101	Input from the accumulator, A
011	Input = 2A (i.e. acc shifted one place left)
111	Input from Programme Selector (on the operator's console (control desk))

Word 3

Bits 4–6: Source (Routing) of ALU (Accumulator) Input 1

000	Zero
100	(Spare, not used)
010	Input from S2

(continued)

Word 3   (continued)

110	Input from S1
001	Input from S3, the constant specified in the present instruction
101	Input from multiplier register, M
011	Input = 2A (i.e. acc shifted one place left)
111	(Spare, not used)

Bits 7–8: Accumulator Function (op code)

00	ADD: input 1 + input 2
10	SUB: input 1 − input 2
01	REVSUB: input 2 − input 1
11	AND: input 1 and input 2 (known originally as *Collate*)

Bits 9–11: Source (Routing) of ALU (Accumulator) Input 2

000	Input from the accumulator, A
100	Input from the number set up on the control-desk handkeys
010	Input from S2
110	Input from S1
001	Input from S3, the constant specified in this instruction
101	Input from the multiplier register, M
011	Input = 2A (i.e. acc shifted one place up)
111	Input = 1/2A (i.e. acc shifted down one place)

Bits 12–13: Operator's Control Console – Numbers Routing Unit

00	Task selector, switches 1
10	Station rejector, switches 2 and Task Reset
01	Station rejector, switches 1
11	Task selector, switches 2 and Tape Self Drive (?)

Bits 14–16: Control for This Instruction

000	Nil (no action)
100	CT negative: jump to address in M if accumulator register is negative
010	Read from disc, using track/location address held in accumulator
110	Mix S2 (?) (logical OR?)
001	Write to disc
101	Set relay tree, in preparation of disc read/write
011	CT zero: jump to address in M if accumulator register is zero
111	Mix S1 (?) (logical OR?)

A1.2.2   An Example of a Complex Instruction

A typical 153 instruction has more potential for useful work than does a typical instruction seen on a modern computer. The following illustrative example is given in [7]. This example is also presented in Chap. 3 but is repeated in this appendix for convenience. A single 153 instruction can be used to achieve the following sequence of operations:

a. Read a character from tape reader 6 and store this in address 12 of S1
b. Transfer the previous contents of the above address to location 5 of S2

c. Multiply the previous contents of location 5 in S2 by $\pi/4$, a constant contained at S3 within the present instruction, holding the result in the multiplier register

d. Add the previous contents of the multiplier register to the previous contents of location 5 in S2 and hold the result in the accumulator

In a modern register-set computer having four working registers, R1–R4, and an accumulator, the above sequence would have to be programmed in about five separate instructions as follows:

R3 := $\pi/4$;
R4 := R2 * R3;
ACC := R2 + R4;
R2 := R1;
R1 := char read from PTR6.

A1.2.3   Operation

The Elliott 153's operator has the possibility of affecting the outcome of a computation by the setting of several handkeys (switches) on a console. One row of handkeys for the 152 computer is called the *number generator*; its value can be read into the accumulator under program control via one combination of the *Acc in 2* bits in instruction-word 3. There is also a set of *Task selector* and *Station rejector* switches, whose interrogation is controlled by the *Task* bits of instruction-word 3. Finally, the *Program selector* handkeys can be fed into the multiplier via one of the combinations of the *Mr in* bits in instruction-word 2.

References

1. HG (Harry) Carpenter: notes taken by Simon Lavington of nine lengthy telephone conversations with Harry Carpenter, during the period 16 May 2000 to 9 Dec 2002. Harry was unwilling to commit his historical anecdotes to paper but was more than happy to talk. Harry's reticence to write down anecdotes about Borehamwood was explained in a letter to Laurence Clarke, dated 10 Nov 1994: 'I have never disguised the fact that I feel the organisational structure of the RLEB [Research Labs of Elliott Brothers] was badly flawed and ill-suited to the kind of development work we were trying to do (with, incidentally, an impossible time-scale)....'if you can't say something nice, don't say anything at all'
2. SE (Ed) Hersom (2000) E-mail to Simon Lavington dated 8 June 2000
3. Maurice Needham (2007) E-mails and telephone conversations with Simon Lavington, June–Oct 2007
4. Williams FC, Kilburn T (1949) A storage system for use with binary digital computing machines. Proc IEE 96 Part 2(30):183–202. Paper read at the IEE on 2 Nov 1948
5. Coales JF (Jan 1972) Computers and the professional engineer. Proc IEE 119(1):1–16
6. Clarke SLH (Aug 1975) The Elliott 400 series and before. Radio Electron Eng 45(8):415–421

7. Bunt JP (1956) The 153 computer, vol 1. Internal report 371(A), dated 1 Jan 1956. Elliott Brothers Ltd., Computing Division, Borehamwood Research Laboratories, London. This Report contains approximately 170 pages of text. The diagrams, consisting of 110 figures and photographs, are bound separately as vol 2, report 371(B), 1 Jan 1956

8. Bunt JP (1956) The 153 computer. Volume 3: test programmes. Internal report 371(C), dated 1 Jan 1956. Elliott Brothers Ltd., Computing Division, Borehamwood Research Laboratories, London

9. Bunt JP, 153 computer: maintenance handbook. Internal report 386, dated 1 Oct 1955–Jan 1956. Elliott Brothers Ltd., Computing Division, Borehamwood Research Laboratories, London

10. Bunt JP (1957) Amendments to report 371: the 153 computer, volumes 1 and 2. Internal report V/1774, dated 30 Sept 1957. Elliott Brothers Ltd., Computing Division, Borehamwood Research Laboratories, London

Appendix 2
Technical Details of the Elliott Nicholas Computer

A2.1 General Overview of the Nicholas Architecture

Nicholas is a 32-bit serial computer, with two 16-bit instructions per word. The instruction format is one-address, with six bits assigned to the function (i.e. op code) and 10 bits assigned to the address-field. The primary memory contains 1K words. There is no secondary memory. Input/output is via 5-track teleprinter equipment (paper tape and teletype).

The above simple description hides the fact that Nicholas was unconventional in a number of respects, due primarily to the project's origin as a one-off computer, designed in a short time by an electronics expert (Charles Owen) who needed to economise on hardware. The initial application involved axis transformations for trajectory calculations.

There are two main topics that reflect the above design constraints and demonstrate that Nicholas was special: firstly, the data representation employed; secondly, the instruction repertoire. As described in Chap. 2 for the Elliott 152 computer, numbers were held as two's complement fractions, with the binary point being *two* places from the most significant end. As explained below, the basic instruction set adopted a complex coding of the six function digits, with many of the notional 64 combinations being of no practical use and/or having unusual side-effects. It was just as well that the Nicholas user was shielded from hardware details by the presence of an Assembler, known as the *Translation Input*. This allowed the user to write instructions in terms of alphabetic letters which were then automatically translated to valid bit-patterns. There was a standard repertoire of 15 single-letter and 15 double-letter Assembler instructions that sufficed for most practical computations – (see Sect. A2.2).

The Nicholas primary memory consists of 1,024 32-bit words, logically arranged as eight 'loops' of 128 words. Nickel magnetostrictive delay lines were employed, each access being to a specified word in a specified loop. In detail, each 'loop' of 128 words physically consisted of eight delay lines, each holding 16 words, electrically connected in series. As described in [1], 'The lines were stored in a tall aluminium cabinet, about 6 feet high [see Fig. A2.1]. Each line was a loosely coiled spiral of nickel wire, held by paper strips about half an inch above an 18 inch square

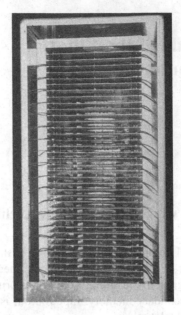

Fig. A2.1 The Nicholas memory cabinet was approximately 6 ft high. Each 'tray' within the cabinet holds a horizontal coil of nickel wire acting as a magnetostrictive delay line, the coils being supported by small strips of white paper which are just visible in the lower trays. The total capacity of the memory was 1,024 32-bit words

aluminium plate. These plates had holes in the centre to facilitate air circulation in the cabinet.'

Since delay lines are by nature sequential, the minimum Nicholas access-time is one word-time, the maximum is 128 word-times and the average is about 64 word-times. Addressing is always to a word boundary, a fact that has to be taken into account when arranging the pairs of instructions that make up a Nicholas program.

An extra 16-word delay line was used for timing purposes, acting as the 'pendulum to the machine's clock' [1]. The digit frequency is given as 330 kHz in [2], though it is more likely to have been 333 kHz so as to correspond to the standard digit period of 3 μs adopted by Borehamwood at that time for the Elliott 400 series computers (and indeed for their near-cousins, the Ferranti Pegasus and Perseus computers). Furthermore, a note on the original Nicholas diagram in [3] (see Fig. A2.2) gives the digit period as 3 μs. Finally, [4] states that the maximum access-time of the memory (128 word-times) is 'about 12.6 ms', implying a digit period of about 3.076 μs.

The duration of each instruction was dependent upon the relative separation of address-requests in the *three-beat* fetch-execute-execute sequence of a pair of instructions [4]. To describe the three Nicholas beats, it is first necessary to introduce the computer's five central registers – which were mostly implemented as

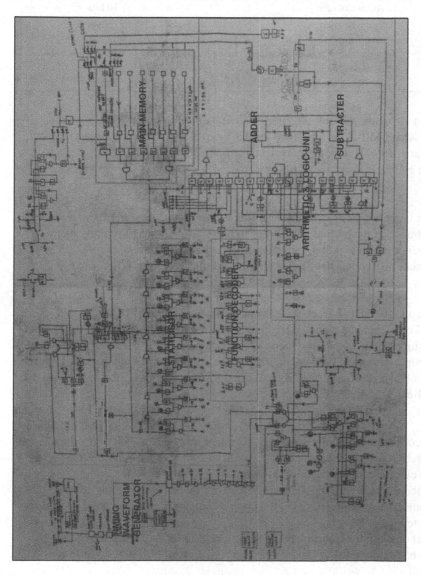

Fig. A2.2 The underlying diagram in this image is Charles Owen's original 1952 logic drawing for Nicholas. Modern annotations have been superimposed on Charles Owen's diagram to show the various sections of the Nicholas CPU. On the left is the timing waveform generator. On the right is the memory, which was shown in more detail on another diagram. In the centre are flip-flops (*staticisors*), feeding the function decoding logic immediately beneath. To the bottom right of the diagram is the ALU, containing an adder and a subtracter

nickel delay lines [3–5]. The Nicholas registers are presented below, using modern terminology and annotated with their conceptual lengths – (the original 1952 terminology and actual lengths are given later, in Sect. A2.4).

PC	Program Counter	10 bits
WR	Working Register	16 bits
ACC	Accumulator	32 bits
AEX	Accumulator extension, used e.g. during multiplication	32 bits (+1 bit)
MR	Multiplicand register	32 bits
CC	Coincidence Counter, for matching addresses	10 bits

PC and ACC are the only registers visible to programmers. The interaction of ACC, AEX and MR at the hardware level are explained in Sect. A2.3 below, when the software *Multiply* subroutine is described.

The three Nicholas beats are as follows:

Beat 1:

a. WR contains the next-instruction address. CC looks for a match between this address and the current position of the circulating loops of primary memory.
b. When a match is found, move the next-instruction address into PC; fetch the current instruction-pair from memory and place them in WR.

Beat 2:

a. Decode the first instruction (held in the least-significant 16 bits of WR). CC looks for a match between the instruction's operand-address and the current position of the circulating loops of primary memory.
b. When a match is found, either obey the instruction (reading or writing to memory if appropriate) or, if a control transfer is indicated, then go to step (a) of Beat 1.

Beat 3:

a. Decode the second instruction (held in the top 16 bits of WR). CC looks for a match between the instruction's operand-address and the current position of the circulating loops of primary memory.
b. When a match is found, either: (i) obey the instruction (reading or writing to memory if appropriate) or (ii) if a control transfer is indicated, then go straight to step (a) of Beat 1.
c. Add one to the next-instruction address held in PC and place it in WR.
d. Go back to step (a) of Beat 1.

Given the need to wait for address-coincidence in each beat, we may calculate the average time for a Nicholas instruction. If the average access-time of the main memory is approximately 6 ms, then the three beats of a pair of orders take a total of $3 \times 6 = 18$ ms, giving 9 ms as the average instruction time for a single order. This corresponds to a rate of about 111 instructions per second – which may be compared with the figure of 80 instructions/s given in [2]. The minimum time for two successive ADD instructions is five word-times, or 240 μs each. The longest time for these two instructions is 384 word-times, or 18.432 ms each.

If two consecutive memory-references are to identical locations modulo 128, then a gap of 128 word-times has to follow the first access before the second access is possible. If two consecutive addresses only differ by 2 (modulo 128), access is achieved in the shortest possible time and so programmers strove to optimise their code to match this condition. Notice that, in step (a) of beats 2 and 3, hardware always looks for an address-match even though some of the Nicholas instructions are monadic (meaning that an operand-address is not required). For this reason, Nicholas programmers were encouraged to put optimal dummy addresses into monadic instructions such as the *Shift one place Left* instruction (see below). In addition, to quote [4], 'it may sometimes be possible, especially if a program has a large number of orders with dummy address, to save time by always putting a transfer [jump] order in the second half of each location and by rearranging the orders to get the addresses into a convenient order; when used in this manner the machine resembles one with a *two-address* order code'.

A2.2   The Nicholas Instruction Set

The format for a pair of instructions is as follows, where the right-hand (less-significant) one is executed first:

<-- *second instr.* -->		<--- *first instr.* - -->	
6	10	6	10
F	N	F	N
Op code	Address	Op code	Address

The Function bits (op code) are divided, for hardware convenience, into two fields as shown in the lists below. Each field may be treated as an octal digit to which the Nicholas Assembler assigns an alphabetic letter. Although the two fields might be imagined as providing a maximum of 64 instructions, far fewer than this have any practical use. The most useful surviving description of the valid instructions will be found in [4] but even this document is silent about many combinations of the F bits. Fortunately, it is not necessary to delve into the hardware details of Charles Owen's decoding of the F bits, though the surviving diagram in [3] (see Fig. A2.2) and the explanation of Sect. A2.4 give the necessary clues. Knowing the high regard in which Charles Owen was held by colleagues [6] – Owen was honoured with a prestigious IBM Fellowship in 1969 – we can be confident that Owen's complex decoding scheme achieved his goal of minimizing the number of standard circuit boards required to implement Nicholas' hardware.

The following (modern) notation is used in describing Nicholas instructions.

a = contents of the accumulator

x = contents of storage location n

t = the current five-bit character as read in from paper tape, placed as the least-significant 5 bits in a 32-bit word.

Primes are used to indicate the new values at the conclusion of an instruction. Operand addresses are denoted by n; dummy addresses in monadic instructions are denoted by m.

The Nicholas instruction set is composed of combinations of the following two groups of basic operations.

F bits	Action		Corresponding Assembler letter
- - - 000	do nothing		O
- - - 001	a' = a + x	(add)	A
- - - 010	jump to n if a < 0		Z
- - - 011	unconditional absolute jump		T
- - - 100	special action (see below)		Y
- - - 101	a' = a + t	(input a character)	I
- - - 110	a' = a × x	(multiplication)	M
- - - 111	x' = a	(write acc to memory)	W
000 - - -	do nothing		O
001 - - -	a' = 0	(clear acc)	C
010 - - -	a' = 2 × a	(arith shift left one place)	D
011 - - -	a' = a/2	(arith shift right one place)	H
100 - - -	special action	(see below)	X
101 - - -	a' = −a	(negate acc)	N
110 - - -	a' = a & x	(logical AND)	L
111 - - -	a' = a − x	(subtract)	S

The actual bit-pattern for the instruction *Add the contents of location 13 to the accumulator* would be: 0000010000001101. In Nicholas Assembler, this would be written as: A 13. Similarly, the bit-pattern for *Arithmetical shift right by one place* would be 011000ΦΦΦΦΦΦΦΦΦΦ where Φ indicates that, for this monadic function, the address digits are irrelevant to the *shift* instruction and therefore may be set to any value that helps to minimise unnecessary time spent in waiting for memory-address coincidence (see above).

The Nicholas Assembler, known as the *Translation Input,* introduced an additional single-letter mnemonic, P, which was a pseudo-instruction translated by software into a call to the library subroutine for printing, as described in Sect. A2.3 below.

Further valid Nicholas instructions may be composed of certain combinations of the above two lists of basic hardware actions. Here are the more useful combinations:

F bits	Action		Corresponding Assembler letters
001001	a' = x	Clear and add (i.e. load)	CA
010001	a' = 2a + x	Double and add	DA
011001	a' = a/2 + x	Halve and add	HA
101001	a' = x − a	Reverse subtract	NA
001111	x' = a; a' = 0	Store acc, then clear acc	WC
010111	x' = a; a' = 2a	Store acc, then double acc	WD
011111	x' = a; a' = a/2	Store acc, then halve acc	WH
101111	x' = a; a' = −a	Store acc, then negate acc	WN
111111	x' = a; a' = a − x	Store acc, then subtract old x	WS
110111	x' = a; a' = a & x	Store acc, then AND with old x	WL
001101	a' = t	Read an input character; step the paper tape reader on to the next row of holes	CI

Each pair of Function Letters, as used in an Assembler program, may be written in any order; the assembler will then compile the pair into the correct bit-pattern at machine-code level as shown above. In hardware terms, the right-hand three F bits mainly affect the serial data paths leading *out of* the accumulator; the left-hand three F bits mainly affect the way the *inputs* to the ALU are logically combined on their way into the accumulator. In [4], certain Assembler letters are termed *Auxiliary Function letters;* these are X, N, D, H and C.

As [4] observes, 'certain other pairs of Function letters [ie Assembler mnemonics] are permissible though of limited utility'. Amongst these are the following:

010110	a' = a(x + 2a)	MD
011110	a' = a(x + a/2)	MH

It is also possible to use an unconditional jump (T) or a conditional jump (Z) in combination with the *Auxiliary Function letters* (X, N, D, H, C) to achieve some curious side-effects concerned with either (a) inhibiting the normal incrementing of the program counter register PC, or (b) forcing the logical effect of the *Auxiliary Function letter* to persist until the next unconditional or conditional jump instruction is encountered. Examples are:

F bits	Action	Inhibit +1 to PC?	Auxiliary Fn persists?	Corresponding Assembler letters
100011	a' = a	Yes	No	TX
101011	a' = −a	Yes	No	TN
010011	a' = 2a	No	Yes	TD
011011	a' = a/2	No	Yes	TH
001011	a' = 0	No	Yes	TC

As [4] points out, 'Great care is needed when using such combinations and it is recommended that their use be avoided until some experience has been gained.' The TX and TN orders are always to be placed in the second (more significant) half of the word containing a pair of instructions. At the conclusion of a sequence of pairs of instructions, the second half of each of which contains TX or TN, control will be returned to the order in the memory location following that which contains the first instruction in the sequence. Such sequences are used in the multiplication and printing subroutines (see Sect. A2.3). When using the TD, TH and TC instructions, the contents of the accumulator will be doubled, halved or cleared respectively *every* time PC is incremented until a successful jump instruction is encountered.

The Function letter X is only intended for use with the Function letters T and Z, as described above. An instruction with X alone (i.e. with F-bits = 100000) has no effect. The Function letter Y is used in the multiplication subroutine to manipulate the accumulator extension register (see below). Multiplication (M) and printing (P) are performed by special subroutines. M and P orders must be placed in the second-half (ms half) of a 32-bit program-word.

A2.3   Nicholas Assembler and Library of Subroutines

The fully-developed system software for Nicholas was largely written by George and Ruth Felton, as described in Chap. 8. Following the example of EDSAC at the University of Cambridge [7], users prepared programs for Nicholas on punched paper tape in terms of alphabetic mnemonics and decimal numbers. A user's program was then read in and converted into binary by the previously-loaded Nicholas Assembler. This Assembler, called the *Translation Input Routine*, occupies locations 0–213 of memory and includes subroutines for multiplication and printing. Locations from 214 upwards then contain various useful addresses and constants. User programs normally start at address 265.

A user might include in his or her program one or more well-tested sections of code, chosen from a library which in due course included the following groups of subroutines [4, 8]:

Division,
Square root and other fractional powers,
Trigonometrical functions,
Exponential functions,
Hyperbolic functions,
Complex numbers,
Logarithms,
Quadrature,
Solution of differential equations,
Floating-point arithmetic,
Matrix manipulation,
Printing and layout.

The floating-point interpreter took about 0.5 s per floating-point instruction, according to its author, George Felton [9]. The Matrix Interpretive Scheme was written by Felton to calculate flutter vibrations in aircraft. The de Havilland factory at Hatfield, where the Comet airliner was being designed, was quite close to Borehamwood, and Elliotts sold a large amount of Nicholas computer-time to Peter Hunt who worked at de Havilland in the aerodynamics department. The general principles of the Nicholas subroutine library and interpretive software were later carried over by Felton into the Ferranti Pegasus Library [9].

It is instructive to give the Print and Multiplication subroutines in full, since these illustrate the more esoteric uses of the TX and TN instructions. The descriptions which follow are taken directly from George Felton' explanation on pages 29 and 30 of [4].

A2.3.1 The Print Subroutine

This closed subroutine, which is stored in locations 138–149 of the *Translation Input Routine,* is called by a *P* pseudo-instruction. P is translated into the binary equivalent of TX 138 during the Assembly phase of a user's program. To quote [4]: 'When the subroutine is entered the accumulator contains the binary equivalent of the teleprinter code for the character it is desired to print. This binary number is tested by the IX orders and doubled between each test until seven mark or space signals have been sent to the teleprinter. These signals have to be sent at intervals of 202 word-times [about 2 milliseconds] to operate the teleprinter correctly; this consideration determines the dummy addresses of the IX and D orders and the sequence of orders. The orders of the subroutine are as follows [as they would appear in written (source) form]':

Address	Lower (First) Instruction		Upper (Second) Instruction	
138	IX	10	TX	144
139	IX	30	TX	143
140	IX	84	TX	142
141	D	15	TX	145
142	D	16	TX	139
143	D	17	TX	147
144	D	18	TX	140
145	IX	124	TX	149
146	IX	50	TX	141
147	IX	104	TX	148
149	D	22	TX	146
149	D	19	IX	70 (absence of TX permits return to the main program)

The appearance of the IX order in the print routine is not fully explained by the surviving source documentation. Commenting many years later, George Felton was still unsure how to explain the action. He recalled [9] that: 'The IX-order has function bits 100101 and is not precisely defined in the original manual [4]. It appears in the Print Subroutine (see Appendix D, page 29, of [4]) but nowhere else, as far as I know. I feel sure that this Print subroutine was devised by Charles Owen. I can't recall using the IX-order but I may have included it in my "uniselector" program for the Initial Orders. My memory is weak on this point and much of the design documentation has now been lost... Appendix A on page 17 of [4] supports a *possible* meaning of the IX-order, namely: "Read the tape and add it to the least significant end of the Accumulator" + "special action". This apparently clashes with its use in the Print routine, since this refers to *output*, not input. Maybe the "special action" has two meanings – but I feel there is little chance of hitting the right one in view of the loss of so much information'.

A2.3.2   The Multiplication Subroutine

This closed subroutine occupies storage locations 0, 2, 4, 5, 7, 9, 82, 84 and 86 of the *Translation Input Routine*. To quote [4], 'When the order M n is obeyed control is transferred to location 0 and the accumulator goes double-length; the number originally in the accumulator occupies one half and the number from location n occupies the other half of this double length accumulator. Orders with an even address will affect the multiplier part of the accumulator and orders with an odd address will affect the multiplicand part. The orders of the subroutine are given below [as they would appear in written (source) form].'

'The orders in locations 0, 2, 4 and 5 change the signs of the numbers to make both positive and the multiplication proper is initiated by one of the orders YC in locations 7 and 9 (depending upon the sign of the product). YC clears one half of the double length accumulator leaving the multiplier in the other half and transfers the multiplicand to a multiplicand register. It also causes the accumulator to increase its length to 2 words plus 1 digit. In the ensuing word times, until coincidence occurs at either 82 or 84, the multiplier is shifted one digit every other word time and simultaneously the multiplicand is added to the other half of the accumulator if there is a digit in the multiplier at the most significant end. Just before coincidence occurs the multiplier has been shifted out and the double length product occupies the whole of the accumulator. On coincidence the accumulator returns to single length but the least significant digit is lost in the process. Order 82 or 84 makes the least-significant digit unity and since there is no TX (or TN) in either order, control is returned to the order immediately after the original multiplication order, M. In this process the least significant digit is always unity but there is, in general, no bias in the rounding-off error. However, if the double length product ends in 32 or more zeros, this extra digit may cause trouble.'

The multiplication subroutine is as follows:

Address	Lower (first) instruction		Upper (second) instruction		
0	ZN	2	TN	4	(Test sign of multiplicand)
2	ZN	5	TN	7	(Test sign of multiplier (negative multiplicand))
4	ZN	7	TN	9	(Test sign of multiplier (positive multiplicand))
5	0	7	TX	9	
7	YC	14	TX	82	
9	YC	16	TX	84	
82	A	86	N	88	(Negative product) (absence of TX or) TN permits return
84	A	86	0	88	(Positive product) to main program
86		1			(Round-off constant = 1×2^{-30})

A2.4 Charles Owen's Original Nicholas Terminology

In what is probably the earliest (1952) surviving description of the Nicholas instruction set [3], Charles Owen used a somewhat different notation to that employed in George Felton's 1953 programming manual [4]. The 1952 and 1953 notations are given in Table A2.1, along with the modern equivalent names as used in the descriptions of Sects. A2.1 and A2.2.

Charles Owen's terminology is clearly related to his engineering design. This is demonstrated in the labelling of the function-bits in his 1952 description of the Nicholas Order Code (i.e. instruction set), where the signal-names A to F correspond with the outputs from the flip-flops shown in the logic diagram of [3]. The decoding of the six function-bits is seen to be incomplete, meaning that far fewer than the 64 possible combinations are distinguished. Owen's specification of each valid instruction is given in Table A2.2, followed by his advisory notes to programmers as set forth in [3].

Reference [3] notes that function numbers 2, 3 or 4 'must not be used with 11 or 12 as this would result in 2, 3 or 4 happening every time the order number was changed thereafter. Actually one could make use of this facility in the initial orders programme to reduce the number of digits in the wired orders by about 20. This method would spread the orders over another ten words.' The *Initial Orders,* given on page 5 of [3], are set out as shown in Table A2.3. Reference [3] then appends the following comment to the list of orders: 'Total of 67 digits shared as input coils'.

Finally, [3] also gives an estimate of 65 standard circuit plates required for the main Nicholas logic. The plates, each conceptually equivalent to a printed-circuit board, are of three types, notionally following the designs of standard Elliott digital circuits presented by Owen in [10].

Table A2.1 Some early names used for the delay-line central registers in Nicholas

Modern name	Name as given in [4]	Name as given in [3]	Annotation given on the diagram in [3]	Length specified in [3], with any tappings noted
PC	Order number Register, ONR	Order number Register, ONR	IAR (annotation is rather indistinct)	30 Digits
WR	Order register, OR	Order register, OR	Inst Reg	31 Digits, tapped at 15
ACC + AEX	Accumulator; Accumulator extension	Accumulator	ACCr	62, Tapped at 29
MR	Multiplicand register	Multiplicand register	M' and reg	32
CC	Coincidence counter	Serial number register	Line addr genr.	30 Digits
–	–	Control	Control line	16 Words
–	–	Clock	Clock line	1 Word

Table A2.2 The original notation and description of Nicholas instructions, as given in [3]

Function number		ABC
1.	000 - - -	Accumulator circulating
2.	001 - - -	Clear accumulator
3.	010 - - -	Double the contents of accumulator
4.	011 - - -	Halve the contents of accumulator
5.	100 - - -	X (Inhibits change of contents of order number register, etc.)
6.	101 - - -	Change sign of contents of accumulator
7.	110 - - -	Collate with incoming number
8.	111 - - -	Subtract incoming number from accumulator
		DEF
9.	- - - 000	Do nothing
10.	- - - 001	Add incoming number to accumulator
11.	- - - 010	Conditional transfer (accumulator negative)
12.	- - - 011	Transfer control
13.	- - - 100	Y (used in multiplication routine with 2)
14.	- - - 101	Read tape and step on one character
15.	- - - 110	Multiply the contents of the accumulator by the number in the location specified. (Note: Must only be used in the second half of an order)
16.	- - - 111	Write contents of accumulator into the store

Table A2.3 The Nicholas *Initial Orders*, as given in [3]

Order number		
1	Clear and read tape	X2 (i.e. Double)
2	X2	X2
3	Read tape	X2
4	X2	X2
5	Read tape	X2
6	X2	X2
7	X2	X2 Read tape
8	X2	X2
9	X2	X2
10	X2 Read tape	X2
11	X2	X2 Read tape
12	X2	X2
13	X2 Read tape	X2
14	X2	X2
15	X2	X2 Read tape
16	32 Write	64 Clear and add
17	32 CT-	16 Clear and add
18	20 Add	16 Write
19	1 Tc	
20	1	

A2.5   Using Nicholas

The further development of the Nicholas programming system by George Felton has been described in Chap. 8. We end this appendix by recounting anecdotes that give a user's view of what it felt like to work with Nicholas.

As a one-off 'hand-built' machine, the reliability of Nicholas was hardly expected to be exemplary. Ed Hersom remembers [11] that 'we were used to storage troubles occurring every few hours... Crashes were usually caused by single bits being picked up in the store and corrupting the stored program. When this happened curious outputs might appear .... It turned out that the teleprinter had come from naval stores (not surprising considering the history of Elliott Bros) and this printer had been fitted with an "answer back" drum so Nicholas, in its aberrant actions, had only to issue the *Who are you?* code and ROYAL NAVY would emerge. It printed this at a noticeably faster rate than the usual output, so sitting in an adjacent office one could hear when this fault had occurred ....

'For several months we would run Nicholas overnight unattended. The runs entailed reading data off a long paper tape, analysing each section and printing out the results. To guard against losing vast amounts of printing paper on the teleprinter should the machine go wrong, the results were output to punched paper tape. It wasn't quite unattended. We had warned the night-watchman that if on his rounds he heard that the tape reader and punch were not maintaining their usual rhythm he should push the *off/single-shot/run* switch from run to off.

'One morning we came in and found, from examining the output tape, that the machine had obviously gone wrong but then had miraculously continued to work correctly! By the time this was discovered the night-watchman had gone off duty so we couldn't quiz him until the following morning. When asked what had happened, he responded with simply "Was it alright?" He, bless the man, had switched to "off" as instructed but then switched back to "run" just to see what might occur! The second remarkable thing was that the fault which had occurred was corrected just on a restart. That night-watchman's action had been most valuable.'

More operational experience of Nicholas, for example the prediction of General Election results for the BBC during which the machine worked without error for several hours, are described in Chap. 8.

References

1. Hersom SE (2002) Nicholas, the forgotten Elliott project. Resurrection, the Bulletin of the Computer Conservation Society, Issue number 27, spring 2002, pp. 10–14
2. Hersom SE (1956) Operating experience with Nicholas. Proc IEE 103 Part B (1–3):276–277 (Lecture delivered at the Convention on Digital Computer techniques, 11 Apr 1956)
3. (a) Anon (1952) Summary of the Nicholas order code. Undated six-page typed note. Contains a section entitled Hardware Required, which strongly suggests that this document was written by Charles Owen some time in the middle of 1952 (b) Large (approximately three feet square) annotated dye-line logic diagram of Nicholas – see Fig. A2.2. These two associated documents came to light in 2009 when Charles Owen's daughter, Sally Whytehead, was sorting through family papers

4. Felton GE (1953) Programming 'Nicholas'. Elliott Brothers Ltd., Borehamwood Research Laboratories, London. Technical report M12 dated 6 July 1953 (35 typed pages)
5. Hill ND (1953) Nicholas. In: Proceedings of the NPL symposium on automatic digital computers, pp 44–45, HMSO, 1954
6. (a) Anon (1984) Obituary for C E Owen, The Times, Saturday 2 June 1984 (b) Conversations between Ian Merry (formerly of Ferranti Ltd.) and Simon Lavington, 1999
7. Wilkes MV, Wheeler DJ, Gill S (1951) The preparation of programs for an electronic digital computer. Addison-Wesley, Cambridge
8. Felton GE (2006) Getting the job done. Resurrection number 38, summer 2006. http://www.cs.man.ac.uk/CCS/res/res38.htm#e
9. GE Felton (2008) E-mail communications with Simon Lavington, Nov 2008
10. Owen CE (1952) Three standard circuits for serial digital computers. Borehamwood Research Laboratory of Elliott Brothers Ltd., London. Internal research report number 301, 2 Sept 1952
11. SE Hersom (2000) Nicholas: reminiscences. Typewritten document sent to Simon Lavington, Jan 2000

Appendix 3
Technical Details of the Elliott 400 Series Computers

A3.1 General Characteristics of the Family

Borehamwood produced four types of computers in the 400 series: the 401, 402, 403 and 405. A paper specification for an Elliott 404 was produced in 1956 [1] but the design never materialised. In any case, the architecture was very similar to that of the 405. The 404's proposed instruction format had one extra bit in the Op code field and one less in the address-field when compared with the 405's format. The instruction set of the 404 was similar in scope to that of the 405 – although the 404 would have allowed for the double modification of operand addresses.

The 400-series machines all had 2's complement serial arithmetic units employing thermionic valves (mostly double-triodes). All machines in the range used basically the same family of Elliott packaged circuits – with some additions to the family as time went on. The rhythm of the CPU was clocked to a timing track on the drum or disc backing store. Central registers and fast storage (where provided) were implemented as nickel magnetostrictive delay lines. Backing storage was via fixed-head magnetic drums or discs.

The Elliott 401 went through a number of modifications in its lifetime, of which the few details to have come to light are presented later, in Sect. A3.3. The description given below is for the original (1953) version of the machine. The description of the 403 has not been easy to verify but is believed to be correct. The descriptions of the 402 (also known as the 402E) and of the 405 are believed to be typical of standard production versions.

Only two machines of the Elliott 400 series had hardware floating-point facilities. These were known as the 402F variant, first delivered to Germany in 1958, for which the floating-point arithmetic unit added a further three cabinets to the normal complement of six cabinets. (Laurence Clarke, who designed the floating-point unit, remembers the floating-point unit as only one extra cabinet [2], but it depends upon whether one only counts fully populated logic cabinets or includes cabinets containing power supplies, cooling fans, etc. See, for example, the photograph in Fig. 5.6). One of the Elliott 402F computers was put to good use for 12 years for optical lens design by the Leitz company, before being retired in 1970 [3]. A second

Fig. A3.1 The photo shows Computing Division staff in 1952, working on the backwiring of the three main racks which formed the CPU of the Elliott 401 computer. It may be deduced that, for Borehamwood, the 401 was more of a prototype than a production machine

402F went to British Rail. Delivery lists for all Elliott 400 series computers are given in Appendix 8.

The general properties of the 400 series computers are compared in Table A3.1. This table should be read in conjunction with the further details that follow. Note, however, that the surviving original Elliott source documentation is not always consistent, specifications evolving during the production life of each type of machine. Note especially that the fine details of the Elliott 401 and its peripheral equipment underwent several improvements during the years 1953–1965, first at Cambridge and then at Rothamsted – see Sect. A3.3 below and Chap. 5. A good first-hand account of the engineering environment in which the 400 series machines were developed at Borehamwood is given by Laurence Clarke in [4].

All the 400 series machines shared the same logic circuits, based on an original design by Charles Owen but converted by Laurence Clarke in 1952 to use the recently-introduced 12AT7 triodes instead of the more expensive (but more reliable) miniature pentodes. Laurence has described the circuit design philosophy as follows [4]. 'The Owen circuits were based on a delay circuit which was very

Table A3.1 General characteristics of Elliott 400 series computers. The figures should be interpreted in the light of the comments given in the text

	401	402E and 402 F	403 (WREDAC)	405
Word length, visible bits	32	32	34	32
Word length incl. gap bits, if any	34	34	34	34
Digit period, microseconds	3	3	3	3
Instruction length	32	32	17	16
Instruction format, addresses	1 + 1	1 + 1	1	1
No. of instructions/word	1	1	1	2
Visible central registers (apart from Acc, Acc extn., Multiplier and handkeys)	2 (X, Y)	7 B-lines	3 B-lines chosen from 12 fast registers	3 B-lines
Fixed-point ADD time, min., milliseconds	0.204	0.204	0.204	0.306
Fixed-point MPY time, min., milliseconds	7	3.3	3.3	3.3
Max. Primary store (*Immediate Access* plus *Quick Access*), words	(none)	15 words	512 words	512 words
Backing store, words, max.	2,944	3K	16K	32K
Typical power requirements	5 kVA	7 kVA (11 kVA for 402F)	15 kVA, plus *??* kVA for WREDOC	?
Date first delivered	1953, 1954	1955	1955	1956

determined. The input was clocked; this caused a valve to make an inductance, which then charged up a condenser. At the end of the next clock period a reset pulse sucked the charge out very rapidly, and that left you with a totally determined pulse. What this enabled us to do was to put it together in very standard forms [ie packages] with a number of other devices – AND gate, OR-gate, digit delay, coincidence gated converter. These were combined to produce a gated delay – the standard circuit which you could then turn into what in other computers of the day was a flip-flop.

'I think this activity was the beginning of the end of suck-it-and see electronics … At Elliotts we started to work in a more methodical fashion. We analysed worst-worst cases for the logic loading rules …'". This led to standard logic packages of predictable performance which could be combined without the logic designer having to worry about the internal circuit details.

A3.2   Elliott 401: Details of Fast Storage and the Instruction Set

The definitive specification of the 401 as it emerged from Borehamwood in 1953 is given in [5]. Note that a set of original 401 drawings was deposited in the Science Museum in London in 1991 [6]. The computer itself, as it existed in its last working state in 1965, is physically preserved in a Science Museum store at the time of writing. An original register-to-register diagram of the 401, and the details of the address-generation mechanism using modern terminology, are given in Figs. A3.2 and A3.3.

The Elliott 401's main (and only) store was a disc (strictly speaking, a fixed-head *drum,* in more recent terminology). When track switching occurred, and when information was written to the disc, the reading amplifiers were temporarily 'paralysed' for three or four word-times. If a program requested a read during a paralysis period, hardware automatically delayed reading for a complete revolution of the disk. One revolution-time equalled 13.1 ms. The 401's CPU had a two-beat fetch-execute rhythm. That is to say, instructions were selected and obeyed alternatively. The basic *beat* was 34 digit-times of 3 μs each (thus allowing for the two-digit gap). The total fetch-execute sequence was therefore basically 204 μs and the basic fixed-point add time was also 204 μs. However, two-successive *ADD* instructions could only be executed at this rate if optimum programming had been used to position these two instructions appropriately on the disk. If the second instruction was 'missed', the disk may have to complete a revolution (13.1 ms) before the required instruction became available. In view of this, and disk paralysis period noted above, it seems reasonable to take an average add time for practical programs of perhaps 3 ms if attempting to compare the 401 with the instruction speeds of other contemporary machines with random-access primary memory. This touches on the art of *optimum programming*, for which the precise location of instructions and operands in a sequentially-accessed memory was important.

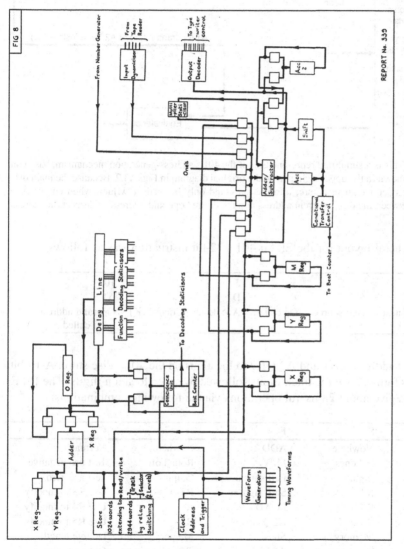

Fig. A3.2 An original diagram, taken from a 1954 Borehamwood research report, shows the layout of the arithmetic unit and central registers of the Elliott 401 computer. The main drum memory is to the left of the diagram and the input/output equipment is on the upper right. The adder/subtracter unit is on the lower right

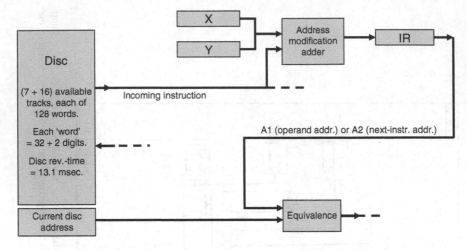

Fig. A3.3 This is a simplified representation of the 401's address-generation mechanism, based on the details shown in the upper-right part of the original diagram in Fig. A3.2. Because the main disc memory was sequential in nature, information could only be read or written when equivalence occurred between the disc's current address and the desired operand-address or instruction-address

The general layout for the Elliott 401's 32-bit instruction was as follows:

10	3	3	3	3	10
A2	**S**	**F**	**D**	**C**	**A1**
Address of next instruction	Acc source	Op code	Acc dest.	Control (K)	Operand address (also called *timing*)

The 10-bit addresses A1 and A2 refer to locations on the 401's disc store. A 10-bit address is formed as three track-digits followed by seven location-digits. The {S, F, D, C} bits give about 28 useful operations via the following combinations:

	S	F	D	C
000	Nowhere	ADD	Nowhere	Normal
001	All ones	MPY	Round off	Test acc negative
010	Input	Left shift n	Output	Test acc zero
011	R3	Shift right n	R3	Use R3 to modify
100	R4	LOAD	R4	Use R4 to modify
101	R5	NEQ	R5	Use R5 to modify
110	Memory	SUB	Memory	Double length
111	Handkeys	AND	Track 7 switch	Optional stop

Some combinations are forbidden, for example {6, –, 6, –} which attempts to specify memory as both the source and destination. The coding of the S, F, D and C fields as given above differs in minor respects from that shown in the original Borehamwood report [5]. The names of the central registers also evolved over the years. Some equivalent names are as follows: R1 = accumulator; R2 = accumulator extension; R3 = Multiplier register, M; R4 = general register X; R5 = general register Y. The main computer, including power supplies and cooling fans, occupied seven cabinets.

Further explanation of some of the Elliott 401 instructions is now given. The *NEQ* instruction is the logical *Not Equivalence* operation, also called *Exclusive OR*. The Handkeys signify a 32-bit value set up manually via switches, originally called the *number generator* by Borehamwood. When shifting the accumulator up or down arithmetically by n places, the value of n is given by the difference (A2 − A1). During multiplication, the contents of R2 are multiplied by the contents of R3, leaving the product (62 digits plus a sign digit) in R1 (more significant half) and R2 (less-significant half). If only the most significant half of a product is required, round off may be used. The product, rounded to 31 binary places, is then placed in R1. The time for multiplication given in Table A3.1 is that for the post-1954 version of the 401 − (the original time was quoted as being 'between 7 and 10 milliseconds, depending upon sign'). When using the *Double Length* indicator, R1 and R2 together form a two-word accumulator. When using the *Optional Stop* indicator, the computer will halt before obeying the instruction and wait until the operator presses the single-shot key on the control console. The machine can be set to ignore *Optional Stop* instructions by depressing a switch on the console.

The original disc store for the Elliott 401 'comprised 8 tracks closely spaced near the outer rim of a 9-inch diameter disc, each track carrying 128 words'. This was soon increased to 23 tracks, each holding 128 words. Since only ten address bits are provided in the 401's instruction, only eight tracks are available to the programmer at any one time. Tracks 0–6 are by convention fixed tracks, and 'track 7' can dynamically be made to refer to any of the 16 remaining tracks, logically numbered 0–15, by means of the *Track 7* instruction. When switching between one *track 7* and another *track 7*, the programmer needed to allow for a full drum revolution of approximately 13 ms.

Selecting the *Input* combination of the S-bits in an Elliott 401 instruction causes a row to be read from the 5-track Tape Reader and the tape to be advanced by one row. The integer represented by the 5-bit combination is placed in the least-significant end of the accumulator. When the *Output* combination of the D-bits is selected, either a paper tape punch or a typewriter (teleprinter) is activated, the choice being determined by the setting of a manual switch on the equipment. In either case, the least-significant five bits of the accumulator are either punched on 5-track paper tape or printed as an alpha-numeric character on a page.

A3.3 The 401 at Rothamsted: Programming and Enhancements

In Tables A3.2 and A3.3 is an example of a library subroutine, as used on the Elliott 401 computer at Rothamsted. The descriptions come from a typewritten computer manual at Rothamsted [7]. The author/date of this particular subroutine is given as M J R Healy, 7 October 1954 and the code implements the square root function.

Table A3.2 The formal description of the square root library subroutine

```
Sub-routine
Square root
y = √x, 0 ≤ x < 1
Addresses occupied: V.64 - V.82
Registers used: All.
Enter at V64, link in R1, x in R4
Result: y in R1 (0 in R4)
Time: 0.1 - 1 sec. approx, longest for small numbers.
Accuracy: The result has two fewer significant (binary) figures than
the original number.
Method: see EDSAC sub-routine S2
a_{n+1} = a_n (1 - ½ c_n)  a_0 = x  a_n -> √x
c_{n+1} = ¼ c_n²(c_n - 3)  c_0 = x - 1  c_n -> 0.
M.J.R.Healy
7 October 1954
```

Table A3.3 The code for the square root library subroutine

```
Programme
Square root
V.64 V.82 4460 V.65
V.82 V.81 0002 V.71 If x = 0, jump to end of programme.
V.81 V.72 6000 V.70 c_0
┌->V.72 V.75 0330 V.73 ¼c_n; c_n to R3
│  V.75 V.77 6600 V.76 ¼c_n - ¾
│  V.77 V.79 4456 V.78
│  V.79 V.66 0110 V.35 a_n c_n
│  V.66 V.68 0300 V.67 ½a_n c_n
│  V.68 V.73 4440 V.69
│  V.73 V.78 4600 V.74 a_{n+1}
│  V.78 V.80 5446 V.79
│  V.80 V.67 0110 V.36
│  V.67 V.74 0006 V.68
│  V.74 V.69 0110 V.38 c_{n+1}
└- V.69 V.72 0002 V.71
V.71 V.65 4440 V.72
V.70 4.00 0000 0.00 ‖ -1
V.76 3.00 0000 0.00 ‖ ¾
V.65 0.12 3456 7.89 ‖ link space.
```

The notation in Table A3.3 is as follows, where <SFDC> are the four octal digits giving the {acc. source, op code, acc. destination and control}:

   <addr. of instr.> <addr. of next instr.> <SFDC> <addr. of operand>

Addresses are given as decimal numbers preceded by V. Table A3.2 contains the original description as found in the Rothamsted manual and Table A3.3 the corresponding program code.

A revealing snap-shot of life as an early user of an early computer is given by Gavin Ross, who programmed the Elliott 401 in machine code at Rothamsted [8]. Gavin writes as follows: 'Frank Yates [Head of Statistics] obtained the agreement that he could use the Elliott 401 for whatever purposes he and his staff thought fit, and although the first priority was to take over the routine analysis of field experiments and surveys, the statisticians who learned to program it wrote more general routines for linear regression, multivariate analysis, nonlinear modelling, biological assay and cluster analysis. Elementary functions like division, square roots, logs and exponentials had to be programmed as subroutines, later supplemented by statistical functions like the Normal Probability Integral. We had to devise our own routines for sorting lists of numbers, for finding our way round multiway tables, for replacing a rectangle of rows and columns by a rectangle of columns and rows, for cleaning up the store, and for numerical analysis procedures such as inverting matrices and finding eigenvalues and eigenvectors, performing integrals and differentials and optimising functions of several variables. These routines died with the machine, and we had to start again with the next computer [a Ferranti Orion].'

The Elliott 401 remained at the Rothamsted Research establishment from 1954 until 1965. As far as can be ascertained [7], the main changes to the hardware during that time were as follows:

- Replacing the character code for digits by a parity-checked code, in 1955.
- A high-speed paper tape reader (a Ferranti Mark II reader) was installed in 1956.
- Replacing the typewriter by a tape punch, to be read by a teleprinter off-line.
- Installing a card reader which was linked to the 401's hand-switches, in 1956. This read 32 columns from 80, at a rate of about 15 cards per minute.
- Adding a controlled sequential addition facility in 1958. This formed the sum of a specified number of consecutive numbers stored on a given track, starting at A1 and ending at A2. Gavin Ross remembers [8] that 'It was supposed to speed things up, but I do not recall it being used by programmers.'
- Adding an extra set of immediate access registers S3–S5, usable instead of R3–R5 without losing information, in 1958.
- The disk was replaced by a drum in 1960.
- Track 6 switching, thereby allowing eight more tracks to become available, was implemented in 1961.

A3.4   Elliott 402: Fast Storage and Instruction Set Details

The Elliott 402 had 15 *Immediate-Access* registers, implemented as single-word nickel delay lines, and faster (electronic) switching of disc tracks. Therefore, the 402's *average* add time would have been faster than that of the Elliott 401. *Immediate-Access* locations 0–7 could be used as index registers (B-lines), with the convention that location 0 always held the value zero.

The Elliott 402's 32-bit instruction had a similar format to that of the 401 given earlier. As before, the format included ten bits of operand-address and ten bits for specifying the address of the next instruction. However, with the 402 the first 16 addresses 1–15 were mapped onto 15 fast registers called the *Immediate-Access Store* and the handkeys were mapped onto address 0. This eliminated the need to refer explicitly to the 401's named registers R4 (X) and R5 (Y) and thus allowed the S-field and the D-field to be reduced in size. The remaining 12 bits of the 402's instruction were re-allocated into five fields, of which the B-field allowed seven of the 15 fast registers to be used for address modification (B = 0 indicating 'no modification'). The layout was as follows.

10	3	3	2	2	10	3
A2	**S**	**F**	**D**	**C**	**A1**	**B**
Next-instruction address	Acc source	Op code	Acc dest	Control	Operand address	Specifies which of the 7 IAS locations is to be used for modification

Actually, the fields were physically arranged in a slightly different order as follows, assuming the least-significant end of the word is at the right-hand side:

    <A2> <S> <F> <D> <A1> <C> <B>

The new repertoire of ALU operations was defined for the Elliott 402 as follows:

	S	**F**	**D**	**C**
000	Zero	ADD	Nowhere	Normal
001	M register	MPY or DIV	M register	Test negative or Divide
010	Memory	Left shift n	Memory	Count
011	Input	Shift right n	Output	Track 7 switch
100		LOAD		
101		AND		
110		SUB		
111		Negate		

As compared to the Elliott 401, the 402 had an improved multiplier design, multiplication taking 3 ms regardless of sign. It also had hardware division, also taking 3 ms, and an improved disc store.

A3.5   Elliott 403 (WREDAC): Fast Storage and Instruction Set Details

The Elliott 403 had a fast, four-word, instruction buffer so that decoding of a following instruction took place whilst the current instruction was being executed. Then the 403 had a comparatively large 512-word *Immediate-Access* store implemented as 12 single-word delay lines (effectively random-access) in the first sub-section, followed by 127 delay lines each of four words. The average add-time was therefore considerably faster than either the Elliott 402 or 405. The Elliott 403 had three visible index registers (B-lines), pre-selected by program from four sets held in the 12 fastest storage locations. For B1 and B2, digits 20–32 are added to the current instruction, thus modifying the Function (op code) and operand-address fields. If B3 is specified, the address of the next instruction (not to be confused with the next word) is added to the current order's address digits.

If the least-significant digit, C, in an Elliott 403 instruction is zero then the instruction refers to arithmetic operations. When C = 1 *input/output transfer* instructions are specified. The format for arithmetic instructions (C = 0) is as follows:

5	9	2	1
F	A	B	C
Op code	Operand-address	Modifier register	Code = 0

There are 32 ALU instructions as specified by the F bits, most of them acting variously on the double-length and single-length accumulators. The accumulator-based repertoire includes:

Add; Subtract; Clear; Clear and Add; Clear and Subtract; Store;
Swap – (i.e. swap the contents of the accumulator with the contents of a store address);
AND; Logical shift left; Logical shift right; Multiply; Divide; Normalize.

Unlike the other computers in the Elliott 400 series, the 403 has three instructions relevant to multiplication, whose action is as follows:

SET MULTIPLIER REGISTER. This loads the multiplier register R with the contents of a specified memory location. This is the only means by which a programmer can refer to the multiplier register.

MULTIPLY and ADD. The contents of a specified memory location is multiplied by the number in the multiplier register R and the 66-digit double-length product is added to the accumulator.

MULTIPLY and SUBTRACT. As above, except that the product is subtracted from the accumulator.

Additionally with C = 0, the Elliott 403 has six *test and jump* instructions involving tests on the contents of the accumulator and two *test, jump and count* instructions involving the contents of modifier registers (B-lines). There are two instructions for loading a value from memory into a selected B-line. Each B-line was 17 bits (defined as the *even* half of a word).

Finally with C = 0, the Elliott 403 has a special *Use Logic* instruction. To quote [9]: 'One special order is reserved in the 0-code orders to determine the mode of operation of the machine. Allowance has been made for up to 8 different modes of operation, each one of which may be sub-classified in 64 ways. Only one mode has been attached to [i.e. implemented in] the machine to date, namely, the "use B-lines" mode'. This instruction configures various B-line options, namely:

a. Specifies the group of three B-lines, from the four available groups, which will be switched to high speed store addresses 1,2,3 respectively;
b. Specifies the B-line to which various *test-and-jump* instructions apply;
c. Specifies the two B-lines which may be added together before being used as modifiers.

Looking back, it is not entirely clear what was in the minds of the Long Range Weapons Establishment and Borehamwood when this instruction was first defined. The option (a) is historically interesting since it hints at what was later to be known as *context-switching*. Option (c) gives double modification.

When C = 1, the machine obeys one of 32 Input/Output instructions as specified by the five F bits. The repertoire includes:

Four instructions for handling slow, 5-bit, input/output;
16 Instructions for handling magnetic tape input/output;
Two instructions for transferring 64-word blocks of data to/from the disc.

The reason why there were as many as 16 magnetic tape instructions is that, originally, the Elliott 403 had a single magnetic tape control channel. A second, independent, channel was then introduced. It was decided to dedicate new instructions to the second channel so as to preserve the integrity of pre-existing program code.

A3.6 Elliott 405: Details of Fast Storage and the Instruction Set

Figure 3.4 shows the overall architecture of an Elliott 405 system, indicating the main data paths. The Elliott 405's CPU had a three-beat rhythm: fetch instruction, read/write from/to store, perform operation. Therefore, the minimum instruction time was 306 μs. The Primary Store had two sections: a fast *Immediate-Access* section and a not-so-fast *Quick-Access* section. The *Immediate-Access Store (IAS)* consisted of either 4 or 20 one-word nickel delay lines. If there were 20 words of IAS, then the *Quick-Access* store had one of its 16-word delay lines replaced by 16 of these 1-word delay lines. The *Quick-Access Store* consisted of at least 20 16-word nickel delay lines (each of total circulation-time 1.6 ms) and up to a maximum of 32 such lines, giving a maximum of 512 words. The actual amount for any specific machine depended upon the physical configuration chosen at installation-time – see Chap. 10. Since it was quite possible to hold a small routine and its working-space in the immediate-access store, it might be thought reasonable to take 306 μs as the Elliott 405's average fixed-point add time. However, the story is not so simple, as is now explained.

The physical addressing of each 16-word delay line in the Elliott 405 is so arranged that the timings of successive words in the *Quick-Access* store differ by

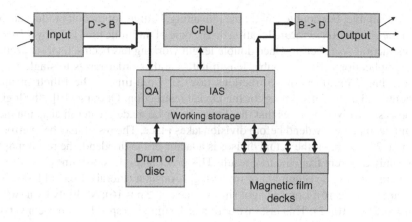

Fig. A3.4 Schematic diagram showing the main sub-sections of an Elliott 405 computer. The programmer could initiate autonomous activity on up to five logically separate local machines: one for input transfers, one for output transfers, one for drum or disc transfers, one for magnetic film transfers, and one for central processing

three word-times in the 16-word cycle. The total time taken by two successive instructions depends very much on the relative positions of the two instructions and their operands in these 16-word delay lines. For example, assuming that a pair of simple ADD instructions is stored at address 4, [10] gives two extreme cases to illustrate how the choice of operand-address can dramatically alter the total time taken by the pair:

	First instruction	Second instruction	Total time taken
Case (a)	Acc = Acc + addr(10)	Acc = Acc + addr(15)	3 word-times (total 0.918 ms)
Case (b)	Acc = Acc + addr(20)	Acc = Acc + addr(5)	35 word-times (total 10.71 ms)

Instructions for the Elliott 405 are packed two to a word. The machine obeys first the one in the most significant half (i.e. the one which occupies digit positions 17–32), and secondly the other which occupies positions 1–16. The Elliott 405 instructions were divided into two groups, distinguished by the setting of the least-significant bit, denoted as C. When C = 0 the format was:

4	9	2	1
F	A	B	C
Op code	Operand address	Modifier register	Code = 0

The Elliott 405 had 16 computational instructions, denoted as *0-codes*, for which C = 0. Briefly, these acted as follows:

a. Operations between the contents of the accumulator and the contents of a memory address: Add, Subtract, Reverse subtract, Multiply, Divide, AND, Swap (i.e. exchange), Load. Note that both single- and double length multiplication are available. For double length, the remaining 31 digits of the full product are left in *Immediate-Access Store* location 3. The type of multiplication is set by a *1-Code* instruction – see below. Once double length working has been set, all subsequent multiplications will be double length until another order resets to single length working. Multiplication instructions take 33 word-times. The Elliott manuals contained a special warning for the Divide instruction. Quoting [10], 'the logical process involved requires that the divisor be or be made greater in absolute magnitude than the dividend before division takes place. The result may be in error by up to 2^{-31} so that if the actual divisor is a factor of the dividend, the result may be slightly different from the true result. This order takes 33 word times.'

b. Operations on the accumulator involving a constant (literal): Logical left shift n times ($1 \le n \le 16$); Logical right shift n times ($1 \ge n \le 16$); Multiply by n (where $n = 0, 2,4,8,10,12$). This last instruction is designed to speed number-conversion in decimal or sterling calculations.

c. Control transfer instructions: unconditional absolute jump; absolute jump if Accumulator is negative; absolute jump if the contents of address (1) is zero and add 2^{-12} to address (1) in any case.

d. Move instructions: these permit any block of 16 words to be moved to any other block-position in primary memory, the size/position being chosen so as to correspond to one of the 16-word nickel delay lines making up the memory. One *Move* instruction covered the address-range 0–255, another *Move* instruction covering the range 256–511. There was an oddity if the lowest block ('line 0') was specified. As explained in [10], locations 0–3 of block 0 are not part of the *Quick-Access Store*, since addresses 0–3 designate the number generator (0) and *Immediate-Access Store* locations 1–3. These four addresses are known as 'ghost locations'. (If the contents of any other block are transferred to block 0, the first four words pass into these ghost locations and remain there unaltered until the whole block is again transferred elsewhere. The only arithmetic functions in which the contents of the ghost locations can take part immediately are Multiplication and Division).

When C = 1, the so-called *1-Code* instructions mostly concerned input/output transfers and backing-store activity. An exception is a group of three *1-Code* instructions that are strictly part of normal computational activity. These three are placed in a group known as *Overall Machine Control* in the Elliott 405 literature, for which the S-bits (see below) are set to the value 7. The three instructions are:

Set single length multiplication.
Set double length multiplication.
Set link. This stored the contents of the Program Counter (called the *Sequence Control Register*) in memory location 1.

The general format for *1-Code* instructions for the Elliott 405 is as follows:

6	3	3	3	1
N	T	F	S	C
			Code = 1	

The S-bits are assigned as follows:

S = 0: a group of instructions for handling input from paper tape and punched cards.

S = 1: a group of instructions for character-based output to paper tape, typewriter or magnetic film.

S = 2: a group of instructions for block transfers (64 words) to/from disc or drum.

S = 3: a group of instructions for block transfers to/from magnetic film.

S = 7: the three *overall machine control* instructions described above.

As can be seen, only some of the possible <N, T, F, S, C> combinations are assigned, thus allowing for future expansion if new devices were to be introduced for the Elliott 405.

A comparison of the relative effectiveness of the Elliott 405's instruction set, when compared to that of its market rival the IBM 705, is given in Sect. A3.9 when discussing a large payroll application for the British army.

A3.7 Elliott 405: General Configurations and Disc Options

The Elliott 400 series computers used fixed-head magnetic drums though, because of their physical shape, they were often called discs. The physical characteristics given in Table A3.4 are for the Elliott 405 computer. However, the 'drum' column is similar to the backing-store arrangement for the Elliott 402 and the 'small disc' column is similar to that of the Elliott 403.

Physically, an Elliott 405 consisted of a number of cabinets [10, 11], each measuring about 6 ft 6 in. high on a 2 ft square base (about 2 m high by 0.6 m²) and each weighing about 320 lb (145 kg). Apart from the operator's console, an installation could be build up from the following units, where *QAS* signifies Quick-Access Storage composed of 16-word nickel delay lines, of which there could be a maximum of 512 words spread throughout the whole computer – (this was in addition to either 4 or 20 single-word lines of Immediate-Access Storage (RAM)).

Table A3.4 Backing-store options for the Elliott 405 computer. A larger disc of capacity 32K words was also available

	Drum	Small disc
Diameter (in.)	8.5	19.25
Width (in.)	1.5	0.5
RPM	4,600	2,300
Tracks	32	64
Sectors	64	256
Words	4,096	16,384
1 rev. time (ms)	13.2	26.4
Packing density (digits/in.)	166	166

Unit and description	No. of cabinets
System Centre (CPU and 128 words of IAS)	2
Drum Store, 4K words (including 128 words of IAS buffer)	2
Disc Store, either 16K or 32K words (incl. 128 words of IAS)	3
35-mm Film Store – Master (incl. 64 words of IAS and 2 decks)	3
35-mm Film Store – Slave (including one film deck)	1
Simple Input/Output (character-at-a-time)	1
Input/Output Compiler (including 16+ words of IAS)	2
Power Supply – master unit	1
Power Supply – slave unit	1

In [12] a small 405 system, such as the one first delivered to Norwich City Council [13], was stated to have nine cabinets and a control console. A medium installation, such as the one used in 1957 at Borehamwood for in-house applications, is believed to have had at least 15 cabinets plus console. In theory the largest Elliott 405 could have 82 cabinets, most of which would be magnetic film units.

An Elliott 405 could have up to four magnetic film *Master* units, controlling a total of up to 16 decks. In addition, there was an off-line output device (called MUF-PUP or MUFPT) which allowed a magnetic film deck to write at high speed to either a lineprinter or to a cluster of paper tape punches or to punched cards. The more demanding, high-performance, lineprinters available for the 405 printed 300 lines/min, with 140 characters per line.

In conclusion, a complete 405 installation gave the programmer several autonomous, programmable, local machines – one for central processing, one for disc or drum memory, one for magnetic film, one for bulk input/output – though it was rare for all to be actively engaged concurrently. The whole assembly of facilities allowed the movement of large amounts of commercial-type data to be overlapped with computation.

A3.8   Input/Output and Bulk Storage
for the Elliott 400 Series

The properties of the common input/output devices for Elliott 400 series computers evolved to some extent over the relevant period 1953–1962. The original input/ output medium for all 400 series computers was 5-track paper tape, based historically on Creed teleprinter equipment. The five bits could sometimes be treated by a computer as four information bits and a parity bit – for example in the encoding of numerals. Different manufacturers used different 5-track conventions. The complete Elliott coding of alphanumeric characters, called Elliott Telecode, is given in Table A3.5 for the Elliott 402, 403 and 405 computers. It may be seen that the numerals all have odd parity for the 402 and 405 conventions. Aside from the desirability of maintaining a conveniently ordered collating sequence for letters and numbers, Table A3.5 indicates that there is some choice in assigning visible characters to bit-patterns.

Table A3.5 Teleprinter codes for various Elliott 400 series computers. The 1's in a telecode character indicate holes in paper tape and the 0's no holes

Telecode character	Letter shift	Figure shift, 402	Figure shift, 403	Figure shift, 405
00000	Blank	Blank	Blank	Blank
00001	A	1	.	1
00010	B	2	*	2
00011	C	*	1	*
00100	D	4	=	4
00101	E	$	2	$ or "
00110	F	=	3	= or £
00111	G	7	;	7
01000	H	8	.	8
01001	I	'	4	'
01010	J	,	5	,
01011	K	+	:	+ or 11
01100	L	:	6	:
01101	M	-	%	-
01110	N	.	;	.
01111	O	%	(	%
10000	P	0	-	0
10001	Q	(	7	(
10010	R	)	8	)
10011	S	3	?	3
10100	T	?	9	?
10101	U	5	/	5
10110	V	6	+	6
10111	W	/	)	/
11000	X	@	0	@ or &
11001	Y	9	£	9
11010	Z	£	@	£ or 10
11011	Figure shift	Figure shift	Figure shift	Figure shift
11100	Space	Space	Space	Space
11101	Carriage return	Carriage return	Carriage return	Carriage return
11110	Line feed	Line feed	Line feed	Line feed
11111	Letter shift	Letter shift	Letter shift	Letter shift

Punched card equipment for input/output was subsequently introduced for the 402 and 405 computers. The 401 was also later equipped with a reduced form of punched card input via an adaptation of the 401's *handkeys* combination of the S-bits of an instruction. For this, any 32 columns out of 80, as selected by means of a plug-board, could be transferred to the accumulator at the rate of 100 cards per minute.

For 400 series computers, the size of a *character* was defined according to the programming context, values of 4, 5 and 6 bits occurring at various points in the Elliott technical literature. There was no generally accepted unit such as an 8-bit *byte* in the 1950s. Practical data transfer rates are dependent upon particular devices when attached to particular computers and it is not easy to generalise and compare performances.

Early paper tape readers for the 400 series computers operated at about 40 chars/s (characters per second), to be followed by the Ferranti paper tape reader at 100 chars/s and, later still, by devices operating at 180 chars/s. In 1958 Borehamwood designed Elliott's fast paper tape reader, capable of transferring information at 1,000 chars/s. Card readers transferred data at the rate of up to 400 eighty-column cards per minute.

The original output teleprinters printed at about 10 chars/s. Paper tape punches worked at about 25 chars/s. Two forms of lineprinter were offered for the Elliott 405. Early machines typically had Bull lineprinters, giving 150 lines per minute with 92 characters per line. Later printers gave 300 lines per minute with 140 characters per line. As mentioned in Chap. 10, these lineprinters were usually driven off-line from magnetic film units because of their demands for high data-rates.

The Elliott 403 had quarter-inch magnetic tape decks and the 405 had 35-mm magnetic film decks, as described in detail in Chap. 10.

We end this account of Borehamwood's 400 series computers by describing the head-to-head evaluation of the Elliott 405 and the IBM 705 in 1956. In that year the Royal Army Pay Corps (RAPC) conducted a procurement exercise to select a digital computing system to replace the hundreds of electro-mechanical desktop machines that were used in the payroll calculations for hundreds of thousands of British soldiers. After sifting through the offerings of 14 UK and US computer manufacturers, the RAPC decided that the only two-candidate EDP systems capable of handling the huge payroll task were the IBM 705 and the Elliott 405. The background to this decision is outlined in Chap. 9. We now continue the detailed comparison of these two computers, based on the contemporary technical evidence contained in [14, 15].

A3.9   Comparison of the Elliott 405 and the IBM 705: The RAPC Procurement

A3.9.1   The Programming Task

The payroll tasks selected by the Royal Army Pay Corps (RAPC) Working Party for automation included [14, 15]:

- Maintenance of records of the soldiers' pay entitlements, tax deductions, dependants' allowances, automatic increments, etc.;
- Preparation of notifications to individuals and to military units of payment details and budget analysis;
- Keeping an up-to-date record of vouchers, army allowance order books, claims and correspondence;
- Production of public audit figures, management statistics and analyses, and internal system checks.

It was planned that input to the computer would be by punched cards, records would be maintained centrally on magnetic tape, and output would be in the form of printed notifications to the military units worldwide. The Working Party decided to specify a data processing system with a minimum capacity of 180,000 soldiers' accounts, expandable to 240,000 accounts, based on single-shift working (nominally 8 h in every 24 h). This would leave the option of further expansion to two- or three-shift working in the event of emergency military mobilisation. The figure of 180,000 was the estimated strength of the regular army by 1960, to which was added 60,000 to cater for the reserve armies.

A3.9.2 Technical Requirements

The main concern of the Working Party was that the proposed payroll computer should have sufficient memory available at electronic speeds. Expressed in physical terms appropriate to the mid-1950s, this set a requirement on the total capacity provided by a combination of fast storage (e.g. nickel delay lines or magnetic cores) and magnetic drums or disks. Such a combination came to be called *on-line storage*, in contrast to the slower bulk storage provided by devices such as de-mountable reels of magnetic tape.

As far as on-line storage is concerned, there was a requirement to hold three types of information readily accessible: (a) look-up tables for rates of pay and other basic data; (b) subroutines in current use; and (c) input/output buffer areas. As an example of rate tables, there were 50 rates of basic pay, 32 rates of additional pay, 33 rates covering standard allowances and deductions, and 800 rates for special allowances for forces serving at various overseas locations. All these rates required the equivalent of a total of 3,550 decimal digits of storage. The subroutines covered input/output procedures, sorting/merging, the central accounting calculations, and various tests and checks. In summary it was estimated that, for the purposes of comparing different computers, the on-line working storage (code and data) required was expressible as follows:

For binary coded decimal or mixed-radix machines:	30,000 decimal digits
For binary machines, the equivalent of:	40,000 decimal digits

A detailed study was then carried out on candidate machines that seemed able to meet these overall requirements. The results, expressed as equivalent decimal digits of storage, for the two computers of special interest were:

Item	IBM 705	Elliott 405
Data: rate tables	3,550	3,500
Budget analysis	1,500	1,500
Input, output and working areas	5,000	4,608
Code: general subroutines	4,700	9,666
Validity tests	6,750	11,812
Sorting and merging subroutines	2,500	2,700

(In 1957 the RAPC used the nomenclature *National/Elliott 405* since, by agreement with Borehamwood, the marketing of the Elliott 405 had become the responsibility of the National Cash Register Co. Ltd. by that time).

For the code items above, each IBM 705 instruction was assumed to occupy five decimal digits and each National/Elliott 405 instruction was assumed to occupy the equivalent of 4.5 decimal digits. The estimated differences in total code space between the two machines was largely accounted for by observed differences in instruction-set efficiency. For example, the number of instructions required for three particular subroutines that showed marked differences in size was:

Subroutine	IBM705	Elliott 405
Comparison of input with record	25	40
Arrears calculations	160	300
Validity tests, each one	90	175

The Working Party was clearly worried about program complexity and the job of training RAPC staff to make use of whichever computer was chosen for the payroll project. Based on preliminary studies, the Working Party states in its report that 'the preparation of programs for the National/Elliott 405 EDP system would be a considerably more complex task, and would take about a year longer, than for the IBM 705 EDP system with the maximum programming staff which could be effectively employed on the project. One factor is that the IBM 705 EDP system has a very much larger high speed store, ie 40,000 positions of core storage as against 512x32 bit words of delay-line storage and employs an autocode assembly program. The [IBM] autocoder system provides facilities for preparation of programs in simple notation with automatic translation into computer language, and the writing of programs with mnemonic operating codes and data that may be referred to by name instead of by absolute address. The overall effect of this facility is to relieve programmers of a great deal of work and to reduce the complexity of programs.'

A3.9.3   Specifications of the IBM 705 and Elliott 405 Proposals

The IBM 705 and the Elliott 405 computers are now compared, noting that, for the army payroll tender, the version of the Elliott machine proposed by the manufacturer was slightly different from a standard 405. Such differences are explained later.

The table below compares single-processor installations. Actually, three Elliott 405 machines, operating concurrently, were required to service the army's minimum stated payroll work-load of 180,000 accounts. A fourth 405 system was required to cope with the upper load of 240,000 accounts.

In order to aid comparison between the two manufacturer's offerings, the original (1956) units of storage for the proposed installations have been translated into equivalent bytes (6-bit and 8-bit bytes respectively). For further information on the IBM 705, see for example [16].

Parameter	IBM705	Elliott 405	See note
Word length	variable	32 bits	a
Instruction-length	30 bits	16 bits	b
Fixed-point *ADD* time	119 μs	306 μs	c
On-line storage	40 KB	2 KB	d
Backing storage, decks	10	8	e

Notes

a. The IBM was a variable-length *decimal* machine. The allowable data types were character strings and fixed-point decimal numbers only
b. Two Elliott 405 instructions were packed into each word
c. The add time for the IBM 705 is given as that for five-digit decimal numbers. The add time for the Elliott 405 assumes an average of three word-times from primary (delay-line) memory
d. For the IBM 705: 40,000 characters or 'positions' (each a 6-bit byte) of core storage. For the 405: 19 single-word and 31 sixteen-word nickel delay lines (total = 515 words, or 2,060 bytes). 32,768 words of magnetic disk storage (equivalent to 128 KB)
e. For the IBM 705: each of ten magnetic tape decks had a maximum transfer rate of 15K chars/s. For the Elliott 405: each of eight magnetic film decks had a maximum transfer rate of approximately 12K chars/s (see below). Each 1,000-ft reel of magnetic film held 282K words

The off-line data preparation equipment for both the IBM and the National/Elliott proposals was basically identical, consisting of 36 card punches and 36 verifiers. Each manufacturer provided for a certain amount of off-line printing from magnetic tape.

As noted in the Working Party's Report, the Elliott 405 system proposed by the manufacturer 'involves changes in logical design and engineering development, and is not the same as systems in current production. On the basis of engineering reports we are reasonably confident that a system as specified could be produced within approximately two years of an order being placed.' The changes proposed by Elliotts to their standard 405 were as follows:

i. Extra immediate-access storage (515 words, instead of 128 words);
ii. Larger-capacity magnetic disk (32K words, instead of 16K words);
iii. Higher-speed magnetic film units (achieved by doubling the tape-speed to 60 in./s and changing to unidirectional reading/writing, thereby raising the instantaneous transfer rate from 300 to 12,000 chars/s);
iv. Facilities for simultaneous reading/writing and checking on rewind;
v. Use of variable-length records (instead of fixed-length blocks);
vi. Provision of special 'screening' hardware which would perform on-the-fly filtering of information being read from magnetic film; for this purpose, each record was to be preceded by a 32-bit tag which was compared on the fly with the contents of a 32-bit interrogand register;
vii. Provision of a universal high-speed card reader.

Of the above seven proposed enhancements, the advice to the Working Party from the Post Office engineers stated that Elliotts 'can reasonably be expected to proceed with the development of the special features incorporated in the proposal, and make them work', but there was an implication that providing higher-speed magnetic film would prove to be technically challenging for the company. More comments on Borehamwood's ideas for magnetic tape and film systems are given in Chap. 10.

The Working Party had little doubt about the technical merit and credibility of the proposed IBM 705 system, noting that 'the [manufacturer's] proposal goes into a great deal of detail and shows a very clear appreciation of the problems to be tackled in this application'. The Working Party was, however, quite anxious about the dollar commitment implied by the choice of an IBM system. In the post-war period and right up to the 1960s, exchange control regulations made it difficult for any UK organisation to make dollar purchases.

A3.9.4   The Costs and Benefits

The principal equipment for the IBM bid consisted of an IBM 705 with 40,000 positions of magnetic core storage and 10 magnetic tape decks. In the case of the Elliott bid, at least three National/Elliott 405 computers, each with 515 words of nickel delay-line storage, 32K words of magnetic disk storage and four magnetic tape decks, were required to meet the computing load. The ancillary equipment (printers, card punches, etc.) for the two installations was somewhat similar in functionality and cost. The IBM equipment was to be rented, whilst that of Elliotts was to be purchased. To compare the bids, the Working Party assumed that capital costs were to be written off over 7 years. In summary, the comparative costs and savings to RAPC worked out as follows.

	IBM 705	Elliott 405
Manpower saved	1,065	1,058
Annual value of staff savings	£777K	£771K
Annual equipment cost[a]	£251K	£323K
Estimated net annual financial saving	£526K	£448K

[a] Hire charges of IBM equipment for 7 years, or purchase price of three Elliott 405 systems amortised over 7 years

It was estimated that the IBM installation could handle 180,000 soldier's accounts in 3 h/day, whilst 240,000 accounts could still be accommodated in single-shift working. Although three Elliott 405 systems could handle 180,000 accounts by single-shift working with 4 h/day spare, a fourth 405 system would be required for 240,000 accounts. In overall account-processing terms, the Working Party estimated that it would take five Elliott 405 systems to equal the full computing capacity of one IBM 705.

Therefore, on both cost and capacity grounds, the Working Party favoured the IBM bid. Additional factors which tended to favour IBM included: more extensive parity checking at the hardware level; a less-complex programming model; ability to pre-test programs on existing IBM 705 systems in the USA whilst the army's 705 was on order; stronger evidence from existing installations about in-service reliability; and greater confidence about the company's ability to meet the stated delivery date. Factors against choosing the IBM bid included: the current UK currency (dollar) restrictions, and the element of risk in employing a single computer, of American manufacture, for handling the accounts of all British soldiers.

A3.9.5   The Chosen System and Its Performance

The IBM bid was accepted officially in 1958, after the RAPC Electronic Computer Investigating Committee had assured itself that IBM 705 systems were reliable. In 1957 an IBM 704 at the UK's Atomic Weapons Research Establishment, Aldermaston, was the only IBM 700 series installation in Europe – though 704s had been operational in America since approximately 1955. However, the Committee had noted that, by the end of 1957, 'the IBM 705 is a standard machine which is coming off the production line at the rate of 7–9 machines a month. Many IBM 705s are in operational use in the USA and their reliability is regarded as proven.'

To quote the Committee's report [14, 15]: 'The following examples, obtained independently, give some indication of the standard of reliability which can be achieved:

a. United States Treasury: one IBM 705 system working 18 hours a day for 7 days a week – 95% effective time.
b. Bureau of Old Age and Survivors Insurance (Baltimore): Two IBM 705 systems working independently on separate functions for two shifts a day – 95% effective time.
c. USAF (Stores Control): One IBM 705 working two shifts a day – 86.3% effective time.
d. Domestic Corporation of New York: one IBM 705; total operating time [to date]: 157,877 hours. During this period, the average observed errors were as follows:
    Tape errors: 0.65 per 8 hour shift;
    Memory errors: 0.06 per 8 hour shift;
    Other errors: 0.18 per 8 hour shift'.

An IBM 705 system was delivered to the RAPC's main establishment at Worthy Down, about 5 miles north of Winchester, at the end of 1960 and beginning of 1961.

References

1. Mills RG (1956) A general description of the Elliott 404 electronic digital computer. Report S64 published by the Computing Machine Division, Elliott Brothers Ltd., Borehamwood, London, May 1956 (42 typed pages)
2. SLH Clarke (2009) E-mail to Simon Lavington dated 14 Oct 2009
3. Pierre-E Mounier-Kuhn (CNRS & Centre de recherches en Histoire de l'Innovation Université Paris-Sorbonne) (2008) E-mails to Simon Lavington, Nov 2008

4. Clarke SLH (1993) Recollections of the Elliott 400 series. Computer Resurrection, the Bulletin of the Computer Conservation Society, Issue number 6, summer 1993, pp. 15–21
5. St Johnston A, Clarke SLH, Muchmore NWW, Devonald CH, Stallworthy BV, Carpenter HG, Bunt JP (1954) 401 Mark I computer. Elliott Brothers Ltd., Borehamwood, London. Internal report 339, 29 March 1954 (116 p, 46 figures)
6. An item entitled Index of 401 Computer Mk 1 documents is held by the Science Museum Library in London, catalogued as ARCH:ELLI. This item embraces a collection of four documents and 312 drawings, believed to have been deposited by W S Elliott in 1991/92. Note that these drawings probably refer to the original (1953) design and do not give any details of subsequent modifications carried out during the working lifetime of the computer
7. Gavin Ross (2002) Letter sent to Simon Lavington dated 19 Dec 2002 and containing photocopies of original programming manuals. The hardware changes listed by Gavin Ross come from John Gower's understanding of entries in the Annual Reports of Rothamsted from 1955 onwards
8. Gavin Ross (2009) E-mails to Simon Lavington in June and July 2009
9. Department of Supply, Weapons Research Establishment, An Introductory coding manual for the WRE digital automatic computer. D L Overheu. Tech. Memo TRD 39. Undated, but probably written in about 1959. An electronic copy is available at: www.ourcomputerheritage.org/wp/
10. Wakefield AJ (1956) Programming the Elliott 405 unit-construction business computing system. Elliott Brothers Ltd., Borehamwood internal report S45, London. At least three editions of this document appeared, the third edition being dated 13 Aug 1956
11. (a) Anon (undated) A specification of an Elliott 405 electronic digital computing system. Elliott Brothers Ltd., Borehamwood internal report L56, London (b) Anon, 405 – A simplified representation of the National-Elliott Electronic Data Processing System. NCR sales leaflet, undated but probably produced in 1959 or 1960. See also section E2X3 of: www.ourcomputerheritage.org/wp/
12. St Johnston A, Clarke SLH (1957) The development of a business computer system. Presented at the convention on electronics in automation, Cambridge, 27 June 1957. Published in the J Br IRE 17(July 1957):351–364
13. Barnard AJ (1958) The first year with a business computer. Comput J 1(1 Apr 1958) (The Elliott 405 at Norwich City Council)
14. Royal Army Pay Corps: Report of the Electronic Computer Investigation Committee. The War Office (F9), Dec 1957
15. Royal Army Pay Corps: Electronic Computer Investigating Committee: Report of Working Party. Application of automatic data-processing to soldiers' pay accounting. The War Office, Aug 1957
16. Blaauw GA, Brooks FP (1997) Computer architecture – concepts and evolution. Addison Wesley, Reading, pp 665–679. ISBN 0-201-10557-8

Appendix 4
Technical Details of the Elliott 800 Series and 503 Computers

A4.1   General Overview of the Family

The hardware implementation of the Elliott 800 series computers was based on germanium junction transistors and ferrite cores. The software-compatible Elliott 503 computer used diode-transistor logic. In architectural terms, Borehamwood departed from the design-philosophy used for the earlier 400 series computers in one major respect: the 800 series and the 503 had hardly any program-visible central registers apart from the accumulator. This is not quite true, as is shown later, but the principle is that *any* primary memory location can be used as an index (modifier) register. This use of main memory for address-generation purposes is achieved without loss of speed for most cases; timing details are given later.

The Elliott 800 series began life with a 33-bit word which soon evolved to 39 bits in the case of the 803 and then for the software-compatible 503. The 803 was a great success in the marketplace, helping to secure Elliott's position by 1961 as the supplier of half the computers sold that year in the UK. A brief family history of the 800 series is now given. This is followed in Sects. A4.2–A4.4 by some specific technical details for the 802, 803 and 503 respectively. In Sect. A4.5 input/output equipment is covered and then, in Sect. A4.6, the complete instruction sets of the 803 and 503 are presented.

The Elliott 801 was an in-house test-rig built at Borehamwood in 1957 primarily to evaluate John Bunt's *transistors-plus-cores* logic circuits and the Mullard core store. The Elliott 802, launched in November 1958 at the Automation Exhibition at Olympia, London, was the production version of the 801. It was a 33-bit word machine, superseded about a year later by the 803A (see below). The 802 had a big L-shaped desk footprint. The 802 was mostly transistorised, except that valves were used for (a) core store drivers and (b) resetting the core logic elements, because the currently available transistors lacked the necessary power for these two tasks. (The shortcomings of early transistors are discussed in Chap. 10). A hardware square-root instruction was later added to the 802 – one of the few computers to incorporate this feature.

Seven 802 computers were delivered between 1958 and 1961 – (see listings in Appendix 8). On grounds of hardware economy, the 802 held its frequently used working registers (including the accumulator (33 bits), instruction-pair register (33 bits) and the 11-bit program counter) in one 102-digit nickel delay line called the *Operations Register*. There was also a 65-digit double-length accumulator used in multiplication, division and shifting instructions. The least-significant 32 bits of the double-length register were called the A*uxiliary Register, AR*, and were visible to the programmer; the upper 33 bits of the double-length register were inaccessible. On the 803A and B computers – (see below) – the Auxiliary Register was 38 bits long and formed the least-significant 38 bits of the 77-bit double-length register. The normal accumulator formed the top 39 bits.

Finally, there was an overflow register. With a digit period of 6 μs, the circulation-time for the main *Operations Register* was 612 μs, which thereby defined the timing of most instructions.

The Elliott 803A was a fully transistorised version of the 802, with the word-length increased to 39 bits. The first 803 worked in 1959; the first delivery to an external customer is believed to have been in November 1959. It had a cabinet-based design. Like the 802, the 803A held all its internal registers as a single bit-stream which generally circulated through the various stages of processing once per instruction. The 803A was a short-lived design, superseded by the 803B. Since arithmetic was serial, the 803A with its longer word-length was in general rather slower than the 802. The Elliott 803B was an enhanced 803A that first worked in 1960. The 803B employed more parallel paths (separate registers) internally instead of the bit-stream approach, and had hardware floating-point. Unless otherwise specified, the majority of '803s' sold would have been 803Bs. The selling price (1963 values) was about £29,000 [1]. The 803B was small by comparison with contemporaries, a company brochure enthusiastically stating that the complete footprint of a minimum installation was *only* 400 ft^2 [2]. The design was simple and completely transistorised, resulting in a power consumption of only 3.6 KW. The computer was said to have been 'an immediate success … the transistor/core logic proved extremely reliable' [3]. A total of about 211 of the 803 systems (including 803A, 803B and the ARCH 8000 Process Control variant) were delivered between 1960 and 1966 – see Appendix 8.

All members of the 800 series family had logic circuits based on a combination of germanium junction transistors and ferrite cores. In the late 1950s, transistor characteristics were not well suited for high-speed logic switching unaided, so John Bunt used ferrite cores as logic elements and (originally) an OC71 transistor for amplification. These two components, plus a resistor, were mounted on 'daughter' printed-circuit boards measuring 1.5 in. × 2.25 in. (later reduced to 1.5 in. × 1.5 in.). About 30 daughter boards were then mounted upon Mother boards measuring 13 in. × 8 in. (about 33 cm × 20 cm). Suitable windings round each core were used to give two basic logic functions: (A *or* B) and (A and not B). Since a logic core had to be in a reset state at the start of each logical operation and then interrogated at the end of an operation, a two-part system was used whereby the state of one core was copied to a following 'slave' core. This yielded a basic digit period of (3 + 3) = 6 μs. Logic could be performed on each of the two parts (*master* and *slave*) of a complete circuit module, resulting in some gains in economy. The final design of the production Elliott 803 was principally based on the Mullard OC84 transistor (see Chap. 10).

The daughter board construction was not used in the Elliott 803B computer, the cores, transistors (OC84) and resistors being mounted directly onto the main board which measured about 10 in. x 17 in. There was no 'master/slave' relationship between cores in the 803B computer. The cores were called 'alpha' and 'beta', depending on the phase of the trigger pulse that reset them. Each board (which had cores on it) had a pair of OC23 power transistors to generate the two trigger pulses for the cores on that board. Alpha and Beta cores had equal status, with logic functions being performed by both phase cores.

The physically larger Elliott 503 computer [4] consists of a number of cabinets, each typically measuring 78 in. in height by 38 in. in width by 24 in. in depth ($2 \times 1 \times 0.6 \text{ m}^3$). A typical installation might consist of seven such cabinets plus the input/output equipment. Many different configuration options are possible. The random-access memory is in two parts: a fast section of 8K words (40 KB) and a backing section of up to 128K words in units of 16K words. Both types of memory consist of ferrite core stores. The cycle time of the fast section is 3.6 μs. Access to the backing section is normally via autonomous transfers to the fast section at 15,800 words/s, though individual words can be accessed from backing store in 71.9 μs.

By the time Borehamwood came to design the Elliott 503, the characteristics of the available transistors had improved; so the 503's logic circuits were based on transistors (for amplifications) and diodes for the logic functions, rather than the earlier transistor-plus-core combination.

The first internal deliveries of the Elliott 503 occurred in 1963, followed by deliveries to external customers from 1964 onwards. From November 1961 a series of amusing and aggressive advertisements for the 503 had begun to appear in the magazine *New Scientist*, of which the text of an advertisement dated 1st November 1962 is typical: 'The new Elliott 503 computer, companion to the famous 803, is probably the greatest computer of its class ever produced. The 503 is remarkably fast, extremely versatile, and surprisingly easy to operate ... The first British designed computer equipped to use Algol is the Elliott 503 ...'.

An overview of the 800/503 family is given in Table A4.1, which should be read in conjunction with the further details provided in the next sections.

A4.2   Further Details of the Elliott 802

The information in this section comes mainly from [5]. Two 16-bit single-address instructions occupy one 33-bit word. They are separated by a one-bit marker called, rather confusingly, the *B-line*. If this B-bit is set to 1, then the second (right hand) instruction of the pair is modified by adding to it the (new) contents of the location specified by the address-part of the first instruction. This facility enables any location in main memory to be used as an index register. Address modification is performed without loss of speed. In many respects the 802's instruction set is identical to that of the 803, which is described in greater detail Sect. A4.6.

The 802's main memory consists of 1,024 words of 33 bits each (thus equivalent to about 4 KB in modern terminology). The first four words contain fixed instructions, used for initialising (boot-up). The memory technology is ferrite cores.

Table A4.1 General characteristics of the Elliott 800/503 family of computers

	802	803A	803B	503
Word length, visible bits	33	39	39	39
Digit period, μs	6	6	6	?
Instruction length	16	19	19	19
Instruction format, addresses	1	1	1	1
No. of instructions/word	2	2	2	2
Basic ALU: serial or parallel?	Serial	Serial	Serial	Parallel
Fixed-point ADD time, unmodified, minimum, μs	612	720	576	7.2
Fixed-point ADD time, modified, max., μs	612	720	576	10.8
Fixed-point MPY time, min, ms or μs	21.4 ms	29.5 ms	1.15 ms	34.8 μs
Hardware floating-point ADD time, min, μs	no	?	864	13.2
Max. Primary store (core), words	1K	4K ?	8K	8K
Core backing store, words, max.	None	None	None	128K
Typical power requirements	2 KVA	1 KVA	3.5 KVA	?
Date first delivered	1958	1960	1960	1963

The 802 requires a single-phase, 2 kVA, ac supply – thus putting it in the class of ordinary domestic appliances in terms of power consumption. The AC mains input is made to trickle-charge a large battery, thus providing (i) some degree of isolation from mains voltage transients, and (ii) time for the computer to perform an orderly shut-down in the event of mains failure. The CPU, main memory, I/O circuitry and control console are together housed in an L-shaped desk, the longer arm of which is 223 cm long and the shorter arm is 159 cm. The power supply is in a separate unit measuring 84 cm by 76 cm. All units are 81 cm high. The 802 can claim to have been the UK's first minicomputer.

A4.3   Further Details of the Elliott 803A and 803B

The 803A was an 802 upgraded in the following respects: fully transistorised core store drivers and logic core reset drivers (now that suitable power transistors had arrived in the marketplace); word length increased to 39 bits so that a larger main memory could be specified by more address-bits per instruction; floating-point hardware as standard; and L-shaped desk format replaced by a cabinet-based physical appearance. As has been mentioned earlier, the 803A was slower than the 802 because the 803A still retained the circulating *Operations register* which had to be increased to 120 bits to accommodate the increased word length. Thus, in order to increase operating speed, the 803B was re-designed by Laurie Bental to incorporate several separate nickel delay lines in place of the main *Operations Register*. In the 803, SCR, IR and ACC were each held in separate delay lines. The machine's rhythm was changed to a two-beat *fetch/execute* sequence. Each beat was 48 digit periods, so that simple instructions took $(2 \times 48 \times 6) = 576$ μs (Fig. A4.1).

The fastest Elliott 803 instructions (Group 4 jumps, see Sect. A4.6) take 288 μs. (Compare this with the 4.5 μs for Group 4 instructions on the much faster, but

Fig. A4.1 Over 200 Elliott 803 computers were sold between November 1959 and the end of 1966. The 803B computer shown in the photo was used by the software house *Vaughan Programming Services (VPS)* before being donated to the computer collection at Bletchley Park in 1994. At the time of writing it is maintained in working order by volunteers at the National Museum of Computing at Bletchley Park. Andrew St Johnston, from 1968 Managing Director of VPS, is seen at the left of the photo

software compatible, Elliott 503 computer.) The Elliott 803 fixed-point operations in Groups 0, 1, 3 and 3 all take 576 µs each. Fixed-point multiply takes from 1.152 to 12.096 ms, depending upon the number of consecutive ones or zeros at the most significant end of the multiplier. Divide takes 12.096 ms each.

Floating-point add takes 864 µs, floating-point multiply takes 4,896 µs (i.e. 17 word-times) and floating-point divide takes a maximum of 9,792 µs (i.e. a maximum of 34 word-times). The short divide (instruction 66) takes 4,608 µs (16 word-times). The square root instruction (67) takes 4,320 µs (15 word-times).

For the input/output instructions in Group 7 (see below), the *prepare* type of orders generally take 864 µs each. The actual input/output transfers then take a variety of milliseconds, according to the characteristics of the device and its state of readiness.

A4.4   Further Details of the Elliott 503

As has been said, the random-access memory for the 503 is in two parts: a fast section of 8K words (approximately equivalent to 40 KB) of 3.6 µs cycle time and a backing section of up to 128K words in units of 16K words. Access to the backing section is normally via autonomous transfers to the fast section, though individual words can be accessed from backing store in 71.9 µs.

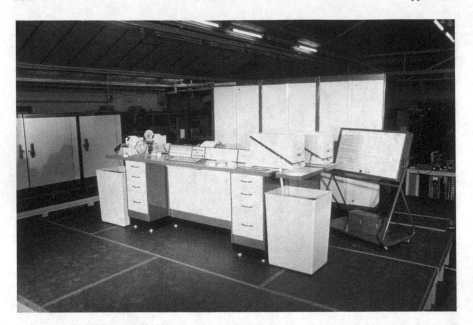

Fig. A4.2 An Elliott 503 computer on the commissioning floor at Borehamwood in 1963. The engineer's display panel in the foreground to the right of the photo is used to indicate the state of various registers during testing and maintenance. Notice the two fast paper tape readers on the control desk to the left and the two paper tape punches (in sound-absorbing white boxes) to the right

The fastest Elliott 503 instructions (group 4 jumps) take 4.5 μs. The fixed-point operations on the 503 take respectively 7.2 μs (group 0), 8.4 μs (groups 1 and 2) and 8.7 μs (group 3). Floating-point add/subtract takes 13.2–30.3 (average 18) μs. The figures for floating-point multiply and divide are respectively: 31.5–41.1 (average 33.8) μs and 60.9–61.8 μs. If the instruction preceding a B-line is in groups 4–7 then its time is increased by 3.6 μs. Details of the instruction set (order code) are given in Sect. A4.6 (Fig. A4.2).

A4.5   Input/Output for the Elliott 803 and 503

The 503 computer, being a more powerful machine designed a couple of years after the 803, naturally allowed for a more up-to-date range of peripheral equipment. Examples are the replacement of magnetic *film* by magnetic *tape* and a richer paper tape character set. The comparative performance of Elliott magnetic film and tape systems is given in Chap. 10. The Elliott 503 included 15 Autonomous Data Transfer (ADT) channels and a repertoire of input/output instructions that differed in detail from those provided for the Elliott 803. The full instruction sets are described in Sect. A4.6.

Elliott 800 series computers used 5-track paper tape, the 803 telecode being the same as for the Elliott 402 (and for the common option for the 405) – see Table A3.3.

Table A4.2 Elliott 503 8-track paper tape code. Some illustrative sample characters from the set of up to 128 possibilities

Binary pattern on 8-track paper tape (the point represents the sprocket hole)	Interpretation, as an alphanumeric character or for printer control
00110.000	0
00010.001	1
00010.010	2
00000.011	3
00010.100	4
00000.101	5
01000.001	A
01000.010	B
01010.011	C
01000.100	D
01010.101	E
11010.001	a
11010.010	b
11000.011	c
11010.100	d
11000.101	e
00101.101	+
00010.010	Newline
10010.000	Space
11111.111	Erase (ignored)
00000.000	Blank run-out (ignored)

Table A4.3 Maximum transfer rates for a selection of input/output devices

	Elliott 803	Elliott 503
Paper tape reader	500 chars/s	1,000 chars/s
Paper tape punch	100 chars/s	100 chars/s
Card reader	340 cards/min	340 cards/min
Card punch	100 cards/min	100 cards/min
Line printer	300 lines/min	1,000 lines/min
Core backing store	None	71.9 µs/word
Magnetic film	4,350 chars/s	Not applicable
Magnetic tape	Not applicable	42,000 chars/s

The Elliott 503 used 8-track paper tape, with a different coding from the previous Elliott 5-track convention. Table A4.2 shows some sample 8-track characters, from which it may be inferred that *even parity* is preserved for all the combinations to which meaning has been assigned.

Internal character representations within the 503 used seven bits, whereas 6-bit internal characters were common for the 803.

In summary, a variety of input/output devices were available for the 803 and for the 503 computers. Table A4.3 gives, for the highest-performance device under each category, the characteristics in terms of the maximum transfer rates for the computer in question.

A4.6   Instruction Sets for the Elliott 803 and 503

For the Elliott 803 and 503, two 19-bit instructions are packed into each 39-bit word. The pair of instructions is separated by a 'B-line' bit. When this bit is set, the second instruction is modified by adding to it the contents of the memory location specified by the address portion of the first instruction of the pair. (For the Elliott 503 only, the scheme was generalized by the 67 instruction – see later.) This B-bit mechanism allows 'any' memory location to be used as an address-modifier (i.e. index register). There are no explicit hardware index registers within in the CPU.

The layout of a pair of instructions for the Elliott 803 and 503 is as follows:

6	13	1	6	13
F	N	B	F	N
Op code	Address, constant or device	B indicator	Op code	Address, constant or device

N can either be a memory address or a constant (literal) or an input/output device specifier, according to the function as specified by the Op code bits. It is always a memory address for instructions in groups 0–4, as shown below. N is used as a constant (literal) for instructions 50, 51, 54, 55. It should be set to 4096 for instruction 65 and as an address in instructions 73 and 77. Its use for other input/output instructions is described later. On the computer's control panel there is an array of 39 hand-switches called the *word generator*. The number set up on these switches may be read into the accumulator via the 70 instruction. By convention, the op code (function bits) for each instruction are written as two octal digits, thereby covering the range 00–77.

Arithmetic is normally single-length, two's complement, with fixed-point values being held in the range $-1 \le x < +1$. The single-length accumulator is extended by an auxiliary register AR for those instructions which involve double-length working. From the programmers' viewpoint, 39-bit floating-point numbers are held in the form:

$$x = a.2^b,$$

where: $-1 \le a < -\frac{1}{2}$ or $a = 0$ or $\frac{1}{2} \le a < 1$ and $-256 \le b < 256$.

Actually, the exponent is held internally as $(b + 256)$, so that $0 \le b < 255$, leading to a more convenient representation of floating-point zero [6].

Instructions in groups 0–3 are symmetrical, the main difference between the groups being the sequence of implied memory operations at the detailed hardware level. The Elliott 803 and 503 have a magnetic core store with destructive-read properties. Thus, a *read* must always be followed by a *write* operation. For group 0 instructions, it is the *old (former)* contents n of the memory location that is written back. For group 1 it is the old contents of acc, a, that is written back. For groups 2 and 3, it is some function of {a,n} that is written back. This hardware symmetry means that many of the instructions in groups 1, 2 and 3 may seem curious to the modern programmer. To emphasise the point, only the mnemonics of instructions

00–37 that would now be regarded as standard practice are emboldened in the description below.

The instruction set(s) which follow come from the two Elliott booklets entitled *803 FACTS* and *503 FACTS* [2 and 7]. The definition of instructions with Op codes 00–65 is identical for the 803 and 503 computers. Instructions in the range 66–77 are concerned with input and output and their definitions differ between the 803 and the 503, as explained later. Actually, the special instructions 66 and 67 are simply described as *not used* in [2], because they were only enabled for Process Control applications of the Elliott 803 computer. Information on the 66 and 67 instructions for the 803 comes from [6, 8].

A4.6.1 Notation

In defining the 00–37 instructions for the Elliott 803 and 503 computers, we employ the following notation. The 'old' and 'new' contents of memory location N are denoted by **n** and **n'** respectively. Similarly, the 'old' and 'new' contents of the accumulator are denoted by **a** and **a'**. For instructions in the range 50–77, the **N** bits are sometimes used as a constant (literal), sometimes as a memory address and sometimes as an extension of the F bits (thereby defining further sub-operations). When used to extend the F bits, N must be given one of a set of specific values, such as 4096, as indicated below. Finally, **AR** denotes the *Auxiliary Register,* used for example in double-length operations.

Op code	a'	n'	Modern mnemonic and explanation	
00	a	n	**NOP**	No operation
01	−a	n	**NEG**	Negate accumulator
02	n + 1	n	**LDINC**	Load acc & inc.
03	a & n	n	**AND**	
04	a + n	n	**ADD**	
05	a − n	n	**SUB**	
06	0	n	**CLR**	Clear acc
07	n − a	n	**REVSUB**	Reverse subtract.
10	n	a	**SWAP**	Swap acc & memory
11	−n	a	SWAPN	Swap & negate
12	n + 1	a	SWINC	Swap & inc.
13	a & n	a	SWAND	Swap & AND
14	a + n	a	SWADD	Swap & ADD
15	a − n	a	SWSUB	Swap & SUB
16	0	a	STCLR	Store & clear
17	n − a	a	SWRSUB	Swap & rev. SUB.
20	a	a	**STO**	Store acc
21	a	−a	**STN**	Store acc negatively
22	a	n + 1	**INCM**	Increment memory
23	a	a &n	STAND	Store & AND memory

(continued)

(continued)

Op code	a'	n'	Modern mnemonic and explanation	
24	a	a + n	STADD	Store & ADD
25	a	a − n	STSUB	Store & SUB
26	a	0	**CLM**	Clear memory
27	a	n − a	STRSUB	Store & rev. SUB.
30	n	n	**LDA**	Load acc
31	n	−n	LDMNEG	Load acc & negate memory
32	n	n + 1	LDMINC	Load acc & inc. memory
33	n	a & n	LDMAND	Load acc & AND into memory
34	n	a + n	LDMADD	Load acc & ADD into memory
35	n	a −n	LDMSUB	Load acc & SUB into memory
36	n	0	LDMCLR	Load acc & clear memory
37	n	n −a	LDMRSUB	Load acc & rev. SUB into memory.
40, 44			JMP	Unconditional jump
41, 45			JNEG	Jump if acc negative
42, 46			JEQ	Jump if acc equals zero
43, 47			JOV	Jump if fxpt overflow, & reset overflow indicator

(40–43 transfer to the first instruction of a pair starting at address N; 44–47 transfer to the second instruction of a pair).

50			SHRD	Arith. shift of the double-length acc right by N places.
51			SHRS	shift acc logically right N times; clear AR.
52	a × n	n	MPYD	Multiply acc by n, giving a double-length product.
53			MPYS	Single-length multiply by n; clear AR.
54			SHLD	Shift the double-length acc left by N places.
55			SHLS	Shift acc left N times; clear AR.
56	a/n	n	DIV	Divide (double-length dividend, single-length quotient). Clear AR.
57			LAR	Read AR to acc.
60	a + n	n	FLADD	Floating-point add; clear AR.
61	a − n	n	FLSUB	floating-point subtract; clear AR
62	n − a	n	FLRSUB	Floating-point reverse-subtract; clear AR
63	a × n	n	FLMPY	Floating-point multiply; clear AR
64	a/n	n	FLDIV	Floating-point divide; clear AR
65		4096	CONFL	Convert the integer in acc to a normalised Floating-point number; clear AR
65		0 -> 39	SHLC	Shift acc circular (end-around) upwards N places.
70			HKY	Read the control-panel handkeys (*word generator*) into the accumulator.
73			SETLNK	Write the address of the present instruction to memory location N. (*Used for subroutine return*).

The action of all of the foregoing instructions is identical for the Elliott 803 and 503 computers. The rest of the instructions are defined differently for each machine, as now explained.

A4.6.2   Instructions in the Range 66–77 for the Elliott 803

66	a/n	n	DIVSH	Divide acc by operand, placing 13-digit quotient in acc. *(NB – only for Process Control applications).*
67			SQRT	Extract square root of acc, placing 13-digit root in acc. *(NB – only for Process Control applications).*

The rest of the Group 7 instructions are specific to the Elliott 803's input/output devices, so have been arranged below accordingly. As remarked in [6], 'The beauty of the Group 7 input/output instructions is that the set is extremely flexible. In general the instruction specifies the function and the address of the device. 72 and 73 were extensively used for process control where there are a large number of transducers etc. 76 and 77 were used for a variety of block transfer devices many of which were not even envisaged when the [803] processor was designed.'

a. 803 Instructions for paper tape reader, punch and teleprinter:

71	0	Read a char. from the first tape reader to accumulator.
71	2048	Read a char. from the second tape reader to accumulator.
74	N	Punch the char. N on the first tape punch.
74	2048 + N	Punch the char. N on the second tape punch
74	4096 + N	Print the char. N on the teleprinter.

(Paper tape reader, punch and teleprinter channels include *busy* line facilities).

Instructions 75, 76 and 77 were used for a variety of input/output devices, as described later from the programmers' viewpoint. First, though, a general engineering description of these instructions is given. The engineering account is taken from [8].

b. Engineering description of 803 instructions 75, 76 and 77.

75	Input or output the 13 least-significant digits to or from the Accumulator. Device and function are specified by the N bits. (In the case of input, the Acc is first cleared). Time taken: two word-times.
76	Output 13-bit Address code and 40-bit store code. (Prepare to input or output into or out of store. Device and function specified by code). Also clear Acc and input control word into 13 least-significant digits of Acc. Time taken: three word-times.
77	Block transfer from peripheral device into or out of store, starting at the address specified. Every 77 instruction must be preceded by a 76 instruction. Timing of block transfer is under peripheral control. The Elliott 803's maximum transfer rate of information is one 39-bit word every 144 µs.

Now follows the programmers' descriptions, as given in the 803 FACTS booklet [2].

c. 80-Column punched-card input and output for the Elliott 803:

76	512	Read card input control word; prepare to read card.
77	N	Read card to store locations N to N + 79.
76	2561	Read card output control word; prepare to punch a card.
77	N	Punch the information held in store locations N to N + 79. (Actual punching takes 600 ms per card).

d. Magnetic film store instructions for the Elliott 803:

75	1027	Read address of last block read or written.
76	1024, 1032, 1040 or 1048	Read handler control word to accumulator; prepare to read on film handler 1, 2, 3 or 4.
76	1025, 1033, 1041 or 1049	Read handler control word to accumulator; prepare to write on handler 1, 2, 3 or 4.
76	1026, 1034, 1042, 1050	Read handler control word to accumulator; prepare to search on handler 1, 2, 3 or 4.
77	N	Read, write or search as prescribed by a 76 instruction.

e. Digital plotter instructions for the Elliott 803:

72	7169, 7170, 7172, 7176	Pen moves in direction E, W, N, S.
72	7173, 7174, 7177, 7178	Pen moves in direction NE, NW, SE, SW.
72	7184, 7200	Pen raise, or pen lower.

f. Anelex Lineprinter instructions for the Elliott 803:

76	3073	Read Anelex control word to accumulator; prepare to print one line.
77	N	Transfer to lineprinter from store locations N to N + 120. The contents, M, of location N controls the lineprinter's paper-feed as follows:
		$M \leq 0 \leq 30$ Feed M + 1 lines and print.
		$M = 31$ or 32 Print on the same line.
		$M \leq 33 \leq 62$ Find channel M and print.
		$M = 63$ Find top of form and print.

A4.6.3   Instructions in the Range 66–77 for the Elliott 503

The 66 and 67 instructions, which are used for special process control purposes in the 803, are re-defined as follows for the 503:

66	SWITCH	Load registers and transfer control. Used for returning from Interrupt. Time taken: 19.5 µs.
67	MOD	Modify the next instruction by adding to it the least-significant 19 digits of n. Time taken: 7.2 µs

The 503 incorporates a fully autonomous facility for controlling the transfer of data between its CPU and its peripheral equipment, via 15 Autonomous Data Transfer (ADT) channels. Provision is made for autonomous transfers from more than one device to take place concurrently. Transfer rates can vary enormously, according to concurrent activity, with a maximum possible rate of about 100,000 words per second [9]. In addition to the usual input/output devices such as paper tape readers/punches, card readers/punches, lineprinters and digital incremental plotters, the Elliott 503's ferrite core backing store is also classed as a peripheral device. Autonomous transfers are used for moving blocks of data between the backing store and the primary store. Alternatively, single words may be transferred between the accumulator and the backing store.

For input/output instructions in group 7 orders, the N bits have the following format:

4	9
Device number	Special mode or control bits

The 15 classes of peripheral device are allocated a fixed priority order. Of the nine special mode bits, the least three significant bits usually specify the operation to be performed whilst the remaining six bits specify the part of the peripheral to which the instruction refers if there is more than one part.

71	N	INCH	Send N to Peripheral Controller. Input a 7-bit character from device N to acc
72	N	OUTW	Send n to Peripheral Controller. Output a word from acc to device N
74	N	SELN	Send N to Peripheral Controller, for selection purposes and for information
75	N	INWD	Send n to Peripheral Controller. Input a Control Word from device N to acc
76	N	PREPAT	Send N to Peripheral Controller. Prepare for an autonomous transfer to/from device N by reading a Control Word from device into acc
77	N	EXAT	Execute the autonomous transfer previously set up via the 76 order, to/from memory location N. The CPU places protective tags on the area of memory involved in the transfer. The most significant part of the accumulator specifies the number of words, M, to be transferred

References

1. National Elliott 803 publicity brochure. Undated, but probably 1963. A document number CS109 is given in very small print at the back. The brochure says: 'A basic machine with paper tape input and output costs only £29,000 including installation, supply of library programmes, and six months' free maintenance'
2. Anon (1964) National Elliott 803 FACTS. Published jointly by the Scientific Computing Division of Elliott Brothers Ltd., Borehamwood, and the NCR Electronics Division of National Cash Register Co. Ltd., London. Various editions of this booklet were issued between 1960 and 1965. The version used in this appendix was issued in Apr 1964

3. Laurie Bental (2001) E-mail to Simon Lavington, Sept 2001
4. Anon (Jan 1962) 503 Ultra high speed digital computer for science and industry. Five-page technical brochure number CP 204, Elliott Computing Division, Borehamwood, London. http://archive.computerhistory.org/resources/text/Elliott_Brothers/Elliott.503.1962.102646077.pdf
5. (a) Anon (undated) National-Elliott 802 – advance information. 5-page undated brochure (b) Anon (1958) Programming the National-Elliott 802 computer – preliminary information. 4-page brochure published by Scientific Computing Division, Elliott Brothers Ltd., Borehamwood, London, Nov 1958. Note that no FACTS booklet was produced for the Elliott 802. (c) Cook RL (1959) Time-sharing on the National-Elliott 802. Comput J 2(4):185–188
6. LJ Bental (2004) Letter to Simon Lavington dated 21 Nov 2004
7. Anon (1963) Elliott 503 FACTS. Elliott Computing Division, Borehamwood, London. Various editions of this booklet were issued between 1963 and 1965. The version used in this appendix was issued in Dec 1963
8. (a) Bental LJ (1961) Arithmetic operations in the 803B computer. Typewritten internal Borehamwood document dated Jan 1961 (b) Bental LJ (1962) A floating point arithmetic unit. Electron Eng March:144–147
9. (a) Interface description for a special peripheral device in the 503 system. Technical manual 5.1.5, Elliott Scientific Computing Division, Undated (b) Williams JWJ, Shaw ML (1964) Data transfers between the 503 and a peripheral device. Typed technical note (13 pages), dated 16 Dec 1964 and stapled to the cover of the above manual

Appendix 5
Technical Details of the Elliott 502 Computer

A5.1 General Overview

The Elliott 502, so named because it was at first conceived in about 1960 as a successor to the Elliott 402, was a high-speed, 'limited-edition' transistorised computer designed for a classified real-time on-line data-processing application. It is believed that the first Elliott 502, delivered in 1963, was the core of the SIMULATOR X project at the Royal Radar Establishment (RRE) located at Malvern. This first Elliott 502 is believed to have supported two lines of research at RRE: (a) simulation and evaluation of the advanced Type 85 defence radar; and (b) development and evaluation of RAF fighter interception techniques (track analysis) for air-defence. A second 502 was delivered to the Air Traffic Control Evaluation Unit at Hurn Airport, near Bournemouth, in 1966, possibly for the EUCLID project. A third 502 is believed to have been delivered to the RAF some time after March 1967, for the SIMULATOR M project which followed on directly from the SIMULATOR X work [1]. It is believed that the various projects which involved 502 computers were part of the *Linesman* and *Mediator* proposals for military and civil control of the UK's air space during the Cold War [2]. A brief discussion of Borehamwood's role in these projects is given in Chap. 8.

The prototype 502 used germanium transistors but the later machines were believed to have been a re-design using silicon transistors which had by then become available [3]. Neil Wiseman had been involved in defining the system architecture (Fig. A5.1).

Apart from using a somewhat similar general form of exterior cabinet construction, the Elliott 502 had no connection with the Elliott 503 computer which was the more powerful version of the Elliott 803 – (see Appendix 4). Furthermore, the latter stages of commissioning the 502 took place at Rochester, rather than at Borehamwood, because the special purpose equipment to interface the 502 to the RRE radar system was being developed at Elliott's Rochester factory [4]. The cost of each Elliott 502 computer is not known but, by comparison with the known figures for an Elliott 503, it is estimated that each Elliott 502 probably cost between £250,000 and £450,000 (1965 prices).

Fig. A5.1 The first Elliott 502 system, photographed at the Royal Radar Establishment (RRE) Malvern in early 1963. The central row of six cabinets is the 502 computer; the rows behind and in front are special purpose interfaces designed by Elliotts at Rochester to interconnect to a radar system. It is believed that three Elliott 502 computers were built, each being used for classified research projects concerned with radar-based monitoring of the UK's air space during the Cold War. The 502 provided hardware support for rapid context-switching and fast response to real-time events

The Elliott 502 was a high-performance parallel, transistorised computer. It was described as 'asynchronous' [5] and as incorporating 'the application of ultra-high-speed techniques to systems in which the time allowed for computing is the actual duration of the related event', resulting in 'making a spectacular increase in the range of systems to which automatic on-line data processing can now be introduced' [6]. The central processor was indeed asynchronous, in the sense of there being no fixed-frequency clock. This was a first for Borehamwood. Iann Barron describes the asynchronous nature of the Elliott 502 as follows [7]: 'There was a central timing system consisting of a chain of delays, which emitted the timing signals for a cycle; the length of the delay was preset (adjustable), but the number of delays (and sequence of delays) was variable, depending on the operation that was occurring, so there was no fixed clock period. The completion of a sub operation was timed by fixed delay appropriate to that sub operation, and not by a completion signal generated by the logic of the suboperation (I am not sure that was true for an arithmetic carry operation).' The use of a chain of delays was also employed in the asynchronous Atlas computer [8], where the delay chain was known as the *Juke Box*.

The 502 had two sections of ferrite core memory: a fast section of 1K 20-bit words (approximately equivalent to 2.5 KB) and a main section extensible 'up to any practical limit' in units of 8K words. The cycle time of the fast section is

1.25 µs and that of the main section is 3 µs. Programs may be obeyed from either store, and operate on data from either store. Input/Output is either via Direct Transfer or via Autonomous Data Transfer. Autonomous data transfers to/from peripheral devices only take place to/from the main section. Provision is made for a maximum of 12 peripheral devices to have independent autonomous data transfer facilities, any simultaneous requests being handled on a priority basis.

A feature of the Elliott 502 is that it allows the apparently simultaneous running of several programs on a time-division basis, according to pre-assigned priorities. Up to eight levels of priority are catered for. A system of interrupts (also called *External Stimuli* or *Programme Stimuli*) allows *Program Breaks*, which enable a high priority program to take precedence over one of lower priority in response to an external event. Seven of the priority levels are associated with external interrupt signals; the eighth level is the default level, applying when no interrupt has been received.

The 502 consists physically of five (double-door?) cabinets [6], the construction allowing the whole assembly to be mounted in a trailer for both transportation and operational use. The suite of five cabinets measures 18 ft long by 2 ft 5 in. deep by 5 ft 9 in. high ($5.5 \times 0.7 \times 1.75$ m³), the total weight being 16 cwt (813 kg). Cooling is via chilled air, employing a separate refrigeration unit. Besides the connections to/from the equipment being controlled and any necessary autonomous data transfers (described below), the 502 has provision for magnetic tape decks and for the following standard input/output equipment: 5-track paper tape reader, transferring at 500 chars/s; 5-track paper tape punch, operating at a maximum speed of 100 chars/s. In addition, Creed type 75 Keyboard teleprinter and transmitter equipment is provided for off-line working.

According to [9], a real-time applications compiler, BASIC CORAL, was working for the Elliott 502 computer from November 1966. The system software details are given in [10].

A5.2   Systems Architecture and Visible Registers

In the Elliott 502, fixed-point numbers of 20 bits are stored as two's complement fractions. Both single-length and double-length fixed-point multiplication and division are provided. There is no floating-point hardware. There is, however, a hardware square root function. The 20-bit instruction format (see Sect. A5.3) is of a conventional one-address type, which includes 6 function bits and 10 operand-address bits.

The central registers included a 20-bit main accumulator (A), a 20-bit auxiliary, or extension, accumulator (R), a 20-bit modifier register (B), a Sequence Control Register or Program Counter (S), a single-bit overflow register (OV) and a Program Control Register (PCR) which contained seven bits, one corresponding to each Interrupt signal or *Program Stimulus*. The function of these seven bits was to enable, or mask, the effect of the corresponding stimulus. The PCR may also have contained other read-only bits providing the states of the stimuli and the current operating priority level, according to Peter Lawrence [11]. The Sequence Control Register, S, contains an extra bit that indicates whether the next instruction is to be fetched from fast RAM or from main RAM.

After obeying each instruction, except for those which have the L (lock) bit set (see Sect. A5.3), there is a check on whether the highest priority level for which both the external stimulus and the PCR bit are set is the same as the current operating priority level. If not the same, then a *Program Break* operation is performed which:

- Stores the current 20-bit working register values, namely S, A, R and B, in memory locations predefined for the current operating priority level;
- Sets the operating priority level to that indicated by the stimulus and PCR states;
- Sets working register values from those stored in locations defined for the new priority level.

Program operation then resumes, as controlled by these new register values. Note that a program can effectively interrupt itself by setting a PCR bit and so unmasking a stimulus already asserted. The *Program Break* operation, more usually referred to as an automatic context-switch, is comparatively very rapid, taking place in under 10 μs.

The Elliott 502's data paths for input and output are interestingly wide. Direct Transfers take place via a 20-bit bi-directional highway; Autonomous Data Transfers take place via a 40-bit bi-directional highway. More details are given later.

A5.3   Elliott 502 Instruction Set

The instruction set for the Elliott 502 offers a rich variety of addressing modes for a relatively straightforward repertoire of ALU operations. Each 20-bit instruction occupies one word, as follows:

1	1	6	2	10
L	M	F	K	N
Interrupt lock	Store mode	Op code	Modifier source	Literal or address

If L = 1 then interrupts are inhibited, or locked, until the succeeding instruction has been obeyed. (Note that, somewhat confusingly, the symbol S was used for this bit in the original Elliott documentation).

M is the *Store Mode* bit, whose interpretation also depends upon the actual instruction being obeyed (as explained below). If M = 0, N represents either an address in fast RAM or N represents a literal (constant). If M = 1, N represents either an address in main RAM or an address in fast RAM that holds the address of an operand in main RAM (i.e. indirect addressing into main RAM).

F is the 6-bit Function (or Op code), specifying two octal digits as used in the tables below.

K specifies the source of the address-modifier, thus:

if K = 0, no modification takes place;
if K = 1, use the contents of the B register;
if K = 2, use the contents of the accumulator, A;
if K = 3, use the contents of the Sequence Control Register (or Program Counter),
    S, which always points to the *next* instruction to be obeyed.

The N bits in the Elliott 502 are generally interpreted in one of four possible ways, depending upon the M bit and the instruction being obeyed, as follows:

For Group 0 and 1 orders:	When M = 0 then N is a positive fraction (i.e. literal)
	When M = 1 then N is a main store address
For Group 2 and 3 orders:	When M = 0 then N is a fast store address
	When M = 1 then the contents of the fast store address
	is used indirectly to address a location in main store
For Group 7 instructions, N is used to specify a peripheral device	

In the Elliott 502 instruction tables given below, the following abbreviations are used:

a, a'	The old and new contents of the accumulator register, A
b, b'	The old and new contents of the modifier register, B
s, s'	The old and new contents of the Sequence Control Register, S
r, r'	The old and new contents of the auxiliary register, R
ar, a'r'	The old and new contents of the double-length accumulator {A,R}
N	The N-bits when used as a constant (i.e. literal)
(N), (N)'	The old and new contents of main store address N
(n), (n)'	The old and new contents of fast store address N
((n)), ((n))'	The old and new contents of main store address (n), i.e. when the main store is being accessed indirectly via a fast store location
OV	The Overflow indicator (a single-bit register)
T	Data (e.g. a 5-bit character) read in from an input device

Instructions in Groups 0–3 include simple short arithmetical operations on the accumulator and on the B register. The action of instructions in Groups 0–3 is dependent upon the setting of the store-mode bit, M, as follows:

Function	When M = 0	When M = 1	Explanation
00	b' = b + N	b' = b + (N)	ADD B
01	b' = b' − N	b' = b − (N)	SUBTRACT B
02	b' = N − b	b' = (N) − b	REVERSE SUBTRACT B

(continued)

(continued)

Function	When M = 0	When M = 1	Explanation
03	b' = N	b' = (N)	LOAD B
04	–	(N)' = b + (N)	ADD B to store
05	–	(N)' = b – (N)	SUBTRACT B from store
06	–	(N)' = (N) – b	REVERSE SUBTRACT B from store
07	–	(N)' = b	STORE B
10	a' = a + N	a' = a + (N)	ADD A
11	a' = a – N	a' = a – (N)	SUBTRACT A
12	a' = N – a	a' = (N) – a	REVERSE SUBTRACT A
13	a' = N	a' = (N)	LOAD A
14	–	(N)' = a + (N)	ADD A to store
15	–	(N)' = a – (N)	SUB A from store
16	–	(N)' = (N) – a	REV SUBTRACT A from store
17	–	(N)' = a	STORE A
20	b' = b +(n)	b' = b + ((n))	ADD B
21	b' = b – (n)	b' = b – ((n))	SUBTRACT B
22	b' = (n) – b	b' = ((n)) – b	REVERSE SUBTRACT B
23	b' = (n)	b' = ((n))	LOAD B
24	(n)' = b + (n)	((n))' = b + ((n))	ADD B to store
25	(n)' = b – (n)	((n))' = b – ((n))	SUBTRACT B from store
26	(n)' = (n) – b	((n))' = ((n)) – b	REVERSE SUBTRACT B from store
27	(n)' = b	((n))' = b	STORE B
30	a' = a + (n)	a' = a + ((n))	ADD A
31	a' = a – (n)	a' = a – ((n))	SUBTRACT A
32	a' = (n) – a	a' = ((n)) – a	REVERSE SUBTRACT A
33	a' = (n)	a' = ((n))	LOAD A
34	(n)' = a + (n)	((n))' = a + ((n))	ADD A to store
35	(n)' = a – (n)	((n))' = a – ((n))	SUBTRACT A from store
36	(n)' = (n) – a	((n))' = ((n)) – a	REVERSE SUBTRACT A from store
37	(n)' = a	((n))' = a	STORE A

Note: for Group 3 instructions, the overflow marker OV is set if the result of any operation is outside the range -1 to $+(1-2^{-19})$.

Group 4 instructions: Transfer of control

40	if b ≠ 0 then b' = b + 1 and s' = N	Jump if b not equal to zero and INC B
41	if b ≠ 0 then b' = b – 1 and s' = N	Jump if b not equal to zero and DEC B
42	if b = 0 then s' = N	Jump if b = 0
43	b' = s and s' = N	Subroutine entry
44	if a ≥ 0 then s' = N	Jump if acc ≥ 0
45	if a < 0 then s' = N	Jump if acc < 0
46	if a = 0 then s' = N	Jump if acc = 0
47	if OV = 1 then s' = N and OV = 0	Jump if overflow

Note: for Group 4 instructions and for instructions 50 and 51, the jump-to address is in fast RAM when M = 0 and in main RAM when M = 1. Following the 43 instruction, the most significant digit of B is 0 if the instruction is in fast RAM and 1 if it is in main RAM.

Group 5 and 6 instructions: Miscellaneous and double-length arithmetic

Function	When M = 0	When M = 1	Explanation
50	s' = (n)	s' = (N)	Absolute unconditional jump
51	s' = s − (n)	s' = (N)	Relative branch
52	a' = a & (n)	s' = a & (N)	Logical AND
53	r' = (n)	r' = (N)	Load R
54	(n)' = (n) + 1	(N)' = (N) + 1	Memory INC
55	(n)' = (n) − 1	(N)' = (N) − 1	Memory DEC
56	(n)' = a & (n)	(N)' = a & (N)	Memory logical AND
57	(n)' = r	(N)' = r	Store R
60	... shift A logically N places left ...		Logical shift left
61	... shift A arith. N places left ...		Arithmetical shift left
62	... shift {A,R} arith. N places left ...		Double-length arithmetical shift
63	a' = SQRT(a + (n))	a = SQRT(a + (N))	Square root
64	a'r' = a x (n)	a'r' = a x (N)	Multiply, double- length
65	a' = a x (n)	a' = (N)	Multiply single-length; R cleared
66	{a,r}/(n) or {a,r}/(N); r' = quotient; a' = rem.		Divide double-length
67	a' = {a,r}/(n)	a' = {a,r}/(N)	Divide single-length; R cleared

Note: at the conclusion of instruction 64, AR holds the product as a 38-bit signed fraction, the most significant bit of R being cleared. At the start of instructions 66 and 67, AR together holds a 38-bit signed fraction

Group 7 instructions: input/output

70	a' = a + T add data from input device N
71	*Unallocated; causes a dynamic stop*
72	*Unallocated; causes a dynamic stop*
73	a' = T read data from input device N
74	*Used to control autonomous transfer devices; no details have yet come to light*
75	*Unallocated; causes a dynamic stop*
76	Causes a Program Break; re-enter at n or N
77	a is output to device N write acc to output device N

Note: for instructions 70, 73, 74 and 77, N specifies the identity of the peripheral device

Amongst the values of N used for standard devices for the 502, the following are known to have applied. Clearly, other peripherals specific to the classified radar application at RRE would have had their own identities.

N = 0 the 502's Operator's Console;
N = 1 the 5-track paper tape reader;
N = 2 the Program Control Register, PCR.

Further details of the PCR are given above in Sect. A5.2. In summary, to quote the Elliott 502's manual [6]: '... PCR contains an indication of where a given program has been prevented from running; instructions 70/2 or 73/2 can be used to determine this, while instruction 77/2 can activate or inhibit a programme'. Note that a Program Break normally occurs as a result of an external demand (interrupt); the 76 instruction is an alternative software method of achieving the same action.

The effect of a 76 instruction is that:

- The S register is set to n or N.
- The stimulus for the current operating priority level is cleared.

This then causes a Program Break. The new priority level will normally be lower than the current one. The address of the 76 instruction will have been stored as the re-entry address to be used when the former priority level is re-stimulated. The 502 console includes switches that can enable or mask each program stimulus (in addition to the control provided by the PCR) and a push-button for emulating each stimulus.

The Elliott 502 was required to handle significant amounts of input/output for the special real-time, on-line applications for which it was designed. The width of the highways for each form of input/output is given below.

Programme Stimuli (i.e. Interrupts):

Demands	7 bits	Into the 502
Replies	7 bits	Out of the 502

Direct Input/Output transfers and device control transfers:

Data	20 bits	Bi-directional
Address	4 bits	Out of the 502
Function (70/73, 74 or 77)	3 bits	Out of the 502
Reply and Busy	2 bits	Into the 502

Autonomous Data Transfers:

Data	40 bits	Bi-directional
Control	12 bits	Out of the 502
Control	12 bits	Into the 502
Priority Control	36 bits	Into the 502
Priority Control	12 bits	Out of the 502

The Elliott 502's autonomous transfer facility, which is similar to techniques referred to in later years as *Direct Memory Access* or *Cycle-stealing,* allows Input/Output to take place in parallel with normal program operation. The mechanism is that when a *Priority Control* signal from a peripheral indicates that transfer of a word is required the computer will, between instructions, automatically access a pointer and a counter held in memory for the peripheral concerned, transfer a word to or from the location indicated by the pointer and then adjust the pointer and counter. Thus, transfer of a block of words is effected without program action. The Elliott 502's 74 instruction is used to indicate to the peripheral the type of action required and to set it in progress. For the Elliott 502, it is up to a program to ascertain the progress of a transfer before using or changing the data concerned. However, on the Elliott 503, for compatibility with 803 programs, an additional memory bit in each word is used to inhibit access to it while the word is involved in an autonomous transfer.

A5.4 Elliott 502 Instruction Times

The approximate times in microseconds for various instructions (see [6]) are as follows:

Instruction(s)	Operand	Instr. in fast RAM		Instr. in main RAM
Groups 0 and 1	Literal operand	2.3		3.8
Groups 0 and 1	Main RAM operand	4.3		8.2
Groups 2 and 3	Fast RAM operand	3.3		4.3
Groups 2 and 3	Main RAM, indirect	4.8		8.2
Group 4; 50 and 51		1.5–3.0		2.5–4.1
52–57	Fast RAM operand	3.3		4.3
52–57	Main RAM operand	4.3		8.2
60 and 61		$(2.8 + 0.5N)$		$(4.0 + 0.5N)$
62		$(3.2 + 0.9N)$		$(4.4 + 0.9N)$
63			33–45	
64–67			18–24	
70, 73, 77			4–6	
76			12–15	
74			5–8	

References

(Note that very few original Elliott 502 source documents have come to light. This is, no doubt, due to the classified nature of the 502's use)

1. Cochrane M (2002) Summary of Elliott projects developed between 1962 and 1969. Three-page typed manuscript, with two-page typed accompanying letter to Simon Lavington dated 9 Feb 2002. Mike Cochrane worked on air defence applications for Elliott's Airspace Control Division (originally Aircraft Direction Division) from mid-1962 to late-1969
2. http://en.wikipedia.org/wiki/Linesman/Mediator
3. Peter Lawrence (2001) E-mail correspondence with Simon Lavington, 3 Dec 2001
4. Iann Barron (2006) Lecture to the Computer Conservation Society at the Science Museum, London, on 4 May 2006, on his career at Elliott Brothers Ltd., London. Iann subsequently

amplified his memories of the 502 project in telephone conversations and e-mails to Simon Lavington in the period 16 to 25 Oct 2006

5. (a) Anon (undated) Features of the Elliott 502 computer. Undated two-page typed document. This was bound in the same folder as (b) Anon (undated) Programming the 502. Undated 14-page typed document. Neither of these two documents has any identifying features, other than that they were both in the possession of D H (Dennis) Rowland, who worked for the Airspace Control Division of Elliot Brothers Ltd., London

6. Anon (1962) 502: General purpose real time on-line data processor. Published by the Mobile Computing Division, Elliott Brothers Ltd., Borehamwood, London, dated Dec 1962. 25 typed pages

7. Iann Barron (2010) E-mail to Simon Lavington on 24 June 2010

8. Kilburn T, Edwards DBG, Lanigan MJ, Sumner FH (Apr 1962) One level storage system. IRE Trans Electron Comput EC-11(2):223–235

9. Article in the magazine Computer Weekly, 24 Nov 1966

10. Anon (1966) Basic coral: specification and 502 compiler system. 59-page manual published by Airspace Control Division, Elliott Brothers Ltd., Borehamwood, London. Issue 2 is dated Oct 1966

11. Peter Lawrence (2004) E-mail correspondence with Simon Lavington, 23 Feb 2004

Appendix 6
Technical Details of Elliott 900 Series Computers

A6.1 General Overview of the Family

The 900 series of computers, which first appeared in 1961, lasted in one form or another until the mid-1980s and was sold in their thousands. Originating from John Bunt's efforts to meet the Army's need for 'mobile computing' for artillery control (see Chap. 8), most of the 900 series derivatives came to be used for aerospace applications – though civil and industrial variants were also successfully produced. Besides John Bunt, the engineers Jim Barrow and Peter Lawrence played a large part in the original 1961 designs.

Starting with an 18-bit word length, 13-bit and 12-bit variants were to appear later. The 900 family of parallel (i.e. not bit serial) computers spanned technologies ranging from discrete transistors to integrated circuits, and from ferrite core memory to semiconductor memory. By the end of the 1970s several of the early commercial users had passed their 900 series computers on to schools and colleges, where they operated happily for some years.

An enthusiastic Elliott company brochure [1], written in 1967/1968 and half way through the 900 series' design life, tells the family's story as follows:

'All the computers in the 900 range are functionally compatible with each other'. Actually, this was not strictly true in the end. All the 18-bit word members of the family (see Table A6.1) had instruction-set compatibility; similarly for all the 12-bit word members (see Table A6.2). However, the 12-bit and 18-bit instruction sets differed, as shown later. There was a single 13-bit variant, the ARCH 102 system.

The brochure continues: 'The series was introduced by the 920A computer, which is in service with the Royal Navy, the Army and the Royal Air Force.' Again, this is not strictly true because there was a 901 experimental computer, designed for an Army tank project, but only one 901 was built. The 920 is described in [2].

Table A6.1 Overall characteristics of some of the 18-bit members of the Elliott 900 family

	903	905	920B	920M	920C	920ATC; MC1800
Primary memory, standard.	8K	8K	8K	8K	8K	16K for ATC
Memory cycle time options, μs	6	1 or 2	6	2 or 5	1	1 for ATC
Max. addressable memory	64K	128K	64K	32K	128K	?
Includes an H register?	No	Yes	No	No	Yes	?
Add time, μs, unmodified	23.5	2.4 or 4.4	23.5	10.6 or 19	2.2	2.2
Multiply time, μs,unmodified	76.5	10.2 or 12.2	76.5	29.6 or 38	9.0	9.0
Basic package, measurements in inches or cubic feet.	Desk, 43 × 26 × 37	Desk, 42 × 24 × 36, or rack-mounted	Military pack, 19 × 9 × 32	Military pack, 12.56 × 7.5 × 7.63	Military pack, 0.5 ->1 cu ft	Military 1 ATR short, incl. power supply

Note: ATR = Air Transport Racking.

Table A6.2 Overall characteristics of the 12-bit members of the Elliott 900 family

	902	102C (or Minim)	ARCH 105	12/12
Primary memory, standard	4K	4K	4K	See text
Memory cycle-time options, microseconds	1 or 2	1 or 2	1 or 2	See text
Max. addressable memory	32K	32K	32K	See text
Add time, μs	2.4 or 4.4	2.4 or 4.4	2.4 or 4.4	See text
Multiply time, μs	11.4 or 13.4	11.4 or 13.4	11.4 or 13.4	See text
Basic package, measurements, in.	Cabinet, $19 \times 42 \times 23$ (rack-mounted)	Military pack, $5 \times 19.63 \times 7.63$	Twin bays, each $23 \times 24 \times 41$	See text

The brochure continues enthusiastically: 'The 920B followed the 920A and with it the first big reduction in cost was achieved. The civil version of the 920B, the 903, is the successor in the title to the highly successful Elliott 803, in its day the most popular and widely applied of all British designed computers... The rapid development of microelectronics ... has led to the design of the 920M... Already an even faster yet equally rugged computer is in production: the 920C, eight times faster than the 920B, which is itself two or three times faster than the 920A. Close on the heels of the 920C have come simplified, lower cost derivatives offering the same high performance capacity over a less extreme temperature range. These are the 902 and the 905, and their "ARCH" equivalents, assembled from a range of rack-mounting units to form highly competitive computer systems for commercial and industrial applications. Newest of all is the microminiature 102C, functionally similar to the 902 but even further scaled down in size to suit military (air, sea and land) mobile installations.'

John Bunt, the 'father' of the 900 series, has added the following comment [3]: 'The 920M was a re-engineered and miniaturized version of the 920B. It was [Elliott's] first significant use of integrated circuits. However, all the connections were welded – discrete components as well as the integrated circuits. Reliability was primarily a matter of standing up to the shock and vibration in the aerospace environment and with the advent of integrated circuits the connections and joints were the cause of most faults.'

The brochure, mentioned above, lists the 30 applications areas to which 900 series computers had been applied by 1968. Of these, projects in five areas predominate: defence, industrial process control, transport-signalling, laboratory research and education. In general terms, the Elliott 903 and 905 were civil variants, the ARCH variants were designed for industrial process control (see Chap. 7) and the rest of the variants were intended for defence applications.

Trying to arrange the family of 900 series computers in chronological order is difficult because: (a) the type-numbering is confusing, (b) there is a scarcity of surviving source-documents, and (c) computer developments proceeded simultaneously in more than one Division of the Elliott-Automation company. Here is an attempt at a rough chronological sequence:

Year	900-Series computers introduced in that year
1961	901
1962	920A
1963	920B
1964	ARCH 102
1965	903, ARCH 9000
1967	920M, 920C
1968	902, 905, 102C/Minim, ARCH105, ARCH 9050
1973	12/12
1976	920ATC, 920 AT
1977	MC1800

We can be a little more precise about the launch of the Elliott 903. Alan Wakefield, who worked as a sales engineer from November 1963 to August 1967, has retained his pocket diaries of the period. He has produced the following estimates [4]. The 903 was presented to sales staff in July 1965, was available for demonstration to customers at Borehamwood from about August 1965 and was exhibited at the Business Efficiency Exhibition, London Olympia, in October 1965. The first 903s were delivered to customers in mid-1966.

Elliott's Mobile Computing Division played a significant part in the early development of the 900 series. Thus, the initials *MCS* were often used in the marketing name of 900 series machines. Examples are: MCS 900, MCS920, MCS920B and MCS920C. Further aliases arose to confuse the uninitiated. For example, an Elliott MCM2 computer was a MCS 290M with 8K words of 5-µs core memory [5].

By 1970 much of the 900-series design emphasis had moved from Borehamwood to Rochester where, as described in Chap. 12, the 920 ATC and the 12/12 Series were to provide the basis of all of Rochester's airborne computer developments until the mid-1980s. By then, not all Rochester's innovations were downwards-compatible with the original 900-series family. For example, the 12/12 computer was designed to have a 12-bit instruction word and also, as far as possible, the same instruction set throughout all the different variants of the machine [6]. However, different length operands were devised to suit different aerospace applications, as described in Sect. A6.3.

Further technical comments on 900 series computers, including sample programs, have been placed on a website by Terry Froggatt – see [7]. Terry worked for Elliotts as a 900 Series programmer from 1966 to 1976. He was the secretary of the 900-users group within the Elliott Computer Users Association.

There now follows instruction-set descriptions of the 18-bit and 12-bit members of the 900-series computers. To remain compatible with the original Elliott documentation, in the following sections digits are numbered from 1 (for the

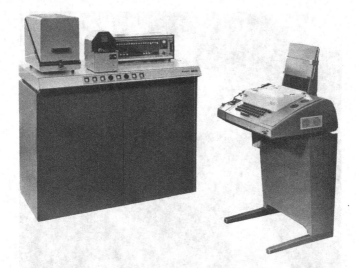

Fig. A6.1 The Elliott 903 computer was the open-market derivative of the Elliott 920 range of compact, mobile military computers. The free-standing device to the right of the photo is an ASR33 Teletype, introduced by the Teletype Corporation of America. It was a low-cost form of keyboard input/output with built-in 8-track paper tape reader/punch. 'ASR' stood for 'automatic send/receive'. From the mid-1960s to late 1970s the *Teletype* formed a ubiquitous and cost-effective device for primitive on-line interactive usage, before Visual Display Units (VDUs) became generally available

right-hand, least-significant, end) through to 12 or 18 for the left-hand, most significant end (Fig. A6.1).

A6.2 The 18-Bit Members of the Family

A6.2.1 The 920A

The Elliott 920A, originally called the MCS920 or simply the 920, was the first full production member of the range. Its instruction set was similar to that which soon became the standard 900, as listed later, except for minor differences in functions 8, 11, no block transfers and only 7-track (not 8-track) paper tape input [8, 9] (Fig. A6.2).

The first 920 system, retrospectively called the 920A, had much slower multiplication and division than subsequent family members. It also offered very limited options for primary memory, namely: (a) 4K words at 6 μs cycle time or (b) 8K words at 8 μs cycle time. The program counter, known as SCR or later simply as S, and the B (modifier) register were actually held in main memory. Thus, the instruction times included the need to access SCR, as well as fetching the instruction and any operand-fetching. Accessing and incrementing SCR (the program counter) took 9 or 11 μs (4K or 8K store). The sample 920A instruction times quoted below

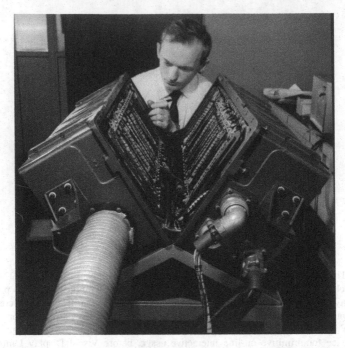

Fig. A6.2 Looking rather like a high-performance racing car engine, the Elliott 920A computer in its ruggedised military chassis was advertised in 1962 as *the first mobile computer*

are without address modification. If modification was called for, then 6 or 8 μs should be added to the times:

Function	Time with 4K 6μ memory	Time with 8K 8μ memory
Add	21 μs	27 μs
Multiply	183 μs	189 μs

No extensions to the basic memory capacity were offered. The 920A was packaged in a box measuring 36 × 12 × 14 in.[3] (military) or 34 × 10 × 33 (civil), and weighing 170 lb (78 kg) military or 80 lb (36 kg) civil. The July 1964 prices for the 920A [10] varied between £21,300 and £26,500, depending upon the choice of memory and packaging options. The power supply unit was extra, typically £750. A complete 920 system with paper tape reader, punch and flexowriter might typically cost £31,534.

A6.2.2   The Other 18-Bit Members of the Elliott 900 Family

The more popular, and compatible, 18-bit 900-series computers are listed in Table A6.1, for which the information comes mainly from the Elliott FACTS booklets for each machine.

The instruction times in Table A6.1 are for unmodified addresses. Modified instructions are naturally slower. For example, the unmodified/modified times for the 920M are: add = 10.6/13.8 μs; multiply = 29.6/32.8 μs. The process of modification is not allowed to change the F bits in a 900-series instruction (unlike the effect of modification in the case of the earlier Elliott 400 and 800 series computers).

The memory cycle times in Table A6.1 are nominal. Minor alterations occurred over the life of each type of machine. For example, in October 1969 an engineer's data sheet specified the following options for a 905:

MC5/13:	16K words at 1.8 μs
MC5/12:	16K words at 1.2 μs
MC/15:	8K words at 1.0 μs

Elliott sales and marketing terminology provides another source of potential confusion for the computer historian. For example, an Elliott MCM2 computer was a 920M with 8K of 5-μs memory.

Other family members compatible with the machines shown in Table A6.1 are now briefly described. The 18-bit ARCH 9000 process-control variant has a similar performance to the 903 and 920B. The 18-bit ARCH 9050 has a similar performance to the 920C and 905. The software-compatible 920ATC and the MC1800 were both 18-bit computers developed during the 1970s specifically for airborne applications. The 920 ATC (Advanced Technology Computer) was developed for aerospace applications at Rochester and was the first 920-derivative to have floating-point hardware. The 920 ATC performed its flight trials in 1976/1977 and went into production in mid-1977. In Chap. 12, Peter Hearne says that 'the 920 ATC and the 12/12 Series provided the basis of all of our future airborne computer developments' – [well, at least until the mid-1980s]. The 12/12 Series computers are described later, since they are part of the 12-bit word branch of the 900 family.

The MC1800 was produced in the mid-1970s by Marconi Space and Defence Systems which, like Elliott Brothers (London) Ltd., became part of the GEC empire in 1968. Quoting from [11], the MC1800 is described as a new product: 'born out of experience gained from the internationally proven 900 series … the MC1800 has been microprogrammed to emulate the 920C to provide compatibility with computers already in service with the Royal Artillery and Field Artillery Computing Equipment (FACE) and the Royal Air Force Jaguar and Nimrod aircraft…. The CPU design is based upon the AMD 2901 bipolar, bit-sliced microprocessor…. The standard CPU accommodates up to 2K of 48-bit words of EPROM of which the 920C emulator occupies approximately 0.5K words.' Several main memory options are available. The CPU interfaces directly to 16K and 32K modules. A 64K module is also available. The MC1800's word length is 18 bits and addressing is up to 128K (using the H register). The add time is 2.1 μs and the multiply time is 9.9 μs. These 1979 speed figures are marginally slower than those quoted in the earlier 1977 edition of the brochure [11], indicating that the MC1800 probably did not go into production until perhaps 1978.

The 18-bit instruction format for all the computers featured in Table A6.1 was as follows:

1	4	13
B	**F**	**N**
Modify	Op code	address

The interpretation of F, the four Op code bits, is listed later, after the central registers have been described. The accumulator, A, the accumulator extension, Q, and the modifier B are all nominally 18-bit registers. S (or SCR, the Program Counter) is 17 bits. H is a one-bit *address mode* register. Physically, it is the 18th bit of S. S and B were actually held in main memory for the Elliott 920B and 903. S, the Program Counter, is incremented just before an instruction is obeyed. Operand addressing may be absolute or may be relative to the address of the current instruction. On a basic machine with 8K words of memory, operand addressing is absolute. On a 920B or 903 with more memory, addressing is relative to the start of the 8K words holding the current instruction. Thus, an operand-address M is made either from $(S + 1 + N)$ or $(S + 1 + N + B)$. Further addressing facilities are made available when programming in the SIR assembly language – see Sect. A6.5.

In the instructions listed below, we denote the contents of address M by m, the contents of A by a and the contents of Q by q. Primes are used to indicate the new contents at the conclusion of an instruction. For $0 \leq F < 14$, N is used as an address. For $F = 14$ or $F = 15$, N is used as a literal (constant). A literal is formed from either N or $(N + B)$. In the following brief description we ignore some of the minor side-effects, for which reference should be made to the original Elliott FACTS booklets and to [7].

A6.2.2.1 Standard Instruction Set for All 18-Bit Elliott 900 Series Computers

F	Principal action(s)	Other effects	Description
0	b' = m	q' = m	Set B register
1	a' = a + m		Add
2	a' = m – a	q' = m	Reverse subtract, i.e. 'negate and add'
3	m' = q	Store Q register	
4	a' = m	Load acc	
5	m' = a	Store acc	
6	a' = a & m		Logical AND
7	if a = 0 then s' = M	Absolute jump if acc zero	
8	s' = M	Unconditional absolute jump	
9	if a < 0 then s' = M	Absolute jump if acc negative	
10	m' = m + 1		Increment memory location
11	m' = s + 1	q' = s + 1	Store link (S incr. at start of instr. anyway)
12	aq' = a × m		Multiply
13	a' = aq/m		Divide – (see also below)

(continued)

(continued)

F	Principal action(s)	Other effects	Description
14	(i) Double-length shift left or right		Depends upon value of N – see below
	(ii) Block transfer		Depends upon value of N – see below
15	(i) Input/output		Depends upon value of N – see below
	(ii) Program termination (i.e. revert to lower priority level).		Depends upon value of N – see below

Note that the *divide* instruction always gives an odd (i.e. not even) answer, never gives a remainder, and is not symmetric about zero

For shifts: if bit 14 of N = 0, then shift left by an amount given by bits 1 -> 6; if bit 14 of N = 1, then shift right. The *shift* instructions still worked with apparently nonsensical amounts, a feature that enabled *shift* orders to be used to achieve the effect of finely tunable delays. Programmers found this very useful when, for example, having to wait for analogue-to-digital converters to settle in between selecting an input and reading in a digitized value. More frivolously, easily tunable delays were of great use in playing music on the computer's console hooter! An Elliott 920A could shift by 4095 places and a 920B by 2047 places.

The Elliott 905 and the 920C are upwards-only compatible in the sense that these two computers allow a greater size of memory to be addressed. They have an Address Mode Indicator register, H. For the Elliott 905 and 920C, extra functions are obtained by two means:

a. By using more N-bit literal combinations for F = 15;
b. By having the actions of certain values of the F bits made dependent upon the state of the address mode indicator H. If H = 0, or if F = {7, 8, 9} then the operand address is within the current block; if H = 1 and if F is not {7, 8, 9} then the operand address is within the first block of store. (Note that {7, 8, 9} are control transfer instructions).

The 18-bit Elliott 900 series of computers had four priority levels: level 1 (highest) -> level 4 (lowest). For the 920C and 905 machines onwards, the currently active S and H are held in fast registers, being automatically stored and replaced by previous stored values when interruption or termination occurs. For all the 900 series computers, B is always held in memory. A and Q must be stored/restored by the programmer. The standard memory locations for the S and B registers are as follows:

Memory address	Contents
0	S1
1	B1
2	S2
3	B2
4	S3
5	B3
6	S4
7	B4

The A and the Q register for each level are stored at addresses chosen by the programmer.

A6.3   The 12-Bit Word Members of the 900 Series Family

These computers, sometimes referred to as the *cut-down* members of the 900 series, necessarily performed arithmetic to 12-bit, rather than 18-bit, precision. They also had a more limited addressing capability, a more cumbersome method for achieving address modification and a reduced number of priority levels. The main 12-bit family members are shown in Table A6.2.

The Elliott 102C was at the heart of the Minim Navigation Management System produced by Elliott Flight Automation Ltd., Airborne Computing Division, in approximately 1968 – see [12, 13]. Hence, the name *Minim* is sometimes used to denote the 102C computer. See also Sect. A6.5 for more comments on the use of these computers for airborne applications.

The 102C was designed from the start for airborne use, to environmental standard DEF 133 class A, which includes an impressive operating temperature range of −40°C to + 85°C. The 102C's case conforms to ATR (Air Transport Racking) ARINC standard for ½ long ATR.

The 12/12 airborne computers started off by being generally compatible with the 12-bit Elliott 900 family, though [6] states that: 'the flexibility can be taken further by extending the data word length to 24 bits'. In Chap. 12, Peter Hearne remarks that 'the 12 series computer was designed to have a 12-bit instruction word and also, as far as possible, the same instruction set throughout all the different variants of the machine. However, different length data words (9, 12, 16, 18, or 24 bits) were provided to suit the particular applications....Whilst the various divisions of Marconi Elliott Avionics were allowed to design and implement their own hardware and system versions of the 12 series machine for use in their various flight control, air data, display and similar applications, the design was closely guarded at the Rochester factory.' The earlier versions of the 12/12 [6] had a 2 µs cycle time, 4K memory. Depending on what interface and power supply options were chosen, the 12/12 was usually packaged in either a ½ ATR Long or a ½ ATR Short chassis.

The Elliott 12/12 came in at an exciting time in airborne computing when the traditionally analogue field of *flight control* (aerodynamic stability, engine control, etc.) was beginning to be influenced by the digital successes in the field of *mission systems* (navigation, weapons-aiming, etc.). By 1972, airborne analogue computing had acquired 'a large background of hard won experience ... bringing digital flight control to the same level of confidence will be no easy task' [14]. In looking ahead at the new, formerly analogue-dominated, tasks to which digital computers such as the 12/12 might be applied, [14] points out the different data word-lengths that would be appropriate. The 12/12P was probably the first production version to be introduced, in 1973. It had a 4K, 2 µs, core memory and instruction times very similar to those quoted for the Elliott 102C/Minim in Table A6.2 (i.e. ADD = 4.4 µs; MULTIPLY = 11.6 µs) – see [15].

Fig. A6.3 An airborne *Programmer Electronic Control* unit of the 1980s, based on a 12/12 computer and hence on the 12-bit version of the Elliott 900 series computers. Units similar to this one may have formed part of the ECM (electronic counter measures) pod for the Tornado strike aircraft

It is not surprising that the 12/12 went through many adaptations. For example, it was most probably the basis for a *Programmer Electronic Control* unit (see Fig. A6.3) at the heart of the Sky Shadow ECM (electronic counter measures) pod for the Tornado GR.1 strike aircraft [16]. Marconi Defence Systems received an initial development contract for Sky Shadow in 1972, produced a demonstration version in 1976 and started delivery to the RAF in 1980. Approximately, 300 Sky Shadow pods had been produced by the time the project was discontinued in 1996.

The 12-bit instruction format for all the computers featured in Table A6.2 is as follows:

4	1	7
F	**M**	**N**
Op code	Mode	Operand addr.

The Mode bit is generally (but not always) used to indicate whether short or long addresses are to be used for operands. When $M = 0$, the address is simply the 7-bit N field of the instruction. When $M = 1$, a 13-bit or 15-bit address is formed from N extended by the pointer register D. In addition to this effect, the N bits or the $(N + D)$ bits can be modified by adding the contents of the B register. To do this, an instruction has to be preceded by a *modify-the-next-instruction* command, (0/0/0). See below for the complete list of op codes. In most cases of modification, the contents of B (as loaded by the preceding instruction) are added to the address. In the case of function 11, the contents of B are used to define a separate store address. Note that since all modified instructions alter the E register contents, modification is not practical with functions 3 and instruction 14/0/32, and should be used with care on functions 13 and 14.

The registers for the 12-bit members of the Elliott 900 family are as follows:

S register (program counter): 13 bits, extensible to 15 for a 32K store;
A register (accumulator): 12 bits;
E register (accumulator extension): 11 bits;
B register (modifier): 12 bits;
D register (pointer): 6 bits, extensible to 8 bits.

D is used with the seven N bits to make a total of 13 (extendable to 15) address bits and in the original documentation V is used to signify [N extended by D]. In the abbreviated notation (N + D), as used in the lists below, remember that D is used to fill the *upper* bits in address calculations.

In the following list, the contents of memory location N is denoted by n. The contents of register N is denoted by N. Where the N-column has been left blank, there are no particular constraints on the value specified by N. The new contents of a register or memory location after an instruction has completed are indicated by a prime. The following list illustrates the action of unmodified instructions, that is when *not* preceded by an order having F = 0. The source of the list is principally the Elliott FACTS brochure for the 902 computer, issue 1, dated October 1968. Extra entries in italics come from the 102C computer's description given in [13].

F	M	N		
0	0	–	b' = n	Modify next instruction
0	1	–	b' = n	Modify next instruction
1	0	–	a' = a + n	Add (7-bit short addr N)
1	1	–	a' = a + n	Add (13-bit or 15-bit long addr (N + D))
2	0	–	a' = n – a	Reverse subtract (7-bit short addr N)
2	1	–	a' = n – a	Reverse subtract (13/15-bit long addr (N + D))
3	0	–	n' = e	Store acc extension E (7-bit short addr N)
3	1	–	n' = e	Store acc extension E (13/15-bit long addr (N + D))
4	0	–	a' = n	Load acc (7-bit short addr N)
4	1	–	a' = n	Load acc (13/15-bit long addr (N + D))
5	0	–	n' = a	Store acc (7-bit short addr N)
5	1	–	n' = a	Store acc (13/15-bit long addr (N + D))
6	0	–	a' = a & n	AND (7-bit short addr N)
6	1	–	a' = a & n	AND (13/15-bit long addr (N + D))
7	0	–	if a = 0, s' = s + N	Rel. jump forwards if acc = 0
7	1	–	if a = 0, s' = s – N	Rel. jump backwards if acc = 0
8	0	–	s' = s + N	Uncond. rel. jump forwards
8	1	–	s' = s – N	Uncond. rel. jump backwards
9	0	–	if a < 0, s' = s + N	Rel. jump forwards if acc < 0

(continued)

(continued)

F	M	N		
9	1	–	if a < 0, s' = s – N	Rel. jump backwards if acc < 0
10	0	–	a' = n + 1; n' = n + 1	Load-and-count (7-bit short addr N)
10	1	–	a' = n + 1; n' = n + 1	Load-and-count (13/15-bit long addr (N + D))
11	0	–	s' = (n, n + 1)	Uncond. indirect jump (via 7-bit short addr N)
11	1	–	s' = (n, n + 1)	Uncond. indirect jump (via13/15-bit long addr)
12	0	–	ae' = a * n	Multiply (double length) (7-bit short addr N)
12	1	–	ae' = a * n	Multiply (double length) (13/15-bit long addr)
13	0	–	a' = ae/n	Divide (7-bit short addr N)
13	1	–	a' = ae/n	Divide (13/15-bit long addr (N + D))
14	0	32	a' = e	Copy acc-extension to acc
14	1	32	e' = a	Copy acc to acc-extension
14	0	64	a' = d	Copy pointer to acc
14	1	64	d' = a	Load pointer
14	*0*	*65*	*a' = s + 1; s' = s+2*	*Load program counter to acc and skip*
14	*1*	*65*	*d' = s + 1; s' = s+2*	*Load program counter to D and skip*
14	*0*	*0 -> 31*	*shift acc left*	Shift acc left by n places
14	*1*	*0 -> 31*	*read*	*a' = word from interface unit, action: N1 –N5*
14	0	96 -> 127	shift acc right	Shift acc right arith by (128 – n) places
14	*1*	*96 -> 127*	*interface control*	*Interface action according to N1 -> N5*
15	0	0		Input char from paper tape reader
15	0	127		Load acc from handkeys
15	0	1 -> 126		Input a word from device n
15	1	0		Punch a char via the paper tape punch
15	1	1 -> 126		Output a word to device n
15	1	127		Interrupt terminate, return to base program

Note that, for instruction 10/0 and 10/1, the hardware action is to read the operand from memory, pass it through the ALU and increment it on its way into the accumulator, and finally to write the new contents of the accumulator back into memory. This action is often referred to generically by engineers as: *read-modify-write*. From the programmer's viewpoint, this indivisible primitive has important implications for synchronising processes. It is believed [17] that the 10/0 and 10/1 instructions were originally of the *Exchange Acc with Memory* variety but that Steve Chubb, the Chief Programmer in the Airborne Computing Division in about 1968, pressed for the instructions to be changed to the *Load and Count* form. Note also that some additional background to instructions 14/0 and 14/1 is given in Sect. A6.5 below.

Subroutine entry is achieved by the following pair of instructions:

0/m	)	Link stored in n, n + 1
11/n	)	Subroutine address held in m', m' + 1

Subroutine exit, and long jumps in general, are achieved by:

11/n	Destination address held in n, n + 1

Interrupt actions for the extended 902 systems are as follows. Upon receipt of an interrupt signal, registers S and D are dumped into main store locations 0 and 1, and re-loaded from two more locations whose addresses are given by (128 + p) and (129 + p), where p = 2, 4, 6, ... 30 – as defined by the signals from peripheral p, one of 15 possible interrupting devices. The interrupt routine ends with an *interrupt terminate* instruction (15/1/127) which restores S and D from memory locations 0 and 1.

As with many members of the Elliott 900 family, an Autonomous Transfer Unit can be added. This allows cycle-stealing peripherals to operate with the 900 series interface.

A6.4   Character Codes for 900 Series 8-Track Paper Tape

The initial Elliott 920 convention, known as 920 Telecode, differed only in minor respects from the 8-track encoding previously adopted by Borehamwood for the Elliott 503 computers, for which see Appendix 4. Sometime later Elliott introduced the 903 Telecode, which was also used by the Elliott 4100 series computers and which is quite similar to what was to become the international standard ASCII code with even parity. In turn, by about 1970, *903 Telecode* was simply being referred to as *900 Telecode*.

In practical terms, any 900-series machine could, by 1970, read tapes in either the 920 Telecode or 903 Telecode. As for standard Elliott software, the tape copy-ing and editing utilities, the Algol system, the SIR assembler and the decimal input/ output routines were all available in two versions, for either Telecode. However, Fortran and Coral were only ever available in 903 Telecode [17]. See [18] for more details of the 900 series character codes.

In Table A6.3 we give some sample characters for 920 Telecode and for 903 Telecode (which was also used for the Elliott 4100 series computers).

A6.5   Programming the Elliott 900 Series Computers

The emphasis of the Elliott 900 series was on robust, physically-small, computers suitable for military applications. Compared with the more-or-less contemporary Elliott 4100 series, the 900 machines were not particularly easy to program. Here are a few observations made by Terry Froggatt, who worked for Elliotts as a 900 Series programmer from 1966 to 1976.

Terry has said [19]: 'The later Minim and the 12-series computers (both 12-bit 900 Series derivatives) were hard to program because, with their short word

Table A6.3 Some illustrative sample characters for Elliott 920 Telecode and 903 Telecode, from the set of up to 128 possibilities

Printable character	Binary pattern on paper tape, for 920 Telecode	Binary pattern on paper tape, for 903 and 4100 Telecode
0	00110.000	00110.000
1	00100.001	10110.001
2	00100.010	10110.010
3	00110.011	00110.011
4	00100.100	10110.100
5	00110.101	00110.101
A	01000.001	01000.001
B	01000.010	01000.010
C	01010.011	11000.011
D	01000.100	01000.100
E	01010.101	11000.101
a	11010.001	11100.001
b	11010.010	11100.010
c	11000.011	01100.011
d	11010.100	11100.100
e	11000.101	01100.101
+	00101.101	00101.011
newline	00010.010	00001.010
space	10010.000	10100.000
erase	11111.111	11111.111
blank	00000.000	00000.000

lengths, only a small part of the memory was directly addressable; this also made it difficult to accumulate any reusable software. In contrast, a 920B with its 18-bit word length and 8192-word memory was easier to program, the whole memory being directly and uniformly addressable. The 900 series fixed-point hardware is optimised for pure fractional working rather than integer working. Division always gives an "odd" answer, never gives a remainder, and is not symmetric about zero. There are no condition codes to indicate *overflow* or *carry*, making it difficult to compare two numbers safely. There is no single *call subroutine* instruction and most 900s had no stack. There are assorted side-effects to watch out for. Usually, there was no way of finding out if there is more tape in the paper-tape reader, or if another character has been typed on the Teletype, without "hanging" the program if there isn't. Also, there is no way for a program to find out how much store is on the machine without "hanging" when it reads past the end.'

There were no *immediate* instructions (i.e. those whose operand was a literal, or constant) – the address bits held the operand address, not the operand value. However, the 900 series Symbolic Assembler, SIR, gave some assistance to programmers in this respect, as shown by the following examples of two SIR multiply commands for the 12-bit members of the family:

12 10	*multiply the accumulator by the contents of location 10*
12 +10	*multiply the accumulator by the constant +10*

For the latter, SIR placed the decimal constant +10 at the end of the program code (possibly to be shared with other uses of the same constant) and placed the address of the constant into the address bits of the object code to be executed at run-time. A similar SIR scheme operated for negative constants.

The following instructions for the 12-bit members of the 900 series family were also designed to facilitate easy loading of values to registers:

14	0	65	$a' = s + 1; s' = s + 2$	Load program counter to acc and skip
14	1	65	$d' = s + 1; s' = s + 2$	Load program counter to D and skip

Before these two instructions were introduced, D could only be loaded by reading a constant, usually from page 0 (i.e. locations 0–127), into the accumulator A and then executing an *Acc-to-D instruction* (14 1:64). Terry Froggatt remembers [20] that Dina St. Johnston, the wife of Andrew and the founder of Vaughan Programming Systems (VPS), came to visit the Airborne Computing Division in about 1968, during the early days of the Elliott 902 computer. VPS had become involved in writing the Fortran compiler for the 902 and had previously written the Fortran compiler for the 920B [21]. Dina 'declared the 902 to be unprogrammable' unless the 14/0:65 and 14/1:65 instructions were added to the machine.

References

1. Anon, 900 series small low-cost computers. 10-page brochure published by Elliott-Automation Ltd., Mobile Computing Division, Borehamwood. Undated but probably 1967 or 1968
2. JP Bunt (1965) A new control computer. Control Feb:63–65
3. JP Bunt (2002) Letter to Simon Lavington dated 1 Feb 2002
4. Alan Wakefield (2009) E-mail to Simon Lavington dated 9 Feb 2009
5. Anon (1967) Digital Computer MCM2: specification. 47-page technical manual published by the Elliott-Automation Mobile Computing Division in Sept 1967
6. Anon (1973) 12/12 Airborne computers. 4-page brochure published by Marconi-Elliott Avionic Systems Ltd., Rochester. Reference number 27732/PL2142/F02
7. In 2004 Terry Froggatt placed technical details of Elliott 900 series computers, including sample programs, on the Computer Conservation Society's Our Computer Heritage website. www.ourcomputerheritage.org/wp/
8. Anon, The Elliott MCS920 computer. 18-page brochure reference MCD/B/2/63 published by Elliott-Automation, Mobile Computing Division. Undated but probably 1963
9. Lawrence PJ (1965) Programming compatibility of 920 series computers. 8-page typed note, reference 322/PJL/JGG, Elliott-Automation Mobile Computing Division, 12 Nov 1965
10. Anon (1964) UK price list, MCS920 general purpose mobile digital computer. 8-page brochure published by Elliott-Automation, Mobile Computing Division. Dated 1 July 1964
11. Anon (1977, 1979) The MC1800 Miniature Processor. Four-page brochure published by Marconi Space and Defence Systems Ltd., Stanmore. First edition, reference LIT2-3SI-1-1, dated 1977. Second edition, reference LIT2-3SI-2-1, dated 1979
12. Anon (1968) Minim navigation management system. 12-page brochure published by Elliott Flight Automation Ltd., Borehamwood, Airborne Computing Division, 'an English Electric Company'. Undated but, with the English Electric annotation, likely to have been 1968

13. Anon (1968) 102C Functional specification. Report number 363/266/A08, issue 2, dated Aug 1968, 12-pages. Published by Elliott Flight Automation Ltd., Borehamwood, Airborne Computing Division, 'an English Electric Company'

14. Ruggles R, Scott EM (1972) Developments in aircraft digital systems. Paper presented to the AGARD Avionics Panel 24th technical meeting on Automation in Manned Aerospace Systems, Dayton, OH, Oct 1972 (Ruggles and Scott were employees of Marconi-Elliott Avionics Systems Ltd., Rochester)

15. Anon (1973) 12/12 Airborne computers. Four-page technical brochure, dated 1973 and produced by Marconi-Elliott Avionic Systems Ltd., Rochester

16. The Sky Shadow project is described at: www.forecastinternational.com/. One of the 12/12 Programmer Electronic Control units was salvaged in 2007 from a sale of government-surplus equipment and restored by Erik Baigar, to whom the author is indebted for information about this project

17. TJ Froggatt (2008) E-mails to Simon Lavington, 9 and 28 Oct 2008

18. Anon, 903/905/920 Useful notes. A bound collection of useful internal reports relating to character codes, including documents dated 1 Dec 1969 and 1 Apr 1970. Airborne Computing Division Library, Elliott Flight Automation, book number 106. http://www.tjfroggatt.plus.com/USEFULNO.PDF

19. TJ Froggatt (2008) Contribution to a computer conservation society seminar on Elliott software, London, 15 May 2008. Written up for Simon Lavington and sent with an explanatory e-mail on 9 Oct 2008

20. TJ Froggatt (2008) E-mail to Simon Lavington on 14 June 2008

21. Lavington SH (May 2009) An appreciation of Dina St Johnston, 1930–2007, founder of the UK's first Software House. Comput J 52(3):378–387

Appendix 7
Technical Details of the Elliott 4100 Series Computers

A7.1 General Overview of the Family

The specification and hardware design for the Elliott 4100 series had largely been completed by the start of 1964 [1]. Alan Wakefield, an Elliott Sales engineer, recalls [2] that 'we, the Sales force, were introduced to the 4100 series, internally, at a three-day sales training course on December 14th, 15th and 16th 1964. Customer visits, demonstrations, seminars and sales campaigns started in earnest early in 1965.' The Elliott 4100's instruction set represented a new direction for Borehamwood, in that it strongly reflected the influence of programmers such as Roger Cook (see also Chap. 8). Roger Cook remembers [3] that: 'we designed the 4120 with NCR in mind and the 4130 for our more technical users. We were also dimly aware that compilers would become the norm.' Evidence of the hardware support for high-level languages is given in Sects. A7.2 and A7.3.

There were two members of the 4100 series family, of which the 4120 was the first to be delivered to an outside customer in 1965. By 31 March 1967, 58 of the 4120 systems (including the ARCH 2020 variant) had been delivered and a further 86 machines were on order [4]. The more powerful Elliott 4130 computer was the next to arrive. By 31 March 1967, 21 of the 4130 systems (including the ARCH 2030 variant) had been ordered but none had yet been delivered to an external customer.

When Elliott-Automation's main computing interests were absorbed into ICL at the end of 1968, the 4100 series were the only Elliott computers to be marketed by ICL, albeit as a poor relation to the more comprehensive and powerful English Electric System 4 and ICT 1900 series machines and to the last of the LEO III computers (LEO III deliveries spanned the period 1962–1969). Many of the surviving 4100 series software technical manuals are held in the ICL Archive [5]. As mentioned in Chap. 13, ICL did at least acknowledge in 1968 that the Elliott 4100 series had been 'most successful in universities, research establishments and for industrial automation schemes. The graphical display system associated with 4100 central processors is a recognized leader in computer design technology' [6].

The Elliott type 4280 Graphical Display Unit had a 10 in. × 10 in. viewing area with 1,024 × 1,024 addressable positions, giving a resolution to within 0.01 of an inch. The image was automatically re-generated ten times per second from a display file held in the computer's main memory, to give a flicker-free picture. Curves or lines could be drawn at the rate of 100 μs per displayed inch. The type 4280 unit included a vector generator for drawing straight lines, a character generator which displayed the alphanumeric characters of the 4100 series internal codes in three sizes (5/64th in., 5/32nd in. or 5/16th in.) and a hand-held *light pen* which enabled the user to identify points on the display. (The light pen achieved the same effect as a modern mouse and cursor.)

Despite its apparent enthusiasm for Elliott's graphical display system, ICL showed little interest in maintaining the existing 4100 machines or their peripherals. Largely because of this, three ex-Elliott-Automation engineers founded Systems Reliability Ltd. (SRL) at Luton in 1968, as described in Chap. 14.

According to [7] manufacture of the 4100 series ceased in 1970. It is not known when the last 4100 was retired from active service but it is likely to have been at the beginning of the 1980s.

The 4100 series machines were based on bit-parallel CPUs employing silicon transistors. For each of the 4120 and 4130 computers, there was originally a choice of ferrite core store: either 2- or 6-μs cycle time. The 4130 had a faster CPU and implemented floating-point operations in hardware. Floating-point was performed by software extracodes in the 4120. The Autonomous Transfer Unit (ATU) was an add-on extra for the 4120 but was built into the main cabinet of a 4130. The comparative figures given in Table A7.1 are taken from [8], which is dated October 1967.

The physical dimensions of a basic Elliott 4130 processor were: height 63.5 in. (161 cm), width 70 in. (178 cm), depth 26 in. (68.5 cm), weight 1,040 lb (450 kg) and power consumption 2 kVA.

Table A7.1 Overall characteristics of Elliott 4100 series computers

	4120	4130
Word length, bits	24	24
Number of instructions per word	1 or 2	1 or 2
Max. installed memory at 2 μs cycle time	64K words	256K words
Fxpt ADD time, direct addressing mode, with 6 μs store	12.0 μs	12.0 μs
Fxpt ADD time, direct addressing mode, with 2 μs store	5.6 μs	4.5 μs
Fxpt MPY time, direct addressing mode, with 6 μs store	67.0 μs	22.0 μs
Fxpt MPY time, direct addressing mode, with 2 μs store	60.6 μs	15.0 μs
Floating-point hardware?	No	Yes
Flpt ADD time, direct addressing mode, with 2 μs store	199 μs	15 μs

A7.2 Systems Architecture and Visible Registers

The Elliott 4100 series' 24-bit word employed two's complement representation for integers, as did all Elliott computers. Single-address format instructions were either short (12 bits) or long (24 bits). A long instruction may be split across two consecutive memory locations, in which case the instruction takes a little longer to execute. The program counter, S, refers to the half-word address of the next instruction. The effect of obeying an instruction in the second half of a word which has just been altered by the instruction in the first half of the same word is not defined. For many applications, four 6-bit characters were stored per word.

Roger Cook has commented retrospectively [3] that: 'I (wrongly?) decided that a 6 bit (rather than 8 bit) character would be cost effective – having been told that memory was "quite expensive"'. When held in memory, floating-point numbers were normally rounded and packed into two words containing 39 bits of mantissa and 9 bits of exponent (see also Sect. A7.3).

As is described later, the Elliott 4100 series had a much more powerful repertoire of addressing modes than previous Borehamwood computers. The series also implemented a neat and comprehensive mechanism for handling the various condition-bits (e.g. accumulator sign, overflow, interrupt, etc.) that contribute to the current status of a computer. Roger Cook has observed [3] that: 'As much as possible of the internal operation was to be available to the programmer (eg interrupts, busy etc) and was to be mathematically consistent'. The concept of a stack, as used for example in block-structured languages, is given hardware support – see the MVE and MVB instructions given in Sect. A7.3. There was hardware assistance for packing and unpacking characters. A distinction was made between the three forms of shift, namely *logical, arithmetic* or *circular*. There was a flexible set of instructions for register-to-register moves. Finally, the Elliott 4100 series had a Standard Interface for all input/output devices, the physical manifestation of which was a standard plug and socket arrangement for all peripherals.

Short instructions for the Elliott 4100 series have six function-bits (i.e. the op code) and six address bits, thus only giving access to the first 64 memory locations for operands.

Short format instructions:

6	6
F	N
Op code	Address

For short instructions, the octal value of the F-bits lies in the range 00–37. Almost all of the 32 short instructions are duplicated by long instructions that offer richer addressing modes. Thus, short instruction op codes 00–27 generally have the same arithmetical or logical definitions as long instructions that have op codes in the range 40–67 (see lists in Sect. A7.3).

The layout of long, 24-bit, instructions is as follows:

Long format instructions:

6	2	1	15
F	**Y**	**Z**	**N**
Op code	Addressing mode	Extracode indicator	Literal or address

For long instructions, the octal value of the F-bits lies in the range 40–77. The values of the Y-bits denote the addressing mode, as follows:

0	Literal (N is treated as a positive integer – i.e. not signed)
1	Direct (N is an absolute address)
2	Modified (the contents of R is added to N to give the final address)
3	Indirect (the contents of memory location N gives the address of the operand)

When using modified or indirect addressing, bits 16–22 of the final address must be zero. This gives the effect of being able to address a maximum of 256K words, in blocks of 64K words.

The Elliott 4100 has the following programmer-accessible registers. When describing digit positions, the 4100 convention is that bit 24 is the left hand (most significant) position and bit 1 is the least-significant position.

	Size, bits	Description
M	24	Main accumulator
R	24	Reserve accumulator, also used as the address-modification register, etc.
S	17	Program-counter, also known as the sequence-control register
K	12	Count register
C	14	Conditions register. Bits 16–7 are unallocated. The remaining C bits are assigned as follows (according to an amalgamation of the information contained in [1, 8])
	$c24$	Result negative, denoted by *Neg* in the instruction listing given below
	$c23$	Result standardized, denoted by *St*
	$c22$	Result non-zero, denoted by *Nz*
	$c21$	Carry out from ms accumulator bit during addition or subtraction, denoted by *Ca*
	$c20$	Arithmetic overflow, denoted by *Of*
	$c19$	Normal interrupt permit
	$c18$	Attention interrupt permit
	$c17$	Invalid information transfer
	$c6 - c1$	These give the state of six manual switches on the operator's console

The C bits can be inspected *in toto* by transferring C into the accumulator, M, by the 700/520 instruction (see below). In some instances, a 24-bit link is formed by adding the current value of the program counter S to bits 24–18 of C, thereby preserving the essential control state of a program in a compact form prior to entering a subroutine.

A7.3 Elliott 4100 Series Instruction Set

In the instructions listed below, m is the contents of M, r is the contents of R, s is the contents of S, and k is the contents of K. Primes indicate the new values at the conclusion of an instruction, a notation chosen in this book to be compatible with the other instruction sets described in Appendices 2–6. It is significant that, in the original Elliott-Automation documentation for the 4100 series [1, 8], the Algol symbol for 'becomes equal to' (:=) was used instead of primes, yet another hint that the architecture of the 4100 series computers was oriented towards the needs of high-level language compiler writers. In the list below, square brackets indicate 'contents of address'; thus, [r] means 'the contents of location addressed by the R register'. There are four 6-bit characters per word; these are denoted by {a, b, c, d}, where a is stored at the most significant end of the word.

There are several choices of operand-addressing for each combination of the F bits (the op code), depending upon how the Y bits are to be interpreted. Rather than showing every option explicitly in the listing below, we show the action for short instructions and then the action for long instructions. For the latter, three possibilities are distinguished in the listing below:

a. The action is independent of the setting of the Y bits.
b. A specific action is defined for the combination Y = 0.
c. A specific action is defined for the cases of Y = 1, 2 or 3.

In the listing below, these three cases are distinguished by filling in the Y column by: (a) nothing, (b) y = 0; and (c) y = 1,3. Finally, the actions for the shift instructions, the register-to-register instructions, the input/output instructions and the extracode instructions also depend upon the values of the N digits. For clarity, these four sub-groups of instructions are listed separately, after the straightforward computational orders have been described. Since the Z field in an instruction is zero for all except extracodes, the Z field has been omitted from all but one of the sub-sections below. The values of the F-bits are given in octal below.

The behind-the-scenes hardware decoding of the F, Y, Z and N fields of a long instruction is complex. For this reason, the documentation issued to users (e.g. [8]) laid emphasis on assembly-language mnemonics, rather than on bit-patterns, when tabulating instructions. The mnemonics, reproduced below, are those used in the NEAT (National Elliott Assembly Technique) and the SAP (Symbolic Assembly Programming language) programming manuals. Roger Cook remembers [3] that: 'The symbolic names for the instruction codes were specified by NCR – (we [at Borehamwood] tended to program using the basic numerical codes).'

Group A: straightforward short and long instructions

F (short)	F (long)	Y	Principal action(s)	Description	Mnemonic
00	40		m' = m + Q	Add, using main accumulator	ADD
01	41		m' = m − Q	Subtract	SUB
02	42		m' = Q − m	Reverse-subtract	NADD

(continued)

(continued)

F (short)	F (long)	Y	Principal action(s)	Description	Mnemonic
03	43		m' = Q	Load accumulator	LD
04	44		r' = Q	Load reserve accumulator	LDR
05			s' = n; c'$_{24-18}$ = n$_{24-18}$	Exit	JIR
	45	y = 0	s' = N	Unconditional jump	J
	45	y = 1,3	s' = Q	Unconditional jump	JI
06	46		m' = m & Q	Logical AND	AND
07	47		m' = m & ⌐Q	Logical AND NOT	ANDN
10	50		r' = r + Q	Add, using reserve accumulator	ADDR
11	51		r' = r − Q	Subtract	SUBR
12	52		r' = Q − r	Reverse subtract	NADR
	53	y = 0	0' = $_{c24-18}$ + s; s' = s + N	Subroutine entry, addr zero for link	JFL
13	53	y = 1-3	0' = $_{c24-18}$ + s; s' = Q	Subroutine entry, addr zero for link	JIL
14	54		k' = Q	Load K, the count register	LDK
15			*Shift instructions – see explanation below*		
	55		compare (m − Q)	Set the conditions register accordingly	COMP
16	56	y = 0	s' = s + N	Unconditional relative jump forwards	JF
	56	y = 1,3	s' = s + Q	Unconditional relative jump forwards	JA
17	57	y = 0	s' = s − N	Unconditional relative jump backwards	JB
	57	y = 1,3	s' = s − Q	Unconditional relative jump backwards	JS
20	60	y = 0	if *Neg* then s' = s + Q	Relative jump forwards if negative	JN
21	61	y = 0	if not *Neg* then s' = s + Q	Relative jump forwards if not negative	JNN
22	62	y = 0	if not *Nz* then s' = s + Q	Relative jump forwards if zero	JZ
23	63	y = 0	if *Nz* then s' = s + Q	Relative jump forwards if non-zero	JNZ
24	64	y = 0	if *St* then s' = s + Q	Relative jump forwards if standardized	JST
25	65	y = 0	if *Of* then s' = s + Q	Relative jump forwards if overflow	JOF
26			(unassigned?)		
27	67	y = 0	k' = k − 1; if k$_{12}$ = 1 then s' = s + Q	Decrement, test and jump if	DKJN
30	60	y = 1,3	Q' = m	Store accumulator	ST
31	61	y = 1,3	Q' = r	Store reserve accumulator	STR
32	62	y = 1,3	Q' = − Q	Negate the contents of memory	NEGS
33	63	y = 1,3	Q' = Q − m	Subtract acc from store	SUBS

(continued)

(continued)

F (short)	F (long)	Y	Principal action(s)	Description	Mnemonic
34	64	y = 1,3	Q' = Q + m	Add acc to store	ADDS
35	65	y = 1,3	Q' = 0	Clear memory location	CLS
36	66	y = 1,3	Q' = Q + 1	Increment memory location	INCS
37	67	y = 1,3	Q' = Q – 1	Decrement memory location	DECS
	70	y = 0	*Register-to-register moves – see explanation below*		
	70	y = 1,3	Q' = Q(bcda); m' = m(abc)Q(a)	Fetch next character	GET
	71	y = 1,3	Q' = Q(bcd)m(d)	Store next character	PUT
	72	y = 1,3	m' = (r,m)/Q	Divide, double-length	DIVM
	73	y = 1,3	(r,m)' = (r,m) x Q	Multiply, double-length	MULM
	74	y = 1,3	m' = Q; [r]' = m; r' = r – 1	Pop up from a stack	MVE
	75	y = 1,3	Q' = m; m' = [r]; r' = r + 1	Push down onto a stack	MVB
	76	y = 1,3	swap Q and m	Exchange values of Q and m	EXC
	77	y = 1,3	swap Q and r	Exchange values of Q and r	EXCR

The input/output instructions, for which the F bits = octal 74–77 and for which the Y bits = 0, are described later.

Group B: shift instructions.

The shift instructions, which are short orders for which the F bits = octal 15, use the N bits to determine the mode of shifting (i.e. left or right, logical, arithmetic or circular) and the K bits to determine the number of places shifted. The list of permitted possibilities is as follows, in which the value of the six N digits is given in octal:

F	N	Action	Mnemonic
15	00	Shift r left arithmetically k places	SRL
15	01	Shift r left circularly k places	SRLA
15	02	Shift r right arithmetically k places	SRR
15	03	Shift r by k 6-bit characters circularly left	SRLC
15	04	Shift m left arithmetically k places	SML
15	05	Shift m left circularly k places	SMLA
15	06	Shift m right arithmetically k places	SMR
15	07	Shift m by k 6-bit characters circularly left	SMLC
15	12	Shift r right logically by k places	SRRL
15	16	Shift m right logically by k places	SMRL
15	20	Shift r until standardized, or k places, whichever is less	SRST
15	24	Shift m until standardized, or k places, whichever is less	SMST
15	40	Shift both m and r arithmetically left k places	SBL
15	42	Shift both m and r arithmetically right k places	SBR
15	52	Shift both m and r logically right k places	SBRL
15	62	Shift m and r until standardized, or k places, whichever is less	SBST

Group C: register-to-register instructions.

The register-to-register instructions, which are long orders for which the F bits = octal 70 and the Y bits = 0, use the N bits to define the registers involved. The list of assigned combinations, for which the value of the 15 N digits is given in octal, is as follows:

F	Y	N	Action	Mnemonic
70	0	00020	r' = k	KTOR
70	0	00402	r' = m	MTOR
70	0	00404	r' = s	STOR
70	0	00441	r' = r + 1 if carry set	CAIR
70	0	00541	r' = r − 1 if carry set	CADR
70	0	01001	m' = r	RTOM
70	0	01003	m' = m OR r	MORR
70	0	01010	m' = c	CTOM
70	0	02001	s' = r	RTOS
70	0	02002	s' = m	MTOS
70	0	04002	c' = m	MTOC
70	0	10001	k' = r	RTOK
70	0	10002	k' = m	MTOK
70	0	10201	k' = − r	RNTK
70	0	21000	m' = interrupt word (see below)	ITOM
70	0	41000	m' = attention word (see below)	ATOM

Group D: input/output instructions.

The input/output instructions, for which the F bits = octal 74–77 and for which the Y bits = 0, use the first three octal digits of N to supplement the F bits. The last two octal digits of N, denoted as *nn* below, define the peripheral channel number. The 4100 Standard Interface normally provides for up to 12 independent, asynchronous, input/output channels (with extra channels as an option, up to 14?). Each channel can call for either of two types of program break: an *Interrupt* or an *Attention*. Two 12-bit locations, the Interrupt word and the Attention word, are provided and each may be inspected by program using the ITOM and ATOM instructions above. Beneath this level, a hardware *Hesitation* (high-priority interrupt) is also provided for use with devices using hardware-assisted autonomous data transfers (ADT) and cycle-stealing.

An optional hardware Autonomous Transfer Unit organizes bulk data transfers via cycle-stealing in a manner independently from the main CPU. Thus, input/output activity could be interleaved with normal computing. Up to three *packed transfer units* and one *unpacked transfer unit* may be included in an Autonomous Transfer Unit.

The 4100 Standard Interface has 8 *data-in* lines, 8 *data-out* lines, 3 interrupt lines and 11 other control, status and timing signals. The input/output instructions for peripheral channel nn are as follows:

F	Y	N	Action	Mnemonic
74	0	000nn	Input data packed repetitive	IDPR
74	0	100nn	Output data packed repetitive	ODPR
74	0	200nn	Input data unpacked repetitive	IDUR
74	0	300nn	Output data unpacked repetitive	ODUR

(continued)

(continued)

F	Y	N	Action	Mnemonic
75	0	000nn	Input status word packed repetitive	ISPR
75	0	100nn	Output control word packed repetitive	OCPR
75	0	200nn	Input status word unpacked repetitive	ISUR
75	0	300nn	Output control word unpacked repetitive	OCUR
76	0	200nn	Input data unpacked single to m	IDUM
76	0	300nn	Output data unpacked single from m	ODUM
77	0	200nn	Input status word unpacked single to m	ISUM
77	0	300nn	Output control word unpacked single from m	OCUM

Group E: Extracodes.

When $Z = 1$ and the F-bits are in the octal range 40–77, an extracode instruction may be indicated, though only about 26 of the available F-bit combinations are allocated as actual extracodes. The action upon encountering an extracode instruction, as deduced from [1], varies according to whether the Y bit (i.e. the address-mode bits) are zero or in the range 1–3, as follows:

Action for literal address mode ($Y = 0$):

a. Place N in memory location 1
b. Place the link ($c_{24-18} + S$) in memory location 2;
c. Jump to a memory location given by twice the value of the F-bits, that is to one of the even-numbered locations in the range 64–126 inclusive. This is then the start of a standard subroutine for implementing the extracode.

Action for other addressing modes ($Y = 1, 2$ or 3):

a. If $Y = 1$ then place N in location 1, or
   If $Y = 2$ then place ($N + r$) in location 1, or
   if $Y = 3$ then place the contents of address N in location 1;
b. Place ($c_{24-18} + S$) in memory location 2;
c. Jump to a memory location given by twice the value of the F-bits plus 1, that is to one of the odd-numbered locations in the range 65–127 inclusive.

The extracodes are now listed, with F, Y, Z and N being given in octal except that, for the Y field, a 'y' indicates any number in the range 1, 2 or 3 and for the N field, an 'n' indicates any valid address. Note that the 14 floating-point extracodes are implemented in hardware on the Elliott 4130. On the 4130 where hardware is used, the mantissa occupies 48 bits within CPU registers and the exponent 12 bits. This *triple* can be accessed collectively via the WUF and FLU extracodes (see below). When held in memory, floating-point numbers are normally rounded and packed into two words containing 39 bits of mantissa and 9 bits of exponent. The following abbreviations are used in the list below:

fpa = floating-point accumulator;
fQ = the floating-point operand held in locations Q, Q + 1;
dQ = the double-length operand held in locations Q, Q + 1;
tQ = the triple-length operand held in locations Q, Q + 1 and Q + 2.

F	Y	Z	N	Action	Mnemonic
40	0	1	0	fpa' = − fpa	FN
40	0	1	2	fpa' = integer m in floating-point form	FCP
40	0	1	4	fpa' = modulus (fpa)	FMOD
40	0	1	6	m' = entier (fpa)	FENT
41	0	1	10	If fpa < 0, m' = − 1; if fpa = 0, m' = 0; if fpa > 0, m' = 1	FSIG
40	y	1	n	fpa' = fQ	FL
41	0	1	0	Copy to lower address	CTLA
41	0	1	1,000	Copy to higher address	CTHA
41	y	1	n	fQ' = fpa	WF
42	y	1	n	fpa' = fpa + fQ	FA
43	y	1	n	fpa' = fpa − fQ	FS
44	y	1	n	fpa' = fpa × fQ	FM
45	y	1	n	fpa' = fpa/fQ	FD
46	y	1	n	set c_{24-22} from (fpa − fQ)	FCP
50	y	1	n	m' = m × Q	MULS
51	y	1	n	m' = m/Q; r' = remainder	DIV
52	y	1	n	(r,m)' = Dq	BL
53	y	1	n	dQ' = (r,m)	WB
54	y	1	n	Jump indirect and restore link	JIRX
55	y	1	n	Jump indirect	JIX
56	y	1	n	Jump indirect, setting link	JILX
57	y	1	n	Access chapter item with index Q, placing its addr in R	INDEX
60	y	1	n	fpa' = tQ (unrounded representation)	FLU
61	y	1	n	(Unrounded representation)	WUF
77	0	1	n	nth letter of alphabet displayed (on console)	TR
77	y	1	n	Q displayed in octal (on console)	CH

The INDEX instruction in the above list assumes that a program's memory-space is organised into *chapters* – see also under SPAN in the next section – and that a particular chapter contains some form of structured data such as an array or table. If an INDEX instruction is issued with the address of a codeword (or descriptor) in R, then the address of the ith element of the data-structure to which the codeword points is placed in R.

A7.4 Operating Systems, Time-Sharing and Multiprogramming Facilities

According to [9], there was originally an intention to provide hardware assistance for multiprogramming. The 4130 was intended to offer two programming environments: *Executive Mode* and *Protected Mode*. Under the latter, which was to be the normal user mode when the multiprogramming system was in operation, a program was restricted to its allocated area of memory and was limited in its use of peripheral devices. An *Alarm Clock* was to be provided that set a limit on the time for which a particular user program could run within Protected Mode before being terminated. Within Protected Mode, core store was to be allocated to a user program via two 10-bit registers that gave the *Base* address and the *Range* of permitted memory. Any attempt to access a location outside the permitted area would cause the user's program to be suspended and Executive Mode entered.

To facilitate the above proposed multiprogramming environment, several additional Elliott 4130 instructions were suggested, including:

EXEN	Enter Executive Mode
PMEN	Load the Base and Range registers and the Alarm Clock setting and then enter Protected Mode

It is believed that the above multiprogramming facilities were seldom activated for the Elliott 4130 computer, except in the KOS operating system described later. An *Alarm Clock*, actually known as the *Real Time Clock*, was, however, provided as standard for the 4130 and as part of the Autonomous Transfer Unit for the 4120. This produced an interrupt once every second and could be set to 'ring' by transferring data after N seconds.

From [10] it is deduced that the default operating system for Elliott 4100 computers in the period from 1965 to 1968 was the Systems Executive known as EASE. This consisted of three sections: NICE (Normal Input and Control Executive), SPAN (Storage Planning and Allocation) and TSS (Time Sharing Supervisor). It is believed that the three sections of EASE constituted independent modules, as follows.

NICE was a simple Executive that enabled an operator to input relocatable binary paper tapes, enter a named program, remove a program, cause a printout of an area of memory, etc.

SPAN handled the housekeeping for information transfers between primary memory (core) and secondary memory (e.g. disc pack). It assumed that a program's storage space was divided into *chapters*, each containing one or more *blocks*, each block containing one or more entry points known as *labels*. A program may call upon one or more of SPAN's routines, which include the following utilities:

ALLOC	asks SPAN to reserve space (in primary memory) for a chapter. This may result in the response *No Room* if SPAN cannot find sufficient space
DELETE	frees up space no longer needed by a chapter
BANISH	move a chapter to secondary storage
RECALL	bring a chapter into primary storage

TSS was available to look after *Interrupts* and *Attentions* coming from each Standard Interface channel, transferring control to a routine appropriate for each peripheral device. The Elliott 4100 series defines three levels of program priority, the highest being called the Interrupt level, the intermediate one being called the Attention level and the lowest level being that of normal computation. There exist appropriate TSS routines running at each level. Transfers to/from a level within TSS occur either as a result of an Interrupt or Attention signal or as a result of subroutine entry/exit. TSS organises queues and buffers as appropriate, for input/output transfers.

An early in-house Elliott 4100 operating system used on the commissioning floor at Borehamwood was called SysD (System D). This offered 'a very simple system control vocabulary, was interactive on the Selectric typewriter, and made it easy to load and run paper tape based programs' [11].

By the 1970s, it is thought that several other operating systems had been implemented for Elliott 4100 series computers. DES (Disc Executive System) was a standalone operating system used by individual large users, for example when working overnight and at weekends. It allowed programs to access the whole of physical memory. DES2 had a 'slave' area of memory where a second program could be run in tandem with the first program. DES BATCH was the batch job operating system, used for example in computing service environments.

DES reflected the fact that the Elliott 4100 series was amongst the first Borehamwood products to offer disc packs as standard peripherals. Disc (or *disk*) memory – in fixed or exchangeable form – was one of the significant innovations of the mid-1960s. Disc storage as an intermediate, *direct-access,* medium between core primary memory and magnetic tape backing store had begun to make its presence felt in the late 1950s, following the trend set by IBM in 1956 with their IBM 305 RAMAC product – as mentioned in Chap. 10. However, a few years were to elapse before disc technology made a significant impact upon the design of standard operating systems. The disc equipment offered for the Elliott 4100 series computers in 1967 consisted of ten disc surfaces, each with 100 tracks split into 16 sectors of 64 words. The on-line capacity was therefore about one million words. The read-write heads took about 100 ms to traverse 33 tracks and, once the desired *cylinder* of tracks had been reached, the mean access-time was 12.5 ms and a sector could be transferred in 1.5 ms [8].

Elliott 4100 series computers were installed at several UK Universities, where they inspired systems software developments by the academic users (see also Sect. 8.5). The University of Kent at Canterbury was especially active, being responsible for the Kent On-line System KOS [12], a simple multi-access operating system which allowed both batch use and on-line terminals simultaneously. KOS, implemented on an Elliott 4130 in the period late 1968 to early 1970, supported a fully conversational incremental BASIC compiler via eight teletype terminals [13]. The development of the BASIC compiler was a joint venture between Kent and the University College of North Wales.

Another, unrelated, on-line multi-access system had come live in 1967 when the functional language POP-2 and Multi-POP was implemented on an Elliott 4120 at the Department of Machine Intelligence and Perception at Edinburgh University [14]. As further evidence of the interest amongst researchers in the Elliott 4130's features, the Institut de Programmation at Orsay (south of Paris) of the Institut Blaise Pacal ordered a 4130 in 1967 'pour le *time sharing et le conversationnel'*. To quote [15], 'We are about to receive an Elliott 4130, equipped for time-sharing use, and possessing a wired structure which will enable us to develop advanced studies on programming systems, memory hierarchy management, handling of virtual memories.'

Returning to KOS, it is worth quoting Peter Brown, the leader of the KOS development team at Kent, because of his appreciation of some of the Elliott 4130's more advanced features [12].

'The 4130 has two modes of operation, namely *executive mode* and *slave mode*. The latter, however, has been completely ignored until very recently and virtually all programs, whether written by the manufacturers or by users, have run in executive mode. The slave mode of operation uses the well-known base and range register technique. There is an important sub-mode of slave mode, called *pure procedure mode*. (The manufacturers call it *common program mode*.) This has influenced the design of KOS more than any other hardware feature. In pure procedure mode the program instruction counter is absolute and it is only data references that are subject to the addition of the base. Using this hardware, a single program can control any number of slaves. A slave is simply an area of workspace, and the slave that is active at any one time is determined by the setting of the base and range registers.

'There is a further hardware feature that allows for pure constants. Each pure procedure can have its own data area which contains all true constants, i.e. all data whose value is set at load time and not subsequently changed. When using pure procedures, it is best to place tables and error messages in this data area, so that there will only be a single copy of them rather than one copy in each slave area.

'The pure procedure mode of the hardware and its ease of use radically changes the economics of time sharing for the 4130. For multi-access work the 4130 is at its most efficient when there are one or more pure procedures, remaining permanently in store while they are in use, being shared by several jobs. For example, there might be two pure procedures in use, a compiler and an application package; three console users and a card-to-printer job might be using the compiler, and four other console users might be using the application package. All should enjoy excellent response time. Moreover, if the pure procedures are always resident in core there is no overhead in providing fully conversational working.'

KOS allowed both the Algol and the Fortran compilers to be resident in the batch stream [16]. Brian Spratt, at the time the Director of the Computing Service at the University of Kent, remembers [16] that KOS proved very successful and was adopted by several of the other UK universities that used Elliott 4130 computers in their Computing Services for running student's programs. 'The Computer Board [which administered UK academic computing resources] was quite pleased and we (ie Kent and nine other universities) all had 64K 2 microsecond store upgrades approved. But our (Ex Elliott) computer manager Des Caul managed to upgrade the system with the original 6 microsecond store to give us a total of 96K memory. The other 4130 sites quickly adopted this arrangement.' In all, Elliott 4100 series machines were delivered to about 18 UK universities and about five technical colleges – see the delivery lists in Appendix 8.

Peter Brown ends his description of KOS by comparing KOS with the Elliott/ICL software currently available in 1971 for the 4130 and states [12] that 'the manufacturers have recently introduced a new multi-programming operating system. Currently this is little used but it will, no doubt, gradually find wider usage'.

In contrast to the enthusiasm at Kent, Leicester University never used KOS on its large 4130 installation consisting of 65K words of 2-μs core store, an Autonomous Transfer Unit and eight magnetic tape decks. Leicester's original operating system was T30C, essentially a batch processor. John Thompson, who ran the Leicester Computing Centre, has commented thus [17]. 'Algol fitted the Elliott software environment perfectly, but the Fortran team were adamant that one could not have a Fortran system in that framework and designed their own from scratch. So T30C essentially had to dump one system and spool in another in order to change language. For speed, we allocated three tape drives to the system because we could afford to. The Fortran compiler was pretty awful (we were finding bugs for ages and Elliott were slow to fix them) and certainly one could not access the top half of the store. (Whether one could in Algol I cannot remember, but most of the big linear algebra calculations were in Fortran, as were imported programs such as IBMOL.) When we finally got hold of the Fortran compiler details - by which I mean a poorly annotated listing - I was able to jury rig the thing so that a particular named COMMON block, /ZZZZ/ actually, resided in the top half of the store.'

References

1. Anon (1964) Elliott 4150 digital computer: functional specification. 44-page typed internal report TIS/4150, published by Scientific Computing Division, Elliott Brothers Ltd., London, dated May 1964. There are hand-written alterations, amending the 4150 to 4120
2. A Wakefield (2009) E-mail to Simon Lavington, 10 Jan 2009
3. Roger Cook (2008) E-mail to Simon Lavington dated 11 Oct 2008
4. Elliott automation: computers and orders, 1947–1966. Booklet published in early 1967 by the Directorate of Information Services, Elliott-Automation Ltd., 21 Portland Place, London W1. Addendum sheet gives the totals at 31 March 1967
5. The ICL Archive, preserved by the National Museum of Science and Industry (London) at its repository at Wroughton, has been catalogued by Hamish Carmichael of the Computer Conservation Society. Elliott 4100 series technical manuals, mostly concerning software, are held as the following ICL Archive item numbers: 38/152 to 38/155, 38/163, 38/181 to 38/201, 38/215
6. Birkett D (1968) ICL Profile, a six-page Press Release issued by the ICT Company Information Officer, Dennis Birkett, dated 10 Aug 1968 (Available as document COM/1993/1433 at the National Museum of Science and Industry, South Kensington, London)
7. Campbell-Kelly M (1989) ICL – a business and technical history. Oxford University Press, Oxford. ISBN 0-19-853918-5
8. Anon (1967) 4100 computer system FACTS booklet, October 1967. Published by Elliott-Automation Computers Ltd. Catalogue number 440 – issue 4
9. (a) Anon, Appendix C: NCR – Elliott 4100 Data processing system: 4130 processor and (b) Anon, Appendix E: 4100 Autonomous Transfer Unit, Functional Specification, Section 2. These two typed appendices were evidently part of a larger internal document produced by Elliott-Automation. Undated but probably written between mid-1965 and October 1967. Documents preserved by D H (Dennis) Rowland, who worked for the Airspace Control Division of Elliot Brothers Ltd., London
10. Anon (1965) NCR Elliott 4100 Electronic Data Processing System FACTS, Apr 1965. Jointly published by (a) Scientific Computing Division, Elliott Brothers Ltd., Borehamwood, London and (b) NCR Electronics, National Cash Register Company Ltd., London. Catalogue number 440
11. David Warman (2010) E-mail to Simon Lavington dated 3 Feb 2010
12. Brown PJ (July 1971) The Kent on-line system. Softw Pract Experience 1(3):269–277
13. Brown PJ (1971) Effective use of batch and on-line facilities for introductory programming courses. Comput Bull Oct:370–372
14. Burstall RM, Collins JS, Popplestone RJ (1971) Programming in POP-2. Edinburgh University Press, Edinburgh
15. Arsac J, A Propos de la Reforme de l'Enseignement. In Progrès et Science, special issue on the Institut de Programmation, 4th trimester, 1967, page 6. Background comments on this article were provided by Pierre Mounier, in an e-mail to Simon Lavington dated 14 Apr 2009. See also the cartoon, reproduced as Fig. 8.9 in Chap. 8, which was drawn by Bernard Robinet, a student at the Institut de Programmation who was writing his dissertation on APL in 1967
16. EB Spratt (2008) E-mail to Simon Lavington, 29 Dec 2008
17. John Thompson (2009) E-mail to Simon Lavington dated 10 Jan 2009

Appendix 8
Elliott Digital Computer Deliveries and Costs

A8.1 Accuracy of the Information

It is difficult, perhaps now impossible, to produce a definitive list of the delivery dates, customers and applications of all the hundreds of Elliott computers designed and manufactured at Borehamwood. The information given in this appendix is a best-guess compilation of data culled from five sources, cited as [1–5]. Although [1, 2, 5] are original Elliott-Automation documents, minor inconsistencies have come to light when their contents have been cross-checked in detail. Reference [4], although anecdotal and often hazy about dates, does give some definite first-hand information about particular installations and this has been useful in judging the accuracy of the other sources. No specific Elliott company sales records (invoices, receipts, etc.) have come to light.

In Sect. A8.2 we list the Elliott digital computers by type, in the order: 400 series, 800 series, 502, 503, 900 series and 4100 series. Small numbers of various ARCH derivatives are most probably included in the lists for the 800 series (e.g. ARCH 8000), 900 series (e.g. ARCH 9000) and 4100 series (e.g. ARCH 2020). Chapter 7 discusses the relationship between the ARCH process control hardware and the standard Elliott general-purpose computers.

Elliott-Automation was effectively taken over by GEC in 1968, as described in Chap. 13. Machines manufactured at Borehamwood and elsewhere by Marconi-Elliott Computers Ltd. and by GEC Computers Ltd. in the period 1968–1989 are not listed in this appendix. General information about these computers will be found in Chap. 14.

A8.2 Delivery Lists

A8.2.1 Elliott 401

Date	Customer	Application and notes
Mar 1954	Agricultural Research Council, Rothamsted	Agricultural research statistics; also scientific and engineering computations by other organisations. Finally switched off in 1965.

A8.2.2 Elliott 402

Date	Customer	Application and notes
1955	Institut Blaise Pascal, Paris, France	Research and numerical analysis
1955	Army Operational Research Group, West Byfleet	Operational research
1956	Imperial Chemical Industries Ltd., Co Durham	Operational research; molecular structures
1957	Bomber Command, RAF High Wycombe	Operational research
1957	Rank, Taylor and Hobson Ltd., Leicester	Optical lens systems design
1958	Rotol Propellers Ltd., Gloucester	Propeller engineering design
1958	British Railways, Derby	Research and statistics
1958	Ernst Leitz GmbH, Wetzlar, Germany	Optical lens systems design
1958	Elliott Bros, Borehamwood	Computing service
1959	British Railways at Wolverton, Bedfordshire	Engineering research

It is believed that ten Elliott 402 computers were built. The above list represents a best guess of their destinations. See Chap. 5 for more details.

A8.2.3 Elliott 403 (WREDAC)

Date	Customer	Application and notes
Sept 1955	Weapons Research Establishment, Salisbury, Australia	Analysis of Woomera guided missile trials and research

A8.2.4 Elliott 405

Date	Customer	Application and notes
July 1956	Elliott Brothers (London) Ltd. Computing Services Division, Borehamwood	Computing service bureau. (By June 1964 this had become a standby computer in the Computer Maintenance Division)
Nov 1956	National Cash Register Co. Ltd., Marylebone Road, London, NW1	Demonstration and computing service No. 1
Feb 1957	City & County of Norwich, City Treasurer's Department	Final reminders for rates, payment of accounts, expenditure analysis, water rates, income costing and loans; eventually also wages and salaries. Replaced by a larger 405 in Oct 1961)
Sept 1957	National Gas Turbine Establishment, Pystock, Farnborough, Hants	* On-line data reduction in engine testing

(continued)

(continued)

Date	Customer	Application and notes
Nov 1957	Unilever Ltd., London	Wide variety of experimental work including linear programming
Dec 1957	Board of Trade, Census Office, Eastcote, Pinner, Middlesex	Census analysis. (Small computer?)
Feb 1958	British Insulated Callender's Cables London, W12	Railway electrification research and design work, payroll, costing
Feb 1958	Littlewoods Mail Order Stores Ltd. Liverpool 23	Mail order provisioning, inventory control
Apr 1958	Siemens (Woolwich) Ltd., London, SE18	Production Planning and control, in association with NRDC. Removed when AEI took over Siemens. This machine then went in February 1962 to the Control Group, Engineering Department, University of Cambridge. Bits of this machine then went to Forest Grammar School, Winnersh, Berks, in August 1966.
May 1958	Newton Chambers & Co Ltd., Sheffield	Payroll and stock control
Aug 1958	Albert E. Reed & Co. Ltd., Alyesford, Kent	Stores ledger control and accounting, payroll
Oct 1958	North Western Gas Board, Manchester	Payroll and gas billing
Oct 1958	Legal & General Assurance Soc. Ltd., Kingswood, Surrey	Payroll, maintaining and processing policy records of group life and pension schemes
Nov 1958	National Cash Register Co. Ltd., Frankfurt, Main, Germany	Demonstration and computing service, civil and constructional engineering calculations
Dec 1958	General Post Office, London	Payroll of 122,000 engineering, postal, telephone, telegraph and office staff in London area (more than £10 million per annum); statistics.
Jan 1959	Joseph Lucas (Sales & Service) Ltd., Birmingham	Sales statistics, order scheduling
Jan 1959	National Cash Register Co. Ltd., (National-Elliott Computing Service No. 2), Neasden, London	Demonstration and computing service, No. 2
Apr 1959	National Cash Register Co. Ltd., (National-Elliott Computing Service No. 3), Neasden, London	Demonstration, training and computing service, number 3
Mar 1959	Reckitt & Sons Ltd., Hull	Order handling, invoicing; sales ledger, sales statistics, depot stock records
May 1959	Courtaulds Ltd., Coventry	Invoicing, sales ledger, sales statistics; payroll; stores stock control maintenance. (This machine was replaced by a larger one in Sept 1960 – see entry below)

(continued)

(continued)

Date	Customer	Application and notes
Aug 1959	British Railways, Midland Region, Wolverton, Bucks.	Payroll, stores accounting, labour and material Analysis. See Note (1) below
Sept 1959	Crosse & Blackwell (Holdings) Ltd. London, SE1	Invoicing, stock control and sales statistics. In 1965 or 1966 this machine was given to Forest Grammar School, Winersh, Berkshire (see Chap. 8).
Sept 1959	General Post Office, London	(Same as for machine installed in Dec 1958)
Oct 1959	Elliott Brothers (London) Ltd. Computing Services Division, Borehamwood, Herts	Computing service bureau; payroll; stock control
Nov 1959	National Cash Register Co. Ltd., Barrack St., Sydney, Australia	Demonstration and computing service. After 1962 this machine was acquired by the Radio Frequency and Microwave Section of the National Standards Lab (part of CSIRO). Then in 1970 this machine was donated to the Powerhouse Museum, Sydney, where parts of it are on display
Dec 1959	Sumitomo Bank, Osaka, Japan	Deposit accounts, discounting of bills of exchange
Jan 1960	Associated British Picture Corporation, London	Payroll, theatre statistics, cinema costing
Sept 1960	Courtaulds Ltd., Coventry	(Replacing the machine installed in May 1959 – see above)
May 1961	North Western Gas Board Altrincham, Cheshire	Payroll and gas billing
Oct 1961	City & County of Norwich	(Replacing the machine installed in February 1957 – see above)
Dec 1960	National Cash Register Co. Ltd., (National-Elliott Computing Service No. 4), Neasden, London	Computing service number 4. (Model 405M).
June 1961	Newton Chambers & Co. Ltd., Sheffield	Payroll and stock control
Apr 1962	Snowy Mountains Hydro-Electric Authority, Australia	Accounting

An asterisk in the above list indicates that the computer was used for on-line control

Note (1). This BR installation is not explicitly recorded in [2]. However, the stated overall total of 405 installations in [2] does include an extra one which could well be the BR installation. Also, *British Transport Commission (London Midland Railway)* is mentioned as an explicit Elliott 405 user at the 31st meeting of the *405 Group*, which took place at NCR's Marylebone Road headquarters in London on 11 July 1961. There is anecdotal evidence from Roger Cook that an Elliott 405 was installed at (or at least assessed for) ICI's Nobel plant at Ardeer, Scotland. No dates are given and no other reference to this machine has thus far been encountered. For example, ICI does not appear in the list of users at the July 1961 meeting of the *405 Group* mentioned above.

A8.2.5   Elliott 802

Date	Customer	Application and notes
1958 Sept	Natural Gas Pipeline Co. of America, Chicago, Illinois, USA	Process control and general computing (via Panellit Inc., Skokie, Illinois?)
1959 Aug	Ministry of Public Works (Belgium)	Hydrodynamic investigations
Dec	Unknown (U.S.S.R.)	Unknown
Dec	N.C.R., Brussels (Belgium)	Computing service
Oct	Elliott-Automation Ltd.	Service engineers training and service testing
1960 July	Serck Radiators Ltd., Birmingham	Heat exchanger design
1961 Jan	British Aluminium Co. Ltd., Gerrards Cross	Simulation studies, operating research and stock control

A8.2.6   Elliott 803 and Elliott ARCH 8000

It is believed that deliveries up to about the end of 1960 were of the 803 model A variety and those from 1961 onwards were 803Bs.

Date	Customer	Application and notes
1959 Nov	E.I. Du Pont de Nemours Inc., Beaumont, Texas, USA	*Control of a nylon process
1960	Southern Electricity Board, Southall, Middlesex	Consumer billing
	E.I. Du Pont de Nemours Inc., Florence, South Carolina, USA	* Process control of Mylar film plant
Jan	Westinghouse Electric Corporation, Cheswick, Pennsylvania, USA	* Simulation studies for closed loop control systems
Feb	Northern Illinois Gas Corporation, Bellwood, USA	* Gas distribution control
	E.I. Du Pont de Nemours Inc., Circleville, Ohio, USA	* Control of nylon process
Sept	N.C.R., Frankfurt (Federal German Republic)	Computer mfg. and service bureau. Computing service
May	Boston Edison Co., Mystic Power Station, Boston, USA	* Generating station control
May	Berlin Gas Works (Federal German Republic)	Statistical and operational research, gas billing
June	Gulf States Utilities, Nelson Station, Westlake, Louisiana, USA	* Generating station control
July	Samuel Fox & Co. Ltd., Stockbridge Works, Sheffield	* Billet cut-up optimization in steel works
July	U.K.A.E.A., Calder Hall, Cumbria	* Reactor data acquisition and analysis

(continued)

(continued)

Date	Customer	Application and notes
July	The Distillers Co. Ltd., Epsom	Chemical eng., analytical and phys. chem. problems, simulation.
Aug	Finnish Cable Works, Helsinki, (Finland)	Cable design, shipbuilding and computing centre
Aug	Information Systems Inc., Los Angeles, USA	Process control for undisclosed customer
	N.C.R., Frankfurt, (Federal German Republic)	Computing service
Sept	Kancelarske Stroje (Skoda) (Czechoslovakia)	Calculations in vehicle design
	Owens-Corning Fibreglass Co., Aiken, South Carolina, USA	* Control of fibreglass production
Sept	N.C.R., Paris (France)	Computing service
Sept	Information Systems Inc., Los Angeles, USA	Process control for undisclosed customer (See Note (6) below)
	NCR-Elliott Computer Workshops Ltd.	Computing workshop service
Dec	Imperial Chemical Industries Ltd. (Billingham)	Off-line process control in ammonia works
	Tidewater Refinery, Delaware City, USA	*Control of petro-chemical process (Naphthalene distillation).
1961	Government Establishment (Admiralty)	Systems development.
	Elliott-Automation Ltd., Rochester	Aircraft and guided weapons research and radar development.
	The Chemical Works Voronezh (USSR)	*Data acquisition, analysis and control in synthetic rubber plant. See also Note (7).
	Applied Ballistics Dept. Ordnance Board, London	Weapon research; fire control; trajectories.
Sept	The Lummus Co. Ltd. (London)	Scientific calculations (chemical and structural)
Sept	G. A. Harvey & Co. Ltd., London	Invoicing and payroll analysis
	Kancelarske Stroje, Prague (Czechoslovakia)	Computing service
Oct	Brunel College of Advanced Technology	Teaching and research
	Prakla G.m.b.H., Hannover, (Federal German Republic)	Geophysical, surveying and prospecting calculations
Oct	Banco Pinto de Magalhais, Oporto (Portugal)	Banking and statistical
	Hawker Siddeley Group	Electrical engineering calculations, linear prog.
Nov	Mullard Ltd., Southampton	Engineering applications, transistor design. (See Note (1) below)
Nov	Mullard Research Labs, Salfords, Surrey	Research into solid-state and vacuum physics
Nov	Royal Radar Establishment, Malvern	Communication satellite experiments
Nov	Richard Thomas & Baldwins Ltd., Newport	Operational research in steel making

(continued)

(continued)

Date	Customer	Application and notes
	Fairey Aviation Division, Westland Aircraft Ltd., Hayes, Middlesex	Helicopter design
March	General Post Office Research, Dollis Hill	Network calculations, electronic design
	Brook Green Laundry	Laundry accounts
April	Technical University of Helsinki (Finland)	Research and teaching
May	Hindustan Aircraft Ltd. (India)	Aircraft design and engineering
May	Philipp Holzmann A.G., Frankfurt, (Federal German Rep).	Structural and civil engineering calculations
June	Electrotechnical Institute, Warsaw, (Poland)	Electrical engineering calculations
July	Godfrey Phillips Ltd., London	Credit notes, stock control, management reports for associated publishing companies, invoicing (for tobacco depots? See Note (3)
	NCR-Elliott Computer Workshops Ltd.	Computing service
Sept	Koch & Mazzuckin, Hannover, (Federal German Republic)	Civil engineering calculations
Sept	TNO/IWECO Institute, Delft (The Netherlands)	Research
Nov	Brush Electrical Engineering Co. Ltd., Loughborough	Electrical engineering calculations; design of motors and transformers. See Note (4)
Dec	General Post Office Goonhilly (Cornwall)	Satellite tracking. See Note (2) below
1962	Energoticky Dispecink (Czechoslovakia)	Electrical network calculations
	Elliott-Automation Ltd.	Systems development
	Ministry of Defence (RAF)	Undisclosed. *(Possibly Ministry of Aviation, for photogrammetric surveying?)*
	Elliott-Automation Ltd.	Program development
	Royal Radar Establishment, Malvern	Experimental applications
	De Havilland Aircraft Co., London	Design/analysis of Blue Streak space launching conversion programme; scientific and engineering service
	United Fuel Gas Co., Charleston, W Virginia, USA	*Gas distribution. 1961?
	Elliott-Automation Ltd.	* Experimental air traffic control system
	Valentine & Sons Ltd., Dundee	Order processing, sales accounting and stock Control; payroll
	Gluckslee Milchgesellschaft GmbH,	Accounting.Hamburg, (Fed. German Rep.)
	Sunderland Technical College	Teaching and research
	Rugby College of Engineering & Technology	Teaching, students' use on open-shop basis to analyse lab results

(continued)

(continued)

Date	Customer	Application and notes
	U.K. Atomic Energy Authority, Experimental Est., Dounreay.	Atomic energy, stores accounting, costing, payroll
	N.C.R. (The Netherlands)	Computing service
	National Gas Turbine Establishment Farnborough	Performance and design calcs. on aircraft & Engines; processing aerodynamic data
	An Foras Taluntais Agricultural Institute, Dublin, (Eire)	Analysis of field crop experiments; agricultural statistics
April	University of Reading	Scientific research, agricultural economics & maths
	Phenix Belge Insurance Co., Antwerp, Belgium	Insurance work.
April	University of Exeter	Research in geophysics, maths, chem., econ. and botany; teaching
	University of Leicester	Chemistry research; structural engineering, re-stressed concrete; sociological surveys; numerical analysis
	Southern Electricity Board (Newbury)	Accounting
	University of Hull	Economic and psychological research; mathematics; physics; timetabling; assistance to local industry
	2 computers: Richard Thomas & Baldwin Ltd., Spencer Works, Llanwern	* (a) Ingot/slab controller on hot-strip steel mill
		* (b) Finishing end scheduler in steelworks
	Northampton County Treasurer's Dept.	Income and expend. anal., costing highways and bridges; school meals; service work
	Kitcat & Aitken Investment control	(Stockbroking) clerical work, clearing returns and ledger control
	Ministry of Heavy Industry (Hungary)	Engineering calculations and bureau service
	National-Elliott Training School	Engineering instruction
	N.C.R., Stockholm (Sweden)	Computing service
	British Broadcasting Corporation, London	Production of day-to-day audience figs. for sound and TV progs.; engineering calculations
	Vickers da Costa & Co. Ltd., London	Preparation of clearing returns and accounting; foreign currency ledgers; valuations
	NCR-Elliott Computer Workshops Ltd. (City)	Computing service work for city firms
	British Petroleum Co. Ltd., Sunbury-on-Thames	Chemical engineering calculations, statistics
	Mills Associates	Service bureau

(continued)

(continued)

Date	Customer	Application and notes
	Crompton Parkinson Ltd., Guiseley, Yorkshire	Accounting and statistical, with sales documents directly linked to control stock at 28 depots
	Nat. Aeronautical & Space Laboratory, Amsterdam, The Netherlands	Aerospace research and design calculations
	Sun Oil Corporation, Marcus Hook, PA, USA	Petro-chemical processing
	Birmingham C.A.T.	Engineering calcs. research in chemical eng.
	University of Wroclaw (Poland)	Teaching and research
	Information Systems Inc., Los Angeles, USA	(For an undisclosed customer)
	Short Bros. & Harland Ltd., Belfast	Analysis of flight test data
	Richard Thomas & Baldwins Ltd.	Systems development by E-A Automation Systems Ltd. for Richard Thomas & Baldwins, Pagefield House, Newport, Mon.
	J. & P. Coates Ltd., Paisley	Dye recipe prediction; statistical work. 1961?
	Bristol College of Science & Tech.	Research in X-ray crystallography, student survey analysis; college administration. (may have been Dec 1961)
	University of Aberdeen	Teaching and research. (May have been Dec 1961).
	Royal Radar Establishment, Malvern	Scientific research
	Potato Marketing Board, Oxford	Market research. 1963?
	Thornber Bros. Ltd., Mytholmroyd, Halifax	Genetic research in chicken breeding. 1961?
	A. B. Matema, Stockholm, (Sweden)	Computing bureau; stock accounting 1961?
	Bedford Computer Services Ltd.	Computing Service 1963?
	Signals Research & Dev. Est., Christchurch	Radio propagation; research on the earth's magnetic field; satellite tracking
	Brown Brothers Ltd., London	Sales Analysis and customer records.
	Technische Hochschule, Darmstadt (Fed. German Rep.)	Civil Engineering calculations.
	Kancerlarske Stroje, Prague, Czechoslovakia	Electric power network calculations. See Note (5) below.
1963	Technoimport, Bucharest (Romania)	* Data acquisition, perf. analysis and control in steel works (the Hunedoara steelworks?)
	Kaiser-Engineers AEC, Hanford, Washington, USA	* Reactor data acquisition and analysis.

(continued)

(continued)

Date	Customer	Application and notes
	NCR-Elliott Computer Workshops Ltd. (Greenford)	Computer bureau and workshop
	NCR-Elliott Computer Workshops Ltd. (Southwark)	Computer bureau and workshop
	NCR, (Berlin, Federal German Republic)	Service bureau
	NASA Plum Brook Reactor Facility, Sandusky, Ohio, USA	* Reactor performance monitoring and control; acquisition of experimental results. Or 1962?
	Tidewater Oil Corp., Avon Refinery, San Francisco, USA	* Plant optimization and performance calculations. Or 1962
	King's College, (London?)	Crystallographic research
	Sovnarhozes, Moscow (U.S.S.R.)	Economic planning
	Associated Octel Ltd., Ellesmere Port	Production planning in chemical processing
	Sovnarhozes (U.S.S.R.)	Economic planning
	Hatfield College of Technology	Teaching and research
	N.C.R. (Norway)	Demonstration and computing service
	Chemical Industries (Czechoslovakia)	Statistics and research work
	Elliott-Automation Ltd.	Development of peripheral equipment
	Royal Institute of Great Britain, London	Crystallographic research, analysis of complex molecules
	London & Hull Maritime Insurance Co. Ltd. London	Insurance work
	Newport & Monmouth Technical College	Teaching
	Monk & Dunstone Ltd., London	Civil and structural engineering, quantity surveying
	Laboratory of Civil Engineering, Lisbon, Portugal	Civil engineering calculations
	Hepworths Ltd., Leeds	Maint. of subscription and accounts of 300 branches
	Imperial Chemical Industries Ltd. (Manchester)	Instrumental colour matching
	Energo Projekt Belgrade (Yugoslavia)	Calculations for power plant and hydro-control systems
	Ministry of Agriculture & Fisheries, Guildford	Statistical work
	Co-operative Wholesale Society, Desborough	Invoicing to 1,600 stores, stock records, accounting and payroll
	Hunting Engineering Ltd., Ampthill, Beds	Project planning
	Lanchester College of Technology	Teaching and research
	University of Durham	Teaching and research
	Elliott-Automation Ltd.	Aircraft systems research (Military Aircraft Controls Division, Borehamwood)

(continued)

(continued)

Date	Customer	Application and notes
	CSIRO Chem. Research Labs. (Australia)	Research into crystallography and chemical processes, nuclear magnetic resonance, chromatography; maths, statistics
	Royal Melbourne Inst. of Technology, jointly with E-A Pty Ltd. Melbourne, Australia	Teaching, using Elliott Autocode & Algol; exam. results, computer service & courses for local industry incl. do-it-yourself Computer Workshop.
	L. & C. Steinmuller GmbH., Gummersbach, (Fed. German Rep.)	Structural engineering and steam boiler and reactor calculations
	Monsanto Research S.A, Zurich. (Switzerland)	Scientific calculations, mainly crystallographic
	C.B.K.O., Gdansk, (Poland)	Ship building and engineering calculations
	N.C.R. (Switzerland)	Computing service
	Institut Blaise Pascal, Paris (France)	Mathematical research
	Draughtsmens & Allied Technicians Association, Richmond, Surrey	Subscription records for 72,000 trade union members; economic research; accounting, statistics
	Steel Company (Hungary)	Process control; data processing
	Technion Institute of Technology, Haifa, (Israel)	Teaching and research
	N.C.R. (Spain)	Computing service
	United Steel Companies Ltd., Swinden Labs Rotherham, Yorkshire	Operational research
1964	Economic Research Inst. Belgrade (Yugoslavia)	Computer mfg. and service bureau
	Independent Computer Service Ltd. (Edinburgh)	Computer mfg. and service bureau. Computing service
	Metalurski Institute (Yugoslavia)	Research
	Slovnaft (Czechoslovakia)	* Control of an ethylene plant
	Royal Air Force	* Fighter interception control
	2 computers: BMEWS-Fylingdales	* Processing of radar data
	Royal Military College of Science	Teaching and research
	Oxford University, Dept. of Biometry	Medical research statistics
	Royal Corps, of Signals	Teaching and research
	N.C.R. (South Africa)	Computing service
	P .U. T .C.O. (South Africa)	Public utilities work
	Inst. Edwardo Torroja de la Construccion y del Cemento (Spain)	Civil engineering
	Ministry of Public Works (Belgium)	Civil engineering
	Joseph Lucas Ltd.	Elec. and mech. engineering, physics and chem.
	University College of N. Wales (Bangor)	Education & research
	Elliott-Automation Ltd.	Medical research and automation

(continued)

(continued)

Date	Customer	Application and notes
	Swiss Bank Corporation, London	Central stock share and securities work
	Crittall Manufacturing Co. Ltd., Braintree, Essex	Stock control
	Optische Industrie (The Netherlands)	Research
	S. Bradford & Sons Ltd.	Production control and sales invoicing records
	Scottish Stock Exchange	Accounting of stocks and shares
	Godfrey Davis Ltd.	Stock control; car hire records and accounts
	RVO/TNO Physics Laboratorium (The Netherlands) Research	
	Mathematical Institute (Yugoslavia)	Calcs for power plant and water regulation
	Portsmouth Technical College	Education and research
	Joseph Lucas Ltd.	Elec. and mech. engineering, physics and chem.
	Richard Sharrock Ltd.	Invoicing, stock control and payroll
	G.I.R.E.C. (Belgium)	Undisclosed
	Ove Arup & Partners Consulting Engineers	Civil engineering calculations
	Imperial College of Science & Technology	Optical instrument design and research. Or 1962
	N. Corah (St. Margaret) Ltd.	Invoicing, stock control
	Ilford Borough Council	Municipal accounting
	London Hospital	Medical research
1965	Ministry of Posts & Telegraphs (India)	Telecommunication calculations
	Government Establishment	Undisclosed
	Edinburgh Medical Automation Centre	Medical computing service
	Technical University of Helsinki (Finland)	Research and teaching
	Overseas customer	Undisclosed
	R.A.F. Locking	Technical apprentice training
	R.A.F. Locking	Technical apprentice training
	John Dalton College	Research
	Liverpool College of Technology	Education and research
	Oulu University (Finland)	Research and teaching
	Albright & Wilson Ltd., (Oldbury)	Chemical engineering, and research
	Ministry of Technology (Warren Spring Lab.)	Scientific and general engineering calculations
	S. Smith & Sons Ltd.	Design and production control, engineering development
	Chesterfield Corporation	Municipal accounting
	E.M.I. Electronics Ltd.	Electronics research
	General Borough of Dewsbury	Municipal accounting
	Cater Bros Ltd.	Invoicing, stock control and payroll

(continued)

(continued)

Date	Customer	Application and notes
	Bath City Council	Municipal accounts rating, payroll
	Amsterdam Ballast Co. (The Netherlands)	Commercial applications
	Bond Worth Ltd.	Stock control order, processing and payroll
	Buxted Chicken Co. Ltd.	Research and accounts
	Chelsea College of Advanced Technology	Education and research
	East Surrey Water Board	Consumer billing
	R.A.F. Locking	Systems development
1966	Ministry of Defence (R.A.F.)	Undisclosed
	Belfast College of Technology	Education and research
	Tampere University (Finland)	Research and teaching
	Ministry of Chemical Industry (U.S.S.R.)	* Control of ammonia plant
	Thomson Newspapers	* Computer typesetting
	Undisclosed Customer (Pakistan)	Undisclosed
	Tillotsons Corrugated Cases Ltd.	Stock control
	Royal Navy Armament Depot	Spare parts control.
	Mills Associates	Service bureau
	Overseas Customer	Undisclosed

An asterisk in the above list indicates that the computer was used for online control

Note (1). [2] gives two 803s for Mullard Ltd. in 1961: one at their Research Labs at Salfords, Surrey; the other at Southampton. Reference [1] gives only one Mullard installation.

Note (2). The first live Telstar transmission from Goonhilly took place on 11 July 1962. Reference [2] gives 1961 for the 803 installation at Goonhilly; Ref. [1] gives 1963; Ref. [3] gives December 1961. See also [6].

Note (3). Godfrey Phillips Ltd., London: Ref. [1] mentions tobacco as the applications-area; Ref. [2] mentions publishing.

Note (4). Brush Electrical is only given in [2].

Note (5). Reference [2] gives this extra Stroje installation in 1962.

Note (6). Reference [5] gives four (not one) computers delivered to Information Systems Inc for 'undisclosed customers'.

Note (7). There are at least three extra Elliott 803 sales, to undisclosed Russian organisations, not mentioned in the above list. They arose as follows. Elliott-Automation had a presence at various trade exhibitions behind the Iron Curtain. At the conclusion of many of these exhibitions, equipment was 'sold' off the stand. This was standard practice for several British companies, being a mutually beneficial way of circumventing bureaucracy. Tony Hoare, who was present at four such exhibitions, has written as follows [7]. 'It's a shame you have no record of the exhibition sales in Moscow. There were at least four. 1960: 803A at the SIMA exhibition. 1961: 803B probably – (see below). I exhibited an early version of our ALGOL compiler, under strict instructions to bring back the paper tape which contained it. Suitcase lost on return flight from Moscow. I wonder whether the goons succeeded in decoding it? There was also in 1962 or 1963 a general 'British Exhibition' at Vystavka, where we exhibited on 803 a process control program written by Dina Vaughan. Khruschev was a visitor. Finally, I recall a 503 in Sokolniki Park in 1964.... Over the same period, there were computers exhibited in Eastern Europe, Poznan, Budapest, etc., which I did not participate in. I think the reason why we kept these sales secret was that we had to observe US export restrictions on sales of US technology to the Soviets. Of course, all our components and most peripherals were of US manufacture.' Actually, some components were of UK manufacture, for example the Mullard transistors. Of the Elliott 803 sold off the stand at Moscow in 1961 (see above), Joseph Roth remembers that this went to the Moscow Tyre Factory [8].

A8.2.7   Elliott 502

Date	Customer	Application and notes
1964	Royal Radar Establishment	* Radar simulation (on-line).
1966	A.T.C. Evaluation Unit	* Air Traffic Control Procedural simulation (on-line).
1967?	Ministry of Aviation	* Simulation (on-line).

An asterisk in the above list indicates that the computer was used for on-line control

A8.2.8   Elliott 503

Date	Customer	Application and notes
1963	Elliott-Automation Ltd.	Service Bureau
	N.C.R.	Service Bureau
	Elliott-Automation Ltd.	Service Bureau
1964	United Steel Co. Ltd.	Operational research production scheduling
	ABW/TNO (The Netherlands)	Government computing centre for industry
	The Hydro-University Computing Centre (Australia)	Scientific computing bureau. (See Note (1))
	Rijkswaterstaat, The Hague (The Netherlands)	Land reclamation calculations
	N.A.T.O. (Italy)	Undisclosed
	Army Operational Research Establishment .	Operational research
	Aircraft & Armaments Experimental Establishment	Evaluation of aircraft performance
	Bristol University	Crystallography and general research
	N.C.R. (Federal German Republic)	Service Bureau
	Soviet Academy of Science (U.S.S.R.)	General scientific computing
1965	Gosplan (U.S.S.R.)	System simulation studies
	Short Bros. & Harland Ltd.	Analysis of flight test data
	State Computing Centre (Finland)	Government computing centre
	Dept. of Scientific & Industrial Res. (N. Zealand)	Meteorological analysis records and highway design
	Rocket Propulsion Establishment	Analysis of rocket firing and design of rocket motors
	Mullard Ltd.	Electronics and physics research
	General Post Office	Operational and communications research
	Elliott-Automation Ltd.	Research & development.
	Battersea College of Advanced Technology (Became University of Surrey in Sept 1966)	Education and research
	Technion Institute of Technology (Israel)	Teaching and research

(continued)

(continued)

Date	Customer	Application and notes
	Prakla G.m.b.H. (Federal German Republic)	Geophysical, surveying and prospecting calculations
	Institute for Data Processing (German Democratic Rep.)	Economic planning and scientific research
	Kancelarske Stroje (Czechoslovakia)	Computing centre for economic planning
1966	Rescona (The Netherlands)	Civil and structural engineering
	Undisclosed (Overseas)	Undisclosed
	Elliott-Automation Ltd.	Systems development
	Elliott-Automation Ltd.	Radar research
	EMI Electronics Ltd.	Research
	Satchwell Controls Ltd.	Data Processing, planning and research

Note (1). This delivery was to 'the University of Tasmania and the Hydro-Electric Commission, Tasmania'. It was almost certainly the first sale of an Elliott 503 to an external customer. The original tender document was dated 18 January 1962. Elliott-Automation opened a Computing Service Centre in Melbourne, based on an 803, early in 1963. The Elliott 503 was installed at the Hydro-University Computing Centre (HUCC), Hobart, Tasmania, in January 1964 and is believed to have become fully operational in June/July of that year. The 503 operated at HUCC until 1977. More information on this computer is given in Sect. A8.3.5.

A8.2.9 Elliott 900 Series: Partial List, up to About March 1967 (Includes Some ARCH 9000 Computers)

Date	Customer	Application and notes
1965	Royal Navy	* Underwater weapon experimental system
	Royal Netherlands Air Force (The Netherlands)	* Fighter interception control
	Services Research & Development Estab.	* On-line communications
	Elliott-Automation Ltd.	Development of peripheral equipment
	War Office	* On-line military systems
	Munich City Council (Federal German Republic)	* Road traffic control
	Elliott-Automation Ltd.	Development of message switching systems
	Elliott-Automation Ltd.	Development of airborne computing system
	Ministry of Aviation	* On-line navigation system
	Ministry of Technology (Warren Spring Lab.)	* Self-adaptive control system research
	National Physical Laboratory	* Far infra-red interferometry
	Distillers Co. Ltd. (Hull)	* Process investigation and control

(continued)

(continued)

Date	Customer	Application and notes
1966	Bolidens Gruv. A.B. (Sweden)	* Analytical process control
	2 computers: Admiralty	Navigation application
	2 computers: Ministry of Aviation	* Airborne application
	Ministry of Aviation	* Mobile radar system
	Elliott-Automation Ltd.	Meteorological data plotting
	University of Birmingham	Traffic survey work
	Royal Air Force	* Fighter interception control
	Finnish Cable Works (Finland)	* Ore cleaning and refining
	12 computers:	Elliott-Automation Ltd. Systems and program development
	Reading Evening Post	* Typesetting
	Royal Liberty School (Romford)	Education and research
	Elliott-Automation Ltd.	Mobile classroom for demos and lectures
	British Glass Industries Research Assoc. (Sheffield) Research into improving strength & properties of moulded glass	
	White Fish Authority (Hull)	Statistical analysis
	Elliott-Automation Ltd.	Development of software
	Trent River Authority (Nottingham)	Control of water resources
On Order, as at the End of 1966		
	British Launderer's Research Association	Design of small electrical systems, off-line control of laundries
	Lucas Gas Turbine Equipment Ltd.	Engine calcs for gas turbine development
	Undisclosed Research Establishment	Unknown
	Scottish Woollen Technical College	Research for Textile Industry
	Elliott-Automation Ltd.	Engineer training
	J. G. L. Poulson Assoc. Pontefract.	Civil and structural engineering. Preparing bills of quantity
	3 Computers: Thomson Regional Newspapers	* Typesetting (at Warminster)
	British Ceramic Research Association	* Control of instruments for structural res.
	An Aviation Company	Control to online plotter
	Machine Tool Industry Research Association	Gear design
	Serck R&D Ltd.	Engineering data reduction, commercial and Technical work.
	Mid Kent College of Technology	Education, teaching and research
	Undisclosed Research Centre	Research
	A laboratory	Monitoring of instruments and data proc.
	A university	* Teaching and research in behavioural sciences
	Girling Ltd.	Design and analysis of braking systems
	U.K.A.E.A.	* Control of X-ray diffractometry
	An oil company	* Control of engine test-beds

(continued)

(continued)

Date	Customer	Application and notes
	East Midlands Gas Board	* Control of light distillate gas-making plant
	41 Computers: Ministry of Defence	* Undisclosed application in defence (operational weapons systems)
	20 Computers: Ministry of Defence	* Undisclosed application in defence (operational weapons systems)
	Printing Works	* Typesetting
	Sheffield University	* Investigation of learning patterns
	9 Computers: Ministry of Defence	Development of defence application
	Eurocontrol (France)	* Air space control
	Royal Netherlands Navy (The Netherlands)	* Tactical training simulator
	A.S.E.A. (Sweden)	* Undisclosed defence application
	Undisclosed customer	* Laboratory instrument control
	B.P. Vohburg, Bavaria	* Refinery monitoring
	A Hospital in South Africa	* Control of air-conditioning plant
	Union International	General computing service
	2 Computers: Admiralty	Development of defence application
	Overseas Agent	Overseas defence application

The number of Elliott 900 series computers delivered by Borehamwood probably exceeded 1,300 by mid-1977 (see Chap. 14). To this should be added the large numbers of 900 series derivatives delivered by various other GEC-Marconi divisions at Rochester and elsewhere for applications in aerospace and defence (see Chap. 12 and Appendix 6). These airborne computers included the 920 (probably 600 or 700 delivered), the 920ATC (550) and the 12 Series (7,000 or more). If *derivatives* of the 12 Series are included, Chap. 12 indicates that sales were in the region of 30,000.

A8.2.10   Elliott 4120 Computers and ARCH 2020: Partial List, up to About March 1967

Date	Customer	Application and notes
1965	G. Maunsell & Partners	Civil engineering calculations
	Elliott-Automation Ltd.	Research and testing peripherals and production tech.
	Elliott-Automation Ltd.	Training maintenance engineers
	Elliott-Automation Ltd.	Software development

(continued)

(continued)

Date	Customer	Application and notes
	British Telecommunications Research	Research in telecommunications
	Aircraft Research Association	Research and design calculations
1966	British Coal Utilisation Research Association	Combustion research
	British Scientific Instrument Research Association Operational research	
	Shoe & Allied Trades Research Association	Production planning, research
	Signals Research & Development Establishment Satellite communications	
	Univ. of Edinburgh (Dept. of Machine	* Advanced programming research Intelligence and Perception) (interactive)
	Dundee Technical College	Research and teaching
	Northern Polytechnic	Teaching and research
	An NCR Customer	Accounts and statistics of telegraph messages
	National Physical Laboratory	* Study of 'conversational' programming
	Elliott-Automation Ltd.	* Training simulator research
	An NCR Customer	Research in nuclear physics
	An NCR Customer	Stock control and victualling
	British Hovercraft Corporation	Hovercraft design and research
	Fisons Fertilisers Ltd.	Simulation and linear programming
	British Petroleum Ltd.	Research
	Humphreys & Glasgow Ltd.	Calculations for chemical, mech. and civil engineering
	NCR Elliott Computer Workshops Ltd.	Bureau service
	NCR	Systems development
	An NCR Customer	Service bureau
	Racal Electronics Ltd.	General electronics research
	An NCR Customer	Investment and securities records. General accounting
	Imperial Tobacco Co.	Research statistics
	2 computers: Ministry of Aviation	* Message switching
	An NCR Customer	Ministry accounting and administration
	NCR Service bureau.	Applications development
	An NCR Customer	Production control
	An NCR Customer	Stock control and customer invoicing
	Schwedt Oil Refinery (German Dem. Rep.)	* Refinery control res. (Vehicle mounted system)
	Elliott-Automation Ltd.	Research and testing peripherals and prod. techniques
	Ministry of Electrical Power (Rumania)	Electrical network calculations
	Australian Sales Research Bureau Ltd. (Australia) Market research	

(continued)

(continued)

Date	Customer	Application and notes
	Undisclosed (Hungary)	Undisclosed
	Elliott-Automation Ltd.	Software development
On Order, as at the End of 1966		
	An NCR Customer	Accounting
	An NCR Customer	Civil engineering calculations
	An NCR Customer	Accounting and statistics
	A Public Utility	* Distribution control system
	Ministry of Defence	* Naval training simulator
	Munich City Council (Federal German Rep.)	* Second system in road traffic control hierarchy
	Elliott-Automation Ltd.	Computing service
	A Public Utility	* Integrated telemetry and control system
	Imperial Smelting Corporation	* Control of zinc smelting plant
	An NCR Customer	Spare parts control
	NCR	Service bureau and inventory control
	An NCR Customer	Local authority applications
	NCR	Service bureau
	An NCR Customer	Financial
	An NCR Customer	Stores control
	An NCR Customer	General accounting
	An NCR Customer	Accounting and statistics
	An NCR Customer	General accounting, stock evaluating etc.
	An NCR Customer	Customers orders, stock records and forecasting
	An NCR Customer	Accounting
	An NCR Customer	Invoicing, sales ledger
	An NCR Customer	Accounting and statistical analysis
	An NCR Customer	Co-ordination of sales and production
	An NCR Customer	Accounting
	An NCR Customer	Accounting
	An NCR Customer	Stamp redemption accounting at branch level
	A Training College	Teaching and research
	Ove Arup & Partners Consulting Engineers	Design calcs., structural analysis., quantity surveying etc.
	Kingston College of Technology	General research, teaching and business studies
	Aberdeen University (Dept. of Natural Philosophy)	* Study of human concept formation processes
	Robert Gordon's Colleges	Research and teaching
	U.K.A.E,A.-Springfield	Undisclosed
	British Paper & Board Industries Res. Assoc.	Data analysis and linear programming on paper trim problems
	Hunting Engineering Ltd.	Project planning
	Motor Industries Research Association	Structural analysis and analysis of wind tunnel tests

(continued)

(continued)

Date	Customer	Application and notes
	Barking College of Technology	Teaching and education
	British Electric Transformer Co. Ltd.	Design, production and organisation control
	An NCR Customer	Analysis of record returns from farmers
	An NCR Customer	Circulation and advertising statistics
	An NCR Customer	Deposit and loan accounting

An asterisk in the above list indicates that the computer was used for on-line control.
Summary of NCR/Elliott 4120 computers and ARCH 2020 Industrial Control Systems, up to the end of 1966: delivered 40; on order: 40; total: 80. After 1968, ICL took over sales of Elliott 4100 series computers. It is believed that the last ones to be manufactured were delivered in about 1972.

A8.2.11   Elliott 4130 Computers: Partial List, up to about March 1967

Date	Customer	Application and notes
1966	Sussex University (Dept. of Exp'l. Psychology)	* Study of animal behaviour
	Csepel (Hungary)	Data processing and production control
	Keele University	Speech analysis and human response studies
	Aberystwyth University	Research and teaching
	Warwick University	Research and teaching
	York University	Administration, teaching and research
	Reading University	Research and teaching
	Bangor University	Research and teaching
	Kent University	Numerical analysis
	Queen's College, Dundee	* Multi-access computing system
	Elliott-Automation Ltd.	Project control management information
	National Research Inst. for Computer	Commercial and scientific data processing
	Techniques & Automation (Czechoslovakia)	
	NCR Bureau & sales calculations	Computing service
	An NCR Customer	Research into computing science
	An NCR Customer	Stock information and vehicle scheduling
	An NCR Customer	Undisclosed
	Elliott-Automation Ltd.	Customer demonstration and software development
	Cambridge University	* Hybrid system for research into process control.
	Leicester University	Advanced research in teaching, space research
	Royal Observatory (Edinburgh)	* Control of telescopes and photographic instruments

An asterisk in the above list indicates that the computer was used for online control

After 1968, ICL took over sales of Elliott 4100 series computers. It is believed that the last ones to be manufactured were delivered in about 1972.

A8.3 Cost Estimates

Very few original company documents have come to light that give the detailed contemporary costs of Elliott digital computers and associated equipment. More generally, as observed by Hendry [9], 'there are many sources of quantitative information on the early British computer industry, very few of which agree with each other'. The following table gives a pragmatic summary of cost estimates for Elliott computers, based on the sources of the data quoted later.

All of the computers featured in Table A8.1 came with various options. In deriving the figure in the bottom row, we have taken account of the probable configurations of machines actually sold to customers so as to deduce an overall average costing.

A8.3.1 Notes on the Above Cost Estimates

A contemporary article in the Computer Bulletin [10] gives the following typical costs for computers: Elliott 402E: £25,000; Elliott 402F: £35,000; Elliott 405: 'price according to specification', but the annual maintenance charge was quoted as '5% of capital cost or £2,500, whichever is the greater', which might imply that a modest 405 could cost in the region of £50,000.

The book by John Hendry [9] draws on information given in the periodical *Computer Survey*. Hendry quotes average system prices at 1963 levels as follows: Elliott 402 = £25K; Elliott 405 = £125K; Elliott 802 = £20K; Elliott 803 = £35K; Elliott 503 = £80K. In his book [11], Martin Campbell-Kelly quotes £80K as an 'average' price for an Elliott 503.

Regarding discounts, R G Wilson, who joined Elliotts in 1962 and was a Sales Engineer from 1964 to 1968, provided the following information [12] in February 2009: 'I'm now fairly sure that 803 (and presumably 503?) systems for educational users qualified for a 20% discount, while 4100 systems attracted discount at 10%. I also believe that we didn't discount 903s at all, on the basis that prices had allegedly been brought down as low as we could go and/or possibly that as they were

Table A8.1 Approximate contemporary selling price of commercially available Elliott computers, 1955–1967

	402	405	800 Series	503	900 Series	4100 Series
Price range	£25K–£35K	£50K–£125K	£20K–£35K	£75K–£400K	£13K–£35K	??
Typical cost	£27K	£85K	£30K	£130K	£25K	£60K

almost all likely to go to educational and small research users we had already taken account of that in our pricing structure. This doesn't, of course, preclude any special deals that might have been negotiated.'

Below we give further Elliott-specific information, including known costs of particular computer installations.

Elliott 402

The first Elliott 402, delivered to the Institut Blaise Pascal in 1955, cost £27,000 [13].

Elliott 405

The cost of the Elliott 405 'and all necessary ancillary equipment' used in the NRDC/ Siemens project in 1957 amounted to £84,000 (see Chap. 5). The purchase price of the large 405 computer installed at Littlewoods in 1958 (described in Chap. 9) was about £110,000 – see [14]. Andrew St Johnston's notebook gives an early (July 1955) estimated cost of a typical basic 405 with drum as £71.4K (or £76.9K with a disc) and the cost of a large 405 at between £109.4K and £114.9K. He added an estimated £7K for 'programming, installation and spares'. In the tender evaluation for the Royal Army Pay Corp's payroll application (see Chap. 9 and Appendix 3) the cost of an Elliott 405 was quoted as £108K in 1956. The average price of £125K for an Elliott 405 as quoted by Martin Campbell-Kelly [11] seems rather high.

Elliott 800 Series

An Elliott 803 was installed at Hatfield Polytechnic in September 1963. After the deduction of 20% educational discount, the basic system cost £23,200, plus floating-point unit at £4,000, plus ancillary data processing equipment at £2,000, yielding a total price of £29,200. This is equivalent to £35K without the educational discount. In a National Elliott 803 glossy brochure number CS109 (undated but probably 1963) the following quotation appears: 'A basic machine with paper tape input and output costs only £29,000 including installation, supply of library programmes, and six months' free maintenance.' The basic cost of an Elliott 803 was quoted as £30,000, according to an article in the *Welwyn & Hatfield Advertiser: 11 January 1963*. Somewhat later, the Elliott-Automation Computing Division pocket diaries for 1964 and 1965 stated that an Elliott 803 'costs from £20,000'.

Elliott 503

An advertisement in the New Scientist dated 27 June 1963 implies that the price of an Elliott 503, for which deliveries to external customers had not yet commenced, would be 'up to £200,000'. The Elliott-Automation Computing Division pocket diaries for 1964 and 1965 state that the Elliott 503 'costs up to £400,000'. The 1966 edition of the diary gives the upper price at £500,000. Alan Wakefield, who joined Elliotts in 1961, worked as a Sales Engineer from 1963–1967. Writing in January 2009, Alan Wakefield says [15]: '£400,000 for 503 would have been just about the maximum expanded configuration with 132K core backing store, full mag.tape and LP peripherals etc etc. A more likely *average* configuration 503 would have been in the range £120K to £150K .... I rather feel that [Martin Campbell-Kelly's figure [see [11]] of £80K is on the low side. I have had £75K in my mind as the starting price for a minimum configuration 503.' Further evidence comes from [16], though it is not entirely clear what weight to place on this. For the Elliott 503, [16] states: 'Selling Price: £56,000 to £416,000; rental per month: £1,017 to £9,200; installation cost: included in price'. The Elliott 503, installed at the Hydro-University Computing Centre (HUCC), Hobart, Tasmania, in January 1964, provides a much more specific case study [17]. The HUCC's basic 503 included an 8K word core store, two tape readers, two tape punches and a control typewriter and cost £73,000. Annual maintenance of this was £2,250 per annum. To the basic machine was added a peripheral transfer control unit, a magnetic tape controller, three Ampex TM4 tape decks and an Anelex high-speed lineprinter, these units bringing the total price for the whole HUCC system to £160,150. The total maintenance for the system was £4,950 per annum. Additional funds were required for various necessary spares and test equipment, amongst which were two relatively expensive items of interest: an engineers' display panel (£2,200) and a Tektronix oscilloscope (£1,460).

Elliott 900 Series

According to the brochure *UK Price List, MCS920 General Purpose Mobile Digital Computer*, published by Elliott-Automation's Mobile Computing Division in July 1964, prices for the 920A varied between £21,300 and £26,500, depending upon the choice of memory and packaging options. The power supply unit was extra, typically £750. A complete Elliott 920 system with paper tape reader, punch and flexowriter might typically cost £31,534. The Mobile Computing Division pocket diary for 1965 quotes £21K for a minimum MCS920. The Elliott-Automation Computing Division pocket diary for 1966 states that the basic Elliott 903 costs £12,750. Alan Wakefield recalled [15] that: 'I sold a number of 903 systems in the period 1966/67, and I recall that the contracted prices ranged from about £15,000 to £35,000 (depending on configuration and peripherals) with an average selling price about £23,000–£25,000'.

Elliott 4100 Series

According to a contemporary internal NCR/Elliott memo [18] the approximate cost of a typical Elliott 4120 system was £60,000.

A8.3.2   Special Computers for Classified Projects

There were other Elliott digital computers, such as the 152, Nicholas and the 401, but they were not commercially available. As described in Chap. 3 and Appendix 8, three further Elliott computers earned revenue for the company although as defence, rather than civilian, projects. The Elliott 153 cost the Admiralty about £125,000 in 1954; the Elliott 403 (WREDAC) cost the Long Range Weapons Establishment £106,625 in 1955; each of three Elliott 502 computers cost the Royal Radar Establishment and the Ministry of Aviation about £300,000 in the years 1964, 1966 and 1967 respectively – though no detailed documentation has come to light to confirm these figures. In Table A8.2, these defence computers have been lumped into a separate column.

A8.3.3   Industrial Control and Automation

As discussed in Chap. 7, many of the Elliott 800 and 900 and ARCH series computers found their way into process control applications. For such applications, the cost of the central processor was often dwarfed by the cost of the surrounding instrumentation and interfacing equipment – all supplied by Elliotts. Two examples will suffice to illustrate this point.

a. *Imperial Smelting Corporation, Avonmouth.* In 1967 an Elliott ARCH 2020 was installed to control a smelting operation. This involved the ARCH 2020 in handling over 500 measurements, more than 800 contact closure signals and over 120 direct digital control (DDC) loops, thus making it 'the largest [DDC] of this type known in the world'. Elliott-Automation supplied the whole of the automation system, including data-logging and materials-handling equipment, bringing the value of the work done at Avonmouth to almost £1 million (1967 prices). The Elliott 4100 series processor that lay at the heart of the ARCH 2020 system probably only represented about 5% of the cost of the whole Avonmouth project.

b. *Dista Products Ltd., Speke, Liverpool.* An Elliott ARCH 102 computer was installed for the control of batch fermentation of antibiotics such as penicillin (see Chap. 7). The system, involving 114 control loops under the direct digital control of the ARCH 102 computer, cost about £100,000 (1967 prices) to implement. The Elliott 902 processor at the heart of the ARCH 102 system probably represented about 20% of the cost of the whole Speke project.

A8.4   Computer Sales Revenues, 1954–1966

The total number of Elliott computers delivered each year is shown in Table A8.2. This includes a few machines used for in-house bureau work by Borehamwood and by NCR, as indicated in the delivery lists presented earlier.

Table A8.2 Probable numbers of Elliott digital computers delivered per year

	Defence computers	402	405	800 Series	503 Series	900 Series	4100 Series
1954	1						
1955	1	2					
1956		1	2				
1957		2	4				
1958		4	9	1			
1959		1	11	4			
1960			3	24			
1961			3	26			
1962			1	53			
1963				42	3		
1964	1			34	10		
1965	1			24	13	12	6
1966	1			10	6	29	34

Table A8.3 Approximate income from the sale of Elliott digital computers, 1954–1966, in £K

	Defence computers	402	405	800 Series	503 Series	900 Series	4100 Series	Total, less def.	Total, incl. def.
1954	125							0	125
1955	107	54						54	161
1956		27	170					197	197
1957		54	340					394	394
1958		108	765	30				903	903
1959		27	935	120				1,082	1,082
1960			255	720				975	975
1961			255	780				1,035	1,035
1962		27	85	1,590				1,675	1,675
1963		54		1,260	390			1,650	1,650
1964	300			1,020	1,300			2,320	2,620
1965	300			720	1,690	300	360	3,070	3,370
1966	300			300	780	725	2,040	3,845	4,145

By multiplying the number of each type of computer by the average cost of each type, we can derive an approximation to total sales income. This is shown in Table A8.3.

The figures for some of the years should possibly be reduced somewhat, to allow for machines that were used in-house for bureau work, etc., rather than being sold to external customers. On the other hand, such machines did generate revenue. Furthermore, the income figures should very probably be increased anyway, to allow for after-sales services such as maintenance, spares, upgrades and software.

Elliott-Automation's approximate income from the sale of computers, as derived above, is discussed in Chap. 13 in the context of the company's overall financial position in the years leading up to the GEC takeover.

References

1. Anon (1967) Elliott Automation: computers and orders, 1947–1966. Brochure published in early 1967 by the Directorate of Information Services, Elliott-Automation Ltd., 21 Portland Place, London W1. A leaflet, inserted in the booklet subsequently, gives the total delivered and on order figures for each computer as at 31 March 1967
2. Anon (1963) Computer and data processing installations. Elliott Computing Division. Issued 31 Aug 1963 by Elliott Brothers Ltd., Borehamwood, London
3. Various issues of the quarterly periodical Computer Survey, which appeared more or less regularly from June 1962
4. Written memoranda from many individuals who had been involved in the design, sales or use of Elliott computers in the period 1947–1970. See also [7] and [8], cited below
5. Anon, ARCH in action: on-line computing and data handling systems. Publication number R31 (48 pages) produced by Elliott Process Automation Limited. Undated but a date of mid-1966 may be deduced
6. Seaman ECH, Thomson WE (1962) Computing and data transmission for prediction steering of aerial. In: IEE international conference on satellite communication, London, Nov 1962
7. CAR (Tony) Hoare (2009) E-mail to Simon Lavington dated 10 Aug 2009. (Describes the sales of Elliott 800 series machines to Russian organizations)
8. Joseph Roth (2008) E-mail communication with Simon Lavington on 24 Feb 2008
9. Hendry J (1990) Innovating for failure: government policy and the early British computer industry. MIT Press, London. ISBN: 0-262-08187-3. This book draws on information given in the periodical Computer Survey
10. Anon (1957) Comparative data on machines available in the United Kingdom for clerical users. Comput Bull Oct:88 onwards
11. Campbell-Kelly M (1989) ICL – a business and technical history. Oxford University Press, Oxford. ISBN: 0-19-853918-5. The source of the computer costs given in this book is stated to be: Williams RH (1976) Early computers in Europe. In: Proceedings of 1976 National Computer Conference, AFIPS Press, Montvale, NJ, pp 21–29, 'with corrections from other sources'
12. RG Wilson (2009) E-mail to Simon Lavington dated 3 Feb 2009
13. Pierre-E Mounier-Kuhn (CNRS & Centre de Recherches en Histoire de l'Innovation Université Paris-Sorbonne) (2008) E-mail to Simon Lavington dated 25 Nov 2008
14. Everitt G (2006) Making money while the world slept. Computer Resurrection, the Bulletin of the Computer Conservation Society, Issue number 37, spring 2006
15. Alan Wakefield (2010) E-mail to Simon Lavington dated 29 Jan 2010
16. Anon (1969) Current computers, 1969. Richard Williams & Partners, Computer Specialists. ISBN-10: 0901407003; ISBN-13: 978-0901407009. Quoted by Nigel Williams on the following website: http://www.retrocomputingtasmania.com/home/projects/elliott-503#TOC-Elliott-503-customer-deliveries
17. Besides the above Retrocomputingtasmania website organised by Nigel Williams, various other HUCC-specific documents have been scanned and made available online by Brian Marriott at: http://www.pdp8user.net/elliott-503/documents
18. Anon (1965) Machine comparisons. NCR/Elliott Information memo number 5, 26 Jan 1965 (Two pages, type-written, internal company document)

Appendix 9
Supplementary Avionics Details

A9.1 A History of Elliott's Rochester Site

The Medway area of Kent could, with some justification, be called the cradle of British aviation. The following account of the origins of the Rochester factory is taken largely from the 1992 booklet *A Brief History of Rochester Airport* [1].

In 1909 the three Short brothers, Oswald, Horace and Eustace, opened the world's first aircraft factory at Leysdown on the Isle of Sheppey, in the Medway estuary. At Leysdown they constructed, under licence, six Wright Flyer machines. It was also at Leysdown that the first successful all-British aircraft, the Short Number 2, flew on 30 October 1909 to win the Daily Mail prize for the first all-British circular flight of 1 mile. In 1913 the Short Brothers moved their Seaplane construction to a more sheltered site at nearby Rochester on the River Medway. Here they continued to build sea and land planes until, by 1933, the lack of a suitable airfield at the riverside site led Shorts and Rochester City Council into a partnership to develop a new Rochester Airport. A 120-acre location was chosen about 2 miles south-east of the centre of the city of Rochester.

Shorts started assembling aeroplanes at Rochester Airport at the end of 1933 and the first air service from the airport commenced in June 1934. In 1937, a flying school to train RAF volunteer reservists was established at the airport, later being enlarged to train Fleet Air Arm personnel. Short Brothers was not the only company to manufacture on the airport site but it quickly became the main player.

By the outbreak of the Second World War, Short's Rochester Airport factory was in full production assembling Stirlings, the RAF's first four-engined bomber.

When the war ended, aircraft production at Rochester was rapidly curtailed and many employees made redundant. In 1946 the British government decided to concentrate all Short's activities at Belfast and their Rochester factory was closed. However, pilot training activities, aircraft maintenance, passenger services and private flying continued at the Airport.

In 1946 the firm of B&P Swift Ltd., together with the subsidiary company Swift and Swallow Ltd., rented space from the government in the main factory at Airport Works. B&P Swift was by that time a general mechanical engineering company; the principle activity of its partner, Swift & Swallow, was the production of scales and food-processing machinery. There was, however, a connection with the aircraft industry because during the war B&P Swift Ltd. had manufactured gearboxes for aircraft controls and flap and undercarriage actuators for Shorts. After the link-up in 1947 between B&P Swift Ltd. and Elliott Brothers (London) Ltd., as described in Chap. 1, Elliott's Rochester factory became the manufacturing base for their aviation products, together with other Elliott industrial equipment such as Fisher control valves.

Rochester lay about 25 miles by road from the main Elliott factory at Lewisham and about 40 miles from Elliott's Borehamwood Research Laboratories. By 1953 Elliotts were renting about 185,000 ft^2 of 'modern single-storey building' at Airport Works from the Ministry of Supply, at an annual rent of £12,200 [2].

A snapshot of Elliott activity at the Rochester site at about that time may be gained from Ron Bristow, who joined Borehamwood in September 1951. Bristow went to Rochester on a day visit from Borehamwood in late 1951 or early 1952, organized by the company, as he says, 'to show us how the other half lived'. Ron remembers [3] Fisher valves being manufactured at Rochester under licence from the American company and the production of Swift and Swallow weighing machines and food processing equipment. Ron continues [3]: 'I saw the food processing business and recall that these were very large industrial-scale machines, floor-standing, certainly not for the kitchen table. There was also a Gear Division, very well equipped with complex machine tools, on a large scale. It was said that Elliotts could make any kind of gear from the largest to the smallest and to the highest degree of accuracy. Later we used instrument gears from this Division in the electro-mechanical part of the Blue Steel inertial navigation computing and in the GPI Mk 6 in the Vulcan and Victor carrying Blue Steel – [see Sect. A9.3]. There was also a Sheet Metal Division, manager Max Lichten, producing large panels, assemblies, and complex structures. Later this Division also supplied complex assemblies for the Blue Steel inertial navigation system. Then there was Fuse Division making I believe proximity shell and missile fuses, though this may have been a little later. I think the manager was a Tony Price. Naval Weapons Division was also at Rochester under a George Smithson. Both these Divisions went to Frimley to become part of Elliott Space and Weapons Automation Ltd. Radio & Radar Division was also at Rochester, in about 1956 or 7. This may have been the production facility for that Division; they had a large coil winding shop which I used on sub-contract.'

Colin Thurston also gives a snapshot of life at Rochester a couple of years after Ron Bristow's visit. Colin remembers [4] that: 'when I first went to work at Elliotts at Rochester in 1954 there were I think four or five Divisions: Fisher Governor, Naval Division, Swift & Swallow, Aviation (I think "Avionics" had not yet been coined) and perhaps a small Radar Division. Elliotts occupied about two thirds of the buildings on the Airfield site; the main very large hangar in the front was occupied by a company called Le Grand Sutcliffe and Gell which made very heavy fabrications for I think the oilfield market. The two largest [Elliott] divisions were Fisher and Swift and Swallow. Fisher made fluid control valves under licence from Fisher Governor in Marshaltown, USA. I remember being told that it was a very good business. Naval Division made Gun Directors for battleships (they were extremely large!) and still made the mechanical 'computers' which were used on board battleships to direct the guns taking into account the many unknowns of speed and weather etc. My memory of them at that age was that they were a very complex assortment of slides, levers and ball resolvers ....

'I worked in [the Swift and Swallow] Division for a while. They were trying to make an automatic scale for shops. Because of the lack of computers or miniature components etc. it was a Heath Robinson device relying on electro mechanical fingers pressing the keys on an electro mechanical calculator. Needless to say it did not work! Dickie Pollard had an office there and was clearly very senior. He seemed to come and go; apparently he suffered badly with heart problems and therefore had to take things easy. I know that he was very involved in the technical side of things. I was told that he was very close to Bagrit and Ross, having been in at the beginning with them in B and P Swift and Swift and Swallow. I was also told that he was the "P" in B & P Swift. I do know from first hand experience that he knew them both well and was often in London speaking to them.'

In early 1954 the Elliott analogue computer AGWAC was being manufactured at Rochester for the Australian Long Range Weapons Establishment – (see Chap. 4).

Sometime between July 1960 and May 1961 Elliott-Automation commenced new building activity at Rochester. By 1964 Elliott-Automation was occupying 560,000 ft^2 of space at Airport Works and a further 295,000 ft^2 were planned – see Fig. A9.1. Ron Bristow, who transferred from Borehamwood to Rochester in 1963,

Fig. A9.1 Elliott-Automation's factory at Rochester Airport, in about 1966. The photo shows a mix of old buildings, some of them dating back to the time of the aircraft manufacturer Short Brothers in the 1930s, and newer buildings erected since B & P Swift Ltd. and Elliott Brothers (London) Ltd began to occupy the site in 1946/1947. The main runway is out of view to the left of the photo

recalls [5] that 'the expansion of the avionics business was handled by transferring it to Rochester over a period of years, division by division, as new buildings were put up there and recruiting also took place there. A very large proportion of the Rochester technical staff, perhaps the majority for many years, came from Borehamwood. At the production level, many employees had worked for Shorts and many came later from the [Royal Naval] Dockyard [at nearby Chatham].'

By 1962 or 1963 Rochester had become the headquarters for Elliott Flight Automation. The move of the aviation activities from Borehamwood was a gradual one, the Transport Aircraft Controls Division being the last to move to Rochester.

The mergers and takeovers of the late 1960s left the aviation sections of Elliott-Automation relatively intact and, under the GEC banner, the spirit of Elliott innovation flourished. By the mid-1980s, the Rochester site was firmly established as a centre of excellence in the international aerospace scene. It remains so to this day, under the banner of BAE Systems. The evolution of the companies occupying the Airport Works, Rochester, over the last 50 years does, however, require a little more explanation.

The name *Elliotts* was retained at Rochester from about 1948 to 1988, surviving the merger between Elliott-Automation and English Electric in 1967 and the take-over of English Electric by GEC in 1968. The old Elliott factory at Lewisham

Fig. A9.2 Units of the automatic flight control and landing system supplied by Elliott-Automation for the Super VC10 airliners, which went into service in 1967. Similar units were supplied for the BAC 111 aircraft

closed in 1989, after a decade of decline. Radar-related R&D continued in one form or another at Borehamwood until in 2003 GEC-Marconi finally ceased all activity at the Borehamwood Laboratories. *Elliott Brothers (London) Ltd.* continued as a registered trading name of GEC Avionics until 1988. The name *Marconi* appears within the GEC empire from 1968 onwards – the original Marconi Company had been absorbed within English Electric in 1946. The formal links between GEC and British Aerospace (BAe) began in 1993. BAe was formed in 1977 as a nationalised corporation by the merger of British Aircraft Corporation, Hawker Siddeley Aviation, Hawker Siddeley Dynamics and Scottish Aviation.

As far as aerospace activity at Airport Works, Rochester, is concerned, a summary of the company name-changes since 1948 is as follows:

1962 Elliott Flight Automation Ltd.
1969 Marconi-Elliott Avionics Systems Ltd.
1978 Marconi Avionics Ltd.
1984 GEC Avionics Ltd.
1993 GEC-Marconi Avionics Ltd.
1999 BAE Systems.

According to the BAE corporate website [6], in 2006 BAE employed 90,000 people in five continents, was the largest European defence company, was amongst the top ten US defence companies, had annual sales of £14.8 billion and spent £1.2 billion per year on R&D. In 2006 the Airport Works, Rochester, housed Electronics and Integrated Solutions, which is part of the BAE Avionic Systems Division.

It is curious to note that, of the three principal sites of Elliott research and manufacturing activity that dominated the 1950s, the oldest established (Lewisham) was the first to dwindle whilst Rochester, the last one to come into the Elliott empire, outlived both Lewisham and Borehamwood. Of course, there were many other Elliott-Automation sites at the company's zenith in the mid-1960s, both in the UK and abroad, as listed in Appendix 11, but none could compare in company folklore with the great triumvirate of Lewisham, Borehamwood and Rochester.

A9.2 An Introduction to Elliott's Flight Automation Activities

The involvement of Elliott Brother (London) Ltd. in the design and manufacture of aircraft instruments dates from about 1911. Up to the end of 1947 this activity was exclusively electro-mechanical in nature and based at Elliott's Lewisham factory. Over the next 10 years, the Elliott company gradually expanded into in two broad areas of aircraft instrumentation:

- *Flight Control*: aerodynamic stability and manoeuvring, engine control, flight and engine instruments;
- *Mission Systems*: navigation, target detection, weapon aiming and delivery.

Aircraft Flight Control and Mission Systems were themselves broad categories, which in due course drew upon other specialities such as precision gyros, head-up displays, tactical radar and electronic counter-measures. The term 'aircraft' came to include 'missile'. The term *Flight Automation* then became the overall description for all the above activities.

Elliott's entry into Flight Automation was almost exclusively via defence contracts for state-of-the-art military projects, though commercial aviation projects rapidly followed. Charting the dates of these projects, and the names and locations of the company's groups that carried out the work, is beyond the scope of this book and is, in any case, a somewhat confusing story owing to the rapidity with which the Elliott-Automation management changed the names of the company's Divisions. Below we give some of the organisational landmarks. These also serve to give some indication of how the Flight Automation activities were distributed between Lewisham, Borehamwood and Rochester.

Early autopilot research at Lewisham, begun in 1947 and mostly sponsored by the Royal Aircraft Establishment (RAE) at Farnborough, was oriented towards the needs of radio-controlled *drone* pilotless aircraft for use as targets in guided weapons trials [7]. In due course this led to a contract for Elliotts to manufacture the control system for the JINDIVIK target aircraft designed by the Australian Ministry of Defence in association with RAE. JINDIVIK enhancements continued until the 1970s. The manufacture of various forms of autostabiliser equipment was continued at Lewisham until about 1952, when the work was transferred to Rochester [7].

Meanwhile, as described in Chaps. 1 and 2, the electronics expertise accumulated at Borehamwood under various Admiralty contracts was finding new outlets associated with RAE and airborne applications. Besides the huge TRIDAC analogue computer, other contracts included *Red Cheeks*, a steerable unpowered bomb designed to give a stand-off capability. It had an inertial guidance system and analogue computing components and was intended for the Canberra bomber. The preliminary trajectory calculations for Red Cheeks were first performed using the Elliott Nicholas computer in 1953 [8]. The Red Cheeks development was eventually cancelled by the government, but not before three prototype control systems had been delivered to RAE in about 1955 [5]. Elliott's experience with the Red Cheeks project led directly to the very important *Blue Steel* guided missile contract, as recounted in Sect. A9.3.

An Aviation Division was formally established at Borehamwood in late 1953 or early 1954, initially managed by W.H. Pearse. A Guided Weapons Division was established at about the same time with W R Thomas as Divisional Manager and taking responsibility for the technical specification of TRIDAC. At about this time the Aviation Division acquired two main contracts: (a) a master reference gyro (MRG B) for V bombers and stand-off guided missiles; (b) an autostabiliser/autopilot system for the English Electric Lightning fighter. The second contract 'was a fully-integrated system with fast-response electro-hydraulic actuators, capable of providing three-axis stabilisation over the full range of supersonic flight and was state of the art at the time' [9]. In Chap. 4 we described some of the Elliott analogue computing equipment associated with this activity. The Lightning autostabiliser also used large numbers of small magnetic amplifiers. Dr. E H Frost-Smith at

Fig. A9.3 An Aviation Division was established at Borehamwood in 1953/1954. Early contracts included a master reference gyro for V bombers and an autostabiliser/autopilot system for the English Electric Lightning supersonic fighter (shown in the photo). The Lightning contract used fast-response electro-hydraulic actuators to providing three-axis stabilization

Borehamwood was generally regarded as possibly the UK's leading expert on magnetic amplifiers [5].

In 1958 the Aviation Division was split into four Divisions: Aircraft Controls, Inertial Navigation, Aircraft Engine Instruments and Aviation Service and Repair [7], all brought together under the joint management of Jack Pateman and Bill Alexander. An Airborne Computing Division was formed in the Flight Automation group at Borehamwood some time before May 1959 and from this grew the digital avionics activities ably described by Peter Hearne in Chap. 12.

In the period 1958–1963 the great majority of Borehamwood's Flight Automation activities were gradually transferred to Rochester. Much of the radar work continued at Borehamwood, as did some of the avionics software development. By the time GEC took over in 1968 Rochester was firmly established as the Flight Automation headquarters.

The digital computing highlights of Elliott's *aircraft mission systems* are fully described in Chap. 12. Selected highlights of Elliott's *aircraft flight control* endeavours, as given in [1], are now listed.

1954–1957	Development of an autostabiliser/autopilot system for the English Electric Lightning fighter
1957–1960	Development of an automatic flight control system for the Blackburn Buccaneer low-level strike aircraft
1960	Electro-mechanical analogue air data computers start to be produced by Elliotts at Rochester

(continued)

(continued)	
1962–1969	Development of a failure-survival automatic landing system for the Vickers VC-10 civil airliner and flight-control systems for the BAC 1-11
1965 onwards	Supply of air data computers for the Lockheed C-5A Galaxy
1976	Aérospatiale-BAC Concorde supersonic airliners start routine automatic landings, using Elliott automatic flight control systems
1976–1977	Elliott and Boeing successfully demonstrate a limited fly-by-wire system for the Boeing YC-14 military transport prototype. (See below for a definition of *Fly-by-Wire*)
1980	First orders for fail-safe digital controls for wing flaps and slats for various models of the European Airbus – (first the A310, then the A300–600, then the A320).
1981–1984	Flight trials for the fly-by-wire system for the Anglo-French Jaguar demonstrator

Peter Hearne [10] has provided the following description of flight control terminology, to explain the meaning of Fly-By-Wire.

Electrical signalling denotes a basic electrical link between a position-pickoff on the pilot's control column and pedals and the electrical control valve on the main hydraulic control actuator. *Stability Augmentation System (SAS)* is a system complex of gyros, computers and actuator elements which measures the unstable motion of the aircraft and provides corrective inputs to the flying control system to ensure that the aircraft's flight responses and manoeuvring characteristics are maintained at an acceptable safe level.

In modern aircraft the combination of *Electrical Signalling and Stability Augmentation Systems* is usually referred to as *Fly-By-Wire*. The combination of the two systems allows aircraft which would otherwise have unacceptably difficult or dangerous handling characteristics to be flown safely and easily, either by the pilot himself or by an additional autopilot module, throughout the whole flight envelope of speed height and aircraft loading.

In the extreme case these systems are referred to as *Active Control Systems* or *Control Configured Vehicles*, where the *Fly-By-Wire* system is used to permit unusual aerodynamic configurations to be used which have valuable overall design advantages but which depend almost entirely upon the artificial stabilisation subsystem for their safe flight operation. Recent publications have shown that the German Industry was considering such concepts as early as 1939/1940 and that at least one of the early German workers in the field later became a member of the co-operative Tornado flight controls design team.

Lastly, *Inner Loop* refers mainly to the short period motion with a frequency range which extends above the third to one fifth of a cycle per second range and is concerned with motion and disturbances arising from the basic dynamic stability of the aircraft and system design.

Outer Loop refers principally to control inputs which are made to the basic stabilised aircraft to cause it to acquire or maintain certain fixed datums or profiles such as altitude, course and airspeed/mach number, or to couple it to radio or navigation system guidance signals.

Finally, returning to the idea that Flight Automation is the umbrella term for both Flight Control and Mission Systems, which themselves are embraced by the wider term *Avionics*, it is important to recall the name of the man who stands out as the initiating personality behind both Borehamwood's and Rochester's endeavours in these fields.

From about 1952 until his retirement in 1989, the leading light in Elliott's Flight Automation activities was undoubtedly J E (Jack) Pateman. Jack was born in 1921, volunteered for the RAF in 1939 and worked on radar systems throughout the war [11]. He joined Belling & Lee as a research engineer in 1946 and then moved to the Circuits Division at Borehamwood in 1948. He became one of the two principal engineers in the newly established Aviation Division in 1953. He was the Division's deputy chairman and joint managing director in 1961, becoming managing director of Elliott Flight Automation from 1971 to 1986. He finished his career as Special Director of GEC, responsible to Arnold Weinstock for many other associated activities in addition to aviation – including the chairmanship of GEC Computers. Jack was appointed CBE in 1970 and in 1981 he was awarded the Royal Aeronautical Society's Gold Medal. He died on 28 August 2004.

To quote from his obituary in *The Times* newspaper of 10 September 2004, 'Jack Pateman was one of the great engineering originals: a gifted and imaginative technician who pioneered a new industry and created a world-class business. He was of a vanishing breed of engineers who made good businessmen, the reverse being seldom, if ever, true…. Under Pateman's leadership, his avionics business won six Queen's Awards for technological achievement and another eight for export, principally in the highly-competitive US market.'

A9.3   The Blue Steel Project

In 1955 Borehamwood was awarded a contract to provide the guidance system for the *Blue Steel* missile. The *Blue Steel* system had been defined in RAE Specification 1132 dated 3 September 1954. The aircraft company AV Roe was responsible for the missile and for the modifications to the V-bombers which would be carrying it. Extensive trials were carried out, mostly in Australia, and the *Blue Steel* system became fully operational in the Royal Air Force in February 1963 – see Fig. A9.4. Six V-bomber squadrons were equipped with *Blue Steel*, which became the UK's nuclear deterrent force until 1969 when the Royal Navy took over this duty with the Polaris submarines.

Ron Bristow recalls that 'The practical limits of analogue computing in aircraft systems were essentially reached in the navigation system for the *Blue Steel* stand-off missile and the V-bombers which carried it' [12]. Here is Ron Bristow's description of the *Blue Steel* analogue computing equipment designed at Borehamwood.

'After its release from the aircraft the missile was guided entirely by inertial navigation; before release the aircraft navigation to the release point used the missile

Fig. A9.4 The *Blue Steel* missile was designed by the aircraft company A V Roe, with Elliott providing the guidance system. The high point in the development of airborne analogue computing was reached in the navigation system for the *Blue Steel* stand-off missiles and the V-bombers which carried them. The missile, which is 35 ft (10.7 m) in length, is seen here next to a Vulcan bomber. The *Blue Steel* system became fully operational in 1963. Six V-bomber squadrons were equipped with *Blue Steel,* which became the UK's nuclear deterrent force until 1969 when the Royal Navy took over this duty with the Polaris submarines

inertial navigation system and the aircraft Doppler radar to give a Doppler – inertial mixed system which was up-dated periodically from H2S position fixes. The aircraft equipment included a special version, Mk VI, of the Ground Position Indicator and a new Ground Speed Resolver. The aircraft system was essentially electro-mechanical using, for example, synchros and precision ball resolvers.

'The missile navigation system used a gyro-stabilised Space Reference Unit carrying precision accelerometers whose output provided the inputs to the integrators of the analogue computing system. The first stage of integration on each channel used a high gain 'drift –corrected' electronic operational amplifier with precision components, the second stage of integration used a velodyne with a high precision tacho-generator and high –gain amplification. Inputs to the integrator channels for Coriolis and latitude corrections and Earth's eccentricity, were computed in separate summing amplifiers and electromechanical multipliers.

'Accuracy and stability of components was of critical importance particularly during the missile's few minutes of flight when no further corrections could be made. The gyros on the Space Reference Unit contained heaters and temperature sensors to maintain their temperature within 1 degree C; even so the ambient temperature was required to be within ± 5 degrees C so that a controlled cooling system was required for the complete assembly. This was greatly to the benefit of the precision components and to the germanium transistors which were by then available and proven for low- power circuitry. Even so, achievement of the overall system accuracy required that the accuracy of individual components including integrator resistors and capacitors, tacho-generators, sine-cos potentiometers and others approached 0.01% and in a small number of instances pre-set adjustments were involved.'

A9.4 Radar History and a Guide to the Bands, Frequencies and Wavelengths Used

The word Radar is an abbreviation of *Radio detection and ranging*. Radar techniques use a family of electromagnetic waves called *microwaves*, defined as having a wavelength from about half a metre down to about 1 mm. Microwaves can be generated at a range of frequencies, where the higher frequencies correspond to the shorter wavelengths.

Detecting objects by radar is essentially a process of transmitting pulses of electro-magnetic energy, hoping that some of these are reflected back to the sender by the target. Accurately interpreting the returning pulses, or *echoes,* in respect of target size, range and bearing, calls for electronic ingenuity. Much research over many years into electronic circuitry and the design of aerials (antennas) for microwave transmitters/receivers was necessary before acceptable operational accuracy was achieved. Indeed, radar innovation is continuing today.

In the 1930s, radar techniques used relatively long wavelengths because of the practical difficulties of generating microwaves at high frequencies. Generally speaking, the shorter the wavelength the more accurate becomes the radar equipment at its job of detecting objects and determining the object's range and bearing. However, the shorter the wavelength the higher the frequency and the more complex is the associated electronics that is required for generating, transmitting and receiving the microwaves. A major advance at the start of the Second World War was the British invention of the *magnetron,* a vacuum tube oscillator that was able for the first time to generate microwaves having a wavelength as small as 10 cm.

Before the magnetron, early experimental radar had been primitive. On the Suffolk coast at Orfordness, R A (later Sir Robert) Watson-Watt and his team of Air Ministry scientists were first able to demonstrate that an aircraft could be detected at a range of about 40 miles. This was in July 1935. Two years later, as the Orfordness experiments advanced and the threat of war grew ever more serious, the British government decided to build a chain of radar stations (CH, or 'Chain Home') round the English coast from St Catherine's Point in the south to the River Tees in the north. The purpose of the CH stations was to give early warning of approaching enemy bombers. At first, no accurate information on aircraft direction or height could be provided by the 25-m wavelength electro-magnetic transmissions then in use. By the time war was declared in September 1939, CH was operating at a wavelength of 10 m, able to detect hostile aircraft at a range of up to 140 miles. The CH radar aerials would seem crude to modern eyes: they consisted of wires suspended from 107-m high lattice towers which looked rather like very tall electricity pylons. Information from the CH stations was fed to Fighter Command, which co-ordinated the RAF's response to approaching enemy aircraft.

In 1940 intensive radar research was conducted in several UK government establishments, particularly TRE and ASE (see Chap. 1). The emphasis was on devising better aerial designs and higher transmitting powers, operating at shorter wavelengths. By mid-1940 the naval radar group under J F Coales had developed their Type 282 sea-going radar set, operating at a wavelength of 50 cm. Orders were

Table A9.1 The division of radar wavelengths into bands

Band name	Approximate wavelength range (cm)	Approximate frequency range (GHz)
L	30–15	1–2
S	15–8	2–4
C	9–4	4–8
X	4–2.5	8–12
K	2.5–0.75	12–40

placed for a first batch of 200 units – under conditions of strict secrecy. For security reasons, the actual production of the 282's sub-units was distributed amongst several British companies rather than being concentrated in one place. The transmitters were to be manufactured by the General Electric Company (GEC), the modulators and generators by British Thomson-Houston (BTH), the receivers by the Marconi company and the CRT displays and consoles by A C Cossor – all under the close supervision of ASE, where the aerial system and feeders were to be designed. In terms of maintaining secrecy, it was the aerial systems that would have provided the quickest clue to the operating frequency of any radar installation.

By the end of 1942, most British ships had been fitted with several types of radar set – each set having a different aerial system and/or operating at a different wavelength, and therefore each giving a different operational benefit in the war at sea. Additional functionality such as Identification Friend or Foe (IFF) and Electronic Counter-Measures (ECM, e.g. *jamming*), were gradually introduced.

By convention, the useful range of microwaves employed in practical radar equipment has now been divided into the following bands. Table A9.1 gives the more common bands (though precise boundaries are a matter of some debate). The nomenclature L, S, C, X, K and Q follows a sequence started during the Second World War – see for example [13].

A9.5   Aviation, Radar and the Cancellation of the Nimrod AEW Project

From time to time in the anecdotes of former Elliott employees, hints appear of a certain rivalry between the radar divisions (latterly centred at Borehamwood) and the aviation divisions (latterly centred at Rochester). Both divisions had state-of-the-art technical capabilities in their respective areas, but as time went by they had different experiences of winning and executing contracts.

In truth, since about 1953 there was bound to be some overlap between the spheres of influence of the two parties. To quote John Kinnear in Chap. 11, 'military aircraft provided by far the most important market for advanced radar technology from the mid-1950s onwards. It is not surprising that, especially within the Marconi Avionics organisation, the various radar divisions became more and more closely linked with the aircraft divisions. There were, however, differences in technical cultures.' One difference lay in the approach to procurement and project management. As described by Peter Hearne in Chap. 12, by the late 1960s the airborne computing divisions at Rochester had begun to direct their efforts towards the American market. Exposure to American methods was to sharpen up Rochester's approach to UK and multi-government European projects.

As the years went by, culture differences became identified with two strong personalities: Peter Mariner who led the radar side and Jack Pateman who led the aviation side. The two teams, not surprisingly, exhibited undying loyalty to their respective hard-working leaders.

At Borehamwood, radar started as a specialist research activity dependent upon high-frequency pulse electronics. Aviation started as a systems instrumentation activity dependent upon analogue techniques. The Aviation group went on to achieve significant market presence rather earlier than did the Radar group, which had to contend with competition from established firms such as Decca, Plessey, Ferranti, EMI and BTH whose radar products were familiar to the Ministry of Defence since the 1940s. It was not until the early 1970s, with applications such as battlefield surveillance, that the Elliott radar divisions began to achieve volume sales. Meanwhile, the aviation divisions' volume sales had begun about 10 years earlier, with auto-stabilisers and air data computers.

There were perhaps two avionics projects where it is conjectured that Rochester and Borehamwood had probably questioned each other's approach to project management. Firstly, when Elliott-Automation Radar Systems and Ferranti Ltd. were funded to study and bid for the Ground Attack and Reconnaissance radar for variable geometry aircraft (VGA) in 1970, there subsequently arose a chance for the two companies to share the work on the total avionics aspects of the aircraft. As is shown in Chap. 11, senior management discussions came to an impasse over which company should be responsible for the Inertial Navigation part of the system. Rough justice was eventually imposed by the government and the Elliott side got substantially nothing.

The second project where questions were asked was the Airborne Early Warning (AEW) system carried by Nimrod aircraft. The technical setbacks of this difficult project, which in one form or another spanned the years 1964–1986, are recounted in detail in Chap. 11. The Nimrod AEW project was cancelled at the end of 1986, amidst great embarrassment to the whole of GEC. Peter Mariner's radar teams tended to get the blame for the embarrassment. This seems rather unfair in retrospect. An informal but detailed history and technical overview of the Nimrod AEW project has appeared [14] which contains much valid criticism of the manner in which the whole project was handled by the Ministry of Defence. This augments the measured account given by John Kinnear in Chap. 11. It is worth quoting extensively from [14], especially since it touches upon the GEC computer technology that lay at the heart of the project.

'The 1976 and 1977 specifications of the Nimrod AEW 3 ASR 400 were, to say the least, very demanding. They called for exceptional detection capabilities of both sea vessels and aircraft over land and sea … and with the ability to automatically initiate and track up to 400 targets. Six operator consoles (four radar, one communications and one for ESM (Electronic warfare Support Measures)) were planned ....

'The heart of the Mission System Avionics was the GEC 4080M computer that received data from the scanners, the Loral ARI-18240/1 ESM system, the Cossor Jubilee Guardsman IFF equipment and the two Ferranti FIN 1012 inertial navigation systems. The computer processed this mass of data and then displayed it on the multi-function display and control consoles where the operators communicated to the various command organizations and operational units through the Automatic Management of Radio and Intercom Systems (AMRICS).

'The fundamental problem was that the computer simply was not powerful enough. The GEC 4080M computer had a storage capacity of [only] 1 megabyte, which could be augmented via a data-bus with an additional 1.4 megabytes, giving a grand total of just 2.4 megabytes total storage capacity, small even by the standards of the time and particularly so given the task it had to perform. The computer quickly showed it was too slow for the task and soon became overloaded, at which point track continuity suffered, this then led to track duplication, which slowly increased and further overloaded the system.'

By way of background information, the GEC 4080M (introduced in 1979) was a ruggedised version of the 4080. The GEC 4000 series first appeared in 1973. The original 1973 versions could support up to 256 KB of core store, although this would have been an unthinkably large amount when the system was developed – the first one was shipped with 64 KB [15]. The data highways were mostly 16 bits, with 32-bit and some 64-bit instructions. Input/output was performed by the BMC, *Basic Multiplexor Channel*, a second dedicated processor. Up to three further I/O processors could be fitted, but for most applications one was perfectly adequate. By 1976 the 256 KB store limit was becoming quite a serious limitation. The 4082 was therefore introduced, which was a 4080 with two extra store address lines, so it could support 1 Mb of core store. The 4080 series was periodically upgraded during the late 1970s.

Continuing the account of the Nimrod AEW from [14]: 'Under test by the MOD(PE) in 1984 the Mission System Avionics (MSA), whilst falling short of the ASR 444 requirements, worked well and showed promise, but it was very unreliable and its performance changed from sortie to sortie .... All the time the costs mounted, with little sign that this grotesque white elephant would ever work as designed. Finally, common sense prevailed and in 1986 the axe finally fell ...'. The cost to the taxpayer is not known. One estimate puts it at about £1 billion [14].

A9.6   The Story of the Elliott Cassegrain Aerial Patent

There were many successful applications worldwide of the Elliott Cassegrain radar aerial, originally developed at Borehamwood. Indeed, the basic idea was so innovative that many sought to copy it – legally and illegally. The following account of how the patent was defended in America was written by the late John Kinnear, the joint author of Chap. 11 of this book, in May 2005 [16].

In 1950 The Royal Navy was considering the possibility of a small homing missile of approximately 9 in. diameter, as part of the Mopsy project – (see Chap. 11). This limited the aerial of the homing eye to approximately 6 in. maximum diameter, and to obtain the necessary tracking accuracy a high operating frequency such as 36 GHz (9 mm wavelength) would be required.

With a conventional front-fed dish aerial a monopulse feed system would obstruct the aperture and seriously degrade the performance. Alec Cochrane and Eric Whitehead came up with the concept of combining a parallel grid main-reflector with a secondary reflector surfaced by the microwave equivalent of a quarter-wave-plate. This would rotate the polarisation of the collimated beam through 90° so that it could then emerge through the main reflector. This became known as the Elliott Twist-reflecting Cassegrain Aerial, by analogy with the generally comparable optical telescope configuration. (In fact, in its originally envisaged form, the roles of Main- and Sub-reflector were reversed).

Contracts were placed in 1951 with the Marconi Research Laboratories for the tracking/illuminating aerial and with Elliott Brothers at Borehamwood for the 9-mm monopulse feed and for the missile homing eye. A team under Eric Whitehead at Borehamwood set about designing and making the instruments and components in the 9-mm band necessary for designing the monopulse feed systems and for testing the aerial. Peter Mariner joined the team early in 1951 with responsibility for the aerials group and John Kinnear, who joined the team soon after, was given the task of putting the invention into practice.

Jigs and templates were made and when the awaited materials arrived test pieces were made for the trans-reflecting parabolic reflector and the twist-reflecting plate. These were individually tested and found to perform well. The elements were then assembled into an experimental aerial and tested in November 1951. Results were encouraging and matched the performance expected of conventional forms of aerial. A prototype aerial was then designed and made, again with very satisfactory results. This confirmed the feasibility of this type of aerial. Over the next few months alternative fabrication methods were evaluated, as was also a successful version of the aerial with a twist-reflecting main reflector and a trans-reflecting sub-reflector – the true Cassgrainian configuration.

In the course of the Elliott company's general interest in cross-licencing, a number of visits by major US electronics companies took place to the Lewisham and Borehamwood sites. In the course of showing the breadth and quality of research being carried out at Borehamwood a prototype Cassegrain scanning aerial was demonstrated to American visitors. Patents were therefore applied for in the United Kingdom and for the United States.

Peter Mariner, who led the Borehamwood radar activities after Cochrane's departure in 1954, made periodic visits to US electronics companies. In the course of a visit in the mid-1960s he gained the impression that one of the US guided weapons embodied the Elliott Cassegrain type of aerial. He reported his suspicions to the Elliott-Automation Board, who decided to instigate infringement proceedings against the US government. A Chicago patent attorney, Louis Bernat, who was an acquaintance of Herzfeld, Elliott-Automation's Finance Director, was engaged to pursue the claim.

At first the validity of the patent was contested on the grounds that the aerial had been invented in the USA. By good fortune, John Kinnear was able to produce the hard-back notebook that included his records of the testing of the first aerial, with dates. These pre-dated any claim of use in the USA and the validity of the patent was accepted.

Patents with a possible military/defence use are kept out of the public domain and Governments have the absolute right to make use of them. Since the projects employing them are likely to be classified secret, the patentee has no knowledge of their use unless the original patenting company is itself involved in the design or manufacture of the equipment.

The process of discovery in the USA was yielding no positive results, so in about 1969 Peter Mariner asked John Kinnear to become personally involved and devote time to pursuing the claim on a technical basis.

The process of discovery in the USA is devious and protracted. The patentee's representative provides his attorney with a question about a possible infringement. The attorney puts this question in a form he thinks appropriate to the US Department of Justice lawyer allotted to the claim. He in turn has to establish what body in the US military or industry would be concerned with the equipment and put the question to it. That body has then to find an expert who is knowledgeable in the field to determine whether or to what extent the security classification permits an answer. The outcome is then relayed back through the chain to the plaintiff.

Since the initial enquiries had given a negative answer, John Kinnear used sources such as the reference books *Janes Warships* and *Janes Weapon Systems* to identify as many as possible of the US weapon systems that appeared to include radar. Many were eliminated because pictures or descriptions showed that different types of aerials were used. A short list of possible offenders was compiled which included systems for Air Defence, the Navy and the Army.

This enabled more specific questions to be asked, couched in a manner aimed at circumventing the likelihood of security barriers being encountered. The US Justice Department obviously had difficulties in locating the experts who could give the answers, so replies could take months. The Justice Department always acted fairly and when it became clear that the claims had substance, illustrations and/or manufacturing drawings of the specified aerial systems were provided under security cover. These confirmed or denied infringement and also enabled Elliott-Automation to estimate the production cost of each aerial which, with the numbers of equipment being ascertained from sources such as those mentioned above, led to the overall value of the infringement being estimated and royalties claimed accordingly. Both army and naval systems were involved.

In 1972, a substantial extent of infringement being by then known, and because Herzfeld needed to close Elliott-Automation's books to complete the takeover by GEC, the company requested its attorney to go to court and a date was set for hearing. At the last moment the Justice Department agreed a settlement and Judgment was given on 28 July 1972 in the sum of $1,150,000. For the above reason, claims against third parties were not taken further.

Ironically, the probing confirmed that the missile suspected by Peter Mariner of using the Elliott aerial which initiated the claim proceedings, did not do so, but that the aerial had, in fact, been included in the proposal of another company which failed to secure the contract.

Following the US judgement and the acceptance of the validity of the patents, a settlement was agreed with the UK Ministry of Defence in respect of British use. French electronics companies had also made extensive use of the Elliott Cassegrain aerial but unfortunately no patent had been taken out in France since, in 1952, no countries other than the UK, USA and The Netherlands were believed to have a significant capability in the radar field.

References

1. Preston J, Moulton MF (Oct 1992) A brief history of Rochester airport, Rev edn. Published by the Royal Aeronautical Society, Medway Branch, and sponsored by GEC Avionics Ltd., Airport Works, Rochester
2. Three-quarter page advertisement on page 11 of The Times newspaper for 11 May 1953, in compliance with the regulations of the Council of the Stock Exchange, London, 'for the purpose of giving information to the Public with regard to the Company'
3. RW (Ron) Bristow (2009) E-mail to Simon Lavington on 4 June 2009
4. Colin Thurston (2009) Elliotts, B & P swift, swift & swallow. One-page typed note prepared for Simon Lavington and dated 3 Dec 2009
5. RW (Ron) Bristow (2005) E-mail to Simon Lavington on 11 July 2005
6. See the BAe Systems corporate website at: www.baesystems.com/aboutus/evolution.htm
7. Anon, Elliott Flight Automation Limited: a brief history. This 30-page typed document gives varying degrees of coverage for the period 1948 to 1985, with some staff listings to 1992. Ron Bristow, who has a long-standing interest in Elliott company history, provided the following further information on the provenance in an e-mail to Simon Lavington in March 2007. 'It is an updated version of the document "Elliott Flight Automation History" by David Broadbent which, in 1970, had the Elliott Archive catalogue number 1004/10/1. Broadbent was a senior engineer and manager in Elliott Brothers (London) Ltd., and in particular in Elliott Flight Automation, for many years in the 1950s and 1960s. After his death, Broadbent's notes were added to by C.R Reese, an engineer and manager in Elliott Flight Automation from about 1955 to 1993, using press releases and company announcements'. The document is now part of the Marconi Archives at the Bodleian Library, Oxford
8. Rose BM (1953) Trajectory calculations for Red Cheeks. Borehamwood Internal Research Report number 328, London, 27 Aug 1953
9. Ince D (1992) Combat and competition. Newton Publishers, Swindon. ISBN 1 872308 23 6
10. Peter Hearne (2008) E-mail to Simon Lavington, 24 July 2008
11. Collinson D (2004) Obituary of Jack Pateman. Institution of Electrical Engineers, IEE Comput Control Eng Oct/Nov:8
12. RW (Ron) Bristow (2009) Analogue computing in the Blue Steel missile. One-page typed manuscript, sent to Simon Lavington on 6 Oct 2009
13. Slotnik MI (1962) Introduction to radar systems. McGraw-Hill, New York
14. Williamson B, BAe Nimrod AEW. http://www.spyflight.co.uk/Nim%20aew.htm – which consists of about a dozen pages of text plus several photographs
15. Gabriel A (1997) GEC computers. www.cucumber.demon.co.uk/geccl/
16. The story of the Cassegrain aerial patent was written by John Kinnear and sent to Simon Lavington on 2 May 2005. It was undecided whether or not to include this material in chapter 11 (on Elliott's radar activities), which was being drafted at the same time by Dr Elizabeth Laverick and John Kinnear. In the event, it was decided to place the Cassegrain patent material in an Appendix

Appendix 10
Historical Notes on Early British and Non-British Computers

A10.1 First Attempts, Worldwide

Table A10.1 gives a selection of early automatic computing machine projects of the 1940s. Not all of these projects resulted in what we would now call *stored-program computers*: some of the machines were deliberately special-purpose. The entries in the table show the speed and storage capacity on the dates when each computer first came into operation. Most machines went through several phases of development, so the performance and facilities may have been enhanced as time went by.

The intention of Table A10.1 is to show that several groups in several locations had been devising aids to automatic computation, both before and immediately after the time when John Coales' group at Borehamwood began designing the Elliott 152 computer in 1947. It is tempting, but definitely erroneous, to think that all designers were aware of all the other projects that preceded their own work. In particular, in 1947 the engineers at Borehamwood were only likely to have been familiar with the ENIAC project – initially classified but publicized in the UK from 1946 by Professor Douglas Hartree [1]. In due course some knowledge of the SSEM, EDSAC and the early stages of the Whirlwind computer projects would also have found its way to Borehamwood.

For completeness, we now give some notes and references for each of the 14 projects featured in Table A10.1. The projects are arranged chronologically.

A10.1.1   Z3

Konrad Zuse (1910–1995), who trained as a civil engineer, worked in the German aircraft industry. He decided to design and build a binary mechanical computer to help with the monotonous calculations that he was asked to perform for aerodynamic structures. The first of four machines, Z1, was completed in 1938. His third machine, Z3, was completed in 1941 and was described by him as 'the first fully operating model' [2]. It used electro-mechanical relays with a clock frequency of 5.33 Hz, held its instructions on perforated recycled 35-mm film stock, and was of

Table A10.1 A selection of the many digital calculating machines which were designed in the 1940s

Computer	Date first operational	Fxpt Add time	Multiplication time	Primary storage capacity	Memory type
Z3 (Konrad Zuse)	1941	0.8 s	3 s	64 words (~ 192 bytes)	E/Mech
ASCC (Harvard Mark I)	1943	0.3 s	6 s	72 words (~792 bytes)	E/Mech
Colossus Mark I (Bletchley Park)	1943	–	–	–	–
ENIAC (Moore School)	1945	0.2 ms	2.8 ms	20 words (~ 100 bytes)	Elect
SSEM (Manchester U.)	1948	1.2 ms	–	32 words (128 bytes)	CRT
EDSAC (Cambridge U.)	1949	1.4 ms	5.4 ms	512 words (2.25 KB)	Delay
CSIRAC (Sydney)	1949	~ 2 ms	–	384 words (~ 860 bytes)	Delay
SEAC (Washington)	1950	864 μs	2.92 ms	512 words (~ 3 KB)	Delay
SWAC (Los Angeles)	1950	62 μs	385 μs	256 words (~ 57 bytes)	CRT
Pilot ACE (NPL)	1950	64 μs	2 ms	352 words (1,408 bytes)	Delay
Ferranti Mark I (Manchester)	1951	1.2 ms	2.16 ms	256 words (1.25 KB)	CRT
UNIVAC I	1951	525 μs	2.15 ms	1000 words (~ 10.5 KB)	Delay
Whirlwind (MIT)	1951	24 μs	36–44 μs	1,024 words (2 KB)	CRT
IAS (Princeton)	1951	62 μs	713 μs	4 K words (20 KB)	CRT

Abbreviations:
For arithmetic speeds: μs = microsecond; ms = millisecond
For memory technology: delay = mercury delay lines; CRT = electrostatic storage using cathode ray tubes; E/Mech = electro-mechanical (e.g. relays or punched paper tape); Elect = electronic (e.g. flip-flops)
Storage capacity is normally quoted in terms of each computer's word-length. To help modern comparisons, the capacity is also given approximately in KB, where 1 byte is taken to be 8 bits

the sequence-controlled calculator family – see the ASCC computer below. Z3 was destroyed in the war but a replica was constructed in 1964 and is now on display at the Deutsche Museum in Munich [3].

A10.1.2   ASCC

The Automatic Sequence-Controlled Calculator (ASCC) was built between 1937 and 1943 by IBM for Harvard University and was familiarly known as the Harvard Mark I [4]. The original requirements for this machine were specified by Howard Aiken. Weighing 5 t, it was an electro-mechanical monster 51 ft long, 8 ft high and 3 ft deep. The 'programs' were punched on loops of 3 in. wide paper tape and, once set going, the machine computed automatically. In this sense, it was probably the first automatic calculating engine (but see Sect. A10.1.1). However, since it had neither a conditional branch instruction nor a means of holding a (normal) program internally in a read-write store, it was not what we would now call a 'universal' computer.

A10.1.3   Colossus

A number of *Rapid Analytical Machines* were built during the war on both sides of the Atlantic, under conditions of strict secrecy, for cryptanalysis. Many of these special-purpose machines were digital but none contained what we would now recognise as internal read/write memory. (There is one possible exception, the Aquarius machine at Bletchley Park, built towards the end of the war – see [5]). The most famous of these aids to code-breaking was the COLOSSUS series of Rapid Analytical Machines that were constructed by the GPO Research Laboratory at Dollis Hill, north London, for installation at the Government Code and Cypher School, Bletchley Park [6–8]. The first COLOSSUS came into operation at Bletchley Park in December 1943. Some months later the first of ten COLOSSUS Mark II machines started work on 1 June 1944, just in time for the Normandy landings. Each COLOSSUS Mark II contained 2,500 thermionic valves (tubes), performed binary logical operations involving 5-bit characters, and contained conditional branching – but no internal read-write memory. The mere existence of COLOSSUS was not public knowledge until the 1970s and details of its internal structure were not generally known until the 1990s. Two Colossus Mark II machines survived the war, being used in the early 1950s [5].

A10.1.4   ENIAC

In 1943 the American military planned to transfer the time-consuming task of producing ballistics tables for artillery to a special-purpose digital electronic computer called ENIAC – Electronic Numerical Integrator and Computer [9–11]. ENIAC, which was designed and built at the Moore School of Electrical Engineering at the University of Pennsylvania, was truly a tour-de-force. Weighing nearly 30 t and containing 17,468 thermionic valves (tubes), it came into operation late in 1945. It was decimal, not binary, and had no internal re-writable memory as we would now understand it. Nevertheless, when it became operational in the autumn of 1945, ENIAC immediately demonstrated the potential of high-speed automatic digital computation and was the inspiration behind most of the modern generation of early stored-program computer projects of the late 1940s. Of particular influence was a series of lectures held at the Moore School during the summer of 1946, during which a stored-program project called EDVAC (Electronic Discrete Variable Automatic Computer) was described [12]. The EDVAC report, though incomplete in minor details, was widely circulated amongst the early computer designers.

A10.1.5   SSEM

In the autumn of 1946 F C Williams, then at the Telecommunications Research Establishment (TRE), invented the *anticipation-pulse* method of storing binary information electrostatically on the phosphor-coated screen of a cathode ray tube (CRT). During the next 18 months he and T Kilburn refined the technique at the University of Manchester to produce a workable random-access memory device called the Williams Tube or, more accurately, the Williams–Kilburn Tube. A prototype stored-program computer known as the Small-Scale Experimental Machine, SSEM, or the 'Baby', was built to give the new memory system a rigorous testing. The SSEM first ran a program on 21 June 1948 [13, 14]. Although the computer was tiny and had very primitive manual input/output, it is believed to have been the first machine to demonstrate the principle of universal high-speed computing. It was enlarged and enhanced during 1948 and 1949, to produce the Manchester University Mark I [15].

A10.1.6   EDSAC

In 1946, after war-time service at TRE, Maurice Wilkes resumed his post as Director of the Mathematical Laboratory at Cambridge. During the summer of 1946 he attended the Moore School lectures (see ENIAC above) and was much influenced by the EDVAC report. Maurice Wilkes led the Cambridge team which produced EDSAC, the world's first fully functional stored-program computer [16]. EDSAC first ran a program on 6 May 1949. The Cambridge team attached great importance to the establishment of a library of subroutines. The EDSAC programming system, and a resulting book, set the standard for computer software in the early days of digital computing [17].

A10.1.7   CSIRAC

Trevor Pearcey graduated in Physics from Imperial College, London University, in 1940 and spent the rest of the war working on radar at the Air Defence Experimental Establishment (ADEE). In late 1945, he moved to Australia to work for the Radiophysics Division of the Commonwealth Scientific and Industrial Research Centre (CSIR) at Sydney. Later at Sydney, Pearcey and colleagues built the CSIR Mark I computer (subsequently re-named CSIRAC), which ran its first test program in November 1949. Development and improvement of the computer continued over the next 2 or 3 years [18].

A10.1.8   SEAC

The 'eastern' (as opposed to 'western') Laboratory of the American National Bureau of Standards, in Washington, started to build SEAC, the Standards' Eastern Automatic Computer, in 1948. The version that worked in May 1950 was probably the first American stored-program computer to become fully operational [19]. A host of American pioneering computers followed, amongst which were SWAC (the Standards' Western Automatic Computer in Los Angeles), the ERA1101, Whirlwind, UNIVAC, ORDVAC, EDVAC, IAS and RAYDAC (see [20]). SEAC was unusual in that the logic circuits of the CPU (central processing unit) were mainly implemented using germanium point-contact diodes (or *crystal diodes*, as they were called). The whole machine contained 10,500 crystal diodes and only 747 thermionic valves (tubes).

A10.1.9   SWAC

The Standards' Western Automatic Computer, designed by a team led by Harry Huskey, was a parallel machine that used the Williams–Kilburn type of CRT storage [21]. Huskey had spent 1947 at the National Physical Laboratory in Teddington in Alan Turing's group, working on modifications to the Pilot ACE design. Huskey had been offered the position at NPL on the recommendation of Professor Douglas Hartree, whom he had met whilst working on the ENIAC project. The SWAC project started in January 1949. It came into operation in August 1950, at which time it was the fastest stored-program computer in existence.

A10.1.10   Pilot ACE

Alan Turing had published a landmark theoretical paper describing the concept of a universal computer in 1936 [22]. Although familiar through personal contact with John von Neumann and the EDVAC and IAS work in America (see below), Turing had no need or inclination to follow anyone else's design for a stored-program computer. Working at the National Physical Laboratory (NPL) at Teddington, near London, on 19 February 1946 Turing presented the Executive Committee of NPL with his complete design for an electronic stored-program computer [23, 24]. The machine, which he called the Automatic Computing Engine (ACE), was estimated by Turing to cost £11,200. Various delays, changes of staff and other factors [25] meant that a Pilot model of ACE did not come into operation until May 1950.

A10.1.11   Ferranti Mark I

The Manchester University Mark I computer was the successor to the SSEM (see Sect. A10.1.5). The Manchester Mark I became fully operational (i.e. with program-controlled input/output and drum transfers) in the autumn of 1949 [15]. The Lancashire-based company Ferranti Ltd. re-engineered this prototype and produced the Ferranti Mark I [26]. The first production machine was delivered to Manchester University in February 1951. One further Ferranti Mark I was delivered (to Canada) and then seven improved Mark I * (*Mark I* Star) computers were produced from 1953 onwards.

A10.1.12   UNIVAC I

Presper Eckert and John Mauchley, the main driving forces of the team which built ENIAC (see above), set up their own computer manufacturing company. Their first contract, from the Northrop Aircraft Company, resulted in a stored-program computer called BINAC [27]. This worked under test conditions in August 1949 but is believed never to have become fully operational at Northrop. Meanwhile, Eckert and Mauchley were designing a much larger machine called UNIVAC. This was intended for commercial data processing, whereas most other early computers focussed on applications in science and engineering. UNIVAC had hardware character-handling facilities and provision for bulk input/output from/to magnetic tape units (called *Uniservos*) in parallel with main computing activities. The first production UNIVAC was delivered to the United States Census Bureau on 31 March 1951 [28].

A10.1.13   Whirlwind

Jay Forrester led a team based in the Servomechanisms Laboratory at the Massachusetts Institute of Technology (MIT) that began work in 1944 on a government-sponsored project called ASCA (Airplane Stability & Control Analyser). The original implementation was analogue but, by 1946, Forrester had persuaded the funding authorities that a general-purpose, real-time, digital computer would be more appropriate. The project was re-named Whirlwind. After much difficulty developing a special 'holding-beam' version of electrostatic CRT storage, Whirlwind was working reliably enough to do useful work by March 1951 [29, 30]. The project's designers placed great emphasis on speed and reliability. Being intended for real-time defence applications, Whirlwind forms a useful yardstick with which to measure the progress of the Elliott 152 computer at Borehamwood – see Chap. 2.

A10.1.14   IAS

John von Neumann's group at the Institute for Advanced Study (IAS), Princeton University, was a source of inspiration for at least five other early computer design groups in America. As part of the arrangements for financial support, IAS regularly sent working drawings to teams at Los Alamos (who produced the MANIAC computer), the University of Illinois (ORDVAC and ILLIAC), Oak Ridge National

Laboratory, Argonne National Laboratory (AVIDAC, ORACLE) and the Rand Corporation (JOHNNIAC). The Institute's own computer, simply called the IAS machine, was parallel, employing Williams–Kilburn CRT storage; it was performing useful computation by the summer of 1951 [31].

Of the above 14 projects, the latter ten were universal stored-program computers. A study of Appendix 1 shows that the internal architecture of the Elliott 152 computer, with its low-level functional parallelism, was rather different from any of the architectures represented by Table A10.1. This was mainly because of Borehamwood's unusual requirements for rapid real-time, on-line computation. Only one of the computers in the Table, namely Whirlwind, had a multiplication time faster than the Elliott 152's figure of 60 μs. The 152's primary storage (RAM) of 256 words, equivalent to 512 bytes, looks small in comparison to other contemporary machines, though the Elliott 152 did have separate read-only memory for instructions.

A10.2 Into the Marketplace: The Rich Heritage of British Designs

To the five British projects featured in Table A10.1 should be added the pioneering efforts at other UK locations, notably at: Birkbeck College, University of London; Imperial College, University of London; the J. Lyons Catering Company, London; the Telecommunications Research Establishment, Malvern; the Post Office Research Laboratory, Dollis Hill; the Atomic Energy Research Establishment, Harwell; and Elliott's own activity at Borehamwood. All these early computing projects are described in [32]. Most of them are featured in Fig. 1.3, indicating the probable influence of war-time electronic know-how on the development of early British computers.

Between the years 1948 and 1970, approximately 80 distinct models of stored-program digital computer were designed in the UK, resulting in nearly 3,000 installed machines of British provenance. It is estimated that the total number of UK-designed computers in operation in Britain rose very approximately as follows:

By 1950 = 4 (all research prototypes);
By 1955 = 30 (the majority in science and engineering applications);
By 1960 = 400;
By 1965 = 1,000;
By 1970 = 2,800 (the majority in business and commercial applications).

The gradual dominance of business applications is a factor that became important during the period of company mergers and takeovers, described in Chap. 13. Notice that the above totals of computers do not include those of foreign manufacture. From the autumn of 1956 American-designed machines, and particularly those of IBM, began to make their presence felt.

Focussing for the moment on production models, we may eliminate from the full list (of 80 British types) various one-off machines that were not made available on the open market. In particular, we eliminate the pioneering computers designed at universities and those designed at government research establishments.

The elimination of all of the one-off models leaves 12 UK companies on the list. Between them they were responsible for approximately 49 computer types that came onto the market between 1951 and 1970, as shown in Table A10.2.

Although *minicomputers* of the size of a large cupboard or chest-of-drawers were beginning to appear by the end of the period under review – the Digital Equipment

Table A10.2 The 12 UK computer companies whose products appeared on the market between 1951 and 1970

Company, computer	Date first working	Approx. number sold, up to 1970
AEI		
Metrovic MV950	1956	6
AEI 1010	1960	10 (?)
Computer Technology Ltd.		
Computer Technology Modular One	1968	30 (?)
Digico		
Digico Digiac	1966	20 (?)
Digico Micro 16	1968	50 (?)
Elliott Brothers (London) Ltd., Borehamwood[a]		
Elliott 401	1953	1
Elliott 402	1955	10
Elliott 405	1956	33
Elliott 802	1958	7
Elliott 803	1959	211
Elliott 900 series	1963	700 (?)
Elliott 503	1963	32
Elliott 502	1964	3
Elliott 4100 series	1966	160 (?)
EMI[b]		
Emidec 1100	1960	21 (?)
Emidec 2400	1961?	20 (?)
English Electric[c]		
Deuce series	1955	33
KDN2	1962	20 (?)
KDP10	1962	5 (?)
KDF6	1963	15 (?)
KDF9	1963	29 (?)
KDF8	1964	5 (?)
KDF7	1965	15 (?)
System 4	1967	?
Ferranti Ltd.[d]		
Ferranti Mark 1	1951	2
Ferranti Mark 1 star	1953	7
Ferranti Pegasus	1956	40
Ferranti Mercury	1957	19

(continued)

Table A10.2 (continued)

Company, computer	Date first working	Approx. number sold, up to 1970
Ferranti Perseus	1959	2
Ferranti Sirius	1961	16
Ferranti Apollo	1961	?
Ferranti Atlas	1962	3[e]
Ferranti Poseidon	1962?	5 (?)
Ferranti Argus series	1963?	150+ (?)
Ferranti Orion	1963	13
GEC		
CDL 1301 (jointly with BTM, see below)	1961	?
GEC 90xx series	1964?	?
GEC S7	1966?	?
ICT/ICL (incorporating BTM)[f]		
BTM HEC	1953	8 (?)
BTM 1200 series	1954?	80 (?)
ICT 1300 series (see also under GEC)	1961	125 (?)
ICT 558 FCC	1962	(?)
ICT 1500	1963?	70 (?)
ICT 1600	1965?	(?)
ICT 1900 series	1964	284 to 15 Feb 1967, plus many more
Leo Computers Ltd.[g]		
Leo II	1957	11
Leo III	1963	94
Marconi		
TAC	1959	7
Myriad I and II	1963, 1968	50 (?)
STC[h]		
Stantec Zebra	1958	45 (?)

[a] The Elliott entry excludes one-off designs (Nicholas, 153, etc.) and special ARCH process-control variants

[b] The EMI entry excludes the EMI Electronic Business Machine, also known as the EMI CP407 or, colloquially, as the *BMC Payroll Computer*. This computer was delivered to BMC's Austin Longbridge factory in 1958

[c] The English Electric System 4 was based on the design of the RCA Spectra, which was compatible with the IBM/360 series of computers

[d] The Ferranti entry excludes the Ferranti Hermes, for which no details have come to hand

[e] In addition to the three Atlas 1 machines, two reduced-facility Atlas 2 computers were delivered

[f] The ICT entry includes the ICT 1500 and ICT 1600, even though these were based on American designs – respectively the RCA 301 and the RCA 3301

[g] The original Leo computer (1951) is excluded because it was a one-off design for in-house use (see also Sect. A10.3)

[h] The Stantec Zebra's design was a collaboration between mathematicians from the Laboratory of the Netherlands Postal and Telecommunications Services at Leidschendam (particularly W L van der Poel) and engineers from STC [33]. The machines were built in STC's Monmouth factory. STC itself was a long-established component manufacturer for the telephone, telegraph, radio and telecommunications industries. The company was owned by ITT of America until the mid-1980s

Corporation's iconic PDP8 machine was available from mid-1965 – most of the computers in Table A10.2 were classed as *mainframes,* the earlier ones occupying a considerable floor area, and represented a considerable investment for the customer. Computers of the 1950s and 1960s were stand-alone: they were not generally interconnected because there were no compelling operational reasons to justify the implied expense of doing this. In any case, incompatibility of manufacturers' input/output interfaces and software made interconnectivity difficult to engineer.

The hardware of the earlier machines in the Table, such as Elliott computers up to the 405 (1956) and Ferranti computers up to Perseus (1959) were based on thermionic valves (tubes). The first machine in Table A10.2 to be based on transistors was the AEI Metrovic MV950 (1956), which was the production version of a Manchester University prototype that first ran a program in November 1953 [15, 34] – believed to have been the world's first transistor computer. The Stantec Zebra (1958) used both valves and transistors in approximately equal numbers [33], illustrating the chronological overlap of technologies. Borehamwood's excursions into transistor technology are recounted in Chap. 10.

It is important to bear in mind the huge range of price and performance represented by the computers listed in Table A10.2 and the consequential differences in targeted market area. At one extreme, the Ferranti Atlas was a supercomputer whose designers at Manchester University had striven to provide the highest computational speeds possible with contemporary technology [15, 35]. The Atlas design group, led by Tom Kilburn, began work in the autumn of 1956 and the first Ferranti production model was inaugurated in December 1962. With a price tag in excess of £1 million, it was considered by many to be the most powerful computer in the world at that time. The Ferranti sales staff equated one Atlas to four IBM 7094 computers in terms of work throughput. Atlas pioneered several technological firsts, including virtual storage and automatic paging for hardware memory management.

Like many ground-breaking projects before and since, the development costs of the Atlas project spiralled. Some idea of the uncertainty can be gauged by Ferranti's estimates of the works cost of the first production model, which rose from £375,000 in February 1959 to £650,000 in November 1960 to £930,000 in October 1962 [15]. Ferranti only built three Atlas computers and three smaller Atlas 2 computers, one of the smaller machines forming the basis of novel work carried out at Cambridge University which resulted in the Cambridge Titan computer. In the harsh light of market reality, Atlas sales were distinctly disappointing.

At the other extreme in Table A10.2, the Metrovic MV950 had a very modest performance and correspondingly modest cost. It used a 4K word drum main store and junction transistors with a pedestrian high-frequency response, necessitating a relatively low clock frequency of 57 kHz. The 32-bit fixed-point multiplication time was 8 ms plus the mean access-time of the drum of 10 ms [34]. Although pioneering in the sense of early use of transistor technology, the MV950's impact on the open market was minimal: all six production MV950s were used internally within the Metropolitan-Vickers group for engineering design purposes.

Although all the earlier computers in Table A10.2 were, in principle, general-purpose machines, their usefulness in terms of cost-effectiveness was primarily to be seen in scientific and engineering applications. This was obviously not the only market area of interest to the manufacturers featured in Table A10.2. By 1965, ICT and Leo Computers Ltd. were forging ahead with business and commercial applications. In the specialized field of industrial control and automation, Elliott-Automation had become the major player in 1965, closely followed by Ferranti and English Electric. Finally, in the military arena Elliott-Automation, Ferranti and Marconi were competing for contracts in defence areas such as aerospace, field artillery control and ship-borne Action Information Systems.

To get the complete picture of UK computer usage, we should of course add imported computers to the list of machines given in Table A10.2. The first non-British computer to reach these shores, an IBM 650, was installed in October 1956. IBM quickly came to dominate the European markets. In Britain, IBM computers accounted for about 18% of all UK installations in 1962 and about 29% by 1967. IBM's market share by value was even more dramatic, having risen to about 40% by 1967 [36]. The spread of American competition was eventually seen as a serious threat by the UK government, which fostered remedial actions in the period 1964–1968 as discussed in Chap. 13.

A10.3 Further Details of Three British Computer Manufacturers

Below we give the historical and technical background to three of the companies featured in Table A10.2. The intention is to add perspective to our main subject, the Elliott group of companies, by sketching the development of computing activity in three organisations that at various times became Elliott's market rivals and/or partners. The politics of the partnerships are described in Chap. 13.

A10.3.1 English Electric Computers and LEO Computers

As far as the *sale* of digital computers is concerned, English Electric and its subsidiary Marconi were rather slower off the mark than either Elliott or Ferranti – (see also Table 6.5 in Chap. 6). However, English Electric first became *interested* in computers relatively early. Sir George Nelson (later Lord Nelson), the CEO of English Electric, was a member of the Executive Council of the National Physical Laboratory (NPL). In January 1949 A C D (Colin) Haley was recruited by English Electric to lead a team of about a dozen engineers and technicians on loan to NPL [37]. The English Electric team co-operated with J H (Jim) Wilkinson, E A (Ted) Newman and others at NPL to complete the implementation of the Pilot ACE computer which first ran a program on 10 May 1950 and went into full-time service at NPL in February 1952. Computer design continued in-house at NPL between 1953 and 1957 on the full (final) version of ACE. The full ACE first ran a program late in 1957 [32].

Table A10.3 Deliveries of English Electric DEUCE computer

Delivery date	Quantity: customer
2/55	1: EE Nelson Research Lab., Stafford
Spring 55	1: National Physical Lab., Teddington
5/55	1: RAE, Farnborough. *This first RAE machine was known as Gert.*
	1: EE NRL, Marconi House, London
	1: EE, Main Works, Stafford. *Used for transformer design*
6/56	2: Bristol Aeroplane Co., Filton
8/56	1: New South Wales University of Technology, Sydney. *Computer known as UTECOM*
9/56	1: Atomic Weapons Research Establishment, Aldermaston
12/56	1: RAE, Farnborough. *This second RAE machine was known as Daisy*
2/57	1: Bristol Siddeley Aero-Engine Co., Patchway *(Some say two computers delivered)*
6/57	1: BP, Aldgate, London
9/57	1: Short Bros & Harland, Belfast
11/57	2: EE Co. (later British Aircraft Corporation), Warton, near Preston
2/58	2: EE Mechanical Engineering Lab., Whetstone, Leicester
?/58	1: Glasgow University
?/58	1: Central Bureau of Statistics, Norsk Regnesentral, Oslo
11/58	1: EE Co., Luton
	3: Ministry of Agriculture, Fisheries & Food, Guildford
?/60	1: Liverpool University *(later (1964) moved to Stafford Technical College)*
	1: Queens University Belfast
	1: National Engineering Labs. (DSIR), East Kilbride
	1: Central Electricity Generating Board, London
	2: EE Computers Bureau, Kidsbrove
	1: UK Atomic Energy Authority, Capenhurst
?/60	1: EE Co., Liverpool
	1: Admiralty Signals Research Establishment, Teddington
	1: EE Co., Stafford
Total:	33 (This is the generally agreed figure, pending further evidence)

First deliveries of the English Electric DEUCE computer, the production version of the NPL Pilot ACE, occurred in 1955. There seems to be no surviving definitive list of DEUCE deliveries but Table A10.3, based on the evidence in [38], gives the general picture. It is interesting that 12 out of the 33 machines remained within the English Electric empire, where they were put to work on a range of engineering problems and computing bureau activity.

As summarised in [32], English Electric developed three smaller computers during the late 1950s. The motivation for these came from the company's involvement with digital data- logging equipment for steel rolling mills and electricity generation plants. The first of these computers, the KDN2, used transistor circuits and was available from 1962. From the KDN2, two further small computers were developed: the KDF7 for general process control applications and the KDF6 for commercial data processing. These were all 16-bit word-length machines and approximately 40 of them were sold. These developments took place at English

Electric's Stafford site and later at a special factory at nearby Kidsgrove. The 'KD' in the above computers' names stood for *Kidsgrove*.

Concurrent with the development of 16-bit machines, English Electric was developing two larger computers [32]. Firstly, and as a result of a long-standing technical arrangement with the RCA company in America, English Electric built a version of the RCA501 known as the KDP10 (later upgraded and known as the KDF8). Intended for commercial data processing, about ten KDP10 and KDP8 machines were sold. Secondly, a team led by A C D Haley designed a high-performance computer of considerable historical interest called the KDF9 [39–41]. First deliveries of the KDF9 occurred in 1963 and approximately 29 were sold between 1964 and 1970 [42].

English Electric's Computer Division merged with Leo Computers Ltd. in April 1963, to form a company called English Electric Leo Computers Ltd. The reasons why this merger made sense for both partners were two-fold. Firstly, English Electric wished to broaden its computer horizons by moving away from reliance on the scientific field and towards participation in the rapidly expanding commercial data-processing market. Leo Computers were well established in the commercial data-processing area. Secondly, the management of Leo Computers realised that the tasks of enhancing their current product, LEO III, and then designing a future replacement for it, were beyond their present technical resources. English Electric was able to gain control of Leo Computers in a reasonably smooth manner.

The origin of Leo computers, which grew out of the J. Lyons' catering company, is a fascinating story [32]. The Leo Computer Company designed and built two follow-on computers, LEO II and LEO III. Briefly, the first LEO II was delivered in May 1957 to J Lyons & Co. Ltd. and the 11th and last machine went in January 1961 to the Ford Motor Co. at Dagenham. In 1962 the first LEO III became a bureau machine at Leo Computers Ltd. in London. The last of 94 LEO III computers was delivered to the London Boroughs Management Service Unit in 1967. Actually, LEO III was enhanced during the period 1962–1967 and three varieties eventually became available:

LEO III	Store access: 13.5 μs; time for a simple instruction: 34 μs
LEO 360	Store access: 6.0 μs; time for a simple instruction: 12 μs
LEO 326	Store access: 5.0 μs; time for a simple instruction: 5 μs

For more on the Leo story, see [43].

In 1964 English Electric Leo Computers Ltd absorbed the computer activities of the Marconi section of English Electric, to form English Electric-Leo- Marconi Computers Ltd. (EELM).

A10.3.2 Marconi Computers

Since 1946 the Marconi company, based in the south-east of England, had developed relatively independently from the main English Electric empire whose manufacturing centre was in the midlands and north-west of the country. Marconi had created its own computer division at Chelmsford for applications relating to radar data processing, air defence and air traffic control. As far as computers are concerned, only two Marconi designs had emerged before the GEC takeover of English Electric in 1968. In 1961 the Chelmsford division produced the Marconi *Transistorised Automatic Computer* or TAC. This was a 20-bit word machine, of which about seven were built. It had a 4K word main memory and was microcoded. The original target application was for a defence project but the TAC subsequently found a use for tasks such as nuclear power station control. In one such role, a TAC remained in operation from 1961 to 2004 [44].

In 1963 came the Marconi Myriad computer, a machine aimed at specialist military and process-control applications. The company had started to produce integrated circuits in 1962 and the Myriad was an early example of the use of integrated circuits in a digital computer. In 1968, the Marconi Myriad II computer was produced, which had the same instruction set as Myriad I but at a lower cost. Both machines had a 24-bit word and offered up to eight levels of interrupt priority and were designed particularly for real-time applications such as air traffic control and message switching [45].

References

1. Hartree DR (1946) The ENIAC, an electronic computing machine. Nature 158(4015), 20 Apr and 12 Oct
2. Zuse K (1980) Some remarks on the history of computing in Germany. In: Metropolis N, Howlett J, Rota G-C (eds) A history of computing in the twentieth century. Academic Press, New York, pp 611–627. ISBN: 0-12-491650-3. This book is a compilation of papers, the original versions of which were presented at the International Research Conference on the History of Computing, Los Alamos, 10–15 June 1976
3. http://user.cs.tu-berlin.de/~zuse/Konrad_Zuse/en/rechner_z3.html
4. Campbell-Kelly M, Aspray W (1996) Computer: a history of the information machine. Basic Books, New York. ISBN 0-465-02989-2
5. Lavington S (Apr/June 2006) In the footsteps of Colossus; a description of Oedipus. IEEE Ann Hist Comput 28(2):44–55
6. Flowers TH (July 1983) The design of Colossus. Ann Hist Comput 5(3):239–252
7. Coombs AWM (July 1983) The making of Colossus. Ann Hist Comput 5(3):253–259
8. Chandler WW (July 1983) The installation and maintenance of Colossus. Ann Hist Comput 5(3):260–262
9. Burks AW, Burks AR (1981) The ENIAC: the first general-purpose electronic computer. Ann Hist Comput 3(4):310–389; commentary on pages 389–399
10. Eckert JP (1980) The ENIAC. In: Metropolis N, Howlett J, Rota G-C (eds) A history of computing in the twentieth century. Academic Press, New York, pp 525–540
11. Mauchley JW (1980) The ENIAC. In: Metropolis N, Howlett J, Rota G-C (eds) A history of computing in the twentieth century. Academic Press, New York, pp 541–550
12. von Neumann J (1945) Report on the EDVAC. Photocopied for distribution, June 1945. Later incorporated in: Burks AW, Goldstine HH, von Neumann J (June 1946) Preliminary discussion of the logical design of an electronic computing instrument. Institute for Advanced Study, Princeton, NJ. Reprinted in Randell B (1973) The origins of digital computers. Springer, Berlin
13. Williams FC, Kilburn T (Sept 1948) Electronic digital computers. Lett Nat 162:487

14. Williams FC, Kilburn T, Tootill GC (Feb 1951) Universal high-speed digital computers: a small-scale experimental machine. Proc IEE 98 Part 2(61):13–28
15. Lavington SH (1975, 1998) A history of Manchester computers. First edition published in 1975 by the National Computing Centre, Manchester. Second edition published by the British Computer Society, Swindon in 1998. ISBN 0-902505-01-8
16. Wilkes MV (July 1975) Early computer developments at Cambridge: the EDSAC. Radio Electron Eng 45:332–335
17. Wilkes MV, Wheeler DJ, Gill S (1951) The preparation of programmes for an electronic digital computer, with special reference to the EDSAC and the use of a library of subroutines. Addison-Wesley, Cambridge
18. McCann D, Thorne P (2000) The last of the first: CSIRAC, Australia's first computer. Department of Computer Science & Software Engineering, University of Melbourne, Melbourne
19. Astin AV (1955) Computer development (SEAC and DYSEAC) at the National Bureau of Standards. National Bureau of Standards Circular 551, U.S. Government Printing Office, Washington, DC, 25 Jan 1955
20. See for example the papers in: Review of electronic digital computers, a joint AIEE/IRE Computer Conference held at Philadelphia, Dec 1951
21. Huskey HD (1980) The SWAC: the National Bureau of Standards Western Automatic Computer. In: Metropolis N, Howlett J, Rota G-C (eds) A history of computing in the twentieth century. Academic, New York, pp 419 – 430
22. Turing AM (1937) On computable numbers, with an application to the Entscheidungsproblem. Proc London Math Soc, Ser 2, 42:230–265. Corrigenda 43:544–546
23. Turing AM (1946) Proposals for the development in the mathematics division of an Automatic Computing Engine (ACE). Report E882, Executive Committee, NPL, Feb 1946. Reprinted Apr 1972 as NPL Report Co. Sci. 57
24. Carpenter BE, Doran RW (Aug 1977) The other Turing machine. Comput J 20(3):269–279
25. Hodges A (1983) Alan Turing: the enigma. Burnett Books, London. ISBN 0-09-152130-0
26. Pollard BW, Lonsdale K (1953) The construction and operation of the Manchester University computer. Proc IEE 100(Part 2):501–512 (Note: this paper refers to the production Ferranti Mark I, installed at Manchester University)
27. Stern N (July 1979) BINAC: a case study in the history of technology. Ann Hist Comput 1(1):9–20
28. Stern N (1981) From ENIAC to UNIVAC: an appraisal of the Eckert-Mauchly computers. Digital Press, Bedford
29. Redmond KC, Smith TM (1980) Whirlwind; the history of a pioneer computer. Digital Press, Bedford. ISBN 0-932376-09-6
30. Everett RR (1980) Whirlwind. In: Metropolis N, Howlett J, Rota G-C (eds) A history of computing in the twentieth century. Academic, New York, pp 365–384
31. Bigelow J (1980) Computer development at the Institute for Advanced Study. In: Metropolis N, Howlett J, Rota G-C (eds) A history of computing in the twentieth century. Academic, New York, pp 291–310
32. Lavington SH (1980) Early British computers. Manchester University Press, Lavington. ISBN: 0-7190-0803-4. Text available at: http://ed-thelen.org/comp-hist/EarlyBritish.html
33. Anon (1957) Stantec Zebra electronic digital computer. 11-page illustrated technical brochure published by Standard Telephones and Cables Ltd., Information Processing Division, Newport, Monmouthshire. Document C/MT -20 Ed 1/3, dated 1957. See: http://archive.computerhistory.org/resources/text/Standard/Standard.StantecZebra.1957.102646083.pdf. See also the later (1961) version at: http://archive.computerhistory.org/resources/text/Standard/Stantec.Zebra.1961.102646082.pdf. Finally, refer to: Davies D (Oct 1975) Whatever happened to the Stantec Zebra? Nature 257(5527):544–546
34. Anon (1957) The Metrovick 950 digital computer. 18-page technical brochure number SP/7655/1. The Metropolitan-Vickers Electrical Co. Ltd., Trafford Park, Manchester

35. Kilburn T, Edwards DBG, Lanigan MJ, Sumner FH (Apr 1962) One level storage system. IRE Trans Electron Comput EC-11(2):223–235

36. Campbell-Kelly M (1989) ICL: a business and technical history. Oxford University Press, Oxford. ISBN 0-19-853918-5

37. Haley ACD (Aug 1975) The inconspicuous computer. Radio Electron Eng 45:409–410

38. The tentative delivery list for DEUCE computers is based on DEUCE information obtained from several sources, principally: http://users.tpg.com.au/eedeuce/ and http://www.old-computers.com/museum/computer.asp?st=1&c=1089 and http://www.members.optusnet.com.au/deucepix/pjwalker.htm

39. Allmark RH, Lucking JR (1962) Design of an arithmetic unit incorporating a nesting store. In: Proceedings of the IFIP Congress, Munich, 1962, pp 694–698. Reprinted in: Bell & Newell (1971) Computer structures. McGraw-Hill, New York

40. Davis GM (1960) The English electric KDF9 computer system. Comput Bull Dec:119–120

41. A 34-page English Electric KDF9 manual is available at: http://archive.computerhistory.org/resources/text/English_Electric/EnglishElectric.KDF9.1961.102641284.pdf

42. A full delivery list is given at the KDF9 section of the Our Computer Heritage website: http://www.ourcomputerheritage.org/wp/upload/CCS-N4X1.pdf

43. See: http://www.leo-computers.org.uk/pageone.htm. This is the website of the LEO 'fan club', contributed to by former LEO employees and users. It contains lots of information including a list of books on the Leo computers

44. John Blackburn, in correspondence with Simon Lavington, July 2007. John described the technical and historical background to the Marconi TAC computer that has been restored to working condition at the National Museum of Computing, Bletchley Park

45. Anon (1970) Myriad II computer system. 40-page technical brochure published in 1970 by Marconi-Elliott Computer Systems, Borehamwood, London

Appendix 11
Elliott-Automation Group Structure and Factories in 1965

A11.1   List of Elliott-Automation Companies as at May 1965

The following is transcribed from the organisational and hierarchical diagram that appears in the booklet entitled *Elliott-Automation Reports and Accounts for the year ended 31 December 1964*. This was presented at the company's Annual General Meeting held on 24 June 1965.

For clarity, the original complex diagram that appeared on pages 4 and 5 of the June 1956 Report has been re-cast as a numbered list, the numbering representing the hierarchical structure. To aid analysis, a distinction is made between:

Companies (denoted in **bold** below);
Divisions or sections within companies;
Research laboratories (denoted in *italics* below).

The original diagram, which is dated May 1965, did not contain any numbering or textual annotations. Where known, the physical location of a company has been added below.

1. **Elliott-Automation Limited**. This is the headquarters company. 16 subsidiary groups of companies (numbered 2–17 below) report directly to this headquarters company. The Elliott-Automation Ltd. headquarters contains the following sections, principally located at 29 Portland Place, London: group accounts; budget co-ordination; internal audit; organisation and methods; group establishment services; group personnel management; legal department; group patents department; information services.

2. **Elliott Process Automation Ltd.** This has the following Divisions:

   a. Chemical and Oil Division
   b. Metals, Paper, Rubber and Plastics Division
   c. Mining and Minerals Division
   d. Power Generation Division
   e. Public Utilities and General Instruments Division
   f. Quality Control Division (Oil and Chemicals)
   g. Quality Control Division (Metals and Minerals)

    h. **Palatine Precision Ltd.**
    i. **Rotameter Manufacturing Company Ltd.**, mostly located at Croydon
    j. Spares and Repairs Division
    k. Systems Research Division
    l. *Fluid Dynamics Laboratory*
    m. (jointly owned) **Rotron Controls Ltd.**
    n. (majority owned) **Hallikainen Instruments Inc. USA**

3. **Elliott Flight Automation Ltd.,** mostly based at Rochester

    a. Transport Aircraft Controls Division
    b. Military Aircraft Controls Division
    c. Aircraft Engine Instruments Division
    d. Inertial Navigation Division
    e. Airborne Computing Division
    f. Airborne Display Division
    g. Flight Instruments Division
    h. Gyro Division
    i. Automatic Test Equipment Division
    j. Precision Test Equipment Division
    k. Aviation Service and Repair Division
    l. *Flight Automation Research Laboratory*
    m. *Fuel Flow Laboratory*

4. **Elliott Space and Weapon Automation Ltd.,** mostly located at Frimley, Surrey

    a. Space and Guided Weapons Division
    b. Naval Weapons Division
    c. Mobile Computing Division
    d. Airspace Control Division
    e. Radar Control Division
    f. Fuze Division
    g. Trainer and Simulator Division
    h. Magnetic Tape Systems Division
    i. *Space Development & Weapons Research Laboratory*

5. **Elliott-Automation Radar Systems Ltd.,** mostly located at Manor Way, Borehamwood

    a. Airborne Radar Division
    b. Airborne Communications Division
    c. Mobile Search Radar Division
    d. Radar & Communications Service & Repair Division
    e. *Radar & Communications Research Laboratory*

6. **Elliott-Automation Nucleonics Ltd.** partly based at Lewisham

    a. Reactor Control Division
    b. **Isotope Developments Ltd.**

c. Baldwin Nuclear Instruments Division
d. Sonics Division

7. **Elliott Medical Automation Ltd.**

a. Medical Data Systems Division
b. Medical Equipment Division; **Godart CPI Ltd.**

8. **A E Dean & Co. (X-Ray Apparatus) Ltd.**

9. **Elliott Brothers (London) Ltd.**

a. Microelectronics Group:

i. Microelectronics Sales Division
ii. Modular Circuits Division
iii. Integrated Circuits Division
iv. *Microelectronics Research Laboratory*

b. Electrical Measurement Division

i. Servo Components Division
ii. Precision Potentiometer Division

c. **E-A Space and Advanced Military Systems Ltd.**
d. **Elliott Marine Automation Ltd.**

i. Marine Systems Division
ii. Marine Equipments Department
iii. Marine Service Department

e. **Elliott Traffic Automation Ltd.**
f. **Elliott Electronic Tubes Ltd.,** mostly located at the Borehamwood main site

i. Telecommunications Division
ii. Radar and Communication Instruments Division

g. Automation Services Group

i. **E-A Technical Services Ltd.**
Technical Centres at: Birmingham, Bramhall, Bristol, East Kilbride, Newcastle, Newport, Sheffield, Southampton
Factory Centres at: Lewisham, Park Royal, Rochester
ii. **Elliott-Automation Services Ltd.**
Installation Division

10. **Londex Ltd.**

11. **E-A Control Valves Ltd.**

a. **Fisher Governor Company Ltd.,** mostly located at Rochester
b. **Farris Engineering Ltd.**
c. **Gordon Valves Ltd.** Continental Division

12. **Elliott-Automation Computers Ltd.,** located at the Borehamwood
    main site

    a. Scientific Computing Division
    b. National Computing Division
    c. Educational Computing Division
    d. Data processing Division
    e. Computing Services Division
    f. Computer Maintenance Division
    g. *Computing Research Laboratory*

13. **Elliott Mechanical Automation Ltd.**

    a. **Spencer (Melksham) Ltd.**
    b. **Spencer-Weatherly Ltd**.
    c. Industrial Weighing Division
    d. Mechanical Automation Division
    e. Mechanical Engineering Division
    f. **Baldwin Fluid Power Ltd.**
    g. **Conveyors & Automation Ltd.**
    h. (associated overseas company) **Spencer (Melksham) SA Pty Ltd.** South
       Africa

14. **Associated Automation Ltd.,** mostly located at Willesden.

    a. **Elliott-Automation Accessories Ltd.**
    b. Post Office Division
    c. Aircraft Relay Division
    d. Relay Division
    e. Office Machines Division
    f. **National Automatic Machines Ltd.**
    g. Stamp and Ticket Machine Division
    h. **Savings Services Ltd.**
    i. Rentals Division
    j. *Metallurgical Laboratory*

15. **Satchwell Controls Ltd.,** mostly located at Slough

    a. **Satchwell Appliance Controls Ltd.**
    b. **Satchwell Control Systems Ltd.**
    c. **Black Automatic Controls Ltd.**
    d. **Perl Controls Ltd.**
    e. (direct overseas subsidiary) **Contactor (PTY) Ltd.,** South Africa
    f. (direct overseas subsidiary) **Satchwell Regulatorer AB** Sweden
    g. (associated overseas company) **Orthotherm Ges.m.b.h.** Austria
    h. (associated overseas company) **A s Orthotherm** Denmark
    i. (associated overseas company) **Deutche Ortho Therm G.m.b.h.** German F R

16. **Elliott-Automation (Overseas) Ltd.**

   a. **Elliott-Automation (Pty) Ltd.** Australia
   b. **Satchwell Controls (Pty) Ltd.** Australia
   c. **Elliott-Automation G.m.b.h** Austria
   d. **Elliott-Automation (Pty) Ltd.** South Africa
   e. **Elliott-Automation AB** Sweden
   f. **Elliott-Automation AG** Switzerland

17. (partly owned) **Elliott-Automation Continental SA**

   a. **Usines Belges Vynckier Frères SA** Belgium, and subsidiaries
   b. **Satchwell Grigson-Page SA** Belgium
   c. **Elliott-Automation (France) S.a.r.l** France
   d. **La Thermostatique SA** France
   e. **Houdec SA** France
   f. **Elliott-Automation Gmbh** German Federal Republic
   g. **Satchwell Regeltechnik Gmbh** German Federal Republic
   h. **Godart Gesellschaft für Elektromedizinische Geräte mbH** German F R
   i. **Elliott-Automation S.p.a.** Italy
   j. **Strumenti Automazione Controllo Impianti Regolazione Spa** Italy
   k. **Elliott-Automation Nederland N.V.,** The Netherlands
   l. **Godart N.V.,** The Netherlands

The above list of companies and divisions in May 1965 gives a reasonable picture of Elliott-Automation close to the high point of its existence as an independent enterprise. No organisational diagram is given in the 1965 Annual Report (presented on 29 June 1966). However, it can be deduced that Elliott-Automation had acquired additional overseas interests by the end of 1965. Under category 16 above, new arrivals during 1965 appear to be:

Elliott-Automation (Ireland) Ltd.;
Elliott-Automation (Singapore) Ltd.

Under category 17 above the new arrivals appear to be:

Koenig Automation SA, France;
Vyncoluxe Presstoff GmbH, German FR;
Deutsche Orthotherm GmbH, German FR;
Handelmaatschappij ZKE Jongstra NV, The Netherlands;
A/S Ortotherm, Denmark.

A11.2 Elliott-Automation Factories

In an illustrated Elliott-Automation company brochure printed in 1964 [1], the Introduction states: 'Elliott-Automation has some 50 factories, Service Centres and Branch Offices in the United Kingdom and a further 40 factories and places of business in Europe, Australia and South Africa. This booklet contains a selection of views of some of the factories.' Photographs are given of 25 of the more important sites (or, at any rate, of those sites for which images were available in 1964). The titles of the photographs, listed in the order in which they appear in the company's booklet, are given below.

1. Head Office: 34 Portland Place, London.	Stated factory floor area, in square feet × 1,000
2. Borehamwood main site	346 + 115 to come in 1965
3. Manor Way, Borehamwood	39
4. Stanmoor	29
5. Willesden	206
6. Park Royal	120
7. Lewisham	222
8. Greenwich	77
9. Dartford	53
10. Rochester	560 + 295 planned
11. Waddon	56
12. Croydon	60
13. Slough	190
14. Frimley	107
15. Melksham	170
16. Treforest	34
17. Maryport	144
18. East Kilbride	200
19. Cowdenbeath	50
20. Hamburgh	84
21. Utrecht	15
22. Ghent	860
23. Milan	26
24. Johannesburg	25
25. Cape Province	30
26. New South Wales	35
Total of the above sites (UK and overseas)	3,738,000 ft^2

The total Elliott-Automation Group's UK factory floor area in 1964 is given as 2.7 million square feet in a graph in the brochure.

The factories at Park Royal and at Maryport deserve some explanation, being associated with a company called the Electroflo Meter Company Ltd. According to [2], this firm was founded at Park Royal in the 1920s to manufacture instruments of American design under licence. Electroflo gradually developed instruments of their own design for applications such as power generation, public utilities and steel production. By the start of the Second World War, Electroflo was said to be amongst the top three industrial instrumentation companies in the UK. A so-called *shadow* factory was built at Maryport in Cumberland, as a safeguard against enemy destruction of the Park Royal factory. In 1956 Electroflo amalgamated with Associated Automation to become part of the Elliott-Automation Group. By 1964 the Electroflo activity had become part of Elliott Process Automation.

References

1. Anon (1964) Elliott-Automation factories. 30-page illustrated booklet, undated by most probably 1964. Elliott-Automation Ltd., London
2. Anon, Electroflo Meter Company Ltd. Two-page typewritten memo number 4.18/2/8, in the Elliott Document Archive assembled by Ron Bristow, a former Elliott employee. This document archive is now part of the Marconi Archive held at the Bodleian Library, University of Oxford, Oxford

Bibliography

General Comments

To date, no other specific books have emerged that deal with the analogue and digital computing activities of the Borehamwood Research Laboratories of Elliott Brothers (London) Ltd. and associated companies. Furthermore, most projects undertaken during the first 8 or so years of the Laboratory's existence were related to classified defence contracts. All staff from the grade of foreman upwards signed the Official Secrets Act. In the phrase of the time, most Borehamwood activity was *hush hush*. The principal evidence of the computer-related work undertaken during this early period exists in the form of Borehamwood Research Reports, each having strictly limited circulation and mostly now probably destroyed. However, microfiche copies of reports numbered 1B to 303 have survived. Relevant items are listed below in the section 'Early Borehamwood Research Reports'.

Documents deposited in The National Archives (formerly known as the *Public Record Office)* at Kew constitute another possible source of early Borehamwood information. Surviving files related to the Admiralty (catalogued as *ADM* and especially within the group *ADM 213*) provide a rather fragmented picture of MRS5 and related Borehamwood activity. A fascinating historical gem, at the time highly sensitive, is document ADM 178/309: *Report on morale and output of Elliot Bros Ltd: suggestions for improvement, 1943*. This deals with the Lewisham factory. Notice the incorrect spelling of 'Elliot', which is a not-infrequent hazard for researchers scanning catalogues.

Between March 1951 and August 1954 an *Elliott Journal* was issued. To quote the front cover, this was intended to be 'a periodical review of developments in engineering and physical science with particular reference to the work of Elliott Brothers (London) Ltd'. In the event, only five issues appeared. The contents of these journals are listed below in the section 'The Elliott Journal'.

After about 1954, articles describing Borehamwood's computer-related projects and products began to appear in scientific journals, along with the distribution of brochures and technical descriptions unfettered by government security restraints. Libraries and the Internet provide pointers to these later sources of Elliott information. Finally, mention should be made of two useful retrospective views of early Borehamwood activity, written by participants:

Coales JF (Jan 1972) Computers and the professional engineer. Proc IEE 119(1):1–16

Clarke SLH (Aug 1975) The Elliott 400 series and before. Radio Electron Eng 45(8):415–421

Early Borehamwood Research Reports

The Borehamwood reports from 1947 to about 1954 that have some bearing on the chapters of *Moving Targets* are listed below. The intention is twofold: to provide activity-dates and names of individuals so as to supplement the material given in the main chapters of this book; to provide a guide to scholars intending to carry out further research. Note that *MRSV* is synonymous with *MRS5* in the titles of reports connected with the Medium Range System.

Each of the reports listed below has an access-annotation: S (*secret*), C (*classified*), R (*restricted*), P&C (*private and confidential*) or U (*unrestricted*). Dates of issue are given in the form: <day>/<month>/<year>. Authors are identified by their initials, the full names being listed later. The abbreviation *PR* in a title stands for 'progress report'.

The many reports that are *not* listed below cover a variety of subjects, varying from 'Interim report of automatic boiler control' to 'The influence of shot noise on the location of a star in daylight by the photo-electric method'. Tempting as it is to explore such subjects further, the criterion for including a report in the following list is simply that it impinges directly on material in Chaps. 2–5 and 8 of this book.

Report no.	Title	Date	Access	Author(s)
4	Comprehensive Display System: PR No. 1	31/7/47	S	CAL
7B	MRSV: PR No. 1	1/10/47	S	JFC
7B	MRSV Appendix to PR No. 1	1/10/47	S	JFC
12	Comprehensive Display System: PR No. 2	5/12/47	S	CAL
14	MRSV: PR No. 2	17/12/47	S	JFC
22	Electrical pulse storage by means of a Cathode Ray Tube	26/2/48	R	MVN
27	MRSV: PR No. 3	5/2/48	S	JFC
38	Comprehensive Display System: PR No. 3	9/6/48	S	CAL
39	Appendix to Report No. 38, CDS. An appreciation.	24/5/48	S	CAL
44	MRSV: PR No. 4	9/6/48	S	JFC
47	MRSV. Appendix to PR No. 4	21/6/48	S	JFC
60	Size of numbers in the MRSV computer	31/8/48	S	SEH
61	MRSV: PR No. 5	2/9/48	S	JFC
62	Comprehensive Display System: PR No. 4	9/9/48	S	CAL
82	MRSV: PR No. 6	25/11/48	S	JFC
84	Comprehensive Display System: PR No. 5	14/12/48	S	CAL
86	Appendix to CDS PR No. 5: Technical Proposals for CDS	31/12/48	S	RB, CAL, MSR

(continued)

(continued)

Report no.	Title	Date	Access	Author(s)
95	MRSV: PR No. 7	21/2/49	S	JFC
99	Electrical pulse storage using a Cathode Ray Tube	1/3/49	R	MVN
111B	A possible marker selection system for CDS employing a permanent and unique code for each marker	5/4/49	C	MSR
113	Comprehensive Display System: PR No. 6	31/3/49	S	CAL
114	MRS5: PR No. 8	27/5/49	S	JFC
122	Comprehensive Display System: PR No. 7	30/6/49	S	MVN
132	Two types of commutator for use in high-speed digital computers	11/8/49	R	JEB, EGL, RCR, PW
133	A subtraction circuit for use in serial high-speed binary digital computers	10/8/49	R	PW, RCR
134	A preliminary trial of a digital data receiver using a binary disc reader	26/8/49	R	RCR
135	MRS5 PR No. 9	14/9/49	S	JFC
142B	Glass printed circuit units	16/10/49	U	DLJ
144	Pulse transformer to handle high duty cycle pulse trains in the logical circuits of computers	11/11/49	R	HGC
145	Investigation into a punched tape system for measuring angular position in binary code	25/10/49	C	JAB
146	Comprehensive Display System: PR No. 8	25/10/49	S	CAL
153	Investigation of miniaturised RF choke design for printed circuit applications	25/11/49	U	CRV, JAC
158	MRS5: PR No. 10	21/12/49	S	JFC
163	Theory of MRS5 computer	3/1/50	S	SEH
165	Comprehensive Display System: PR No. 9	31/1/50	S	CAL
166	A desk calculator in binary scale	11/1/50	R	DSE
168	The present position of automatic computing machine development in England	10/1/50	U	WSE
173	Pilot production of printed circuit units	26/4/50	C	DLJ, JAC
182	A digital-analogue converter for servomechanism applications	20/2/50	R	JB, RCR,
183B	A scale-of-two controller for computer operations	7/3/50	R	DSE, LCSW
184B	20 Kc/s plug-in flip flop	7/3/50	R	DSE
186	Investigation and design of chassis and racking for printed circuit plates with forced air cooling	26/5/50	C	RFT, JJP
189	Comprehensive Display System: PR No. 10	31/3/50	S	CAL
193	MRS5 PR No. 11 (No. 1 of 905)	5/4/50	S	JFC
195	MRS5 computer programme	25/5/50	S	SEH
196B	Estimated cost of production for printed circuit units	1/5/50	U	DLJ

(continued)

(continued)

Report no.	Title	Date	Access	Author(s)
197	An improved analogue-digital converter for use in a position control system	5/5/50	R	JB, RCR
199B	Equipment and programme for 'Netting' trials 1950	9/6/50	C	CAC, ARC
200	Comprehensive Display System: PR No. 11	13/6/50	C	CAL
202	'Netting' progress report No.2	7/7/50	S	JFC
203	Three-dimensional simulator PR No.1	14/7/50	S	JFC
207	A trial decimal to binary converter	25/8/50	C	DSE, JHB
208	A cathode ray tube digital store and accumulator	8/8/50	C	RCR
209	A clock pulse generator for series-working binary digital computer	9/8/50	C	EGL
213	Comprehensive Display System: PR No. 12	18/9/50	S	CAL
214	Three-dimensional simulator PR No. 2	10/10/50	S	JFC
215	'Netting' PR No. 3	11/10/50	S	JFC
217	Digital computing machine components of universal application	5/12/50	U	WSE
219B	Power supplies for 'Netting' trials	8/12/50	C	GAE
220	A digital data transmission system suitable for use with a binary digital computer of the serial type	13/12/50	C	RCR
223B	A decimal to binary converter	15/1/51	C	DSE, JMTC
224	Three-dimensional simulator PR No. 3	23/1/51	S	JFC
225	RAE simulator – preliminary report on mechanical design of simulators in the USA	22/2/51	S	WHP
226	The Elliott differential analyser	24/2/51	R	KLS
227	Automatic circuit checker for circuit plates	25/2/51	C	HDJ, JAB, AVH
232	'Netting' PR No. 4	3/4/51	S	JFC
233	A local control signal distributor for operating digital reading heads situated at a distance from a controlling computer	4/4/51	C	AGWE
237	Three-dimensional simulator PR No. 4	23/4/51	R	JFC
238	Comprehensive Display System: PR No. 13	25/4/51	S	CAL
241	Investigation of resistor and conductor coatings for printed circuits	4/5/52	U	RFA, JAC, DLJ
245	'Netting' PR No. 5	23/7/51	S	JFC
246	Design proposals for D/F calculator	29/7/51	S	BB
247B	Proposals for a general-purpose mathematical electronic digital computer	3/8/51	U	CHD, CEO
249	UDE weapon plot: progress report No. 1	29/8/51	S	JEP
251	Three-dimensional simulator PR No. 5	11/9/51	R	JFC

(continued)

(continued)

Report no.	Title	Date	Access	Author(s)
252	CDS X-Models vols. 1–5	3/5/51	S&D	MVN
253	'Netting' progress report No. 6	9/10/51	S	JFC
254	A note on the use of germanium delay filaments as digital store devices	13/8/51	P&C	JBG
255	CDS PR No. 14	16/10/51	S	CAL
263	Three-dimensional simulator PR No. 6	11/12/51	R	JFC
267	A general-purpose calculating machine for the National Research Development Corporation	30/1/52	P&C	WSE, NDH, SEH, CHD, BMR
271	Three-dimensional simulator PR No. 7	3/3/52	R	JFC
272	Some pulse tests on magnetic specimens having rectangular hysteresis loops	3/5/52	P&C	PFD
275	Preliminary study of the overall accuracy of the simulator	3/3/52	R	AJW
276	A general-purpose calculating machine for the National Research Development Corporation (subsid. report)	4/4/52	P&C	SEH
281	An experimental three-dimensional display	29/4/52	R	REF, WPM
283	An investigation of the causes of drift in Order Generators with proposals for the design of an improved Order Generator.	29/4/52	R	SLHC
285	Three-dimensional simulator (Tridac) PR No. 8	29/5/52	R	JFC
286	The design of the axis resolution unit and relative motion computer for Tridac	29/5/52	R	CHD, AVH, AJW
290	Basic study of the overall accuracy of the simulator (Tridac)	27/6/52	R	AJW
292	The 'Netting' servo systems	26/6/52	S	AVH, PGB,
295	'Netting' – Director design	17/7/52	S	WHP, JGL
298	'Netting' trials – Final Report	5/6/53	S	CAC
299	Three-dimensional simulator (Tridac) PR No. 9	8/9/52	R	HMG
300	A voltage-to-binary digital converter	9/9/52	U	AGWE, RCR
301	Three standard circuits for serial digital computers	2/9/52	U	CEO
302	A CRT store for sixty 14-digit binary numbers with a digit period of 3 µs	6/9/52	U	PW, RCR
303	The development of a range of digital computer components with special reference to packaged circuit units	27/10/52	P&C	WSE, HGC, CEO
307	Guidance and control sections of Tridac	15/12/52	S	AVH, AJW
309	Magnetostriction delay line storage	30/12/52	P&C	JRH, RCR
313	Structural stiffness of the 'Netting' Director	13/2/53	S	JGL, JRP, PDB

(continued)

(continued)

Report no.	Title	Date	Access	Author(s)
315	Test problems for Tridac on beam-riding and homing missiles	27/5/53	S	RWH, AJW
316	Netting trials tabulated results	10/4/53	S	CAC
321	Netting study: collection of technical notes	30/6/53	S	AEDB
322	Netting study: final report	5/8/53	S	ARC
325	Magnetostriction delay lines	22/7/53	P&C	RM
328	Trajectory calculations for Red Cheeks	27/8/53	S	BMR
330	Electrical servos used in Tridac and the RAE single-phase flight simulator	14/4/54	R	DJWM, GAW
331	Tridac control desk and programme unit	1/6/56	R	JCN, REH
332	Non-linear diode units and high-speed multiplier for Tridac	20/4/54	R	RWH, JCN
333	Power supply for Tridac	3/2/56	R	RCG
334	Tridac monitoring and protection circuits	2/1/56	R	REH
335	High-speed hydraulic servos for Tridac	1/1/55	R	RWH, PW
336	Test gear for Tridac	?	?	JCN, AJI
337	The standard DC amplifier in Tridac (Mark II amplifier)	8/2/54	R	DJWM, JCN
338	Frequency and voltage references in Tridac	1/8/54	R	DJWM
339	401 Mark I computer	29/3/54	P&C	ASJ, SLHC, NWWM, CHD, BVS, HGC, JPB
346	Introduction to Tridac, Vols. 1, 2, 3	16/11/53	R	AVH, RWH, AJW,
347	The plotting tables and paper recorders in Tridac	23/2/54	R	DJWM, GAW, REH
348	Mathematics of the D/F calculator programme	5/2/54	S	AJW
351	A magnetic amplifier computer for axes conversion	4/5/54	S	JHA, EHFS
358	A solid delay line for use as a short or long-line store	18/9/54	P&C	AGWE
364	Preliminary study of a digital computer for a one-plane homing simulator	18/8/54	R	AJW, JPB
371A	The 153 computer volume 1	1/1/56	S	JPB
371B	The 153 computer volume 2	1/1/56	S	JPB
371C	The 153 computer volume 3	1/1/56	P&C	JPB
379	A CRT store for use with a high-speed digital computer	2/4/56	P&C	GGB
386	153 computer maintenance handbook	1/10/55	S	JPB
471	Computer study on reactor power control	9/6/59	R	JHA
533	Design study of a field artillery computing equipment	12/7/65	C	?

Borehamwood issued three other report-categories whose access was less restricted than that of the main research category:

T series	Technical notes
M series	Technical manuals
S series	Industrial case studies

The S series embraced, for example, applications-specific studies for the Elliott 405 computer, as described in Chap. 9. A few illustrative examples of T series and M series reports that are relevant to early Elliott computer projects are now given.

T11	Technical notes on 401 Mk I – a general-purpose computer for NRDC.	2/9/52	P&C	ASJ
T12	Technical notes on digital storage using ferro-magnetic materials.	2/9/52	U	PFD
T13	Technical notes on standardised printed circuit units for digital computers.	2/9/52	U	DLJ

M12	Programming 'Nicholas'	6/7/53	U	GEF
M30	Manual of the Elliott 402 Electronic digital computer	31/10/55	P&C	HLSO
M31	Handbook for the Elliott 403 computer, Part 1	30/9/55	P&C	IHG

The identification of authors for all of the previously listed reports is shown below. This list might be taken as identifying the 70 or so scientists and engineers who contributed to the design of the analogue and digital computing aspects of the projects being pursued by the Borehamwood Research Laboratories of Elliott Brothers (London) Ltd. in the period 1947 to 1955. The largely unsung efforts of these individuals helped to create Borehamwood's reputation as a centre for innovation.

JHA	J H Aird	RFA	R F Armitage
JHB	J H Bach	GGB	G G Ballard
BB	B Bambrough	JEB	J E Barrow
RB	R Benjamin (of ASE)	JAB	J A Bolton
JB	J Boothroyd	PDB	P D Boyer
JAB	J A Bradley	PGB	P G Briggs
JPB	J P Bunt	ARC	A R Cameron
HGC	H G Carpenter	JAC	J A Chitty
JMTC	J M T Clark	SLHC	S L H Clarke
JFC	J F Coales	CAC	C A Cochrane
GBC	G B Cole	AEDB	A E de Barr
CHD	C H Devonald	PFD	P F Dorey
AGWE	A G W Edmunds	RE	R Elkins
WSE	W S Elliott	GAE	G A Emery
DSE	D S Evans	GEF	G E Felton
REF	R E Ford	EHFS	E H Frost-Smith
HMG	H M Gale	RCG	R C Gold
IHG	I H Gould	JBG	J B Gunn
JRH	J R Halsey	REH	R E Hare

(continued)

(continued)

AVH	A V Hemingway	SEH	S E Hersom
NDH	N D Hill	RWH	R W Hynes
AJI	A J Ide	DLJ	D L Johnston
HDJ	H D Joyner	CAL	C A Laws
JGL	J G Lubbock	EGL	E G (Tom) Ludlow
JEL	J E Ludlow	DJWM	D J W Marsh
WPM	W P Melling	RM	R Millership
NWWM	N W W Muchmore	MVN	M V Needham
JCN	J C Nutter	HLSO	H L S Orde
CEO	C E Owen	JRP	J R Parish
JEP	J E Pateman	WHP	W H Pearse
JJP	J J Pickering	MSR	M S Richards
RCR	R C Robbins	BMR	B M Rose
KLS	K L Selig	ASJ	A St Johnston
BVS	B V Stallworthy	RFT	R F Taylor
EACV	E A C Vincent	CRV	C R Vincent
AJW	A J Wakefield	GAW	G A White
PW	P Wilde	LCSW	L C S Wilmot

The Elliott Journal

This publication was issued for a limited period, as follows:

Volume 1: no. 1, March 1951; no. 2, September 1951; no. 3, July 1952; no. 4, May 1953.
Volume 2: no. 1, August 1954.

The first issue of the *Elliott Journal* had a foreword written by Sir Ben Lockspeiser, in his capacity as Secretary, Department of Scientific and Industrial Research. The main articles in the five issues are as follows:

Vol/no.	*Title*	*Author(s)*
1/1	150 years of instrument making	Anon
1/1	Magnetic amplifiers and their application to industrial purposes.	H M Gale
1/1	Pulsed circuits for resistance strain gauges	J G Yates
1/1	Application of the force-balance principle to pneumatic instruments for process control	D T Broadbent
1/1	A photo-electric curve follower	K L Selig
1/1	Precision alternating current measurement with a DC/AC comparator	G F Shotter, H D Hawkes
1/1	A phase front plotter for testing microwave aerials	C A Cochrane
1/1	A precision sine-cosine potentiometer	W H Pearse
1/1	Thermal fluctuation of charge in linear circuits	E A N Whitehead
1/2	Some developments in electronic magnetometers	A W Brewer, J Squires, H McG Ross

(continued)

(continued)

Vol/no.	Title	Author(s)
1/2	A general-purpose differential analyzer. Part 1 – description of the machine	G L Ashdown. K L Selig
1/2	Circuit standardisation in series-working high-speed digital computers	W S Elliott
1/2	Dynamic force reactions in double-ported control valves	G F Brockett, C F King
1/2	A microwave swept-frequency impedance meter	E A N Whitehead
1/2	A new procedure in accurate calculation of orifice plates	K Goitein, K F Shrubb
1/3	Instruments and industrial design	Alec Davis
1/3	A general-purpose differential analyzer. Part 2 – application of machine	S E Hersom, K L Selig
1/3	Ferromagnetism and ferroelectricity	A E De Barr
1/3	Measurement and recording of liquid steel temperature	Anon
1/3	Recent developments in instruments	E C Klepp
1/3	A new integrator for analogue computers	J E Pateman
1/3	A laboratory for hydraulic research	J D Davies
1/4	Graphic recorders – some historical notes	W Phillips
1/4	Note on the optimum input winding resistance of a magnetic amplifier employing voltage feedback	P D Atkinson
1/4	Automatic control of hot blast temperature	G Olah, R Andrews
1/4	The application of sampling methods to analogue integrators	J E Pateman
1/4	Reflecting dynamometer instruments of the suspended ironless type	H D Hawkes, D G H Jones
1/4	A phase shifter for use from 10–100 Mc/s	W P Melling
1/4	Digital storage using ferromagnetic materials	A E DE Barr
1/4	A self-balancing strain gauge bridge for use in wind tunnel tests	P G Briggs
2/1	Elliott instruments in the museum of the Cavendish Laboratory	Anon
2/1	The characteristics and limitations of rotary amplifiers	G Ashdown
2/1	Zero stabilization of directly-coupled amplifiers	E H Frost-Smith, A R B Churcher
2/1	An estimation of the discontinuities introduced by flange couplings in rectangular waveguides	R B Nichols
2/1	Analysis and design of a linear differential transformer	P D Atkinson
2/1	An introduction to information theory	N D Hill

Index

12/12. *See* Elliott digital computers
102C. *See* Elliott digital computers
152. *See* Elliott digital computers
153. *See* Elliott digital computers
311. *See* OEDIPUS
401. *See* Elliott digital computers
402. *See* Elliott digital computers
403. *See* Elliott digital computers
405. *See* Elliott digital computers
502. *See* Elliott digital computers
503. *See* Elliott digital computers
802. *See* Elliott digital computers
803. *See* Elliott digital computers
901. *See* Elliott digital computers
902. *See* Elliott digital computers
903. *See* Elliott digital computers
905. *See* Elliott digital computers
920. *See* Elliott digital computers
4120. *See* Elliott digital computers
4130. *See* Elliott digital computers

A

AB Dick company, 489, 491
Accounting and Tabulating Machine
    Company, 448
ACE computer, 55, 181, 184, 215, 218, 341,
    656, 659
Acorn computer, 475
A7 Corsair, 422
Action Information Organisation (AIO), 8,
    10–12
Ada language, 425, 426
Address modification, 343–345, 536, 540,
    557, 584, 588, 600
ADEE. *See* Air Defence Experimental
    Establishment

Admiralty
    admiralty fire control boxes (AFCB), 116,
        119–120
    admiralty fire control clocks, 115–118
    admiralty fire control tables (AFCT), 9–11,
        36, 114–124
    admiralty gunnery establishment (AGE),
        12, 51
    ARL, Teddington, 12, 81, 82, 135
    ASE, 5–8, 10–13, 20, 33, 35–36, 41, 57,
        72, 134, 174, 647, 648, 685
    AUWE, 383
Admiralty research laboratory (ARL),
    Teddington, 12, 81, 82, 135
Admiralty signal establishment (ASE), 5–8,
    10–13, 20, 33, 35–36, 41, 57, 72, 134,
    174, 647, 648, 685
Admiralty underwater weapons establishment
    (AUWE), 383
AEI. *See* Associated Electrical Industries Ltd.
AEI-Elliott process automation, 484
AERE. *See* Atomic Energy Research
    Establishment
AEW. *See* Airborne Early Warning (AEW)
    System
AGWAC (Australian Guided Weapons
    Analogue Computer). See Analogue
    Computers, Elliott designs
AIO. *See* Action Information Organisation
Airborne Early Warning (AEW) System, 381,
    383–385, 388–494
Airbus series of aircraft, 113, 393, 644
Aircraft Landing Monitoring System
    (ALMS), 383
Aircraft Mission Systems, 588, 641–643, 645
Air data computer, 398, 420, 423, 643,
    644, 649

Air Defence Experimental Establishment (ADEE), 5, 658
Airplane Stability and Control Analyser (ASCA) project, 660
Air transport racking (ATR), 404, 407, 414, 415, 580, 588
Aitken, H., 54, 618
Alexander, B., 389, 406, 419, 643
ALGOL, 281–287, 289–291, 293, 295, 300, 329, 367, 557, 592, 601, 609–610
ALMS. See Aircraft Landing Monitoring System
ALPHA. See GEC computers
Alvey (the Alvey programme of collaborative research), 492–493
Analogue computers, Elliott designs
    AGWAC, 99, 133–139, 142, 164, 639
    air data computers, 398, 420, 423, 643, 644, 649
    differential analyser, 123–126, 155, 262, 402, 682
    GPAC, 140–143, 286
    ND111, 139–140
    nuclear reactor computers and simulators, 23, 139, 140
    small analogue computer, 140–143
    TRIDAC (the three-dimensional simulator), viii–ix, 39, 52, 74, 113, 122, 123, 125–140, 142, 339, 642
Analogue computers vs. digital computers, viii, ix, 113–114
Analogue-to-digital conversion, 226, 587
AN/APS 20. See Radar, airborne
Anschultz floated mercury gyro, 432
Anticipation-pulse CRT storage, 59–60, 149, 337, 338, 506–507, 657
Anti-submarine warfare (ASW), 407, 427, 428, 430, 431
Apollo computer, 59, 85, 663
Applications of Elliott computers, 230–250, 256, 261, 294. See also Elliott computers, delivery lists
Applications of Elliott computers to
    aircraft, vii–ix, 43, 44, 182, 212, 366, 398, 405, 406, 413–414, 609, 612
    army gunnery control, 294
    chemicals industries, 242–244
    electricity (power) generation, 235–236
    ground-based air defence, 294–299
    mail order companies, 272–273
    oil refining and related activities, 231, 241–242
    paper mills, 244–246, 253
    payroll (RAPC), 316–319, 548–549
    radar systems, 374, 375, 385

    road traffic control, 231, 246–247, 629
    schools and education, 301, 601
    ships and shipping, 244
    steel and other metals processing, 231–235
    typesetting, 244–246
    UK government research establishments, 231, 236–241
    universities and colleges, 299–300, 474
AQS901 radar, 427–428
Archer-Thomson, H., 34, 37, 47, 61, 92
ARCH (articulated control hierarchy) process control computers. See Elliott digital computers
Argus computer. See Ferranti computers
ARL. See Admiralty Research Laboratory (ARL), Teddington
Arpanet, 476
ASCA project. See Airplane Stability and Control Analyser (ASCA) project
ASCC. See Automatic Sequence-Controlled Calculator (ASSC), aka Harvard Mark I
ASE. See Admiralty Signal Establishment
Associated automation, 202, 209, 223, 240, 280, 439
Associated Electrical Industries Ltd. (AEI), 12, 28, 187, 445, 446, 450–452, 454, 471, 480, 484, 613, 662, 664
Associative or CAM (content-addressable memory), 89, 90, 96–97
ASW. See Anti-submarine warfare
Asynchronous computer design, 570
Atkinson, P.D., 35, 129, 164, 165, 168, 687
Atlas. See Ferranti computers
Atomic Energy Research Establishment (AERE), 171, 238, 350, 661
Atomic Weapons Research Establishment, Aldermaston (AWRE), 155, 171, 553, 666
ATR. See Air Transport Racking
Australian Guided Weapons Analogue Computer (AGWAC). See Analogue computers, Elliott designs
Autocode, 280–283, 286, 293, 300, 343, 550, 621
Automatic Sequence-Controlled Calculator (ASSC), aka Harvard Mark I, 54, 656
Autonetics, the North American Aviation's electronic systems group, 399, 402–405
Autopilot, 23, 135, 143, 400–401, 413, 419, 421, 429, 642–644
AUWE. See Admiralty Underwater Weapons Establishment
Avery company (W & T Avery Ltd.), 17, 26, 28, 29
AVIDAC computer, 661

AWACS, 385, 389, 391, 393, 394
AWRE. *See* Atomic Weapons Research
    Establishment, Aldermaston (AWRE)
Axis-conversion, 44, 58, 261, 337, 506, 508

B
Babbage, Charles, 54
BAe. *See* British Aerospace
BAE Systems, ix, xi, 1, 24, 294, 397, 406,
    418, 452, 457, 464, 483, 488, 640, 641
Bagrit, Sir Leon, v, xii, 17–20, 22–30, 38, 40,
    45, 51, 64, 66–75, 148, 149, 156, 169,
    173, 175, 176, 189, 195, 196, 198, 201,
    202, 204–206, 209–211, 217, 220, 225,
    236, 252, 256, 276, 278, 279, 289, 314,
    324, 325, 339, 351, 377, 381, 432,
    436–438, 440, 443, 453, 457–461,
    469–473, 480, 484, 499–503
    arrival at the Lewisham factory, 22
    biographical details, 17–20, 25–30, 502
    foresees World Wide Web, 502
    retirement, 30, 502
    Times newspaper articles, 499
    transient ischemic attack (TIA), 202
Ballard, G.G. (Geoff), 81–82, 252, 685
Bambrough, B., 82, 263, 267, 685
Barltrop, D., 421
Barron, I., xii, 352, 353, 355, 356, 498, 570
Barrow, J.E. (Jim), 39, 61, 62, 164, 278, 297,
    351, 352, 508, 579, 685
Bartolome, T., xii, 496, 497
BBC. *See* British Broadcasting Corporation
Bell Telephone Laboratories, 37, 57
Bendix Aviation Corporation, 205
Benjamin, R., 41, 685
Bennett, J.M. (John), 56
Bennett, W.E. (Ben), 39, 52–53
Bental, Laurie, xii, 23, 278, 352, 353, 355,
    366, 469, 484, 558
BETA. *See* GEC computers
Biggs, A., 137, 138
BINAC computer, 660
Binary encoding disk, 49
Birkbeck College, University of London, 26,
    27, 171–172, 218, 661
Birkett, D., 472
Blackett, P.M.S (Patrick) (later Lord Blackett),
    156
Bletchley Park, 5, 6, 54, 89, 90, 559, 656, 657
Blind Landing Experimental Unit (BLEU) at
    Bedford, 383
Bloodhound guided missile, 133, 137, 220
Blue Steel stand-off nuclear missile, 75, 389,
    638, 642, 645–646

Blue Streak fixed-site ballistic missile, 126, 133
BMC computer. *See* EMI computers
Boeing YC-14, 644
Borehamwood Laboratories of Elliott Brothers
    (London) Ltd.
    closure, 466
    employee numbers, 39
    financial position for 1948/9, 68
    new buildings, 632
    original research agenda, 171
    origins, 373–374
Bowden, Vivian, Lord Bowden, 22, 56, 340
Bowie, J., 104
B & P Swift Ltd. *See* Swift, B & P Ltd.
Bradshaw, M., 480
Braunholtz, T.G.H., 168
Bristol's Instrument Company, 201,
    205–206
Bristow, H.R. (Ron), xi, xii, 16, 638–640, 645
British Aerospace (BAe), 390, 392, 393, 397,
    401, 452, 457, 641
British Aluminium Company, 275, 276, 615
British Broadcasting Corporation (BBC), v,
    25, 43, 178, 193–194, 264, 270–272,
    301, 475, 501, 503, 528
British Computer Society (BCS), 287, 474
British instrument industry, 16, 17, 64, 200
British Railways, 178, 179, 612, 614
British Tabulating Machine Co. Ltd. (BTM),
    xi, 6, 214, 218–220, 274, 316–319,
    330, 435, 446–448, 454, 461, 663
British Telecom (BT), 475, 493, 494, 628
British Thomson-Houston (BTH), 13, 214,
    450, 452, 454, 648, 649
Broadhurst, S.W., 91
Brooker, R.A. (Tony), 156
Brown, P., 608, 609
Brunt Committee on High Speed Calculating
    Machines, 154
Brunt, Sir David, 56, 154, 171
BT. *See* British Telecom
BTH. *See* British Thomson-Houston
BTM. *See* British Tabulating Machine Co. Ltd.
BTM1400 computer, 318
Buccaneer aircraft, 384, 389, 390, 394, 401,
    419, 643
Bunt, J.P. (John), xii, 35, 36, 39, 61, 62, 81,
    164–166, 168, 174, 179, 206, 209, 210,
    223, 277, 278, 297, 351, 353, 414, 415,
    465, 469–470, 477, 479, 482, 483, 555,
    556, 579, 581, 685
Burroughs Class 9 Simplex accounting
    machines, 314, 316
Burton, A.J. (Joe), 274, 310, 311
Byte magazine, 474–475

C

CADET computer, 350

Calder Hall nuclear power station, Cumbria, 203, 240

Calpine, C.A., 50

CAM. *See* Associative or CAM (content-addressable memory); Content-addressable memory

Cambridge University, 6, 38, 46, 54, 62, 72, 103, 108, 154, 168, 170–173, 185, 187, 218, 265–267, 269, 299, 301, 311, 338–340, 432, 492, 499, 522, 613, 630, 664

Cameron, R., 53, 140

Caminer, D., 465

Canberra aircraft, 387, 401, 455–456, 642

Cane, J.E. (Johnnie), 61, 81–82, 104, 164

Caravan guided weapon project, 141

Card Random Access Memory (CRAM), 320–321, 329, 330, 366

Carpenter, H.G. (Harry), xii, 5, 39, 51, 60–61, 91–94, 99, 159, 164–166, 168, 169, 171, 174, 180–182, 268, 337, 346, 493, 505, 507, 508, 685

Cassegrain radar aerial, 51, 74, 376–380, 384, 386–388, 390, 478, 650–653

Cathode Ray Tube (electrostatic) memory, 42, 56, 57, 59, 61, 62, 80–82, 93, 94, 98, 149–151, 158, 337, 338, 357, 506, 507, 656–661, 683, 684

Cavendish Laboratory, University of Cambridge, 38, 56, 687

CCS. *See* Computer Conservation Society

CDC. *See* Control Data Corporation

CDL. *See* Computer Developments Ltd.

CDS. *See* Comprehensive Display System

CEGB. *See* Central Electricity Generating Board

Central Electricity Generating Board (CEGB), 235, 236, 269, 666

Central Tactical System (CTS), 415, 416, 429

Century Works, Lewisham, 14–15, 21–24

Chelmsford (Marconi site), 456, 457, 464, 478–481, 483, 489, 497, 498, 667–668

Cheltenham (GCHQ site), 79, 89, 93, 171, 217, 219, 247

Chinn, P., 140, 286

Chisholm, K., 479

Clarke, J., 470

Clarke, M., 470

Clarke, S.L.H. (Laurence), xi, xii, 30, 36, 72, 88–89, 104–107, 152, 159–161, 164–169, 174, 175, 178, 179, 201, 209, 253, 267, 277, 278, 311, 313, 315, 324, 331, 338, 339, 343, 346, 356, 361, 362, 407, 415, 454, 471, 480, 482, 486–490, 493, 531, 532, 680, 685

Clayden, R.T. (Ron), 354

Clayton, Sir Robert, 378, 482, 483

Coales, J.F. (John), 4–8, 11, 12, 14, 16, 19, 20, 24, 26, 33–49, 52, 55, 61–63, 66–75, 91, 92, 113, 121, 127, 128, 134, 149, 151, 155, 156, 174, 176, 187, 201, 216, 217, 372–374, 377, 395, 432, 451, 483, 499–503, 505, 506, 647, 680, 685

automatic control group at Cambridge, 72, 500

biographical details, 72, 174

disagreements with Bagrit, 324

Oakwood (house), 34, 35

war-time work in naval radar, 4–8, 11, 72, 647

Cobber (familiar name for Elliott 403 computer), 100–101, 104

COBOL language, 319, 326, 329

Cochrane, C.A. (Alec), 5, 35–38, 44, 48, 50–51, 72–73, 122, 123, 374, 376, 377, 651, 685, 686

Cold War, v, vi, 83, 126–127, 130, 195, 295, 569, 570

Cole, B., 105, 108–110, 278, 685

Coleur, J., 491

Colossus cryptanalysis machine, 54, 89, 657

Comet aircraft, 182, 183, 267, 385, 386, 405, 415, 419, 523

Comish, D., 471

Command and Control system, 3, 11, 43, 485, 492, 506

Commonwealth Scientific and Industrial Research Centre (CSIR), Australia, 54, 102, 103, 135, 658

Communications and Radar Research Laboratory (CRRL) at Borehamwood, 379, 380, 672

Comparative financial positions of selected companies, 71, 151, 325

Comparative performance of selected computers, 319, 328, 342, 560

Comparative prices of selected computers, 328, 342, 552

Comparison between the Elliott and Ferranti companies, 15, 87, 215, 217, 341, 342, 346

Composite Signals Organisation (CSO), 83

Comprehensive Display System (CDS), 8, 10–12, 39–43, 69, 73, 139, 251, 373, 680–683

Computer Conservation Society (CCS), 172–173
Computer Developments Ltd. (CDL), 454, 663
Computer history pre-1950, 5, 38, 42, 53–57, 138, 655–657
Computer Research Corporation, 313
Computer Technology Ltd., 356, 486, 662
Computer Weekly, 474
Computing Research Laboratory, Borehamwood, 278, 279, 439, 674
Compu-Tronic. *See* NCR Compu-Tronic accounting machine
Comrie, L.J., 56
Concorde aircraft, 405, 410–412, 430, 644
Content-addressable memory (CAM), 89, 90, 96–97
Control Data Corporation (CDC), 229, 431
Cook, R.L. (Roger), xii, 254–256, 266, 267, 269–273, 277, 278, 280, 281, 283, 285–287, 291, 302, 303, 311, 319, 320, 352, 366, 469, 471, 597, 599, 601, 614
Cook, W.R. (Bill), 52
CORAL language, 293, 571, 592
Cossor company, 372, 648, 650
Couffignal, L., 178
Coventry site of GEC, 454, 457, 464, 481, 483, 494
Cox, J.W. (John), 274, 310, 311
CP407. *See* EMI computers
CRAM. *See* Card Random Access Memory
Crawley, H.J. (John), xii, 56, 110, 147–149, 151, 152, 155, 163–165, 169, 173, 177, 180, 183, 214
Creed teleprinters, 83, 546, 571
Cross, G., 301, 489–491, 615
CRRL. *See* Communications and Radar Research Laboratory
CRT store. *See* Cathode Ray Tube memory
CSIR. *See* Commonwealth Scientific and Industrial Research Centre, Australia
CSIRAC computer, 54, 656, 658
CSO. *See* Composite Signals Organisation
Cudmore, B., 104, 164
Cyclone analogue computer, 127

D
Data General Company, 486, 487
Data links, 384, 387, 475, 494
Data-loggers, data logging, 23, 195–197, 223, 226–227, 230, 235, 236, 239, 241–243, 249, 333, 355, 634, 666

Davies, D., 475–476
Dayton, Ohio (NCR site), 312–315, 319, 320, 331
DDA. *See* Digital differential analyzer
DDC. *See* Direct Digital Controller
De Barr, A.E., 38, 685, 687
DEC. *See* Digital Equipment Corporation
Decca Company, 108, 294, 317, 362, 372, 388, 395, 649
Defence budget, vi, vii, 126
Defence Teleprinter Network (DTN), 80, 83
De Havilland aircraft company, 180, 182–184, 267, 300, 385, 523, 617
Delivery lists, x, 184, 218, 219, 248, 268, 288, 299–300, 319, 532, 609, 611–631, 635
Demise of, 15, 24, 58, 189, 201, 254, 387, 436, 469, 478, 488, 489, 496–499
Department of Scientific and Industrial Research (DSIR), 56, 154, 237–238, 666, 686
Department of Trade and Industry (DTI), 371, 486
DES. *See* Disc Executive System
DEUCE. *See* English Electric computers
Devonald, C.H. (Hugh), 128, 159, 165, 166, 168, 169, 267, 268, 340, 685
Dexan computer, 402
DF computer. *See* Elliott digital computers
Differential analyser, ix, 123–126, 155, 262, 682
Digico computer, 486, 487, 662
DIGITAC computer, 213
Digital differential analyzer (DDA), 126, 402, 417
Digital Equipment Corporation (DEC), 333, 366, 410, 412, 469, 474, 475, 484, 486–487, 492, 574, 575, 662–664
Digital Equipment Corporation computers
PDP1, 366
PDP8, 333, 475, 486, 662–664
PDP11, 474, 486
VAX, 492
Digital plotter, 114, 366, 566, 567
Digital-to-analogue conversion, 15, 137–138, 226, 681
Digital *vs.* analogue computing, viii, 113–114, 122, 194, 196, 242, 410, 588
Dijkstra, E., 283, 285
Dimbleby, R., 271–272
Direct Digital Controller (DDC), 224–226, 229, 230, 235, 238, 242, 243, 485, 634, 635
Direction finding (DF) systems, 6, 79–89, 150, 267, 337, 505

Directly-coupled (dc) amplifiers, 125,
    130–132, 139–141, 684, 687
Director (for naval gunnery), 1, 33, 36, 44,
    261, 372, 505
Disc Executive System (DES), 608
Dista Products Ltd., 243, 244, 635
Dollis Hill (Post Office Research Station),
    90–91, 617, 657, 661
Double triodes, 84, 105, 107, 152, 157, 158,
    338, 341, 346, 531
Dragon nuclear reactor, 239, 241
DSIR. See Department of Scientific and
    Industrial Research
DTI. See Department of Trade and Industry
DTN. See Defence Teleprinter Network
Dumaresq naval calculator, 15, 114
Dunstable site of GEC, 483–489, 492, 493
DYSEAC computer, 214

E
Eadie, N., xii, 465, 471
EARS. See Elliott Automation Radar Systems
    Ltd.
EASE (Systems Executive for the Elliott 4100
    series computers), 607
Eastwood, Dr. (Marconi Research Director),
    480, 483
EBRL (Elliott Borehamwood Research
    Laboratory). See Borehamwood
Eccles (familiar name for Elliott 402
    computer), 178
Eckert, P., 186, 660
ECMA. See European Computer
    Manufacturers Association
Edmunds, A.G.W., 93, 159, 164, 685
EDSAC. See Electronic Delay Storage
    Automatic Calculator Computer
Edwards, D.B.G. (Dai), xii, 114
EELM. See English Electric Leo Marconi
    company
EFA. See Elliott Flight Automation
Egg-box lens (for radar), 48, 50,
    58, 375
EI DuPont de Nemours Inc., 206, 207,
    211, 243
E.K. Cole company (ECKO), 372
ELDO. See European Launcher Development
    Organisation
Electric and Musical Industries Ltd. (EMI),
    13, 214, 274, 317, 318, 330, 351,
    353–354, 360, 361, 365, 372, 388,
    427, 446–448, 450–451, 463, 625,
    649, 662, 663

Electroflo company, 676
Electromethods company, 17, 19, 64
Electronic Delay Storage Automatic
    Calculator (EDSAC) computer,
    6, 54, 55, 57, 160, 185, 218, 262,
    265, 299, 338, 360, 522, 538, 655,
    656, 658
Electronic Discrete Variable Automatic
    Computer (EDVAC), 657–659
Electronic Numerical Integrator and Computer
    (ENIAC), 45–46, 54, 655–660
Electrostatic memory. See Cathode Ray Tube
    memory
Elliott and Elliott-Automation Company
    Divisions
    computing division, 38, 39, 55, 73, 81
    Guided Weapons (GW) Division, 51, 75,
        91, 126–127, 141, 142, 266–267, 286,
        373–374, 616, 642, 672
    Mobile Computing Division (MCS), 39,
        278–280, 297, 439, 582, 633, 672
    Nuclear Instrumentation Division, 139
Elliott Automation Computers Ltd.
    senior staff list, 278, 469
    sub-divisions of, 228
Elliott-Automation Ltd.
    financial information for, 25, 50, 68,
        73, 175, 188, 325, 334, 356–357,
        440, 443, 448–460, 462, 466, 478,
        479, 635
    formation of, 201, 330, 378, 436, 472
    group companies, 14, 15, 18, 24, 26, 75,
        276, 277, 279, 325, 381, 436, 444, 462,
        464, 469–471, 476, 478, 484, 490, 498,
        503, 581–582, 671–676
    shares and dividends, 15, 28, 65, 66, 73,
        201, 206, 438, 440, 445, 459, 460
    take-over of, v, 18, 24, 223, 246, 247, 275,
        303, 397, 406, 436, 443, 461, 472, 478,
        481, 500, 635, 640, 652
Elliott Automation Radar Systems (EARS)
    Ltd., 371–395, 439, 649, 672
Elliott Brothers (London) Ltd.
    Board members in 1945, 14, 65
    demise of, 201, 436, 478
    financial information for, 25, 50, 149
    origins of, v, x, 65, 313
    shares and dividends, 460
Elliott computers
    comparative market share, 228–229, 438,
        445, 463
    delivery lists, 184, 319, 532, 609,
        611, 635
    selling price of, 552, 631, 633

Elliott digital computers

12/12, 260, 412, 415, 489, 575, 576, 579, 582, 585

152 (DF computer), vii, x, 3, 6, 8, 39, 44, 47, 53, 58–63, 72, 79–81, 84–86, 91–94, 123, 148–150, 152, 154, 157, 158, 174, 250–251, 259–263, 268, 297, 337, 338, 352, 361, 400, 505–513, 515, 634, 655, 660, 661

153, viii, 6, 74, 79–89, 93, 98, 110, 129, 152, 154, 165, 177, 259, 260, 267, 337–339, 341, 344, 347–352, 505–513, 634, 663, 681, 684

311 (see OEDIPUS)

401, viii, x, 6, 74, 81, 82, 93, 94, 107, 110, 152–153, 157, 159–166, 168, 170–177, 179–184, 189, 198, 218, 219, 260, 263, 268, 272, 338–346, 348, 349, 354, 364, 508, 531–540, 547, 611, 634, 662, 684, 685

402, viii, 6, 75, 82, 100, 105–108, 110, 159, 163, 168, 169, 173–179, 181, 184, 218, 219, 260, 267–274, 294, 296, 309, 311, 339–344, 346–349, 361, 444, 531–533, 539–541, 545–547, 560–561, 569, 612, 631, 632, 634, 635, 662, 685

403 (WREDAC), viii, 6, 75, 79, 80, 100, 103–105, 107–108, 110, 114, 135–136, 138, 168, 173, 174, 177, 184, 219, 259, 260, 272, 309, 337–339, 344, 345, 348, 349, 357, 358, 360, 361, 495, 531, 533, 540–542, 545–548, 612, 634, 685

404, 184, 531

405, viii, 105, 106, 110, 127, 168, 173–174, 184–187, 189, 210, 211, 219–220, 227, 236–238, 259, 260, 272–275, 301, 302, 309–335, 337–344, 348–350, 353, 358, 360–363, 444, 447, 531, 533, 540–552, 560–561, 612–614, 631, 632, 634, 635, 662, 664, 685

502, viii, 174, 228, 234, 260, 278, 293, 296, 319, 344, 347–349, 355, 356, 569–577, 611, 624, 634, 662

503, viii, 174, 224, 234, 249, 260, 277, 284, 285, 288–293, 296, 300, 302–303, 319, 333, 341, 344, 347–349, 359, 363, 366, 438, 444, 445, 555–567, 569, 577, 592, 611, 623–625, 631–635, 662

802, 179, 207, 209–210, 251, 254, 270, 275, 276, 281, 285–287, 319, 352–354, 356, 402, 495, 555–558, 615, 631, 662

803, 176, 178, 188, 203, 206–211, 224, 227, 228, 232–234, 236, 240–241, 243, 249, 251, 252, 254–255, 270, 272, 275, 276, 279, 281–289, 293, 295, 296, 299–300, 319, 323, 325, 326, 335, 341, 344, 347–349, 351, 353–355, 359, 363, 366, 436, 438, 447–448, 471, 495, 555–563, 565–566, 569, 577, 581, 615–623, 625, 631, 632, 662

901, 297, 405, 579, 582

902, 224, 226, 244, 252–253, 260, 297, 488, 581, 582, 590, 592, 594, 635

903, 9, 224, 247, 249, 260, 277, 288, 289, 301–302, 359, 363, 407, 488, 580–583, 585, 586, 592, 593, 631, 633, 635

905, 10, 50, 224, 246, 247, 249, 260, 277, 465, 481, 488, 489, 580–582, 585, 587, 681

4120, viii, 228, 246, 260, 300, 303, 319, 327–330, 334, 349, 363, 365, 437, 472, 597, 598, 607, 608, 627–630, 633

4130, viii, 178, 228, 260, 293–295, 300, 303, 319, 327, 330, 334, 349, 437, 465, 472, 474, 481, 500, 597, 598, 605–609, 630–631

803A, 210, 353, 354, 366, 551, 552, 554–555, 615

920A, 297, 405, 407, 414, 488, 579, 581–584, 587, 633

ARCH, 148, 188, 189, 212, 220, 224–230, 233–236, 238, 241–249, 252–253, 255, 260, 278, 303, 437, 443, 556, 579, 581, 582, 585, 597, 611, 615–623, 625–630, 634–635, 663

920AT, 582

920ATC, 430, 488, 489, 580, 582, 585, 627

803B, 210, 227, 233–234, 319, 349, 351, 353, 354, 366, 556–559, 615, 623

920B, 298, 405–409, 414, 416, 428, 429, 488, 580–582, 585–587, 593, 594

102C, 581, 582, 588, 590

920C, 414, 415, 488, 580–582, 585, 587

DF, 80–89, 150, 337

402E, 175, 179, 531, 533, 631

402F, 107, 175, 179, 270, 271, 349, 531–533, 631

405M, 319, 606

920M, 297, 405–409, 414, 416–418, 422, 488, 580–582, 585

MC1800, 580, 582, 585

MCM2, 582, 585

Minim, 407, 410, 414, 422, 489, 581, 582, 588, 592

Nicholas, viii, 6, 59, 74, 81, 85, 159, 180, 183, 250–251, 260–267, 270–272, 338–339, 344, 347–349, 356, 515–528, 634, 642, 663, 685

Panellit 609, 203, 208, 211, 224, 228, 240

Elliott Flight Automation (EFA), 279–280,
    294, 381, 386, 388, 389, 395, 397, 439,
    482, 588, 640, 641, 645, 672
Elliott Instrument Company, v
Elliott ND111. *See* Analogue computers,
    Elliott designs
Elliottomation Ltd., 201–202
Elliottronic, 23, 150, 195, 196
Elliott, W. (Eighteenth-century apprentice
    instrument maker), 14–20, 27–28, 201
Elliott, W.S. (Bill), 5, 14, 21, 37–39, 55, 61,
    73, 81, 152, 156, 159, 163, 164,
    166–169, 174, 261, 268, 339, 340
  biographical information, 38, 174, 502
  plans to take staff from Borehamwood, 209
Ellis, F.S. (Stuart), 164, 311, 471–472
Elphinstone, G.K.E, Sir Keith, 14–15, 65
Elstree film studios, 1, 361, 409
E-mail, 250–252
Emery, G., 168
EMI. *See* Electric and Musical Industries Ltd.
EMI computers
  BMC, 354, 650, 663
  CP407, 354, 663
  EMIDEC 1100, 274, 317, 318, 353, 354,
    363–365, 448, 662
  EMIDEC 2400, 274, 448, 662
EMIDEC computers. *See* EMI computers
English Electric Co. Ltd.
  origins, 455
English Electric computers
  DEUCE, 6, 87, 103, 215, 218, 219, 342,
    662, 666
  KDF6, 662, 666
  KDF7, 464, 481, 662, 666
  KDF9, 285, 345, 482, 662, 667
  KDN2, 228, 233, 464, 662, 666
  KDP10, 448, 662, 667
  System 4, 457, 458, 462–465, 470–472,
    597, 662, 663
English Electric Leo Marconi company
    (EELM), 447, 457–458, 470–471, 667
ENIAC. *See* Electronic Numerical Integrator
    and Computer
Epsylon Research & Development Co. Ltd., 360
ERA 1101 computer, 650
ERA 1103 computer, 214
Ernst Leitz GmbH, 178, 270, 612
ESPRIT Research Programme of the European
    Community, 493
Ethernet, 491–492
Eton College, 301–302
EURATOM. *See* European Atomic Energy
    Community

European Atomic Energy Community
    (EURATOM), 239, 241
European Computer Manufacturers
    Association (ECMA), 286, 363
European Launcher Development Organisation
    (ELDO), 133, 297
Evans, D.S., 61, 685
Evans, I.P. (Iorweth), 488
Everitt, G., xii, 272–273, 289
Extracodes, 349, 350, 598, 600,
    601, 605

F
FACE. *See* Field artillery computing
    equipment
FACTS booklets of Elliott computers, 366,
    563, 584, 586, 590
Fairchild camera and instrument corporation,
    436
Fairclough, J.W., 168
F16 aircraft, 424–426
Felton, G.E. (George), xii, 168, 169, 261,
    262, 264–267, 339, 340, 346,
    522–525, 528, 685
Felton, R., 265, 267, 339, 522
Ferranti computers
  Argus, 220, 229, 233, 446, 486, 487, 663
  Atlas, 283, 292, 299, 333, 343, 345, 363,
    445, 663, 664
  Ferut, 159
  FPC/1 (Pegasus), 177
  Hermes, 663
  Mark I, 6, 54, 56, 96, 103, 149, 155, 156,
    159, 160, 167, 184, 217, 219, 281, 299,
    340–343, 346, 656, 659–660, 662
  Mark I* (Mark I Star), 6, 87, 89, 96, 184,
    217–219, 341, 342, 660, 662
  Mercury, 87, 114, 270, 299, 340, 362, 662
  Newt, 355
  Orion, 445–446, 539, 663
  Pegasus, 87, 165, 168–170, 187, 219–220,
    267, 282, 317, 333, 338, 340–343, 345,
    346, 362, 516, 523, 662
  Perseus, 165, 317, 338, 447, 516, 663, 664
  Poseidon, 663
  Sirius, 333, 355, 447, 663
Ferranti Ltd.
  company history, xi, 213
  final demise, 488
  London Computer Centre, 219–220,
    340, 345
  take-over of main computer interests,
    446, 447

Ferrite cores, 210, 297, 338, 353, 355, 422, 555–557, 567, 570, 579, 598
Ferut. *See* Ferranti computers
Festival of Britain, 123–125
Field artillery computing equipment (FACE), 298, 299, 480, 585, 684
Fielding, L.P. (Peter), xii, 30, 202
Fire Brigade air defence system, 295–296
Fire control in ships, ix, 8, 43, 45, 46, 65, 116–118, 121
Fisher control valves, 638
Fisher Governor Co. Ltd., 205, 638, 673
Flatt, L., 421, 423
Flight Control, ix, 113, 143, 182, 383, 397, 398, 400, 401, 410–413, 419, 421, 429–431, 588, 640–645
Flowers Report, 300
Flowers, T.H. (Tommy), 90, 91, 93
Flutter problem, 182–184, 267, 273
Fly-By-Wire, 398, 411, 413, 416, 429–430, 644
Flyplane predictor, 51–52, 118–122
Fog Box, 72–73
Folk dancing, 33, 267
Ford Instrument Company Inc., 44–45, 118
Forest Grammar School, 301, 302, 613–614
Forrester, J.W. (Jay), 660
Foxhunter radar, 384, 389, 390, 395, 415, 431, 496
FPC 1. *See* Ferranti computers
Fraser, A., 482, 483, 489, 491
Freeman, P., xii, 91
Frimley, Surrey, 278, 280, 294, 381, 442, 672
Froggatt, Terry, xii, 397, 407, 422, 582, 592, 594
Frost-Smith, E.H., 642–643, 685, 687
Fujitsu Company, 447, 466
Functional parallelism, 59, 84, 337, 348, 507, 510, 661
Fuse factory, 3, 19–20, 36, 39, 277

G
Gabriel, A., xii, 481, 484, 485, 497
Gale, H.M. (Harry), 38, 122, 127–128, 685, 686
GAMMA. *See* GEC computers
Gammage, N., 480, 482
GCHQ. *See* Government Communications Headquarters
GEC. *See* General Electric Company Ltd.
GECCL. *See* GEC Computers Co. Ltd.
GEC Communications Company, 483, 484, 494–495

GEC computers
2050, 465, 477, 479, 481
4080, 465, 477, 481, 487, 650
ALPHA, 284, 481, 482, 557
BETA, 284, 481, 482, 487, 557
GAMMA, 284, 481, 482
4080M, 431, 492, 650
Series 63, 489–493, 495
GEC Computers Co. Ltd.
financial information, 483–484, 486
proposed merger with Ferranti Ltd., 487
sales information, 485, 494
GEC-EA. *See* GEC Elliott-Automation
GEC Elliott-Automation (GEC-EA)
financial information, 478–479
GEC-Elliott Traffic Automation, 484
GECnet, 485
GE 412 computer, 233–234, 254
GEC-Plessey Telecommunications (GPT), 454, 484–486, 494–495
GEC Research Laboratory at Stanmore, 377, 378, 402
General Election, 264, 270, 271, 528
General Electric Company Ltd. (GEC), ix, 7, 13, 24, 37, 113, 140, 214, 226, 246, 247, 249, 255, 259, 261, 277, 284, 316, 357, 371, 378, 381, 388, 397, 402, 406, 429, 436, 449–457, 463–466, 470–473, 476–497, 500, 585, 611, 635, 640, 641, 645, 648–652, 668
General register-set architecture, 344, 345
Gillies, Donald, 171, 180, 183, 184
Gill, Stanley, 265–266
Glass printed-circuit boards, 63, 86, 91, 268, 338, 681
Glenrothes site (microelectronics), 356–357, 409, 478, 481, 483
Glint, 33–75, 375
Goddard, P., 105
Google, 485
Government Communications Headquarters (GCHQ), x, 5, 6, 74, 79, 81–83, 88–99, 150, 155, 166, 171, 217, 219, 267, 339, 505
GPAC. *See* Analogue computers, Elliott designs
GPT. *See* GEC-Plessey Telecommunications (GPT)
Graf Spee german battleship, 4
Graphical display unit, 365, 366, 470, 597–598
Great Depression, the, 28
Grimsdale, R.L. (Dick), 350

Guided weapons (GW), guided missiles, 51,
        75, 91, 93, 99, 118, 119, 126–131, 133,
        135, 136, 140–142, 204, 219, 263,
        266–267, 286, 373–374, 380, 612, 616,
        642, 651, 672

H

HACS. *See* High Angle Control System
Haley, A.C.D. (Colin), 665, 667
Hall Telephone Accessories Ltd., 202
Halsbury, 3rd Earl of, 149
Halsey, J., 129, 164
Halsey, J.R., 165, 166, 168, 311, 685
Harben, D.C., 65, 66
Hartree, D.R. (Douglas), 46, 56, 193, 362,
        655, 659
Harvard Mark I. *See* Automatic Sequence-
        Controlled Calculator (ASSC), aka
        Harvard Mark I
Harwell, location of the UK's Atomic Energy
        Authority (UKAEA), 238–239, 241
Hatfield school, 300
Hawkes, H.D., 20, 36, 38, 686, 687
Head-up display (HUD), 399, 412, 418–426,
        642
Healy, M., xii, 172
Hearne, P.A. (Peter), xii, 325, 397, 401, 406,
        495, 585, 588, 643–644, 649
HEC. *See* Hollerith electronic computer
Hemingway, A.V. (Arthur), 36, 38, 127–128,
        130, 686
Hennessey, D., 147–149
Henville, R., xii, 84
Herbert, A.J., 28
Herbert & Sons, weighing machine
        manufacturer, 25, 26, 28, 29
Hersom, S.E. (Ed.), xii, 2, 44, 58, 59, 61,
        127–129, 167, 168, 226, 250–253, 256,
        261–263, 265–267, 271, 311, 337, 469,
        528, 686, 687
Herzfeld, E.O. (Edgar), 18, 25, 67, 68, 278,
        311, 356, 381, 473, 478, 480, 651, 652
Hewlett-Packard company, 486, 487
Higginson and Company of Bishopsgate,
        merchant bank, 16, 64, 200
Higginsons (Higginson & Co.), 26, 28, 64
High Angle Control System (HACS),
        12, 46, 118
Hillmore, J., 283–285
Hill, N.D. (Norman), 38, 43, 45, 52–53, 55,
        58, 59, 64, 73, 91–92, 129, 259, 267,
        274, 309, 311, 353, 354, 686, 687
Hinchliffe, G., 489

Hirst, H. (Lord Hirst), 451, 453
Hirst Research Laboratories (GEC, Wembley),
        37, 497
HMAS Tobruk, 120–121
HMS Belfast, 8, 10, 117
HMS Cavalier, 119, 120
HMS Dreadnought, 139, 239
HM Signal School (HMSS), 4, 8, 33
Hoare, C.A.R. (Sir Tony), xii, 278, 281,
        283–287, 290, 292, 469, 498, 623
Hogg, D., 168
Hollerith electronic computer (HEC), 218, 663
Hollerith, H., 448
Hollingdale, S.H., 154
Holt, R., 267
Honeyman, A.D. (Doug), 274, 310, 311
Honeywell company, 229, 320
Honeywell 200 computer, 329
Honeywell 800 computer, 448
Hounsfield, Sir Godfrey, 354
Howard, R.W. (Ron), xii, 113, 141–143,
        397, 400, 401, 405, 406, 412, 413,
        419, 420, 430, 461
Howarth, D., 292–293
HUD. *See* Head-up display
Hunter, D. (Paddy), 278, 480, 482
Hunt, P.M. (Peter), 183, 184, 267, 278, 480,
        482, 523
Huskey, H.D. (Harry), 56, 659
Hydraulic servos, 23, 48, 132, 133, 137, 684
Hynes, R.W. (Roy), xii, 125, 128, 129, 686

I

IAS. *See* Institute of advanced study, Princeton
IBM company, 229, 317, 360, 445, 446, 457,
        463, 465, 475
IBM computers
        370/168, 106
        650, 87, 178, 220, 665
        701, 104
        704, 87, 95–96, 104, 270, 337–338, 343, 553
        705, 309, 314, 317–319, 362, 447, 545,
                548–553
        1401, 138, 327, 448
        7090, 106, 138, 448
        305 RAMAC, 359, 608
        system/360, 327, 333, 457
ICI. *See* Imperial Chemical Industries
ICL. *See* International Computers Limited
ICL/ICT computers
        1900 series, 326, 327, 333, 365, 457, 462,
                465, 472, 486, 597, 663
        2900 series, 465, 486

ICT. *See* International Computers and
Tabulators
ILAAS. *See* Integrated Low Attack Avionic
System
Imperial Chemical Industries (ICI), 178, 179,
220, 242–243, 369, 612, 614, 616, 620
Imperial College, London, 30, 140, 160,
171–172, 174, 180, 492, 495, 501,
658, 661
Imperial Smelting Corporation, 235, 238,
443, 629, 634–635
Ince, D., 175
Industrial Reorganisation Corporation (IRC),
189, 449, 459, 461, 462
Inertial navigation, 75, 389, 398–399, 403,
409, 416–417, 426–428, 432, 638, 643,
645–646, 649, 650
Information Systems Inc. (ISI), 207, 209, 210,
616, 619, 623
Initial orders (IOs), 85, 165, 263–265, 268,
524, 525, 527
Inmos Ltd., 356
Institut Blaise Pascal, 178, 219, 269, 295, 612,
621, 632
Institute of advanced study (IAS), Princeton,
55, 656, 660–661
Instrument Society of America, 207–209,
224–225
Integrated Low Attack Avionic System
(ILAAS), 418–422
Intel, 449, 475
Interference test set, 268
International Computers and Tabulators (ICT)
origins of, 327, 328, 333, 365, 445–448,
458, 462, 463
International Computers Limited (ICL), xi,
220, 254, 266, 293, 299, 300, 326, 330,
335, 367, 435, 436, 444, 445, 447, 449,
457, 458, 463–466, 470–472, 476, 480,
482, 486, 487, 489, 491, 597, 598, 630,
631, 663
International Computers (Holdings) Ltd., 463
International Signal and Control, 488
Internet, 449, 457, 473, 476, 485, 679
Intruder detection systems, 382
IOs. *See* Initial orders
IPC. *See* Iraq Petroleum Company
Iraq Petroleum Company (IPC), 245, 269
IRC. *See* Industrial Reorganisation
Corporation
Irish, M., xii, 319, 320
Irton Moor, Scarborough, 79, 83, 84,
87–88, 267
ISI. *See* Information Systems Inc.

J
Jacobs Instrument Company (JAINCOMP)
computer, 214
Jacquard loom, 193
Jaguar aircraft, 297, 416–418, 585
JAINCOMP computer. *See* Jacobs Instrument
Company (JAINCOMP) computer
J & E Stone of Deptford, 16
Jindivik pilot-less target airplane, 135, 642
J Lyons & Co. Ltd., 56, 185, 218, 247, 667
JOHNNIAC computer, 660–661
Johnson, M.H. (Harry), 160, 200
Johnston, D.L. (Dennis), 60, 61, 63, 91,
268, 686
Jovial language, 293, 424–426

K
Kent On-line System (KOS), 293–294,
607–609
Kidsgrove (English Electric site), 464, 478,
479, 482, 666–667
Kilburn, Tom, 5, 59, 138, 158, 338, 343, 506,
507, 657–658, 664
Kinetheodolite film analysis, 101
King, P., xii, 269, 270, 275, 277, 283, 285,
288, 469
Kinnear, J.A.C. (John), xii, 371, 372, 376–378,
380, 386, 389, 390, 395, 648–652
Kitz, B., 82–83
Korean War, vi, 35, 121, 126
KOS. *See* Kent On-line System

L
Lam, M., 486, 487
Lamorna (an Elliott company house in
Radlett), 35
Language H, 293, 319, 320, 329
Laurence Scott & Electromotors Ltd.,
119, 120
Laverick, E. (Betty), xii, 159, 371, 373, 377,
378, 381, 388, 390, 395
Lawrence, P., xii, 277, 278, 407, 571–572, 579
Laws, C.A. (Coppy), 5, 35–36, 38, 41, 47,
251, 252, 311, 686
Lea Valley Water Company, 252–253
Lee, G.R., 16–17, 19, 20, 24, 28, 40, 64–66,
69, 71
LEO computers. *See* Lyons Electronic Office
(LEO) computers
Leo Computers Ltd., 185, 218, 317, 318, 663,
665, 667
Lewis, B. (later Bobby Hersom), 262, 267

Lewisham factory of Elliott Brothers (London)
Ltd.
final closure, 24, 373
origins, 66
range of products in the mid-1950s,
viii, 23, 24, 73, 74, 114, 116, 147,
216, 217, 325
Lightning aircraft, 13, 142, 401, 455–456
Light pen, 365, 367, 598
Linesman air defence system, 294
Ling temco vought (LTV), 422–423, 426
Littlewoods Mail Order Company, 272–273,
310–312, 613
Llanwern. *See* Spencer Steelworks
Lockspeiser, Sir Ben, 56, 686
Logabax, 148–149
Lonergan, J.P. (Jack), xii, 135, 136
Long Range Weapons Establishment (LRWE)
and Organisation, South Australia, 79,
99, 102, 103, 107, 108, 110, 128,
134–136, 177, 309, 542, 634, 639
Long Range Weapons Organisation (LRWO),
99, 100, 134, 135
Long Shot experimental missile, 51
LRWO. *See* Long Range Weapons
Organisation
LTV. *See* Ling temco vought
Ludlow, E.G. (Tom), 5, 43, 61, 164, 686
Lyons Electronic Office (LEO) computers
LEO 260, 667
LEO 360, 667
LEO II, 185, 218, 317, 318, 447, 448,
663, 667
LEO III, 597, 663, 667

M
MACE. *See* Master Control Executive
Mack, E.S. (Ed), 491
Mackintosh, I.M. (Ian), 356
Magnetic amplifier, 122, 139, 143, 642–643,
684, 686–687
Magnetic film store, 359–363, 447–448, 543,
545, 546, 548, 551, 560, 561
Magnetic Ink Character Recognition (MICR),
320–321, 365, 387–388
Magnetostrictive delay line. *See* Nickel delay
line
MAL. *See* Mills Associates Ltd.
Malvern. *See* Telecommunications Research
Establishment (TRE), Malvern
Manchester University, 54, 56, 57, 59,
147, 149, 150, 154–156, 171–172,
184, 217, 219, 292, 299, 338, 340,

342–343, 350, 357, 474, 506,
658–660, 664
Manchester University computers
Baby (familiar name for the Small-Scale
Experimental machine), 54, 658
Mark I, 54, 56, 149, 155, 184, 217, 219,
281, 299, 340, 342–343, 357, 656,
658–660
Meg, 340
Small-Scale Experimental Machine
(SSEM), 6, 54, 506, 656–659
Manhattan project, 206
MANIAC computer, 660–661
Marconi company
activities, xi, 406, 455, 464, 484, 641
history, 24, 457
name changes, 406, 452, 456, 457, 477, 641
Marconi computers
M2100 series, 479
Myriad I, 663, 668
Myriad II, 479–480, 663, 668
Transistorised Automatic Computer (TAC),
663, 668
Marconi-Elliott Computer Systems Limited
(MECS), 39, 246, 456, 464, 465, 477,
479, 483, 484
Marconi Space and Defence Systems (MSDS),
410, 456, 488, 585
Mariner, P.F. (Peter), 371, 375–381, 386,
388–390, 392, 395, 406, 649, 651–653
Maritime Aircraft Systems Division (MASD),
407, 426, 428, 429
Maritime reconnaissance (MR), 385, 386, 407,
426–428, 518, 526
Mark 37 FCS (fire control system), 46, 118
Mark II software (for the Elliott 503
computer), 290–292
Mark I Star computer. *See* Ferranti computers
Marlow, D.H., 170, 178
Mars confectionary company, 309
MASD. *See* Maritime Aircraft Systems
Division
Massachusetts Institute of Technology (MIT),
44, 55–57, 59, 85, 127, 291, 351, 366,
656, 660
Master Control Executive (MACE), 241,
287–288
Master reference gyro (MRG B), 43–44,
642, 643
Matrix interpretive scheme, 265, 343, 523
Mauchley, J., 186, 660
Maudsley, B.G. (Brian), 168
MC1800 computer. *See* Elliott digital
computers

McGregor Ross, H., 71, 72
MCM2 computer. *See* Elliott digital computers
MCS. *See* Mobile Computing Division of
    Elliott-Automation
MECS. *See* Marconi-Elliott Computer
    Systems Limited
Mediator air defence system, 569
Medium Range System (MRS) of naval
    gunnery
    MRS3, 9, 10, 118–119
    MRS4, 9–10, 118–119
MEG. *See* Manchester University computers
Mercury computer. *See* Ferranti computers
Merry, I.W. (Ian), xii, 168
Merton, C., xii, 186
Metropolitan-Vickers Co. Ltd., 13, 214, 220,
    350, 451, 452, 454, 664
Met-Vic or Metro-Vick (common abbreviations
    for Metropolitan-Vickers Co. Ltd.),
    9–10, 214, 450, 452, 454, 662, 664
MI5. *See* Military Intelligence, Section 5
Michaelson, R.L. (Ronnie), 274
MICR. *See* Magnetic Ink Character
    Recognition
Microelectronics Group of Elliott-Automation,
    279–280, 356–357, 439–440, 476, 478
Microelectronics Research Laboratory of
    Elliott-Automation, 439, 476, 478, 673
Military Intelligence, Section 5 (MI5), 66
Millership, R.W. (Ron), 158, 166, 173, 686
Millis, B.G. (Brian), xii, 186, 187
Mills Associates Ltd. (MAL), 326, 618, 623
Mills, R.G. (Gerry), xii, 269, 274, 277–278,
    310, 311, 318, 324–326, 438
Miniature pentodes, 60, 63, 80, 84–86, 98,
    152, 157, 158, 268, 337–339, 346, 532
Minilog, 226, 341, 352, 355
Minim computer. *See* Elliott digital computers
Minim navigation management system, 588
Ministry of Supply (MOS), vi, 58, 68, 69, 99,
    126–127, 134, 135, 138, 153, 155, 198,
    219, 401, 638
Ministry of Technology, 189, 235, 449,
    461–463, 482, 493, 501, 622, 625
Ministry of Transport, 246
Missiles, viii–x, 50–51, 74, 75, 79, 93,
    99–103, 106, 118, 119, 125–127,
    129–131, 133, 135–138, 141–142, 204,
    208–209, 219, 220, 234, 286, 295, 296,
    376, 380, 383, 389, 402–404, 419,
    423–425, 612, 638, 642, 645–646,
    651–653, 684
Missile tracking equipment, 101–103, 380,
    402, 651

MIT. *See* Massachusetts Institute of
    Technology
Mitchell, H., 311
Mobile Computing Division of Elliott-
    Automation, 39, 278, 280, 295, 302,
    325, 439, 470, 496, 498, 581–582,
    633, 635, 672
Modular One computer, 356, 475, 486, 662
Monk, G.W. (Geoff), 407, 480–483
Monopulse static-split radar technique, 375
Moore School, University of Pennsylvania,
    54, 57, 657
Mopsy project, 74, 376–377, 651
Morris, S., 34, 47, 252, 267, 271, 471, 500
MOS. *See* Ministry of Supply
MOSAIC computer, 6, 102
Moscow, 210–211, 283, 284, 620, 623
Motorola company, 356, 485
Mounier, P., xii, 178, 269
MR. *See* Maritime reconnaissance
MRG B. *See* Master reference gyro
MRS5 project (also sometimes written MRSV)
    cancellation, 47, 50–52
    requirements, 13, 57, 58, 374
MSDS. *See* Marconi Space and Defence Systems
MUC (early abbreviation for 'Manchester
    University Computer,' usually
    signifying the Ferranti Mark I installed
    at Manchester University in 1951),
    54, 56, 155, 156, 184, 217, 219,
    299, 340–343, 656, 659–660, 662
Muchmore, N.W.W. (Norman), 61, 129,
    159, 164–166, 168, 686
MUFPT (engineers' name for a unit of an
    Elliott 405 computer for transferring
    data between magnetic film storage
    and a printer), 546
MUF-PUP (engineers' name for a unit of an
    Elliott 405 computer for transferring
    data between magnetic film storage
    and a printer), 546
Mullard company, 13, 63, 164, 210. 351–354,
    372, 555, 556, 616, 623, 624
Multics, 291
Munich City Council, 246, 625, 629
MV950 computer, 220, 350, 662, 664
Myriad Marconi. *See* Marconi computers

N
NAHC. *See* National Archive for the History
    of Computing
Nash, H.E.C. (Eddie), 274, 277–278, 286,
    311–312, 324, 326, 438

National Archive for the History of Computing (NAHC), 147, 189
National Cash Register Co. Ltd. (NCR), viii, 230, 259, 273, 286, 312–316, 549, 612–614
  end of marketing agreement with Elliotts, 315–316
  marketing agreement with Elliotts, 313–314, 471
National Computing Centre (NCC), 486
National Economic Development Office, 487
National Elliott Assembly Technique (NEAT) Assembly language, 320, 329, 601
National-Elliott Computers. See Elliott digital computers
National-Elliott Computing Service, 315, 613, 614
National Enterprise Board, 487
National Gas Turbine Establishment (NGTE), Pyestock, Farnborough, 127, 220, 227, 236–237, 612, 618
National Motorways Communication System, 246, 255
National Physical Laboratory (NPL), 6, 46, 54–56, 138, 154–156, 160, 167, 171, 181, 215, 218, 237–238, 283–284, 340, 341, 475–476, 618, 620, 625, 628, 656, 659, 660, 665, 666
National Research Development Corporation (NRDC), xii, 56, 58, 72, 94, 110, 111, 147, 150, 163, 165, 189, 195, 214, 228, 267, 311, 339, 346, 360, 683
  NRDC contracts for Elliott computers, 339
  NRDC Siemens project, 185, 187, 632
Naur, P., 283–285
Naval radar, origins of, 4–12
Naval Radar Systems. See Sea-going radar
Naval Weapons Division of Elliott-Automation, 638, 672
Navigation Attack Weapon Aiming System (NAVWAS), 416
NAVWAS. See Navigation Attack Weapon Aiming System
NCC. See National Computing Centre
NCR. See National Cash Register
NCR 315 computer, 230–231, 260, 278, 313, 319, 320, 322, 329–331, 366, 438, 439, 445
NCR Compu-Tronic accounting machine, 322
NCR Elliott Computer Workshops Ltd., 323, 616–618, 620, 628
ND111, 139–140
Needham, M.V. (Maurice), xii, 5, 41, 43, 59–61, 116, 139, 140, 252, 506, 507, 686

Nellie (familiar name for one particular Elliott 405 computer), 301
Netting project
  data-capture (for glint assessment), 53, 62
  fly-past tests, 53
Neuron logic circuit, 355
Newey, Roger, xii, 482, 491, 493
Newman, M.A.H. (Max), 343
New Range (common name for the ICL 2900 series of computers). See ICL/ICT computers
Newt test-bed for neuron circuits, 355
Nicholas. See Elliott digital computers
Nicholls, L.H.F. (Leslie), 81, 82
Nickel (magnetostrictive) delay line memory, 158, 166, 263, 338, 515, 516, 531
Nimrod aircraft, 386–387, 407, 585, 649
Normal Input and Control Executive (NICE) for 4100 series computers, 607
Northamptonshire County Council, 323, 485
Norwich City Council, 320, 321, 546
NPL. See National Physical Laboratory
NRDC. See National Research Development Corporation
Nuclear Instrumentation Division. See Elliott and Elliott-Automation Company Divisions
Nuclear Reactor Computers and Simulators. See Analogue computers, Elliott designs
Nucleus (the hardwired central executive of the 4000 series computers), 488
Nutter, J.C.N. (Jack), 128, 129, 140, 686

O

Oakley, B., 493
OEDIPUS computer, 6, 74, 79, 89–99, 171, 339
Oil refining and related activities, 231, 241–242
One-Time Pads (OTP), 89, 90, 94, 95, 99
Optimum programming, 87, 172, 341, 342, 534
ORACLE computer, 660–661
Orde, H.L.S. (Henry), 267, 269, 286, 310, 311, 469, 686
ORDVAC computer, 659–661
Orion. See Ferranti computers
OS4000 (a GEC operating system), 485
OTP. See One-Time Pads
Ovenstone, J.A. (John), 102–106
Owen, C.E. (Charles), xii, 81, 164, 165, 167–169, 173, 178, 263–265, 268, 338–340, 346, 515, 517, 519, 524–527, 532, 534, 616, 686

P

PACE analogue computer, 141, 500
Package technology, 268
Packet-switching, 475–476, 485
Panellit 609, 203, 208, 211, 224, 228, 240
Panellit computers. *See* Elliott digital
    computers
Panellit Division of Elliott-Automation,
    240, 278
Panellit Inc. (an American company),
    207–209, 615
Panellit Ltd. (a company within the
    Elliott-Automation group), 209, 224
Paper mills, 231, 244–246, 253
Parallelism, 59, 84, 86, 154, 155, 337, 348,
    507, 510, 661
Parliamentary Select Committee on Science
    and Technology, 444
Pasley-Tyler, H. (Henry), 19, 25, 35, 73, 122,
    128, 129, 170, 174, 176, 381, 386, 388,
    443, 473, 480
PASS. *See* Precision Angulation and Support
    System
Pateman, J.E. (Jack), xii, 38, 142, 325, 381,
    388, 389, 402, 406, 415, 419, 420,
    422–424, 431, 494, 643, 645, 649,
    686, 687
Patents, 4, 14, 15, 29, 41, 49, 51, 58, 59, 147,
    149, 150, 171, 173, 206, 208, 215, 216,
    343, 376–379, 478, 506, 650–653, 671
Payroll (RAPC), 316–319
PC. *See* Personal computer
PDP1. *See* Digital Equipment Corporation
    computers
PDP8. *See* Digital Equipment Corporation
    computers
PDP11. *See* Digital Equipment Corporation
    computers
Pearcey, T., 103, 135, 658
Pearse, W.H. (Bill), 35, 125–126, 129,
    642, 686
Peenemunde (engineers from), 35, 125
Pegasus. *See* Ferranti computers
Pentecost, D., xii, 275
Peripheral equipment characteristics, 138, 333,
    355, 363–367, 447–448, 532, 560, 567,
    620, 625
Perseus. *See* Ferranti computers
Personal computer (PC), 161–162, 166, 270,
    301, 332, 344, 466, 474–475
Personal Computer World magazine, 474–475
Philco Corporation, 351
Phillips, C.F. (Chris), 36, 81, 165, 166, 168
Phoenix, Arizona, 233, 491

Pilot ACE, 6, 54, 55, 155, 160, 167, 171, 181,
    184, 215, 218, 341, 656, 659, 665, 666
Pinkerton, J.M.M., 56
Plessey company, 214, 463, 470
Pollard, D., 29, 639
POP-2 language, 608
Poppelbaum, W.J. (Ted), 355, 480
Popsy missile project, 376
Port Arthur Refinery, Texas, 241
Poseidon. *See* Ferranti computers
Powers-Samas company, 148, 214, 447, 448
Precision Angulation and Support System
    (PASS), 382
Predictors (for naval gunnery), 44
Prestel, 485
Preston, D.M. (Des), 274, 310, 311
Prime computer, 65, 234
Project R, 489–491
Project Wavell, 492
Pye Ltd., 108, 360–361
Pyestock. *See* National Gas Turbine
    Establishment (NGTE), Pyestock,
    Farnborough
Pymm, J., 281

R

Radar, airborne
    AI type 23, 389
    AI type 24, 390
    Foxhunter, 384, 389, 390, 395, 415,
        431, 496
    type AN/APS 20, 381, 383, 387
Radar, definitions and principles, 3–12, 37–38,
    43, 47–50, 57, 120, 386–387, 505,
    647–648
Radar, sea-going
    type 274, 7, 8, 11, 117
    type 275, 7, 8, 119–121
    type 282, 7, 647–648
    type 285, 7
    type 903, 9
    type 904, 9–10
    type 905, 10, 50
RAE. *See* Royal Aircraft Establishment,
    Farnborough
Rank Cintel company, 419
Rank, Taylor and Hobson Ltd., 178, 612
RAPC. *See* Royal Army Pay Corps
Rapid Analytical Machines, 6, 112, 657
Rapier Blind-fire anti-aircraft missile
    system, 383
Rayner, Paul, xii, 105, 109, 110, 397, 402,
    405, 413, 417, 422, 427, 494, 495

RCA company, 457, 472, 667
RCA Spectra 70 computer, 457, 472, 663
Real time computing systems, 58, 401
Real-time interaction via joystick, 42
Red Cheeks guided bomb, 287, 642
Reed International Company, 245, 253
Rees-Mogg, W. (Lord Rees-Mogg), xii,
    501–502
Reffen, P., 277–278, 483
Reith lectures (broadcast by the BBC),
    v, 193–195, 198, 501, 503
Research Laboratory, Elliott Brothers (RLEB).
    See Borehamwood
Richard Thomas & Baldwin Ltd. See Spencer
    Steelworks
RLEB. See Borehamwood
Roadrunner project, 489
Road traffic control, 231, 246–247, 625, 629
Robbins, R.C., 60, 61, 82, 164, 165, 168, 686
Rochester Airport, 64, 136, 198–199, 637, 639
Rochester factory of Elliott-Automation, 64,
    137, 199, 413, 422, 569, 588, 637–638
Rock-Carling, F., 38, 93
Rose, B.M. (Brighid), 168, 264, 265, 267, 686
Ross, L.L. Dr. (Lotti or Lawrence), 17–19, 22,
    23, 25, 64, 66–68, 71–72, 136, 139,
    160, 169, 170, 186, 195, 197–198, 202,
    209, 210, 217, 223, 339, 356, 381, 469,
    473, 480
Rothamsted Research Station (Agricultural),
    94, 171, 172, 218, 219, 536, 611
Roth, J.F. (Joseph), xii, 105, 204, 211,
    231–232, 234, 240, 248
Rotol Propellers Ltd., 178, 612
Royal Aircraft Establishment (RAE),
    Farnborough, 74, 99, 126–137, 154,
    171, 219, 236, 263, 339, 362, 400, 402,
    642, 645, 646, 657
Royal Army Pay Corps (RAPC), 314–319,
    326, 362, 447, 548–553, 632
Royal Artillery, 297, 585
Royal Liberty School, 301–302, 626
Royal Radar Establishment (RRE), successor
    to TRE at Malvern, 296, 387, 389, 569,
    570, 575, 616, 617, 619, 624, 634
RRE. See Royal Radar Establishment,
    successor to TRE at Malvern
Ruth, D., 491

S
Sale of Elliott computers to America,
    261, 275, 309, 315, 332–333,
    445, 446, 631

Sales and deliveries of Elliott computers, viii,
    x, 79, 184, 218, 261, 275, 276, 309,
    315, 332–333, 444–446, 631
Salisbury, near Adelaide, 99, 101, 134
Samuel Fox & Co. Ltd., 227, 232, 233,
    251, 615
SAP. See Symbolic Assembly Program
Scammell, G., xii, 485, 497
Scarborough, 79, 82–83, 88, 267, 351
Scarrott, G.G. (Gordon), 56
Schools and education, 26, 300–302, 626
Science and Engineering Research Council
    (SERC), 492–493, 499
Scotland, proposed computer for, 171, 244
Scott, N., 473
Scott, W., 470–471
SCOW. See Steel Company of Wales Ltd.
SEAC. See Standards Eastern Automatic
    Computer
Sea Cat missile, 118, 133
Sea-going radar
    type 274, 7, 8, 11, 117
    type 275, 7, 8, 119–121
    type 282, 7, 647–648
    type 285, 7
    type 903, 9
    type 904, 9–10
    type 905, 10, 50
Selig, K.L., 123, 125, 686, 687
Selling price of, vii, 163, 556, 631, 633
SERC. See Science and Engineering Research
    Council
Series 63. See GEC computers
SGCS. See Siemens GEC Communication
    Systems
Shackleton, P., 274, 284, 310, 311
Shares and dividends, 15, 16, 28, 65, 66, 68,
    73, 201, 206, 440, 459, 460, 487, 544,
    564, 622
Ships and shipping, 3, 6–8, 11, 12, 46, 52, 65,
    114, 118–121, 205, 231, 244, 384, 385,
    425, 648
Short Brothers (aircraft company), 64, 141,
    198, 637, 639
Short nickel line accumulating register
    calculator (SNARC), 158, 159, 268
Siemens Brothers & Co Ltd., 15–16,
    27–28, 65
Siemens Brothers, shares in Elliott Brothers
    (London) Ltd.
    adverse effects of, 15
    buy-out of shares, 16, 65
Siemens Edison Swan and NRDC project,
    185, 187, 311

Siemens Edison Swan factory at Woolwich, 185, 187, 311
Siemens GEC Communication Systems (SGCS), 484
SIGINT. *See* Signals Intelligence
Signals Intelligence (SIGINT), 81, 99
Simmonds, K., 136
SIMULATOR X air defence project, 296, 569
Sinclair, J., xii, 471, 472
Single-shot data preparation, 321
Sirius. *See* Ferranti computers
Sir Leon Bagrit Memorial Trust, 501
SIR symbolic assembler, 586, 592–594
Sky Shadow, 589
Sleight, R., 426
Small analogue computer, 140–143
Smith company. *See* S Smith & Sons Ltd.
Smith, L.W., 14, 16, 18, 65, 66
Smith, R.O., 14, 65, 66
Smith, W.O., 14
SNARC. *See* Short nickel line accumulating register calculator
Social consequences of automation, 195, 204
Space and Weapon Automation Ltd. (an Elliott-Automation group company), 278, 280, 298, 381, 439, 442, 672
SPAN. *See* Storage Planning and Allocation (SPAN) system software for the Elliott 4100 series
Spencer Steelworks of Richard Thomas & Baldwin at Llanwern near Newport, 211, 253
Sperry, A.F. (Al), 9, 197, 206–211, 418–420, 422
Spratt, E.B., xii, 609
Square root (hardware), 348, 349, 555, 571
Square root (software), 172, 281, 522, 537–539, 559
SRL. *See* Systems Reliability Ltd.
SSEM. *See* Manchester University computers
S Smith & Sons Ltd., 36, 622
STAAG. *See* Stabilised Tachymetric Anti Aircraft Gun
Stabilised Tachymetric Anti Aircraft Gun (STAAG) system, 9
Stallworthy, B., 129, 159, 164–166, 168, 686
Standards Eastern Automatic Computer (SEAC), 54, 214, 656, 658–659
Standards Western Automatic Computer (SWAC), 54, 56, 656, 659
Standard Telephones and Cables Ltd. (STC), xi, 155, 255, 274, 317, 359, 372, 446, 494, 663

Stanmore. *See* GEC Research Laboratory at Stanmore
STANTEC Zebra computer, 333, 663, 664
STC. *See* Standard Telephones and Cables Ltd.
Steel and other metals processing, 231–235
Steel Company of Wales Ltd. (SCOW), 228, 233–235, 469
St. Johnston, Andrew, 5, 38, 43, 61, 81, 88, 93, 104, 108, 110, 129, 142, 159, 164–166, 168, 170, 174–176, 178, 209–211, 240, 266, 273, 277, 279, 289, 292, 303, 309, 311, 325, 339, 343, 350, 351, 361, 402, 405, 413, 415, 464–465, 469, 471, 482, 493, 496, 498, 508, 559, 632
biographical information, 174
Storage Planning and Allocation (SPAN) system software for the Elliott 4100 series, 607
Strachey, Christopher, 56, 154–156, 159, 160, 165, 167–169, 171, 186, 189, 268, 284, 343, 346
biographical information, 155
Sunbeam car, 33, 34
SUN workstations, 492
Super-enciphered intercepts, 89–91, 94, 99
SWAC. *See* Standards Western Automatic Computer
Swann, B.B. (Bernard), 446, 449
Swift and Swallow Ltd., 637–639
Swift, B & P Ltd.
reverse take-over of Elliotts, 25, 28, 66, 198–200, 453, 638–639
Symbolic Assembly Program (SAP), 293, 329, 593
System 4. *See* English Electric computers
System/360. *See* IBM computers
Systems Reliability Ltd. (SRL), 465, 471–472, 598, 603
System X telephone exchange, 494

T
TAC. *See* Marconi computers
Telecommunications Research Establishment (TRE), Malvern, 5, 99, 102, 171, 661
Telent company, 457
Telent Technology Services Ltd., 485, 497
Teleprinter codes, 263, 264, 523, 547
Telford, Sir Robert (Bob), 388, 471, 480, 486, 489
Terrain Referenced Navigation (TRN), 425
Thomas, W.R., 128, 136, 195, 211–212, 233, 236, 252, 253, 616, 618, 619, 642

Thompson-Ramo-Wooldridge (TRW)
    company, 213, 229, 454
Thomson Regional Newspapers, 245–246, 626
Three-dimensional simulator (early name for
    TRIDAC). *See* Analogue computers,
    Elliott designs
Thurston, Colin, xii, 489, 491, 638
TI. *See* Translation Input
Tidewater Refinery, USA, 206–207, 211,
    241, 616
Time Sharing Supervisor (TSS), 607
Tootill, G.C. (Geoff), 343
Tornado aircraft, 390, 411, 418, 426–427,
    429, 589, 644
Toronto University, 159, 217, 219, 346
TRADIC. *See* TRAnsistor DIgital Computer
TRANSAC S-1000 computer, 351
TRAnsistor DIgital Computer (TRADIC),
    350–351
Transistors, 43, 57, 155, 207, 210, 254–255,
    318, 341, 348, 350–357, 402, 404, 447,
    454, 495, 555–558, 569, 579, 598, 616,
    623, 646, 664, 666
Translation Input (TI) (for Nicholas com-
    puter), 265, 515, 520
Transmitting station (TS), 10, 116, 117, 119
Transputers, 356
TREAC computer, 153
TRIDAC. *See* Analogue computers, Elliott
    designs
TRN. *See* Terrain Referenced Navigation
TRW. *See* Thompson-Ramo-Wooldridge
TS. *See* Transmitting station
TSR 2 aircraft (TSR stood for 'Tactical
    Strike and Reconnaissance'), vii,
    143, 380, 387, 389, 399–402, 404,
    416, 419, 495
TTL integrated circuits, 226, 352
Tunnel diodes, 341, 353, 355–356, 480
Turing, A.M. (Alan), 46, 55, 61,
155, 659
TX-0 computer, 351
Tyndale, J., 61, 62
Typhoon aircraft, 430
Typhoon analogue computer, 127, 133

U
UNIVAC computer, 186, 317, 340, 345, 359,
    448, 465, 656, 659, 660
UNIX operating system, 332, 489, 491–492
Upper Terrace House, Hampstead, 22, 501–502
Uttley, A.M. (Pete), 5, 46, 56, 153

V
Vaughan, Aldrina (Dina) (later Dina
    St. Johnston), xii, 82, 129, 241, 246,
    254, 255, 266, 267, 273, 287, 310–312,
    465, 469, 594, 623
    biographical information, 266
Vaughan Programming Services (VPS), 233,
    235, 240–241, 246, 249, 254, 266,
    287–289, 303, 312, 464–465, 471, 489,
    559, 594
Vaughan Systems Ltd., 174, 246, 255,
    464–465, 483, 489
VAX. *See* Digital Equipment Corporation
    computers
V-bombers, 383, 642, 643, 645, 646
Venona, 99
VERDAN computer. *See* Versatile digital
    analyzer (VERDAN) computer
Versatile digital analyzer (VERDAN)
    computer, 126, 399, 402–405, 407,
    414, 495
Vickers (an informal abbreviation for
    Vickers-Armstrong Ltd.), 9–10, 12, 14,
    247, 463
Vickers-Armstrong Ltd., 12, 14, 247
Vickers VC10 aircraft, 143, 401, 405,
    411, 644
Viewdata, 485
Virtual storage, 664
Visualisation, 11, 30, 82, 113–114, 503
VPS. *See* Vaughan Programming Services

W
Wakefield, A.J. (Albert), 82, 128, 129, 251,
    267, 268, 273, 310, 311, 686
Wakefield, M.A. (Alan), xii, 333–335, 582,
    597, 633
Warman, D., xii, 472
Warren, K.R. (Sir Kenneth), 419–421
Warren Spring Laboratory, Hertfordshire, 235,
    238, 622, 625
Warwick Road building, Borehamwood,
    177, 477, 485
Watford Technical College, 179
Watson-Watt, R.A. (Sir Robert), 4–5, 647
Weapons Research Establishment (WRE),
    99–106, 134, 136–138, 612
Weinstock, A. (Lord Weinstock), 431,
    451–455, 457, 461, 479, 483, 486,
    491, 494, 497, 645
    biographical information, 451–455
Wellingborough, GEC's factory, 485

Wembley. *See* Hirst Research Laboratories

Whetstone Algol, 285

Whirlwind computer, 56, 57, 213, 214, 655, 656, 659–661

Whitehead, E.A.N. (Eric), 38, 48, 50, 53, 61, 266, 374, 375, 377, 379, 388, 389, 651, 686, 687

Wilkes, M.V. (Sir Maurice), 5, 38, 46, 55, 56, 108, 138, 154, 168, 171, 172, 311, 658

Wilkinson, J.H. (Jim), 138, 665

Williams, F.C. (Sir Frederik), 5, 56, 149, 150, 154, 155, 343, 506, 507, 657–658

Williams-Kilburn Tube (a truer description of the Williams Tube), 658

Williams, M.G.D. (Mike), xi

Williams Tube, 59, 98, 507, 658

Willis, D., 108, 360, 362

Wilson, H. (Prime Minister), 211, 449, 461, 501

Wilson, R.G. (Ron), xii, 359, 363–364, 631

Wiltshire, J., 454, 473, 480, 482–484, 489

Witley, Surrey, 5, 33

Wolvercote mill, 245, 253

Womersley, J.R., 46

Woomera rocket range, South Australia, 99, 100, 127, 134, 309

World Wide Web (WWW), 476, 485

Worthy Down, near Winchester, 318, 553

WRE. *See* Weapons Research Establishment

WREDAC (Weapons Research Establishment Digital Automatic Computer, aka Elliott 403). *See* Elliott digital computers

WRE Digital Output Converter (WREDOC) for WREDAC, 78, 104, 105, 107–111, 309, 358, 495, 533

Wright, Dr. (managing director of Siemens Brothers), 16–17

WWW. *See* World Wide Web

Wykeham, W.A.P. (Bill), 72, 156

Wythenshawe, site of a Ferranti factory, 220, 446, 486, 487

X

X-band radar, 44, 48

X25 packet-switched systems, 485

Y

Yates, F., 172, 180, 181, 539

Y station, 83

Z

Zebra. *See* STANTEC Zebra computer

Zuse, K., 54, 270, 271, 655, 656

Picture Credits

	Figure numbers
BAE Systems	5.12, 11.5, 11.6, 12.2, 12.8, 12.10, 12.11, 12.12, A9.3
BAE Systems (via Bruce Williamson)	11.7
Baigar, Erik	A6.3
Barron, Iann and successors to Elliott-Automation	5.1, 10.1
Beeldbank Rijkswaterstaat (via Eric van der Meer)	8.7
HMS Belfast, Imperial War Museum (photo Simon Lavington)	4.2
Birkbeck College, University of London (via Keith Harrison)	1.12
Blatt, Russell www.lifeinlegacy.com	13.7
Briggs, Jeremy	A9.4
Bunt, John and Monica	14.4
Campbell-Kelly, Martin	5.9
Carpenter, Harry and Frances Morley	3.5
Chatham Historic Dockyard Trust (photos & diagram Simon Lavington)	4.3
Clarke, Laurence	5.3, 5.7, 14.6, A3.1
Crown Copyright, by permission of Director GCHQ (via Peter Freeman)	3.8
Defence Archive Unit/RAF Holmpton (via James Fox)	8.10
Elliott-Automation's successors (BAE Systems & Telent plc)	1.2, 1.4, 1.8, 1.9, 1.10, 2.2, 2.4, 2.6, 2.7, 2.8, 2.9, 3.2, 3.3, 3.11, 3.12, 3.13, 4.1, 4.5, 4.6, 4.7, 4.9, 4.10, 4.11, 4.12, 4.13, 4.14, 4.15, 4.16, 5.2, 5.5, 5.6, 5.10, 6.1, 6.2, 6.3, 6.4, 6.5, 6.6, 6.7, 6.9, 6.10, 7.1, 7.2, 7.3, 7.4, 7.7, 7.8, 7.9, 7.10, 7.11, 8.2, 8.3, 8.4, 8.5, 8.8, 8.11, 8.12, 8.13, 9.3, 9.4, 9.5, 10.4, 10.5, 10.6, 10.7, 10.8, 10.9, 10.10, 11.3, 11.4, 12.1, 12.3, 12.4, 12.5, 12.6, 12.7, 12.9, 13.1, 14.1, 14.5, A2.1, A3.2, A4.2, A5.1, A6.1, A6.2, A9.1, A9.2

(continued)

(continued)

	Figure numbers
Farnborough Air Sciences Trust, copyright RAE	4.8
Farnborough Air Sciences Trust (via A T Hills & Qinetic)	7.5, 7.6
Felton, George	8.1
International Society of Automation, copyright ISA 1995	6.8
Kahan, Alex	1.13
King's College London, Archives & Corporate Records, (via Frances Pattman)	14.2
Kinnear, John	11.1
Laverick, Elizabeth	11.2
Lavington, Simon	1.3, 2.3, 2.10, 3.1, 3.4, 3.6, 3.7, 3.9, 9.2, 13.3, 13.4, 13.6, A1.1, A1.2, A3.3, A3.4
Lewisham Local History & Archives Centre (via John Coulter)	1.11
Manchester University, Dept. of Computer Science (via Bernard Strutt)	5.4
Merry, Ian	5.8
Museum of Science & Industry, Manchester (via Jan Hicks)	10.2
National Library of Australia (via John Deane)	3.10
The National Museum of Computing, Bletchley Park (via Kevin Murrell)	10.3, A4.1
National Portrait Gallery copyright. Photo by Keith Herschell, Bassano & Vandyk	14.8
National Portrait Gallery copyright. Photo by Elliott & Fry	1.7
NCR UK Retirement Fellowship (via Ian Ormerod)	9.1, 9.8
Ordnance Survey, with permission. (via Ed Hersom)	1.1
Oxford University Press (via Mary Bergin-Cartwright)	13.5
Robinet, Mme Nicole, (via Pierre-E. Mounier-Kuhn)	8.9
Royal Australian Navy Sea Power Centre (via John Perryman)	4.4
Bernard Lee Schwartz Foundation, Inc. Photo by Bernard Lee Schwartz	14.9
Science Museum Library & Archives, Wroughton; copyright Fujitsu Services Ltd.	9.6, 9.7, 13.2
St Johnston, Harriet	14.7
St. Modwen Properties PLC (via Menna Rees-Steer)	14.3
Steer, Alison	2.1, 2.5
Times' Series newspapers, Newsquest (London) Ltd. (via Andrew St Johnston)	5.11
Wakefield, Alan and successors to Elliott-Automation	8.6
Whytehead, Sally & Elliott-Automation, with annotations by Simon Lavington	A2.2
Wikimedia Commons, Rémi Kaupp.	1.5
Wikimedia Commons, U.S. Naval Historical Center	1.6